State of

ROSTER *of* SOLDIERS

IN THE

WAR *of* 1812-14

Prepared and published under the direction of
HERBERT T. JOHNSON
The Adjutant General
1933

CLEARFIELD

Originally published
St. Albans, Vermont, 1933

Reprinted for
Clearfield Company, Inc. by
Genealogical Publishing Co., Inc.
Baltimore, Maryland
1995

International Standard Book Number: 0-8063-4596-9

Made in the United States of America

FOREWORD

Napoleon, dominating Europe after the tremendous battle of Austerlitz in 1805, issued decrees declaring the continent closed to British goods, and ordered all vessels seized that touched at a British port. England, still master of the seas when Admiral Nelson shattered the combined fleets of France and Spain off Cape Trafalgar in October of the same year, retaliated by seizing all merchant vessels which did not touch at British ports; and in consequence American ocean trade, caught between these two orders, was so heavily reduced that in 1808-1809, President Madison tried by desperate diplomacy to bribe England and France to bid against each other for our trade. It happened at this time that British seamen deserted to the higher paid and better treated American merchantmen; and England, contemptuous of American naval weakness, exercised the "right of search" on American vessels to recover her sorely needed seamen. In May 1811, our frigate *President*, chasing a British cruiser on which a Massachusetts citizen was impressed, was fired upon by a British sloop of war. American indignation was great. After Governor Harrison of the Northwest Territory had reported British ammunition in the hands of Indians, and Henry Clay's brilliant oratory had stirred great popular excitement, President Madison wrote a fiery message against British outrages, and on June 18, 1812, Congress declared war.

The United States was woefully unprepared. The regular army numbered less than seven thousand men, many of them raw recruits. Our fifteen ships had to match England's one thousand. Much went amiss. The commander at Detroit was courtmartialed and sentenced to death for timid abandonment of his post, and the generals at the other end of Lake Erie fought duels over mutual charges of cowardice instead of advancing against the enemy. Clay had boasted that the Conquest of Canada could be accomplished by a small body of militia, but events proved that except for the victory of Perry's little Lake Erie fleet and Macdonough's brilliant manoeuvers on Lake Champlain, we could hardly have been saved from a disastrous British invasion from Canada. Cheered by Perry's famous dispatch "We have met the enemy and they are ours," Harrison recaptured Detroit, but in August, 1814, a small British force raided Washington and burned the city. Fortunately for us, however, England was principally engaged in fighting France, so that the United States had had time to build a few necessary ships. Though our Navy was still small, the exploits of such frigates as *Old Ironsides* proved the genius of American seamanship, and by a series of surprising triumphs kept the country in a fever of rejoicing. The war was disastrous to American exports, but fortunately our Navy in two years had captured some 2000 British merchantmen,[1] and England, worn by trouble on all sides, signed peace with us at Ghent on Christmas eve, 1814.

Such in brief are the facts relating to the War of 1812. Vermont's position as a state bordering both on Lake Champlain and Canada laid her open to especial danger, and made her part in the campaigns particularly important. When British impressment of American seamen had first stirred the nation in 1807, the Vermont Legislature adopted, by a vote of 169 to 1, a resolution which they forwarded to President Jefferson in which they declared: "And we do further for ourselves and our constituents declare that, fearless of the dangers to [which] we may be exposed as a frontier state, we shall be ever ready to obey the call of our common country, whenever it shall be necessary either for the purposes of redress or vengeance." [Vt. Assembly Journal 1807 p. 230.] Jefferson, though not needing the help of Vermonters at the time, replied that their sentiments were "worthy of their known patriotism." Again in 1809, after further outrages, the Legislature sent a similar message to President Madison, who received it with equal gratitude. Consequently when Madison issued his proclamation of war, Governor Jonas Galusha and the legis-

[1] D. S. Muzzey, American History p. 221.

lature sustained the government and passed laws immediately to prohibit intercourse with Canada.

But it must be understood that, though Vermonters could be stirred to patriotic fury by British indignities on the high seas, they were not all so eager to see their livelihood endangered by laws forbidding commerce with Canada. In consequence Galusha and the Democratic legislature were opposed in the 1813 elections by the Federalists who succeeded by a hotly contested vote of 112 to 111 in declaring Martin Chittenden as governor—a man who opposed the war.

Yet there was no doubt as to the loyalty of the state as a whole. At the outbreak of the war, after Congress had authorized the President to detach and organize 100,000 men for federal service, and the Secretary of War had apportioned 3000 to Vermont, the state promptly responded to the requisition, and Adjutant General David Fay, by command of Governor Galusha, ordered out four regiments of ten companies each, which were in service at Plattsburgh by September, 1812.

Their loyalty did not blind them to their interests and better judgments, for the state was not in sympathy with all of President Madison's policies, and on November 2, 1812, the Vermont House of Representatives adopted a resolution by a substantial majority to be sent to the President, in which they declared "that this assembly have the fullest confidence that the constituted authorities will at all times be anxious to bring the said war to a close, when it can be done consistently with the honor and interest of our country," and "that although this assembly deem it their duty to give to the general government every aid in their power, in the prosecution of the present just and necessary war, yet they will with great pleasure hail the happy day when the war shall be brought to an honorable conclusion." [Vt. Assembly Journal 1812 p. 179.] Acting in harmony with the Federal Government, the state legislature of 1812-13 passed acts to forbid unauthorized traffic through or from Vermont into Canada, but resentment against financial losses resulting from such laws was so widespread that the acts were repealed in November, 1813.

Within the state the people were not prepared for war. The northern towns lived in constant fear of Indian incursions from Canada, and many citizens abandoned their houses and farms. Though the fear seems to have been unfounded, a small detachment of troops was stationed at North Troy, and the selectmen of several towns furnished and supported guards for the frontier villages of Troy, Derby, and Canaan.

On November 6, 1812, the legislature authorized the raising of a volunteer corps of sixty-eight companies (two brigades) for the service of the Federal Government, and by 1814 the entire male population of Vermont—aged from sixteen to sixty—volunteered for service on the occasion of the invasion of Plattsburg, though only those who lived nearby reached Plattsburg in time to engage in the battle. But there were scattering detachments that saw service elsewhere outside the state, principally in the campaign of 1814 on the Niagara frontier; and such men as were in that campaign served in the brigade under the immediate command of General Winfield Scott in the battles of Chippewa Plain and Lundy's Lane, and under Major General Brown in the terrific night battle of Fort Erie, August 15, 1814.[1] For the most part, the Vermonters who served in the Regular Army were in the 11th, 26th, 30th and 31st Infantry. The 11th was organized in 1812, and served for the duration of the war—nearly three years. The other three were organized in the spring of 1813, to serve for one year, though a remnant of the 30th and 31st was in the Battle of Plattsburg in September, 1814.

The plan of the 1812 campaign was to garrison coast fortifications with local militia together with some Regulars, while the main forces invaded Canada from Detroit and Niagara. The Plattsburg army was designed to protect the Vermont and New York frontiers, and, therefore, nearly one-half its strength was recruited from Vermont. The year 1813, as far as Vermont was concerned, was given over to a vigorous

[1] For detailed accounts of Vermonters engaged in these battles, see *Spooner's Vermont Journal* of August 5, 1814; and particularly the letter probably written by Lieut. F. A. Sawyer of Burlington in the *Northern Sentinel* of August 19, 1814.

but futile enforcement of the non-intercourse act of November 6, 1812, and to repelling the British incursions from the north. A British force of fifty-two boats and fourteen hundred men under Colonel Murry set out on a marauding expedition up and down Lake Champlain. Major General Wade Hampton with three or four thousand men stationed himself at Burlington where he repeatedly called for but did not receive additional aid. Fortunately, however, the British demonstration against Burlington on August 2, 1813, was of small importance, and the invading troops moved on to Swanton where they did minor damage. Again on December 27th, British troops destroyed public storehouses and barracks at Derby.

In November, 1813, a portion of the militia of the third brigade and third division of Vermont militia, under Lieutenant Colonel Luther Dixon, crossed the Lake into New York and put themselves under Hampton's command. But Governor Chittenden, who was opposed to the war in the first place, and who believed that the militia should be employed only within the state "to suppress insurrections and repel invasions," ordered them to return. But the entire militia was thoroughly disgusted with the Governor's proclamation, and Captain Sanford Gadcomb drew up a reply, signed by all the officers, in which he spoke in part as follows:[1]

> "We shall take the liberty to state to your Excellency, plainly, our sentiments on this subject. We consider your proclamation as a gross insult to the officers and soldiers in service, inasmuch as it implies that they are so *ignorant* of their rights as to believe that you have authority to command them in their present situation, or so *abandoned* as to follow your insidious advice. We cannot regard your proclamation in any other light than as an unwarrantable stretch of executive authority, issued from the worst of motives, to effect the basest purposes. It is, in our opinion, a renewed instance of that spirit of disorganization and anarchy which is carried on by a faction to overwhelm our country with ruin and disgrace. We cannot perceive what other object your

[1] For the complete text of the Governor's proclamation, together with the reply from the officers of the militia, see the *Records of the Governor and Council of the State of Vermont*, Vol. VI, pp. 492-494.

Excellency could have in view than to embarrass the operations of the Army, to excite mutiny and sedition among the soldiers and induce them to desert, that they might forfeit the wages to which they are entitled for their patriotic services."

Nevertheless the militia returned before their service had expired, and no further notice was taken of the transaction. Without more notable incident the northern campaign of 1813 ended.

Through the early months of 1814 there were frequent British marauding expeditions upon the northern frontier, but never did the encounters break into extensive hostilities. On the Lake, however, the war assumed a serious complexion. On May 14th, the British fleet opened fire on the battery at the mouth of Otter Creek, where Commander Macdonough, descending the river with his sloop of war and several galleys, forced the enemy to retreat without losing a man. A few days later Macdonough entered the Lake with his fleet and anchored at Cumberland Bay. At the same time Vermonters were enlisting in the Plattsburg army, attached to the 30th and 31st U. S. Regulars, and on the 11th of September the double battle—on land and water—took place. The ridiculously small and ill-trained land forces astonished the nation and the world by defeating a superior British force; and Commander, now Captain, Macdonough in a naval battle which still ranks as one of the major sea encounters in American history, effectively put an end to the British expectations of success across the American frontier, and thus hastened the treaty of peace which was signed on December 24th of the same year.

T. H. J.

For those who may care to investigate the subject of the War of 1812 further, and especially Vermont's part in it, the following sources and histories are suggested:

Vermont newspapers: The Vermont Republican
                    The Washingtonian
                    Spooner's Vermont Journal
                    The Northern Sentinel

Records of the Governor and Council of the State of Vermont.
    Volumes 5 and 6.

Vermont Assembly Journals, 1805-1815.

Vermont Historical Magazine.

H. Adams, History of the United States during the Administrations of Jefferson and Madison. 9 volumes.

W. H. Crockett, History of Vermont. 4 volumes.

B. J. Lossing, Pictorial Field Book of the War of 1812.

J. B. McMaster, History of the People of the United States.
    Volumes 3 and 4.

P. S. Palmer, History of Lake Champlain from 1609 to the close of the year 1814.

J. B. Wilbur, Ira Allen. 2 volumes.

WAR GOVERNORS AND THEIR COUNCILS

THIRTY-FIFTH COUNCIL
October 1811 to October 1812

JONAS GALUSHA, Shaftsbury, Governor.
PAUL BRIGHAM, Norwich, Lieut. Governor.

Councillors:

BERIAH LOOMIS, Thetford,
NOAH CHITTENDEN, Jericho,
ELIAS KEYES, Stockbridge,
JOSIAH WRIGHT, Pownal,
EZRA BUTLER, Waterbury,
FREDERICK BLISS, Georgia,

GILBERT DENISON, Guilford,
SAMUEL C. CRAFTS, Craftsbury,
HORATIO SEYMOUR, Middlebury,
WILLIAM HUNTER, Windsor,
PLINY SMITH, Orwell,
JOHN CAMERON, Ryegate,

ROLLIN C. MALLARY, Castleton, Secretary.
ISRAEL P. DANA, Danville, Sheriff.

Jonas Galusha, born in Norwich, Conn., Feb. 11, 1753, came to Shaftsbury in 1775. He was captain of a militia company from 1777 to 1780. In 1777 there were two companies in the town, one of which seems to have taken part in the battle of Hubbardton, where Amos Huntington, its captain, was captured by the British. Captain Galusha was thereupon assigned to the command of both companies, and he led them in the battle of Bennington. He represented Shaftsbury in the Legislature of 1800; was Councillor from Oct. 1793 until Oct. 1799, and also from Oct. 1801 until Oct. 1806; Sheriff of Bennington county from 1781 to 1787; Judge of the County Court from 1795 until 1798, and again from 1801 until 1807; Judge of the Supreme Court in 1807 and 1808; and Governor from 1809 until 1813, and from 1815 until 1820. He was an elector of President and Vice President in 1808, 1820, and 1824; one of the Council of Censors in 1792; and a member of the Constitutional Conventions of 1814 and 1822, and President of both. His services in civil offices covered forty years. "He possessed a mild, benevolent, and philosophic turn of mind, and a comprehensive understanding. He was not a dealer in many words, gave his reasons with openness and candor, and always made them plain to the meanest capacity. Like Cincinnatus he delighted to retire from the toils of war and labors of state, to return again to the comforts of society and follow his plough."—Vt. Hist. Magazine, Vol. I, p. 234. Like many of his day in Vermont, among them several excellent and notable men, he was both farmer and innkeeper. Gov. Galusha, though not a member of any church, was, "in the estimation of those competent to judge, a true Christian. He maintained family worship in all its forms, was known to observe private devotions, was an habitual attendant upon public worship and at social meetings, and frequently took an active part in the latter. In his daily life he was also such as a Christian should be, modest, amiable, upright, faithful to every obligation. * * * When nearly seventy-nine years of age, he attended a protracted meeting at Manchester, and took an active part in its exercises; as the result of which he was aroused to a sense of the duty of making a public profession of religion, and announced his intention to do so, but was prevented from accomplishing his purpose by a stroke of paralysis, which he experienced soon after, and from which he never recovered. * * * By his first wife, Mary, (daughter of Gov. Thomas Chittenden,) he had five sons and four daughters. His children were well trained, and all of them who survived childhood became professors of religion; one of them, Elon, an eminent minister in the Baptist denomination."—Memoirs of Jonas Galusha, by Rev. Pliny H. White. In publishing the death of Gov. Galusha, which occurred on the 24th of Sept. 1834, the Vermont Watchman and State Gazette characterized him as "a decided and unwavering republican, an honest man, and a veteran of the revolution."

THIRTY-SIXTH COUNCIL
October 1812 to October 1813

JONAS GALUSHA, Shaftsbury, Governor.
PAUL BRIGHAM, Norwich, Lieut. Governor.
Councillors:

BERIAH LOOMIS, Thetford,
ELIAS KEYES, Stockbridge,
JOSIAH WRIGHT, Pownal,
EZRA BUTLER, Waterbury,
FREDERICK BLISS, Georgia,
SAMUEL C. CRAFTS, Craftsbury,

HORATIO SEYMOUR, Middlebury,
WILLIAM HUNTER, Windsor,
PLINY SMITH, Orwell,
JOHN CAMERON, Ryegate,
WM. C. BRADLEY, Westminster,
WM. C. HARRINGTON, Burlington.

ROLLIN C. MALLARY, Castleton, Secretary.
JOHN PECK, Waterbury, Sheriff.

THIRTY-SEVENTH COUNCIL
October 1813 to October 1814

MARTIN CHITTENDEN, Jericho, Governor.
WILLIAM CHAMBERLAIN, Peacham, Lieut. Governor.
Councillors:

SAMUEL FLETCHER, Townshend,
SOLOMON MILLER, Williston,
BERIAH LOOMIS, Thetford,
ELIAS KEYES, Stockbridge,
DANIEL DANA, Guildhall,
JOSIAH WRIGHT, Pownal,

FREDERICK BLISS, Georgia,
HORATIO SEYMOUR, Middlebury,
WILLIAM HUNTER, Windsor,
WM. C. HARRINGTON, Burlington,
GAMALIEL PAINTER, Middlebury,
MARK RICHARDS, Westminster.

ROLLIN C. MALLARY, Castleton, Secretary until Oct. 26, 1813.
SAMUEL SWIFT, Middlebury, Secretary from Oct. 26, 1813.
JOHN PECK, Waterbury, Sheriff.

Martin Chittenden, the second son of Gov. Thomas Chittenden, was born in Salisbury, Conn., March 12, 1769, and graduated at Dartmouth College in 1789. He represented Jericho in the General Assembly 1790 and subsequently for eight years, and Williston two years; was Clerk of Chittenden County Court four years, and Judge ten; Judge of Probate two years; delegate in the Constitutional Conventions of 1791 and 1793; Member of Congress from 1803 to 1813, ten years; and Governor in 1813 and '14. He died Sept. 5, 1840, in his seventy-second year, having been for about thirty years employed in public service.—Drake's Dictionary of American Biography; Vt. Historical Magazine, Vol. I; Deming's Catalogue; and Vt. Watchman & State Journal of Sept. 21, 1840.

MEMBERS OF CONGRESS

1812-14

SENATE

Jonathan Robinson 1807-1815
Stephen R. Bradley 1801-1813
Dudley Chase 1813-1817

REPRESENTATIVES

Martin Chittenden 1803-1813
Samuel Shaw 1808-1813
James Fisk 1810-1815
William Strong 1810-1815
William C. Bradley 1813-1815
Ezra Butler 1813-1815
Richard Skinner 1813-1815
Charles Rich 1813-1815

ROSTER WAR 1812-14

*Verified by War Department Records.
‡Verified by Pension Bureau Records.

ABBETT, JOHN
Served in War of 1812 and was captured by troops Sept. 17, 1814 at Fort Erie. Discharged Nov. 8th. Ref: Records of ·Naval Records and Library, Navy Department.

‡*ABBEY, DANIEL
Served in Captain Mason's Company, Col. Fifield's Regt., Detached Militia in U. S. service 5 months and 16 days in 1812. Lived in Holland. Pension Certificate No. 3140.

*ABBEY, EBENEZER
Served in company commanded by Lieut James S. Morton in Col. W. B. Sumner's Regt. Enlisted April 12, 1814. Discharged April 21, 1814.

‡*ABBEY, SAMUEL
Served in Captain Mason's Company, Col. Fifield's Regt., Detached Militia in U. S. service 3 months and 15 days in 1812. Pension Certificate No. 3318.

ABBOTT, MOREHOUSE, Ridgebury, Conn. Enlisted May 28, 1813 in Captain James Taylor's Company, 30th Regt. Re-enlisted March 1, 1814 at Plattsburgh and promoted to sergeant. Also served in Captain William Miller's Company, 30th Regt. and Captain Gideon Spencer's Company, 30th Regt. Ref: R. & L. 1812, AGO Pages 52-53-54-55-56-58.

ABBOTT, BENJAMIN
Served in company commanded by Capt. John McNeil Jr., 11th Regt.; on pay roll of company for January and February, 1813. Ref: R. & L. 1812, AGO Page 17.

‡ABBOTT, DANIEL
Served in Captain Rockwood's Company. Pension Certificate No. 6998.

‡ABBOTT, EBENEZER
Volunteered to go to Plattsburgh in September, 1814, and served 7 days in company commanded by Capt. Frederick Griswold, raised in Brookfield, Vt. Pension Certificate of widow, Sally, No. 31127.

ABBOTT, JAMES, Strafford. Volunteered to go to Plattsburgh in September, 1814, and served 5 days in company commanded by Capt. Cyril Chandler. Ref: Book 52, AGO Page 42.

*ABBOTT, JOB
Served in 1st Regiment (Judson's) Vermont Militia.

ABBOTT, JOHN
Enlisted February 3, 1813 in Detachment of Recruits under command of Capt. John McNeil, Jr., 11th Regt. Died April 13, 1813. Ref: R. & L. 1812, AGO Page 16.

ABBOTT, LESTER
Volunteered to go to Plattsburgh in September, 1814, and served 7 days in company commanded by Capt. Frederick Griswold, raised in Brookfield, Vt. Ref. Book 52, AGO Page 52.

*ABBOTT, SAMUEL, Stowe. Enlisted Feb. 10, 1813 in Detachment of Recruits under the command of Capt. John W. Weeks, 11th Regt. Ref: R & L. 1812, AGO Pages 4 and 5. Also served at the Battle of Plattsburgh in September, 1814, in company commanded by Capt. Nehemiah Perkins, 4th Regt. (Peck's). Ref: Book 51, AGO Pages 214 and 251.

ABBOTT, WILLIAM, Thetford. Volunteered to go to Plattsburgh in September, 1814, and went as far as Bolton, Vt. Served 6 days in company commanded by Capt. Salmon Howard, 2nd Regt. Ref: Book 52, AGO Pages 15 and 16.

ABBY, JEREMIAH, Huntington. Served at the Battle of Plattsburgh in September, 1814, in company commanded by Capt. Josiah M. Barrows. Ref: Book 51, AGO Page 77.

*ABEL, BANNISTER
Enlisted Sept. 25, 1813 in Capt. N. B. Eldridge's Company, Col. Dixon's Regt. Transferred to Capt. Asahel Langworthy's Company, Col. Isaac Clark's Rifle Corps, Sept. 28, 1813 and served therein 1 month and 14 days. Ref: Book 52, AGO Pages 260 and 267; Book 53, AGO Page 111.

ABEL, EDWARD
Served in Capt. Haig's Corps of Light Dragoons from May 1, 1814 to June 30, 1814. Ref: R. & L. 1812, AGO Page 20.

‡*ABEL, THEOPHILUS
Enlisted Sept. 25, 1813 in Capt. N. B. Eldridge's Company, Col. Dixon's Regt. Transferred to Capt Asahel Langworthy's Company, Col. Isaac Clark's Rifle Corps, Sept. 28, 1813 and served therein 1 month and 20 days. Pension Certificate of widow, Minerva, No. 35602. Ref: Book 52, AGO Pages 260 and 267; Book 53, AGO Page 108.

ABEL, WYLLYS, Orwell. Volunteered to go to Plattsburgh in September, 1814, and served 11 days in company commanded by Capt. Wait Branch. Ref: Book 51, AGO Pages 16 and 32.

ABELL, BARRILLA, Sergeant. Enlisted April 26, 1813 in Capt. James Taylor's Company, 30th Regt. Transferred to Capt. Gideon Spencer's Company, 30th Regt., and served to May 2, 1814. Ref: R. & L. 1812, AGO Pages 52, 56 and 58.

ABENS, SILAS.
Served in Company of Infantry under the command of Capt. White Youngs, 15th Regt., April 30, 1812 to April 30, 1817. Name appears on Muster Roll from Aug. 31, 1814 to Dec. 31, 1814. Ref: R. & L. 1812, AGO Page 27.

*ABERNETHY, JOHN.
Served in company commanded by Capt. Eseck Sprague, Col. Sumner's Regt., from April 12, 1814 to April 21, 1814.

*ABOT, ELIPHLET.
Served in Captain Howard's Company, Vermont Militia.

ABRAHAM, CHARLES, Poultney or St. Albans. Served in Capt. John Wires' Company, 30th Regt., from May 1, 1813 to April 30, 1814. Ref: R. & L. 1812, AGO Page 40.

*ADAMS, ABEL, Captain,
Served in 3rd Regt., Vermont Militia, commanded by Col. Jonathan Williams.

‡ADAMS, ABIJAH.
Aged 28 years; 5 feet 10 inches high; dark complexion; brown hair; blue eyes; by profession a farmer; born in Killington, Conn. Enlisted at Addison April 4, 1814 for period of war; discharged at Burlington in 1815. Name appears on Muster Roll of Capt. Gideon Spencer's Company, 30th Regt. from Dec. 30, 1813 to June 30, 1814; joined June 1, 1814. Name also appears on Muster Roll of Capt. William Miller's Company, 30th Regt., to Aug. 31, 1814 and on Muster Roll of Capt. James Taylor's Company, 30th Regt., from Feb. 28, 1814. Pension Certificate of widow, Submit, No. 1601. Ref: R. & L. 1812, AGO Pages 53-54-55-56.

ADAMS, ALANSON.
Served in company commanded by Lieut. V. R. Goodrich, 11th Regt. Name appears on Pay Roll of company for January and February, 1813. Ref: R. & L. 1812, AGO Page 11.

*ADAMS, ANSON,   Randolph.
Volunteered to go to Plattsburgh in September, 1814, in company commanded by Capt. Lebbeus Egerton.

*ADAMS, ASA,
Served in Capt. Rogers' Company, Col. Fifield's Regt., Detached Militia, in U. S. service 4 months and 2 days in 1812.

‡ADAMS, BENJAMIN.
Served in Capt. Azro Buck's Company. Pension Certificate No. 1334.

*ADAMS, BILDAD.
Served in Capt. Parsons' Company, Col. Jonathan Williams' Regt., Detached Militia, in U. S. service 2 months and 13 days, 1812.

*ADAMS, DAVID,   Waterbury.
Volunteered to go to Plattsburgh in September, 1814, and served 11 days in company commanded by Capt. George Atkins in 4th Regt., Vermont Militia, commanded by Col. John Peck.

*ADAMS, EBENEZER, Corporal.
Served in company commanded by Capt. Jonathan P. Stanley, Col. W. B. Sumner's Regt., from April 12, 1814 to April 18, 1814.

*ADAMS, FRIEND.
Served in company commanded by Capt. Othniel Jewett, Col. Sumner's Regt., from April 19, 1814 to April 21, 1814.

ADAMS, GARDNER.
Enlisted Jan. 28, 1813 in company commanded by Lieut. V. R. Goodrich, 11th Regt. Name appears on Pay Roll of company for January and February, 1813. Ref: R. & L. 1812, AGO Page 11.

ADAMS, GEORGE.
Enlisted May 12, 1812 for a period of 5 years in Company of Infantry under the command of Capt. White Youngs, 15th Regt. Name appears on Muster Roll from Aug. 31, 1814 to Dec. 31, 1814. Ref: R. & L. 1812, AGO Page 27.

*ADAMS, IRA.
Served with Hospital Attendants, Vermont.

ADAMS, JAMES.
Appointed 3rd Lieutenant, 31st Infantry, April 30, 1813. Died Nov. 22, 1813. Ref: Heitman's Historical Register and Dictionary USA.

ADAMS, JEDUTHAN.
Served in company commanded by Capt. Jonathan P. Stanley, Col. W. B. Sumner's Regt., from April 12, 1814 to April 18, 1814. Ref: Book 52, AGO Page 287.

‡*ADAMS, JEREMIAH.
Served in Capt. Richardson's Company, Col. Martindale's Regt., Detached Militia, in U. S. service 2 months and 13 days, 1812. Pension Certificate No. 12669.

*ADAMS, JOHN.
Served in Capt. Preston's Company, Col. Jonathan Williams' Regt., Detached Militia, in U. S. service 2 months and 6 days, 1812. Served in Capt. Noyce's Company, Col. Jonathan Williams' Regt., Detached Militia, in U. S. service 2 months and 6 days, 1812. Volunteered to go to Plattsburgh in September, 1814, and served in company commanded by Capt. Frederick Griswold, raised in Brookfield, Vt.

*ADAMS, JOSEPH.
Enlisted in Capt. Shubael Wales Company, Col. W. B. Sumner's Regt., April 12, 1814; transferred to Capt. Salmon Foster's Company, Sumner's Regt., April 13, 1814; discharged April 21, 1814.

ADAMS, LYMAN,   Randolph.
Volunteered to go to Plattsburgh, September, 1814, in company commanded by Capt. Lebbeus Egerton. Ref: Book 52, AGO Page 82.

*ADAMS, LYNDA,   Roxbury.
Volunteered to go to Plattsburgh in September, 1814 and served about 6 days in Capt. Lebbeus Egerton's Company.

‡ADAMS, NATHAN, Grand Isle?
Served in Captain Allen's Company.
Pension Certificate of widow, Caroline,
No. 27561.

‡*ADAMS, NEWEL.
Served in Capt. Preston's Company,
Col. Jonathan Williams' Regt., Detached Militia, in U. S. service 2
months and 6 days, 1812. Pension
Certificate No. 11966. Pension Certificate of widow, Mary A., No. 12229.

ADAMS, PAUL. Ensign,
Served in Artillery of Detached Militia of Vermont in the service of the
United States at Champlain for 2
days commencing Nov. 18 and ending Nov. 19, 1812.

‡*ADAMS, SAMUEL.
Served in Capt. Parson's Company,
Col. Jonathan Williams' Regt., Detached Militia, in U. S. service 2
months and 13 days, 1812. Also served
in Capt. Haig's Corps of Light Dragoons from May 1st to June 30, 1814.
Also served in Capt. Keeler's Company, Col. Martindale's Regt. Pension Certificate No. 287. Pension Certificate of widow, Alice, No. 31770.

ADAMS, SILAS.
Served in Capt. Simeon Wright's
Company from May 1, 1813 to Aug. 2,
1814. Ref: R. & L. 1812, AGO Page 51.

‡*ADAMS, STEPHEN.
Served in Capt. Durkee's Company,
Col. Fifield's Regt., Detached Militia,
in U. S. service 2 months and 16 days,
1812. Pension Certificate No. 9148.
Pension Certificate of widow, Rhoda,
No. 3544.

*ADAMS, STERLING.
Enlisted Sept. 25, 1813 in company
commanded by Capt. Jonathan Prentiss Jr., Col. Dixon's Regt.

ADAMS, THOMAS, Corporal,
Enlisted June 3, 1812 for a period of
five years in Company of Infantry
under the command of Capt. White
Youngs, 15th Regt. Name appears on
Muster Roll from Aug. 31, 1814 to
Dec. 31, 1814. Ref: R. & L. 1812,
AGO Page 27.

*ADAMS, WILLIAM.
Served in company commanded by
Capt. Jonathan P. Stanley, Col. W.
B. Sumner's Regt., from April 12, 1814
to April 15, 1814.

‡ADAMS, ZOPHEO.
Served in Captain Gordon's Company.
Pension Certificate No. 2173.

ADCOCK, WILLIAM, Burlington.
Served in Capt. Sanford's Company,
30th Inf., from Sept. 1, 1814 to June
16, 1815. Ref: R. & L. 1812, AGO
Page 23.

ADKINS, JOSEPH, Sergeant,
Enlisted April 22, 1813 for 1 year in
Capt. Daniel Farrington's Company,
30th Regt. Ref: R. & L. 1812, AGO
Page 50.

AGER, HIRAM, Shoreham.
Enlisted with his father, Jason Ager,
and accompanied him, sharing the
same dangers. In one of the battles
he was shot through the left foot.
He returned and afterwards resided

in St. Lawrence County, N. Y. Ref:
Rev. J. F. Goodhue's History of
Shoreham, Page 101.

AGER, JASON. Shoreham.
Entered the army under Capt. Samuel
H. Holly, was ordered to the Niagara
frontier, participated in all the severe
and dangerous service under Generals
Scott, Brown and Ripley in that quar-
ter; at the sortie of Fort Erie, September 17, 1814, was wounded by a
ball which shivered his right ankle
so that it was necessary to amputate
the foot. He returned home and died
on Chilson Hill, Ticonderoga. Ref:
Rev. J. F. Goodhue's History of
Shoreham, Page 101.

*AHLE, WILLIAM W.
Served with Hospital Attendants, Vermont.

AIKENS, ASA, Captain.
Appointed Captain, 31st Infantry,
April 30, 1813. Honorably discharged
June 15, 1815. Ref: Heitman's His-
torical Register and Dictionary, USA.

‡*AIKENS, JOHN.
Served in Capt. Morrill's Company,
Col. Fifield's Regt., Detached Militia,
in U. S. service 2 months and 18
days, 1812. Also served in Captain
Beard's Company. Pension Certificate of widow, Phebe, No. 20126.

AIKENS, SOLOMON, Barnard.
Enlisted June 9, 1813 in Capt. Nehemiah Noble's Company, 31st U. S. Infantry. Ref: Wm. N. Newton's History of Barnard, Vol. 1, Page 95 (Vt.
Historical Society).

AILSWORTH, PHILIP.
Enlisted May 1, 1812 for 5 years in
Company of Infantry under the com-
mand of Capt. White Youngs, 15th
Regt. Name appears on Muster Roll
from Aug. 31, 1814 to Dec. 31, 1814.
Ref: R. & L. 1812, AGO Page 27.

*AINSWORTH, AMASA, Calais.
Volunteered to go to Plattsburgh in
September, 1814, and served 10 days
in company commanded by Capt.
Gideon Wheelock.

*AINSWORTH, DANFORTH, Montpelier
or Calais. Served in Capt. Durkee's
Company, Col. Fifield's Regt., Detached Militia, in U. S. service 2 months
and 26 days, 1812. Also served in
Col. Fifield's Regt. in U. S. service
from Dec. 8, 1812 to March 18, 1813.

AINSWORTH, LUTHER.
Volunteered to go to Plattsburgh in
September, 1814, and served 7 days
in company commanded by Capt.
Frederick Griswold, raised in Brookfield, Vt. Ref: Book 52, AGO Pages
52 and 64.

AINSWORTH, SAMUEL, Woodbury.
Volunteered to go to Plattsburgh in
September, 1814, and served 7 days.
No organization given. Ref: Book
52, AGO Page 210.

*AINSWORTH, WILLARD, Sergeant,
Highgate. Served in Capt. Saxe's
Company, Col. William Williams'
Regt., Detached Militia, in U. S. serv-
ice 4 months and 24 days, 1812. Sta-
tioned at Swanton Falls.

*AIRS, JAMES.
Served in 1st Regiment, Vermont Militia, commanded by Col. Judson.

*AKELY, FRANCIS
Served in Capt. Briggs' Company, Col. Jonathan Williams' Regt., Detached Militia, in U. S. service 2 months and 13 days, 1812.

ALBEE, ELKANAH,   Highgate.
Volunteered to go to Plattsburgh in September, 1814, and served 5 days in company commanded by Capt. Conrad Saxe in Col. William Williams' Regt. Ref: Book 51, AGO Pages 100 and 101.

ALBEY, JOSEPH.
Served in company commanded by Capt. Shubael Wales, Col. W. B. Sumner's Regt., from April 12, 1814 to April 21, 1814. Ref: Book 52, AGO Page 289.

ALBRIGHT, ELIJAH, Corporal, Franklin County. Enlisted June 17, 1812 for a period of 5 years in Company of Infantry under the command of Capt. White Youngs, 15th Regt. Name appears on Muster Roll from Aug. 31, 1814 to Dec. 31, 1814. Ref: R. & L. 1812, AGO Page 27.

ALBRO, J. E.
Appointed Ensign, 31st Infantry, March 28, 1814; appointed 2nd lieutenant Sept. 30, 1814. Ref: Governor and Council Vt. Vol. 6, Page 478 (Vt. State Library).

ALBROUGH, WILLIAM.
Served from May 1, 1814 to July 6, 1814. Name appears on Pay Roll but no organization is given. Ref: R. & L. 1812, AGO Page 29.

ALDEN, HENRY.
Served in Capt. Weeks' Company, 11th Regt. Name appears on Pay Roll of company for January and February, 1813. Ref: R. & L. 1812, AGO Page 5.

ALDEN, HORACE.
Served in Capt. O. Lowry's Company, Col. William Williams' Regt., Detached Militia, in U. S. service 4 months and 26 days, 1812. Ref: Book 53, AGO Page 10.

*ALDERS, ENOCH.
Served in company commanded by Capt. Jonathan P. Stanley, Col. W. B. Sumner's Regt., from April 12, 1814 to April 15, 1814.

ALDRICH, CALVIN JR.
Enlisted March 17, 1813 in Detachment of Recruits under command of Capt. John McNeil Jr. 11th Regt. Name appears on Pay Roll for advance pay and retained bounty to May 31, 1813. Ref: R. & L. 1812, AGO Page 16.

ALDRICH, EBEN.
Served in company commanded by Capt. Samuel H. Holly, 11th Regt., from Dec 23, 1812 to Feb. 28, 1813. Ref: R. & L. 1812, AGO Page 25.

ALDRICH, JACOB.
Served in company commanded by Capt. Samuel H. Holly, 11th Regt. Name appears on Pay Roll for January and February, 1813. Ref: R. & L. 1812, AGO Page 25.

ALDRICH, LUTHER.
Enlisted May 27, 1813 in Capt. James Taylor's Company, 30th Regt. Transferred to Capt. Gideon Spencer's Company, 30th Regt., and served to May 26, 1814. Ref: R. & L. 1812, AGO Pages 52, 56, 59.

ALDRICH, SYLVANUS,   Barre.
Volunteered to go to Plattsburgh in September, 1814, and served 10 days in company commanded by Capt. Warren Ellis. Ref: Book 52, AGO Page 242.

ALDRICH, TIMOTHY, Ensign.
Served in company of Capt. John McNeil, Jr., 11th Regt., from Nov. 1, 1812 to Feb. 28, 1813. Ref: R. & L. 1812, AGO Page 17.

ALDRIDGE, DAVID.
Enlisted Jan. 10, 1814 for period of war in company of late Capt. J. Brooks, commanded by Lieut. John I. Cromwell, Corps of U. S. Artillery. Name appears on Muster Roll of company from April 30, 1814 to June 30, 1814. Ref: R. & L. 1812, AGO Page 18.

*ALEOT, WILLIAM.
Enlisted Sept. 25, 1813 in company commanded by Capt. Amos Robinson, Col. Dixon's Regt.

*ALEXANDER, AMOS.
Served in Company of Militia commanded by Capt. Stephen Brown, 3rd Regt. (Tyler's). Joined Oct. 12, 1813. Name appears on Muster Roll to Oct. 17, 1813.

*ALEXANDER, EMERY.
Enlisted Sept. 23, 1813 in Capt. Amasa Mansfield's Company, Col Dixon's Regt. Transferred to Capt. Asahel Langworthy's Company, Col. Isaac Clark's Rifle Corps, Sept. 27, 1813, and served to November, 1813.

*ALEXANDER, GEORGE.
Served in 1st Regiment, Vt. Militia, commanded by Col. Judson.

*ALEXANDER, LEE.
Served in 3rd Regiment, Vt. Militia, commanded by Col. Jonathan Williams.

ALEXANDER, ROBERT.
Volunteered to go to Plattsburgh in September, 1814, and went as far as Bolton, Vt. Served 4 days in company commanded by Lieut. Phineas Kimball, West Fairlee. Ref: Book 52, AGO Page 46.

ALFORD, AMMI,   St. Albans.
Volunteered to go to Plattsburgh in Sept., 1814 and was present at the battle on September 11th. No organization given. Ref: Book 51, AGO Pages 117 and 122.

ALFORD, JACK.
Enlisted March 17, 1813 for period of war in Capt. Simeon Wright's Company. Ref: R. & L. 1812, AGO Page 51.

*ALFORD, SAMUEL,   Fairfield.
Served 6 months in 1812 in Company of Infantry commanded by Capt. George W. Kindall, Col. William Williams' Regt.

*‡ALFORD, SAMUEL JR.
Served in Capt. Kindall's Company, Col. William Williams' Regt., Detached Militia, in U. S. service 4 months and 23 days, 1812. Pension Certificate No. 286.

ALFRED, JOHN,   Sheldon.
Served in Capt. Sanford's Company, 30th Inf., from April 1, 1814 to June 16, 1815. Ref: R. & L. 1812, AGO Page 23.

ALGER, GEORGE, Sergeant,
Served in Corps of Artillery from March 30 to June 30, 1814. Ref: R. & L. 1812, AGO Page 31.

ALGIER, GEORGE.
Served in company commanded by Lieut. V. R. Goodrich, 11th Regt., from Nov. 1, 1812 to Feb. 28, 1813. Ref: R. & L. 1812, AGO Page 11.

ALLANSON, ALLEN.
Appointed Ensign, 31st Infantry, Dec. 12, 1814; appointed 3rd Lieutenant January, 1815; honorably discharged June 15, 1815. Ref: Heitman's Historical Register & Dictionary USA.

ALLARD, AARON,   Franklin County.
Volunteered to go to Plattsburgh Sept. 11, 1814 and served in the 15th or 22nd Regt. Ref: Hemenway's Vt. Gazetteer, Vol. 2, Page 391.

ALLARD, HENRY.
Enlisted Feb. 19, 1813 in Detachment of Recruits under the command of Capt. Edgerton, 11th Regt. Name appears on Pay Roll to May 18, 1813. Ref: R. & L. 1812, AGO Page 3.

ALLARD, HENRY.
Served in Detachment of Recruits under the command of Capt. Jonathan Starks, 11th Regt., from March 22, 1813 to June 21, 1813. Ref: R. & L. 1812, AGO Page 19.

ALLARD, JACOB.
Enlisted March 1, 1813 in Detachment of Recruits under command of Capt. Edgerton, 11th Regt. Name appears on Pay Roll to May 31, 1813. Ref: R. & L. 1812, AGO Page 3.

ALLARD, JAMES.
Served in company commanded by Capt. John McNeil Jr., 11th Regt. Name appears on Pay Roll of company for January and February 1813. Ref: R. & L. 1812, AGO Page 17.

ALLEN, ABIJAH,   Shelburne.
Volunteered to go to Plattsburgh in September, 1814 and served in Major Luman Judson's command. Ref: Book 51, AGO Page 78.

ALLEN, ALANSON, Corporal, Montpelier
Volunteered to go to Plattsburgh in September, 1814, and served 8 days in company commanded by Capt. Timothy Hubbard. Ref: Book 52, AGO Page 256.

*ALLEN, ALFRED B.
Served in Capt. Edmund B. Hill's Company, Sumner's Regt., from April 12, 1814 to April 21, 1814.

ALLEN, ALONZO, Lieutenant.
Appointed Ensign, 31st Infantry, Nov. 8, 1814; appointed 3rd Lieutenant Jan. 1, 1815. Ref: Governor and Council Vt., Vol. 6, Page 478 (Vt. State Library).

*ALLEN, ALVA,   Enosburgh.
Served in Capt. Asahel Scoville's Company, Col. Clark's Regiment of Riflemen, from Oct. 15, 1813 to Nov. 17, 1813.

*ALLEN, AMASA.
Served in Capt. Mason's Company, Col. Fifield's Regt., Detached Militia, in U. S. service 6 months in 1812.

*ALLEN, ASAPH, Sergeant,   Middlesex.
Volunteered to go to Plattsburgh in September, 1814, and served 10 days in company by Capt. Holden Putnam, 4th Regt. (Peck's) Vermont Militia.

*ALLEN, CHARLES S.
Served in 4th Regt. Vt. Militia, commanded by Col. John Peck.

ALLEN, DAN.
Served from Sept. 1, 1813 to Feb. 28, 1814 and from May 1, 1814 to May 18, 1814. No organization given. Ref: R. & L. 1812, AGO Page 29.

*ALLEN, DAVID.
Enlisted Dec. 19, 1812 for a period of 5 years in company of late Capt. J. Brooks, commanded by Lieut. John I. Cromwell, Corps of U. S. Artillery. Name appears on Muster Roll of company from April 30, 1814 to June 30, 1814. Ref: R. & L. 1812, AGO Page 18. Also served in Capt. Eseck Sprague's Company, Sumner's Regt., from April 12, 1814 to April 21, 1814.

*ALLEN, EBEN W.
Served in Capt. Eseck Sprague's Company, Sumner's Regt., from April 12, 1814 to April 21, 1814.

*ALLEN, EBENEZER, Sergeant, Chelsea.
Served in Capt. Wheatly's Company, Col. Fifield's Regt., Detached Militia, in U. S. service 2 months and 21 days in 1812. Also served in company of Militia commanded by Lieut. Bates from June 11, 1813 to June 14, 1813. Also volunteered to go to Plattsburgh in September, 1814, and served 6 days; no organization given.

ALLEN, ELISHA, Corporal.
Served in 1st Regt. of Detached Militia of Vermont in the service of the United States at Champlain for 2 days commencing Nov. 18, 1812 and ending Nov. 19, 1812.

ALLEN, ELISHA R.
Served in company commanded by Capt. Samuel H. Holly; 11th Regt., from Nov. 1, 1812 to Feb. 28, 1813. Ref: R. & L. 1812, AGO Page 25.

*ALLEN, ERASTUS, Sergeant and Ensign, Whiting. Served in company commanded by Capt. Salmon Foster, Col. Sumner's Regt., from April 13, 1814 to April 21, 1814; volunteered to go to Plattsburgh in September, 1814, and served 9 days in same company.

ALLEN, ETHAN,   Tunbridge. Volunteered to go to Plattsburgh in September, 1814 and served in Capt. David Knox's Company. Ref: Book 52, AGO Page 117.

ALLEN, ETHAN AUGUSTUS. Appointed Cadet, Military Academy, Dec. 10, 1804 (22); 2nd Lieutenant, Artillery, Nov. 14, 1806; 1st Lieutenant Oct. 1, 1809; transferred to Corps Artillery May 12, 1814; Captain July 25, 1814; honorably discharged June 15, 1815; reinstated May 17, 1816; honorably discharged June 1, 1821; died Jan. 6, 1855. Ref: Heitman's Historical Register and Dictionary USA.

ALLEN, FRANCIS, Sergeant. Served from May 1, 1814 to June 30, 1814 in Corps of Artillery comanded by Capt. Alexander S. Brooks. Ref: R. & L. 1812, AGO Page 31.

ALLEN, HANIBAL MONTESCUE. Appointed Cadet, Military Academy, June 15, 1803 (2); 2nd Lieutenant, Artillery, June 27, 1804; 1st Lieutenant Jan. 31, 1806; Captain Jan. 29, 1811; died May 11, 1813. Ref: Heitman's Historical Register and Dictionary USA.

ALLEN, HIRAM,   Shoreham. Volunteered to go to Plattsburgh in September, 1814, and served about 6 days in company commanded by Capt. Samuel Hand. Ref: Rev. J. F. Goodhue's History of Shoreham, Page 108.

‡*ALLEN, HORACE. Served in Capt. Lowery's Company, 4th Regt. (Williams') Vt. Militia. Pension Certificate No. 6333. Pension Certificate of widow, Mary, No. 6708.

‡ALLEN, IRA. Served in Captain Pettis' Company. Pension Certificate of widow, Cornelia A., No. 22018.

*ALLEN, IRA. Served in Lieut. Justus Foote's Company, Sumner's Regt., from April 12, 1814 to April 15, 1814.

ALLEN, IRA. Enlisted May 5, 1813 for 1 year in Capt. Daniel Farrington's Company, 30th Regt. Re-enlisted May 5, 1814 in Capt. James Taylor's Company, 30th Regt. Transferred to 29th Regt. April 6, 1814. Ref: R. & L. 1812, AGO Pages 50-51-53.

ALLEN, IRA C. Enlisted July 27, 1812 for a period of 5 years in company of late Capt. J. Brooks, commanded by Lieut. John I. Cromwell, Corps of U. S. Artillery Name appears on Muster Roll of company from April 30, 1814 to June 30,

1814. Served as Artificer. Ref: R. & L. 1812, AGO Page 18.

*ALLEN, IRAD. Served in Capt. Pettes' Company, Col. William Williams' Regt., Detached Militia, in U. S. service 4 months and 17 days in 1812.

*ALLEN, ISAAC,   Randolph. Volunteered to go to Plattsburgh in September, 1814, and served in company commanded by Capt. Lebbeus Egerton.

*ALLEN, James,   Franklin County. Served in Capt. Strait's Company, Col. Martindale's Regt., Detached Militia, in U. S. service 2 months and 13 days, 1812. Also volunteered to go to Plattsburgh September 11, 1814 and served in 15th or 22nd Regt. Ref: Hemenway's Vt. Gazetteer, Vol. 2, Page 392.

ALLEN, JAMES,   Montpelier. Volunteered to go to Plattsburgh in September, 1814, and served 8 days in company commanded by Capt. Timothy Hubbard. Ref: Book 52, AGO Pages 246 and 256.

ALLEN, JEREMIAH. Served in Capt. William Miller's Company, 30th Regt. Name appears on Muster Roll to Aug. 31, 1814. Servant to Ensign John Gilbert from July 11, 1814 to Aug. 31, 1814. Ref: R. & L. 1812, AGO Page 54.

‡ALLEN, JESSY. Served in Captain A Partridge's Company. Pension Certificate No. 4319.

‡ALLEN, JOEL,   Grand Isle. Volunteered to go to Plattsburgh in September, 1814, and served in company commanded by Capt. Abner Keeler. Pension Certificate of widow, Lara, No. 27153.

ALLEN, JOEL, JR. Volunteered to go to Plattsburgh in September, 1814, and served in company commanded by Capt Jonathan Jennings. Ref: Book 52, AGO Page 79.

*ALLEN, JOHN, Corporal. Served in company commanded by Capt. John Hackett, Col. Sumner's Regt., from April 12, 1814 to April 15, 1814.

ALLEN, JONATHAN. Served in Corps of Artillery commanded by Capt. Alexander S. Brooks. Name appears on Pay Roll to June 30, 1814. Discharged June 14, 1814. Ref: R. & L. 1812, AGO Page 31.

*ALLEN, JOSEPH. Served in company commanded by Capt. Salmon Foster, Col. Sumner's Regt., from April 13, 1814 to April 21, 1814.

ALLEN, JOSIAH,   Barre. Volunteered to go to Plattsburgh, September, 1814, and served 10 days in company commanded by Capt. Warren Ellis. Ref: Book 52, AGO Page 242.

*ALLEN, JOSIAH J.
Served in Capt. Persons' Company,
Col. Jonathan Williams Regt., Detached Militia, in U. S. service 2
months and 13 days, 1812.

ALLEN, JULIUS.
Volunteered to go to Plattsburgh,
September, 1814, and served in com-
pany commanded by Capt. Jonathan
Jennings of Chelsea. Ref: Book 52,
AGO Pages 79 and 81.

*ALLEN, LEVI.
Served in Capt. Daniel Farrington's
Company, 30th Regt. (also commanded
by Capt. Simeon Wright) from April
26, 1813 to April 26, 1814. Also served in Tyler's Regt., Vermont Militia.
Ref: R. & L. 1812, AGO, Pages 50-51.

ALLEN, LYMAN.
Served in Corps of Artillery commanded by Capt. Alexander S. Brooks
from May 1, 1814 to June 30, 1814.
Ref: R. & L. 1812, AGO Page 31.

*ALLEN, MOSES. Ensign
Served in Capt. John Palmer's Company of Militia, 1st Regt., 2nd Brig.,
3rd Div. Name appears on Muster
Roll from June 11, 1813 to June 14,
1813 and from Oct. 4, 1813 to Oct. 13,
1813.

ALLEN, NATHAN,   Enosburgh.
Volunteered to go to Plattsburgh, Sep-
tember, 1814. No organization given.
Ref: Book 51, AGO Page 188.

ALLEN, OBED.
Volunteered to go to Plattsburgh,
September, 1814, and served in com-
pany commanded by Capt. Jonathan
Jennings of Chelsea. Ref: Book 52,
AGO Pages 79 and 104.

*ALLEN, PETER. L., Lieutenant.
Served in 3rd Regiment, Vermont
Militia, commanded by Col. Tyler.

ALLEN, REUBEN,   Sudbury.
Volunteered to go to Plattsburgh,
September, 1814, and served 6 days
in company commanded by Capt.
Thomas Hall. Ref: Book 52, AGO
Page 122.

ALLEN, REUBEN,   Goshen.
Volunteered to go to Plattsburgh,
September, 1814, and served 5 days in
company commanded by Capt. Dur-
ham Sprague. Ref: Book 52, AGO
Page 129.

ALLEN, RICHARD, Adjutant.
Volunteered to go to Plattsburgh,
September, 1814, and served 6 days
in 2nd Regt., Vermont Militia. Ref:
Book 52, AGO Page 159.

*ALLEN, ROBERT.
Served in Capt. Mason's Company,
Col. Fifield's Regt., Detached Militia,
in U. S. service 3 months and 16
days, 1812.

*ALLEN, RUSSELL.
Served in Corning's Detachment, Vermont Militia.

ALLEN, SAMUEL,   Chelsea.
Enlisted June 15, 1813 for a period

of 5 years in company of late Capt.
J. Brooks, commanded by Lieut. John
I. Cromwell, Corps of U. S. Artillery.
Name appears on Muster Roll of com-
pany from April 30, 1814 to June 30,
1814. Also volunteered to go to
Plattsburgh, September, 1814 and serv-
ed in company commanded by Capt.
Jonathan Jennings. Ref: R. & L.
1812, AGO Page 18; Book 52, AGO
Pages 79 and 81.

*ALLEN, SETH.
Served in Capt. Wheeler's Company,
Col. Fifield's Regt., Detached Militia,
in U. S. service 6 months and 4 days,
1812.

*ALLEN, SETH.
Served in Capt. Start's Company, Col.
Martindale's Regt., Detached Militia,
in U. S. service 1 month and 5 days,
1812.

ALLEN, SILAS.
Enlisted Sept. 17, 1813 in Capt.
Daniel Farrington's Company, 30th
Regt. (also commanded by Capt.
Simeon Wright). Name appears on
Muster Roll from March 1, 1814 to
April 30, 1814. Ref: R. & L. 1812,
AGO Pages 50 and 51.

‡ALLEN, SIMON.
Served in Detachment of Recruits under the command of Lieut. V. R.
Goodrich, 11th Regt., from May 2,
1813 to Aug. 1, 1813. Pension Certificate No. 6909.

ALLEN, STEPHEN.   Franklin County.
Volunteered to go to Plattsburgh
September 11, 1814 and served in the
15th or 22nd Regt. Ref: Hemenway's
Vt. Gazetteer, Vol. 2, Page 391.

‡*ALLEN, THOMAS.
Served in Capt. Barns' Company, Col.
William Williams' Regt., Detached
Militia, in U. S. service 5 months,
1812. Also served in company of
Militia commanded by Capt. John M.
Eldridge, 1st Regt. 2nd Brig., 3rd
Div., from June 11, 1813 to June 14,
1813. Pension Certificate No. 10990.

*ALLEN, VIAL,   Calais.
Volunteered to go to Plattsburgh,
September, 1814, and served 8 days
in company commanded by Capt.
Gideon Wheelock.

*‡ALLEN, WILLIAM,   Vergennes.
Served in Capt. Mason's Company,
Col. Fifield's Regt., Detached Militia,
in U. S. service 6 months, 1812. Enlisted April 6, 1814 in Capt. Gideon
Spencer's Company, 30th Regt., and
transferred to 29th Regt. on same
date. Served in Capt. Eseck Sprague's
Company, Col. Sumner's Regt., from
April 12, 1814 to April 21, 1814. Volunteered to go to Plattsburgh, September, 1814, served 10 days in company commanded by Capt. Gideon
Spencer, and took part in the battle.
Pension Certificate No. 123. Pension
Certificate of widow, Lucretia, No.
13524.

*ALLICE, ARAD.
Served in 4th Regt., Vermont Militia,
commanded by Col. William Williams.

*ALLIS, ABEL A.
Served in Capt. Amos Robinson's
Company, Col. Dixon's Regt., from
Sept. 25, 1813 to Nov. 12, 1813.

‡*ALLIS, OREB.
Served in 4th Regt. Vt. Militia commanded by Col. William Williams, Detached Militia in U. S. service in 1812.
Also served in Captain Gunbring's
Company. Pension Certificate of
widow, Lucinda, No. 19551.

ALLISON, J. S., 1st Lieutenant and Aid,
Served on General Staff of the Northern Army commanded by Maj. Gen.
George Izard from July 1st to 31st,
1814. Ref: R. & L. 1812, AGO Page
28.

*ALLISON, WILLIAM.
Served in 1st Regt., Vt. Militia, commanded by Col. Martindale.

*ALMEN, BENNET.
Served in 1st Regt., Vt. Militia, commanded by Col. Martindale.

ALSTON, WILLIAM.
Served in Capt. Wright's Company,
Col. Martindale's Regt., Detached
Militia, in U. S. service 11 days, 1812.
Ref: Book 53, AGO Page 48.

ALVERSON, THOMAS.
Enlisted April 2, 1813 in Detachment
of Recruits under the command of
Capt. John W. Weeks, 11th Regt.
Name appears on Pay Roll to July 1,
1813. Ref: R. & L. 1812, AGO Page 4.

‡*AMBLER, FREDERIC.
Served in Capt. Lowry's Company,
Col. William Williams' Regt., De-
tached Militia, in U. S. service 4
months and 25 days, 1812. Pension
Certificate No. 6258.

*AMBLER, JAMES, Ensign,
Served in 3rd Regt., Vt. Militia, commanded by Col. Tyler.

AMBLER, JOHN, Huntington.
Volunteered to go to Plattsburgh,
September, 1814, and served at the
battle in company commanded by
Capt. Josiah N. Barrows. Ref: Book
51, AGO Page 77.

*AMBLER, SELEH.
Served in company of Cavalry commanded by Capt. John Munson, 3
Regt. (Tyler's) Vt. Militia, from Oct.
11, 1813 to Oct. 17, 1813.

AMBROME, JOHN, Franklin County.
Volunteered to go to Plattsburgh
Sept. 11, 1814 and served in 15th or
22nd Regt. Ref: Hemenway's Vt.
Gazetteer, Vol. 2, Page 391.

AMBROSE, RICHARD, Sergeant.
Enlisted June 2, 1812 for a period
of 5 years in company of late Capt.
J. Brooks, commanded by Lieut. John
I. Cromwell, Corps of U. S. Artillery.
Name appears on Muster Roll from
April 30, 1814 to June 30, 1814. Ref:
R. & L. 1812, AGO Page 18

*AMES, ABSOLOM.
Served in Capt. Walker's Company,
Col. Fifield's Regt., Detached Militia,
in U. S. service 2 months and 26
days, 1812.

*AMES, ISAAC, Montpelier.
Volunteered to go to Plattsburgh,
September, 1814 and served 8 days
in company commanded by Capt.
Timothy Hubbard. Also served with
Hospital Attendants, Vermont.

*AMES, RUSSELL, Shoreham.
Served in Capt. Robbins' Company,
Col. William Williams' Regt., Detached Militia, in U. S. service 4 months
and 29 days, 1812.

*AMES, SAMUEL.
Enlisted Jan. 23, 1813 in Detachment
of Recruits commanded by Capt. John
McNeil, Jr., 11th Regt. Name ap-
pears on Pay Roll to May 31, 1813.
Also served in Sumner's Regiment,
Vt. Militia. Ref: R. & L. 1812, AGO
Page 16.

AMES, THOMAS.
Served as private in the War of 1812
and was captured by troops July 5,
1813 at Fort Sclusher. Discharged
Oct. 31, 1814. Ref: Records of Naval
Records and Library, Navy Department.

*AMES, WALTER, Sergeant.
Served in company of Militia com-
manded by Lieut. Bates in 1st Regt.
(Judson's), from June 11, 1813 to
June 14, 1813.

AMES, WELLS.
Served in Detachment of Recruits un-
der command of Capt. John Mc-
Neil, Jr., 11th Regt. Name appears
on Pay Roll to May 31, 1813. Ref:
R. & L. 1812, AGO Page 16.

*AMES, WILLIAM.
Served in 2nd Regt., Vt. Militia, commanded by Col. Fifield.

*AMES, WILLIAM.
Served in company of Militia com-
manded by Lieut. Bates in 1st Regt.
(Judson's), from June 11, 1813 to
June 14, 1813.

*AMIDON, ALFRED, Randolph.
Served in company commanded by
Captains Wheatly and Wright in Col.
Fifield's Regt., Detached Militia, in
U. S. service 6 months, 1812. Volunteered to go to Plattsburgh, September, 1814, and served in company
commanded by Capt. Lebbeus Egerton.

*AMIDON, DYER.
Served in Col. Fifield's Regt., Detached Militia, in U. S. service 6
months, 1812. Volunteered to go to
Plattsburgh, September, 1814, and
served 7 days in company commanded
by Capt. Frederick Griswold, raised
in Brookfield, Vt.

AMIDON, ELIJAH, Sergeant, Braintree.
Volunteered to go to Plattsburgh
Sept. 10, 1814 and was at the battle.
Served in company commanded by
Capt. Lot Hudson. Ref: Book 52,
AGO Pages 24 and 28; Book 51, AGO
Page 295.

AMIDON, ROYAL, Braintree.
Volunteered to go to Plattsburgh
Sept. 10, 1814 and was at the battle.
Served about 10 days in company
commanded by Capt. Lot Hudson.
Ref: Book 52, AGO Pages 24 and 27

AMLING, EZRA.
Served in the War of 1812 and was captured by troops Dec. 19, 1813 at Fort Niagara. Died June 3, 1814. Ref: Records of Naval Records and Library, Navy Dept.

*****AMSDEN, ABEL.**
Enlisted in Capt. Shubael Wales' Company, Col. W. B. Sumner's Regt., April 12, 1814; transferred to Capt. Salmon Foster's Company, Sumner's Regt., April 13, 1814 and served to April 21, 1814.

*****AMSDEN, ABRAHAM.**
Served in Corning's Detachment, Vt. Militia.

*****AMSDEN, BENJAMIN.**
Served in Captain Howard's Company, Vt. Militia.

AMSDEN. DOWNING, Corporal.
Served in Captain Dodge's Company, Col. Fifield's Regt., Detached Militia, in U. S. service 2 months and 21 days, 1812. Ref: Book 53, AGO Page 12.

*****AMSDEN, LEVI.**
Served in Corning's Detachment, Vt. Militia.

*****AMSDON, ABRAM JR.**
Served in Corning's Detachment, Vt. Militia.

AMY, HEMAN, JR.
Volunteered to go to Plattsburgh, September, 1814, and served 7 days in company commanded by Capt. Asaph Smith. Ref: Book 51, AGO Page 20.

‡*AMY, JOHN.
Served in company commanded by Captains Durkee and Walker, Col. Fifield's Regt., Detached Militia, in U. S. service 6 months, 1812. Volunteered to go to Plattsburgh, September, 1814, and served 7 days in company commanded by Capt. Asaph Smith. Pension Certificate of widow, Cynthia G., No. 13425.

‡*ANDERSON, JAMES.
Served in Capt. Richardson's Company, Col. Martindale's Regt., Detached Militia, in U. S. service 2 months and 13 days, 1812. Pension Certificate No. 4157. Pension Certificate of widow, Amanda, No. 35123.

*****ANDERSON, JAMES.**
Enlisted Sept. 20, 1813 in company commanded by Capt. John Weed in Col. Isaac Clark's Regt. of Riflemen.

ANDERSON, JAMES.
Enlisted July 25, 1813 for a period of 5 years in company of late Capt. J. Brooks, commanded by Lieut. John I. Cromwell, Corps of U. S. Artillery. Name appears on Muster Roll of company from April 30, 1814 to June 30, 1814. Ref: R. & L. 1812, AGO Page 18.

ANDERSON, JOHN.
Appointed Cadet. Military Academy, Oct. 9, 1806 (3); 2nd Lieutenant Artillery Dec. 9, 1807; resigned May 1, 1811; 1st Lieutenant 19th Infantry July 6, 1812; Captain March 16, 1813; brevet Major Topographical Engineer April 12, 1813; honorably discharged June 15, 1815; reinstated May 2, 1816; brevet Lt. Colonel April 12, 1823 for 10 years faithful service in one grade; died Sept. 14, 1834. Ref: Heitman's Historical Register & Dictionary USA. Served as Major Topographical Engineer on General Staff of the Northern Army commanded by Maj. Gen. George Izard. Name appears on Pay Roll to July 31, 1814. Ref: R. & L. 1812, AGO Page 28.

ANDERSON, JOHN W.
Served in Detachment of Recruits under the command of Capt. Charles Follett, 11th Regt., from Feb. 17, 1813 to May 16, 1813. Ref: R. & L. 1812, AGO Page 13.

*****ANDERSON, JOSEPH.**
Served in Capt. Sabin's Company, Col. Jonathan Williams' Regt., Detached Militia, in U. S. service 2 months and 6 days, 1812.

ANDERSON, MATTHEW, Captain.   Ira.
Volunteered to go to Plattsburgh, September, 1814. Commanded Company from Ira. Ref: Hemenway's Vt. Gazetteer, Vol. 3, Page 783.

‡ANDERSON, NATHANIEL.
Served in Captain Caleb Hendee's Company. Pension Certificate of widow, Eunice, No. 38004.

*****ANDERSON, ROBERT JR.**
Served in company commanded by Capt. John Weed, Col. Isaac Clark's Regiment of Riflemen. Enlisted Sept. 20, 1813, and served to November, 1813.

*****ANDERSON, WILLIAM.**
Served in Capt. Hotchkiss' Company, Col. Martindale's Regt., Detached Militia, in U. S. service 2 months and 13 days, 1812.

ANDREWS, AMOS.   Montpelier.
Volunteered to go to Plattsburgh, September, 1814, and served 8 days in company commanded by Capt. Timothy Hubbard. Ref: Book 52. AGO Page 256.

‡ANDREWS. ASA.
Volunteered to go to Plattsburgh, September, 1814, and served 7 days in company commanded by Capt. Frederick Griswold, raised in Brookfield. Vt. Pension Certificate No. 32503.

ANDREWS, FRANCIS S.
Served in Regt. of Light Dragoons from Feb. 24, 1814 to June 30, 1814. Ref: R & L. 1812, AGO Page 21.

ANDREWS, GEORGE,   Franklin County.
Volunteered to go to Plattsburgh, Sept. 11, 1814 and served in 15th or 22nd Regt. Ref: Hemenway's Vt. Gazetteer, Vol. 2, Page 392.

ANDREWS, HIRAM.
Enlisted March 31, 1814 for period of the war in Capt. Gideon Spencer's

Company, 30th Regt. In Provost Guard. Joined June 1, 1814. Name appears on Muster Roll Dec. 30, 1813 to June 30, 1814. Ref: R. & L. 1812, AGO Page 56.

‡*ANDREWS, JACOB T.
Served in Capt. Walker's Company, Col. Fifield's Regt., Detached Militia, in U. S. service 6 months and 3 days, 1812. Volunteered to go to Plattsburgh, September, 1814, and served 7 days in company commanded by Capt. Frederick Griswold, raised in Brookfield, Vt. Pension Certificate of widow, Mary F., No. 9651.

*ANDREWS, JOHN,   Fairfax.
Served in Capt. Pettes' Company, Col. William Williams' Regt., Detached Militia, in U. S. service 4 months and 17 days, 1812. Volunteered to go to Plattsburgh, September, 1814, and served 8 days in company commanded by Capt. Josiah Grout.

ANDREWS, JOSEPH,   Johnson.
Volunteered to go to Plattsburgh, September, 1814, and served 4 days in Capt. Thomas Waterman's Company, Dixon's Regt. Ref: Book 51, AGO Page 208.

*ANDREWS, JOSEPH,   Montpelier.
Served in Capt. E. Walker's Company, Col. Fifield's Regt., Detached Militia, in U. S. service 6 months 5 days, 1812. Volunteered to go to Plattsburgh, September, 1814, and served 8 days in company commanded by Capt. Timothy Hubbard. Also served with Hospital Attendants, Vermont.

ANDREWS, SAMUEL, Corporal,
Served in company of late Capt. J. Brooks, commanded by Lt. John I. Cromwell, Corps of U. S. Artillery. Name appears on Muster Roll of company from April 30, 1814 to June 30, 1814. Ref: R. & L. 1812, AGO Page 18.

ANDREWS, SAMUEL M.
Served as a carpenter in Company of Artificers commanded by Alexander Parris from May 1, 1814 to June 30, 1814. Ref: R. & L. 1812, AGO Page 24.

ANDREWS, SETH.
Served in Detachment of Recruits under the command of Capt. Charles Follett, 11th Regt., from March 18, 1813 to June 17, 1813. Ref: R. & L. 1812, AGO Page 13.

ANDRUS, BRADFORD,   Pittsford.
Volunteered to go to Plattsburgh, September, 1814, and served 8 days in company commanded by Capt. Caleb Hendee. Ref: Book 52, AGO Page 124.

ANDRUS, ETHAN,   Cornwall.
Volunteered to go to Plattsburgh, September, 1814, and served in company commanded by Capt Edmund B. Hill, Sumner's Regt. Ref: Rev. Lyman Mathews' History of Cornwall, Page 344.

*ANDRUS, JOSEPH B., Musician.
Enlisted Sept. 25, 1813 in company commanded by Capt. N. B. Eldridge, Col. Dixon's Regt.

ANDRUS, NATHANIEL K.   Pittsford.
Volunteered to go to Plattsburgh, September, 1814, and served 8 days in company commanded by Capt. Caleb Hendee. Ref: Book 52, AGO Page 124.

*ANDRUS, ORRIN.
Served in company commanded by Capt. Shubael Wales, Col. W. B. Sumner's Regt., from April 12, 1814 to April 21, 1814.

ANGEL, JAMES, C, Corporal,
Served in Capt. Taylor's Company, 30th Inf., from May 7, 1814 to June 19, 1815. Ref: R. & L. 1812, AGO Page 23.

ANGEL, NEWELL, Ensign, West Haven.
Volunteered to go to Plattsburgh, September, 1814 and served 4 days in Capt. David B. Phippeney's Company. Ref: Book 52, AGO Page 146.

*ANGELL, JAMES.
Served in Capt. Cross' Company, Col. Martindale's Regt. Detached Militia, in U. S. service 2 months and 13 days, 1812.

‡ANGEVINE, OLIVER L.,   Poultney.
Volunteered to go to Plattsburgh, September, 1814, and served 3 days in company commanded by Capt. Briant Ransom. Pension Certificate of widow, Sally, No. 27370.

ANGEVINE, STEPHEN. Poultney or St. Albans. Served in Capt. John Wires' Company, 30th Regt., from June 1, 1813 to May, 1814. Ref: R. & L. 1812, AGO Page 40.

*ANNICE JOSEPH.
Served in Capt. Barns' Company, Col. William Williams' Regt. Detached Militia, in U. S. service 5 months, 1812.

*ANNING, ROBERT.
Served in Capt. Edmund B. Hill's Company, Col. Sumner's Regt., from April 12, 1814 to April 21, 1814.

‡*ANNIS, JAMES,   Corinth.
Served in Capt. Rogers' Company, Col Fifield's Regt. Detached Militia, in U. S. service 2 months and 10 days, 1812. Volunteered to go to Plattsburgh, September, 1814, and served 7 days in company commanded by Capt Frederick Griswold, raised in Brookfield, Vt. Pension Certificate No. 4639. Pension Certificate of widow, Betsey, No. 29526.

‡ANNIS, JOSEPH.
Served in Capt. Hezekiah Barnes' Company, 1st Regt. Pension Certificate No. 7237.

ANNIS, SOLOMON.
Volunteered to go to Plattsburgh, September, 1814, and served 7 days in company commanded by Capt. Frederick Griswold, raised in Brookfield, Vt. Ref: Book 52, AGO Page 52.

ANNIS, THOMAS.   Thetford.
Volunteered to go to Plattsburgh,
September, 1814, and went as far as
Bolton, Vt. Served 6 days in com-
pany commanded by Capt. Salmon
Howard, 2nd Regt. Ref: Book 52,
AGO Page 15.

*ANNIS, WILLIAM.
Served in Capt. Rogers' Company,
Col. Fifield's Regt. Detached Militia,
in U. S. service 5 months and 2 days,
1812.

*ANNON, ROBERT.
Served in Sumner's Regt., Vt. Militia.

ANTHON, PETER.
Served in Corps of Artillery command-
ed by Capt. Alexander S. Brooks from
Sept. 1, 1813 to June 30, 1814. Ref:
R. & L. 1812, AGO Page 31.

APES, WILLIAM.
Served in Corps of Artillery commanded by Capt. Alexander S. Brooks
from May 1 to June 30, 1814. Ref:
R. & L. 1812, AGO Page 31.

ARBUCKLE, JAMES,   Montpelier.
Volunteered to go to Plattsburgh,
September, 1814 and served in com-
pany commanded by Capt. Timothy
Hubbard. Ref: Book 52, AGO Pages
212 and 256.

*ARBUCKLE, JOHN.
Served in 4th Regt. Vt. Militia, commanded by Col. John Peck.

ARBUCKLE, WILLIAM,   Barre.
Volunteered to go to Plattsburgh,
September, 1814, and served 9 days
in company commanded by Capt.
Warren Ellis. Ref: Book 52, AGO
Pages 224 and 242.

*ARCHER, ASA.
Served in Capt. Richardson's Company, Col. Martindale's Regt. Detached Militia, in U. S. service 2 months
and 13 days, 1812. Enlisted May 25,
1813 for 1 year in Capt. Daniel Farrington's Company (also commanded
by Capt. Simeon Wright), 30th Regt.
Name appears on Muster Roll from
March 1, 1814 to April 30, 1814. Ref:
R. & L. 1812, AGO Pages 50-51.

ARDAWAY, NEHEMIAH.
Served in Capt. Amos Robinson's
Company, Dixon's Regt., from Sept.
25, 1813 to Nov. 12, 1813. Ref: Book
52, AGO Page 271.

*ARDIN, TABOR.
Served in 1st Regt. Vt. Militia, commanded by Col. Martindale.

ARLIN, JOHN.
Enlisted Feb. 2, 1813 in Detachment
of Recruits under the command of
Capt. Edgerton, 11th Regt. Name ap-
pears on Pay Roll to May 1, 1813.
Ref: R. & L. 1812, AGO Page 3.

*ARMINGTON, HEZEKIAH.
Served in Capt. Wheeler's Company,
Col. Fifield's Regt. Detached Militia,
in U S. service 6 months, 1812.

ARMORY, JOSEPH,   Franklin County.
Volunteered to go to Plattsburgh,
Sept. 11, 1814 and served in the 15th
or 22nd Regt. Ref: Hemenway's Vt.
Gazetteer, Vol. 2, Page 392.

*ARMS, JESSE.
Served in Corning's Detachment, Vt.
Militia.

ARMSTRONG, AMOS.
Age 24 years; 5 feet 9½ inches high;
light complexion; light hair; blue
eyes; by profession a farmer; born
in Ballstown, N. Y. Enlisted at Ballstown, N. Y. May 27, 1814; discharged at Burlington, Vt. 1815. Name
appears on Muster Roll of Capt.
Gideon Spencer's Company, 30th
Regt. from Dec. 30, 1813 to June 30,
1814; joined June 30, 1814. Name
appears on Muster Roll of Capt.
Miller's Company, 30th Regt., to Aug.
31, 1814. Ref: R. & L. 1812, AGO
Pages 54-55-56.

*ARMSTRONG, CHAUNSEY,   Shoreham.
Served in company commanded by
Capt. James Gray, Jr., Sumner's
Regt., from April 12, 1814 to May 20,
1814. Volunteered to go to Platts-
burgh, September, 1814, and served
6 days in Capt. Samuel Hand's Com-
pany. Ref: Book 52, AGO Page 279;
Rev. J. F. Goodhue's History of
Shoreham, Page 108.

‡ARMSTRONG, CHESTER.
Served under Captains Cutting, Hand,
Halliday and Plimpton. Pension Certificate No. 26739. Pension Certificate
of widow, Eunice, No. 42234.

*ARMSTRONG, ELLIOTT,   Shoreham.
Served in company commanded by
Capt. James Gray, Jr., Sumner's
Regt., from April 12, 1814 to May 20,
1814. Also served in Capt. John Robbins' Company, Col. William Williams' Regt. Ref: Book 52, AGO
Page 279; Rev. J. F. Goodhue's History of Shoreham, Page 107.

‡ARMSTRONG, IRA.
Served with his team. Pension Certificate No. 32686.

*ARMSTRONG, JOHN.
Served in Capt. George Fisher's Company, Sumner's Regt., from April 12,
1814 to May 20, 1814.

‡*ARMSTRONG, PHINEAS,   Pawlet.
Served in Capt. Scovell's Company,
Col. Martindale's Regt. Detached
Militia, in U. S. service 2 months and
21 days, 1812. Also served in Capt.
Scofield's Company. Pension Certifi-
cate of widow, Eunice, No. 385.

ARMSTRONG, RICHARD.
Aged 44 years; 5 feet 10 inches high;
light complexion; brown hair; blue
eyes; by profession a farmer; born
in Bedford, N. Y. Enlisted April
29, 1814 at Ballstown, N. Y. Discharged at Burlington, Vt. in 1815.
Name appears on Muster Roll of
Capt. Gideon Spencer's Company, 30th
Regt., from Dec. 30, 1813 to June 30,
1814; joined June 30, 1814. Name
appears on Muster Roll of Capt. William Miller's Company to Aug. 31,
1814. Ref: R. & L. 1812, AGO Pages
54-55-56.

‡*ARNOLD, ANDREW, Lieutenant and
Captain.
Appointed 1st Lieutenant 31st Inf.
April 30, 1813; Captain Jan. 11, 1814;

honorably discharged June 15, 1815. Served as lieutenant in 2nd Regt. (Fifield's) and also served in Capt. Edgerton's Company. Pension Certificate No. 13979.

*ARNOLD, GAMALIN, Ensign.
Served in 2nd Regt. Vt. Militia, commanded by Col. Fifield.

ARNOLD, LEMUEL, Franklin County.
Volunteered to go to Plattsburgh, Sept. 11, 1814 and served in 15th or 22nd Regt. Ref: Hemenway's Vt. Gazetteer, Vol. 2, Page 392.

*ARNOLD, LEVI.
Enlisted Sept. 18, 1813 in Capt. Isaac Finch's Company, Col. Isaac Clark's Rifle Corps and served until November, 1813.

*ARNOLD, LUTHER, Pawlet.
Served in Capt. Hotchkiss' Company, Col. Martindale's Regt. Detached Militia, in U. S. service 2 months and 13 days, 1812.

*ARNOLD, NATHAN.
Served in Capt. Roswell Hunt's Company, 3rd Regt. (Tyler's), from Oct. 5, 1813 to Oct. 16, 1813.

ARNOLD VANZELLEA, Eaton, N. Y.
Served in Capt. Lynd's Company, 29th Inf., from May 1, 1814 to July 9, 1814. Ref: R. & L. 1812, AGO Page 30.

*ASA, LEWIS.
Served in Corning's Detachment, Vt. Militia.

ASH, JOSHUA.
Served in Capt. Haig's Corps of Light Dragoons from May 1, 1814 to June 30, 1814. Ref: R. & L. 1812, AGO Page 20.

*ASHLEY, ARCHIBALD, Sergeant.
Enlisted Sept. 25, 1813 in Capt. Prentiss' Company, Col. Dixon's Regt. Detached Militia, and served 1 month and 23 days.

ASHLEY, CALVIN.
Volunteered to go to Plattsburgh, September, 1814 and went as far as Bolton, Vt. Served 4 days in company commanded by Lieut. Phineus Kimball, West Fairlee. Ref: Book 52, AGO Page 46.

ASHLEY, ELISHA.
Appointed 1st Lieutenant, 11th Inf., April 17, 1812; resigned March 13, 1813. Ref: Governor and Council, Vt., Vol. 6, Page 473.

‡*ASHLEY, ELISHA JR.
Enlisted Sept. 25, 1813 in company commanded by Capt. Jonathan Prentiss, Jr., Col. Dixon's Regt. Pension Certificate of widow, Harriet M., No. 11174.

*ASHLEY, ISAAC.
Served in Capt. Ormsbee's Company, Col. Martindale's Regt. Detached Militia, in U. S. service 2 months and 14 days, 1812.

ASHLEY, JONAS.
Served as private in War of 1812 and was captured by troops Sept. 17, 1814 at Fort Erie. Discharged Nov. 8th. Ref: Records of Naval Records and Library, Navy Department.

ASHLEY, TIMOTHY.
Enlisted May 24, 1813 in Capt. James Taylor's Company, 30th Regt. Transferred to Capt. Gideon Spencer's Company, 30th Regt. and served to May 24, 1814. Ref: R. & L. 1812, AGO Pages 52-56-58.

‡*ASHLEY, WILLIAM.
Served in Capt. Dodge's Company, Col. Fifield's Regt. Detached Militia, in U. S. service 2 months and 21 days, 1812. Enlisted Sept. 25, 1813 in company commanded by Capt. Jonathan Prentiss, Jr., Dixon's Regt. Pension Certificate No. 5274. Pension Certificate of widow, Lucinda L., No. 31969.

*ASKEY, JOHN.
Served in 1st Regt., Vt. Militia, commanded by Col. Martindale

*ASSELTINE, BARTIS.
Enlisted Sept 28, 1813 in Capt. Asahel Langworthy's Company, Col. Isaac Clark's Rifle Corps and served to November, 1813. Also served in 2nd Regt. Vt. Militia commanded by Col. Fifield.

ASTER, ISAAC.
Served in Capt. Rogers' Company, Col. Fifield's Regt. Detached Militia, in U. S. service 4 months and 3 days, 1812. Ref: Book 53, AGO Page 18.

*ATCHINSON, JOHN.
Enlisted Sept. 25, 1813 and served 1 month and 23 days in Capt. Birge's Company, Col. Dixon's Regt. Detached Militia in U. S. service.

*ATHERTON, CHESTER, Huntington.
Volunteered to go to Plattsburgh, September, 1814, was present at the battle, and served in company commanded by Capt. Josiah N. Barrows. Also served in 1st Regt. Vt. Militia, commanded by Col. Judson. Ref: Book 51, AGO Page 77.

‡*ATHERTON, ELIHU.
Served in Capt. O. Lowry's Company, Col. William Williams' Regt. Detached Militia, in U. S. service 4 months and 26 days, 1812. Also served in Capt. Oliver Sonney's Company. Pension Certificate No. 6335.

*ATHERTON, ELIHU, JR.
Served in 4th Regt. Vt. Militia commanded by Col. John Peck.

*ATHERTON, JOSEPH.
Served in 1st Regt. Vt. Militia commanded by Col. Judson.

ATHERTON, JOSEPH H., Brattleboro.
Appointed Ensign 31st Inf., March 28, 1814; 3rd Lieutenant May 2, 1814; honorably discharged June 15, 1815. Ref: Heitman's Historical Register & Dictionary USA; Governor and Council Vt. Vol. 6, Page 478.

*ATHERTON, OBEDIAH.
Served in 1 Regt. Vt. Militia commanded by Col. Judson.

*ATKINS, GEORGE, Captain, Waterbury.
Volunteered to go to Plattsburgh,
September, 1814.. Served 11 days and
took part in the battle. Commanded
company in 4th Regt. (Peck's) Vt.
Militia, raised at Waterbury.

*ATKINS, HORATIO G.
Served in 4th Regt. Vt. Militia, commanded by Col. John Peck.

‡*ATKINS, IRA,   Cabot.
Served in Capt. Hezekiah Barns' Com-
pany, 1st Regt., 2nd Brig., 3rd Div.,
from June 11, 1813 to June 14, 1813.
Volunteered to go to Plattsburgh,
September, 1814, and served 4 days
in Capt. Anthony Perry's Company.
Pension Certificate of widow, Betsey,
No. 21303.

*ATKINS, JOHN.
Served in Capt. S. Pettes' Company,
Col. William Williams' Regt. Detached Militia, in U. S. service 4 months
and 19 days, 1812.

*ATKINS, JOHN JR.
Served in Corning's Detachment, Vt.
Militia.

ATKINS, JOSIAH, Sergeant.
Served in Capt. Simeon Wright's Company from April 22, 1813 to April
21, 1814. Ref: R. & L. 1812, AGO
Page 51.

ATWATER, SIMEON.
Served from March 24, 1813 to June
23, 1813 in Detachment of Recruits
commanded by Capt. Charles Follett,
11th Regt. Ref: R. & L. 1812, AGO
Page 13.

*ATWATER, THOMAS.
Served from June 11, 1813 to June 4,
1813 in Capt. Moses Jewett's Company of Militia, 1st Regt., 2nd Brig.,
3rd Div. Ref: R. & L. 1812, AGO
Page 42.

ATWOOD, AMASA,   Shoreham.
Volunteered to go to Plattsburgh,
September, 1814 and served about 6
days in company commanded by
Capt. Samuel Hand. Ref: Rev. J. F.
Goodhue's History of Shoreham, Page
108.

‡*ATWOOD, BENJAMIN.
Served from April 12th to April 21,
1814 in Capt. Shubael Wales' Company. Col. W. B. Sumner's Regt. Volunteered to go to Plattsburgh, September, 1814 and served in Capt. Edmund B. Hill's Company. Sumner's
Regt. Pension Certificate No. 32046.

ATWOOD, DANIEL.
Enlisted in Capt. Benjamin Bradford's
Company. Name appears on Muster
Roll from May 31, 1813 to Aug. 31,
1813. On command on board the
scows. Ref: R. & L. 1812, AGO Page
26.

*ATWOOD, EBENEZER,   Barnard.
Served from April 12, 1814 to May
20, 1814 in company of Capt. James
Gray Jr., Col. Sumner's Regt.

ATWOOD, JACOB, Sergeant,   Shoreham.
Volunteered to go to Plattsburgh,
September, 1814, and served about 6
days in Captain Samuel Hand's Company. Ref: Rev. J. F. Goodhue's History of Shoreham, Page 107.

ATWOOD, JOHN.
Appointed 3rd Lieutenant, 31st Inf.,
April 30, 1813; resigned Jan. 11, 1814.
Ref: Heitman's Historical Register
and Dictionary USA.

ATWOOD, JOSEPH,   Shoreham.
Served in Capt. Benjamin Bradford's
Company of Infantry. Name ap-
pears on Muster Roll from May 31,
1813 to Aug. 31, 1813. Volunteered
to go to Plattsburgh, September, 1814
and served 6 days in Capt. Samuel
Hand's Company. Ref: R. & L. 1812,
AGO Page 26; Rev. J. F. Goodhue's
History of Shoreham, Page 107.

ATWOOD, PARKER,   Shoreham.
Volunteered to go to Plattsburgh,
September, 1814 and served about 6
days in Capt. Samuel Hand's Com-
pany. Ref: Rev. J. F. Goodhue's
History of Shoreham, Page 108.

ATWOOD, THOMAS,   Shoreham.
Volunteered to go to Plattsburgh,
September, 1814, and served about a
week in Capt. Samuel Hand's Company. Ref: Book 51, AGO Page 63.

*AUBERY, JOHN F.
Served in Tyler's Regiment, Vt.
Militia.

*AUBERY, OLIVER M.
Served in Capt. Rogers' Company,
Col. Fifield's Regt. Detached Militia,
in U. S. service 2 months and 18
days, 1812.

*AUDWAY, NEHEMIAH.
Served in Dixon's Regiment, Vt. Militia.

AUSTIN, ABIEL, 2nd Lieutenant, Bethel.
Volunteered to go to Plattsburgh,
September, 1813, and served 8 days
in company commanded by Capt. Ne-
hemiah Noble. Ref: Book 51, AGO
Pages 218 and 219.

‡*AUSTIN, ASA,   Waterbury.
Volunteered to go to Plattsburgh,
September, 1814, and was at the
battle. Served 11 days in Capt.
George Atkins' Company, 4th Regt.
(Peck's). Pension Certificate No.
21402.

*AUSTIN, BENJAMIN, Corporal, Rich-
ford. Served from Sept. 25, 1813 to
Nov. 3, 1813 in Captain Martin D.
Follett's Company, Col. Dixon's Regt.

*AUSTIN, BENJAMIN.
Served from Sept. 25, 1813 to Nov.
14, 1813 in company commanded by
Capt. N. B. Eldridge in Col. Dixon's
Regt.

AUSTIN, CHARLES,   Franklin County.
Volunteered to go to Plattsburgh
Sept. 11, 1814 and served in 15th or
22nd Regt. Ref: Hemenway's Vt.
Gazetteer, Vol. 2, Page 392.

*AUSTIN, DANIEL H.,   Waterbury.
Volunteered to go to Plattsburgh,
September, 1814 and served 11 days
in Capt. George Atkins' Company,
4th Regt. (Peck's).

*AUSTIN, DAVID.   Waterbury.
Volunteered to go to Plattsburgh,
September, 1814 and served 11 days
as waiter in Capt. George Atkins'
Company, 4th Regt. (Peck's).

‡AUSTIN, ELIJAH.
Served in Capt. Ephraim Hackett's
Company. Pension Certificate No.
34558.

*AUSTIN, ETHAN.
Enlisted Sept. 25, 1813 in company
commanded by Capt. Jonathan Prentiss Jr., Col. Dixon's Regt.

AUSTIN, FREDERICK,   Georgia.
Volunteered to go to Plattsburgh,
September, 1814, and served 8 days.
No organization given. Ref: Book
51, AGO Pages 105 and 183.

*AUSTIN, GEORGE W.
Served from April 12, 1814 to April
21, 1814 in Lieut. Justus Foote's
Company, Sumner's Regt.

*AUSTIN, HENRY.
Enlisted Sept. 25, 1813 in company
commanded by Capt. Jonathan Prentiss Jr., Col. Dixon's Regt.

*AUSTIN, ISAAC,   Marshfield.
Served in 2 Regt. (Fifield's) Vt. Militia.

AUSTIN, JOHN.
Served in Captain Chadwick's Com-
pany. Ref: R. & L. 1812, AGO
Page 32.

AUSTIN, LEVI,   Stowe.
Volunteered to go to Plattsburgh,
September, 1814 and served in Capt.
Nehemiah Perkins' Company, 4th
Regt. (Peck's). Ref: Hemenway's Vt.
Gazetteer Vol. 2, Page 742.

‡*AUSTIN, LYMAN, Musician.
Served from Sept. 25, 1813 to Oct. 25,
1813 in Capt. N. B. Eldridge's Company, Dixon's Regt. Pension Certificate of widow, Hannah, No. 28650.

‡*AUSTIN, NATHANIEL.
Served in Capt. Bingham's Company,
Col. Jonathan Williams' Regt. Detached Militia, in U. S. service 2
months and 9 days, 1812. Pension
Certificate of widow, Emily, No.
8172.

‡*AUSTIN, ORIN,   Waterbury.
Volunteered to go to Plattsburgh,
September, 1814, and was at the
battle. Served 11 days in Capt.
George Atkins' Company, 4 Regt.
(Peck's). Pension Certificate No.
22382.

*AUSTIN, PHINEAS.
Served in Capt. Durkee's Company,
Col. Fifield's Regt. Detached Militia,
in U. S. service 2 months and 21
days, 1812.

*AUSTIN, RAYMOND, Drummer, Rich-
ford. Enlisted Sept. 25, 1813 and
served 1 month and 23 days in Capt.
Martin D. Follett's Company, Col.
Dixon's Regt.

AUSTIN, RUFUS, Fairfax, Swanton, or
Highgate. Served in Capt. Conrad
Saxe's Company, Col. William Wil-
liams' Regt., 3 months and 4 days,
1812. Enlisted Aug. 8, 1812 in com-
pany commanded by Capt. Joseph
Beeman Jr., 11th Regt. U. S. Inf.
under Col. Ira Clark. Served in
Lieut. V. R. Goodrich's Company,
11th Regt.; name appears on Pay
Roll of company for January and
February, 1813, and for period from
July 15th to Dec. 8, 1813. Ref: R.
& L. 1812, AGO Page 11; Book 53,
AGO Page 50; Hemenway's Vt. Ga-
zetteer, Vol. 2, Pages 402 and 444.

AUSTIN, SAMUEL.
Enlisted Apr. 24, 1813 in Capt. James
Taylor's Company, 30th Regt.; name
appears on Muster Roll from Nov.
30, 1813 to Dec. 31, 1813; transferred
to Capt. Gideon Spencer's Company,
30th Regt., and served to April 25,
1814. Ref: R. & L. 1812, AGO Pages
52, 56, 59.

*AUSTIN, SOLOMON.
Enlisted in Capt. James Taylor's Company, 30th Regt., April 24, 1813; name
appears on Muster Roll of company
from Nov. 30, 1813 to Dec. 31, 1813;
transferred to Capt. Gideon Spencer's
Company and served to April 25, 1814.

AUSTIN, STEPHEN, Corporal.
Enlisted in U. S. Marine Corps May
21, 1812 at New York. Ref: Book 52,
AGO Page 294.

*AUSTIN, THOMAS.
Served in Capt. Wright's Company,
Col. Fifield's Regt. Detached Militia,
in U. S. service 6 months, 1812.

AUSTIN, TIMOTHY,   Georgia.
Volunteered to go to Plattsburgh,
September, 1814, and served 8 days.
No organization given. Ref: Book
51, AGO Pages 105 and 183.

*AVEREST, DUDLEY, 3rd Lieutenant.
Served in Capt. George Fisher's Company, Sumner's Regt., from April 12,
1814 to May 20, 1814.

AVERILL, DAVID W.,   Barre.
Volunteered to go to Plattsburgh,
September, 1814, and served 9 days
in Capt. Warren Ellis' Company. Ref:
Book 52, Pages 233 and 242.

‡*AVERILL, GIDEON.
Served in 1 Regt. (Judson's) Vt. Militia. Also served in Captain Kinney's
Company. Pension Certificate of
widow, Samatha, No. 27419.

AVERILL, JESSE, Corporal, Waitsfield.
Volunteered to go to Plattsburgh,
September, 1814, and served 4 days
in Capt. Mathias S. Jones, Company.
Ref: Book 52, AGO Pages 170 and 207.

‡AVERILL, JOHN,   Waitsfield.
Volunteered to go to Plattsburgh,
September, 1814, and served 4 days

in Capt. Mathias S. Jones' Company. Also served in Captain Walker's Company. Pension Certificate No. 33575.

AVERILL, JOSEPH.
Enlisted May 11, 1813 in Capt. James Taylor's Company, 30th Regt.; name appears on Muster Roll from Nov. 30, 1813 to Dec. 31, 1813; transferred to Capt. Gideon Spencer's Company, 30th Regt., and served to May 12, 1814. Ref: R. & L. 1812, AGO Pages 52, 56, 58.

AVERILL, OLIVER, Corporal, Williamstown. Volunteered to go to Plattsburgh, September, 1814, and served 8 days in Captain David Robinson's Company. Ref: Book 52, AGO Page 9.

‡AVERILL, ROBERT.
Served in Capt. J. Kinney's Company and Capt. Barton's Company. Pension Certificate No. 21403. Pension Certificate of widow, Acsah, No. 29329.

*AVERILL, SAMUEL, Corporal.
Served in company commanded by Capt. James Gray, Jr., Sumner's Regt., from April 12, 1814 to May 20, 1814.

*AVERILL, TRUMAN.
Served in Capt. Roswel Hunt's Company, 3rd Regt., from Oct. 5, 1813 to Oct. 16, 1813.

AVERY, ABRAHAM, Cornwall.
Volunteered to go to Plattsburgh, September, 1814, and was at the battle. Served in Capt. Edmund B. Hill's Company, Sumner's Regt. Ref: Book 51, AGO Page 13.

AVERY, ALEXANDER.
Enlisted April 28, 1813 in Capt. James Taylor's Company, 30th Regt.; name appears on Muster Roll from Nov. 30, 1813 to Dec. 31, 1813; transferred to Capt. Gideon Spencer's Company, 30th Regt. and served to May 27, 1814. Ref: R. & L. 1812, AGO Pages 52, 56,59.

AVERY, CHRISTOPHER, Lieutenant, Corinth. Volunteered to go to Plattsburgh, September, 1814, and served in company commanded by Capt. Abel Jackman. Ref: Book 52, AGO Page 44.

*‡AVERY, DANIEL. Cornwall.
Served in Capt. Edmund B. Hill's Company, Sumner's Regt., from April 12, 1814 to April 21, 1814; also took part in the Battle of Plattsburgh, September, 1814, with the same company. Pension Certificate No. 29737.

*AVERY, GEORGE W.
Served in Capt. Rogers' Company, Col. Fifield's Regt. Detached Militia, in U. S. service 5 months and 27 days, 1812.

*AVERY, JACOB.
Served from March 8, 1813 to June 7, 1813 with Detachment of Recruits under the command of Capt. Jonathan Starks, 11th Regt. Also served with Hospital Attendants, Vermont. Ref: R. & L. 1812, AGO Page 19.

AVERY, JOHN. Cornwall.
Served in Capt. Asahel Scovell's Company, Col. Clark's Rifle Regt., from Oct. 15, 1813 to Nov. 17, 1813. Volunteered to go to Plattsburgh, September, 1814, and served in Capt. Edmund B. Hill's Company, Sumner's Regt. Ref: R. & L. 1812, AGO Page 22; Book 51, AGO Page 13.

AVERY, MATTHIAS.
Served from March 4, 1813 to June 3, 1813 in Detachment of Recruits under the command of Capt. Jonathan Starks, 11th Regt. Ref: R. & L. 1812, AGO Page 19.

AVERY, NEWELL W.
Served from May 1, 1814 to June 30, 1814 in Capt. Alexander Brooks' Corps of Artillery. Ref: R. & L. 1812, AGO Page 31.

*AVERY, ROBERT.
Served in 1st Regt., Vt. Militia, under Col. Judson.

AVERY, ROGER, Cornwall.
Volunteered to go to Plattsburgh, September, 1814, and was at the battle. Served in Capt. Edmund B. Hill's Company, Sumner's Regt. Ref: Book 51, AGO Page 13.

AVERY, SHEDRAH.
Served from March 10, 1813 to June 9, 1813 in Detachment of Recruits under the command of Capt. Jonathan Starks, 11th Regt. Ref: R. & L. 1812, AGO Page 19.

*AVERY, SIMEON.
Served in Capt. Rogers' Company, Col. Fifield's Regt. Detached Militia, in U. S. service 5 months and 27 days, 1812. Ref: Book 53, AGO Page 30.

*AVORY, JOHN, Enosburgh.
Served in Regiment of Riflemen, Vermont Volunteers, September-November, 1813.

*AVREL, ROBERT, Shelburne.
Volunteered to go to Plattsburgh, September, 1814, and served in 1st Regt., Major Luman Judson's command.

*AYER, JOHN.
Served in Capt. Briggs' Company, Col. Jonathan Williams Regt. Detached Militia, in U. S. service 2 months and 13 days, 1812.

‡*AYERS, BENJAMIN. Fairfield.
Served in Capt. Kendall's Company, Col. William Williams' Regt. Detached Militia, in U. S. service 4 months and 23 days, 1812. Also served in Capt. George Kimball's Company. Pension Certificate of widow, Sally, No. 30826.

AYERS, ELIJAH.
Enlisted June 18, 1812 for a period of 5 years in Company of late Capt. J. Brooks, commanded by Lieut. John I. Cromwell, Corps of U. S. Artillery. Name appears on Muster Roll from April 30, 1814 to June 30, 1814. Ref: R. & L. 1812, AGO Page 18.

*AYERS, JOEL.
Served in Capt. Shubael Wales Company, Col. W. B. Sumner's Regt., from April 12, 1814 to April 21, 1814.

‡AYERS, JOHN P.,   Plainfield.
Volunteered to go to Plattsburgh, September, 1814, and served 9 days in company commanded by Capt. James English. Pension Certificate of widow, Sally, No. 23595.

‡AYERS, JOSEPH,   Plainfield.
Enlisted March 27, 1813 in Company of late Captain J. Brooks, commanded by Lieut. John I. Cromwell, Corps of U. S. Artillery; name appears on Muster Roll of Company from April 30, 1814 to June 30, 1814. Volunteered to go to Plattsburgh, September, 1814, and served 9 days in Capt. James English's Company. Also served in Captain Bachelder's Company. Pension Certificate of widow, Anna B., No. 13698.

AYRES, JACOB,   Franklin County.
Volunteered to go to Plattsburgh Sept. 11, 1814 and served in 15th or 22nd Regt. Ref: Hemenway's Vt. Gazetteer, Vol. 2, Page 392.

*AZETTIN, BATES.
Served in 2nd Regiment, Vt. Militia, commanded by Col. Fifield.

*BABBITT, JACOB.
Served in Capt. Mason's Company, Col. Fifield's Regt. Detached Militia, in U. S. service 6 months in 1812.

*BABCOCK, AUGUSTUS.
Served in Capt. Bingham's Company, Col. Jonathan Williams' Regt. Detached Militia, in U. S. service 2 months and 9 days, 1812.

*BABCOCK, BENJAMIN,   Richmond.
Served in Capt. Hezekiah Barns' Company, 1st Regt., 2nd Brig., 3rd Div., from June 11, 1813 to June 14, 1813. Volunteered to go to Plattsburgh, September, 1814, and served 9 days in Capt. Roswell Hunt's Company, 3rd Regt. (Tyler's).

BABCOCK, ELIAS, Sheldon or Berkshire.
Volunteered to go to Plattsburgh, September, 1814, and served 8 days in company commanded by Capt. Samuel Weed. Ref: Book 51, AGO Pages 125, 143, 152.

*BABCOCK, PELEG,   Highgate.
Served in Capt. Saxe's Company, Col. William Williams' Regt., Detached Militia, in U. S. service 4 months and 24 days, 1812.

*BABCOCK, SIMON, Corporal.
Served in Capt. Pettes' Company, Col. William Williams' Regt. Detached Militia, in U. S. service 4 months and 17 days, 1812.

*BABCOCK, THOMAS.
Served in Capt. Othniel Jewett's Company, Sumner's Regt., from April 17, 1814 to April 21, 1814.

BABCOCK, WILLIAM,   Franklin County.
Volunteered to go to Plattsburgh, Sept. 11, 1814 and served in 15th or 22nd Regt. Ref: Hemenway's Vt. Gazetteer, Vol. 2, Page 391.

BACH, ISAAC D.
Served in Capt. Barns' Company, Col. William Williams' Regt. Detached Militia, in U. S. service 5 months, 1812. Ref: Book 53, AGO Page 9.

‡BACHELDOR, JOSEPH.
Served in Captain Oliver Taylor's Company. Pension Certificate No. 12241.

*BACHELLOR, AARON.
Served in 4th Regt. Vt. Militia commanded by Col. Williams.

*BACHELOR, HENRY.
Served in Capt. George Fisher's Company, Sumner's Regt. from April 12, 1814 to May 20, 1814.

*BACHELOR, SAMUEL.
Served in Capt. Thomas Dorwin's Company of Vt. Militia, 1st Regt., 2nd Brig., 3rd Div., from June 11, 1813 to June 14, 1813.

‡BACHUS, GARDEN B.
Served in Captain Gideon Spencer's Company. Pension Certificate of widow, Lucy, No. 29900.

BACKUS, CHARLES, Sergeant.
Served in Capt. Samuel H. Holly's Company, 11th Regt. Name appears on Pay Roll for January and February, 1813. Ref: R. & L. 1812, AGO Page 25.

BACKUS, JOHN.
Served in Lieut. William S. Foster's Company, 11th Regt. Name appears on Pay Roll of Company for January and February, 1813. Ref: R. & L. 1812, AGO Page 7.

*BACKUS, SHUBAL.
Served in Capt Phelps' Company, Col. Jonathan Williams' Regt. Detached Militia, in U. S. service 2 months and 21 days, 1812.

BACON, ABIJAH,   Williamstown.
Volunteered to go to Plattsburgh, September, 1814, and served 8 days in Capt. David Robinson's Company. Ref: Book 52, AGO Pages 8 and 10.

BACON, CHARLES,   Shoreham.
Volunteered to go to Plattsburgh, September, 1814, and served about 6 days in Capt. Samuel Hand's Company. Ref: Rev. J. F. Goodhue's History of Shoreham, Page 108.

BACON, DANIEL,   Shelburne.
Volunteered to go to Plattsburgh, September, 1814, and served in 1st Regt., Major Luman Judson's command. Ref: Book 51, AGO Page 78.

BACON, EDMUND,   Williamstown.
Was in the Battle of Plattsburgh Sept. 11, 1814 and served about 8 days in Capt. David Robinson's Company. Ref: Book 52, AGO Page 2.

‡BACON, HARLOW.
Pension Certificate of widow, Philena, No. 40308. No organization given.

*BACON, JAMES.
Served in Capt. Brown's Company, Col. Martindale's Regt. Detached Militia, in U. S. service 2 months and 14 days, 1812.

*BACON, JESSE.
Served as drummer in 3rd Regt. Vt.
Militia commanded by Col. Tyler.

BACON, JOHN   Shelburne.
Volunteered to go to Plattsburgh,
September, 1814, and served in 1st
Regt., Major Luman Judson's com-
mand. Ref: Book 51, AGO Page 78.

*BACON, JOSEPH.
Enlisted Sept. 25, 1813 in Capt.
Thomas Waterman's Company, Dix-
on's Regt.

BACON, LEVI,   Brandon.
Volunteered to go to Plattsburgh,
September, 1814, and served 8 days
in Capt. Micah Brown's Company.
Ref: Book 52, AGO Page 131.

BACON, NATHAN.
Served as private in War of 1812 and
was captured by troops June 26, 1813
at Beaver Dams. Discharged Aug.
10th. Ref: Records of Naval Records
and Library, Navy Dept.

BACON, NATHANIEL,   Orwell.
Volunteered to go to Plattsburgh,
September, 1814, and served 11 days
in Capt. Wait Branch's Company.
Ref: Book 51, AGO Page 16.

*BACON, WILLIAM.
Served in 1st Regt. Vt. Militia, commanded by Col. Judson.

BADGER, EPHRAIM J.
Served as private in War of 1812 and
was captured by troops June 26, 1813
at Beaver Dams. Discharged Aug.
10th. Ref: Records of Naval Records
and Library, Navy Dept.

*BADGER, LUNNS.
Served in Capt. Ithiel Stone's Company of Vt. Militia, 1st Regt., 2nd
Brig., 3rd Div., from June 11, 1813
to June 14, 1813.

*BADGER, NATHANIEL.
Served in companies of Capt. Wheatly
and Capt. Wright, Col. Fifield's Regt.
Detached Militia, in U. S. service
6 months, 1812.

‡*BADGER, SAMUEL.
Served in Capt. Morrill's Company,
Col. Fifield's Regt. Detached Militia,
in U. S. service 2 months and 18 days,
1812. Pension Certificate of widow,
Cynthia, No. 4310.

*BAGLE, JEREMIAH.
Served in 3rd Regt., Vt. Militia, commanded by Col. Williams.

‡BAGLEY, AARON,   Barre.
Volunteered to go to Plattsburgh, Sep-
tember, 1814, and served in Captain
Ellis' Company. Pension Certificate
No. 32997.

BAGLEY, BENJAMIN, Corporal, Brookfield. Volunteered to go to Plattsburgh, September, 1814, and served
7 days in company commanded by
Capt. Frederick Griswold. Ref: Book
52, AGO Pages 52 and 56.

‡BAGLEY, DANIEL.
Enlisted July 4, 1812 and served to
Jan. 5, 1814. Enlisted at Hartland.

Engaged in Chantanqua River battle.
Served in Capt. Phineas Williams'
Company, 11th Regt., from Jan. 1st
to Feb. 28, 1813. Ref: R. & L. 1812,
AGO Page 15; Book 51, AGO Page 1.

BAGLEY, DAVID.
Volunteered to go to Plattsburgh,
September, 1814, and served 3 days
in company of Capt. James George
of Topsham. Ref: Book 52, AGO
Pages 67 and 70.

‡BAGLEY, EDWARD.
Served in Captain Laben Edgerton's
Company. Pension Certificate No.
6045.

‡BAGLEY, JOHN.
Served in Captain George's Company.
Pension Certificate No. 17507.

BAGLEY, MOSES,   Washington.
Served in Capt. Walker's Company,
Col. Fifield's Regt. Detached Militia,
in U. S. service 2 months and 24
days, 1812. Volunteered to go to
Plattsburgh, September, 1814, and
served in Capt. Amos Stiles' Company.
Ref: Book 52, AGO Page 36. Book 53,
AGO Page 33.

‡BAGLEY, PERKINS.
Served in Captain Bacon's Company
Pension Certificate No. 19596.

BAGLEY, RUSSIA.
Volunteered to go to Plattsburgh,
September, 1814 and served 7 days
in company of Capt. Frederick Gris-
wold, raised in Brookfield, Vt. Ref:
Book 52, AGO Page 52.

BAGLEY, SAMUEL JR.
Volunteered to go to Plattsburgh,
September, 1814, and served 7 days
in company of Capt. Frederick Gris-
wold, raised in Brookfield, Vt. Ref:
Book 52, AGO Page 52.

‡BAGLEY, THOMAS JR.
Served in Capt. R. B. Brown's Com-
pany. Pension Certificate of widow,
Nancy, No. 9065.

BAIL, EBENEZER.
Served in Capt. Weeks' Company,
11th Regt. Name appears on Pay
Roll for January and February, 1813.
Ref: R. & L. 1812, AGO Page 5.

*BAILEY, ABEL.
Served in company of Capt. James
Gray, Jr., Sumner's Regt., from April
12, 1814 to May 20, 1814.

BAILEY, ABIAL,   Corinth.
Volunteered to go to Plattsburgh,
September, 1814, and served in company commanded by Capt. Abel Jackman. Ref: Book 52, AGO Page 44.

BAILEY, CALEB. Corporal.
Served in Capt. Charles Follett's Company, 11th Regt., from Jan. 26, 1813
to May 24, 1813. Ref: R. & L. 1812,
AGO Page 12.

‡BAILEY, CEPHUS.
Served in Captain Tobias' Company.
Pension Certificate No. 13181.

*BAILEY. CHARLES, Sergeant, Winhall.
Served in Capt. Richardson's Company, Col. Martindale's Regt. Detached Militia, in U. S. service 2
months and 13 days, 1812. Served
as sergeant in 1st Regt. of Detached
Militia of Vermont in the service of
the U. S. at Champlain for 2 days
commencing Nov. 18 and ending Nov.
19, 1812.

BAILEY, COBB, Corporal.
Enlisted Jan. 26, 1813, in Detachment of Recruits under the command of Capt. Charles Follett, 11th
Regt. Name appears on Pay Roll
to May 31, 1813. Ref: R. & L. 1812,
AGO Page 13.

*BAILEY, CYRUS.
Served in Capt. Richardson's Company, Col. Martindale's Regt. Detached Militia, in U. S. service 2
months and 13 days, 1812.

BAILEY, DANIEL, Sergeant.
Served in Capt. Weeks' Company,
11th Regt. Name appears on Pay
Poll for January and February, 1813.
Ref: R. & L. 1812, AGO Page 5.

*BAILEY, EBENEZER JR.,   Berlin?
Served in Capt. Edmund B. Hill's
Company, Sumner's Regt, from April
12, 1814 to April 21, 1814.

BAILEY, ENOS JR., Drummer. Pittsford.
Served in Capt. Daniel Farrington's
Comany (also commanded by Capt
Simeon Wright), 30th Regt., from
April 27, 1813 to April 27, 1814.
Volunteered to go to Plattsburgh.
September 1814 and served 8 days
in Capt. Caleb Hendee's Company.
Ref: R. & L. 1812, AGO Pages 50 and
51; Book 52, AGO Page 124.

‡*BAILEY, HARLOW, Drummer.
Served in Capt. Wheeler's Company,
Col. Fifield's Regt. Detached Militia,
in U. S. service 3 months and 16
days, 1812. Pension Certificate No.
6910. Pension Certificate of widow.
Apphia B., No. 31174.

BAILEY, IRA,   Rochester.
Volunteered to go to Plattsburgh.
September, 1814 and served 7 days
in Capt. Oliver Mason's Company.
Ref: Book 51, AGO Page 269.

*BAILEY, JAMES, Corporal, Quarter-
master Sergeant. Served in Capt.
Rogers' Company, Col. Fifield's Regt.
Detached Militia, in U. S. service
5 months and 27 days, 1812.

‡BAILEY, JONATHAN.
Served from March 16, 1813 to June
15, 1813 in Capt. Charles Follett's
Company, 11th Regt. Also served in
Capt. Wool's Company. Pension Cer-
tificate of widow. Bethany, No.
13495. Ref: R. & L. 1812, AGO
Page 13.

‡*BAILEY, JOSHUA JR.
Served in Capt. Rogers' Company,
Col. Fifield's Regt. Detached Militia,
in U. S. service 4 months and 28
days, 1812. Pension Certificate of
widow, Sarah J., No. 2438.

BAILEY, PHILANDER.   Danville.
Served in Capt. Morrill's Company,
Col. Fifield's Regt Detached Militia,
in U. S. service 2 months and 18
days, 1812. Served at Troy from
July 4th to 16th, 1812 in company
commanded by Major A. Warner.
Ref: Book 53, AGO Page 36; Vol.
51 Vt. State Papers, Page 107.

BAILEY, SAMUEL,   Troy.
Served in Capt. Mason's Company,
Col. Fifield's Regt. Detached Militia,
in U. S. service 3 months and 27
days, 1812. Served at Troy from July
4th to 16th, 1812 in company commanded by Major A. Warner. Ref:
Book 53, AGO Page 39; Vol. 51, Vt.
State Papers, Page 107.

*BAILEY, TIMOTHY.
Served in Capt. Thomas Dorwin's
Company of Vt. Militia. 1st Regt.,
2nd Brig., 3rd Div., from June 11,
1813 to June 14, 1813.

BAILEY, WILLIAM.
Served in Capt. Alexander Brook's
Corps of Artillery from April 23rd
to June 30, 1814. Ref: R. & L.
1812, AGO Page 31.

BAILEY, WILLIAM W., Corporal.
Served in Capt. Weeks' Company,
11th Regt. Name appears on Pay
Roll for January and February, 1813.
Ref: R. & L. 1812, AGO Page 5.

BAILY. WILLIAM, Corporal, Shoreham.
Volunteered to go to Plattsburgh,
September, 1814, and served 6 days
in Capt. Samuel Hand's Company.
Ref: Rev. J. F. Goodhue's History
of Shoreham, Page 107.

BAION, PHINEAS E.
Served from Feb. 17, 1813 to May 16,
1813 in Detachment of Recruits under the command of Lieut. V. R.
Goodrich, 11th Regt. Ref: R. & L.
1812, AGO Page 10.

*BAIRD, DANIEL,   Shoreham.
Volunteered to go to Plattsburgh,
September, 1814, and served in Capt.
Samuel Hand's Company. Also serv-
ed in Sumner's Regt. Ref: Rev. J. F.
Goodhue's History of Shoreham, Page
107.

*BAIRD, JOHN.
Served in Sumner's Regiment. Vt.
Militia.

*BAIRD, THADEUS, Ensign.
Served in 1st Regt., Vt. Militia, commanded by Col. Martindale.

BAIRD, THOMAS, Ensign.
Served in 1st Regt. of Detached Mili-
tia of Vermont in the service of the
United States at Champlain for 2
days commencing Nov. 18 and ending
Nov. 19, 1812.

*BAKER, ADOLPHUS.
Served in Capt Edmund B. Hill's
Company, Sumner's Regt., from April
12, 1814 to April 21, 1814.

*BAKER, ALMERIN.
Served in Capt. Hezekiah Barns' Company, 1st Regt., 2nd Brig., 3rd Div.,
Militia. Name appears on Pay Roll
from June 11, 1813 to June 14, 1813.

‡BAKER, ALPHEUS.
Served in Captain Hill's Company.
Pension Certificate No. 32998.

*BAKER, ANDREW.
Served in Capt. Taylor's Company.
Col. William Williams' Regt. Detached Militia, in U. S. service 4 months
and 24 days, 1812.

*BAKER, ASA.
Appointed 2nd Lieutenant, 31st Inf.,
April 30, 1813; 1st Lieutenant Jan. 11,
1814; honorably discharged June 15,
1815. Served with Hospital Attendants, Vermont. Ref: Heitman's Historical Register & Dictionary USA.

BAKER, ASA.   Wicassett.
Served from May 1, 1814 to July 4,
1814 in Capt. Poland's Company, 34th
Inf. Ref: R & L. 1812, AGO Page 30.

BAKER, BENJAMIN T.
Served in Capt. Weeks' Company, 11th
Regt. Name appears on Pay Roll for
January and February, 1813   Ref:
R. & L. 1812, AGO Page 5.

*BAKER, CHARLES,   Georgia.
Enlisted in Capt Shubael Wales' Company, Col. W. B. Sumner's Regt.,
April 12, 1814; transferred to Capt.
Salmon Foster's Company, same regiment. April 13, 1814 and served to
April 21, 1814. Volunteered to go to
Plattsburgh. September, 1814, and
served in Capt. Jesse Post's Company,
Dixon's Regt.

BAKER, DANIEL.
Ensign 16th Inf. Jan. 8, 1799; 2nd
Lieutenant March 3, 1799; honorably
discharged June 15, 1800; 2nd
Lieutenant 3rd Inf. Feb. 16, 1801;
transferred to 1st Inf. April 1, 1802;
1st Lieutenant Aug. 11, 1806; Captain
March 12, 1812; Major 45th Inf. April
15, 1814; retained May 17, 1815 as
Captain 8th Inf. with brevet rank of
Major from April 15, 1814; transferred to 3rd Inf. Dec. 2, 1815; Major 7th Inf. June 1, 1819; transferred
to 3rd Inf. June 1, 1821; Lt. Colonel
6th Inf. May 1, 1829; brevet Major
Aug. 9, 1812 for distinguished service
in the battle of Brownstown Maguago,
Michigan; died Oct. 30, 1836. Ref:
Heitman's Historical Register & Dictionary USA.

*BAKER, EBENEZER.
Served in Capt. Needham's Company,
Col. Martindale's Regt. Detached
Militia, in U. S. service 1 month· and
10 days, 1812.

BAKER, ELIJAH,   Stockbridge.
Volunteered to go to Plattsburgh,
September, 1814, and served 7 days
in Capt. Elias Keyes' Company. Ref:
Book 51, AGO Page 237.

*BAKER, ELIJAH, Sergeant,   Georgia.
Served in Capt. Sabin's Company, Col.
Jonathan Williams' Regt. Detached
Militia, in U. S. service 2 months and
6 days, 1812.

*BAKER, ELIJAH JR., Ensign, Georgia.
Enlisted Sept. 25, 1813 in Capt. Jesse
Post's Company, Col. Luther Dixon's

Regt. Volunteered to go to Plattsburgh, September, 1814, and served
8 days in Capt. Jesse Post's Company,
Dixon's Regt.

*BAKER, ELISHA.   Sheldon.
Served in Capt. Phelps' Company, Col.
William Williams' Regt. Detached
Militia, in U. S. service 5 months,
1812. Volunteered to go to Plattsburgh, September, 1814, and served
about 6 days in Capt. Samuel Weed's
Company.

BAKER, EZRA, Sergeant.
Enlisted June 12, 1812 for a period
of five years in company of Capt.
White Youngs, 15th Regt. Name appears on Muster Roll from Aug. 31.
1814 to Dec. 31, 1814. Ref: R. & L.
1812, AGO Page 27.

BAKER, HEZEKIAH,   Berlin.
Volunteered to go to Plattsburgh,
September, 1814 and served 8 days
in Capt. Cyrus Johnson's Company.
Ref: Book 52, AGO Pages 184 and 202.

*BAKER, IRA.
Served in Capt. Ormsbee's Company,
Col. Martindale's Regt. Detached Militia, in U. S. service 2 months and
14 days, 1812.

BAKER, ISAAC.
Served in Capt. Haig's Corps of Light
Dragoons from May 1st to June 30th,
1814. Ref: R. & L. 1812, AGO Page 20.

‡BAKER, JACOB,   Fairfax.
Enlisted Aug. 8, 1812 in company commanded by Capt. Joseph Beeman, Jr.,
11th Regt. U. S.; Inf. under Col. Ira
Clark. Served in Lieut. V. R. Goodrich's Company, 11th Regt. Name appears on Pay Roll of company for
January & February, 1813. Pension
Certificate of widow, Abigail, No.
31996.

*BAKER, JAMES,   Enosburgh.
Served in Capt. Asahel Scovell's Company, Col. Clark's Regt. of Riflemen,
from Oct. 15th to Nov. 17th, 1813.

*BAKER, JOHN (alias John Bacon).
Served in Capt. Richardson's Company, Col. Martindale's Regt. Detached Militia, in U. S. service 2 months
and 13 days, 1812.

*BAKER, JOHN K.
Served in Capt. Moses Jewett's Company of Militia, 1st Regt., 2nd Brig.,
3rd Div., from June 11, 1813 to June
14, 1813.

BAKER, JONATHAN.
Served in Capt. Charles Follett's Company, 11th Regt., from Feb. 7, 1813
to May 6, 1813. Ref: R. & L. 1812,
AGO Pages 12 and 13.

*BAKER, JOSEPH, Ensign.
Served in 2nd Regt. Vt. Militia commanded by Col. Fifield.

*BAKER, LUTHER.
Served in Capt. Dorrance's Company,
Col. William Williams' Regt., Detached Militia, in U. S. service 4 months
and 24 days, 1812. Also served in
Dixon's Regt. Vt. Militia.

‡*BAKER, LYMAN.
Enlisted Oct. 2, 1813 in Capt. Asahel
Langworthy's Company, Col. Isaac
Clark's Rifle Corps; transferred Oct.
3, 1813 to Capt. Jesse Post's Company,
Dixon's Regt. Pension Certificate No.
25666.

*BAKER, MEDAD, Sergeant,   Georgia.
Enlisted Sept. 25, 1813 and served
1 month and 23 days in 1813 in Capt.
Jesse Post's Company, Col. Dixon's
Regt. Volunteered to go to Plattsburgh, September, 1814, and served
8 days in same company.

BAKER, MOSES.
Served in Capt. Samuel H. Holly's
Company, 11th Regt. Name appears
on Pay Roll for January and Febru-
ary, 1813. Ref: R. & L. 1812, AGO
Page 25.

*BAKER, OZI.
Served in Capt. Strait's Company, Col.
Martindale's Regt. Detached Militia,
in U. S. service 2 months and 13
days, 1812.

‡BAKER, PHILIP,   Whiting.
Volunteered to go to Plattsburgh,
September, 1814 and served 9 days
in Capt. Salmon Foster's Company.
Pension Certificate of widow, Betsey,
No. 32319.

*BAKER, SAMUEL.
Served in Lieut. Bates' Company, 1st
Regt., from June 11th to 14th, 1813.

BAKER, SOLOMON, Lieutenant, Huntington. Volunteered to go to Plattsburgh, September, 1814, and was at
the battle. Served in Capt. Josiah
N. Barrow's Company. Ref: Book 51,
AGO Page 77.

*BAKER, STEPHEN.
Served with Hospital Attendants, Vermont.

BAKER, THOMAS.
Served in Capt. Alexander Brooks'
Corps of Artillery from May 1st to
June 30th, 1814. Ref: R. & L. 1812,
AGO Page 31.

BAKER, WARREN.
Enlisted June 2, 1813 in Capt. Simeon
Wright's Company. Died of wounds
April 24, 1814. Ref: R. & L. 1812,
AGO Page 51.

BAKER, WILLARD,   Georgia.
Served as a Plattsburgh volunteer,
September, 1814, in Capt. Jesse Post's
Company, Dixon's Regt. Ref: Hemen-
way's Vt. Gazetteer, Vol. 2, Page 417.

BAKER, ZENAS, Corporal,   St. Albans.
Enlisted April 27, 1813 for one year
in Capt. John Wires' Company, 30th
Regt. Ref: R. & L. 1812, AGO Page 40.

*BALCH, HART.
Served in Capt. Richardson's Company, Col. Martindale's Regt. Detached Militia in U. S. service 2
months and 13 days, 1812.

BALCH, ISRAEL,   Shrewsbury.
Volunteered to go to Plattsburgh,
September, 1814, and served 4 days
in Capt. Robert Reed's Company.
Ref: Book 52, AGO Pages 138 and 140.

*BALCH, SIMEON.
Served in Capt. Shubael Wales' Com-
pany, Col. W. B. Sumner's Regt., from
April 12th to April 21st, 1814.

BALDING, G. H.
Appointed Ensign, 31st Inf., March 28,
1814. Ref: Governor and Council,
Vt., Vol. 6, Page 478.

*BALDING, TREAT.
Served in Capt. Shubael Wales' Com-
pany, Col. W. B. Sumner's Regt., from
April 12, 1814 to April 21, 1814..

BALDWIN, ANDREW M.,   Whiting.
Volunteered to go to Plattsburgh,
September, 1814, and served 9 days in
Capt. Salmon Foster's Company. Ref:
Book 51, AGO Pages 7 and 9.

*‡BALDWIN, ASA.
Served in companies of Captains
Walker and Taylor, Col. Fifield's
Regt., 6 months. Volunteered to go
to Plattsburgh, September, 1814, and
went as far as Bolton, Vt. Served
4 days in company commanded by
Lieut. Phineus Kimball, West Fair-
lee. Pension Certificate of widow,
Milcah G., No. 12960.

BALDWIN, CALVIN.
Volunteered to go to Plattsburgh,
September, 1814, and went as far as
Bolton, Vt. Served 4 days in com-
pany commanded by Lieut. Phineus
Kimball, West Fairlee. Ref: Book
52, AGO Pages 46-47.

BALDWIN, CALVIN.
Volunteered to go to Plattsburgh,
September, 1814, and served 4 days
in Capt. Aaron Kidder's Company.
Ref: Book 52, AGO Page 65.

*BALDWIN, DANIEL.
Served in 3rd Regt. Vt. Militia, com
manded by Col. Williams.

*BALDWIN, DAVID.
Served in company of Capt. James
Gray, Jr., Sumner's Regt., from April
12, 1814 to May 20, 1814.

*BALDWIN, ELEAZER.
Served in Lieut. Justus Foote's Company, Sumner's Regt., from April 12,
1814 to April 15, 1814.

*BALDWIN, EZRA.
Served in Capt. Burnap's Company,
Col. Jonathan Williams' Regt. Detached Militia, in U. S. service 2 months
and 13 days, 1812.

*BALDWIN, ISAAC.
Served in company of Capt. John
McNeil Jr., 11th Regt. Name appears
on Pay Roll of Company for Janu-
ary & February, 1813. Also served in
Sumner's Regt. Vt. Militia. Ref: R.
& L. 1812, AGO Page 17.

*BALDWIN, JAMES,   Randolph.
Volunteered to go to Plattsburgh,
September, 1814, and served in Capt.
Lebbeus Egerton's Company.

BALDWIN, JAMES,   Orange.
Volunteered to go to Plattsburgh
Sept. 11, 1814 and served 5 days in
Capt. David Rising's Company. Ref:
Book 52, AGO Page 19.

*BALDWIN, JOHN.
Served in company commanded by
Capt. James Gray, Jr., Sumner's
Regt., from April 12, 1814 to May
20, 1814.

BALDWIN, JOHN.   Newark.
Enlisted March 20, 1814 in Capt.
James Taylor's Company, 30th Regt.;
joined Capt. Gideon Spencer's Company, 30th Regt., June 1, 1814; transferred to Capt. Sanford's Company,
30th Inf. and name appears on Pay
Roll of discharged men to Dec. 30,
1815 as having served from Sept. 1,
1814 to June 16, 1815. Ref: R. & L.
1812, AGO Pages 53, 57, 23.

BALDWIN, JOHN,   Roxbury.
Volunteered to go to Plattsburgh,
September, 1814, and served 8 days
in Capt. Samuel M. Orcutt's Company. Ref: Book 52, AGO Page 250.

BALDWIN, JOHN,   West Fairlee.
Volunteered to go to Plattsburgh,
September, 1814, and served in Capt.
Aaron Kidder's Company. Ref: Book
52, AGO Pages 107 and 108.

*BALDWIN, JOHN C.
Served in Capt. Adams' Company,
Col. Jonathan Williams' Regt. Detached Militia, in U. S. service 2 months
and 7 days, 1812.

‡BALDWIN, LYMAN.
Served in Capt. Patridge's Company.
Pension Certificate No. 15690.

BALDWIN, SOLOMON, Franklin County.
Volunteered to go to Plattsburgh,
Sept. 11, 1814 and served in 15th or
22nd Regt. Ref: Hemenway's Vt.
Gaz., Vol. 2, Page 392.

‡BALDWIN, STEPHEN.
Volunteered to go to Plattsburgh,
September, 1814 and went as far as
Bolton, Vt. Served 4 days in com-
pany of Lieut. Phineus Kimball, West
Fairlee. Pension Certificate No.
32506.

*BALDWIN, STEPHEN JR.
Served in company commanded by
Capt. James Gray, Jr., Sumner's
Regt., from April 12, 1814 to May 20,
1814.

*BALDWIN, THOMAS, Corporal.
Served in company commanded by
Capt. James Gray, Jr., Sumner's
Regt., from April 12, 1814 to May 20,
1814.

*BALDWIN, TREAT.
Served in Capt. Salmon Foster's Company, Sumner's Regt., from April 13,
1814 to April 21, 1814.

*BALDWIN, WILLIAM.
Served in company of Capt. James
Gray Jr., Sumner's Regt., from April
12, 1814 to May 20, 1814.

BALL. DANIEL.
Served in Lieut. William S. Foster's
Company, 11th Regt. Name appears
on Pay Roll for January and Febru-
ary, 1813. Ref: R. & L. 1812, AGO
Page 7.

BALL, DAVID.
Served in Capt. Charles Follett's Company, 11th Regt., from March 6, 1813
to May 8, 1813. Ref: R. & L. 1812,
AGO Page 13.

BALL, GEORGE
Served in Capt. Benjamin Bradford's
Company. Name appears on Muster
Roll from May 31, 1813 to Aug. 31,
1813. Ref: R. & L. 1812, AGO Page 26.

BALL, HORACE,   Shoreham.
Volunteered to go to Plattsburgh,
September, 1814, and served about 6
days in Capt. Samuel Hand's Company. Ref: Rev. J. F. Goodhue's History of Shoreham, Page 108.

BALL, JAMES V., Major and Lieuten-
ant-Colonel.
Served in Corps of Light Dragoons.
Name appears on Pay Roll to June
30, 1814. Ref: R. & L. 1812, AGO
Page 20.

BALL, JESSE.
Volunteered to go to Plattsburgh,
September, 1814, and went as far as
Bolton, Vt. Served 4 days in com-
pany of Lieut. Phineus Kimball, West
Fairlee. Ref: Book 52, AGO Page 46.

*BALL, JOHN.
Served in Capt. Adams' Company, Col.
Jonathan Williams' Regt. Detached
Militia, in U. S. service 2 months and
7 days, 1812.

BALL, JOSEPH,   Shoreham.
Volunteered to go to Plattsburgh,
September, 1814, and served about 6
days in Capt. Samuel Hand's Com-
pany. Ref: Rev. J. F. Goodhue's
History of Shoreham, Page 107.

*BALL, NATHAN,   Shoreham.
Served in company of Capt. James
Gray Jr., Sumner's Regt., from April
12, 1814 to May 20, 1814.

BALLARD, JAMES.
Age 30 years; 5 feet 7 inches high;
light complexion; brown hair; blue
eyes; by profession a farmer; born
in Lindage, Westershire, England. Enlisted Dec. 19, 1813 at Plattsburgh
in 30th Regt., U. S. Inf. Served in
Capt. William Miller's Company and
Captain Gideon Spencer's Company
in said Regiment. Discharged at Burlington, Vermont, in 1815. Ref: R.
& L. 1812, AGO Pages 54, 55, 57.

BALLARD, JOHN.
Served in Capt. Samuel Gordon's
Company, 11th Regt. Name appears
on Pay Roll of company for January
and February, 1813. Ref: R. & L.
1812, AGO Page 9.

BALLARD, NATHAN.
Enlisted March 8, 1814 for a period
of 5 years in Capt. James Taylor's
Company, 30th Regt.; transferred to
Capt. Gideon Spencer's Company, 30th
Regt., and served until discharged by
reason of old age June 3, 1816, at
Burlington. Ref: R. & L. 1812, AGO
Pages 53 and 57.

BALLARD, STEPHEN.
Served in Capt. John W. Weeks' Company, 11th Regt., from Jan. 9, 1813 to May 10, 1813. Ref: R. & L. 1812, AGO Page 4.

‡BALLON, WILLIAM.
Served in Capt. Oliver Lowery's Company, 4th Regt. (Williams'). Pension Certificate No. 283.

BALLOU, WILLIAM,   Richmond.
Served in 6th Company, 3rd Regt., 2nd Brigade, commanded by Brig. Gen. Newhall, for a period of 3 months beginning in September, 1812. Ref: Vol. 50 Vt. State Papers, Page 85.

BALLOU, WILLIAM,   Tunbridge.
Volunteered to go to Plattsburgh, September, 1814, and served 4 days in Capt. Ephraim Hackett's Company. Ref: Book 52, AGO Pages 71 and 72.

BAMFORD, MOSES,   Northfield.
Served in Capt. Goodenu's Company, 33rd Inf., from May 1, 1814 to July 4, 1814. Ref: R. & L. 1812, AGO Page 30.

‡BAMSEY, JOHN.
Served in Capt. Levall's Company. Pension Certificate No. 14531.

*BANCROFT, BENJAMIN,   Calais.
Volunteered to go to Plattsburgh, September, 1814, and served 8 days in Capt. Gideon Wheelock's Company.

BANCROFT, C., Sergeant,   Barre.
Volunteered to go to Plattsburgh, September, 1814, and served in Capt. Warren Ellis' Company. Ref: Hemenway's Vt. Gazetteer, Vol. 4, Page 41.

BANCROFT, CHARLES,   Marshfield.
Volunteered to go to Plattsburgh, September, 1814, and served 9 days in Capt. James English's Company. Ref: Book 52, AGO Pages 199, 200, 248.

BANCROFT, JOHN,   Barre.
Volunteered to go to Plattsburgh, September, 1814, and served 9 days in Capt. Warren Ellis' Company. Ref: Book 52, AGO Pages 223 and 242.

‡BANCROFT, JONATHAN,   Barre.
Volunteered to go to Plattsburgh, September, 1814, and served 9 days in Capt. Warren Ellis' Company. Pension Certificate No. 30811.

BANCROFT, LAWSON,   Marshfield.
Volunteered to go to Plattsburgh, September, 1814, and served 9 days in Capt. James English's Company. Ref: Book 52, AGO Page248.

BANCROFT, NATHANIEL, Franklin County Volunteered to go to Plattsburgh, September 11, 1814, and served in 15th or 22nd Regt. Ref: Hemenway's Vt. Gazetteer, Vol. 2, Page 392.

‡BANCROFT, NATHANIEL, Montpelier.
Volunteered to go to Plattsburgh, September, 1814, and served 10 days in Capt. Timothy Hubbard's Company. Pension Certificate of widow, Elizabeth, A., No. 32320.

*BANCROFT, NATHANIEL,   Calais.
Volunteered to go to Plattsburgh, September, 1814, and served 10 days in Capt Gideon Wheelock's Company. Ref: Book 52, AGO Page 247.

*BANEHORN, ENOCH.
Served in 1st Regt. Vt. Militia, commanded by Col. Judson.

*BANFIELD, SAMUEL D.
Served in Capt. Rogers' Company, Col. Fifield's Regt. Detached Militia, in U. S. service 2 months and 18 days, 1812.

BANGER, NICHOLAS, Franklin County.
Volunteered to go to Plattsburgh, September 11, 1814 and served in 15th or 22nd Regt. Ref: Hemenway's Vt. Gazetteer, Vol. 2, Page 391.

*BANGS, ADOLPHUS, Corporal.
Served in Capt. Shubael Wales' Company, Col. W. B. Sumner's Regt., from April 12, 1814 to April 21, 1814.

BANGS, OLIVER, 2nd Lieutenant.
Served in Capt. Alexander Brook's Corps of Artillery. Name appears on Pay Roll from June 1st to 30th, 1814. Ref: R. & L. 1812, AGO Page 31.

‡BANGS, THEOPHILUS,   Grand Isle?
Served in Capt. Farnsworth's Company. Pension Certificate of widow, Charlotte, No. 20925.

*BANISTER, SIMEON.
Served in Capt. Bingham's Company, Col. Jonathan Williams' Regt. Detached Militia, in U. S. service 2 months and 9 days, 1812. Ref: Book 53, AGO Page 46.

BANKS, BENTLY,   Corinth.
Volunteered to go to Plattsburgh, September, 1814, and served 3 days in Capt. Abel Jackman's Company. Ref: Book 52, AGO Pages 44 and 45.

BANKS, ELIAS,   Franklin County.
Volunteered to go to Plattsburgh, Sept. 11, 1814, and served in 15th or 22nd Regt. Ref: Hemenway's Vt. Gazetteer, Vol. 2, Page 391.

BANKS, JOHN,   Franklin County.
Volunteered to go to Plattsburgh, Sept. 11, 1814 and served in 15th or 22nd Regt. Ref: Hemenway's Vt. Gazetteer, Vol. 2, Page 391.

BANKS, JONATHAN B., Franklin County.
Volunteered to go to Plattsburgh, Sept. 11, 1814 and served in 15th or 22nd Regt. Ref: Hemenway's Vt. Gazetteer, Vol. 2, Page 391.

BANKS, LITTLETON,   Franklin County.
Volunteered to go to Plattsburgh, Sept. 11, 1814 and served in 15th or 22nd Regt. Ref: Hemenway's Vt. Gazetteer, Vol. 2, Page 391.

BANKS, THOMAS.   Corinth.
Volunteered to go to Plattsburgh, September, 1814, and served in Capt. Abel Jackman's Company. Ref: Book 52, AGO Page 44.

BANNEL, CHESTER.
Served in Capt. Week's Company, 11th Regt. Name appears on Pay Roll for January and February, 1813. Ref: R. & L. 1812, AGO Page 5.

BAPTIST, JOHN, Carpenter.
Served in Company of Artificers commanded by Alexander Parris from May 1st to June 30, 1814. Ref: R. & L. 1812, AGO Page 24.

BARBER, ANSEL,   Shoreham.
Volunteered to go to Plattsburgh, September, 1814, and served 6 days in Capt. Samuel Hand's Company. Ref: Rev. J. F. Goodhue's History of Shoreham, Page 108.

*BARBER, AUGUSTUS.
Served in Capt. Isaac Finch's Company, Col. Clark's Regt. of Riflemen, from Oct. 6, 1813 to Nov. 18, 1813.

‡BARBER, BENJAMIN F.,   Orwell.
Volunteered to go to Plattsburgh, September, 1814, and served 11 days in Capt. Wait Branch's Company. Pension Certificate No. 22824.

‡BARBER, BERIAH.
Enlisted Aug. 9, 1813 in Capt. Daniel Farrington's Company (also commanded by Capt. Simeon Wright), 30th Regt. Name appears on Muster Roll from March 1, 1814 to April 30, 1814. Pension Certificate No. 14096.

BARBER, CYRUS,   Barre.
Volunteered to go to Plattsburgh, September, 1814, and served 9 days in Capt. Warren Ellis' Company. Ref: Book 52, AGO Pages 233 and 242.

‡BARBER, E. C.
Served in Capt. Brown's Company. Pension Certificate No. 25585.

‡BARBER, ELIHU,   Richmond.
Volunteered to go to Plattsburgh, September, 1814, and served 9 days in Capt. Roswell Hunt's Company, 3 Regt. (Tyler's). Pension Certificate of widow, Elizabeth, No. 28864.

*BARBER, FRANKLIN.
Served in 4th Regt. Vt. Militia, commanded by Col. Williams.

BARBER, GIDEON,   Richmond.
Volunteered to go to Plattsburgh, September, 1814, and served 9 days in Capt. Roswell Hunt's Company, 3 Regt. (Tyler's). Ref: Book 51, AGO Page 82.

BARBER, HORATIO,   Hubbardton.
Volunteered to go to Plattsburgh, September, 1814, and served 6 days as a Teamster in Capt. Henry J. Horton's Company. Ref: Book 52, AGO Page 142.

*BARBER, ISAAC R.
Served in company of Capt. James Gray Jr., Sumner's Regt., from April 12, 1814 to May 20, 1814.

‡*BARBER, ISRAEL.
Served in Capt. Eseck Sprague's Company, Sumner's Regt., from April 12, 1814 to April 21, 1814. Pension Certificate No. 25034. Pension Certificate of widow, Olive S., No. 32056.

*BARBER, JAMES B.
Served in Capt. Ormsbee's Company, Col. Martindale's Regt. Detached Militia, in U. S. service 1 month and 17 days, 1812.

‡BARBER, JAMES H.
Served in Captain Spencer's Company, 30th Regt. Pension Certificate No. 25304.

BARBER, JESSE, Carpenter,   Fairfax.
Enlisted Sept. 12, 1813 in Capt. Asa Wilkins' Company, Col. Dixon's Regt. Ref: Hemenway's Vt. Gazetteer,, Vol. 2, Page 402.

*BARBER, JOHN, Fifer-Musician.
Served in Capt. Stephen Brown's Company of Militia, 3 Regt. (Tyler's) from Oct. 5, 1813 to Oct. 17, 1813.

BARBER, JOSEPH.
Enlisted Sept. 25, 1813 in Capt. Daniel Farrington's Company (also commanded by Capt. Simeon Wright), 30th Regt. Transferred to 29th Regt. April 6, 1814. Ref: R. & L. 1812, AGO Pages 50 and 51.

BARBER, JOSIAH.
Served in Capt. Chadwick's Company. Ref: R. & L. 1812, AGO Page 32.

‡*BARBER, MARTIN, JR.,   Richmond.
Volunteered to go to Plattsburgh, September, 1814, and served 9 days in Capt. Roswell Hunt's Company, 3rd Regt. Pension Certificate of widow, Fanna, No. 26199.

*BARBER, OLIVER.
Served in Capt. Stephen Brown's Company of Militia, 3 Regt. (Tyler's), from Oct. 8, 1813 to Oct. 17, 1813.

‡BARBER, ORESTUS H.
Served in Capt. Curtis Munson's Company. Pension Certificate No. 32692.

*BARBER, ROBERT, Ensign.
Served in 3 Regt. Vt. Militia commanded by Col. Bowdish.

BARBER, RUSSELL,   Middletown.
Volunteered to go to Plattsburgh, September, 1814, and served 4 days in Capt. Reuben Wood's Company. Ref: Book 52, AGO Page 143.

*BARBER, SHUBEL.
Served in Capt. Roswell Hunt's Company of Militia, 3 Regt. (Tyler's) from Oct. 5, 1813 to Oct. 16, 1813. Also served in Corning's Detachment, Vt. Militia.

*BARBER, WILLARD
Served in Capt. Robbins' Company. Col. William Williams' Regt. Detached Militia, in U. S. service 19 days, 1812.

*BARBERS, PAUL.
Served in Sumner's Regt., Vt. Militia.

*BARGE, ALEXANDER, Corporal.
Served in 1st Regt. Vt. Militia commanded by Col. Martindale.

*BARKER, ASA, Corporal.
Enlisted Sept. 25, 1813 and served 1 month and 23 days in Capt. Amos Robinson's Company, Col. Dixon's Regt.

BARKER, DANIEL,   Barre.
Volunteered to go to Plattsburgh, September, 1814, and served 10 days in Capt. Warren Ellis' Company. Ref: Book 52, AGO Page 242.

*BARKER, JESSE.
Served in Capt. Mason's Company,
Col. Fifield's Regt. Detached Militia,
in U. S. service 2 months and 14
days, 1812. Ref: Book 53, AGO
Page 60.

‡BARKER, JOHN.
Pension Certificate of widow, Mary
S., No. 44107. No. organization given.

BARKER, JOHN,   Litchfield. Conn.
Served in Capt. Conkling's Company,
4th Inf., from May 1, 1814 to July 9,
1814. Ref: R. & L. 1812, AGO Page
30.

*BARKER, JOHN.
Served in Capt. George Fisher's Company, Sumner's Regt., from April 12,
1814 to May 20, 1814.

*BARKER, JOHN JR.
Served in Capt. Jonathan P. Stanley's Company, Col. W. B. Sumner's
Regt.. from April 12, 1814 to April
15, 1814.

'BARKER. JONAS.
Served in Capt. Wright's Company.
Col. Martindale's Regt. Detached
Militia, in U. S. service 2 months and
14 days, 1812.

BARKER, JONATHAN.
Served in Capt. Daniel Farrington's
Company (also commanded by Capt.
Simeon Wright), 30th Regt., from
April 21, 1813 to April 30, 1814. Ref:
R. & L. 1812, AGO Pages 50, and 51.

BARKER, JONATHAN JR.
Served in Capt. Benjamin Bradford's
Company. Name appears on Muster
Roll from May 31, 1813 to Aug. 31,
1813. Ref: R. & L. 1812, AGO Page
26.

*BARKER. ROBERT.
Served in Capt. Jonathan P. Stanley's
Company, Col. W. B. Sumner's Regt.,
from April 12, 1814 to April 15, 1814.

*BARKER, WILLIAM.
Served in Capt. John Palmer's Company of Militia, 1st Regt., 2nd Brig.,
3rd Div., from June 11th to 14th,
1813.

BARLOW, LEWIS.   Pittsford.
Volunteered to go to Plattsburgh,
September, 1814, and served 8 days
as a Waggoner in Capt. Caleb Hen-
dee's Company. Ref: Book 52, AGO
Page 125.

*BARLOW, PELEG C.
Served in 1st Regt. Vt. Militia, commanded by Col. Martindale.

BARLOW. THOMAS, Corporal. Pittsford.
Volunteered to go to Plattsburgh,
September, 1814, and served 8 days
in Capt Caleb Hendee's Company.
Ref: Book 52, AGO Page 124.

*BARLOW, WILLIAM W. JR.. Pittsford.
Volunteered to go to Plattsburgh,
September, 1814, and served 8 days
in Capt. Caleb Hendee's Company.
Also served in 3rd Regt. Vt. Militia
under Col. Tyler. Ref: Book 52, AGO
Page 124.

*BARNARD, ASA,   Hyde Park?
Served in Capt. Taylor's Company,
Col. Fifield's Regt. Detached Militia,
in U. S. service 6 months, 1812.

‡*BARNARD, ISAAC G.,
Served in Capt Dorrance's Company,
4 Regt. (Williams). Pension Certificate No. 12168.

*BARNARD, NATHANIEL,   Randolph.
Volunteered to go to Plattsburgh,
September, 1814, and served in Capt.
Lebbeus Egerton's Company.

BARNARD, STEPHEN,   Townshend.
Served from Feb. 9, 1813 to May 8,
1813 in Capt Charles Follett's Company, 11th Regt. Ref: R. & L. 1812,
AGO Page 13.

BARNARD, TIMOTHY.
Served in Lieut. William S. Foster's
Company, 11th Regt. Name appears
on Pay Roll for January and Feb-
ruary, 1813. Ref: R. & L. 1812, AGO
Page 7.

*BARNES. ALONZO.
Served from April 12, 1814 to May
20, 1814 in company of Capt. James
Gray Jr., Sumner's Regt.

*BARNES. AVERY,   Randolph.
Volunteered to go to Plattsburgh,
September, 1814, and served in Capt.
Lebbeus Egerton's Company.

BARNES, BENJAMIN,   Bakersfield.
Volunteered and was at the Battle
of Plattsburgh Sept. 11, 1814. Served
in Capt. M. Stearns' Company. Ref:
Hemenway's Vt. Gazetteer, Vol. 2,
Page 394.

*BARNES. CYRUS, Corporal.
Enlisted April 26, 1813 in Capt. James
Taylor's Company, 30th Regt.; name
appears on Muster Roll from Nov. 30,
1813 to Dec. 31, 1813. Transferred
to Capt. Gideon Spencer's Company,
30th Regt., and served to April 25,
1814. Also served in 4th Regt. commanded by Col. Williams. Ref: R.
& L. 1812, AGO Pages 52, 56, 58.

*BARNES. HARRY.
Served in 1st Regt. Vt. Militia commanded by Col. Judson.

BARNES, JEFFERY,   Pittsford.
Volunteered to go to Plattsburgh,
September, 1814, and served 8 days
in Capt. Caleb Hendee's Company.
Ref: Book 52, AGO Page 124.

BARNES, JOEL, Captain,   Chelsea.
Volunteered to go to Plattsburgh,
September, 1814, and served 4 days
in command of company raised in
Chelsea. Ref: Book 52, AGO Pages
69, 77, 78; Book 51, AGO Page 295.

BARNES. JOHN JR.
Served from April 12, 1814 to April
21, 1814 in Capt. Othniel Jewett's
Company, Sumner's Regt. Ref: Book
52, AGO Page 265.

‡BARNES. JOHN JR., Sergeant, Pittsford.
Served in Capt Daniel Farrington's
Company, 30th Regt., from April 23,
1813 to April 26, 1814. Also served
in Capt. Liby's Company. Pension
Certificate No. 14244. . Pension Certificate of widow, Electa, No. 4214.

*BARNES, JOSHUA JR.
Served in Sumner's Regiment, Vt.
Militia.

*BARNES, SAMUEL.
Served from April 17, 1814 to April
21, 1814 in Capt. Othniel Jewett's
Company, Sumner's Regt.

*BARNES, STEPHEN.
Served from April 12, 1814 to April
15, 1814 in Capt. John Hackett's Company, Sumner's Regt.

*BARNES, WILLIAM.
Served in 2nd Regt Vt. Militia commanded by Col. Fifield.

BARNET, JAMES.
Served from May 18, to June 30,
1814 in Regt. of Light Dragoons.
Ref: R. & L. 1812, AGO Page 21.

BARNET, JOB.
Served from Sept. 1, 1812 to Jan.
12, 1813 in Capt. Weeks' Company,
11th Regt. Died Jan. 12, 1813. Ref:
R. & L. 1812, AGO Page 5.

*BARNET, JOB JR.
Served in 4th Regt. Vt. Militia commanded by Col. Peck.

*‡BARNET, JOHN.
Served in Capt. Solomon Clark's Company. Pension Certificate No. 5720.
Also served in Tyler's Regt., Vt. Militia.

BARNET, JOSEPH,   Middlesex.
Volunteered to go to Plattsburgh,
September, 1814, and served 10 days
in Capt. Holden Putnam's Company.
Ref: Book 52, AGO Page 251.

*BARNET, MOSES, Sergeant.
Served from Oct. 11, 1813 to Oct. 17,
1813 in Capt. Stephen Brown's Company, 3rd Regt. (Tyler's).

*BARNET, SMITH.
Served in Capt. Lowry's Company,
Col. William Williams' Regt. Detach-
ed Militia, in U. S. service 4 months
and 26 days, 1812. Also served in
Corning's Detachment, Vt. Militia.

*BARNET, WILLIAM.
Served in Tyler's Regt., Vt. Militia.

BARNETT, ELISHA.
Served in Capt. Briggs' Company,
Col. Jonathan Williams' Regt. Detach-
ed Militia, in U. S. service 2 months
and 13 days, 1812. Ref: Book 53,
AGO Page 99.

BARNETT, JOB.
Enlisted Jan. 29, 1813 in Capt.
Phineas Williams' Company. 11th
Regt. Name appears on Pay Roll for
January and February, 1813, and Pay
Roll to May 31, 1813. Ref: R. & L.
1812, AGO Pages 14 and 15.

BARNETT, JOHN, Seaman.
Captured by Earl Moira Aug. 10,
1813 on Lake Ontario. Discharged
Sept. 18th. Ref: Records of Naval
Records and Library, Navy Dept.

BARNETT, JOHN.
Served from May 1, 1813 to April 30,
1814 in Capt. Simeon Wright's Company. Ref: R. & L. 1812, AGO
Page 51.

BARNETT, JOHN.
Served from May 18, 1813 to May 17,
1814 in Capt. Simeon Wright's Company. Ref: R. & L. 1812, AGO
Page 51.

*BARNETT, NEHEMIAH JR.
Served in 4th Regt., Vt. Militia, com
manded by Col. Peck.

*BARNETT, SAMUEL,   Middlesex.
Served in Capt Holden Putnam's Company, 4 Regt. (Peck's) Vt. Militia.

‡BARNETT, WILLIAM.
Served in Capt. Sinclair's Company.
Pension Certificate of widow, Malinda,
No. 33020.

*BARNEY, CALVIN.
Served in 1st Regt. Vt. Militia, commanded by Col. Martindale.

*BARNEY, ELKANAH.
Served in Capt. Cross' Company, Col.
Martindale's Regt. Detached Militia,
in U. S. service 2 months and 14
days, 1812.

*BARNEY, HEMAN.
Served in Tyler's Regt. Vt. Militia.

BARNEY, JACOB, Musician.
Enlisted Jan. 17, 1814 for a period
of 5 years in company of late Capt.
J. Brooks, commanded by Lieut. John
I. Cromwell, Corps of U. S. Artillery.
Name appears on Muster Roll of company from April 30, 1814 to June 30,
1814. Paroled prisoner transferred
from Capt. Collins Co. Ref: R. & L.
1812, AGO Page 18.

BARNEY, LEMUEL, Highgate or Swanton. Volunteered to go to Plattsburgh, September, 1814, and served 6
days in Capt. A. J. Brown's Company. Ref: Book 51, AGO Pages 130,
139, 148, 169.

*BARNEY, MATTHEW.
Served from Oct. 8, 1813 to Oct. 17,
1813 in Capt. Stephen Brown's Company, 3 Regt. (Tyler's).

*BARNEY, RUFUS L., Corporal.
Served in Capt. Prentiss' Company,
Col. Dixon's Regt. Detached Militia,
in U. S. service 1 month and 23 days,
1813.

BARNEY, WILLIAM.
Appointed 1st Lieutenant 30th Inf.
April 30, 1813; Captain June 23, 1814;
honorably discharged June 15, 1815.
Ref: Heitman's Historical Register &
Dictionary U. S. A.

BARNEY, WILLIAM.
Enlisted Dec. 7, 1813 for a period of
5 years in company of late Capt. J.
Brooks, commanded by Lieut. John I.
Cromwell, Corps of U. S. Artillery.
Name appears on Muster Roll from
April 30, 1814 to June 30, 1814. Trans-
ferred from Capt Collins' Company.
Ref: R. & L. AGO Page 18.

BARNHAM, ENOCH.
Served from June 11, 1813 to June 14,
1813 in Capt. Thomas Dorwin's Com-
pany of Vt. Militia, 1st Regt. 2nd
Brig., 3rd Div. Ref: R. & L. 1812,
AGO Pages 45 and 46.

*BARNS, ALEXANDER F.
Served from June 11, 1813 to June 14, 1813 in Capt. Hezekiah Barns' Company, 1st Regt, 2nd Brig., 3rd Div.

*BARNS, BENJAMIN F.,   Fairfield.
Served in Capt. George W. Kindall's Company 6 months in 1812. Served in Capt. Kendall's Company, Col. William Williams' Regt. Detached Militia, in U. S. service 4 months and 23 days, 1812.

BARNS, BENJAMIN J.
Served in Capt. George W. Kindall's Company of Infantry. Name appears on Muster Roll from Aug. 31 to Oct. 31, 1812 and from Nov. 1 to Dec. 8, 1812. Ref: R. & L. 1812, AGO Pages 37 and 38.

*BARNS, CALVIN.
Served in Capt. Needham's Company, Col. Martindale's Regt. Detached Militia, in U. S. service 2 months and 11 days, 1812.

*BARNS, EBENEZER.
Served in Capt. Strait's Company, Col. Martindale's Regt. Detached Militia, in U. S. service 2 months and 13 days, 1812. Served in Capt. Benjamin Bradford's Company; name appears on Muster Roll from May 31, 1813 to Aug. 31, 1813; discharged by reason of disability Aug. 11, 1813.

*BARNS, ELIJAH, Leiutenant.
Served in 3rd Regt. Vt. Militia commanded by Col. Bowdish.

*BARNS, HEZEKIAH, Captain, Charlotte.
Served from June 11, 1813 to June 14, 1813 in command of company of Militia in 1st Regt., 2nd Brig., 3rd. Div.

*BARNS, HEZEKIAH JR., Captain Paymaster, Charlotte. Served in 4th Regt. Vt. Militia commanded by Col. Williams.

*BARNS, JAMES.
Served from April 20, 1814 to April 21, 1814 in Capt. Eseck Sprague's Company, Sumner's Regt.

*BARNS, LEONARD.
Served in Capt. Hopkins' Company, Col. Martindale's Regt. Detached Militia in U. S. service 2 months and 13 days, 1812.

BARNS, THOMAS.
Served in Lieut. William S. Foster's Company, 11th Regt. Name appears on Pay Roll for January and February, 1813. Ref: R. & L. 1812, AGO Page 7.

*BARNUM, ABIJAH, Quartermaster Sergeant. Served 5 months and 3 days in Capt. Willson's Company, Col. Williams' Regt. of Detached Militia stationed at Swanton Falls in 1812.

*BARNUM, JOB, Ensign.
Served from April 12, 1814 to April 21, 1814 in Capt. Othniel Jewett's Company, Sumner's Regt.

*BARNUM, LEWIS.
Served in Sumner's Regt. Vt. Militia.

*BARNUM, OLIVER W.
Served from April 12, 1814 to April 21, 1814 in Capt. Edmund B. Hill's Company, Sumner's Regt.

BARNUM, TRUMAN,   Shoreham.
Volunteered to go to Plattsburgh, September, 1814, and served about 6 days in Capt. Samuel Hand's Company. Ref: Rev. J. F. Goodhue's History of Shoreham, Page 108.

BARNY, JOHN JR., Sergeant. Pittsford.
Volunteered to go to Plattsburgh, September, 1814, and served 8 days in Capt. Caleb Hendee's Company. Ref: Book 52, AGO Page 124.

*BARR, ALEXANDER.
Served in Capt. Brown's Company, Col. Martindale's Regt. Detached Militia, in U. S. service 16 days, 1812.

‡BARR, EBENEZER N.
Served in Captain Barr's Company. Pension Certificate No. 23150.

*BARR, SAMUEL T.
Served from Oct. 5, 1813 to Oct. 16, 1813 in Capt. Roswell Hunt's Company, 3 Regt. (Tyler's).

BARR, TRUMAN,   Sudbury.
Volunteered to go to Plattsburgh, September, 1814, and served 6 days in Capt. Thomas Hall's Company. Ref: Book 52, AGO Page 122.

*BARRELL, PHINEHAS.
Served in 2nd Regt. Vt. Militia commanded by Col. Fifield.

BARRET, ALEXANDER.
Served from May 21, 1813 to May 20, 1814 in Capt. Simeon Wright's Company. Ref: R. & L. 1812, AGO Page 51.

BARRETT, ALFRED.
Served in Capt. Phineas Williams' Company, 11th Regt Name appears on Pay Roll of company for January and February, 1813. Ref: R. & L 1812, AGO Page 15.

*BARRETT, ANDREW.
Served from Sept. 25, 1813 to Nov. 12, 1813 in Capt. Amos Robinson's Company, Dixon's Regt.

BARRETT, ASA.
Volunteered to go to Plattsburgh, September, 1814, and served 4 days in Capt. Aaron Kidder's Company. Ref: Book 52, AGO Page 65.

‡*BARRETT, BENJAMIN.
Enlisted Sept. 25, 1813 and served 1 month and 23 days in Capt. N. B. Eldridge's Company, Dixon's Regt. Also served in Captain Wilson's Company Pension Certificate No. 14235. Pension Certificate of widow, Fanny, No. 11727.

*BARRETT, ELISHA.
Enlisted Oct. 2, 1813 and served 78 days in Capt. John Weed's Company, Col. Clark's Regt.

*BARRETT, GARRARD, Drum Major.
Served in 1st Regt. Vt Militia commanded by Col. Judson.

BARRETT, JOHN.
Served from March 18th to June 17th,
1813 in Capt. Charles Follett's Company, 11th Regt. Ref: R. & L. 1812,
AGO Page 13.

BARRETT, JOSEPH,   Strafford.
Volunteered to go to Plattsburgh
and served in company of Capt. Jedediah H. Harris. Ref: Hemenway's
Vt. Gazetteer, Vol. 2, Page 1083.

BARRETT, OFFIN.
Served as saddler from May 1, 1814
to Aug. 31, 1814 in Capt. Haig's
Corps of Light Dragoons. R. & L.
1812, AGO Pages 20 and 29.

BARRETT, PHINEAS.
Served in Capt. Dodge's Company,
Col. Fifield's Regt. Detached Militia,
in U. S. service 26 days, 1812. Ref:
Book 53, AGO Page 15.

*BARRETT, SAMUEL.
Served in Capt Mason's Company,
Col. Fifield's Regt. Detached Militia
in U. S. service 2 months and 14
days, 1812.

‡*BARREY, NATHAN.
Served in Capt. Mason's Company,
Col. Fifield's Regt. Detached Militia,
in U. S. service 2 months and 14
days, 1812. Pension Certificate of
widow, Olive, No. 28466.

‡BARRON, BENJAMIN.
Served in Captain John Butler's Company. Pension Certificate No. 14980.

BARRON, ELIZUS,   Washington.
Volunteered to go to Plattsburgh,
September, 1814, and served in Capt
Amos Stiles' Company. Ref: Book
52, AGO Pages 36, 37, 38.

BARRON, JOSEPH,   Ferrisburgh.
Served from April 9th to June 30th,
1814 in Regiment of Light Dragoons.
Served in U. S. Navy Dept. on Lake
Champlain as Pilot on the "Saratoga" and was mortally wounded during battle of Sept. 11, 1814. Ref:
R. & L. 1812, AGO Page 21; Vol.
51 Vt. State Papers, Page 146.

‡BARROWS, ALFRED,   Thetford.
Volunteered to go to Plattsburgh,
September, 1814, and served in Capt.
Joseph Barrett's Company, 2nd Regt.
Pension Certificate No. 25150.

BARROWS, AMOS,   Sharon, Conn.
Age 29; eyes, blue; hair, brown; com-
plexion, light; occupation, farmer;
height, 5 feet 9 inches; born in
Sharon, Conn. Enlisted in Capt. Wil-
liam Miller's Company, 30th Regt.
March 18, 1814 for a period of five
years. Transferred to Capt. Gideon
Spencer's Company, 30th Regt. Ref:
R. & L. 1812, AGO Pages 54, 55, 57.

*BARROWS, ERASTUS.
Served from April 12, 1814 to May
20, 1814 in Company of Capt. James
Gray Jr., Sumner's Regt.

‡*BARROWS, FREDERICK.
Served in Capt. Taylor's Company,
Col. Fifield's Regt. Detached Militia,

in U. S. service 6 months, 1812. Pension Certificate No. 11927.

BARROWS, ISAAC G.
Served 4 months and 29 days, 1812,
in Capt. Dorrance's Company, Col.
William Williams' Regt. Ref: Book
53, AGO Page 95.

BARROWS, JONATHAN P.   Pittsford.
Volunteered to go to Plattsburgh,
September, 1814 and served 8 days in
Capt. Caleb Hendee's Company. Ref:
Book 52, AGO Page 124.

*BARROWS, JOSIAH N., Capt. & 2nd
Lieutenant, Huntington. Served from
Oct. 5, 1813 to Oct. 17, 1813 in Capt.
John Munson's Company, 3rd Regt.
commanded by Col. Tyler. Volunteered to go to Plattsburgh, September, 1814, and served at the battle
in command of a company raised in
Huntington and Hinesburg.

*BARROWS, PRINCE.
Served from April 12, 1814 to May
20, 1814 in company of Capt. James
Gray Jr., Sumner's Regt.

BARROWS, ROSS,   Shoreham.
Volunteered to go to Plattsburgh,
September, 1814 and served about 6
days in company of Cavalry under
Capt. Nathaniel North. Ref: Rev.
J. F. Goodhue's History of Shoreham,
Page 107.

‡BARROWS, ZOROASTER.
Served in Captain M. Worth's Company. Pension Certificate No. 30851.

BARTHOLOMEW, CHARLES, Shrewsbury. Volunteered to go to Plattsburgh, September, 1814, and served
4 days in Capt. Robert Reed's Company. Ref: Book 52, AGO Pages
138 and 140.

BARTHOLOMEW, ERASTUS,   Chelsea.
Volunteered and went to Plattsburgh,
September 11, 1814. Served 6 days
in company of Capt. David Robinson
raised in Williamstown and vicinity.
Ref: Book 52, AGO Pages 5 and 14.

BARTHOLOMEW, PETER.
Served from May 1st to June 30th,
1814 in Capt. Haig's Corps of Light
Dragoons. Ref: R. & L. 1812, AGO
Page 20.

*BARTHOLOMEW, SHELDON.
Served in Capt. Burnap's Company,
Col. Jonathan Williams' Regt. Detached Militia, in U. S. service 2
months and 13 days, 1812.

*BARTLETT, ANDREW.
Served in Capt. Robbins' Company,
Col. Williams' Regt. Detached Militia, in U. S. service 4 months and
29 days, 1812.

*BARTLETT, CHRISTOPHER, Sergeant,
Waitsfield. Volunteered to go to
Plattsburgh, September, 1814 and
served 4 days in Capt. Mathias Jones'
Company. Also, served as sergeant
in Corning's Detachment, Vt. Militia.
Ref: Book 52, AGO Page 170.

*BARTLETT, DAVID.
Served in Capt. Preston's Company,
Col. Jonathan Williams' Regt Detached Militia, in U. S. service 2
months and 6 days, 1812.

*BARTLETT, EBENEZER.
Served in 3rd Regt. Vt. Militia commanded by Col. Tyler.

BARTLETT, EBER.   Jericho.
Took part in the Battle of Platts-
burgh. Ref: History of Jericho,
Page 142.

‡*BARTLETT, HOOKER.
Served in Capt. Robbins' Company,
Col. William Williams' Regt. Detached Militia, in U. S. service 4
months and 29 days, 1812. Pension
Certificate of widow, Hannah, No.
10693.

BARTLETT, JOEL,   Orange.
Volunteered to go to Plattsburgh
Sept. 11, 1814 and served 5 days in
Capt. David Rising's Company. Ref:
Book 52, AGO Page 19.

*BARLETT, LOTAN.
Served in company of Capt. John Mc-
Neil Jr., 11th Regt. Name appears
on Pay Roll of company for January and February, 1813. Also served
with Hospital Attendants, Vt. Ref:
R. & L. 1812, AGO Page 17.

*BARTLETT, ORSON.
Enlisted Sept. 25, 1813 and served 1
month and 23 days in Capt. Jesse
Post's Company, Col. Dixon's Regt.

*BARTLETT, SAMUEL.   Highgate.
Served in Capt. Saxe's Company, Col.
William Williams' Regt. Detached
Militia, in U. S. service 3 months and
24 days, 1812. Enlisted Sept. 25,
1813 and served 1 month and 23 days
in Capt. Amos Robinson's Company,
Col. Dixon's Regt. Ref: Book 52,
AGO Page 271; Book 53, AGO Pages
88 and 107.

*BARTLETT, SAMUEL JR.
Served in Capt. L. Robinson's Company, Col. Dixon's Regt. Detached
Militia, U. S. service 1 month and 18
days, 1813.

‡BARTLETT, WILLIAM.
Served in Capt. Ethan Burnap's Com-
pany, 3rd Regt. Pension Certificate
No. 8754.

BARTON, ANTHONY,   Vergennes.
Volunteered to go to Plattsburgh,
September, 1814, was at the battle
and served 10 days in Capt. Gideon
Spencer's Company. Ref: Book 51,
AGO Page 1.

BARTON, BENJAMIN, 1st Sergeant,
Orange. Volunteered to go to Plattsburgh Sept. 11, 1814, and served 5
days in Capt. David Rising's Company. Ref: Book 52, AGO Pages 19
and 21.

*BARTON, CALEB JR.
Served from June 11, 1813 to June
14, 1813 in Ithiel Stone's Company
of Vt Militia, 1st Regt., 2nd Brig.,
3rd Div.

*BARTON, CALEB B. (or E.)
Served in 1st Regt. Vt. Militia commanded by Col. Judson.

BARTON, DANIEL,   Pittsford.
Volunteered to go to Plattsburgh,
September, 1814, and served 8 days
in Capt. Caleb Hendee's Company.
Ref: Book 52, AGO Page 124.

BARTON, DAVID, Corporal, Montpelier.
Volunteered to go to Plattsburgh,
September, 1814, and served 8 days
in Capt. Timothy Hubbard's Company.
Ref: Book 52, AGO Page 256.

BARTON, JEREMIAH, Sergeant.
Enlisted April 11, 1813 in Company
of late Capt. J. Brooks, commanded
by Lieut. John I. Cromwell, Corps
of U. S. Artillery. Name appears
on Muster Roll from April 30, 1814
to June 30, 1814. Ref: R. & L. 1812,
AGO Page 18.

*BARTON, JOHN D.
Served in Sumner's Regt. Vt. Militia.

BARTON, JOSEPH O.
Enlisted Dec. 20, 1813 in company of
late Capt. J. Brooks, commanded by
Lieut. John I. Cromwell, Corps of
U. S. Artillery. Name appears on
Muster Roll from April 30, 1814 to
June 30, 1814. Transferred from
Capt. Leonard's Company. Ref: R.
& L. 1812, AGO Page 18.

BARTON, ROBERT,   Franklin County.
Volunteered to go to Plattsburgh
Sept. 11, 1814 and served in 15th or
22nd Regt. Ref: Hemenway's Vt.
Gazetteer, Vol. 2, Page 392.

‡BARTON, WILLIAM.
Served in Captain Stone's Company.
Pension Certificate of widow, Ann,
No. 28192.

BASCOM, ELISHA,   Shoreham.
Volunteered to go to Plattsburgh,
September, 1814, and served about 6
days in Capt. Samuel Hand's Com-
pany. Ref: Rev. J. F. Goodhue's
History of Shoreham, Page 107.

*BASCOMB, JOSIAH, Sergeant, Enos-
burgh. Served from Oct. 14, 1813 to
Nov. 17, 1813 in Capt. Asahel Scovell's
Company, Col. Clark's Regt.

BASHFORD, JAMES.
Served from March 29, 1813 to June
28, 1813 in Capt. Samul Gordon's
Company, 11th Regt. Ref: R. & L.
1812, AGO Page 8.

BASS, JOEL, Sergeant,   Williamstown.
Served at the Battle of Plattsburgh
Sept. 11, 1814 and was in Capt. David
Robinson's Company. Served about 8
days. Ref: Book 52, AGO Pages 2
and 9.

*BASS, JONATHAN,   Randolph.
Volunteered to go to Plattsburgh,
September, 1814, and served in Capt.
Lebbeus Egerton's Company.

‡BASS, ZACHEUS.
Served as a surgeon. No organization given. Pension Certificate No.
31718.

*BASSET. HORACE. Drummer.
Served in 2nd Regt. Vt. Militia commanded by Col. Fifield.

‡BASSETT. ARBA.
Served under Captain Hendrickson or Captain Mead. Pension Certificate of widow, Mary, No. 27283.

BASSETT, JAMES.
Served from Dec. 21, 1812 to July 6, 1813 in Capt. Edgerton's Company, 11th Regt. Ref: R. & L. 1812, AGO Pages 2 and 3.

BASSETT, WILLIAM,   Barre.
Volunteered to go to Plattsburgh, September, 1814, and served 10 days in Capt. Warren Ellis' Company. Ref: Book 52, AGO Page 242.

*BASSFORD, DAVID, Lieutenant.
Appointed Sept. 23, 1813 and served in Capt. Amasa Mansfield's Company, Dixon's Regt.

*BASSFORD, JOHN, Sergeant.
Enlisted Sept. 23, 1813 and served 1 month and 23 days in Capt. Amasa Mansfield's Company, Col. Dixon's Regt.

*BASTO, ELISHA, 3rd Sergeant.
Served from June 11, 1813 to June 14, 1813 in Capt. Moses Jewett's Company of Militia, 1st Regt., 2nd Brig., 3rd Div.

*BASTO, GILBERT.
Served from June 11, 1813 to June 14, 1813 in company commanded by Capt. John M. Eldridge, 1st Regt., 2nd Brig., 3rd Div., Vt. Militia.

*BASTO, HENRY, Corporal.
Served in 1st Regt. Vt. Militia commanded by Col. Judson.

*BASTWICK, GEORGE T., Sergeant.
Served in 1st Regt. Vt. Militia commanded by Col. Judson.

BATCHELDER, BENJAMIN.
Volunteered to go to Plattsburgh, September, 1814 and served in Capt. Ebenezer Spencer's Company, of Vershire. Ref: Book 52, AGO Page 48.

*BATCHELDER, HENRY.
Served in Capt. Richardson's Company, Col. Martindale's Regt. Detached Militia, in U. S. service 2 months and 13 days, 1812. Ref: Book 53, AGO Page 83.

BATCHELDER, JOSEPH,   Marshfield.
Volunteered to go to Plattsburgh, September, 1814, and served 9 days in Capt. James English's Company. Ref: Book 52, AGO Page 248.

BATCHELDER, JOSEPH,   Barre.
Volunteered to go to Plattsburgh, September, 1814, and served 9 days in Capt. Warren Ellis' Company. Ref: Book 52, AGO Pages 222 and 242.

BATCHELDER, NATHANIEL,   Barre.
Volunteered to go to Plattsburgh, September, 1814, and served 5 days in Capt. Warren Ellis Company. Ref: Book 52, AGO Pages 168 and 242.

BATCHELDER, NATHANIEL JR., Barre.
Volunteered to go to Plattsburgh, September, 1814, and served 5 days in Capt Warren El'is' Company. Ref: Hemenway's Vt. Gazetteer, Vol. 4, Page 42.

‡BATCHELDER, PARLEY,   Barre.
Volunteered to go to Plattsburgh, September, 1814, and served in Captain Warren Ellis' Company. Pension Certificate No. 30848.

BATCHELDER, WILLIAM,   Barre.
Volunteered to go to Plattsburgh, September, 1814, and served 10 days in Capt. Warren Ellis' Company. Ref: Book 52, AGO Page 242.

‡*BATCHELDOR, ZEPHANIA.
Served in Capt. Wheatley's Company, Col. Fifield's Regt. Detached Militia, in U. S. service 2 months and 21 days, 1812. Pension Certificate of widow, Ruth, No. 1471.

BATEMAN, LUTHER, Sergeant, Shoreham. Volunteered to go to Plattsburgh, September, 1814, and served 6 days in Capt. Samuel Hand's Company. Ref: Rev. J. F. Goodhue's History of Shoreham, Page 107.

BATEMAN, THOMAS,   Shoreham.
Volunteered to go to Plattsburgh, September, 1814 and served 6 days in Capt. Samuel Hand's Company. Ref: Rev. J. F. Goodhue's History of Shoreham, Page 107.

*BATES, ALPHEUS.
Served from June 11, 1813 to June 14, 1813 in Lieut. Bates' Company, 1 Regt. (Judson's).

BATES, BENJAMIN, Lieutenant.
Served in 1st Regt. of Detached Militia of Vermont in the service of the United States at Champlain for 2 days commencing Nov. 18 and ending Nov. 19, 1812.

BATES, CARVER,   Barre.
Volunteered to go to Plattsburgh, September, 1814, and served 10 days in Capt. Warren Ellis' Company. Ref: Book 52, AGO Page 242.

BATES, D. W., Corporal.
Served from March 8, 1813 to June 7, 1813 in Capt. Samul Gordon's Company, 11th Regt. Ref: R. & L. 1812, AGO, Page 8.

*BATES, DAVID.
Served in Capt. Ormsbee's Company, Col. Martindale's Regt. Detached Militia, in U. S. service 2 months and 14 days, 1812.

‡BATES, ELIHU,   Richmond.
Volunteered to go to Plattsburgh, September, 1814, and served 9 days in Capt. Roswell Hunt's Company, 3 Regt. (Tyler's). Pension Certificate of widow, Nancy, No. 26097.

*BATES, ELIPHALET,   Randolph.
Served under Captains Wheatly and Wright, Col. Fifield's Regt. Vt. Militia, in U. S. service 4 months and 26 days, 1812. Volunteered to go to Plattsburgh, September, 1814, and served in Capt. Lebbeus Edgerton's Company. Also served in 4 Regt. (Williams') Vt. Militia.

BATES, GEORGE,   Fairfax.
Enlisted Aug. 8, 1812 in company of
Capt. Joseph Beeman, Jr. 11th Regt.
U. S. Inf. under Col. Ira Clark. Ref:
Hemenway's Vt. Gazetteer, Vol. 2,
Page 402.

*‡BATES, JACOB, Corporal Sergeant.
Served from June 11, 1813 to June
14, 1813 in Lieut. Moses Bates' Company, 1st Regt. (Judson's). Pension
Certificate No. 15030. Pension Certificate of widow, Rowanna, No. 25897.

*BATES, JOHNSON,   Waterbury.
Volunteered to go to Plattsburgh,
September, 1814, and served 11 days
in Capt. George Atkins' Company, 4
Regt. (Peck's). Also served in Corn-
ing's Detachment, Vt. Militia.

*BATES, LEVI, Musician.
Served in Capt. Adams' Company,
Col. Jonathan Williams' Regt. Detached Militia, in U. S. service 2 months
and 7 days, 1812.

BATES, MARTIN.
Enlisted April 22, 1813 in Capt. James
Taylor's Company, 30th Regt. Trans-
ferred to Capt. Gideon's Spencer's
Company, 30th Regt. and served to
April 25, 1814. Ref: R. & L. 1812,
AGO Pages 57 and 58.

*BATES, MOSES, Lieutenant Captain
Served from June 11, 1813 to June
14, 1813 in Lieut. Bates' Company,
Col. Dixon's Regt.

*BATES, MOSES.
Served from Sept. 25, 1813 to Oct. 4,
1813 in Capt. Elijah Birge's Company,
Dixon's Regt.

*BATES, PETER,   Randolph.
Volunteered to go to Plattsburgh,
September, 1814, and served in Capt.
Lebbeus Egerton's Company.

*BATES, REUBEN.
Served in Capt. Scovell's Company,
Col. Martindale's Regt. Detached
Militia, in U. S. service 1 month and
14 days, 1812.

*BATES, ROBERT B.
Served in Lieut. Justus Foote's Company, Sumner's Regt. from April 12,
1814 to April 15, 1814.

BATES, ROSWELL.
Served from Jan. 1st to June 30,
1814 in Capt. Haig's Corps of Light
Dragoons. Ref: R. & L. 1812, AGO
Page 20.

‡*BATES, SIMEON, Corporal, Montpelier.
Served in Capt. Walker's Company,
Col. Fifield's Regt. Detached Militia,
in U. S. service 6 months and 3 days,
1812. Volunteered to go to Plattsburgh, September, 1814, and served
8 days in Capt. Timothy Hubbard's
Company. Pension Certificate No.
11869 Pension Certificate of widow,
Emily, No. 33253.

*BATES, SOLOMON.
Served in 1st Regt. Vt. Militia commanded by Col. Martindale.

BATES, WILLIAM,   Fairfax.
Served in 1813 and 1814 in Capt.
Joseph Beeman's Company. Ref:
Hemenway's Vt. Gazetteer, Vol. 2,
Page 402.

BATINEAU, LEWIS,   Franklin County.
Volunteered to go to Plattsburgh
Sept. 11, 1814 and served in 15th or
22nd Regt. Ref: Hemenway's Vt. Gazetteer, Vol. 2, Page 392. .

*BATTIE, WILLIAM.
Served in 1 Regt. Vt. Militia commanded by Col. Judson.

*BATTIS, JOHN.
Served from Sept. 25, 1813 to Oct. 31,
1813 in Capt. Jesse Post's Company,
Dixon's Regt.

*BATTIST, JOHN JR.
Served in Dixon's Regt. Vt. Militia.

‡BATTLES, JAMES B.
Served in Capt. Lot Hudson's Company. Pension Certificate No. 33909.

‡BAULCH, NATHANIEL.
Served in Capt. E. C. Burnap's Com-
pany, 3rd Regt. Pension Certificate
No. 16914.

BAVIL, SAMUEL,   Georgia.
Served about 5½ months in Col. Wil-
liam Williams' Regt. Ref: Vol 50
Vt. State Papers, Page 204.

‡*BAXTER, DAVID.
Served in Capt. Robbins' Company,
Col. William Williams' Regt. Detached Militia, in U. S. service 4 months
and 29 days, 1812. Pension Certificate No. 12421.

‡BAXTER, ELIHU B.,   Cornwall.
Volunteered to go to Plattsburgh,
September, 1814, and served in Capt.
Edmund B. Hill's Company, Sumner's
Regt. Was present at the battle.
Pension Certificate No. 28612.

BAXTER, GIDEON,   Sudbury.
Volunteered to go to Plattsburgh,
September, 1814, and served 6 days
in Capt. Thomas Hall's Company.
Ref: Book 52, AGO Page 122.

BAXTER, HORACE.
Appointed 2nd Lieutenant, Infantry,
(probably 11th Regt.) March, 1812.
Ref: Governor and Council Vt., Vol.
6, Page 473.

‡*BAXTER, IRA.
Served in Capt. Taylor's Company,
Col. Fifield's Regt. Detached Militia,
in U. S service 2 months and 21 days,
1812. Pension Certificate No. 12477.

*BAXTER, THOMAS,   Clarendon.
Served in Capt. Needham's Company,
Col. Martindale's Regt. Detached Militia, in U. S. service 2 months and
13 days, 1812. Enlisted Sept. 21,
1813 in Capt. Daniel Farrington's
Company, 30th Regt. Transferred to
31st Regt. Ref: R. & L. 1812, AGO
Pages 50 and 51.

BAY, MARTIN.
Enlisted Jan. 8, 1813 in Capt. John
W. Weeks' Company, 11th Regt. Never
joined. Ref: R. & L. 1812, AGO
Page 4.

BAYDEN, EBENEZER JR.
Enlisted Sept 25, 1813 in Capt. Jesse Post's Company, Col. Dixon's Regt. Ref: Book 52, AGO Page 290.

*BAYES, WILLIAM.
Served in Dixon's Regt. Vt. Militia.

BAYLE, JEREMIAH.   ..
Served in Capt. Preston's Company, Col. Jonathan Williams' Regt. Detached Militia, in U. S. service 2 months and 6 days, 1812. Ref: Book 53, AGO Page 77.

*BAYLEY, DANIEL.
Served in Capt. Rogers' Company, Col. Fifield's Regt. Detached Militia, in U. S service 10 days, 1812. Also served in Capt. Burnap's Company, Col. Jonathan Williams' Regt. Detached Militia, in U. S. service 15 days, 1812.

BAYLEY, EBEN,   Berlin.
Volunteered to go to Plattsburgh. September, 1814, and served 7 days in Capt. Cyrus Johnson's Company. Ref: Book 52, AGO Pages 202 and 255.

*BAYLEY, JACOB 4th.
Served in Capt. Rogers' Company, Col. Fifield's Regt. Detached Militia, in U. S. service 5 months and 27 days, 1812.

BAYLEY, JESSE, Sergeant.
Served in Capt. Morrill's Company, Col. Fifield's Regt. Detached Militia, in U. S. service 6 months and 5 days, 1812. Ref: Book 53, AGO Page 36.

‡BAYLEY, JOHN.
Served in Capt. Rogers' Company, Col. Fifield's Regt. Detached Militia, in U. S. service 2 months and 22 days, 1812. Pension Certificate No. 18044. Pension Certificate of widow, Martha Powers, No. 28772.

BAYLEY, JOHN.
Enlisted Jan. 18, 1813 in Lieut. V. R. Goodrich's Company, 11th Regt. and served until date of death, April 6, 1813. Ref: R. & L., 1812, AGO Pages 10 and 11.

BAYLEY, JOHN.
Appointed Major, 30th Inf. Feb. 23, 1813; Lt. Colonel 34th Inf. May 15, 1814; transferred to 24th Inf. Sept. 28, 1814; honorably discharged June 15, 1815. Ref: Heitman's Historical Register & Dictionary USA; Governor and Council, Vt., Vol. 6, Page 475.

*BAYLEY, JOHN 2nd.
Served in 2nd Regt. Vt Militia commanded by Col. Fifield.

*BAYLEY, JOSEPH 2nd.
Served in Capt. Rogers' Company, Col. Fifield's Regt. Detached Militia, in U. S. service 2 months, 1812.

*BAYLEY, MOSES.
Served in 2nd Regt. Vt. Militia commanded by Col. Fifield.

‡BAYLEY, SAMUEL S.
Served in Capt. Rufus Stenard's Company. Pension Certificate No. 9261.

*BEACH, AMBROSE.
Served in Sumner's Regt. Vt. Militia.

*BEACH, AMOS.
Served in Sumner's Regt. Vt. Militia.

BEACH, GASHAM.   Salisbury.
Volunteered to go to Plattsburgh, September, 1814, and served 4 days in Capt. John Morton's Company. Ref: Book 52, AGO Page 141.

‡BEACH, GERSHAM,   Pittsford.
Volunteered to go to Plattsburgh, September, 1814, and served 8 days in Capt. Caleb Hendee's Company. Pension Certificate of widow, Rebecca, No. 26740.

‡*BEACH, HOMER, Musician.
Served in Capt. J. M. Eldridge's Company, 1st Regt. (Judson's). Pension Certificate No. 23752.

BEACH, LAPHER.
Served in Capt. Stephen Brown's Company, Tyler's Regt. from Oct. 5, 1813 to Oct. 17, 1813. Ref: R. & L. 1812, AGO Page 34.

*BEACH, LINUS.
Served from April 12, 1814 to April 15, 1814 in Lieut. Justus Foote's Company, Sumner's Regt.

*BEACH, MATTHEW,   Fairfield.
Served in Capt. Kendall's Company, Col. William Williams' Regt. Detached Militia, in U. S. service 4 months and 23 days, 1812.

BEACH, ROBERT,   Huntington.
Volunteered to go to Plattsburgh, September, 1814, and served in Capt. Josiah N. Barrow's Company. Was present at the battle. Ref: Book 51, AGO Page 77.

*BEACH, SHERMAN,   Huntington.
Served from Oct. 11, 1813 to Oct. 17, 1813 in Capt. John Munson's Company, 3 Regt. (Tyler's). Volunteered to go to Plattsburgh, September, 1814, and served in Capt. Josiah N. Barrows' Company. Was at the battle.

BEACH, SILAS.
Enlisted April 22, 1813 in Capt. James Taylor's Company, 30th Regt. Transferred to Capt. Gideon Spencer's Company, 30th Regt. and served until discharged April 25, 1814. Ref: R. & L. 1812, AGO Pages 52, 57, 58.

BEACH, THOMAS.
Served from June 11, 1813 to June 14, 1813 in Capt. John M. Eldridge's Company, 1st Regt., 2nd Brig., 3rd Div. Vt. Militia. Ref: R. &. L. 1812, AGO Page 35.

*BEACH, ZOPHER.
Served in 3rd Regt. Vt. Militia commanded by Col. Tyler.

BEACHER, GAD.
Served from March 10, 1813 to May 31, 1813 in Capt. John Weeks' Company, 11th Regt. Ref: R. & L. 1812, AGO Page 4.

BEACHER, MARCUS.
Served from May 1st to June 30th,
1814, in Capt. Haig's Corps of Light
Dragoons. Ref: R. & L. 1812, AGO
Page 20.

*BEADEN, ALPHEUS P.
Served from April 12, 1814 to April
21, 1814 in Capt. Shubael Wales' Company, Col. W. B. Sumner's Regt.

BEAL, ABEL.
Served in Capt. Chadwick's Company.
Ref: R. & L. 1812, AGO Page 32.

*BEALS, GEORGE.
Served in Capt. Adams Company, Col.
Jonathan Williams' Regt. Detached
Militia, in U. S. service 15 days, 1812.
Served from Sept. 25, 1813 to Oct. 22,
1813 in Capt. N. B. Eldridge's Com-
pany, Dixon's Regt. Served from
Nov. 1, 1812 to Feb. 28, 1813 in Lieut.
V. R. Goodrich's Company, 11th Regt.

*BEAL, LUTHER, Corporal.
Served in Capt. Taylor's Company.
Col. William Williams' Regt. Detached Militia, in U. S. service 4 months
and 24 days, 1812.

*BEAL, SHEPARD, 2nd Lieutenant.
Enlisted Sept. 25, 1813 in Capt. N. B.
Eldridge's Company, Dixon's Regt.

BEALS, DANIEL.
Served in Capt. Samuel H. Holly's
Company, 11th Regt. Name appears
on Pay Roll for January and Feb-
ruary, 1813. Ref: R. & L. 1812, AGO
Page 25.

‡*BEALS, LEVI.
Served from Sept. 25, 1813 to Sept.
28, 1813 in Capt. Amos Robinson's
Company, Dixon's Regt. Also served
in Captain Gilman's Company. Pension Certificate No. 28485.

*BEALS, NATHAN.
Enlisted Sept. 25, 1813 in Capt. N. B.
Eldridge's Company, Dixon's Regt.

BEALS, WILLIAM JR., Fifer, Pittsford.
Volunteered to go to Plattsburgh,
September, 1814, and served 8 days
in Capt. Caleb Hendee's Company.
Ref: Book 52, AGO Page 124.

*BEAN, AARON.
Served with Hospital Attendants, Vt.

‡BEAN, CLIFFORD.
Volunteered to go to Plattsburgh,
September, 1814, and served in com-
pany commanded by Capt. Jonathan
Jennings of Chelsea. Pension Certi-
ficate of widow, Nancy B., No. 36995.

BEAN, DAVID,   Strafford.
Volunteered to go to Plattsburgh,
September, 1814, and served in Capt.
Joseph Barrett's Company, 2nd Regt.
Ref: Book 52, AGO Page 41.

BEAN, DAVID.
Volunteered to go to Plattsburgh,
September, 1814, and served 7 days
in company commanded by Capt.
Frederick Griswold, raised in Brook-
field, Vt. Ref: Book 52, AGO Page 52.

‡*BEAN, DAVID, Sergeant.
Served from June 11, 1813 to June
14, 1813 in Lieut. Bates' Company of
Militia, 1st Regt. (Judson's). Pension Certificate of widow, Maria, No.
28063.

*BEAN, JOHN, 1st Sergeant.
Volunteered to go to Plattsburgh,
September, 1814 and served in com-
pany commanded by Capt. Jonathan
Jennings of Chelsea. Also served in
3 Regt. Vt. Militia commanded by
Col. Williams. Ref: Book 52, AGO
Pages 79 and 104.

*BEAN, JOHN JR.
Served from Sept. 23, 1813 to Nov. 14,
1813 in Capt. Amasa Mansfield's Company, Dixon's Regt.

*BEAN, JOHN R.
Served from Sept. 23, 1813 to Nov. 8,
1813 in Capt. Amasa Mansfield's Company, Dixon's Regt.

*‡BEAN, LEVI.
Served in Capt. Bingham's Company,
Col. Jonathan Williams' Regt. Detached Militia, in U. S. service 2
months and 9 days, 1812. Volunteered to go to Plattsburgh, September,
1814, and served in company commanded by Capt. Jonathan Jennings
of Chelsea. Pension Certificate No.
6158.

BEAN, RICHARD, 1st Lieutenant.
Served in company of Capt. John Mc-
Neil Jr., 11th Regt. Name appears
on Pay Roll for January and February, 1813, as Quartermaster of the
11th Regt. Ref: R. & L. 1812, AGO
Page 17.

‡*BEAN, WENTWORTH.
Served in Capt. Walker's Company
Col. Fifield's Regt. Detached Militia,
in U. S. service 2 months and 26 days,
1812. Volunteered to go to Plattsburgh, September, 1814, and served
6 days in Capt. Cyrus Johnson's Company. Pension Certificate No. 18633.

BEAN, WILLIAM.
Served from May 1st to June 30,
1814 in Capt. Alexander Brooks Corps
of Artillery. Ref: R. & L. 1812, AGO
Page 31.

*BEARCE, E. C.
Served in 4th Regt.Vt. Militia commanded by Col. Williams.

BEARD, JOHN H.,   Orange.
Volunteered to go to Plattsburgh,
Sept. 11, 1814, and served 5 days
in Capt. David Rising's Company. Ref:
Book 52, AGO Pages 19 and 20.

BEARDSLEY, LEVI, Sergeant, St. Albans.
Served from May 14, 1813 to May,
1814, in Capt. John Wires' Company,
30th Regt. Ref: R. & L. 1812, AGO
Page 40.

*BEARDSLEY, NATHANIEL B., Fairfield.
Served in Capt. Kendall's Company,
Col. William Williams' Regt. Detached Militia, in U. S. service 4 months
and 10 days, 1812.

*BEARDSLEY. ROSWELL.
Served in Capt. Willson's Company,
Col. William Williams' Regt. Detached Militia, in U. S. service 5 months,
1812.

‡BEARDSLEY. WILLIAM. Sergeant,
Shaftsbury. Born in Shaftsbury, Vt.;
aged 21 years; 5 feet 9 inches high;
light complexion; sandy hair; grey
eyes; by profession a farmer. Enlisted at Plattsburgh, Feb. 22, 1814
in Capt. Danforth's Company 30th
Regt. U. S. Inf.; discharged at Burlington, 1815. Name appears on
Descriptive Roll of Capt. William
Miller's Company, 30th Regt. Also
served in Capt. Cross' Company, Col.
Martindale's Regt. Detached Militia,
in U. S. service 2 months and 14
days, 1812. Ref: R. & L. 1812, AGO
Page 55. Pension Certificate No. 12497.

BEATTY, JOHN.
Enlisted Aug. 31. 1812 for a period
of 5 years in Capt. White Youngs'
Company. 15th Regt. Name appears
on Muster Roll from Aug. 31, 1814
to Dec. 31, 1814. Ref: R. & L. 1812,
AGO Page 27.

BEBEE. PETER.   St. Albans.
Served from Oct. 14, 1813 to Oct.,
1814 in Capt. John Wires' Company.
30th Regt. Ref: R. & L. 1812, AGO
Page 40.

BECKETT. SETH.   Barre.
Volunteered to go to Plattsburgh,
September. 1814. and served 10 days
in Capt. Warren Ellis' Company. Ref:
Book 52. AGO Page 242.

*BECKFORD. THOMAS.
Enlisted Oct. 2, 1813 in Capt. Asahel
Langworthy's Company, Col. Isaac
Clark's Rifle Corps.

‡BECKLEY, HORACE.   Barre.
Volunteered to go to Plattsburgh,
September, 1814, and served 9 days
in Capt. Warren Ellis' Company.
Also served in Captain March's Com-
pany and Captain Stacy's Company.
Pension Certificate No. 19574. Pen-
sion Certificate of widow, Hannah,
No. 13197.

*BECKLEY, ORAMEL.   Barre.
Volunteered to go to Plattsburgh,
September. 1814, and served 10 days
in Capt. Warren Ellis' Company. Also
served under Captains Rockwood and
Stacy. Pension Certificate No. 1805.

BECKLEY, ZEBEDEE.   Barre.
Volunteered to go to Plattsburgh,
September, 1814, and served 8 days
as a teamster in Capt. Warren Ellis'
Company. Ref: Book 52, AGO Pages
219 and 242.

BECKWITH. BENJAMIN.
Served from Jan. 28, 1813 to April 1,
1813 in Lieut. William S. Foster's
Company. 11th Regt. Ref: R. & L.
1812. AGO Page 6.

‡BECKWITH. JOSIAH.   Williamstown.
Volunteered to go to Plattsburgh,
September. 1814. and served 8 days
in Capt. David Robinson's Company.
Pension Certificate No. 6890.

*BECKWITH. SILAS.
Served in 1st Regt. Vt. Militia commanded by Col. Judson.

*BECKWORTH, ABRAM.
Served from April 12, 1814 to May
20, 1814 in company of Capt. James
Gray Jr., Sumner's Regt.

BEDEL. HAZEN, Sergeant.
Served in company of Capt. John
McNeil Jr., 11th Regt. Name appears
on Pay Roll for January and Febru-
ary, 1813. Ref: R. & L. 1812, AGO
Page 17.

BEEBE. DAVID L.,   Pittsford.
Volunteered to go to Plattsburgh,
September. 1814, and served 8 days
in Capt. Caleb Hendee's Company.
Ref: Book 52, AGO Page 124.

*BEEBE, EPHRAIM JR.
Served from Sept. 20, 1813 to November, 1813, in Capt. John Weed's Company, Col. Clark's Rifle Regt.

*BEEBE, HENRY.
Served in Capt. Strait's Company, Col.
Martindale's Regt. Detached Militia,
in U. S. service 2 months and 13 days,
1812.

‡*BEEBE. LOTHROP.
Served from April 12. 1814 to April
21, 1814 in Lieut. James S. Morton's
Company. Col. W. B. Sumner's Regt.
Pension Certificate No. 34460.

*BEEBE, PETER.
Enlisted Sept. 25, 1813 in Capt. Elijah
W. Woods Company, Dixon's Regt.

*BEEBE, POTTER.
Served in Dixon's Regt. Vt. Militia.

BEEBE. REUBEN.
Enlisted Feb. 24, 1813 in Capt. Charles
Follett's Company, 11th Regt. Name
appears on Pay Roll to May 31,
1813. Ref: R. & L. 1812, AGO Page
13.

*BEECHER. LYMAN.
Served in 1st Regt. Vt. Militia commanded by Col. Judson.

*BEEDE, AARON,   Corinth.
Served under Captains Taylor and
Rogers. Col. Fifield's Regt. Detached
Militia, in U. S. service 6 months,
1812. Volunteered to go to Plattsburgh, September, 1814, and served
in Capt. Abel Jackman's Company.

*BEEDE. AARON 2d.,   Strafford.
Served under Captains Taylor and
Rogers. Col. Fifield's Regt. Detached Militia, in U. S. service 2 months
and 21 days, 1812. Volunteered to
go to Plattsburgh, September, 1814,
and served 7 days in Capt. Joseph
Barrett's Company.

*BEEDLE. SAMUEL.
Served with Hospital Attendants, Vt.

‡BEEMAN, ALMON.
Served in Captain Jewett's Company
Pension Certificate of widow, Elmira,
No. 25308.

BEEMAN, BERIAH,   Fairfax.
Served in 1813 and 1814 in Capt.
Joseph Beeman's Company. Ref:
Hemenway's Vt. Gazetteer, Vol. 2,
Page 402.

BEEMAN, FRIEND,   Bridport.
Served in Capt. Sanford's Company,
30th Inf. Name appears on Pay
Roll of discharged men to Dec. 30,
1815. Ref: R. & L 1812, AGO Page 23.

BEEMAN, JOSEPH, Captain,   Fairfax.
Was in U. S. service as a Captain in
the 11th Regt. Ref: Vol. 58 Vt. State
Papers, Page 218; Hemenway's Vt.
Gazetteer Vol. 2, Pages 178 and 179.

BEEMAN, JOSEPH JR.,   Fairfax.
Appointed Captain, 11th Inf. March
12, 1812 and served as Captain of
Fairfax company in 11th Regt. under Col. Ira Clark, beginning Aug. 8,
1812. Ref: Book 51, AGO Pages 120
and 127; Heitman's Historical Register & Dictionary USA; Hemenway's
Vt. Gazetteer, Vol. 2, Page 402.

*BEERS, ELNATHAN B.
Served in Sumner's Regt. Vt. Militia.

BEERS, JAMES.
Born in Dorset, Vermont. Enlisted
March 5, 1814 in Dorset; served as
private in Capt. Foster's Company,
11th Regt. U. S. Inf.; was taken prisoner on board the schooner "Somers"
on Lake Erie, Aug. 12, 1814; was
conveyed as a prisoner of war to
Melville Island, Nova Scotia, and was
discharged Aug. 20, 1815; was allowed
pension on his application executed
March 6, 1871 while a resident of
New London (New Lisbon) Otsego
County, N. Y. at which place he resided in 1852. He was 76 years of
age at the time he made application
for pension. Married April 2, 1814
in Pownal, Vt., Hannah Butterfield.
No reference to children in the papers
in this claim. Ref: Pension Claim
S. C. 14103 on file at Pension Bureau,
Veterans Administration, Washington, D. C.

*BEERS, JOSEPH.
Served in Capt. Phelps' Company, Col.
William Williams' Regt. Detached
Militia, in U. S. service 5 months,
1812.

BEERS, NATHAN.
Enlisted April 30, 1813 for 1 year in
Capt. Simeon Wright's Company.
Ref: R. & L. 1812, AGO Page 51.

*BEERS, NEHEMIAH.
Served in Capt. Phelps' Company,
Col. William Williams' Regt. Detached Militia, in U. S. service 5 months
in 1812. Ref: Book 53, AGO Page 27.

BEHONON, JOSEPH.
Served in Capt. Walker's Company,
Col. Fifield's Regt. Detached Militia,
in U. S. service 6 months and 3 days,
1812. Ref: Book 53, AGO Page 23.

BELAMY, ABNER.
Served from Oct. 5, 1813 to Oct. 17,
1813 in Capt. Stephen Brown's Company, Tyler's Regt. Ref: R. & L.
1812, AGO Page 34.

BELCHER, JOHN.
Enlisted May 12, 1812 for a period
of 5 years in Capt. White Youngs'
Company, 15th Regt. Name appears

on Muster Roll from Aug. 31, 1814
to Dec. 31, 1814. Ref: R. & L. 1812,
AGO Page 27.

BELDEN, CHARLES W. JR., St. Albans.
Enlisted May 3, 1813 for 1 year in
Capt. John Wires' Company, 30th
Regt. Ref: R. & L. 1812, AGO Page
40.

‡*BELDING, ASA.
Served in Capt. Briggs' Company,
Col. Jonathan Williams' Regt. Detached Militia, in U. S. service 2
months and 13 days, 1812. Pension
Certificate No. 12549. Pension Certificate of widow, Lydia, No. 6125.

BELDING, ERETUS.
Served in Capt. Benjamin S. Edgerton's Company, 11th Regt. Name appears on Pay Roll for September and
October, 1812 and January and February, 1813. Ref: R. & L. 1812,
AGO Pages 1 and 2.

BELDING, GODFREY, H., Sergeant.
Served in Capt. Phineas Williams'
Company, 11th Regt. Name appears
on Pay Roll for January and Febru-
ary 1813. Ref: R. & L. 1812, AGO
Page 15.

BELDING, JONATHAN JR.
Served in Capt. Samuel H. Holly's
Company, 11th Regt. Name appears
on Pay Roll for January and Febru-
ary, 1813. Ref: R. & L. 1812, AGO
Page 25.

BELDING, WILLIAM C., Corporal.
Served in Lieut. William S. Foster's
Company, 11th Regt. Name appears
on Pay Roll for January & Feb-
ruary, 1813. Ref: R. & L. 1812, AGO
Page 7.

BELL, ALEXANDER.
Served from March 4th to June 30th,
1814 in Regt. of Light Dragoons. Ref:
R. & L. 1812, AGO Page 21.

*BELL, ANTHONY.
Served from Sept. 18, 1813 to November, 1813, in Capt. Isaac Finch's Company, Col. Clark's Regt.

‡*BELL, CHARLES.
Served from March 25, 1813 to June
24, 1813 in Capt. Samul Gordon's Com-
pany, 11th Regt. Also served in Capt.
Hotchkiss' Company, Martindale's
Regt. Pension Certificate No. 3025.
Ref: R. & L. 1812, AGO Page 8.

BELL, DAVID, Musician.
Enlisted May 31, 1813 for 1 year in
Capt. Benjamin Bradford's Company.
Name appears on Muster Roll to
Aug. 31, 1813. Ref: R. & L. 1812,
AGO Page 26.

*BELL, FRANCIS.
Served from Oct. 8, 1813 to Nov. 18,
1813 in Capt. Isaac Finch's Company,
Col. Clark's Regt.

*BELL, HARVY JR., Sergeant.
Served from April 12, 1814 to April
21, 1814 in Lieut. Justus Foote's Company, Sumner's Regt.

BELL. ISAAC, Corporal.
Enlisted May 31, 1813 for 1 year in
Capt. Benjamin Bradford's Company.
Name appears on Muster Roll to Aug.
31, 1813. Ref: R. & L. 1812, AGO
Page 26.

*BELL, JOHN.
Served in Capt. Samuel H. Holly's
Company, 11th Regt. from Nov. 1,
1812 to Feb. 28, 1813. Served from
Sept. 25, 1813 to Sept. 29, 1813 in
Capt. Amos Robinson's Company,
Dixon's Regt. R. & L. 1812, AGO
Page 25.

‡BELL, LYMAN.
Served in Capt. Samuel Hand's Com-
pany. Pension Certificate of widow,
Betsey, No. 11214.

‡*BELL, MOOR.
Served from April 12, 1814 to May
20, 1814 in Capt. George Fisher's Company, Sumner's Regt. Also served
in 46th Regt. Vt. Militia. Pension
Certificate No. 1589. Pension Certificate of widow, Annis, No. 21445.

*BELL, NORMAN.
Served from April 12, 1814 to April
15, 1814 in Capt. John Hackett's Company, Sumner's Regt.

‡BELL, ORLANDO.
Served in Capt. Reynolds' Company.
Pension Certificate No. 25999.

BELL, ORLEAN.
Served from Feb. 10, 1813 to May 9,
1813 in Capt. Samul Gordon's Company, 11th Regt. Ref: R. & L. 1812,
AGO Page 8.

*BELL, SAM,   Enosburgh.
Served in Capt. George W. Kindall's
Company, 4 Regt. (Williams). Name
appears on Muster Roll Nov. 1 to
Dec. 8, 1812 and Muster Roll to Oct.
31, 1812; detached July 15th and ar-
rived in Camp Sept. 23rd. Ref: R.
& L. 1812, AGO Pages 38 and 39;
Vol. 52, Vt. State Papers, Page 50.

*BELL, SIMPSON,   Johnson.
Enlisted Sept. 25, 1813 and served 1
month and 23 days, 1813. Volunteered to go to Plattsburgh, September,
1814, and served in same company.

*BELLAMY, ABNER.
Served in 3 Regt. Vt. Militia, commanded by Col. Tyler.

*BELLAMY, CHAUNCY H.
Served in Sumner's Regt. Vt. Militia.

*BELLAMY, HIRAM, Corporal.
Served from April 12, 1814 to April
21, 1814 in Capt. Eseck Sprague's
Company, Sumner's Regt.

‡BELLAMY, SAMUEL J.
Served in Capt. Gideon Spencer's
Company, 30th Regt. Pension Certi-
ficate No. 19151.

BELLOWS, ADONIJAH.
Enlisted May 18, 1813 for 1 year in
Capt. James Taylor's Company, 30th
Regt.; name appears on Muster Roll
from Nov. 30, 1813 to Dec. 31, 1813.

Transferred to Capt. Gideon Spencer's
Company, 30th Regt.; name appears
on Muster Roll from Dec. 30, 1813
to June 30, 1814. Ref: R. & L. 1812,
AGO Pages 52 and 57.

BELLOWS, ELA, Captain,   Fairfax.
Served with 24 men in 1812. Ref:
Hemenway's Vt. Gazetteer, Vol. 2,
Page 403.

‡BELLUS, DANIEL.
Served in Captain Clark's Company.
Pension Certificate No. 3862.

‡*BELLUS, EBENEZER,   Fairfax.
Enlisted Sept. 25, 1813 in Capt. Asa
Wilkins' Company, Dixon's Regt. and
transferred to Capt. Asahel Langworthy's Company, Col. Isaac Clark's
Rifle Corps, Oct. 26, 1813; served in
Detached Militia 1 month. Volunteered to go to Plattsburgh, September, 1814, and served 8 days in Capt.
Josiah Grout's Company. Also served
in Captain Taylor's Company, 4th
Regt. (Williams'). Pension Certificate of widow, Lovica, No. 1893.

*BELON, STEPHEN.
Served in Sumner's Regt. Vt. Militia.

*BELSTIR, BAREAH, Corporal.
Served in 1st Regt. Vt. Militia commanded by Col. Martindale.

*BELUE, WILLIAM.
Served in 4 Regt. Vt. Militia commanded by Col. Williams.

*BEMAS, ABNER.
Served from April 20, 1814 to April
21, 1814 in Capt. Eseck Sprague's
Company, Sumner's Regt.

BEMENT, HIRAM,   Tunbridge.
Volunteered to go to Plattsburgh,
September, 1814, and served 5 days
in Capt. David Knox's Company. Ref:
Book 52, AGO Page 117.

‡*BEMIS, ABIJAH,   Marshfield.
Served in Capt. Rogers' Company,
Col. Fifield's Regt. Detached Militia,
in U. S. service 5 months and 27
days, 1812. Volunteered to go to
Plattsburgh, September, 1814 and
served in Capt. James English's Company. Pension Certificate No. 4638.
Ref: Book 52, AGO Page 248.

BEMIS, DANIEL, Pittsford or Salisbury.
Served from Aug. 5, 1814 to June 19,
1815 in Capt. Taylor's Company, 30th
Inf. Ref: R. & L. 1812, AGO Page 23.

‡BEMIS, DAVID.
Served in Captain Richardson's Company and transferred to Bemis' Company. Pension Certificate No. 5097.

*BEMIS, OBEDIAH,   Marshfield.
Served in Capt. Rogers' Company, Col.
Fifield's Regt. Detached Militia, in
U. S. service 5 months and 27 days,
1812. Volunteered to go to Plattsburgh,
September, 1814, and served 9 days
in Capt. James English's Company.
Ref: Book 52, AGO Pages 199 and 248.

‡*BEMIS, PHINEAS.   Marshfield.
Served in Capt. Rogers' Company, Col.
Fifield's Regt. Detached Militia, in

U. S. service 2 months and 18 days,
1812. Pension Certificate of widow,
Lucy, No. 6741. Pension Certificate
of soldier, No. 12622.

BEMONT, EDMOND.
Served from May 1st to 31st, 1814
in Company of Artificers commanded
by Alexander Parris. Ref: R. & L.
1812, AGO Page 24.

*BEN, JOSEPH.
Enlisted Sept. 27, 1813 in Capt. Asahel
Langworthy's Company, Col. Isaac
Clark's Rifle Corps. Served in Regt.
of Light Dragoons; name appears on
Pay Roll showing service from May
4th to June 30, 1814.

*BENEDICT, ABEL, Sergeant,   Cornwall.
Served from April 12, 1814 to April
21, 1814 in Capt. Shubael Wales Company, W. B. Sumner's Regt. Volunteered to go Plattsburgh, September,
1814, and was in the battle, serving
in Capt. Edmund B. Hill's Company,
Sumner's Regt.

*BENEDICT, JOHN, Corporal.
Served from April 12, 1814 to April
21, 1814 in Capt. Shubael Wales' Company, Col. W. B. Sumner's Regt.

*BENEDICT, JONAS N., Corporal and
Sergeant, Bridport. Served in Capt.
Robbins' Company, Col. William Wil-
liams' Regt. Detached Militia, in U.
S. service 4 months and 29 days, 1812.

*BENEDICT, NATHANIEL.
Served in Col. Clark's Regt. of Riflemen September to November, 1813.

*BENETT, DAVID.
Served in 1st Regt. Vt. Militia commanded by Col. Martindale.

*BENHAM, JOHN.
Served in Sumner's Regt. Vt. Militia
and in 3rd Regt. Vt. Militia commanded by Col. Tyler.

‡BENHAM, JOHN T.
Served at the Battle of Plattsburgh.
No organization given. Pension Cer-
tificate No. 26144.

*BENHAM, PHILANDER.
Enlisted Sept. 25, 1813 in Capt. Jesse
Post's Company, Dixon's Regt. Also
served at Plattsburgh, September,
1814.

*BENHAM, SAMUEL JR.,   Tinmouth.
Served in 1st Regt. Vt. Militia commanded by Col. Martindale.

‡*BENHAM, SILAS
Served in 3rd Regt. Vt. Militia commanded by Col. Tyler. Also served
in Capt. Loury's Company. Pension
Certificate of widow, Lovisa, No.
28566.

BENJAMIN, JOSEPH,   Fair Haven.
Volunteered to go to Plattsburgh,
September, 1814, and served 4 days
in Capt. Colton's Company. Ref:
Book 52, AGO Page 145.

BENJAMIN, JOSIAH,   Montpelier.
Volunteered to go to Plattsburgh,
September, 1814, and served 8 days
in Capt. Timothy Hubbard's Company.
Ref: Book 52, AGO Page 256.

*BENJAMIN, LUMBARD.
Served in 1st Regt. Vt. Militia commanded by Col. Martindale.

BENNET, ALMON.
Served in Capt. Hotchkiss' Company,
Col. Martindale's Regt. Detached Militia, in U. S. service 1 month and 22
days, 1812. Ref: Book 53, AGO Page
64.

BENNET, DANIEL.
Served in Capt. Weeks' Company, 11th
Regt. Name appears on Pay Roll
for January and February, 1813. Ref:
R. & L. 1812, AGO Page 5.

‡*BENNET, ELIJAH.
Served in Capt. Hotchkiss' Company,
Col. Martindale's Regt. Detached Militia, in U. S. service 2 months and 13
days, 1812. Pension Certificate of
widow, Dema, No. 4035.

‡*BENNET, JOSIAH.
Served in Capt. A. Scovil's Company,
1st Regt. (Martindale's) Vt. Militia.
Pension Certificate of widow, Cyrena,
No. 24952.

*BENNET, SANFORD S.
Served in 1st Regt. Vt. Militia (Judson's).

BENNET, ZERAH.
Served in Capt. Weeks' Company,
11th Regt. Name appears on Pay
Roll for January and February, 1813.
Ref: R. & L. 1812, AGO Page 5.

*BENNETT, ADAM.
Served in 3rd Regt. Vt. Militia, commanded by Col. Tyler.

*BENNETT, AMERIAH.
Enlisted Sept. 20, 1813 in Capt. John
Weed's Company, Col. Clarks' Regt.
and served to November, 1813.

BENNETT, ANDREW, Sergeant, Tunbridge. Volunteered to go to Plattsburgh, September, 1814, and served
4 days in Capt. Ephraim Hackett's
Company. Ref: Book 52, AGO Page
71.

*BENNETT, CHARLES, Captain.
Entered service Sept. 25, 1813 and
commanded a company in Col. Luther
Dixon's Regt.

BENNETT, DANIEL,   Richmond.
Volunteered to go to Plattsburgh,
September, 1814, and served 9 days
in Capt. Roswell Hunt's Company, 3
Regt. Vt. Militia. Ref: Book 51, AGO
Page 82.

BENNETT, DANIEL,   Tunbridge.
Volunteered to go to Plattsburgh,
September, 1814, and served 4 days
in Capt. Ephraim Hackett's Company.
Ref: Book 52, AGO Pages 71 and 72.

BENNETT, FREEMAN, Franklin County.
Volunteered to go to Plattsburgh
Sept. 11, 1814 and served in 15th or
22nd Regt. Ref: Hemenway's Vt. Gazetteer, Vol. 2, Page 391.

*BENNETT, HUMPHREY,   Randolph.
Volunteered to go to Plattsburgh,
September, 1814, and served in Capt.
Lebbeus Egerton's Company.

*BENNETT, JAMES.
Served in Sumner's Regt. Vt. Militia.

BENNETT, JAMES,   Montpelier.
Volunteered to go to Plattsburgh,
Septebmber. 1814, and served 8 days
in Capt. Timothy Hubbard's Company.
Ref: Book 52, AGO Page 256.

*BENNETT, JOSEPH,   Stowe.
Volunteered to go to Plattsburgh,
September, 1814, and was at the
battle, serving in Capt. Nehemiah
Perkins' Company, 4 Regt. (Peck's)
Vt. Militia.

BENNETT, LEBBEUS,   Chelsea.
Volunteered to go to Plattsburgh,
September, 1814, and served 6 days.
No organization given. Ref: Book 52,
AGO Page 175.

BENNETT, NATHANIEL.
Served from April 17, 1813 to July 16,
1813 in Capt. John W. Weeks Company, 11th Regt. Ref: R. & L. 1812,
AGO Page 4.

*BENNETT, SEELEY, Adjutant.
Served in 1st Regt. Vt. Militia commanded by Col. Judson.

BENNETT, SELAH.
Appointed Ensign 11th Inf. March 12.
1812; struck off Sept. 2, 1812. Ref:
Heitman's Historical Register & Dictionary USA.

*BENNETT, SELDEN.
Served from April 12, 1814 to May 20,
1814 in Capt. George Fisher's Company, Sumner's Regt.

*BENNETT, THOMAS.
Served in 3 Regt. Vt. Militia commanded by Col. Tyler.

‡BENNETT, WILLIAM,   Tunbridge.
Volunteered to go to Plattsburgh,
September, 1814, and served 4 days
in Capt. Ephraim Hackett's Company.
Pension Certificate No. 30847.

*BENSON, DAVID,   Danby.
Served in Capt. Brown's Company.
Col. Martindale's Regt. Detached
Militia, in U. S. service 16 days, 1812.
Served from April 4, 1813 to July 13,
1813 in Capt. Samul Gordon's Com-
pany, 11th Regt. Ref: R. & L. 1812,
AGO Page 8.

BENSON, DAVID JR.
Served in Capt. Samuel H. Holly's
Company, 11th Regt. Name appears
on Pay Roll for January and Febru-
ary, 1813. Ref: R. & L. 1812, AGO
Page 25.

*BENSON, DUTY.
Served in Capt. Brown's Company,
Col. Martindale's Regt. Detached Militia. in U. S. service 2 months and 14
days, 1812.

‡BENSON, FREEMAN.
Served in Capt. Nason Ormsby's Com-
pany. Pension Certificate of widow,
Sally, No. 15336.

BENSON, HENRY,   Strafford.
Volunteered to go to Plattsburgh,
September, 1814, and served in Capt.
Cyril Chandler's Company. Ref: Book
52, AGO Page 42.

*BENSON, JOHN.
Served in Capt. Willson's Company,
Col. William Williams' Regt. Detached Militia, in U. S. service 4 months
and 23 days, 1812.

‡*BENSON, JOSEPH JR., Corporal,
Stowe. Volunteered to go to Plattsburgh, September, 1814, and served
in Capt. Nehemiah Perkins' Company, 4th Regt. (Peck's) Vt. Militia.
Also served in Corning's Detachment,
Vt. Militia. Pension Certificate of
widow, Eliza, No. 25380.

‡*BENSON, NOAH.
Served in Capt. Phelps' Company, Col.
Jonathan Williams' Regt. Detached
Militia, in U. S. service 2 months and
21 days, 1812. Pension Certificate of
widow, Linda, No. 1325.

BENSON, PETER,
Enlisted Aug. 16, 1812 for a period
of five years in Capt. White Youngs'
Company of Infantry, 15th Regt.
Name appears on Muster Roll from
Aug. 31, 1814 to Dec. 31, 1814. Ref:
R. & L. 1812, AGO Page 27.

*BENSON, RUFUS.
Served in Capt. Brown's Company,
Col. Martindale's Regt. Detached
Militia, in U. S. service 25 days, 1812.

BENSON, SENECA.
Enlisted May 9, 1813 for 1 year in
Capt. Simeon Wright's Company. Ref:
R. & L. 1812, AGO Page 51.

*BENSON, WILLIAM.
Served in Capt. Phelps' Company,
Col. Jonathan Williams' Regt. Detached Militia, in U. S. service 2
months and 21 days, 1812.

*BENTLEY, HENRY.
Served in Capt. Phineas Wiliams'
Company, 11th Regt.; name appears
on Pay Roll for January and Febru-
ary, 1813. Served from Sept. 14,
1813 to November, 1813 in Capt. Isaac
Finch's Company, Col. Clark's Regt.
Ref: R. & L. 1812, AGO Page 15.

*BENTLEY, IRA.
Served from Sept. 25, 1813 to Sept. 29,
1813 in Capt. Amos Robinson's Company, Dixon's Regt.

*BENTLEY, LEVI.
Served from Sept. 25, 1813 to Oct. 11,
1813 in Capt. N. B. Eldridge's Company, Dixon's Regt.

BENTLEY, THOMAS,   St. Albans.
Served in company of Capt. John
McNeil Jr., 11th Regt. Name appears on Pay Roll of company for
January and February, 1813. Served
from May 7, 1814 to June 16, 1815
in Capt. Sanford's Company, 30th
Inf. Ref: R. & L. 1812, AGO Pages
17 and 23.

*BENTLY, ABISHA.
Served in Capt. Needham's Company,
Col. Martindale's Regt. Detached
Militia, in U. S. service 2 months and
14 days, 1812.

BENTON, ALEXANDER,   Barton.
Enlisted April 27, 1813 for 1 year in
Capt. James Taylor's Company, 30th

Regt.; name appears on Muster Roll from Nov. 30, 1813 to Dec. 31, 1813. Transferred to Capt. Gideon Spencer's Company, 30th Regt. and served to April 28, 1814. Ref: R. & L. 1812, AGO Pages 52, 57, 59.

BENTON, ELIJAH,   Cornwall. Volunteered to go to Plattsburgh, September, 1814, and was at the battle, serving in Capt. Edmund B. Hill's Company, Sumner's Regt. Ref: Book 51, AGO Page 13.

BENTON, FELIX,   Cornwall. Volunteered to go to Plattsburgh, September, 1814, and was at the battle. Served in Capt. Edmund B. Hill's Company, Sumner's Regt. Ref: Book 51, AGO Pages 13 and 15.

*BENTON, JOHN H. Served in 3 Regt. Vt. Militia commanded by Col. Williams.

BENTON, JOSEPH D., Franklin County, Volunteered to go to Plattsburgh, Sept. 11, 1814 and served in 15th or 22nd Regt. Ref: Hemenway's Vt. Gazetteer, Vol. 2, Page 391.

*BENTON, NOAH L.,   Cornwall. Served from April 12, 1814 to April 21, 1814 in Capt. Shubael Wales' Company, Col. W. B .Sumner's Regt. Volunteered to go to Plattsburgh, September, 1814, and was at the battle, serving in Capt. Edmund B. Hill's Company, Sumner's Regt.

BENTON, SEYMOUR,   Barton. Enlisted April 27, 1813 for 1 year in Capt. James Taylor's Company, 30th Regt. Ref: R. & L. 1812, AGO Page 59.

‡*BENTON, TOLMAN. Enlisted Sept. 29, 1813 and served 1 month and 19 days in Capt. Asahel Langworthy's Company, Col. Isaac Clark's Rifle Corps. Pension Certificate of widow, Margaret, No. 7011.

*BENTON, WILLIAM. Served in Sumner's Regt. Vt. Militia.

BERGON, WILLIAM. Volunteered to go to Plattsburgh, September, 1814, and served 4 days in Capt. Aaron Kidder's Company. Ref: Book 52, AGO Page 65.

BERKLEY, PHILIP. Enlisted Dec. 22, 1812 for a period of 5 years in Capt. White Youngs' Company, 15th Regt. Name appears on Muster Roll from Aug. 31, 1814 to Dec. 31, 1814. Ref: R. & L. 1812, AGO Page 27.

*BERRY, ALONZO. Served in Sumner's Regt. Vt. Militia.

*BERRY, BENJAMIN. Served from May 1st to June 30, 1814 in Corps of Artillery, commanded by Capt. Alexander Brooks. Also served in Corning's Detachment, Vt. Militia. Ref: R. & L. 1812, AGO Page 31.

*BERRY, JOHN,   Barnard. Served in Capt. Phelps' Company, Col. Jonathan Williams' Regt. Detached

Militia, in U. S. service 2 months and 21 days, 1812. Also served as Quartermaster in 1 Regt. (Judson's) Vt. Militia.

BERRY, PELEG,   West Fairlee. Volunteered to go to Plattsburgh, September, 1814, and served in Lieut. P. Kimball's Company. Ref: Book 52, AGO Page 109.

*BERRY, SAMUEL. Served in Dixon's Regt. Vt. Militia.

‡*BERRY, STEPHEN. Served in Capt. Prentice's Company, Dixons' Regt. Pension Certificate No. 24829.

BERSONS, BETA,   Franklin County. Volunteered to go to Plattsburgh, Sept. 11, 1814 and served in 15th or 22nd Regt. Ref: Hemenway's Vt. Gazetteer, Vol. 2, Page 392.

BERT, WILLIAM. Served in Capt. Benjamin S. Edgerton's Company, 11th Regt. Enlisted Sept. 30, 1812 and appears on Pay Roll for September and October, 1812. Ref: R. & L. 1812, AGO Page 1.

BESSE, ANTHONY, Enosburgh or Richford. Enlisted Sept. 25, 1813 and served 1 month and 23 days in Capt. Martin D. Folett's Company, Col. Dixon's Regt. Ref: Book 52, AGO Page 268; Book 53, AGO Page 106.

*BESSE, HOLMES, Corporal. Served in Capt. Phelps' Company, Col. Jonathan Williams' Regt. Detached Militia in U. S. service 2 months and 21 days, 1812.

BEVERSTOCK, SILAS, Sergeant, Shrewsbury. Enlisted May 10, 1813 for 1 year in Capt. Daniel Farrington's Company (also commanded by Capt. SimeonWright), 30th Regt.; name appears on Muster Roll from March 1, 1814 to April 30, 1814. Served as sergeant from May 16, 1814 to June 19, 1815 in Capt. Taylor's Company, 30th Inf. Ref: R. & L. 1812, AGO Pages 23 and 51.

BEWELS, BENJAMIN. Enlisted April 29, 1814 for period of the war and served in 30th Regt. in companies of Capt. William Miller, Capt. Gideon Spencer and Capt. James Taylor. Ref: R. & L. 1812, AGO Pages 53, 54, 57.

BICKFORD, ISAAC. Served from Jan. 8, 1813 to June 21, 1813 in Capt. Jonathan Starks' Company, 11th Regt. Ref: R. & L. 1812, AGO Page 19.

*BICKFORD, JOHN,   Danville. Served in Capt. Morrill's Company, Col. Fifield's Regt. Detached Militia in U. S. service 6 months and 5 days, 1812.

*BICKFORD, SAMUEL. Served with Hospital Attendants, Vt.

‡BICKFORD, THOMAS. Served in Captain Calton's Company. Pension Certificate of widow, Elizabeth, No. 28452.

BICKLEY, JOHN.
Enlisted Dec. 25, 1812 for five years in company of late Capt. J. Brooks, commanded by Lieut. John I. Cromwell, Corps of U. S. Artillery. Name appears on Muster Roll of company from April 30, 1814 to June 30, 1814. Ref: R. & L. 1812, AGO Page 18.

BICKNELL, JOHN S., Captain, Barnard.
Appointed 1st Lieutenant 31st Inf. April 30, 1813; Captain Jan. 11, 1814; honorably discharged June 15, 1815. Went to Plattsburgh, September, 1814, as captain of a company from Barnard. Ref: Heitman's Historical Register and Dictionary USA; Wm. M. Newton's History of Barnard, Page 96.

‡*BIDWELL, BENJAMIN.
Served in Capt. O. Lowry's Company, Col. William Williams' Regt. in U. S. service 4 months and 26 days, 1812. Pension Certificate No. 23670.

BIDWELL, JOSIAH,   Barre.
Volunteered to go to Plattsburgh, September, 1814, and served 10 days in Capt. Warren Ellis' Company. Ref: Book 52, AGO Page 242.

*BIGELOW, ALPHEUS.
Served from April 12, 1814 to April 15, 1814 in Capt. John Hackett's Company, Sumner's Regt.

BIGELOW, ASA, Musician.
Volunteered to go to Plattsburgh, September, 1814, and served 7 days in company of Capt. Frederick Griswold, raised in Brookfield, Vt. Ref: Book 52, AGO Page 52.

BIGELOW, DANIEL,   Hubbardton.
Served from April 26, 1813 to April 27, 1814 in Capt. Daniel Farrington's Company. (also commanded by Capt. Simeon Wright) 30th Regt. Ref: R. & L 1812, AGO Pages 50 and 51.

BIGELOW, ELIJAH.
Served in Capt. Benjamin S. Edgerton's Company, 11th Regt. Name appears on Pay Roll for September and October, 1812, and January and February, 1813. Ref: R. & L. 1812, AGO Pages 1 and 2.

*BIGELOW, ISAAC, Drummer, Fairfield.
Served in Capt. George W. Kindall's Company, 4th Regt. commanded by Col. William Williams. Name appears on Pay Roll to Sept. 10, 1812, Muster Roll from Aug. 31 to Oct. 31, 1812, and Muster Roll from Nov. 1 to Dec. 8, 1812.

*BIGELOW, JAMES.
Served from April 12, 1814 to April 21, 1814 in Lieut. James S. Morton's Company, Col. W. B. Sumner's Regt.

BIGELOW, JOSIAH JR.
Volunteered to go to Plattsburgh, September, 1814, and served 7 days in Capt. Frederick Griswold's Company, raised in Brookfield, Vt. Ref: Book 52, AGO Page 52.

BIGELOW, WATERS L.
Volunteered to go to Plattsburgh, September, 1814, and served 7 days in Capt. Frederick Griswold's Company, raised in Brookfield, Vt. Ref: Book 52, AGO Pages 52 and 64.

BIGFORD, JOHN.
Served from Feb. 15, 1813 to May 10, 1813 in Capt. John W. Weeks' Company, 11th Regt. Ref: R. & L. 1812, AGO Page 4.

BIGSBY, SAMUEL,   Fairfax.
Volunteered to go to Plattsburgh, September, 1814, and served 8 days in Capt. Josiah Grout's Company. Ref: Book 51, AGO Page 103.

*BIGSBY, SAMUEL JR.   Vershire.
Served about 3 months from September, 1812, in Capt. Oliver Taylor's Company, of Thetford, in Col. Fifield's Regt. Died in December, 1812.

BIGSBY, SOLOMON.
Volunteered to go to Plattsburgh, September, 1814, and served 7 days in Capt. Frederick Griswold's Company, raised in Brookfield, Vt. Ref: Book 52, AGO Page 52.

*BILGOOD, BENJAMIN.
Served in 1st Regt. Vt. Militia commanded by Col. Judson.

*BILL, DANIEL JR.
Served in 3 Regt. Vt. Mililtia commanded by Col. Tyler.

‡BILL, SILAS.
Served in Captain Perry's Company. Pension Certificate of widow, Lucy, No. 27816.

BILLINGS, ABEL,   Stockbridge.
Volunteered to go to Plattsburgh, September, 1814, and served 7 days in Capt. Elias Keyes' Company. Ref: Book 51, AGO Page 240.

*BILLINGS, EBENEZER.
Served from April 12, 1814 to April 21. 1814 in Lieut. Justus Foote's Company, Sumner's Regt.

‡BILLINGS, EZEKIEL.
Served from Feb. 15th to June 30, 1814 in Capt. McFarland's Regt. of Light Dragoons. Pension Certificate No. 20447.

‡BILLINGS, ISAAC,   Highgate.
Served in Capt. Charles Follett's Company, 11th Regt. Name appears on Pay Roll for January and February, 1813. Volunteered to go to Plattsburgh, September, 1814 and served 5 days in Capt. Conrad Saxe's Company, Col. William Williams' Regt. Pension Certificate of widow, Anstice, No. 4689.

BILLINGS, JONATHAN.
Served in company of late Capt. J. Brooks, commanded by Lieut. John I. Cromwell, Corps of U. S. Artillery. Name appears on Muster Roll from April 30, 1814 to June 30, 1814. Ref: R. & L. 1812, AGO Page 18.

BILLINGS, NATHANIEL, Franklin County. Volunteered to go to Plattsburgh Sept. 11, 1814 and served in 15th or 22nd Regt. Ref: Hemenway's Vt. Gazetteer, Vol. 2, Page 391.

*BILLINGS, WILLIAM.
Served in Capt. Wheeler's Company,
Col. Fifield's Regt. Detached Militia,
in U. S. service 3 months and 16 days,
1812.

BILLINGS, ZEBINA.
Served from May 1st to May 22nd,
1814, in Company of Artificers commanded by Alexander Parris. Carpenter. Ref: R. & L. 1812, AGO
Page 24.

BILLOWS, EBENEZER.
Served in Capt. Taylor's Company,
Col. Wm. Williams' Regt. Detached
Militia, in U. S. service 4 months and
24 days, 1812. Ref: Book 53, AGO
Page 12.

*BILLS, CHESTER.
Served in 3 Regt. Vt. Militia commanded by Col. Tyler.

*BILLS, DANIEL.
Served in Tyler's Regt. Vt. Militia.

BILLS, NATHANIEL.
.Served from Dec. 9, 1812 to Feb. 28,
1813 in Capt. Phineas Williams' Company, 11th Regt. Ref: R. & L. 1812,
AGO Page 15.

BINGEN, JOHN J.
Served from March 3, 1813 to June
2, 1813 in Capt. John W. Weeks'
Company, 11th Regt. Ref: R. & L.
1812, AGO Page 4.

*BINGHAM, ASA.
Served in 3 Regt. Vt. Militia commanded by Col. Tyler.

*BINGHAM, ASAHEL, Sergeant, Corn-
wall. Volunteered to go to Plattsburgh, September, 1814, and served
in Capt. Edmund B. Hill's Company,
Sumner's Regt.

*BINGHAM, BENJAMIN.
Served from April 12, 1814 to May
20, 1814 in Capt. George Fisher's Company, Sumner's Regt.

BINGHAM, CALVIN.
Served in Capt. Samuel H. Holly's
Company, 11th Regt. Name appears
on Pay Roll for January and Feb-
ruary, 1813. Ref: R. & L. 1812, AGO
Page 25.

BINGHAM, ELDREDGE, Highgate.
Enlisted Sept. 1, 1812 in Capt. Conrad Saxe's Company, Col. Wm. Williams' Regt. Ref: Hemenway's Vt.
Gazetteer, Vol. 2, Page 420.

*BINGHAM, ELIAS, Stowe.
Volunteered to go to Plattsburgh,
September, 1814, and served in Capt.
Nehemiah Perkins' Company, 4 Regt.
(Peck's).

‡*BINGHAM, HARRY.
Served in Capt. Bingham's Company,
Col. Jonathan Williams' Regt. Detached Militia in U. S. service 2 months
and 9 days, 1812. Pension Certificate
of widow, Marcia, No. 28214.

BINGHAM, JAMES P.
Served in Capt. Samuel H. Holly's
Company, 11th Regt. Name appears

on Pay Roll for January and February, 1813. Ref: R. & L. 1812,
AGO, Page 25.

BINGHAM, JEREMIAH 2d.
Served in Capt. Samuel H. Holly's
Company, 11th Regt. from Nov. 2,
1812 to Feb. 28, 1813. Ref: R. & L.
1812, AGO Page 25.

BINGHAM, JOSEPH.
Served in Capt. Samuel H. Holly's
Company, 11th Regt. Name appears
on Pay Roll for January and Feb-
ruary, 1813. Ref: R. & L. 1812, AGO
Page 25.

BINGHAM, LUTHER G., Cornwall.
Volunteered to go to Plattsburgh,
September, 1814 and served in Capt.
Edmund B. Hill's Company, Sumner's
Regt. Ref: Rev. Lyman Mathew's His-
tory of Cornwall, Page 345.

BINGHAM, NATHAN, Shoreham.
Served from April 12, 1814 to May 20,
1814 in Capt. George Fisher's Company, Sumner's Regt. Volunteered to
go to Plattsburgh, September, 1814,
and served 6 days in Capt. Samuel
Hand's Company. Ref: Book 52, AGO
Page 278; Rev. J. F. Goodhue's History of Shoreham, Page 108.

*BINGHAM, REUBEN.
Served from April 12, 1814 to April
21, 1814 in Capt. Shubael Wales' Company, Col. W. B. Sumner's Regt.

*BINGHAM, WILLIAM.
Appointed 1st Lieutenant 31st Inf.
April 30, 1813; resigned Jan. 11, 1814.
Served as Captain in 3 Regt. commanded by Col. Williams. Ref: Heitman's Historical Register & Dictionary USA.

*BIRCH, BENJAMIN.
Served in 1 Regt. Vt. Militia commanded by Col. Judson.

BIRCH, DAVID, Franklin County.
Volunteered to go to Plattsburgh
Sept. 11, 1814 and served in 15th or
22nd Regt. Ref: Hemenway's Vt.
Gazetteer, Vol. 2, Page 391.

*BIRCH, HYSON.
Served in 1 Regt. Vt. Militia commanded by Col. Judson.

*BIRCH, SILAS.
Served in 1 Regt. Vt. Militia commanded by Col. Judson.

BIRD, JOSEPH, Bristol.
Volunteered to go to Plattsburgh,
September, 1814, and served 10 days.
No organization given. Ref: Book
51, AGO Page 48.

BIRDSLEY, NATHANIEL B. Swanton.
Served in Capt. George W. Kindal's
Company, Col. William Williams'
Regt. 6 months in 1812. Ref: Book
51, AGO Page 199.

BIRGE, ANSEL, Sergeant.
Served in Capt. Charles Follett's Company, 11th Regt. Name appears on
Pay Roll for January and February,
1813. Ref: R. & L. 1812, AGO Page 12.

‡BIRGE, CYRUS.
Served in Capt. Birge's Company. Pension Certificate of widow, Adeline, No. 30554.

*BIRGE, ELIJAH, Captain,   Underhill.
Appointed Sept. 25, 1813 for 3 months to command a company in Col. Luther Dixon's Regt.

*BIRGE, HORACE P.
Served from April 12, 1814 to April 21, 1814 in Capt. Othniel Jewett's Company, Sumner's Regt. Ref: Book 52, AGO Page 264.

*BIRGE, JAMES.
Enlisted Sept. 25, 1813 in Capt. Elijah Birge's Company, Col. Dixon's Regt. and served 1 month and 23 days.

*BIRGE, WARREN, Corporal.
Enlisted Sept. 25, 1813 and served 1 month and 23 days in Capt. Elijah Birge's Company, Col. Dixon's Regt.

BIRMINGHAM, THOMAS.
Born in Villbaron, Ireland. Enlisted at Plattsburgh, April 19, 1814 for a period of five years in Capt. William Miller's Company, 30th Regt. Name appears on Muster Roll to Aug. 31, 1814. Ref: R. & L. 1812, AGO Pages 54 and 55.

*BISBEE, ELISHA.
Served in Sumner's Regt. Vt. Militia.

BISBEE, NATHAN.
Volunteered to go to Plattsburgh, September, 1814, and served 7 days in Capt. Frederick Griswold's Company, raised in Brookfield, Vt. Ref: Book 52, AGO Page 52.

*BISHOP, AMOS B.
Served from June 11, 1813 to June 17, 1813 in Capt. John Munson's Company of Cavalry, 3 Regt. (Tyler's).

*BISHOP, BENJAMIN, Sergeant.
Served in Sumner's Regt. Vt. Militia.

*BISHOP, ELEAZER.
Served in Corning's Detachment, Vt. Militia, and in 4 Regt. Vt. Militia commanded by Col. Peck.

*BISHOP, ELIHU, Drummer.
Served in Capt. Needham's Company, Col. Martindale's Regt. Detached Militia, in U. S. service 2 months and 14 days, 1812.

‡*BISHOP, EPHRAIM,   Richmond.
Served in Capt. Barns' Company, Col. Wm. Williams Regt. Detached Militia, in U. S. service 5 months, 1812. Served from June 11, 1813 to June 14, 1813 in Capt. Thomas Dorwin's Company, 1st Regt. 2nd Brig., 3rd Div. Volunteered to go to Plattsburgh, September, 1814, and served 9 days in Capt. Roswell Hunt's Company, 3 Regt. (Tyler's). Pension Certificate No. 21035. Pension Certificate of widow, Lucy, No. 27641.

‡BISHOP, IRA, Corporal.
Served in Capt. Phelps' Company, Col. Jonathan Williams' Regt. Detached Militia, in U. S. service 2 months and 21 days, 1812. Pension Certificate No. 5877.

*BISHOP, JESSE.
Served in Capt. Phelps' Company, Col. Jonathan Williams Regt. Detached Militia in U. S. service 1 month and 15 days, 1812.

BISHOP, JOB, Corporal.
Served as corporal in War of 1812 and was captured by troops Sept. 17, 1814 at Fort Erie. Discharged Nov. 8th. Ref: Records of Naval Records and Library, Navy Dept.

*BISHOP, JOHN.
Served in Capt. Phelps' Company, Col. Jonathan Williams' Regt. Detached Militia, in U. S. service 21 days, 1812. Served in Capt. H. Mason's Company, Col. Fifield's Regt. Detached Militia in U. S. service 5 months and 29 days, 1812, for which he was paid $19.93. Served from Nov. 1, 1812 to Feb. 28, 1813 in Capt. Samul Gordon's Company, 11th Regt. Ref: R. & L. 1812, AGO Page 9.

BISHOP, JOSHUA.
Served from May 1 to Aug. 18, 1814. No organization given. Ref: R. & L. 1812, AGO Page 29.

*BISHOP, LEMUEL, Musician.
Served in 1 Regt. Vt. Militia commanded by Col. Judson.

‡BISHOP, LEVI, Corporal.   St. Albans.
Enlisted April 24, 1813 for 1 year in Capt. John Wires' Company, 30th Regt. Also served in Captain Sanford's Company, 30th Regt. Pension Certificate of widow, Sarah, No. 10885.

*BISHOP, LUTHER.
Served in 4 Regt. Vt. Militia commanded by Col. Williams.

*BISHOP, PUTNAM, Sergeant.
Served from April 12, 1814 to April 21, 1814 in Capt. Othniel Jewett's Company, Sumner's Regt.

*BISSA, ANTHONY.
Served in Dixon's Regt. Vt. Militia.

BISSELL, AARON.
Served from March 25, 1813 to June 24, 1813 in Capt. Charles Follett's Company, 11th Regt. Ref: R. & L. 1812, AGO Page 13

*BISSELL, BENJAMIN, Shoreham or Enosburgh. Served from Oct. 15, 1813 to Nov. 17, 1813 in Capt. Asahel Scovell's Company, Col. Clark's Regt. of Riflemen. Volunteered to go to Plattsburgh, September, 1814, and served 3 days in company of Militia Cavalry. Also served in Capt. John Robbins' Company, Col. Wm. Williams' Regt.

BISSELL, DANIEL, Brig. Gen.
Served from May 1st to June 30, 1814 on General Staff of the Northern Army commanded by Maj. Gen. George Izard. Ref: R. & L. 1812, AGO Page 28.

BISSELL, JOHN JR.,   Fairfax.
Enlisted Aug. 8, 1812 in company of Capt. Joseph Beeman Jr. 11th Regt.

U. S. Inf. under Col. Ira Clark. Name appears on Pay Roll for Lieut. V. R. Goodrich's Company, 11th Regt., for January and February, 1813. Ref: R. & L. 1812, AGO Page 11; Hemenway's Vt. Gazetteer, Vol. 2, Page 402.

BISSELL, THOMAS,   Shoreham.
Volunteered to go to Plattsburgh, September, 1814, and served 3 days in Company of Militia Cavalry. Ref: Book 51, AGO Page 33.

BISSELL, WILLIAM,   Franklin County.
Volunteered to go to Plattsburgh, Sept. 11, 1814 and served in 15th or 22nd Regt. Ref: Hemenway's Vt. Gazetteer, Vol. 2, Page 391.

*BITGOOD, BENJAMIN.
Served from June 11, 1813 to June 14, 1813 in Capt. Samuel Blinn's Company, 1 Regt. (Judson's). Ref: R. & L. 1812, AGO Page 49.

*BITT, DAVID.
Served in 3 Regt. Vt. Militia commanded by Col. Tyler.

*BITTERBUSH, WILLIAM.
Served in Dixon's Regt. Vt. Militia.

BITTS, JOHN.
Enlisted May 11, 1813 for 1 year in Capt. Simeon Wright's Company. Ref: R. & L. 1812, AGO Page 51.

*BIXBE, AARON.
Served in Capt. Strait's Company, Col. Martindale's Regt. Detached Militia in U. S. service 2 months and 13 days, 1812.

*BIXBY, DAVID.
Served in Capt. Sabins' Company, Col. Jonathan Williams' Regt. Detached Militia, in U. S. service 2 months and 6 days, 1812.

*BIXBY, IRA.
Served in 3 Regt. Vt. Militia commanded by Col. Tyler.

BIXBY, JOEL.
Served from Feb. 15, 1813 to May 14, 1813 in Capt Charles Follett's Company, 11th Regt. Ref: R. & L. 1812, AGO Page 13.

*BIXBY, JOSEPH.
Served in Capt. Adams' Company, Col. Jonathan Williams' Regt. Detached Militia, in U. S. service 2 months and 7 days, 1812.

BIXBY, ROBERT,   Shrewsbury.
Volunteered to go to Plattsburgh, September, 1814 and served 4 days in Capt. Robert Reed's Company. Ref: Book 52, AGO Page 138.

*BIXBY, SALMON.
Enlisted Sept. 25, 1813 in Capt. Elijah Birge's Company, Dixon's Regt.

*BIXBY, SAMUEL.
Served in 2 Regt. Vt. Militia commanded by Col. Fifield.

*BISBEE, SOLOMON,   Chelsea.
Served in Capt. Wheatley's Company, Col. Fifield's Regt. Detached Militia,

in U. S. service 2 months and 21 days, 1812. Volunteered to go to Plattsburgh, September, 1814, and served 6 days; no organization given.

*BIXBY, THEOPHILUS.
Served in 4 Regt. Vt. Militia commanded by Col. Peck.

BLACK, ARCHIBALD.
Served from March 13, 1813 to June 12, 1813 in Capt. Charles Follett's Company, 11th Regt. Ref: R. & L. 1812, AGO Page 13.

BLACK, DAVID.
Enlisted Jan. 11, 1813 in Capt. Charles Follett's Company, 11th Regt. Name appears on Pay Roll to May 31, 1813. Ref: R. & L. 1812, AGO Page 13.

BLACK, JOHN, Lieutenant.
Served in Capt. Hopkins' Company, Col. Martindale's Regt. Detached Militia in U. S. service 1 month and 3 days in 1812. Enlisted Sept. 20, 1813 as a sergeant in Capt. John Weed's Company. Appointed 2nd Lieutenant 26 Inf. April 21, 1814; 1st Lieutenant Nov. 15, 1814; honorably discharged June 15, 1815. Ref: Heitman's Historical Register & Dictionary USA; Book 52, AGO Page 292; Book 53, AGO Page 24.

*BLACK, JOHN, Sergeant.
Served as sergeant in Regt. of Riflemen from September to November, 1813. Served as private in 1 Regt. Vt. Militia commanded by Col. Martindale.

BLACK, NATHANIEL, Corporal.
Served in Lieut. William S. Foster's Company, 11th Regt. Name appears on Pay Roll for January and February, 1813. Ref: R. & L 1812, AGO Page 7.

BLACK, SILAS,   Berlin.
Volunteered to go to Plattsburgh, September, 1814, and served 8 days in Capt. Cyrus Johnson's Company. Ref: Book 52, AGO Page 202.

BLACK, WILLIAM.   Swanton.
Served from July 15th to Dec. 8, 1813 in Capt. V. R. Goodrich's Company, 11th Regt. and was in action at the battle of Lundy's Lane. Ref: Hemenway's Vt. Gazetteer, Vol. 2, Page 444.

*BLACKMAN, JAMES H..   St. Albans.
Served in Capt. Ormsbee's Company, Col. Martindale's Regt. Detached Militia in U. S. service 1 month and 17 days, 1812. Enlisted June 1, 1813 for 1 year in Capt. Sanford's Company, 30th Regt.; also served in Capt. John Wires' Company, 30th Regt. Ref: R. & L. 1812, AGO Pages 1 and 40.

BLACKMAN, SAMUEL, 1st Sergeant,

Washington. Volunteered to go to Plattsburgh, September, 1814, and served in Capt. Amos Stiles Company. Ref: Book 52, AGO Page 36.

*BLACKMOR, JONATHAN, Suregon's Mate. Served in 1 Regt. Vt. Militia commanded by Col. Martindale.

*BLAIR. JAMES JR.
Served in Capt. Barns' Company, Col.
Wm. Williams' Regt. Detached Militia in U. S. service 5 months, 1812.
Served in Lieut. Bates' Company from
June 11, 1813 to June 14, 1813.

*BLAISDALE, JOHN.
Served from April 12, 1814 to May 20,
1814 in Capt. George Fisher's Company, Sumner's Regt.

BLAISDELL, DAVID.   Deerfield.
Served from May 1, 1814 to Aug. 1,
1814 in Capt. Goodenou's Company,
33rd Inf. Ref: R. & L. 1812, AGO
Page 30.

BLAISDELL, HUGH.
Served in Capt. Benjamin Bradford's
Company. Name appears on Muster
Roll from May 31, 1813 to Aug. 31,
1813; joined by transfer July 22, 1813.
Ref: R. & L. 1812, AGO Page 26.

BLAISDELL, JACOB,   Strafford.
Volunteered to go to Plattsburgh,
September, 1814, and served 6 days
in Capt. Jedediah H. Harris' Company. Ref: Book 52, AGO Pages 43
and 101.

BLAISDELL, JACOB,   Strafford.
Volunteered to go to Plattsburgh,
September, 1814, and served 6 days
in Capt. Joseph Barret's Company.
Ref: Book 52, AGO Page 101.

*BLAISDELL, JAMES P.,   Strafford.
Served in Capt. Taylor's Company
and Capt. Rogers' Company, Col.
Fifield's Regt. Detached Militia in U.
S. service 6 months in 1812. Volunteered to go to Plattsburgh, September, 1814, and served 6 days in Capt.
Jedediah H. Harris' Company.

BLAISDELL, JOHN,   Strafford.
Volunteered to go to Plattsburgh,
September, 1814, and served 6 days
in Capt. Jedediah H. Harris' Company. Ref: Book 52, AGO Page 43.

‡*BLAISDELL, JONATHAN M. St. Albans.. Served from Sept. 25, 1813
to Oct. 1, 1813 in Capt. Amos Robinson's Company, Dixon's Regt. Volunteered to go to Plattsburgh, September, 1814, and served 7 days in Capt.
Samuel Farnsworth's Company. Pension Certificate of widow, Peggy, M.,
No. 27262.

BLAISDELL, JOSHUA, Franklin County.
Volunteered to go to Plattsburgh
Sept. 11, 1814 and served in 15th or
22nd Regt. Ref: Hemenway's Vt. Gazetteer, Vol, 2, Page 392.

BLAISDELL, MARSHALL K.,
Served from April 24, 1813 to July 23,
1813 in Capt. Charles Follett's Company, 11th Regt. Ref: R. & L. 1812,
AGO Page 13.

*BLAISDELL, PARRET.
Served in 4 Regt. Vt. Militia commanded by Col. Peck.

BLAISDELL, PARROT JR.,   Montpelier.
Volunteered to go to Plattsburgh,
September, 1814, and served 8 days
in Capt. Timothy Hubbard's Company. Ref: Book 52, AGO Page 256.

BLAISDELL, WELLS,   Strafford.
Volunteered to go to Plattsburgh,
September, 1814, and served 6 days
in Capt. Jedediah H. Harris' Company. Ref: Book 52, AGO Page 43.

BLAISDELL, WILLIAM,   Cambridge.
Volunteered to go to Plattsburgh,
September, 1814, and served 8 days
in Capt. Salmon Green's Company.
Ref: Book 51, AGO Page 207.

BLAISDELL, WILLIAM K.
Served in Capt. Alvah Warner's Company. Pension Certificate No. 32281.

‡*BLAKE, ENOCH.
Served in Capt. Morrill's Company,
Col. Fifield's Regt. Detached Militia
in U. S. service 6 months and 3 days,
1812. Pension Certificate of widow,
Anna, No. 3105.

BLAKE, HARVEY.
Enlisted Jan. 8, 1813 in Capt. Charles
Follett's Company, 11th Regt. Name
appears on Pay Roll for advance pay
and retained bounty to May 31, 1813.
Ref: R. & L. 1812, AGO Page 13.

BLAKE, HENRY JONES, Captain.
Appointed 2nd Lieutenant 11th Inf.
May 1, 1812; 1st Lieutenant June 26,
1813; Captain Sept. 1, 1814; transferred to Artillery Corps May 17,
1815; resigned Feb. 8, 1816. Ref:
Heitman's Historical Register & Dictionary USA.

BLAKE, HENRY T., 2nd Lieutenant.
Served in Capt. Charles Follett's Company, 11th Regt. Name appears on
Pay Roll for January and February,
1813. Ref: R. & L. 1812, AGO Page
12.

BLAKE, JEREMIAH.
Served from May 1st to June 30, 1814
in Capt. Alexander Brooks' Corps of
Artillery. Ref: R. & L. 1812, AGO
Page 31.

BLAKE, JOHN,   Georgia.
Served in 1813 in Capt. Jesse Post's
Company, Dixon's Regt. Ref: Hemenway's Vt. Gazetteer, Vol. 2, Page 417.

*BLAKE, JOHN.
Served in Capt. Rogers' Company,
Col. Fifield's Regt. Detached Militia
in U. S. service 5 months and 27
days, 1812. Served in Company of
Capt. John McNeil, Jr., 11th Regt.;
name appears on Pay Roll for January and February, 1813. Ref: R. &
L. 1812, AGO Page 17.

*BLAKE, JONATHAN,   Georgia.
Enlisted Sept. 25, 1813 and served 1
month and 23 days in Capt. Jesse
Post's Company, Dixon's Regt. Volunteered to go to Plattsburgh, September, 1814, and served 8 days in
same company.

BLAKE, MESHACK W.
Served from May 1, 1813 to Feb. 28,
1814. No organization given. Ref:
R. & L. 1812, AGO Page 29.

‡BLAKE, PAGE.
Served in Capt. Jones' Company. Pension Certificate No. 11702.

‡BLAKE, TIMOTHY.
Enlisted Jan. 8, 1813 in Capt. Charles Follett's Company, 11th Regt. Name appears on Pay Roll to May 31, 1813. Pension Certificate No. 34942. Pension Certificate of widow, Ann, No. 3.

BLAKE, WILLIAM, Sergeant, Fairfax.
Enlisted Aug. 8, 1812 in company of Capt. Joseph Beeman Jr. 11th Regt. U. S. Inf. under Col. Ira Clark. Ref: Hemenway's Vt. Gazetteer, Vol. 2, Page 402.

BLAKE, WILLIAM.
Served as private in War of 1812 and was captured by troops Oct. 23, 1814 at Fort Erie. Discharged March 13, 1815. Ref: Naval Records and Library, Navy Dept.

*BLAKELEY, JAMES.
Served in Sumner's Regt. Vt. Militia.

‡BLAKELY, MOSES.
Enlisted April 22, 1813 for 1 year in Capt. Simeon Wright's Company. Pension Certificate of widow, Irene, No. 4999.

*BLAKELY, WILLIAM.
Served in Capt. Barns' Company, Col. Wm. Williams' Regt. Detached Militia in U. S. service 5 months, 1812.

*BLAKLEY, JOSEPH.
Served with Hospital Attendants, Vt.

*BLANCHARD, AARON, Sergeant.
Served in Capt. Richardson's Company, Col. Martindale's Regt. Detached Militia in U. S. service 2 months and 13 days, 1812. Also served in 1st Regt. Detached Militia of Vt. in U. S. service at Champlain for 2 days commencing Nov. 18 and ending Nov. 19, 1812, with rank of sergeant.

‡BLANCHARD, AMASA, Brookfield.
Volunteered to go to Plattsburgh, September, 1814, and served 7 days in Capt. Frederick Griswold's Company. Also served in Capt. John Wheatley's Company. Pension Certificate No. 8950.

*BLANCHARD, AMOS.
Served in Capt. Walker's Company, Col. Fifield's Regt. Detached Militia in U. S. service 2 months and 24 days, 1812. Volunteered to go to Plattsburgh, September, 1814, and served 7 days in Capt. Frederick Griswold's Company, raised in Brookfield, Vt. Book 52, AGO Page 52.

BLANCHARD, ASA, Barre.
Volunteered to go to Plattsburgh, September, 1814, and served 9 days in Capt. Warren's Ellis' Company. Ref: Book 52, AGO Pages 218 and 256.

*BLANCHARD, ASEL 2nd.
Served from April 12, 1814 to April 21, 1814 in Capt. Othniel Jewett's Company, Sumner's Regt.

*BLANCHARD, BARNARD.
Served in Col. Fifield's Regt. Detached Militia in U. S. service 6 months, 1812.

*BLANCHARD, CHARLES.
Served from July 22nd to Dec. 9, 1812 in Capt. Pettes' Company, Col. Wm. Williams' Regt. Detached Militia.

BLANCHARD, DAVID.
Served from Nov. 1, 1812 to Feb. 28, 1813 in Capt. Samuel H. Holly's Company, 11th Regt. Ref: R. & L. 1812, AGO Page 25.

BLANCHARD, GATES.
Enlisted Dec. 30, 1812 in Capt. Edgerton's Company, 11th Regt.; name appears on Pay Roll to July 1, 1813. Ref: R. & L. 1812, AGO Page 3.

‡*BLANCHARD, GEORGE D.
Served in Capt. Bingham's Company, Col. Jonathan Williams' Regt. Detached Militia in U. S. service 2 months and 9 days, 1812. Pension Certificate of widow, Anna, No. 18051.

BLANCHARD, ISAAC.
Service from May 1st to June 30, 1814 in Corps of Light Dragoons. Ref: R. & L. 1812, AGO Page 20.

‡BLANCHARD, JAMES.
Served in Captain Perry's Company. Pension Certificate of widow, Susan E., No. 33061.

BLANCHARD, JOHN.
Served from March 26, 1813 to June 25, 1813 in Capt. Benjamin S. Edgerton's Company, 11th Regt. Ref: R. & L. 1812, AGO Page 3.

*BLANCHARD, JONATHAN.
Served in Capt. Wheeler's Company, Col. Fifield's Regt. Detached Militia, in U. S. service 2 months and 18 days, 1812.

*BLANCHARD, JOSEPH.
Served in 1 Regt. Vt. Militia commanded by Col. Judson.

‡*BLANCHARD, MOSES, Calais.
Volunteered to go to Plattsburgh, September, 1814, and served 10 days in Capt. Gideon Wheelock's Company. Also served in Captain Burnap's Company. Pension Certificate of widow, Editha, No. 8887.

BLANCHARD, ORLIN, Sergeant, Isle-La-Motte. Served from July 22nd to Dec. 9, 1812 in Capt Pettes' Company, Col. Wm. Williams' Regt. Detached Militia. Ref: Book 53, AGO Page 1.

*BLANCHARD, PHILIP, Ensign, Highgate. Enlisted Sept. 1, 1812 in Capt. Conrad Saxe's Company, 4 Regt. (Williams') Vt. Militia.

BLANCHARD, RUFUS.
Volunteered to go to Plattsburgh, September, 1814, and went as far as Bolton. Served 4 days in Lieut. Phineus Kimball's Company, West Fairlee. Ref: Book 52, AGO Page 46.

*BLANCHARD, WARREN.
Served in Capt. Burnap's Company, Col. Jonathan Williams' Regt. Detached Militia in U. S. service 2 months and 13 days, 1812.

BLANCHARD, WILLIAM.
Volunteered to go to Plattsburgh.
September, 1814, and served 7 days
in Capt. Frederick Griswold's Company. Ref: Book 52, AGO Page 52.

BLANCHER, BENJAMIN.
Served from March 9, 1813 to June 8,
1813 in Capt. Charles Folletts' Company, 11th Regt. Ref: R. & L. 1812,
AGO Page 13.

BLANDE, DANIEL.
Enlisted Jan. 19, 1813 in Lieut. V. R.
Goodrich's Company, 11th Regt. Name
appears on Pay Roll to May 31, 1813.
Ref: R. & L. 1812, AGO Page 10.

BLAXTON, THOMAS, Franklin County.
Volunteered to go to Plattsburgh,
Sept. 11, 1814 and served in 15th or
22nd Regt. Ref: Hemenway's Vt. Gazetteer, Vol. 2, Page 392.

*BLIN, CHESTER, Sergeant, Shelburne.
Served from June 11, 1813 to June 14,
1813 in Capt. Samuel Blinn's Company of Militia, 1st Regt.   Volunteered to go to Plattsburgh, September, 1814, and served in Major Luman
Judson's command.

*BLIN, SAMUEL, Captain.
Served in 1st Regt Vt Militia commanded by Col Judson

*BLIN, THEODORE.
Served in 1st Regt. Vt. Militia commanded by Col. Martindale.

BLIN, WILLIAM,   Shelburne.
Volunteered to go to Plattsburgh,
September, 1814, and served in Ma-
jor Luman Judson's command. Ref:
Book 51, AGO Page 78.

*BLIN, ZADOCK,   Huntington.
Served from Oct. 11, 1813 to Oct. 17,
1813 in Capt. John Munson's Company of Cavalry, 3rd Regt. (Tyler's).
Volunteered to go to Plattsburgh,
September, 1814, and was at the
battle, serving in Capt. Josiah N. Barrows' Company.

*BLINN, ANDREW.
Served from June 11, 1813 to June 14,
1813 in Capt. Samuel Blinn's Company of Militia, 1st Regt.

*BLINN, JONATHAN.
Served from June 11, 1813 to June 14,
1813 in Capt. Samuel Blinn's Company of Militia, 1st Regt.

*BLINN, SAMUEL, Captain.
Served as Captain of Company of
Militia from June 11, 1813 to June
14, 1813. Ref: R. & L. 1812, AGO
Page 49.

BLINN, THEODORE.
Served in Capt. Cross' Company, Col.
Martindale's Regt. Detached Militia.
in U. S. service 2 months and 13
days, 1812. Ref: Book 53, AGO
Page 3.

‡*BLISS, ABNER,   Georgia.
Served in Capt. L. Robinson's Com-
pany, Col. Dixon's Regt. Detached
Militia, in U. S. service 1 month and
19 days, 1813.   Pension Certificate
No. 25335.

*BLISS, AMOS, Captain.
Served in 3 Regt. (Tyler's) Vt. Militia as a Captain.

*BLISS, BILLY.
Served in Tyler's Regt. Vt. Militia.

BLISS, BRADLEY,   St. Albans.
Enlisted May 5, 1813 for 1 year in
Capt. John Wires' Company, 30th
Regt. Ref: R. & L. 1812, AGO Page
40.

BLISS, CALVIN,   Shoreham.
Volunteered to go to Plattsburgh,
September, 1814, and served 8 days.
No organization given. Ref: Book
51, AGO Page 43.

‡BLISS, CHESTER.
Served in Capt. J Kinney's Company.
Pension Certificate of widow, Mary
Ann, No. 28959.

*BLISS, ELIAS.
Served in 3 Regt. (Tyler's) Vt. Militia.

‡*BLISS, GALON, Sergeant.
Served in Capt. Walker's Company,
Col. Fifield's Regt. Detached Militia
in U. S. service 6 months and 5 days,
1812. Pension Certificate of widow,
Linda, No. 1642.

*BLISS, HENRY, Sergeant.
Served in 3 Regt. Vt. Militia commanded by Col. Tyler.

*BLISS, IRA, Sergeant.
Served in 3 Regt. Vt. Militia commanded by Col. Tyler.

BLISS, JOHN, 1st Lieutenant.
Served in Capt. Weeks' Company,
11th Regt.; name appears on Pay
Roll for January and February, 1813.
Served from Oct. 5, 1813 to Oct. 17,
1813 as sergeant in Capt. John Mun-
son's Company of Cavalry, 3 Regt.
(Tyler's).

*BLISS, JOSHUA JR.,   Calais.
Volunteered to go to Plattsburgh,
September, 1814, and served 10 days
in Capt. Gideon Wheelock's Company.

*BLISS, JULIUS,   Jericho.
Served in 3 Regt. Vt. Militia commanded by Col. Tyler. Also took
part in the Battle of Plattsburgh.
Ref: History of Jericho, Page 142.

*BLISS, MOSES.
Enlisted Sept. 25, 1813 in Capt. Elijah
W. Wood's Company, Col. Dixon's
Regt.

*BLISS, ORRIN (or Aaron).
Enlisted Sept. 25, 1813 and served 1
month and 23 days in Capt. Jesse
Post's Company, Col. Dixon's Regt.

*BLISS, PELATIAH,   Essex.
Volunteered to go to Plattsburgh,
September, 1814, and served in Ty-
ler's Regt. Vt. Militia.

*BLISS, REUBEN,   Georgia.
Enlisted Sept. 25, 1813 and served 1
month and 23 days in Capt. Jesse
Post's Company, Dixon's Regt.

‡*BLISS, STEPHEN.
Enlisted Sept. 25, 1813 and served 1
month and 23 days in Capt. Jesse
Post's Company, Col. Dixon's Regt.
Pension Certificate of widow, Ange-
line, No. 7585.

*BLODGETT, AMOS.
Served from Sept. 25, 1813 to Sept.
27, 1813 in Capt. Amos Robinson's
Company, Col. Dixon's Regt.

*BLODGETT, AUGUSTUS, Corporal, Ran-
dolph. Volunteered to go to Plattsburgh, September, 1814, and served
in Capt. Lebbeus Egerton's Company.

*BLODGETT, CYRUS.
Served under Captains Durkee and
Wright, Col. Fifield's Regt. Detached
Militia, in U. S. service 3 months and
9 days, 1812.

*BLODGETT, DAN,   Randolph.
Volunteered to go to Plattsburgh,
September, 1814, and served in Capt.
Lebbeus Egerton's Company.

*BLODGETT, ELI,   Randolph.
Volunteered to go to Plattsburgh,
September, 1814, and served in Capt.
Lebbeus Egerton's Company.

*BLODGETT, FREDERICK,   Randolph.
Volunteered to go to Plattsburgh,
September, 1814, and served in Capt.
Lebbeus Egerton's Company.

‡*BLODGETT, HARVEY.
Served from April 12, 1814 to April
21, 1814 in Capt. Shubael Wales' Company, Col. W. B. Sumner's Regt. Also
served in Capt. M. Brown's Company.
Pension Certificate No. 25158. Pension Certificate of widow, Hannah,
No. 32212.

*BLODGETT, HEMAN,   Randolph.
Volunteered to go to Plattsburgh,
September, 1814, and served in Capt.
Lebbeus Egerton's Company.

*BLODGETT, JOSEPH,   Randolph.
Served in Capt. Morrill's Company,
Col. Fifield's Regt. Detached Militia in
U. S. service 6 months and 5 days,
1812. Volunteered to go to Plattsburgh, September, 1814, and served
in Capt. Lebbeus Egerton's Company.

*BLODGETT, PARLEY,   Randolph.
Volunteered to go to Plattsburgh,
September, 1814 and served in Capt.
Lebbeus Egerton's Company.

*BLODGETT, SYLVANUS, Fifer-Musician.
Jericho. Served in 3 Regt. Vt. Militia
commanded by Col. Tyler. Also took
part in the Battle of Plattsburgh.
Ref: History of Jericho, Page 142.

*BLOOD, ISAAC.
Served in Tyler's Regt. Vt. Militia
and in 4th Regt. Vt. Militia commanded by Col. Williams.

*BLOOD, JAMES, Corporal Sergeant.
Served in Capt. Pettes' Company, Col.
Wm. Williams' Regt. Detached Militia, in U. S. service 4 months and
17 days, 1812. Also served as sergeant
in 3rd Regt. Vt. Militia commanded
by Col. Tyler.

*BLOOD, JOHN.
Served in Tyler's Regt. Vt. Militia.

*BLOOD, MARVIN.
Served in Capt. Phelps' Company,
Col. Jonathan Williams' Regt. Detached Militia in U. S. service 2
months and 21 days, 1812.

*BLOOD, MOODY.
Served in Tyler's Regt. Vt. Militia.

*BLOOD, NATHANIEL.
Served from Oct. 11, 1813 to Oct. 17,
1813 in Capt. John Munson's Company, 3 Regt. (Tyler's).

‡*BLOOD, NATHANIEL JR.
Served in Tyler's Regt. Vt. Militia
and also in Capt. J. Sinclair's Company. Pension Certificate of widow,
Lucinda, No. 30776.

‡*BLOOD, SAMUEL, Corporal.
Served in Capt. Dodge's Company,
Col. Fifield's Regt. Detached Militia,
in U. S. service 2 months and 21
days, 1812. Pension Certificate of
widow, Eliza, No. 4789.

*BLOOD, WILLIAM JR.
Served in 3rd Regt. Vt. Militia commanded by Col. Tyler.

*BLOOMFIELD, JOSEPH.
Served in Capt. Robbins' Company,
Col. Wm. Williams' Regt. Detached
Militia, in U. S. service 4 months and
29 days, 1812.

‡BLOSSOM, WILLIAM R.
Volunteered to go to Plattsburgh,
September, 1814. Served in Captain
Keyes' Company. Pension Certificate
No. 33261.

BLOW, FRANCIS.
Served in Capt. Alexander Brooks'
Corps of Artillery. Name appears on
Pay Roll to June 30, 1814. Ref:
R. & L. 1812, AGO Page 31.

*BLOWERS, SOLOMON.
Served in 1st Regt. Vt. Militia commanded by Col. Martindale.

‡BLOWERS, WILLIAM.
No organization given. Pension Certificate of widow, Mary Ann, No.
10546.

BLUE, JOHN,   Shepardstown.
Served from May 1, 1814 to Aug. 10,
1814 in Capt. Morgan's Company,
Rifle Regt. Ref: R. & L. 1812, AGO
Page 30.

*BLUE, WILLIAM.
Served in 4 Regt. Vt. Militia commanded by Col. Williams.

BLUNT, EPHRAIM,   Danville.
Volunteered to go to Plattsburgh,
September, 1814, and served 3 days
in Capt. Solomon Langmaid's Company. Ref: Book 51, AGO Pages 75
and 76.

BLUNT, WILLIAM,   Danville.
Volunteered to go to Plattsburgh,
September, 1814, and served 3 days
in Capt. Solomon Langmaid's Company. Ref: Book 51, AGO Pages 75
and 76.

BLUSH, HENRY,   Burlington.
Volunteered to go to Plattsburgh,
September, 1814, and served 10 days
in Capt. Henry Mayo's Company. Ref:
Book 51, AGO Page 81.

‡*BLUSH, OLIVER.
Served in 1st Regt. Vt. Militia commanded by Col. Judson. Also served
under Captains Page and Grout. Pension Certificate of widow, Clarissa
E., No. 28093.

BLUSH, WILLIAM,   Burlington.
Volunteered to go to Plattsburgh,
September, 1814, and served 10 days
in Capt. Henry Mayo's Company. Ref:
Book 51, AGO Page 81.

*BLY, WILLIAM.
Served in Capt. Burnap's Company,
Col. Jonathan Williams' Regt. Detached Militia, in U. S. service 1
month and 26 days.

*BOARDMAN, HENRY.
Served in 1st Regt. Vt. Militia commanded by Col. Judson.

*BOARDMAN, JONATHAN.
Served from June 11, 1813 to June
14, 1813 in Lieut. Bates' Company,
1 Regt. (Judson's).

BOBB, JOSEPH.
Served in Capt. Benjamin Bradford's
Company; name appears on Muster
Roll from May 31, 1813 to Aug. 31,
1813. Ref: R. & L. 1812, AGO Page
26.

*BODWELL, RANSOM.
Served in Capt. Wheeler's Company,
Col. Fifield's Regt. Detached Militia,
in U. S. service 6 months and 4 days,
1812.

BOGGS, JAMES,   Franklin County.
Enlisted May 13, 1812 for 5 years
in Capt. White Youngs' Company,
15th Regt. Name appears on Muster
Roll from Aug. 31, 1814 to Dec. 31,
1814. Ref: R. & L. 1812, AGO Page
27.

‡BOGLE, JEREMIAH.
Served in Captain Preston's Company,
3 Regt. Pension Certificate No. 19928.

BOHANNON, JOSIAH.
Enlisted May 13, 1813 for 1 year in
Capt. James Taylor's Company, 30th
Regt. Transferred to Capt. Gideon
Spencer's Company, 30th Regt. and
served to May 13, 1814. Ref: R. & L.
1812, AGO Pages 52, 57, 59.

BOHONNON, EBEN W., Sergeant.
Served in Capt. Benjamin S. Edgerton's Company, 11th Regt. Name appears on Pay Roll for September and
October, 1812, and January and February, 1813. Ref: R. & L. 1812, AGO
Pages 1 and 2.

BOHONON, EBENEZER W.
Appointed Ensign 31 Inf. April 30,
1814; 3rd Lieutenant May 1, 1814;
honorably discharged June 15, 1815;
Ref: Heitman's Historical Register
& Dictionary USA.

BOHONON, ELEAZER.
Appointed Ensign 31 Inf. March 28,
1814; 3rd Lieutenant May 1, 1814;
honorably discharged June 15, 1815.
Ref: Governor and Council Vt. Vol.
6, Page 478.

BOLLES, JOHN.
Served from March 22, 1813 to June
21, 1813 in Capt. Edgerton's Company,
11th Regt. Ref: R. & L. 1812, AGO
Page 3.

BOLSTER, BARACH,   Londonderry.
Served in Capt. Richardson's Company, Col. Martindale's Regt. Detached Militia in U. S. service 2 months
and 13 days, 1812. Ref: Book 53,
AGO Page 58; Vol. 50 Vt. State
Papers, Page 115.

*BOLSTER, JOHN.
Served in Capt. Noyes' Company, Col.
Jonathan Williams' Regt. Detached
Militia in U. S. service 2 months and
6 days, 1812.

*BOND, DANIEL.
Served in Capt. George Fisher's Company, Sumner's Regt. from April 12,
1814 to May 20, 1814.

BOND, ELIAB, Corporal.
Served in Capt. Samul Gordon's Company, 11th Regt. Name appears on
Pay Roll for January and February,
1813. Ref: R. & L. 1812, AGO Page 9.

*BOND, ELIJAH.
Served from April 12, 1814 to April
15, 1814 in Lieut. Justus Foote's Company, Sumner's Regt.

*BOND, JOHN.
Served from April 12, 1814 to May
20, 1814 in Capt. George Fisher's Company, Sumner's Regt.

‡*BOND, JOSIAH.
Served in Capt. Needham's Company,
Col. Martindale's Regt. Detached
Militia in U. S. service 2 months and
14 days, 1812. Pension Certificate of
widow, Morilla, No. 1689.

‡BOND, MOSES.
Served in Captain Gordon's Company,
11th Regt. Pension Certificate No.
2207.

BOND, NATHAN, Sergeant.
Served in Cavalry of Detached Mili-
tia of Vermont in the service of the
United States at Champlain for 2
days commencing Nov. 18 and ending
Nov. 19, 1812.

*BONNETT, JOHN.
Served in Capt. Morrill's Company,
Col. Fifield's Regt. Detached Militia
in U. S. service 4 months and 6 days,
1812.

*BOOGE, ALEXANDER, Corporal.
Served in Capt. Needham's Company,
Col. Martindale's Regt. Detached Militia in U. S. service 2 months and 14
days, 1812.

‡BOOGE, HARRIS, 2nd Lieutenant, Pittsford. Served in Capt. Caleb Hendee's Company. Volunteered to go to
Plattsburgh and served 8 days. Pension Certificate of widow, Laura, No.
16676.

‡*BOORN, JESSE, Fifer.
Served in Capt. Richardson's Company, Col. Martindale's Regt. Detached Militia in U. S. service 2 months and 13 days, 1812. Pension Certificate No. 5557.

‡BOORN, STEPHEN.
Served in Capt. Richardson's Company, Col. Martindale's Regt. Detached Militia in U. S. service 2 months and 5 days, 1812. Pension Certificate of widow, Polly S., No. 4642.

‡BOOSHE, JOHN.
Served in Captain Isaac Holt's Company. Pension Certificate of widow, Abigail G., No. 30020.

BOOTH, BENJAMIN.
Served from Feb. 14th to June 30th, 1814 in Regt. of Light Dragoons. Ref: R. & L. 1812, AGO Page 21.

*BOOTH, ELISHA JR.
Served from June 11, 1813 to June 14, 1813 in Capt. Thomas Dorwin's Company of Vt. Militia, 1st Regt. 2nd Brig., 3rd Div.

BOOTH, SIMEON, Randolph.
Served in Capt. Wright's Company, Col. Fifield's Regt. Detached Militia in U. S. service 6 months, 1812. Volunteered to go to Plattsburgh, September, 1814, and served in Capt. Lebbeus Egerton's Company. Ref: Book 53, AGO Page 23; Book 52, AGO Pages 82 and 85.

*BORDMAN, TIMOTHY, Sergeant.
Served from April 12, 1814 to April 21, 1814 in Lieut. Justus Foote's Company, Sumner's Regt.

*BORDWELL, AMASA.
Served in Corning's Detachment, Vt. Militia.

BOSTON, JACOB.
Served from April 21, 1813 to April 24, 1814 in Capt. Daniel Farrington's Company (also commanded by Capt. Simeon Wright) 30th Regt. Ref: R. & L. 1812, AGO Pages 50 and 51.

‡*BOSTWICK, ANSON, Ensign.
Served from April 25, 1813 to Nov. 8, 1813 in Capt. Elijah Birge's Company, Dixon's Regt. Pension Certificate of widow, Sarepta, No. 34208.

BOSTWICK, ARTHUR.
Appointed 2nd Lieutenant 30 Inf. April 30, 1813; regimental Quartermaster 1813; 1st Lieutenant Feb. 18, 1814; honorably discharged June 15, 1815. Ref: Heitman's Historical Register & Dictionary USA.

*BOSTWICK, GILBERT.
Served in Capt. Barns' Company, Col. Wm. Williams' Regt. Detached Militia in U. S. service 5 months, 1812. Served in Capt. John Eldridge's Company, 1st Regt. 2nd Brig. 3rd Div. from June 11, 1813 to June 14, 1813. Ref: Book 53, AGO Page 9.

*BOSWORTH, ALANSON.
Served in Capt. Mason's Company, Col. Fifield's Regt. Detached Militia in U. S. service 5 months and 15 days, 1812.

*BOSWORTH, IRA, 2nd Lieutenant, Bridport. Served from April 12, 1814 to May 20, 1814 in company of Capt. James Gray Jr., Sumner's Regt.

BOSWORTH, NATHANIEL.
Volunteered to go to Plattsburgh, September, 1814, and served 7 days in Capt. Frederick Griswold's Company, raised in Brookfield, Vt. Ref: Book 52, AGO Page 52.

*BOSWORTH, WILLIAM, Sergeant.
Served from April 12, 1814 to May 20, 1814 in company of Capt. James Gray Jr., Col. Wm. B. Sumner's Regt.

BOTTLES, HENRY, Berne, N. Y.
Served from Sept. 1, 1814 to June 19, 1815 in Capt. Taylor's Company, 30th Inf. Ref: R. & L. 1812, AGO Page 23.

BOTTLES, WILLIAM, Berne, N. Y.
Served from Sept. 4, 1814 to June 19, 1815 in Capt. Taylor's Company, 30th Inf. Ref: R. & L. 1812, AGO Page 23.

BOTTUM, BISHOP, Orwell.
Volunteered to go to Plattsburgh, September, 1814, and served 15 days in Capt. Asahel Scovell's Company. Ref: Book 51, AGO Page 22.

*BOTTUM, DYER, Corporal, Enosburgh.
Served from Oct. 14th to Nov. 17, 1813 in Capt. Asahel Scovell's Company, Col. Clark's Rifle Corps.

‡BOTTUM, ROSWELL, Orwell.
Volunteered to go to Plattsburgh, September, 1814 and served 11 days in Capt. Wait Branch's Company. Pension Certificate of widow, Elan, No. 24116.

BOUKER, WILLIAM.
Served in Capt. Alexander Brooks' Corps of Artillery. Name appears on Pay Roll to June 30, 1814. Ref: R. & L. 1812, AGO Page 31.

‡BOUTELL, SAMUEL.
Served in Capt. R. Scott's Company. Pension Certificate of widow, Caroline, No. 37000.

*BOUTON, STEPHEN, Ensign.
Served from June 11, 1813 to June 14, 1813 in Capt. Ithiel Stone's Company, 1st Regt. 2nd Brig. 3rd Div.

*BOUTWELL, CHARLES.
Served in Capt. Parsons' Company, Col. Jonathan Williams' Regt. Detached Militia, in U. S. service 2 months and 13 days, 1812.

‡*BOUTWELL, ELI, Drummer, Barre.
Served in Capt. E. Walker's Company, Col. Fifield's Regt. Detached Militia in U. S. service 2 months and 24 days, 1812. Pension Certificate No. 5831. Pension Certificate of widow, Love, No. 6790.

BOUTWELL, HENRY.
Served from Jan. 30, 1813 to July 29, 1813 in Lieut. Wm. S. Foster's Company, 11th Regt. Ref: R. & L. 1812, AGO Page 6.

BOUTWELL. JAMES,   Marshfield.
Volunteered to go to Plattsburgh,
September, 1814, and served 9 days
in Capt. James English's Company.
Ref: Book 52, AGO Page 248.

*BOUTWELL. JOHN.
Served from Oct. 5, 1813 to Dec. 23,
1813 in Capt. Asahel Langworthy's
Company, Col. Isaac Clark's Rifle
Corps. Ref: Book 52, AGO Page 260.

*BOUTWELL, KENDALL.
Served in Capt. Walker's Company,
Col. Fifield's Regt. Detached Militia,
in U. S. service 2 months and 24 days,
1812.

BOUTWELL, NEHEMIAH,   Barre.
Volunteered to go to Plattsburgh,
September, 1814, and served 9 days
in Capt. Warren Ellis' Company. Ref:
Book 52, AGO Pages 233 and 242.

*BOWDISH, JOSEPH. Colonel.
Served in 3rd Regt. (Bowdish) Vt.
Militia.

BOWE, TERRY,   Franklin County.
Volunteered to go to Plattsburgh
Sept. 11, 1814 and served in 15th or
22nd Regt. Ref: Hemenway's Vt.
Gazetteer, Vol. 2, Page 391.

*BOWEN, EZRA. Lieutenant.
Enlisted Sept. 25, 1813 in Capt. Thom-
as Waterman's Company, Col. Dixon's
Regt.

BOWEN. JOSH. .
Served as Corporal in War of 1812
and was captured by Troops May 5,
1814 at Rappids. Exchanged May 4,
1815. Ref: Records of Naval Records
and Library, Navy Dept.

*BOWEN. NATHAN.
Served with Hospital Attendants, Vt.

BOWEN, SAMUEL,   Bethel.
Volunteered to go to Plattsburgh,
September, 1814, and served 8 days
in Capt. Nehemiah Noble's Company.
Ref: Book 51, AGO Page 236.

*BOWEN, THOMAS.
Enlisted Sept. 25, 1813 in Capt. Amos
Robinson's Company, Col. Dixon's
Regt.

BOWERS, BENJAMIN,   Swanton.
Volunteered to go to Plattsburgh,
September, 1814, and served 7 days,
no organization given. Ref: Book
51, AGO Pages 136, 137, 138.

*BOWERS, JOHN.
Enlisted Sept. 25, 1813 in Capt. Amos
Robinson's Company, Dixon's Regt.
and served as waiter for Major Hathaway.

BOWKER, DAVID H., Corporal
Served from May 1 to June 30, 1814
in Capt Alexander Brooks' Corps of
Artillery. Ref: R. & L. 1812, AGO
Page 31.

*BOWKER, ELIAS, Sergeant Major,
Georgia. Served in Capt. Wood's
Company, Col. Dixon's Regt. Detach-
ed Militia, in U. S. service 1 month

and 23 days, 1813. Vounteered to
go to Plattsburgh, September, 1814,
and served 8 days in Capt. Post's
Company, Dixon's Regt. Appointed
Sergeant Sept. 25, 1813; promoted to
Sergeant Major Oct. 25, 1813.

BOWKER, JACOB,   Swanton.
Served in Capt. V. R. Goodrich's
Company, Col. Isaac Clark's Rifle
Corps. Ref: Book 52, AGO Page 260.
8, 1813; was in action at the battle
of Lundy's Lane. Ref: Hemenway's
Vt. Gazetteer, Vol. 2, Page 444.

*BOWKER JOSEPH, Corporal, Georgia.
Served in Capt. Saxe's Company,
Col. Wm. Williams' Regt. Detached
Militia in U. S. service 4 months
and 24 days, 1812. Served in
Capt. Wood's Company, Col. Dix-
on's Regt. Detached Militia in U. S.
service 1 month and 23 days, 1813;
appointed corporal Sept. 25, 1813.
Volunteered to go to Plattsburgh,
September, 1814, and served in Capt.
Jesse Post's Company, Dixon's Regt.
8 days.

BOWKER, NATHANIEL,   Georgia.
Volunteered to go to Plattsburgh,
September, 1814, and served 8 days
in Capt. Jesse Post's Company, Dixon's Regt. Ref: Book 51, AGO Pages
102 and 173.

*BOWLEY. JERMAN, Musician.
Served in 1st Regt. Vt. Militia commanded by Col. Judson.

‡BOWMAN, HENRY.
Served in Captain Birge's Company,
Dixon's Regt. Pension Certificate of
widow, Narcissus, No. 34666.

BOWMAN, JOHN.
Enlisted May 22. 1813. Served in Capt.
James Taylor's Company, Capt.
Gideon Spencer's Company, Capt.
William Miller's Company and Lieut.
Phelps Smith's Company, all in the
30th Regt. Ref: R. & L. 1812, AGO
Pages 52, 53, 54, 57, 59.

*BOWMAN, SAMUEL.
Served in Capt. O. Lowry's Company,
Col. Wm. Williams' Regt. Detached
Militia, in U. S. service 4 months and
26 days, 1812. Also served in Corn-
ing's Detachment, Vt. Militia.

‡*BOWMAN, WILLIAM,   Fairfax.
Enlisted Oct. 22. 1813 in Capt. Asahel
Langworthy's Company, Col. Isaac
Clark's Rifle Corps; transferred to
Capt. Birge's Company, Dixon's Regt.
and served 29 days. Served in Capt.
Joseph Beeman's Company in 1813
and 1814. Pension Certificate No.
1771.

BOWTELL, HENRY.
Enlisted Feb. 6, 1813 in Lieut. Wm.
S. Foster's Company, 11th Regt.; on
Pay Roll for January and February,
1813.

BOWTELLE, NATHANIEL.
Served in Lieut. Wm. S. Foster's
Company, 11th Regt.; on Pay Roll
for January and February, 1813. Ref:
R. & L. 1812, AGO Page 7.

*BOYCE, JOHN.
Served from April 12, 1814 to April
15, 1814 in Capt. John Hackett's Company of Militia. Sumner's Regt.

*BOYCE, JOSEPH.
Served from April 12, 1814 to April
15, 1814 in Capt. John Hackett's Company, Sumner's Regt.

‡*BOYCE, SAMUEL.
Served in Capt. Rogers' Company,
Col. Fifield's Regt. Detached Militia
in U. S. service 2 months and 18
days, 1812. Pension Certificate of
widow, Cynthia, No. 9409.

BOYD, WILLIAM.
Enlisted May 6, 1812 for 5 years in
Capt. White Youngs' Company, 15th
Regt. Name appears on Muster Roll
from Aug. 31, 1814 to Dec. 31, 1814.
Ref: R. & L. 1812, AGO Page 27.

BOYDEN, DARIUS,   Montpelier.
Volunteered to go to Plattsburgh,
September, 1814, and served 8 days
in Capt. Timothy Hubbard's Company.
Ref: Book 52, AGO Pages 246 and
256.

*BOYDEN, EBENEZER, Lieutenant,
Georgia. Served from Sept. 25 to
Oct. 13, 1813 in Capt. Jesse Post's
Company, Dixon's Regt.

*BOYDEN, EBENEZER JR.
Served in Capt. Post's Company, Col.
Dixon's Regt. Detached Militia in U.
S. service 1 month and 23 days, 1813.

BOYES, SAMUEL,   Johnson.
Volunteered to go to Plattsburgh,
September, 1814, and served 8 days
in Capt. Thomas Waterman's Com-
pany, Dixon's Regt. Ref: Book 51,
AGO Page 208.

*BOYES, WILLIAM.
Enlisted Sept. 25, 1813 and served 1
month and 23 days, in Capt. Waterman's Company, Col. Dixon's Regt.

*BOYINGTON, DAVID.
Served from April 12, 1814 to April
21, 1814 in Capt. Shubael Wales' Company, Col. W. B. Sumner's Regt.

*BOYINGTON, DAVID 2d.
Served in Sumner's Regt. Vt. Militia.

*BOYINGTON, JEDEDIAH.
Served in 1st Regt. Vt. Militia commanded by Col. Judson.

BOYINGTON, RICHARD.
Served in Capt. Phineas Williams'
Company, 11th Regt.; on Pay Roll for
January and February, 1813. Ref:
R. & L. 1812, AGO Page 15.

*BOYINGTON, WILLIAM.
Served from April 12, 1814 to April
21, 1814 in Capt. Shubael Wales' Company, Col. W. B. Sumner's Regt.

BOYLE, DANIEL,   Franklin County.
Volunteered to go to Plattsburgh,
September. 11, 1814 and served in 15th
or 22nd Regt. Ref: Hemenway's Vt.
Gazetteer, Vol. 2, Page 392.

‡BOYLE, JEREMIAH F.
Served in Captain Preston's Company,
3rd Regt. Pension Certificate No.
27626.

‡*BOYNTON, ABRAM.
Served in Capt. Durkee's Company,
Col. Fifield's Regt. Detached Militia
in U. S. service 2 months and 16
days, 1812. Pension Certificate No.
9139.

*BOYNTON, ANJOS.
Served in Corning's Detachment, Vt.
Militia.

*BOYNTON, ANSON,   Richmond.
Served from Oct. 5th to Oct. 17, 1813
in Capt. Roswell Hunt's Company, 3
Regt. (Tyler's). Volunteered to go
to Plattsburgh, September, 1814.

‡BOYNTON, DANIEL.
Served in Captain Wales' Company.
Pension Certificate of widow, Thank-
ful, No. 9.

*BOYNTON, E. W.
Served in 4 Regt. Vt. Militia commanded by Col. Williams.

‡*BOYNTON, JOHN, Corporal.
Served in Capt. Morrill's Company,
Col. Fifield's Regt. Detached Militia
in U. S. service 2 months and 18
days, 1812. Pension Certificate No.
4318. Pension Certificate of daughter,
Lydia B. Ferris, No. 35488.

*BOYNTON, JOSIAH.
Served in 1 Regt. Vt. Militia commanded by Col. Judson.

*BOYNTON, MILO.
Served from June 11 to 14, 1813 and
from Oct. 4 to 13, 1813 in Capt.
John Palmer's Company, 1st Regt.
2nd Brig., 3rd Div.

*BOYNTON, SAMUEL.
Served from Feb. 17, 1813 to May 16,
1813 in Lieut. V. R. Goodrich's Com-
pany, 11th Regt. Also served in 4
Regt. Vt. Militia commanded by Col.
Williams.

*BOYNTON, STEPHEN.
Served from June 11, 1813 to June
14, 1813 in Capt. Thomas Dorwin's
Company of Vt. Militia, 1st Regt. 2nd
Brig. 3rd Div.

BOYNTON, THOMAS.
Appointed Ensign 31st Inf. Nov. 8,
1814; 3rd Lieutenant Jan. 1, 1815;
honorably discharged June 15, 1815.
Ref: Governor and Council Vt. Vol.
6, Page 478; Heitman's Historical
Register and Dictionary USA.

*BOYSE, HENRY D.
Served with Hospital Attendants, Vt.

‡*BRACKETT, HENRY,   Braintree.
Served under Captains Wheatly and
Wright, Col. Fifield's Regt. Detached
Militia, in U. S. service 6 months
in 1812. Marched to Plattsburgh
Sept. 10, 1814 and served about 10
days in Capt. Lot Hudson's Company.
Pension Certificate No. 2034.

*BRACKETT, JOSEPH, 1st Sergeant.
Served from April 12, 1814 to April
15, 1814 in Capt. John Hackett's Company, Sumner's Regt.

BRADBURY, JESSE,   Franklin County.
Volunteered to go to Plattsburgh
Sept. 11, 1814 and served in 15th
or 22nd Regt. Ref: Hemenway's Vt.
Gaz., Vol. 2, Page 391.

*BRADFORD, ANDREW.
Enlisted Sept. 28, 1812 in Capt. Benjamin S. Edgerton's Company, 11th
Regt.; on Pay Roll for September
and October, 1812 and January and
February 1813. Also served in 1st
Regt. Vt. Militia commanded by Col.
Martindale. Ref: R. & L. 1812, AGO
Pages 1 and 2.

BRADFORD, BENJAMIN, Captain.
Served in Capt. Benjamin Bradford's
Company; on Muster Roll from May
31 to Aug. 31, 1813. Ref: R. & L.
1812, AGO Page 26.

BRADFORD, BEZABEL, Corporal.
Served in Capt. Benjamin S. Edgerton's Company, 11th Regt.; on Pay
Roll for September and October, 1812
and January and February 1813. Enlisted April 23, 1813 for 1 year in
Capt. Daniel Farrington's Company
(also commanded by Capt. Simeon
Wright) 30th Regt.; on Muster Roll
March 1, 1814 to April 30, 1814.
Sick Absent. Ref: R. & L. 1812,
AGO Pages 1, 2, 50, 51.

BRADFORD, BEZILLA,   Tunbridge.
Served from Sept. 1, 1814 to June 16,
1815 in Capt. Sanford's Company,
30th Inf. Ref: R. & L. 1812, AGO
Page 23.

BRADFORD, TIMOTHY.
Served from March 23, 1813 to June
22, 1813 in Detachment of Recruits under Capt. Phineas Williams, 11th
Regt. Ref: R. & L. 1812, AGO
Page 14.

BRADFORD, WILLIAM,   Barre.
Volunteered to go to Plattsburgh,
September, 1814, and served 9 days
in Capt. Warren Ellis' Company. Ref:
Book 52, AGO Pages 233 and 242.

*BRADISH, EDMOND.
Served in 1 Regt. Vt. Militia commanded by Col. Martindale.

BRADISH, THOMAS,   Cabot.
Volunteered to go to Plattsburgh,
September, 1814, and served 4 days
in Capt. Anthony Perry's Company.
Ref: Book 52, AGO Page 179.

*BRADLEY, ABRAM.
Enlisted Oct. 11, 1813 in Capt. Elijah
W. Wood's Company, Dixon's Regt.

*BRADLEY, BUNYON.
Served in 3 Regt. Vt. Militia commanded by Col. Tyler.

*BRADLEY, EBEN.
Served in 3 Regt. Vt. Militia commanded by Col. Tyler.

*BRADLEY, HARRY.
Served in 1 Regt. Vt. Militia commanded by Col. Judson.

BRADLEY, ISAAC,   Franklin County.
Volunteered to go to Plattsburgh
Sept. 11, 1814 and served in 15th or
22nd Regt. Ref: Hemenway's Vt. Gazetteer, Vol. 2, Page 392.

*BRADLEY, JEREMY, 1st Lieut.
Served from April 12, 1814 to April
15, 1814 in Capt. John Hackett's Company, Sumner's Regt.

‡*BRADLEY, JOHN, Swanton or Fairfield. Served in Capt. Geo. W. Kindal's Company, 4th Regt. 6 months
in 1812. Served in Capt. Kindal's
Company, Col. Wm. Williams' Regt.
Detached Militia in U. S. service 3
months and 28 days, 1812. Pension
Certificate of widow, Polly, No. 2858.

*BRADLEY, JOHN.
Served in Capt. Scovell's Company,
Col. Martindale's Regt. Detached
Militia, in U. S. service 2 months
and 21 days, 1812.

*BRADLEY, JOY.
Served in 3 Regt. Vt. Militia commanded by Col. Tyler.

*BRADLEY, NATHAN.
Enlisted Sept. 25, 1813 in Capt. N.
B. Eldridge's Company, Dixon's Regt.

*BRADLEY, PETER, Corporal.
Served in Capt. Phelps' Company,
Col. Wm. Williams' Regt. Detached
Militia in U. S. service 5 months
in 1812.

BRADLEY, ROBERT A.
Served in Capt. Benjamin Bradford's
Company; on Muster Roll from May
31, 1813 to Aug. 31, 1813; joined by
transfer July 22, 1813. Ref: R. & L.
1812, AGO Page 26.

‡BRADLEY, SALMON.
Served in Capt. B. Wooster's Company. Pension Certificate No. 30846.

*BRADLEY, THERON.
Served in Tyler's Regt. Vt. Militia.

*BRADLEY, TIMOTHY, Surgeon's Mate.
Served in Col. Isaac Clark's Volunteer Rifle Corps; appointed Surgeon's
Mate Sept. 25, 1813.

*BRADLEY, WRIGHT.
Served from April 12, 1814 to April
21, 1814 in Capt. Edmund B. Hill's
Company, Sumner's Regt.

*BRADSBEE, WILLIAM.
Served in 1 Regt. Vt. Militia commanded by Col. Martindale.

BRADSHAW, JOSIAH.
Volunteered to go to Plattsburgh,
September, 1814, and served 7 days
in Capt. Frederick Griswold's Company, raised in Brookfield, Vermont.
Ref: Book 52, AGO Page 52.

BRADWAY, WILLIAM.
Born in Cheshire, Mass.; aged 38
years; 5 ft. 10 in. high; dark complexion; brown hair; grey eyes; by
profession a farmer; enlisted March
30, 1814 in Capt. Miller's Company,
30th Regt.; discharged at Burlington,

Vt. in 1815. Also served in Capt. Gideon Spencer's Company, Capt. James Taylor's Company, both in 30th Regt. Ref: R. & L. 1812, AGO Pages 53 to 57.

BRAGDON, JOSIAH,   Franklin County. Volunteered to go to Plattsburgh Sept. 11, 1814 and served in 15th or 22nd Regt. Ref: Hemenway's Vt. Gazetteer, Vol. 2, Page 392.

BRAGG, WILLIAM. Volunteered to go to Plattsburgh, September, 1814, and went as far as Bolton, Vt.; in service 4 days in Lieut. Phineus Kimball's Company. West Fairle. Ref: Book 52, AGO Page 46.

*BRAINARD, DAVID. Corporal. Served in Capt. Wheeler's Company, Col. Fifield's Regt. Detached Militia in U. S. service 6 months and 4 days, 1812.

BRAINARD, EBENEZER. Served from March 10, 1813 to May 31, 1813 in Capt. John W. Weeks' Company, 11th Regt. Ref: R. & L. 1812, AGO Page 4.

‡*BRAINARD, JOHN. Served from March 10, 1813 to May 31, 1813 in Capt. John W. Weeks' Company, 11th Regt. Served from April 12, 1814 to May 20, 1814 in company of Capt. James Gray Jr., Sumner's Regt. Pension Certificate of widow, Harriet, No. 4189. Ref: R. & L. 1812, AGO Page 4.

*BRAINARD, LAWRENCE, Sergeant. Served from Sept. 25, 1813 to Oct. 7th in Capt. N. B. Eldridge's Company, Dixon's Regt.

‡*BRAINARD, LOUDON,   Randolph. Volunteered to go to Plattsburgh, September, 1814, in Capt. Lebbeus Egerton's Company. Pension Certificate of widow, Hetta, No. 35356.

BRAN, DANIEL O., Sergeant. Served from June 11, 1813 to June 14, 1813 in Capt. John M. Eldridge's Company, 1st Regt. 2nd Brig., 3rd Div. Ref: R. & L. 1812, AGO Page 35.

BRANCH, DARIUS,   Castleton. Volunteered to go to Plattsburgh, September, 1814, and served 9 days with two horse team. No organization given. Ref: Book 52, AGO Page 154.

BRANCH, ELIJAH, Corporal. Served from Sept. 1, 1812 to Feb. 28, 1813 in Capt. Samul Gordon's Company, 11th Regt. Ref: R. & L. 1812, AGO Page 9.

‡BRANCH, JASPER. Served in Capt. Alden Partridge's Company. Pension Certificate No. 16908.

BRANCH, SAMUEL, Corporal. Served in 1st Regt. of Detached Militia of Vermont in the service of the United States at Champlain for 2 days commencing Nov. 18 and ending Nov. 19, 1812.

BRANCH, Wait, Captain,   Orwell. Volunteered to go to Plattsburgh, September, 1814, and served 11 days in command of company raised at Orwell. Ref: Book 51, AGO Page 16.

*BRAND, CALEB. Served in Capt. Barns' Company, Col. Wm. Williams' Regt. Detached Militia, in U. S. service 5 months, 1812. Served from June 11, 1813 to June 14, 1813 in Capt. Thomas Dorwin's Company, 1st Regt. 2nd Brig., 3rd Div.

*BRAND, DAVID. Served from June 11, 1813 to June 14, 1813 in Capt. Thomas Dorwin's Company, 1st Regt. 2nd Brig., 3rd Div.

*BRAND, NATHAN. Served from June 11, 1813 to June 14, 1813 in Capt. Thomas Dorwin's Company, 1st Regt. 2nd Brig. 3rd Div.

*BRASEE, PETER. Served in Sumner's Regt. Vt. Militia.

*BRASTEAD, BENJAMIN. Served from Oct. 15th to Nov. 17, 1813 in Capt. Asahel Scovell's Company, Col. Clark's Rifle Corps.

‡BRASTED, WILLIAM. Served in Captain Gray's Company. Pension Certificate of widow, Anna, No. 25775.

BRASTWICK, GEORGE T., Sergeant. Served in Capt. John M. Eldridge's Company, 1st Regt. 2nd Brig. 3rd Div., from June 11, 1813 to June 14, 1813. Ref: R. & L. 1812, AGO Page 35.

BRAW, ROBERT. Served in Capt. Wheeler's Company, Col. Fifield's Regt. Detached Militia in U. S. service 6 months and 4 days, 1812. Ref: Book 53, AGO Page 67.

‡BRAYTON, RUFUS. Served in Capt. John D. Reynolds' Company. Pension Certificate of widow, Anna, No. 14431.

BRAYTON, STEPHEN. Served from May 27, 1813 to Jan. 26, 1814 in Capt. Daniel Farrington's Company (also commanded by Capt. Simeon Wright), 30th Regt. Ref: R. & L. 1812, AGO Pages 50 and 51.

*BREAKNEY, FRANCIS, Sergeant. Served in 1 Regt. Vt. Militia commanded by Col. Martindale.

BRECKENBRIDGE.   Sergeant. Served in 1st Regt. of Detached Militia of Vt. in the service of the U. S. at Champlain for 2 days commencing Nov. 18 and ending Nov. 19, 1812.

BREAKENRIDGE, FRANCIS. Served in Capt. Cross' Company, Col. Martindale's Regt. Detached Militia, in U. S. service 2 months and 14 days, 1812. Ref: Book 53, AGO Page 70.

‡*BREAKENRIDGE, JAMES.
Served in Capt. Dorrance's Company,
Col. Wm. Williams' Regt. Detached
Militia in U. S. service 4 months and
29 days. 1812. Pension Certificate of
widow, Clarissa, No. 18188.

*BRESEE, PETER.
Served in Sumner's Regt. Vt. Militia.

‡BREVORT, HENRY.
Served in Capt. George Fisher's Company. Pension Certificate No. 32708.

‡BREVORT, SAMUEL,   St. Albans.
Enlisted May 11, 1813 for 1 year
in Capt. John Wires' Company, 30th
Regt. Also served in Capt. Sanford's Company, 30th Regt. Pension
Certificate No. 10227. Ref: R. & L.
1812, AGO Page 40.

BREWER, ALONZO.
Appointed Cadet, Military Academy,
July 13, 1813 (16); 3rd Lieutenant
Corps Artillery March 2, 1815; re-
signed Oct. 16, 1816; died 1823. Ref:
Heitman's Historical Register & Dic-
tionary USA.

BREWER, ANDREW.
Served from Feb. 8, 1813 to Feb. 27,
1813 in Capt. Edgerton's Company,
11th Regt. Ref: R. & L. 1812, AGO
Page 3.

*BREWER, DAVID,   Sutton.
Served in Capt. Wheeler's Company,
Col. Fifield's Regt. Detached Militia
in U. S. service 6 months and 4 days,
1812.

*BREWER, JACOB.
Served in Capt. Taylor's Company,
Col. Wm. Williams' Regt. Detached
Militia in U. S. service 4 months and
24 days, 1812.

*BREWER, JAMES.
Served in 4 Regt. Vt. Militia commanded by Col. Williams.

*BREWER, MOSES.
Served in Capt. Wheeler's Company,
Col. Fifield's Regt. Detached Militia
in U. S. service 6 months and 4 days,
1812.

*BREWER, PETER,   Highgate.
Served in Capt. Saxe's Company, Col.
Wm. Williams' Regt. Detached Militia in U. S. service 3 months and 24
days, 1812.

BREWETT, PAUL.
Enlisted June 3, 1812 for a period
of 5 years in company of late Capt.
J. Brooks commanded by Lieut. John
I. Cromwell, Corps of U. S. Artillery;
on Muster Roll from April 30, 1814
to June 30, 1814. Ref: R. & L. 1812,
AGO Page 18.

‡BREWSTER, ALBE.
Served in Captain Taylor's Company.
Pension Certificate No. 11722. Pen-
sion Certificate of widow, Lydia M.,
No. 28011.

*BREWSTER, ASA.
Served in Capt. Burnap's Company,
Col. Jonathan Williams' Regt. Detached Militia in U. S. service 2 months
and 13 days, 1812.

*BREWSTER, CHARLES,   Huntington
Volunteered to go to Plattsburgh,
September, 1814, and was at the
battle, serving in Capt. Josiah N. Barrows' Company, 3rd Regt. Also served in 4 Regt. Vt. Militia commanded
by Col. Williams.

BREWSTER, CHARLES 2nd, Huntington.
Volunteered to go to Plattsburgh,
September, 1814, and was at the
battle, serving in Capt. Josiah N. Barrows' Company, 3 Regt. Ref: Book
51, AGO Page 77,

*BREWSTER, COMFORT.
Served in 3 Regt. Vt. Militia com-
manded by Col. Tyler; served in 4
Regt. Vt. Militia commanded by Col.
Williams.

‡*BREWSTER, DYER.
Served in Capt. Burnap's Company,
Col. Jonathan Williams' Regt. Detached Militia in U. S. service 2
months and 13 days, 1812. Also served in Capt. Burnett's Company. Pension Certificate No. 9744.

BREWSTER, EPHRAIM.
Served as Surgeon's Mate 2nd Inf.
April 14, 1812; died Sept. 11, 1812.
Ref: Heitman's Historical Register
and Dictionary USA.

*BREWSTER, ETHAN A.
Served in Corning's Detachment, Vt.
Militia.

*BREWSTER, FREDERICK.
Served in 1 Regt. Vt. Militia commanded by Col. Judson.

*BREWSTER, JACOB.
Served in 4 Regt. Vt. Militia commanded by Col. Williams.

*BREWSTER, JONATHAN, Lieutenant.
Served as 1st and 2nd Lieutenant
in Cavalry of Detached Militia of
Vermont in the service of the U. S.
at Champlain for 2 days commencing Nov. 18 and ending Nov. 19, 1812.

‡*BREWSTER, LEONARD.
Served in Capt. Taylor's Company,
Col. Wm. Williams' Regt. Detached
Militia, in U. S. service 4 months
and 24 days, 1812. Pension Certifi-
cate No. 22738.

*BREWSTER, LORIN, Corporal.
Served from April 12, 1814 to April
15, 1814 in Capt. John Hackett's Company, Sumner's Regt.

BREWSTER, PAUL,   Woodstock.
Served from March 22, 1813 to June
21, 1813 in Capt. Phineas Williams'
Company, 11th Regt. Ref: R. & L.
1812, AGO Page 14.

BREWSTER, SAMUEL,   Huntington.
Volunteered to go to Plattsburgh,
September, 1814, and was present at
the battle, serving in Capt. Josiah
N. Barrows' Company. Ref: Book
51, AGO Page 77.

*BREWSTER, WILLIAM.
Served from Oct. 11, 1813 to Oct. 17,
1813 in Capt. John Munson's Company, 3 Regt.

*BRIANT, SAMUEL F., Corporal.
Served in Capt. Needham's Company,
Col. Martindale's Regt. Detached
Militia in U. S. service 2 months
and 14 days, 1812.

‡BRICE, ALEX.
Served in Capt. Wright's Company.
Pension Certificate No. 7824.

*BRIDGE, ALFRED.
Served in Capt. E. Walker's Company, Col. Fifield's Regt. Detached
Militia in U. S. service 6 months and
3 days, 1812.

‡BRIDGE, BARZALEEL.
Enlisted Aug. 12, 1813 for 1 year
in Capt. Simeon Wright's Company.
Pension Certificate of widow, Almira,
No. 3245.

BRIDGE, JEREMIAH.
Served in Capt. Richardson's Company, Col. Martindale's Regt. Detached Militia in U. S. service 2 months
and 13 days, 1812. Ref: Book 53,
AGO Page 58.

*BRIDGE, JONAS, Enosburgh.
Served from Oct. 15, 1813 to Nov. 17,
1813 in Capt. Asahel Scovell's Company, Col. Clark's Regt. of Riflemen.

BRIDGES, BORABREL. Franklin County.
Volunteered to go to Plattsburgh,
Sept. 11, 1814 and served in 15th or
22nd Regt. Ref: Hemenway's Vt. Gazetteer, Vol. 2, Page 392.

BRIDGES, CALEB.
Enlisted Jan. 20, 1813 in Company of
John McNeil Jr., 11th Regt.; on Pay
Roll to May 31, 1813. Ref: R. & L.
1812, AGO Page 16.

BRIDGES, JOSIAH.
Served from Jan. 14, 1813 to June
21, 1813 in Capt. Jonathan Starks'
Company, 11th Regt. Ref: R. & L.
1812, AGO Page 19.

BRIGGS, ABNER.
Enlisted May 17, 1813 for 1 year
in Capt. Simeon Wright's Company.
Ref: R. & L. 1812, AGO Page 51.

*BRIGGS, ALFRED.
Served in 2 Regt. Vt. Militia commanded by Col. Fifield.

BRIGGS, AMASA, Williamstown.
Volunteered to go to Plattsburgh,
September, 1814, and went as far as
Burlington, serving in Capt. David
Robinson's Company. Ref: Book 52,
AGO Pages 2 and 12.

*BRIGGS, ASA B., Barnard.
Served in Capt. Phelps' Company, Col.
Jonathan Williams' Regt. Detached
Militia in U. S. service 2 months and
21 days, 1812.

*BRIGGS, ASA JR., Captain.
Served in 3 Regt. Vt. Militia commanded by Col. Williams.

*BRIGGS, BENJAMIN.
Served from April 12, 1814 to May
20, 1814 in Capt. George Fisher's Company, Sumner's Regt.

BRIGGS, CALEB.
Served in company of Capt. John
McNeil Jr. 11th Regt.; on Pay Roll
for January and February, 1813.
Ref: R. & L. 1812, AGO Page 17.

*BRIGGS, E. D., Rochester.
Volunteered to go to Plattsburgh,
September, 1814. Ref: Book 51, AGO
Page 249.

BRIGGS, EPHRAIM, Captain, Barnard.
Served in Col. J. Williams' Regt.
on detached service from December,
1812 to May, 1814. Ref: Wm. M.
Newton's History of Barnard, Vol. 1,
Page 96.

*BRIGGS, ISAAC N.
Appointed Ensign 31 Inf. April 30,
1813; 2nd Lieutenant May 1, 1814;
honorably discharged June 15, 1815.
Also served in 3 Regt. Vt. Militia
commanded by Col. Williams. Ref:
Heitman's Historical Register & Dictionary USA.

BRIGGS, JAMES.
Enlisted May 28, 1813 for 1 year
in Capt. Simeon Wright's Company.
Ref: R. & L. 1812, AGO Page 51.

*BRIGGS, JESSE.
Served in Capt. Phelps' Company, Col.
Jonathan Williams Regt. Detached
Militia in U. S. service 2 months and
21 days, 1812.

BRIGGS, JOHN P., Surgeon, Franklin
County. Volunteered to go to Plattsburgh Sept. 11, 1814 and served in
15th or 22nd Regt. Ref: Hemenway's
Vt. Gaz. Vol. 2, Page 391.

*BRIGGS, ROYAL.
Served from Oct. 5, 1813 to Oct. 17,
1813 in Capt. Stephen Brown's Company, 3 Regt. (Tyler's).

*BRIGGS, SAMUEL JR.
Served in Capt. Briggs' Company,
Col. Jonathan Williams' Regt. Detached Militia in U. S. service 2
months and 13 days, 1812.

*BRIGGS, SIMEON, Barre.
Served in Capt. Walker's Company,
Col. Fifield's Regt. Detached Militia in U. S. service 2 months and
24 days, 1812.

‡*BRIGGS, WILLIAM.
Served in Capt. Benjamin S. Edgerton's Company, 11th Regt.; on Pay
Roll for September and October, 1812
and January and February, 1813.
Served from April 12, 1814 to April
21, 1814 in Capt. Edmund B. Hill's
Company, Sumner's Regt. Also served in Captain Saxted's Company. Was
in battle at Chrystler's Farm Nov.
11, 1813 and reported missing after
the battle. Ref: R. & L. 1812, AGO
Pages 1 and 2; Governor and Council, Vt. Vol. 6, Page 490. Pension
Certificate No. 25232.

BRIGHAM, ABNER, 1st Lieutenant, Morristown. Volunteered to go to Plattsburgh, September, 1814, and served
8 days in Capt. Denison Cook's Company. Ref: Book 51, AGO Pages
202 and 206.

*BRIGHAM, ASA.
Served in 3 Regt. Vt. Militia commanded by Col. Tyler.

*BRIGHAM, ASAHEL, Sergeant.
Served from April 12, 1814 to April 21, 1814 in Capt. Shubael Wales' Company, Col. W. B. Sumner's Regt.

BRIGHAM, CYRUS,   Montpelier.
Volunteered to go to Plattsburgh, September, 1814, and served 8 days in Capt. Timothy Hubbard's Company. Ref: Book 52, AGO Page 256.

*BRIGHAM, ELDRIDGE.
Served in Capt. Saxe's Company, Col. Wm. Williams' Regt. Detached Militia in U. S. service 3 months and 24 days, 1812. Served in Capt. Willson's Company, Col. Wm. Williams' Regt. Detached Militia in U. S. service 4 months and 24 days, 1812.

*BRIGHAM, MILLER.
Enlisted Sept. 25, 1813 in Company of Capt. Jonathan Prentiss Jr. Dixon's Regt.

*BRIGHAM, NATHAN.
Served in Sumner's Regt. Vt. Militia.

*BRIGHAM, PIERPOINT,   St. Albans.
Enlisted Sept. 25, 1813 and served 1 month and 23 days in Capt. Eldridge's Company, Col. Dixon's Regt. Volunteered to go to Plattsburgh and was at the battle Sept. 11, 1814, serving in Capt. Samuel H. Farnsworth's Company. Ref: Hemenway's Vt. Gazetteer, Vol. 2, Page 434.

*BRIGHAM, RUFUS.
Enlisted Sept. 25, 1813 in company of Capt. Jonathan Prentiss, Jr., Dixon's Regt.

*BRIGHAM, SILAS.
Enlisted Sept. 25, 1813 in company of Capt. Jonathan Prentiss, Jr., Dixon's Regt.

BRIGHAM, THOMAS.
Served from March 26, 1813 to June 23, 1813 in Capt. John W. Weeks' Company, 11th Regt. Ref: R. & L. 1812, AGO Page 4.

*BRIGHAM, URIEL.
Served in Tyler's Regt. Vt. Militia.

BRIMMINGHAM, THOMAS, Franklin County. Volunteered to go to Plattsburgh Sept. 11, 1814 and served in 15th or 22nd Regt. Ref: Hemenway's Vt. Gazetteer, Vol. 2, Page 391.

‡*BRINK, JAMES, JR.
Served in Capt. Burnap's Company, Col. Jonathan Williams' Regt. Detached Militia in U. S. service 2 months and 13 days, 1812. Pension Certificate of widow, Millie, No. 10400.

BRINK, ORISON.
Served in Capt. V. R. Goodrich's Company, 11th Regt.; on Pay Roll for January and February, 1813. Ref: R. & L. 1812, AGO Page 11.

BRINK, ORSON.
Was born at Oxford and served as a private in the War of 1812; captured by boats and troops June 13, 1813 on Lake Champlain; discharged Oct. 31st. Ref: Records of Naval Records and Library, Navy Dept.

*BRINTNALL, THOMAS, Corporal.
Served in Capt. Dorrance's Company, Col. Wm. Williams' Regt. Detached Militia, in U. S. service 4 months and 29 days, 1812.

*BRISTOL, AARON W.
Served from April 12, 1814 to April 21, 1814 in Capt. Othniel Jewett's Company, Sumner's Regt.

BRITTAN, JAMES JR.,   Barre.
Volunteered to go to Plattsburgh, September, 1814, and sreved 10 days in Capt. Warren Ellis' Company. Ref: Book 52, AGO Page 242.

*BRITTELL, CLAUDIUS.
Served in Capt. Wright's Company, Col. Martindale's Regt. Detached Militia in U. S. service 2 months and 14 days, 1812.

*BRITTON, CLAUDIUS.
Served from April 12, 1814 to April 21, 1814 in Capt. Shubael Wales'.Company, Col. W. B. Sumner's Regt.

*BRITTON, SAMUEL J. (or S.) Weybridge. Served from July 20 to Dec. 8, 1812 in Capt. Dorrance's Company, Col. Wm. Williams' Regt.

*BRITTON, SAMUEL S.
Served from April 12, 1814 to April 15, 1814 in Capt. John Hackett's Company, Sumner's Regt.

BRITTON, WILLIAM, Franklin County. Volunteered to go to Plattsburgh Sept. 11, 1814 and served in 15th or 22nd Regt. Ref: Hemenway's Vt. Gazetteer, Vol. 2, Page 392.

BROADWELL, JOHN.
Enlisted March 22, 1814, during the war in Capt. James Taylor's Company, 30th Regt. Ref: R. & L. 1812, AGO Page 53.

BRONAUGH. I. C., Hospital Surgeon. Served on General Staff of the Northern Army commanded by Major General George Izard; on Pay Roll to July 31, 1814. Ref: R. & L. 1812, AGO Page 28.

*BRONNEL. JEREMIAH. Ensign.
Served in 1 Regt. Vt. Militia commanded by Col. Judson.

BRONSDON. JOSEPH B., Mas. Carp. Served from May 1st to June 30, 1814 in Company of Artificers commanded by Alexander Parris. Ref: R. & L. 1812, AGO Page 24.

‡BROOKINS. PHILETUS, Corporal, St. Albans. Enlisted April 23, 1813 for 1 year in Capt. John Wires' Company, 30th Regt. Also served in Capt. Sanford's Company, 30th Regt. Pension Certificate of widow, Desire, No. 2131. Ref: R. & L. 1812, AGO Page 40.

‡BROOKINS, SILAS JR.,   Shoreham.
Served from Oct. 15, 1813 to Nov.
17, 1813 in Capt. Asahel Scoville's
Company, Col. Clark's Rifle Regt.
Also served in Capt. Scofield's Com-
pany. Served from April 12, 1814
to May 20, 1814 in company of Capt.
James Gray, Jr., Sumner's Regt.
Ref: R. & L. 1812, AGO Page 22;
Book 52, AGO Page 274; Book 52,
AGO Page 280. Pension Certificate
No. 19949.

BROOKS, AARON,   Franklin County.
Volunteered to go to Plattsburgh
Sept. 11, 1814 and served in 15th or
22nd Regt. Ref: Hemenway's Vt.
Gazetteer, Vol. 2, Page 392.

BROOKS, ALEXANDER S., Captain.
Served in Capt. Alexander Brooks'
Corps of Artillery; on Pay Roll to
June 30, 1814. Ref: R. & L. 1812,
AGO Page 31.

*BROOKS, BEZABELL.
Served from April 12, 1814 to April
21, 1814 in Capt. Othniel Jewett's
Company, Sumner's Regt.

*BROOKS, CEPHUS.
Served from April 12, 1814 to April
15, 1814 in Lieut. Justus Foote's
Company, Sumner's Regt.

BROOKS, EBENEZER, Corporal.
Served from May 1 to June 30, 1814
in Capt. Alex'r Brooks' Corps of
Artillery. Ref: R. & L. 1812, AGO
Page 31.

BROOKS, HOSEA, Surgeon, Cornwall.
Volunteered to go to Plattsburgh,
September, 1814 and was at the battle,
serving in Capt. Edmund B. Hill's
Company, Sumner's Regt. Ref: Book
51, AGO Page 13.

BROOKS, JAMES,   Franklin County.
Volunteered to go to Plattsburgh
Sept. 11, 1814 and served in 15th or
22nd Regt. Ref: Hemenway's Vt.
Gazetteer, Vol. 2, Page 391.

BROOKS, JONAS G.
Appointed Ensign. Volunteers, 1812;
Ensgin 45 Inf. April 21, 1814; 3 Lieut.
Aug. 1, 1814; 2 Lieut. Jan. 1, 1815;
honorably discharged June 15, 1815.
Ref: Heitmans' Historical Register
& Dictionary USA.

BROOKS, JONATHAN, Captain.
Commanded company of U. S. Artil-
lery; on Muster Roll from April 30,
1814 to June 30, 1814; disbanded
June 1, 1814. Ref: R. & L. 1812,
AGO Page 18.

BROOKS, JOSH.
Served as private in War of 1812
and was captured by troops Sept.
17, 1814 at Fort Erie. Discharged
Nov. 8th. Ref: Records of Naval Records and Library, Navy Dept.

‡*BROOKS, JOSEPH.
Served in Capt. Needham's Company,
Col. Martindale's Regt. Detached
Militia in U. S. service 2 months
and 14 days, 1812. Pension Certifi-
cate of widow, Sally, No. 31206.

*BROOKS, JOSHUA.
Served in Capt. Wright's Company,
Col. Fifield's Regt. Detached Militia in U. S. service 2 months and
21 days, 1812.

‡*BROOKS, NATHANIEL,   Strafford.
Served in Capt. Taylor's Company,
Col. Fifield's Regt. Detached Militia, in U. S. service 6 months in
1812. Also served in Capt. Rodgers'
Company. Pension Certificate No.
6855.

‡*BROOKS, OSMUND, Corporal, Bethel.
Volunteered to go to Plattsburgh,
September, 1814, and served 8 days
in Capt. Nehemiah Noble's Company,
3 Regt. (Williams'). Pension Certificate of widow, Louisa, No. 27555.

‡BROOKS, PARDON A.
Served in Capt. Noble's Company.
Pension Certificate of widow, Lavinia,
No. 39604.

BROOKS, PELEG L.
Served in Capt. Benjamin Bradford's
Company; on Muster Roll from May
31, 1813 to Aug. 31, 1813. Ref: R.
& L. 1812, AGO Page 26.

*BROOKS, SETH.
Served from April 12, 1814 to April
21, 1814 in Lieut. Justus Foote's Company, Sumner's Regt.

BROOKS, SILAS JR.,   Enosburgh.
Served from Oct. 14, 1813 to Nov.
17, 1813 in Capt. Asahel Scovel's
Company, Col. Clark's Rifle Corps.
Ref: Hemenway's Vt. Gazetteer, Vol.
2, Page 398.

BROOKS, THOMAS,   Montpelier.
Volunteered to go to Plattsburgh,
September, 1814, and served 8 days
in Capt. Timothy Hubbard's Company. Ref: Book 52, AGO Page 256.

*BROUGHTON, DANIEL, Captain, Wil-
liston. Served in Capt. Wheeler's
Company, Col. Fifield's Regt. Detach-
ed Militia, in U. S. service 3 months
and 16 days, 1812. Enlisted in Capt.
James Taylor's Company, 30th Regt.,
April 26, 1813; transferred to Capt.
Gideon Spencer's Company, 30th
Regt. and served to April 25, 1814.
Volunteered to go to Plattsburgh,
September, 1814 and served 11 days
as a Captain. Ref: R. & L. 1812,
AGO Page 52; Book 52, AGO Page
150.

BROUGHTON, HORACE.
Appointed 2nd Lieutenant 26 Inf.
April 21, 1814; 1st Lieutenant Dec.
10, 1814; honorably discharged June
15, 1815; Captain 6 Inf. Feb.
19, 1817; transferred to Rifle Regt.
May 8, 1817; 1st Lieutenant July 31,
1817; resigned April 5, 1818. Ref:
Heitman's Historical Register & Dictionary USA.

‡*BROUGHTON, JOHN S., Sergeant.
Served in Capt. Mason's Company,
Col. Fifield's Regt. Detached Militia
in U. S. service 5 months and 26
days, 1812. Enlisted April 26, 1813
and served in Capt. Gideon Spen-

cer's Company and Capt. James Taylor's Company, both in 30th Regt.; held rank of Sergeant in Capt. Taylor's Company; discharged April 25, 1814. Also served in Capt. A. S. Brown's Company. Pension Certificate No. 17607.

BROWER, JAMES.
Enlisted Nov. 6, 1812 for 5 years in company of late Capt. J. Brooks commanded by Lt. John I. Cromwell, Corps of U. S. Artillery; on Muster Roll from April 30, 1814 to June 30, 1814. Ref: R. & L. 1812, AGO Page 18.

‡*BROWN, ABEL.
Served in Capt. Parson's Company, Col. Jonathan Williams' Regt; Detached Militia in U. S. service 2 months and 13 days, 1812. Pension Certificate of widow, Priscilla, No. 481.

BROWN, ABRAHAM, Franklin County.
Volunteered to go to Plattsburgh, Sept. 11, 1814, and served in 15th or 22nd Regt. Ref: Hemenway's Vt. Gazetteer, Vol. 2, Page 391.

BROWN, ABRAHAM, Strafford.
Volunteered to go to Plattsburgh, September, 1814, and served 5 days in Capt. Joseph Barrett's Company. Ref: Book 52, AGO Page 41.

BROWN, ALBERT.
Served from May 1 to June 30, 1814 in Capt. Alexander Brooks' Corps of Artillery. Ref: R. & L. 1812, AGO Page 31.

BROWN, AMASA J., Captain, Swanton.
Appointed Captain 30 Inf. April 30, 1813; dismissed Jan. 31, 1814. Volunteered to go to Plattsburgh and was at the battle Sept. 11, 1814 in command of a company from Swanton. Ref: Heitman's Historical Register & Dictionary USA; Hemenway's Vt .Gazetteer, Vol. 2, Page 444.

*BROWN, AMOS, Corporal.
Enlisted Sept. 23, 1813 in Capt. Amasa Mansfield's Company, Dixon's Regt.

*BROWN, AMOS.
Served in 3 Regt. Vt. Militia commanded by Col. Tyler.

BROWN, AMOS W.
Appointed 2 Lieutenant 31 Inf. April 30, 1813; 1st Lieutenant Jan. 11, 1814; struck off Oct. 25, 1814; reinstated March 6, 1815; honorably discharged June 15, 1815. Ref: Heitman's Historical Register & Dictionary USA.

BROWN, AQUILLA, Sergeant.
Served from May 1 to June 30, 1814 in Corps of Light Dragoons. Ref: R. & L. 1812, AGO Page 20.

‡BROWN, ARCHELAUS S., Fifer, East Montpelier. Volunteered to go to Plattsburgh, September, 1814, and served 4 days in Capt. Timothy Hubbard's Company. Pension Certificate No. 29901.

*BROWN, ASA.
Served with Hospital Attendants, Vt.

‡BROWN, BARNA.
Served in Captain Howard's Company, 2nd Regt. Pension Certificate No. 5876.

*BROWN BENJAMIN.
Served in Capt. Ormsbee's Company, Col. Martindale's Regt. Detached Militia, in U. S. service 2 months and 14 days, 1812. Served from Feb. 20, 1813 to May 9, 1813 in Capt. Edgerton's Company, 11th Regt. Ref: R. & L. 1812, AGO Page 3.

‡*BROWN, BRADISH, Richmond. Volunteered to go to Plattsburgh, September, 1814, and served 9 days in Capt. Roswell Hunt's Company, 3 Regt. Also served in 4 Regt. (Williams') Vt. Militia and in Capt. Stephen Jones' Company. Pension Certificate of widow, Eliza, No. 21675.

BROWN, CALEB, Sergeant.
Served in 1st Regt. of Detached Militia of Vermont in the service of the United States at Champlain for 2 days commencing Nov. 18 and ending Nov. 19, 1812.

*BROWN, CHARLES.
Served in Capt. Preston's Company, Col. Jonathan Williams' Regt. Detached Militia in U. S. service 2 months and 6 days, 1812.

BROWN, CHAUNCY, Richford.
Served in Capt. Willson's Company, Col. Wm. Williams' Regt. Detached Militia in U. S. service 4 months and 24 days, 1812. Served in Capt. Martin D. Folett's Company, Dixon's Regt., on duty on Canadian Frontier in 1813. Ref: Book 53, AGO Page 73; Hemenway's Vt. Gazetteer, Vol. 2, Page 428.

*BROWN, CHENEY.
Served in 4 Regt. Vt. Militia commanded by Col. Williams.

‡*BROWN, CYREL J.
Served in Capt. Brown's Company, Col. Martindale's Regt. Detached Militia in U. S. service 2 months and 14 days, 1812. Pension Certificate No. 13588. Pension Certificate of widow, Ann D., No. 33871.

*BROWN, DANIEL.
Served in 3 Regt. Vt. Militia commanded by Col. Tyler.

*BROWN, DANIEL.
Served from April 12, 1814 to April 21, 1814 in Capt. Eseck Sprague's Company, Sumner's Regt.

*BROWN, DANIEL.
Served from April 12, 1814 to April 21, 1814 in Capt. Othniel Jewett's Company, Sumner's Regt.

*BROWN, DANIEL, Sergeant.
Served in Capt. Taylor's Company, Col. Fifield's Regt. Detached Militia in U. S. service 6 months, 1812. Served as sergeant in Capt. Brown's Company, Col. Martindale's Regt. Detached Militia in U. S. service 2 months and 14 days, 1812.

BROWN, DAVID, Corporal.
Served from Nov. 1, 1812 to Jan.
26, 1813 in Capt. Charles Follett's
Company. 11th Regt. Ref: R. & L.
1812, AGO Page 12.

BROWN, DAVID, Sergeant.
Served in 1st Regt. Detached Militia
of Vt. in the service of the U. S.
at Champlain for 2 days commencing Nov. 18 and ending Nov. 19,
1812. Served from Jan. 12, 1813
to June 30, 1813 in Lieut. Wm. S.
Foster's Company, 11th Regt. Ref:
R. & L. 1812, AGO Page 6.

BROWN, DERICK, Sergeant, Pownal.
Served from April 27, 1814 to June
16, 1815 in Capt. Sanford's Company,
30th Inf. Ref: R. & L. 1812, AGO
Page 23.

BROWN, EBEN.
Served from Feb. 17, 1813 to May 16,
1813 in Capt. Samul Gordon's Company, 11th Regt. Ref: R. & L. 1812,
AGO Page 8.

*BROWN, EBENEZER.
. Served in 1 Regt. Vt. Militia commanded by Col. Martindale.

BROWN, ELIADA, Montpelier or Berlin.
Volunteered to go to Plattsburgh,
September, 1814, and served 8 days
in Capt. Timothy Hubbard's Company. Ref: Book 52, AGO Page 256.

‡*BROWN, ELISHA, Randolph. Volunteered to go to Plattsburgh, September, 1814, and served in Capt. Lebbeus Egerton's Company. Also served in Captain Gaes' Company. Pension Certificate of widow, Mahetibel,
No. 7814.

BROWN, ENOCH,   Strafford.
Volunteered to go to Plattsburgh,
September, 1814, and served 4 days
in Company of Militia from Town of
Strafford. Ref: Book 52, AGO Page
101.

BROWN, ENOS E., Fletcher or Swanton.
Volunteered to go to Plattsburgh,
September, 1814, and served 7 days
in Capt. A. J. Brown's Company.
Ref: Book 51, AGO Pages 141 and 147.

BROWN, EPHRAIM.
Served from March 8, 1813 to June 7,
1813 in Lieut. V. R. Goodrich's Company, 11th Regt. Ref: R. & L. 1812,
AGO, Page 10.

*BROWN, EPHRAIM.
Served from March 15, 1813 to June
14, 1813 in Capt. Charles Follett's
Company, 11th Regt.

*BROWN, ERASTUS,   St. Albans.
Enlisted May 1, 1813 for 1 year in
Capt. John Wires' Company, 30th
Regt. Also served in 1 Regt. (Mar-
tindale's) Vt. Militia. Ref: R. & L.
1812, AGO Page 40.

*BROWN, ETHAN.
Served in Capt. Wheeler's Company,
Col. Fifield's Regt. Detached Militia
in U. S. service 2 months and 25
days, 1812.

*BROWN, EZRA.
Served from April 12, 1814 to April
21, 1814 in Capt. Eseck Sprague's
Company, Sumner's Regt.

*BROWN, EZRA. 1st Lieutenant.
Served in Dixon's Regt. Vt. Militia.

*BROWN, FRANCIS.
Enlisted May 15, 1813 in Capt. James
Taylor's Company, 30th Regt. Trans-
ferred to Capt. Gideon Spencer's Com-
pany, 30th Regt. and served to May
15, 1814. Also served as Fifer in 4
Regt. (Williams') Vt. Militia. Ref:
R. & L. 1812, AGO Pages 52, 56, 59.

BROWN, HAREN,   Thetford.
Marched for Plattsburgh, September,
1814, and went as far as Bolton, Vt.,
serving 6 days in Capt. Salmon Howard's Company, 2nd Regt. Ref: Book
52, AGO Page 15.

*BROWN, IRA.
Served in Capt. Briggs' Company,
Col. Jonathan Williams' Regt. Detached Militia in U. S. service 2
months and 13 days, 1812. Volunteered to go to Plattsburgh, September, 1814, and served 10 days in Capt.
Gideon Wheelock's Company.

*BROWN, ISAAC.
Served in Capt. Walker's Company,
Col. Fifield's Regt. Detached Militia,
in U. S. service 14 days, 1812. Served
in Capt. Samul Gordon's Company,
11th Regt.; on Pay Roll for January
and February, 1813. Ref: R. & L.
1812, AGO Page 9.

BROWN, JACOB,   Wolfsborough.
Appointed Ensign 11th Inf. April 11,
1814 and 2nd Lieutenant Sept. 1, 1814.
Served from Sept. 1, 1814 to June 16,
1815 in Capt. Sanford's Company,
30th Inf. Ref: R. & L. 1812, AGO
Page 23; Governor and Council Vt.
Vol. 6, Page 478.

‡BROWN, JAMES,   Richford.
Enlisted Jan. 17, 1813 in Capt.
Charles Follett's Company, 11th Regt.;
on Pay Roll to May 31, 1813. Served
in Capt. Benjamin Bradford's Com-
pany as musician; on Muster Roll
from May 31, 1813 to Aug. 31, 1813.
Enlisted Sept. 25, 1813 and served 1
month and 23 days, 1813, in Capt.
Follett's Company, Col. Dixon's Regt.
Pension Certificate of widow, Harriet,
No. 15939. Ref: R. & L. 1812, AGO
Page 26; Book 52, AGO Page 268;
Book 53, AGO Page 106.

‡BROWN, JAMES.
Served in Capt. John Barney's Company. Pension Certificate No. 15449.

‡BROWN, JAMES.
Served in Capt. Grout's Company. Pension Certificate No. 21749.

*BROWN, JAMES.
Served in Capt. Langworthy's Com-
pany. Col. Dixon's Regt. Detached
Militia in U. S. service 19 days,
1813. Enlisted Oct. 30, 1813 in Capt.
Asahel Langworthy's Company, Col.
Isaac Clark's Regt.

BROWN, JAMES, Corporal.
Enlisted May 1, 1813 for 1 year in
Capt. Simeon Wright's Company. Ref:
R. & L. 1812, AGO Page 51.

BROWN, JAMES,   Franklin County.
Volunteered to go to Plattsburgh,
Sept. 11, 1814, and served in 15th or
22nd Regt. Ref: Hemenway's Vt. Gazetteer, Vol. 2, Page 392.

BROWN, JAMES DUNBAR.
Appointed Ensign 25 Inf. Jan. 22,
1813; 3 Lieutenant March 1, 1813; 2nd
Lieutenant Aug. 15, 1813; 1st Lieutenant May 2, 1814; honorably discharged June 15, 1815; reinstated Dec. 2,
1815; 2nd Lieutenant Corps Artillery
with brevet of 1st Lieutenant from
May 2, 1814; died May 13, 1817. Ref:
Heitman's Historical Register and
Dictionary USA.

‡*BROWN, JAMES 1st Sergeant.
Served from June 11, 1813 to June 14,
1813 in Capt. Moses Jewett's Company of Militia, 1st Regt. 2nd Brig.
3rd Div. Pension Certificate of widow,
Harriet, No. 20778.

*BROWN, JARED R.
Served in Capt. Wright's Company,
Col. Martindale's Regt. Detached Militia in U. S service 1 month and 16
days, 1812.

*BROWN, JENKS.
Served in Capt. Ormsbee's Company,
Col. Martindale's Regt. Detached
Militia in U. S. service 2 months and
14 days, 1812.

*BROWN, JERRY.
Served in Capt. Strait's Company,
Col. Martindale's Regt. Detached Militia in U. S. service 2 months and 13
days, 1812.

*BROWN, JOEL, Sergeant.
Enlisted Sept. 25, 1813 and served 1
month and 23 days in Capt. Birge's
Company, Col. Dixon's Regt.

BROWN, JOHN,   Georgia.
Volunteered to go to Plattsburgh,
September, 1814, and served 8 days
in Capt. Jesse Post's Company, Dixon's Regt. Ref: Book 51, AGO Page
102.

BROWN, JOHN,   St. Albans.
Enlisted April 23, 1813 in Capt. John
Wires' Company, 30th Regt. for 1
year. Ref: R. & L. 1812, AGO
Page 40.

BROWN, JOHN, M. D.,   Salisbury.
In Regular Army in 1812 according
to History of Salisbury.

BROWN, JOHN.
Enlisted Jan. 1, 1813 in Lieut. V. R.
Goodrich's Company, 11th Regt.; on
Pay Roll to May 31, 1813. Ref: R.
& L. 1812, AGO Page 10.

BROWN, JOHN.
Served in Capt. Weeks' Company,
11th Regt.; on Pay Roll for January
and February, 1813. Ref: R. & L.
1812, AGO Page 5.

BROWN, JOHN,   Fairfax.
Served in Capt. Joseph Beeman's
Company in 1813 and 1814. Ref:
Hemenway's Vt. Gazetteer, Vol. 2,
Page 402.

*BROWN, JOHN. Musician,   Putney?
Served in Capt. Adams' Company,
Jonathan Williams' Regt. Detached
Militia in U. S. service 2 months
and 7 days, 1812.

BROWN, JOHN,   Corinth.
Volunteered to go to Plattsburgh,
September, 1814, and served 3 days
in Capt. Abel Jackman's Company.
Ref: Book 52, AGO Pages 44, 45, 49.

BROWN, JOHN,   Montpelier.
Volunteered to go to Plattsburgh,
September, 1814, and served 8 days
in Capt. Timothy Hubbard's Company. Ref: Book 52, AGO Page 256.

‡*BROWN, JOHN.
Served in Capt. Hotchkiss' Company,
1 Regt. (Judson's). Pension Certificate No. 25314. Pension Certificate of widow, Lucinda, No. 28004.

*BROWN, JOHN.
Served in Capt. Phelps' Company,
Col. Wm. Williams' Regt. Detached
Militia in U. S. service 5 months,
1812.

*BROWN, JOHN,   Calais.
Volunteered to go to Plattsburgh,
September, 1814, and served 10 days
in Capt. Gideon Wheelock's Company.

*BROWN, JOHN JR., Lieutenant, Salis-
bury. Served from Oct. 5, 1813 to
Oct. 17, 1813 in Capt. Stephen
Brown's Company, 3rd Regt.

BROWN, JOHN M., Franklin County.
Volunteered to go to Plattsburgh,
Sept. 11, 1814 and served in 15th
or 22nd Regt. Ref: Hemenway's
Vt. Gazetteer, Vol. 2, Page 391.

BROWN, JOHN O.
Served from March 2, 1813 to May
31, 1813 in Capt. Edgerton's Company,
11th Regt. Ref: R. & L. 1812, AGO
Page 3.

*BROWN, JOHNSON.
Served from Sept. 25-30, 1813 in
Capt. Elijah Birge's Company, Dixon's
Regt.

‡BROWN, JONAS.
Served in Capt. Burknap's Company.
Pension Certificate No. 2778.

BROWN, JONATHAN.
Served from April 12, 1814 to April
21, 1814 in Capt. Eseck Sprague's
Company, Sumner's Regt. Ref:
Book 52, AGO Page 263.

BROWN, JOSEPH,   St. Albans.
Enlisted April 26, 1813 for 1 year
in Capt. John Wires' Company, 30th
Regt.; sick at home, furloughed by
Dr. Day. Ref: R. & L. 1812, AGO
Page 40.

BROWN, JOSEPH, Teamster, Jericho.
Was drafted into service with his
team at Plattsburgh, March 12, 1813.
Pension was granted his widow, Polly
Brown. Ref: History of Jericho,
Page 143.

*BROWN, JOSHUA N.
Served from April 12, 1814 to April
21, 1814 in Capt. Eseck Sprague's
Company, Sumner's Regt. Also served in 4 Regt. (Williams') Vt. Militia.

BROWN, JUDE M., Waitsfield.
Volunteered to go to Plattsburgh,
September, 1814, and served 4 days
in Capt. Mathias S. Jones' Company.
Ref: Book 52, AGO Page 170.

BROWN, LABON, Enosburgh.
Served in Capt. Martin D. Folett's
Company. Ref: Hemenway's Vt. Ga-
zetteer, Vol. 2, Page 155.

*BROWN, LANCASTER.
Served with Hospital Attendants, Vt.

*BROWN, LEMUEL.
Served in 4 Regt. Vt. Militia commanded by Col. Peck.

BROWN, LEVI, Vershire.
Volunteered to go to Plattsburgh,
September, 1814, and served in Capt.
Ira Corse's Company's. Ref: Book
52, AGO Page 103.

*BROWN, LIMAN.
Sumner's Regt. Vt. Militia.

*BROWN, MICAH, Captain, Brandon.
Served in 1st Regt. (Martindale's) Detached Militia of Vt. in U. S. service
at Champlain for 2 days commencing
the 18th of November and ending
Nov. 19, 1812. Volunteered to go to
Plattsburgh, September, 1814, and
served 8 days in command of company raised at Brandon.

*BROWN, MIRAM.
Served in Capt. Bingham's Company,
Col. Jonathan Williams' Regt. Detached Militia, in U. S. service 2
months and 9 days 1812.

*BROWN, MOSES.
Served in Captain Howard's Company,
Vt. Militia.

BROWN, MOSES JR., Bakersfield.
Volunteered and was at the battle
of Plattsburgh Sept. 11, 1814 in Capt.
M. Stearns' Company. Ref: Hemenway's Vt. Gazetteer, Vol. 2, Page
394.

BROWN, N., Captain, Rochester.
Volunteered to go to Plattsburgh,
September, 1814. No organization
given. Ref: Book 51, AGO Page 249.

BROWN, NATHAN. Franklin County.
Volunteered to go to Plattsburgh
Sept. 11, 1814 and served in 15th or
22nd Regt. Ref: Hemenway's Vt.
Gazetteer, Vol. 2, Page 391.

*BROWN, NATHANIAL, Ensign.
Served in 2 Regt. Vt. Militia commanded by Col. Fifield.

‡BROWN, NATHANIEL.
Served from Feb. 8, 1813 to May 7,
1813 in Capt. Charles Follett's Company, 11th Regt. Pension Certificate
of widow, Jemima, No. 4293.

*BROWN, NELSON, Corporal, Richford.
Enlisted Sept. 25, 1813 and served 1
month and 23 days in Capt. Martin
D. Follett's Company, Col. Dixon's
Regt.

BROWN, NOAH.
Enlisted Sept. 12, 1813 in Capt. James
Taylor's Company, 30th Regt. Transferred to Capt. Gideon Spencer's Company, 30th Regt. and served to Feb.
8, 1814. Ref: R. & L. 1812, AGO
Pages 52, 57, 59.

BROWN, OLIVER, Pittsford.
Volunteered to go to Plattsburgh,
September, 1814, and served 8 days
in Capt. Caleb Hendee's Company.
Ref: Book 52, AGO Page 124.

BROWN, PETER, Strafford.
Volunteered to go to Plattsburgh,
September, 1814, and served in Capt.
Jedediah H. Harris' Company. Serv-
ed from Sept. 28, 1814 to June 19,
1815 as a corporal in Capt. Taylor's
Company, 30th Regt. Ref: Book 52,
Page 43; R. & L. 1812, AGO Page 23.

*BROWN, PHINEAS.
Enlisted Sept. 30, 1813 in Capt. Isaac
Finch's Company, Col. Clark's Regt.
of Riflemen.

*BROWN, PRESTON, Johnson.
Enlisted Sept. 25, 1813 and served 1
month and 23 days in Capt. Thomas
Waterman's Company, Dixon's Regt.
Volunteered to go to Plattsburgh,
September, 1814, in the same com-
pany.

*BROWN, PURCHASE JR., Highgate.
Served in Capt. Saxe's Company, Col.
Wm. Williams' Regt. Detached Militia in U. S. service 3 months and
27 days, 1812.

BROWN, RETURN B.
Appointed Captain 4 Inf. March 18,
1809; Major 31 Inf. March 9, 1814;
honorably discharged June 15, 1815.
Ref: Heitman's Historical Register &
Dictionary USA.

*BROWN, REUBEN, Fairfield.
Served in Capt. Kendall's Company,
Col. Wm. Williams' Regt. Detached
Militia in U. S. service 4 months and
23 days, 1812. Served 6 months in
Capt. George W. Kindall's Company,
4 Regt. commanded by Col. Wm. Wil-
liams.

BROWN, REUBEN, Fairfax.
Enlisted Aug. 8, 1812 in Company of
Capt. Joseph Beeman Jr., 11th Regt.
U. S. Inf. under Col. Ira Clark.
Ref: Hemenway's Vt. Gazetteer, Vol.
2. Page 402.

*BROWN, RICHARD.
Served in Capt. Brown's Company,
Col. Martindale's Regt. Detached Militia in U. S. service 2 months and 14
days, 1812.

*BROWN, ROBERT.
Served in Capt. Wheeler's Company,
2 Regt. (Fifield's) Vt. Militia.

BROWN, ROSWELL H.,   Whiting.
Volunteered to go to Plattsburgh,
September, 1814, and served 9 days
in Capt. Salmon Foster's Company.
Ref: Book 51, AGO Pages 7 and 8.

BROWN, RUFUS.
Served as private in War of 1812.
Was captured by troops Sept. 17, 1814
at Fort Erie. Discharged Nov. 8th.
Ref: Records of Naval Records and
Library, Navy Dept.

BROWN, SALMON.
Served from March 15, 1813 to June
14, 1813 in Capt. Charles Follett's
Company, 11th Regt. Ref: R. & L.
1812, AGO Page 13.

BROWN, SAMUEL,   Strafford.
Volunteered to go to Plattsburgh,
September, 1814, and served 4 days
in Company of Militia from Strafford. Ref: Book 52, AGO Page 101.

‡*BROWN, SAMUEL R.
Served from April 12, 1814 to May 20,
1814 in Capt. George Fisher's Company, Sumner's Regt. Pension Certificate of widow, Hannah L., No.
39446.

‡BROWN, SAMUEL.
Served in Capt. Nathaniel Brown's
Company. Pension Certificate No.
24029. Pension Certificate of widow,
Louisa, No. 34493.

*BROWN, SIMEON.
Served from June 11 to June 14, 1813
in Lieut. Bates' Company, 1st Regt.

*BROWN, SIMON.
Appointed 2nd Lieutenant 31 Inf.
April 30, 1813; 1st Lieutenant Jan.
11, 1814; honorably discharged June
15, 1815. Served as Lieutenant in 2
Regt. Vt. Militia commanded by Col.
Fifield. Ref: Heitman's Historical
Register & Dictionary USA.

BROWN, SIMON.
Served from April 12 to April 21,
1814 in Lieut. James S. Morton's
Company, Col. W. B. Sumner's Regt.
Served from May 1 to June 30, 1814
as corporal in Corps of Light Dra-
goons. Ref: Book 52, AGO Page 286;
R. & L. 1812, AGO Page 20.

*BROWN, STEPHEN, Captain.
Served from Oct. 5, 1813 to Oct. 17,
1813 in Capt. Stephen Brown's Company, 3rd Regt.

BROWN, STEPHEN S.,   Swanton.
Volunteered to go to Plattsburgh,
September, 1814, and served 6 days
under Capt. Amasa I. Brown. Ref:
Book 51, AGO Pages 114, 142, 123,
159.

‡*BROWN, STILLMAN,   Whiting.
Enlisted April 12, 1814 in Capt. Shu-
bael Wales' Company, Col. W. B.
Sumner's Regt.; transferred to Capt.
Salmon Foster's Company, Sumner's
Regt. April 13, 1814 and served to

April 21, 1814; volunteered to go to
Plattsburgh, September, 1814, and
served 9 days in Capt. Foster's Company. Pension Certificate of widow,
Betsey, No. 30819.

*BROWN, STOREY.
Served in Capt. Cross's Company,
Col. Martindale's Regt. Detached Militia in U. S. service 2 months and 14
days, 1812.

BROWN, STUART,   Washington.
Volunteered to go to Plattsburgh,
September, 1814, and served in Capt.
Amos Stiles' Company. Ref: Book 52,
AGO Page 36.

‡BROWN, THOMAS,   Washington.
Was in battle of Plattsburgh, Sept.
11, 1814, serving in Capt. David Robinson's company, raised in Williamstown and vicinity. Pension Certificate No. 28375.

BROWN, THOMAS, Corporal.
Enlisted May 2, 1814 for period of
war in company of late Capt. J.
Brooks commanded by Lt. John I.
Cromwell, Corps of U. S. Artillery;
on Muster Roll from April 30, 1814
to June 30, 1814; promoted from
private June 1, 1814. Ref: R. & L.
1812, AGO Page 18.

BROWN, THOMAS,   Morristown.
Volunteered to go to Plattsburgh,
September, 1814, and served 8 days
in Capt. Denison Cook's Company.
Ref: Book 51, AGO Pages 202 and 206.

‡BROWN, THOMAS G.
Served in Captain Andrew's Company. Pension Certificate No. 33271.

*BROWN, WAREHAM JR.
Served from April 19, 1814 to April
21, 1814 in Capt. Othniel Jewett's
Company, Sumner's Regt.

*BROWN, WARHAM.
Served in Capt. Robbins' Company,
Col. Wm. Williams' Regt. Detached
Militia in U. S. service 4 months and
29 days, 1812.

BROWN, WARREN.
Served from March 13, 1813 to June
12, 1813 in Capt. Charles Follett's
Company, 11th Regt. Ref: R. & L.
1812, AGO Page 13.

BROWN, WILDER,   Putney.
Enlisted Jan. 13, 1813 in Lieut. V. R.
Goodrich's Company, 11th Regt.; on
Pay Roll to May 31, 1813. Ref: R. &
L. 1812, AGO Page 10.

‡*BROWN, WILLIAM, Williston or Jeri-
cho. Served from June 11, 1813 to
June 14, 1813 in Lt. Bates' Company,
1st Regt.; volunteered to go to
Plattsburgh, September 1814 in same
company. Also served in 4 Regt.
(Peck's) Vt. Militia. Capt. Myron
Reed's Company and Lieut. Allen's
Company. Pension Certificate No.
25499. Pension Certificate of widow,
Annie B., No. 33191.

*BROWN, ZELOTES.
Served in 1 Regt. Vt. Militia commanded by Col. Martindale.

*BROWNELL, DAVID.
Served in Capt. Briggs' Company,
Col. Jonathan Williams' Regt. Detached Militia in U. S. service 2
months and 13 days, 1812.

*BROWNELL, IRA.
Served in 3 Regt. Vt. Militia commanded by Col. Tyler.

*BROWNELL, ISAAC.
Served in 1 Regt. Vt. Militia commanded by Col. Martindale.

*BROWNELL, JEREMIAH. Ensign.
Served in Lieut. Bates' Company. 1st
Regt. from June 11, 1813 to June 14,
1813. Also served in 4 Regt. (Williams') Vt. Militia.

*BROWNELL, JOSEPH JR.
Served in Capt. Briggs' Company,
Col. Jonathan Williams' Regt. Detached Militia in U. S. service 2
months and 13 days, 1812.

*BROWNELL, SAMUEL A.
Served in 3 Regt. Vt. Militia commanded by Col. Tyler.

‡BROWNELL, THOMAS,   Colchester.
Volunteered to go to Plattsburgh.
September, 1814, and served 8 days;
no organization given.   Served in
Capt. Bates' Company. Pension Cer-
tificate of widow, Mary H., No. 21363.

BROWNING, THOMAS,   Barre.
Volunteered to go to Plattsburgh,
September, 1814, and served in Capt.
Warren Ellis' Company. Ref: Hemen-
way's Vt. Gazetteer, Vol. 4, Page 41.

BROWNSON, ASA.   Richmond.
Volunteered to go to Plattsburgh,
September, 1814, and served 9 days
in Capt. Roswell Hunt's Company, 3
Regt. (Tyler's). Ref: Book 51, AGO
Page 82.

BROWNSON, ELI,   Richmond.
Volunteered to go to Plattsburgh,
September, 1814, and served 9 days
in Capt. Roswell Hunt's Company, 3
Regt. (Tyler's). Ref: Book 51, AGO
Pages 82, 86, 277.

*BROWNSON. GIDEON.
Appointed 2nd Lieutenant 30 Inf.
April 30, 1813; 1st Lieutenant Aug.
15, 1813; honorably discharged June
15, 1815. Also served as Lieutenant
in 1 Regt. (Martindale's). Ref: Heitman's Historical Register & Dictionary USA.

‡*BROWNSON, GILBERT,   Richmond.
Served 3 months beginning September,
1812, in 6th Company, 3rd Regt. Inf.
2nd Brig. commanded by Brig. Gen.
Newell. Also served in Capt. Oliver
Lowery's Company, 4 Regt. (Williams'). Pension Certificate No. 7399.

*BROWNSON, HARRY,   Richmond.
Volunteered to go to Plattsburgh,
September, 1814, and served 9 days
in Capt. Roswell Hunt's Company,
3rd Regt.

BROWNSON. HENRY.
Served from Oct. 12, 1813 to Oct. 16,
1813 in Capt. Roswell Hunt's Company, 3rd Regt. Ref: R. & L. 1812,
AGO Page 41.

‡*BROWNSON, JOEL,   Richmond.
Served in Capt. Lowry's Company,
Col. Wm. Williams' Regt. Detached
Militia, U. S. service 4 months and
26 days, 1812. Pension Certificate
No. 1964.

*BROWNSON, JOEL JR., Corporal Rich-
mond. Served from Oct. 4, 1813 to
Oct. 16, 1813 in Capt. Roswell Hunt's
Company of Militia, 3 Regt. (Tyler's).

BROWNSON, JOHN.
Appointed Ensign 1 Inf. June 28.
1804; 2nd Lieutenant Jan. 31, 1807;
1st Lieutenant Dec. 8, 1808; Captain
Jan. 31, 1814; honorably discharged
June 15, 1815. Ref: Heitman's Historical Register and Dictionary USA.

*BROWNSON. SAMUEL.
Served in 4 Regt. Vt. Militia commanded by Col. Williams.

*BROWNSON, THERON,   Randolph.
Volunteered to go to Plattsburgh,
September, 1814, and served in Capt.
Lebbeus Egerton's Company.

‡BRUCE. ABNER.
Served in Capt. L. Edgerton's Com-
pany, 2nd Regt. Pension Certificate
No. 15692.

BRUCE. ALEXANDER.
Enlisted May 17, 1813 for 1 year in
Capt. Daniel Farrington's Company
(also commanded by Capt. Simeon
Wright), 30th Regt. On Muster Roll
March 1, 1814 to April 30, 1814. Ref:
R. & L. 1812, AGO Pages 50 and 51.

BRUCE, ANTHONY.
Served from Feb. 16th to June 30,
1814 in Regt. of Light Dragoons.
Ref: R. & L. 1812, AGO Page 21.

BRUCE, CHRISTOPHER, Corporal.
Served in 1st Regt. of Detached Militia of Vermont in the U. S. service
at Champlain commencing Nov. 18
and ending Nov. 19, 1812.

*BRUCE. HEMAN.
Served in Corning's Detachment Vt.
Militia.

BRUCE, JAMES.
Volunteered to go to Plattsburgh,
September, 1814, and served 7 days
in Capt. Frederick Griswold's Com-
pany, raised in Brookfield, Vt. Ref:
Book 52, AGO Page 52.

‡BRUCE, JONAS.
Served in Capt. S. Edgerton's Com-
pany. Pension Certificate of widow,
Abigail F., No. 26854.

*BRUCE. JONATHAN, Corporal.
Served in 1 Regt. Vt. Militia commanded by Col. Martindale.

BRUCE, SAMUEL,   Brookfield.
Volunteered to go to Plattsburgh,
September, 1814, and served in Capt.
Frederick Griswold's Company, 7
days. Ref: Book 52, AGO Pages 52
and 54.

*BRUNSON, THOMAS.
Served in Corning's Detachment, Vt.
Militia.

*BRUSH, EBENEZER.
Served from Sept. 25, 1813 to Oct.
1st in Capt. Charles Bennett's Company, Dixon's Regt.

*BRUSH. EPENETUS. Fairfax.
Served from April 12, 1814 to April
21, 1814 and volunteered to go to
Plattsburgh, September, 1814, in Company of Lieut. James S. Morton, Col.
W. B. Sumner's Regt.

BRUSH, ISIAH.
Enlisted May 6, 1813 for 1 year in
Capt. James Taylor's Company, 30th
Regt.; on Muster Roll Nov. 30, 1813
to Dec. 31, 1813. Ref: R. & L. 1812,
AGO Page 52.

BRUSH, JOHN.
Served from March 1st to June 30,
1814 in Corps of Artillery. commanded
by Capt. Alexander S. Brooks. Ref:
R. & L. 1812, AGO Page 31.

BRUSH. JONATHAN, Fairfax.
Served from April 23, 1813 to May
15. 1814 in Capt. Gideon Spencer's
Company and Capt. James Taylor's
Company. 30th Regt. Served in Capt.
Joseph Beeman's Company in 1813
and 1814. Ref: R. & L. 1812, AGO
Pages 56 and 58; Hemenway's Vt.
Gazetteer, Vol. 2, Page 402.

‡*BRUSH, JOSHUA, Lieutenant, Fairfax.
Appointed Sept. 25, 1813. Capt. Asa
Wilkins Company, Dixon's Regt. Pension Certificate No. 21122. Pension
Certificate of widow, Sarah, No. 6600.

*BRUSH, JOSIAH, Fairfax or St. Albans.
Served in Capt. Taylor's Company,
Col. Wm. Williams' Regt. Detached
Militia in U. S. service 4 months and
24 days, 1812. Served from May 6,
1813 to May 24, 1813 in Capt. Gideon
Spencer's Company, 30th Regt.

BRUSH, ORLIN.
Served in Capt. Chadwick's Company.
Ref: R. & L. 1812, AGO Page 32.

BRUSH. ORSON, Swanton.
Served in Capt. V. R. Goodrich's
Company, 11th Regt.; on Pay Roll
from July 15 to Dec. 8, 1813; in action at the battle of Lundy's Lane.
Ref: Hemenway's Vt. Gazetteer, Vol.
2. Page 444.

*BRUSH, SMITH, Fairfax.
Enlisted Sept. 25, 1813 in Capt. Asa
Wilkins' Company, Col. Dixon's Regt.;
transferred to Capt. Asahel Langworthy's Company, Col. Isaac Clark's
Rifle Corps; unfit for duty.

BRUSTER. LUNAN.
Served in Capt. Chadwick's Company.
Ref: R. & L. 1812, AGO Page 32.

BRUTON, WILLIAM.
Born in Herrifordshire, England. Enlisted Jan. 1, 1814 at Plattsburgh for
5 years in Capt. James Taylor's Company. 30th Regt.; on Muster Roll Feb.
28, 1814. On board Navy. Ref: R.
& L. 1812, AGO Pages 53 and 55.

BRYAN. JEREMIAH.
Served from June 11, 1813 to June 14,
1813 in Lieut. Bates' Company of
Militia. Ref: R. & L. 1812, AGO
Page 33.

*BRYANT, CHANDLER.
Served in Capt. Ormsbee's Company.
Col. Martindale's Regt. Detached
Militia in U. S. service 1 month and
17 days, 1812.

BRYANT, DANIEL C.
Appointed 1st Lieutenant 31 Inf.
April 30, 1813; Captain Dec. 1, 1814;
honorably discharged June 15, 1815.
Ref: Heitman's Historical Register &
Dictionary USA.

*BRYANT, DUDLEY.
Served in Capt. Taylor's Company,
Col. Fifield's Regt. Detached Militia
in U. S. service 6 months, 1812. Ref:
Book 53, AGO Page 22.

BRYANT, HUGH, Franklin County.
Volunteered to go to Plattsburgh
Sept. 11, 1814 and served in 15th or
22nd Regt. Ref: Hemenway's Vt.
Gazetteer, Vol. 2, Page 392.

*BRYANT, JAMES.
Served in Capt. Dodge's Company,
Col. Fifield's Regt. Detached Militia
in U. S. service 2 months and 21
days, 1812.

BRYANT, JOHN.
Served in Capt. Benj. Bradford's
Company; joined by transfer July 22,.
1813; on Muster Roll from May 31,
1813 to Aug. 31, 1813. Ref: R. & L.
1812, AGO Page 26.

*BRYANT, JONATHAN.
Served in Capt. Phelps' Company,
Col. Jonathan Williams' Regt. Detached Militia in U. S. service 2
months and 21 days, 1812.

BRYANT, JOSEPH H.
Served in Capt. Samuel H. Holly's
Company, 11th Regt.; on Pay Roll for
January and February, 1813. Ref: R.
& L. 1812, AGO Page 25.

*BRYANT, JOSEPH Sergeant.
Served in Detached Militia, Capt.
Rogers' Company, Col. Fifield's Regt.,
in U. S. service 5 months and 27
days, 1812.

BRYANT, ORSON, Fairfax.
Enlisted Aug. 8, 1812 in company of
Capt. Joseph Beeman Jr. 11th Regt.
U. S. Inf. under Col. Ira Clark.
Ref: Hemenway's Vt. Gazetteer, Vol.
2, Page 402.

*BRYANT, SAMUEL.
Served in Capt. Phelps' Company,
Col. Jonathan Williams' Regt. Detached Militia in U. S. service 2
months and 21 days, 1812. Also served in Corning's Detachment and 3
Regt. (Williams') Vt. Militia. Ref:
Book 53, AGO Page 34.

‡BRYANT. SAMUEL JR.
Served in Capt. Rufus Stewart's Company. Pension Certificate No. 9545.

*BRYDIE, DAVID JR.
Served from April 12, 1814 to April
21, 1814 in Capt. Eseck Sprague's
Company, Sumner's Regt.

*BUCHANAN, JAMES.
Served in 2 Regt. Vt. Militia commanded by Col. Fifield.

*BUCHANAN, JOSEPH.
Served in 2 Regt. Vt. Militia commanded by Col. Fifield.

*BUCK, AMOS.
Served from April 12, 1814 to April 21, 1814 in Capt. Eseck Sprague's Company, Sumner's Regt.

*BUCK, ANSON,   Fairfield.
Served in Capt. Dorrance's Company, Col. Wm. Williams' Regt. Detached Militia in service 4 months and 24 days, 1812. Volunteered to go to Plattsburgh, September, 1814, and served 8 days in Capt. Benjamin Wooster's Company. Ref: Book 51, AGO Pages 160 and 179.

*BUCK, ASAHEL.
Served in Capt. Wright's Company, Col. Fifield's Regt. Detached Militia in U. S. service 6 months, 1812.

BUCK, CYRUS A.,   St. Albans.
Enlisted April 27, 1813 for 1 year in Capt. John Wires' Company, 30th Regt. Ref: R. & L. 1812, AGO Page 40.

BUCK, DANIEL AZRO ASHLEY.
Appointed Cadet, Military Academy, July 9, 1806 (1); 2nd Lieutenant Engineers Jan. 25, 1808; resigned Aug. 31, 1811; 2nd Lieutenant 3rd Artillery Oct. 17, 1812; Captain 31 Inf. April 30, 1813; hon. disch. June 15, 1815; died Dec. 24, 1841. Ref: Governor and Council Vt. Vol. 6, Page 476.

BUCK, FELLOWS,   Williamstown.
Was in battle of Plattsburgh, Sept. 11, 1814, serving in Capt. David Robinson's Company 8 days. Ref: Book 52, AGO Page 2.

‡BUCK, IRA,   Bethel.
Volunteered to go to Plattsburgh, September, 1814, and served 8 days in Capt. Nehemiah Noble's Company, 4 Regt. Pension Certificate of widow, Polly, No. 16213.

*BUCK, ISAAC D.,   Sergeant.
Served from June 11, 1813 to June 14, 1813 in Capt. John M. Eldridge's Company, 1st Regt. 2nd Brig. 3rd Div.

BUCK, JAMES, Waggoner,   Pittsford.
Volunteered to go to Plattsburgh, September, 1814, and served 8 days in Capt. Caleb Hendee's Company: Ref: Book 52, AGO Page 125.

*BUCK, LEMUEL.
Served in Capt. Dorrance's Company, Col. Wm. Williams' Regt. Detached Militia in U. S. service 4 months and 24 days, 1812.

BUCK, LONDUS L.
Appointed Cadet, Military Academy, June 15, 1808 (3); 1st Lieutenant 6 Inf. Jan. 3, 1812; Captain Apr. 19, 1814; honorably discharged June 15, 1815; died July 13, 1817. Ref: Heitman's Historical Register & Dictionary USA.

‡BUCK, PHILIP.
Served in Capt. Colton's Company. Pension Certificate No. 9802.

*BUCK, SUPPLY.
Served in Capt. Cross' Company. Col. Martindale's Regt. Detached Militia in U. S. service 2 months and 14 days, 1812.

*BUCK, WILLIAM.
Served from April 12, 1814 to May 20, 1814 in company of Capt. James Gray Jr., Sumner's Regt.

BUCKER, LYMAN.
Served from June 11, 1813 to June 14, 1813 in Capt. John M. Eldridge's Company, 1st Regt. 2nd Brig., 3rd Div. Vt. Militia. Ref: R. & L. 1812, AGO Page 35.

BUCKHAM, JONATHAN, Franklin County. Volunteered to go to Plattsburgh Sept. 11, 1814 and served in 15th or 22nd Regt. Ref: Hemenway's Vt. Gazetteer, Vol. 2, Page 392.

BUCKLAND, HIRAM,   Brandon.
Volunteered to go to Plattsburgh, September, 1814, and served 8 days in Capt. Micah Brown's Company. Ref: Book 52, AGO Page 132.

*BUCKLAND, JOSEPH M.
Served in Capt. Bingham's Company, Col. Jonathan Williams' Regt. Detached Militia in U. S. service 2 months and 9 days, 1812.

BUCKLEY, EZRA,   Franklin County.
Volunteered to go to Plattsburgh Sept. 11, 1814, and served in 15th or 22nd Regt. Ref: Hemenway's Vt. Gazetteer, Vol. 2, Page 391.

BUCKLEY, ROGER,   Berlin.
Volunteered to go to Plattsburgh, September, 1814, and served 7 days in Capt. Cyrus Johnson's Company. Ref: Book 52, AGO Page 255.

‡BUCKLIN, RUFUS JR.,   Wallingford.
Appointed 2nd Lieutenant 11th Inf. March 12, 1812; 1st Lieutenant Aug. 15, 1813; out Sept. 1, 1814. Served in Capt. Samul Gordon's Company, 11th Regt.; on Pay Roll for January and February, 1813. Pension Certificate of widow, Harriet, No. 1957. Ref: Governor and Council Vt. Vol. 6, Page 473; R. & L. 1812, AGO Page 9.

‡BUCKMAN, CALVIN,   Bethel.
Volunteered to go to Plattsburgh, September, 1814, and served 9 days in Capt. Nehemiah Noble's Company. Pension Certificate No. 30555.

BUDD, ERTIA E., Sergeant. Franklin County. Volunteered to go to Plattsburgh Sept. 11, 1814 and served in 15th or 22nd Regt. Ref: Hemenway's Vt. Gazetteer, Vol. 2, Page 391.

BUEL, BENJAMIN.
Enlisted April 29, 1814 for period of the war in Capt. Miller's Company, 30th Regt. Ref: R. & L. 1812, AGO Page 1.

*BUEL, DRAYNE, Corporal.
Served in Tyler's Regt. Vt. Militia.

‡*BUEL, JOHN.　　　Corporal.
Served in Capt. Bingham's Company,
Col. Jonathan Williams' Regt. De-
tached Militia in U. S. service 2
months and 9 days, 1812. Pension
Certificate of widow, Anna, No. 13612.

*BUELL, JARED.
Served in Capt. Wood's Company,
Col. Dixon's Regt. Detached Militia
in U. S. service 18 days, 1813. Serv-
ed in Capt. Langworthy's Company,
Col. Dixon's Regt. Detached Militia
in U. S. service 1 month and 8 days,
1813. Enlisted Oct. 29, 1813 in Capt.
Asahel Langworthy's Company, Col.
Isaac Clark's Regt.

*BUELL. ORANGE.　　　Trumpeter.
Served from Oct. 11, 1813 to Oct. 17,
1813 in Capt. John Munson's Company, 3 Regt. (Tyler's).

‡*BUELL. SAMUEL,　　　Brandon?
Served in Capt. Saxe's Company, Col.
Wm. Williams' Regt. Detached Mili-
tia in U. S. service 3 months and 24
days, 1812. Volunteered to go to
Plattsburgh, September, 1814, and
served 8 days in Capt. Micah Brown's
Company. Pension Certificate No.
29387. Pension Certificate of widow,
Martha, No. 11027.

BUELL, WILLIAM,　　　Corporal.
Enlisted Aug. 3, 1813 at New York
in U. S. Marine Corps. Ref: Book
52, AGO Page 294.

*BUFFUM, JONATHAN.
Served from June 11, 1813 to June 14,
1813 in Capt. Hezekiah Barns' Company, 1st Regt. 2nd Brig., 3rd Div.

BUFUM. DANIEL.
Served from June 11, 1813 to June
14, 1813 in Capt. Ithiel Stone's Company, 1st Regt. 2nd Brig., 3rd Div.
Ref: R. & L. 1812, AGO Page 44.

BUGBEE, ALVIN,　　　Trumpeter.
Served from May 1st to June 30, 1814
in Capt. Haig's Corps of Light Dragoons. Ref: R. & L. 1812, AGO
Page 20.

*BUGBEE, LUTHER.　　　Danville.
Appointed 3rd Lieutenant April 30,
1813; Regimental Adjutant 1813—
March. 1814; resigned March 29,
1814. Served as Ensign in Capt.
Joseph Morrill's Company, Col. Fifield's Regt. Ref: Heitman's Historical Register & Dictionary USA.

‡*BUGBEE, OLIVER.
Served in Capt. Burnap's Company,
Col. Jonathan Williams' Regt. Detached Militia in U. S. service 2
months and 13 days, 1812. Served
from Nov. 1, 1812 to Feb. 28, 1813
in Capt. Samul Gordon's Company,
11th Regt. Pension Certificate No.
6159. Ref: R. & L. 1812, AGO Page 9.

*BUGBEE. PRESTON.
Served in Capt. Rogers Company,
Col. Fifield's Regt. Detached Militia
in U. S. service 5 months and 27
days, 1812.

*BUHONNAN, JOSEPH,　　Washington.
Volunteered and was in the battle of
Plattsburgh, September, 1814, serving
in Capt. David Robinson's Company.
Also served in 2 Regt.- (Fifield's) Vt.
Militia according to War Dept. Rec-
ords. Ref: Book 52, AGO Page 2.

‡*BUKER, SILAS.
Enlisted Sept. 25, 1813 and served 1
month and 23 days in Capt. Charles
Bennett's Company, Dixon's' Regt.
Pension Certificate No. 13555.

‡BULIS, TOBIAS.
Served in Capt. Joseph Hazen's Com-
pany. Pension Certificate of widow,
Charlotte, No. 12208.

*BULL. JEREMIAH.
Served from Oct. 4, 1813 to Oct. 13,
1813 in Capt. John Palmer's Company, 1st Regt. 2nd Brig., 3rd Div.

*BULL, JOSHUA.
Served in 1st Regt. Vt. Militia commanded by Col. Judson.

BULLARD, BENJAMIN, Physician, Addison. Volunteered to go to Plattsburgh, September, 1814, and served
9 days in Capt. George Fisher's Company. Ref: Book 51, AGO Page 5.

‡*BULLARD, HEZEKIAH.
Served in Capt. Cross' Company, Col.
Martindale's Regt. Detached Militia
in U. S. service 2 months and 14
days, 1812. Pension Certificate No.
12921.

*BULLARD, JESSE.
Served in 1 Regt. Vt. Militia commanded by Col. Judson.

*BULLARD, JOHN,　　Drum Major.
Served as private in 1 Regt. (Judson's) Vt. Militia and as drum major
in 1 Regt. (Martindale's) Vt. Militia.

*BULLARD, LYMAN,　　　Newfane.
Served in Capt. Parsons' Company,
Col. Jonathan Williams' Regt. Detached Militia in U. S. service 2
months and 13 days, 1812.

BULLARD, MARTIN,　　　Fifer.
Served from April 12, 1814 to April
21, 1814 in Capt. Shubael Wales'
Company, Col. W. B. Sumner's Regt.
Ref: Book 52, AGO Page 288.

*BULLARD, NATHAN.
Served in Capt. Walker's Company,
Col. Fifield's Regt. Detached Militia
in U. S. service 13 days, 1812.

*BULLARD, SAMUEL,　　　Captain.
Served in 1 Regt., 3 Brig., 3 Div. Vt.
Militia.

*BULLARD, STEPHEN.
Enlisted Jan. 29, 1813 in Capt. Weeks'
Company, 11th Regt.; on Pay Roll for
January and February, 1813. Also
served in 4 Regt. (Williams') Vt.
Militia. Ref: R. & L. 1812, AGO
Page 5.

*BULLARD, THURSTIN, Fifer, Addison.
Volunteered to go to Plattsburgh,
September, 1814, and served 9 days
in Capt. George Fisher's Company,
Sumner's Regt. Was at the battle.

*BULLEN, JOEL.
    Served in 1 Regt. Vt. Militia com-
    manded by Col. Judson.

*BULLETT, JOHN.
    Enlisted Sept. 25, 1813 in Capt. Elijah
    W. Wood's Company, Dixon's Regt.

*BULLIS, GUMAN.
    Served from April 12, 1814 to April
    21, 1814 in Capt. Othniel Jewett's
    Company, Sumner's Regt.

BULLIS, ISAAC,   Fifer.
    Served from March 9, 1813 to June
    8, 1813 in Capt. Charles Follett's Com-
    pany, 11th Regt. Ref: R. & L. 1812,
    AGO, Page 13.

BULLISS, JOHN.
    Served from April 5, 1813 to July 4,
    1813 in Capt. Charles Follett's Com-
    pany, 11th Regt. Ref: R. & L. 1812,
    AGO Page 13.

BULLISS, JOSEPH.
    Served from April 9, 1813 to July 8,
    1813 in Capt. Charles Follett's Com-
    pany, 11th Regt. Ref: R. & L. 1812,
    AGO Page 13.

BULLOCK, SHUBAL,   St. Albans.
    Enlisted April 27, 1813 for 1 year in
    Capt. John Wires' Company, 30th
    Regt. Ref: R. & L. 1812, AGO Page
    40.

BULLOCK, ZENAS,   Marshfield.
    Volunteered to go to Plattsburgh,
    September, 1814, and served 9 days
    in Capt. James English's Company.
    Ref: Book 52, AGO Page 248.

BULLOON, JOHN,   Franklin County.
    Volunteered to go to Plattsburgh,
    Sept. 11, 1814 and served in 15th or
    22nd Regt. Ref Hemenway's Vt. Ga-
    zetteer, Vol. 2, Page 391.

‡BUMP, CYRUS,   Salisbury.
    Volunteered to go to Plattsburgh,
    September, 1814, and served 9 days.
    No organization given. Ref: Book
    51, AGO Pages 64, 65, 67. Served
    in Capt. John Morton's Company.
    Pension Certificate No. 31919.

‡BUMP, HARRY, Captain, Salisbury.
    Volunteered to go to Plattsburgh,
    September, 1814, and served 9 days.
    No organization given. Ref: Book
    51, AGO Pages 55, 64, 65. Also serv-
    ed as Captain of a company. Pension
    Certificate No. 32711.

*BUMP, ZENAS.
    Served in Capt. Needham's Company,
    Col. Martindale's Regt. Detached
    Militia in U. S. service 2 months and
    14 days, 1812.

*BUNKER, DAVID.
    Served from April 12, 1814 to April
    21, 1814 in Capt. Eseck Sprague's
    Company, Sumner's Regt.

*BUNKER, EBEN.
    Served in 3 Regt. Vt. Militia com-
    manded by Col. Tyler.

*BUNT, JOHN.
    Served in 1 Regt. Vt. Militia com-
    manded by Col. Martindale.

*BUNT, JOHN JR.
    Enlisted Sept. 20, 1813 in Capt. John
    Weed's Company, Col. Clark's Rifle
    Corps.

*BUNT, RICHARD.
    Enlisted Sept. 20, 1813 in Capt. John
    Weed's Company, Col. Clark's Rifle
    Regt.

*BUNT, SAMUEL.
    Enlisted Sept. 20, 1813 in Capt. John
    Weed's Company, Col. Clark's Rifle
    Regt.

BURBANK, DANIEL.
    Served in Capt. Weeks' Company,
    1th Regt. On Pay Roll for January
    and February 1813. Ref: R. & L.
    1812, AGO Page 5.

BURBANK, HAZEN.
    Served in Capt. Weeks' Company,
    11th Regt. On Pay Roll for January
    and February, 1813. Ref: R. & L.
    1812, AGO Page 5.

‡*BURBANK, JOHN.
    Served from June 11, 1813 to June
    14, 1813 in Capt. Moses Jewett's Com-
    pany, 1st Regt. 2nd Brig. 3rd Div.
    Pension Certificate No. 9810.

*BURBANK, NAHUM.
    Served in 1 Regt. Vt. Militia com-
    manded by Col. Judson.

BURBANK, SILAS,   Montpelier.
    Volunteered to go to Plattsburgh,
    September, 1814, and served 8 days
    in Capt. Timothy's Hubbard's Com-
    pany. Ref: Book 52, AGO Page 256.

BURBANK, SOLOMON B.
    Served from Feb. 20-28, 1813 in Capt.
    Samuel H. Holly's Company, 11th
    Regt. Ref: R. & L. 1812, AGO Page
    25.

BURBANK, WILLIAM,   Bethel.
    Volunteered to go to Plattsburgh,
    September, 1814, and served 9 days
    in Capt. Nehemiah Noble's Company.
    Ref: Book 51, AGO Page 233.

BURBECK, WILLIAM.
    Born in Boston, Mass.; aged 41 years;
    5 feet 7½ inches high; dark com-
    plexion; brown hair; brown eyes; by
    profession a blacksmith. Enlisted at
    Plainfield May 1, 1814 in Capt. Wm.
    Miller's Company, 30th Regt.; served
    in Capt. Gideon Spencer's Company,
    30th Regt. and Capt. James Taylor's
    Company, 30th Regt.; discharged at
    Burlington, Vt. in 1815. Ref: R. &
    L. 1812, AGO Pages 1, 53, 54, 55, 57.

*BURCHARD, BENJAMIN.
    Served in Sumner's Regt. Vt. Militia.

*BURCHARD, LEVI O.
    Served from April 12, 1814 to May
    20, 1814 in Capt. George Fisher's
    Company, Sumner's Regt.

*BURCHARD, NATHAN,   Drummer.
    Served from April 12, 1814 to May
    20, 1814 in Capt. George Fisher's
    Company, Sumner's Regt.

BURDET, DANIEL.
Enlisted June 8, 1813 for 1 year in Capt. Daniel Farrington's Company (also commanded by Capt. Simeon Wright), 30th Regt.; on Muster Roll March 1, 1814 to April 30, 1814. Ref: R. & L. 1812, AGO Pages 50 and 51.

BURDET, ISRAEL,   Pittsford.
Served from April 26, 1813 to April 27, 1814 in Capt. Daniel Farrington's Company (also commanded by Capt. Simeon Wright), 30th Regt. Ref: R. & L. 1812, AGO Pages 50 and 51.

BURDICK, ELNATHAN,   Fairfax.
Served in 1813 and 1814 in Capt. Joseph Beeman's Company. Volunteered to go to Plattsburgh, September, 1814, and served 7 days in Capt. Josiah Grout's Company. Ref: Hemenway's Vt. Gazetteer, Vol. 2, Pages 402 and 403; Book 51, AGO Pages 133, 134, 185.

‡*BURDICK, MAXON.
Enlisted Sept. 25, 1813 in Company of Capt. Jonathan Prentiss Jr. Dixon's Regt. Pension Certificate No. 33731.

BURDICK, NATHANIEL.
Enlisted April 22, 1813 in Capt. James Taylor's Company, 30th Regt.; transferred to Capt. Gideon Spencer's Company, 30th Regt. and served to April 25, 1814. Ref: R. & L. 1812, AGO Pages 52, 57, 58.

*BURDICK, NATHANIEL,   Fairfax.
Served in Capt. Dorrance's Company, Col. Wm. Williams' Regt. Detached Militia in U. S. service 3 months and 11 days, 1812 .Enlisted Sept. 27, 1813 in Capt. Asahel Langworthy's Company, Col. Isaac Clark's Rifle Corps. Served in 1813 and 1814 in Capt. Joseph Beeman's Company. Ref: Hemenway's Vt. Gazetteer Vol. 2, Page 402.

BURDICK, TIMOTHY, Fairfax or Swanton. Served in Lieut. V. R. Goodrich's Company, 11th Regt.; on Pay Roll for January and February, 1813. Enlisted Aug. 8, 1812 in Company of Capt. Joseph Beeman Jr., 11th Regt. U. S. Inf. under Col. Ira Clark. Ref: R. & L. 1812, AGO Page 11; Hemenway's Vt .Gazetteer, Vol. 2, Page 402.

BURDITT, GEORGE,   Pittsford.
Volunteered to go to Plattsburgh, September, 1814, and served 8 days in Capt. Caleb Hendee's Company. Ref: Book 52, AGO Page 124.

*BURDOCK, AMOS.
Served in Sumner's Regt. Vt. Militia.

*BURDOCK, ASA.
Served in Sumner's Regt. Vt. Militia.

BURGAN, JOHN.
Born at Chester, N. H. Enlisted at Fairlee April 2, 1814 during the war and served in Capt. Wm. Miller's Company, Capt. Gideon Spencer's Company, and Capt. James Taylor's Company, all in the 30th Regt. Ref: R. & L. 1812, AGO Pages 53, 54, 55, 57.

*BURGESS, ABNER.
Served in Capt. Wright's Company, Col. Fifield's Regt. Detached Militia, in U. S. service 6 months, 1812.

BURGESS, ANTHONY,   Montpelier.
Volunteered to go to Plattsburgh, September, 1814, and served 8 days in Capt. Timothy Hubbard's Company. Ref: Book 52, AGO Page 256.

BURGESS, HENRY.
Served in Capt. Samuel H. Holly's Company, 11th Regt.; on Pay Roll for January and February, 1813. Ref: R. & L. 1812, AGO Page 25.

BURGESS, ISAIAH,   Montpelier.
Volunteered to go to Plattsburgh, September, 1814, and served 8 days in Capt. Timothy Hubbard's Company. Ref:: Book 52, AGO Page 256.

BURGIS, ELISHA.
Served in Capt. Chadwick's Company. Ref: R. & L. 1812, AGO Page 32.

BURGISS, JOSIAH.
Served from Feb. 27, 1813 to March 4, 1813 in Capt. Jonathan Starks' Company, 11th Regt. Ref: R. & L. 1812, AGO Page 19.

‡BURGOIN, WILLIAM.
Served in Capt. Miller's Company. Pension Certificate No. 17253.

‡BURKE, ASAHEL, Musician, Morristown. Volunteered to go to Plattsburgh, September, 1814, and served 8 days in Capt. Denison Cook's Company. Pension Certificate of widow, Zeriah, No. 18429.

BURKE, BENJAMIN,   Barre.
Volunteered to go to Plattsburgh, September, 1814, and served in Capt. Warren Ellis' Company. Ref: Hemenway's Vt. Gazetteer Vol. 4, Page 41.

BURKE, DANIEL.
Enlisted at Boston April 18, 1814 in U. S. Marine Corps. Ref: Book 52, AGO Page 294.

BURKE, EDWARD.
Served as private in War of 1812 and was captured by troops Sept. 17, 1814 at Fort Erie. Discharged Nov. 8th. Ref: Records of Naval Records and Library Navy Dept.

‡BURKE, IRA.
Served in Capt. Sabin's Company, Col. Jonathan Williams' Regt. Detached Militia, in U. S. service 2 months and 6 days, 1812. Pension Certificate of widow, Roxana, No. 27925.

‡BURKE, JOSEPH,   Morristown.
Served in company of Capt. John McNeil Jr., 11th Regt.; on Pay Roll of company for January and February, 1813. Enlisted May 6, 1813 for 1 year in Capt. James Taylor's Company, 30th Regt. Volunteered to go to Plattsburgh, September, 1814, and served 8 days in Capt. Denison Cook's Company. Pension Certificate No. 32290. Ref: R. & L. 1812, AGO Page 17 and page 59.

BURKE, MELZOR B..   Sergeant.
Served from April 1. 1813 to June
30, 1813 in Capt. Charles Follett's
Company. 11th Regt. Ref: R. & L.
1812, AGO Page 13.

*BURKE, SETH.
Enlisted April 12, 1814 in Capt.
Shubael Wales' Company, Col. W. B.
Sumner's Regt.; transferred April 13,
1814 to Capt. Salmon Foster's Company, same Regt., and served to April
21, 1814.

BURKE, WILLIAM.
Served in Capt. Benjamin S. Edger-
ton's Company 11th Regt.; on Pay
Roll for January and February, 1813.
Ref: R. & L. 1812, AGO Page 2.

BURKES, THOMAS.
Served in Capt. Benjamin S. Edgerton's Company, 11th Regt.; on Pay
Roll for September and October, 1812,
and January and February, 1813.
Ref: R. & L. 1812, AGO Pages 1
and 2.

BURKELEY, PHILO,   Franklin County.
Volunteered to go to Plattsburgh
Sept. 11, 1814 and served in 15th or
22nd Regt. Ref: Hemenway's Vt.
Gazetteer, Vol. 2, Page 392.

BURL, NATHANIEL,   Lansingburgh.
Served from Oct. 8, 1814 to June 19,
1815 in Capt. Taylor's Company, 30th
Inf. Ref: R. & L. 1812, AGO Page
23.

BURLAND, JNO.
Served in War of 1812 and was cap-
tured by troops Dec. 19, 1813 at Fort
Niagara. Died April 20, 1814. Ref:
Records of Naval Records and Li-
brary, Navy Dept.

BURLEY, JEREMIAH,   Sanborton.
Served from July 1 to Aug. 31, 1813,
and from May 1 to July 4, 1814, in
Capt. Poland's Company, 34th Inf.
Ref:: R. & L. 1812, AGO Page 30.

*BURMAN, JOHN H.,   Johnson.
Served 1 month and 23 days, 1813, in
Capt. Thomas Waterman's Company,
Dixon's Regt. Volunteered to go to
Plattsburgh, September, 1814, in same
company.

BURMAN, JONATHAN,   Johnson.
Volunteered to go to Plattsburgh,
September, 1814, and served in Capt.
Thomas Waterman's Company, Dix-
on's Regt. Ref: Book 51, AGO Page
208.

BURN, AARON,   Lieutenant.
Served in Capt. George W. Kindall's
Company; on Pay Roll to Sept. 10,
1812; on Muster Roll from Nov. 1
to Dec. 8, 1812; appointed Adjutant
Nov. 4. Ref: R. & L. 1812, AGO
Pages 37, 38, 39.

‡BURNAP. CALVIN.
Appointed Ensign 31 Inf. Nov.
8, 1814; 3rd Lieutenant Jan. 1, 1815;
honorably discharged June 15, 1815.
Served as private in Capt. Burnap's
Company, Col. Jonathan Williams'
Regt. Detached Militia in U. S. serv-

ice 2 months and 13 days. 1812. Also
served in Captain Stewart's Company.
Pension Certificate No. 2465. Ref:
Governor and Council, Vt., Vol. 6,
Page 478; Heitman's Historical Reg-
ister & Dictionary USA; Book 53,
AGO Page 41.

BURNAP, ETHAN.
Appointed Captain 31 Inf. April 30,
1813; honorably discharged June 15,
1815. Ref: Heitman's Historical Register & Dictionary USA.

‡*BURNAP, JACOB.
Served in Capt. Wright's Company.
Col. Martindale's Regt. Detached
Militia in U. S. service 2 months and
14 days, 1812. Served from April 12,
1814 to April 21, 1814 as Ensign in
Lieut. James S. Morton's Company,
Sumner's Regt. Pension Certificate of
widow, Lillah, No. 4117.

*BURNAP, JOSEPH.
Served from April 12, 1814 to April
21, 1814 in Lieut. James S. Morton's
Company, Sumner's Regt.

BURNAP. JOSIAH.   Salisbury.
Volunteered to go to Plattsburgh,
September, 1814, and served 4 days
in Capt. John Morton's Company.
Ref: Book 52, AGO Page 141.

*BURNELL, NATHAN.
Served in Capt. Wilkins' Company,
Col. Dixon's Regt. Detached Militia
in U. S. service 1 month and 23
days, 1813.

BURNES, JOHN.
Served from March 3, 1813 to June 2,
1813 in Capt. John W. Weeks' Company, 11th Regt. Ref: R. & L. 1812,
AGO Page 4.

*BURNETT, ELISHA,   Musician.
Served in 3 Regt. Vt. Militia commanded by Col. Williams.

‡*BURNETT, SAMUEL.
Served in 4 Regt. (Peck's) Vt. Militia. Also served in Capt. Micah
Brown's Company. Pension Certificate No. 31921.

*BURNHAM, ASAHEL,   Thetford.
Volunteered to go to Plattsburgh,
September, 1814, and went as far as
Bolton, Vt., serving 6 days in Capt.
Salmon Howard's Company, 2nd Regt.

BURNHAM, BAILEY,   Sergeant.
Served in Capt. Chadwick's Com-
pany. Ref: R. & L. 1812, AGO
Page 32.

*BURNHAM, CHARLES.
Served in 1 Regt. Vt. Militia commanded by Col. Judson.

BURNHAM, ENOCH,   Williamstown.
Volunteered to go to Plattsburgh,
September, 1814, and served 8 days
in Capt. David Robinson's Company.
Ref: Book 52, AGO Pages 8 and 10.

BURNHAM, ERASTUS,   Cabot.
Volunteered to go to Plattsburgh,
September, 1814, and served 3 days
in Capt. Anthony Perry's Company.
Ref: Book 52, AGO Pages 253 and 254.

BURNHAM, EZEKIEL.
Served in Capt. Benjamin Bradford's
Company; on Muster Roll from May
31, 1813 to Aug. 31, 1813; joined by
transfer July 22, 1813. Ref: R. & L.
1812, AGO Page 26.

*BURNHAM, FREDERICK,   Swanton.
Served from Aug. 8, 1812 in company
of Capt. Joseph Beeman Jr., 11th
Regt. U. S. Inf. under Col. Ira
Clark. Served in Lieut. V. R. Good-
rich's Company, 11th Regt.; on Pay
Roll for January and February, 1813.
Also served with Hospital Attend-
ants, Vt. Ref: R. & L. 1812, AGO
Page 11; Hemenway's Vt. Gazetteer,
Vol. 2, Page 402.

BURNHAM, HARRIS.
Served in Capt. Chadwick's Company. Ref: R. & L. 1812, AGO Page
32.

*BURNHAM, JAMES.
Served in Capt. Wright's Company,
Col. Fifield's Regt. Detached Militia
in U. S. service 6 months, 1812.

*BURNHAM, JOHN, Corporal, Strafford.
Enlisted Sept. 25, 1813 in Capt. Amos
Robinson's Company, Dixon's Regt.,
as a Corporal. Also served in Capt.
Thomas Waterman's Company, Dix-
on's Regt. Volunteered to go to
Plattsburgh, September, 1814, and
served 7 days in Capt. Joseph Bar-
rett's Company. Ref: Book 52, AGO
Page 41.

*BURNHAM, JOSEPH,   Thetford.
Volunteered to go to Plattsburgh,
September, 1814, and went as far as
Bolton, Vt., serving 6 days in Capt.
Salmon Howard's Company, 2nd Regt.

BURNHAM, JOSHUA P.
Appointed Sergeant 11th Inf. June 1,
1812 to July, 1814; Ensign July 1,
1814; 3rd Lieutenant Sept. 1, 1814;
resigned Dec. 4, 1814. Served in
Capt. Benjamin S. Edgerton's Company, 11th Regt.; on Pay Roll for
September and October, 1812, and on
Pay Roll for January and February,
1813 showing service from Nov. 1 to
Dec. 31, 1812. Ref: Heitman's Historical Register & Dictionary USA;
R. & L. 1812, AGO Pages 1 and 2.

BURNHAM, JOSIAH,   Corinth.
Volunteered to go to Plattsburgh,
September, 1814, and served 3 days
in Capt. Abel Jackman's Company.
Ref: Book 52, AGO Pages 44 and 45.

*BURNHAM, MICHAEL,   Thetford.
Volunteered to go to Plattsburgh,
September, 1814, and went as far as
Bolton, Vt. serving 6 days in Capt.
Salmon Howard's Company, 2nd Regt.

BURNHAM, N.,   Fairfax.
In U. S. service from Sept. 12, 1813
in Capt. Asa Wilkins' Company, Dixon's Regt. Ref: Hemenway's Vt. Gazetteer, Vol. 2, Page 402.

*BURNHAM, OLIVER W.,   Lincoln.
Volunteered to go to Plattsburgh,
September, 1814, and was at the bat-
tle. Served 9 days in Capt. Jehiel
Saxton's Company, Sumner's Regt.

*BURNHAM, PHILANDER .
Enlisted Sept. 25, 1813 in Capt. Robinson's Company, Col. Dixon's Regt.
and served 1 month and 23 days.
Also served 1 month and 23 days,
1813, in Capt. Post's Company, Col.
Dixon's Regt.

*BURNHAM, RILEY,   Sergeant.
Enlisted Sept. 25, 1813 and served 1
month and 23 days in Capt. Waterman's Company, Col. Dixon's Regt.

BURNHAM, SAMUEL.
Served in Capt. Hotchkiss' Company,
Col. Martindale's Regt. Detached
Militia in U. S. service 2 months and
13 days, 1812. Volunteered to go to
Plattsburgh, September, 1814, and
served in Capt. Ebenezer Spencer's
Company, Vershire. Ref: Book 53,
AGO Page 77; Book 52, AGO Page 48.

*BURNHAM, TIMOTHY.
Served in 1 Regt. Vt. Militia commanded by Col. Judson; served in
Capt. Howard's Company, Vt. Militia.

BURNHAM, WILLIAM, Franklin County.
Volunteered to go to Plattsburgh
Sept. 11, 1814 and served in 15th or
22nd Regt. Ref: Hemenway's Vt.
Gazetteer, Vol. 2, Page 391.

*BURNS, DAVID.
Served from Sept. 25, 1813 to Oct. 6,
1813 in Capt. Elijah Birge's Company,
Dixon's Regt.

‡BURNS, JOHN.
Served under Captains Reed and
Allen. Pension Certificate of widow
Roenay, No. 35078.

*BURNS, LEONARD.
Served in 1 Regt. Vt. Militia com
manded by Col. Martindale.

BURNS, NATHAN.
Enlisted Sept. 25, 1813 in Capt. Asa
Wilkins' Company, Dixon's Regt. Ref:
Book 52, AGO Page 272.

*BURNS, WILLIAM.
Served in Capt. Durkee's Company,
Col. Fifield's Regt. Detached Militia
in U. S. service 1 month and 11 days,
1812. Served from June 11, 1813 to
June 14, 1813 in Capt. Hezekiah
Barns' Company, 1st Regt. Ref:
Book 53, AGO Page 53.

*BURPEE, EMERY.
Served in Capt. Adams' Company,
Col. Jonathan Williams' Regt. Detached Militia in U. S. service 2
months and 7 days, 1812.

*BURR, AARON. Lieutenant-Adjutant-
Captain, Fairfield. Served in Capt.
George W. Kindal's Company, 4th
Regt. 6 months in 1812. Volunteered to go to Plattsburgh, September,
1814, and served 8 days in Capt. Benjamin Wooster's Company. Also
served in 3 Regt. Vt. Militia commanded by Col. Bowdish.

‡*BURR, ASAHEL,   Sudbury
Served in Capt. Adams' Company,
Col. Jonathan Williams' Regt. Detach-

ed Militia in U. S. service 2 months
and 7 days, 1812. Pension Certificate No. 8474.

‡BURR,ASAHEL.
Volunteered to go to Plattsburgh,
September, 1814, and served 6 days
in Capt. Thomas Hall's Company.
Pension Certificate No. 33913.

BURR, JAMES, Sudbury.
Volunteered to go to Plattsburgh,
September, 1814, and served 6 days
in Capt. Thomas Hall's Company.
Ref: Book 52, AGO Page 122.

BURR, JOHN, Sergeant.
Enlisted Nov. 21, 1812 for 5 years in
company of late Capt. J. Brooks,
commanded by Lt. John I. Cromwell,
Corps of U. S. Artillery; on Muster
Roll from April 30, 1814 to June 30,
1814. Ref: R. & L. 1812, AGO Page
18.

BURRELL, JESSE.
Enlisted April 26, 1814 during the
war in Capt. Wm. Miller's Company,
30th Regt. On Muster Roll to Aug.
31, 1814; sick in hospital. Ref: R.
& L. 1812, AGO Page 54.

*BURRELL, JOHN.
Served in 4 Regt. Vt. Militia commanded by Col. Williams.

BURRETT, JOHN.
Served in Capt. Willson's Company,
Col. Wm. Williams' Regt. Detached
Militia in U. S. service 5 months,
1812. Ref: Book 52, AGO Page 22.

BURRIDGE, JACOB, Musician, Braintree.
Marched to Plattsburgh, Sept. 10,
1814, serving under Capt. Lot Hudson. Ref: Book 52, AGO Pages 24
and 26.

*BURRILL, EZRA A.
Served from April 12, 1814 to April
21, 1814 in Capt. Othniel Jewett's
Company, Sumner's Regt.

*BURRIT, GERRAD, Musician.
Served from June 11, 1813 to June 14,
1813 in Lieut. Bates' Company, 1st
Regt. Volunteered to go to Platts-
burgh, September, 1814, serving in
Major Luman Judson's command.

BURRITT, REUBEN, Shelburne.
Volunteered to go to Plattsburgh,
September, 1814, serving in Major Luman Judson's command. Ref: Book
51, AGO Page 78.

*BURROUGHS, DAVID D.
Served in Capt. Wright's Company,
Col. Fifield's Regt. Detached Militia
in U. S. service 6 months, 1812.

*BURROUGHS, ELIJAH, Cabot.
Served in Capt. Mason's Company,
Col. Fifield's Regt. Detached Militia
in U. S. service 3 months and 16
days, 1812.

BURROUGHS, JOEL, Sergeant, Pittsford.
Volunteered to go to Plattsburgh,
September, 1814, and served 8 days
in Capt. Caleb Hendee's Company.
Ref: Book 52, AGO Page 124.

BURROUGHS, TIMOTHY JR., Corporal.
Volunteered to go to Plattsburgh,
September, 1814, and served 7 days
in Capt. Frederick Griswold's Com-
pany, raised in Brookfield, Vt. Ref:
Book 52, AGO Pages 52 and 56.

‡*BURROUGHS, ZEBULON, Coventry.
Served in Capt. Mason's Company,
Col. Fifield's Regt. Detached Militia
in U. S. service 2 months and 12
days, 1812. Pension Certificate No.
18769.

*BURROWS, ABNER.
Served in 2 Regt. Vt. Militia commanded by Col. Fifield.

BURROWS, NATHAN.
Served from May 1 to June 30, 1814
in Capt. Alexander Brooks' Corps of
Artillery. Ref: R. & L. 1812, AGO
Page 31.

*BURT, ASAHEL JR.
Served in Capt. Wheeler's Company,
Col. Fifield's Regt. Detached Militia
in U. S. service 6 months and 4
days, 1812.

BURT, JOHN.
Served in Capt. Strait's Company,
Col. Martindale's Regt. Detached
Militia in U. S. service 2 months and
13 days, 1812. Ref: Book 53, AGO
Page 25.

*BURT, SAMUEL.
Served in Capt. Burnap's Company,
Col. Jonathan Williams' Regt. Detached Militia in U. S. service 1
month and 22 days, 1812.

*BURTEH, RUFUS.
Served in 4 Regt. Vt. Militia commanded by Col. Williams.

*BURTON, CALEB.
Served in Capt. Willson's Company,
Col. Wm. Williams' Regt. Detached
Militia in U. S. service 5 months
1812.

‡BURTON, ELIJAH JR., Sergeant.
Served from April 23, 1813 to April
24, 1814 in Capt. Daniel Farrington's
Company (also commanded by Capt.
Simeon Wright), 30th Regt. Pension
Certificate of widow, Abbey P., No.
8079. Ref: R. & L. 1812, AGO Pages
50 and 51.

‡BURTON, HARVEY.
Served in Lieut. J. Major's Company.
Pension Certificate of widow, Harriet,
No. 19123.

BURTON, JACOB, Washington.
Volunteered to go to Plattsburgh,
September, 1814, and served in Capt.
Amos Stiles' Company. Ref: Book
52, AGO Page 36.

BURTON, JEDEDIAH.
Served from April 26, 1813 to April
26, 1814 in Capt. Gideon Spencer's
Company, 30th Regt. and Capt. James
Taylor's Company, 30th Regt. Ref:
R. & L. 1812, AGO Pages 52, 57, 59.

BURTON, JOHN.
Enlisted June 19, 1813 for 1 year in
Capt. Daniel Farrington's Company

(also commanded by Capt. Simeon Wright), 30th Regt. On Muster Roll March 1, 1814 to April 30, 1814. Ref: R. & L. 1812, AGO Pages, 50 and 51.

*BURTON, JOHN H.
Served in Capt. Burnap's Company, Col. Jonathan Williams' Regt. Detached Militia in U. S. service 2 months and 13 days, 1812. Appointed 2nd Lieut. 30 Inf. April 30, 1813; 1st Lieutenant Dec. 13, 1813; Regimental Adjutant July 13, to June 15; honorably discharged June 15, 1815. Ref: Heitman's Historical Register & Dictionary USA; Governor and Council, Vt., Vol. 6, Page 475.

‡*BURTON, JOSEPH, Sergeant, Manchester. Served as sergeant in Capt. Scovell's Company, Col. Martindale's Regt. Detached Militia in U. S. service 2 months and 21 days, 1812. Served as corporal in Cavalry of Detached Militia of Vt. in U. S. service at Champlain commencing Nov. 18th and ending Nov. 19, 1812. Pension Certificate of widow, Anna, No. 17389.

BURTON, OLIVER GEORGE, Irasburgh. Appointed Cadet, Military Academy, March 20, 1807 (7); 1st Lieutenant 4 Inf. June 18, 1808; Captain Aug. 25, 1811; Major 33 Inf. June 15, 1814; honorably discharged June 15, 1815; M S K at West Point 1816 to 1820; died Feb. 22, 1821. Ref: Heitman's Historical Register & Dictionary USA; Governor and Council Vt. Vol. 6, Page 478.

BURWELL, REUBEN A.
Served in Capt. Benjamin S. Edgerton's Company, 11th Regt., from Nov. 1, 1812 to date of death, Jan. 3, 1813. Ref: R. & L. 1812, AGO Pages 1 and 2.

BUSELLS, JOHN,　　　　Fairfax.
Served from Aug. 8, 1812 in Company of Capt. Joseph Beeman Jr. 11th Regt. U. S. Inf. under Col. Ira Clark. Ref: Hemenway's Vt. Gazetteer, Vol. 2, Page 402.

BUSH, DAVID.
Served from Sept. 1, 1813 to Feb. 28, 1814 and from May 1, 1814 to Aug. 10, 1814 in 12th Infantry. Ref: R. & L. 1812, AGO Page 30.

BUSH, EBENEZER, Lieutenant, Shoreham. Served as lieutenant of company of Cavalry from Shoreham. Volunteered to go to Plattsburgh, September, 1814, marched to Burlington and crossed the lake but did not take part in the battle. Ref: Rev. J. F. Goodhue's History of Shoreham, Page 104.

*BUSH, ELI W., Corporal, Fairfield. Served in Capt. Kendall's Company, Col. Wm. Williams' Regt. Detached Militia in U. S. service 4 months and 23 days, 1812. Served from April 29, 1813 to April 29, 1814 in Capt. James Taylor's Company, 30th Regt. and Capt. Gideon Spencer's Company, 30th Regt. Ref: R. & L. 1812, AGO Pages 52, 56, 58.

*BUSH, JOHN JR., Corporal.
Served in Sumner's Regt. Vt. Militia.

*BUSH, JOSIAH.
Served in 4 Regt. Vt. Militia commanded by Col. Williams.

BUSH, LYMAN, Drummer, Rochester. Enlisted May 1, 1813 for 1 year in Capt. Simeon Wright's Company. Volunteered to go to Plattsburgh, September, 1814, and served 7 days in Capt. Oliver Mason's Company. Ref: R. & L. 1812, AGO Page 51; Book 51, AGO Pages 249, 264.

*BUSH, NATHAN.
Served in 1 Regt. Vt. Militia commanded by Col. Martindale.

*BUSH, SETH.
Served in Sumner's Regt. Vt. Miltia.

BUSH, STEPHEN,　　　　Carpenter .
Served from May 1 to May 25, 1814 in company of Artificers commanded by Alexander Parris. Ref: R. & L. 1812, AGO Page 24.

*BUSH, WILLIAM.
Served in 1 Regt. Vt. Militia commanded by Col. Martindale.

BUSHEE, WILLIAM L.
Enlisted Nov. 5, 1813 for 1 year and served in Capt. Wm. Miller's Company, Capt. Gideon Spencer's Company, Capt. James Taylor's Company and Capt. Daniel Farrington's Company, all in the 30th Regt. Ref: R. & L. 1812, AGO, Pages 50, 51, 53, 54, 57.　　..

*BUSHLY, EPHRAIM W.
Served in 1 Regt. Vt. Militia commanded by Col. Martindale.

*BUSHNELL, JAMES,　　　Corporal.
Served from April 12, 1814 to April 21, 1814 in Col. W. B. Sumner's Regt.

*BUSHNELL, SEGWICK, 2nd Sergeant.
Served from April 12, 1814 to April 21. 1814 in Capt. Eseck Sprague's Company, Sumner's Regt.

*BUSHNELL, SIMEON.
Served in Sumner's Regt. Vt. Militia.

BUSKIRK, GARNET.
Served from March 1 to June 30, 1814 in Capt. Alexander Brooks' Corps of Artillery. Ref: R. & L. 1812, AGO Page 31.

BUSS, JOSEPH.
Served in company of Capt. John McNeil Jr., 11th Regt.; on Pay Roll for January and February, 1813. Ref: R. & L. 1812, AGO Page 17.

BUSSELL, LEONARD M.,　　　Barre.
Volunteered to go to Plattsburgh, September, 1814, and served in Capt. Warren Ellis' Company. Ref: Hemenway's Vt. Gazetteer, Vol. 4, Page 42.

BUSWELL, JESSE.
Enlisted April 26, 1814 during the war in Capt. Gideon Spencer's Company, 30th Regt.; on Muster Roll Dec. 30, 1813 to June 30, 1814; joined June 1, 1814. Ref: R. & L. 1812, AGO Page 57.

*BUTCHER, BENJAMIN.
Enlisted Sept. 14, 1813 in Capt.
Isaac Finch's Company, Col. Clark's
Regt. of Riflemen. Served in com-
pany of Capt. John McNeil Jr. 11th
Regt.; on Pay Roll for January and
February, 1813.

‡*BUTLER, AMMI R. R.
Enlisted Sept. 25, 1813 and served 1
month and 23 days in Capt. Amos
Robinson's Company, Dixon's Regt.
Also served as Aide to Colonel Bow-
dish. Pension Certificate of widow,
Matildah, No. 8110.

BUTLER, ABEL.
Appointed Ensign 31 Inf. April 30,
1813; resigned Sept. 4, 1813. Ref:
Heitman's Historical Register & Dictionary USA.

BUTLER, CALVIN,   Richmond.
Volunteered to go to Plattsburgh,
September, 1814, and served 9 days
in Capt. Roswell Hunt's Company, 3
Regt. Ref: Book 51, AGO Page 82.

BUTLER, DAVID.
Served from March 22, 1813 to June
1, 1813 in Lieut. V. R. Goodrich's
Company, 11th Regt. Ref: R. & L.
1812, AGO Page 10.

*BUTLER, ELDAD S.,   Adjutant.
Served in 4 Regt. Vt. Militia commanded by Col. Williams.

*BUTLER, EZRA P., Corporal, Water-
bury. Volunteered to go to Plattsburgh, September, 1814, and was in
the battle, serving 11 days in Capt.
George Atkins' Company, 4 Regt.
(Peck's).

BUTLER, IRA.
Served from March 11, 1813 to May
23, 1813 in Capt. Phineas Williams'
Company, 11th Regt. Ref: R. & L.
1812, AGO Page 14.

*BUTLER, ISAAC H.,   Captain.
Served in 3 Regt. Vt. Militia commanded by Col. Bowdish.

‡BUTLER. JACOB,   Ira.
Volunteered to go to Plattsburgh,
September, 1814, and served 4 days
in Capt. Matthew Anderson's Com-
pany. Pension Certificate of widow,
Amanda, No. 25674.

BUTLER. JAMES.
Served from June 1, 1813 to June 30,
1814 in Regt. of Light Dragoons.
Ref: R. & L. 1812, AGO Page 21.

*BUTLER, JAMES.   Richmond.
Served from April 12, 1814 to May
20, 1814 in Capt. George Fisher's Company, Sumner's Regt. Volunteered to
go to Plattsburgh, September, 1814,
served in Capt. Roswell Hunt's Company, 3 Regt. (Tyler's). Ref: Book
51, AGO Page 82.

BUTLER, JOEL.
Served from June 11, 1813 to June 14,
1813 in Lt. Bates' Company, 1st
Regt. Ref: R. & L. 1812, AGO Page
33.

*BUTLER, JOHN.
Served in 3 Regt. Vt. Militia commanded by Col. Tyler.

*BUTLER, JOSEPH M.,   Fairfax.
Served from Aug. 8, 1812 in Com-
pany of Capt. Joseph Beeman Jr.
11th Regt. U. S. Inf. under Col. Ira
Clark. Served in Lieut. V. R. Good-
rich's Company, 11th Regt.; on Pay
Roll for January and February, 1813.
Served with Hospital Attendants, Vt.
Ref: R. & L. 1812, AGO Page 11;
Hemenway's Vt. Gazetteer, Vol. 2,
Page 402.

*BUTLER, LEONARD.
Served from March 11, 1813 to June
10, 1813 in Capt. Charles Follett's
Company, 11th Regt. Ref: R. & L.
1812, AGO Page 13.

*BUTLER, ORANGE.
Served from Sept. 25, 1813 to Oct. 13,
1813 in Capt. Jesse Post's Company,
Dixon's Regt.

BUTLER, REUBEN.
Enlisted April 21, 1813 for 1 year in
Capt. Simeon Wright's Company.
Ref: R. & L. 1812, AGO Page 51.

‡BUTLER, SAMUEL.
Served in Capt. Stephen Pettit's Company. Pension Certificate No. 25362.

*BUTLER, SAMUEL S., Surgeon's Mate.
Served in 3 Regt. Vt. Militia commanded by Col. Bowdish.

*BUTLER, SETH.
Served with Hospital Attendants, Vt.

*BUTLER, WILLIAM.
Served from Oct. 11, 1813 to Oct. 17,
1813 in Capt. John Munson's Company of Cavalry, 3 Regt.

*BUTTERFIELD, AUGUSTUS.
Enlisted Nov. 9, 1813 in Capt. Asahel
Langworthy's Company, Col. Isaac
Clark's Regt.

*BUTTERFIELD, DAVID.
Served in Capt. Adams' Company,
Col. Jonathan Williams' Regt. Detached Militia in U. S. service 13
days, 1812.

*BUTTERFIELD. SAMUEL,   Topsham.
Served in Capt. Rogers' Company,
Col. Fifield's Regt. Detached Militia
in U. S. service 2 months and 18
days, 1812. Volunteered to go to
Plattsburgh, September, 1814, and
served 4 days in Capt. James George's
Company.

BUTTERFIELD. SAMUEL JR.
Volunteered to go to Plattsburgh,
September, 1814, and served 4 days
in Capt. James George's Company
from Topsham. Ref: Book 52, AGO
Page 70.

*BUTTERFIELD. THOMAS.
Served in Capt. Richardson's Company, Col. Martindale's Regt. Detached Militia in U. S. service 2
months and 13 days, 1812.

‡BUTTERFIELD, WELLBEE.
Served in Capt. James George's Company. Pension Certificate of widow, Eliza F., No. 27315.

*BUTTERFIELD, WILLIAM.
Served in Capt. Brown's Company. Col. Martindale's Regt. Detached Militia in U. S. service 1 month and 13 days, 1812.

*BUTTOLPH, DAVID.
Served from April 12, 1814 to April 21, 1814 in Lieut. Justus Foote's Company, Sumner's Regt.

BUTTOLPH, JOSEPH.
Volunteered to go to Plattsburgh, September, 1814, and served in Capt. Elijah Parker's Company. Ref: Book 51, AGO Page 42.

BUTTON, ELIJAH.
Served in 1st Regt. of Detached Militia of Vermont in U. S. service at Champlain commencing Nov. 18 and ending Nov. 19, 1812.

‡*BUTTON, GARDNER.
Served in 1 Regt. Vt. Militia commanded by Col. Martindale. Pension Certificate of widow, Lydia, No. 1960.

*BUXTON, DANIEL.
Served from Sept. 25, 1813 to Oct. 4, 1813 in Capt. Elijah Birge's Company, Dixon's Regt.

BUXTON, JOSEPH.
Served in Capt. Brown's Company, Col. Martindale's Regt. Detached Militia in U. S. service 2 months and 14 days, 1812. Ref: Book 53, AGO Page 90.

BUZZELL, JOSHUA.
Served in Capt. H. Mason's Company, Col. Fifield's Regt. Detached Militia in U. S. service 2 months and 20 days, 1812. Served from May 1 to June 30, 1814 in Capt. Haig's Corps of Light Dragoons at Champlain. Wounded. Ref: Book 53, AGO Page 12; R. & L. 1812, AGO Page 20.

BYOM, SOLOMON,   Braintree.
Marched to Plattsburgh, Sept. 10, 1814 in company of Capt. Lot Hudson. Ref: Book 52, AGO Pages 24 and 26.

‡*BYRD, AMOS.
Served from April 12, 1814 to April 21, 1814 in Capt. Eseck Sprague's Company, Sumner's Regt. Also served in Captain Jewett's Company, Sumner's Regt. Pension Certificate of widow, Randilla, No. 27183.

*BYRON, JEREMIAH.
Served in 1 Regt. Vt. Militia commanded by Col. Judson.

BYSLEY, SAMUEL.
Served in Capt. Taylor's Company, Col. Fifield's Regt. Detached Militia in U. S. service 2 months and 21 days, 1812. Ref: Book 53, AGO Page 74.

*CABLE, TRS. (See also Robinson, Nathaniel). Served in 3 Regt. Vt. Militia commanded by Col. Williams.

CABOT, HUBBARD S.
Appointed Ensign 31 Inf. March 28, 1814; 3rd Lieutenant May 2, 1814; died Sept. 4, 1814. Ref: Heitman's Historical Register & Dictionary USA; Governor and Council Vt. Vol. 6, Page 478.

*CADWELL, BENJAMIN JR.
Served in Capt. Brown's Company, Col. Martindale's Regt. Detached Militia, in U. S. service 8 days, 1812.

CADWELL, JOHN.
Served from March 23, 1814 to June 3, 1814 in Capt. James Taylor's Company, 30th Regt. and Capt. Gideon Spencer's Company, 30th Regt. Ref: R. & L. 1812, AGO Pages 53 and 57.

*CADWELL, MILO.
Served in Sumner's Regt. Vt. Militia.

CADY, ALITHA,   Fairfax.
Served from Sept. 12, 1813 in Capt. Asa Wilkins' Company, Dixon's Regt. Ref: Hemenway's Vt. Gazetteer, Vol. 2, Page 402.

CADY, BUEL,   Cambridge.
Volunteered to go to Plattsburgh, September, 1814, and served 8 days in Capt. Salmon Green's Company. Ref: Book 51, AGO Page 207.

CADY, CALVIN,   Granville.
Volunteered to go to Plattsburgh, September, 1814, and served 7 days in Capt. Asaph Smith's Company. Ref: Book 51, AGO Page 20.

*CADY, ELISHA,   Corporal.
Served in Corning's Detachment, Vt. Militia.

‡*CADY, ERASTUS,   Corporal.
Served in Capt. Dodge's Company, Col. Fifield's Regt. Detached Militia in U. S. service 2 months and 21 days, 1812. Pension Certificate of widow, Deborah, No. 8895.

*CADY, EZEKIEL.
Served from Sept. 25, 1813 to Oct. 24, 1813 in Capt. N. B. Eldridge's Company, Dixon's Regt.

*CADY, HIRAM.
Served in Capt. Willson's Company, Col. Wm. Williams' Regt. Detached Militia in U. S. service 4 months and 24 days, 1812. Enlisted Sept. 25, 1813 and served 1 month and 2 days in Capt. N. B. Eldridge's Company, Col. Dixon's Regt.

‡*CADY, IRA, Corporal,   Stowe.
Served in Capt. Dorrance's Company, Col. Wm. Williams' Regt. Detached Militia in U. S. service 4 months and 6 days, 1812. Volunteered to go to Plattsburgh, September, 1814, and was at the battle, serving in Capt. Nehemiah Perkins' Company, 4th Regt. (Peck's). Pension Certificate No. 17678.

CADY, ISAAC,   Granville.
Volunteered to go to Plattsburgh, September, 1814, and served 7 days in Capt. Asaph Smith's Company. Ref: Book 51, AGO Page 20.

CADY, ISAAC JR.,   Granville.
Volunteered to go to Plattsburgh,
September, 1814, and served 7 days
in Capt. Asaph Smith's Company.
Ref: Book 51, AGO Page 20.

*CADY, JASON.   Waterbury.
Volunteered to go to Plattsburgh,
September, 1814, and was at the
battle, serving 11 days in Capt.
George Atkins' Company 4 Regt.
(Peck's).

CADY, JOHN,   Granville.
Volunteered to go to Plattsburgh,
September, 1814, and served 7 days
in Capt. Asaph Smith's Company.
Ref: Book 51, AGO Page 20.

*CADY, NATHANIEL.
Enlisted May 6, 1814 for 5 years in
Capt. White Youngs' Company, 15th
Regt.; on Muster Roll from Aug. 31,
1814 to Dec. 31, 1814. Also served
in 4 Regt. (Williams') Vt. Militia.
Ref: R. & L. 1812, AGO Page 27.

CADY, PARLEY,   Granville.
Volunteered to go to Plattsburgh,
September, 1814, and served 7 days
in Capt. Asaph Smith's Company.
Ref: Book 51, AGO Page 20.

*CAHOON, JOHN,   Lieutenant.
Served in 2 Regt. Vt. Militia commanded by Col. Fifield.

CAIN, JOHN.
Served in Capt. Richardson's Company, Col. Martindale's Regt. Detached Militia in U. S. service 2 months
and 13 days, 1812. Ref: Book 53,
AGO Page 24.

CAIN, WILLIAM.
Enlisted May 25, 1813 for 1 year in
Capt. Simeon Wright's Company.
Ref: R. & L. 1812, AGO Page 51.

CALDER, JOSEPH L.
Enlisted Feb. 16, 1814 during the
war in company of late Capt. J.
Brooks, commanded by Lt. John I.
Cromwell, Corps of U. S. Artillery.
On Muster Roll of Company from
April 30, 1814 to June 30, 1814;
transferred from Capt. Collins' Com-
pany. Ref: R. & L. 1812, AGO
Page 18.

CALDWELL, AARON.
Served from March 31, 1813 to June
30, 1813 in Capt. Edgerton's Company,
11th Regt. Ref: R. & L. 1812, AGO
Page 3.

*CALDWELL, CHARLES.
Enlisted Sept. 25, 1813 and served
1 month and 23 days in Capt. Elijah
W. Wood's Company, Col. Dixon's
Regt. Served from April 12, 1814
to April 21, 1814 in Capt. Eseck
Sprague's Company, Sumner's Regt.
Also served in 1 Regt. (Judson's) Vt.
Militia.

CALDWELL, JACOB,   Corporal.
Served from May 1 to June 30, 1814
in Capt. Alexander Brooks' Corps
of Artillery. Ref: R. & L. 1812,
AGO Page 31.

CALDWELL, JAMES,   Montpelier.
Volunteered to go to Plattsburgh,
September, 1814, and served 8 days
in Capt. Timothy Hubbard's Company. Ref: Book 52, AGO Page 256.

*CALDWELL, JOHN.
Served from April 12, 1814 to April
21, 1814 in Capt. Eseck Sprague's
Company, Sumner's Regt.

CALDWELL, JOHN,   Sergeant.
Appointed Sergeant Light Dragoons
Feb. 13, 1813 to March, 1814; Cor-
poral 2 Light Dragoons March 11,
1814; transferred to Light Dragoons
May 12, 1814; honorably discharged
June 15, 1815. Ref: Heitman's His-
torical Register & Dictionary USA;
R. & L. 1812, AGO Page 20.

*CALDWELL, MATHEW.
Served in 1 Regt. Vt. Militia commanded by Col. Judson.

*CALDWELL, MOSES.
Served in Capt. Taylor's Company,
Col. Fifield's Regt. Detached Militia in U. S. service 2 months and
21 days, 1812.

‡*CALDWELL, NOAH D.
Enlisted Sept. 25, 1813 in Capt.
Charles Bennett's Company, Col.
Dixon's Regt. Volunteered to go to
Plattsburgh, September, 1814, and
served 10 days in Capt. Thomas
Waterman's Company, Col. Dixon's
Regt. Pension Certificate No. 13938.
Ref: Book 51, AGO Pages 208 and
209.

*CALEB, ELIAS W.
Served in Corning's Detachment, Vt.
Militia.

*CALF, WILLIAM.
Served from June 11, 1813 to June
14, 1813 in Lt. Bates' Company, 1
Regt. (Judson's).

CALFE, CUTTING S.,   Washington.
Volunteered to go to Plattsburgh,
September, 1814, and served in Capt.
Amos Stiles' Company. Ref: Book
52, AGO Page 36.

CALFE, JOSEPH,   Washington.
Volunteered to go to Plattsburgh,
September, 1814, and served in Capt.
Amos Stiles' Company. Ref: Book
52, AGO Page 36.

*CALKINS, ELIAS,   Corporal.
Served from June 11, 1813 to June
14, 1813 in Capt. John M. Eldridge's
Company, 1st Regt. 2nd Brig., 3rd
Div. Vt. Militia.

CALKINS, GEORGE,   St. Albans.
Volunteered and was in the battle
at Plattsburgh Sept. 11, 1814, serving
in Capt. Samuel H. Farnsworth's
Company. Ref: Hemenway's Vt. Gazetteer, Vol. 2, Page 434.

CALKINS, JONAS,   St. Albans.
Volunteered and was in the battle
at Plattsburgh Sept. 11, 1814, serving
in Capt. Samuel H. Farnsworth's
Company. Ref: Hemenway's Vt. Gazetteer, Vol. 2, Page 434.

*CALL, CYREL.
Served in Capt. Taylor's Company.
Detached Militia in U. S. service 4
months and 24 days, 1812. Enlisted
Sept. 25, 1813 in Capt. Asa Wilkins'
Company, Dixon's Regt. Volunteered
to go to Plattsburgh, September, 1814,
and served 8 days in Capt. Josiah
Grout's Company. Ref: Book 52, AGO
Page 272; Book 51, AGO Page 103;
Hemenway's Vt. Gazetteer, Vol. 2,
Pages 402 and 403.

*CALL, ERASTUS.
Served in Capt. Durkee's Company,
Col. Fifield's Regt. Detached Militia
in U. S. service 2 months and 21
days, 1812.

‡CALL, EZRA D.
Served in Capt. Steward's Company.
Pension Certificate No. 13885.

‡CALL, PHILIP.
Served in Capt. Hall's Company. Pension Certificate of widow, Sally, No.
6315.

*CALL, ROYAL.
Served in Capt. Willson's Company,
Col. Wm. Williams' Regt. Detached
Militia in U. S. service 5 months,
1812.

*CALL, RUFUS,   Fairfax.
Transferred from Capt. Asa Wilkins'
Company, Col. Dixon's Regt., to Capt.
Asahel Langworthy's Company, Col.
Isaac Clark's Rifle Corps Oct. 23,
1813.

CALL, WILLIAM R.,   Woodstock.
Enlisted March 18, 1813 in Capt.
Phineas Williams' Company, 11th
Regt.; on Pay Roll to May 31, 1813.
Ref: R. & L. 1812, AGO Page 14.

CALLAN, J. (or P.)
Appointed 1st Lieutenant May 20,
1814; transferred from 2nd Light
Dragoons to 26th Regt. of Riflemen.
Ref: Governor and Council, Vt., Vol.
6, Page 477.

CALLAR, DAVID,   Sudbury.
Volunteered to go to Plattsburgh,
September, 1814, and served 6 days
in Capt. Thomas Hall's Company.
Ref: Book 52, AGO Page 122.

*CALLEMORE, SAMUEL, Musician.
Served from June 11, 1813 to June
14, 1813 in Capt. John M. Eldridge's
Company, 1st Regt. 2nd Brig., 3rd
Div.

CALLENDER, HENRY B.
Served from May 1 to June 30,
1814 in Company of Artificers commanded by Capt. Alexander Parris,
as Sad. Har. Ref: R. & L. 1812,
AGO Page 24.

*CALLENDER, SAMUEL,   Fifer.
Served in Capt. Barns' Company,
Col. Wm. Williams' Regt. Detached
Militia in U. S. service 5 months,
1812.

‡*CALVIN, ALPHEUS R.
Served from June 11, 1813 to June
14, 1813 in Capt. Moses Jewett's

Company, 1st Regt. 2nd. Brig. 3rd
Div. Also served in Capt. Steward's
Company. Pension Certificate No.
26866.

‡*CALVIN, ISRAEL P.,   Danby.
Served in Capt. Hotchkiss' Company,
Col. Martindale's Regt. Detached
Militia in U. S. service 1 month and
19 days, 1812. Pension Certificate
No. 17258.

CAMP, JARED,   Fairfax.
Served from Aug. 8, 1812 in company of Capt. Joseph Beeman, Jr.,
11th Regt. U. S. Inf. under Col. Ira
Clark. Ref: Hemenway's Vt. Gazetteer, Vol. 2, Page 402.

*‡CAMP, JOB G.
Served from Nov. 1, 1812 to Feb. 28,
1813 in Lt. V. R. Goodrich's Company, 11th Regt. Also served in 3
Regt. (Williams'). Pension Certificate No. 4425.

CAMP, JOHN.
Served from May 1st to June 30, 1814
as a Saddler in Capt. Haig's Corps
of Light Dragoons. Ref: R. & L.
1812, AGO Page 20.

*CAMP, JOHN R.
Served in Capt. Burnap's Company,
Col. Jonathan Williams' Regt. Detached Militia in U. S. service 1
month and 13 days, 1812.

*CAMP, RIVERIUS, Lieutenant-Quarter-
master, Stowe. Volunteered to go to
Plattsburgh, September, 1814, and
was at the battle, serving in Capt.
Nehemiah Perkins' Company 4 Regt.
(Peck's). Also served 8 days in
April, 1814, in Col. John Peck's Regt.

CAMPBELL, CHARLES.
Enlisted Feb. 21, 1814 and served in
Capt. Wm. Miller's Company, Capt.
Gideon Spencer's Company and Capt.
James Taylor's Company, 30th Regt.;
on board Navy. Volunteered from
Franklin County to go to Platts-
burgh, September, 1814, and served
in either the 15th or 22nd Regt. Ref:
R. & L. 1812, AGO Pages 53, 54, 57;
Hemenway's Vt. Gazetteer, Vol. 2,
Page 392.

CAMPBELL, DANIEL.
Served in Capt. Benjamin Bradford's
Company; on Muster Roll from May
31, 1813 to Aug. 31, 1813. Ref: R. &
L. 1812, AGO Page 26.

CAMPBELL, DAVID,   Ensign.
Served in Capt. Benjamin Bradford's
Company; on Muster Roll from May
31, 1813 to Aug. 31, 1813. Ref: R. &
L. 1812, AGO Page 26.

CAMPBELL, ELICK,   Washington.
Volunteered to go to Plattsburgh,
September, 1814, and served in Capt.
Amos Stiles' Company. Ref: Book
52, AGO Page 36.

*CAMPBELL, ELIJAH.
Served in 1 Regt. Vt. Militia commanded by Col. Martindale.

CAMPBELL, GEORGE Middletown or St.
Albans. Enlisted May 3, 1813 for 1
year in Capt. John Wires Company,
30th Regt. Served from Sept. 1,
1814 to June 16, 1815 in Capt. Sanford's Company, 30th Inf. Ref: R. &
L. 1812, AGO Page 23 and Page 40.

*CAMPBELL, GEORGE.
Served from April 12, 1814 to April
21, 1814 in Capt. Eseck Sprague's
Company, Sumner's Regt.

‡CAMPBELL, HORACE.
Pension Certificate of widow, Sally,
No. 3235. No organization given.

*CAMPBELL, ISAIAH.
Enlisted Sept. 23, 1813 in Capt.
Amasa Mansfield's Company, Dixon's
Regt.

*CAMPBELL, JOHN,   Captain.
Served in Corning's Detachment, Vt.
Militia. Also served in 4 Regt. Vt.
Militia commanded by Col. Peck.

CAMPBELL, JOHN,   Williamstown.
Volunteered to go to Plattsburgh,
September. 1814, and served 7 days
in Capt. David Robinson's Company.
Ref: Book 52, AGO Pages 10 and 11.

*CAMPBELL, JOHN.
Enlisted Sept. 25, 1813 in Capt. Elijah
W. Wood's Company, Dixon's Regt.

CAMPBELL, JOSEPH,   Benson.
Served from Sept. 1, 1814 to June 16,
1815 in Capt. Sanford's Company,
30th Inf. Ref: R. & L. 1812, AGO
Page 23.

*CAMPBELL, ROBERT.
Served from Sept. 25-29, 1813 in
Capt. Elijah W. Wood's, Company,
Dixon's Regt.

CAMPBELL, SOLOMON M.,   St. Albans.
Enlisted May 5, 1813 for 1 year in
Capt. John Wires' Company, 30th
Regt. Ref: R. & L. 1812, AGO
Page 40.

CAMPBELL, T. H. (or J. H.) 1st Lieuten-
ant. Enlisted Sept. 25, 1813 in Capt.
N. B. Eldridge's Company, Dixon's
Regt.

*CAMPBELL, THOMAS.
Served in Capt. Briggs' Company,
Col. Jonathan Williams' Regt. Detached Militia in U. S. service 2
months and 13 days, 1812.

CAMPBELL, WILLIAM.
Appointed 1st Lieutenant, Light
Artillery, Dec. 12, 1808; Captain May
30, 1810; Major Aug. 31, 1814; honorably discharged June 15, 1815. Ref:
Heitman's Historical Register & Dictionary USA.

CAMPFIELD, JESSE.
Served as carpenter in Company of
Artificers commanded by Alexander
Parris; on Pay Roll for May and
June, 1814. Ref: R. & L. 1812, AGO
Page 24.

CANADA, A.
Served in Capt. James Taylor's Company, 30th Regt.; on Muster Roll
to Feb. 28, 1814. Ref: R. & L. 1812,
AGO Page 53.

*CANADA, HUGH.
Served from April 12. 1814 to April
21, 1814 in Capt. Shubael Wales'
Company, Col. W. B. Sumner's
Regt. Ref: Book 52, AGO Page 289.

*CANADA, JOHN.
Served in 4 Regt. Vt. Militia commanded by Col. Peck.

CANDOR, JOHN,   Franklin County.
Volunteered to go to Plattsburgh
Sept. 11, 1814 and served in 15th or
22nd Regt. Ref: Hemenway's Vt.
Gazetteer, Vol. 2, Page 392.

*CANE, JOHN.
Served in 1 Regt. Vt. Militia commanded by Col. Martindale.

*CANFIELD, LEVI.
Served from June 11, 1813 to June
14, 1813 in Capt. Thomas Dorwin's
Company, 1st Regt. 2nd Brig. 3rd
Div., under Col. Isaac Clark.

CANFIELD, LEVI JR.
Served from June 11, 1813 to June 14,
1813 in Capt. Thomas Dorwin's Company, 2nd Brig., 3rd Div. Ref: R. &
L. 1812, AGO Page 46.

CANFIELD, SILAS,   Sergeant.
Enlisted April 30, 1813 for 1 year
in Capt. Simeon Wright's Company.
Ref: R. & L. 1812, AGO Page 51.

CANIER, LEBBINS.
Volunteered to go to Plattsburgh,
September, 1814, and went as far as
Bolton, Vt., serving 4 days in Lieut.
Phineus Kimball's Company, West
Fairlee. Ref: Book 52, AGO Pages
46 and 47.

*CANNON, JOHN.
Served in Col. Wm. Williams' Regt.
Detached Militia in U. S. service 3
months and 25 days, 1812. Also
served in 1 Regt. (Judson's) Vt.
Militia. Ref: Book 53, AGO Page 11.

CANNY, PETER.
Served from March 16, 1813 to June
15, 1813 in Capt. Charles Follett's
Company, 11th Regt. Ref: R. & L.
1812, AGO Page 13.

*CANSERT, NATHAN.
Served from June 11, 1813 to June
14, 1813 in Capt. John M. Eldridge's
Company, 1st Regt. 2nd Brig., 3rd
Div. (Name spelled "Consor" on
War Dept. Records.)

*CANSOR, JOSEPH.
Served from June 11, 1813 to June
14, 1813 in Capt. John M. Eldridge's
Company, 1st Regt., 2nd Brig., 3rd
Div.

CANVASS, JAMES,   Fairfield.
Served in Capt. Geo. Kimball's Company, stationed at Swanton in 1812.
Ref: Hemenway's Vt. Gazetteer, Vol.
2, Page 408.

CAPLIN, ORIN.   Braintree.
Went to Plattsburgh, Sept. 10, 1814,
in Capt. Lot Hudson's Company.
Ref: Book 52, AGO Page 24.

CAPRON, ABIJAH,   Williamstown.
Volunteered and was at the battle
of Plattsburgh Sept. 11, 1814, serving in Capt. David Robinson's Company. Ref: Book 52, AGO Page 2.

*CAPRON, JOSEPH JR.
Served from April 12, 1814 to April
15, 1814 in Capt. Jonathan P. Stanley's Company, Col. W. B. Sumner's
Regt.

*CAPRON, SAMUEL.
Served in 1 Regt. Vt. Militia commanded by Col. Martindale.

*CARD, GEORGE, Corporal Sergeant.
Served in Cavalry of Detached Militia of Vt. in U. S. service at Champlain commencing Nov. 18 and ending
Nov. 19, 1812.

CARLEY, ELIJAH.
Served from March 30th to June 30,
1814 in Regt. of Light Dragoons.
Ref: R. & L. 1812, AGO Page 21.

‡CARLEY, HUGH G.
Served from March 30 to June 30,
1814 in Regt. of Light Dragoons.
Also served in Capt. Hopkins' Com-
pany. Pension Certificate No. 31292.
Ref: R. & L. 1812, AGO Page 21.

CARLEY, JOEL,   Highgate.
Served in New York State from
Sept. 25, to Nov. 14, 1813. No or-
ganization given. Ref: Vol. 50, Vt.
State Papers, Page 94.

*CARLIN, JOHN.
Enlisted Sept. 25, 1813 and served
1 month and 23 days in Capt. Wood's
Company, Col. Dixon's Regt.

CARLISLE, JAMES.
Enlisted May 8, 1812 for 5 years
in Capt. White Youngs' Company,
15th Regt.; on Muster Roll from
Aug. 31, 1814 to Dec. 31, 1814;
killed Sept. 11, 1814. Ref: R. & L.
1812, AGO Page 27.

CARLISLE JAMES.
Served in Corps of Light Dragoons
under Capt. Haig; on Pay Roll to
June 30, 1814. Ref: R. & L. 1812,
AGO Page 20.

‡CARLISLE, MARTIN,   Goshen.
Volunteered to go to Plattsburgh,
September, 1814, and served 5 days
in Capt. Durham Sprague's Company.
Pension Certificate of widow, Abigail,
No. 24422.

CARLTON, EBENEZER.
Served in Lieut. Wm. S. Foster's
Company, 11th Regt.; on Pay Roll
for January and February, 1813.
Ref: R. & L. 1812, AGO Page 7.

CARLTON, ENOCH,   Cambridge.
Volunteered to go to Plattsburgh,
September, 1814, and served 8 days
in Capt. Salmon Green's Company.
Ref: Book 51, AGO Page 207.

*CARLTON, GEORGE, Corporal, St. Al-
bans. Served in Capt. Brown's Company, Col. Martindale's Regt. Detached Militia in U. S. service 2
months and 14 days, 1812. Served

in Capt. Chadwick's Company, 2
Regt. Served from May 1, 1813 to
April, 1814, as corporal in Capt.
John Wires' Company, 30th Regt.
Ref: R. & L. 1812, AGO Page 32
and Page 40.

*CARLTON, PHINEAS.
Served in 1 Regt. Vt. Militia commanded by Col. Martindale.

*CARMAN, JOHN,   Highgate.
Served from Sept. 1, 1812 in Capt.
Conrade Saxe's Company, 4 Regt.
(Williams'). Ref: Hemenway's Vt.
Gazetteer, Vol. 2, Page 420.

*CARNEY, MOSES C.,   Fifer.
Served in 2 Regt. Vt. Militia commanded by Col. Fifield.

*CARPENTER, ABEL, Quartermaster
Sergeant. Served with Detachment of
Militia sent to Derby from Caledonia
County in July 1812. Served in Corn-
ing's Detachment, Vt. Militia. Volun-
teered to go to Plattsburgh, Septem-
ber, 1814, and went as far as Bolton,
Vt., serving in Lieut. Phineas Kim-
ball's Company, West Fairlee. Ref:
Vol. 49 Vt. State Papers, Page 223;
Book 52, AGO Pages 46 and 47.

‡*CARPENTER, ALANSON, Sergeant,
Middlesex. Served in Capt. Holden
Putnam's Company, 4 Regt. (Peck's).
Pension Certificate No. 23741.

*CARPENTER, ALMON,   Sergeant.
Served in Capt. Burnap's Company,
Col. Jonathan Williams' Regt. Detached Militia in U. S. service 2
months and 1 day, 1812.

‡*CARPENTER, AMOS.
Served in Capt. Sabin's Company,
Col. Jonathan Williams' Regt. Detached Militia in U. S. service 2
months and 6 days, 1812. Pension
Certificate No. 9651. Pension Certificate of widow, Delam, No. 14093.

CARPENTER, BENJAMIN,   Franklin
County.
Volunteered to go to Plattsburgh
Sept. 11, 1814 and served in 15th
or 22nd Regt. Ref: Hemenway's Vt.
Gazetteer, Vol. 2, Page 391.

*CARPENTER, BOSWELL, Lieutenant.
Served in Dixon's Regt. Vt. Militia.

CARPENTER, CALEB,   Pittsford.
Volunteered to go to Plattsburgh,
September, 1814 and served 8 days
in Capt. Caleb Hendee's Company.
Ref: Book 52, AGO Page 124.

*CARPENTER, CEPHAS, Adjutant-Cap-
tain. Served 8 days in April, 1814 in
Col. John Peck's Regt. Ref: Vol. 50,
Vt. State Papers, Page 220.

*CARPENTER, CHARLES,   Randolph.
Volunteered to go to Plattsburgh,
September, 1814, and served in Capt.
Lebbeus Egerton's Company.

‡*CARPENTER, CHESTER, Sergeant.
Served in Capt. Mason's Company,
Col. Fifield's Regt. Detached Militia
in U. S. service 6 months, 1812.

Served in Capt. J. Morrill's Company. Served in company of Capt. John McNeil Jr. 11th Regt. Pension Certificate No. 9044. Pension Certificate of widow, Betsey, No. 22361. Ref: R. & L. 1812, AGO Page 17.

*CARPENTER, COMFORT.
Enlisted April 12, 1814 in Capt. Shubael Wales' Company, Col. W. B. Sumner's Regt.; transferred to Capt. Salmon Foster's Company, same Regt.; April 13, 1814 and served to April 21, 1814.

CARPENTER, DANIEL,   Jericho.
Enlisted July 9, 1813 for 1 year in Capt. Simeon Wright's Company; transferred to Capt. Clark's Company, 30th Inf. about March 1, 1814 and served to July 9, 1814. Ref: R. & L. 1812, AGO Pages 30 and 51.

‡CARPENTER, EBENEZER.
Pension Certificate of widow, Sally, No. 44653. No organization given.

CARPENTER, EDWARD,   Ira.
Volunteered to go to Plattsburgh, September, 1814, and served 4 days in Capt. Matthew Anderson's Company. Ref: Book 52, AGO Page 144.

*CARPENTER, ELIAS, Corporal-Sergeant, Randolph. Served in Capt. Wright's Company, Col. Fifield's Regt. Detached Militia in U. S. service 6 months, 1812. Volunteered to go to Plattsburgh, September, 1814, and served as sergeant in Capt. Lebbeus Egerton's Company.

CARPENTER, EPHRAIM, Ensign, Strafford. Volunteered to go to Plattsburgh, September, 1814, and served 5 days in Capt. Cyril Chandler's Company. Ref: Book 52, AGO Page 42.

‡CARPENTER, GEORGE,   Guilford.
Served in Capt. E. Burnap's Company (3 Regt.). Pension Certificate No. 10947.

*CARPENTER, GIDEON.
Served from April 12, 1814 to May 20, 1814 in Capt. George Fisher's Company, Sumner's Regt. Volunteered to go to Plattsburgh, September, 1814, and served 9 days in same company; was at the battle.

CARPENTER, GUY.
Served from May 1, 1814 to July 5, 1814 in Capt. Smythe's Company, Rifle Regt. Ref: R. & L. 1812, AGO Page 30.

CARPENTER, HENRY.
Served from Feb. 4, 1813 to May 3, 1813 in Lieut. V. R. Goodrich's Company. 11th Regt. Ref: R. & L. 1812, AGO Pages 10 and 11.

CARPENTER, ISRAEL, Musician, Ira. Volunteered to go to Plattsburgh, September, 1814, and served in Capt. Matthew Anderson's Company. Ref: Hemenway's Vt. Gazetteer, Vol. 3, Page 783.

*CARPENTER, JESSE.
Served in 4 Regt. Vt. Militia commanded by Col. Peck.

*CARPENTER, JOEL, Ensign.
Served in 2 Regt., 3rd Brig., 3 Div. Vt. Militia. Also served in Capt. Chadwick's Company. Ref: R. & L. 1812, AGO Page 32.

*CARPENTER, JOHN,   Williamstown.
Served in Capt. Walker's Company, Col. Fifield's Regt. Detached Militia in U. S. service 6 months and 3 days, 1812. Served from June 11, 1813 to June 14, 1813 in Capt. Hezekiah Barns' Company, 1st Regt. 2nd Brig., 3rd Div. Volunteered to go to Plattsburgh, September, 1814, and served in Capt. David Robinson's Company; went as far as Burlington.

*CARPENTER, JOSEPH.
Served in Capt. Durkee's Company, Col. Fifield's Regt. Detached Militia in U. S. service 2 months and 21 days, 1812.

CARPENTER, LUTHER,   Orange.
Marched for Plattsburgh Sept. 11, 1814 but only went part way, serving as wagoner in Capt. David Rising's Company. Ref: Book 52, AGO Pages 19 and 22.

‡CARPENTER, MARCUS.
Served in Capt. Edward White's Company. Pension Certificate of widow, Hannah, No. 30042.

*CARPENTER, MARSHALL,   Randolph.
Volunteered to go to Plattsburgh, September, 1814, and served in Capt. Lebbeus Egerton's Company.

*CARPENTER, NATHAN, Sergeant.
Served from April 12, 1814 to April 15, 1814 in Capt. John Hackett's Company, Sumner's Regt.

*CARPENTER, NATHANIEL, Middlesex.
Served in Capt. Holden Putnam's Company, 4 Regt. (Peck's).

*CARPENTER, OLIVER,   Randolph.
Volunteered to go to Plattsburgh, September, 1814, and served in Capt. Lebbeus Egerton's Company.

*CARPENTER, ORIN,   Randolph.
Volunteered to go to Plattsburgh, September, 1814, and served in Capt. Lebbeus Egerton's Company.

CARPENTER, PARKER,   Strafford.
Volunteered to go to Plattsburgh, September, 1814, and served in Capt. Joseph Barrett's Company. Ref: Book 52, AGO Page 41.

*CARPENTER, PHINEHAS,   Sergeant, Fairfax. Enlisted Sept. 25, 1813 and served 1 month and 23 days in Capt. Wilkins' Company, Col. Dixon's Regt.

‡CARPENTER, ROSWELL, Lieutenant.
Served from Sept. 25, 1813 to Oct. 14, 1813 in Capt. Asa Wilkins' Company, Dixon's Regt. Also served in Capt. Brush's Company. Pension Certificate of widow, Lucy, No. 23369.

CARPENTER, STEPHEN,   Barre.
Volunteered to go to Plattsburgh, September, 1814, and served in Capt. Warren Ellis' Company. Ref: Hemenway's Vt. Gazetteer, Vol. 4, Page 41.

CARPENTER, SULLIVAN,   Strafford.
Volunteered to go to Plattsburgh,
September, 1814, and served in Capt.
Cyril Chandler's Company. Ref: Book
52 AGO Page 42.

*CARPENTER, THOMAS.
Served in Capt. Barns' Company,
Col. Wm. Williams. Regt. Detached
Militia in U. S. service 5 months.
Served from June 11, 1813 to June
14, 1813 in Capt. Thomas Dorwin's
Company, 1st 'Regt. 2nd Brig., 3rd
Div.

CARPENTER, WILSON,   Ira.
Volunteered to go to Plattsburgh,
September, 1814, and served 4 days
in Capt. Matthew Anderson's Company. Ref: Book 52, AGO Page 144.

*CARR ABNER.
Served in Capt. Rogers' Company,
Col. Fifield's Regt. Detached Militia
in U. S. service 3 months and 9 days,
1812.

CARR, JESSE.
Served in Capt. John W. Weeks'
Company, 11th Regt. Ref: R. & L.
1812, AGO Page 4.

‡CARR. JOHN.
Served in Capt. Langmaid's Com-
pany. Pension Certificate of widow,
Sally, No. 25689.

CARR, MERRIT A.
Enlisted April 22, 1813 in Capt.
James Taylor's Company, 30th Regt.;
transferred to Capt. Gideon Spencer's Company and served to April
25, 1814. Ref: R. & L. 1812, AGO
Pages 52, 57, 58.

CARR, ROBERT,   Corinth.
Volunteered to go to Plattsburgh,
September, 1814, and served in Capt.
Abel Jackman's Company. Ref: Book
52, AGO Page 44.

*CARR, TIMOTHY.
Served with Hospital Attendants, Vt.

CARR, WILLIAM.
Volunteered to go to Plattsburgh,
September, 1814, and served in company of Capt. Ebenezer Spencer, Vershire. Ref: Book 52, AGO Page 48.

*CARREL, SIMEON.
Served in Capt. Sabin's Company,
Col. Jonathan Williams' Regt. Detached Militia in U. S. service 2
months and 6 days, 1812.

CARRIER, JOHN, Ensign,   Vershire.
Volunteered to go to Plattsburgh,
September, 1814, and served in Capt.
Ebenezer Spencer's Company, Ver-
shire. Ref: Book 52, AGO Pages 48
and 120.

CARTER, ABEL, 1st Sergeant, Williamstown. Took part in the Battle of
Plattsburgh, Sept. 11, 1814 and served 8 days in Capt. David Robinson's
Company. Ref: Book 52, AGO Pages
2 and 9.

*CARTER, FRANCIS.
Served in Sumner's Regt. Vt. Militia.

*CARTER, JOHN.
Enlisted Sept. 25, 1813 and served
in Capt. Thomas Waterman's Company, Dixon's Regt.

*CARTER, JOHN.
Served with Hospital Attendants, Vt.

*CARTER, JOHN,   Groton.
Served in Capt. Rogers' Company,
Col. Fifield's Regt. Detached Militia
in U. S. service 2 months and 18
days, 1812.

CARTER, JOHN JR.,   Johnson.
Volunteered to go to Plattsburgh,
September, 1814, and served in Capt.
Thomas Waterman's Company, Dix-
on's Regt. Ref: Book 51, AGO Page
208.

‡CARTER, JOHN L.
Served in Capt. Thornton's Company.
Pension Certificate No. 19614.

CARTER, JOSEPH.   Groton.
Served from April 9, 1814 to June
16, 1815 in Capt. Sanford's Company, 30th Inf. Ref: R. & L. 1812,
AGO Page 23.

CARTER, JOSIAH.   Franklin County.
Volunteered to go to Plattsburgh
Sept. 11, 1814 and served in 15th or
22nd Regt. Ref: Hemenway's Vt.
Gazetteer, Vol. 2, Page 391.

CARTER, LYMAN W., Corporal, Morristown. Volunteered to go to Plattsburgh, September, 1814, and served
8 days in Capt. Denison Cook's Company. Ref: Book 51, AGO Pages
202 and 206.

*CARTER, RUFUS.
Served from April 12, 1814 to May
20, 1814 in company of Capt. James
Gray Jr., Sumner's Regt.

CARTER, SAMUEL,   Groton.
Served from April 9, 1814 to June
16, 1815 in Capt. Sanford's Company,
30th Inf. Ref. R. & L. 1812, AGO
Page 23.

*CARTER, THOMAS.
Served from April 17, 1814 to April
21, 1814 in Capt. Othniel Jewett's
Company, Sumner's Regt.

CARTIER, AMON,   Vergennes.
Volunteered to go to Plattsburgh,
September, 1814, and was at the
battle, serving 10 days in Capt.
Gideon Spencer's Company. Ref:
Book 51, AGO Pages 1, 280, 289.

*CARTRIGHT, SAMUEL.
Served in 2 Regt. Vt. Militia commanded by Col. Fifield.

CARTTE, DAVID.
Served from Oct. 11, 1813 to Oct. 17,
1813 in Capt. John Munson's Company of Cavalry, 3 Regt. (Tyler's).
Ref: R. & L. 1812, AGO Page 36.

CARVEY, OWEN.
Served from May 1 to June 30, 1814
in Capt. Alexander Brooks' Corps
of Artillery. Ref: R. & L. 1812,
AGO Page 31.

*CARY, AMOS.
Served in 3 Regt. Vt. Militia commanded by Col. Williams.

*CARY, ASA.
Served from April 12, 1814 to May 20, 1814 in Capt. George Fisher's Company, Sumner's Regt.

*CARY, C. SIMEON.
Served in 3 Regt. Vt. Militia commanded by Col. Williams.

CARY, DANIEL.
Served in Lieut. Wm. S. Foster's Company, 11th Regt.; on Pay Roll for January and February, 1813. Ref: R. & L. 1812, AGO Page 7.

CARY, DANIEL H.
Served in Capt. Alexander Brooks' Corps of Artillery; on Pay Roll to June 30, 1814. Ref: R. & L. 1812, AGO Page 31.

CARY, EDWARD,   Swanton.
Served in Capt. V. R. Goodrich's Company, 11th Regt.; on Pay Roll from July 15 to Dec. 8, 1813; in action at the battle of Lundy's Lane. Ref: Hemenway's Vt. Gazetteer, Vol. 2, Page 444.

CARY, LEVI.
Served from May 12, 1813 to April 18, 1814 in Capt. Daniel Farrington's Company, (also commanded by Capt. Simeon Wright), 30th Regt. Ref: R. & L. 1812, AGO Pages 50 and 51.

CARY, SETH.
Enlisted May 26, 1813 in Capt. James Taylor's Company, 30th Regt.; transferred to Capt Gideon Spencer's Company, 30th Regt. and served to May 26, 1814. Ref: R. & L. 1812, AGO Pages 52, 57, 59.

*CARY, WILLIAM, Ensign.
Served in 4 Regt. Vt. Militia commanded by Col. Williams.

*CASE, ABRAHAM.
Served in Capt. Robbins' Company, Col. Wm. Williams' Regt. Detached Militia in U. S. service 4 months and 29 days, 1812.

*CASE, ISAAC,   Addison or Bristol.
Served in Capt. Robbins' Company, Col. Wm. Williams' Regt. Detached Militia in U. S. service 4 months and 29 days, 1812. Served from April 12, 1814 to May 30, 1814 in Capt. George Fisher's Company, Sumner's Regt.; volunteered to go to Plattsburgh, September, 1814, and was in the battle, serving 9 days in said Fisher's Company. (This name may possibly be "Chase").

CASE, JESSE.
Served from Feb. 13, 1813 to May 12, 1813 in company of Capt. John McNeil, Jr., 11th Regt. Ref: R. & L. 1812, AGO Page 16.

‡CASE, LUMAN,   Bristol.
Volunteered to go to Plattsburgh, September, 1814, and was at the battle, serving 9 days in Capt. Jehiel Saxton's Company, Sumner's Regt.

Also served in Capt. Phelps' Company. Pension Certificate No. 25563. Pension Certificate of widow, Abigail, No. 34501. Ref: Book 51, AGO Page 18.

*CASE, LUTHER.
Served in Capt. Taylor's Company, Col. Wm. Williams' Regt. Detached Militia in U. S. service 4 months and 24 days, 1812.

*CASTLE, AMOS.
Served from June 11-14, 1813 in Capt. John Palmer's Company, 2nd Brig., 3rd Div.

*CASTLE, ANSON.
Served from Oct. 4, 1813 to Oct. 13, 1813 in Capt. John Palmer's Company, 1st Regt. 2nd Brig., 3rd Div.

‡*CASTLE, AUGUSTUS.
Served in Capt. S. Pettees' Company, Col. Wm. Williams' Regt. Detached Militia in U. S. service 3 months and 9 days, 1812. Pension Certificate No. 8904. Pension Certificate of widow, Elizabeth, No. 30261.

*CASTLE, DAVID.
Served in 3 Regt. Vt. Militia commanded by Col. Tyler.

*CASTLE, HEMAN.
Served from Sept. 25, 1813 to Oct. 1, 1813 in Capt. Elijah Birge's Company, Dixon's Regt.

*CASTLE, JOEL, Corporal.
Served in 3 Regt. Vt. Militia commanded by Col. Tyler.

*CASTLE, JONATHAN, 2nd Lieutenant.
Served in Tyler's Regt. Vt. Militia.

*CASTLE, NATHAN.
Served in 1 Regt. Vt. Militia commanded by Col. Judson.

*CASTLE, NATHAN JR.
Served from June 11, 1813 to June 14, 1813 in Capt. Ithiel Stone's Company, 1st Regt., 2nd Brig., 3rd Div.

*CASTLE, RODNEY.
Served in 1 Regt. Vt. Militia commanded by Col. Judson.

‡*CASTLE, SETH, Corporal.
Appointed corporal Sept. 25, 1813 in Capt. Wood's Company, Col. Dixon's Regt. Pension Certificate No. 18249.

*CASTLE, SEYMOUR.
Served from Sept. 25, 1813 to Oct. 1, 1813 in Capt. Elijah Birge's Company, Dixon's Regt.

‡CASTER, WILLIAM.
Served in Capt. Hopkins' Company. Pension Certificate No. 25772. Pension Certificate of widow, Catharine, No. 23659.

‡*CASWELL, NATHAN.
Served in Capt. Saxe's Company, Col. Wm. Williams' Regt. Detached Militia in U. S. service 4 months and 24 days, 1812. Pension Certificate No. 12495.

CASWELL, SAMUEL.
Served in company of Capt. John
McNeil Jr., 11th Regt.; on Pay Roll
for January and February, 1813.
Ref: R. & L. 1812, AGO Page 17.

CASWELL, ZEBULON.
Served in Capt. Weeks' Company,
11th Regt.; on Pay Roll for January
and February, 1813. Ref: R. & L.
1812, AGO Page 5.

CASY, AMOS,   Fairfax.
Served from Aug. 8, 1812 in company
of Capt. Joseph Beeman Jr., 11th
Regt. U. S. Inf. under Col. Ira
Clark. Ref: Hemenway's Vt. Gazet-
teer, Vol. 2, Page 402.

CATE, CHARLES,   Marshfield.
Volunteered to go to Plattsburgh,
September, 1814, and served 9 days
in Capt. James English's Company.
Ref: Book 52, AGO Page 248.

CATE, EARL,   Montpelier.
Volunteered to go to Plattsburgh,
September, 1814, and served 8 days
in Capt. Timothy Hubbard's Company. Ref: Book 52, AGO Page 256.

*CATLIN, IRA, Corporal.
Served from June 11, 1813 to June
14, 1813 in Capt. Hezekiah Barns'
Company, 1st Regt. 2nd Brig., 3rd
Div.

*CATLIN, JAMES.
Served in 1 Regt. Vt. Militia commanded by Col. Judson.

*CATLIN, THEODORE, Lieutenant.
Served in 4 Regt. Vt. Militia commanded by Col. Williams.

*CAVENDEE, WILLIAM.
Served in Sumner's Regt. Vt. Militia.

*CAY, CALVIN.
Served from June 11, 1813 to June 14,
1813 in Capt. Thomas Dorwin's Company, 1st Regt. 2nd Brig., 3rd Div.

*CEALY, JONATHAN JR.
Served in Sumner's Regt. Vt. Militia.

*CENSOR, NATHAN.
Served in 1 Regt. Vt. Militia commanded by Col. Judson.

CENTER, ISAAC.
Volunteered to go to Plattsburgh,
September, 1814, and went as far as
Bolton, serving 4 days in Lieut.
Phineus Kimball's Company, West
Fairlee. Ref: Book 52, AGO Page
46.

CHADWICK, AMOS, Sheldon or Berkshire. Volunteered to go to Plattsburgh, September, 1814, and served
7 days in Capt. Samuel Weed's Company. Ref: Book 51, AGO Pages 152
and 172.

‡*CHADWICK, BENJAMIN, Randolph.
Volunteered to go to Plattsburgh,
September, 1814, and served in Capt.
Lebbeus Egerton's Company. Pension
Certificate of widow, Olive, No. 11955.

*CHADWICK, DAVID, Captain.
Commanded company in 2 Regt., 3
Brig., 3 Div. Vt. Volunteers.

CHADWICK, DAVID, Musician.
Enlisted March 10, 1813 for 5 years
in company of late Capt. J. Brooks,
commanded by Lieut. John I. Crom-
well, Corps of U. S. Artillery; on
Muster Roll from April 30, 1814 to
June 30, 1814; paroled prisoner. Ref:
R. & L. 1812, AGO Page 18.

*CHADWICK, SYLVESTER.
Served in Capt. Rogers' Company,
Col. Fifield's Regt. Detached Militia
in U. S. service 3 months and 9
days, 1812.

CHAFEE, JOEL.
Served in Capt. Preston's Company,
Col. Jonathan Williams' Regt. Detached Militia in U. S. service 2
months and 6 days, 1812. Ref: Book
53, AGO Page 92.

CHAFFEE, ALVA,   Belvidere.
Volunteered to go to Plattsburgh,
September, 1814, and served 7 days
in company of Capt. Moody Shattuck. Ref: Book 51, AGO Pages 210
and 213.

CHAFFEE, CHESTER, Corporal, Belvidere. Volunteered to go to Plattsburgh, September, 1814, and served
7 days in Capt. Moody Shattuck's
Company. Ref: Book 51, AGO Page
210.

CHAFFEE, CYRUS.
Volunteered to go to Plattsburgh,
September, 1814, and served 7 days
in company of Capt. Frederick Gris-
wold, Brookfield, Vt. Ref: Book 52,
AGO Page 52.

‡CHAFFEE, JARVELL.
Served from March 20, 1813 to June
19, 1813 in Capt. Charles Follett's
Company, 11th Regt. Also served in
Capt. John Bliss' Company. Pension
Certificate of widow, Elizabeth, No.
30913. Ref: R. & L. 1812, AGO
Page 13.

*CHAFFEE, JASPER.
Served in Capt. Dorrance's Company,
Col. Wm. Williams' Regt. Detached
Militia in U. S. service 4 months and
24 days, 1812.

*CHAFFEE, JOSEPH, Sergeant.
Served in Capt. Cross' Company, Col.
Martindale's Regt. Detached Militia
in U. S. service 2 months and 14
days, 1812.

CHAFFEE, OTIS.
Served from March 13, 1813 to June
12, 1813 in Capt. John Weeks' Company, 11th Regt. Ref: R. & L. 1812,
AGO Page 4.

*CHAFFEE, WARREN.   Fairfield.
Served in Capt. Geo. W. Kindall's
Company, Col. Wm. Williams' Regt.
in U. S. service 4 months and 23
days, 1812.

CHAFFEY, JOHN,   Montpelier.
Volunteered to go to Plattsburgh,
September, 1814, and served 8 days
in Capt. Timothy Hubbard's Company. Ref: Book 52, AGO Page 256.

‡*CHAFFIN, JOHN H.
Served in Capt. Hubbard's Company.
Pension Certificate No. 21455. Pension Certificate of widow, Susanna, No. 42368.

*CHAMBERLAIN, BARNARD.
Served in Capt. Robbins' Company, Col. Wm. Williams' Regt. Detached Militia in U. S. service 4 months and 29 days, 1812.

*CHAMBERLAIN, HEMAN.
Served in Sumner's Regt. Vt. Militia.

CHAMBERLAIN, HENRY, Lieutenant.
Volunteered to go to Plattsburgh, September, 1814, and served in Capt. Jonathan Jennings' Company, Chelsea. Ref: Book 52, AGO Page 79.

CHAMBERLAIN, HIRAM.
Served from April 20, 1814 to April 21, 1814 in Capt. Eseck Sprague's Company, Sumner's Regt. Ref: Book 52, AGO Page 263.

*CHAMBERLAIN, HOSEA.
Served in 1 Regt. Vt. Militia commanded by Col. Judson.

‡CHAMBERLAIN, JOHN.
Served in Abner Keeler's Company. Pension Certificate of widow, Nancy, No. 32778.

*CHAMBERLAIN, JOHN, Quartermaster-Sergeant. Appointed Quartermaster-Sergeant Sept. 25, 1813 and served until Oct. 29, 1813 in Col. Luther Dixon's Regt. Vt. Militia.

*CHAMBERLAIN, JOSEPH, Corporal-Nurse, Tunbridge. Served in Capt. Rogers' Company, Col. Fifield's Regt. Detached Militia in U. S. service 4 months and 24 days, 1812. Belonged to Light Infantry Company of Tunbridge; started for Plattsburgh, September, 1814, with Capt. David Knox and Lieut. Smith and went as far as Bolton, serving 4 days.

*CHAMBERLAIN, JOSHUA.
Served in 1 Regt. Vt. Militia commanded by Col. Judson.

*CHAMBERLAIN, LUTHER.
Served in Capt. Colton's Company. Pension Certificate No. 32071.

CHAMBERLAIN, RUFUS,   Middlesex.
Volunteered to go to Plattsburgh, September, 1814, and served 10 days in Capt. Holden Putnam's Company. Ref: Book 52, AGO Page 251.

CHAMBERLIN, ASA.   Barnard.
Served in Capt. Barns' Company, Col. Wm. Williams' Regt. Detached Militia in U. S. service 5 months, 1812. Ref: Book 53, AGO Page 19; Vol. 50 Vt. State Papers, Page 250.

CHAMBERLIN, BLANCHARD.
Volunteered to go to Plattsburgh, September, 1814, and served 4 days in company of Capt. James George of Topsham. Ref: Book 52, AGO Page 70.

CHAMBERLIN, CYRUS.
Served from Sept. 1, 1812 to Feb. 28, 1813 in Capt. Benjamin S. Edgerton's Company, 11th Regt.; on Pay Roll for September and October, 1812, and January and February, 1813. Ref: R. & L. 1812, AGO Pages 1 and 2.

*CHAMBERLIN, CYRUS,   Thetford.
Marched for Plattsburgh, September, 1814, and went as far as Bolton, Vt., serving 6 days in Capt. Salmon Howard's Company, 2nd Regt.

CHAMBERLIN, EBENEZER.
Served from March 17, 1813 to June 16, 1813 in Capt. Edgerton's Company, 11th Regt. Ref: R. & L. 1812, AGO Page 3.

CHAMBERLIN, ELISHA,   Barnard.
Volunteered to go to Plattsburgh, September, 1814, and served 8 days in Capt. John S. Bicknell's Company. Ref: Book 51, AGO Page 250.

‡*CHAMBERLIN, FREEMAN,   Barnard.
Served in Capt. Bingham's Company, Col. Jonathan Williams' Regt. Detached Militia in U. S. service 1 month and 26 days, 1812. Also served in Capt. Starks Bicknell's Company. Pension Certificate No. 10073. Pension Certificate of widow, Almyra.

CHAMBERLIN, HENRY,   Montpelier.
Volunteered to go to Plattsburgh, September, 1814, and served 8 days in Capt. Timothy Hubbard's Company. Ref: Book 52, AGO Pages 246 and 256.

CHAMBERLIN, ISAAC,   Stockbridge.
Volunteered to go to Plattsburgh, September, 1814, and served 7 days in Capt. Elias Keyes' Company. Ref: Book 51, AGO Page 238.

*CHAMBERLIN, JEHIEL.
Served in Sumner's Regt. Vt. Militia.

*CHAMBERLIN, JOHN,   Richmond.
Served from March 10, 1813 to June 9, 1813 in Capt. Edgerton's Company, 11th Regt. Served in Corning's Detachment, Vt. Militia. Served from Oct. 5, 1813 to Oct. 16, 1813 in Capt. Roswell Hunt's Company, 3 Regt. (Tyler's); volunteered to go to Plattsburgh, September, 1814, in same company.

CHAMBERLIN, JOSEPH J., Corporal.
Served in Capt. Benjamin S. Edgerton's Company, 11th Regt.; on Pay Roll for September and October, 1812 and January and February, 1813. Ref: R. & L. 1812, AGO Pages 1 and 2.

*CHAMBERLIN, MOSES M., Captain.
Served in 3 Regt. Vt. Militia commanded by Col. Bowdish.

*CHAMBERLIN, MOSES W., Corporal.
Served in Capt. Rogers' Company, Col. Fifield's Regt. Detached Militia in U. S. service 2 months and 18 days, 1812.

CHAMBERLIN, RALPH,   Marshfield.
Volunteered to go to Plattsburgh,
September. 1814, and served 9 days
in Capt. James English's Company.
Ref: Book 52, AGO Page 248.

*CHAMBERLIN, SAMUEL.
Served in 3 Regt. Vt. Militia commanded by Col. Williams.

CHAMBERLIN, SYLVANUS, Stockbridge.
Volunteered to go to Plattsburgh,
September, 1814, and served 8 days
in Capt. Elias Keyes' Company. Ref:
Book 51, AGO Page 239.

CHAMBERLIN, THOMAS.
Volunteered to go to Plattsburgh,
September, 1814, and served 4 days
in Company of Capt. James George
of Topsham.   Ref: Book 52, AGO
Page 70.

‡CHAMBERLIN, WASHINGTON, Stockbridge. Volunteered to go to Plattsburgh, September, 1814, and served
10 days in Capt. Elias Keyes' Company. Pension Certificate of widow,
Asenath, No. 17941.

CHAMBERLIN, WILLIAM,   Strafford.
Volunteered to go to Plattsburgh,
September, 1814, and served in Capt.
Joseph Barrett's Company. Ref: Book
52, AGO Page 41.

*CHAMPION, JOHN.
Served from April 12, 1814 to April
21, 1814 in Capt. Othniel Jewett's
Company, Sumner's Regt.

CHANDLER, CYRIL, Lieutenant or Captain, Strafford. Volunteered to go to
Plattsburgh, September, 1814. Appears
to have served as 2nd Lieutenant in
Capt. Joseph Barrett's Company and
as Captain of a company of his own.
Ref: Book 52, AGO Pages 41 and 42.

*CHANDLER, ELIJAH.
Served in Capt. Briggs' Company,
Col. Jonathan Williams' Regt. Detached Militia in U. S. service 2
months and 13 days, 1812.

*CHANDLER, ISAAC.
Served in Capt. Pettes' Company,
Col. Wm. Williams' Regt. Detached
Militia in U. S. service 3 months
and 9 days, 1812.

CHANDLER, JOHN,   Franklin County.
Volunteered to go to Plattsburgh
Sept. 11, 1814 and served in 15th or
22nd Regt. Ref: Hemenway's Vt. Gazetteer, Vol. 2, Page 391.

*CHANDLER, JOSEPH, Sergeant, Tun-
bridge. Served from June 11, 1813
to June 14, 1813 in Lieut. Bates'
Company, 1 Regt. (Judson's). Volunteered to go to Plattsburgh, September, 1814, and served in Capt. David
Knox's Company.
CHANDLER, JOSIAH.

Served in Capt. Chadwick's Company.
2nd Regt. Ref: R. & L. 1812, AGO
Page 32.

CHANDLER, LEMUEL,   Strafford.
Volunteered to go to Plattsburgh,
September, 1814, and served in Capt.
Cyril Chandler's Company. Ref: Book
52, AGO Page 42.

CHANDLER, RUFUS,   Strafford.
Volunteered to go to Plattsburgh,
September, 1814, and served 5 days
in Capt. Joseph Barrett's Company.
Ref: Book 52, AGO Page 41.

*CHANEY, CLAUDIUS T.
Served in 2 Regt. Vt. Militia commanded by Col. Fifield.

*CHAPIN, CALVIN, Sergeant.
Served in Capt. Phelps' Company, Col.
Jonathan Williams' Regt. Detached
Militia in U. S. service 2 months
and 21 days, 1812.

*CHAPIN, JOEL.
Served in 3 Regt. Vt. Militia commanded by Col. Williams.

*CHAPIN, JOSEPH JR., Sergeant.
Served in 4 Regt. Vt. Militia commanded by Col. Peck.

*CHAPIN, LEVI, Corporal.
Served in 3 Regt. Vt. Militia commanded by Col. Tyler.

*CHAPIN, MYRON,   Jericho.
Served in 3 Regt. (Tyler's) Vt. Mili-
tia. Took part in the Battle of
Plattsburgh. Ref: History of Jericho,
Page 142.

CHAPLIN, JONATHAN G.
Volunteered to go to Plattsburgh,
September, 1814, and served in Capt.
Warren Ellis' Company. Ref: Hem-
enway's Vt. Gazetteer, Vol. 4, Page
42.

CHAPMAN, ELIJAH, Fairfax or Swanton. Served from Aug. 8, 1812 in
company of Capt. Joseph Beeman, Jr.
11th Regt. U. S. Inf. under Col.
Ira Clark. Served from Nov. 1, 1812
to Feb. 28, 1813 in Lieut. V. R.
Goodrich's Company, 11th Regt. Ref:
R. & L. 1812, AGO Page 11; Hemenway's Vt. Gazetteer, Vol. 2, Page
402.

CHAPMAN, ISAAC.
Served from May 1 to June 30, 1814
in Capt. Alexander Brooks' Corps of
Artillery. Ref: R & L. 1812, AGO
Page 31.

‡CHAPMAN, JONATHAN W.
Served in Capt. Morrill's Company.
Pension Certificate No. 18389.

CHAPMAN, JOSEPH.
Served from Nov. 1, 1812 to Feb. 28,
1813 in company of Capt. John Mc-
Neil Jr., 11th Regt. Ref: R. & L.
1812, AGO Page 17.

CHAPMAN, JOSEPH,   Clarendon.
Volunteered to go to Plattsburgh,
September, 1814, and served 4 days
in Capt. Durham Sprague's Company.
Ref: Book 52, AGO Page 128.

CHAPMAN, PHINEAS,   Fairfax.
Volunteered to go to Plattsburgh,
September, 1814, and served 8 days
in Capt. Josiah Grout's Company.
Ref: Book 51, AGO Page 103.

CHAPMAN, RODMAN. Drummer.
Served from April 12, 1814 to April
21, 1814 in Lieut. Justus Foote's
Company, Sumner's Regt. Ref: Book
52, AGO Page 285.

‡*CHAPMAN, ROSWELL.
Served in Capt. Sabin's Company, Col.
Jonathan Williams' Regt. Detached
Militia in U. S. service 2 months and
6 days, 1812. Pension Certificate
No. 14210.

CHAPMAN, THOMAS.
Enlisted June 1, 1812 for 5 years
in Capt. White Youngs' Company,
15th Regt.; on Muster Roll from
Aug. 31, 1814 to Dec. 31, 1814. Ref:
R. & L. 1812, AGO Page 27.

‡CHAPPEL, ELIAS.
Born in Bowman, N. Y.; aged 17
years; 5 feet 9 inches high; light
complexion; light hair; black eyes;
by profession a farmer. Enlisted at
Pawlet April 19, 1814 for period of
the war and served in Capt. Wm.
Miller's Company, Capt. Gideon Spencer's Company and Capt. James Taylor's Company, all in the 30th Regt.;
discharged at Burlington, Vt., 1815.
Pension Certificate No. 3457. Ref:
R. & L. 1812, AGO Pages 53, 54, 55,
57.

CHAPPEL, HYRAM.
Born at Old Canaan, Conn. Enlisted
at Pawlet April 11, 1814 during the
war and served in Capt. Wm. Miller's Company, Capt. Gideon Spencer's Company and Capt. James Taylor's Company, all in the 30th Regt.
Ref: R. & L. 1812, AGO Pages 53,
54, 55, 57.

‡*CHAPPELL, DAVID, Corporal.
Appointed Corporal Sept. 27, 1813
in Capt. Langworthy's Company, Col.
Isaac Clark's Rifle Corps and served
1 month and 21 days. Pension Certificate No. 15485.

*CHAPPELL, HENRY,   Highgate.
Served 3 months and 25 days beginning Sept. 1, 1812, in Capt. Conrade Saxe's Company, Col. Wm. Williams' Regt.; volunteered to go to
Plattsburgh, September, 1814, and
served 5 days in same company.

*CHAPPELL, WILLIAM, Corporal.
Appointed corporal Sept. 27, 1813 and
served 1 month and 21 days in Capt.
Asahel Langworthy's Company, Col.
Isaac Clark's Rifle Regt.

*CHASE, ABNER, Sergeant.
Served in Sumner's Regt. Vt. Militia.

*CHASE, ABRAHAM.
Served in Capt. Preston's Company,
Col. Jonathan Williams' Regt. Detached Militia in U. S. service 2
months and 6 days, 1812.

*CHASE, ALEX.
Served from March 11, 1813 to June
10, 1813 in Capt. Samul Gordon's
Company, 11th Regt. Ref: R. & L.
1812, AGO Page 8.

*CHASE, BENJAMIN.
Served in Sumner's Regt. Vt. Militia.

CHASE, CALEB.   Braintree.
Marched to Plattsburgh Sept. 10, 1814,
serving in Capt. Lot Hudson's Company. Ref: Book 52, AGO Pages 24
and 26.

CHASE, DANIEL.
Served in Capt. Benjamin Bradford's
Company; on Muster Roll from May
31, 1813 to Aug. 31, 1813; joined by
transfer July 22, 1813. Ref: R. & L.
1812, AGO Page 26.

CHASE, ELISHA.
Appointed Ensign 31 Inf. March 8,
1814; 3rd Lieutenant May 1, 1814;
2 Lieutenant Dec. 1, 1814; honorably discharged July 15, 1815. Ref:
Heitman's Historical Register & Dictionary USA; Governor and Coun-
cill Vt. Vol. 6, Page 478.

*CHASE, EZRA,   Calais.
Volunteered to go to Plattsburgh,
September, 1814, and served 10 days
in Capt. Gideon Wheelock's Company.

*CHASE, ISAAC.
Served in Sumner's Regt. Vt. Militia.

*CHASE, JACOB,   Salisbury.
Served from May 1 to June 26, 1814;
no organization given. Also served
in 1 Regt. (Judson's) Vt. Militia.

*CHASE, JAMES.
Served in Capt. Durkee's Company,
Col. Fifield's Regt. Detached Militia
in U. S. service 2 months and 21
days, 1812. Served in Capt. Wright's
Company, Col. Fifield's Regt. Detached Militia in U. S. service 3 months
and 9 days, 1812. Served from April
12, 1814 to April 21, 1814, in Lieut.
Justus Foote's Company, Sumner's
Regt.

*CHASE, JOHN.
Served from June 11, 1813 to June
14, 1813 in Lieut. Bates' Company,
1st Regt. (Judson's).

CHASE, JOHN.
Enlisted March 25, 1813 for 1 year
and 6 months in company of late
Capt. J. Brooks, commanded by Lieut.
John I. Cromwell, Corps of U. S.
Artillery; on Muster Roll from April
30, 1814 to June 30, 1814. Ref: R.
& L. 1812, AGO Page 18.

*CHASE, JOHN, Sergeant.
Served in Capt. Hiram Mason's Company, Col. Fifield's Regt. Detached
Militia in U. S. service 6 months
in 1812.

*CHASE, JONATHAN, Lieutenant-Quar-
termaster, Guilford. Served in 3
Regt. Vt. Militia commanded by Col.
Williams.

‡CHASE, JOSHUA.
Volunteered to go to Plattsburgh,
September, 1814, and served 4 days
in Capt. James George's Company of
Topsham. Pension Certificate No.
33021.

‡*CHASE, NATHAN,   Calais.
Volunteered to go to Plattsburgh,
September, 1814, and served 10 days
in Capt. Gideon Wheelock's Com-
pany. Pension Certificate of widow,
Naomi, No. 25323.

CHASE, NATHANIEL.
Served from May 1 to May 31, 1814
as Master Carpenter in Company of

Artificers commanded by Alexander Parris. Ref: R. & L. 1812, AGO Page 24.

*CHASE, NELSON A., Lieutenant, Calais.
Volunteered to go to Plattsburgh, September, 1814, and served 10 days in Capt. Gideon Wheelock's Company.

CHASE, SAMUEL.
Volunteered to go to Plattsburgh, September, 1814, and served in company of Capt. Ebenezer Spencer of Vershire. Ref: Book 52, AGO Page 48.

CHASE, SETH, Randolph.
Volunteered to go to Plattsburgh, September, 1814, and went as far as Burlington with a 2 horse team to carry guns, serving in Capt. Lebbeus Egerton's Company. Ref: Book 52, AGO Page 94.

CHASE, SILAS W. C., Sergeant.
Served from March 10, 1813 to Aug. 9. 1813 in Lieut. Wm. S. Foster's Company, 11th Regt. Ref: R. & L. 1812, AGO Page 6.

CHASE, STEPHEN.
Enlisted Nov. 1, 1812 in Capt. Weeks' Company, 11th Regt.; on Pay Roll for January and February, 1813. Ref: R. & L. 1812, AGO Page 5.

*CHASE, STEPHEN, JR.
Served in Capt. Rogers' Company, Col. Fifield's Regt. Detached Militia in U. S. service 10 days in 1812.

*CHASE, THEODORE.
Served in Capt. Noyce's Company, Col. Jonathan Williams' Regt. Detached Militia in U. S. service 2 months and 6 days, 1812.

*CHASE, THUSTIN.
Served in Sumner's Regt. Vt. Militia.

*CHASE, TRUMAN, Ensign.
Served in 2 Regt. 3 Brig., 3 Div., Vt. Militia.

CHASE, WILLIAM, Corporal.
Served in Capt. Benjamin Bradford's Company; on Muster Roll from May 31, 1813 to Aug. 31, 1813; joined by transfer July 22, 1813. Ref: R. & L. 1812, AGO Page 26.

‡CHASE, ZENAS.
Served in Capt. Wright's Company. Pension Certificate of widow, Elizabeth, No. 10499.

CHATTERTON, BENJAMIN, Middlesex.
Volunteered to go to Plattsburgh, September, 1814, and served in Capt. Holden Putnam's Company, 4th Regt. (Peck's). Ref: Hemenway's Vt. Gazetteer, Vol. 4, Page 250.

*CHATTERTON, HOYT.
Served in Regt. of Riflemen, Vt. Volunteers, from September to November, 1813.

‡*CHATTERTON, LEVERETT, Sergeant.
Served in Capt. Brown's Company. Col. Martindale's Regt. Detached

Militia in U. S. service 2 months and 14 days, 1812. Pension Certificate No. 1214. Pension Certificate of widow, Mary Jackson, No. 11630.

CHATTERTON, SAMUEL.
Appointed 3 Lieutenant April 21, 1814; 2nd Lieutenant Aug. 1, 1814; honorably discharged June 15, 1815. On Pay Roll of Corps of Light Dragoons to June 30, 1814; promoted to 2nd Lieutenant 48th Regt. Inf. Ref: Heitman's Historical Register and Dictionary USA; R. & L. 1812, AGO Page 20.

*CHATTERTON, WAIT.
Enlisted Sept. 14, 1813 in Capt. Isaac Finch's Company, Col. Isaac Clark's Rifle Regt.; transferred to Capt. Asahel Scovell's Company, same Regiment, Oct. 25, 1813, and served to Nov. 8, 1813.

*CHEENEY, JAMES.
Served in Sumner's Regt. Vt. Militia.

CHEENEY, WILLIAM A., Pownal.
Served from Sept. 1, 1814 to June 16, 1815 in Capt. Sanford's' Company, 30th Inf. Ref: R. & L. 1812, AGO Page 23.

CHENEY, PAUL J., Waterford.
Served from July 25, 1814 to June 16, 1815 in Capt. Sanford's Company, 30th Inf. Ref: R. & L. 1812, AGO Page 23.

*CHEEVER, NATHANIEL.
Served in Capt. Mason's Company, Col. Fifield's Regt. Detached Militia in U. S. service 2 months and 14 days, 1812.

‡CHELLIS, JOHN, Shoreham.
Volunteered to go to Plattsburgh, September, 1814, and served 6 days in Capt. Samuel Hand's Company. Pension Certificate of widow, Sally, No. 27333.

*CHELLIS, SETH.
Served from April 12, 1814 to May 20, 1814 in Company of Capt. James Gray Jr., Sumner's Regt.

*CHELLIS, STEWART, Enosburgh.
Served from Oct. 14, 1813 to Nov. 9, 1813 in Capt. Asahel Scoville's Company, Col. Clark's Rifle Regt.

‡CHENEY, ABIATHAR.
Served in Capt. Micah Brown's Company. Pension Certificate of widow, Catharine, No. 21404.

‡CHENEY, DANIEL, Washington.
Was at the battle of Plattsburgh Sept. 11, 1814, serving in Capt. David Robinson's Company. Pension Certificate of widow. Sophronia, No. 30790.

CHENEY, ELISHUA.
Served in War of 1812 and was captured by Troops Sept. 17, 1814 at Fort Erie. Discharged Nov. 8th. Ref: Records of Naval Records and Library, Navy Dept.

CHENEY, EPHRAIM, Brandon.
Volunteered to go to Plattsburgh, September, 1814, and served 8 days

in Capt. Micah Brown's Company.
Ref: Book 52, AGO Pages 132 and
163.

CHENEY, GILES,   Washington.
Volunteered to go to Plattsburgh,
September, 1814, and served in Capt.
Amos Stiles' Company. Ref: Book
52, AGO Page 36.

*CHENEY, HOWARD.
Served in Capt. Strait's Company,
Col. Martindale's Regt. Detached
Militia in U. S. service 2 months and
13 days, 1812.

CHENEY, J. W.,   St. Albans.
Enlisted April 28, 1813 for 1 year in
Capt. John Wires' Company, 30th
Regt. Ref: R. & L. 1812, AGO Page
40.

*CHENEY, JONAS.
Served in Sumner's Regt. Vt. Militia.

*CHENEY, JOSEPH,   Washington.
Served in Capt. Walker's Company,
Col. Fifield's Regt. Detached Militia
in U. S. service 6 months and 3
days, 1812. Enlisted Sept. 29, 1813
and served 1 month and 19 days as
sergeant in Capt. Bennett's Company,
Col. Dixon's Regt. Volunteered to
go to Plattsburgh, September, 1814,
and served in Capt. Amos Stiles'
Company.

*CHENEY, PAUL D., Surgeon, Addison.
Served with Hospital Attendants, Vt.

CHENEY, SAMUEL,   Brandon.
Volunteered to go to Plattsburgh,
September, 1814, and served 8 days
in Capt. Micah Brown's Company.
Ref: Book 52, AGO Pages 132 and 133.

*CHENEY, THOMAS.
Served in Capt. Briggs' Company,
Col. Jonathan Williams' Regt. Detached Militia in U. S. service 2
months and 13 days, 1812. Served
from April 12, 1814 to May 20, 1814
in Capt. George Fisher's Company,
Sumner's Regt.

‡*CHENEY, WILLIAM, Corporal.
Served in Capt. Wheeler's Company,
Col. Fifield's Regt. Detached Militia
in U. S. service 6 months and 4
days, 1812. Served from March 3,
1813 to June 2, 1813 in Capt. Phineas
Williams' Company, 11th Regt. Pension Certificate of widow, Palace D., No.
17706. Ref: R. & L. 1812, AGO Page
14.

*CHERRY, ABNER T.
Served in Capt. Daimeville's Company. Pension Certificate No. 18483.

CHESLEY, JONATHAN,   Vershire.
Volunteered to go to Plattsburgh,
September, 1814, and served 3 days
in Capt. Ira Corse's Company. Ref:
Book 52, AGO Page 91.

*CHESLEY, PHILIP G.
Served in Capt. Taylor's Company,
Col. Fifield's Regt. Detached Militia
in U. S. service 6 months, 1812.

*CHESTER, DANIEL.
Served in Capt. Parsons' Company,
Col. Jonathan Williams' Regt. Detached Militia in U. S. service 2
months and 13 days, 1812.

*CHICKERING, ZACKERIAH.
Served in Capt. Morrill's Company,
Col. Fifield's Regt. Detached Militia
in U. S. service 6 months and 5
days, 1812.

*CHILD, ALEXANDER.
Served in Capt. Walker's Company,
Col. Fifield's Regt. Detached Militia
in U. S. service 3 months and 9 days,
1812.

*CHILD, EZRA, Surgeon's Mate.
Served in 2 Regt. Vt. Militia commanded by Col. Fifield.

‡CHILD, JOHN,   Shoreham.
Volunteered to go to Plattsburgh,
September, 1814 and served 6 days
in Capt. Samuel Hand's Company.
Also served in Capt. S. Wright's
Company. Pension Certificate of
widow, Mahala, No. 31792. Ref: Rev.
J. F. Goodhue's History of Shore-
ham, Page 108.

*CHILD, RUFUS.
Served in Corning's Detachment, Vt.
Militia.

*CHILDS, ALEXANDER.
Served in Capt. Dorrance's Company,
Col. Wm. Williams' Regt. Detached
Militia in U. S. service 4 months and
24 days, 1812.

CHILDS, BENJAMIN, Corporal.
Served from Nov. 1, 1812 to Feb.
28, 1813 in Capt. Phineas Williams'
Company, 11th Regt. Ref: R. & L.
1812, AGO Page 15.

‡CHILDS, DANIEL, H.
Enlisted May 1, 1813 for 1 year in
Capt. Simeon Wright's Company.
Pension Certificate of widow, Mary,
No. 33356.

CHILDS, EBENEZER,   Brandon.
Volunteered to go to Plattsburgh,
September, 1814, and served 6 days;
no organization given. Ref: Book
51, AGO Page 273.

*CHILDS, GARDNER, Corporal.
Served Sept. 27-28, 1813, in Capt.
Elijah W. Wood's Company, Dixon's
Regt.

*CHILDS, JACOB.
Served in Capt. Wheeler's Company,
Col. Fifield's Regt. Detached Militia
in U. S. service 3 months and 16
days, 1812.

CHILDS, NATHANIEL.
Enlisted May 21, 1813 for 1 year in
Capt. Simeon Wright's Company.
Ref: R. & L. 1812, AGO Page 51.

CHILDS, RHODOLPHUS R.
Appointed Ensign 30 Inf. April 30,
1813, and served in Capt. Simeon
Wright's Company; 3rd Lieutenant
March 5, 1814; honorably discharged
June 15. 1815. Ref: Heitman's His-
torical Register & Dictionary USA;
R. & L. 1812, AGO Page 51.

*CHILSON, DANIEL.
Served in Capt. Phelps' Company,
Col. Wm. Williams' Regt. Detached
Militia in U. S. service 4 months,
1812.

*CHILSON, OLIVER.
Served in Capt. Dorrance's Company,
Col. Wm. Williams' Regt. Detached
Militia in U. S. service 4 months and
29 days, 1812.

*CHIPMAN, LEVI, Corporal.
Served in 2 Regt. Vt. Militia commanded by Col. Fifield.

*CHIPMAN, NORMAN.
Served in Capt. Thompson's Company.
Pension Certificate No. 34413.

*CHIPMAN, THOMAS.
Served in Tyler's Regt. Vt. Militia.

*CHIPMAN, THOMAS, Captain.
Served in 3 Regt. (Tyler's) Vt. Militia.

CHIPMAN, TIMOTHY F., Brig. Gen.
Volunteered to go to Plattsburgh,
September, 1814; crossed the lake
from Burlington but was not in the
battle; went with Company of Cavalry
made up of men from Shoreham and
Bridport. Ref: Rev. J. F. Goodhue's
History of Shoreham. Page 104;
also biographical sketch in Hemenway's Vt. Gazetteer, Vol. 1, Page
100.

*CHISMORE, WILLIAM.
Served in Capt. Mason's Company,
Col. Fifield's Regt. Detached Militia
in U. S. service 4 months and 21
days, 1812.

CHITTEN, STEWART, Waggoner.
Served from Oct. 14, 1813 to Nov.
10, 1813 in Capt. Asahel Scovell's
Company, Col. Clark's Rifle Regt. Ref:
Book 52, AGO Page 274.

CHITTENDEN, BATES,   Fairfax.
Served from Aug. 8, 1812 in com-
pany of Capt. Joseph Beeman Jr. 11th
Regt. U. S. Inf. under Col. Ira
Clark. Ref: Hemenway's Vt. Ga-
zetteer, Vol. 2, Page 402.

*CHITTENDEN, CLER.
Served from April 12, 1814 to April
15, 1814 in Lieut. Justus Foote's Company, Sumner's Regt.

CHITTENDEN, EBNER.
Served in Capt. Jewett's Company.
Pension Certificate No. 9025.

*CHITTENDEN, GILES.
Served from Oct. 11, 1813 to Oct. 17,
1813 in Capt. John Munson's Company, 3 Regt. (Tyler's).

CHITTENDEN, JOSEPH H.
Volunteered to go to Plattsburgh,
September, 1814, serving 11 days in
Capt. Wait Branch's Company. Ref:
Book 51, AGO Page 16.

*CHITTENDEN, MIRAN.
Served in Sumner's Regt. Vt. Militia.

CHITTENDEN, THOMAS, Lieutenant.
Appointed Ensign 30 Inf. April 30,
1813; 3rd Lieutenant Aug. 15, 1813;
2nd Lieutenant July 10, 1814; Regt.
Paymaster Jan. 1815; honorably discharged June 15, 1815. Ref: Heitman's Historical Register & Dictionary USA.

CHOICE, JAMES,   Franklin County.
Volunteered to go to Plattsburgh
Sept. 11, 1814 and served in 15th or
22nd Regt. Ref: Hemenway's Vt. Gazetteer, Vol. 2, Page 391.

CHRISTIAN, LEVI H.
Served in Capt. Weeks' Company,
11th Regt.; on Pay Roll of company
for January and February, 1813. Ref:
R. & L. 1812, AGO Page 5.

CHRISTIE, DANIEL.
Served in Capt. Charles Follett's Com-
pany, 11th Regt.; on Pay Roll for
January and February, 1812. Ref: R.
& L. 1812, AGO Page 12.

CHRISTIE, ROBERT, Lieutenant, Marshfield. Volunteered to go to Plattsburgh, September, 1814, and served
9 days in Capt. James English's Company. Ref: Book 52, AGO Page 248.

CHUBB, ALBY, Corporal.
Served in 1st Regt. Detached Militia
of Vt. in U. S. service at Champlain
commencing Nov. 18 and ending Nov.
19, 1812.

‡*CHUBB, ARBA, Corporal.
Served in Capt. Ormsbee's Company,
Col. Martindale's Regt. Detached Militia in U. S. service 2 months and
14 days, 1812. Pension Certificate
No. 422. Pension Certificate of
widow, Sarah, No. 30932. (1st name
may possibly be Hervey or Herby).

CHUBB, JOHN,   Corinth.
Volunteered to go to Plattsburgh,
September, 1814, and served in Capt.
Abel Jackman's Company. Ref: Book
52, AGO Page 44.

CHUBB, JOSEPH,   Corinth.
Volunteered to go to Plattsburgh,
September, 1814, and served in Capt.
Abel Jackman's Company. Ref: Book
52, AGO Page 44.

CHUBB, WILLIAM,   Barre.
Volunteered to go to Plattsburgh,
September, 1814, and served 10 days
in Capt. Warren Ellis' Company. Ref:
Book 52, AGO Page 242.

*CHUNN, ZACHERIAH.
Served with Hospital Attendants, Vt.

*CHURCH, DAVID.
Enlisted Sept. 27, 1812 in Capt.
Charles Follett's Company, 11th Regt.;
on Pay Roll for advance pay and retained bounty to May 31, 1813. Served
in 1 Regt. (Martindale's) Vt. Militia. Ref: R. & L. 1812, AGO Page
13.

*CHURCH, ERASTUS, Cambridge or Fair-
field. Enlisted Sept. 25, 1813 and
served 1 month and 23 days in Capt.
Charles Bennett's Company, Dixon's

Regt. Volunteered to go to Plattsburgh, September, 1814, and served 8 days in Capt. Salmon Green's Company.

CHURCH, HARVEY, 1st Lieutenant, Fair Haven. Volunteered to go to Plattsburgh, September, 1814; no organization given. Ref: Hemenway's Vt. Gazetteer, Vol. 3, Page 711.

*CHURCH, IRA. Served in Capt. Chas. Bennett's Company, Col. Dixon's Regt. Detached Militia in U. S. service 1 month and 2 days, 1813; date of enlistment Sept. 25, 1813.

CHURCH, IRA, Swanton or St. Albans. Enlisted Sept. 25, 1813 and served 1 month and 23 days as a Musician in Capt. Eldridge's Company, Col. Dixon's Regt. Volunteered to go to Plattsburgh, September, 1814, and served in Capt. Samuel H. Farnsworth's Company.

*CHURCH, ISAAC. Served from June 11, 1813 to June 14, 1813 in Capt. Thomas Dorwin's Company, 1st Regt. 2nd Brig., 3rd Div.

CHURCH, JACOB JR. Volunteered to go to Plattsburgh, September, 1814, and went as far as Bolton, Vt., serving 4 days in Lieut. Phineus Kimball's Company, West Fairlee. Ref: Book 52, AGO Page 46.

CHURCH, JOHN. Volunteered to go to Plattsburgh, September, 1814, and served 4 days in Capt. James George's Company of Topsham. Ref: Book 52, AGO Page 70.

CHURCH, LEMUEL. Volunteered to go to Plattsburgh, September, 1814, and went as far as Bolton, Vt., serving 4 days in Lieut. Phineus Kimball's Company, West Fairlee. Ref: Book 52, AGO Pages 46 and 47.

CHURCH, MOSES. Enlisted Jan. 22, 1813 in Capt. Edgerton's Company. 11th Regt.; died March 2, 1813. Ref: R. & L. 1812, AGO Pages 2 and 3.

*CHURCH, NEHEMIAH, Lieutenant. Served in 3 Regt. Vt. Militia commanded by Col. Williams.

*CHURCH, NOAH, Drummer. Served as Drummer in 1 Regt. Vt. Militia commanded by Col. Martindale.

*CHURCH, ORREN. Served in Capt. Phelps' Company, Col. Wm. Williams' Regt. Detached Militia in U. S. service 5 months, 1812.

CHURCH, RUEL. Volunteered to go to Plattsburgh, September, 1814, and went as far as Bolton, Vt., serving 4 days in Lieut. Phineus Kimball's Company, West Fairlee. Ref: Book 52, AGO Page 46.

‡CHURCH, SAMUEL J. Served in Capt. McEntosh's Company. Pension Certificate of widow, Polly, No. 42926.

CHURCH, SIMON. Served from April 13, 1814 to April 21, 1814 in Capt. Salmon Foster's Company, Sumner's Regt. Ref: Book 52, AGO Page 284.

CHURCH, WILLARD, Fifer, Vershire. Volunteered to go to Plattsburgh, September, 1814, and served 3 days in Capt. Ira Corse's Company. Ref: Book 52, AGO Page 91.

‡*CHURCHILL, ALVA, Enosburgh. Served from Oct. 15, 1813 to Nov. 17, 1813 in Capt. Asahel Scovell's Company, Col. Clark's Rifle Regt. Pension Certificate of widow, Elmira S., No. 27483.

*CHURCHILL, DARIUS, Enosburgh. Enlisted Oct. 15, 1813 and served to Nov. 17, 1813 in Capt. Asahel Scovell's Company, Col. Clark's Rifle Corps.

CHURCHILL, EPHRAIM, Franklin County. Volunteered to go to Plattsburgh Sept. 11, 1814 and served in 15th or 22nd Regt. Ref: Hemenway's Vt. Gazetteer, Vol. 2, Page 391.

CHURCHILL, FRANCIS W. Volunteered to go to Plattsburgh, September, 1814, and went as far as Bolton, Vt. serving 4 days in Lieut. Phineus Kimball's Company, West Fairlee. Ref: Book 52, AGO Pages 46 and 47.

‡*CHURCHILL, GILBERT. Served from June 11, 1813 to June 14, 1813 in Lieut. Bates' Company, 1st Regt. Pension Certificate No. 27909.

‡CHURCHILL, ISAAC. Served in Capt. Phelps' Company. Pension Certificate of widow, Julia A., No. 31138.

‡CHURCHILL, ISAAC. Served in Capt. N. S. Clark's Company. Pension Certificate of widow, Arvilla, No. 38190.

CHURCHILL, ISAAC, Woodstock. Served from March 27, 1813 to June 26, 1813 in Capt. Phineas Williams' Company, 11th Regt. Ref: R. & L. 1812, AGO Page 14.

*CHURCHILL, JAMES JR. Served in Dixon's Regt. Vt. Militia.

CHURCHILL, JANNA JR. Served from Sept. 25, 1813 to Oct. 2, 1813 in Capt. Elijah W. Wood's Company, Dixon's Regt. Ref: Book 52, AGO Page 273.

CHURCHILL, JOHN. Born in Berne, N. Y. Served from Sept. 10, 1814 to June 19, 1815 in Capt. Taylor's Company, 30th Regt. Ref: R. & L. 1812, AGO Page 23.

CHURCHILL, NATHANIEL, Hubbardton. Enlisted May 15, 1813 for 1 year. On Muster Roll of Capt. Daniel Farrington's Company, 30th Regt. (also commanded by Capt. Simeon Wright) from March 1, 1814 to April 30, 1814. Pay Roll of discharged men of Capt. Taylor's Company, 30th Regt. shows service from March 1, 1814 to July 14, 1814. Ref: R. & L. 1812, AGO Pages 23, 50, 51.

*CHURCHILL, NOAH, Lieutenant.
Served in Corning's Detachment, Vt. Militia.

CHURCHILL, ROBERT W.
Volunteered to go to Plattsburgh, September, 1814, and served 4 days in Capt. Aaron Kidder's Company or Lieut. Phineus Kimball's Company, West Fairlee. Ref: Book 52, AGO Pages 46 and 65.

*CHURCHILL, SETH.
Served in 3 Regt. Vt. Militia commanded by Col. Williams.

CHURCHILL, SILAS,   Hubbardton.
Volunteered to go to Plattsburgh, September, 1814, and served 6 days in Capt. Henry J. Horton's Company as a teamster. Ref: Book 52, AGO Page 142.

CHURCHILL, SYLVESTER.
Appointed 1st Lt. 3 Artillery March 12, 1812; Captain Aug. 15, 1813; transferred to Artillery Corps May 12, 1814; Major, Asst. Inspector General Aug. 29, 1813 to June 15, 1815; retained May 17, 1815 as Captain Corps Artillery. Resided in Montpelier for a few years previous to 1809 when he removed to Windsor and became one of the proprietors of the Vt. Republican Newspaper. Ref: Heitman's Historical Register & Dictionary; Hemenway's Vt. Gazetteer, Vol. 4, Page 297.

*CHURCHILL, THOMAS F.
Enlisted Sept. 25, 1813 and served 1 month and 23 days in Capt. Wood's Company, Col. Dixon's Regt.

*CHURCHILL, WILLIAM L., Ensign.
Volunteered to go to Plattsburgh, September, 1814, and served 5 days in Capt. Aaron Kidder's Company. Also served in 4 Regt. (Peck's). Ref: Book 52, AGO Page 65.

*CILLEY, WILLIAM.
Served in Capt. Birge's Company, Col. Dixon's Regt. Detached Militia in U. S. service 1 month and 23 days, 1813.

*CISCO, JERRY.
Served in Capt. Sanford's Company. Pension Certificate No. 30893.

CISCO, URIAH.
Enlisted Sept. 25, 1813 in Capt. Amos Robinson's Company, Dixon's Regt.; transferred to Rifle Corps Oct. 3, 1813. Ref: Book 52, AGO Page 271.

‡CLAFLIN, JONATHAN G.,   Barre.
Volunteered to go to Plattsburgh, September, 1814, and served 9 days in Capt. Warren Ellis Company. Pension Certificate No. 31025.

CLAFLIN, NATHAN, Ensign,   Hancock.
Volunteered to go to Plattsburgh, September, 1814, and served 7 days under Capt. Asaph Smith. Ref: Book 51, AGO Pages 20, 21, 27.

*CLAFLIN, OBED.
Served in Capt. O. Lowry's Company, Col. William William's Regt. Detached Militia in U. S. service 4 months and 26 days, 1812.

*CLAFLIN, SYLVANUS.
Served in Capt. Phelps' Company, Col. Jonathan Williams' Regt. Detached Militia in U. S. service 2 months and 21 days, 1812.

CLAFLIN, TIMOTHY P.
Volunteered to go to Plattsburgh, September, 1814, and served 7 days in Capt. Asaph Smith's Company. Ref: Book 51, AGO Page 20.

CLAFLIN, WILLIAM.
Volunteered to go to Plattsburgh, September, 1814, and served 7 days in Capt. Asaph Smith's Company. Ref: Book 51, AGO Page 20.

CLAIR, RICHARD M.
Served in Capt. Alexander Brooks' Corps of Artillery; on Pay Roll to June 30, 1814. Ref: R. & L. 1812, AGO Page 31.

*CLAPP, EZEKIEL, Sergeant.
Served as Sergeant in Corning's Detachment, Vt. Militia and as Ensign in 4 Regt. (Peck's) Vt. Militia.

*CLAPP, LEONARD.
Served in Corning's Detachment, Vt. Militia.

*CLAPP, RUFUS, Sergeant.
Served in 4 Regt. Vt. Militia commanded by Col. Peck.

‡*CLAPP, SEARS.
Served with Hospital Attendants, Vt. Also served in Capt. Burnap's Company. Pension Certificate of widow, Phebe, No. 25466.

CLARE, WILLIAM.
Served in Capt. Haig's Corps of Light Dragoons; on Pay Roll to June 30, 1814; prisoner of war. Ref: R. & L. 1812, AGO Page 20.

*CLARK, A. W.
Served in Capt. Dorrance's Company. Col. Wm. Williams' Regt. Detached Militia in U. S. service 4 months and 23 days, 1812.

*CLARK, ABEL, Fifer, Musician.
Served from April 12, 1814 to May 29, 1814 in Capt. George Fisher's Company, Sumner's Regt.

CLARK, AMASA W.,   Huntington.
Served from Oct. 11, 1813 to Oct. 17, 1813 in Capt. John Munson's Company of Cavalry, 3rd Regt. Volunteered to go to Plattsburgh, September, 1814, and was at the battle, serving in Capt. Josiah N. Barrows' Company. Ref: R. & L. 1812, AGO Page 36; Book 51, AGO Page 77.

‡*CLARK, AMOS, Sergeant, Highgate. Served in Capt. Saxe's Company, Col. Wm. Williams' Regt. Detached Militia in U. S. service 3 months and 24 days, 1812. Served from June 11, 1813 to June 14, 1813 in Capt. Ithiel Stone's Company of Militia, 1st Regt. 2nd Brig., 3rd Div., as a sergeant. Also served in Capt. John Gilbert's Company. Pension Certificate No. 6490.

*CLARK, AMOS W. Served in 3 Regt. Vt. Militia commanded by Col. Tyler.

CLARK, ANDREW. Served from March 1 to June 30, 1814 in Capt. Alexander Brooks' Corps of Artillery. Ref: R. & L. 1812, AGO Page 31.

*CLARK, ASAHEL, Addison. Volunteered to go to Plattsburgh, September, 1814, and served 9 days in Capt. George Fisher's Company, Sumner's Regt.; was in the battle; served from April 12, 1814 to May 20, 1814 in same company.

*CLARK, B. Served in 1 Regt. Vt. Militia commanded by Col. Judson.

*CLARK, BARTLET B., Sergeant. Served under Captains Durkee and Wright, Col. Fifield's Regt. Detached Militia in U. S. service 6 months, 1812.

CLARK, CALVIN, Corporal. Volunteered to go to Plattsburgh, September, 1814, and served in Capt. Jonathan Jennings' Company, Chelsea. Ref: Book 52, AGO Pages 79 and 81.

CLARK, CHARLES P. Served in Capt. Barns' Company, Col. Wm. Williams' Regt. Detached Militia in U. S. service 5 months, 1812. Ref: Book 53, AGO Page 13.

CLARK, CHARLES W. Served from April 14, 1814 to June 3, 1814 in Capt. Gideon Spencer's Company and Capt. James Taylor's Company, 30th Regt. Ref: R. & L. 1812, AGO Pages 53 and 57.

CLARK, CHESTER, Corporal. Served in 1st Regt. Detached Militia of Vt. in U. S. service at Champlain commencing Nov. 18 and ending Nov. 19, 1812.

CLARK, DAVID, Barnard. Served from May 31, 1813 in Capt. Nehemiah Noble's Company, 31st U. S. Inf. Ref: Wm. M. Newton's History of Barnard, Vol. 1, Page 95.

*CLARK, DAVID, Whiting. Served from July 9 to Dec. 8, 1812 in Capt. Robbins' Company, Col. Wm. Williams' Regt. Enlisted Sept. 25, 1813 and served 1 month and 23 days in Capt. Amos Robinson's Company, Col. Dixon's Regt. Served from April 13, 1814 to April 21, 1814 and also served 9 days in September, 1814, as a Plattsburgh volunteer in Capt. Salmon Foster's Company. Sumner's Regt.

*CLARK, EBENEZER, Fife Major. Served in 3 Regt. Vt. Militia commanded by Col. Williams.

CLARK, ELAM, Williamstown. Enlisted from Jan. 9, 1813, to February, 1813, in Capt. Edgerton's Company, 11th Regt. Ref: R. & L. 1812, AGO Page 3. Volunteered to go to Plattsburgh, September, 1814, and was in the battle Sept. 11th, serving 5 days in Capt. David Robinson's Company. Ref: Book 52, AGO Pages 2 and 10.

*CLARK, ELI. Served in Capt. Noyes' Company, Col. Jonathan Williams' Regt. Detached Militia in U. S. service 2 months and 6 days, 1812. Volunteered to go to Plattsburgh, September, 1814, and served 7 days in Capt. Oliver Mason's Company as a substitute for Asa Eaton of Rochester.

CLARK, ELIHUE. Served from April 30, 1813 to April 30, 1814 in Capt. Daniel Farrington's Company (also commanded by Capt. Simeon Wright) 30th Regt. Ref: R. & L. 1812, AGO Pages 50 and 51.

*CLARK, ELISHA, Pawlet. Served in Capt. Scovell's Company, Col. Martindale's Regt. Detached Militia in U. S. service 1 month and 14 days, 1812. Also served in Sumner's Regt. Vt. Militia.

*CLARK, FRANCIS L. Served from June 11, 1813 to June 14, 1813 in Capt. Ithiel Stone's Company, 1st Regt. 2nd Brig., 3rd Div.

*CLARK, FREDERICK. Served from Oct. 11, 1813 to Oct. 17, 1813 in Capt. Stephen Brown's Company, 3rd Regt. (Tyler's).

CLARK, GUY. Served from Jan. 13, 1813 to June 8, 1813 in Capt. John W. Weeks' Company, 11th Regt. Ref: R. & L. 1812, AGO Pages 4 and 5.

‡*CLARK, HIRAM. Enlisted Sept. 25, 1813 and served 1 month and 23 days in Capt. A. Robinson's Company, Col. Dixon's Regt. Also served in Capt. Robins' Company. Pension Certificate No. 21123.

CLARK, ISAAC, Bennington. Appointed Colonel 11 Inf. March 12, 1812; transferred to 48 Inf. April 27, 1814; 26th Inf. May 12, 1814; honorably discharged June 15, 1815; died Jan. 31, 1822. Ref: Heitman's Historical Register & Dictionary USA.

CLARK, ISAAC JR. Appointed Ensign 11 Inf. Dec. 31, 1812; 3rd Lieutenant May 1, 1813; 2nd Lieutenant Aug. 14, 1813; 1st Lieutenant Sept., 1814; honorably discharged June 15, 1815; reinstated Dec. 2, 1815 in 5 Inf.; transferred to 6 Inf. May 17, 1816; Captain Aug. 27, 1822; Major, Quartermaster July 7, 1838; brevet Major Aug. 7, 1832 for 10 years faithful service in 1 grade; drowned July 22, 1842. Ref: Heitman's Historical Register & Dictionary USA.

ROSTER WAR 1812-14   103

CLARK, ISAAC,   Pittsford.
Served from Feb. 15, 1813 to May
14, 1813 in Capt. Charles Follett's
Company, 11th Regt. Volunteered to
go to Plattsburgh, September, 1814,
and served 8 days in Capt. Caleb
Hendee's Company. Ref: R. & L. 1812,
AGO Page 13; Book 52, AGO Pages
125 and 150.

*CLARK, JAMES.
Served with Hospital Attendants, Vt.

*CLARK, JAMES W.
Served in 1 Regt. Vt. Militia commanded by Col. Judson.

‡*CLARK, JESSE.
Served in Corning's Detachment, Vt.
Militia and 4 Regt. (Peck's). Vt.
Militia. Also served in Capt. Mon-
son's Company. Pension Certificate
of widow, Sarepta, No. 7317.

CLARK, JOHN, Sergeant, Franklin County. Enlisted April 22, 1812 for 5
years in Capt. White Youngs' Company, 15th Regt.; on Muster Roll
from Aug. 31, 1814 to Dec. 31, 1814.
Ref: R. & L. 1812, AGO Page 27.

CLARK, JOHN.
Served in Capt. Phineas Williams'
Company, 11th Regt.; on Pay Roll of
company for January and February,
1813. Ref: R. & L. 1812, AGO
Page 15.

‡*CLARK, JOHN F.
Served in Capt. S. Pettes' Company,
Col. Wm. Williams' Regt. Detached
Militia in U. S. service 3 months and
14 days, 1812. Pension Certificate
of widow, Susanna, No. 5558.

‡CLARK, JOHN H.
Served in Capt. Thomas Waterman's
Company. Pension Certificate No.
18492. Pension Certificate of widow,
Eunice D., No. 33141.

CLARK, JONATHAN,   Strafford.
Served in Capt. Benjamin S. Edgerton's Company, 11th Regt.; on Pay
Roll for September and October, 1812,
and January and February, 1813.
Ref: R. & L. 1812, AGO Pages 1
and 2.

*CLARK, JOSEPH.
Served from April 12, 1814 to April
21, 1814 in Capt. Eseck Sprague's
Company, Sumner's Regt.

CLARK, JOSEPH P., Fairfax or Swanton. Served in Company of Capt.
Joseph Beeman Jr., 11th Regt. U.
S. Inf. under Col. Ira Clark, from
Aug. 8, 1812. Served in Lieut. V.
R. Goodrich's Company, 11th Regt.;
on Pay Roll for January and February, 1813, and from July 15 to Dec.
8, 1813. Served in Capt. Sanford's
Company, 30th Inf. from Sept. 1,
1814 to June 16, 1815. Ref: R. & L.
1812, AGO Pages 11 and 23; Hemenway's Vt. Gazetteer, Vol. 2, Pages
402 and 444.

CLARK, JOSIAH, Corporal. Woodstock.
Served in Capt. Phineas Williams'
Company, 11th Regt.; on Pay Roll

for January and February, 1813;
absent with leave, not paid. Ref:
R. & L. 1812, AGO Page 15.

*CLARK, JUDSON. Drummer.
Served from June 11, 1813 to June
14, 1813 in Capt. Hezekiah Barns'
Company, 1st Regt. 2nd Brig., 3rd
Div.

*CLARK, JULIUS C. (or D.), Sergeant,
Tinmouth. Served in Capt. Hotchkiss' Company, Col. Martindale's
Regt. Detached Militia in U. S. service 2 months and 13 days, 1812.
Appointed Quartermaster Sergeant
Sept. 15, 1813 in Col. Isaac Clark's
Volunteer Rifle Corps. Served as sergeant in 1st Regt. Detached Militia
of Vt. in U. S. service at Champlain
commencing Nov. 18 and ending Nov.
19, 1812.

*CLARK, LEVI,   Johnson.
Enlisted Sept. 25, 1813 and served
1 month and 23 days in Capt. Thomas
Waterman's Company, Col. Dixon's
Regt.; volunteered to go to Plattsburgh, September, 1814, and served
10 days in same company.

‡CLARK, LYMAN, Corporal, Addison.
Volunteered to go to Plattsburgh,
September, 1814, and served 9 days
in Capt. George Fisher's Company,
Sumner's Regt.; was in the battle.
Pension Certificate No. 32728.

CLARK, MOSES A.,   Orwell.
Volunteered to go to Plattsburgh,
September, 1814, and served in Capt.
Wait Branch's Company. Ref: Book
51, AGO Page 16.

CLARK, N., Orderly Sergeant.
Served in 1st Regt. Detached Militia
of Vt. in U. S. service at Champlain
commencing Nov. 18 and ending Nov.
19, 1812.

*CLARK, NAHUM.
Served in Capt. Brown's Company,
Col. Martindale's Regt. Detached
Militia in U. S. service 2 months and
14 days, 1812.

‡*CLARK, NATHANIEL,   Barnard.
Served in Capt. Phelps' Company,
Col. Jonathan Williams' Regt. Detached Militia in U. S. service 2
months and 21 days, 1812. Also
served in Capt. Philips' Company.
Pension Certificate No. 12535.

CLARK, NEWMAN S.
Born at Bolton, Vt.; appointed Ensign 11 Inf. March 12, 1812; 2nd
Lieut. March 13, 1813; 1st Lieutenant Aug. 15, 1813; Regimental Adjutant Aug., 1813 to June, 1814;
Captain Oct. 1, 1814; transferred to
6 Inf. May 17, 1815; transferred to
2 Inf. March 22, 1819; Major July
21, 1834; Lt. Colonel 8 Inf. July 7,
1838; Colonel 6 Inf. June 29, 1846;
brevet Captain July 25, 1814 for his
gallantry and good conduct in the
battle of Niagara; died Oct. 17, 1860.
Served as Adjutant, 11th Regt., Capt.
Phineas Williams' Company; on Pay
Roll for January and February, 1813.
Ref: Heitman's Historical Register &
Dictionary; R. & L. 1812, AGO Page
15.

*CLARK, NORTHROP, Sergeant.
Served in Capt. Ormsbee's Company,
Col. Martindale's Regt. Detached
Militia in U. S. service 2 months and
14 days, 1812.

‡*CLARK, OLIVER,   Thetford.
Marched for Plattsburgh, September,
1814, and went as far as Bolton, Vt.,
serving 6 days in Capt. Salmon Howard's Company, 2nd Regt. Pension
Certificate of widow, Mehitabel, No.
4221.

‡CLARK, ORANGE,   Williamstown.
Volunteered to go to Plattsburgh,
September, 1814, and served 8 days
in Capt. David Robinson's Company.
Pension Certificate No. 30874.

‡CLARK, ORANGE S.
Served in Capt. Hall's Company.
Pension Certificate No. 24893.

‡*CLARK, RODOLPHOS.
Served in 1 Regt. (Judson's) Vt. Militia; Corning's Detachment, Vt. Militia; and 4 Regt. (Peck's) Vt. Militia.
Also served in Capt. Caleb Munson's
Company. Pension Certificate No.
1597.

CLARK, SABIN,   Rochester.
Volunteered to go to Plattsburgh,
September, 1814, and served 7 days
in Capt. Oliver Mason's Company.
Ref: Book 51, AGO Page 254.

CLARK, SALMON.
Appointed Captain 30th Inf. April
30, 1813; resigned Aug. 1, 1814. Ref:
Governor and Council Vt. Vol. 6,
Page 475.

*CLARK, SAMUEL.
Served from April 20, 1814 to April
21, 1814 in Capt. Eseck Sprague's
Company, Sumner's Regt.

CLARK, SATTERLEE.
Appointed Cadet Military Academy
May 15, 1805; 2 Lieutenant Artillery
Dec. 9, 1807; 1st Lieutenant July 10,
1811 to Dec. 31, 1813; District Paymaster Aug. 15, 1810; honorably discharged June 15, 1815; died March
1, 1848. Ref: Heitman's Historical
Register & Dictionary USA.

CLARK, SETH.
Served in Capt. Weeks' Company,
11th Regt.; on Pay Roll for January and February, 1813. Ref: R.
& L. 1812, AGO Page 5.

*CLARK, SETH, Surgeon,   Johnson.
Served as Surgeon's Mate in 4 Regt.
(Williams') Vt. Militia. Volunteered
to go to Plattsburgh, September, 1814,
and served 4 days in Capt. Thomas
Waterman's Company, Dixon's Regt.

*CLARK, SETH JR., Surgeon's Mate.
Appointed Surgeon's Mate Sept. 25,
1813 in Col. Dixon's Regt. Vt. Militia
in U. S. service.

*CLARK, SIMON.
Served in 1 Regt. (Judson's) Vt. Militia. Enlisted Nov. 1, 1812 in Capt.
Samul Gordon's Company, 11th Regt.;
on Pay Roll for January and February, 1813. Ref: R. & L. 1812, AGO
Page 9.

CLARK, SOLOMON.
Served in Capt. Benjamin S. Edgerton's Company, 11th Regt.; on Pay
Roll for September and October, 1812,
and January and February, 1813.
Served from March 24, 1813 to June
23, 1813 in Capt. John W. Weeks'
Company, 11th Regt. Ref: R. & L.
1812, AGO Pages 1, 2, 4.

CLARK, THEOPHELUS, East Montpelier.
Volunteered to go to Plattsburgh,
September, 1814, and served 5 days
in Capt. Timothy Hubbard's Com-
pany, as a teamster. Ref: Book 52,
AGO Pages 174 and 245.

*CLARK, THOMAS.
Served in Capt. Briggs' Company,
Col. Jonathan Williams' Regt. De-
tached Militia in U. S. service 16
days. Served in Capt. Phineas Wil-
liams' Company, 11th Regt.; on Pay
Roll for January and February, 1813.
Served from April 12, 1814 to April
21, 1814 in Capt. Eseck Sprague's
Company, Sumner's Regt. Ref: R. &
L. 1812, AGO Page 15.

CLARK, THOMAS A.
Served from May 1st to June 30,
1814 in Capt. Haig's Corps of Light
Dragoons. Ref: R. & L. 1812, AGO
Page 20.

*CLARK, THOMPSON.
Served from April 20, 1814 to April
21, 1814 in Capt. Eseck Sprague's
Company, Sumner's Regt.

‡CLARK, TRUMAN.
Pension Certificate of widow, Martha
W., No. 7240. No organization given.

*CLARK, WILLIAM.   Thetford.
Marched for Plattsburgh, September,
1814, and went as far as Bolton, Vt.,
serving 6 days in Capt. Salmon Howard's Company, 2nd Regt. Ref: Book
52, AGO Page 15.

*CLARK, WILLIAM M., Sergeant.
Appointed sergeant Sept. 14, 1813 in
Capt. Asahel Langworthy's Company,
Col. Isaac Clark's Rifle Regt., in U.
S. service.

‡*CLARK, WILLIAM T.
Served in Capt. Brown's Company,
Col. Martindale's Regt. Detached
Militia in U. S. service 23 days, 1812.
Also served in Capt. Scoville's Com-
pany. Pension Certificate No. 21461.
Pension Certificate of widow, Hen-
rietta, No. 27185.

CLARK, ZIBA.
Volunteered to go to Plattsburgh,
September, 1814, and served 7 days
in Capt. Frederick Griswold's Com-
pany, raised in Brookfield, Vt. Ref:
Book 52, AGO Page 52.

‡CLARY, CALVIN.
Served in Capt. Jesse Post's Company,
Dixon's Regt. Pension Certificate of
widow, Laura, No. 28072.

‡*CLARY, MOSES.
Enlisted Sept. 25, 1813 and served
1 month and 23 days in Capt. Wood's
Company, Col. Dixon's Regt. Pen-
sion Certificate No. 25919. Pension
Certificate of widow, Olive No. 8730.

*CLAY, JAMES.
Served in Capt. Parsons' Company,
Col. Jonathan Williams' Regt. Detached Militia in U. S. service 2
months and 13 days, 1812.

*CLAYE, FRANKLIN.
Served from April 12, 1814 to May 20,
1814 in company of Capt. James
Gray Jr., Sumner's Regt.

CLAYES, ELIJAH,   Brandon.
Volunteered to go to Plattsburgh,
September, 1814, and served 8 days
in Capt. Micah Brown's Company.
Ref: Book 51, AGO Page 37; Book
52, AGO Page 135.

CLAYTON, FARMER.
Served in War of 1812 and was cap-
tured by troops Sept. 17, 1814 at Fort
Erie. Discharged Nov. 8, 1814. Ref:
Records of Naval Records and Li-
brary, Navy Dept.

*CLEAVES, LUTHER, Corporal, Water-
bury. Volunteered to go to Plattsburgh, September, 1814, and served
11 days in Capt. George Atkins' Company, 4th Regt. (Peck's); was in
the battle.

‡*CLEMENT. CYRUS H.
Served in Capt. Rogers' Company,
Col. Fifield's Regt. Detached Militia
in U. S. service 6 months, 1812. Also
served in Capt. Taylor's Company.
Pension Certificate No. 5214. (On
Pension Records the last name is
given as Clemens.)

*CLEMENT, JAMES, Corporal, Tunbridge.
Served in 1st Regt. of Detached Militia of Vt. in U. S. service at Champlain commencing Nov. 18 and ending Nov. 19, 1812. Volunteered to
go to Plattsburgh, September, 1814,
and served in Capt. David Knox's
Company.

CLEMENT, JOB,   Corinth.
Volunteered to go to Plattsburgh,
September, 1814, and served in Capt.
Abel Jackman's Company. Ref: Book
52, AGO Page 44.

*CLEMENT, MERRILL, (or Morrell)
Served with Hospital Attendants, Vt.

*CLEMENT, OBEDIAH, Corporal.
Served in Capt. Walker's Company,
Col. Fifield's Regt. Detached Militia
in U. S. service 2 months and 21
days, 1812.

CLEMENT, WILLIAM,   Tunbridge.
Volunteered to go to Plattsburgh,
September, 1814, and served in Capt.
David Knox's Company. Ref: Book
52, AGO Page 117.

CLEMONS, BENJAMIN.
Served in company of Capt. John
McNeil Jr., 11th Regt. On Pay Roll
for January and February, 1813. Ref:
R. & L. 1812, AGO Page 17.

CLEVELAND, BERIAH, Sergeant.
Enlisted May 28, 1813 for 1 year and
served in Capt. James Taylor's Com-
pany, 30th Regt. and Capt. Gideon
Spencer's Company. 30th Regt. Ref:
R. & L. 1812, AGO Pages 52, 56, 58.

CLEVELAND, CHARLES E.,   Bethel.
Volunteered to go to Plattsburgh,
September, 1814, and served 8 days
in Capt. Nehemiah Noble's Company.
Ref: Book 51, AGO Page 235.

CLEVELAND, ENOCH,   Braintree.
Marched to Plattsburgh Sept. 10, 1814
and served in Capt. Lot Hudson's
Company. Ref: Book 52, AGO Page
24.

‡CLEVELAND, FASSETT.
Served in Capt. Ransom's Company.
Pension Certificate No. 34918.

‡CLEVELAND, JOHN.
Served in Capt. Fassett's Company.
Pension Certificate of widow, Abi,
No. 10455.

‡*CLEVELAND, JOHN, Surgeon, Pawlet.
Served in Lieut. R. J. Strong's Com-
pany, 1st Regt. (Martindale's) Vt.
Militia. Pension Certificate No. 21642.

‡*CLEVELAND, JOHN D., Georgia or
Highgate. Served in Capt. Saxe's
Company, Col. Wm. Williams' Regt.
Detached Militia in U. S. service 3
months and 24 days, 1812. Pension
Certificate of widow, Mary L., No.
13411.

*CLEVELAND, SAMUEL.   Tunbridge.
Served in Capt. Bingham's Company,
Col. Jonathan Williams' Regt. De-
tached Militia in U. S. service 3 days.

CLEVELAND, SAMUEL JR.
Enlisted Sept. 22, 1812 in Capt. Ben-
jamin S. Edgerton's Company, 11th
Regt.; on Pay Roll for September
and October, 1812 and January and
February, 1813. Ref: R. & L. 1812,
AGO Pages 1 and 2.

*CLICK, WILLIAM, Corporal.
Served in Sumner's Regt. Vt. Militia.

CLIFFORD, EDWARD,   Pittsford.
Volunteered to go to Plattsburgh,
September, 1814, and served 8 days
in Capt. Caleb Hendee's Company.
Ref: Book 52, AGO Page 124.

*CLIFFORD, JOHN, Sergeant,   Corinth.
Served in Capt. Rogers' Company,
Col. Fifield's Regt. Detached Militia
in U. S. service 2 months and 21
days, 1812. Volunteered to go to
Plattsburgh, September, 1814, and
served in Capt. Ebenezer Spencer's
Company, Vershire.

*CLIFFORD, JOSEPH, Sergeant.
Served in Capt. Walker's Company,
Col. Fifield's Regt. Detached Militia
in U. S. service 6 months and 3
days, 1812.

CLINTON, THOMAS.
Served from May 1 to May 31, 1814
as a carpenter in a company of Artificers commanded by Alexander Parris. Ref: R. & L. 1812, AGO Page
24.

CLINTON, WRIGHT, 2nd Lieutenant.
Served in Corps of Light Dragoons;
on Pay Roll to June 30, 1814. Ref:
R. & L. 1812, AGO Page 20.

CLOGSTON. SAMUEL.
Served in Capt. Benjamin Bradford's
Company; on Muster Roll from May
31, 1813 to Aug. 31, 1813. Ref: R.
& L. 1812, AGO Page 26.

CLOGSTON, THOMAS.   Strafford.
Volunteered to go to Plattsburgh,
September, 1814, and served in Capt.
Cyril Chandler's Company. Ref: Book
52, AGO Page 42.

CLOICE, ELIJAH.   Franklin County.
Volunteered to go to Plattsburgh
Sept. 11, 1814 and served in 15th or
22nd Regt. Ref: Hemenway's Vt. Gazetteer, Vol. 2, Page 392.

*CLOSSON, JOHN.
Served in Capt. Wheeler's Company,
Col. Fifield's Regt. Detached Militia
in U. S. service 6 months and 4
days, 1812.

*CLOSSON, WILLIAM.
Served from April 12, 1814 to April
21, 1814 in Lieut. Justus Foote's Company, Sumner's Regt.

CLOUGH, EZEKIEL.
Enlisted Jan. 24, 1813 in Lieut. V.
R. Goodrich's Company, 11th Regt.;
on Pay Roll for January and Febru-
ary, 1813. Ref: R. & L. 1812, AGO
Page 11.

CLOUGH, JEREMIAH.
Enlisted Jan. 9, 1813 in Capt. John
W. Weeks' Company, 11th Regt.; on
Pay Roll to June 8, 1813. Ref: R.
& L. 1812, AGO Pages 4 and 5.

CLOUGH, JOSEPH.   Chelsea.
Served from May 9, 1813 to May 24,
1814 in Capt. James Taylor's Company and Capt. Gideon Spencer's
Company, 30th Regt. Ref: R. & L.
1812, AGO Pages 52, 57, 58.

CLOUGH, JOSIAH,   Strafford.
Volunteered to go to Plattsburgh,
September, 1814, and served 6 days
in Capt. Jedediah H. Harris' Company. Ref: Book 52, AGO Page 43.

‡*CLOUGH, REUBEN.
Served in Capt. Taylor's Company,
Col. Fifield's Regt. Detached Militia
in U. S. service 14 days, 1812. Served in Capt. Phineas Williams' Company, 11th Regt.; on Pay Roll for
January and February, 1813. Served
in Capt. Goodrich's Company. Pension Certificate of widow, Betsey E.,
No. 3183.

‡CLOUGH, WINTHROP.
Served in Capt. Poteedge's Company.
Pension Certificate No. 15714.

*CLUM, GREENE.
Served in 4 Regt. Vt. Militia commanded by Col. Williams.

*CLUMB, WILLIAM.
Served from April 12. 1814 to April
21, 1814 in Capt. Eseck Sprague's
Company, Sumner's Regt.

CLUTE. JOHN.
Served from Feb. 12, 1813 to May
11, 1813 in Lieut. V. R. Goodrich's
Company, 11th Regt. Ref: R. & L.
1812, AGO Pages 10 and 11.

*COATS, DENISON.
Served in Capt. Hiram Mason's Company, Col. Fifield's Regt. Detached
Militia in U. S. service 5 months
and 17 days, 1812.

COATS, PRENTISS, Musician.
Served in Capt. Samul Gordon's Company, 11th Regt.; on Pay Roll of
company of January and February,
1813. Ref: R. & L. 1812, AGO
Page 9.

COATS, THOMAS, Corporal.
Served from Nov. 1, 1812 to Feb.
28, 1813 in Capt. Charles Follett's
Company, 11th Regt. Ref: R. & L.
1812, AGO Page 12.

COBB. CALVIN D., Corporal.
Served from April 29, 1813 to April
30, 1814 in Capt. James Taylor's
Company and Capt. Gideon Spen-
cer's Company, 30th Regt. Ref: R.
& L. 1812, AGO Pages 52, 56, 58.

COBB, CYRUS.
Served from May 1 to June 30, 1814
in company of Artificers commanded
by Alexander Parris. Ref: R. & L.
1812, AGO Page 24.

COBB, DANIEL,   Strafford.
Volunteered to go to Plattsburgh,
September, 1814, and served 6 days
in Capt. Jedediah H. Harris' Company. Ref: Book 52, AGO Page 43.

COBB, EBEN, Corporal, Franklin County.
Volunteered to go to Plattsburgh
Sept. 11, 1814 and served .in 15th or
22nd Regt. Ref: Hemenway's Vt. Gazetteer, Vol. 2, Page 391.

*COBB, EBENEZER.
Served from June 11, 1813 to June
14, 1813 in Capt. Moses Jewett's Company, 1st Regt. 2nd Brig., 3rd Div.

*COBB, ERIEL.
Served in Capt. Mason's Company,
Col. Fifield's Regt. Detached Militia
in U. S. service 2 months and 14
days, 1812.

*COBB, HARRY.
Served from April 12, 1814 to April
21, 1814 in Capt. Eseck Sprague's
Company, Sumner's Regt.

*COBB, ISAAC.
Served in Capt. Thomas Tupper's
Company. Pension Certificate No.
34273.

COBB, JAMES D.
Appointed Cadet Military Academy
March 8, 1808 (6); 2nd Lieutenant
Light Artillery March 1, 1811; 1st
Lieutenant April 1, 1812; dismissed
March 9, 1814. Ref: Heitman's His-
torical Register & Dictionary USA.

‡COBB, JOHN C.,   Randolph.
Served in Capt. Chase's Company.
Volunteered to go to Plattsburgh,
September, 1814, and served in Capt.
Lebbeus Egerton's Company. Pension
Certificate No. 30886.

‡*COBB, NATHANIEL,   Coventry.
Served in Capt. Hiram Mason's Company, Col. Fifield's Regt. Detached

Militia in U. S. service 3 months and 15 days, 1812; served from Sept. 16, 1812 to March 15, 1813, being stationed at Derby, part of the time by substitute Timothy Hammond. Pension Certificate No. 1281.

COBB. OBIAH, Franklin County. Volunteered to go to Plattsburgh Sept. 11, 1814 and served in 15th or 22nd Regt. Ref: Hemenway's Vt. Gazetteer, Vol. 2, Page 392.

COBB, PHILO. Served in Capt. Weeks' Company, 11th Regt.; on Pay Roll for January and Februray, 1813. Died Feb. 22, 1813. Ref: R. & L. 1812, AGO Page 5.

‡*COBB, REUEL. Served in Capt. Mason's Company, Col. Fifield's Regt. Detached Militia in U. S. service 6 months, 1812. Pension Certificate No. 16376. Pension Certificate of widow, Nancy, No. 25378.

*COBB, STEPHEN C. Served in Capt. Brown's Company, Col. Martindale's Regt. Detached Militia in U. S. service 10 days, 1812. Served from Sept. 1, 1814 to June 16, 1815 in Capt. Sanford's Company, 30th Inf.; on this Pay Roll soldier's residence is given as Schoghtecoke, N. Y. Ref: R. & L. 1812, AGO Page 23.

*COBB, TISDALE, Lieutenant, Coventry. Served from Sept. 16, 1812 to March 15, 1813 in Capt. Hiram Mason's Company, 2 Regt. (Fifield's) Detached Militia, stationed at Derby.

*COBB, WILLARD. 1st Lieutenant, Pawlet. Served as 2nd Lieutenant in 1 Regt. (Martindale's) Vt. Militia and as 1st Lieutenant in Artillery of Detached Militia in U. S. service at Champlain commencing Nov. 18 and ending Nov. 19, 1812.

COBURN, CHARLES. Volunteered to go to Plattsburgh, September. 1814, and went as far as Bolton. Vt., serving 4 days in Lieut. Phineus Kimball's Company, West Fairlee. Ref: Book 52, AGO Pages 46 and 47.

COBURN, CHEENEY. Served from Feb. 15, 1813 to May 14, 1813 in Capt. Edgerton's Company, 11 Regt. Ref: R. & L. 1812, AGO Page 3.

COBURN, GEORGE. Volunteered to go to Plattsburgh, September, 1814, and went as far as Bolton, Vt., serving 4 days in Lieut. Phineus Kimball's Company, West Fairlee. Ref: Book 52, AGO Page 46.

COBURN, HENRY. Volunteered to go to Plattsburgh, September, 1814, and served 4 days in Capt. Aaron Kidder's Company or Lieut. Phineas Kimball's Company. West Fairlee. Ref: Book 52, AGO Pages 46, 47, 65.

*COBURN, JAMES. Served in Capt. Mason's Company, Col. Fifield's Regt. Detached Militia in U. S. service 6 months, 1812.

COBURN, JOHN, Highgate. Served in New York state from Sept. 25 to Nov. 18, 1813; no organization given. Ref: Vol. 50 Vt. State Papers, Page 94.

COBURN, LEMUEL. Volunteered to go to Plattsburgh, September, 1814, and went as far as Bolton, Vt., serving 4 days in Lieut. Phineus Kimball's Company, West Fairlee. Ref: Book 52, AGO Pages 46, 47, 109.

*COBURN, PHINEAS, Randolph. Volunteered to go to Plattsburgh, September, 1814, and served in Capt. Lebbeus Egerton's Company.

*COBURN, STEPHEN. Served in Capt. Mason's Company, Col. Fifield's Regt. Detached Militia in U. S. service 5 months and 12 days, 1812.

*COCHRAN, DAVID. Enlisted Sept. 29, 1813 in Capt. Asahel Langworthy's Company, Col. Isaac Clark's Rifle Corps.

*COCHRAN, HENRY. Served with Regt. of Riflemen, Vt. Volunteers, from September to November, 1813.

COCHRAN, JOHN, Fifer. Served in Capt. Chadwick's Company, 2nd Regt. Ref: R. & L. 1812, AGO Page 32.

‡COCHRAN, NATHANIEL, Sergeant. Plainfield. Served in Capt. Walker's Company. Volunteered to go to Plattsburgh, September, 1814, and served 9 days in Capt. James English's Company. Pension Certificate of widow, Abagail, No. 4224. Ref: Book 52, AGO Pages 195, 199, 248.

COCHRAN, ROBERT. Served in Capt. Chadwick's Company, 2nd Regt. Ref: R. & L. 1812, AGO Page 32.

*COCHRAN, SETH. Served as Sergeant in Capt. Taylor's Company, Col. Wm. Williams' Regt. Detached Militia in U. S. service 4 months and 24 days, 1812, stationed at Swanton Falls. Appointed Sergeant in Capt. Asahel Langworthy's Company, Col. Clark's Rifle Regt. Oct. 2, 1813. Served in Capt. Chadwick's Company, 2nd Regt.

COCKLE, ROBERT. Served from March 12, 1813 to June 11, 1813 in Lieut. V. R. Goodrich's Company. 11th Regt. Ref: R. & L. 1812, AGO Page 10.

CODDING. ABIATHER, Belvidere. Served in Capt. Brush's Company, Col. Dixon's Regt. Detached Militia in U. S. service 1 month and 23 days, 1813. Enlisted Sept. 25, 1813 in Capt. Asa Wilkins' Company, Dixon's Regt. Volunteered to go to Plattsburgh, September, 1814, and served 7 days in Capt. Moody Shattuck's Company.

*COFFIN, MOSES,   Waterbury.
Served in Capt. Lowry's Company, Col. Wm. Williams' Regt. Detached Militia in U. S. service 4 months and 26 days, 1812. Volunteered to go to Plattsburgh, September, 1814, and served 11 days in Capt. George Atkins' Company, 4 Regt. Peck's; was in the battle. Lived on Blush Hill with his wife, Lydia Dustin Coffin, his two sons, Moses, Jr., and Daniel, and a daughter, Electa. The two sons died in the 2nd year of the War of 1812, one, (Moses, Jr.) at Fort George, Upper Canada, and the other (Daniel) at Plattsburgh, N. Y., Nov. 15, 1813. Ref: Theo. G. Lewis' History of Waterbury, Page 45.

*COFFREY, JOHN.
Served in Capt. Parsons' Company, Col. Jonathan Williams' Regt. Detached Militia in U. S. service 2 months and 13 days, 1812.

*COFFEE, JOHN.
Served from Sept. 25, 1813 to Oct. 7, 1813 in Capt. Elijah W. Wood's Company, Dixon's Regt.

*COFFRIN, JACOB.
Served from June 11, 1813 to June 14, 1813 in Lieut. Bates' Company, 1st Regt.

*COFFRIN, JOHN.
Served from June 11, 1813 to June 14, 1813 in Lieut. Bates' Company, 1st Regt. (Judson's).

*COFRAN, JOSEPH, Corporal, Wheelock.
Served in Capt. Wheeler's Company, Detached Militia, Col. Fifield's Regt., 6 months in 1812.

COGGSWELL, MANSON S.
Served in Capt. Benjamin Edgerton's Company, 11th Regt. at battle of Chrystler's Farm Nov. 11, 1813, and was reported missing after the battle. Ref: Governor and Council Vt. Vol. 6, Page 490.

COGSWELL, ALANSON S.
Served in Capt. Benjamin S. Edgerton's Company, 11th Regt.; on Pay Roll for September and October, 1812, and January and February, 1813. Was captured by troops Dec. 19, 1813 at Fort Niagara; died March 5, 1814. Ref: R. & L. 1812, AGO Pages 1 and 2; Records of Naval Records and Library, Navy Dept.

COLBAUGH, MICHAEL.
Served in Capt. Haig's Corps of Light Dragoons; on Pay Roll to June 30, 1814; prisoner of war. Ref: R. & L. 1812, AGO Page 20.

*COLBETH, WINTHROP.
Served in 4 Regt. Vt. Militia commanded by Col. Peck.

*COLBURN, BENJAMIN.
Served in Capt. Wheeler's Company, Col. Fifield's Regt. Detached Militia in U. S. service 5 months and 26 days, 1812.

*COLBURN, DAVID.
Served from Sept. 25, 1813 to Nov. 15, 1813 in Capt. Jesse Post's Company, Dixon's Regt.

*COLBURN, EBENEZER JR., Randolph.
Volunteered to go to Plattsburgh, September, 1814, and served in Capt. Lebbeus Egerton's Company.

‡COLBURN, ELLIS.
Served in Capt. Read's Company. Pension Certificate of widow, Lucy W., No. 25718.

*COLBURN, FOSTER.
Served in 1 Regt. Vt. Militia commanded by Col. Martindale.

*COLBURN, JONATHAN L.
Served in Capt. Robbins' Company. Col. Wm. Williams' Regt. Detached Militia in U. S. service 4 months and 29 days, 1812. Also served in 1 Regt. (Judson's).

*COLBURN, JOSEPH.
Served in 1 Regt. Vt. Militia commanded by Col. Judson.

COLBURN, LEWIS.
Enlisted May 7, 1813 for 1 year in Capt. Daniel Farrington's Company (also commanded by Capt. Simeon Wright) 30th Regt.; on Muster Roll from March 1, 1814 to April 30, 1814. Ref: R. & L. 1812, AGO Page 50 and Page 51.

*COLBURN, ROSWELL.
Served in 3 Regt. Vt. Militia commanded by Col. Williams.

*COLBURN, WASHINGTON.
Enlisted Sept. 25, 1813 and served 1 month and 23 days in Capt. Birge's Company, Col. Dixon's Regt.

COLBY, AARON.
Served in Capt. Benjamin Bradford's Company; on Muster Roll from May 31, 1813 to Aug. 31, 1813. Ref: R. & L. 1812, AGO Page 26.

COLBY, ENOCH.
Served from Feb. 8, 1813 to Feb. 15. 1813 in Capt. Jonathan Stark's Company, 11th Regt. Ref: R. & L. 1812, AGO Page 19.

*COLBY, EPHRAIM, Drummer.
Served in Capt. Rogers' Company. Col. Fifield's Regt. Detached Militia in U. S. service 5 months and 27 days, 1812.

*COLBY, HARTLEY.
Served with Hospital Attendants, Vt.

*COLBY, HEZEKIAH.
Served in Capt. Bingham's Company, Col. Jonathan Williams' Regt. Detached Militia in U. S. service 2 months and 9 days, 1812.

COLBY, JOHN.   Tunbridge.
Volunteered to go to Plattsburgh, September, 1814, and served 4 days in Capt. Ephraim Hackett's Company. Ref: Book 52, AGO Page 71.

COLBY. JOHN B., Tunbridge.
Volunteered to go to Plattsburgh,
September, 1814, and served 4 days
in Capt. Ephraim Hackett's Company.
Ref: Book 52, AGO Pages 71 and 72.

COLBY, JONATHAN, Corinth.
Volunteered to go to Plattsburgh,
September, 1814, and served 3 days
in Capt. Abel Jackman's Company.
Ref: Book 52, AGO Pages 44 and 45.

‡*COLBY. LEVI.
Served in Capt. Wheatley's Company,
Col. Fifield's Regt. Detached Militia
in U. S. service 2 months and 21
days, 1812. Pension Certificate No.
11791.

COLBY, MOSES. Fairfax.
Served in 1813 and 1814 in Capt.
Joseph Beeman's Company. Ref: Hemenway's Vt. Gazetteer, Vol. 2, Page
402.

‡COLBY, THOMAS, Thetford.
Volunteered to go to Plattsburgh,
September, 1814, and served 6 days
in Capt. Orange Hubbard's Company.
Pension Certificate of widow, Olive,
No. 30034.

*COLDWELL. CHARLES.
Served in Dixon's Regt. Vt. Militia.

*COLE. ABRAL.
Served in Capt. Jones' Company.
Pension Certificate No. 7464.

*COLE, AMOS.
Served from April 12, 1814 to April
18, 1814 in Capt. Jonathan P. Stanley's Company's Col. W. B. Sumner's
Regt.

‡*COLE, DANIEL.
Served in Capt. Bingham's Company,
Col. Jonathan Williams' Regt. De-
tached Militia in U. S. service 2
months and 9 days, 1812. Pension
Certificate No. 11791.

*COLE. DANIEL.
Served in Capt. Phelps' Company,
Col. Wm. Williams' Regt. Detached
Militia in U. S. service 5 months,
1812.

COLE. DAVID, Berlin.
Volunteered to go to Plattsburgh,
September, 1814, and served 8 days
in Capt. Cyrus Johnson's Company.
Ref: Book 52, AGO Page 201.

COLE, ELIJAH, Franklin County.
Volunteered to go to Plattsburgh
Sept. 11, 1814 and served in 15th or
22nd Regt. Ref: Hemenway's Vt. Gazetteer, Vol. 2, Page 391.

COLE, ENOS. 2nd Lieutenant, Morristown.
Volunteered to go to Plattsburgh,
September, 1814, and served 8 days
in Capt. Denison Cook's Company.
Ref: Book 51, AGO Pages 202 and
206.

*COLE. HENRY.
Served in Capt. Mason's Company,
Col. Fifield's Regt. Detached Militia
in U. S. service 3 months and 22
days, 1812.

*COLE, JABEZ.
Served in 1 Regt. Vt. Militia commanded by Col. Judson.

COLE, JAMES, Musician.
Served in company of late Capt. J.
Brooks, commanded by Lieut. John
I. Cromwell, Corps of U. S. Artillery;
on Muster Roll of company from
April 30, 1814 to June 30, 1814;
paroled prisoner and on furlough.
Ref: R. & L. 1812, AGO Page 18.

*COLE, JONATHAN, Sergeant.
Served from June 11, 1813 to June
14, 1813 in Capt. John Palmer's Company, 1st Regt. 2nd Brig., 3rd Div.

COLE, "PRIEST", Middlesex.
Volunteered to go to Plattsburgh,
September, 1814, and served in Capt.
Holden Putnam's Company, 4th Regt.
(Peck's). Ref: Hemenway's Vt. Ga-
zetteer, Vol. 4, Page 250.

COLE, SAMUEL W., Morristown.
Volunteered to go to Plattsburgh,
September, 1814, and served 4 days
in Capt. Denison Cook's Company.
Ref: Book 51, AGO Page 204.

*COLE, TIMOTHY JR.
Served in Capt. Rogers' Company,
Col. Fifield's Regt. Detached Militia
in U. S. service 5 months and 27
days, 1812.

*COLE, TISDEL.
Served from April 12, 1814 to May
20, 1814 in Capt. George Fisher's Company, Sumner's Regt.

COLEFIX, JOHN.
Served from May 18, 1813 to May 22,
1814 in Capt. James Taylor's Company and Capt. Gideon Spencer's
Company. 30th Regt. Ref: R. & L.
1812, AGO Pages 52, 57, 59.

‡COLEMAN, ABEL H.
Served in Capt. Buck's Company.
Pension Certificate of widow, Lucinda,
No. 7224.

COLEMAN, ERASTUS, Lieutenant, West
Haven. Volunteered to go to Plattsburgh, September, 1814, and served 4
days in Capt. David B. Phippeney's
Company. Ref: Book 52, AGO Page
146.

COLES, GRIFFIN. Sergeant.
Served from May 1 to June 30, 1814
in Capt. Alexander Brooks' Corps of
Artillery. Ref: R. & L. 1812, AGO
Page 31.

COLFIX, JOHN.
Served from Feb. 8, 1813 to May 7,
1813 in Lieut. V. R. Goodrich's Company, 11th Regt. Ref: R. & L. 1812,
AGO Page 10.

COLICE, DANIEL W., Fairfax.
Served from Aug. 8, 1812 in company
of Capt. Joseph Beeman Jr. 11th
Regt. U. S. Inf. under Col. Ira
Clark. Ref: Hemenway's Vt. Ga-
zetteer, Vol. 2, Page 402.

COLICE, JAMES. Fairfax.
Served from Aug. 8, 1812 in company
of Capt. Joseph Beeman, Jr. 11th

Regt. U. S. Inf. under Col. Ira Clark. Ref: Hemenway's Vt. Gazetteer, Vol. 2, Page 402.

*COLLAMER, JACOB, Ensign.
Served in 4 Regt. Vt. Militia commanded by Col. Williams.

COLLAR, JOSEPH, Drummer, Addison.
Volunteered to go to Plattsburgh, September, 1814, and served 9 days in Capt. George Fisher's Company, Sumner's Regt.; was in the battle. Ref: Book 51, AGO Page 5.

*COLLER, ABEL.
Served in Sumner's Regt. Vt. Militia.

COLLER, RUFUS.
Served from Feb. 9, 1813 to May 8, 1813 in Capt. Charles Follett's Company, 11th Regt. Ref: R. & L. 1812, AGO Page 13.

*COLLER, WILLIAM JR.
Enlisted Sept. 25, 1813 in Capt. Martin D. Follett's Company, Dixon's Regt.

COLLIER, DANIEL.
Served from May 5, 1813 to May 5, 1814 in Capt. James Taylor's Company and Capt. Gideon Spencer's Company, 30th Regt. Ref: R. & L. 1812, AGO Pages 52, 56, 59.

COLLIER, JAMES.
Served in Lieut. V. R. Goodrich's Company, 11th Regt.; on Pay Roll of company for January and February, 1813. Ref: R. & L. 1812, AGO Page 11.

*COLLINGS, ALSON.
Served in 4 Regt. Vt. Militia commanded by Col. Williams.

‡*COLLINS, ALPHONZO, Burlington.
Served from June 11, 1813 to June 14, 1813 in Capt. Moses Jewett's Company, 1st Regt. 2nd Brig., 3rd Div. Pension Certificate of widow, Louisa, E., No. 19923. Volunteered to go to Plattsburgh, September, 1814, and served 10 days in Capt. Henry Mayo's Company.

*COLLINS, ALSON.
Served in Sumner's Regt. Vt. Militia.

‡COLLINS, BARTON, Ira.
Volunteered to go to Plattsburgh, September, 1814, and served 4 days in Capt. Matthew Anderson's Company. Pension Certificate of widow, Annahritta, No. 24456.

COLLINS, CHARLES.
Served from Feb. 27, 1813 to May 26, 1813 in Capt. John W. Weeks' Company, 11th Regt. Ref: R. & L. 1812, AGO Pages 4 and 5.

COLLINS, DANIEL.
Served from Jan. 9, 1813 to Feb. 10, 1813 in Capt. Jonathan Starks' Company, 11th Regt. Ref: R. & L. 1812, AGO Page 19.

*COLLINS, ELIJAH.
Enlisted Dec. 23, 1813 for period of the war in company of late Capt. J.

Brooks, commanded by Lt. John I. Cromwell, Corps U. S. Artillery; on Muster Roll from April 30, 1814 to June 30, 1814; transferred from Capt. Leonard's Company. Also served in Tyler's Regt. Vt. Milita. Ref: R. & L. 1812, AGO Page 18.

COLLINS, GEORGE.
Served in Capt. Alexander Brooks' Corps of Artillery; on Pay Roll to June 30, 1814. Ref: R. & L. 1812, AGO Page 31.

COLLINS, JAMES, Swanton.
Served in Capt. V. R. Goodrich's Company, 11th Regt.; on Pay Roll from July 15 to Dec. 8, 1813; was in action at the battle of Lundy's Lane. Ref: Hemenway's Vt. Gazetteer, Vol. 2, Page 444.

COLLINS, JOHN.
Served in Capt. Weeks' Company. 11th Regt.; on Pay Roll for January and February, 1813. Ref: R. & L. 1812, AGO Page 5.

COLLINS, JOHN.
Served in Capt. Samul Gordon's Company, 11th Regt.; enlisted Feb. 12, 1813; died March 23, 1813. Ref: R. & L. 1812, AGO Pages 8 and 9.

*COLLINS, JOHN.
Served in Capt. Rogers' Company, Col. Fifield's Regt. Detached Militia in U. S. service 10 days, 1812.

*COLLINS, JOHN.
Served in Capt. Morrill's Company, Col. Fifield's Regt. Detached Militia in U. S. service 5 months, 1812.

‡*COLLINS, JOHN JR.
Served in Capt. Hotchkiss' Company, Col. Martindale's Regt. Detached Militia in U. S. service 22 days, 1812. Pension Certificate of widow, Lydia, No. 28555.

COLLINS, JOHN J.
Enlisted Sept. 29, 1812 in Capt. Benjamin S. Edgerton's Company, 11th Regt.; on Pay Roll for September and October, 1812, and January and February, 1813. Ref: R. & L. 1812, AGO Pages 1 and 2.

COLLINS, JOSEPH JR.
Volunteered to go to Plattsburgh, September, 1814, and served 4 days in Capt. Matthew Anderson's Company. Ref: Book 52, AGO Page 144.

*COLLINS. LEMUEL.
Served in Capt. Richardson's Company, Col. Martindale's Regt. Detached Militia in U. S. service 2 months and 13 days, 1812. Enlisted Sept. 20, 1813 in Capt. John Weed's Company, Col. Clark's Regt. of Riflemen.

*COLLINS, NATHAN, 2nd Major.
Served in Sumner's Regt. Vt. Militia.

COLLINS, NATHAN, Ira.
Volunteered to go to Plattsburgh, September, 1814, and served 4 days in Capt. Matthew Anderson's Company. Ref: Book 52, AGO Page 144.

*COLLINS, SALVIN.
Served in 4 Regt. Vt. Militia commanded by Col. Peck.

‡COLLINS, DR. SAMUEL, Surgeon.
Pension Certificate of widow, Susanah M., No. 39455; no organization given.

*COLLINS, SERENO.
Served in 1 Regt. Vt. Militia commanded by Col. Judson.

*COLLINS, THOMAS.
Served in Capt. Morrill's Company, Col. Fifield's Regt. Detached Militia in U. S. service 6 months and 5 days, 1812.

COLLINS, TIMOTHY.
Served from May 1 to June 19, 1814; no organization given. Ref: R. & L. 1812, AGO Page 29.

*COLLINS, WINTHROP.
Served in Capt. Weeks' Company, 11th Regt.; on Pay Roll for January and February, 1813. Also served in 2 Regt. (Fifield's) Vt. Militia. Ref: R. & L. 1812, AGO Page 5.

COLMAND, ANTHONY, Franklin County.
Volunteered to go to Plattsburgh Sept. 11, 1814 and served in 15th or 22nd Regt. Ref: Hemenway's Vt. Gazetteer, Vol. 2, Page 391.

‡COLSON, WILLIAM,   Mt. Tabor?
Served in Capt. Foster's Company. Pension Certificate No. 7119.

COLTON, DAN C.,   Hubbardton?
Served from May 11, 1813 to May 1, 1814 in Capt. Daniel Farrington's Company (also commanded by Capt. Simeon Wright) 30th Regt. Ref. R. & L. 1812, AGO Pages 50 and 51.

*COLTON, HARVY,   Georgia.
Enlisted Sept. 25, 1813 in Capt. Jesse Post's Company, Dixon's Regt.; volunteered to go to Plattsburgh, September, 1814. and served 8 days in same company.

COLTON, JOSEPH,   Franklin County.
Volunteered to go to Plattsburgh Sept. 11, 1814 and served in 15th or 22nd Regt. Ref: Hemenway's Vt. Gazetteer, Vol. 2, Page 392.

*COLTON, LORENZO.
Served in Capt. Ormsbee's Company, Col. Martindale's Regt. Detached Militia in U. S. service 2 months and 14 days, 1812.

COLTON, PHINEHAS.
Served in Capt. Needham's Company. Col. Martindale's Regt. Detached Militia in U. S. service 2 months and 14 days, 1812. Ref: Book 53, AGO Page 72.

COLTON, WILLIAM,   Richford.
Served in Capt. Martin D. Follett's Company, Col. Dixon's Regt., on duty on Canadian Frontier in 1813. Served from April 12, 1814 to April 21, 1814 in Capt. Shubael Wales' Company, Col. W. B. Sumner's Regt. Ref: Hemenway's' Vt. Gazetteer, Vol. 2, Page 426; Book 52, AGO Page 289.

COMBS, ELIAS,   South Richford.
Served from March 29, 1813 to June 28, 1813 in Capt. Samul Gordon's Company, 11th Regt. Ref: R. & L. 1812, AGO Page 8. This man was a grandson of Hezekiah Goff, Senior.

COMFORT, ELIJAH.
Served from April 12, 1814 to May 20, 1814 in company of Capt. James Gray, Jr., Sumner's Regt. Ref: Book 52, AGO Page 279.

*COMOO, BENJAMIN.
Served in Capt. Morrill's Company, Col. Fifield's Regt. Detached Militia in U. S. service 6 months and 5 days, 1812.

*COMOO, JOHN.
Served in 2 Regt. Vt. Militia commanded by Col. Fifield.

‡COMSTOCK, JOSHUA.
Served in Capt. Joseph Houland's Company. Pension Certificate No. 24909.

‡*COMSTOCK, LEVI,   Shelburne.
Served in Capt. James Kinney's Company. Volunteered to go to Plattsburgh, September, 1814, and served in Major Luman Judson's command. Pension Certificate No. 11791.

‡COMSTOCK, ORANGE, Ensign, Vershire.
Volunteered to go to Plattsburgh, September, 1814, and served 3 days in Capt. Ira Corse's Company. Pension Certificate No. 33287.

CONANT, ANDREW,   Barre.
Volunteered to go to Plattsburgh, September, 1814, and served in Capt. Warren Ellis' Company. Ref: Hemenway's Vt. Gazetteer Vol. 4, Page 41.

CONANT, AUGUSTUS.
Appointed Cadet, Military Academy, June 15, 1808 (2); 1st Lieutenant 6 Inf. Jan. 3, 1812; resigned Oct. 31, 1812. Ref: Heitman's Historical Register & Dictionary USA.

*CONANT, DAVIS,   Shoreham.
Served in Capt. Robbins' Company. Col. Wm. Williams' Regt. Detached Militia in U. S. service 4 months and 29 days, 1812. Was a brother of Stephen Conant who was also in the service. Ref: Rev. J. F. Goodhue's History of Shoreham, Page 101.

CONANT, GEORGE.
Served from March 5, 1813 to June 4, 1813 in Capt. Edgerton's Company, 11th Regt. Ref: R. & L. 1812, AGO Page 3.

*CONANT, GEORDAN.
Served in 1 Regt. Vt. Militia commanded by Col. Judson.

*CONANT, HORATIO, Corporal.
Served from April 12, 1814 to April 21, 1814 in Lieut. Justus Foote's Company, Sumner's Regt.

*CONANT, ISAAC.
Served in Capt. Walker's Company, Col. Fifield's Regt. Detached Militia in U. S. service 6 months and 3 days, 1812.

CONANT, JOHN, Lieutenant, Brandon or Pawlet. Volunteered to go to Plattsburgh, September, 1814, and served 3 days in Capt. Micah Brown's Company. Ref: Book 52, AGO Pages 130, 131, 133, 134.

CONANT, JONATHAN.
Enlisted July 20, 1813 for 1 year in Capt. James Taylor's Company, 30th Regt.; on Muster Roll Nov. 30, 1813 to Dec. 31, 1813. Ref: R. & L. 1812, AGO Page 52.

CONANT, SAMUEL S., Sergeant, Brandon. Served from April 20, 1813 to April 28, 1814 in Capt. Daniel Farrington's Company, 30th Regt. (also commanded by Capt. Simeon Wright). Volunteered to go to Plattsburgh, September, 1814, and served 8 days in Capt. Micah Brown's Company. Pension Certificate of widow, Elizabeth, No. 26679. Book 52, AGO Page 131.

*CONANT, STEPHEN,   Shoreham. Served from April 12, 1814 to May 20, 1814 in company of Capt. James Gray Jr., Sumner's Regt. Enlisted as a fifer at fifteen, was sent home as too young for the army, stayed 4 months and re-entered the service as a soldier, and remained till the peace. He and his brother, Davis, belonged to the 2 Regt. Light Artillery, and took part in the hotly contested battle of Williamsburgh on the St. Lawrence, Nov. 11, 1813. Ref: Rev. J. F. Goodhue's History of Shoreham, Page 101.

CONE, ENOCH,   Poultney. Volunteered to go to Plattsburgh, September, 1814, and served 2 days in Capt. Briant Ransom's Company. Ref: Book 52, AGO Page 147.

*CONE, GUSTAVIS A.
Pension Certificate No. 26473; no organization given.

CONELLY, THOMAS, Sergeant. Lived in Plattsburgh, N. Y. Served from Aug. 10, 1814 to June 19, 1815 in Capt. Taylor's Company, 30th Inf. Ref: R. & L. 1812, AGO Page 23.

*CONGDON, JOB.
Served in Capt. Brown's Company. Pension Certificate No. 31164.

*CONGDON, JOHN.
Served from March 27, 1813 to June 26, 1813 in Capt. Charles Follett's Company, 11th Regt. Also served with Hospital Attendants, Vt. Ref: R. & L. 1812, AGO Page 13.

*CONGDON, JOSEPH.
Served in Capt. Needham's Company, Col. Martindale's Regt. Detached Militia in U. S. service 2 months and 14 days, 1812.

*CONGER, DANIEL.
Served from June 11, 1813 to June 14, 1813 in Capt. Thomas Dorwin's Company, 1st Regt. 2nd Brig., 3rd Div.

*CONGER, POTTER.
Enlisted Sept. 28, 1813 and served 1 month and 11 days in Capt. Asahel Langworthy's Company, Col. Isaac Clark's Rifle Corps.

*CONGER, REUBEN.
Enlisted Sept. 25, 1813 and served 1 month and 23 days in Capt. Eldridge's Company, Col. Dixon's Regt.

CONK, JOHN H.
Enlisted Oct. 6, 1812 for 5 years in Capt. White Youngs' Company, 15th Regt.; on Muster Roll from Aug. 31, 1814 to Dec. 31, 1814. Ref: R. & L. 1812, AGO Page 27.

CONKEY, PLINEY.
Was born at Orvel and served in the War of 1812; captured by troops Feb. 22, 1813 at Hogdensburgh; discharged Aug. 10, 1813. Ref: Records of Naval Records and Library, Navy Dept.

CONKEY, ZEBINA.
Was born at Orwell and served in the War of 1812; captured by troops Feb. 22, 1813 at Stoney Point; discharged Aug. 10, 1813. Ref: Records of Naval Records and Library, Navy Dept.

CONKLIN, DANIEL.
Enlisted March 11, 1813 for 5 years in company of late Capt. J. Brooks commanded by Lt. John I. Cromwell, Corps of U. S. Artillery; on Muster Roll from April 30, 1814 to June 30, 1814. Ref: R. & L. 1812, AGO Page 18.

CONNELLY, THOMAS,   Ogdensburg. Served from May 1, 1814 to July 12, 1814 in Capt. Smyth's Company, Rifle Regt. Ref: R. & L. 1812, AGO Page 30.

CONNER, EDMUND,   Williamstown. Volunteered to go to Plattsburgh and was in the battle Sept. 11, 1814, serving 8 days in Capt. David Robinson's Company. Ref: Book 52, AGO Page 2.

*CONNER, JOSIAH.
Served in Capt. Morrill's Company, Col. Fifield's Regt. Detached Militia in U. S. service 4 months and 27 days, 1812. Served from Feb. 11th to May 10, 1813 in Capt. Samul Gordon's Company, 11th Regt.

*CONNER, STEPHEN.
Served from June 11, 1813 to June 14, 1813 in Capt. Moses Jewett's Company, 1st Regt. 2nd Brig. 3rd Div.

CONNER, THOMAS O., Corporal. Served from Dec. 24, 1814 to June 19, 1815 in Capt. Taylor's Company, 30th Inf. Ref: R. & L. 1812, AGO Page 23.

CONNERY, ISAAC,   Wiscassett. Served from May 1, 1814 to May 27, 1814 in Capt. Binney's Company, 4th Inf. Ref: R. & L. 1812, AGO Page 30.

CONNET, LUTHER.
Enlisted May 7, 1812 for 5 years in Capt. White Young's Company, 15th Regt.; on Muster Roll from Aug. 31, 1814 to Dec. 31, 1814. Ref: R. & L. 1812, AGO Page 27.

*CONNOR, JOSEPH.
Served in Capt. Benjamin Bradford's Company; on Muster Roll from May 31, 1813 to Aug. 31, 1813; joined by transfer July 22, 1813. Also served in 2 Regt. (Fifield's) Vt. Militia. Ref: R. & L. 1812, AGO Page 26.

*CONNOR, STEPHEN.
Served in 1 Regt. Vt. Militia commanded by Col. Judson.

CONOLLY, WILLIAM, Sergeant, Franklin County. Enlisted June 26, 1812 for 5 years in Capt. White Young's Company, 15th Regt.; on Muster Roll from Aug. 31, 1814 to Dec. 31, 1814. Ref: R. & L. 1812, AGO Page 27.

*CONVERSE, ABEL.
Served from April 12, 1814 to May 20, 1814 in company of Capt. James Gray Jr., Sumner's Regt.

*CONVERSE, ALFRED.
Served in Capt. Willson's Company, Col. Wm. Williams' Regt. Detached Militia in U. S. service 5 months, 1812.

*CONVERSE, BARNARD.
Served with Hospital Attendants, Vt.

CONVERSE, CALVIN.
Volunteered to go to Plattsburgh, September, 1814, and served 7 days in Capt. Asaph Smith's Company. Ref: Book 51, AGO Page 20.

*CONVERSE, DANIEL G., Sergeant.
Served in Capt. Wheatley's Company and Capt. Wright's Company, Col. Fifield's Regt. Detached Militia in U. S. service 6 months, 1812.

‡CONVERSE, FRANCIS.
Pension Certificate of widow, Lydia, No. 5682; no organization given.

*CONVERSE, JAMES, Corporal, Swanton. Served in Capt. Kendall's Company, Col. Wm. Williams' Regt. Detached Militia in U. S. service 4 months and 23 days, 1812. Served in Capt. Alexander Brooks' Corps of Artillery; on Pay Roll to June 30, 1814 as corporal. Ref: R. & L. 1812, AGO Page 31.

*CONVERSE, JESSE.
Served in 1 Regt. Vt. Militia commanded by Col. Judson.

‡*CONVERSE, SANFORD, Sergeant.
Served in Capt. Robbins' Company, Col. Wm. Williams' Regt. Detached Militia in U. S. service 4 months and 29 days, 1812. Pension Certificate of widow, Alice, No. 4555.

*CONVERSE, WILLIAM D.
Served in 1 Regt. Vt. Militia commanded by Col. Judson.

*COOK, AMOS.
Served in Capt. Hotchkiss' Company, Col. Martindale's Regt. Detached Militia in U. S. service 2 months and 13 days, 1812.

*COOK, ARCHIBALD.
Enlisted Sept. 25, 1813 in company of Capt. Prentiss, Jr., Col. Dixon's

Regt. and served 1 month and 23 days; Elias Howard served as substitute from Sept. 30, 1813.

*COOK, BENAIAH.
Served in Capt. Dorrance's Company, Col. Wm. Williams' Regt. Detached Militia in U. S. service 4 months and 29 days, 1812.

COOK, BENJAMIN.
Served from April 22, 1813 to April 28, 1814 in Capt. Simeon Wright's Company. Ref: R. & L. 1812, AGO Page 51.

‡COOK, CHAUNCEY,   Cornwall.
Served in Capt. Michael Brown's Company. Volunteered to go to Plattsburgh, September, 1814, and served 7 days; no organization given. Pension Certificate of widow, Betsey, No. 15405. Ref: Book 51, AGO Pages 49 and 51.

COOK, CHESTER,   Morristown.
Volunteered to go to Plattsburgh, September, 1814, and served 8 days in Capt. Denison Cook's Company. Ref: Book 51, AGO Pages 202, 203, 206.

*COOK, DANIEL.
Served in 2 Regt. Vt. Militia commanded by Col. Fifield.

*COOK, DANIEL 2d.
Served in Capt. Rogers' Company, Fifield's Regt. Detached Militia in U. S. service 5 months and 27 days, 1812.

*COOK, DANIEL D., Cornet.
Served from April 12, 1814 to April 15, 1814 in Capt. John Hackett's Company, Sumner's Regt.

‡COOK, DENISON, Captain, Morristown.
Volunteered to go to Plattsburgh, September, 1814, and served 8 days in company raised at Morristown. Pension Certificate of widow, Margaret, No. 11900.

COOK, DOAN,   Barre.
Volunteered to go to Plattsburgh, September, 1814, and served 9 days in Capt. Warren Ellis' Company. Ref: Book 52, AGO Pages 233 and 242.

*COOK, EDMOND.
Served from April 13, 1814 to April 21, 1814 in Capt. Salmon Foster's Company, Sumner's' Regt.

COOK, ELIAS.
Served from May 1 to May 31, 1814 as blacksmith in company of Artificers commanded by Alexander Parris. Ref: R. & L. 1812, AGO Page 24.

COOK, ELISHA,   Franklin County.
Volunteered to go to Plattsburgh Sept. 11, 1814 and served in 15th or 22nd Regt. Ref: Hemenway's Vt. Gazetter, Vol. 2, Page 391.

‡COOK, GEORGE.
Served in Capt. M. D. Follett's Company. Pension Certificate of widow, Betsey, No. 23702.

COOK, JAMES,   Addison.
Enlisted March 28, 1813 in Capt.
Jonathan Starks' Company, 11th
Regt.; on Pay Roll to May 31, 1813.
Volunteered to go to Plattsburgh,
September, 1814, and served 9 days;
no organization given. Ref: R. &
L. 1812, AGO Page 19; Book 51,
AGO Page 62.

*COOK, JAMES, Corporal.
Served in Capt. Robbins' Company,
Col. Wm. Williams' Regt. Detached
Militia in U. S. service 18 days,
1812. Enlisted Nov. 1, 1812 in Capt.
Samuel Gordon's Company, 11th
Regt.; died Jan. 5, 1813. Ref: Book
53, AGO Page 22; R. & L. 1812, AGO
Page 9.

‡*COOK, JONATHAN, Corporal, Morristown. Served in Capt. Hiram Mason's Company, Col. Fifield's Regt.
Detached Militia in U. S. service 2
months and 20 days, 1812. Also
served in Capt. William Mason's Company. Pension Certificate No. 12984.
Pension Certificate of widow, Sarah,
No. 3548.

‡*COOK, NATHAN,   Highgate.
Served in Capt. Saxe's Company,
Col. Wm. Williams' Regt. Detached
Militia in U. S. service 4 months and
24 days, 1812. Pension Certificate
No. 3822; Pension Certificate of
widow, Minerva, No. 11275.

COOK, NATHANIEL.
Enlisted Jan. 9, 1813 in Capt. Jonathan Starks' Company, 11th Regt.;
died April 25, 1813. Ref: R. & L.
1812, AGO Page 19.

COOK, NATHANIEL JR.
Enlisted Jan. 11, 1813 in Capt. Jonathan Starks' Company, 11th Regt.;
on Pay Roll to May 31, 1813. Ref:
R. & L. 1812, AGO Page 19.

‡*COOK, NICHOLAS.
Served in Capt. Needham's Company,
Col. Martindale's Regt. Detached
Militia in U. S. service 2 months and
14 days, 1812. Pension Certificate
No. 11852.

*COOK, OLIVER JR., Corporal, Vernon.
Served in Capt. Noyes' Company,
Col. Jonathan Williams' Regt. Detached Militia, in U. S. service 2
months and 6 days, 1812.

*COOK, OTIS, Corporal.
Served in Capt. Adams' Company,
Col. Jonathan Williams' Regt. Detached Militia in U. S. service 2
months and 7 days, 1812.

COOK, PAUL,   St. Albans.
Enlisted June 1, 1813 for 1 year in
Capt. John Wires' Company, 30th
Regt. Ref: R. & L. 1812, AGO Page
40.

COOK. REUBEN,   Shoreham.
Volunteered to go to Plattsburgh,
September, 1814, and served 6 days
in Capt. Samuel Hand's Company.
Ref: Rev. J. F. Goodhue's History
of Shoreham, Page 107.

‡*COOK, ROBERT.
Enlisted Sept. 25, 1813 in company
of Capt. Jonathan Prentiss Jr., Dixon's' Regt.; served by Alpheus Hall,
Substitute. Pension Certificate No.
9849.

COOK, ROBERT.
Enlisted July 4, 1813 for 1 year in
Capt. James Taylor's Company, 30th
Regt. Ref: R. & L. 1812, AGO Page
58.

*COOK, SAMUEL, Fife Major, Pittsford.
Served in Col. Wm. Williams' Regt.
Detached Militia in U. S. service 4
months and 26 days, 1812.

COOK, SAMUEL,   Barre.
Volunteered to go to Plattsburgh,
September, 1814, and served 9 days
in Capt. Warren Ellis' Company.
Ref: Book 52, AGO Pages 233 and 242.

COOK, SHUBALL.
Served from March 30, 1813 to June
10, 1813 in Capt. Charles Follett's
Company, 11th Regt. Ref: R. & L.
1812, AGO Page 13.

‡*COOK, SIMEON, Corporal.
Served in Capt. Charles Follett's
Company, 11th Regt.; on Pay Roll
for January and February, 1813.
Served in Capt. Hotchkiss' Company,
1st Regt. (Martindale's). Pension
Certificate No. 8946.

*COOK, TRUMAN, Corporal.
Served in Capt. Stephen Brown's Company, 3 Regt. (Tyler's) from Oct. 5,
1813 to Oct. 17, 1813.

*COOK, WILLIAM, Musician, .Cornwall.
Served from April 12, 1814 to May 20,
1814 in company of Capt. James
Gray Jr., Sumner's Regt. Volunteered to go to Plattsburgh, September,
1814, and was at the battle, serving
in Capt. Edmund B. Hill's Company,
Sumner's Regt.

COOK, WILLIAM.
Served in company of late Capt. J.
Brooks commanded by Lieut. John
I. Cromwell, Corps of U. S. Artillery;
on Muster Roll from April 30, 1814
to June 30, 1814 as Lieut. Cromwell's
private waiter. Ref: R. & L. 1812,
AGO Page 18.

*COOLE, PHILIP K.
Served from April 12, 1814 to April
21. 1814 in Capt. Eseck Sprague's
Company. Sumner's Regt.

COOLE, WILLIAM,   Franklin County.
Volunteered to go to Plattsburgh,
Sept. 11, 1814 and served in 15th or
22nd Regt.; Ref: Hemenway's Vt.
Gazetteer, Vol. 2, Page 392.

COOLEDGE, ISAIAH,   Addison.
Volunteered to go to Plattsburgh,
September, 1814, and was in the
battle, serving 9 days in Capt. George
Fisher's Company, Sumner's Regt.
Ref: Book 51, AGO Page 5.

*COOLEY. ALFRED JR.
Served from April 12, 1814 to May
20, 1814 in company of Capt. James
Gray Jr., Sumner's Regt.

*COOLEY, ISRAEL.
Served in Capt. Taylor's Company,
Col. Fifield's Regt. Detached Militia
in U. S. service 2 months and 21
days, 1812.

‡COOLEY, LEONARD.
Served in Capt. D. Buck's Company.
Pension Certificate No. 9065.

*COOLEY, LOOK.
Served in Dixon's Regt. Vt. Militia.

COOLEY, MARTIN.
Served from March 27, 1813 to June
26, 1813 in Capt. Charles Follett's
Company, 11th Regt. Ref: R. & L.
1812, AGO Page 13.

*COOLEY, PHILLIP R.
Served in Sumner's Regt. Vt. Militia.

COOMBS, JOHN.
Enlisted July 3, 1813 for 1 year in
Capt. Daniel Farrington's Company
(also commanded by Capt. Simeon
Wright) 30th Regt.; on Muster Roll
March 1, 1814 to April 30, 1814. Ref:
R. & L. 1812, AGO Pages 50 and 51.

COOMS, JOHN,   Benson.
Served from March 1, 1814 to July 2,
1814 in Capt. Wright's Company,
30th Regt. Ref: R. & L. 1812, AGO
Page 30.

*COOPER, AMOS B., 1st Lieutenant.
Served from Oct. 5, 1813 to Oct. 7,
1813 in Capt. Roswell Hunt's Company, 3 Regt. (Tyler's).

COOPER, ASHLEY,   Shoreham.
Volunteered to go to Plattsburgh,
September, 1814, and served about
6 days in Capt. Samuel Hand's Com-
pany. Ref: Rev. J .F. Goodhue's
History of Shoreham, Page 108.

COOPER, DARIUS,   Shoreham.
Volunteered to go to Plattsburgh,
September, 1814, and served 6 days
in Capt. Samuel Hand's Company.
Ref: Rev. J. F. Goodhue's History
of Shoreham, Page 108.

*COOPER, ELIJAH,   Richford.
Served from April 12, 1814 to May
20, 1814 in Capt. George Fisher's
Company, Sumner's Regt. Served in
Capt. Martin D. Follett's Company,
Dixon's Regt., on duty on Canadian
Frontier in 1813.

COOPER, ELIJAH,   Richmond.
Volunteered to go to Plattsburgh,
September, 1814, and served 9 days
in Capt. Roswell Hunt's Company,
3 Regt. (Tyler's). Ref: Book 51,
AGO Page 82.

COOPER, ENOCH, Sergeant, Shoreham.
Served from Nov. 1, 1812 to Feb. 28,
1813 in Capt. Samuel H. Holly's
Company, 11th Regt. Served in battles
of Chippewa and Bridgewater. In
official report of battle at Bridgewater is found the following: "11th
Inf. officers wounded 2nd Lt. Cooper,
slightly, contusion in the breast."
After his return home he married
and removed to Orwell where he re-
sumed his trade of journeyman wheel-
wright. Later he moved to Palmyra,
N. Y. where he died. Ref: R. & L.
1812, AGO Page 25; Ref: J. F.
Goodhue's History of Shoreham, Page
101.

COOPER, ENOCH,   Marshfield.
Volunteered to go to Plattsburgh,
September, 1814, and served 9 days
in Capt. James English's Company.
Ref: Book 52, AGO Page 248.

COOPER, ENOCH.
Enlisted May 4, 1813 for 1 year in
Capt. James Taylor's Company, 30th
Regt. Ref: R. & L. 1812, AGO
Page 58.

COOPER, JASON.
Enlisted May 4, 1813 for 1 year in
Capt. James Taylor's Company, 30th
Regt. Ref: R. & L. 1812, AGO
Page 58.

COOPER, MOSES.
Enlisted Feb. 23, 1813 in Capt. John
W. Weeks' Company, 11th Regt. Ref:
R. & L. 1812, AGO Pages 4 and 5.

*COOPER, MOSES B., Lieutenant.
Served in 3 Regt. Vt. Militia commanded by Col. Tyler.

COOPER, PHINEAS S.,   Rochester.
Volunteered to go to Plattsburgh,
September, 1814, and served 9 days
in Capt. Oliver Mason's Company.
Ref: Book 51, AGO Pages 257 and 261.

*COOPER, SAMUEL, 2nd Lieutenant,
Richford. Served from April 12,
1814 to May 20, 1814 in Capt. George
Fisher's Company, Sumner's Regt.
Served in Capt. Martin D. Follett's
Company, Dixon's Regt. on duty on
Northern Frontier in 1813.

*COOPER, SAMUEL,   Richmond.
Volunteered to go to Plattsburgh,
September, 1814, and served 9 days
in Capt. Roswell Hunt's Company,
3 Regt. (Tyler's).

COOPER, STEPHEN,   Franklin County.
Volunteered to go to Plattsburgh
Sept. 11, 1814 and served in 15th or
22nd Regt. Ref: Hemenway's Vt.
Gazetteer, Vol. 2, Page 392.

*COOPER, WILLIAM, Sergeant.
Served from April 12, 1814 to May
20, 1814 in Capt. George Fisher's
Company, Sumner's Regt. Volunteered to go to Plattsburgh, September,
1814, and served 6 days in Capt.
Samuel Hand's Company.

COOPER, ZEBEDEE,   Pittsford.
Volunteered to go to Plattsburgh,
September, 1814, and served 8 days
in Capt. Caleb Hendee's Company.
Ref: Book 52, AGO Page 124.

COOPER, ZEBEDEE JR., Fifer, Pittsford. Volunteered to go to Plattsburgh, September, 1814, and served
8 days in Capt. Caleb Hendee's Company. Ref: Book 52, AGO Page 124.

‡COPELAND. OTIS.
Pension Certificate of widow, Rebecca
Skinner, No. 26321; no organization
given.

*COPELAND, RUFAS, Lieutenant.
Served in 3 Regt. Vt. Militia commanded by Col. Williams.

*COPELAND, SAMUEL.
Served in 3 Regt. Vt. Militia commanded by Col. Williams.

COPELAND, SAMUEL, Williamspoit.
Served from May 1, 1814 to July 10, 1814 in Capt. Montgomery's Company, 14th Inf. Ref: R. & L. 1812, AGO Page 30.

*COPELAND, SMITH.
Served in Capt. Preston's Company, Col. Jonathan Williams' Regt. Detached Militia in U. S. service 2 months and 6 days, 1812. Ref: Book 53, AGO Page 64.

COPELAND, WEEKS, Corporal, Salisbury. Enlisted May 1, 1813 for 1 year in Capt. Simeon Wright's Company. Ref: R. & L. 1812, AGO Page 51.

COPHRIN, JOSEPH.
Enlisted May 31, 1813 for 1 year in Capt. Benjamin Bradford's Company; died July 29, 1813. Ref: R. & L. 1812, AGO Page 26.

COPLEY, HARVEY, Brandon.
Volunteered to go to Plattsburgh, September, 1814, and served 8 days in Capt. Micah Brown's Company. Ref: Book 52, AGO Page 137.

COPLIN, ORIN, Braintree.
Volunteered to go to Plattsburgh, September, 1814, and served in Capt. Lot Hudson's Company. Ref: Book 52, AGO Page 24.

*COPP, JOHN C.
Served in Capt. Edgerton's Company, Vt. Volunteers.

COPPS, JOHN.
Enlisted March 14, 1813 for 5 years in company of late Capt. J. Brooks commanded by Lt. John I. Cromwell, Corps of U. S. Artillery; on Muster Roll from April 30, 1814 to June 30, 1814. Ref: R. & L. 1812, AGO Page 18.

CORBIN, ASA.
Served from May 1 to June 30, 1814 in Capt. Alexander Brooks' Corps of Artillery. Ref: R. & L. 1812, AGO Page 31.

*CORBY, RUFAS.
Served in 3 Regt. Vt. Militia commanded by Col. Williams.

COREY, AMOS.
Served. in Lieut. V. R. Goodrich's Company, 11th Regt.; on Pay Roll for January and February, 1813. Ref: R. & L. 1812, AGO Page 11.

*COREY, CHARLES.
Served in 2 Regt. Vt. Militia commanded by Col. Fifield.

‡*COREY, HENRY, Surgeon's Mate.
Served in Capt. Smead's Company. Also served in 2 Regt. (Fifield's) Vt. Militia. Pension Certificate No. 13709.

COREY, JOHN.
Served from June 11, 1813 to June 14, 1813 in Capt. Moses Jewett's Company, 1st Regt. 2nd Brig., 3rd Div. Ref: R. & L. 1812, AGO Page 42.

*COREY, RUSSELL, Stowe.
Volunteered to go to Plattsburgh, September, 1814, and was present at the battle serving in Capt. Nehemiah Perkins' Company, 4 Regt. (Peck's).

‡*COREY, WILLIAM, Lieutenant Enosburgh. Served from Oct. 14 to Nov. 17, 1813 in Capt. Asahel Scovell's Company, Col. Clark's Rifle Regt. Served from April 12, 1814 to May 20, 1814 as 3rd Lieutenant in company of Capt. James Gray Jr., Sumner's Regt. Volunteered to go to Plattsburgh, September, 1814, and served 10 days as Lieutenant in Capt. William H. Pickett's Company, Sumner's Regt. Also served in 4 Regt. (Williams) and under Captains Standish and Burnap. Pension Certificate No. 11105.

*COREY, ZOPHER.
Served from April 12, 1814 to May 20, 1814 in company of Capt. James Gray Jr., Sumner's Regt.

‡CORKINS, GEORGE.
Served in Capt. Farnsworth's Company. Pension Certificate of widow Louisa, No. 28151.

‡CORKINS, JONAS.
Served in Capt. Eldridge's Companv. Pension Certificate No. 22520.

‡CORLEW, DANIEL.
Served in Capt. Corlew's Company. Pension Certificate No. 3317.

‡*CORLISS, JOHN.
Served in Capt. Rogers' Companv, Col. Fifield's Regt. Detached Militia in U. S. service 5 months and 27 days, 1812. Pension Certificate No. 3537.

‡*CORLISS, SAMUEL, Fairfield.
Served in Capt. Kendall's Company, Wm. Williams' Regt. Detached Militia in U. S. service 4 months and 23 days, 1812. Served from March 30, 1813 to June 29, 1813 in Capt. Samul Gordon's Company, 11th Regt. Served in Capt. B. Smead's Company. Pension Certificate of widow, Sally, No. 29295.

*CORLISS, THOMAS.
Served in Capt. Rogers' Company, Col. Fifield's Regt. Detached Militia in U. S. service 2 months and 18 days, 1812.

CORMICK, B., Franklin County.
Volunteered to go to Plattsburgh Sept. 11, 1814 and served in 15th or 22nd Regt. Ref: Hemenway's Vt. Gazetteer, Vol. 2, Page 392.

*CORNELL, BURGESS.
Served in 4 Regt. Vt. Militia commanded by Col. Williams.

*CORNING, JAMES JR.
Served in Corning's Detachment, Vt. Militia.

*CORNING, JOHN S.,Ensign.
Served in 3 Regt. Vt. Militia commanded by Col. Tyler.

CORNING, MALACHI.
Appointed 1 Lieutenant 11 Inf. March 12, 1812; Captain Aug. 15, 1813; honorably discharged June 15, 1815. Served as 1st Lieutenant in Capt. Phineas Williams' Company, 11th Inf.; on Pay Roll for January and February, 1813. Ref: Heitman's Historical Register & Dictionary USA; R. & L. 1812, AGO Page 15.

*CORNING, RICHARD.
Served from June 11, 1813 to June 14, 1813 in Capt. Moses Jewett's Company, 1st Regt. 2nd Brig., 3rd Div.

*CORNING, RUSSELL, Major.
Serving in Corning's Detachment, Vt. Militia.

CORNISH, JOSHUA, Corporal, Franklin County. Volunteered to go to Plattsburgh Sept. 11, 1814 and served in 15th or 22nd Regt. Ref: Hemenway's Vt. Gazetteer, Vol. 2, Page 391.

*CORSER, NICHOLS.
Served in Capt. Burnap's Company, Col. Jonathan Williams' Regt. Detached Militia in U. S. service 1 month and 13 days, 1812.

CORSE, IRA, Captain,   Vershire.
Volunteered to go to Plattsburgh, September, 1814, and served 3 days in command of company from Vershire. Ref: Book 52, AGO Pages 91 and 92.

*CORSON, JONATHAN.
Served in 2 Regt. Vt. Militia commanded by Col. Fifield.

CORSS, EBEN,   Waitsfield.
Volunteered to go to Plattsburgh, September, 1814, and served 4 days in Capt. Mathias S. Jones' Company. Ref: Book 52, AGO Page 170.

CORY, AMOS.
Served in Capt. Briggs' Company, Col. Jonathan Williams' Regt. Detached Militia in U. S. service 13 days. Ref: Book 53, AGO Page 97.

*CORY, LAWTON.
Served in Capt. Wheeler's Company, Col. Fifield's Regt. Detached Militia in U. S. service 6 months, 1812.

COTTER, ABEL.
Served from April 12, 1814 to April 21, 1814 in Lieut. Justus Foote's Company, Sumner's Regt. Ref: Book 52, AGO Page 285.

*COTTMAN, ELIJAH, Corporal.
Served in 3 Regt. Vt. Militia commanded by Col. Tyler.

*COTTON, BEBE L., 2nd Lieutenant, Randolph. Volunteered to go to Plattsburgh, September, 1814, and served in Capt. Lebbeus Egerton's Company.

COTTON, HARVEY.
Served in Capt. Post's Company, Col. Dixon's Regt. Detached Militia in U. S. service 1 month and 23 days, 1813. Ref: Book 53, AGO Page 110.

COTTON, HORACE,   Shoreham.
Volunteered to go to Plattsburgh, September, 1814, and served 6 days in Capt. Samuel Hand's Company. Ref: Rev. J. F. Goodhue's History of Shoreham, Page 108.

‡COTTON, JACOB.
Served in Capt. Wilson's Company. Pension Certificate No. 26765.

*COTTON, JOHN.
Served in 4 Regt. Vt. Militia commanded by Col. Peck.

COTTON, SALMON C.
Appointed Ensign 11 Inf. July 19, 1813; 2nd Lieutenant Nov. 19, 1813; Captain 26 Inf. April 21, 1814; honorably discharged June 15, 1815. Ref: Heitman's Historical Register & Dictionary USA.

COTTON, SOLOMON.
Volunteered to go to Plattsburgh, September, 1814, and went as far as Bolton, Vt., serving 4 days in Lieut. Phineus Kimball's Company, West Fairlee. Ref: Book 52, AGO Page 46.

*COTTON, WADLEY.
Served in 4 Regt. Vt. Militia commanded by Col. Peck.

*COTTON, WILLIAM.
Served in Sumner's Regt. Vt. Militia.

COUCH, SAMUEL.
Served from March 20, 1813 to June 9, 1813 in Capt. Charles Follett's Company, 11th Regt. Ref: R. & L. 1812, AGO Page 13.

*COULBURN, JONATHAN.
Served in 1 Regt. Vt. Militia commanded by Col. Judson.

COULT, BENJAMIN.
Volunteered to go to Plattsburgh, September, 1814, and served 7 days in Capt. Frederick Griswold's Company, raised in Brookfield, Vt. Ref: Book 52, AGO Page 52.

COUMIER, JOHN, Marine.
Volunteered at Vergennes, Vt., Aug. 1. 1814 and served until honorably discharged Sept. 15, 1814 at Plattsburgh, N. Y. Served under Capt. George Robbins in the command of Commodore MacDonough. Ref: Book 51, AGO Page 113.

COURRIER, CALEB.
Served in company of Capt. John McNeil Jr., 11th Regt.; on Pay Roll for January and February, 1813. Ref: R. & L. 1812, AGO Page 17.

COURRIER, JAMES.
Served in company of Capt. John McNeil Jr., 11th Regt., from Jan. 1, 1813 until date of death, Feb. 5, 1813. Ref. R. & L. 1812, AGO Page 17.

COURRIER, SYLVANUS.
Served from March 22, 1813 to June 8, 1813 in Capt. John W. Weeks' Company, 11th Regt. Ref: R. & L. 1812, AGO Page 4.

COURRIER, WILLIAM.
Served in Capt. Phineas Williams'
Company, 11th Regt.; on Pay Roll
for January and February, 1813. Ref:
R. & L. 1812, AGO Page 15.

*COURSER, NICHOLS.
Served in 3 Regt. Vt. Militia commanded by Col. Williams.

COURSIER, BENJAMIN.
Volunteered to go to Plattsburgh,
September, 1814, and went as far as
Bolton, Vt., serving 4 days in Lieut.
Phineus Kimball's Company. West
Fairlee. Ref: Book 52, AGO Pages
46 and 47.

*COVAL, CALVIN.
Served in Capt. Lowry's Company,
Col. Wm. Williams' Regt. Detached
Militia in U. S. service 4 months and
26 days, 1812.

*COVEL, SIMEON.
Served from Oct. 5, 1813 to Oct. 17,
1813 in Capt. Stephen Brown's Company, 3 Regt. (Tyler's).

COVINHOON, WILLIAM, Franklin County. Volunteered to go to Plattsburgh
Sept. 11, 1814 and served in 15th or
22nd Regt. Ref: Hemenway's Vt.
Gazetteer, Vol. 2, Page 392.

*COWDRY, LUTHER,   Randolph.
Volunteered to go to Plattsburgh,
September, 1814, and served in Capt.
Lebbeus Egerton's Company.

COWDRY, STEPHEN, Sergeant,   Wells.
Enlisted at Middletown March 24,
1814 for 1 year and served in Capt.
Wm. Miller's Company, Capt. Gideon
Spencer's Company and Capt. James
Taylor's Company, all in the 30th
Regt. Ref: R. & L. 1812, AGO Pages
53, 54, 55, 56.

COWELL, ANSELL.
Served from May 1 to June 30, 1814
in Capt. Alexander Brooks' Corps of
Artillery. Ref: R. & L. 1812, AGO
Page 31.

COWLES, CHARLES W.
Enlisted at Sackets Harbour April
22, 1815 in U. S. Marine Corps. Ref:
Book 52, AGO Page 294.

‡COWLES, JABEZ.
Served in Capt. Chapell's Company.
Pension Certificate No. 8310.

COWLES, JOHN,   Franklin County.
Volunteered to go to Plattsburgh
Sept. 11, 1814 and served in 15th or
22nd Regt. Ref: Hemenway's Vt. Gazetteer, Vol. 2, Page 392.

*COWLES, STOLEN.
Served from April 12, 1814 to April
21, 1814 in Lieut. James S. Morton's
Company, Col. W. B. Sumner's Regt.

COX, DANIEL S.
Volunteered to go to Plattsburgh,
September, 1814 and went as far as
Bolton, Vt., serving 4 days in Lieut.
Phineus Kimball's Company. West
Fairlee. Ref: Book 52, AGO Page 46.

COX, ELISHA.   Pittsford.
Enlisted May 6, 1813 for 1 year in
Capt. Simeon Wright's Company.
Ref: R. & L. 1812, AGO Page 51.

‡*COX, EZEKIEL,   Richmond.
Served 3 months beginning September,
1812, in 6th Company, 3d Regt. 2nd
Brig. commanded by Brig. Gen.
Newell. Served in 4 Regt. (Wil-
liams') Vt. Militia. Volunteered to
go to Plattsburgh, September, 1814,
and served 9 days in Capt. Roswell
Hunt's Company, 3 Regt. Pension
Certificate of widow, Anna, No. 5830.

‡COX, GARDNER,   Barnard.
Served in Capt. Bicknell's Company.
Pension Certificate of widow, Char-
lotte D., No. 39157.

*COX, JOSEPH,   Fairfax.
Served in Capt. Taylor's Company,
Col. Wm. Williams' Regt. Detached
Militia in U. S. service 4 months and
24 days, 1812. Volunteered to go
to Plattsburgh, September, 1814, and
served 8 days in Capt. Josiah Grout's
Company.

*COX, LEVI,   Woodstock.
Appointed 2nd Lieutenant 31 Inf.
April 30, 1813; 1st Lieutenant Jan.
11, 1814; honorably discharged June
15, 1815. Served in 3 Regt. Vt. Mili-
tia commanded by Col. Williams.
Ref: Heitman's Historical Register &
Dictionary USA.

COX, THOMAS.
Served from May 1st to June 30,
1814 in Capt. Haig's Corps of Light
Dragoons. Ref: R. & L. 1812, AGO
Page 20.

COY, CALVIN.
Served from Sept. 4, 1813 to March
1, 1814 in Capt. James Taylor's Company and Capt. Gideon Spencer's
Company, 30th Regt. Ref: R. & L.
1812, AGO Pages 52, 53, 57, 59.

COZZENS, JOHN,   Shoreham.
Volunteered to go to Plattsburgh,
September, 1814, and served 6 days
in Capt. Samuel Hand's Company.
Ref: Rev. J. F. Goodhue's History
of Shoreham, Page 108.

CRAIGEN, SAMUEL A.
Served from Feb. 9, 1813 to May 8,
1813 in Capt. John W. Weeks' Company, 11th Regt. Ref: R. & L. 1812,
AGO Page 4.

‡CRAIN, ELIJAH.
Served in Capt. John Wheatley's Com-
pany. Pension Certificate No. 1931.
Pension Certificate of widow, Emily,
No. 18566.

‡CRAM, CALEB.
Served in Capt. Richardson's Company, Col. Martindale's Regt. Detached
Militia in U. S. service 2 months and
13 days, 1812. Pension Certificate of
widow, Sarah, No. 8975.

CRAM, HUMPHREY,   Tunbridge, Vt.
Born in Stoddard, N. H.; aged 19
years; 5 feet 4 inches high; dark
complexion; dark eyes; dark hair;

by profession a farmer. Enlisted at Tunbridge, Vt. May 6, 1813 in the Army of the U. S. for the period of 1 year unless sooner discharged. Ref: Paper in the custody of the Vt. Historical Society.

CRAM, JONATHAN.   Roxbury.
Volunteered to go to Plattsburgh September, 1814, and served 8 days in Capt. David Robinson's Company, raised in Williamstown and vicinity. Ref: Loose Rolls, Book 52, AGO.

CRAM, JONATHAN, Sergeant, Roxbury.
Volunteered to go to Plattsburgh, September, 1814, and served 7 days in Capt. Samuel M. Orcutt's Company. Ref: Book 52, AGO Pages 167 and 250.

‡CRAM, NATHAN.
Served in Capt. Smead's Company. Pension Certificate No. 5753.

‡*CRAM, PHILIP, Corporal, Roxbury.
Served in Capt. John Wheatly's Company, 2 Regt. (Fifield's). Volunteered to go to Plattsburgh, September, 1814, and served 8 days in Capt. Samuel M. Orcutt's Company. Pension Certificate No. 5459. Pension Certificate of widow, Aptha, No. 43004.

CRAM, ROBERT,   Roxbury.
Volunteered to go to Plattsburgh, September, 1814, and served in Capt. Samuel M. Orcutt's Company. Ref: Book 52, AGO Pages 166 and 250.

*CRAMPTON, DANIEL T.
Served from April 12, 1814 to May 20, 1814 in Capt. George Fisher's Company, Sumner's Regt.

CRANDALL, AARON.
Served in Capt. Phineas Williams' Company, 11th Regt.; on Pay Roll for January and February, 1813. Ref: R. & L. 1812, AGO Page 15.

CRANDALL, GEORGE W., Franklin County. Volunteered to go to Plattsburgh Sept. 11, 1814 and served in 15th or 22nd Regt. Ref: Hemenway's Vt. Gazetteer, Vol. 2, Page 391.

CRANDEL, MARQUIS G.
Served in Capt. Chadwick's Company. 2 Regt. Ref: R. & L. 1812, AGO Page 32.

*CRANDELL, M. D.
Enlisted Oct. 2, 1813 in Capt. Asahel Langworthy's Company, Col. Isaac Clark's Regt.

*CRANE, AARON.
Served from April 12, 1814 to April 15, 1814 in Lieut. Justus Foote's Company, Sumner's Regt.

CRANE, ABIAH,   Williamstown.
Volunteered to go to Plattsburgh September, 1814, and served in Capt. David Robinson's Company 8 days; was at the battle Sept. 11, 1814. Ref: Book 52, AGO Pages 2 and 10.

*CRANE, CALEB, Corporal.
Served in 1 Regt. Vt. Militia commanded by Col. Martindale.

*CRANE, CHARLES.
Served from April 12, 1814 to April 15, 1813 in Lieut. Justus Foote's Company, Sumner's Regt.

‡*CRANE, ELIJAH.
Served in 2 Regt. (Fifield's) Vt. Militia. Served from April 12, 1814 to May 20, 1814 in company of Capt. James Gray Jr., Sumner's Regt. Pension Certificate of widow, Eliza C., No. 12757.

*CRANE, MILTON, 1st Sergeant.
Served from April 12, 1814 to April 21, 1814 in Capt. Eseck Sprague's Company, Sumner's Regt.

*CRANE, THADEUS.
Served in Corning's Detachment, Vt. Militia.

CRANE, WILLIAM.
Volunteered to go to Plattsburgh, September, 1814, and served 8 days in Capt. Josiah Grout's Company. Ref: Book 51, AGO Page 103.

CRANFORD, DAVID, 2nd Lieutenant.
Served in Lieut. V. R. Goodrich's Company, 11th Regt.; on Pay Roll for January and February, 1813. Ref: R. & L. 1812, AGO Page 11.

CRAPON, SAMUEL.
Served from May 1 to June 30, 1814 in company of Artificers commanded by Alexander Parris. Ref. R. & L. 1812, AGO Page 24.

‡CRAW, IRA.
Served in Capt. Aaron Burr's Company. Pension Certificate No. 34718.

CRAW, JOSEPH, M.
Served from April 12, 1814 to May 20, 1814 in company of Capt. James Gray Jr., Sumner's Regt. Ref: Book 52, AGO Page 280.

CRAW, PHILIP.
Served in Col. Fifield's Regt. Detached Militia in U. S. service 6 months, 1812. Ref: Book 53, AGO Page 10.

CRAWFORD, DANIEL,   Swanton.
Served in Capt. Valentine R. Goodrich's Company, 11th Regt.; on Pay Roll from July 15 to Dec. 8, 1813; in action at the Battle of Lundy's Lane. Ref: Hemenway's Vt. Gazetteer, Vol. 2, Page 444.

CRAWFORD, DAVID, Captain, Putney.
Appointed 2nd Lieutenant 11 Inf. May 7, 1812; 1st Lieutenant June 26, 1813; Captain Sept. 17, 1814; honorably discharged June 15, 1815. Distinguished in the battle of Niagara Falls; Brigadier Major, distinguished in Gen. Brown's sortie at Fort Erie, Sept. 17, 1814 in which he was wounded. Ref: Heitman's Historical Register & Dictionary USA; Hemenway's Vt. Gazetteer, Vol. 5, Part 1, Page 226.

‡CRAWFORD, ELIJAH.
Served in Capt. Gray's Company. Pension Certificate of widow, Sarah C., No. 31184.

*CRAWFORD, JOHN.
Served in Capt. Cross' Company,
Col. Martindale's Regt. Detached
Militia in U. S. service 2 months
and 14 days, 1812.

*CRAWFORD, MARIUS.
Served in Capt. Sabin's Company,
Col. Jonathan Williams' Regt. Detached Militia in U. S. service 17
days.

CREAMER, JOHN W.
Served in Capt. W. Haig's Corps of
Light Dragoons; on Pay Roll to June
30, 1814. Ref: R. & L. 1812, AGO
Page 20.

*CRIPPEN, SAMUEL.
Served in Capt. Robinson's Company,
Col. Dixon's Regt. Detached Militia
in U. S. service 1 month and 23
days, 1813; enlisted Sept. 25, 1813.

CRISSEY, JOHN,   Fairfax or Sheldon.
Volunteered to go to Plattsburgh,
September, 1814, and served in either
Capt. Joseph Beeman's Company or
Capt. Josiah Grout's Company. Ref:
Book 51, AGO Page 120.

CRISSEY, SAMUEL,   Fairfax.
Volunteered to go to Plattsburgh,
September, 1814, and served 8 days
in Capt. Josiah Grout's Company.
Ref: Book 51, AGO Page 103.

CRISSEY, SYLVANUS,   Fairfax.
Volunteered to go to Plattsburgh,
September, 1814, and served 8 days
in Capt. Josiah Grout's Company.
Ref: Book 51, AGO Page 103.

‡CRITCHETT, JEDEDIAH,   Georgia.
Volunteered to go to Plattsburgh,
September, 1814, and served 8 days
in Capt. Jesse Post's Company, Dixon's Regt. Pension Certificate of
widow, Harriet, No. 28268.

CRITCHETT, JEDEDIAH,   Milton.
Volunteered to go to Plattsburgh,
September, 1814, and served 8 days
in Capt. Samuel Farnsworth's Company. Ref: Book 51, AGO Page 87.

*CROCK, CYRUS.
Served in Capt. Howard's Company,
Vt. Militia.

CROCKER, CYRUS.   Thetford.
Marched for Plattsburgh, September,
1814, and went as far as Bolton, Vt.,
serving 6 days in Capt. Salmon Howard's Company. Ref: Book 52, AGO
Page 15.

*CROCKER, EZRA.
Served in Corning's Detachment, Vt.
Militia.

*CROCKER, JAMES, D., Sergeant.
Served in 2 Regt. Vt. Militia commanded by Col. Fifield.

*CROCKER, JESSE.
Served in Capt. Burnap's Company,
Col. Jonathan Williams' Regt. Detached Militia in U. S. service 1
month and 15 days, 1812.

*CROCKER, SETH,   Randolph.
Volunteered to go to Plattsburgh,
September, 1814, and served in Capt.
Lebbeus Egerton's Company.

*CROCKER, ZIBA.
Served in Capt. Lowry's Company,
Col. Wm. Williams' Regt. Detached
Militia in U. S. service 4 months
and 26 days, 1812. Also served in 1
Regt. (Peck's) Vt. Militia and Corn-
ing's Detachment, Vt. Militia.

*CROFOOT, ELIJAH JR.
Served in Sumner's' Regt. Vt. Militia.

CROFT, JAMES.
Enlisted Feb. 28, 1812 for 5 years in
Capt. White Youngs' Company, 15th
Regt.; on Muster Roll from Aug.
31, 1814 to Dec. 31, 1814. Ref. R.
& L. 1812, AGO Page 27.

CROMWELL, JOHN S., 2nd Lieutenant.
Enlisted Nov. 23, 1812 in company
of Capt. J. Brooks, commanded by
Lieut. John I. Cromwell, Corps of
U. S. Artillery; appointed conductor
of Artillery May 12, 1814; on Muster
Roll from April 30, 1814 to June 30,
1814. Ref: R. & L. 1812, AGO Page
18.

*CROMWELL, LEONARD.
Served in 3 Regt. Vt. Militia commanded by Col. Williams.

*CRONK, AARON.
Served in 1st Regt. Vt. Militia commanded by Col. Judson.

CRONKHITE, GEORGE.
Served in Capt. Haskins' Company.
Pension Certificate No. 21845.

CROOK, JAMES,   Salisbury.
Volunteered to go to Plattsburgh,
September, 1814, and served 4 days
in Capt. John Morton's Company.
Ref: Book 52, AGO Page 141.

*CROOK, SAMUEL S.
Served from April 12, 1814 to April
15, 1814 in Capt. John Hackett's
Company, Sumner's Regt.

*CROOK, WILLIAM.
Served in Capt. Rogers' Company,
Col. Fifield's Regt. Detached Militia
in U. S. service 5 months and 2
days, 1812.

CROOKER, JAMES D.
Served in Capt. Taylor's Company,
Col. Fifield's Regt. Detached Militia
in U. S. service 2 months and 21
days, 1812. Ref: Book 53, AGO Page
61.

‡*CROOKER, NOAH JR.,   Woodstock.
Served in Capt. Phelps' Company,
Col. Jonathan Williams' Regt. De-
tached Militia in U. S. service 2
months and 21 days, 1812. Pension
Certificate No. 15824.

*CROSBY, JEREMIAH.
Served in Capt. Burnap's Company,
Col. Jonathan Williams' Regt. Detached Militia in U. S. service 2
months and 13 days, 1812.

CROSBY, JONATHAN, Franklin County.
Volunteered to go to Plattsburgh
Sept. 11, 1814 and served in 15th cr
22nd Regt. Ref: Hemenway's Vt.
Gazetteer, Vol. 2, Page 392.

CROSBY, THOMAS, Corporal, Franklin County. Volunteered to go to Plattsburgh Sept. 11, 1814 and served in 15th or 22nd Regt. Ref: Hemenway's Vt. Gazetteer, Vol. 2, Page 391.

*CROSIER, ALEXANDER, Belvidere or Fairfax. Served in Capt. Brush's Company, Col. Dixon's Regt. Detached Militia in U. S. service 1 month and 23 days, 1813. Enlisted Sept. 25, 1813 in Capt. Asa Wilkins' Company, Dixon's Regt. Volunteered to go to Plattsburgh, September, 1814, and served in Capt. Moody Shattuck's Company.

‡*CROSIER, SAMUEL, Lieutenant. Served in Capt. Preston's Company, 3 Regt. (Williams') Vt. Militia. Pension Certificate of widow, Rhoda, No. 1637.

CROSS, BENJAMIN. Served from Feb. 11, 1813 to May 10, 1813 in Capt. John Weeks' Company, 11th Regt. Ref: R. & L. 1812, AGO Page 4.

*CROSS, DANIEL. Served from Feb. 13, 1813 to May 12, 1813 in Capt. Edgerton's Company, 11th Regt. Served from April 12, 1814 to April 14, 1814 in Capt. Jonathan Stanley's Company, Col. W. B. Sumner's Regt. Ref: R. & L. 1812, AGO Page 3.

CROSS, ELEAZER. Served from May 7, 1813 to Feb. 27, 1814 in Capt. Simeon Wright's Company. Ref: R. & L. 1812, AGO Page 51.

*CROSS, ELIHU, Major. Served in 1st Regt. of Detached Militia of Vermont in the service of the U. S. at Champlain commencing Nov. 18 and ending Nov. 19, 1812.

*CROSS, PETER.   Barton. Served in Capt. Mason's Company, Col. Fifield's Regt. Detached Militia in U. S. service 5 months and 26 days, 1812.

‡*CROSS, REAL, Corporal,   Barton. Served in Capt. Mason's Company, Col. Fifield's Regt. Detached Militia in U. S. service 5 months and 27 days, 1812. Pension Certificate No. 2177.

*CROSS, SAMUEL, Captain. Served as 1st Lieutenant and Captain in 1st Regt. of Detached Militia of Vt. in U. S. service at Champlain commencing Nov. 18 and ending Nov. 19, 1812.

*CROSSETT, JASON, Sergeant. Served in Corning's Detachment, Vt. Militia.

CROSSLEY, THOMAS. Enlisted Nov. 7, 1812 for 5 years in Capt. White Youngs' Company, 15th Regt.; on Muster Roll from Aug. 31, 1814 to Dec. 31, 1814. Ref: R. & L. 1812, AGO Page 27.

CROSSMAN, ALLEN. Enlisted April 20, 1812 for 5 years in Capt. White Youngs' Company, 15th Regt.; on Muster Roll from Aug. 31, 1814 to Dec. 31, 1814. Ref: R. & L. 1812, AGO Page 27.

CROSSMAN, JACOB,   Montpelier. Volunteered to go to Plattsburgh, September, 1814, and served 8 days in Capt. Timothy Hubbard's Company. Ref: Book 52, AGO Pages 246 and 256.

*CROSSMAN, SILAS C.,   Johnson. Enlisted Sept. 25, 1813 and served 1 month and 23 days in Capt. Waterman's Company, Col. Dixon's Regt. Volunteered to go to Plattsburgh, September, 1814, and served 11 days in same company.

*CROUCH, AARON. Served in 1 Regt. Vt. Militia commanded by Col. Judson.

‡CROWELL, SAMUEL, Johnson or Hyde Park. Volunteered to go to Plattsburgh, September, 1814, and served 15 days in Capt. Thomas Waterman's Company, Dixon's Regt. Pension Certificate No. 19393.

*CUDWORTH, DAVID,   Shoreham. Served in Capt. Robbins' Company, Col. Wm. Williams' Regt. Detached Militia in U. S. service 4 months and 29 days, 1812. Volunteered to go to Plattsburgh, September, 1814, and served 6 days in Capt. Samuel Hand's Company.

*CUDWORTH, JOHN. Served from April 12, 1814 to April 21, 1814 in Capt. Eseck Sprague's Company, Sumner's Regt.

‡CULVER, JEREMIAH,   Berlin. Volunteered to go to Plattsburgh, September, 1814, and served 7 days in Capt. Cyrus Johnson's Company. Also served in Capt. Samuel Tillerson's Company. Pension Certificate No. 30228. Pension Certificate of widow, Lydia, No. 29572.

*CULVER, LOT. Served in Sumner's Regt. Vt. Militia.

*CULVER, OLIVER B., Sergeant. Served in Capt. Dorrance's Company, Col. Wm. Williams' Regt. Detached Militia in U. S. service 4 months and 29 days, 1812, as corporal and sergeant. Ref: Book 53,, AGO Page 59.

‡*CULVER, SALMON. Served in Capt. Burnap's Company. Col. Jonathan Williams' Regt. Detached Militia in U. S. service 2 months and 13 days, 1812. Pension Certificate of widow, Sally, No. 2144.

CULVER, SAMUEL,   Shoreham. Volunteered to go to Plattsburgh, September, 1814, and served 6 days in Capt. Samuel Hand's Company. Ref: Rev. J. F. Goodhue's History of Shoreham, Page 107.

*CUMBER, WALTER. Served in 4 Regt. Vt. Militia commanded by Col. Williams.

*CUMINGS, ISON.
Served in Capt. Howard's Company,
Vt. Militia.

*CUMINGS, ISRAEL.
Served in Capt. Howard's Company,
Vt. Militia.

*CUMMINGS, EBEN,   Thetford.
Marched for Plattsburgh, September,
1814, and went as far as Bolton, Vt.,
serving 6 days in Capt. Salmon Howard's Company, 2nd Regt. Ref: Book
52, AGO Page 16.

*CUMMINGS, EZRA,   Thetford.
Marched for Plattsburgh, September,
1814, and went as far as Bolton, Vt.,
serving 6 days in Capt. Salmon Howard's Company, 2nd Regt. Ref: Book
52, AGO Page 15.

CUMMINGS, ISAAC,   Thetford.
Marched for Plattsburgh, September,
1814, and went as far as Bolton, Vt.,
serving 6 days in Capt. Salmon Howard's Company, 2nd Regt. Ref: Book
52, AGO Page 15.

CUMMINGS, JAMES.
Served in Capt. Benjamin S. Edgerton's Company, 11th Regt.; on Pay
Roll for September and October, 1812,
and January and February, 1813.
Ref: R. & L. 1812, AGO Pages 1
and 2.

*CUMMINGS, JAMES JR.
Served in Corning's Detachment, Vt.
Militia.

*CUMMINGS, JEREMIAH, Fifer, Thet-
ford. Marched for Plattsburgh, September, 1814, and went as far as
Bolton, Vt., serving 6 days in Capt.
Salmon Howard's Company, 2nd Regt.

‡*CUMMINGS, JOHN,   Barnard.
Served in Capt. Phelps' Company,
Col. Jonathan Williams' Regt. Detached Militia in U. S. service 2
months and 21 days, 1812. Volunteered to go to Plattsburgh, September, 1814, and served 8 days in Capt.
John S. Bicknell's Company, 3 Regt.
(Williams'). Pension Certificate No.
10162.

CUMMINGS, LEONARD. Highgate or
Swanton. Volunteered to go to Plattsburgh, September, 1814, and served
in Capt. A. J. Brown's Company.
Ref: Book 51, AGO Page 130.

*CUMMINGS, PETER.
Served in Capt. Richardson's Company, Col. Martindale's Regt. Detached Militia in U. S. service 10
days, 1812.

CUMMINGS, SHERMAN,   Marshfield.
Volunteered to go to Plattsburgh,
September, 1814, and served 9 days
in Capt. James English's Company.
Ref: Book 52, AGO Page 248.

CUMMINGS, SIMON,   Montpelier.
Volunteered to go to Plattsburgh,
September, 1814, and served 8 days
in Capt. Timothy Hubbard's Company. Ref: Book 52, AGO Page 256.

CUMMINGS, STEPHEN.
Served in Lieut. Wm. S. Foster's
Company, 11th Regt.; on Pay Roll
for January and February, 1813. Ref:
R. & L. 1812, AGO Page 7.

*CUMMINGS, WILLIAM.
Served from April 12, 1814 to April
21, 1814 in Capt. Edmund B. Hill's
Company, Sumner's Regt.

CUMMINGS, WILLIAM. Adjutant Gen-
eral. Served on General Staff of
Northern Army commanded by Major
Gen. George Izard; on Pay Roll to
July 31, 1814. Ref: R. & L. 1812,
AGO Page 28.

*CUMMINS, JOHN.
Served in Capt. Strait's Company,
Col. Martindale's Regt. Detached
Militia in U. S. service 10 days, 1812.

CUMMINS, JOHN.
Enlisted Nov. 19, 1812 in Capt.
Weeks' Company, 11th Regt.; died
Dec. 15, 1812. Ref: R. & L. 1812,
AGO Page 5.

CUMMINS, JOHN.
Served in Capt. Phineas Williams'
Company, 11th Regt.; on Pay Roll
of company for January and Febru-
ary, 1813. Ref: R. & L. 1812, AGO
Page 15.

*CUMMINS, NATHAN.
Served in 3 Regt. Vt. Militia commanded by Col. Williams.

*CUNE, JOHN.
Served with Hospital Attendants, Vt.

CUNNELL, CHESTER,   Warren, Conn.
Served from Sept. 1, 1814 to June 16,
1815 in Capt. Sanford's Company,
30th Inf. Ref: R. & L. 1812, AGO
Page 23.

CUNNINGHAM, ISAAC S., Stockbridge.
Volunteered to go to Plattsburgh,
September, 1814, and served 8 days
in Capt. Elias Keyes' Company. Ref:
Book 51, AGO Page 239.

CUNNINGHAM, JAMES.
Volunteered to go to Plattsburgh,
September, 1814, and served 4 days
in company of Capt. James George
of Topsham. Ref: Book 52, AGO
Page 68.

*CURLER, BENJAMIN.
Served in Sumner's Regt. Vt. Militia.

CURLEY, RUFUS.
Served in Capt. Preston's Company,
Col. Jonathan Williams' Regt. Detached Militia in U. S. service 2
months and 6 days, 1812. Ref: Book
53, AGO Page 64.

CURLEY, WILLIAM.
Served in company of late Capt. J.
Brooks, commanded by Lieut. John
I. Cromwell, Corps of U. S. Artillery; on Muster Roll from April 30,
1814 to June 30, 1814; paroled prisoner. Ref: R. & L. 1812, AGO Page
18.

CURRIER, ANDREW,   Barre.
Volunteered to go to Plattsburgh,
September, 1814, and served 10 days
in Capt. Warren Ellis' Company. Ref:
Book 52, AGO Page 242.

*CURRIER, ANDREW, Fifer.
Served in Capt. John Palmer's Company, 1st Regt., 2nd Brig., 3rd Div.;
on Muster Roll from June 11-14, 1813
and from Oct. 4 to Oct. 13, 1813.

CURRIER, JOSEPH.
Served in 2 Regt. Vt. Militia commanded by Col. Fifield.

CURRIER, SAMUEL,   Berlin.
Volunteered to go to Plattsburgh,
September, 1814, and served 7 days
in Capt. Cyrus Johnson's Company.
Ref: Book 52, AGO Page 255.

*CURRIER, WILLIAM.
Served in 1 Regt. Vt. Militia commanded by Col. Martindale.

CURRIN, JAMES,   Franklin County.
Volunteered to go to Plattsburgh
Sept. 11, 1814 and served in 15th or
22nd Regt. Ref: Hemenway's Vt.
Gazetteer, Vol. 2, Page 392.

CURRY, ARCHIBALD.
Enlisted March 13, 1813 in Capt.
Charles Follett's Company, 11th Regt.;
died April 5, 1813. Ref: R. & L.
1812, AGO Page 13.

‡CURRY, SAMUEL P.
Served in Capt. J. Kinney's Com-
pany. Pension Certificate of widow,
Mary R., No. 26186.

CURRY, WILLIAM.
Enlisted Feb. 18, 1812 for five years
in Capt. White Youngs' Company
of Infantry, 15th Regt. Ref: R. &
L. 1812, AGO Page 27.

CURTIS, AARON,   Richmond.
Volunteered to go to Plattsburgh,
September, 1814, and served 9 days
in Capt. Roswell Hunt's Company, 3
Regt. (Tyler's) Ref: Book 51, AGO
Page 82.

CURTIS, ANSON,   Richford.
Served in Capt. Martin D. Follett's
Company, Dixon's Regt. on duty on
Canadian Frontier in 1813. Ref:
Hemenway's Vt. Gazetteer, Vol. 2,
Page 428.

⁻CURTIS, BENJAMIN A.
Served from April 12, 1814 to April
21, 1814 in Capt. Eseck Sprague's
Company, Sumner's Regt.

CURTIS, BRADFORD T.   Bridport.
Volunteered to go to Plattsburgh,
September, 1814, and served 21 days;
no organization given. Ref: Book 51,
AGO Page 38.

*CURTIS, CHARLES C.
Served from April 20, 1814 to April
21, 1814 in Capt. Eseck Sprague's
Company, Sumner's Regt.

*CURTIS, DAVID.
Served in 1 Regt. Vt. Militia commanded by Col. Martindale.

*CURTIS, EBENEZER.
Served from April 12, 1814 to April
21, 1814 in Capt. Eseck Sprague's
Company, Sumner's Regt.

*CURTIS, ELDAD K.
Served in Capt. Lowry's Company,
Col. Wm. Williams' Regt. Detached
Militia in U. S. service 4 months
and 26 days, 1812.

*CURTIS, FREDERICK.
Served in 1 Regt. Vt. Militia commanded by Col. Judson.

*CURTIS, HENRY,   Bridport.
Served in Capt. Robbins' Company,
Col. Wm. Williams' Regt. Detached
Militia in U. S. service 4 months and
29 days, 1812.

CURTIS, JAMES,   Addison.
Volunteered to go to Plattsburgh,
September, 1814, and served 9 days
in Capt. George Fisher's Company,
Sumner's Regt.; was in the battle.
Ref: Book 51, AGO Page 5.

CURTIS, JOSEPH H.,   Ira.
Served in Capt. Benj. Bradford's
Company; on Muster Roll from May
31, 1813 to Aug. 31, 1813. Volunteered to go to Plattsburgh September,
1814, and served 4 days in Capt.
Matthew Anderson's Company. Ref:
R. & L. 1812, AGO Page 26; Book
52, AGO Page 144.

*CURTIS, LUTHER,   Richmond.
Served 3 months beginning September,
1812, in 6th Company, 3rd Regt. 2nd
Brig., commanded by Brig. Gen.
Newell. Served from Oct. 5, 1813
to Oct. 16, 1813 in Capt. Roswell
Hunt's Company, 3 Regt. (Tyler's).
Ref: Vol. 50, Vt. State Papers, Page
85.

*CURTIS, PHILO.
Served in Sumner's Regt. Vt. Militia.

*CURTIS, PLINY, Corporal.
Volunteered to go to Plattsburgh,
September, 1814, and served 10 or
12 days in Capt. Gideon Wheelock's
Company.

‡*CURTIS, RANSOM,   Orange.
Served in Capt. Rogers' Company,
Col. Fifield's Regt. Detached Militia
in U. S. service 2 months and 18
days, 1812. Served in Capt. Burnap's
Company. Pension Certificate No.
15170. Pension Certificate of widow,
Anna, No. 16873.

CURTIS, T.,   Richmond.
Volunteered to go to Plattsburgh,
September, 1814, and served 9 days
in Capt. Roswell Hunt's Company,
3rd Regt. Ref: Book 51, AGO Page
82.

CURTIS, THADEUS.
Enlisted Aug. 1, 1813 for 1 year in
Capt. James Taylor's Company, 30th
Regt.; transferred to Capt. Gideon
Spencer's Company, 30th Regt.;
transferred to Capt. Clark's Company,
30th Regt., June 2, 1814; discharged
Aug. 1, 1814. Ref: R. & L. 1812,
AGO Pages 29, 52, 57, 59.

*CURTIS, TIMOTHY B.
Served from April 20, 1814 to April
21, 1814 in Capt. Eseck Sprague's
Company, Sumner's Regt.

CURTIS, ZIBA.
Served in Capt. Benjamin Bradford's
Company; on Muster Roll from May
31, 1813 to Aug. 31, 1813. Ref: R.
& L. 1812, AGO Page 26.

*CUSHING, CHARLES, Fifer,   Burke.
Served in Capt. Wheeler's Company,
Col. Fifield's Regt. Detached Militia
in U. S. service 6 months and 4
days, 1812.

*CUSHING, DENNIS, Corporal.
Served in Capt. Robbins' Company,
Col. Wm. Willions' Regt. Detached
Militia in U. S. service 4 months and
29 days, 1812.

*CUSHING, JOHN.
Served with Hospital Attendants, Vt.

‡*CUSHMAN, ABIAL.
Served in Capt. Phelps' Company,
Col. Wm. Williams' Regt. Detached
Militia in U. S. service 5 months,
1812. Also served in Capt. Feet's
Company. Pension Certificate of
widow, Tabitha, No. 8733 .

CUSHMAN, ARTEMUS, 1st Lieutenant,
Braintree. Marched to Plattsburgh,
Sept. 10, 1814 and served 10 days in
Capt. Lot Hudson's Company. Ref:
Book 52, AGO Pages 24 and 33; Book
51, AGO Page 295.

CUSHMAN, D. S.
Served from March 25, 1813 to June
24, 1813 in Capt. Samul Gordon's
Company, 11th Regt. Ref: R. & L.
1812, AGO Page 8.

CUSHMAN, JEREMIAH.
Born in Plymton, Mass.; age 28
years; height 5 feet 10½ inches;
complexion, dark; hair, brown; eyes,
hazel; by profession a carpenter.
Enlisted May 22, 1814 for period of
war in Capt. Wm. Miller's Company,
30th Regt.; enlisted at Pownal; discharged at Burlington, 1815. Ref:
R. & L. 1812, AGO Pages 54 and 55.

CUSHMAN, NATHANIEL.
Enlisted May 6, 1813 for 1 year in
Capt. Simeon Wright's Company.
Ref: R. & L. 1812, AGO Page 51.

*CUSHMAN, SALMON.
Served in Capt. Post's Company, Col.
Dixon's Regt. Detached Militia in
U. S. service 1 month and 23 days;
enlisted Sept. 25, 1813.

*CUSHMAN, SETH, Brig. Major and In-
spector. Served with General and
Staff (Orms') Vt. Militia.

CUSHMAN, WILLARD S.,   Tunbridge.
Volunteered to go to Plattsburgh,
September, 1814, and served in Capt.
David Knox's Company. Ref: Book
52, AGO Page 116.

CUSHMAN, WILLIAM, Sergeant, Pittsford. Volunteered to go to Plattsburgh, September, 1814, and served
8 days in Capt. Caleb Hendee's Company. Ref: Book 52, AGO Page 124.

*CUSHMAN, ZABINA.
Served in Sumner's Regt. Vt. Militia.

CUTHBERT, JOHN W.
Served in Capt. Benjamin S. Edgerton's Company, 11th Regt.; on Pay
Roll for September and October, 1812,
and January and February, 1813.
Ref: R. & L. 1812, AGO Pages 1
and 2.

CUTLER, EBENEZER.
Volunteered to go to Plattsburgh,
September, 1814, and served 7 days
in company of Capt. Frederick Gris-
wold, raised in Brookfield, Vt. Ref:
Book 52, AGO Pages 52 and 53.

*CUTLER, EPHRAIM, Sergeant.
Served in Capt. Willson's Company,
Col. Wm. Williams' Regt. Detached
Militia in U. S. service 4 months and
24 days, 1812.

CUTLER, ISAAC, Sergeant.
Served in Capt. Willson's Company,
Col. Wm. Williams' Regt. stationed
at Swanton Falls in 1812. Ref: Vol.
49 Vt. State Papers, Page 119.

CUTLER, JAMES,   Marlboro?
Enlisted Feb. 2, 1813 in Capt. Charles
Follett's Company, 11th Regt.; deserted Feb. 2, 1813. Ref: R. & L.
1812, AGO Page 13.

CUTLER, JONATHAN JR.,   Montpelier.
Volunteered to go to Plattsburgh,
September, 1814, and served 8 days
in Capt. Timothy Hubbard's Company. Ref: Book 52, AGO Page 256.

‡CUTLER, JOSHUA.
Served in Capt. Sumner's Company.
Pension Certificate of widow, Ladisa,
No. 43577.

CUTLER, LEONARD.
Served in the War of 1812 and was
captured by troops May 6, 1814 at
Oswago; discharged Oct. 8, 1814.
Ref: Records of Naval Records and
Library, Navy Dept.

*CUTLER, MOSES, Fifer.
Served in Capt. Mason's Company,
Col. Fifield's Regt. Detached Militia
in U. S. service 3 months and 15
days, 1812.

*CUTLER, RICHARD.
Served from June 11, 1813 to June
14, 1813 in Capt. Hezekiah Barns'
Company, 1st Regt. 2nd Brig., 3rd
Div.

CUTLER, SALEM,   East Montpelier.
Volunteered to go to Plattsburgh,
September, 1814, and served 4 days;
no organization given. Ref: Book
52, AGO Pages 173 and 192.

*CUTTING, CLARK.
Served in Capt. Briggs' Company,
Col. Jonathan Williams' Regt. Detached Militia in U. S. service 1
month and 27 days, 1812.

*CUTTING, DAVID,   Marshfield.
Served in Capt. Rogers' Company,
Col. Fifield's Regt. Detached Militia
in U. S. service 2 months and 18
days, 1812.

CUTTING, GEORGE, Ensign, Shoreham. Volunteered to go to Plattsburgh. September, 1814, and served 6 days in Capt. Samuel Hand's Company. Ref: Rev. J. F. Goodhue's History of Shoreham, Page 107.

*CUTTING, JEREMIAH, Shoreham. Served from April 12, 1814 to May 20, 1814 in company of Capt. James Gray Jr., Sumner's Regt. Also served in Capt. John Robbins' Company, Col. Wm. Williams' Regt. Volunteered to go to Plattsburgh, September, 1814, and served 6 days in Capt. Samuel Hand's Company. Ref: Rev. J. F. Goodhue's History of Shoreham, Page 107.

CUTTING, JONAS, Lt. Colonel. Appointed Lt. Colonel 25 Inf. March 12, 1812; resigned Sept. 1, 1814; died April 5, 1834. Ref: Heitman's Historical Register & Dictionary USA.

DAGGETT, ARTHUR JR, Montpelier. Volunteered to go to Plattsburgh, September, 1814, and served 8 days in Capt. Timothy Hubbard's Company. Ref: Book 52, AGO Pages 246, 249, 256.

*DAGGETT, DAVID, Calais. Volunteered to go to Plattsburgn, September, 1814, and served 10 days in Capt. Gideon Wheelock's Company.

*DAGGETT, HENRY. Served from April 12, 1814 to April 21, 1814 in Capt. Shubael Wales' Company, Col. W. B. Sumner's Regt.

DAGGETT, ISRAEL. Served from Jan. 15, 1813 to July 1, 1813 in Capt. Edgerton's Company, 11th Regt. Ref: R. & L. 1812, AGO Page 3.

DAGGETT, ORA. Served in Capt. John Palmer's Company, 1st Regt. 2nd Brig.; 3rd Div.; on Muster Roll June 11 to June 14, 1813 and Oct. 4, to Oct. 13, 1813. Ref: R. & L. 1812, AGO Pages 47 and 48.

DAGGETT, SIMEON, Montpelier. Volunteered to go to Plattsburgh, September, 1814, and served 8 days in Capt. Timothy Hubbard's Company. Ref: Book 52, AGO Page 256.

DAILIN, JACOB, Burlington. Volunteered to go to Plattsburgh, September, 1814, and served in Capt. Henry Mayo's Company. Ref: Book 51, AGO Page 81.

*DAINES, JOHN. Served in 1 Regt. Vt. Militia commanded by Col. Judson.

DAKE, ARNOLD B., Lieutenant. Appointed Ensign 30 Inf. April 30, 1813; 3 Lieutenant Jan. 31, 1814; 2 Lieutenant Sept. 13, 1814; transferred to 5th Inf. May 17, 1815; resigned Jan. 1, 1817. Ref: Heitman's Historical Register & Dictionary USA.

*DAKE, BENJAMIN. Served in Capt. Brigham's Company, Col. Jonathan Williams' Regt. Detached Militia in U. S. service 2 months and 9 days, 1812.

DAKE, BENJAMIN. Volunteered to go to Plattsburgh, September, 1814, and served in Capt. Ebenezer Spencer's Company, Vershire. Ref: Book 52, AGO Page 48.

‡DAKE, BENJAMIN F., St. Albans. Enlisted June 15, 1813 for 1 year in Capt. John Wires' Company, 30th Regt. Pension Certificate of widow, Clarissa, No. 18002.

*DAKE, JOSEPH, Stowe. Volunteered to go to Plattsburgh, September, 1814, and was at the battle, serving in Capt. Nehemiah Perkins' Company, 4 Regt. (Williams').

DALTON, JOHN P. Served from Sept. 1, 1814 to June 16, 1815 in Capt. Sanford's Company, 30th Inf. Ref: R. & L. 1812, AGO Page 23.

*DALY, WILLIAM, Corporal. Served in Capt. Briggs' Company, Col. Jonathan Williams' Regt. Detached Militia in U. S. service 2 months and 13 days, 1812.

DAMON, GARY, Shoreham. Volunteered to go to Plattsburgh, September, 1814, and served 6 days in Capt. Samuel Hand's Company. Ref: Rev. J. F. Goodhue's History of Shoreham, Page 107.

‡DAMON, MARTIN R. Served in Capt. A. B. Rogers' Company. Pension Certificate No. 30897.

DAMON, ZACARIAH. Served from May 1st to June 30, 1814 as carpenter in a company of Artificers commanded by Alexander Parris. Ref: R. & L. 1812, AGO Page 24.

DANA, AUSTIN, Cornwall. Volunteered to go to Plattsburgh, September, 1814, and was at the battle, serving in Capt. Edmund B. Hill's Company, Sumner's Regt. Ref: Book 51, AGO Page 13.

*DANA, DANIEL, Colonel. Served as Colonel in 31 Inf. Feb. 23, 1813; honorably discharged June 15, 1815. Served as Major in 3 Regt. (Williams') Vt. Militia. Ref: Heitman's Historical Register & Dictionary USA.

*DANA, DANIEL. Served in Capt. Hotchkiss' Company, Col. Martindale's Regt. Detached Militia in U. S. service 1 month and 7 days, 1812.

*DANA, FOSTER. Served in Corning's Detachment, Vt. Militia.

*DANA, HENRY, C. Served in Capt. Adams' Company, Col. Jonathan Williams' Regt. Detached Militia in U. S. service 2 months and 7 days, 1812.

*DANBY, JOHN W., Randolph. Volunteered to go to Plattsburgh, September, 1814, and served in Capt. Lebbeus Egerton's Company.

*DANFORTH, CHARLES.
Served in 1 Regt. Vt. Militia commanded by Col. Judson.

‡DANFORTH, DANIEL C., Sergeant.
Fairfax. Enlisted Sept. 25, 1813 and served 1 month and 23 days in Capt. Asa Wilkins' Company, Dixon's Regt. Also served in Capt. Partridge's Company. Pension Certificate No. 6981.

‡*DANFORTH, DAVID, Sergeant, Fairfax. Enlisted Sept. 25, 1813 in Capt. Asa Wilkins' Company, Dixon's Regt. Pension Certificate No. 20829.

*DANFORTH, DAVID JR.
Enlisted Sept. 25, 1813 and served 1 month and 23 days in Capt. Jesse Post's Company, Dixon's Regt.

*DANFORTH, ELKANAH.
Served in Capt. Morrill's Company, 2 Regt. (Fifield's) Detached Militia in U. S. service 2 months and 18 days, 1812.

*DANFORTH, ELKANAH JR., Randolph.
Volunteered to go to Plattsburgh, September, 1814, and served in Capt. Lebbeus Egerton's Company.

*DANFORTH, HENRY, Sergeant.
Served from Sept. 25, 1813 to Oct. 2, 1813 in Capt. N. B. Eldridge's Company, Dixon's Regt.

DANFORTH, ISAAC, Fairfax.
Served in 1813 and 1814 in Capt. Joseph Beeman's Company. Ref: Hemenway's Vt. Gazetteer, Vol. 2, Page 402.

*DANFORTH, JONATHAN JR .
Served in Capt. Saxe's Company, Col. Wm. Williams' Regt. Detached Militia in U. S. service 4 months and 24 days, 1812.

*DANFORTH, LEVI, Fairfax.
Enlisted Sept. 25, 1813 and served 1 month and 23 days in Capt. Asa Wilkins' Company, Col. Dixon's Regt.

DANFORTH, SAMUEL.
Served in Lieut. Wm. S. Foster's Company, 11th Regt.; on Pay Roll for January and February, 1813. Ref: R. & L. 1812, AGO Page 7.

DANFORTH, SYLVANUS, Pownal?
Appointed Captain 30 Inf. April 30, 1813; honorably discharged June 15, 1815. Ref: Heitmans' Historical Register & Dictionary USA.

*DANFORTH, WARREN, Fairfield.
Served in Capt. Kendall's Company. Col. Wm. Williams' Regt. Detached Militia in U. S. service 4 months and 23 days, 1812.

*DANFORTH, WILLIAM, Sergeant.
Enlisted Sept. 25, 1813 and served 1 month and 23 days in Capt. Amos Robinson's Company, Col. Dixon's Regt.

‡*DANIELS, CLARK.
Served in Capt. Morrill's Company. Col. Fifield's Regt. Detached Militia in U. S. service 3 months and 17

days, 1812. Pension Certificate No. 8694.

*DANIELS, CLEMENT, Corporal.
Served in Capt. Wheeler's Company, Col. Fifield's Regt. Detached Militia in U. S. service 6 months and 4 days, 1812.

*DANIELS, FRANCIS.
Served in Capt. Ormsby's Company. Col. Martindale's Regt. Detached Militia in U. S. service 2 months and 14 days, 1812. Served from May 1 to June 30, 1814 in Capt. Alexander Brooks' Corps of Artillery. Ref: R. & L. 1812, AGO Page 31.

DANIELS, GAD, Fifer, Vershire.
Volunteered to go to Plattsburgh. September, 1814, and served 3 days in Capt. Ira Corse's Company. Ref: Book 52, AGO Page 91.

*DANIELS, GEORGE.
Served in Capt. Ormsby's Company. Col. Martindale's Regt. Detached Militia in U. S. service 13 days, 1812.

DANIELS, GROSVENOR, Fifer, Vershire.
Volunteered to go to Plattsburgh. September, 1814, and served 3 days in Capt. Ira Corse's Company. Ref: Book 52, AGO Page 91.

DANIELS, JOHN., Utica, N. Y.
Served from Oct. 6, 1814 to June 19, 1815 in Capt. Taylor's Company, 30th Inf. Ref: R. & L. 1812, AGO Page 23.

DANIELS, JOHN JR., Sergeant.
Served from April 29, 1813 to April 28, 1814 in Capt. Daniel Farrington's Company, 30th Regt. (also commanded by Capt. Simeon Wright.) Ref: R. & L. 1812, AGO Pages 50 and 51.

*DANIELS, LEAVITT, Danville.
Served in Capt. Morrill's Company, Col. Fifield's Regt. Detached Militia in U. S. service 6 months and 5 days, 1812.

*DANIELS, SAMUEL.
Served in Lieut. Wm. S. Foster's Company, 11th Regt.; on Pay Roll for January and February, 1813. Also served in 4 Regt. (Peck's) Vt. Militia. Ref: R. & L. 1812, AGO Page 7.

‡DANIELS, THEODORE.
Served in Capt. Thornton's Company. Pension Certificate No. 21090.

*DANIELS, ZATHA, Corporal, Jamaica.
Served in Capt. Preston's Company, Col. Jonathan Williams' Regt. Detached Militia in U. S. service 2 months and 6 days, 1812.

DANTER, THOMAS, Georgia.
Served in Capt. Jesse Post's Company, Dixon's Regt., in 1814. Ref: Hemenway's Vt. Gazetteer, Vol. 2, Page 417.

DANTON, GEORGE W., Burlington.
Served from Sept. 1, 1814 to June 16, 1815 in Capt. Sanford's Company, 30th Inf. Ref: R. & L. 1812, AGO Page 23.

DANTZ, JOHN,
Served from Feb. 2, 1813 to Feb. 28, 1813 in Capt. Samuel H. Holly's Company, 11th Regt. Ref: R. & L. 1812, AGO Page 25.

DARBY, BENJAMIN, Lieutenant.
Appointed 3 Lieutenant 30 Inf. April 30, 1813; 2 Lieutenant Sept. 18, 1813; 1 Lieutenant Aug. 1, 1814; honorably discharged June 15, 1815. On Muster Roll of Capt. Wm. Miller's Company, 30th Regt. to Aug. 31, 1814. Ref: Heitman's Historical Register and Dictionary USA; Governor and Council, Vt. Vol. 6, Page 475; R. & L. 1812, AGO Page 54.

‡DARBY, GEORGE.
Served in Capt. J. W. Reynolds' Company. Pension Certificate of widow, Rebecca, No. 24477.

DARBY, JOHN.
Enlisted June 16, 1813 for 1 year in Capt. Simeon Wright's Company. Ref: R. & L. 1812, AGO Page 51.

DARBY, JOHN W.,   Randolph.
Volunteered to go to Plattsburgh, September, 1814, and served in Capt. Lebbeus Egerton's Company. Ref: Hemenway's Vt. Gazetteer, Vol. 2, Page 999.

‡DARBY, RODERICK.
Volunteered to go to Plattsburgh, September, 1814, and went as far as Bolton, Vt., serving 4 days in Lieut. Phineus Kimball's Company, West Fairlee.. Also served in Capt. Ebenezer Spencer's Company. Pension Certificate No. 32539. Ref: Book 52, AGO Pages 46, 48, 49.

DARK, LEVI.
·Served from Oct. 14 to Nov. 17, 1813 in Capt. Asahel Scoville's Company. Ref: R. & L. 1812, AGO Page 22.

*DARLING, CALVIN.
Served in Capt. Richardson's Company, Col. Martindale's Regt. Detached Militia in U. S. service 2 months and 13 days, 1812.

*DARLING, EBENEZER.
Served in Capt. Wheeler's Company, Col. Fifield's Regt. Detached Militia in U. S. service 2 months and 18 days, 1812.

*DARLING, EBENEZER.
Served in Capt. Dorrance's Company, Col. Wm. Williams' Regt. Detached Militia in U. S. service 4 months and 29 days, 1812.

DARLING, ELI.
On Pay Roll of Capt. Weeks' Company, 11th Regt. for January and February, 1813; deserted Jan. 1, 1813; never mustered or paid. Ref: R. & L. 1812, AGO Page 5.

*DARLING, JACOB.
Served in Capt. Lowry's Company. Col. Wm. Williams' Regt. Detached Militia in U. S. service 4 months and 26 days. 1812.

*DARLING, JOHN, Sergeant.
Served in Capt. Rogers' Company, Col. Fifield's Regt. Detached Militia in U. S. service 5 months and 27 days, 1812.

DARLING, LEVI,   Hancock.
Volunteered to go to Plattsburgh, September, 1814, and served 7 days in Capt. Asaph Smith's Company. Ref: Book 51, AGO Pages 20 and 21.

*DARLING, MESHACK.
Served in Capt. Wheeler's Company, Col. Fifield's Regt. Detached Militia in U. S. service 6 months and 4 days, 1812.

*DARLING, PETER.
Name appears on Pay Roll of Capt. Phineas Williams' Company, 11th Regt., for January and February, 1813; absent, not paid. Enlisted Feb. 27, 1813 in Capt. Charles Follett's Company, 11th Regt.; on Pay Roll to May 31, 1813. Also served in 1 Regt. (Martindale's) Vt. Militia. Ref: R. & L. 1812, AGO Pages 13 and 15.

DARLING, SAMUEL,   Corinth.
Volunteered to go to Plattsburgh, September, 1814, and served in Capt. Abel Jackman's Company. Ref: Book 52, AGO Page 44.

*DARLING, SIMEON,   Fairfield.
Served in Capt. Kendall's Company, Col. Wm. Williams' Regt. and Capt. Wright's Company, Col. Fifield's Regt. Detached Militia in U. S. service 8 months and 2 days, 1812. Served from May 1 to June 30, 1814 as corporal in Capt. Alexander Brooks' Corps of Artillery. Ref: R. & L. 1812, AGO Page 31.

*DART, LEVI,   Enosburgh.
Enlisted Oct. 15, 1813 in Capt. Asahel Scovell's Company, Col. Clark's Rifle Corps.

‡*DARTT, OLIVET.
Served in Capt. Scovell's Company, Col. Martindale's Regt. Detached Militia in U. S. service 23 days, 1812. Served from May 1, 1813 to April 30, 1814 in Capt. Simeon Wright's Company. Pension Certificate No. 445.

DAUD, ORRIN.
Served from April 12, 1814 to April 21, 1814 in Capt. Eseck Sprague's Company, Sumner's Regt. Ref: Book 52, AGO Page 263.

DAVENPORT, ABEL.
Served from Feb. 16, 1813 to May 15, 1813 in Lieut. V. R. Goodrich's Company, 11th Regt. Ref: R. & L. 1812, AGO Pages 10 and 11.

‡DAVENPORT, AMOS,   Williamstown.
Pension Certificate of widow, Loretta, No. 14560; no organization given.

DAVENPORT, B.,   Williamstown.
Volunteered to go to Plattsburgh, September, 1814, and served 8 days in Capt. David Robinson's Company. Ref: Book 52, AGO Page 10.

DAVENPORT, ELI.
Enlisted Feb. 10, 1813 in Capt. John
W. Weeks' Company, 11th Regt.; on
Pay Roll for January and February,
1813. Ref: R. & L. 1812, AGO Pages
4 and 5.

‡DAVENPORT, LEMUEL.
Served in Capt. Dickenson's Company. Pension Certificate No. 13941.

*DAVENPORT, LEVI, Ensign.
Served from June 11, 1813 to June
14, 1813 in Capt. John M. Eldridge's
Company 1st Regt. 2nd Brig. 3rd
Div.

DAVENPORT, PHINEAS.
Served in Capt. Weeks' Company,
11th Regt.; on Pay Roll for January and February. 1813. Ref: R.
& L. 1812, AGO Page 5.

DAVENPORT, WILLIAM H., Franklin
County. Volunteered to go to Plattsburgh, Sept. 11, 1814 and served in
15th or 22nd Regt. Ref: Hemenway's
Vt. Gazetteer, Vol. 2, Page 391.

DAVID, JOHN.
Served from April 12, 1814 to April
21, 1814 in Capt. Eseck Sprague's
Company, Sumner's Regt. Ref: Book
52, AGO Page 263.

*DAVIDS, LYMAN.
Served from June 11, 1813 to June
14, 1813 in Capt. Samuel Blinn's Company, 1st Regt.

*DAVIDS, TRUMAN.
Served from June 11, 1813 to June
14, 1813 in Capt. Samuel Blinn's
Company, 1st Regt.

DAVIDSON, CHESTER, Franklin County.
Volunteered to go to Plattsburgh
Sept. 11, 1814 and served in 15th or
22nd Regt. Ref: Hemenway's Vt. Gazetteer, Vol. 2, Page 391.

DAVIES, CHARLES T.,   St. Albans.
Enlisted May 22, 1813 for 1 year in
Capt. John Wires' Company, 30th
Regt.; served as Artificer at Bur-
lington. Ref: R. & L. 1812, AGO
Page 40.

DAVIS, ABNER.
Served from March 10, 1813 to June
9, 1813 in Lieut. V. R. Goodrich's
Company, 11th Regt. Ref: R. & L.
1812, AGO Page 10.

DAVIS, ABRAHAM.
Served in Capt. Benjamin Bradford's
Company; on Muster Roll from May
31, 1813 to Aug. 31, 1813; on com-
mand on board the scows. Ref: R.
& L. 1812, AGO Page 26.

*DAVIS, ANDREW.
Served from June 11, 1813 to June
14, 1813 in Lieut. Bates' Company,
1st Regt.

*DAVIS, ASA.
Served in 4 Regt. Vt. Militia commanded by Col. Williams.

‡*DAVIS, BENJAMIN.
Served in Capt. Adams' Company,
Col. Jonathan Williams' Regt. De-

tached Militia in U. S. service 2
months and 7 days, 1812. Pension
Certificate No. 10699.

DAVIS, BENJAMIN.
Served from Nov. 1, 1812 to Feb. 28,
1813 in company of Capt. John Mc-
Neil Jr., 11th Regt. Served from
March 18, 1813 to June 17, 1813 in
Capt. Charles Follett's Company, 11th
Regt. Ref: R. & L. 1812, AGO Pages
13 and 17.

*DAVIS, BENJAMIN.
Served in Capt. Sabin's Company,
Col. Jonathan Williams' Regt. Detached Militia in U. S. service 2
months and 6 days, 1812.

*DAVIS, CALEB.
Served in Capt. Phelps' Company,
Col. Jonathan Williams' Regt. Detached Militia in U. S. service 1
month and 16 days, 1812.

*DAVIS, CHARLES, 1st Sergeant.
Served from April 12, 1814 to April
21, 1814 in Lieut. Justus Foote's
Company, Sumner's Regt.

DAVIS, CHARLES I.
Enlisted June 4, 1813 for 1 year in
Capt. Sanford's Company, 30th Regt.
Ref: R. & L. 1812, AGO Page 1.

DAVIS, CHESTER,   Franklin County.
Volunteered to go to Plattsburgh
Sept. 11, 1814 and served in 15th or
22nd Regt. Ref: Hemenway's Vt. Gazetteer, Vol. 2, Page 392.

*DAVIS, EDMAN.
Served with Hospital Attendants, Vt.

*DAVIS, ELEAZER, Lieutenant.
Appointed 3 Lieutenant 31 Inf. April
30, 1813; 1 Lieutenant May 1, 1814;
resigned Sept. 30, 1814. Served as
Ensign in 3 Regt. (Williams') Vt.
Militia. Ref: Heitman's Historical
Register & Dictionary USA.

‡*DAVIS, ELIJAH.
Served in Capt. Lowry's Company,
Col. Wm. Williams' Regt. Detached
Militia in U. S. service 4 months
and 26 days, 1812. Also served in
Corning's Detachment, Vt. Militia.
Pension Certificate of widow, Deborah,
No. 468.

DAVIS, FRANCIS,   St. Albans.
Volunteered to go to Plattsburgh,
September, 1814, and served 7 days
in Capt. Farnsworth's Company.
Ref: Book 51, AGO Pages 116 and
196.

‡DAVIS, FRANCIS JR.
Volunteered to go to Plattsburgh,
September, 1814, and served 7 days
in Capt. Frederick Griswold's Company, raised in Brookfield, Vt. Pension Certificate No. 22663.

‡DAVIS, GEORGE.
Served under Captains Hazen and
Pettit. Pension Certificate of widow,
Eunice, No. 30353.

DAVIS, GRINDAL,   Goshen.
Volunteered to go to Plattsburgh,
September, 1814, and served 5 days
in Capt. Durham Sprague's Company.
Ref: Book 52, AGO Page 129.

*DAVIS, ISAAC B., Lieutenant.
Served in Capt. Saxe's Company,
Col. Wm. Williams' Regt. Detached
Militia in U. S. service 4 months
and 24 days, 1812. Served from
April 27, 1813 to July 2, 1813 in
company of Capt. John McNeil Jr.,
11th Regt. Appointed Ensign 11 Inf.
April 15, 1814; 3 Lieutenant May 1,
1814; 2 Lieutenant Sept. 17, 1814;
died Sept. 28, 1814 of wounds re-
ceived in action at Fort Erie U. C.
Ref: Heitman's Historical Register
& Dictionary USA; R. & L. 1812,
AGO Page 16.

DAVIS, JACOB JR.,   Montpelier.
Carried guns from Montpelier to Burlington at time of Plattsburgh invasion, September, 1814, serving 5 or
6 days; did not join any company.
Ref: Book 52, AGO Page 213.

DAVIS, JAMES.
Enlisted Nov. 1, 1812 in company of
Capt. John McNeil Jr. 11th Regt.;
died Jan. 18, 1813. Ref: R. & L.
1812, AGO Page 17.

‡DAVIS, JOHN.
Served in Capt. Myron Reed's Company, 3 Regt. (Tyler's). Pension Certificate of widow, Mary L., No. 8626.

DAVIS, JOHN, Fifer,   Pittsfield.
Served in Capt. Durkee's Company,
Col. Fifield's Regt. Detached Militia
in U. S. service 2 months and 21
days, 1812. Ref: Book 53, AGO Page
70; Vol. 51, Vt. State Papers, Page
94.

*DAVIS, JOHN Corporal.
Served in Capt. Sabin's Company.
Col. Jonathan Williams' Regt. Detached Militia in U. S. service 2
months and 6 days, 1812.

*DAVIS, JOHN JR.
Served in Capt. E. Walker's Company, Col. Fifield's Regt. Detached
Militia in U. S. service 6 months
and 5 days, 1812.

‡DAVIS, JOHN P.   Montpelier.
Volunteered to go to Plattsburgh,
September, 1814, and served 8 days
in Capt. Tiomthy Hubbard's Com-
pany. Pension Certificate of widow,
Asenath, No. 36120.

‡DAVIS, JONATHAN.
Volunteered to go to Plattsburgh,
September, 1814, and served in Capt.
Ebenezer Spencer's Company, Ver-
shire. Also served in Capt. D. A. A.
Buck's Company. Pension Certificate
No. 21248. Ref: Book 52, AGO
Pages 48 and 97.

*DAVIS, JOSEPH, Sergeant.
Served in Capt. Sabins' Company,
Col. Jonathan Williams' Regt. Detached Militia in U. S. service 2
months and 6 days, 1812.

DAVIS, JOSIAH.
Served from May 1 to Aug. 19, 1814;
no organization given. Ref: R. &
L. 1812, AGO Page 29.

‡DAVIS, MARK,   Barnard.
Served from May 17, 1813 to Sept.
17, 1813 in Capt. Nehemiah Noble's
Company, 31st U. S. Inf. Also serv-
ed in Capt. Atkins' Company. Pen-
sion Certificate No. 14693. Ref: Wm.
N. Newton's History of Barnard,
Vol. 1, Page 95.

DAVIS, MOSES.
Served from Feb. 18, 1813 to May
10, 1813 in Capt. John W. Weeks'
Company, 11th Regt. Also served in
Capt. Chadwick's Company, 2nd Regt.
Ref: R. & L. 1812, AGO Pages 4 and
5; R. & L. 1812, AGO Page 32.

*DAVIS, MOSES,   Barnard.
Served in Capt. Taylor's Company,
Col. Wm. Williams' Regt. Detached
Militia in U. S. service 4 months
and 24 days, 1812.

*DAVIS, MOSES.
Enlisted Sept. 25, 1813 and served 1
month and 23 days in Capt. Waterman's Company, Col. Dixon's Regt.

*DAVIS, NATHAN.
Served in Capt. Bingham's Company,
Col. Jonathan Williams Regt. Detached Militia in U. S. service 2
months and 9 days, 1812.

DAVIS, OLIVER J.
Served from Feb. 26, 1813 to May
25, 1813 in Lieut. V. R. Goodrich's
Company, 11th Regt. Ref: R. & L.
1812, AGO Page 10.

*DAVIS, ORIN,   St. Albans.
Enlisted Sept. 25, 1813 in Capt. Robinson's Company, Col. Dixon's Regt.;
transferred to Capt. Langworthy's
Company, Dixon's Regt. Oct. 30, 1813
and served therein 19 days. Volunteered to go to Plattsburgh and was
at the battle Sept. 11, 1814, serving
in Capt. Samuel H. Farnsworth's
Company. Ref: Hemenway's Vt. Gazetteer, Vol. 2, Page 434.

*DAVIS, REUBIN.
Served in 1 Regt. Vt. Militia commanded by Col. Martindale.

DAVIS, SAMUEL,   Montpelier.
Volunteered to go to Plattsburgh,
September, 1814, and served 8 days
in Capt. Timothy Hubbard's Company. Ref: Book 52, AGO Pages 246
and 256.

DAVIS, SAMUEL J.,   Marshfield.
Volunteered to go to Plattsburgh,
September, 1814, and served 9 days
in Capt. James English's Company.
Ref: Book 52, AGO Page 248.

*DAVIS, SAMUEL.
Served in Capt. Morrill's Company,
Col. Fifield's Regt. Detached Militia
in U. S. service 6 months and 3
days, 1812.

‡*DAVIS, SAMUEL I.
Served in Capt. Rogers' Company,
Col. Fifield's Regt. Detached Militia
in U. S. service 5 months and 27
days, 1812. Pension Certificate No.
15230.

DAVIS, SIMON C.,   Goshen.
Volunteered to go to Plattsburgh,
September, 1814, and served 5 days
in Capt. Durham Sprague's Company.
Ref: Book 52, AGO Page 129.

DAVIS, SOLOMON.
Served from April 3, 1813 to July 2,
1813 in Capt. Jonathan Starks' Company, 11th Regt. Ref: R. & L. 1812,
AGO Page 19.

*DAVIS, STEPHEN.
Served in Capt. Briggs' Company,
Col. Jonathan Williams' Regt. Detached Militia in U. S. service 2
months and 13 days, 1812.

*DAVIS, STEPHEN.
Served in Burnap's Company, Col.
Jonathan Williams' Regt. Detached
Militia in U. S. service 2 months
and 13 days, 1812.

‡*DAVIS, STEPHEN S.
Served in Capt. Cross' Company, Col.
Martindale's Regt. Detached Militia
in U. S. service 5 days, 1812. Pension Certificate No. 19785.

DAVIS, STEPHEN.
Served in Lieut. Wm. S. Foster's
Company, 11th Regt.; on Pay Roll
for January and February, 1813. Ref:
R. & L. 1812, AGO Page 7.

*DAVIS, TASKER,   Corinth.
Served in Capt. Rogers' Company,
Col. Fifield's Regt. Detached Militia
in U. S. service 2 months and 18
days, 1812.

DAVIS, THOMAS.
Served in Capt. Samul Gordon's Com-
pany, 11th Regt.; on Pay Roll for
January and February, 1813. Ref: R.
& L. 1812, AGO Page 9.

DAVIS, WASHINGTON,   Pittsford.
Volunteered to go to Plattsburgh,
September, 1814, and served 8 days
as substitute for John Kingsley in
Capt. Caleb Hendee's Company. Ref:
Book 52, AGO Page 125.

*DAVIS, WILLIAM Y.
Enlisted Sept. 25, 1813 and served
1 month and 23 days in Capt. Jesse
Post's Company, Col. Dixon's Regt.

DAVISON, ASAHEL.
Enlisted March 5, 1813 in Lieut. V.
R. Goodrich's Company, 11th Regt.;
died April 2, 1813. Ref: R. & L.
1812, AGO Page 10.

‡*DAVISON, JOSEPH.
Served in Capt. Briggs' Company,
Col. Jonathan Williams' Regt. De-
tached Militia in U. S. service 2
months and 13 days, 1812. Pension
Certificate No. 4724.

‡*DAVISON, PAUL. Drummer.
Served in Capt. Wheeler's Company,
Col. Fifield's Regt. Detached Militia
in U. S. service 3 months and 16
days, 1812. Pension Certificate of
widow, Melissa C. D. Wyman, No.
18370.

DAVISON, WILLIAM,   Jamaica?
Served in Capt. Preston's Company.
Col. Jonathan Williams' Regt. Detached Militia in U. S. service 2
months and 6 days, 1812. Ref: Book
53, AGO Page 92.

DAY, ADAM.
Enlisted April 26, 1813 for 5 years
in company of late Capt. J. Brooks,
commanded by Lieut. John I. Cromwell, Corps of U. S. Artillery; on
Muster Roll April 30, 1814 to June
30, 1814. Ref: R. & L. 1812, AGO
Page 18.

*DAY, BENJAMIN.
Served in 3 Regt. Vt. Militia commanded by Col. Tyler.

*DAY, CHILDS,   Huntington.
Served in Capt. Dorrance's Company,
Col. Wm. Williams' Regt. Detached
Militia in U. S. service 4 months
and 23 days, 1812. Served from
Oct. 11, 1813 to Oct. 17, 1813 in
Capt. John Munson's Company of
Cavalry, 3 Regt. Volunteered to go
to Plattsburgh, September, 1814, and
was present at the battle serving in
Capt. Josiah N. Barrows' Company.
Ref: Book 51, AGO Page 77.

*DAY, DANIEL.
Served in 1 Regt. Vt. Militia commanded by Col. Judson.

DAY, ELIPHALET.
Served in Capt. Weeks' Company,
11th Regt.; on Pay Roll for January
and February, 1813. Ref: R. & L.
1812, AGO Page 5.

DAY, EZRA,   Pittsford.
Enlisted May 17, 1813 for 1 year in
Capt. Simeon Wright's Company.
Ref: R. & L. 1812, AGO Page 51.

*DAY, HORATIO.
Served in Tyler's Regt. Vt. Militia.

DAY, IRA,   Barre.
Volunteered to go to Plattsburgh,
September, 1814, and served 9 days
in Capt. Warren Ellis' Company.
Ref: Book 52, AGO Page 233.

DAY, JAMES,   Franklin County.
Volunteered to go to Plattsburgh
Sept. 11, 1814 and served in 15th or
22nd Regt. Ref: Hemenway's Vt. Ga-
zeetter, Vol. 2, Page 392.

DAY, JEREMIAH,   Addison.
Volunteered to go to Plattsburgh,
September, 1814, and served 9 days
in Capt. George Fisher's Company,
Sumner's Regt.; was in the battle.
Ref: Book 51, AGO Page 5.

*DAY, JOSEPH JR.
Served in Capt. Cross' Company, Col.
Martindale's Regt. Detached Militia
in U. S. service 2 months and 14
days, 1812.

‡DAY, OLIVER.
Served in Capt. Bebee's Company.
Pension Certificate No. 34531.

*DAY, RESOLVED, Fifer.   Addison.
Served in Capt. Robbins' Company,
Col. Wm. Williams' Regt. Detached

Militia in U. S. service 4 months and 29 days, 1812. Volunteered to go to Plattsburgh, September, 1814, and served 9 days in Capt. George Fisher's Company, Sumner's Regt.; was in the battle.

*DAY, SAMUEL, Sergeant,   Addison.
Served in Capt. Robbins' Company, Col. Wm. Williams' Regt. Detached Militia in U. S. service 4 months and 29 days, 1812; stationed at Swanton Falls. Served from May 1 to June 30, 1814 in Capt. Alexander Brooks' Corps of Artillery. Volunteered to go to Plattsburgh, September, 1814, and was in the battle, serving 9 days in Capt. George Fisher's Company, Sumner's Regt. Ref: Book 51, AGO Page 5; R. & L. 1812, AGO Page 31.

*DAY, STEPHEN.
Served in 3 Regt. Vt. Militia commanded by Col. Tyler.

DAY, SYLVESTER, Surgeon, Montpelier.
Appointed Surgeon 4 Inf. March 13, 1813; transferred to 5 Inf. May 17, 1815; Post Surgeon April 18, 1818; died Feb. 20, 1851. Ref: Heitman's Historical Register & Dictionary USA; Hemenway's Vt. Gazetteer, Vol. 4, Page 296.

*DAYTON, ISAAC JR.
Served in Sumner's Regt. Vt. Militia.

‡*DAYTON, JACOB, Shoreham or Enosburgh. Enlisted Oct. 15, 1813 in Capt. Asahel Scovell's Company, Regt. of Riflemen, and served to November, 1813. Served from April 12, 1814 to May 20, 1814 in Capt. George Fisher's Company, Sumner's Regt. Pension Certificate No. 11536. Pension Certificate of widow, Esther, No. 32951. Ref: Book 52, AGO Page 278.

*DEALING, PHILIP.
Served in 2 Regt. Vt. Militia commanded by Col. Fifield.

‡DEAN, CHARLES.
Served in Capt. Saxton's Company. Pension Certificate of widow, Prudence F., No. 27642.

*DEAN, DUDLEY.
Served in 1 Regt. Vt. Militia commanded by Col. Martindale.

*DEAN, ELIJAH.
Served in Capt. Ormsbee's Company, Col. Martindale's Regt. Detached Militia in U. S. service 2 months and 14 days, 1812.

DEAN, EZRA JR., Lieutenant.
Appointed Ensign 11 Inf. April 20, 1814; 3 Lieutenant May 2, 1814; 2 Lieutenant Oct. 10, 1814; honorably discharged June 15, 1815; died Jan. 25, 1872. Ref: Heitman's Historical Register & Dictionary USA; Governor and Council Vt. Vol. 6, Page 478.

DEAN, GEORGE.
Served in Capt. Phineas Williams' Company, 11th Regt.; on Pay Roll for January and February, 1813. Ref: R. & L. 1812, AGO Page 15.

*DEAN, HARRY.
Served in Sumner's Regt. Vt. Militia.

DEAN, JAMES.
Appointed Ensign 4 Inf. July 19, 1813; 3 Lieutenant Aug. 15, 1813; 2 Lieutenant June 28, 1814; honorably discharged June 15, 1815; died 1842. Ref: Heitman's Historical Register & Dictionary USA.

DEAN, JOHN.
Served as Forage Master on General Staff of the Northern Army commanded by Maj. Gen. George Izard; on Pay Roll to July 31, 1814. Ref: R. & L. 1812, AGO Page 28.

DEAN, JOHN.
Served in Capt. Benjamin Edgerton's Company, 11th Regt.; on Pay Roll for January and February, 1813. Ref: R. & L. 1812, AGO Page 2.

DEAN, JOHN, Fifer,   Pittsford.
Served from April 27, 1813 to April 27, 1814 in Capt. Daniel Farrington's Company (also commanded by Capt. Simeon Wright) 30th Regt. Ref: R. L. 1812, AGO Pages 50 and 51.

*DEAN, JOHN.   Bethel.
Volunteered to go to Plattsburgh, September, 1814, and served in Capt. Nehemiah Noble's Company, 3 Regt. (Williams'). Also served in 1 Regt. (Judson's) Vt. Militia.

DEAN, LEMUEL.
Enlisted April 27, 1813 for 1 year in Capt. Simeon Wright's Company. Ref: R. & L. 1812, AGO Page 51.

*DEAN, LEWIS B.
Served in Sumner's Regt. Vt. Militia.

DEAN, LUKE,   Pittsford.
Volunteered to go to Plattsburgh, September, 1814, and served 8 days in Capt. Caleb Hendee's Company. Ref: Book 52, AGO Page 124.

*DEAN, NATHANIEL JR.
Served from April 20, 1814 to April 21, 1814 in Capt. Eseck Sprague's Company, Sumner's Regt.

*DEAN, RUSSELL Sergeant.
Served in Capt. Richardson's Company, Col. Martindale's Regt. Detached Militia in U. S. service 2 months and 13 days, 1812.

*DEAN, WILLIAM.
Served in Sumner's Regt. Vt. Militia.

DEARBORN, WINTHROP S.,   Candia.
Served from July 1 to Aug. 31, 1813 and May 1 to July 4, 1814 in Capt. Chadwick's Company, 34th Inf. Ref: R. & L. 1812, AGO Page 30.

DEAVERIX, JOHN,   Richmond.
Volunteered to go to Plattsburgh, September, 1814, and served 9 days in Capt. Roswell Hunt's Company, 3rd Regt. Ref: Book 51, AGO Page 82.

DEARBORN, HENRY,   Vershire.
Volunteered to go to Plattsburgh, September, 1814, and served 3 days in Capt. Ira Corse's Company. Ref: Book 52, AGO Page 91.

*DEARBORN, NATHAN.
Served in Capt. Rogers' Company, Col. Fifield's Regt. Detached Militia in U. S. service 1 month and 23 days, 1812.

‡DEARBORN, NEHEMIAH, Strafford.
Volunteered to go to Plattsburgh, September, 1814, and served in Capt. Joseph Barrett's Company. Pension Certificate of widow, Judith, No. 25814.

*DEAVREX, ALANSON.
Served from Oct. 5, 1813 to Oct. 8, 1813 in Capt. Roswell Hunt's Company, 3 Regt. (Tyler's).

‡DEBAR, JOSEPH.
Served in Capt. Wick's Company. Pension Certificate No. 18969.

DECOUS, STEPHEN.
Enlisted April 1, 1814 for period of the war and served in Capt. Wm. Miller's Company, Capt. Gideon Spencer's Company and Capt. James Taylor's Company, 30th Regt.; served as nurse in General Hospital at Burlington. Ref: R. & L. 1812, AGO Pages 53, 54, 55, 57.

*DEE, ELIJAH JR., Brig Major, Georgia.
Appointed Brig. Major Oct. 28, 1813 on Staff of Gen. Elias Fasset in U. S. service. Also served as 1 Major in Dixon's Regt. Vt. Militia. (For biographical sketch, see Hemenway's Vt. Gazetteer, Vol. 2, Page 240).

*DEE, JEREMIAH.
Enlisted Sept. 25, 1813 in Capt. Jesse Post's Company, Dixon's Regt.

DEFAW, JOHN.
Served in Benjamin S. Edgerton's Company, 11th Regt.; on Pay Roll for September and October, 1812, and January and February, 1813. Ref: R. & L. 1812, AGO Pages 1 and 2.

DEJOY, JOHN.
Enlisted Dec. 23, 1813 for period of the war in Capt. Simeon Wright's Company. Ref: R. & L. 1812, AGO Page 51.

DELAND, PHILIP, Marshfield.
Served in Capt. Rogers' Company, Col. Fifield's Regt. Detached Militia in U. S. service 2 months and 18 days, 1812. Ref: Book 53, AGO Page 6.

*DELANO, RANSOM.
Enlisted Sept. 18, 1813 in Capt. Isaac Finch's Regt. of Riflemen.

DELONG, JOSEPH, Auburn.
Served from May 1, 1814 to July 1, 1814 in Capt. Spencer's Company. 29th Inf. Ref: R. & L. 1812, AGO Page 30.

DEMEAR, PHILIP.
Enlisted Sept. 9, 1813 for 5 years in company of late Capt. J. Brooks commanded by Lieut. John I. Cromwell, Corps of U. S. Artillery; on Muster Roll from April 30, 1814 to June 30, 1814. Ref: R. & L. 1812, AGO Page 18.

‡DEMERITT, DANIEL.
Served in Capt. Allen's Company. Pension Certificate of widow, Rachael, No. 26444.

*DEMERY, DAVID, Shoreham or Enosburgh. Served in Capt. Dorrance's Company, Col. Wm. Williams' Regt. Detached Militia in U. S. service 4 months and 29 days, 1812. Served from Oct. 14th to Nov. 17, 1813 in Capt. Asahel Scoville's Company, Col. Clark's Regt. of Riflemen.

‡DEMING, ELBRIDGE G.
Served in Capt. Hand's Company. Pension Certificate of widow, Sally B., No. 44180.

DEMING, JEDEDIAH, Sheldon.
Volunteered to go to Plattsburgh, September, 1814, and served 6 days in Capt. Samuel Weed's Company. Ref: Book 51, AGO Page 155.

*DEMING, LEONARD, Sergeant.
Served from April 12, 1814 to April 21, 1814 in Capt. Edmund B. Hill's Company, Sumner's Regt. Volunteered to go to Plattsburgh, September, 1814, and served 7 days in Capt. Silas Wright's Company.

*DEMMEN, BENJAMIN, Sergeant.
Served in 4 Regt. Vt. Militia commanded by Col. Peck.

*DEMMON, DANIEL, Waterbury.
Volunteered to go to Plattsburgh, September, 1814, and served 11 days in Capt. George Atkins' Company, 4 Regt. (Peck's).

DEMPSEY, ISAAC.
Enlisted April 5, 1813 for period of the war in company of late Capt. J. Brooks, commanded by Lieut. John I. Cromwell, Corps of U. S. Artillery; on Muster Roll from April 30, 1814 to June 30, 1814. Ref: R. & L. 1812, AGO Page 18.

‡DENIO, ARIAL.
Served in Capt. Cross' Company, Col. Martindale's Regt. Detached Militia in U. S. service 2 months and 14 days, 1812. Pension Certificate of widow, Lovina, No. 1879.

‡*DENIO, CONRAD, Isle-La-Motte.
Served in Capt. Pettees' Company, Col. Wm. Williams' Regt. Detached Militia in U. S. service from July 22 to Dec. 9, 1812. Pension Certificate No. 9029.

*DENIO, EBENEZER.
Served in Capt. Hopkins' Company, Col. Martindale's Regt. Detached Militia in U. S. service 2 months and 13 days, 1812.

‡DENIO, IRA, Enosburgh.
Volunteered to go to Plattsburgh, September, 1814, and served in Capt. Farnsworth's Company. Pension Certificate of widow, Harriet, No. 28634.

DENIO, JOHN, Swanton.
Volunteered and was at the battle of Plattsburgh Sept. 11, 1814, serving in Capt. Amasa J. Brown's Company. Ref: Hemenway's Vt. Gazetteer, Vol. 2, Page 445.

*DENIO, JONATHAN.
Served in 1 Regt. Vt. Militia commanded by Col. Judson.

*DENISON, ABISHA.
Served in Capt. Preston's Company, Col. Jonathan Williams' Regt. Detached Militia in U. S. service 2 months and 6 days, 1812.

*DENISON, DANIEL.
Served in 3 Regt. Vt. Militia commanded by Col. Williams.

*DENISON, LEWIS.
Served in Capt. Needham's Company. Col. Martindale's Regt. Detached Militia in U. S. service 2 months and 13 days, 1812.

*DENNET, LOVE.
Served in Capt. Wheeler's Company, Col. Fifield's Regt. Detached Militia in U. S. service 6 months and 4 days, 1812. Served from March 5, 1813 to June 4, 1813 in Capt. Edgerton's Company, 11th Regt. Ref: R. & L. 1812, AGO Page 3.

*DENNETT, THOMAS R., Sergeant.
Served in Capt. Mason's Company, Col. Fifield's Regt. Detached Militia in U. S. service 1 month and 12 days, 1812.

DENNICE, THOMAS, Franklin County.
Volunteered to go to Plattsburgh Sept. 11, 1814 and served in 15th or 22nd Regt. Ref: Hemenway's Vt. Gazetteer, Vol. 2, Page 391.

*DENNIS, ELEAZER.
Served in 1 Regt. Vt. Militia commanded by Col. Martindale.

DENNIS, GEORGE.
Served from Feb. 25, 1813 to May 4, 1813 in Capt. Charles Follett's Company, 11th Regt. Ref: R. & L. 1812, AGO Page 13.

*DENNIS, ISAAC.
Served in 1 Regt. Vt. Militia commanded by Col. Judson.

DENNIS, ROYAL, Fair Haven.
Volunteered to go to Plattsburgh, September, 1814; no organization given. Ref: Hemenway's Vt. Gazetteer, Vol. 3, Page 711.

DENNIS, SAMUEL, Corporal.
Served in Capt. Benjamin Bradford's Company; on Muster Roll from May 31, 1813 to Aug. 31, 1813. Ref: R. & L. 1812, AGO Page 26.

‡DENNY, HENRY C.
Served in Capt. Adams' Company. Pension Certificate of widow, Sally, No. 9289.

*DENSAMORE, WILLIAM.
Served with Hospital Attendents, Vt.

‡DENSMORE, JOEL.
Served in Capt. Samul Gordon's Company, 11th Regt.; on Pay Roll for January and February, 1813. Pension Certificate No. 21468.

*DENSMORE, JOHN R., Calais.
Volunteered to go to Plattsburgh, September, 1814, and served 9 days in Capt. Gideon Wheelock's Company.

DEPUIRS, JONEW.
Served in Lieut. Wm. F. Foster's Company, 11th Regt.; on Pay Roll for January and February, 1813. Ref: R. & L. 1812, AGO Page 7.

DEPUTRIN, JAMES.
Served from Jan. 1, 1813 to July 1, 1813 in Lieut. Wm. S. Foster's Company, 11th Regt. Ref: R. & L. 1812, AGO Page 6.

DEPUTRIN, JOHN.
Enlisted Feb. 27, 1813 in Lieut. Wm. S. Foster's Company, 11th Regt.; died April 20, 1813. Ref: R. & L. 1812, AGO Page 6.

‡DEPUTRIN, JONAS.
Served in Capt. Balch's Company. Pension Certificate of widow, Christian, No. 15642.

DERBY, ABRAHAM.
Served from May 1st to June 30, 1814 in Alexander Parris' Company of Artificers as a carpenter. Ref: R. & L. 1812, AGO Page 24.

DERBY, JOHN, Burlington.
Served from June 17, 1813 to May 31, 1814 in Capt. Clark's Company, 30th Inf. Ref: R. & L. 1812, AGO Page 30.

‡*DERBY, REUBEN.
Served in Capt. A. Farr's Company, 3 Regt. (Tyler's). Pension Certificate No. 34242.

*DERBY, RUFUS R.
Served from April 12, 1814 to May 20, 1814 in Capt. George Fisher's Company, Sumner's Regt. Ref: Book 52, AGO Page 278.

DEREY, BENJAMIN J., Braintree.
Marched to Plattsburgh Sept. 10, 1814 and served in Capt. Lot Hudson's Company. Ref: Book 52, AGO Page 24.

*DERIVAGE, FRANCIS.
Served from Sept. 25 to Sept. 30, 1813 in Capt. Amos Robinson's Company, Dixon's Regt.

DERUSSEY, EDWARD, 1st Lieutenant Engineers. Served on General Staff of the Northern Army commanded by Maj. Gen. George Izard; on Pay Roll to July 31, 1814. Ref: R. & L. 1812, AGO Page 28.

*DERY, TYLER, Brookline?
Served in Capt. Noyce's Company, Col. Jonathan Williams' Regt. Detached Militia in U. S. service 2 months and 6 days, 1812.

*DEWEY, ALANSON.
Served in Capt. Phelps' Company, Col. Wm. Williams' Regt. Detached Militia in U. S. service 5 months, 1812.

DEWEY, ANDREW, Barre.
Volunteered to go to Plattsburgh, September, 1814, and served 10 days in Capt. Warren Ellis' Company. Ref: Book 52, AGO Page 242.

DEWEY, CHARLES,   Franklin County.
Volunteered to go to Plattsburgh
Sept. 11, 1814 and served in 15th or
22nd Regt. Ref: Hemenway's Vt.
Gazetteer, Vol. 2, Page 391.

DEWEY, DAVID.
Volunteered to go to Plattsburgh,
September, 1814, and served 7 days
in Capt. Frederick Griswold's Com-
pany, raised in Brookfield, Vt. Ref:
Book 52, AGO Page 52.

*DEWEY, ENOCH.   Middlebury.
Served from April 12, 1814 to April
15, 1814 in Capt. John Hackett's
Company, Sumner's Regt. Volunteered to go to Plattsburgh, September,
1814, and served 6 days in Capt.
Elias Keyes' Company.

‡DEWEY, GEORGE W.
Served in Capt. Brewer's Company.
Pension Certificate No. 33845.

‡*DEWEY, JOHN, Ensign.
Served from April 6, 1813 to July
5, 1813 in Capt. Charles Follett's
Company, 11th Regt. Also served in
Capt. J. Prentiss' Company, Dixon's
Regt. Pension Certificate of widow,
Emily A., No. 28895.

DEWEY, SIMEON,   Berlin.
Volunteered to go to Plattsburgh,
September, 1814, and served 5 days
in Capt. Cyrus Johnson's Company,
as a teamster. Ref: Book 52, AGO
Page 185.

*DEWEY, STILLMAN.
Served from April 12, 1814 to April
21, 1814 in Capt. Edmund B. Hill's
Company, Sumner's Regt.

*DEWEY, TRUMAN, Sergeant.
Served from April 12, 1814 to April
21, 1814 in Lieut. James S. Morton's
Company, Sumner's Regt.

*DEWOLFE, JOHN,   Waterbury.
Volunteered to go to Plattsburgh,
September, 1814, and was in the
battle, serving 11 days in Capt.
George Atkins' Company, 4 Regt.
(Peck's).

*DEXTER, BENJAMIN.
Served from April 12, 1814 to April
21, 1814 in Lieut. Justus Foote's Company, Sumner's Regt.

‡DEXTER, JABEZ.   Washington, N. H.
Served from July 14, 1814 to June
19, 1815 in Capt. Taylor's Company,
30th Inf. Ref: R. & L. 1812, AGO
Page 23.   Pension Certificate No.
14018.

*DEXTER, OLIVER, Sergeant.
Served in Capt. Phelps' Company,
Col. Wm. Williams' Regt. Detached
Militia in U. S. service 5 months,
1812, at Swanton Falls.

DEXTER, OLIVER R.,   Highgate.
Served in Capt. Saxe's Company,
Col. Wm. Williams' Regt. Detached
Militia in U. S. service 3 months
and 16 days, 1812. Served in Capt.
Weeks' Company 11th Regt.; on Pay
Roll for January and February, 1813.

Ref: Book 53, AGO Page 30; R. & L.
1812, AGO Page 5.

DIAMOND, HENRY.
Served from May 1 to July 18, 1814;
no organization given. Ref: R. & L.
1812, AGO Page 29.

DIAMOND, THOMAS, Franklin County.
Volunteered to go to Plattsburgh
Sept. 11, 1814 and served in 15th or
22nd Regt. Ref: Hemenway's Vt. Gazetteer, Vol. 2, Page 391.

DIBBLE, ASA.
Served from May 1 to June 30, 1814
as a laborer in Alexander Parris'
Company of Artificers. Ref: R. &
L. 1812, AGO Page 24.

*DIBBLE, BENJAMIN.
Served from Sept. 20, 1813 to Nov. 7,
1813 in Capt. John Weed's Company,
Regt. of Riflemen.

DIBILL, JOHN,   Franklin County.
Volunteered to go to Plattsburgh
Sept. 11, 1814 and served in 15th or
22nd Regt. Ref: Hemenway's Vt. Gazetteer, Vol. 2, Page 392.

DICE, HENRY.
Enlisted May 2, 1812 for 5 years in
Capt. White Youngs' Company, 15th
Regt.; on Muster Roll from Aug. 31,
1814 to Dec. 31, 1814. Ref: R. & L.
1812, AGO Page 27.

*DICKENSON, JOHN.
Served in 1 Regt. Vt. Militia commanded by Col. Judson.

DICKENSON, SILAS.
Appointed Captain 31 Inf. April 30,
1813; honorably discharged June 15,
1815. Ref: Heitman's Historical Register & Dictionary USA.

*DICKENSON, STRONG, Corporal, Geor-
gia or Highgate. Served in Capt.
Saxe's Company, Col. Wm. Williams'
Regt. Detached Militia in U. S. service 4 months and 24 days, 1812.

DICKERSON, HARRY (or Dickenson,
Henry), Philadelphia, Pa. Enlisted
at Burlington April 8, 1814 for 5
years and served in Capt. James
Taylor's Company, Capt. Wm. Mil-
ler's Company, and Capt. Gideon
Spencer's Company, all in the 30th
Regt. (This soldier was a Negro).
Ref: R. & L. 1812, AGO Pages 53,
54, 55, 57.

*DICKERSON (or Dickenson), MOSES,
Weybridge. Served from June 11 to
June 14, 1813 in Capt. Moses Jewett's
Company, 1st Regt. 2nd Brig., 3rd
Div.

DICKEY, DAVID.
Served in Capt. Samuel H. Holly's
Company, 11th Regt.; on Pay Roll
for January and February, 1813. Ref:
R. & L. 1812, AGO Page 25.

DICKEY, SAMUEL,   Franklin County.
Volunteered to go to Plattsburgh
Sept. 11, 1814 and served in 15th or
22nd Regt. Ref: Hemenway's Vt. Gazetteer, Vol. 2, Page 391.

DICKEY, THOMAS, Sergeant.
Served in company of Capt. John
McNeil Jr., 11th Regt.; on Pay Roll
for January and February, 1813.
Ref: R. & L. 1812, AGO Page 17.

*DICKINSON, BETHER.
Served in 4 Regt. Vt. Militia commanded by Col. Peck.

*DICKINSON, CALVIN.
Served in Capt. Noyce's Company,
Col. Jonathan Williams' Regt. Detached Militia in U. S. service 2
months and 6 days, 1812.

DICKINSON, GIDEON.   Williamstown.
Volunteered to go to Plattsburgh
September, 1814, but only went to
Burlington. Served in Capt. David
Robinson's Company. Ref: Book 52,
AGO Page 2.

*DICKINSON, HENRY.
Served in Capt. Morrill's Company,
Col. Fifield's Regt. Detached Militia
in U. S. service 2 months and 18
days, 1812.

‡DICKINSON, IRA, St. Albans or Cambridge. Enlisted May 1, 1813 for 1
year in Capt. John Wires' Company,
30th Regt. Served in Capt. Chadwick's Company, 2nd Regt. Volunteered to go to Plattsburgh, September, 1814, and served 8 days in Capt.
Salmon Green's Company. Ref: R.
& L. 1812, AGO Pages 32 and 40;
Book 51, AGO Page 207. Pension
Certificate No. 8685.

DICKINSON, JOHN,   West Haven.
Volunteered to go to Plattsburgh,
September, 1814, and served 4 days
in Capt. David B. Phippeney's Company. Ref: Book 52, AGO Page 146.

DICKINSON, THOMAS,   Swanton.
Served in Lieut. V. R. Goodrich's
Company, 11th Regt.; on Pay Roll
for January and February, 1813; on
Pay Roll from July 15 to Dec. 8,
1813; was in action at the battle of
Lundy's Lane. Ref: R. & L. 1812,
AGO Page 11; Hemenway's Vt. Ga-
zetteer, Vol. 2, Page 444.

*DICKINSON, THOMAS J.
Served in 4 Regt. Vt. Militia commanded by Col. Williams.

*DIKE, ELISHA.
Served in Capt. Mason's Company,
Col. Fifield's Regt. Detached Militia
in U. S. service 5 months and 13
days, 1812.

DIKE, JONATHAN, Ensign,   Pittsford.
Volunteered to go to Plattsburgh,
September, 1814, and served 8 days
in Capt. Caleb Hendee's Company.
Ref: Book 52, AGO Pages 124 and 126.

*DIKE, LINUS.
Enlisted Sept. 25, 1813 and served 1
month and 23 days in Capt. Thomas
Waterman's Company, Col. Dixon's
Regt.

‡*DIKE, REUBEN.
Served in Capt. Parsons' Company,
Col. Jonathan Williams' Regt. De-

tached Militia in U. S. service 2
months and 13 days, 1812. Also served in Capt. Cutting's Company. Pension Certificate No. 27029.

DIKEMAN, AZER, Corporal, Pittsford.
Volunteered to go to Plattsburgh,
September, 1814, and served 8 days
in Capt. Caleb Hendee's Company.
Ref: Book 52, AGO Page 124.

*DIKEMAN, CALEB,   St. Albans.
Served in Capt. Ormsby's Company,
Col. Martindale's Regt. Detached
Militia in U. S. service 2 months and
14 days, 1812. Served from April
23, 1813 to April, 1814, in Capt. John
Wires' Company, 30th Regt. Ref: R.
& L. 1812, AGO Page 40.

*DILL, EBENEZER.
Served in Capt. Noyes' Company, Col.
Jonathan Williams' Regt. Detached
Militia in U. S. service 2 months and
6 days, 1812. Enlisted at Guilford
Feb. 14, 1814 in Capt. E. Burnap's
Company 31st U. S. Inf. under Col.
D. Dana. Born at Groton, Conn.
and died in service Aug. 1, 1814.

‡DILLINGHAM, AJALON.
Served in Capt. Vance's Company.
Pension Certificate No. 28376.

*DIMICK, HORACE, Corporal.
Served in Capt. Scovell's Company,
Col. Martindale's Regt. Detached
Militia in U. S. service 2 months and
21 days, 1812.

DIMICK, JUSTIN.
Cadet, Military Academy, Oct. 18,
1814. Ref: Heitman's Historical Register & Dictionary USA.

‡*DIMMICK, LOREN.
Served from Oct. 5, 1813 to Oct. 17,
1813 in Capt. Stephen Brown's Company, 3 Regt. (Tyler's). Pension
Certificate of widow, Sybile, No. 21399.

DIMMOCK, DEXTER, Musician.
Served in Capt. Phinea Williams'
Company, 11th Regt.; on Pay Roll of
company for January and February,
1813. Ref: R. & L. 1812, AGO Page
15.

DIMON, JOHN,   Fairfield.
Volunteered to go to Plattsburgh,
September, 1814, and served 6 days
in Capt. Amasa I. Brown's Company.
Ref: Book 51, AGO Pages 124 and 126.

DIMON, JOHN,   St. Albans.
Volunteered to go to Plattsburgh
and was at the battle Sept. 11, 1814,
serving in Capt. Samuel H. Farnsworth's Company. Ref: Hemenway's
Vt. Gazetteer, Vol. 2, Page 434.

DIMON, MOSES.   St. Albans.
Volunteered and was in action at
Plattsburgh Sept. 11, 1814, serving
in Capt. Samuel H. Farnsworth's
Company. Ref: Hemenways' Vt. Ga-
zetteer, Vol. 2, Page 434.

*DIMOND, ELY,   Highgate.
Served in Capt. Conrade Saxe's Company, 4 Regt. (Williams') Vt. Militia from Sept. 1, 1812. Ref: Hemenway's Vt. Gazetteer Vol. 2, Page 420.

DIMOND, JOHN.
Volunteered to go to Plattsburgh,
September, 1814, and went as far as
Bolton, Vt., serving 4 days in Lieut.
Phineus Kimball's Company. West
Fairlee. Ref: Book 52, AGO Page 46.

DINESHA, JONATHAN.
Served in Capt. Waterman's Company,
Col. Dixon's Regt. Detached Militia
in U. S. service 1 month and 23 days,
1813. Ref: Book 53, AGO Page 111.

DINGLEY, JOHN.
Enlisted Sept. 24, 1813 for 5 years
in company of late Capt. J. Brooks,
commanded by Lieut. John I. Crom-
well, Corps of U. S. Artillery; on
Muster Roll from April 30, 1814 to
June 30, 1814. Ref: R. & L. 1812,
AGO Page 18.

DINON, JARAD JR.,   Westford.
Served with Detached Militia in U.
S. service in 1812; went to Tinmouth.
Ref: Vol. 52, Vt. State Papers, Page
101.

*DIRGE, SOLOMON.
Served in Capt. Shubael Wales' Company, Col. W. B. Sumner's Regt.
from April 12, 1814 to April 21, 1814.

DIX, SILAS.
Served in Capt. Preston's Company,
Col. Jonathan Williams' Regt. Detached Militia in U. S. service 2
months and 6 days, 1812. Ref: Book
53, AGO Page 64.

*DIX, WILES.
Served in 3 Regt. Vt. Militia commanded by Col. Williams.

*DIXON, BARNET.
Served in 1 Regt. Vt. Militia commanded by Col. Martindale.

*DIXON, GIDEON O., Lieutenant.
Served in Capt. Charles Bennett's
Company, Dixon's Regt.; enlisted
Sept. 25, 1813.

*DIXON, JARED.
Served in Capt. Pettees' Company,
Col. Wm. Williams' Regt. Detached
Militia in U. S. service 4 months
and 17 days, 1812.

*DIXON, LUTHER, Lieut. Colonel.
Appointed Lieutenant Colonel of Consolidated Regiment of Vt. Militia
in U. S. service, Sept. 25, 1813.

*DOANE, ISAIAH.
Served in Capt. Willson's Company,
Col. Wm. Williams' Regt. Detached
Militia in U. S. service 4 months and
24 days, 1812.

DOANE, JOHN,   Bakersfield.
Volunteered and was at the battle
of Plattsburgh Sept. 11, 1814, serving
in Capt. M. Stearns' Company. Ref:
Hemenway's Vt. Gazetteer, Vol. 2,
Page 393.

*DOANE, JOSEPH,   Johnson.
Enlisted Sept. 25, 1813 and served
1 month and 23 days in Capt. Thomas
Waterman's Company, Dixon's Regt.;
volunteered to go to Plattsburgh, September, 1814, and served 8 days in
same company.

‡*DOANE, JOSIAH,   Bakersfield.
Enlisted Oct. 18, 1813 and served 62
days in Capt. John Weed's Company,
Regt. of Riflemen. Volunteered and
was at the battle of Plattsburgh
Sept. 11, 1814, serving in Capt. M.
Stearns' Company. Pension Certifi-
cate of widow, Adelia, No. 14319.

DOCKHAM, WILLIAM.
Served in Capt. Benjamin Bradford's
Company; on Muster Roll from May
31, 1813 to Aug. 31, 1813; joined by
transfer July 22, 1813. Ref: R. &
L. 1812, AGO Page 26.

DODD, AMBROSE.
Served from May 1 to June 30, 1814
in Capt. Alexander Brooks' Corps of
Artillery. Ref: R. & L. 1812, AGO
Page 31.

DODGE, ANDREW,   Montpelier.
Served in Capt. Walker's Company,
Col. Fifield's Regt. Detached Militia
in U. S. service 6 months and 5
days, 1812. Volunteered to go to
Plattsburgh, September, 1814, and
served 10 days in Capt. Timothy Hubbard's Company. Ref: Book 53, AGO
Page 4; Book 52, AGO Pages 198 and
256.

*DODGE, ANDREW, Captain, Hartland.
Served from Sept. 5 to Dec. 8, 1812
in Col. Fifield's Regt., in U. S. service.

*DODGE, ASA,   Barre.
Served from April 12, 1814 to April
21, 1814 in Capt. Shubael Wales' Company, Col. W. B. Sumner's Regt.
Volunteered to go to Plattsburgh,
September, 1814, and served 10 days
in Capt. Warren Ellis' Company.

DODGE, BENJAMIN R., Sergeant, St.
Albans. Enlisted April 29, 1813 for
1 year in Capt. John Wires' Company, 30th Regt. Ref: R. & L. 1812,
AGO Page 40.

*DODGE, DANIEL, Ensign Adjutant,
Johnson. Served as Ensign in 4 Regt.
(Williams') Vt. Militia. Appointed
Ensign in Capt. Thomas Waterman's
Company, Dixon's Regt., Sept. 25,
1813; appointed Adjutant Nov. 8,
1813; volunteered to go to Plattsburgh, September, 1814, and served
9 days in same company.

DODGE, DAVID,   Johnson.
Volunteered to go to Plattsburgh,
September, 1814, and served in Capt.
Thomas Waterman's Company, Dix-
on's Regt. Ref: Book 51, AGO Page
208.

DODGE, ELIJAH,   Brandon.
Volunteered to go to Plattsburgh,
September, 1814, and served 8 days
in Capt. Micah Brown's Company.
Ref: Book 52, AGO Pages 132 and 134.

*DODGE, ELISHA, Sergeant, Johnson.
Enlisted Sept. 25, 1813 and served
1 month and 23 days as Sergeant
in Capt. Thomas Waterman's Company. Col. Dixon's Regt. Detached
Militia in U. S. service 1 month and
23 days, 1813. Volunteered to go to

Plattsburgh, September, 1814, and served 9 days in Capt. Waterman's Company.

DODGE, HENRY.
Served from March 21, 1813 to June 21, 1813 in company of Capt. John McNeil Jr., 11th Regt. Ref: R. & L. 1812, AGO Page 16.

DODGE, JACOB F., Sergeant, Montpelier.
Volunteered to go to Plattsburgh, September, 1814, and served 8 days in Capt. Timothy Hubbard's Company. Ref: Book 52, AGO Page 256.

*DODGE, JAMES.
Served in Capt. Walker's Company, Col. Fifield's Regt. Detached Militia in U. S. service 2 months and 26 days, 1812.

*DODGE, JAMES.
Enlisted Sept. 25, 1813 and served 1 month and 23 days in Capt. Thomas Waterman's Company, Col. Dixon's Regt.

DODGE, JAMES JR., Johnson.
Volunteered to go to Plattsburgh, September, 1814, and served in Capt. Thomas Waterman's Company, Dixon's Regt. Ref: Book 51, AGO Page 208.

*DODGE, JOEL.
Served in Capt. Cross' Company, Col. Martindale's Regt. Detached Militia in U. S. service 2 months and 14 days, 1812.

*DODGE, JOHN.
Served from April 12, 1814 to April 21, 1814 in Capt. Shubael Wales' Company, Col. W. B. Sumner's Regt.

DODGE, JOHN.
Served from Feb. 27, 1813 to July 16, 1813 in Capt. John W. Weeks' Company, 11th Regt. Ref: R. & L. 1812, AGO Pages 4 and 5.

*DODGE, JOHN, Weybridge.
Served from June 11, 1813 to June 14, 1813 in Capt. Moses Jewett's Company, 1st Regt. 2nd Brig., 3rd Div.

‡DODGE, JOSEPH, Barre.
Served from March 15, 1813 to June 14, 1813 in Capt. Phineas Williams' Company, 11th Regt. Volunteered to go to Plattsburgh, September, 1814, and served 9 days in Capt. Warren Ellis' Company. Pension Certificate of widow, Electa M., No. 16030. Ref: R. & L. 1812, AGO Page 14.

*DODGE, JOSIAH.
Served with Hospital Attendants, Vt.

*DODGE, MALICHI. Fairfax.
Enlisted Sept. 25, 1813 and served 1 month and 23 days in Capt. Asa Wilkins' Company, Col. Dixon's Regt.

DODGE, NATHANIEL. Marshfield.
Volunteered to go to Plattsburgh, September, 1814, and served 9 days in Capt. James English's Company. Ref: Book 52, AGO Page 248.

DODGE, NATHANIEL B., Barre.
Volunteered to go to Plattsburgh. September, 1814, and served 10 days in Capt. Warren Ellis' Company. Ref: Book 52, AGO Page 242.

DODGE, PHINEAS, Montpelier.
Volunteered to go to Plattsburgh, September, 1814, and served 8 days in Capt. Timothy Hubbard's Company. Ref: Book 52, AGO Page 256.

DODGE, PHINEAS, Johnson.
Volunteered to go to Plattsburgh, September, 1814, and served in Capt. Thomas Waterman's Company, Dixon's Regt. Ref: Book 51, AGO Page 208.

DODGE, PHINEAS.
Volunteered to. go to Plattsburgh, September, 1814, and served 3 days in Capt. Aaron Kidder's Company. Ref: Book 52, AGO Page 65.

*DODGE, ROBERT, Montpelier.
Served in Capt. Walker's Company, Col. Fifield's Regt. Detached Militia in U. S. service 6 months and 5 days, 1812. Volunteered to go to Plattsburgh, September, 1814, and served 8 days in Capt. Timothy Hubbard's Company.

DODGE, SALMON, Richford.
Served in Capt. Martin D. Follett's Company, Col. Dixon's Regt., on duty on Canadian Frontier in 1813. Ref: Hemenway's Vt. Gazetteer, Vol. 2, Page 427.

DODGE, SAMUEL.
Volunteered to go to Plattsburgh, September, 1814, and served 3 days in Capt. Aaron Kidder's Company. Ref: Book 52, AGO Page 65.

*DODGE, SAMUEL, Johnson.
Enlisted Sept. 25, 1813 and served 1 month and 23 days in Capt. Waterman's Company, Col. Dixon's Regt. Detached Militia in U. S. service. Volunteered to go to Plattsburgh, September, 1814, and served in same company.

*DODGE, SOLOMON.
Enlisted Sept. 25, 1813 in Capt. Martin D. Follett's Company, Dixon's Regt.

DODGE, THOMAS, Lieutenant.
Served in 1st Regt. of Detached Militia of Vt. in U. S. service at Champlain commencing Nov. 18 and ending Nov. 19, 1812.

*DODGE, WILLIAM.
Enlisted Sept. 25, 1813 and served 1 month and 23 days in Capt. Waterman's Company, Col. Dixon's Regt. Detached Militia in U. S. service.

DODGE, ZUNNER.
Served from March 25, 1813 to June 24, 1813 in Capt. John W. Weeks' Company, 11th Regt. Ref: R. & L. 1812, AGO Page 4.

DODNEY, CLAYTON, Franklin County.
Enlisted July 18, 1812 for 5 years in Capt. White Youngs' Company,

15th Regt.; on Muster Roll from Aug. 31, 1814 to Dec. 31, 1814. Ref: R. & L. 1812, AGO Page 27.

DOE, DAVID.
Appointed Ensign July 6, 1814 and 3d Lieutenant Oct. 1, 1814, 26th Regt. of Riflemen. Ref: Governor and Council Vt. Vol. 6, Page 477.

*DOGET, HENRY.
Served in Sumner's Regt. Vt. Militia.

DOLBEAR, NATHAN.
Volunteered to go to Plattsburgh, September, 1814, and served 7 days in Capt. Asaph Smith's Company. Ref: Book 51, AGO Page 20.

DOLBEAR, SAMUEL.
Volunteered to go to Plattsburgh, September, 1814, and served 7 days in Capt. Asaph Smith's Company. Ref: Book 51, AGO Page 20.

DOLE, EBEN M.,   Berlin.
Volunteered to go to Plattsburgh, September, 1814, and served 7 days in Capt. Cyrus Johnson's Company. Ref: Book 52, AGO Page 255.

*DOLLEY, WILLIAM.
Served with Hospital Attendants, Vt.

DON, ROBERT.
Served from April 12, 1814 to April 15, 1814 in Capt. Jonathan P. Standley's Company, Col. W. B. Sumner's Regt. Ref: Book 52, AGO Page 287.

*DONE, ISAIAH.
Served in 1 Regt. Vt. Militia commanded by Col. Judson.

*DONE, JOHN.
Served in Sumner's Regt. Vt. Militia.

*DONE, JOSIAH.
Served in 1 Regt. Vt. Militia commanded by Col. Judson.

*DONE, ORRIN.
Served in Sumner's Regt. Vt. Militia.

*DONE, SIMEON.
Served in Capt. Hopkins' Company, Col. Martindale's Regt. Detached Militia in U. S. service 1 month and 3 days, 1812.

DONNELL, JOSHUA P.,   Portland.
Served from July 3 to Aug. 31, 1813 and from May 1 to July 11, 1814 in Capt. Crossman's Company, 34th Inf. Ref: R. & L. 1812, AGO Page 30.

DONSKEE, EDWARD.
Served in Capt. Phelps' Company, Col. Wm. Williams' Regt. Detached Militia in U. S. service 5 months, 1812. Ref: Book 53, AGO Page 22.

DOOLITTLE, ABRAHAM, Corporal.
Served in company of Capt. John McNeil Jr., 11th Regt.; on Pay Roll for January and February, 1813. Ref: R. & L. 1812, AGO Page 17.

*DOOLITTLE, JOEL. Adjutant.
Served in Sumner's Regt. Vt. Militia.

DOREMUS, CORNELIUS.
Enlisted Dec. 1, 1812 for 5 years in company of late Capt. J. Brooks, commanded by Lieut. John I. Cromwell, Corps of U. S. Artillery; on Muster Roll from April 30, 1814 to June 30, 1814. Ref: R. & L. 1812, AGO Page 18.

DORR, JOHN, Sergeant.
Enlisted April 5, 1812 for 5 years in Capt. White Youngs' Company, 15th Regt.; on Muster Roll from Aug. 31, 1814 to Dec. 31, 1814. Ref: R. & L. 1812, AGO Page 27.

*DORRANCE, JOSEPH, Captain.
Served in 4 Regt. Vt. Militia commanded by Col. Williams.

*DORRILL, WILLIAM.
Served in Capt. Hopkins' Company, Col. Martindale's Regt. Detached Militia in U. S. service 2 months and 13 days, 1812.

*DORWIN, LYMAN, Lieutenant.
Served from June 11, 1813 to June 14, 1813 in Capt. Thomas Dorwin's Company, 1st Regt. 2nd Brig., 3rd Div.

*DORWIN THOMAS M., Captain.
Commanded company in 1st Regt. 2nd Brig., 3rd Div. from June 11, 1813 to June 14, 1813.

*DOTEN, ISAAC JR.
Served from April 12, 1814 to April 21, 1814 in Capt. Othniel Jewett's Company, Sumner's Regt.

DOTEY, DANIEL,   Vershire, Vt.
Born in the City of New York; aged 45 years; 5 feet 9½ inches high; light complexion; blue eyes; brown hair; by profession a shoemaker. Enlisted at Vershire May 6, 1813 in the Army of the U. S. for the period of 1 year unless sooner discharged. Ref: Paper in the custody of the Vt. Historical Society.

DOTY, ABRAHAM,   Schohani, N. Y.
Served from Sept. 18, 1814 to June 19, 1815 in Capt. Taylor's Company, 30th Inf. Ref: R. & L. 1812, AGO Page 23.

*DOTY, IRA A., Corporal.
Served in Capt. Pettes' Company, Col. Wm. Williams' Regt. Detached Militia in U. S. service 4 months and 17 days, 1812. Served from Feb. 25, 1813 to May 24, 1813 in Capt. Charles Follett's Company, 11th Regt.

DOTY, JEDUTHAN.   Montpelier.
Volunteered to go to Plattsburgh, September, 1814, and served 8 days in Capt. Timothy Hubbard's Company. Ref: Book 52, AGO Pages 198 and 256.

*DOTY, JOHN.
Served from April 13, 1814 to April 21, 1814 in Capt. Salmon Foster's Company, Sumner's Regt.

‡*DOTY, MARSHALL S.
Served from April 12, 1814 to May 20, 1814 in company of Capt. James Gray Jr., Sumner's Regt. Pension Certificate No. 31522.

‡DOTY, SIMON.
Served in Capt. Reynolds' Company.
Pension Certificate No. 26642.

*DOUBTY. JOHN.
Served from April 12, 1814 to April
21, 1814 in Capt. Shubael Wales'
Company, Col. W. B. Sumner's Regt.

‡DOUD, EBENEZER.
Served in Capt. Seneca Page's Company. Pension Certificate No. 803.

DOUGHERTY, BENJAMIN, Franklin
County. Enlisted Oct. 21, 1812 for 5
years in Capt. White Youngs' Company, 15th Regt.; on Muster Roll
from Aug. 31, 1814 to Dec. 31, 1814.
Ref: R. & L. 1812, AGO Page 27.

DOUGHERTY, CHARLES, Sandy Hill,
N. Y. Served from Oct. 22, 1814
to June 19, 1815 in Capt. Taylor's
Company, 30th Inf. Ref: R. & L.
1812, AGO Page 23.

DOUGHERTY, ISAAC,   Sudbury.
Volunteered to go to Plattsburgh,
September, 1814, and served 6 days
in Capt. Thomas Hall's Company.
Ref: Book 52, AGO Page 122.

*DOUGHTEY, ISAAC.
Served in Capt. Brown's Company,
Col. Martindale's Regt. Detached
Militia in U. S. service 2 months and
14 days, 1812.

*DOUGHTY (or Doty) SPENCER, Enos-
burgh. Served from Oct. 15, 1813
to Nov. 17, 1813 in Capt. Asahel
Scoville's Company, Col. Clark's Regt.
of Riflemen.

DOUGLAS, CALEB.
Served in War of 1812 and was captured by troops Sept. 6, 1814 at
Plattsburgh;   discharged   Oct.   8,
1814. Ref: Records of Naval Records and Library, Navy Dept.

DOUGLAS, GEORGE, Franklin County.
Volunteered to go to Plattsburgh
Sept. 11, 1814 and served in 15th or
22nd Regt. Ref: Hemenway's Vt. Gazetteer, Vol. 2, Page 391.

DOUGLAS, JOHN,   Richmond.
Volunteered to go to Plattsburgh,
September, 1814, and served 9 days
in Capt. Roswell Hunt's Company,
3 Regt. Ref: Book 51, AGO Page 82.

*DOUGLAS, JOSEPH.
Served from Oct. 5, 1813 to Oct. 8,
1813 in Capt. Roswell Hunt's Company, 3 Regt. (Tyler's).

DOUGLAS, LUTHER.
Served in War of 1812 and was cap-
tured by troops Sept. 17, 1814 at
Fort Erie; discharged Nov. 8, 1814.
Ref: Records of Naval Records and
Library, Navy Dept.

*DOUGLAS, RICHARD.
Served from Oct. 5, 1813 to Oct. 16,
1813 in Capt. Roswell Hunt's Company, 3 Regt. (Tyler's).

*DOUGLAS, SAMUEL.
Served from Oct. 5, 1813 to Oct. 16,
1813 in Capt. Roswell Hunt's Company, 3 Regt. (Tyler's).

*DOUGLAS. WILLIAM JR., Richmond.
Served from Oct. 11, 1813 to Oct. 16,
1813 in Capt. Roswell Hunt's Company, 3 Regt. (Tyler's); volunteered
to go to Plattsburgh, September, 1814,
and served 9 days in same company.
Also served in Regt. of Riflemen, September to November, 1813.

DOUGLAS, W. MIAM.
Served from Oct. 8, 1813 to Nov. 18,
1813 in Capt. Isaac Finch's Company,
Rifle Regt. Ref: Book 52, AGO Page
276.

*DOUSE, JOHN,   Thetford.
Marched for Plattsburgh, September,
1814, and went as far as Bolton,
Vt., serving 6 days in Capt. Salmon
Howard's Company, 2nd Regt.

DOUTY, THOMAS C.
Served from May 1st to June 30,
1814 in Capt. Haig's Corps of Light
Dragoons. Ref: R. & L. 1812, AGO
Page 20.

DOUX, EBENEZER.
Served in Capt. S. Pettes' Company,
Col. Wm. Williams' Regt. Detached
Militia in U. S. service 3 months and
9 days, 1812. Ref: Book 53, AGO
Page 8.

*DOW, EBENEZER.
Served in 4 Regt. Vt. Militia commanded by Col. Williams.

DOW, ELISHA B.
Enlisted May 21, 1813 for 1 year in
Capt. Simeon Wright's Company. Ref:
R. & L. 1812, AGO Page 51.

‡*DOW, JAMES H.
Served in Capt. Howard's Company,
Vt. Militia. Pension Certificate No.
23515.

DOW, JOHN,   Franklin County.
Volunteered to go to Plattsburgh
Sept. 11, 1814 and served in 15th or
22nd Regt. Ref: Hemenway's Vt. Gazetteer, Vol. 2, Page 392.

DOW, JONATHAN.
Served in company of Capt. John Mc-
Neil Jr., 11th Regt. on Pay Roll
for January and February, 1813.
Ref: R. & L. 1812, AGO Page 17.

DOW, MELVIN.
Served from July 1 to July 31, 1814
as Wagon Master on General Staff
of the Northern Army commanded
by Maj. Gen. George Izard. Ref: R.
& L. 1812, AGO Page 28.

*DOW, ROBERT.
Served in Sumner's Regt. Vt. Militia.

DOWNER, CUSHMAN.
Served in Capt. Benjamin S. Edgerton's Company, 11th Regt.; on Pay
Roll for September and October, 1812,
and January and February, 1813.
Ref: R. & L. 1812, AGO Pages 1
and 2.

‡*DOWNER, RICHARD.
Served in Capt. Mason's Company,
Col. Fifield's Regt. Detached Militia
in U. S. service 1 month and 17 days,
1812. Pension Certificate of widow,
Catharine. No. 7753.

DOWNEY, HENRY, Sergeant.
Served in Capt. Phelps' Company,
Col. Wm. Williams' Regt. stationed
at Swanton Falls in 1812. Ref: Vol.
49 Vt. State Papers, Page 119.

DOWNEY, HORACE,   Pittsford.
Volunteered to go to Plattsburgh,
September, 1814, and served 8 days
in Capt. Caleb Hendee's Company.
Ref: Book 52, AGO Page 125.

*DOWNEY, JAMES.
Served in Capt. Phelps' Company,
Col. Wm. Williams' Regt. Detached
Militia in U. S. service 4 months and
5 days, 1812. Also served in Sum-
ner's Regt. Vt. Militia.

DOWNEY, JOHN,   Pittsford.
Volunteered to go to Plattsburgh,
September, 1814, and served 8 days
in Capt. Caleb Hendee's Company.
Ref: Book 52, AGO Page 124.

DOWNEY, PATRICK, Sergeant, Sandy
Hill, N. Y. Served from Oct. 11,
1814 to June 19, 1815 in Capt. Taylor's Company, 30th Inf. Ref: R. &
L. 1812, AGO Page 23.

DOWNEY, WILLIAM, Corporal.
Enlisted May 8, 1813 for 1 year in
Capt. Simeon Wright's Company.
Ref: R. & L. 1812, AGO Page 51.

DOWNING, CALEB.
Served from Feb. 11, 1813 to April
14, 1813 in Capt. Jonathan Starks'
Company, 11th Regt. Ref: R. & L.
1812, AGO Page 19.

*DOWNING, ELISHA.
Served in Capt. Wright's Company,
Col. Fifield's Regt. Detached Militia
in U. S. service 3 months and 11
days, 1812.

*DOWNING, GEORGE.
Served from June 11, 1813 to June
14, 1813 in Lieut. Bates' Company,
1 Regt. (Judson's).

DOWNING, GEORGE.
Enlisted May 16, 1813 for 1 year and
served in Capt. Gideon Spencer's Company, Capt. James Taylor's Company,
30th Regt.; discharged May 15, 1814.
Ref: R. & L. 1812, AGO Pages 52,
57, 59.

DOWNING, GIDEON,   Washington.
Volunteered to go to Plattsburgh,
September, 1814, and served in Capt.
Amos Stiles' Company. Ref: Book 52,
AGO Pages 36 and 220.

DOWNING, GIDEON,   Barre.
Volunteered to go to Plattsburgh,
September, 1814, and served in Capt.
Warren Ellis' Company. Ref: Hemen-
way's Vt. Gazetteer Vol. 4, Page 41.

DOWNING, JOHN,   Jericho.
Took part in the Battle of Plattsburgh. Ref: History of Jericho, Page
142.

‡*DOWNING, LUTHER C.
Served in Capt. Bingham's Company,
Col. Jonathan Williams' Regt. De-
tached Militia in U. S. service 2
months and 9 days, 1812. Pension
Certificate of widow, Sarah, No. 207.

DOWNING, PERKINS.
Volunteered to go to Plattsburgh,
September, 1814, and served in Capt.
Joel Barnes' Company of Chelsea.
Ref: Book 52, AGO Page 77.

‡DOWNING, SAMUEL,   Washington.
Volunteered to go to Plattsburgh,
September, 1814, and served in Capt.
Amos Stiles' Company. Pension Cer-
tificate of widow, Lucinda, No. 22859.

‡DOWNING, SAM P.
Pension Certificate of widow, Sally
A., No. 7045. No organization given.

*DOWNS, DAVID,   West Haven.
Volunteered to go to Plattsburgh,
September, 1814, and served 4 days
in Capt. David B. Phippeney's Company. Also served with Hospital Attendants, Vt. Ref: Book 52, AGO
Page 146.

DOX, PETER,   Stillwater.
Served from May 1, 1814 to July 11,
1814 in Capt. Lynd's Company, 29th
Inf. Ref: R. & L. 1812, AGO Page
30.

DOXEY, JOHN.
Served in 1 Regt. Vt. Militia commanded by Col. Judson.

‡*DOYLE, JOHN M.
Served in Capt. Durkee's Company,
Col. Fifield's Regt. Detached Militia
in U. S. service 2 months and 21
days, 1812. Also served in Capt.
Smeed's Company. Pension Certificate No. 4950.

DRAIN, DANIEL.
Served from Feb. 8, 1813 to May 7,
1813 in Capt. Charles Follett's Company, 11th Regt. Ref: R. & L. 1812,
AGO Page 13.

DRAIN, DAVID.
Served in Capt. Charles Follett's Com-
pany, 11th Regt.; on Pay Roll for
January and February, 1812. Ref:
R. & L. 1812, AGO Page 12.

DRAINS, JOHN.
Served in Capt. Blinn's Company of
Militia; on Muster Roll from June
11, 1813 to June 14, 1813. Ref: R.
& L. 1812, AGO Page 49.

DRAKE, DANIEL, Corporal, Clarendon.
Served from Jan. 16, 1815 to June
19, 1815 in Capt. Taylor's Company,
30th Inf. Ref: R. & L. 1812, AGO
Page 23.

DRAKE, DANIEL,   St. Albans.
Served from May 25, 1813 to May,
1814, in Capt. John Wires' Company,
30th Regt. Ref: R. & L. 1812, AGO
Page 40; Hemenway's Vt. Gazetteer,
Vol. 2, Page 433.

*DRAKE, DANIEL.
Served in Capt. Needham's Company,
Col. Martindale's Regt. Detached
Militia in U. S. service 2 months
and 14 days, 1812.

*DRAKE, DANIEL.
Served in Capt. Burnap's Company,
Col. Jonathan Williams' Regt. Detached Militia in U. S. service 2
months and 13 days, 1812.

*DRAKE. ELIAS.   Calais.
Volunteered to go to Plattsburgh,
September, 1814, and served 8 days
in Capt. Gideon Wheelock's Company. Ref: Book 52, AGO Pages
180 and 247.

*DRAKE, ELIJAH. Sergeant.
Served from April 12, 1814 to April
21, 1814 in Capt. Othniel Jewett's
Company, Sumner's Regt.

*DRAKE. SOLOMON, Lieutenant, Bristol.
Volunteered to go to Plattsburgh,
September, 1814, and was at the
battle, serving 9 days in Capt. Jehiel
Saxton's Company, Sumner's Regt.

*DRAPER. SIMEON.
Served in Capt. Start's Company,
Col. Martindale's Regt. Detached
Militia in U. S. service 1 month
and 5 days, 1812.

DRAYTON, WILLIAM, Inspector General.
Served on General Staff of the North-
ern Army commanded by Major Gen-
eral George Izard; on Pay Roll to
July 31, 1814. Ref: R. & L. 1812,
AGO Page 28.

*DRESSER, RESOLVED.
Served in Capt. Pettes' Company,
Col. Wm. Williams' Regt. Detached
Militia in U. S. service 3 months
and 17 days, 1812.

*DREW. ELISHA.
Served from June 11, 1813 to June 14,
1813 in Capt. Moses Jewett's Company, 1st Regt. 2nd Brig. 3rd Div.

*DREW, ISAAC, Corporal.
Served in 1 Regt. Vt. Militia commanded by Col. Judson.

DREW. JAMES.
Volunteered to go to Plattsburgh,
September, 1814, and served 4 days
in Capt. Aaron Kidder's Company.
Ref: Book 52, AGO Page 65.

*DREW, PAUL.
Served from April 12, 1814 to April
21, 1814 in Capt. Othniel Jewett's
Company, Sumner's Regt.

DREW. SAMUEL.   Rochester, N. H.
Enlisted at Fairlee April 2, 1814 for
the period of the war and served
in Capt. Wm. Miller's Company,
Capt. Gideon Spencer's Company and
Capt. James Taylor's Company, all in
the 30th Regt. Ref: R. & L. 1812,
AGO Pages 53, 54, 55, 57.

DREW, SMITH.   Franklin County.
Volunteered to go to Plattsburgh
Sept. 11, 1814 and served in 15th or
22nd Regt. Ref. Hemenway's Vt.
Gazetteer, Vol. 2, Page 392.

DREW. THOMAS.
Enlisted Jan. 6, 1813 in Capt. Jonathan Starks' Company, 11th Regt.;
on Pay Roll to May 31, 1813. Ref:
R. & L. 1812, AGO Page 19.

*DREW. ZACHEUS.
Served from June 11, 1813 to June
14, 1813 in Capt. Samuel Blinn's Company, 1st Regt. (Judson's).

DROUT, JOHN.
Served from July 1 to Aug. 31, 1813
and from May 1 to July 4, 1814; no
organization given. Ref: R. & L.
1812, AGO Page 29.

DROWN, MOSES.
Enlisted Jan. 13, 1813 in Capt. Jonathan Starks' Company, 11th Regt.;
on Pay Roll to May 31, 1813. Ref:
R. & L. 1812, AGO Page 19.

DROWN, SAMUEL.
Enlisted Jan. 1, 1813 in Capt. Jonathan Starks' Company, 11th Regt.;
on Pay Roll to May 31, 1813. Ref: R.
& L. 1812, AGO Page 19.

DRUMMOND, JOHN.
Enlisted May 23, 1812 for 5 years
in Capt. White Youngs' Company,
15th Regt.; on Muster Roll from
Aug. 31, 1814 to Dec. 31, 1814. Ref:
R. & L. 1812, AGO Page 27.

DRURY. AMOS, Corporal,   Pittsford.
Volunteered to go to Plattsburgh,
September, 1814, and served 8 days
in Capt. Caleb Hendee's Company.
Ref: Book 52, AGO Page 124.

*DRURY, DAVID.
Served from April 12, 1814 to April
21, 1814 in Capt. Shubael Wales' Company, Col. W. B. Sumner's Regt.

DRURY, JOHN W., Sergeant, Holden,
Mass. or St. Albans. Enlisted April
23, 1813 for 1 year in Capt. John
Wires' Company. 30th Regt. Served
from July 11. 1814 to June 16, 1815
in Capt. Sanford's Company, 30th
Inf. Ref: R. & L. 1812, AGO Page
40 and Page 23.

DUCLOS, NICHOLAS, Corporal, Swan-
ton. Enlisted in American Army in
February, 1813. Served in Corps of
Light Dragoons from May 1st to June
30, 1814. Ref: R. & L. 1812, AGO
Page 20; Vol. 51 Vt. State Papers,
Page 23.

DUDLEY, ABIJAH.   Franklin County.
Volunteered to go to Plattsburgh
Sept. 11, 1814 and served in 15th or
22nd Regt. Ref: Hemenway's Vt.
Gazetteer, Vol. 2, Page 391.

*DUDLEY, JOHN, Sergeant.
Served in Capt. Richardson's Company, Col. Martindale's Regt. Detached Militia in U. S. service 2
months and 13 days, 1812.

‡DUDLEY. JONATHAN.   Montpelier.
Volunteered to go to Plattsburgh,
September, 1814 and served 8 days
in Capt .Timothy Hubbard's Company. Pension Certificate No. 32757.

*DUDLEY, PHENEHAS.
Enlisted Sept. 25. 1813 in Company
of Capt. Jonathan Prentiss Jr., Dixon's Regt.

*DUDLEY, SAMUEL R.
Served in Capt. Briggs' Company,
Col. Jonathan Williams' Regt. Detached Militia in U. S. service 2
months and 13 days, 1812.

*DUDLEY, SEANDER (probably Lean-der). Served in 3 Regt. (Tyler's) Vt. Militia.

DUDLY, TIBBITS, Corporal.
Served from Feb. 4, 1813 to May 3, 1813 in Lieut. Wm. S. Foster's Company, 11th Regt. Ref: R. & L. 1812, AGO Page 6.

DUFER, ABEL.
Served in Capt. Benjamin Bradford's Company. Muster Roll from May 31, 1813 to Aug. 31, 1813. Ref: R. & L. 1812, AGO Page 26.

DUFER, SILAS.
Served in Capt. Benjamin Bradford's Company; on Muster Roll from May 31, 1813 to Aug. 31, 1813. Ref: R. & L. 1812, AGO Page 26.

*DUGAR, JOSEPH.
Enlisted Sept. 25, 1813 in Capt. Thomas Waterman's Company, Dixon's Regt.

DUGGET, JAMES JR.
Served in Capt. Chadwick's Company, 2nd Regt. Ref: R. & L. 1812, AGO Page 32.

DUKE, ENOCH, Musician.
Enlisted Sept. 23, 1813 in Capt. Amasa Mansfield's Company, Dixon's Regt. Ref: Book 52, AGO Page 269.

DUKEMAN, THOMAS,   Fairfax.
Served from Aug. 8, 1812 in company of Capt. Joseph Beeman Jr. 11th Regt. U. S. Inf. under Col. Ira Clark. Ref: Hemenway's Vt. Gazetteer, Vol. 2, Page 402.

*DUN, PETER, Fife Major.
Served in 1 Regt. Vt. Militia commanded by Col. Judson.

DUNCAN, JOHN.
Served in Capt. Rogers' Company, Col. Fifield's Regt. Detached Militia in U. S. service 2 months and 18 days, 1812. Ref: Book 53, AGO Page 17.

*DUNCAN, THOMAS.
Served in Dixon's Regt. Vt. Militia.

DUNCAN, WILLIAM R., Lieutenant and Brig. Major. Served on General Staff of the Northern Army commanded by Maj. Gen. George Izard. Ref: R. & L. 1812, AGO Page 28.

DUNEHER, WILLIAM.
Enlisted Sept. 25, 1813 in Company of Capt. Jonathan Prentiss Jr., Dixon's Regt. Ref: Book 52, AGO Page 270.

*DUNHAM, HORACE, Sergeant.
Served from April 12, 1814 to April 21, 1814 in Lieut. Justus Foote's Company, Sumner's Regt.

"DUNHAM, JOSIAH.
Enlisted March 4, 1813 for 5 years in company of late Capt. J. Brooks commanded by Lieut. John I. Cromwell. Corps of U. S. Artillery; on Muster Roll from April 30, 1814 to June 30, 1814. Also served with Hospital Attendants, Vt.

‡DUNHAM, OTHANIEL, Lieutenant, Stockbridge. Volunteered to go to Plattsburgh, September, 1814, and served 8 days in Capt. Elias Keyes' Company. Pension Certificate of widow, Emily, No. 17920.

*DUNKIN, JOHN.
Served in 2 Regt. Vt. Militia commanded by Col. Fifield.

DUNKING, JOSEPH.
Served from Feb .22, 1813 to May 21, 1813 in Lieut. V. R. Goodrich's Company, 11th Regt. Ref: R. & L. 1812, AGO Page 10.

*DUNKINS, THOMAS.
Served in 2 Regt. Vt. Militia commanded by Col. Fifield.

DUNLAP, JOHN.
On Pay Roll of Capt. Weeks' Company, 11th Regt., for January and February, 1813; doing duty and paid in the 21st Regt. Infantry. Ref: R. & L. 1812, AGO Page 5.

*DUNLAP, ROBERT.
Served in 3 Regt. Vt. Militia commanded by Col. Williams.

DUNN, JOHN,   Sandy Hill, N. Y.
Served from Sept. 24, 1814 to June 19, 1815 in Capt. Taylor's Company, 30th Infantry. Ref: R. & L. 1812, AGO Page 23.

DUNN, JOSEPH.
Served from May 1 to June 30, 1814 as master saddler in company of Artificers commanded by Alexander Parris. Ref: R. & L. 1812, AGO Page 24.

DUNN, JOSHUA.
Served from May 1 to June 30, 1814 as Sad. Har. in company of Artificers commanded by Alexander Parris. Ref: R. & L. 1812, AGO Page 24.

‡DUNNING, ABEL.
Served in Capt. Danforth's Company. Pension Certificate of widow, Cyntha, No. 30550.

‡*DUNNING, CEPHAS, Drummer.
Served in Capt. Cross' Company, Col. Martindale's Regt. Detached Militia in U. S. service 2 months and 13 days, 1812. Pension Certificate No. 8227.

*DUNNING, JOHN.
Served from April 12, 1814 to April 15, 1814 in Capt. John Hackett's Company, Sumner's Regt.

*DUNSHEE, EDWARD.
Served in 4 Regt. Vt. Militia commanded by Col. Williams.

DUNSHEE, JOHN,   Bristol.
Volunteered to go to Plattsburgh, September, 1814, and was at the battle, serving 9 days in Capt. Jehiel Saxton's Company, Sumner's Regt. Ref: Book 51, AGO Page 18.

‡*DUNSHEE, JONATHAN T., Cambridge.
Enlisted Sept. 25, 1813 in Capt. Thomas Waterman's Company, Dix-

on's Regt. Volunteered to go to Plattsburgh, September, 1814, and served 8 days in Capt. Salmon Green's Company. Also served in Capt. Chadwick's Company. Pension Certificate No. 5626.

‡*DUNSHEE, WILLIAM, Bristol. Volunteered to go to Plattsburgh, September, 1814, and was at the battle, serving 9 days in Capt. Jehiel Saxton's Company, Sumner's Regt. Also served in Dixon's Regt. Vt. Militia. Pension Certificate of widow, Almeda, No. 26207.

DUNTON, EZEKIEL, Brig. General, Bristol. Served as Brig. Gen. in 2nd Regt. 1st Brig., 3rd Div., Vt. Militia. Took command of a volunteer company from Bristol as their Captain and was at the battle of Plattsburgh. Ref: Hemenway's Vt. Gazetteer, Vol. 1, Page 22.

‡*DUNTON, THOMAS, Sergeant. Appointed Sergeant Sept. 28, 1813 in Capt. Asahel Langworthy's Company, Col. Isaac Clark's Regt. of Volunteer Riflemen. Volunteered to go to Plattsburgh, September, 1814, and served 8 days in Capt. Jesse Post's Company, Dixon's Regt. Also served in Capt. Sabin's Company. Pension Certificate of widow, Aurora B., No. 28152.

*DUNTON, WILLIAM. Enlisted Sept. 25, 1813 in Capt. Elijah W. Wood's Company, Dixon's Regt.

DURAND, AARON. Served from May 1 to June 30, 1814 in Capt. Alexander Brooks' Corps of Artillery. Ref: R. & L. 1812, AGO Page 31.

DURFEY, ELIJAH, Cornwall. Volunteered to go to Plattsburgh, September, 1814, and served in Capt. Edmund B. Hill's Company, Sumner's Regt. Ref: Rev. Lyman Mathews' History of Cornwall, Page 345.

DURFEY, PROSPER, Lincoln. Volunteered to go to Plattsburgh, September, 1814, and was at the battle, serving 9 days in Capt. Jehiel Saxton's Company, Sumner's Regt. Ref: Book 51, AGO Page 18.

*DURGEE, RANSOM. Enlisted Sept. 29, 1813 in Capt. Asahel Langworthy's Company, Col. Isaac Clark's Rifle Corps.

*DURGEY, CHARLES. Served in Dixon's Regt. Vt. Militia.

DURGIN, SAMUEL. Volunteered to go to Plattsburgh, September, 1814, and served in Capt. Ebenezer Spencer's Company at Vershire. Ref: Book 52, AGO Pages 48 and 49.

*DURHAM, RUSSELL. Enlisted Sept. 25, 1813 in Company of Capt. Jonathan Prentiss Jr., Dixon's Regt.

*DURHAM, ZEBA. Enlisted Sept. 23, 1813 in Capt. Amasa Mansfield's Company, Dixon's Regt.

DURKEE, ASA W., Pittsford. Enlisted April 25, 1813 for 1 year in Capt. Simeon Wright's Company. Served from March 10, 1814 to June 16, 1815 in Capt. Sanford's Company. 30th Inf. Ref: R & L. 1812, AGO Pages 23 and 51.

DURKEE, ASHEL. Volunteered to go to Plattsburgh, September, 1814, and served 7 days in Capt. Frederick Griswold's Company, raised in Brookfield, Vt. Ref: Book 52, AGO Page 52.

DURKEE, CHARLES, Swanton. Volunteered to go to Plattsburgh, September, 1814; no organization given. Ref: Book 51, AGO Pages 137 and 165.

DURKEE, DAVID, Pittsford. Served from April 25, 1813 to April 27, 1814 in Capt. Simeon Wright's Company. Served from June 20, 1814 to June 19, 1815 in Capt. Taylor's Company, 30th Inf. Ref: R. & L. 1812, AGO Pages 23 and 51.

DURKEE, JOHN, Tunbridge. Volunteered to go to Plattsburgh, September, 1814, and served 4 days in Capt. Ephraim Hackett's Company, Sumner's Regt. Ref: Book 52, AGO Page 71.

*DURKEE, NATHAN, Drummer. Served under Captains Durkee and Wright, Col. Fifield's Regt. Detached Militia in U. S. service 6 months.

*DURKEE, ORIN, Captain. Served in 2 Regt. Vt. Militia commanded by Col. Fifield.

‡DURKEE, RANSOM. Served in Capt. Langworthy's Company, Col. Dixon's Regt. Detached Militia in U. S. service 1 month and 19 days, 1813. Pension Certificate No. 10219.

DURKEE, SAMUEL, Williamstown. Volunteered to go to Plattsburgh, September, 1814, and was in the battle, serving 8 days in Capt. David Robinson's Company. Ref: Book 52, AGO Page 2.

DURKEE, ZALA. Volunteered to go to Plattsburgh, September, 1814, and served 7 days in Capt. Frederick Griswold's Company, raised in Brookfield, Vt. Ref: Book 52, AGO Page 52.

DURKEY, CHARLES. Enlisted Sept. 25, 1813 in Capt. Amos Robinson's Company, Dixon's Regt. Ref: Book 52, AGO Page 271.

‡DURLAM, FREDERICK. Served in Capt. Stewart's Company. Pension Certificate No. 10319.

DURR, JOHN, Franklin County. Volunteered to go to Plattsburgh Sept. 11, 1814 and served in 15th or 22nd Regt. Ref: Hemenway's Vt. Gazetteer, Vol. 2, Page 391.

DURRAND, M. F.
Served from May 28, 1813 to July 31,
1814 as Barrack Master on Staff of
the Northern Army commanded by
Maj. Gen. George Izard. Ref: R. &
L. 1812, AGO Page 28.

*DUSTIN, ELIPHALET.
Served in Capt. Rogers' Company,
Col. Fifield's Regt. Detached Militia
in U. S. service 5 months and 27
days, 1812.

DUSTIN, PETER,   Tunbridge.
Volunteered to go to Plattsburgh,
September, 1814, and served in Capt.
David Knox's Company. Ref: Book
52, AGO Page 116.

DUTCHER, DANIEL, Lieutenant, Swanton or St. Albans. Volunteered to
go to Plattsburgh, September, 1814,
and served in Capt. S. W. Farnsworth's Company. Ref: Book 51, AGO
Page 128.

*DUTCHER, DAVID, Captain.
Served in Capt. Cross' Company, Col.
Martindale's Regt. Detached Militia
in U. S. service 2 months and 14
days, 1812. Served as Captain of company of volunteers from St. Albans
at time of Plattsburgh battle in September, 1814.

DUTTON, AMZI.
Enlisted Aug. 22, 1812 in Capt.
Samul Gordon's Company, 11th Regt.;
on Pay Roll for company for Janu-
ary and February, 1813. Ref: R.
& L. 1812, AGO Page 9.

'DUTTON, EBENEZER,   Shoreham.
Served from April 12, 1814 to May
20, 1814 in company of Capt. James
Gray Jr., Sumner's Regt. Volunteer-
ed to go to Plattsburgh, September,
1814, and served 6 days in Capt.
Samuel Hand's Company. Ref: Rev.
J. F. Goodhue's History of Shoreham,
Page 108.

*DUTTON, EPHRAIM.
Served in 1 Regt. Vt. Militia commanded by Col. Judson.

*DUTTON, JAMES.
Served from April 12, 1814 to April
21, 1814 in Capt. Edmund B. Hill's
Company, Sumner's Regt.

DUTTON, JOHN P.
Enlisted Dec. 23, 1813 during the
war in Capt. Simeon Wright's Company. Ref: R. & L. 1812, AGO Page
51.

DUTTON, SALMON.
Enlisted April 19, 1813 for 1 year in
Capt. Daniel Farrington's Company
(also commanded by Capt. Simeon
Wright), 30th Regt. Ref: R. & L.
1812, AGO Pages 50 and 51.

‡*DUTTON, SAMUEL, Cabot or Walden.
Served in Captain Mason's Company,
Col. Fifield's Regt. Detached Militia in
U. S. service 6 months, 1812. Volun-
teered to go to Plattsburgh, Septem-
ber, 1814, and served 4 days in Capt.
Major Robinson's Company. Also
served in Capt. Morrill's Company.

Pension Certificate No. 17654. Pension Certificate of widow, Olive, No.
11632.

DUTTON, THOMAS,   St. Albans.
Served at the Battle of Plattsburgh
Sept. 11, 1814 in Capt. Samuel H.
Farnsworth's Company. Ref: Hemen-
way's Vt. Gazetteer, Vol. 2, Page
434.

DUTTON, WILLIAM,   Walden.
Volunteered to go to Plattsburgh,
September, 1814, and served 4 days
in Capt. Major Robinson's Company.
Ref: Book 51, AGO Page 74.

DUVEY, JOHN, Ensign.
Appointed Ensign Sept. 25, 1813 in
company of Capt. Jonathan Prentiss,
Jr., Dixon's Regt. Ref: Book 52, AGO
Page 270.

DUVEY, JOHN M.
Enlisted Sept. 25, 1813 in company
of Capt. Jonathan Prentiss Jr., Dixon's Regt. Ref: Book 52, AGO Page
270.

DWINELL, AMOS,   Tunbridge.
Volunteered to go to Plattsburgh,
September, 1814, and served 4 days
in Capt. Ephraim Hackett's Com-
pany, Sumner's Regt. Ref: Book 52,
AGO Page 71.

‡DWYER, JOHN.
Served in Capt. Parker's Company.
Pension Certificate of widow, Lydia,
No. 28851.

‡DWYER, WILLIAM.
Served in Capt. Kimball's Company.
Pension Certificate No. 21138.

DYER, DYSON.
Served from June 9 to June 30, 1814
in Capt. Alexander Brooks' Corps of
Artillery. Ref: R. & L. 1812, AGO
Page 31.

*DYER, SOLOMON.
Served from April 13, 1814 to April
21, 1814 in Capt. Salmon Foster's Company, Sumner's Regt.

‡*DYER, THOMAS N.
Served in Capt. Wheatly's Company,
Col. Fifield's Regt. Detached Militia
in U. S. service 2 months and 21
days, 1812. Pension Certificate No.
7916. Pension Certificate of widow,
Mary, No. 27792.

DYKE, ENOCH.
Served in Capt. Mansfield's Company,
Col. Dixon's Regt. Detached Militia
in U. S. service 1 month and 23
days, 1813. Ref: Book 53, AGO Page
109.

*DYKE, ENOS, Drummer.
Served in Dixon's Regt. Vt. Militia.

*DYKE, JOSEPH, Drummer.
Served in 3 Regt. Vt. Militia commanded by Col. Tyler.

EADES, THOMAS.
Served in Capt. Haig's Corps of
Light Dragoons; on Pay Roll to June
30, 1814; prisoner of war. Served

from June 1, 1813 to July 31, 1814.
Ref: R. & L. 1812, AGO Pages 20
and 29.

EAGER, HIRAM.
Served from Dec. 24, 1812 to Feb.
28, 1813 in Capt. Samuel H. Holly's
Company, 11th Regt. Ref: R. & L.
1812, AGO Page 25.

EAGER, JASON.
Served from Dec. 18, 1812 to Feb.
28, 1813 in Capt. Samuel H. Holly's
Company, 11th Regt. Ref: R. & L.
1812, AGO Page 25.

*EAMES, ISAAC, 1st Lieutenant, Dover.
Served in 3 Regt. Vt. Militia commanded by Col. Williams.

‡EASTERBROOK, MARSHALL.
Served in Capt. Smead's Company.
Pension Certificate No. 8498.

*EASTMAN, BENJAMIN, Corporal.
Served in Capt. Briggs' Company,
Col. Jonathan Williams' Regt. Detached Militia in U. S. service 2
months and 13 days, 1812.

‡*EASTMAN, CALVIN JR.
Served from April 12, 1814 to April
21, 1814 in Capt. Edmund B. Hill's
Company, Sumner's Regt. Pension
Certificate of widow, Clarissa, No.
26662.

EASTMAN, CHILLIS.
Served in Company of Capt. John
McNeil Jr., 11 Regt.; died Jan. 3,
1813. Ref: R. & L. 1812, AGO Page
17.

‡EASTMAN, DANIEL,   Clarendon.
Volunteered to go to Plattsburgh,
September, 1814, and served 7 days
in Capt. Durham Sprague's Company.
Pension Certificate of widow, Try-
phena, No. 22864.

EASTMAN, EZRA,   Fairfax.
Served from Aug. 8, 1812 in company
of Capt. Joseph Beeman, Jr. in 11th
Regt. U. S. Inf. under Col. Ira
Clark. Served in Lieut. V. R. Good-
rich's Company, 11th Regt.; on Pay
Roll for January and February, 1813.
Ref: Hemenway's Vt. Gazetteer, Vol.
2, Page 402; R. & L. 1812, AGO
Page 11.

*EASTMAN, ELIAS.
Enlisted Sept. 20, 1813 in Capt. John
Weed's Company, Regt. of Rifle-
men.

‡*EASTMAN, ELISHA.
Enlisted Sept. 20, 1813 in Capt. John
Weed's Company, Regt. of Riflemen.
Also served in Capt. D. Sprague's
Company. Pension Certificate No.
34905.

*EASTMAN, ENOCH.
Enlisted Sept. 20, 1813 in Capt. John
Weed's Company, Regt. of Riflemen.

‡*EASTMAN, HARRY, Drummer.
Served in Capt. Phelps' Company,
Col. Wm. Williams' Regt. Detached
Militia in U. S. service 5 months,
1812. Pension Certificate No. 8273.

EASTMAN, HENRY, Sergeant.
Served from Feb. 2, 1813 to April
6, 1813 in company of Capt. John
McNeil Jr., 11th Regt. Ref: R. &
L. 1812, AGO Page 16.

*EASTMAN, JOHN,   Corinth.
Served in Capt. Rogers' Company,
Col. Fifield's Regt. Detached Militia
in U. S. service 1 month and 23
days, 1812. Volunteered to go to
Plattsburgh, September, 1814, and
served 3 days in Capt. Abel Jackman's Company.

EASTMAN, JOHN,   Cortland, N. H.
Enlisted at Burlington Sept. 14, 1814
for duration of war in Capt. Wm.
Miller's Company, 30th Regt. Ref:
R. & L. 1812, AGO Page 55.

EASTMAN, JOHN C.
Served from March 9, 1813 to April
15, 1813 in Lieut. Wm. S. Foster's
Company, 11th Regt. Ref: R. & L.
1812, AGO Page 6.

‡EASTMAN, JONATHAN, Lieutenant.
Appointed Lieutenant 1 Artillery
March 12, 1812; honorably discharged
June 1, 1814. Pension Certificate of
widow, Philanda, No. 12502. Heitman's Historical Register & Dictionary USA.

*EASTMAN, JUSTIN.
Served in Capt. Strait's Company,
Col. Martindale's Regt. Detached
Militia in U. S. service 2 months
and 13 days, 1812.

‡EASTMAN, LUTHER.
Served in Capt. J. Saxton's Company.
Pension Certificate No. 1207.

*EASTMAN, PETER, Sergeant.
Served in 1 Regt. Vt. Militia commanded by Col. Judson.

*EASTMAN, RUSSELL.
Served from April 12, 1814 to April
21, 1814 in Capt. Othniel Jewett's
Company, Sumner's Regt.

*EASTMAN, SILAS N., Fifer.
Served from June 11, 1813 to June
14, 1813 in Capt. Ithiel Stone's Company, 1st Regt. 2nd Brig., 3rd Div.

*EASTMAN, STEPHEN JR.
Enlisted Sept. 20, 1813 in Capt. John
Weed's Company, Regt. of Riflemen.

EASTMAN, WILLIAM,   Strafford.
Volunteered to go to Plattsburgh,
September, 1814, and served in Capt.
Joseph Barrett's Company. Ref: Book
52, AGO Page 41.

EASTON, JULIAN,   Canajohaire.
Served from May 1, 1814 to July 9,
1814 in Lieut. Hanson's Company,
29th Inf. Ref: R. & L. 1812, AGO
Page 30.

*EATON, ABIJAH.
Served in Capt. Richardson's Company, Col. Martindale's Regt. Detached Militia in U. S. service 2
months and 13 days, 1812. Served
from Feb. 22, 1813 to May 21, 1813
in Capt. Charles Follett's Company,
11th Regt. Ref: R. & L. 1812, AGO
Page 13.

EATON, ABNA.
Enlisted Jan. 9. 1813 in Capt. Phineas Williams' Company. 11th Regt.; on Pay Roll to May 31, 1813. Ref: R. & L. 1812, AGO Page 14.

‡*EATON, ADNA, Sergeant,   Barnard.
Served in Capt. Briggs' Company, Col. Jonathan Williams' Regt. Detached Militia in U. S. service 2 months and 13 days, 1812. Pension Certificate No. 10772. Pension Certificate of widow, Lucy, No. 32496. Volunteered to go to Plattsburgh, September, 1814, and served 8 days in Capt. John S. Bicknell's Company. Ref: Book 51, AGO Page 250.

EATON, AIDORE,   Castleton.
Volunteered to go to Plattsburgh, September, 1814, and served 9 days; no organization given.   Ref: Book 52, AGO Page 154.

EATON, DAVID, Quartermaster.
Volunteered to go to Plattsburgh, September, 1814, and served 7 days in Capt. Asaph Smith's Company. Ref: Book 51, AGO Pages 20 and 21.

‡*EATON, GORDON.
Served in Capt. Richardson's Company, Col. Martindale's Regt. Detached Militia in U. S. service 2 months and 13 days, 1812. Pension Certificate of widow, Roxanna, No. 3849.

*EATON, HALLOT.
Served in Capt. Richardson's Company, Col. Martindale's Regt. Detached Militia in U. S. service 2 months and 13 days, 1812.

EATON, HUMPHRY.
Served in Capt. Benjamin Bradford's Company; on Muster Roll from May 31, 1813 to Aug. 31, 1813; joined by transfer July 22, 1813. Ref: R. & L. 1812, AGO Page 26.

EATON, JACOB F.
Served from Feb. 2, 1813 to May 1, 1813 in Capt. Samul Gordon's Company, 11th Regt. Served from June 10 to June 30, 1814 in company of Artificers commanded by Alexander Parris, as an Armorer. Ref: R. & L. 1812, AGO Pages 8, 9, 24.

*EATON, JAMES.
Served from Sept. 25, 1813 to Sept. 29, 1813 in Capt. Amos Robinson's Company, Dixon's Regt.

*EATON, JOHN.
Served in Capt. Saxe's Company, Col. Wm. Williams' Regt. Detached Militia in U. S. service 4 months and 24 days, 1812. Enisted May 10. 1813 in Capt. James Taylor's Company, 30th Regt.; transferred to Capt. Gideon Spencer's Company, 30th Regt. and served to May 10, 1814. Ref: R. & L. 1812, AGO Pages 52, 57, 59.

*EATON, JONATHAN J., Corporal.
Served in Capt. Brown's Company. Col. Martindale's Regt. Detached Militia in U. S. service 2 months and 14 days, 1812. Enlisted Sept. 25. 1813 and served 1 month and 23 days

in Capt. Birge's Company, Col. Dixon's' Regt.

EATON. JOSHUA,   Tunbridge.
Volunteered to go to Plattsburgh, September, 1814, and served in Capt. David Knox's Company. Ref: Book 52, AGO Page 116.

EATON, MOSES,   Johnson.
Volunteered to go to Plattsburgh, September, 1814, and served in Capt. Thomas Waterman's Company, Dixon's Regt. Ref: Book 51, AGO Page 208.

*EATON, PARLEY, Sergeant.
Enlisted Sept. 25, 1813 in Capt. Charles Bennett's Company, Dixon's Regt.

EATON. PETER,   Corinth.
Volunteered to go to Plattsburgh, September, 1814, and served 7 days in Capt. Ebenezer Spencer's Company, Vershire. Ref: Book 52, AGO Pages 48, 49, 120.

EATON, TIMOTHY B.,   Tunbridge.
Volunteered to go to Plattsburgh, September, 1814, and served in Capt. David Knox's Company. Ref: Book 52, AGO Page 116.

*EATON. WILLIAM.
Served in Capt. Adams' Company, Col. Jonathan Williams' Regt. Detached Militia in U. S. service 2 months and 7 days, 1812. Served from June 1 to June 30, 1814 in Company of Artificers commanded by Alexander Parris. Ref: R. & L. 1812, AGO Page 24; Book 53, AGO Page 62.

EATY. WILLIAM,   Shepardstown.
Served from May 1, 1814 to Aug. 15, 1814 in Capt. Morgan's Company, Rifle Regt. Ref: R. & L. 1812, AGO Page 30.

*EDDY, DAVID.
Served from June 11, 1813 to June 14, 1813 in Capt. Thomas Dorwin's Company, 1st Regt. 2nd Brig., 3rd Div.

*EDDY, EBENEZER.
Served in 3 Regt. Vt. Militia commanded by Col. Williams.

EDDY, ELAM.
Served in Capt. Bingham's Company, Col. Jonathan Williams' Regt. Detached Militia in U. S. service 2 months and 9 days, 1812. Ref: Book 53, AGO. Page 46.

*EDDY, JOHN, Sergeant Corporal, Clarendon. Served in Capt. Sabins' Company, Col. Jonathan Williams' Regt. Detached Militia in U. S. service 2 months and 6 days, 1812. Served from June 11 to June 14, 1813 and from Oct. 4 to Oct. 13, 1813 in Capt. John Palmer's Company of Militia. 1st Regt. 2nd Brig., 3rd Div. Volunteered to go to Plattsburgh. September, 1814, and served in Capt. Durham Sprague's Company. Ref: Book 52. AGO Page 128.

EDDY, JONATHAN, Lieutenant, Montpelier. Appointed 3 Lieutenant 31 Inf. April 30, 1813; 2 Lieutenant Jan. 11, 1814; 1 Lieutenant Sept. 30, 1814; honorably discharged June 15, 1815. Ref: Heitman's Historical Register & Dictionary USA.

EDDY, PELEG.   Clarendon.
Volunteered to go to Plattsburgh, September, 1814, and served 7 days in Capt. Durham Sprague's Company. Ref: Book 52, AGO Page 128.

EDDY, THOMAS,   Burlington.
Volunteered to go to Plattsburgh, September, 1814, and served in Capt. Henry Mayo's Company. Ref: Book 51, AGO Page 81.

‡*EDDY, WILLIAM,   Bristol.
Served from June 11, 1813 to June 14, 1813 in Capt. Moses Jewett's Company, 1st Regt. 2nd Brig., 3rd Div.

EDGARS, HUGH.
Enlisted May 14, 1812 for 5 years in Capt. White Youngs' Company, 15th Regt.; on Muster Roll from Aug. 31, 1814 to Dec. 31, 1814. Ref: R. & L. 1812, AGO Page 27.

EDGERTON, ANDREW,   Cabot.
Volunteered to go to Plattsburgh, September, 1814, and served 4 days in Capt. Anthony Perry's Company. Ref: Book 52, AGO Pages 179, 252, 254.

EDGET, HORAN.
Served in War of 1812 and was captured by troops Sept. 17, 1814 at Fort Erie. Discharged Nov. 8, 1814. Ref: Records of Naval Records and Library, Navy Dept.

EDGETY, MOSES.
Served in Capt. Chadwick's Company, 2nd Regt. Ref: R. & L. 1812, AGO Page 32.

EDMONDS, ASA M.
Served from March 25, 1813 to June 24, 1813 in Capt. Samul Gordon's Company, 11th Regt. Appointed Ensign, 11th Inf. April 18, 1814. Ref: R. & L. 1812, AGO Page 8; Governor and Council Vt. Vol. 6, Page 478.

EDMONDS, THOMAS.
Served from May 1 to June 30, 1814 in Capt. Alexander Brooks' Corps of Artillery. Ref: R. & L. 1812, AGO Page 31.

EDMUNDS, JAMES,   Clarendon.
Volunteered to go to Plattsburgh, September, 1814, and served 4 days in Capt. Durham Sprague's Company. Ref: Book 52, AGO Page 128.

*EDMUNDS, WILLIAM.
Served in 4 Regt. Vt. Militia commanded by Col. Peck.

EDSON, AMASA, Ensign,   Brookfield.
Volunteered to go to Plattsburgh, September, 1814, and served 7 days in Capt. Frederick Griswold's Company, from Brookfield. Ref: Book 52, AGO Pages 52, 56, 121.

EDSON, CALVIN.
Served from March 25, 1813 to June 24, 1813 in Capt. Edgerton's Company, 11th Regt. Ref: R. & L. 1812, AGO Page 3.

*EDSON, ELIJAH.
Served in Capt. Taylor's Company, Col. Fifield's Regt. Detached Militia in U. S. service 3 months and 9 days, 1812.

*EDSON, JOHN, Sergeant,   Randolph.
Volunteered to go to Plattsburgh, September, 1814, and served in Capt. Lebbeus Egerton's Company. Also served in 2 Regt. (Fifield's) Vt. Militia.

EDSON, JOSIAH,   Bakersfield.
Volunteered and was at the Battle of Plattsburgh Sept. 11, 1814, serving in Capt. M. Stearns' Company. Ref: Hemenway's Vt. Gazetteer, Vol. 2, Page 394.

*EDSON, JOSIAH JR.,   Randolph.
Volunteered to go to Plattsburgh, September, 1814, and served in Capt. Lebbeus Egerton's Company.

*EDSON, LEONARD, Lieutenant.
Served in 2 Regt. Vt. Militia commanded by Col. Fifield.

EDUNITER, DAVID,   Franklin County.
Volunteered to go to Plattsburgh Sept. 11, 1814 and served in 15th or 22nd Regt. Ref: Hemenway's Vt. Gazetteer, Vol. 2, Page 391.

EDWARDS, CARY,   Fairfax.
Served from Aug. 8, 1812 in company of Capt. Joseph Beeman Jr. 11th Regt. U. S. Inf. under Col. Ira Clark. Served in Lieut. V. R. Goodrich's Company, 11th Regt. Ref: R. & L. 1812, AGO Page 11; Hemenway's Vt. Gazetteer, Vol. 2, Page 402.

*EDWARDS, EBENEZER.
Served in 2 Regt. Vt. Militia commanded by Col. Fifield.

*EDWARDS, EDWARD.
Served in 1 Regt. Vt. Militia commanded by Col. Judson.

EDWARDS, ISAAC, Corporal, Hanover, N. J. Enlisted at Panton March 28, 1814 during the war and served in Capt. Wm. Miller's Company, Capt. James Taylor's Company and Capt. Gideon Spencer's Company, 30th Regt. Ref: R. & L. 1812, AGO Pages 53, 54, 55, 56.

EDWARDS, JOHN.
Enlisted Feb. 1, 1813 for 5 years in company of late Capt. J. Brooks, commanded by Lieut. John I. Cromwell. Corps of U. S. Artillery; on Muster Roll from April 30, 1814 to June 30, 1814. Served from September, 1813, to April 27, 1814; no organization given. Ref: R. & L. 1812, AGO Pages 18 and 29.

EDWARDS, RICE.
Served from May 1 to Sept. 25, 1814; no organization given. Ref: R. & L. 1812, AGO Page 29.

EDWARDS, ROLAND, East Montpelier. Volunteered to go to Plattsburgh, September, 1814, and served 8 days in Capt. Timothy Hubbard's Company. Ref: Book 52, AGO Pages 241, 246, 256.

EDWARDS, WILLIAM. Served from May 1 to July 28, 1814; no organization given. Ref: R. & L. 1812, AGO Page 29.

EELLS, O. J., Doctor,   Cornwall. Hearing that there were wounded in need of surgical attention, this doctor and Dr. Ford started for Plattsburgh. When they reached Burlington they learned their services were not needed and returned home; did not join any organization. Ref: Rev. Lyman Mathews' History of Cornwall, Page 345.

EGERTON, BENJAMIN S., Captain. Appointed Captain 11 Inf. March 12, 1812; resigned Dec. 12, 1813. Commanded company in 11th Regt.; on Pay Roll for September and October, 1812 and January and February, 1813. Ref: Heitman's Historical Register & Dictionary USA; R. & L. 1812, AGO Pages 1 and 2.

*EGERTON, LEBBEUS, Captain, Randolph. Appointed Capt. 31 Inf. April 30, 1813; resigned Jan. 11, 1814. Volunteered to go to Plattsburgh, September, 1814. and commanded company raised in Randolph. Also served as Adjutant in 2 Regt. (Fifield's) Vt. Militia.

*EGGLESTON, MICHAEL. Served in Capt. Wright's Company, Col. Martindale's Regt. Detached Militia in U. S. service 2 months and 14 days, 1812.

EGLESTON, ROGER,   Pittsford. Volunteered to go to Plattsburgh, September, 1814, and served 8 days in Capt. Caleb Hendee's Company. Ref: Book 52, AGO Page 125.

ELBERT, JOHN L., 3rd Lieutenant. Served in Corps of Light Dragoons; on Pay Roll to June 30, 1814. Ref: R. & L. 1812, AGO Page 20.

*ELDRED, JESSE. Served from Nov. 1, 1812 to Feb. 28, 1813 in Capt. Charles Follett's Company, 11th Regt. Also served in 1 Regt. (Martindale's) Vt. Militia. Ref: R. & L. 1812, AGO Page 12.

*ELDRED, JOHN. Served from April 12, 1814 to April 21, 1814 in Capt. Eseck Sprague's Company, Sumner's Regt.

ELDREDGE, WILLIAM. Served from May 1st to June 30, 1814 in Capt. Haig's Corps of Light Dragoons. Ref: R. & L. 1812, AGO Page 20.

*ELDRIDGE, BELA. Served from April 12, 1814 to April 21, 1814 in Capt. Othniel Jewett's Company, Sumner's Regt.

*ELDRIDGE, CHARLES M. Served in 1 Regt. Vt. Militia commanded by Col. Judson.

‡ELDRIDGE, DANIEL. Served in Capt. Robbins' Company, Col. Wm. Williams' Regt. Detached Militia in U. S. service 4 months and 29 days, 1812. Pension Certificate No. 4458.

*ELDRIDGE, GILES R. Served in 4 Regt. Vt. Militia commanded by Col. Peck.

*ELDRIDGE, JOHN M., Captain. Served from June 11, 1813 to June 14, 1813 in Capt. John M. Eldridge's Company, 1st Regt. 2nd Brig., 3rd Div.

*ELDRIDGE, JOSEPH W. Served in 4 Regt. Vt. Militia commanded by Col. Peck.

*ELDRIDGE, NATHANIEL B., Captain. Entered service Sept. 25, 1813 as captain of company in Lt. Col. Luther Dixon's Regt.

*ELDRIDGE, OLIVER, Corporal. Served in Capt. Robbins' Company, Col. Wm. Williams' Regt. Detached Militia in U. S. service 4 months and 29 days, 1812.

‡*ELDRIDGE, WILLIAM A., Shoreham. Served from April 12, 1814 to May 20, 1814 in company of Capt. James Gray Jr., Sumner's Regt. Also served on the Niagara frontier under Generals Brown and Scott. His son (1st name not given) served with him in Canada. Pension Certificate of widow, Emily, No. 31099. Ref: Rev. J. F. Goodhue's History of Shoreham, Page 101.

‡ELITHORP, DANFORTH,   Orwell. Volunteered to go to Plattsburgh, September, 1814, and served 11 days in Capt. Wait Branch's Company. Pension Certificate of widow, Edna E., No. 30458.

ELITHORP, JACOB,   Shoreham. Volunteered to go to Plattsburgh, September, 1814, and served 6 days in Capt. Nathaniel North's Company of Cavalry. Ref: Rev. J. F. Goodhue's History of Shoreham, Page 107.

*ELITHORP, JOHN, Ensign Lieutenant, Sheldon. Volunteered to go to Plattsburgh, September, 1814, and served in Capt. Samuel Wead's Company. Served as Lieutenant in 3 Regt. (Bowdish) Vt. Militia. Ref: Book 51, AGO Pages 109, 125, 152.

*ELITHORP, JOHN Y. Served in Sumner's Regt., Vt. Militia.

‡ELKINS, CURTIS. Served in Capt. Stewart's Company. Pension Certificate No. 18942.

‡*ELKINS, JOHN, Adjutant. Served in 3 Regt. Vt. Militia commanded by Col. Fifield. Pension Certificate No. 9429.

ELKINS, JONATHAN.
On Pay Roll of Capt. Haig's Corps of Light Dragoons to June 30, 1814; unfit for service. Ref: R. & L. 1812, AGO Page 20.

ELLAR, DAVID,   Rowan Co. N. H.
Served from May 1, 1814 to July 3, 1814 in Capt. Nelson's Company, 10th Inf. Ref: R. & L. 1812, AGO Page 30.

ELLENWOOD, DANIEL.
Served in Capt. Benjamin Bradford's Company; on Muster Roll from May 31, 1813 to Aug. 31, 1813. Ref: R. & L. 1812, AGO Page 26.

*ELLENWOOD, JAMES, Corporal Sergeant, Johnson. Enlisted Sept. 25, 1813 and served 1 month and 23 days in Capt. Thomas Waterman's Company, Dixon's Regt. Volunteered to go to Plattsburgh, September, 1814, and served 10 days as a Sergeant in same company.

‡*ELLENWOOD, RALPH,   Johnson.
Served in Capt. Taylor's Company, Col. Wm. Williams' Regt. Detached Militia in U. S. service 4 months and 24 days, 1812. Enlisted Sept. 25, 1813 and served 1 month and 23 days in Capt. Thomas Waterman's Company, Dixon's Regt.; volunteered to go to Plattsburgh, September, 1814, and served 4 days in same company. Pension Certificate No. 8564.

ELLENWOOD, THOMAS,   Johnson.
Volunteered to go to Plattsburgh, September, 1814, and served in Capt. Thomas Waterman's Company, Dixon's Regt. Ref: Book 51, AGO Page 208.

ELLERY, JOSEPH.
Served from Feb. 12, 1813 to May 11, 1813 in Capt. Benjamin S. Edgerton's Company, 11th Regt. Ref: R. & L. 1812, AGO Pages 2 and 3.

*ELLES, THOMAS W.
Served from April 12, 1814 to April 18, 1814 in Capt. Jonathan P. Stanley's Company, Col. W. B. Sumner's Regt.

‡ELLIOTT, BENJAMIN.
Served in Capt. Timothy Fairchild's Company. Pension Certificate No. 30754.

ELLIOTT, JAMES, Captain.
Appointed 2 Lieutenant 1 Inf. Feb. 16, 1801; honorably discharged June 1, 1802; Captain 3 Artillery April 9, 1812; resigned Dec. 1, 1812. Ref: Heitman's Historical Register & Dictionary USA.

ELLIOTT, JOSIAH.   Franklin County.
Volunteered to go to Plattsburgh Sept. 11, 1814 and served in 15th or 22nd Regt. Ref: Hemenway's Vt. Gazetteer, Vol. 2, Page 391.

ELLIOTT, ROBERT. Captain.
Served from July 1 to July 31, 1814 on General Staff of the Northern Army commanded by Maj. Gen. George Izard. Ref: R. & L. 1812, AGO Page 28.

*ELLIOTT, SAMUEL.
Served in 3 Regt. Vt. Militia commanded by Col. Williams.

*ELLIOTT, WILLIAM, Corporal.
Served from April 12, 1814 to April 21, 1814 in Capt. Eseck Sprague's Company, Sumner's Regt.

*ELLIS, ABIJAH JR.
Served in 3 Regt. Vt. Militia commanded by Col. Tyler.

ELLIS, ABRAHAM,   Franklin County.
Volunteered to go to Plattsburgh Sept. 11, 1814 and served in 15th or 22nd Regt. Ref: Hemenway's Vt. Gazetteer, Vol. 2, Page 391.

*ELLIS, ANDREW.
Served in 1 Regt. Vt. Militia commanded by Col. Judson.

*ELLIS, AUGUSTUS.
Served in 4 Regt. Vt. Militia commanded by Col. Peck.

*ELLIS, DANIEL.
Served in Capt. Bingham's Company, Col. Jonathan Williams' Regt. Detached Militia in U. S. service 2 months and 9 days, 1812. Served in Lieut. Wm. S. Foster's Company, 11th Regt., from Feb. 6, 1813 to date of death April 10, 1813. Ref: R. & L. 1812, AGO Page 6.

*ELLIS, DAVID.
Served in Capt. Cross' Company, Col. Martindale's Regt. Detached Militia in U. S. service 2 months and 13 days, 1812.

ELLIS, ELIJAH,   Roxbury.
Volunteered to go to Plattsburgh, September, 1814, and served 8 days in Capt. Samuel M. Orcutt's Company. Ref: Book 52, AGO Page 250.

ELLIS, ELNATHAN.
Served from May 16, 1813 to May 15, 1814 in Capt. James Taylor's Company and Capt. Gideon Spencer's Company, 30th Regt. Ref: R. & L. 1812, AGO Pages 52, 57, 59.

‡*ELLIS, EPHRAIM C.
Served in Capt. Mason's Company, Col. Fifield's Regt. Detached Militia in U. S. service 6 months, 1812. Pension Certificate of widow, Fanny, No. 20658.

ELLIS, JEREMIAH,   Barre.
Volunteered to go to Plattsburgh, September, 1814, and served 9 days in Capt. Warren Ellis' Company. Ref: Book 52, AGO Pages 233 and 242.

*ELLIS, JOHN.
Served in 1 Regt. Vt. Militia commanded by Col. Martindale.

*ELLIS, JOSEPH.
Served in 3 Regt. Vt. Militia commanded by Col. Tyler.

ELLIS, JUDAH,   Cambridge.
Volunteered to go to Plattsburgh, September, 1814, and served 8 days in Capt. Salmon Green's Company. Ref: Book 51, AGO Pages 98 and 207.

‡ELLIS, LYMAN.
Served in Capt. M. Bates' Company.
Pension Certificate of widow, Anna,
No. 26226.

ELLIS, OREB.
Served in Capt. Taylor's Company,
Col. Wm. Williams' Regt. Detached
Militia in U. S. service 4 months
and 24 days, 1812. Also served in
Capt. Chadwick's Company, 2nd Regt.
Ref: Book 53, AGO Page 73; R. & L.
1812, AGO Page 32.

ELLIS, SAMUEL.
Enlisted Oct. 22, 1812 for 5 years
in company of late Capt. J. Brooks,
commanded by Lieut. John I. Crom-
well, Corps of U. S. Artillery; on
Muster Roll from April 30, 1814 to
June 30, 1814. Ref: R. & L. 1812,
AGO Page 18.

‡ELLIS, STEPHEN,   Barnard.
Volunteered to go to Plattsburgh,
September, 1814, and served 8 days
in Capt. John S. Bicknell's Com-
pany. Pension Certificate of widow,
Betsey, No. 24493.

ELLIS, WARREN, Captain,   Barre.
Volunteered to go to Plattsburgh,
September, 1814, and served 10 days
in command of Barre company. Ref:
Book 52, AGO Page 242.

*ELLIS, WILLIAM, Corporal.
Served from June 11, 1813 to June
14, 1813 in Lieut. Bates' Company,
1st Regt.

ELLIS, ZEPHARIAH,   New Haven.
Served from Sept. 1, 1814 to June
16, 1815 in Capt. Sanford's Company,
30th Inf. Ref: R. & L. 1812, AGO
Page 23.

ELLISE, JOHN,   Cabot.
Volunteered to go to Plattsburgh,
September, 1814, and served 3 days
in Capt. Anthony Perry's Company.
Ref: Book 52, AGO Pages 253 and 254.

*ELLSWORTH, BENJAMIN W.
Served in 1 Regt. Vt. Militia commanded by Col. Martindale.

ELLSWORTH, EDWARD.
Volunteered to go to Plattsburgh,
September, 1814, and served 7 days
in Capt. Asaph Smith's Company.
Ref: Book 51, AGO Page 20.

‡ELLSWORTH, ERASTUS B., St. Albans.
Enlisted May 7, 1813 for 1 year in
Capt. John Wires' Company, 30th
Regt. Pension Certificate No. 8654.

*ELLSWORTH, JESSE.   Cornwall.
Served from April 12, 1814 to April
21, 1814 in Capt. Edmund B. Hill's
Company, Sumner's Regt.; volunteered to go to Plattsburgh, September,
1814, and was at the battle, serving
in the same company.

‡ELLSWORTH, JOHN M.,   Bristol.
Volunteered to go to Plattsburgh,
September, 1814, and was at the
battle, serving 9 days in Capt. Jehiel
Saxton's Company. Sumner's Regt.
Pension Certificate of widow, Par-
melia. No. 26201.

ELLSWORTH, JOSEPH,   Fairfax.
Served in Capt. Joseph Beeman's
Company in 1813 and 1814. Volunteered to go to Plattsburgh, September, 1814, and served 8 days in Capt.
Josiah Grout's Company. Ref: Hemenway's Vt. Gazetteer, Vol. 2, Pages
402 and 403; Book 51, AGO Page 103.

ELLSWORTH, JOSEPH.
Served in Capt. Taylor's Company,
Col. Wm. Williams' Regt. Detached
Militia in U. S. service 4 months and
24 days, 1812. Ref: Book 53, AGO
Page 42.

*ELLSWORTH, LEWIS W.,   Cornwall.
Served from April 12, 1814 to April
21, 1814 in Capt. Edmund B. Hill's
Company. Sumner's Regt.; volunteered to go to Plattsburgh, September,
1814, and was at the battle, serving
in same company.

‡*ELLSWORTH, WILLIAM.
Served in Capt. Burnap's Company,
Col. Jonathan Williams' Regt. De-
tached Militia in U. S. service 1
month and 5 days, 1812. Pension
Certificate No. 13297.

ELLSWORTH, WILLIAM JR.
Volunteered to go to Plattsburgh,
September, 1814, and served in Capt.
Asaph Smith's Company 7 days. Ref:
Book 51, AGO Pages 20 and 21.

*ELLSWORTH, WILLIAM C., Adjutant.
Served in 3 Regt. Vt. Militia commanded by Col. Bowdish.

*ELMER, CHESTER,   Addison.
Served from April 12, 1814 to May
20, 1814 in Capt. George Fisher's
Company, Sumner's Regt.; volunteered to go to Plattsburgh, September,
1814, and was in the battle, serving
9 days in same company.

*ELMORE, IRA.
Served in Capt. Mason's Company,
Col. Fifield's Regt. Detached Militia
in U. S. service 3 months and 8
days, 1812.

*ELMS, BARTLETT, Corporal.
Served in Corning's Detachment, Vt.
Militia.

*ELSWORTH, JOSEPH.
Served in 4 Regt. Vt. Militia commanded by Col. Williams.

ELTON, MOSES, Lieutenant.
Served in 1st Regt. Detached Militia
of Vermont in U. S. service at Champlain commencing Nov. 18 and ending Nov. 19, 1812.

‡*ELWELL, HARVEY, Drummer.
Served in Capt. Strait's Company,
Col. Martindale's Regt. Detached
Militia in U. S. service 2 months
and 13 days, 1812. Pension Certifi-
cate No. 16301.

‡EMERSON, HENRY.
Served in Capt. Brown's Company.
Pension Certificate of widow, Dorcas,
No. 5615.

‡EMERSON. JONATHAN.   Thetford.
Volunteered to go to Plattsburgh,
September, 1814. and served 7 days
in Capt. Joseph Barrett's Company.
Also served in Capt. Partridge's Company. Pension Certificate No. 2950.

‡EMERSON. LYMAN.   Rochester.
Volunteered to go to Plattsburgh,
September, 1814. and served 7 days
in Capt. Oliver Mason's Company.
Pension Certificate of widow, Olive.
No. 20661.

‡*EMERSON. MOSES P.
Served in Capt. Wheeler's Company.
Col. Fifield's Regt. Detached Militia
in U. S. service 6 months and 4
days, 1812. Served in Capt. Samuel
H. Holly's Company. 11th Regt.;
on Pay Roll for January and February. 1813. Ref: R. & L. 1812. AGO
Page 25. Pension Certificate No.
7702.

EMERSON, OLIVER. Corporal,   Danby.
Served in Capt. Samul Gordon's Company, 11th Regt.; on Pay Roll for
January and February. 1813. Ref: R.
& L. 1812, AGO Page 9.

*EMERSON, PAUL, Drum Major, Montpelier. Served in Capt. Walker's
Company, Col. Fifield's Regt. Detached Militia in U. S. service 6
months and 5 days, 1812. Volunteered to go to Plattsburgh. September, 1814, and served 8 days in Capt.
Timothy Hubbard's Company.

*EMERSON, SAMUEL.
Served from Jan. 11, 1813 to July 1,
1813 in Lieut. Wm. S. Foster's Company, 11th Regt. Also served with
Hospital Attendants. Vt. Ref: R. &
L. 1812, AGO Page 6.

EMERSON, TIMOTHY,   Roxbury.
Volunteered to go to Plattsburgh,
September. 1814, and served 8 days
in Capt. Samuel M. Orcutt's Company. Ref: Book 52, AGO Page 250.

‡EMERY, EDWARD.
Enlisted June 27, 1812 for 5 years
in company of late Capt. J. Brooks,
commanded by Lieut. John I. Cromwell. Corps of U. S. Artillery; on
Muster Roll from April 30, 1814 to
June 30, 1814. Also served in Capt.
Churchill's Company. Pension Certificate of widow, Julia Ann, No.
19020.

‡*EMERY, JAMES.
Served in Capt. Bingham's Company,
Col. Jonathan Williams' Regt. Detached Militia in U. S. service 2
months and 9 days, 1812. Also served in Capt. Pennock's Company. Pension Certificate of widow, Betsey, No.
27768.

‡EMERY. JOHN C.
Served in Capt. Burnap's Company.
Pension Certificate No. 15280. Pension Certificate of widow, Mary Ann,
No. 31300.

EMERY, JONATHAN.   Orange.
Volunteered to go to Plattsburgh,
September, 1814, and went part way.
serving 5 days in Capt. David Rising's Company. Ref: Book 52, AGO
Page 19.

EMERY, JOSEPH.
Served from Feb. 15, 1813 to May
14, 1813 in Capt. Charles Follett's
Company, 11th Regt. Served from
May 1 to June 30, 1814 in company
of Artificers commanded by Alexander
Parris. Ref: R. & L. 1812, AGO
Pages 13 and 24.

*EMERY, NATHANIEL. Sergeant.
Served in 3 Regt. Vt. Militia commanded by Col. Tyler.

*EMERY, RUSSELL.
Served in Capt. Saxe's Company, Col.
Wm. Williams' Regt. Detached Militia in U. S. service 3 months and
1 day, 1812.

*EMERY, SAMUEL. Fifer.
Served in Capt. Prentiss' Company,
Col. Dixon's Regt. Detached Militia
in U. S. service 1 month and 23
days, 1813.

EMMONS, ELISHA, Lieutenant.
Appointed 3 Lieutenant 31 Inf. April
30, 1813; Regimental Quartermaster
July, 1813 to May, 1814; 1 Lieutenant May 1, 1814; honorably discharged June 15, 1815. Ref: Heitman's Historical Register & Dictionary USA.

EMMONS, ELLIHU, Sergeant.
Served in Capt. Phineas Williams'
Company, 11th Regt.; on Pay Roll
for January and February, 1813. Ref:
R. & L. 1812, AGO Page 15.

EMMONS, HORATIO, Corporal.
Served from March 14, 1813 to June
13, 1813 in Capt. Samul Gordon's
Company, 11th Regt.; appointment as
Corporal confirmed May 8, 1813. Ref:
R. & L. 1812, AGO Page 8.

EMMONS, JOSEPH.
Served from May 1 to June 30, 1814
in Capt. Alexander Brooks' Corps of
Artillery. Ref: R. & L. 1812, AGO
Page 31.

EMORY, JOHN,   Washington.
Volunteered to go to Plattsburgh,
September, 1814. and served in Capt.
Amos Stiles' Company. Ref: Book 52,
AGO Page 36.

*ENGLAND, SILAS, Fifer.
Served in Capt. Wilson's Company,
Col. Wm. Williams' Regt. Detached
Militia in U. S. service 4 months and
24 days, 1812.

‡*ENGLISH, ALEXANDER,   Randolph.
Served under Captains Wheatly and
Wright, Col. Fifield's Regt. Detached
Militia in U. S. service 6 months,
1812. Volunteered to go to Plattsburgh, September, 1814, and served in
Capt. Lebbeus Egerton's Company.
Pension Certificate No. 1933. Pension Certificate of widow, Annie, No.
8757.

ENGLISH, JAMES. Captain.   Marshfield.
Volunteered to go to Plattsburgh,
September, 1814, and served 9 days
in command of company raised at
Marshfield. Ref: Book 52, AGO Page
248.

*ENGLISH, JOHN.
Served in Capt. O. Lowry's Company, Col. Wm. Williams' Regt. Detached Militia in U. S. service 4 months and 26 days, 1812. Also served in Corning's Detachment, Vt. Militia.

ENGLISH, JOHN SR.,   Waitsfield.
Enlisted March 9, 1813 in Capt. John W. Weeks' Company, 11th Regt.; on Pay Roll to June 8, 1813; died in service soon after May, 1813. Ref: R. & L. 1812, AGO Page 4; M. B. Jones' History of Waitsfield, Page 79.

*ENGLISH, THOMAS,   Randolph.
Volunteered to go to Plattsburgh, September, 1814, and served in Capt. Lebbeus Egerton's Company.

ENGLISH, WOOSTER,   Tunbridge.
Volunteered to go to Plattsburgh, September, 1814, and served 5 days in Capt. David Knox's Company. Ref: Book 52, AGO Page 117.

*ENO, MARTIN, Corporal.
Served from April 12, 1814 to April 21, 1814 in Capt. Othniel Jewett's Company, Sumner's Regt.

*ENO, WILLIAM.
Served from April 17, 1814 to April 21, 1814 in Capt. Othniel Jewett's Company, Sumner's Regt.

ENOS, ABNER,   Leicester.
Volunteered to go to Plattsburgh, September, 1814, and served 8 days in Capt. Ebenezer Jenney's Company. Ref: Book 52, AGO Page 160.

ENOS, DAVID,   Hartford, Conn.
Enlisted at Plattsburgh Dec. 20, 1813 during the war and served in Capt. Wm. Miller's Company and Capt. Gideon Spencer's Company, 30th Regt. Born in Simsbury, Conn.; age 54 years; height 5 feet 8 inches; complexion light; hair brown; eyes blue; farmer. Discharged at Burlington, Vt., in 1815. Ref: R. & L. 1812, AGO Pages 54, 55, 57.

ENOS, DAVID K.
Born in Ferrisburgh; aged 17 years; height 5 feet 5 inches; complexion light; hair light; eyes blue; by profession a carpenter. Enlisted at Plattsburgh Jan. 3, 1815 in Capt. Wm. Miller's Company for period of the war; discharged at Burlington, Vt., in 1815. Ref: R. & L. 1812, AGO Pages 1 and 55.

ERWIN, JOHN.
Enlisted Sept. 30, 1813 for 1 year in Capt. Gideon Spencer's Company, 30th Regt.; on Muster Roll Dec. 30, 1813 to June 30, 1814; joined June 30, 1814. Ref: R. & L. 1812, AGO Page 56.

ESSEX, R.,   Richford.
Served in Capt. Martin D. Follett's Company, Dixons' Regt., on duty on Canadian Frontier in 1813. Ref: Hemenway's Vt. Gazetteer, Vol. 2, Page 428.

ESTABROOKS, T. W.,   Sherburne.
Volunteered to go to Plattsburgh and served 10 days in September, 1814; no organization given. Ref: Book 52, AGO Pages 164 and 165.

*ESTERBROOK, ABRA JR.
Served in Capt. Sabin's Company, Col. Jonathan Williams' Regt. Detached Militia in U. S. service 2 months and 6 days, 1812.

ESTERBROOKS, LEVI.
Served from Jan. 1, 1813 to July 1, 1813 in Lieut. Wm. S. Foster's Company, 11th Regt. Ref: R. & L. 1812, AGO Page 6.

‡*ESTUS, BENJAMIN HALL.
Served from Aug. 8, 1812 in company of Capt. Joseph Beeman Jr., 11th Regt. U. S. Inf. under Col. Ira Clark. Also served in Capt. Dike's Company and in 3 Regt. (Tyler's) Vt. Militia. Pension Certificate of widow, Esther, No. 10233.

ESTUS, EZRA,   Swanton.
Served in Capt. V. R. Goodrich's Company, 11th Regt.; on Pay Roll from July 15 to Dec. 8, 1813; was in action at the battle of Lundy's Lane. Ref: Hemenway's Vt. Gazetteer, Vol. 2, Page 444.

*ESTUS, NATHAN.
Served from April 12, 1814 to May 20, 1814 in Company of Capt. James Gray Jr., Sumner's Regt.

ESTUS, RICHARD,   Fairfax.
Served from Aug. 8, 1812 in company of Capt. Joseph Beeman Jr., 11th Regt. U. S. Inf. under Col. Ira Clark. Served in Lieut. V. R. Goodrich's Company, 11th Regt.; on Pay Roll for January and February, 1813. Ref: R. & L. 1812, AGO Page 11; Hemenway's Vt. Gazetteer, Vol. 2, Page 402.

ESTY, JOHN,   Lincoln.
Volunteered to go to Plattsburgh, September, 1814; no organization given. Ref: Book 51, AGO Page 59.

EUSTACE, RICHARD,   Swanton.
Served in Capt. V. R. Goodrich's Company, 11th Regt.; on Pay Roll from July 15 to Dec. 8, 1813; was in action at the battle of Lundy's Lane. Ref: Hemenway's Vt. Gazetteer, Vol. 2, Page 444.

*EVANS, CALVIN R.
Served in Capt. Scovell's Company, Col. Martindale's Regt. Detached Militia in U. S. service 1 month and 15 days, 1812.

*EVANS, JOSEPH.
Served from Oct. 5, 1813 to Oct. 17, 1813 in Capt. Stephen Brown's Company, 3 Regt. (Tyler's).

*EVANS, JOSHUA.
Served in Capt. Taylor's Company, Col. Wm. Williams' Regt. Detached Militia in U. S. service 4 months and 24 days, 1812.

*EVANS, OTIS.
Served in Capt. Wheeler's Company,
Col. Fifiled's Regt. Detached Militia
in U. S. service 6 months and 4
days, 1812.

‡*EVANS, STEPHEN.
Served in Capt. Dodge's Company,
Col. Fifield's Regt. Detached Militia
in U. S. service 2 months and 21
days, 1812. Pension Certificate No.
10238.

EVENS, ABIATHER,   Schohani, N. Y.
Served from Sept. 8, 1814 to June
19, 1815 in Capt. Taylor's Company,
30th Inf. Ref: R. & L. 1812, AGO
Page 23.

*EVENS, CALVIN R.
Served in 1 Regt. Vt. Militia commanded by Col. Martindale.

‡*EVEREST, DUDLEY, Lieutenant.
Served as 3 Lieutenant in Capt.
Fisher's Company, Sumner's Regt.
Pension Certificate of widow, Try-
phena, No. 26376.

*EVEREST, HIRAM, Sergeant.
Served from April 12, 1814 to April
21, 1814 in Col. W. B. Sumner's
Regt.

*EVERETTS, HORATIO, Corporal.
Served in 4 Regt. Vt. Militia commanded by Col. Peck.

EVERTS, AMAZIAH.
Enlisted April 29, 1813 for 1 year
in Capt. James Taylor's Company,
30th Regt.; transferred to Capt.
Gideon Spencer's Company, 30th Regt.
and served to April 29, 1814. Acted
as servant to Lieut. Kendall. Ref:
R. & L. 1812, AGO Pages 52, 57, 59.

*EVERTS, GEORGE.
Served from April 12, 1814 to May
20, 1814 in Capt. George Fisher's
Company, Sumner's Regt.

*EVERTS, WILLIAM, Lieutenant.
Served in Capt. Lowry's Company,
Col. Wm. Williams' Regt. Detached
Militia in U. S. service 4 months and
26 days, 1812. Also served as Lieut-
enant in Corning's Detachment, Vt.
Militia.

*EVRET (or Everet) JAMES.
Served in Capt. Dodge's Company,
Col. Fifield's Regt. Detached Militia
in U. S. service 2 months and 21
days, 1812.

EWING, DANIEL S., Corporal, Clarendon. Volunteered to go to Plattsburgh, September, 1814, and served
7 days in Capt. Durham Sprague's
Company. Ref: Book 52, AGO Page
128.

*EWINGS, WILLIAM, Corporal, Whiting.
Served from April 12, 1814 to April
21, 1814 in Capt. Shubael Wales'
Company, Col. W. B. Sumner's Regt.
Volunteered to go to Plattsburgh,
September, 1814, and served 9 days
in Capt. Salmon Foster's Company,
Sumner's Regt.

EXTELL, SAMUEL.   Shoreham.
Entered the service and died soon
afterward. Ref: Rev. J. F. Goodhue's History of Shoreham, Page 101.

‡FADDEN, NATHANIEL.
Served in Capt. Hill's Company. Pension Certificate of widow, Mary, No.
9715.

*FAIRBANKS, CALVIN, Captain, Bar-
nard, Vt. Commanded company of
Militia that started for the Battle
of Plattsburgh, September, 1814; went
as far as Burlington, Vt., and learned that the battle was over; remained at Burlington a short time and
then returned home. Also served as
Ensign in 3 Regt. (Williams') Vt.
Militia. Ref: Book 52, AGO Page
156.

FAIRBANKS, CHARLES.
Served in Capt. Benjamin Bradford's
Company; on Muster Roll from May
31, 1813 to Aug. 31, 1813. Ref: R.
& L. 1812, AGO Page 26.

‡*FAIRBANKS, CHESTER.
Served in 3 Regt. Vt. Militia commanded by Col. Williams. Also served in Capt. Ripley's Company. Pension Certificate of widow, Betsey, No.
4069.

*FAIRBANKS, DAVID.
Served in Capt. Phelps' Company,
Col. Jonathan Williams' Regt. Detached Militia in U. S. service 2
months and 21 days, 1812.

FAIRBANKS, DEXTER, Sergeant.
Served in Capt. Benjamin Bradford's
Company; on Muster Roll from May
31, 1813 to Aug. 31, 1813. Ref: R.
& L. 1812, AGO Page 26.

FAIRBANKS, JOHN, Sergeant. Brandon.
Volunteered to go to Plattsburgh,
September, 1814, and served 8 days
in Capt. Micah Brown's Company.
Ref: Book 52, AGO Page 131.

*FAIRBANKS, LYNDE.
Served in Capt. Sabins' Company, Col.
Jonathan Williams' Regt. Detached
Militia in U. S. service 2 months
and 6 days, 1812.

*FAIRBANKS, SAMUEL,   Georgia.
Enlisted Sept. 25, 1813 in Capt.
Thomas Waterman's Company, Col.
Dixon's Regt. Volunteered to go to
Plattsburgh, September, 1814, and
served 8 days in Capt. Jesse Post's
Company, Dixon's Regt.

*FAIRFIELD, DAVID.
Served from April 12, 1814 to May
20, 1814 in Capt. George Fisher's
Company, Sumner's Regt.

*FAIRCHILD, HENRY.
Served from June 11, 1813 to June
14, 1813 in Capt. Moses Jewett's Company, 1st Regt. 2nd Brig., 3rd Div.

*FAIRCHILD, LEVI, Sergeant.
Served in 4 Regt. Vt. Militia commanded by Col. Williams.

*FAIRCHILD, PHILEMON,   Bridport.
Served in Capt. Robbins' Company,
Col. Wm. Williams' Regt. Detached
Militia in U. S. service 4 months
and 29 days. 1812. Volunteered to
go to Plattsburgh, September, 1814,
and served 10 days in Capt. William
H. Pickett's Company, Col. Sumner's
Reg. Ref: Book 51, AGO Pages 25
and 41.

*FAIREFIELD, DAVID (or Fairchild,
David). Served in Sumner's Regt.
Vt. Militia.

FAIRFIELD, WILLIAM.
Served from Nov. 1, 1812 to Feb. 28,
1813 in Capt. Charles Follett's Company, 11th Regt. Ref: R. & L. 1812,
AGO Page 12.

FALCH, JOHN.
Served in Capt. Benjamin Bradford's
Company; on Muster Roll from May
31, 1813 to Aug. 31, 1813. Ref: R.
& L. 1812, AGO Page 26.

FALKENBURG, HAYES.
Served from May 1 to June 30, 1814
in Capt. Haig's Corps of Light Dragoons. Ref: R. & L. 1812, AGO
Page 20.

FALL, MOSES.
Served from Feb. 12, 1813 to May
11, 1813 in Capt. Jonathan Starks'
Company, 11th Regt. Ref: R. & L.
1812, AGO Page 19.

*FANKNER, JACOB.
Served with Hospital Attendants, Vt.

FARGO, JABEZ,   Huntington.
Volunteered to go to Plattsburgh,
September, 1814, and was at the
battle, serving in Capt. Josiah N.
Barrows' Company. Ref: Book 51,
AGO Page 77.

*FARGO, LEONARD D.,   Pittsford.
Served in Capt. Scovell's Company,
Col. Martindale's Regt. Detached
Militia in U. S. service 1 month
and 15 days, 1812.

FARLEY, AMOS,   Montpelier.
Volunteered to go to Plattsburgh,
September, 1814, and served 8 days
in Capt. Timothy Hubbard's Company. Ref: Book 52, AGO Page 256.

FARMAN, BENJAMIN H.,   Franklin.
Served in Capt. Kendall's Company,
Col. Wm. Williams' Regt. Detached
Militia in U. S. service 4 months
and 23 days, 1812. Ref: Book 53,
AGO Page 73; Vol. 50 Vt. State
Papers, Page 223.

*FARMAN, JOHN.
Served in Capt. Lowry's Company,
Col. Wm. Williams' Regt. Detached
Militia in U. S. service 4 months
and 26 days, 1812. Also served in
3 Regt. (Tyler's) Vt. Militia.

*FARMER, BENJAMIN H.,   Fairfield.
Served 6 months in 1812 in Capt.
George W. Kindall's Company, 4
Regt .(Williams') Vt. Militia. Served
from April 12, 1814 to April 21, 1814
in Capt. Othniel Jewett's Company,
Sumner's Regt.

FARMER, JAMES,   Middlebury.
Served from May 1, 1814 to July 13,
1814 in Capt. Spencer's Company,
30th Inf. Ref: R. & L. 1812, AGO
Page 30.

FARNAM, ASA.
Served from April 21, 1813 to April
25, 1814 in Capt. Daniel Farrington's Company (also commanded by
Capt. Simeon Wright), 30th Regt.
Ref: R. & L. 1812, AGO Pages 50
and 51.

*FARNHAM, AARON A.
Served in 3 Regt. Vt. Militia commanded by Col. Tyler.

FARNHAM, ALFRED,   Richmond.
Volunteered to go to Plattsburgh,
September, 1814, and served 9 days
in Capt. Roswell Hunt's Company,
3rd Regt. Ref: Book 51, AGO Page
82.

FARNHAM, EBENEZER, Corporal, Pownal. Served from April 16, 1814
to June 19, 1815 in Capt. Taylor's
Company, 30th Inf. Ref: R. & L.
1812, AGO Page 23.

*FARNHAM, JOHN,   St. Albans.
Enlisted May 22, 1813 for 1 year in
Capt. Sanford's Company, 30th Regt.
Also served in Capt. John Wires'
Company, 30th Regt. and in Corn-
ing's Detachment, Vt. Militia. Ref:
R. & L. 1812, AGO Pages 1 and 40.

FARNHEM, JOSEPH, Corporal.
Served in 1st Regt. of Detached
Militia of Vt. in U. S. service at
Champlain commencing Nov. 18 and
ending Nov. 19, 1812.

*FARNSWORTH, ALDEN. .
Served in Capt. Mason's Company,
Col. Fifield's Regt. Detached Militia
in U. S. service 5 months and 28
days, 1812. Served from Feb. 11,
1813 to May 10, 1813 in Capt. Edgerton's Company, 11th Regt.

‡*FARNSWORTH, ANDREW, Bakersfield
or Richford. Enlisted Sept. 25, 1813
and served 1 month and 23 days in
Capt. Follett's Company, Col. Dixon's
Regt. Pension Certificate No. 18907.
Volunteered to go to Plattsburgh
Sept. 11, 1814 and was at the battle,
serving under Capt. M. Stearns.
Ref: Hemenway's Vt. Gazetteer, Vol.
2, Page 394.

FARNSWORTH, ASAHEL, Fairfield, Fairfax or Sheldon. Volunteered to go
to Plattsburgh, September, 1814, and
served 6 days in Capt. Arad Merrill's Company. Ref: Book 51, AGO
Pages 168 and 185.

‡*FARNSWORTH, EBENEZER (or Ebenezer Jr.) Served in Capt. Richardson's Company, Col. Martindale's
Regt. Detached Militia in U. S. service 2 months and 13 days, 1812. Pension Certificate of widow, Rebeckah,
No. 14266.

FARNSWORTH. HOLDEN,   Burlington.
Volunteered to go to Plattsburgh,
September, 1814, and served 10 days
in Capt. Henry Mayo's Company.
Ref: Book 51, AGO Page 81.

‡FARNSWORTH, HORACE, Fairfax. Served in Capt. Joseph Beeman's Company in 1813 and 1814. Pension Certificate No. 12398.

‡*FARNSWORTH, ISAAC, Drummer, Thetford. Served in Capt. Taylor's Company, Col. Fifield's Regt. Detached Militia in U. S. service 2 months and 21 days, 1812. Marched for Plattsburgh, September. 1814, and went as far as Bolton, Vt., serving 6 days in Capt: Salmon Howard's Company, 2nd Regt. Pension Certificate of widow, Deborah, No. 34410.

FARNSWORTH, JOSEPH D., Surgeon, Fairfax. "He was holding court, Sept. 11, 1814, when the boom of the cannon at Plattsburgh announced that the fight had begun. He adjourned the court and departed for the scene of action; volunteered his services as surgeon, was accepted, and served for 4 days in that office." Ref: Hemenway's Vt. Gazetteer, Vol. 2, Page 179.

*FARNSWORTH, MOSES. Served from June 11, 1813 to June 14, 1813 in Capt. Moses Jewett's Company, 1st Regt. 2nd Brig., 3rd Div.

FARNSWORTH, PRENTICE, Bakersfield. Volunteered and was at the battle of Plattsburgh, Sept. 11, 1814 serving in Capt. M. Stearns' Company. Ref: Hemenway's Vt. Gazetter, Vol. 2, Page 394.

*FARNSWORTH, SAMUEL H., Captain, St. Albans. Volunteered to go to Plattsburgh, September, 1814, and served in Col. Dixon's Regt. Also served as Ensign in 1 Regt. 3 Brig. 3 Div. Vt. Militia. Ref: Book 51, AGO Page 128.

‡FARNSWORTH, SIMEON. Served in Capt. R. Stewart's Company. Pension Certificate No. 8355.

*FARNSWORTH, WILLIAM. Appointed Captain 26 Inf. April 21, 1814; resigned Aug. 1, 1814. Served as Sergeant in Capt. Strait's Company. Col. Martindale's Regt. Detached Militia in U. S. service 2 months and 13 days, 1812. Ref: Heitman's Historical Register & Dictionary USA.

*FARNUM, JAMES. Served in 1 Regt. Vt. Militia commanded by Col. Judson.

*FARR, AMOS. Served in Capt. Rogers' Company, Col. Fifield's Regt. Detached Militia in U. S. service 5 months and 27 days, 1812.

*FARR, ARTEMUS, Captain. Served in 3 Regt. Vt. Militia commanded by Col. Tyler.

*FARR, IRA. Served from April 12, 1814 to April 21, 1814 in Capt. Othniel Jewett's Company, Sumner's Regt.

‡*FARRAND, CYRUS. Served in Capt. Bates' Company, 1 Regt. (Judson's) Vt. Militia. Pension Certificate No. 23719.

‡FARRAND, IRA. Pension Certificate of widow, Sarah, No. 43694; no organization given.

*FARRAND, SAMUEL. Served from April 12, 1814 to May 20, 1814 in Capt. George Fisher's Company, Sumner's Regt.

FARRAND, THOMAS. Served from March 3, 1813 to June 2, 1813 in Capt. Charles Follett's Company, 11th Regt. Ref: R. & L. 1812, AGO Page 13.

*FARRAND, WILLIAM. Served from April 12, 1814 to April 21, 1814 in Lieut. Justus Foote's Company, Sumner's Regt.

*FARRAR, SAMUEL, Sergeant. Enlisted Sept. 20, 1813 in Capt. John Weed's Company, Regt. of Riflemen.

FARRER, ISAAC. Served in Capt. Benjamin Bradford's Company; on Muster Roll from May 31, 1813 to Aug. 31, 1813. Ref: R. & L. 1812, AGO Page 26.

FARRER, NOAH. Served in Capt. Benjamin Bradford's Company; on Muster Roll from May 31, 1813 to Aug. 31, 1813. Ref: R. & L. 1812, AGO Page 26.

FARRINGTON, DANIEL, Captain, Brandon. Appointed Captain 30 Inf. April 30, 1813; honorably discharged June 15, 1815. Commanded company in 30th Regt.; on Muster Roll from March 1, 1814 to April 30, 1814. Ref: Heitman's Historical Register & Dictionary USA; R. & L. 1812, AGO Page 50.

FARRON, MICHAEL. Served from March 1 to June 30, 1814 in Capt. Alexander Brooks' Corps of Artillery. Ref: R. & L. 1812, AGO Page 31.

FARWELL, ABEL, Lieutenant. Served as 2nd Lieutenant 11 Inf. March 12, 1812; resigned June 20, 1813. Served in Capt. Phineas Williams' Company, 11th Regt.; on Pay Roll for January and February, 1813. Ref: Heitman's Historical Register & Dictionary USA; R. & L. 1812, AGO Page 15.

*FARWELL, BENJAMIN. Served in Capt. Rogers' Company, Col. Fifield's Regt.; Detached Militia in U. S. service 4 months and 6 days, 1812.

FARWELL, DANIEL. Served from March 20, 1813 to June 19, 1813 in Lieut. V. R. Goodrich's Company, 11th Regt. Ref: R. & L. 1812, AGO Page 10.

*FARWELL, HENRY JR. Served in Capt. Phelps' Company, Col. Jonathan Williams' Regt. Detached Militia in U. S. service 2 months and 21 days, 1812.

FARWELL, JOHN,   Barre.
Volunteered to go to Plattsburgh,
September, 1814, and served 10 days
in Capt. Warren Ellis' Company.
Ref: Book 52, AGO Page 242.

FARWELL, JOHN, Lieutenant.
Appointed 2 Lieutenant 31 Inf. April
30, 1813; 1 Lieutenant January 31,
1814; resigned Sept. 30, 1814. Ref:
Heitman's Historical Register & Dictionary USA.

FARWELL, SOLOMON,   Poultney.
Volunteered to go to Plattsburgh,
September, 1814, and served 2 days
in Capt. Briant Ransom's Company.
Ref: Book 52, AGO Page 147.

*FARWELL, WILLIAM, Sergeant.
Appointed Sergeant Sept. 28, 1813 in
Capt. Asahel Langworthy's Company,
Col. Isaac Clark's Regt. of Volun-
teer Riflemen.

FARWELL, WILLIAM JR.
Served in Capt. Langworthy's Com-
pany, Col. Dixon's Regt. Detached
Militia in U. S. service 1 month and
20 days, 1813. Ref: Book 53, AGO
Page 110.

*FASSETT, ALVIN, Sergeant, Enosburgh
or Richford. Enlisted Sept. 25, 1813
as corporal in Capt. Martin D. Follett's Company, Col. Dixon's Regt.
and served 1 month and 23 days;
volunteered to go to Plattsburgh, September, 1814, and served 6 days as
Sergeant in same company.

FASSETT, AMOS, Sergeant,   Hancock.
Volunteered to go to Plattsburgh,
September, 1814, and served 7 days
in Capt. Asaph Smith's Company.
Ref: Book 51, AGO Pages 20 and 21.

‡*FASSETT, AMOS I.
Served in Capt. Charles Bennett's
Company, Dixon's Regt.; served from
Sept. 25, 1813 to Oct. 13, 1813. Pen-
sion Certificate of widow, Julia A.,
No. 17600.

FASSETT, ANSON, Enosburgh, Richford
or Sheldon. Volunteered to go to
Plattsburgh, Sept. 1814 and served
6 days in Capt. Martin D. Follitt's
Company, Dixon's Regt. Ref: R. & L.
1812, AGO Page 106.

FASSETT, BENJAMIN, Lieutenant, Cambridge or St. Albans. Appointed 3
Lieutenant 30 Inf. April 30, 1813;
2 Lieutenant Dec. 1, 1813; honorably
discharged June 15, 1815. Served
from April 10, 1813 in Capt. John
Wires' Company, 30th Regt. Ref:
Heitman's Historical Register & Dictionary U S A; Ref: R. & L. 1812,
AGO Page 40.

*FASSETT, ELIAS, Colonel, Bennington.
Appointed Colonel 30 Inf. Feb. 23,
1813; honorably discharged June 15,
1815. Served from Sept. 25, 1813 to
Nov. 7, 1813 as Brigadier General
in 3 Brig., 3 Div. Vt. Militia in
U. S. service.

‡*FASSETT, HIRAM, Fifer, Enosburgh or
Fairfield. Served in Capt. Kendall's
Company, Col. Wm. Williams' Regt.

Detached Militia in U. S. service 4
months and 23 days, 1812. Pension
Certificate of widow, Cynthia A., No.
13964.

FASSETT, JOHN.
Volunteered to go to Plattsburgh,
September, 1814, and served 7 days
in Capt. Asaph Smith's Company.
Ref: Book 51, AGO Page 20.

*FASSETT, JOHN, Surgeon.
Appointed Surgeon Sept. 25, 1813 in
Consolidated Regt. of Vt. Militia in
U. S. service under Col. Dixon.

‡FASSETT, JOSEPH.
Served in Capt. Churchill's Company.
Pension Certificate of widow, Vodisa,
No. 18184.

FAXON, FRANCIS, Corporal, Burlington.
Volunteered to go to Plattsburgh,
September, 1814, and served in Capt.
Henry Mayo's Company. Ref: Book
51, AGO Page 81.

*FAY, EDWARD 2nd.
Served in 3 Regt. Vt. Militia commanded by Col. Tyler.

*FAY, ELIJAH JR.
Served in 1 Regt. (Martindale's) Vt.
Militia.

FAY, HEMAN ALLEN.
Appointed 1 Lieutenant Artillery,
Dec. 23, 1811; transferred to Artillery Corps May 12, 1814; honorably
discharged June 15, 1815; Ref: Heitman's Historical Register & Dictionary USA.

*FAY, HENRY.
Served in Capt. Dorrance's Company,
Col. Wm. Williams' Regt. Detached
Militia in U. S. service 4 months and
7 days, 1812.

FAY, IRA,   Barnard.
Volunteered to go to Plattsburgh,
September, 1814, and served 8 days
in Capt. John S. Bicknell's Company.
Ref: Book 51, AGO Page 251.

*FAY, JEDEDIAH,   Calais.
Volunteered to go to Plattsburgh,
September, 1814, and served 10 days
in Capt. Gideon Wheelock's Company.

*FAY, JOHN,   Huntington.
Volunteered to go to Plattsburgh,
September, 1814, and was at the
battle, serving in Capt. Josiah N.
Barrows' Company, 3 Regt. (Tyler's).

FAY, JONATHAN,   Bakersfield.
Volunteered to go to Plattsburgh,
Sept. 11, 1814 and served in Capt.
M. Stearns' Company; was at the
battle. Ref: Hemenway's Vt. Gazet-
teer, Vol. 2, Page 394.

‡*FAY, NATHAN, Fifer.
Served from Oct. 5, 1813 to Oct. 16,
1813 in Capt. Roswell Hunt's Company, 3 Regt. Pension Certificate of
widow, Polly, No. 24224.

FAY, SAFFORD,   Richmond.
Volunteered to go to Plattsburgh,
September, 1814, and served 9 days
in Capt. Roswell Hunt's Company,
3 Regt. Ref: Book 51, AGO Page 82.

FAY, SALMON.   Jericho.
Took part in the Battle of Plattsburgh. Ref: History of Jericho, Page
142.

*FAY, SALMON JR.
Served in 3 Regt. Vt. Militia commanded by Col. Tyler.

FAY, SANFORD,   Richford.
Served in Capt. Martin D. Follett's
Company, Dixon's Regt., on duty on
Canadian Frontier in 1813. Ref:
Hemenway's Vt. Gazetteer, Vol. 2,
Page 428.

FELCH, FRANCIS,   Cavendish.
Served in Detached Militia in U. S.
service in September, 1812. Ref: Vol.
52 Vt. State Papers, Page 38.

FELCH, HEZEKIAH.
Volunteered to go to Plattsburgh,
September, 1814, and served 4 days
in Capt. James George's Company
of Topsham. Ref: Book 52, AGO
Pages 67 and 70.

FELCHER, JOHN,   Morristown.
Volunteered to go to Plattsburgh,
September, 1814, and served 8 days
in Capt. Denison Cook's Company.
Ref: Book 51, AGO Pages 202 and
206.

FELLER, WILLIAM.
Enlisted Jan. 22, 1813 in Capt.
Charles Follett's Company, 11th Regt.;
on Pay Roll to May 31, 1813. Ref:
R. & L. 1812, AGO Page 13.

FELLOWS, CHASE.
Volunteered to go to Plattsburgh,
September, 1814, and served 4 days
in company of Capt. James George
of Topsham. Ref: Book 52, AGO
Pages 67, 68, 70.

‡FELLOWS, JOHN,   Corinth.
Volunteered to go to Plattsburgh,
September, 1814, and served in company of Capt. Ebenezer Spencer, Vershire. Also served in Capt. Dickinson's Company. Pension Certificate
of widow, Dorothy, No. 3728. Ref:
Book 52, AGO Pages 48 and 49.

*FELLOWS, JONATHAN,   Richmond.
Served 3 months beginning September,
1812, in 6th Company, 3 Regt. 2
Brig., commanded by Brig. Gen.
Newell. Also served in 4 Regt. (Wil-
liams') Vt. Militia. Ref: Vol. 50
Vt. State Papers, Page 85.

‡FELLOWS, MERRILL, Corporal, Richmond. Volunteered to go to Plattsburgh, September, 1814, and served
9 days in Capt. Roswell Hunt's Company, 3 Regt. (Tyler's); served from
Oct. 5, 1813 to Oct. 16, 1813 in same
company. Pension Certificate of
widow, Betsey, No. 28294.

*FELLOWS, MERRITT.
Served in 3 Regt. Vt. Militia commanded by Col. Tyler.

FELLOWS, SAMUEL,   Corinth.
Volunteered to go to Plattsburgh,
September, 1814, and served in company of Capt. Ebenezer Spencer, Vershire. Ref: Book 52, AGO Pages 48
and 49.

FELT, WILLIAM.
Enlisted May 12, 1813 for 1 year in
Capt. Daniel Farrington's Company,
30th Regt. (also commanded by Capt.
Simeon Wright); on Muster Roll from
March 1, 1814 to April 30, 1814. Ref:
R. & L. 1812, AGO Pages 50 and 51.

*FELTON, JOSEPH.
Served from Sept. 25, 1813 to Oct.
3, 1813 in Capt. Elijah Birge's Company, Dixon's Regt.

*FELTON, WILLIAM, Ensign Lieutenant,
Swanton or Fairfield. Served in
Capt. George W. Kindall's Company,
4 Regt. (Williams') 6 months in 1812.
Also served in 3 Regt. (Bowdish)
Vt. Militia, as a Lieutenant.

*FENDERSON, REUBEN.
Served with Hospital Attendants, Vt.

*FENN, CHESTER,   Cornwall.
Served from April 12, 1814 to April
21, 1814 in Capt. Edmund B. Hill's
Company, Sumner's Regt. Volunteered to go to Plattsburgh, September,
1814, and was at the battle, serving in same company.

*FENN, DANIEL,   Shoreham.
Served from April 12, 1814 to May
20, 1814 in Capt. George Fisher's Company, Sumner's Regt. Volunteered to
go to Plattsburgh, September, 1814,
and served 6 days in Capt. Samuel
Hand's Company.

*FENN, ETHAN.
Served from April 12, 1814 to April
21, 1814 in Capt. Edmund B. Hill's
Company, Sumner's Regt.

FENSBY, JEREMIAH,   Tunbridge.
Volunteered to go to Plattsburgh,
September, 1814, and served 3 days
in Capt. David Knox's Company. Ref:
Book 52, AGO Page 117.

FENTON, CORNWELL,   Wells.
Enlisted Feb. 28, 1814 for period of
the war in Capt. Clark's Company,
30th Regt. Served from Sept. 1,
1814 to June 16, 1815 in Capt. Sanford's Company, 30th Inf. Ref: R.
& L. 1812, AGO Pages 1 and 23.

*FENTON, ORIN.
Served in 1 Regt. Vt. Militia commanded by Col. Judson.

*FENTON, THOMAS.
Served from April 12, 1814 to May
20, 1814 in company of Capt. James
Gray Jr., Sumner's Regt.

*FERGUSON, BARTEMAS.
Served from April 12, 1814 to April
21, 1814 in Capt. Edmund B. Hill's
Company, Sumner's Regt.

FERGUSON, HENRY, Corporal.
Served in company of Capt. John
McNeil Jr., 11th Regt.; on Pay Roll
for January and February, 1813. Ref:
R. & L. 1812, AGO Page 17.

FERGUSON, JESSE. Trumpeter.
Served from May 1 to June 30, 1814
in Capt. Haig's Corps of Light Dragoons. Ref: R. & L. 1812, AGO Page
20.

FERGUSON, WILLIAM.
Volunteered to go to Plattsburgh,
September, 1814, and went as far as
Bolton, Vt., serving 4 days in Lieut.
Phineus Kimball's Company, West
Fairlee. Ref: Book 52, AGO Page 46.

FERREN, WILLIAM,   Strafford.
Volunteered to go to Plattsburgh,
September, 1814, and served in Capt.
Joseph Barrett's Company. Ref: Book
52, AGO Page 41.

*FERRIAL, ALEXANDER.
Served from Oct. 26, 1813 to Nov. 18,
1813 in Capt. Isaac Finch's Company,
Col. Clark's Rifle Regt.

*FERRIS, ARCHIBALD.
Served from April 19, 1814 to April
21, 1814 in Capt. Othniel Jewett's
Company, Sumner's Regt.

‡*FERRIS, DARIUS (or Darius Jr.)
Served in Capt. Robbins' Company,
Col. Wm. Williams' Regt. Detached
Militia in U. S. service 4 months and
29 days, 1812. Pension Certificate No.
2041. Pension Certificate of widow,
Hannah, No. 13193.

*FERRIS, JAMES.
Served from Oct. 15, 1813 to Nov. 17,
1813 in Capt. Asahel Scoville's Company, Col. Clark's Rifle Regt. Served
from April 12, 1814 to April 21, 1814
in Capt. Edmund B. Hill's Company,
Sumner's Regt. Ref: Book 52, AGO
Page 282.

FERRIS, JONAS,   Enosburgh.
Served from Oct. 14, 1813 to Nov.
17, 1813 in Capt. Asahel Scovel's
Company, Col. Clark's Rifle Corps.
Ref: Hemenway's Vt. Gazetteer, Vol.
2, Page 398.

*FERRIS, LYMAN.
Served from April 12, 1814 to April
21, 1814 in Capt. Othniel Jewett's
Company, Sumner's Regt.

*FERRIS, MELANCTON.
Served from April 12, 1814 to April
21, 1814 in Capt. Othniel Jewett's
Company, Sumner's Regt.

‡*FERRIS, WILLIAM.
Served from April, 1814, to May 20,
1814 in company of Capt. James Gray
Jr., Sumner's Regt. Pension Certificate No. 10245.

FERRIS, WILLIAM B., Lieutenant.
Appointed Ensign 30 Inf. April 30,
1813; 3 Lieutenant June 23, 1814;
honorably discharged June 15, 1815.
Served as Ensign in Capt. Gideon
Spencer's Company and Capt. Wm.
Miller's Company, 30th Regt. Ref:
Heitman's Historical Register & Dic-
tionary USA; R. & L. 1812, AGO
Pages 54 and 56.

*FERRY, CHARLES.
Served in 4 Regt. Vt. Militia commanded by Col. Williams.

*FERRY, DANIEL.
Enlisted Sept. 25, 1813 and served
1 month and 23 days in Capt. Waterman's Company, Col. Dixon's Regt.

‡FERRY, EBENEZER,   Johnson.
Volunteered to go to Plattsburgh,
September, 1814, and served in Capt.
Thomas Waterman's Company, Col.
Dixon's Regt. Pension Certificate of
widow, Caroline, No. 37112.

*FERRY, JOSEPH.
Enlisted Sept. 25, 1813 in Capt.
Thomas Waterman's Company, Dix-
on's Regt.

FESSON, MOSES M.
Enlisted Jan. 27, 1813 in Capt.
Phineas Williams' Company, 11th
Regt.; on Pay Roll for January and
February, 1813. Ref: R. & L. 1812,
AGO Page 15.

*FIELD, AMOS.
Served from April 12, 1814 to April
21, 1814 in Capt. Edmund B. Hill's
Company, Sumner's Regt.

*FIELD, AUSTIN, Drummer.
Served in 3 Regt. Vt. Militia commanded by Col. Tyler.

*FIELD, EDWARD.
Served in Sumner's Regt. Vt. Militia.

‡FIELD, ELIJAH H.,   Northfield.
Served from Aug. 17, 1814 to June
16, 1815 in Capt. Sanford's Company,
30th Inf. Also served in Capt. Farrington's Company. Pension Certificate No. 1392.

FIELD, ELISHA,   Bakersfield.
Volunteered and was at the Battle
of Plattsburgh Sept. 11, 1814, serving in Capt. M. Stearns' Company.
Ref: Hemenway's Vt. Gazetteer, Vol.
2, Page 394.

*FIELD, FARRAND.
Served in Capt. Preston's Company,
Col. Jonathan Williams' Regt. Detached Militia in U. S. service 2
months and 6 days, 1812.

‡FIELD, FRANCIS.
Served in Capt. Strait's Company,
Col. Martindale's Regt. Detached
Militia in U. S. service 2 months and
13 days, 1812.

‡*FIELD, GEORGE, Corporal.
Served in Sumner's Regt. Vt. Militia. Also served in Capt. Spencer's
Company. Pension Certificate of
widow, Sally, No. 20020.

*FIELD, HARVEY.
Served in 3 Regt. Vt. Militia commanded by Col. Tyler. Took part
in the Battle of Plattsburgh and was
granted a pension. Ref: History of
Jericho, Page 142.

*FIELD, HENRY.
Served in 3 Regt. Vt. Militia commanded by Col. Tyler.

FIELD, JOSEPH.
Enlisted May 5, 1813 for 1 year in
Capt. Daniel Farrington's Company
(also commanded by Capt. Simeon
Wright), 30th Regt.; on Muster Roll
from March 1, 1814 to April 30, 1814;
re-enlisted and transferred to 29th
Regt. April 6th. Ref: R. & L. 1812,
AGO Pages 50 and 51.

*FIELD, LEVI.
Served in 1 Regt. Vt. Militia commanded by Col. Judson.

*FIELD, OLIVER.
Served in Capt. Adams' Company, Col. Jonathan Williams' Regt. Detached Militia in U. S. service 2 months and 7 days, 1812. Also served in 4 Regt. (Peck's) Vt. Militia.

‡*FIELD, ORRIN,   Cornwall.
Served from April 12, 1814 to April 21, 1814 in Capt. Edmund B. Hill's Company, Sumner's Regt.; volunteered to go to Plattsburgh, September, 1814, and was at the battle, serving in the same company. Pension Certificate No. 25234; Pension Certificate of widow, Rhoda, No. 32708.

‡FIELD, RODOLPHUS.
Served in Capt. Alexander Brooks' Corps of Artillery; on Pay Roll to June 30, 1814; on duty with Asst. Insp. Gen. Also served in Capt. Churchill's Company. Pension Certificate No. 2643.

‡FIELD, SETH P.,   Berlin.
Volunteered to go to Plattsburgh, September, 1814, and served 7 days in Capt. Cyrus Johnson's Company. Pension Certificate of widow, Nancy, No. 30616.

*FIELD, SILAS.
Served from April 17, 1814 to April 21, 1814 in Capt. Othniel Jewett's Company, Sumner's Regt.

FIELD, SYLVESTER.
Enlisted June 3, 1813 for 1 year in Capt. Daniel Farrington's Company, 30th Regt. (also commanded by Capt. Simeon Wright); on Muster Roll from March 1, 1814 to April 30, 1814. Ref: R. & L. 1812, AGO Pages 50 and 51.

‡*FIELD, WALDO H.,   Waterbury.
Volunteered to go to Plattsburgh, September, 1814, and served 11 days in Capt. George Atkins' Company, 4 Regt. (Peck's) Vt. Militia. Also served in Sumner's Regt. Vt. Militia. Pension Certificate No. 23962. Pension Certificate of widow, Louisa, No. 34012.

‡*FIELD, WILLIAM.
Served in Capt. Richardson's Company, Col. Martindale's Regt. Detached Militia in U. S. service 2 months and 13 days, 1812. Enlisted Sept. 20, 1813 in Capt. John Weed's Company, Col. Clark's Regt. of Riflemen. Pension Certificate No. 8364.

*FIFE, JOHN.
Served from April 12, 1814 to April 21, 1814 in Lieut. James S. Morton's Company, Col. W. B. Sumner's Regt.

FIFER, FREDERICK.
Served from May 1 to Aug. 23, 1814; no organization given. Ref: R. & L. 1812, AGO Page 29.

*FIFIELD, ANDREW.
Served in Capt. Rogers' Company, Col. Fifield's Regt. Detached Militia in U. S. service 2 months and 18 days, 1812. Ref: Book 53, AGO Page 33.

*FIFIELD, DAVID.
Served in Capt. Rogers' Company, Col. Fifield's Regt. Detached Militia in U. S. service 5 months and 27 days, 1812.

*FIFIELD, EDWARD, Lt. Colonel, Wheelock. Served on northern frontier from Sept. 18, 1812 to March 17, 1813 as Lieutenant Colonel Commandant of 2nd Regt. Detached Militia in U. S. service.

*FILLMORE, DANIEL, Sergeant.
Served in Capt. Wood's Company. Col. Dixon's Regt. Detached Militia in U. S. service 1 month and 23 days, 1813; appointed Sergeant Sept. 25, 1813.

*FILLMORE, JOHN, Sergeant.
Served in Capt. Brown's Company, Col. Martindale's Regt. Detached Militia in U. S. service 2 months and 14 days, 1812. Served as a corporal in 1st Regt. of Detached Militia of Vt. in U. S. service at Champlain commencing Nov. 18 and ending Nov. 19, 1812.

‡FILLMORE, JOHN ADAM.
Served in Capt. Robinson's Company. Pension Certificate of widow, Martha, No. 10894.

*FILLMORE, LOREN.
Served from April 12, 1814 to April 21, 1814 in Lieut. Justus Foote's Company, Sumner's Regt.

*FILMORE, FAYETTE.
Served from April 12, 1814 to April 21, 1814 in Lieut. Justus Foote's Company, Sumner's Regt.

FINCH, HENRY.
Served in company of late Capt. J. Brooks, commanded by Lieut. John I. Cromwell, Corps of U. S. Artillery; on Muster Roll from April 30, 1814 to June 30, 1814. Ref: R. & L. 1812, AGO Page 18.

*FINCH, IRA, Sergeant.
Enlisted Sept. 18, 1813 in Capt. Isaac Finch's Company, Col. Clark's Rifle Regt.

*FINCH, ISAAC, Captain.
Served from Sept. 18, 1813 to Nov. 18, 1813 in command of a company in Col. Isaac Clark's Regt. Appointed Major, 26th Regt. June 6, 1814. Ref: Governor and Council, Vt., Vol. 6, Page 477.

*FINCH, JOHN, Sergeant Major.
Appointed Sergeant Major Sept. 15, 1813 for 60 days in Volunteer Rifle Corps commanded by Col. Isaac Clark.

FINCH, NOAH.
Served from Feb. 5, 1813 to May 4, 1813 in Capt. Charles Follett's Company, 11th Regt. Ref: R. & L. 1812, AGO Page 13.

*FINCH, WILLIAM.
Served from Oct. 11, 1813 to Nov. 18, 1813 in Capt. Isaac Finch's Company, Col. Clark's Rifle Corps.

*FINCH, ZIMRI, Lieutenant.
Served from Sept. 18, 1813 to Nov.
18, 1813 in Capt. Isaac Finch's Company, Col. Clark's Rifle Corps.

FINNEY, LEVI,   Shrewsbury.
Volunteered to go to Plattsburgh,
September, 1814, and served 4 days
in Capt. Robert Reed's Company.
Ref: Book 52, AGO Pages 138 and
140.

*FIRMAN, SMITH.
Served from April 12, 1814 to April
21, 1814 in Lieut. Justus Foote's Company, Sumner's Regt.

FISH, ASAHEL.
Served in Capt. Wilkins' Company,
Col. Dixon's Regt. Detached Militia
in U. S. service 1 month and 12
days, 1813. Ref: Book 53, AGO Page
109.

*FISH, CHRISTOPHER.
Served from April 12, 1814 to April
21, 1814 in Capt. Eseck Sprague's
Company, Sumner's Regt.

‡*FISH, DANIEL.
Served from April 12, 1814 to April
15, 1814 in Capt. Jonathan P. Stanley's Company, Col. W. B. Sumner's
Regt. Also served in Capt. Ebenezer
Jenney's Company. Pension Certificate of widow, Sarah, No. 31207.

*FISH, ELIJAH, Fifer.
Served in 3 Regt. Vt. Militia commanded by Col. Tyler.

*FISH, ELISHA, Fifer.
Served in 3 Regt. Vt. Militia commanded by Col. Tyler.

*FISH, GEORGE M.,   Shrewsbury.
Served from April 12, 1814 to April
15, 1814 in Capt. Jonathan P. Stanley's Company, Col. W. B. Sumner's
Regt. Volunteered to go to Plattsburgh, September, 1814, and served
4 days in Capt. Robert Reed's Company.

*FISH, JONATHAN.
Served in 4 Regt. Vt. Militia commanded by Col. Williams.

FISH, JOSEPH JR.
Served in Capt. Mason's Company,
Col. Fifield's Regt. Detached Militia
in U. S. service 6 months, 1812.
Ref: Book 53, AGO Page 41.

FISH, LEONARD,   Ira.
Volunteered to go to Plattsburgh,
September, 1814, and served 4 days
in Capt. Matthew Anderson's Company. Ref: Book 52, AGO Page 144.

*FISH, NATHANIEL,   Randolph.
Served under Captains Wheatly and
Wright, Col. Fifield's Regt. Detached Militia in U. S. service 6 months,
1812. Volunteered to go to Plattsburgh, September, 1814, and served
in Capt. Lebbeus Egerton's Company.
Book 53, AGO Page 10.

FISH, RUSSELL,   Ira.
Volunteered to go to Plattsburgh,
September, 1814, and served 4 days
in Capt. Matthew Anderson's Company. Ref: Book 52, AGO Page 144.

*FISH, SILAS,   Randolph.
Served under Captains Wheatly and
Wright, Col. Fifield's Regt. Detached Militia in U. S. service 6 months,
1812. Volunteered to go to Plattsburgh, September, 1814, and served
in Capt. Lebbeus Egerton's Company.

*FISH, STEPHEN,   Randolph.
Volunteered to go to Plattsburgh,
September, 1814, and served in Capt.
Lebbeus Egerton's Company.

‡*FISH, WINSLOW,   Randolph.
Volunteered to go to Plattsburgh,
September, 1814, and served in Capt.
Lebbeus Egerton's Company. Pension
Certificate of widow, Jerusha, No.
6131.

FISHER, ALLEN, Corporal, Hinsdale,
N. H. Enlisted at Bristol April 4,
1814 during the war and served in
Capt. Wm. Miller's Company, Capt.
Gideon Spencer's Company, and Capt.
James Taylor's Company, all in the
30th Regt. Ref: R. & L. 1812, AGO
Pages 53, 54, 55, 56.

*FISHER, AMOS.
Served in 2 Regt. Vt. Militia commanded by Col. Fifield.

FISHER, ASA.
Served in Capt. Walker's Company,
Col. Fifield's Regt. Detached Militia
in U. S. service 6 months and 3
days, 1812. Ref: Book 53, AGO Page
43.

*FISHER, BARNABAS.
Served in Sumner's Regt. Vt. Militia.

FISHER, BENJAMIN.
Volunteered to go to Plattsburgh,
September, 1814, and went as far as
Bolton, Vt., serving 4 days in Lieut.
Phineus Kimball's Company, West
Fairlee. Ref: Book 52, AGO Page
46.

FISHER, EZRA.   St. Albans.
Enlisted May 12, 1813 for 1 year in
Capt. John Wires' Company, 30th
Regt. Ref: R. & L. 1812, AGO
Page 40.

FISHER, FRANCIS.
Enlisted June 4, 1812 for 5 years in
Capt. White Youngs' Company, 15th
Regt.; on Muster Roll from Aug. 31,
1814 to Dec. 31, 1814. Ref: R. & L.
1812, AGO Page 27.

FISHER, GARDNER.
Enlisted April 25, 1813 for 1 year in
Capt. Daniel Farrington's Company,
30th Regt. (also commanded by Capt.
Simeon Wright); discharged May 1,
1814. Ref: R. & L. 1812, AGO Pages
50 and 51.

FISHER, GEORGE.
Served from April 4 to June 30, 1814
in Capt. Alexander Brooks' Corps of
Artillery. Ref: R. & L. 1812, AGO
Page 31.

*FISHER, GEORGE, Captain, Addison.
Served from April 12, 1814 to May
20, 1814 in command of company in
Col. W. B. Sumner's Regt.; volun-

teered to go to Plattsburgh, September, 1814, and served 9 days with same company, taking part in the battle.

*FISHER, HENRY,   Addison.
Served from April 12, 1814 to May 20, 1814 in Capt. George Fisher's Company, Sumner's Regt.; volunteered to go to Plattsburgh, September, 1814, and served 9 days in same company; was in the battle. Served in 1 Regt. (Judson's) Vt. Militia.

FISHER, ISAAC L.,   Cornwall.
Volunteered to go to Plattsburgh, September, 1814, and was at the battle, serving in Capt. Edmund B. Hill's Company, Sumner's Regt. Ref: Book 51, AGO Page 13.

FISHER, JAMES,   Ziedfield.
Served in Capt. Charles Follett's Company, 11th Regt.; on Pay Roll for January and February, 1812. Served from March 1, 1814 to April 27, 1814 in Capt. Chadwick's Company, 34th Inf. Ref: R. & L. 1812, AGO Pages 12 and 30.

FISHER, JOHN (or John L.)
Served in Capt. Benjamin S. Edgerton's Company, 11th Regt.; on Pay Roll for September and October, 1812, and January and February, 1813. Also served from April 5, 1813 to July 4, 1813 in Lieut. Wm. S. Foster's Company, 11th Regt. Ref: R. & L. 1812, AGO Pages 1, 2, 6.

*FISHER, JONATHAN.
Served in 4 Regt. Vt. Militia commanded by Col. Peck.

*FISHER, JOSHUA.
Served in Capt. Mason's Company, Col. Fifield's Regt. Detached Militia in U. S. service 5 months and 28 days, 1812.

‡*FISHER, ORRIN.
Enlisted Sept. 25, 1813 in Capt. Amos Robinson's Company, Dixon's Regt. Also served in Capt. Saxe's Company. Pension Certificate No. 18463. Pension Certificate of widow, Huldah, No. 5573. Volunteered to go to Plattsburgh and was at the battle Sept. 11, 1814, serving in Capt. Samuel H. Farnsworth's Company.

FISHER, SILAS B.
Served in Capt. Samuel H. Holly's Company, 11th Regt.; on Pay Roll for January and February, 1813. Ref: R. & L. 1812, AGO Page 25.

‡FISHER, SILVANUS MARTIN, Chelsea.
Born in Guilford, Vt.; aged 29 years; 5 feet 9½ inches high; dark complexion; black eyes; dark brown hair; by profession a shoemaker. Enlisted at Chelsea, Vt. May 1, 1813 in the Army of the U. S. for 1 year unless sooner discharged. Served in Capt. Buck's Company. Pension Certificate No. 1919.

FISHER, SIMEON.
Volunteered to go to Plattsburgh September, 1814, and went as far as Bolton, Vt., serving 4 days in Lieut.

Phineus Kimball's Company, West Fairlee. Ref: Book 52, AGO Pages 46 and 47.

FISHER, WILSON.
Served in Capt. Phineas Williams' Company, 11th Regt.; on Pay Roll for Jan. and Feb., 1813. Ref: R. & L. 1812. AGO Page 15.

FISK, AMOS,   Fairfax.
Volunteered to go to Plattsburgh, September, 1814, and served 8 days in Capt. Josiah Grout's Company. Ref: Book 51, AGO Page 103.

*FISK, ASEL.
Served from Sept. 25, 1813 to Nov. 5, 1813 in Capt. Asa Wilkins' Company, Dixon's Regt.

*FISK, BENJAMIN, Sergeant, Williamstown. Volunteered to go to Plattsburgh, September, 1814, and went as far as Burlington, serving in Capt. David Robinson's Company. Served as Sergeant in 4 Regt. (Peck's) Vt. Militia.

*FISK, DANIEL.
Served in Corning's Detachment, Vt. Militia.

FISK, DAVID,   Williamstown.
Volunteered to go to Plattsburgh, September, 1814, and served 8 days in Capt. David Robinson's Company. Ref: Book 52, AGO Page 8.

FISK, EBEN.   Canterbury, N. H.
Born in Canterbury, N. H.; aged 28 years; 5 feet 8½ inches high; light complexion; light hair; blue eyes; by profession a farmer. Enlisted March 29, 1814 for the period of the war and served in Capt. Wm. Miller's Company and Capt. Gideon Spencer's Company, 30th Regt. Ref: R. & L. 1812, AGO Pages 54, 55, 57. Discharged at Burlington in 1815; enlisted at Groton.

*FISK, EBENEZER,   Groton.
Served in Capt. Morrill's Company, Col. Fifield's Regt. Detached Militia in U. S. service 3 months and 19 days, 1812.

FISK, JOHN.
Served from March 11 to June 10, 1813 in Capt. Samul Gordon's Company, 11th Regt. Ref: R. & L. 1812, AGO Page 8.

*FISK, JOSEPH JR.
Served in 2 Regt. Vt. Militia commanded by Col. Fifield.

FISK, PERRI B.,   Montpelier.
Volunteered to go to Plattsburgh, September, 1814, and served 8 days in Capt. Timothy Hubbard's Company. Ref: Book 52, AGO Page 256.

FISK, SAMUEL,   Northfield.
Volunteered to go to Plattsburgh and was at the battle Sept. 11, 1814, serving 8 days in Capt. David Robinson's Company. Ref: Book 52, AGO Page 2.

FISK, WILLIAM, Ensign, Williamstown.
Volunteered to go to Plattsburgh,
September, 1814, and served 8 days
in Capt. David Robinson's Company.
Ref: Loose Rolls, Book 52, AGO; Page
10, Book 52, AGO.

FISKE, NATHAN.
Volunteered to go to Plattsburgh,
September, 1814, and served 7 days
in Capt. Frederick Griswold's Com-
pany, raised in Brookfield, Vt. Ref:
Book 52, AGO Page 52.

FISKE, STEPHEN.
Volunteered to go to Plattsburgh,
September, 1814, and served 7 days
in Capt. Frederick Griswold's Com-
pany, raised in Brookfield, Vt. Ref:
Book 52, AGO Page 52.

*FITCH, BARNABAS.
Served from April 12, 1814 to May
20, 1814 in company of Capt. James
Gray, Jr., Sumner's Regt.

*FITCH, FRANCIS.
Served in 3 Regt. Vt. Militia commanded by Col. Williams..

*FITCH, FREDERICK.
Served in 3 Regt. Vt. Militia commanded by Col. Tyler.

*FITCH, HENRY, Musician.
Served from April 12, 1814 to April
21, 1814 in Capt. Othniel Jewett's
Company, Sumner's Regt.

FITCH, JABEZ.
Served from May 1 to June 30, 1814
in Capt. Alexander Brooks' Corps of
Artillery. Ref: R. & L. 1812, AGO
Page 31.

FITCH, JOHN,   Huntington.
Volunteered to go to Plattsburgh,
September, 1814, and served 10 days
in Capt. Artemus Farr's Company, 3
Regt. (Tyler's). Ref: Book 51, AGO
Page 93.

FITCH, LYMAN, Colonel,   Thetford.
Colonel of Regiment recruited in
Orange County. A portion of his regiment assembled for defense against
the British the evening before the
Battle of Plattsburg and marched as
far as Waterbury when they heard
of the defeat of the British and,
therefore, returned to their homes.

FITCH, NATHAN.
Served in Lieut. Wm. S. Foster's
Company, 11th Regt.; on Pay Roll
for January and February, 1813. Ref:
R. & L. 1812, AGO Page 7.

*FITTS, ANSELL.
Served in Sumner's Regt. Vt. Militia.

FITTS, ANSETT.
Served from April 12, 1814 to April
15, 1814 in Capt. Jonathan P. Stanley's Company, Col. W. B. Sumner's
Regt. Ref: Book 52, AGO Page 287.

FITTS, ARTEMUS, Lieutenant, Braintree.
Marched for Plattsburgh Sept. 10,
1814 and served about 8 days in
Capt. Lot Hudson's Company. Ref:
Book 52, AGO Pages 24 and 33; Book
51, AGO Page 300.

FITTS, JOHN,   Braintree.
Marched for Plattsburgh Sept. 10,
1814 and served in Capt. Lot Hudson's Company. Ref: Book 52, AGO
Pages 24 and 26.

FITZGERALD, AARON, Franklin County.
Volunteered to go to Plattsburgh
Sept. 11, 1814 and served in 15th or
22nd Regt. Ref: Hemenway's Vt.
Gazetteer, Vol. 2, Page 391.

FITZGERALD, JOHN.
Served from May 1 to June 30, 1814
in Capt. Alexander Brook's Corps of
Artillery. Ref: R. & L. 1812, AGO
Page 31.

FITZPATRICK, EDWARD.
Served in company of late Capt. J.
Brooks, commanded by Lieut. John
I. Cromwell, Corps of U. S. Artil-
lery; on Muster Roll from April 30,
1814 to June 30, 1814; transferred
from Capt. Leonard's Company. Ref:
R. & L. 1812, AGO Page 18.

FITZPATRICK, PATRICK.
Served from May 1 to June 30, 1814
in Capt. Alexander Brook's Corps of
Artillery. Ref: R. & L. 1812, AGO
Page 31.

*FLAGG, ARTEMUS,   Richmond.
Served from Oct. 5, 1813 to Oct. 16,
1813 in Capt. Roswell Hunt's Company, 3 Regt. (Tyler's); volunteered
to go to Plattsburgh, September, 1814,
and served in same company.

*FLAGG, GERSHAM (or Gosham) Drum-
mer. Served from Oct. 5, 1813 to
Oct. 16, 1813 in Capt. Roswell Hunt's
Company, 3 Regt. (Tyler's); volunteered to go to Plattsburgh, September, 1814, and served 9 days in same
company.

‡*FLAGG, JAMES, Sergeant, Enosburgh.
Served from Oct. 14 to Nov. 17, 1813
in Capt. Asahel Scoville's Company,
Col. Clark's Rifle Corps. Pension
Certificate No. 5972; Pension Certifi-
cate of widow, Anna, No. 15439.

*FLAGG, NAHUM.
Served in 1 Regt. Vt. Militia commanded by Col. Judson.

‡FLANDERS, DAVID.
Volunteered to go to Plattsburgh,
September, 1814, and went as far as
Bolton, Vt., serving 4 days in Lieut.
Phineus Kimball's Company, West
Fairlee. Pension Certificate of widow,
Laura, No. 24240.

‡FLANDERS, GEORGE.
Served in Capt. Brown's Company.
Pension Certificate of widow, Esther,
No. 7692.

FLANDERS, JACOB,   Berlin.
Volunteered to go to Plattsburgh,
September, 1814, and served 8 days
in company of Capt. Cyrus Johnson.
Ref: Book 52, AGO Pages 202 and
255.

FLANDERS, JACOB JR.
Volunteered to go to Plattsburgh,
September, 1814, and served in com-

pany of Capt. Joel Barnes of Chelsea. Ref: Book 52, AGO Pages 69 and 77.

FLANDERS, JEREMIAH.
Volunteered to go to Plattsburgh, September, 1814, and went as far as Bolton, Vt., serving 4 days in Lieut. Phineus Kimball's Company, West Fairlee. Ref: Book 52, AGO Pages 46 and 47.

*FLANDERS, JOHN.
Served from Sept. 25, 1813 to Sept. 30, 1813 in Capt. Amos Robinson's Company, Dixon's Regt.

*FLANDERS, JOSEPH.
Served in Capt. Brigham's Company, Col. Jonathan Williams' Regt. Detached Militia in U. S. service 2 months and 9 days, 1812.

FLANDERS, JOSIAH, Franklin County.
Volunteered to go to Plattsburgh Sept. 11, 1814 and served in 15th or 22nd Regt. Ref: Hemenway's Vt. Gazetteer, Vol. 2, Page 391.

FLANDERS, MOSES, Corporal.
Served in company of Capt. John McNeil Jr., 11th Regt.; on Pay Roll for January and February, 1813. Ref: R. & L. 1812, AGO Page 17.

*FLANDERS, NATHANIEL.
Served in Capt. Rogers' Company, Col. Fifield's Regt. Detached Militia in U. S. service 5 months and 27 days, 1812.

‡*FLANDERS, SAMUEL S.
Served in Capt. Rogers Company, Col. Fifield's Regt. Detached Militia in U. S. service 5 months and 27 days, 1812. Also served in Capt. Brooks' Company. Pension Certificate No. 34289. Pension Certificate of widow, Hannah, No. 29950.

FLANDERS, STEPHEN.
Volunteered to go to Plattsburgh, September, 1814, and went as far as Bolton, Vt., serving 4 days in Lieut Phineus Kimball's Company, West Fairlee. Ref: Book 52, AGO Pages 46 and 47.

‡*FLANDERS, ZEBULON.
Served in Capt. Lowry's Company, 4 Regt. (Williams') Vt. Militia. Pension Certificate No. 18455. Pension Certificate of widow, Tamor, No. 10268.

FLEMING, BAPTIST.
Served in Capt. Benjamin S. Edgerton's Company, 11th Regt.; on Pay Roll for September and October, 1812, and January and February, 1813. Ref: R. & L. 1812, AGO Pages 1 and 2.

FLEMING, JOHN.
Enlisted May 4, 1814 for 5 years in company of late Capt. J. Brooks, commanded by Lieut. John I. Cromwell, Corps of U. S. Artillery; on Muster Roll from April 30, 1814 to June 30, 1814. Ref: R. & L. 1812, AGO Page 18.

*FLEMING, JOSEPH.
Served in 4 Regt. Vt. Militia commanded by Col. Williams.

FLEMING, ODLE (or Odell) Shoreham.
Served in Capt. Samuel H. Holly's Company, 11th Regt.; on Pay Roll for January and February, 1813. Fought at Chippewa, Bridgwater and Fort Erie. Ref: R. & L. 1812, AGO Page 25; Rev. J. F. Goodhue's History of Shoreham, Page 101.

*FLETCH, JOSEPH.
Served in Capt. Howard's Company, Vt. Militia.

*FLETCHER, ABEL.
Enlisted Sept. 28, 1812 in Capt. Benjamin S. Edgerton's Company, 11th Regt.; on Pay Roll for September and October, 1812, and January and February, 1813. Also served in 1 Regt. (Martindale's) Vt. Militia. Ref: R. & L. 1812, AGO Pages 1 and 2.

FLETCHER, DANIEL.
Enlisted March 20, 1813 for 5 years in company of late Capt. J. Brooks, commanded by Lieut. John I. Cromwell, Corps of U. S. Artillery; on Muster Roll from April 30, 1814 to June 30, 1814. Ref: R. & L. 1812, AGO Page 18.

FLETCHER, JAMES, Franklin County.
Enlisted May 23, 1812 for 5 years in Capt. White Youngs' Company, 15th Regt. On Muster Roll from Aug. 31, 1814 to Dec. 31, 1814. Ref: R. & L. 1812, AGO Page 27.

‡FLETCHER, JOHN.
Served in Capt. Kendall's Company. Pension Certificate No. 8762.

‡FLETCHER, JOSEPH.
Served in Capt. Waterman's Company, Dixon's Regt. Pension Certificate No. 12875.

*FLETCHER, LUKE, Corporal.
Served in Capt. Walker's Company, Col. Fifield's Regt. Detached Militia in U. S. service 3 months and 9 days, 1812.

FLETCHER, PAUL.
Enlisted April 30, 1813 for 1 year in Capt. Daniel Farrington's Company (also commanded by Capt. Simeon Wright), 30th Regt.; re-enlisted and transferred to 29th Regt. April 6th. Ref: R. & L. 1812, AGO Pages 50 and 51.

*FLETCHER, STEPHEN.
Served in Capt. Needham's Company, Col. Martindale's Regt. Detached Militia in U. S. service 2 months and 14 days, 1812.

FLING, ERASTUS.
Served from Feb. 13, 1813 to May 12, 1813 in Capt. Charles Follett's Company, 11th Regt. Ref: R. & L. 1812, AGO Page 13.

*FLING, SYRREL.
Served in 3 Regt. (Williams') Vt. Militia.

FLINN, MICHAEL,   Bethel.
Volunteered to go to Plattsburgh,
September, 1814, and served 11 days
in Capt. Nehemiah Noble's Company.
Ref: Book 51, AGO Page 230.

‡*FLINT, AUGUSTUS.   Braintree.
Served in Capt. John Wheatley's Com-
pany, Col. Fifield's Regt. Detached
Militia in U. S. service 6 months,
1812. Pension Certificate No. 2742.
Pension Certificate of widow, Mariah,
No. 18808.

‡*FLINT, BENJAMIN.
Served in Corning's Detachment, Vt.
Militia. Also served in Capt. At-
kins' Company, 4 Regt. (Peck's). Pen-
sion Certificate of widow, Harriet,
No. 26661.

*FLINT, EDWARD.
Served from April 12, 1814 to April
21, 1814 in Capt. Eseck Sprague's
Company, Sumner's Regt.

FLINT, GIDEON,   Roxbury.
Volunteered to go to Plattsburgh,
September, 1814, and served 5 days
in Capt. Samuel M. Orcutt's Company. Ref: Book 52, AGO Pages 166
and 250.

FLINT, JOEL,   Williamstown.
Volunteered to go to Plattsburgh,
September, 1814, and went as far as
Burlington, serving 4 days in Capt.
David Robinson's Company. Ref:
Book 52, AGO Pages 2, 8, 12.

*FLINT, JOHN, Enosburgh or Richford.
Enlisted Sept. 25, 1813 and served 1
month and 23 days in Capt. Martin
D. Follett's Company, Col. Dixon's
Regt.

*FLINT, MARTIN, Lieutenant. Randolph.
Volunteered to go to Plattsburgh,
September, 1814, and served in Capt.
Lebbeus Egerton's Company. For
biographical sketch see Hemenway's
Vt. Gazetteer, Vol. 2, Page 1058.

‡FLINT, NATHANIEL,   Braintree.
Marched to Plattsburgh Sept. 10,
1814, serving in Capt. Lot Hudson's
Company. Pension Certificate of
widow, Polly, No. 13743.

*FLINT, PORTER.
Served in Capt. Hotchkiss' Company,
Col. Martindale's Regt. Detached
Militia in U. S. service 1 month and
7 days, 1812.

*FLINT, SAMUEL JR.,   Randolph.
Volunteered to go to Plattsburgh,
September, 1814, and served in Capt.
Lebbeus Egerton's Company.

‡*FLINT, WILLIAM JR.,   Braintree.
Served in Capt. John Wheatley's
Company, Col. Fifield's Regt. Detached Militia in U. S. service 6 months,
1812. Marched to Plattsburgh Sept.
10, 1814 and served in Capt. Lot
Hudson's Company. Pension Certificate No. 1929. Pension Certificate of
widow, Anna, No. 27600.

FLOHR, CHARLES.
Served from Jan. 1, to June 30, 1814
in Regt. of Light Dragoons. Ref: R.
& L. 1812, AGO Page 21.

FLOOD, AMOS.
Volunteered to go to Plattsburgh,
September, 1814, and served in Capt.
Ebenezer Spencer's Company, Ver-
shire. Ref: Book 52, AGO Page 48.

FLOOD, DANIEL.
Enlisted May 18, 1813 for 1 year in
Capt. James Taylor's Company, 30th
Regt.; transferred to Capt. Gideon
Spencer's Company, 30th Regt. and
served to May 18, 1814. Ref: R. & L.
1812, AGO Pages 52, 57, 58.

‡FLOOD, ISAAC,   Fairfax.
Served in Capt. Beeman's Company
in 1813 and 1814. Pension Certificate of widow, Meribah, No. 28223.

*FLOOD, MARK,   Fairfax.
Enlisted Sept. 25, 1813 and served
1 month and 23 days in Capt. Asa
Wilkins' Company, Col. Dixon's Regt.

*FLOWER, ANDREW.
Served from April 12, 1814 to April
21, 1814 in Capt. Edmund B. Hill's
Company, Sumner's Regt.

*FLOWER, JOSEPH, Drummer.
Served in Regt. of Riflemen from
September to November, 1813.

*FLOWER, LUTHER.
Served in Sumner's Regt. Vt. Militia.

*FLOWER, MARTIN.
Enlisted Sept. 30, 1813 in Capt. Isaac
Finch's Company, Col. Clark's Regt.
of Riflemen.

*FLOWER, SEYMOUR, Corporal.
Served from April 12, 1814 to April
21, 1814 in Capt. Shubael Wales' Company, Col. W. B. Sumner's Regt.

FLOYD, IRA.
Served from May 1 to July 31, 1814
in company of Artificers commanded
by Alexander Parris. Ref: R. & L.
1812, AGO Page 24.

FLOYD, JAMES,   Boston.
Served from May 1, 1814 to July 2,
1814 in Capt. Chadwick's Company,
34th Inf. Ref: R. & L. 1812, AGO
Page 30.

*FLY, JAMES (or James, Jr.) Sergeant.
Served in Capt. H. Mason's Company,
Col. Fifield's Regt. Detached Militia
in U. S. service 5 months 29 days,
1812. Served from May 1 to June
30, 1814 as Sergeant in Corps of Light
Dragoons.

FOBES, SOLOMON, Corporal.
Volunteered to go to Plattsburgh,
September, 1814, and served 7 days
in Capt. Frederick Griswold's Com-
pany, raised in Brookfield, Vt. Ref:
Book 52, AGO Page 52.

FOGG, PHINEAS.
Enlisted May 22, 1812 in Lieut. Wm.
S. Foster's Company, 11th Regt.; on
Pay Roll for January and February,
1813. Ref: R. & L. 1812, AGO Page
7.

FOGG, WILLIAM,   Franklin County.
Volunteered to go to Plattsburgh
Sept. 11, 1814 and served in 15th or
22nd Regt. Ref: Hemenway's Vt.
Gazetteer, Vol. 2, Page 391.

FOLET, ANSEL,   Fairfax.
Served from Aug. 8, 1812 in company
of Capt. Joseph Beeman, Jr., 11th
Regt. U. S. Inf. under Col. Ira
Clark. Ref: Hemenway's Vt. Gazet-
teer, Vol. 2, Page 402.

FOLLANSBEE, TIMOTHY.
Served from May 1 to June 30, 1814
as Ship Carpenter in company of Artificers commanded by Alexander Parris. Ref: R. & L. 1812, AGO Page
24.

*FOLLET, BRADBURY.
Served with Hospital Attendants, Vt.

FOLLET, GILES.
Enlisted Feb. 28, 1814 during the
war in Capt. Gideon Spencer's Company, 30th Regt.; on Muster Roll
Dec. 30, 1813 to June 30, 1814; mustered for discharge at Burlington June
3, 1814. Ref: R. & L. 1812, AGO
Page 57.

‡*FOLLET, HENRY, Enosburgh or Richford. Enlisted Sept. 25, 1813 and
served 1 month and 23 days in Capt.
Martin D. Follett's Company, Dixon's
Regt. Volunteered to go to Plattsburgh, September, 1814, and served
in Lieut. Benjamin Follett's Company, Col. Dixon's Regt. Pension
Certificate No. 3352. Pension Certificate of widow, Clarissa, No. 22864.

*FOLLET, JOHN, Enosburgh or Fairfield.
Served in Capt. Kendall's Company,
Col. Wm. Williams' Regt. Detached
Militia in U. S. service 4 months and
23 days, 1812. Volunteered to go
to Plattsburgh, September, 1814, and
served in Lieut. Benjamin Follett's
Company, Dixon's Regt.

FOLLETT, AMASA.   Swanton.
Served from Nov. 1, 1812 to Feb.
28, 1813 in Lieut. V. R. Goodrich's
Company, 11th Regt. Ref: R. & L.
1812, AGO Page 11.

*FOLLETT, BENJAMIN.   Lieutenant,
Enosburgh or Richford. Entered
service Sept. 25, 1813 in Capt. Martin D. Follett's Company, Dixon's
Regt.

FOLLETT, CHARLES, Captain.
Appointed Captain 11 Inf. March 12,
1812; resigned Sept. 1, 1814. On Pay
Roll as captain of company in the
11th Regt. for January and February, 1813. Ref: Governor and Council Vt., Vol. 6, Page 473; R. & L.
1812, AGO Page 12.

*FOLLETT, JOHN.
Served in Capt. Burnap's Company,
Col. Jonathan Williams' Regt. Detached Militia in U. S. service 9
days.

*FOLLETT, MARTIN D., Captain, Enos-
burgh or Richford. Commissioned
Captain Sept. 25, 1813 for 3 months
in Lt. Col. Luther Dixon's Regt.

*FOLLETT, MARTIN D. JR., Richford.
Enlisted Sept. 25, 1813 and served
1 month and 23 days in Capt. Martin D. Follett's Company, Dixon's
Regt.

FOLLETT, SAMUEL.
Served in Capt. Benjamin Bradford's
Company; on Muster Roll from May
31, 1813 to Aug. 31, 1813; joined by
transfer July 22, 1813. Ref: R. &
L. 1812, AGO Page 26.

‡FOLSOM, DAVID.
Served in Capt. Hackett's Company.
Pension Certificate of widow, Mehit-
able, No. 25846.

FOLSOM, JOSIAH.
Served from March 13, 1813 to June
12, 1813 in Capt. Charles Follett's
Company, 11th Regt. Ref: R. & L.
1812, AGO Page 13.

*FOLSOM, MATTHIAS, Sergeant, Tun-
bridge. Served in Capt. Bingham's
Company, Col. Jonathan Williams'
Regt. Detached Militia in U. S. service 2 months and 9 days, 1812. Volunteered to go to Plattsburgh, September, 1814, and served 4 days in Capt.
Ephraim Hackett's Company.

FOOD, JAMES.
Served from March 17, 1813 to June
16, 1813 in Capt. Charles Follett's
Company, 11th Regt. Ref: R. & L.
1812, Page 13.

FOOT, ALVIN.
Served in Capt. Barns' Company, Col.
Wm. Williams' Regt. Detached Mili-
tia in U. S. service 1 month and
23 days, 1812. Ref: Book 53, AGO
Page 78.

‡*FOOT, CLARK, Corporal.
Served in Capt. Dorrance's Company,
Col. Wm. Williams' Regt. Detached
Militia in U. S. service 4 months
and 29 days, 1812. Served from
April 12, 1814 to April 15, 1814 in
Capt. John Hackett's Company, Sum-
ner's Regt., as a corporal. Pension
Certificate No. 1783.

*FOOT, DANIEL M.
Served from April 12, 1814 to April
15, 1814 in Capt. John Hackett's
Company, Sumner's Regt.

*FOOT, ELIJAH, Sergeant,   Cornwall.
Served in Capt. Wright's Company,
Col. Martindale's Regt. Detached
Militia in U. S. service 2 months
and 14 days, 1812. Served from
April 12, 1814 to April 21, 1814 in
Capt. Edmund B. Hill's Company,
Sumner's Regt.; volunteered to go to
Plattsburgh, September, 1814, and was
at the battle, serving as sergeant in
same company.

FOOT, JOHN.
Served from April 12, 1814 to April
21, 1814 in Capt. Eseck Sprague's
Company, Sumner's Regt. Ref: Book
52, AGO Page 263.

*FOOT, JOHNSON, Ensign,   Charlotte.
Served from June 11, 1813 to June
14, 1813 in Capt. Hezekiah Barns'
Company. 1st Regt. 2nd Brig., 3rd
Div. Volunteered to go to Plattsburgh, September, 1814, and served
8 days in Capt. Daniel Hough's Company.

*FOOT, JUSTUS, Lieutenant.
Served from April 12, 1814 to April 21, 1814 in command of a company in Col. Wm. B. Sumner's Regt.

*FOOT, MARTIN, Corporal, Middlebury.
Served from April 12, 1814 to April 21, 1814 in Capt. Edmund B. Hill's Company, Sumner's Regt. Volunteered to go to Plattsburgh, September, 1814, and served in Capt. John Hackett's Company, Sumner's Regt.

*FOOT, RUSSELL, Cornwall.
Served from April 12, 1814 to April 21, 1814 in Capt. Edmund B. Hill's Company, Sumner's Regt.; volunteered to go to Plattsburgh, September, 1814, and was at the battle, serving in same company.

FOOT, WILLIAM, Lieutenant, Middlebury. Volunteered to go to Plattsburgh, September, 1814, and served 9 days in Capt. Silas Wright's Company. Ref: Book 51, AGO Pages 10 and 57.

FOP, NATHANIEL.
Served in Capt. Morrill's Company, Col. Fifield's Regt. Detached Militia in U. S. service 6 months and 5 days, 1812. Ref: Book 53, AGO Page 36.

*FORBES, GEORGE.
Enlisted Nov. 1, 1812 in Capt. Samul Gordon's Company, 11th Regt.; on Pay Roll for January and February, 1813. Also served in 1 Regt. (Martindale's)

*FORBES, LUTHER, Sergeant.
Served in Sumner's Regt. Vt. Militia.

*FORD, ALDEN.
Served in Sumner's Regt. Vt. Militia.

*FORD, ALVA.
Served in Sumner's Regt. Vt. Militia.

‡FORD, AMBROSE.
Served in Capt. Stone's Company. Pension Certificate of widow, Finelia, No. 27818.

*FORD, DANIEL.
Served in Capt. Dorrance's Company, Col. Wm. Williams' Regt. Detached Militia in U. S. service 4 months and 29 days, 1812. Served from April 12, 1814 to April 21, 1814 in Capt. Shubael Wales' Company, Col. W. B. Sumner's Regt.

*FORD, DAVID.
Served in Sumner's Regt. Vt. Militia.

*FORD, EBENEZER.
Served from April 12, 1814 to April 21, 1814 in Lieut. Justus Foote's Company Sumner's Regt. Volunteered to go to Plattsburgh, September, 1814, and went as far as Bolton, Vt., serving 4 days in Lieut. Phineas Kimball's Company, W. Fairlee. Ref: Book 52, AGO Page 46.

FORD, ELISHA, Braintree.
Marched to Plattsburgh, Sept. 10, 1814, serving in Capt. Lot Hudson's Company. Ref: Book 52, AGO Pages 24 and 34.

FORD, ELISHA, 2nd, Sergeant, Braintree.
Marched to Plattsburgh, Sept. 10, 1814 and served 9 days in Capt. Lot Hudson's Company. Ref: Book 52, AGO Pages 24 and 26.

FORD, FREDERICK, Doctor, Cornwall.
Hearing that there were wounded in need of surgical attention, this man and Dr. Eells started for Plattsburgh. When they reached Burlington they learned their services were not needed and returned home. Ref: Rev. Lyman Mathews' History of Cornwall, Page 345.

FORD, JAMES, Franklin County.
Volunteered to go to Plattsburgh Sept. 11, 1814 and served in 15th or 22nd Regt. Ref: Hemenway's Vt. Gazetteer, Vol. 2, Page 392.

FORD, JOHN, Sergeant, Corinth.
Volunteered to go to Plattsburgh, September, 1814, and served 3 days in Capt. Abel Jackman's Company. Ref: Book 52, AGO Pages 44 and 45.

FORD, JONATHAN, Hancock.
Volunteered to go to Plattsburgh, September, 1814, and served 7 days in Capt. Asaph Smith's Company. Ref: Book 51, AGO Page 20.

FORD, SAMUEL, Roxbury.
Volunteered to go to Plattsburgh, September, 1814, and served 8 days in Capt. Samuel M. Orcutt's Company. Ref: Book 52, AGO Page 250.

FORD, WARREN, Jericho.
Took part in the Battle of Plattsburgh. Ref: History of Jericho, Page 142.

*FORD, WILLIS.
Served from April 12, 1814 to April 21, 1814 in Lieut. Justus Foote's Company, Sumner's Regt.

FORDHAM, JAMES.
Served from Feb. 9, 1813 to May 8, 1813 in Capt. Charles Follett's Company, 11th Regt. Ref: R. & L. 1812, AGO Page 13.

FORE, CHANCEY.
Served from Feb. 5, 1813 to Feb. 28, 1813 in Capt. Samuel H. Holly's Company, 11th Regt. Ref: R. & L. 1812, AGO Page 25.

FOREST, ROBERT, Ensign, Tunbridge.
Volunteered to go to Plattsburgh, September, 1814, and served 4 days in Capt. Ephraim Hackett's Company. Ref: Book 52, AGO Page 71.

FORREST, ISAIAH.
Appointed Ensign June 25, 1814; 3 Lieutenant Oct. 1, 1814, 26th Regt. Ref: Governor and Council Vt., Vol. 6, Page 477.

FOSEFORD, ROYCE.
Served from Oct. 4, 1813 to Oct. 13, 1813 in Capt. John Palmer's Company, 1st Regt. 2nd Brig. 3rd Div. Ref: R. & L. 1812, AGO Page 48.

‡*FOSS, JACOB.
Served in Capt. Wheeler's Company,
Col. Fifield's Regt. Detached Militia
in U. S. service 6 months and 4
days, 1812. Pension Certificate of
widow, Sally S., No. 2898.

‡*FOSS, JOSHUA.
Served in Capt. Morrill's Company,
Col. Fifield's Regt. Detached Militia
in U. S. service 6 months and 5
days, 1812. Pension Certificate No.
25870.

‡*FOSS, NATHANIEL, Danville or Irasburgh. Served in Capt. Morrill's
Company, 2nd Regt. (Fifield's) Vt.
Militia. Volunteered to go to Plattsburgh, September, 1814, and served
2 days in company from Danville
under Col. Rankin. Pension Certificate No. 17354.

FOSTER, AARON.
Served in company of Capt. John
McNeil Jr., 11th Regt.; on Pay Roll
for January and February, 1813. Ref:
R. & L. 1812, AGO Page 17.

FOSTER, BARTY,   Franklin County.
Volunteered to go to Plattsburgh
Sept. 11, 1814 and served in 15th or
22nd Regt. Ref: Hemenway's Vt.
Gazetteer, Vol. 2, Page 392.

‡FOSTER, CHESTER.
Served in Capt. Brown's Company.
Pension Certificate No. 34622.

*FOSTER, COLBURN.
Served in Capt. Needham's Company,
Col. Martindale's Regt. Detached
Militia in U. S. service 2 months
and 14 days, 1812.

*FOSTER, DANIEL,   Berkshire.
Served in Capt. Briggs' Company,
Col. Jonathan Williams' Regt. Detached Militia in U. S. service 2
months and 13 days, 1812. Enlisted
Sept. 25, 1813 and served 1 month
and 23 days in Capt. Thomas Waterman's Company, Col. Dixon's Regt.
Pension Certificate No. 18744.

FOSTER, DAVID,   Sheldon.
Volunteered to go to Plattsburgh,
September, 1814, and served 5 days
in Capt. Samuel Weed's Company.
Ref: Book 51, AGO Pages 125, 152,
172, 176.

FOSTER, EBENEZER,   Sudbury.
Volunteered to go to Plattsburgh,
September, 1814, and served 6 days
in Capt. Thomas Hall's Company.
Ref: Book 52, AGO Page 122.

FOSTER, FREDERICK.
Served from May 19, 1813 to May 21,
1814 in Capt. Gideon Spencer's Company and Capt. James Taylor's Company, 30th Regt. Ref: R. & L. 1812,
AGO Pages 52, 57, 58, 59.

FOSTER, GEORGE W., Sergeant, Swanton. Enlisted April 26, 1813 for 1
year in Capt. James Taylor's Company, 30th Regt. Volunteered to go
to Plattsburgh and was at the battle
Sept. 11, 1814, serving in Capt. Amasa
J. Brown's Company. Ref: R. & L.

1812, AGO Page 58; Book 51, AGO
Page 142.

FOSTER, GORDAN.
Enlisted March 20, 1813 in company
of Capt. John McNeil Jr., 11th Regt.;
on Pay Roll to May 31, 1813. Ref:
R. & L. 1812, AGO Page 16.

FOSTER, JOEL,   Sudbury.
Volunteered to go to Plattsburgh,
September, 1814, and served 6 days
in Capt. Thomas Hall's Company.
Ref: Book 52, AGO Page 122.

*FOSTER, JOHN.
Served from April 12, 1814 to April
21, 1814 in Capt. Shubael Wales' Com-
pany, Col. W. B. Sumner's Regt.
Served in 3 Regt. (Williams') Vt.
Militia.

*FOSTER, JOHN JR., Corporal.
Served in Corning's Detachment, and
4 Regt. (Peck's) Vt. Militia.

FOSTER, JOHN M., Quartermaster, Lyndon. Served at Derby, Vt., from
Sept. 16, 1812 to March 16, 1813 in
detachment commanded by Major
Huckens Storrs, being a part of the
2nd Regt. commanded by Col. Edward Fifield. Ref: Vol. 50, Vt. State
Papers, Page 19.

*FOSTER, JOHN S.
Served from April 13, 1814 to April
21, 1814 in Capt. Salmon Foster's
Company, Sumner's Regt.

‡*FOSTER, JOSEPH.
Enlisted Sept. 25, 1813 and served
1 month and 23 days in Capt. Thomas
Waterman's Company, Col. Dixon's
Regt. Pension Certificate No. 18230.

‡FOSTER, LARNARD.
Served in Lieutenant Harvey White's
Company. Pension Certificate No.
34549.

FOSTER, LEMUEL,   Orange.
Volunteered to go to Plattsburgh,
September, 1814, and served in Capt.
David Rising's Company. Ref: Hem-
enway's Vt. Gazetteer, Vol. 2, Page
969.

*FOSTER, MOSES. Lieutenant.
Served in 4 Regt. Vt. Militia commanded by Col. Williams.

FOSTER, NATHAN P.,   Montclair.
Served from May 1, 1814 to Aug. 1,
1814 in Capt. Lynd's Company, 29th
Inf. Ref: R. & L. 1812, AGO Page
30.

*FOSTER, NATHANIEL.
Served from April 12, 1814 to April
21, 1814 in Lieut. Justus Foote's
Company, Sumner's Regt.

*FOSTER, SALMON, Captain, Whiting.
Served from April 13, 1814 to April
21, 1814 in command of a company
in Col. Wm. B. Sumner's Regt.;
volunteered to go to Plattsburgh, September, 1814, and served with same
company.

FOSTER, SAMUEL,   Orange.
Served from Feb. 20, 1813 to May
19, 1813 in Lieut. V. R. Goodrich's
Company, 11th Regt. Volunteered to
go to Plattsburgh Sept. 11, 1814 and
went part way, serving 5 days in
Capt. David Rising's Company. Ref:
R. & L. 1812, AGO Page 10; Book
52, AGO Page 19.

FOSTER, STEPHEN, Ensign, Montpelier.
Volunteered to go to Plattsburgh,
September, 1814, and served 8 days
in Capt. Timothy Hubbard's Company. Ref: Book 52, AGO Pages 212
and 256.

*FOSTER, THEODORE.
Served in Capt. Bingham's Company,
Col. Jonathan Williams' Regt. Detached Militia in U. S. service 2
months and 9 days.

*FOSTER, THOMAS M.
Served in Capt. Walker's Company,
Col. Fifield's Regt. Detached Militia
in U. S. service 3 months and 9
days, 1812. Served in Capt. Durkee's
Company. Col. Fifield's Regt. Detached Militia in U. S. service 2
months and 26 days, 1812. Enlisted
Sept. 7, 1813 in Capt. Asahel Langworthy's Company, Col. Isaac Clark's
Rifle Corps.

*FOSTER, WILLIAM,   St. Albans.
Served from Sept. 25, 1813 to Sept.
30, 1813 in Capt. Amos Robinson's
Company, Dixon's Regt. Served from
April 13, 1814 to April 16, 1814 in
Capt. Salmon Foster's Company, Sumner's Regt. Volunteered and was in
the action at Plattsburgh Sept. 11,
1814, serving in Capt. Samuel H.
Farnsworth's Company. Ref: Hemenway's Vt. Gazetteer, Vol. 2, Page
434.

FOSTER, WILLIAM S., Lieutenant.
Commanded company of Infantry in
11th Regt.; on Pay Roll of Company
for January and February, 1813. Ref:
R. & L. 1812, AGO Page 7.

FOWLER, ABRAHAM C., Sergeant, Man-
chester. Enlisted Nov. 5, 1813 for 1
year in Capt. Daniel Farrington's
Company (also commanded by Capt.
Simeon Wright) 30th Regt.; on Mus-
ter Roll March 1, 1814 to April 30,
1814. Name also appears on Pay
Roll (no organization given) from
March 1 to July 9, 1814. Ref: R.
& L. 1812, AGO Pages 29, 50, 51.

FOWLER, AMOS C., Sergeant.
Enlisted Nov. 5, 1813 for 1 year in
Capt. Gideon Spencer's Company,
30th Regt.; on Muster Roll Dec. 30,
1813 to June 30, 1814; doing duty in
Inspector General's Office; re-enlisted
Feb. 2, 1814 for duration of war.
Ref: R. & L. 1812, AGO Page 56.

*FOWLER, CLARK.
Served in Capt. Ormsbee's Company,
Col. Martindale's Regt. Detached
Militia in U. S. service 2 months
and 14 days, 1812; also served in
1 Regt. of Detached Militia of Vermont in U. S. service at Champlain
for 2 days commencing Nov. 18 and
ending Nov. 19, 1812.

*FOWLER, JACOB (or Jacob Jr)
Served in Capt. Rogers' Company,
Col. Fifield's Regt. Detached Militia
in U. S. service 2 months and 18
days, 1812.

FOX, CHARLES.
Served from March 17, 1813 to June
16, 1813 in Capt. Edgerton's Company,
11th Regt. Ref: R. & L. 1812, AGO
Page 3.

FOX, EPHRAIM,   Portland.
Served from May 1, 1814 to July 5,
1814 in Capt. Brooks' Company, Corps
of Artillery. Ref: R. & L. 1812, AGO
Pages 30 and 31.

*FOX, JAMES.
Served in 3 Regt. Vt. Militia commanded by Col. Williams.

FOX, JOHN,   Fairfax or Swanton.
Served from Aug. 8, 1812 in company
of Capt. Joseph Beeman Jr., 11th
Regt. U. S. Inf. under Col. Ira
Clark. Also served in Lieut. V. R.
Goodrich's Company, 11th Regt.; on
Pay Roll for January and February,
1813. Ref: R. & L. 1812, AGO Page
11; Hemenway's Vt. Gazetteer, Vol.
2, Page 402.

*FOX, SAMUEL.
Served in Capt. Preston's Company,
Col. Jonathan Williams' Regt. Detached Militia in U. S. service 2
months and 6 days, 1812.

FRANCIS, CYRUS K.,   Pownal.
Served from Sept. 19, 1814 to June
19, 1815 in Capt. Taylor's Company,
30th Inf. Ref: R. & L. 1812, AGO
Page 23.

*FRANCIS, FREDERIC.
Served with Hospital Attendants, Vt.

*FRANCIS, JOSEPH, Sergeant.
Served in Capt. Willson's Company,
Col. Wm. Williams' Regt. Detached
Militia in U. S. service 5 months in
1812; stationed at Swanton Falls.

*FRANK, JOHN,   Gray, Mass.
Served from July 10 to Aug. 31,
1813, and from May 1 to July 9, 1814,
in Capt. Poland's Company, 34th Inf.
Also served with Hospital Attendants,
Vt. Ref: R. & L. 1812, AGO Page 30.

FRANKLIN, JOHN W.
Served from Jan. 11, 1813 to July 4,
1813 in Lieut. Wm. S. Foster's Company, 11th Regt. Ref: R. & L. 1812,
AGO Page 6.

FRANKLIN, OTIS, Corporal, Williamstown. Served in Capt. Benjamin S.
Edgerton's Company, 11th Regt.; on
Pay Roll for September and October,
1812 and January and February
1813. Volunteered to go to Plattsburgh, September, 1814, and served
8 days in Capt. David Robinson's
Company. Ref: R. & L. 1812, AGO
Pages 1 and 2; Book 52, AGO Page
10 and Loose Rolls.

FRANKLIN, SAMUEL,   Williamstown.
Volunteered to go to Plattsburgh,
and was at the battle Sept. 11, 1814,

serving 8 days in Capt. David Robinson's Company. Ref: Book 52, AGO Pages 2 and 10.

FRANKLING, G.
Served in War of 1812 and was captured by troops Sept. 17, 1814 at Fort Erie; discharged Nov. 8, 1814. Ref: Records of Naval Records and Library, Navy Dept.

FRANSISCO, BOWMAN,   West Haven.
Volunteered to go to Plattsburgh, September, 1814, and served 4 days in Capt. David B. Phippeney's Company. Ref: Book 52, AGO Page 146.

FRANSISCO, JOHN,   West Haven.
Volunteered to go to Plattsburgh, September, 1814, and served 4 days in Capt. David B., Phippeney's Company. Ref: Book 52, AGO Page 146.

*FRARY, ALMOND.
Served in Capt. Strait's Company, Col. Martindale's Regt. Detached Militia in U. S. service 23 days, 1812.

*FRARY, SPENCER W.
Served from Sept. 25, 1813 to Oct. 8, 1813 in Capt. Jesse Post's Company, Dixon's Regt.

*FRASIER, ALEXANDER, Sergeant.
Served in 3 Regt. Vt. Militia commanded by Col. Tyler.

*FRAZER, ANSON.
Enlisted Nov. 26, 1812 in Capt. Benjamin S. Edgerton's Company, 11th Regt.; on Pay Roll for January and February, 1813. Also served in 2 Regt. (Fifield's) Vt. Militia.

FRAZIER, DANIEL,   Sacketts' Harbor.
Served from May 1, 1814 to July 16, 1814 in Capt. Haig's Company, Light Dragoons. Ref: R. & L. 1812, AGO Pages 20 and 30.

*FRAZIER, JOHN.
Served from June 11 to June 14, 1813 and from Oct. 4 to Oct. 13, 1813 in Capt. John Palmer's Company, 1st Regt. 2nd Brig. 3rd Div. Also served in 4 Regt. (Williams') Vt. Militia.

FREDGE, THOMAS,   Franklin County.
Volunteered to go to Plattsburgh Sept. 11, 1814 and served in 15th or 22nd Regt. Hemenway's Vt. Gazetteer, Vol. 2, Page 391.

*FREELOVE, JOHN JR.
Served from April 12, 1814 to April 21, 1814 in Capt. Othniel Jewett's Company, Sumner's Regt.

FREEMAN, ALLEN,   Huntington.
Volunteered to go to Plattsburgh, September, 1814, and was at the battle, serving in company of Capt. Josiah N. Barrows. Ref: Book 51, AGO Page 77.

‡*FREEMAN, BRINTON, Fairfield or Swanton. Served in Capt. Kendall's Company, Col. Wm. Williams' Regt. Detached Militia in U. S. service 4 months and 23 days, 1812. Enlisted Sept. 25, 1813 in Capt. A. Robin-

son's Company. Col. Dixon's Regt. and served 1 month and 23 days. Volunteered to go to Plattsburgh, September, 1814, and served 6 days in Capt. Amasa I. Brown's Company. Pension Certificate No. 12205. Ref: Book 51, AGO Pages 124, 125, 198.

FREEMAN, EDMOND.
Served from Jan. 11, 1813 to July 4, 1813 in Lieut. Wm. S. Foster's Company, 11th Regt. Ref: R. & L. 1812, AGO Page 6.

*FREEMAN, EZRA.
Served in Capt. Wright's Company, Col. Martindale's Regt. Detached Militia in U. S. service 12 days, 1812.

*FREEMAN, JAMES.
Served in Capt. Briggs' Company, Col. Jonathan Williams' Regt. Detached Militia in U. S. service 2 months and 13 days, 1812.

*FREEMAN, JARVIS.
Served from May 15, 1813 to May 15, 1814 in Capt. Gideon Spencer's Company and Capt. James Taylor's Company, 30th Regt. Also served in 4 Regt. (Williams') Vt. Militia. Ref: R. & L. 1812, AGO Pages 52, 57, 59.

‡FREEMAN, JOHN.
Served in Capt. Valentine Goodrich's Company, 11th Regt. Pension Certificate No. 2171.

‡*FREEMAN, JOHN, Fifer.
Served in 3 Regt. (Williams') Vt. Militia, Capt. Phelps' Company. Pension Certificate No. 14726. Pension Certificate of widow, Clarissa, No. 30522.

*FREEMAN, LUTHER.
Served in Capt. Barns' Company, Col. Wm. Williams' Regt. Detached Militia in U. S. service 5 months, 1812. Also served in 3 Regt. (Tyler's) Vt. Militia.

FREEMAN, NICHOLAS,   Highgate?
Served in Capt. Joseph Beeman's Company, 11th Regt.; killed at Battle of Chippeway; was the son of John Bettis Freeman. Ref: Book 58, Vt. State Papers, Page 218.

FREEMAN, SETH.   Plainfield.
Volunteered to go to Plattsburgh, September, 1814, and served 5 days as a teamster; no organization given. Ref: Book 52, AGO Page 195.

FREEMAN, STEPHEN,   Barre.
Volunteered to go to Plattsburgh, September, 1814, and served 8 days in Capt. Warren Ellis' Company. Ref: Book 52, AGO Page 237.

‡FREEMAN, THOMAS.
Served in Capt. Burnap's Company, Pension Certificate of widow, Rebecca, No. 18696.

*FREEMAN, WALTER, Corporal.
Served from Oct. 11, 1813 to Oct. 17, 1813 in Capt. John Munson's Company, 3 Regt. (Tyler's).

FREEMAN, WELCOME.
Served from May 3, 1813 to May 5, 1814 in Capt. Gideon Spencer's Company and Capt. James Taylor's Company, 30th Regt. Ref: R. & L. 1812. AGO Pages 52, 57, 59.

FRELEIGH, SAMUEL D.
Enlisted July 1, 1812 for 5 years in company of late Capt. J. Brooks, commanded by Lieut. John I. Cromwell, Corps of U. S. Artillery; on Muster Roll from April 30, 1814 to June 30, 1814. Ref: R. & L. 1812, AGO Page 18.

FRENCH, ABIAL, Montpelier.
Volunteered to go to Plattsburgh, September, 1814, and served 8 days in Capt. Timothy Hubbard's Company. Ref: Book 52, AGO Page 256.

*FRENCH, ABRAM.
Served in 1st Regt. Vt. Militia commanded by Col. Judson.

FRENCH, BARTHOLOMEW, Sergeant, Barre. Volunteered to go to Plattsburgh, September, 1814, and served 10 days in Capt. Warren Ellis' Company. Ref: Book 52, AGO Page 242. (According to Hemenway's Vt. Gazetteer—Vol. 4, Page 41—Bartholomew French and Bartholomew French Jr. both served in the war and were buried in the Barre Cemetery).

‡*FRENCH, BARZILLA, Glover.
Served in Capt. Mason's Company, Col. Fifield's Regt. Detached Militia in U. S. service 6 months, 1812. Pension Certificate No. 10985.

FRENCH, BRADLEY, Corporal.
Served in company of Capt. John McNeil Jr., 11th Regt.; on Pay Roll for January and February, 1813. Ref: R. & L. 1812, AGO Page 17.

*FRENCH, DANIEL.
Served in Capt. Charles Follett's Company, 11th Regt.; on Pay Roll for January and February, 1813. Served with Hospital Attendants, Vt. Ref: R. & L. 1812, AGO Page 12.

FRENCH, DAVID, Barre?
Served in Capt. Benjamin S. Edgerton's Company, 11th Regt.; on Pay Roll for September and October, 1812, and January and February, 1813. Ref: R. & L. 1812, AGO Pages 1 and 2.

*FRENCH, ELDAD.
Served in Capt. Burnap's Company, Col. Jonathan Williams' Regt. Detached Militia in U. S. service 15 days.

*FRENCH, ENOCH.
Served in Tyler's Regt. Vt. Militia.

FRENCH, HAINS, Major.
Appointed Major 30 Inf. Feb. 23, 1813; died in service Sept. 4, 1814. Ref: Governor and Council Vt. Vol. 6, Page 475.

‡FRENCH, HASKIL.
Served in Capt. Marston's Company. Pension Certificate No. 8562.

*FRENCH, JAMES, Fairfax.
Served in Capt. Weeks' Company, 11th Regt.; on Pay Roll for January and February, 1813. Enlisted Sept. 25, 1813 and served 1 month and 23 days in Capt. Asa Wilkins' Company, Col. Dixon's Regt. Also served in 2 Regt. (Fifield's) Vt. Militia.

*FRENCH, JEDEDIAH, Randolph.
Volunteered to go to Plattsburgh, September, 1814, and served in Capt. Lebbeus Egerton's Company.

*FRENCH, JOHN, Lieutenant.
Served from March 8, 1813 to June 7, 1813 in Capt. John W. Weeks' Company, 11th Regt. Enlisted June 8, 1813 for 1 year in Capt. Daniel Farrington's Company (also commanded by Capt. S. Wright) 30th Regt. on Muster Roll March 1, 1814 to April 30, 1814. Volunteered to go to Plattsburgh, September, 1814 no organization given. Served in 2 Regt. (Fifield's) Vt. Militia, as Lieutenant. Ref: R. & L. 1812, AGO Pages 4, 50, 51; Book 52, AGO Page 35.

*FRENCH, JONAH.
Served in Capt. Mason's Company, Col. Fifield's Regt. Detached Militia in U. S. service 3 months and 16 days, 1812.

*FRENCH, JONATHAN.
Enlisted June 8, 1813 for 1 year in Capt. Daniel Farrington's Company (also commanded by Capt. Simeon Wright) 30th Regt. Also served in 3 Regt. (Tyler's) Vt. Militia, Ref: R. & L. 1812, AGO Pages 50 and 51.

FRENCH, JONATHAN F.
Served from Feb. 5, 1814 to March 9, 1814 in Capt. Gideon Spencer's Company, 30th Regt. Ref: R. & L. 1812, AGO Page 57.

*FRENCH, JOSEPH W., Randolph.
Volunteered to go to Plattsburgh, September, 1814, and served in Capt. Lebbeus Egerton's Company.

‡FRENCH, LEMUEL.
Served in Capt. A. Farr's Company. Pension Certificate of widow, Laura, No. 27877.

*FRENCH, MANLY.
Served in Capt. Wheeler's Company, Col. Fifield's Regt. Detached Militia in U. S. service 2 months and 18 days, 1812.

*FRENCH, NATHANIEL, Braintree.
Marched to Plattsburgh Sept. 10, 1814 and served about 9 days in Capt. Lot Hudson's Company. Also served with Hospital Attendants, Vt. Ref: Book 52, AGO Pages 24 and 34.

FRENCH, NOAH, Corporal.
Served in Capt. Charles Follett's Company, 11th Regt.; on Pay Roll for January and February, 1813; joined Feb. 6, 1813. Ref: R. & L. 1812, AGO Page 12.

*FRENCH, OLIVER.
Served in Capt. Briggs' Company, Col. Jonathan Williams' Regt. Detached Militia in U. S. service 2 months and 13 days, 1812.

‡*FRENCH, OTIS,   Barre.
Served in Capt. E. Walker's Company, Col. Fifield's Regt. Detached Militia in U. S. service 6 months and 3 days, 1812. Volunteered to go to Plattsburgh, September, 1814, and served 10 days in Capt. Warren Ellis' Company. Pension Certificate No. 8385. Ref: Book 52, AGO Pages 217 and 242.

*FRENCH, SAMUEL B.,   Randolph.
Volunteered to go to Plattsburgh, September, 1814, and served in Capt. Lebbeus Egerton's Company .

FRENCH, SEBE,   Clarendon.
Volunteered to go to Plattsburgh, September, 1814, and served 4 days in Capt. Durham Sprague's Company. Ref: Book 52, AGO Page 128.

*FRENCH, SILAS,   Glover.
Served in Capt. Mason's Company, Col. Fifield's Regt. Detached Militia in U. S. service 2 months and 14 days, 1812.

*FRENCH, SILAS C.
Served in Capt. E. Walker's Company, Col. Fifield's Regt. Detached Militia in U. S. service 2 months and 26 days, 1812.

FRENCH, STEPHEN.
Served from Feb. 23, 1813 to April 14, 1813 in Capt. Charles Follett's Company. 11th Regt. Ref: R. & L. 1812, AGO Page 13.

FRENCH, THOMAS, Lieutenant.
Appointed 2 Lieutenant 26 Inf. April 21, 1814; 1 Lieutenant Aug. 1, 1814; resigned Dec. 10, 1814. Ref: Heitman's Historical Register & Dictionary USA.

FRESHET, NOEL.
Served in Lieut. V. R. Goodrich's Company, 11th Regt.; on Pay Roll for January and February, 1813. Ref: R. & L. 1812, AGO Page 11.

FRIEND, SEBASTIAN.
Enlisted May 18, 1812 for 5 years in Capt. White Youngs' Company, 15th Regt.; on Muster Roll from Aug. 31, 1814 to Dec. 31, 1814. Ref: R. & L. 1812, AGO Page 27.

*FRIMMER, NICHOLAS.
Served in Lieut. V. R. Goodrich's Company, 11th Regt.; on Pay Roll for January and February, 1813. Also served in 4 Regt. (Williams') Vt. Militia.

*FRINK, CONSIDER.   Danby.
Served in Capt. Hotchkiss' Company, Col. Martindale's Regt. Detached Militia in U. S. service 13 days, 1812.

‡FRIP, JOEL.
Served in Capt. Atkins' Company, 4 Regt. (Peck's). Pension Certificate of widow, Nancy, No. 31014.

FRISBEE, ISRAL W.. Corporal.
Served from May 1 to Aug. 21, 1814; no organization given. Ref: R. & L. 1812, AGO Page 29.

*FRISBEE, THADDEUS.
Served from April 12, 1814 to April 21. 1814 in Capt. Edmund B. Hill's Company, Sumner's Regt.

‡FRISBIE, IRA B.
Served from April 22, 1813 to April 26, 1814 in Capt. Gideon Spencer's Company and Capt. James Taylor's Company, 30th Regt. Pension Certificate of widow, Thirza S., No. 1279.

FRISBIE, JARED.
Served from April 22, 1813 to April 26, 1814 in Capt. Gideon Spencer's Company and Capt. James Taylor's Company, 30th Regt. Ref: R. & L. 1812, AGO Pages 52, 57, 58.

‡FRISBIE, JARED P.
Served in Capt. Barnes' Company. Pension Certificate No. 3400.

FRISBIE, JOSIAH, Corporal.
Served from April 22, 1813 to April 25, 1814 in Capt. James Taylor's Company and Capt. Gideon Spencer's Company, 30th Regt. Ref: R. & L. 1812, AGO Pages 52, 56, 58.

FRISKET, NOEL,   Fairfax.
Served from Aug. 8, 1812 in company of Capt. Joseph Beeman Jr., 11th Regt. U. S. Inf. under Col. Ira Clark. Ref: Hemenway's Vt. Gazetteer, Vol. 2, Page 402.

*FRIZZLE, APPOLLAS, Drummer.
Served from April 12, 1814 to May 20, 1814 in company of Capt. James Gray Jr., Sumner's Regt.

*FRIZZLE, ELIAKIM.
Served in Capt. Taylor's Company, Col. Fifield's Regt. Detached Militia in U. S. service 2 months and 21 days, 1812.

FROHAWK, DANIEL.
Served in Capt. Benjamin Bradford's Company; on Muster Roll from May 31, 1813 to Aug. 31, 1813. Ref: R. & L. 1812, AGO Page 26.

FROHAWK, WILLIAM.
Served in Capt. Benjamin Bradford's Company; on Muster Roll from May 31, 1813 to Aug. 31, 1813. Ref: R. & L. 1812, AGO Page 26.

FROST, ABRAHAM, Captain, Bridport.
Volunteered to go to Plattsburgh, September, 1814, and served 6 days in command of a company in Col. Lyman's Regt. Ref: Book 51, AGO Page 60.

FROST, CHARLES.   Franklin County.
Volunteered to go to Plattsburgh Sept. 11, 1814 and served in 15th or 22nd Regt. Ref: Hemenway's Vt. Gazetteer, Vol. 2, Page 391.

*FROST, JOEL JR.
Served from April 12, 1814 to May 20, 1814 in company of Capt. James Gray Jr., Sumner's Regt.

*FROST, LORING,   Glover.
Served in Capt. Mason's Company, Col. Fifield's Regt. Detached Militia in U. S. service 5 months and 26 days, 1812.

‡FROST, MOSES,   Groton.
Served in Capt. Hessick's Company.
Pension Certificate No. 12102.

FROST, SOLOMON.   Troy, N. Y.
Served from Sept. 26, 1814 to June
16, 1815 in Capt. Sanford's Company,
30th Inf. Ref: R. & L. 1812, AGO
Page 23.

FRUFONT, JOSEPH.
Served from April 20, 1813 to March
28, 1813 in Lieut. Wm. S. Foster's
Company, 11th Regt. Ref: R. & L.
1812, AGO Page 6.

*FULINGTON, JONATHAN.
Served in Dixon's Regt. Vt. Militia.

*FULLER, ABNER, Fifer.
Served in Corning's Detachment, Vt.
Militia.

*FULLER, ABRAHAM, Sergeant.
Served from April 30 to July 29,
1813 in Lieut. Wm. S. Foster's Com-
pany, 11th Regt. Enlisted Oct. 5,
1813 in Capt. Asahel Langworthy's
Company, Col. Isaac Clark's Rifle
Corps. Ref: R. & L. 1812, AGO
Page 6.

FULLER, ABSALOM,   Orwell.
Volunteered to go to Plattsburgh,
September, 1814, and served 11 days
in Capt. Wait Branch's Company.
Ref: Book 51, AGO Page 16.

*FULLER, ALMAN.
Enlisted Sept. 25, 1813 and served
1 month and 23 days in Capt. Amos
Robinson's Company, Col. Dixon's
Regt.

FULLER, AMBROSE,   Franklin County.
Volunteered to go to Plattsburgh
Sept. 11, 1814 and served in 15th or
22nd Regt. Ref: Hemenway's Vt. Gazetteer, Vol. 2, Page 392.

FULLER, AMOS,   Franklin County.
Volunteered to go to Plattsburgh
Sept. 11, 1814 and served in 15th or
22nd Regt. Ref: Hemenway's Vt.
Gazetteer, Vol. 2, Page 392.

*FULLER, BENJAMIN.
Served from April 12, 1814 to April
15, 1814 in Lieut. Justus Foote's Company, Sumner's Regt.

FULLER, CALVIN.
Served in Capt. John W. Weeks'
Company, 11th Regt. from March 2,
1813 to date of death April 17, 1813.
Ref: R. & L. 1812, AGO Page 4.

FULLER, CHAUNCEY W., Corporal.
Served from May 1, 1814 to June 30,
1814 in Corps of Light Dragoons.
Ref: R. & L. 1812, AGO Page 20.

FULLER, CHESTER.
Served in War of 1812 and was captured by troops July 25, 1814 at
Londers Lane; discharged Oct. 8,
1814. Ref: Records of Naval Records
and Library, Navy Dept.

*FULLER, CORNELIUS,   Stowe.
Volunteered to go to Plattsburgh,

September, 1814, and was at the
battle, serving in Capt. Nehemiah
Perkins' Company, 4 Regt. (Peck's).

FULLER, DANIEL, Corporal.
Served from May 1, 1813 to May 1,
1814 in company of Capt. Gideon
Spencer and Capt. James Taylor, 30th
Regt. Ref: R. & L. 1812, AGO Pages
52, 56, 58.

‡*FULLER, DANIEL S.
Served in Capt. Pettes' Company,
Col. Wm. Williams' Regt. Detached
Militia in U. S. service in 1812. Pen-
sion Certificate No. 4623. Pension
Certificate of widow, Eliza A., No.
8446.

FULLER, DAVID.
Served in Capt. Pettes' Company,
Col. Wm. Williams' Regt. Detached
Militia in U. S. service 4 months and
17 days, 1812. Ref: Book 53, AGO
Page 70.

*FULLER, DAVID.
Served from June 11, 1813 to June
14, 1813 in Capt. Hezekiah Barns'
Company, 1st Regt. 2nd Brig., 3rd
Div.

FULLER, DAVID.
Served from April 7, 1813 to July 6,
1813 in Capt. Samul Gordon's Company, 11th Regt. Ref: R. & L. 1812,
AGO Page 8.

*FULLER, EBENEZER.
Served in 1 Regt. Vt. Militia commanded by Col. Judson.

FULLER, ELISHA.
Served from March 16 to June 30,
1814 in Regt. of Light Dragoons. Ref:
R. & L. 1812, AGO Page 21.

FULLER, EMERY,   Barre.
Volunteered to go to Plattsburgh,
September, 1814, and served 10 days
in Capt. Warren Ellis' Company. Ref:
Book 52, AGO Page 242.

FULLER, GEORGE,   Woodstock.
Served from Nov. 1, 1812 to Feb. 28,
1813 in Capt. Phineas Williams' Company, 11th Regt. Ref: R. & L. 1812,
AGO Page 15.

‡FULLER, HEMAN.
Served in Capt. Sproul's Company.
Pension Certificate of widow, Amelia,
No. 30158.

‡*FULLER, IRA.
Enlisted Sept. 20, 1813 in Capt. John
Weed's Company, Col. Clark's Regt.
of Riflemen. Pension Certificate No.
16823.

FULLER, JAMES, Sergeant,   Vershire.
Volunteered to go to Plattsburgh,
September, 1814, and served 3 days
in Capt. Ira Corse's Company. Ref:
Book 52, AGO Pages 91 and 92.

FULLER, JEREMIAH.
Served from March 22, 1813 to June
21, 1813 in Capt. John W. Weeks'
Company, 11th Regt. Volunteered to
go to Plattsburgh, September, 1814.

and served 4 days in Lieut. Phineus Kimball's Company, West Fairlee. Ref: R. & L. 1812, AGO Page 4; Book 52, AGO Page 46.

FULLER, JOHN, Franklin County. Volunteered to go to Plattsburgh Sept. 11, 1814 and served in 15th or 22nd Regt. Ref: Hemenway's Vt. Gazetteer, Vol. 2, Page 392.

*FULLER, JOHN, Fifer. Served in Capt. Burnap's Company, Col. Jonathan Williams' Regt. Detached Militia in U. S. service 2 months and 13 days, 1812. Also served in Corning's Detachment, Vt. Militia.

FULLER, JOHN, Major. Appointed Major Rifle Dec. 12, 1808; resigned Aug. 1, 1812; died Feb. 4, 1839. Ref: Heitman's Historical Register & Dictionary USA.

FULLER, JOHN C., Orwell. Volunteered to go to Plattsburgh, September, 1814, and served 11 days in Capt. Wait Branch's Company. Ref: Book 51, AGO Page 16.

‡*FULLER, JONAS. Served in Capt. Phelps' Company, Col. Wm. Williams' Regt. Detached Militia in U. S. service 5 months, 1812. Pension Certificate No. 11004. Pension Certificate of widow, Clarissa, No. 32884.

¬FULLER, JONATHAN. Served in 1 Regt. (Martindale's) Vt. Militia.

‡*FULLER, JOSEPH. Served from Feb. 6, 1813 to May 5, 1813 in Lieut. Wm. S. Foster's Company, 11th Regt. Also served in Corning's Detachment and in Capt. Perkins' Company (4 Regt). Pension Certificate No. 30495. Ref: R. & L. 1812, AGO Page 6.

*FULLER, LAVANDER. Served in Capt. Sabin's Company, Col. Jonathan Williams' Regt. Detached Militia in U. S. service 2 months and 6 days, 1812.

FULLER, LEMUEL. Served from Feb. 28, 1813 to May 27, 1813 in Capt. John W. Weeks' Company, 11th Regt. Ref: R. & L. 1812, AGO Page 4.

FULLER, LUTHER. Served from Jan. 29, 1813 to May 10, 1813 in Capt. John W. Weeks' Company, 11th Regt. Ref: R. & L. 1812, AGO Page 4.

‡FULLER, NATHAN E. Served in Capt. Smead's Company, 11th Regt. Pension Certificate No. 9042.

*FULLER, ORREN, Sergeant. Served in Capt. Dorrance's Company, Col. Wm. Williams' Regt. Detached Militia in U. S. service 4 months and 29 days, 1812.

FULLER, REUBEN, Woodstock. Served in Capt. Phineas Williams' Company, 11th Regt.; on Pay Roll for January and February, 1813. Ref: R. & L. 1812, AGO Page 15.

FULLER, SAMUEL, Franklin County. Volunteered to go to Plattsburgh Sept. 11, 1814 and served in 15th or 22nd Regt. Ref: Hemenway's Vt. Gazetteer, Vol. 2, Page 391.

*FULLER, SAMUEL, Stowe. Volunteered to go to Plattsburgh, September, 1814, and was at the battle, serving in Capt. Nehemiah Perkins' Company, 4 Regt. (Peck's).

‡*FULLER, SAMUEL, Calais. Volunteered to go to Plattsburgh, September, 1814, and served 10 days in Capt. Gideon Wheelock's Company. Pension Certificate No. 23096.

*FULLER, SAMUEL. Served from April 17, 1814 to April 21, 1814 in Capt. Othniel Jewett's Company, Sumner's Regt.

*FULLER, SIMEON. Served in Capt. Mason's Company, Col. Fifield's Regt. Detached Militia in U. S. service 5 months and 27 days, 1812. Volunteered to go to Plattsburgh, September, 1814, and served 7 days in Capt. Frederick Griswold's Company, raised in Brookfield, Vt. Ref: Book 52, AGO Pages 52 and 64.

FULLER, SQUIRE. Volunteered to go to Plattsburgh, September, 1814, and served 7 days in company of Capt. Frederick Griswold; raised in Brookfield, Vt. Ref: Book 52, AGO Pages 52 and 64.

‡*FULLER, STEPHEN. Volunteered to go to Plattsburgh, September, 1814, and served 7 days in Capt. Frederick Griswold's Company, raised in Brookfield, Vt. Also served in Capt. Pettis' Company, 4 Regt. (Williams'). Pension Certificate No. 19240.

*FULLER, THOMAS, Ensign. Served as Quartermaster, Ensign and Adjutant in 3 Regt. (Bowdish) Vt. Militia.

FULLER, TIMOTHY. Served in Capt. John W. Weeks' Company, 11th Regt. from Feb. 26, 1813 to date of death May 15, 1813. Ref: R. & L. 1812, AGO Page 4.

‡*FULLER, WILLIAM. Enlisted Sept. 25, 1813 and served 1 month and 23 days in Capt. Amos Robinson's Company, Dixon's Regt. Pension Certificate of widow, Eliza, No. 12603.

‡FULLER, WILLIAM. Served in Capt. Gilman's Company. Pension Certificate No. 19906.

*FULLER, WILLIAM JR. Served in 1 Regt. Vt. Militia commanded by Col. Judson.

FULLINGTON, EPH.
Served in Capt. Chadwick's Company.
Ref: R. & L. 1812, AGO Page 32.

*FULLINGTON, JAMES, Lieutenant and
Quartermaster. Appointed Sept. 25,
1813 lieutenant and quartermaster in
Col. Dixon's Consolidated Regt. of
Vt. Militia in U. S. service.

FULLINGTON, JONATHAN, Bakersfield.
Served from Sept. 25, 1813 to Oct. 3,
1813 in Capt. Asa Wilkins' Company,
Dixon's Regt. Volunteered and was
at the Battle of Plattsburgh Sept.
11, 1814. Ref: Book 52, AGO Page
272; Hemenway's Vt. Gazetteer, Vol.
2, Page 394.

FULLINGTON, JOTHAM,   Fairfax.
Served from Sept. 12, 1813 in Capt.
Asa Wilkins' Company, Dixon's Regt.
Ref: Hemenway's Vt. Gazetteer, Vol.
2, Page 402.

‡FULLINGTON, MOSES.
Served in Capt. David Chadwick's
Company. Original Pension Applica-
tion No. 32040. Pension Certificate
No. 2289. Pension Certificate of
widow, Hannah M., No. 43276.

FULLUM, C.
Volunteered to go to Plattsburgh,
September, 1814, and served in company of Capt. Joel Barnes of Chelsea. Ref: Book 52, AGO Page 77.

FULLUM, FOSTER.
Volunteered to go to Plattsburgh,
September, 1814, and served in com-
pany of Capt. Joel Barnes of Chelsea.
Ref: Book 52, AGO Page 69.

FULLUM, LEVI.
Volunteered to go to Plattsburgh,
September, 1814, and served in com-
pany of Capt. Joel Barnes of Chelsea.
Ref: Book 52, AGO Pages 69 and 77.

*FULSOM, JONATHAN.
Served from April 12, 1814 to April
15, 1814 in Lieut. Justus Foote's
Company, Sumner's Regt.

FULSOM, JOSHUA, Ensign,   Corinth.
Volunteered to go to Plattsburgh,
September, 1814, and served in Capt.
Abel Jackman's Company. Ref: Book
52, AGO Page 44.

FULTON, JAMES.
Served from Feb. 1st to June 30,
1814 in Regt. of Light Dragoons.
Ref: R. & L. 1812, AGO Page 21.

*FURBUSH, RUFUS, Sergeant.
Served in Capt. Briggs' Company, Col.
Jonathan Williams' Regt. Detached
Militia in U. S. service 2 months and
13 days, 1812.

*FURGESON, BARTEMAS.
Served in Sumner's Regt. Vt. Militia.

FURMAN, JOHN.
Enlisted Feb. 21, 1814 during the
war in Capt. Gideon Spencer's Company, 30th Regt.; on Muster Roll Dec.
30, 1813 to June 30, 1814; wounded
at Lacole Mill. Ref: R. & L. 1812,
AGO Page 57.

FURNHAM, JOEL.
Served from March 9, 1813 to June 8,
1813 in Capt. John W. Weeks' Company, 11th Regt. Ref: R. & L. 1812,
AGO Page 4.

*GABY, GEORGE.
Served in 1 Regt. Vt. Militia commanded by Col. Martindale.

*GADCOMB, SANFORD, Captain and A.
D. C., St. Albans. Served from
Sept. 25, 1813 to Nov. 7, 1813 on
Staff of Brig. Gen. Elias Fasset. Appointed Captain and Regimental Paymaster Nov. 17, 1813 in Dixon's Regt.
of Vt. Militia in U. S. service. Volunteered to go to Plattsburgh and
was at the battle Sept. 11, 1814 serving in Capt. Samuel H. Farnsworth's
Company. Ref: Hemenway's Vt. Gazetteer, Vol. 2, Page 434.

*GADLEY, WILLIAM.
Enlisted Sept. 20, 1813 in Capt. John
Weed's Company, Regt. of Riflemen.

*GAFFIELD, JOHN.
Served in 3 Regt. Vt. Militia commanded by Col. Tyler.

*GAGE, ABRAM,   Jamaica.
Served in Capt. Preston's Company,
Col. Jonathan Williams' Regt. Detached Militia in U. S. service 1
month and 6 days, 1812.

GAGE, ALIS.
Served from April 28, 1813 to April
27, 1814 in Capt. Daniel Farrington's
Company (also commanded by Capt.
Simeon Wright) 30th Regt. Ref: R.
& L. 1812, AGO Pages 50 and 51.

*GAGE, CHASE (or Gaige) Ferrisburgh.
Volunteered to go to Plattsburgh,
September, 1814, and served 9 days;
no organization given. Also served
in Sumner's Regt. Vt. Militia. Ref:
Book 51, AGO Page 57.

GAGE, ELLIS,   Sudbury.
Volunteered to go to Plattsburgh,
September, 1814, and served 6 days
in Capt. Thomas Hall's Company.
Ref: Book 52, AGO Page 122.

*GAGE, FRANCIS.
Served from April 19, 1814 to April
21, 1814 in Capt. Othniel Jewett's
Company, Sumner's Regt.

‡GAGE, JOHN,   Sudbury.
Volunteered to go to Plattsburgh,
September, 1814, and served 6 days
in Capt. Thomas Hall's Company.
Also served in Capt. Munson's Com-
pany. Pension Certificate No. 25456.
Pension Certificate of widow, Hannah,
No. 30336. Ref: Book 52, AGO Page
122.

*GAGE, JOSEPHUS, Musician.
Served in Capt. Dorrance's Company,
Col. Wm. Williams' Regt. Detached
Militia in U. S. service 4 months and
24 days, 1812. Also served in Dixon's
Regt. Vt. Militia.

GAGE, NATHANIEL JR.
Served in Capt. Barns' Company, Col.
Wm. Williams' Regt. Detached Mili-

tia in U. S. service 4 months and 27 days, 1812. Ref: Book 53, AGO Page 13.

*GAGE, PRESERVE.
Served in Capt. Phelps' Company, Col. Wm. Williams' Regt. Detached Militia in U. S. service 5 months, 1812.

*GAGE, SAMUEL.
Served from April 12, 1814 to April 21, 1814 in Capt. Eseck Sprague's Company, Sumner's Regt.

‡GAGE, WILLIAM,   Dorset.
Served from Sept. 1, 1814 to June 16, 1815 in Capt. Sanford's Company, 30th Inf. Pension Certificate No. 12894. Pension Certificate of widow, Phebe, No. 33233.

GAIGE, ABRAHAM, Sergeant,   Bristol.
Volunteered to go to Plattsburgh, September, 1814, and was at the battle, serving 9 days in Capt. Jehiel Saxton's Company, Sumner's Regt. Ref: Book 51, AGO Page 18.

*GAIGE, JOHN.
Served in Sumner's Regt. Vt. Militia.

*GAIGE, WILLIAM W.
Served in Sumner's Regt. Vt. Militia.

GALE, ABRAM,   Middlesex.
Volunteered to go to Plattsburgh, September, 1814, and served in Capt. Holden Putnam's Company, 4 Regt. (Peck's). Ref: Hemenway's Vt. Gazetteer, Vol. 4, Page 250.

*GALE, AMOS.
Served from June 11, 1813 to June 14, 1813 in Lieut. Bates' Company, 1 Regt. (Judson's).

GALE, EBENEZER B.,   Barre.
Volunteered to go to Plattsburgh, September, 1814, and served 10 days in Capt. Warren Ellis' Company. Ref: Book 52, AGO Page 242.

*GALE, EPHRAIM,   Guilford?
Served in Capt. Parson's Company, Col. Jonathan Williams' Regt. Detached Militia in U. S. service 2 months and 13 days, 1812.

GALE, GEORGE,   Bridport.
Volunteered to go to Plattsburgh, September, 1814, and was at the battle, serving in Capt. Edmund B. Hill's Company, Sumner's Regt. Ref: Book 51, AGO Page 14.

‡GALE, ISAAC,   Barre.
Volunteered to go to Plattsburgh, September, 1814, and served 8 days in Capt. Warren Ellis' Company. Pension Certificate of widow, Sally, No. 22895.

GALE, JOHN,   Barre.
Volunteered to go to Plattsburgh, September, 1814, and served 8 days in Capt. Warren Ellis' Company. Ref: Book 52, AGO Pages 233 and 242.

GALE, JOSEPH,   Fairfax.
Served from Aug. 8, 1812 in company of Capt. Joseph Beeman Jr.,

11th Inf. under Col. Ira Clark. Ref: Hemenway's Vt. Gazetteer, Vol. 2, Page 402.

*GALE, PETER,   Burlington.
Served in Capt. Walker's Company, Col. Fifield's Regt. Detached Militia in U. S. service 2 months and 24 days, 1812. Volunteered to go to Plattsburgh, September, 1814, and served in Capt. Henry Mayo's Company.

*GALE, PHINEHAS.
Served in Capt. Robbins' Company, Col. Wm. Williams' Regt. Detached Militia in U. S. service 4 months and 29 days, 1812.

GALE, SENECA, Corporal, Franconia, N. H. Enlisted at Poultney Feb. 14, 1814 for 5 years and served in Capt. Wm. Miller's Company and Capt. Gideon Spencer's Company, 30th Regt. Ref: R. & L. 1812, AGO Pages 1, 54, 55, 56.

GALE, SOMERS, Major,   Cornwall.
Volunteered to go to Plattsburgh, September, 1814, and commanded company of volunteers from Cornwall and vicinity. Ref: Rev. Lyman Mathews' History of Cornwall, Page 344.

GALE, STEPHEN.
Served in company of Capt. John McNeil Jr., 11th Regt.; on Pay Roll for January and February, 1813. Ref: R. & L. 1812, AGO Page 17.

‡*GALE, TIMOTHY.
Served from June 11, 1813 to June 14, 1813 in Lieut. Bates' Company, 1 Regt. (Judson's). Pension Certificate of widow, Ruth, No. 28225.

GALLAGHER, JAMES.
Enlisted May 8, 1812 for 5 years in Capt. White Youngs' Company, 15th Regt.; on Muster Roll from Aug. 31, 1814 to Dec. 31, 1814. Ref: R. & L. 1812, AGO Page 27.

GALLAHER, JOSEPH, Franklin County.
Volunteered to go to Plattsburgh Sept. 11, 1814 and served in 15th or 22nd Regt. Ref: Hemenway's Vt. Gazetteer, Vol. 2, Page 392.

GALLAUGH, ANTHONY, Franklin County. Volunteered to go to Plattsburgh Sept. 11, 1814 and served in 15th or 22nd Regt. Ref: Hemenway's Vt. Gazetteer, Vol. 2, Page 392.

GALLUP, JOSEPH,   Cambridge.
Volunteered to go to Plattsburgh, September, 1814, and served in Capt. Salmon Green's Company. Also served in Capt. Chadwick's Company. Ref: Book 51, AGO Page 207; R. & L. 1812, AGO Page 32.

*GALUSHA, AMOS, Lieutenant, Pawlet.
Served in 1 Regt. of Detached Militia of Vermont in U. S. service commencing Nov. 18 and ending Nov. 19, 1812.

*GALUSHA, EZRA.
Served in Tyler's Regt. Vt. Militia.

*GALUSHA, OLIVER.
Served in Capt. Phineas Williams'
Company, 11th Regt.; on Pay Roll
for January and February, 1813.
Also served in 2 Regt. (Fifield's) Vt.
Militia. Ref: R. & L. 1812, AGO
Page 15.

‡*GAMBELL, JOSEPH, Fifer, Newfane?
Served in Capt. Noyce's Company,
Col. Jonathan Williams' Regt. De-
tached Militia in U. S. service 2
months and 6 days, 1812. Pension
Certificate No. 1891.

GAMSBY, PETER, Corporal.
Served in Capt. Weeks' Company,
11th Regt.; on Pay Roll for January and February, 1813. Ref: R. &
L. 1812, AGO Page 5.

*GANSON, JOHN, Sergeant Major.
Served in Capt. Wright's Company,
Col. Martindale's Regt. Detached Militia in U. S. service 2 months and
14 days, 1812. Served as Sergeant
Major in 3 Regt. (Bowdish) Vt. Militia.

GARDNER, AARON, Musician.
Served in Capt. Phineas Williams'
Company, 11th Regt.; on Pay Roll
for January and February, 1813. Ref:
R. & L. 1812, AGO Page 15.

GARDNER, HOWLAND.
Served from May 1, 1813 to May 10,
1814 in Capt. James Taylor's Company and Capt. Gideon Spencer's Company, 30th Regt. Ref: R. & L. 1812,
AGO Pages 52, 57, 58.

GARDNER, J. L., Lieutenant and Aid.
Served from May 1 to July 31, 1814
as 2nd Lieutenant and Aid on General Staff of the Northern Army commanded by Maj. Gen. George Izard.
Ref: R. & L. 1812, AGO Page 28.

‡GARDNER, JOHN.
Served in Capt. Aiken's Company.
Pension Certificate of widow, Maryett,
No. 34522.

GAREY, OLIVER,   Thetford.
Marched for Plattsburgh, September,
1814, and went as far as Bolton,
serving 6 days in Capt. Salmon Howard's Company, 2 Regt. Ref: Book
52, AGO Pages 15 and 16.

GARFIELD, BENJAMIN JR.
Served from April 12, 1814 to April
15, 1814 in Capt. Jonathan P. Stanley's Company, Col. W. B. Sumner's
Reg. Ref: Book 52, AGO Page 297.

GARFIELD, DEXTER.
Served from April 12, 1814 to April
15, 1814 in Capt. Jonathan P. Stanley's' Company, Col. W. B. Sumner's
Regt. Ref: Book 52, AGO Page 287.

*GARFIELD, SALMON, Corporal.
Served from April 12, 1814 to April
15, 1814 in Capt. Jonathan P. Stanley's Company, Col. W. B. Sumner's
Regt.

GARGE, JONATHAN,   Fairfax.
Served in 1813 and 1814 in Capt.
Joseph Beeman's Company. Ref: Hemenway's Vt. Gazetteer, Vol. 2, Page
402.

GARLAND, WILLIAM,   Fairfax.
Served from Aug. 8, 1812 in company of Capt. Joseph Beeman Jr.
11th Regt. U. S. Inf. under Col.
Ira Clark. Ref: Hemenway's Vt. Gazetteer, Vol. 2, Page 402.

GARLS, JOHN C.,   Baltimore.
Served from May 1, 1813 to July 6,
1814 in Capt. McDonald's Company,
14th Inf. Ref: R. & L. 1812, AGO
Page 30.

*GARREL, ELISHA, J.
Served in 1 Regt. Vt. Militia commanded by Col. Martindale.

*GARRET, ELISHA J.
Served in 1 Regt. Vt. Militia commanded by Col. Martindale.

*GARNER, PHINEHAS.
Served from April 19, 1814 to April
21, 1814 in Capt. Othniel Jewett's
Company, Sumner's Regt.

*GARTNER, ELEZEAR.
Served in Capt. Howard's Company,
Vt. Militia.

GARVIN, EPHRAIM.
Served from March 30, 1813 to June
29, 1813 in Capt. Charles Follett's
Company, 11th Regt. Ref: R. & L.
1812, AGO Page 13.

*GARVIN, JEREMIAH.
Served in Capt. Bingham's' Company,
Col. Jonathan Williams' Regt. Detached Militia in U. S. service 2
months and 9 days, 1812.

*GARVIN, MOSES.
Enlisted Sept. 25, 1813 in Capt.
Thomas Waterman's Company, Dix-
on's Regt.

GARVIN, SAMUEL,   Vershire.
Volunteered to go to Plattsburgh,
September, 1814, and served in Capt.
Ebenezer Spencer's Company. Ref:
Book 52, AGO Pages 48 and 50.

GARVIN, SAMUEL,   Vershire.
Volunteered to go to Plattsburgh,
September, 1814, and served 3 days
in Capt. Ira Corse's Company. Ref:
Book 52, AGO Page 91.

‡GARY, ELI B.
Served from June 11, 1813 to June
14, 1813 in Capt. Ithiel Stone's Com-
pany, 1st Regt. 2nd Brig. 3rd Div.
Pension Certificate of widow, Frances
O., No. 9504 .

GARZEE, ELISHA T.
Served in Capt. Richardson's Company, Col. Martindale's Regt. Detached Militia in U. S. service 2
months and 13 days, 1812. Ref: Book
53, AGO Page 24.

GASHWAY, GEORGE.
Enlisted April 29, 1814 during the
war in Capt. White Youngs' Company,
15th Regt.; on Muster Roll from
Aug. 31, 1814 to Dec. 31, 1814. Ref:
R. & L. 1812, AGO Page 27.

*GASKILL, ASA.
Served with Hospital Attendants, Vt.

*GASKILL, GEORGE.
Served with Hospital Attendants, Vt.

‡GATES, ALVIN,   Tunbridge, Vt.
Born in Barre, Mass.; aged 17 years;
5 feet 6 inches high; blue eyes; light
complexion; brown hair; by profession a farmer. Enlisted at Tunbridge, Vt. June 9, 1813 in the Army
of the U. S. for 1 year unless sooner discharged. Served in Capt. Edgerton's Company, 11th Regt. Pension Certificate No. 17379.

*GATES ARDELL.
Served in Sumner's Regt. Vt. Militia.

GATES, CHARLES.
Served in Capt. Benjamin Bradford's
Company; on Muster Roll from May
31, 1813 to Aug. 31, 1813; on com-
mand on board the row galleys. Ref:
R. & L. 1812, AGO Page 26.

*GATES, GROSS, Shoreham or Enos-
burgh. Served from Oct. 15, 1813
to Nov. 17, 1813 in Capt. Asahel
Scoville's Company, Col. Clark's Regt.
of Riflemen. Volunteered to go to
Plattsburgh, September, 1814, and
served 6 days in Capt. Samuel Hand's
Company. Ref: Rev. J. F. Goodhue's History of Shoreham, Page 107.

*GATES, HORACE,   Richford.
Enlisted Sept. 25, 1813 and served
1 month and 23 days in Capt. Martin
D. Folett's Company, Col. Dixon's
Regt.

*GATES, JEHIAL, Sergeant, Shoreham or
Enosburgh. Served from Oct. 14,
1813 to Nov. 17, 1813 in Capt. Asahel
Scovell's Company, Regt. of Riflemen. Served from April 12, 1814
to May 20, 1814 in company of Capt.
James Gray Jr., Sumner's Regt.

GATES, JONAS, Lieutenant.
Appointed 3 Lieutenant 31 Inf. April
30, 1813; resigned Jan. 11, 1814. Ref:
Heitman's Historical Register & Dic-
tionary USA; Governor and Council
Vt., Vol. 6, Page 476.

*GATES, SILAS, Sergeant.
Served from Sept. 25, 1813 to Oct. 9,
1813 in Capt. N. B. Eldridge's Company, Dixon's Regt.

GAY, ABNER.
Served in Capt. Weeks' Company,
11th Regt.; on Pay Roll for January and February, 1813. Ref: R. &
L. 1812, AGO Page 5.

GAY, DANIEL JR.,   Stockbridge.
Volunteered to go to Plattsburgh,
September, 1814, and served 8 days
in Capt. Elias Keyes' Company. Ref:
Book 51, AGO Page 242.

*GAY, EZRA.
Served from Oct. 8, 1813 to Nov. 18,
1813 in Capt. Isaac Finch's Company,
Col. Clark's Rifle Corps.

*GAY, ISAIAH.
Served in 4 Regt. (Williams') Vt.
Militia.

*GAY, JAMES, Sergeant.
Served from April 12, 1814 to April
21, 1814 in Capt. Eseck Sprague's
Company, Sumner's Regt.

GAY, JOHN.
Served from Oct. 11, 1813 to Oct. 17,
1813 in Capt. John Munson's Company, 3 Regt. (Tyler's). Ref: R. &
L. 1812, AGO Page 36.

*GAY, JONATHAN, Corporal.
Served from April 12, 1814 to April
21, 1814 in Capt. Eseck Sprague's
Company, Sumner's Regt.

GAY, JOSEPH.
Served in Capt. Phelps' Company,
Col. Wm. Williams' Regt. Detached
Militia in U. S. service 5 months,
1812. Ref: Book 53, AGO Page 67.

*GAY, ZEBULON.
Served in 3 Regt. Vt. Militia commanded by Col. Tyler.

‡GAYLORD, ASA.
Served in Capt. E. Johnson's Com-
pany. Pension Certificate of widow,
Eleanor C., No. 28274.

GAYLORD, ELIJAH.
Volunteered to go to Plattsburgh,
September, 1814, and served 7 days
in Capt. Frederick Griswold's Com-
pany, raised in Brookfield, Vt. Ref:
Book 52, AGO Page 52.

*GAYLORD, THEODORE.
Served in 3 Regt. Vt. Militia commanded by Col. Tyler.

GAYLORD, WILLIAM,   Shoreham.
Volunteered to go to Plattsburgh,
September, 1814, and served 6 days
in Capt. Samuel Hand's Company.
Ref: Rev. J. F. Goodhue's History
of Shoreham, Page 108.

GEDDINGS, REUBEN.
Served from Nov. 1, 1812 to Feb. 28,
1813 in Capt. Samul Gordon's Company, 11th Regt. Ref: R. & L. 1812,
AGO Page 9.

‡*GEER, AMOS C.
Served in Corning's Detachment, Vt.
Militia and in Capt. R. Hunt's Company (3 Regt.). Pension Certificate
of widow, Harriet, No. 27332.

*GEER, ISAAC T., Corporal.
Served in 1 Regt. Vt. Militia commanded by Col. Judson.

*GELLET, JEDEDIAH, Sergeant.
Served in 1 Regt. Vt. Militia commanded by Col. Judson.

*GELLY, SAMUEL.
Served from June 11, 1813 to June
14, 1813 in Capt. John M. Eldridge's
Company, 1st Regt. 2nd Brig., 3rd
Div.

*GEMMING, GIDEON.
Served from April 12, 1814 to May
20, 1814 in Company of Capt. James
Gray Jr., Sumner's Regt.

‡GEORGE, ASA.
Served in Capt. Amos Styles' Company. Pension Certificate No. 30920.

*GEORGE, BENAIAH.
Served in Capt. Rogers' Company, Col. Fifield's Regt. Detached Militia in U. S. service 5 months and 27 days, 1812.

GEORGE, CLINTON.   Swanton.
Served in Capt. V. R. Goodrich's Company, 11th Regt.; on Pay Roll from July 31 to Dec. 8, 1813; was in action at the Battle of Lundy's Lane. Ref: Hemenway's Vt. Gazetteer, Vol. 2,, Page 444.

GEORGE, DANIEL S.
Enlisted April 15, 1813 during the war in company of late Capt. J. Brooks, commanded by Lieut. John I. Cromwell, Corps of U. S. Artillery; on Muster Roll from April 30, 1814 to June 30, 1814; transferred from Capt. Leonard's Company. Ref: R. & L. 1812, AGO Page 18.

‡*GEORGE, EBENEZER,   Strafford.
Served under Captains Taylor and Rogers, Col. Fifield's Regt. Detached Militia in U. S. service 2 months and 21 days 1812. Pension Certificate No. 10984.

GEORGE, EDMUND.
Volunteered to go to Plattsburgh, September, 1814, and served 4 days in company of Capt. James George of Topsham. Ref: Book 52, AGO Pages 67 and 70.

*GEORGE, ISAAC.
Enlisted Sept. 18, 1813 in Capt. Isaac Finch's Company, Col. Clark's Rifle Corps.

GEORGE, JAMES, Captain. Topsham, Vt.
Volunteered to go to Plattsburgh, September, 1814, and served 4 days in command of Topsham company. Ref: Book 52, AGO Pages 67, 68, 70.

*GEORGE, JOHN, Corporal.
Enlisted Sept. 18, 1813 in Capt. Isaac Finch's Company, Col. Clark's Regt. of Riflemen.

*GEORGE, JONATHAN, Sergeant.
Enlisted Sept. 18, 1813 in Capt. Isaac Finch's Company, Col. Clark's Regt. of Riflemen.

GEORGE, JOSHUA,   Corinth.
Volunteered to go to Plattsburgh, September, 1814, and served in Capt. Abel Jackman's Company. Ref: Book 52, AGO Page 44.

GEORGE, MICAH,   Vershire.
Volunteered to go to Plattsburgh, September, 1814, and went as far as Burlington, serving 5 days; did not join any organization. Ref: Book 52, AGO Pages 48 and 95.

GEORGE, MICAH JR.,   Vershire.
Volunteered to go to Plattsburgh, September, 1814, and served in company of Capt. Ebenezer Spencer. Ref: Book 52, AGO Pages 48, 49, 95.

*GEORGE, MOSES.
Served in Capt. Walker's Company, Col. Fifield's Regt. Detached Militia in U. S. service 2 months and 24 days, 1812. Served from April 7, 1813 to July 6, 1813 in Lieut. Wm. S. Foster's Company, 11th Regt.

‡GEORGE, WILLIAM.
Volunteered to go to Plattsburgh, September, 1814, and served 4 days in company of Capt. James George of Topsham. Also served in Capt. Buck's Company. Pension Certificate No. 9043.

GERALDS, THOMAS.
Enlisted May 1, 1813 for 1 year in Capt. Simeon Wright's Company. Ref: R. & L. 1812, AGO Page 51.

*GEERY, ELI B.
Served in 1 Regt. Vt. Militia commanded by Col. Judson.

*GERSHORN, DANIEL.
Served in 1 Regt. Vt. Militia commanded by Col. Judson.

‡GETCHELL, ISAAC.
Served in Capt. B. Adams' Company. Pension Certificate No. 3146.

GIBBS, ABEL.
Appointed 2 Lieutenant 30 Inf. April 30, 1813; resigned March 5, 1814. Served in Capt. James Taylor's Company, 30th Regt. Ref: Heitman's Historical Register & Dictionary USA; R. & L. 1812, AGO Page 58.

*GIBBS, ABEL, JR. (or Abiel, Jr.)
Served from June 11, 1813 to June 14, 1813 in Capt. Ithiel Stone's Company, 1st Regt. 2nd Brig., 3rd Div.

*GIBBS, HARRY (or Harvey).
Served in Capt. Wright's Company. Col. Martindale's Regt. Detached Militia in U. S. service 2 months and 14 days, 1812.

*GIBBS, HENRY, Corporal,   Georgia.
Enlisted Sept. 25, 1813 and served 1 month and 23 days in Capt. Jesse Post's Company, Col. Dixon's Regt.

*GIBBS, JOHN.
Served from April 12, 1814 to April 15, 1814 in Lieut. Justus Foote's Company, Sumner's Regt.

*GIBBS, JOSEPHUS.
Served in 1 Regt. Vt. Militia commanded by Col. Judson.

‡GIBBS, JULIUS.
Served in Capt. Jared Jewitt's Company. Pension Certificate No. 8823.

‡GIBBS, SETH.
Served in Capt. Asa Aikens' Company. Pension Certificate No. 4815.

*GIBBS, THOMAS.
Served in Dixon's Regt. Vt. Militia.

*GIBBS, THOMAS JR.
Served in Dixon's Regt. Vt. Militia.

*GIBBS, TRUMAN C.,   Cornwall.
Served from April 12, 1814 to April 21, 1814 in Capt. Edmund B. Hill's Company, Sumner's Regt. Volunteered to go to Plattsburgh September, 1814, and was at the battle, serving in the same company.

*GIBBS, USEVINS.
Served in 1 Regt. Vt. Militia commanded by Col. Judson.

GIBSON, ABEL,   Ashby, Mass.
Born in Ashby, Mass.; aged 30 years; 5 feet 6 inches high; light complexion; light hair; blue eyes; by profession a carpenter. Enlisted at Bridport March 1, 1814 for period of the war and served in Capt. William Miller's Company and Capt. Gideon Spencer's Company, 30th Regt.; discharged at Burlington, Vt. in 1815. Ref: R. & L. 1812, AGO Pages 54, 55, 57.

*GIBSON, ABEL JR., Sergeant.
Served in 3 Regt. Vt. Militia commanded by Col. Williams.

*GIBSON, JAMES.
Served from April 12, 1814 to April 21, 1814 in Lieut. James S. Morton's Company, Col. W. B. Sumner's Regt.

*GIBSON, JOHN JR.,   Enosburgh.
Served from Oct. 15, 1813 to Nov. 17, 1813 in Capt. Asahel Scovell's Company, Col. Clark's Rifle Corps.

‡*GIBSON, OLIVER, Sergeant.
Served as Corporal in Capt. Wright's Company, Col. Martindale's Regt. Detached Militia in U. S. service 2 months and 14 days, 1812. Served from April 12, 1814 to April 15, 1814 as Sergeant in Capt. Jonathan P. Stanley's Company, Col. W. B. Sumner's Regt. Pension Certificate No. 9525. Pension Certificate of widow, Barbara, No. 29575.

*GIBSON, RIAH, (or Rial).
Served in 3 Regt. Vt. Militia commanded by Col. Williams.

GIBSON, SAMUEL.
Served from Feb. 8, 1813 to May 7, 1813 in Capt. Samul Gordon's Company, 11th Regt. Ref: R. & L. 1812, AGO Pages 8 and 9.

‡*GIBSON, THOMAS.
Served in Capt. Hopkins' Company. Col. Martindale's Regt. Detached Militia in U. S. service 2 months and 13 days, 1812. Pension Certificate No. 6160.

GIFFIN, DAVID, Sergeant.
Served from April 23, 1813 to April 25, 1814 in Capt. Gideon Spencer's Company and Capt. James Taylor's Company, 30th Regt. Ref: R. & L. 1812, AGO Pages 56 and 58.

GIFFIN, JOHN M.
Served in Capt. Alexander Brooks' Corps of Artillery; on Pay Roll to June 30, 1814. Ref: R. & L. 1812, AGO Page 31.

GIFFORD, GEORGE,   Montpelier.
Volunteered to go to Plattsburgh, September, 1814, and served 8 days in Capt. Timothy Hubbard's Company. Ref: Book 52, AGO Page 256.

GIFFORD, JOSEPH,   Barnard.
Volunteered to go to Plattsburgh, September, 1814, and served 8 days in Capt. John S. Bicknell's Company. Ref: Book 51, AGO Page 250.

*GIFFORD, NOAH,   Danby.
Served in 1 Regt. Vt. Militia commanded by Col. Martindale.

GIFFORD, NOAH, Sergeant, Pawlet, Vt.
Born in Pawlet, Vt.; aged 22 years; 5 feet 11 inches high; light complexion; brown hair; blue eyes; by profession a joiner. Enlisted at Pawlet April 6, 1814 and served in Capt. Miller's Company, Capt. Gideon Spencer's Company and Capt. James Taylor's Company, all in 30th Regt. Discharged at Burlington, Vt., 1815. Ref: R. & L. 1812, AGO Pages 53, 54, 55, 56. For biographical sketch see Hemenway's Vt. Gazetteer, Vol. 3, Page 915.

GILBERT, ARIEL,   Cabot.
Volunteered to go to Plattsburgh, September, 1814, and served 4 days in Capt. Anthony Perry's Company. Ref: Book 52, AGO Pages 177 and 254.

*GILBERT, ASA JR.
Served in 3 Regt. Vt. Militia commanded by Col. Tyler.

*GILBERT, DANIEL B.
Served in 1 Regt. Vt. Militia commanded by Col. Judson.

*GILBERT, DEXTER.
Served in Sumner's Regt. Vt. Militia.

*GILBERT, ELI.
Served from June 11, 1813 to June 14, 1813 in Lieut. Bates' Company, 1st Regt.

*GILBERT, EZRA,   Braintree.
Served in Col. Fifield's Regt. Detached Militia in U. S. service 6 months, 1812.

‡GILBERT, GEORGE NYE, Surgeon's Mate, Pittsford. Volunteered to go to Plattsburgh, September, 1814, and served in Capt. Caleb Hendee's Company 8 days. Pension Certificate of widow, Lucy E., No. 31053.

GILBERT, HEZEKIAH, Hadley, N. Y.
Served from May 1, 1814 to July 7, 1814 in Capt. Spencer's Company, 29th Inf. Ref: R. & L. 1812, AGO Page 30.

*GILBERT, HIRAM.
Enlisted Oct. 24, 1813 in Capt. Asahel Langworthy's Company, Col. Isaac Clark's Regt. Also served in Dixon's Regt. Vt. Militia.

*GILBERT, JOHN, Lieutenant.
Served in Capt. Cross' Company, Col. Martindale's' Regt. Detached Militia in U. S. service 2 months and 14 days, 1812. Served in 1st Regt. of Detached Militia of Vt. in U. S. service at Champlain commencing Nov. 18 and ending Nov. 19, 1812. Appointed Ensign 30 Inf. Feb. 10, 1814; 3 Lieutenant July 10, 1814; honorably discharged June 15, 1815. Entered service as Ensign in Capt. Wm. Miller's Company, 30th Regt. March 11, 1814; on Muster Roll to Aug. 31, 1814. Ref: Governor and Council Vt. Vol. 6, Page 478; R. & L. 1812, AGO Page 54.

*GILBERT, LUCAS.
Served in 3 Regt. Vt. Militia commanded by Col. Williams.

*GILBERT, MOSES H., Sergeant.
Served in Dixon's Regt. Vt. Militia.

GILBERT, STEPHEN,   Salisbury.
Served from April 12, 1814 to April
21, 1814 in Lieut. James S. Morton's
Company, Col. W. B. Sumner's Regt.
Ref: Book 52, AGO Page 286.

GILBERT, ZERAH, Sergeant, Ballstown,
N. Y. Born in Newton, Conn; aged
22 years; 5 feet 5 inches high; by
profession a Cardwainer; light complexion; dark eyes; brown hair. Enlisted at Ballstown, N. Y. May 3,
1814 and served in Capt. Wm. Miller's Company and Capt. Gideon Spencer's Company, 30th Regt.; discharged at Burlington, Vt., in 1815. Ref:
R. & L. 1812, AGO Pages 54, 55, 56.

*GILCHRIST, JAMES. Sergeant.
Served in Capt. Wheeler's Company,
Col. Fifield's Regt. Detached Militia
in U. S. service 3 months and 5
days, 1812.

*GILCHRIST, JOHN.
Served in Capt. Sabin's Company,
Col. Jonathan Williams' Regt. Detached Militia in U. S. service 2
months and 6 days, 1812.

GILCHRIST, THOMAS.
Served in Capt. Wheeler's Company,
Col. Fifield's Regt. Detached Militia
in U. S. service 2 months and 18
days, 1812. Ref: Book 53, AGO Page
71.

GILE, D. WILLIAM,   Leicester.
Volunteered to go to Plattsburgh,
September, 1814, and served 8 days
in Capt. Ebenezer Jenney's Company.
Ref: Book 52, AGO Page 160.

GILE, DANIEL B.
Served from May 1 to June 30, 1814
in Capt. Haig's Corps of Light Dragoons. Ref: R. & L. 1812, AGO
Page 20.

*GILE, WILLIAM, Surgeon's Mate.
Served in Sumner's Regt. Vt. Militia.

*GILES, EPHRAIM.
Served in Capt. Hotchkiss' Company,
Col. Martindale's Regt. Detached
Militia in U. S. service 1 month and
7 days, 1812.

GILES, JNO.
Served in War of 1812 and was captured by troops Aug. 12, 1814 at
Fort Erie; discharged Oct. 8, 1814.
Ref: Records of Naval Records and
Library, Navy Dept.

GILES, JOHN.
Served from March 9, 1813 to June
8, 1813 in Capt. Edgerton's Company,
11th Regt. Ref: R. & L. 1812, AGO
Page 3.

GILKEY, LEVI.
Volunteered to go to Plattsburgh,
September, 1814, and served in Capt.
Ebenezer Spencer's Company of Vershire. Ref: Book 52, AGO Page 48.

*GILLET, ASA JR.
Served from Oct. 5, 1813 to Oct. 16,
1813 in Capt. Roswell Hunt's Company, 3 Regt. Also served in Corning's Detachment, Vt. Militia. Ref:
R. & L. 1812, AGO Page 41.

*GILLET, CALEB.
Served from Oct. 10, 1813 to Nov.
11, 1813 in Capt. Asahel Langworthy's
Company, Col. Isaac Clark's Rifle
Corps.

*GILLET, ELIPHALET.
Served from June 11, 1813 to June
14, 1813 in Capt. Hezekiah Barns'
Company, 1st Regt. 2nd Brig. 3rd
Div.

GILLET, FRANCIS.
Enlisted July 20, 1812 for 5 years
in company of late Capt. J. Brooks,
commanded by Lieut. John I. Cromwell, Corps of U. S. Artillery; on
Muster Roll from April 30, 1814 to
June 30, 1814. Ref: R. & L. 1812,
AGO Page 18.

*GILLET, FREDERICK C.
Served in Capt. Cross Company, Col.
Martindale's Regt. Detached Militia
in U. S. service 1 month and 25
days, 1812.

*GILLET, JEDEDIAH, Sergeant.
Served from June 11, 1813 to June
14, 1813 in Capt. Hezekiah Barns'
Company, 1st Regt. 2nd Brig., 3rd
Div. Ref: R. & L. 1812, AGO Page
43.

*GILLET, JONATHAN JR.
Served from June 11, 1813 to June
14, 1813 in Capt. Ithiel Stone's Company, 1st Regt. 2nd Brig. 3rd Div.

‡*GILLETT, CYREL,   Thetford.
Marched for Plattsburgh, September,
1814, and went as far as Bolton,
Vt., serving 6 days in Capt. Salmon
Howard's Company, 2nd Regt. Pension Certificate of widow, Octavia W.,
No. 22662.

*GILLETT, DANIEL B.
Served from June 11, 1813 to June
14, 1813 in Capt. John M. Eldridge's
Company, 1st Regt. 2nd Brig. 3rd
Div.

‡*GILLETT, HENRY,   Thetford.
Marched for Plattsburgh in September, 1814 and went as far as Bolton,
Vt., serving 6 days in Capt. Salmon
Howard's Company, 2nd Regt. Pension Certificate No. 33310.

GILLETT, JOHN A.,   Pittsford.
Volunteered to go to Plattsburgh,
September, 1814, and served 8 days
in Capt. Caleb Hendee's Company.
Ref: Book 52, AGO Page 125.

‡GILLETT, LUCAS.
Served in Capt. Preston's Company,
Col. Jonathan Williams' Regt. Detached Militia in U. S. service 2
months and 6 days, 1812. Pension
Certificate No. 5867.

GILLETT, REUBEN,   Cornwall.
Volunteered to go to Plattsburgh,
September, 1814, and was at the
battle, serving in Capt. Edmund B.
Hill's Company, Sumner's Regt. Ref:
Book 51, AGO Pages 13 and 14.

GILLIGAN, ANTHONY, Gilliam Ireland.
Enlisted at Plattsburgh April 19, 1814
for 5 years in Capt. Wm. Miller's
Company, 30th Regt. Ref: R. & L.
1812, AGO Page 55.

*GILLMAN, JOHN, Captain.
Served in 1 Regt. 3 Brig. 3 Div. Vt.
Militia.

GILLSON, ABEL JR.
Served in Capt. Briggs' Company, Col.
Jonathan Williams' Regt. Detached
Militia in U. S. service 2 months
and 12 days, 1812. Ref: Book 53,
AGO Page 72.

*GILLSON, ABNER K.
Served in Capt. Morrill's Company,
Col. Fifield's Regt. Detached Militia
in U. S. service 6 months and 5
days, 1812.

*GILLSON, RIAH.
Served in Capt. Sabin's Company,
Col. Jonathan Williams' Regt. Detached Militia in U. S. service 2
months and 6 days, 1812.

‡*GILMAN, ANDREW.
Served in Capt. Walker's Company,
Col. Fifield's Regt. Detached Militia
in U. S. service 2 months and 2
days, 1812. Also served in Capt.
Simmon's Company. Pension Certificate No. 15893.

GILMAN, AVERY, Sergeant, Marshfield.
Volunteered to go to Plattsburgh,
September, 1814, and served 9 days
in Capt. James English's Company.
Ref: Book 52, AGO Pages 195 and 248.

*GILMAN, HARVEY, Lieutenant.
Appointed Ensign 31 Inf. April 30,
1813; 2 Lieutenant Jan. 31, 1814;
1 Lieutenant 20 Inf. April 21, 1814;
honorably discharged June 15, 1815.
Served with Militia stationed at
Swanton in 1812 as Ensign.

*GILMAN, JOHN.
Enlisted Feb. 20, 1813 in Capt. Jonathan Starks' Company, 11th Regt.;
on Pay Roll to May 31, 1813. Also
served in 4 Regt. (Williams') Vt.
Militia. Ref: R. & L. 1812, AGO
Page 19.

‡*GILMAN, NEHEMIAH.
Served in Capt. Walker's Company,
Col. Fifield's Regt. Detached Militia
in U. S. service 6 months and 3
days, 1812. Pension Certificate of
widow, Abigail, No. 30620.

*GILMAN, ROGER S., Musician, Calais.
Volunteered to go to Plattsburgh,
September, 1814, and served 10 days
in Capt. Gideon Wheelock's Company.

*GILMAN, THOMAS.
Served in Capt. Taylor's Company,
Col. Fifield's Regt., Detached Militia

in U. S. service 6 months, 1812.
Volunteered to go to Plattsburgh,
September, 1814, and served in company of Capt. Ebenezer Spencer, Vershire. Ref: Book 52, AGO Page 48.

GILMORE, JOHN.
Served in Capt. Phelps' Company, Col.
Wm. Williams' Regt. Detached Mili-
tia in U. S. service 5 months, 1812.
Ref: Book 53, AGO Pages 22 and 76.

*GILSON, JOHN 2nd.
Served in Capt. Wheeler's Company,
Col. Fifield's Regt. Detached Militia
in U. S. service 6 months and 4
days, 1812.

*GILSON, JOHN F.
Served in Capt. Parsons' Company,
Col. Jonathan Williams' Regt. Detached Militia in U. S. service 2
months and 13 days, 1812.

GITCHELL, PARKER G.
Volunteered to go to Plattsburgh,
September, 1814, and served 4 days
in Capt. Aaron Kidder's Company.
Ref: Book 52, AGO Page 65.

*GLADDING, JOSIAH, Drummer.
Served from April 12, 1814 to April
21, 1814 in Capt. Eseck Sprague's
Company, Sumner's Regt.

*GLADDING, RICHARD.
Served in Capt. Briggs' Company,
Col. Jonathan Williams' Regt. Detached Militia in U. S. service 2
months and 13 days, 1812.

‡GLADING, SOLOMON.
Pension Certificate of widow, Pamelia,
No. 11220; no organization given.

GLASPIE, CHARLES.
Served from May 31 to June 30, 1814
in Capt. Alexander Brooks' Corps of
Artillery. Ref: R. & L. 1812, AGO
Page 31.

*GLEASON, JONATHAN,   Brookfield.
Served in Col. Fifield's Regt. Detached Militia in U. S. service 2
months and 21 days, 1812. Volunteered to go to Plattsburgh, September, 1814, and served in company of
Capt. Frederick Griswold, raised in
Brookfield, Vt. Ref: Book 52, AGO
Pages 52 and 61.

*GLEASON, LUTHER, Sergeant.
Served in Capt. Ormsbee's Company,
Col. Martindale's Regt. Detached
Militia in U. S. service 2 months and
14 days, 1812. Served from April
20, 1813 to April 24, 1814 as Sergeant
in Capt. Simeon Wright's Company,
commanded by Capt. Daniel Farrington, 30th Regt. Ref: R. & L. 1812,
AGO Pages 50 and 51.

*GLEASON, NATHAN, (or Nathaniel)
Served in Capt. Adams' Company,
Col. Jonathan Williams' Regt. Detached Militia in U. S. service 2
months and 7 days, 1812.

GLEASON, REUBEN.
Volunteered to go to Plattsburgh,
September, 1814, and served 4 days
in Capt. James George's Company,

of Topsham. Ref: Book 52, AGO Pages 68 and 70.

‡GLEASON, SHERMAN C.
Served in Capt. Thornton's Company. Pension Certificate of widow, Rhoda, No. 24301.

GLIDDEN, JAMES.
Served from March 6 to April 6, 1813 in Lieut. Wm. S. Foster's Company, 11th Regt. Ref: R. & L. 1812, AGO Page 6.

GLIDDEN, JOSEPH,   Barre.
Volunteered to go to Plattsburgh, September, 1814, and served 9 days in Capt. Warren Ellis Company. Ref: Book 52, AGO Pages 222, 233, 242.

GLINES, ABNER.
Served from March 13 to June 12, 1813 in Capt. Samul Gordon's Company, 11th Regt. Ref: R. & L. 1812, AGO Page 8.

*GLINES, ASA,   Danville.
Served in Capt. Morrill's Company, Col. Fifield's Regt. Detached Militia in U. S. service 2 months and 18 days, 1812.

GLINES, JOHN.
Served from March 5, 1813 to June 4, 1813 in Capt. Jonathan Starks' Company, 11th Regt. Ref: R. & L. 1812, AGO Page 19.

GLINES, MARTIN.
Served from March 13 to June 12, 1813 in Capt. Samul Gordon's Company, 11th Regt. Ref: R. & L. 1812, AGO Page 8.

GLINES, SAMUEL, Corporal, Franklin County. Volunteered to go to Plattsburgh Sept. 11, 1814 and served in 15th or 22nd Regt. Ref: Hemenway's Vt. Gazetteer, Vol. 2, Page 391.

‡GLYNN, HORATIO.
Served in Capt. Foster's Company. Pension Certificate No. 5033.

GLYNN, JOHN.
Served from March 3, 1813 to June 2, 1813 in Capt. Charles Follett's Company, 11th Regt. Ref: R. & L. 1812, AGO Page 13.

GLYNN, SAMUEL A.
Enlisted March 10, 1814 during the war in company of late Capt. J. Brooks, commanded by Lieut. John I. Cromwell, Corps of U. S. Artillery; on Muster Roll from April 30, 1814 to June 30, 1814. Ref: R. & L. 1812, AGO Page 18.

GLYNN, TIMOTHY,   St. Albans.
Enlisted May 18, 1813 for 1 year in Capt. John Wires' Company, 30th Regt. Ref: R. & L. 1812, AGO Page 40.

*GODDARD, WILLIAM, Highgate or Swanton. Served in Capt. Saxe's Company, Col. Wm. Williams' Regt. Detached Militia in U. S. service 3 months and 4 days, 1812. Served in Lieut. V. R. Goodrich's Company, 11th Regt.; on Pay Roll for January and February, 1813.

*GODFREY, GEORGE JR.
Served in Capt. Cross' Company, Col. Martindale's Regt. Detached Militia in U. S. service 2 months and 14 days, 1812.

GODFREY, HENRY,   Corinth.
Volunteered to go to Plattsburgh, September, 1814, and served in Capt. Abel Jackman's Company. Ref: Book 52, AGO Page 44.

GODFREY, SAMUEL E.
Served in Capt. Samul Gordon's Company, 11th Regt.; on Pay Roll for January and February, 1813. Ref: R. & L. 1812, AGO Page 9.

GODFREY, STEPHEN.
Enlisted June 7, 1813 for 1 year and served in Capt. James Taylor's Company and Capt. Gideon Spencer's Company, 30th Regt. Ref: R. & L. 1812, AGO Pages 52, 57, 58.

‡GODFRY, MOSES.
Volunteered to go to Plattsburgh, September, 1814, and went as far as Bolton, Vt., serving 4 days in Lieut. Phineus Kimball's Company, West Fairlee. Pension Certificate No. 32568.

*GODWIN, SIMEON, Sergeant.
Served in 1 Regt. Vt. Militia commanded by Col. Judson.

GOELLET, JOSEPH.
Enlisted June 14, 1814 for 5 years in company of late Capt. J. Brooks, commanded by Lieut. John I. Cromwell, Corps of U. S. Artillery; on Muster Roll from April 30, 1814 to June 30, 1814. Ref: R. & L. 1812, AGO Page 18.

GOFF, HEZEKIAH,   South Richford.
Served from March 29, 1813 to June 29, 1813 in Capt. Samul Gordon's Company, 11th Regt. Died at Richford Feb., 1848, aged 95. Ref: R. & L. 1812, AGO Page 8.

GOFF, JONATHAN,   South Richford.
Served from March 29 to June 28, 1813 in Capt. Samul Gordon's Company, 11th Regt. Ref: R. & L. 1812, AGO Page 8. (Was a son of Hezekiah Goff, senior.)

GOFF, SETH, Musician, South Richford.
Served in company of late Capt. J. Brooks, commanded by Lieut. John I. Cromwell, Corps of U. S. Artillery; period of enlistment, May 7, 1813 to Nov. 7, 1814; on Muster Roll from April 30, 1814 to June 30, 1814. Ref: R. & L. 1812, AGO Page 18; Hemenway's' Vt. Gazetteer, Vol. 2, Page 287. (Was a son of Hezekiah Goff, senior.)

GOFF, WILLIAM,   Sheldon.
Volunteered to go to Plattsburgh, September, 1814, and served in Capt. Samuel Weed's Company. Ref: Book 51, AGO Pages 125, 152, 155.

*GOLD, REUBEN.
Served in 1 Regt. Vt. Militia commanded by Col. Martindale.

GOLDSBURY, WILLIAM,   Barre.
Volunteered to go to Plattsburgh,
September, 1814, and served in Capt.
Warren Ellis' Company. Ref: Hemen-
way's Vt. Gazetteer, Vol. 4, Page 41.

GOLDTHWAIT, JOHN, Lieutenant.
Appointed Ensign 31st Inf. March 28,
1814; 2nd Lieutenant June 23, 1814.
Ref: Governor and Council Vt., Vol.
6, Page 478.

GOMANS, JAMES.
Served in Capt. Samuel H. Holly's
Company, 11th Regt.; on Pay Roll
for January and February, 1813;
died Feb. 9, 1813. Ref: R. & L.
1812, AGO Page 25.

GONIA, JOSEPH.
Served from June 8, 1813 to Feb. 24,
1814 in Capt. Gideon Spencer's Company and Capt. James Taylor's Company, 30th Regt. Ref: R. & L. 1812,
AGO Pages 52, 57, 59.

*GOOCH, SAMUEL, Randolph or Brain-
tree. Volunteered to go to Plattsburgh, September, 1814, in Capt. Lebbeus Egerton's Company. Marched to
Plattsburgh Sept. 10, 1814 in Capt.
Lot Hudson's Company. Ref: Book
52, AGO Pages 24 and 82.

*GOOCH, THATCHER, Randolph or Brain-
tree. Volunteered to go to Plattsburgh, September, 1814, in Capt. Lebbeus Egerton's Company. Marched to
Plattsburgh Sept. 10, 1814 in Capt.
Lot Hudson's Company. Ref: Book
52, AGO Pages 24 and 82.

GOODALE, CHAUNCEY.
Volunteered to go to Plattsburgh,
September, 1814, and served 7 days
in Capt. Frederick Griswold's Com-
pany, raised in Brookfield, Vt. Ref:
Book 52, AGO Page 52.

*GOODALE, EPAPHRAS E.
Served from April 12, 1814 to May 20,
1814 in Capt. George Fisher's Company, Sumner's Regt.

GOODALE, FRANCIS C.,   Pittsford.
Volunteered to go to Plattsburgh,
September, 1814, and served 8 days
in Capt. Caleb Hendee's Company.
Ref: Book 52, AGO Page 125.

*GOODALE, AARON.
Served in 1 Regt. Vt. Militia commanded by Col. Martindale.

*GOODEL, ELISHA.
Served in Sumner's Regt. Vt. Militia.

*GOODELL, JOHN.
Served in Capt. O. Durkee's Company, Col. Fifield's Regt. Detached
Militia in U. S. service 2 months and
26 days, 1812.

GOODEN, HILLS.
Enlisted Feb. 11, 1813 in Capt. John
W. Weeks' Company, 11th Regt. Ref:
R. & L. 1812, AGO Page 4.

*GOODENOUGH, SAMUEL.
Served in Capt. Mason's Company,
Col. Fifield's Regt. Detached Militia
in U. S. service 3 months and 16
days, 1812.

*GOODENOW, ISAAC.
Served from April 12, 1814 to May
20, 1814 in company of Capt. James
Gray Jr., Sumner's Regt.

GOODHUE, JAMES, Sergeant.
Served from Jan. 1 to Feb. 10, 1813
in Capt. Samul Gordon's Company,
11th Regt.; appointed Quartermaster
Sergeant Feb. 1, 1813. Ref: R. & L.
1812, AGO Page 9.

GOODHUE, JEREMIAH,   Berlin.
Volunteered to go to Plattsburgh,
September, 1814, and served 7 days
in Capt. Cyrus Johnson's Company.
Ref: Book 52, AGO Pages 202 and 255.

GOODHUE, JOSEPH.
Appointed Garrison Surgeon's Mate
Feb. 8, 1803; Post Surgeon Aug. 5,
1816. Ref: Heitman's Historical Register & Dictionary USA.

*GOODMAN, ISAIAH.
Served in Sumner's Regt. Vt. Militia.

‡GOODNO, ASA.
Served in Capt. Smith's Company.
Pension Certificate No. 32777.

‡GOODNO, WILLIAM,   Rochester.
Volunteered to go to Plattsburgh,
September, 1814, and served 7 days
in Capt. Oliver Mason's Company.
Also served in Capt. Mann's Company.
Pension Certificate No. 32776. Ref:
Book 51, AGO Page 268.

*GOODNOUGH, CALVIN.
Served from April 12, 1814 to April
21, 1814 in Lieut. Justus Foote's
Company, Sumner's Regt.

*GOODNOUGH, JESSE.
Served from April 12, 1814 to April
21, 1814 in Capt. Shubael Wales' Company, Col. W. B. Sumner's Regt.

GOODNOUGH, LIBERTY.
Served in Capt. Charles Follett's Company, 11th Regt. from Nov. 1, 1812
to date of death Jan. 22, 1813. Ref:
R. & L. 1812, AGO Page 12.

‡*GOODNOW, ASHER.
Served from April 12, 1814 to May 20,
1814 in company of Capt. James
Gray Jr., Sumner's Regt. Also served in Capt. Hand's Company. Pension Certificate No. 28085.

*GOODNOW, ISAIAH, Corporal.
Served from Nov. 1, 1812 to Feb. 28,
1813 in Capt. Samuel H. Holly's
Company, 11th Regt. Also served in
Sumner's Regt. Vt. Militia. Died
about 1857 in Steuben County, N. Y.
Ref: R. & L. 1812, AGO Page 25;
Rev. J. F. Goodhue's History of
Shoreham, Page 101.

GOODNOW, JOSEPH, Corporal.
Enlisted in U. S. Marine Corps May
30, 1815 at New York. Ref: Book 52,
AGO Page 294.

GOODRICH, BENJAMIN B.,   Pittsford.
Served from April 28, 1813 to April
29, 1814 in Capt. Simeon Wright's
Company. Served from June 20, 1814

to June 19, 1815 in Capt. Taylor's Company, 30th Inf. Ref: R. & L. 1812, AGO Pages 23 and 51.

*GOODRICH, BETHUEL,   Middlebury. Served from April 12, 1814 to April 21, 1814 in Lieut. Justus Foote's Company, Sumner's Regt.

‡GOODRICH, CHAUNCEY. Served in Capt. Colton Ormes' Company. Pension Certificate of widow, Phebe, No. 12535.

*GOODRICH, DANIEL. Served from Oct. 11, 1813 to Oct. 16, 1813 in Capt. Roswell Hunt's Company, 3 Regt. (Tyler's).

*GOODRICH, EDMUND O., Sergeant, Fairfax or Georgia. Served from Sept. 25, 1813 to Oct. 19, 1813 in Capt. Jesse Post's Company, Col. Dixon's Regt. Served 1 month and 23 days, 1813,, in Capt. Prentiss' Company, Col. Dixon's Regt. Served in 1813 and 1814 in Capt. Joseph Beeman's Company. Ref: Hemenway's Vt. Gazetteer, Vol. 2, Page 402.

*GOODRICH, ELIZIER, Lieutenant. Served in 1 Regt. 3 Brig. 3 Div. Vt. Militia.

*GOODRICH, HENRY, Corporal Sergeant. Served in Cavalry in 1st Regt. Detached Militia of Vt. in U. S. service at Champlain 2 days commencing Nov. 18 and ending Nov. 19, 1812.

*GOODRICH, IRA. Served in Capt. Wright's' Company, Col. Martindale's Regt. Detached Militia in U. S. service 2 months and 14 days, 1812.

GOODRICH, JAMES,   Pittsfield. Volunteered to go to Plattsburgh, September, 1814, and served 7 days in Capt. Elias Keyes' Company. Ref: Book 52, AGO Page 156.

*GOODRICH, JOHN. Served in 1 Regt. Vt. Militia commanded by Col. Martindale.

GOODRICH, LEVI L.,   Sudbury. Volunteered to go to Plattsburgh, September, 1814, and served 6 days in Capt. Thomas Hall's Company. Ref: Book 52, AGO Page 122.

*GOODRICH, LUNEL. Served in 4 Regt. Vt. Militia commanded by Col. Williams.

GOODRICH, MOSES,   Middlebury. Volunteered to go to Plattsburgh, September, 1814, and served in Capt. Elias Keyes' Company. Ref: Book 51, AGO Pages 35, 52, 53.

GOODRICH, NOAH. Served in Capt. Samuel H. Holly's Company, 11th Regt.; on Pay Roll for January and February, 1813. Ref: R. & L. 1812, AGO Page 25.

*GOODRICH, OTIS. Served from April 12, 1814 to April 21, 1814 in Lieut. Justus Foote's Company, Sumner's Regt.

GOODRICH, PETER. Served in Capt. Phineas Williams' Company, 11th Regt.; on Pay Roll for January and February, 1813. Ref: R. & L. 1812, AGO Page 15.

GOODRICH, PETER, B. Served in Capt. Samul Gordon's Company, 11th Regt.; on Pay Roll of company for January and February, 1813. Ref: R. & L. 1812, AGO Page 9.

GOODRICH, VALENTINE R., Captain, Swanton. Appointed 1 Lieutenant 11th Inf. March 12, 1812; Captain June 26, 1813; killed July 25, 1814 in battle of Niagara Falls. Commanded company in 11th Regt.; on Pay Roll for January and February, 1813. Ref: Heitman's Historical Register & Dictionary USA; R. & L. 1812, AGO Page 11.

‡GOODRIDGE, IRA. Served in Capt. Morrell's Company. Pension Certificate of widow, Chloe, No. 5658.

*GOODSPEED, HOSEA,   Ira. Served in 1 Regt. Vt. Militia commanded by Col. Martindale.

GOODSPEED, LUTHER, Franklin County. Volunteered to go to Plattsburgh Sept. 11, 1814 and served in 15th or 22nd Regt. Ref: Hemenway's Vt. Gazetteer, Vol. 2, Page 391.

*GOODSPEED, ZENAS,   Pawlet. Served in Capt. Hotchkiss' Company, Col. Martindale's Regt. Detached Militia in U. S. service 2 months and 13 days, 1812.

*GOODWIN, ARON. Served from June 11, 1813 to June 14, 1813 in Capt. Moses Jewett's Company, 1st Regt. 2nd Brig. 3rd Div.

GOODWIN, DAVID, Fife Major, St. Albans. Enlisted May 20, 1813 for 1 year in Capt. John Wires' Company, 30th Regt. Ref: R. & L. 1812, AGO Page 40.

‡GOODWIN, JAMES,   Tunbridge. Served from Feb. 12, 1813 to May 11, 1813 in Capt. Jonathan Starks' Company, 11th Regt. Also served in Capt. David's Company. Pension Certificate No. 33075. Ref: R. & L. 1812, AGO Page 19. Volunteered to go to Plattsburgh, September, 1814, and served in Capt. David Knox's Company. Ref: Book 52, AGO Page 116.

GOODWIN, JOHN. Served from March 4, 1813 to June 3, 1813 in Capt. Edgerton's Company, 11th Regt. Ref: R. & L. 1812, AGO Page 3.

‡GOODWIN, LEVI B. Served in Capt. David Sandford's Company. Pension Certificate No. 2186. Pension Certificate of widow, Eunice M., No. 34396.

GOODWIN, MOSES,   Tunbridge. Volunteered to go to Plattsburgh, September, 1814, and served in Capt. David Knox's Company. Ref: Book 52, AGO Page 116.

GOODWIN, NATHAN.   Tunbridge.
Volunteered to go to Plattsburgh,
September, 1814, and served in Capt.
David Knox's Company. Ref: Book
52, AGO Page 117.

*GOODWIN, RICHARD,   Glover.
Served in Capt. Mason's Company,
Col. Fifield's Regt. Detached Militia
in U. S. service 6 months, 1812.

*GOODWIN, SIMEON, Sergeant.
Served from June 11 to June 14, 1813
and from Oct. 4 to Oct. 14, 1813 in
Capt. John Palmer's Company, 1st
Regt. 2nd Brig. 3rd Div.

*GOODWIN, THOMAS.
Served in Capt. Ormsbee's Company,
Col. Martindale's Regt. Detached
Militia in U. S. service 2 months and
14 days, 1812. Served from March
15 to June 14, 1813 in Capt. Samul
Gordon's Company, 11th Regt.

GOODWIN, WELLS.
Served in Capt. Weeks' Company,
11th Regt.; on Pay Roll for January
and February, 1813. Ref: R. & L.
1812, AGO Page 5.

*GOODYEAR, DANIEL.
Served from April 12, 1814 to April
21, 1814 in Capt. Shubael Wales' Company, Col. W. B. Sumner's Regt.

GOODYEAR, JAMES,   Cornwall.
Enlisted Dec. 22, 1813 for period of
the war in Capt. Simeon Wright's
Company. Re-enlisted and served
from Sept. 1, 1814 to June 16, 1815
in Capt. Sanford's Company, 30th
Inf. Ref: R. & L. 1812, AGO Pages
23 and 51.

‡GOOLD, FREDERICK H.
Served in Capt. Sabine's Company.
Pension Certificate No. 15016.

GOOLET, JOSEPH.
Served from January 15, 1813 to
February, 1813 in Capt. Edgerton's
Company, 11th Regt. Ref: R. & L.
1812, AGO Page 3.

*GORDON, DANIEL.
Served from April 12, 1814 to April
21, 1814 in Capt. Shubael Wales'
Company, Col. W. B. Sumner's Regt.

GORDON, FOSTER.
Enlisted March 20, 1813 in company
of Capt. John McNeil Jr., 11th Regt.;
on Pay Roll to May 31, 1813. Ref:
R. & L. 1812, AGO Page 16.

*GORDON, LEWIS,   Isle-La-Motte.
Enlisted Oct. 11, 1813 in Capt. Asahel
Langworthy's Company, Col. Isaac
Clark's Rifle Corps.

GORDON, ORRIN.
Volunteered to go to Plattsburgh,
September, 1814, and served 7 days
in Capt. Asaph Smith's Company. Ref:
Book 51, AGO Page 20.

*GORDON, ROBERT.
Served in Capt. Rogers' Company,
Col. Fifield's Regt. Detached Militia
in U. S. service 2 months and 18
days, 1812.

GORDON, SAMUEL.
Appointed Captain 11th Inf. March
12, 1812; honorably discharged June
15, 1815; on Pay Roll of his company
for January and February 1813. Ref:
Heitman's Historical Register & Dictionary USA; R. & L. 1812, AGO
Page 9.

*GORDON, WILLIAM H.
Served with Hospital Attendants, Vt.

GORHAM, DANIEL.
Served from June 11 to June 14, 1813
in Capt. John M. Eldridge's Company, 1st Regt. 2nd Brig. 3rd Div.
Ref: R. & L. 1812, AGO Page 35.

GORHAM, HUMPHREY,   St. Albans.
Enlisted April 23, 1813 for 1 year
in Capt. John Wires' Company, 30th
Regt. Ref: R. & L. 1812, AGO Page
40.

*GOSHARN, DANIEL.
Served in 1 Regt. Vt. Militia commanded by Col. Judson.

GOSS, CARVER, Corporal.
Enlisted May 5, 1813 for 1 year in
Capt. Daniel Farrington's Company
(also commanded by Capt. Simeon
Wright), 30th Regt.; on Muster Roll
from March 1, 1814 to April 30, 1814.
Ref: R. & L. 1812, AGO Pages 50
and 51.

GOSS, CHESTER, Ensign,   Brandon.
Volunteered to go to Plattsburgh,
September, 1814, and served 8 days
in Capt. Micah Brown's Company.
Ref: Book 52, AGO Pages 130, 131,
133, 134.

GOSS, MARK, Corporal,   Montpelier.
Volunteered to go to Plattsburgh,
September, 1814, and served 2 weeks
in Capt. Timothy Hubbard's Company. Ref: Book 52, AGO Pages 214
and 256.

GOTHAM, ROBERT.
Served from Jan. 22, 1813 to May 10,
1813 in Capt. John W. Weeks' Company, 11th Regt. Served from May 1
to July 30, 1814; no organization
given. Ref: R. & L. 1812, AGO
Pages 4 and 29.

‡GOTHAM, SAMUEL.
Served from Jan. 28, 1813 to May 10,
1813 in Capt. John W. Weeks' Company, 11th Regt. Pension Certificate
of widow, Susan, No. 32620.

‡GOUDY, JOHN.
Served under Captains Howe and
Pomeroy. Pension Certificate of
widow, Elizabeth, No. 8327.

GOULD, AARON,   Montpelier.
Volunteered to go to Plattsburgh,
September, 1814, and served in Capt.
Timothy Hubbard's Company. Ref:
Book 52, AGO Page 256.

GOULD, ABBOTT.
Enlisted Feb. 1, 1813 in Capt. Phineas
Williams' Company, 11th Regt.; on
Pay Roll to May 31, 1813. Ref: R.
& L. 1812, AGO Page 14.

‡*GOULD, AMOS F., Corporal.
Served in Capt. Preston's Company,
Col. Jonathan Williams' Regt. De-
tached Militia in U. S. service 2
months and 6 days, 1812. Pension
Certificate of widow, Polly, No. 14155.

GOULD, ASA.
Enlisted June 9, 1813 for 1 year in
Capt. Daniel Farrington's Company
(also commanded by Capt. Simeon
Wright) 30th Regt.; on Muster Roll
from March 1, 1814 to April 30, 1814.
Ref: R. & L. 1812, AGO Pages 50
and 51.

GOULD, DAVID,   East Montpelier.
Volunteered to go to Plattsburgh,
September, 1814, and served 4 days;
no organization given. Ref: Book 52,
AGO Page 192.

*GOULD, ELMA.
Enlisted Sept. 25, 1813 in company
of Capt. Jonathan Prentiss Jr., Dixon's Regt.

*GOULD, HILLEMAN.
Served in Capt. Sabin's Company,
Col. Jonathan Williams' Regt. Detached Militia in U. S. service 2
months and 6 days, 1812.

‡*GOULD, JAMES,   Barton.
Served in Capt. Mason's Company,
Col. Fifield's Regt. Detached Militia
in U. S. service 2 months and 10
days, 1812. Pension Certificate No.
14658.

GOULD, JAMES,   East Montpelier.
Volunteered to go to Plattsburgh,
September, 1814, and served 4 days;
no organization given. Ref: Book
52, AGO Page 192.

*GOULD, JOHN,   East Montpelier.
Enlisted Oct. 2, 1813 and served 78
days in Capt. John Weed's Company, Col. Clark's Rifle Corps.

‡*GOULD, JOSEPH.
Served in Capt. Rogers' Company,
Col. Fifield's Regt. Detached Militia
in U. S. service 5 months and 27
days, 1812. Also served in 4 Regt.
(Peck's). Pension Certificate of widow,
Susan, No. 6049.

*GOULD, NATHAN,   Barton.
Served in Capt. Mason's Company,
Col. Fifield's Regt. Detached Militia
in U. S. service 5 months and 26
days, 1812.

GOULD, NATHANIEL.
Served from Nov. 1, 1812 to Feb. 28,
1813 in Capt. Phineas Williams' Company, 11th Regt.; on Pay Roll for
January and February, 1813. Served
from March 20, 1814 to June 3, 1814
in Capt. Gideon Spencer's Company,
30th Regt.

‡*GOULD, PAGE,   Richford.
Enlisted Sept. 25, 1813 in Capt. Mar-
tin D. Folett's Company, Dixon's
Regt. Also served in Capt. Dunnin's
Company. Pension Certificate No.
25035. Pension Certificate of widow,
Sarah P., No. 30102.

GOULD, REUBEN.
Served in Capt. Hotchkiss' Company,
Col. Martindale's Regt. Detached
Militia in U. S. service 1 month and
7 days, 1812. Ref: Book 53, AGO
Page 70.

*GOULD, RUFUS.
Served in 2 Regt. Vt. Militia commanded by Col. Fifield.

GOULD, SAMUEL F.,   Clarendon.
Volunteered to go to Plattsburgh,
September, 1814, and served 7 days
in Capt. Durham Sprague's Company.
Ref: Book 52, AGO Page 128.

*GOULD, WARD.
Served in 3 Regt. Vt. Militia commanded by Col. Williams.

GOULDING, HENRY,   Franklin County.
Volunteered to go to Plattsburgh
Sept. 11, 1814 and served in 15th or
22nd Regt. Ref: Hemenway's Vt. Gazetteer, Vol. 2, Page 391.

‡GOURLEY, ABEL.
Served in Capt. E. Marks' Company.
Pension Certificate No. 6938.

GOUYD, ANTHONY.
Enlisted May 18, 1813 for 1 year and
served in Capt. James Taylor's Company and Capt. Gideon Spencer's
Company, 30th Regt. Ref: R. & L.
1812, AGO Pages 52, 57, 59.

GOUYD, JAMES.
Served from May 12, 1813 to May 12,
1814 in Capt. James Taylor's Company and Capt. Gideon Spencer's
Company, 30th Regt. Ref: R. & L.
1812, AGO Pages 52, 57, 59.

*GOUYD, JOHN.
Served in Col. Wm. Williams' Regt.
Detached Militia in U. S. service 4
months and 26 days, 1812. Served
in Capt. Simeon Wright's Company,
30th Regt., from April 26, 1813 to
March 30, 1814 when he was killed
in action. Ref: R. & L. 1812, AGO
Page 51.

GOVE, ENOS,   Strafford.
Volunteered to go to Plattsburgh,
September, 1814, and served 2 days
in Capt. Cyril Chandler's Company.
Ref: Book 52, AGO Page 42.

GOVER, DANIEL, Corporal.
Enlisted Feb. 22, 1813 for 5 years
in company of late Capt. J. Brooks,
commanded by Lieut. John I. Crom-
well, Corps of U. S. Artillery; on
Muster Roll from April 30, 1814 to
June 30, 1814. Ref: R. & L. 1812,
AGO Page 18.

*GOVERNOR, TIMOTHY.
Served in Sumner's Regt. Vt. Militia.

GOWAN, JOHN M.,   Franklin County.
Volunteered to go to Plattsburgh
Sept. 11, 1814 and served in 15th or
22nd Regt. Ref: Hemenway's Vt. Gazetteer, Vol. 2, Page 392.

GOWSLEY, ABJAH, Corporal.
Served in 1st Regt. Detached Militia
of Vt. in U. S. service at Champlain commencing Nov. 18 and ending Nov. 19, 1812.

‡GRAHAM, ALEXANDER.
Served in Capt. Duncan Taylor's Company, 4th Regt. Pension Certificate No. 24340.

GRAHAM, HARVEY, Sergeant.
Served from May 1, 1814 to June 30, 1814 in Corps of Light Dragoons. Ref: R. & L. 1812, AGO Page 20.

‡*GRAHAM, JOHN.
Served in Capt. Adams' Company, 8 Regt. (Williams') Vt. Militia. Pension Certificate No. 9318.

GRAHAM, JOHN H., Lieutenant, Burlington. Appointed Midshipman in the Navy June 18, 1812 and Lieutenant March 5, 1817; was a native of Vt.; his warrant was sent to him at Burlington. In August, 1812, he was attached to the Frigate JOHN ADAMS which was off New York. In September he Volunteered his services to Commodore Chauncey who commanded the Naval forces on the Great Lakes and repaired with others to Lake Erie; on the night of November 27, 1812 made a descent upon Canada under Lieut. Angus; was wounded in the left leg below the knee and being a compound fracture had to be amputated. January 8, 1813 was ordered by Commodore Chauncey to report to the Commandant of the New York Navy Yard as soon as convenient. July 15, 1814 ordered by the Navy Department to report to Commodore MacDonough on Lake Champlain; was attached to the SARATOGA when the action took place Sept. 11, 1814. October 25th was transferred to the Navy Yard at New York. January 25, 1815 was ordered to the Frigate UNITED STATES at New London, Conn.; remained on her until March 6, 1816. Was retired April 4, 1867 with the rank of Commodore; died March 15, 1878. Ref: Bureau of Navigation Records, Washington, D. C., Naval Records and Library, Navy Dept.

GRAIN, ELIJAH.
Served in Capt. Wheatly's Company, Col. Fifield's Regt. Detached Militia in U. S. service 2 months and 21 days, 1812. Ref: Book 53, AGO Page 28.

GRANDRICKER, MICHAEL, Franklin County. Volunteered to go to Plattsburgh Sept. 11, 1814 and served in 15th or 22nd Regt. Ref: Hemenway's Vt. Gazetteer, Vol. 2, Page 391.

GRANDU, FRANCIS.
Served from Feb. 18 to Feb. 28, 1813 and from March 6 to June 5, 1813 in Lieut. V. R. Goodrich's Company, 11th Regt. Ref: R. & L. 1812, AGO Pages 10 and 11.

GRANDU, JOSEPH.
Enlisted Feb. 18, 1813 in Lieut. V. R. Goodrich's Company, 11th Regt.; on Pay Roll from January and February, 1813 and Pay Roll to May 31, 1813. Ref: R. & L. 1812, AGO Pages 10 and 11.

*GRANDY, ASA.
Served in Capt. Daniel Farrington's Company (also commanded by Capt. Simeon Wright) 30th Regt., from June 1, 1813 to date of death April 12, 1814. Also served in 1 Regt. (Martindale's) Vt. Militia. Ref: R . & L. 1812, AGO Pages 50 and 51.

GRANDY, DAVID,   Goshen.
Volunteered to go to Plattsburgh, September, 1814 and served 5 days in Capt. Durham Sprague's Company. Ref: Book 52, AGO Page 129.

‡GRANDY, ELIJAH,   Panton.
Volunteered to go to Plattsburgh, September, 1814, and served 8 days in Capt. Moulton's Company. Also served in Capt. G. Spencer's Company. Pension Certificate of widow, Esther, No. 27982. Ref: Book 51, AGO Page 29.

‡*GRANDY, LEVI.
Served in Capt. Briggs' Company, Col. Jonathan Williams' Regt. Detached Militia in U. S. service 2 months and 13 days, 1812. Pension Certificate No. 11981.

*GRANDY, LUTHER.
Served in Sumner's Regt. Vt. Militia.

*GRANDY, ROBERT.
Served in Capt. Phelps' Company, Col. Wm. Williams' Regt. Detached Militia in U. S. service 5 months, 1812.

*GRANDY, SANFORD.
Served in Capt. Robbins' Company, Col. Wm. Williams' Regt. Detached Militia in U. S. service 4 months and 29 days, 1812.

GRANDY. SANFORD.   Pawlet.
Born in Pawlet, Vt.; aged 22 years; 5 feet 8½ inches high; dark complexion; brown hair; blue eyes; by profession a farmer. Enlisted Feb. 20, 1814 at Plattsburgh for the period of the war, in Capt. Wm. Miller's Company, 30th Regt. U. S. Inf.; discharged at Burlington, Vt., 1815. Ref: R. & L. 1812, AGO Page 55.

GRANDY. SANFORD.
Enlisted June 12, 1813 for 1 year in Capt. Daniel Farrington's Company (also commanded by Capt. Simeon Wright) 30th Regt.; on Muster Roll from March 1. 1814 to April 30, 1814. Ref: R. & L. 1812, AGO Pages 50 and 51.

GRANDY, SANFORD, Franklin County.
Volunteered to go to Plattsburgh Sept. 11, 1814 and served in 15th or 22nd Regt. Ref: Hemenway's Vt. Gazetteer, Vol. 2, Page 392.

*GRANGER, JOHN,   Randolph.
Volunteered to go to Plattsburgh, September, 1814, and served in Capt. Lebbeus Egerton's Company. Ref: Book 52, AGO Page 82.

GRANT, ASA,   Sheldon.
Volunteered to go to Plattsburgh, September, 1814 and served in Capt. Samuel Weed's Company. Ref: Book 51, AGO Pages 125, 152, 172.

*GRANT, AZARIAH.
Served in Capt. E. Walker's Company, Col. Fifield's Regt. Detached Militia in U. S. service 2 months and 26 days, 1812.

GRANT, ELIHU,   Cornwall.
Volunteered to go to Plattsburgh, September, 1814, and served in Capt. Edmund B. Hill's Company, Sumner's Regt. Ref: Rev. Lyman Mathews' History of Cornwall, Page 344.

GRANT, JOHN,   Washington.
Volunteered to go to Plattsburgh, September, 1814 and served in Capt. Amos Stiles' Company. Ref: Book 52, AGO Pages 36 and 40.

GRANT, JOHN,   Corinth.
Volunteered to go to Plattsburgh, September, 1814, and served in Capt. Abel Jackman's Company. Ref: Book 52, AGO Page 44.

*GRANT, JOHN S., Lieutenant.
Appointed 1st Lieutenant in Capt. Asahel Langworthy's Company, Col. Isaac Clark's Rifle Corps, Sept. 14, 1813. Appointed Adjutant in Col. Clark's Rifle Corps Nov. 11, 1813. Aupointed Ensign 11 Inf. April 15, 1814; 3 Lieutenant May 1, 1814; 2 Lieutenant Sept. 28, 1814; honorably discharged June 15, 1815. Ref: Heitman's Historical Register & Dictionary USA; Book 52, AGO Page 259.

*GRANT, JOSHUA.
Served with Hospital Attendants, Vt.

*GRANT, WILLIAM.
Served in 1 Regt. Vt. Militia commanded by Col. Judson.

*GRASS, WILLIAM.
Served in 4 Regt. Vt. Militia commanded by Col. Williams.

GRAVES, ABNER,   Strafford.
Volunteered to go to Plattsburgh, September, 1814, and served 5 days in Capt. Cyril Chandler's Company. Ref: Book 52, AGO Page 42.

*GRAVES, AUGUSTUS, Corporal.
Served from April 12, 1814 to April 21, 1814 in Lieut. James S. Morton's Company, Sumner's Regt.

GRAVES, BARNABAS,   Sheldon.
Volunteered to go to Plattsburgh, September, 1814, and served 6 days in Capt. Samuel Weed's Company. Ref: Book 51, AGO Pages 155 and 172.

‡GRAVES, CHASE S.
Served in Capt. Thompson's Company. Pension Certificate of widow, Lucinda, No. 5074.

GRAVES, DAVID, Sergeant, Brookfield.
Volunteered to go to Plattsburgh, September, 1814, and served 7 days in company of Capt. Frederick Griswold. Ref: Book 52, AGO Pages 52 and 56.

GRAVES, FRANCIS, Sergeant.
Served from May 1 to June 30, 1814 in Capt. Alexander Brooks' Corps of Artillery. Ref: R. & L. 1812, AGO Page 31.

‡GRAVES, HARLEY H.
Served in Capt. Talbot's Company. Pension Certificate of widow, Edith, No. 28636.

‡GRAVES, HARMON.
Served in Capt. Sperry's Company. Pension Certificate of widow, Betsey, No. 19002.

*GRAVES, HIRAM.
Served from April 12, 1814 to April 21, 1814 in Lieut. James S. Morton's Company, Col. W. B. Sumner's Regt.

GRAVES, INCREASE,   Whiting.
Served from July 9 to Dec. 8, 1812 in Capt. Robbins' Company, Col. Wm. Williams' Regt. Detached Militia in U. S. service 29 days. Ref: Book 53, AGO Page 59; Vol. 50, Vt. State Papers, Page 175.

*GRAVES, INCREASE JR.,   Bridport.
Served 6 months ending Dec. 7, 1812 in Capt. John Robbins' Company, 4 Regt (Williams').

‡*GRAVES, IRA.
Enlisted Sept. 25, 1813 and served 1 month and 23 days in Capt. Birge's Company, Col. Dixon's Regt. Pension Certificate No. 14493.

*GRAVES, JACOB,   Enosburgh.
Served from Oct. 15 to Nov. 17, 1813 in Capt. Asahel Scovell's Company, Col. Clark's Rifle Corps.

*GRAVES, JAMES,   Corinth.
Volunteered to go to Plattsburgh, September, 1814, and served in Capt. Abel Jackman's Company. Also served in Sumner's Regt. Vt. Militia. Ref: Book 52, AGO Page 44.

‡*GRAVES, JAMES A.
Served in Capt. B. Strait's Company, Col. Martindale's Regt. Detached Militia in U. S. service from Sept. 17 to Nov. 30, 1812. Pension Certificate of widow, Hermione, No. 22021.

*GRAVES, JAMES B.
Served in 4 Regt. Vt. Militia commanded by Col. Williams.

GRAVES, JOSHUA,   Salisbury.
Served from Feb. 1 to Feb. 28, 1813 in Capt. Samuel H. Holly's Company, 11th Regt.; Ref: R. & L. 1812, AGO Page 25.

‡*GRAVES, LUTHER, Fifer.
Served in Capt. Saxton's Company, Sumner's Regt. Pension Certificate No. 25549.

*GRAVES, MORRIS, Sergeant.
Served from April 12, 1814 to April 21, 1814 in Lieut. James S. Morton's Company, Sumner's Regt.

GRAVES, RUFUS.
Served in Lieut. Wm. S. Foster's Company, 11th Regt.; on Pay Roll for January and February, 1813. Ref: R. & L. 1812, AGO Page 7.

*GRAVES, SILAS.
Served in Capt. Needham's Company, Col. Martindale's Regt. Detached Militia in U. S. service 2 months and 14 days, 1812.

GRAVES, SILENTS.
Served from March 22, 1813 to June 21, 1813 in Capt. Charles Follett's Company, 11th Regt. Ref: R. & L. 1812, AGO Page 13.

*GRAY, BENJAMIN.
Served in Capt. Wheeler's Company, Col. Fifield's Regt. Detached Militia in U. S. service 6 months and 4 days, 1812.

*GRAY, DANIEL, Sergeant.
Served from April 12, 1814 to May 20, 1814 in company of Capt. James Gray Jr., Sumner's Regt.

*GRAY, ELI B.
Served in 1 Regt. Vt. Militia commanded by Col. Judson.

*GRAY, ELIJAH, Lieutenant, Charlotte.
Served in 1 Regt. Vt. Militia commanded by Col. Judson.

‡GRAY, GEORGE.
Served in Capt. Bean's Company. Pension Certificate of widow, Hannah, No. 22672.

*GRAY, ISAIAH.
Served in 4 Regt. Vt. Militia commanded by Col. Williams.

*GRAY, JAMES JR., Captain, Bridport.
Served from April 12, 1814 to May 20, 1814 in command of a company in Col. Wm. B. Sumner's Regt.

*GRAY, JOSHUA W.
Served in Capt. Sabin's Company, Col. Jonathan Williams' Regt. Detached Militia in U. S. service 2 months and 6 days, 1812.

‡GRAY, OLIVER.
Served in Capt. Ezra Strong's Company. Pension Certificate of widow, Adelia, No. 26674.

‡GRAY, PADDOCK.
Served in Capt. Straight's Company. Pension Certificate of widow, Elizabeth, No. 32609.

‡GRAY, TRUMAN.
Served in Capt. Hendee's Company. Pension Certificate of widow, Polly, No. 35348.

‡*GRAY, WILLIAM.
Served in Capt. Wheeler's Company, Col. Fifield's Regt. Detached Militia in U. S. service 3 months and 16 days, 1812. Also served in Capt. Morrell's Company. Pension Certificate No. 9372.

GREELEY, JOEL.
Enlisted Jan. 29, 1813 in Capt. Phineas Williams' Company, 11th Regt.; on Pay Roll to May 31, 1813. Ref: R. & L. 1812, AGO Pages 14 and 15.

*GREELY, ASHBEL.
Served in Capt. Wright's Company, Col. Fifield's Regt. Detached Militia in U. S. service 6 months, 1812.

GREEN, ALANSON,   Clarendon.
Volunteered to go to Plattsburgh, September, 1814, and served 7 days in Capt. Durham Sprague's Company. Ref: Book 52, AGO Page 128.

GREEN, BENJAMIN,   Rochester.
Volunteered to go to Plattsburgh, September, 1814; no organization given. Ref: Book 51, AGO Page 249.

GREEN, BENJAMIN.
Born in Munsey, Pa.; aged 26 years; 5 feet 7½ inches high; light complexion; brown hair; blue eyes; by profession a blacksmith. Enlisted at Burlington March 15, 1814 for the period of the war and served in Capt. Wm. Miller's Company and Capt. Gideon Spencer's Company, 30th Regt.; discharged at Burlington, Vt., 1815. Ref: R. & L. 1812, AGO Pages 54, 55, 57.

*GREEN, CALEB,   St. Albans.
Served in Capt. Robinson's Company, Col. Dixon's Regt. Detached Militia in U. S. service 1 month, 1813. Enlisted Oct. 30, 1813 and served 19 days in Capt. Asahel Langworthy's Company, Col. Dixon's Regt. and Col. Isaac Clark's Regt. Volunteered to go to Plattsburgh and was at the battle Sept. 11, 1814 serving in Capt. Samuel H. Farnsworth's Company. Ref: Hemenway's Vt. Gazetteer, Vol. 2, Page 434.

‡GREEN, CALVIN,   Barnard.
Enlisted May 17, 1813 in Capt. Nehemiah Noble's Company, 31st U. S. Inf. Also served in Capt. Burnap's Company. Pension Certificate of widow, Nancy, No. 13523. Ref: Wm. N. Newton's History of Barnard, Vol. 1, Page 95.

‡GREEN, CHARLES,   Bethel.
Volunteered to go to Plattsburgh, September, 1814, and served 8 days in Capt. Nehemiah Noble's Company. Pension Certificate No. 31785.

‡GREEN, CYRIL,   Williamstown.
Volunteered to go to Plattsburgh, September, 1814, and served 6 days in Capt. David Robinson's Company. Pension Certificate No. 22396.

‡*GREEN, DAVID, Corporal,   Calais?
Served in Capt. Barns' Company, Col. Wm. Williams' Regt. Detached Militia in U. S. service 5 months, 1812. Served from April 12, 1814 to April 21, 1814 as a private in Capt. Othniel Jewett's Company, Sumner's Regt. Pension Certificate No. 1247.

GREEN, EBENEZER.
Served from Nov. 1, 1812 to Feb. 28, 1813 in Capt. Samuel H. Holly's Company, 11th Regt. Ref: R. & L. 1812, AGO Page 25.

*GREEN, EDO, Corporal.
Served from Oct. 5, 1813 to Oct. 16, 1813 in Capt. Roswell Hunt's Company, 3 Regt. (Tyler's).

GREEN, EDWARD.
Served in Capt. Samuel H. Holly's Company, 11th Regt.; on Pay Roll for January and February, 1813. Ref: R. & L. 1812, AGO Page 25.

*GREEN, ELISHA P., Sergeant.
Served in Capt. Pettes' Company, Col. Wm. Williams' Regt. Detached

Militia in U. S. service 4 months and 17 days, 1812. Served from Jan. 18, 1813 to June 8, 1813 in Capt. John W. Weeks' Company, 11th Regt. Ref: R. & L. 1812, AGO Page 4.

‡*GREEN, GEORGE, Sergeant, Highgate. Served in Capt. Saxe's Company, Col. Wm. Williams' Regt. Detached Militia stationed at Swanton Falls, in U. S. service 4 months and 24 days, 1812. Served in Capt. Hotchkiss' Company, Col. Martindale's Regt. Detached Militia in U. S. service 16 days, 1812. Also served as Ensign in 1st Regt. Pension Certificate No. 3142. Pension Certificate of widow, Polly, No. 2209.

‡*GREEN, HEMANS, Sergeant, St. Albans. Served in Capt. Robinson's Company, Col. Dixon's Regt. Detached Militia in U. S. service 1 month, 1813. Served from Sept. 25, 1813 to Oct. 26, 1813 in Capt. Amos Robinson's Company, Dixon's Regt. Volunteered to go to Plattsburgh, September, 1814, and served 10 days; no organization given. Pension Certificate of widow, Nellie, No. 6724.

'GREEN, HENRY. Enlisted Oct. 8, 1813 for 5 years in company of late Capt. J. Brooks, commanded by Lieut. John I. Cromwell, Corps of U. S. Artillery; on Muster Roll from April 30, 1814 to June 30, 1814; transferred from Capt. Collins' Company. Ref: R. & L. 1812, AGO Page 18.

*GREEN, HENRY C., Corporal, Cornwall. Served from April 12, 1814 to April 21, 1814 in Capt. Edmund B. Hill's Company, Sumner's Regt. Volunteered to go to Plattsburgh, September, 1814, and was at the battle serving in same company.

‡*GREEN, HENRY G., Corporal, Enosburgh. Appointed Corporal Oct. 14, 1813 in Capt. Asahel Scoville's Company, Col. Clark's Rifle Corps; served to Nov. 17, 1813. Pension Certificate of widow, Myra, No. 10908.

*GREEN, IDO,   Richmond. Served in 6th Company, 3rd Regt. 2nd Brig. 3 months beginning September, 1812. Served in 4 Regt. (Williams') Vt. Militia. Volunteered to go to Plattsburgh, September, 1814, and served in Capt. Roswell Hunt's Company, 3rd Regt. Ref: Book 51, AGO Page 82; Vol. 50, Vt. State Papers, Page 85.

*GREEN, ISAAC F., Corporal. Served in 1 Regt. Vt. Militia commanded by Col. Judson.

'GREEN, JAMES, 2nd Lieutenant. Served in Capt. Weeks' Company, 11th Regt.; on Pay Roll for January and February, 1813. Ref: R. & L. 1812, AGO Page 5.

'GREEN, JEREMIAH,   Monkton. Volunteered to go to Plattsburgh, September, 1814, and served 4 days in Capt. R. H. Gallet's Company. Ref: Book 51, AGO Page 68.

*GREEN, JESSE JR. Served from Oct. 11, 1813 to Oct. 17, 1813 in Capt. Roswell Hunt's Company, 3 Regt. (Tyler's).

GREEN, JOHN. Served from Feb. 15, 1813 to May 14, 1813 in Capt. Edgerton's Company, 11th Regt. Ref: R. & L. 1812, AGO Pages 2 and 3.

GREEN, JOSEPH U. Enlisted March 17, 1814 during the war in Capt. Clark's Company, 30th Regt. Ref: R. & L. 1812, AGO Page 1.

GREEN, JOSEPH W.,   Hanover, N. H. Served from Sept. 1, 1814 to June 16, 1815 in Capt. Sanford's Company, 30th Inf. Ref: R. & L. 1812, AGO Page 23.

*GREEN, MILTON, Sergeant. Served in Sumner's Regt. Vt. Militia.

*GREEN, MOSES, Corporal. Enlisted Sept. 20, 1813 in Capt. John Weed's Company, Col. Clark's Rifle Corps.

*GREEN, NATHAN. Served in Capt. Preston's Company, Col. Jonathan Williams' Regt. Detached Militia in U. S. service 2 months and 6 days, 1812.

GREEN, NOEL P.,   St. Albans. Enlisted May 3, 1813 for 1 year in Capt. John Wires' Company, 30th Regt. Ref: R. & L. 1812, AGO Page 40.

‡GREEN, ORRIN,   St. Albans. Volunteered to go to Plattsburgh, September, 1814, and served 9 days; no organization given. Also served in Capt. Farnsworth's Company. Pension Certificate of widow, Phebe, No. 31115.

GREEN, SALMON, Captain, Cambridge. Volunteered to go to Plattsburgh, September, 1814, and served 8 days in command of Cambridge company. Ref: Book 51, AGO Page 207.

GREEN, SIMON, Sergeant,   Strafford. Volunteered to go to Plattsburgh, September, 1814, and served in Capt. Cyril Chandler's Company. Served as sergeant in 1st Regt. of Detached Militia of Vt. in U. S. service at Champlain beginning Nov. 18 and ending Nov. 19, 1812.

GREEN, STODDARD. Enlisted Jan. 18, 1813 in Lieut. V. R. Goodrich's Company, 11th Regt.; on Pay Roll for January and February, 1813. Ref: R. & L. 1812, AGO Page 11.

‡GREEN, THOMAS W. Pension Certificate of widow, Elizabeth, No. 7329; no organization given.

‡GREEN, TRUMAN H. Served in Capt. Phelps' Company, 3rd Regt. Pension Certificate No. 32783.

GREEN, WALLACE, Corporal.
Served in 1st Regt. of Detached Militia of Vt. in U. S. service at Champlain for 2 days commencing Nov. 18 and ending Nov. 19, 1812.

‡*GREEN, WALTER, Sergeant.
Served in Capt. Needham's Company, Col. Martindale's Regt. Detached Militia in U. S. service 2 months and 14 days, 1812. Pension Certificate of widow, Levina, No. 6059.

*GREEN, WILLIAM.
Served from June 7, 1813 to June 7, 1814 in Capt. James Taylor's Company and Capt. Gideon Spencer's Company, 30th Regt. Also served in 1 Regt. (Judson's) Vt. Militia. Ref: R. & L. 1812, AGO Pages 30, 52, 57, 59.

GREEN, WINTHROP,   Vershire.
Volunteered to go to Plattsburgh, September, 1814, and served 3 days in Capt. Ira Corse's Company. Ref: Book 52, AGO Page 91.

*GREEN, ZERAH, Corporal.
Served in Capt. Noyce's Company, Col. Jonathan Williams' Regt. Detached Militia in U. S. service 2 months and 6 days, 1812. Served from Jan. 24, 1813 to April 28, 1813 in Lieut. V. R. Goodrich's Company, 11th Regt.

GREENLEAF, JEREMIAH, Lieutenant, Guilford. Appointed Ensign 31 Inf. April 30, 1813; 3 Lieutenant Jan. 11, 1814; 2 Lieutenant May 2, 1814; honorably discharged June 15, 1815. Served in Capt. Parson's Company, Col. Jonathan Williams' Regt. Detached Militia in U. S. service 2 months and 13 days, 1812, as sergeant. Ref: Heitman's Historical Register & Dictionary USA; Book 53, AGO Page 50. (For biographical sketch see Hemenway's Vt. Gazetteer, Vol. 5, Part 2, Page 47).

GREENLIEF, WILLIAM.
Served in Capt. Benjamin Bradford's Company; on Muster Roll from May 31, 1813 to Aug. 31, 1813. Ref: R. & L. 1812, AGO Page 26.

*GREER, AMOS F.
Served in Corning's Vt. Militia.

GREGG, DANIEL, 1st Lieutenant.
Served in Capt. Benjamin Bradford's Company; on Muster Roll from May 31, 1813 to Aug. 31, 1813. Ref: R. & L. 1812, AGO Page 26.

GREGG, ENOS.
Served from May 1 to June 30, 1814 as a ship carpenter in Alexander Parris' Company of Artificers. Ref: R. & L. 1812, AGO Page 24.

‡*GREGG, JOHN.
Served in Corning's Detachment, Vt. Militia. Served as a musician in 4 Regt. (Peck's) Vt. Militia. Served in Capt. Stephen Jones' Company. Pension Certificate of widow, Joanna, No. 29881.

*GREGG, JOSEPH.
Served in 4 Regt. Vt. Militia commanded by Col. Peck.

*GREGG, LESLIE, Corporal.
Serving in Corning's Detachment Vt. Militia and in 4 Regt. ((Peck's) Vt. Militia.

GREGORY, ALEX T.
Served from March 22, 1813 to June 21, 1813 in Lieut. V. R. Goodrich's Company, 11th Regt. Ref: R. & L. 1812, AGO Page 10.

GREGORY, LEVI,   St. Albans.
Enlisted May 10, 1813 for 1 year in Capt. John Wires' Company, 30th Regt. Ref: R. & L. 1812, AGO Page 40.

GREGORY, PHILANDER,   St. Albans.
Enlisted May 21, 1813 for 1 year in Capt. John Wires' Company, 30th Regt. Ref: R. & L. 1812, AGO Page 40.

*GREGORY, SAMUEL.
Served in Capt. Taylor's Company, Col. Wm. Williams' Regt. Detached Militia in U. S. service 4 months and 24 days, 1812.

*GRENELL, HEMAN.
Served from April 12, 1814 to April 21, 1814 in Capt. Eseck Sprague's Company, Sumner's Regt.

*GRENELL, REUBEN.
Served from April 12, 1814 to April 21, 1814 in Capt. Eseck Sprague's Company, Sumner's Regt.

GREY, DAVID,   Montpelier.
Volunteered to go to Plattsburgh, September, 1814, and served 8 days in Capt. Timothy Hubbard's Company. Ref: Book 52, AGO Page 256.

GREY, JOHN,   Franklin County.
Volunteered to go to Plattsburgh Sept. 11, 1814 and served in 15th or 22nd Regt. Ref: Hemenway's Vt. Gazetteer, Vol. 2, Page 392.

*GRIFFIN, DANIEL,   Richmond.
Served in 6th Company, 3rd Regt. 2nd Brig. commanded by Brig. Gen. Newell, for 3 months beginning September, 1812. Served in 4 Regt. (Williams') Vt. Militia. Served from Jan. 6, 1813 to June 6, 1813 in Capt. Edgerton's Company, 11th Regt. Ref: Vol. 50, Vt. State Papers, Page 85; R. & L. 1812, AGO Pages 2 and 3.

*GRIFFIN, ERASTUS.
Served in 3 Regt. Vt. Militia commanded by Col. Tyler.

*GRIFFIN, ISAAC.
Served in Capt. Burnap's Company, Col. Jonathan Williams' Regt. Detached Militia in U. S. service 2 months and 13 days, 1812.

GRIFFIN, JAMES.
Served from Jan. 2, 1813 to July 6, 1813 in Capt. Edgerton's Company, 11th Regt. Ref: R. & L. 1812, AGO Pages 2 and 3.

GRIFFIN, JOHN.
Served from April 22, 1813 to April 28, 1814 in Capt. James Taylor's Company and Capt. Gideon Spencer's Company, 30th Regt. Ref: R. & L. 1812, AGO Pages 52, 57, 58.

*GRIFFIN, JASPER (or Josper) Sergeant.
Served in 3 Regt. (Tyler's) Vt. Militia.

GRIFFIN, MILTON,   Sudbury.
Volunteered to go to Plattsburgh, September, 1814, and served 6 days in Capt. Thomas Hall's Company. Ref: Book 52, AGO Page 122.

GRIFFIN, RICHARD.
Served from Jan. 2, 1813 to July 6, 1813 in Capt. Benjamin S. Edgerton's Company, 11th Regt. Ref: R. & L. 1812, AGO Pages 2 and 3.

*GRIFFIN, SAMUEL.
Served in 3 Regt. Vt. Militia commanded by Col. Tyler.

*GRIFFIN, THOMAS M., Corporal.
Served in Capt. Taylor's Company, 4 Regt. (Williams') Detached Militia in U. S. service 4 months and 24 days, 1812. Served from April 22, 1813 to April 25, 1814 in Capt. James Taylor's Company and Capt. Gideon Spencer's Company, 30th Regt. Ref: R. & L. 1812, AGO Pages 52, 56, 58.

*GRIGGS, EPHRAIM.
Served in Capt. Briggs' Company, Col. Jonathan Williams' Regt. Detached Militia in U. S. service 1 month and 15 days, 1812.

GRIM, ISAAC.
Enlisted July 27, 1813 for 5 years in company of late Capt. J. Brooks commanded by Lieut. John I. Cromwell, Corps of U. S. Artillery; on Muster Roll from April 30, 1814 to June 30, 1814. Ref: R. & L. 1812, AGO Page 18.

GRIMES, ASA, Lieutenant.
Appointed 1st Lieutenant 31st Inf. April 30, 1813 (probably did not accept). Ref: Governor and Council Vt., Vol. 6, Page 478.

GRIMES, JAMES J.
Served in Capt. Benjamin S. Edgerton's Company, 11th Regt.; on Pay Roll for September and October, 1812 and January and February 1813. Ref: R. & L. 1812, AGO Pages 1 and 2.

*GRINOLD, ABRAM.
Served in Capt. Needham's Company, Col. Martindale's Regt. Detached Militia in U. S. service 2 months and 14 days, 1812.

*GRISWOLD, ABEL,   Enosburgh.
Served from Oct. 15 to Nov. 17, 1813 in Capt. Asahel Scovell's Company, Col. Clark's Rifle Corps.

*GRISWOLD, ANSON, Orwell or Enosburgh. Served from Oct. 15, to Nov. 17, 1813 in Capt. Asahel Scovell's Company, Col. Clark's Rifle Corps. Volunteered to go to Platts-burgh, September, 1814, and served 11 days in Capt. Wait Branch's Company. Ref: Book 51, AGO Page 16.

GRISWOLD, ASAPH,   Waltham.
Volunteered to go to Plattsburgh, September, 1814, and was in the battle, serving 10 days in Capt. Gideon Spencer's Company. Ref: Book 51, AGO Pages 2 and 4.

‡*GRISWOLD, ASAPH,   Orwell.
Served in Capt. Ormsbee's Company, Col. Martindale's Regt. Detached Militia in U. S. service 2 months and 15 days, 1812. Served from Oct. 15, 1813 to Nov. 17, 1813 in Capt. Asahel Scoville's Company, Col. Clark's Rifle Corps. Volunteered to go to Plattsburgh, September, 1814, and served 11 days in Capt. Wait Branch's Company. Pension Certificate of widow, Lodema, No. 16709.

‡*GRISWOLD, BENJAMIN.
Enlisted Sept. 25, 1813 and served 1 month and 23 days in Capt. Waterman's Company, Col. Dixon's Regt. Pension Certificate No. 14204.

GRISWOLD, BENJAMIN JR.
Served in Capt. Chadwick's Company. Ref: R. & L. 1812, AGO Page 32.

*GRISWOLD, COTTON.
Served in Capt. E. Walker's Company, Col. Fifield's Regt. Detached Militia in U. S. service 6 months and 3 days, 1812.

GRISWOLD, DANIEL, Lieutenant.
Appointed Ensign 30 Inf. April 30, 1813; 3 Lieutenant March 5, 1814; honorably discharged June 15, 1815. Served in Capt. Taylor's Company, Col. Wm. Williams' Regt. Detached Militia in U. S. service 4 months and 24 days, 1812. Ref: Heitman's Historical Register & Dictionary USA.

‡GRISWOLD, DAVID E.
Served in Capt. Jewett's Company. Pension Certificate of widow, Ann No. 29339.

GRISWOLD, FREDERICK, Captain, Brookfield. Volunteered to go to Plattsburgh, September, 1814, and commanded company from Brookfield, Vt. Ref: Book 52, AGO Pages 52, 56, 121.

GRISWOLD, HENRY.
Served in Capt. Scovell's Company, Col. Martindale's Regt. Detached Militia in U. S. service 2 months and 14 days, 1812. Ref: Book 53, AGO Page 100.

*GRISWOLD, ISAAC, Drummer.
Enlisted Sept. 25, 1813 and served 1 month and 23 days in Capt. Thomas Waterman's Company, Col. Dixon's Regt.

*GRISWOLD, JOHN.
Served in Capt. Waterman's Company, Col. Dixon's Regt. Detached Militia in U. S. service 1 month and 6 days, 1813.

GRISWOLD, JOHN JR.
Enlisted Sept. 25, 1813 in Capt. Thomas Waterman's Company, Dixon's Regt. Ref: Book 52, AGO Page 291.

‡*GRISWOLD, NATHAN, Corporal.
Served in Sumner's Regt. Vt. Militia.
Also served in Capt. Munson's Company. Pension Certificate No. 8871.

*GRISWOLD, ROBERT.
Served in Capt. Eldridge's Company, Col. Dixon's Regt. Detached Militia in U. S. service 1 month and 23 days, 1813. Enlisted Oct. 26, 1813 in Capt. Asahel Langworthy's Company, Col. Isaac Clark's Regt.

*GRISWOLD, SAMUEL.
Enlisted Sept. 25, 1813 in Capt. Thomas Waterman's Company, Dixon's Regt.

GRISWOLD, SAMUEL, JR., Orwell.
Volunteered to go to Plattsburgh, September, 1814, and served 11 days in Capt. Wait Branch's Company. Ref: Book 51, AGO Page 16.

*GRISWOLD, VINCENT.
Served from April 12, 1814 to April 21, 1814 in Lieut. Justus Foote's Company, Sumner's Regt.

*GRISWOLD, EBER.
Served from April 12, 1814 to April 15, 1814 in Lieut. Justus Foote's Company, Sumner's Regt.

GRISWOULD, ELISHA.
Served from Feb. 20, 1813 to May 19, 1813 in Capt. Charles Follett's Company, 11th Regt. Ref: R. & L. 1812, AGO Page 13.

‡GRONSBECK, NICHOLAS.
Served in Captain Bryant's Company. Pension Certificate No. 31334.

GROSSE, SAMUEL.
Served from May 1 to Aug. 11, 1814 in Capt. Morgan's Company. Rifle Regt. Ref: R. & L. 1812, AGO Pages 29 and 30.

*GROSSE, WILLIAM.
Served from Nov. 1 to Dec. 8, 1812 in Capt. George W. Kindall's Company, 4 Regt. (Williams'); also appears on Muster Roll from Aug. 31 to Oct. 31, 1812.

*GROSVENEUR, DAVID, Corporal.
Served from April 12, 1814 to April 21, 1814 in Capt. Shubael Wales' Company, Col. W. B. Sumner's Regt.

‡GROSVENOR, DANIEL.
Served in Capt. Josiah Grout's Company. Pension Certificate of widow, Frances, No. 28309.

‡*GROSVENOR, ROYALL.
Served in Capt. Wilson's Company, 4 Regt. (Williams') Vt. Militia. Pension Certificate No. 15165. Pension Certificate of widow, Maheteble, No. 18932.

GROUT, BRIDGMAN, Corporal, St. Albans. Enlisted June 1, 1813 in Capt. John Wires' Company, 30th Regt. Volunteered to go to Plattsburgh, September, 1814, and served 8 days as a corporal in Capt. Salmon Green's Company. Ref: R. & L. 1812, AGO Page 40; Book 51, AGO Page 207.

*GROUT, DANIEL.
Served in Capt. Adams' Company, Col. Jonathan Williams' Regt. Detached Militia in U. S. service 2 months and 7 days, 1812.

*GROUT, ELHANAH.
Served in Capt. Adams' Company, Col. Jonathan Williams' Regt. Detached Militia in U. S. service 2 months and 7 days, 1812.

*GROUT, ELIHU, Cornwall.
Served from April 12, 1814 to April 21, 1814 in Capt. Edmund B. Hill's Company, Sumner's Regt.; volunteered to go to Plattsburgh, September, 1814, and served in same company.

*GROUT, ENOS.
Served in Capt. Taylor's Company, Col. Wm. Williams' Regt. Detached Militia in U. S. service 4 months and 24 days, 1812. Enlisted Sept. 25, 1813 as a corporal in Capt. Thomas Waterman's Company, Dixon's Regt. Also served in Capt. Chadwick's Company, 2 Regt. Ref: R. & L. 1812, AGO Page 32.

*GROUT, JOSIAH, 2nd Major, Fairfax.
Appointed Major in Consolidated Regt. of Vt. Militia in U. S. service Sept. 25, 1813. Volunteered to go to Plattsburgh, September, 1814, and served as captain of a company in service at Plattsburgh.

‡GROVER, BERIAH.
Pension Certificate of widow, Ruth Anna,, No. 332; no organization given.

*GROVER, DAVID, Corporal.
Served from April 13, 1814 to April 16, 1814 in Capt. Salmon Foster's Company, Sumner's Regt.

*GROVER, EDMOND, Sergeant.
Served in Artillery of Detached Militia of Vt. in U. S. service at Champlain commencing Nov. 18 and ending Nov. 19, 1812. Also served in Capt. Hopkins' Company, Col. Martindale's Regt. Detached Militia in U. S. service 2 months and 13 days, 1812.

*GROVER, ELIJAH.
Served in Capt. Noyes' Company, Col. Jonathan Williams' Regt. Detached Militia in U. S. service 2 months and 6 days, 1812.

*GROVER, HENNING.
Served from April 12, 1814 to April 21, 1814 in Capt. Shubael Wales' Company, Col. W. B. Sumner's Regt.

‡GROVER, JOSEPH.
Enlisted Sept. 20, 1813 in Capt. John Weed's Company, Col. Clark's Rifle Corps. Pension Certificate No. 23656.

*GROVER, KENY.
Served from April 13, 1814 to April 21, 1814 in Capt. Salmon Foster's Company, Sumner's Regt.

*GROVER, ZERA.
Served in 1 Regt. Vt. Militia commanded by Col. Martindale.

GROW, ASA, Tunbridge.
Volunteered to go to Plattsburgh,
September, 1814, and served in Capt.
David Knox's Company. Ref: Book
52, AGO Page 117.

GROW, EDWARD, Tunbridge.
Volunteered to go to Plattsburgh,
September, 1814, and served in Capt.
David Knox's Company. Ref: Book
52, AGO Page 116.

GROW, IRA, Tunbridge.
Volunteered to go to Plattsburgh,
September, 1814, and served in Capt.
David Knox's Company. Ref: Book
52, AGO Pages 116 and 117.

‡GROW, JONATHAN.
Served in Capt. Knox's Company.
Pension Certificate of widow, Patty,
No. 25882.

GRUNENDIKE, ABRAHAM.
Served from May 1 to June 30, 1814
in Capt. Haig's Corps of Light Dragoons. Ref: R. & L. 1812, AGO
Page 20.

*GUBTAIL (Guptil), HUMPHREY, Water-
bury. Volunteered to go to Plattsburgh, September, 1814, and was at
the battle, serving 11 days in Capt.
George Atkins' Company, 4 Regt.
(Peck's). (For biographical sketch
see Theo. G. Lewis' History of Waterbury, Page 46).

‡GUBTAIL (or Guptil?) JOHN.
Served from March 26, 1813 to June
25, 1813 in Capt. Phineas Williams'
Company, 11th Regt. Also served in
Lieut. Corning's Company. Pension
Certificate No. 16137. Ref: R. & L.
1812, AGO Page 14.

*GUBTAIL (Guptil) NATHANIEL, Water-
bury. Volunteered to go to Plattsburgh, September, 1814, and was in
the battle, serving 11 days in Capt.
George Atkins' Company, 4 Regt.
(Peck's). (For biographical sketch
see Theo. G. Lewis' History of Waterbury, Page 46).

GUIFORD, NOAH.
Served in Capt. Hotchkiss' Company.
Col. Martindale's Regt. Detached
Militia in U. S. service 2 months and
13 days, 1812. Ref: Book 53, AGO
Page 25.

GUIGAS, JOHN A.
Served from March 1 to June 30,
1814 in Capt. Alexander Brooks' Corps
of Artillery. Ref: R. & L. 1812, AGO
Page 31.

*GUILD, RUFUS, Coventry.
Served in Capt. Mason's Company,
Col. Fifield's Regt. Detached Militia
in U. S. service 5 months and 28
days, 1812.

GUILFORD, JOHN.
Served in Capt. Chadwick's Company.
Ref: R. & L. 1812, AGO Page 32.

*GUILFORD, JOSHUA.
Served from June 11, 1813 to June
14, 1813 in Capt. Moses Jewett's Company, 1st Regt. 2nd Brig. 3rd Div.

GUINN, RICHARD.
Served from March 1 to June 30, 1814
in Capt. Alexander Brooks' Corps of
Artillery. Ref: R. & L. 1812, AGO
Page 31.

GUN, CHESTER.
Enlisted Aug. 26, 1813 for 1 year in
Capt. Daniel Farrington's Company,
30th Regt.; on Muster Roll from
March 1, 1814 to April 30, 1814; re-
enlisted and transferred. Ref: R. &
L. 1812, AGO Pages 50 and 51.

GUSHAWAY, GEORGE, Franklin County.
Volunteered to go to Plattsburgh,
Sept. 11, 1814 and served in 15th or
22nd Regt. Ref: Hemenway's Vt.
Gazetteer, Vol. 2, Page 392.

*GUSTIN, SEBRA.
Served in Capt. Wright's Company,
Col. Fifield's Regt. Detached Militia
in U. S. service 2 months and 21
days, 1812.

HABER, PETER.
Enlisted Feb. 21, 1814 for period of
the war and served in Capt. Wm.
Miller's Company and Capt. Gideon
Spencer's Company, 30th Regt. Ref:
R. & L. 1812, AGO Pages 54 and 57.

HACKET, WALLOR.
Enlisted April 29, 1813 for 1 year
in Capt. James Taylor's Company.
30th Regt. Ref: R. & L. 1812, AGO
Page 58.

‡HACKETT, EBENEZER, Tunbridge.
Volunteered to go to Plattsburgh,
September, 1814, and served in Capt.
Ephraim Hackett's Company 4 days.
Pension Certificate of widow, Sally,
No. 25357.

HACKETT, EPHRAIM, Captain, Tunbridge. Volunteered to go to Plattsburgh, September, 1814, and served
4 days in command of Tunbridge
company. Ref: Book 52, AGO Page
71.

*HACKETT, JOHN, Captain.
Served from April 12, 1814 to April
15, 1814 in command of a company
in Col. Wm. B. Sumner's Regt.

HACKETT, JONATHAN.
Served in Capt. Benjamin Bradford's
Company; on Muster Roll from May
31, 1813 to Aug. 31, 1813; joined by
transfer July 22, 1813. Ref: R. & L.
1812, AGO Page 26.

HACKETT, JOSEPH.
Served from Feb. 24, 1813 to May
23, 1813 in company of Capt. John
McNeil Jr., 11th Regt. Ref: R. & L.
1812, AGO Page 16.

HACKETT, JOSIAH, Franklin County.
Volunteered to go to Plattsburgh
Sept. 11, 1814 and served in 15th or
22nd Regt.; Ref: Hemenway's Vt.
Gazetteer, Vol. 2, Page 392.

‡HACKETT, TRUE W., Strafford.
Volunteered to go to Plattsburgh,
September, 1814, and served 5 days
in Capt. Cyril Chandler's Company.

Also served in Capt. Dickerson's Company. Pension Certificate of widow, Adah, No. 1036.

HADDEN, WILLIAM.
Enlisted Nov. 21, 1812 for 5 years in company of late Capt. J. Brooks, commanded by Lieut. John I. Cromwell, Corps of U. S. Artillery; on Muster Roll from April 30, 1814 to June 30, 1814. Ref: R. & L. 1812, AGO Page 18.

*HADLEY, JAMES.
Served from June 11, 1813 to June 14, 1813 in Capt. Hezekiah Barns' Company, 1st Regt. 2nd Brig. 3rd Div.

*HADLEY, JOHN.
Served from June 11, 1813 to June 14, 1813 in Capt. Samuel Blinn's Company, 1st Regt.

*HADLOCK, LEVI.
Served in Capt. Morrill's Company, Col. Fifield's Regt. Detached Militia in U. S. service 6 months and 5 days, 1812.

HAFF, JAMES, Sudbury.
Volunteered to go to Plattsburgh, September, 1814, and served 6 days in Capt. Thomas Hall's Company. Ref: Book 52, AGO Pages 122 and 123.

HAFF, LAURENCE, Sudbury.
Volunteered to go to Plattsburgh, September, 1814, and served 6 days in Capt. Thomas Hall's Company. Ref: Book 52, AGO Page 122.

*HAGAR, THOMAS.
Served from April 12, 1814 to April 21, 1814 in Capt. Edmund B. Hill's Company, Sumner's Regt.

HAGER, AMOS, Marshfield.
Volunteered to go to Plattsburgh, September, 1814, and served 10 days in Capt. James English's Company. Ref: Book 52, AGO Pages 176 and and 248.

‡HAGER, JONAS, St. Albans.
Enlisted May 5, 1813 for 1 year in Capt. John Wires' Company, 30th Regt. Also served in Capt. Sanford's Company. Pension Certificate No. 19505. Ref: R. & L. 1812, AGO Page 40.

HAGER, REUBEN, Marshfield.
Volunteered to go to Plattsburgh, September, 1814, and served 10 days in Capt. James English's Company. Ref: Book 52, AGO Pages 176 and 248.

‡*HAGGET, JOHN.
Served in Capt. Adams' Company, Col. Jonathan Williams' Regt. Detached Militia in U. S. service 2 months and 6 days, 1812. Pension Certificate of widow, Rebecca, No. 27848.

HAIG, GEORGE, Captain.
Served in command of Corps of Light Dragoons; on Pay Roll to June 30, 1814. Ref: R. & L. 1812, AGO Page 20.

HAIGHT, DANIEL.
Enlisted April 22, 1813 for 1 year in Capt. James Taylor's Company, 30th Regt.; on Muster Roll Nov. 30, 1813 to Dec. 31, 1813. Ref: R. & L. 1812, AGO Page 52.

HAIL, WILLIAM F., Lieutenant.
Appointed Ensign 11 Inf. May 27, 1812; 2 Lieutenant March 13, 1813; 1 Lieutenant Aug. 15, 1813; transferred to 6 Inf. May 17, 1815. Served in Capt. Samuel H. Holly's Company, 11th Regt.; on Pay Roll for January and February, 1813. Ref: Heitman's Historical Register & Dictionary USA; R. & L. 1812, AGO Page 25.

HAINES, JOHN. St. Albans.
Volunteered to go to Plattsburgh Sept. 11, 1814 and served in 15th or 22nd Regt. or in Capt. Samuel H. Farnsworth's Company. Ref: Hemenway's Vt. Gazetteer, Vol. 2, Pages 392 and 434.

‡*HAINS, NATHANIEL C.
Enlisted Sept. 25, 1813 and served 1 month and 23 days in Capt. Amos Robinson's Company, Col. Dixon's Regt. Also served in Capt. Gillman's Company. Pension Certificate No. 22234.

*HALE, ALANSON N.
Served in Capt. Wright's Company, Col. Martindale's Regt. Detached Militia in U. S. service 2 months and 14 days, 1812.

*HALE, BENJAMIN, Enosburgh.
Served from Oct. 15, 1813 to November, 1813 in Capt. Asahel Scovell's Company, Col. Clark's Rifle Corps.

HALE, CALVIN, Montpelier.
Volunteered to go to Plattsburgh, September, 1814, and served 8 days in Capt. Timothy Hubbard's Company. Ref: Book 52, AGO Page 256.

HALE, DANIEL.
Enlisted May 9, 1813 for 1 year and served in Capt. Gideon Spencer's Company and Capt. James Taylor's Company, 30th Regt.; discharged May 10, 1814. Ref: R. & L. 1812, AGO Pages 52, 57, 59.

‡HALE, DAVID.
Served in Capt. Taylor's Company. Pension Certificate No. 8672.

*HALE, ELISHA.
Enlisted Sept. 25, 1813 and served 1 month and 23 days in Capt. Jesse Post's Company, Col. Dixon's Regt.

HALE, H., Franklin County.
Volunteered to go to Plattsburgh Sept. 11, 1814 and served in 15th or 22nd Regt.; Ref: Hemenway's Vt. Gazetteer, Vol. 2, Page 391.

HALE, HARRY.
Served in Capt. Wright's Company, Col. Martindale's Regt. Detached Militia in U. S. service 1 month and 16 days, 1812. Ref: Book 53, AGO Page 39.

196   ROSTER WAR 1812-14

HALE, HORACE, Lieutenant.
Appointed 1 Lieutenant 11 Inf.
March 12, 1812; Captain Aug. 15,
1813. Killed Sept. 17, 1814 in action at Fort Erie U. C. On Pay Roll
of Capt. Benj. S. Edgertons' Company, 11th Regt., for January and
February, 1813. Ref: Heitman's Historical Register & Dictionary USA;
R. & L. 1812, AGO Page 2.

HALE, IRA,   Barre?
Enlisted May 23, 1813 for 1 year in
Capt. Daniel Farrington's Company
(also commanded by Capt. Simeon
Wright), 30th Regt.; on Muster Roll
from March 1, 1814 to April 30, 1814.
Ref: R. & L. 1812, AGO Pages 50
and 51.

*HALE, JAMES.
Served in Capt. Robbins' Company,
Col. Wm. Williams' Regt. Detached
Militia in U. S. service 4 months and
29 days, 1812. Served from April 12,
1814 to April 21, 1814 in Capt. Othniel
Jewett's Company, Sumner's Regt.
Volunteered to go to Plattsburgh,
September, 1814, and served 9 days
in Capt. Warren Ellis' Company. Ref:
Book 52, AGO Pages 223 and 242.

HALE, JAMES,   Franklin County.
Volunteered to go to Plattsburgh
Sept. 11, 1814 and served in 15th or
22nd Regt. Ref: Hemenway's Vt.
Gazetteer, Vol. 2, Page 391.

*HALE, LEVI, Corporal.
Served in Capt. Brown's Company,
Col. Martindale's Regt. Detached
Militia in U. S. service 2 months and
13 days, 1812.

*HALE, NATHAN.
Served in 1 Regt. Vt. Militia commanded by Col. Martindale.

HALE, PHILIP.
Served in Capt. L. Robinson's Company, Col. Dixon's Regt. Detached
Militia in U. S. service 2 months,
1813. Ref: Book 53, AGO Page 108.

‡HALE, SAMUEL.
Enlisted Sept. 25, 1813 and served 1
month and 23 days in Capt. Martin
D. Follett's Company, Col. Dixon's
Regt. Pension Certificate No. 5464.

HALE, WILLIAM,   Franklin County.
Volunteered to go to Plattsburgh
Sept. 11, 1814 and served in 15th or
22nd Regt. Ref: Hemenway's Vt.
Gazetteer, Vol. 2, Page 392.

*HALE, WILLIAM S., Corporal, Pittsford. Served from June 20, 1814 to
June 19, 1815 in Capt. Taylor's Company, 30th Inf. Also served in 1
Regt. Vt. Militia commanded by Col.
Martindale. Ref: R. & L. 1812, AGO
Page 23.

*HALEY, REUBEN.
Served in Capt. Taylor's Company,
Col. Fifield's Regt. Detached Militia
in U. S. service 2 months and 21
days, 1812.

HALL, ABNER,   Tunbridge.
Volunteered to go to Plattsburgh,
September, 1814, and served 4 days
in Capt. Ephraim Hackett's Company.
Ref: Book 52, AGO Page 71.

HALL, ALBARO,   Franklin County.
Volunteered to go to Plattsburgh
Sept. 11, 1814 and served in 15th or
22nd Regt. Ref: Hemenway's Vt.
Gazetteer, Vol. 2, Page 392.

HALL, ALVAH.
Enlisted Oct. 27, 1812 for 5 years in
Capt. White Youngs' Company, 15th
Regt.; on Muster Roll from Aug. 31,
1814 to Dec. 31, 1814. Ref: R. & L.
1812, AGO Page 27.

HALL, AMASON,   Sudbury.
Volunteered to go to Plattsburgh,
September, 1814, and served 6 days
in Capt. Thomas Hall's Company.
Ref: Book 52, AGO Page 122.

HALL, ANTIPAS D.
Served in Capt. Benjamin S. Edgerton's Company, 11th Regt.; on Pay
Roll for September and October, 1812.
Ref: R. & L. 1812, AGO Page 1.

*HALL, ALPHEUS.
Served in Dixon's Regt. Vt. Militia.

*HALL, BENJAMIN,   Tunbridge.
Served in Capt. H. Mason's Company, Col. Fifield's Regt. Detached
Militia in U. S. service 2 months and
21 days, 1812. Served in company
of Capt. John McNeil Jr., 11th Regt.;
on Pay Roll for January and February, 1813. Volunteered to go to
Plattsburgh, September, 1814, and
served in Capt. David Knox's Company. Ref: Book 52, AGO Page 117;
R. & L. 1812, AGO Page 17.

HALL, BURGESS,   Shelburne.
Volunteered to go to Plattsburgh,
September, 1814, and served in Major
Luman Judson's command. Ref:
Book 51, AGO Page 78.

*HALL, CHANDLER.
Served in Capt. Preston's Company,
Col. Jonathan Williams' Regt. Detached Militia in U. S. service 2
months and 6 days, 1812.

*HALL, DANIEL.
Served in 1st Regt. (Martindale's)
Vt. Militia. Was captured by troops
Sept. 17, 1814 at Fort Erie; discharged Nov. 8, 1814. Ref: Records of
Naval Records and Library, Navy
Dept.

*HALL, DAVID, Corporal.
Enlisted Feb. 1, 1813 for 5 years in
company of late Capt. J. Brooks commanded by Lieut. John I. Cromwell, Corps of U. S. Artillery; on
Muster Roll of company from April
30, 1814 to June 30, 1814; promoted
from private May 1, 1814. Also served in Sumner's Regt. Vt. Militia.
Ref: R. & L. 1812, AGO Page 18.

*HALL, EDMOND, Corporal.
Served in Sumner's Regt. Vt. Militia.

*HALL, EDWARD,   Randolph.
Volunteered to go to Plattsburgh,
September, 1814, and served in Capt.
Lebbeus Egerton's Company.

*HALL, FRANKLIN,   Tunbridge.
Served in Capt. Dodge's Company,
Col. Fifield's Regt. Detached Militia
in U. S. service 2 months and 21
days, 1812. Volunteered to go to
Plattsburgh, September, 1814, and
served in Capt. David Knox's Company.

*HALL, HAMILTON.
Served from April 12, 1814 to April
21, 1814 in Capt. Othniel Jewett's
Company, Sumner's Regt.

*HALL, HARRY, Lieutenant.
Appointed Lieutenant Sept. 25, 1813
in Capt. Elijah W. Wood's Company,
Dixon's Regt.

HALL, HENRY.
Served from Feb. 27, 1813 to May
26, 1813 in Capt. John W. Weeks'
Company, 11th Regt. Ref: R. & L.
1812, AGO Page 4.

*HALL, HILAND.
Served from April 12, 1814 to April
21, 1814 in Capt. Eseck Sprague's
Company, Sumner's Regt.

HALL, JAMES,   Orwell.
Volunteered to go to Plattsburgh,
September, 1814, and served 11 days
in Capt. Wait Branch's Company.
Ref: Book 51, AGO Page 16.

*HALL, JOEL.
Served in Sumner's Regt. Vt. Militia.

*HALL, JOHN,   IRA.
Served in Capt. Lowry's Company,
Col. Wm. Williams' Regt. Detached
Militia in U. S. service 4 months and
26 days, 1812. Served in Capt. Ben-
jamin S. Edgerton's Company, 11th
Regt.; on Pay Roll for September
and October, 1812 and January and
February, 1813. Volunteered to go
to Plattsburgh, September, 1814, and
served 4 days in Capt. Matthew An-
derson's Company. Also served in
Sumner's Regt. Vt. Militia. Ref:
Book 53, AGO Page 82; Book 52, AGO
Page 144; R. & L. 1812, AGO Pages
1 and 2.

*HALL, JOSEPH JR.,   Richmond.
Served from Oct. 5, 1813 to Oct. 16,
1813 in Capt. Roswell Hunt's Company, 3 Regt. (Tyler's). Volunteered to go to Plattsburgh, September,
1814, and served 9 days in same
company.

*HALL, JOTHUM H.
Served from Oct. 12, 1813 to Oct. 17,
1813 in Capt. Stephen Brown's Company, 3 Regt. (Tyler's).

‡*HALL, MARTIN, Corporal.
Served in Capt. Preston's Company,
Col. Jonathan Williams' Regt. De-
tached Militia in U. S. service 2
months and 6 days, 1812. Pension
Certificate No. 7806.

HALL, MOSES,   Tunbridge.
Volunteered to go to Plattsburgh,
September, 1814, and served in Capt.
David Knox's Company. Ref: Book
52, AGO Page 116.

HALL, MOSES.
Served in Capt. Benjamin S. Edger-
ton's Company, 11th Regt.; on Pay
Roll for September and October, 1812,
and January and February, 1813. Ref:
R. & L. 1812, AGO Pages 1 and 2.

‡HALL, NATHAN.
Served in Capt. Brown's Company,
Col. Martindale's Regt. Detached
Militia in U. S. service 2 months and
14 days, 1812. Pension Certificate of
widow, Abigail, No. 1622.

*HALL, NATHAN.
Served in Capt. H. Mason's Company, Col. Fifield's Regt. Detached
Militia in U. S. service 5 months
and 29 days, 1812.

HALL, NATHAN,   Sudbury.
Volunteered to go to Plattsburgh,
September, 1814, and served 6 days
in Capt. Thomas Hall's Company.
Ref: Book 52, AGO Page 122.

HALL, NATHANIEL.
Served from Feb. 23, 1813 to May 22,
1813 in Capt. Charles Follett's Company, 11th Regt. Ref: R. & L. 1812,
AGO Page 13.

HALL, OBEDEDAM.
Served in Capt. Benjamin S. Edger-
ton's Company, 11th Regt.; on Pay
Roll for September and October, 1812
and January and February, 1813;
was at battle of Chrystler's Farm
Nov. 11, 1813 and reported missing
after the battle. Ref: R. & L. 1812,
AGO Pages 1 and 2; Governor and
Council, Vt., Vol. 6, Page 490.

HALL, ORRA.   St. Albans.
Volunteered and was at the action
at Plattsburgh Sept. 11, 1814 serving
in Capt. Samuel H. Farnsworth's
Company. Ref: Hemenway's Vt. Gazetteer, Vol. 2, Page 434.

‡*HALL, PHILIP, Corporal.
Served in Capt. Robinson's Company,
Dixon's Regt. Pension Certificate of
widow, Achsah, No. 1768.

*HALL, REUBIN.
Served from Oct. 5, 1813 to Oct. 17,
1813 in Capt. Stephen Brown's Company, 3 Regt. (Tyler's).

‡*HALL, SAMUEL,   Richford.
Served in Capt. Needham's Company,
Col. Martindale's Regt. Detached
Militia in U. S. service 2 months and
14 days, 1812. Served from March 29,
1813 to July 3, 1813 in Lieut. Wm.
S. Foster's Company, 11th Regt. En-
listed Sept. 25, 1813 in Capt. Elijah
W. Wood's Company, Dixon's Regt.
Served in Capt. Martin D. Folett's
Company, Col. Dixon's Regt. on duty
on Canadian Frontier in 1813. Pen-
sion Certificate No. 22374. Pension
Certificate of widow, Louisa, No.
34843.

HALL, SETH, Lieutenant.
Appointed 2 Lieutenant 26 Inf. April
21, 1814; honorably discharged June
15, 1815. Ref: Heitman's Historical
Register & Dictionary USA.

HALL, SEWEL.
Enlisted April 29, 1813 for 1 year in
Capt. Simeon Wright's Company. Ref:
R. & L. 1812, AGO Page 51.

‡*HALL, THOMAS.   Fairfield.
Served in Capt. Kindall's Company,
Col. Wm. Williams' Regt. Detached
Militia in U. S. service 4 months and
23 days, 1812. Pension Certificate of
widow, Rosanna, No. 1085.

HALL, THOMAS, Captain,   Sudbury.
Commanded a company of Plattsburgh
Volunteers from Sudbury, September,
1814. Commissioned Captain by Gov-
ernor Jonas Galusha Jan. 1, 1813.
Ref: Book 52, AGO Pages 122 and 123.

HALL, THOMAS,   Poultney.
Enlisted March 19, 1814 for period
of the war in Capt. Clark's Company, 30th Regt. Served from Sept.
1, 1814 to June 16, 1815 in Capt.
Sanford's Company, 30th Inf. Ref:
R. & L. 1812, AGO Pages 1 and 23.

*HALL, TIMOTHY, Musician.
Served as drummer in Capt. Richardson's Company, Col. Martindale's
Regt. Detached Militia in U. S. service in 1812.

*HALL, WELCOME.
Served in Capt. Preston's Company,
Col. Jonathan Williams' Regt. Detached Militia in U. S. service 2
months and 6 days, 1812.

HALL, WILLIAM S.
Served in Capt. Brown's Company,
Col. Martindale's Regt. Detached
Militia in U. S. service 2 months and
14 days, 1812. Ref: Book 53, AGO
Page 56.

*HALLADAY, THEODORE, 1st Lieuten-
ant. Shoreham. Volunteered to go to
Plattsburgh, September, 1814. and
served 7 days in Capt. Samuel Hand's
Company. Also served as 2nd Lieutenant in Sumner's Regt. Vt. Militia.
Ref: Book 51, AGO Page 63.

*HALLOCK, AMOS.
Served in 3 Regt. (Tyler's) Vt. Militia.

*HALLOCK, ANSON.   Richmond.
Served from Oct. 12, 1813 to Oct. 16,
1813 in Capt. Roswell Hunt's Company, 3 Regt. Volunteered to go to
Plattsburgh, September, 1814, and
served 9 days in same company. Also
served in Corning's Detachment, Vt.
Militia. Ref: R. & L. 1812, AGO
Page 41; Book 51, AGO Page 82.

*HALLOCK, ISAAC.
Served from Oct. 5, 1813 to Oct. 16,
1813 in Capt. Roswell Hunt's Company, 3 Regt. (Tyler's).

HALLOCK, JOHN.
Served from April 28, 1813 to June
3, 1814 in Capt. James Taylor's Company and Capt. Gideon Spencer's
Company, 30th Regt. Ref: R. & L.
1812, AGO Pages 52, 57, 59.

HALLOCK, JOSEPH D.,   St. Albans.
Enlisted April 29, 1813 for 1 year in
Capt. John Wires' Company, 30th
Regt. Ref: R. & L. 1812, AGO
Page 40.

*HALLOCK, STEPHEN JR.
Served from Oct. 12, 1813 to Oct. 16,
1813 in Capt. Roswell Hunt's Company, 3 Regt. (Tyler's). Ref: R. &
L. 1812, AGO Page 41.

HALLOWAY, THEODORE, Lieutenant.
Served from April 12, 1814 to April
21, 1814 as 2nd Lieutenant in Lieut.
Justus Foote's Company, Sumner's
Regt. Ref: Book 52, AGO Page 285.

HALSEY, HENRY,   Shoreham.
Volunteered to go to Plattsburgh,
September, 1814, and served 6 days
in Capt. Samuel Hand's Company.
Ref: Rev. J. F. Goodhue's History
of Shoreham, Page 108.

*HAM, EPHRAIM,   Stowe.
Volunteered to go to Plattsburgh,
September, 1814, and was at the
battle, serving in Capt. Nehemiah
Perkins' Company, 4 Regt. (Peck's).

HAM, JOSEPH.
Enlisted Jan. 30, 1813 in Capt. Jonathan Starks' Company 11th Regt.;
on Pay Roll to May 31, 1813. Ref:
R. & L. 1812, AGO Page 19.

HAMBLIN, BARNABAS.
Served from May 14. 1813 to May
14, 1814 in Capt. James Taylor's Company and Capt. Gideon Spencer's
Company, 30th Regt. Ref: R. & L.
1812, AGO Pages 52, 57, 58.

*HAMBLIN, ELEAZER.
Served with Hospital Attendants, Vt.

HAMBLIN, ENOS,   Cornwall.
Volunteered to go to Plattsburgh,
September, 1814, and was at the
battle, serving in Capt. Edmund B.
Hill's Company, Sumner's Regt. Ref:
Book 51, AGO Page 13.

*HAMBLIN, IRA.
Served from April 12, 1814 to April
21, 1814 in Capt. Edmund B. Hill's
Company, Sumner's Regt.

HAMBLIN, JAMES, Corporal. Brookfield.
Volunteered to go to Plattsburgh,
September, 1814. and served 7 days
in Capt. Frederick Griswold's Company. Ref: Book 52, AGO Pages 52
and 56.

*HAMBLIN, JOHN.
Served from April 12, 1814 to April
21, 1814 in Capt. Edmund B. Hill's
Company, Sumner's Regt.

*HAMBLIN, JOSEPH.
Served in 3 Regt .(Tyler's) Vt. Militia.

HAMDEN, OLIVER.
Served in Capt. Dorrance's Company,
Col. Wm. Williams' Regt. Detached
Militia in U. S. service 4 months and
29 days, 1812. Ref: Book 53, AGO
Page 59.

HAMES, JOHN.
Enlisted April 8, 1814 for period of the war in Capt. Gideon Spencer's Company, 30th Regt.; mustered for discharge at Burlington June 3, 1814. (This man was a negro). Ref: R. & L. 1812, AGO Page 57.

*HAMET, BENJAMIN.
Served in Capt. Wheatley's Company, Col. Fifield's Regt. Detached Militia in U. S. service 6 months, 1812.

*HAMILTON, ALEXANDER.
Served in Capt. Start's Company, Col. Martindale's Regt. Detached Militia in U. S. service 21 days, 1812.

*HAMILTON, BELA.
Served from June 11, 1813 to June 14, 1813 in Capt. Thomas Dorwin's Company, 1st Regt. 2nd Brig. 3rd Div. Also served in 4 Regt. (Williams') Vt. Militia.

*HAMILTON, DANIEL.
Served in 1 Regt. Vt. Militia commanded by Col. Martindale.

*HAMILTON, DAVID, Sergeant.
Served in 3 Regt. Vt. Militia commanded by Col. Tyler.

*HAMILTON, EBER, Corporal.
Served in Tyler's Regt. Vt. Militia.

*HAMILTON, GEORGE.
Served in Corning's Detachment, Vt. Militia. Served in 4 Regt. (Peck's) Vt. Militia.

HAMILTON, HUGH,   Shepardstown.
Served from May 1, 1814 to Aug. 11, 1814 in Capt. Morgan's Company, Rifle Regt. Ref: R. & L. 1812, AGO Page 30.

‡HAMILTON, JAMES.
Served in Capt. Johnson's Company. Pension Certificate No. 12297.

HAMILTON, JAMES, Captain.
Served from July 1 to July 31, 1814 on General Staff of the Northern Army commanded by Maj. Gen. George Izard. Ref: R. & L. 1812, AGO Page 28.

HAMILTON, JOHN, Sergeant, Bridport.
Served from May 4, 1813 to May 5, 1813 in Capt. Simeon Wright's Company. Served from April 12, 1814 to May 20, 1814 as sergeant in company of Capt. James Gray Jr., Sumner's Regt. Ref: R. & L. 1812, AGO Page 51; Book 52, AGO Page 279.

*HAMILTON, JOSEPH.
Served in 4 Regt. Vt. Militia commanded by Col. Peck.

HAMILTON, PETER.
Served in company of Capt. John McNeil Jr., 11th Regt.; on Pay Roll for January and February, 1813. Ref: R. & L. 1812, AGO Page 17.

HAMILTON, ROBERT, Sergeant. Franklin County. Volunteered to go to Plattsburgh Sept. 11, 1814 and served in 15th or 22nd Regt. Ref: Hemenway's Vt. Gazetteer, Vol. 2, Page 391.

*HAMILTON, SETH.
Served from April 12, 1814 to May 20, 1814 in company of Capt. James Gray Jr., Sumner's Regt.

*HAMILTON, STEWART.
Served in 4 Regt. (Peck's) Vt. Militia.

‡*HAMILTON, STODDARD.
Served in Capt. Sinclair's Company. Also served in Tyler's Regt. Vt. Militia. Pension Certificate of widow, Mary, No. 28323.

*HAMILTON, WILLIAM, Lieutenant, Cornwall. Served as 1 Lieutenant in 1st Regt. (Martindale's) Vt. Militia in U. S. service at Champlain from Nov. 18 to Nov. 19, 1812. Served from April 12 to April 21, 1814 as 2 Lieutenant in Capt. Edmund B. Hill's Company, Sumner's Regt.; volunteered to go to Plattsburgh, September, 1814, and was at the battle, serving as 1st Lieutenant in same company.

‡HAMILTON, WILLIAM,   Sudbury.
Volunteered to go to Plattsburgh, September, 1814 and served 6 days in Capt. Thomas Hall's Company. Pension Certificate of widow, Zeriah, No. 6738.

*HAMLIN, DANIEL (or Hamblin, Daniel Jr.), Sergeant. Served in Capt. Robbins' Company, Col. Wm. Williams' Regt. Detached Militia in U. S. service 3 months.

HAMLIN, EZRA.
Served in Capt. Samuel H. Holly's Company, 11th Regt.; on Pay Roll for January and February, 1813. Ref: R. & L. 1812, AGO Page 25.

*HAMLIN, HIRAM.
Served from April 12, 1814 to May 20, 1814 in company of Capt. James Gray, Jr., Sumner's Regt.

*HAMLIN, ISAAC B.
Served from April 12, 1814 to May 20, 1814 in Company of Capt. James Gray Jr., Sumner's Regt.

HAMLIN, JAMES.
Volunteered to go to Plattsburgh, September, 1814, and served in company of Capt. Joel Barnes of Chelsea. Ref: Book 52, AGO Page 77.

*HAMLIN, JOEL, Sergeant, Brookfield.
Served in Capt. Wright's Company, Col. Fifield's Regt. Detached Militia in U. S. service 6 months, 1812. Volunteered to go to Plattsburgh, September, 1814, and served 7 days as a Sergeant in company of Capt. Frederick Griswold of Brookfield.

HAMLIN, JOEL,   Jay.
Served from May 1, 1814 to July 7, 1814 in Capt. Spencer's Company, 29th Inf. Ref: R. & L. 1812, AGO Page 30.

HAMLIN, LEVI,   Willsboro.
Served from May 1, 1814 to June 25, 1814 in Lieut. Hanson's Company, 29th Inf. Ref: R. & L. 1812, AGO Page 30.

*HAMLIN, LORIN Sergeant,   Pawlet.
Served in Capt. Hotchkiss' Company.
Col. Martindale's Regt. Detached
Militia in U. S. service 2 months
and 13 days, 1812. Also served in
1st Regt. of Detached Militia of Vt.
in U. S. service at Champlain from
Nov. 18 to Nov. 19, 1812.

*HAMLIN, NATHANIEL, Quartermaster.
Served in 1st Regt. of Detached Mili-
tia of Vermont in U. S. service at
Champlain Nov. 18 to Nov. 19, 1812.

HAMMETT, MICHAEL,   Montpelier.
Volunteered to go to Plattsburgh,
September, 1814, and served 8 days
in Capt. Timothy Hubbard's Company. Ref: Book 52, AGO Page 256.

*HAMMOND, CONSIDER, Sergeant.
Served in Capt. Pettes' Company, Col.
Wm. Williams' Regt. stationed at
Swanton Falls in 1812.

HAMMOND, EDWARD.
Served from March 12 to June 30,
1814 in Regt. of Light Dragoons. Ref:
R. & L. 1812, AGO Page 21.

*HAMMOND, ELISHA.
Served in Capt. Morrill's Company,
Col. Fifield's Regt. Detached Militia
in U. S. service 4 months and 27
days, 1812. Served from Feb. 11,
1813 to May 10, 1813 in Capt. Samul
Gordon's Company, 11th Regt.

HAMMOND, GERMAN,   Pittsford.
Volunteered to go to Plattsburgh,
September, 1814, and served 8 days
as a waggoner in Capt. Caleb Hen-
dee's Company. Ref: Book 52, AGO
Page 125.

‡*HAMMOND, IRA.
Served in Capt. S. Pettes' Company,
Col. Wm. Williams' Regt. Detached
Militia in U. S. service 4 months and
17 days, 1812. Pension Certificate
No. 17864.

*HAMMOND, JAMES.
Served in Corning's Detachment, Vt.
Militia.

*HAMMOND, JEDEDIAH.
Served in Capt. Sabin's Company,
Col. Jonathan Williams' Regt. Detached Militia in U. S. service 2
months and 6 days, 1812.

HAMMOND, SIMEON,   Westminster.
Served from July 29, 1814 to June
19, 1815 in Capt. Taylor's Company,
30th Inf. Ref: R. & L. 1812, AGO
Page 23.

*HAMMOND, THOMAS D., Sergeant.
Served in 1st Regt. of Detached Militia of Vt. in the service of the U. S.
at Champlain from Nov. 18 to Nov.
19, 1812. Also served in Capt. Needham's Company, Col. Martindale's
Regt. Detached Militia in U. S. service 2 months and 14 days, 1812.

HAMMOND, TIMOTHY,   Coventry.
Served in Capt. Hiram Mason's Company, Col. Fifield's Regt. as a substitute for Nathaniel Cobb at Derby
in 1812. Ref: Vol. 51, Vt. State
Papers, Page 24.

HAMNOR, GEORGE,   Franklin County.
Volunteered to go to Plattsburgh
Sept. 11, 1814 and served in 15th or
22nd Regt. Ref: Hemenway's Vt.
Gazetteer, Vol. 2, Page 391.

*HAMPTON, DANIEL.
Served in Sumner's Regt. Vt. Militia.

*HANCHETT, JOHN P.
Served from April 12, 1814 to April
21, 1814 in Capt. Othniel Jewett's
Company, Sumner's Regt.

*HANCOCK, AMASA,   Pawlet.
Served in Capt. Hopkins' Company,
Col. Martindale's Regt. Detached
Militia in U. S. service 1 month and
19 days, 1812.

HANCOCK, JOSEPH, Musician, Montpelier. Volunteered to go to Plattsburgh, September, 1814, and served
8 days in Capt. Timothy Hubbard's
Company. Ref: Book 52, AGO Pages
246 and 256.

HAND, ANSON.
Volunteered to go to Plattsburgh,
September, 1814, and served 7 days
in company of Capt. Frederick Griswold of Brookfield. Ref: Book 51,
AGO Page 299; Book 52, AGO Pages
52 and 121.

HAND, SAMUEL, Captain,   Shoreham.
Volunteered to go to Plattsburgh,
September, 1814, and served 6 days
in command of company of Infantry.
Ref: Rev. J. F. Goodhue's History
of Shoreham, Page 107.

*HANDFORD, SHUBEL.
Served in Sumner's Regt. Vt. Militia.

*HANDY, DAVID.
Served in 1 Regt. Vt. Militia commanded by Col. Judson.

*HANDY, JOSEPH.
Served with Hospital Attendants, Vt.

HANKINGS, ROBERT.
Enlisted Nov. 1, 1812 in Capt. Weeks'
Company, 11th Regt.; on Pay Roll
for January and February, 1813. Ref:
R. & L. 1812, AGO Page 5.

HANKINS, GILBERT, Sergeant, Knoxville.
Served from May 1, 1813 to July 3,
1814 in Capt. Hopkins' Company,
Light Dragoons. Ref: R. & L. 1812,
AGO Page 30.

*HANKS, ANSEL,   Addison.
Served from April 12, 1814 to May
20, 1814 in Capt. George Fisher's Company, Sumner's Regt. Volunteered to
go to Plattsburgh, September, 1814,
and served 9 days in same company;
was at the battle.

HANKS, JARVIS, Musician,   Pawlet.
Served from March 31, 1813 to June
30, 1813 in Capt. Samul Gordon's
Company, 11th Regt. Ref: R. & L.
1812, AGO Page 8.

HANKS, ORIN,   Thetford.
Marched for Plattsburgh, September,
1814, and went as far as Bolton, Vt.,
serving 6 days in Capt. Salmon Howard's Company, 2nd Regt. Ref: Book
52, AGO Pages 15 and 16.

HANNA, JAMES,   Franklin County.
Volunteered to go to Plattsburgh
Sept. 11, 1814 and served in 15th or
22nd Regt. Ref: Hemenway's Vt.
Gazetteer, Vol. 2, Page 391.

HANNAFORD, DAVID.
Enlisted April 24, 1813 for 5 years
in company of late Capt. J. Brooks,
commanded by Lieut. John I. Crom-
well, Corps of U. S. Artillery; on
Muster Roll from April 30, 1814 to
June 30, 1814. Ref: R. & L. 1812,
AGO Page 18.

HANNAN, NATHANIEL, Franklin County. Volunteered to go to Plattsburgh Sept. 11, 1814 and served in
15th or 22nd Regt. Ref: Hemenway's Vt. Gazetteer, Vol. 2, Page
392.

‡HANNIBAL, WALDO.
Served in Capt. George Atkins' Company. Pension Certificate No. 31559.

*HANSEL, THOMAS.
Served in Capt. Sabins' Company, Col.
Jonathan Williams' Regt. Detached
Militia in U. S. service 2 months and
6 days, 1812.

*HANSINGER, BENJAMIN. Sergeant.
Served in 4 Regt. (Williams') Vt.
Militia.

HANSON, EBENEZER.
Volunteered to go to Plattsburgh,
September, 1814, and served 7 days
in company of Capt. Frederick Gris-
wold of Brookfield. Ref: Book 52,
AGO Page 52.

*HANSON, ISAAC,   Calais.
Volunteered to go to Plattsburgh,
September, 1814, and served 10 days
in Capt. Gideon Wheelock's Company.

*HAPGOOD, CHARLES, Sergeant.
Served in Capt. Taylor's Company,
Col. Wm. Williams' Regt. Detached
Militia in U. S. service 4 months and
24 days, 1812. Served from April 22,
1813 to April 25, 1814 in Capt. James
Taylor's Company and Capt. Gideon
Spencer's Company, 30th Regt. Ref:
R. & L. 1812, AGO Pages 52, 56, 58.

*HAPGOOD, ELMORE.
Enlisted Sept. 25, 1813 and served
1 month and 23 days in Capt. Elijah
Birge's Company, Col. Dixon's Regt.

HAPGOOD, LEVI, Sheldon or Berkshire.
Volunteered to go to Plattsburgh,
September, 1814, and served 7 days
in Capt. Samuel Weed's Company.
Ref: Book 51, AGO Pages 125, 152,
172.

‡HARADEN, BENJAMIN.
Served in Capt. Burnap's Company.
Pension Certificate No. 10624.

*HARD, ERASTUS.
Served in Sumner's Regt. Vt. Militia.

HARD, ORESTES,   Shoreham.
Volunteered to go to Plattsburgh,
September, 1814, and served 6 days
in Capt. Samuel Hand's Company.

Ref: Rev. J. F. Goodhue's History
of Shoreham, Page 108.

*HARDERSON, NATHANIEL.
Served with Hospital Attendants, Vt.

HARDING, RANSOM.
Served from April 30, 1813 to May 1,
1814 in Capt. Daniel Farrington's
Company (also commanded by Capt.
Simeon Wright) 30th Regt. Ref: R.
& L. 1812, AGO Pages 50 and 51.

*HARDY, DAVID W.
Served in Capt. Sabin's Company,
Col. Jonathan Williams' Regt. Detached Militia in U. S. service 2
months and 6 days, 1812.

HARDY, EPHRAIM,   Sudbury.
Volunteered to go to Plattsburgh,
September, 1814, and served 6 days
in Capt. Thomas Hall's Company.
Ref: Book 52, AGO Page 122.

*HARDY (or Harding) ELISHA.
Served in Capt. Lowry's Company,
Col. Wm. Williams' Regt. Detached
Militia in U. S. service 4 months
and 26 days, 1812.

HARDY, ELISHA.
Served in Capt. Phineas Williams'
Company, 11th Regt.; on Pay Roll
for January and February, 1813. Ref:
R. & L. 1812, AGO Page 15.

‡*HARDY, TRUMAN.
Served from April 17, 1814 to April
21, 1814 in Capt. Othniel Jewett's
Company, Sumner's Regt. Also served in Capt. Saxton's Company (Sumner's Regt.). Pension Certificate of
widow, Elizabeth, No. 26588.

*HAREN, JEDEDIAH, Drummer.
Served in 4 Regt. Vt. Militia commanded by Col. Williams. .

HARFORD, SHUBAEL.
Served from April 12, 1814 to April
21, 1814 in Capt. Eseck Sprague's
Company, Sumner's Regt. Ref: Book
52, AGO Page 263.

HARGRAVE, JAMES,   Franklin County.
Volunteered to go to Plattsburgh
Sept. 11, 1814 and served in 15th or
22nd Regt. Ref: Hemenway's Vt.
Gazetteer, Vol. 2, Page 392.

*HARIS, NATHANIEL.
Served in Dixon's Regt. Vt. Militia.

HARKINS, CHESTER.
Served from April 12, 1814 to April
21, 1814 in Capt. Othniel Jewett's
Company, Sumner's Regt. Ref: Book
52, AGO Page 264.

*HARLBUT, HARRY, Sergeant.
Served in Tyler's Regt. Vt. Militia.

*HARLOW, WILLIAM.
Served with Hospital Attendants, Vt.

HARMAN, JESSE.
Enlisted April 1, 1812 for 5 years
in Capt. White Youngs' Company,
15th Regt.; on Muster Roll from Aug.
31, 1814 to Dec. 31, 1814. Ref: R.
& L. 1812, AGO Page 27.

*HARMON, BENJAMIN JR.
Enlisted Sept. 20, 1813 in Capt. John
Weed's Company, Col. Clark's Rifle
Corps.

*HARMON, GAD.
Enlisted Sept. 25, 1813 and served
1 month and 23 days in Capt. Elijah
Birge's Company, Col. Dixon's Regt.

HARMON, REUBEN.
Served in Capt. Barns' Company, Col.
Wm. Williams' Regt. Detached Mili-
tia in U. S. service 5 months, 1812.
Ref: Book 53, AGO Page 9.

*HARNDEN, OLIVER,   Shoreham.
Volunteered to go to Plattsburgh,
September, 1814, and served 6 days
in Capt. Nathaniel North's Company
of Cavalry. Also served in 4 Regt.
(Williams') Vt. Militia. Ref: Rev.
J. F. Goodhue's History of Shore-
ham, Page 107.

HARNDON, JOHN.
Served from May 1st to June 30,
1814 in company of Artificers commanded by Alexander Parris. Ref:
R. & L. 1812, AGO Page 24.

*HARNISTAN, JAMES.
Served in 1 Regt. Vt. Militia commanded by Col. Martindale.

*HARNS, THOMAS.
Served in 1 Regt. Vt. Militia commanded by Col. Martindale.

HARNY, ROGER,   Highgate.
Served from Sept. 1, 1812 in Capt.
Conrade Saxe's Company, Col. Wm.
Williams' Regt. Ref: Hemenway's
Vt. Gazetteer, Vol. 2, Page 420.

HARPER, CHARLEY,   Franklin County.
Volunteered to go to Plattsburgh
Sept. 11, 1814 and served in 15th or
22nd Regt. Ref: Hemenway's Vt.
Gazetteer. Vol. 2. Page 391.

HARRINGTON, AMI,   Cornwall.
Enlisted May 1, 1813 for 1 year in
Capt. Simeon Wright's Company.
Volunteered to go to Plattsburgh,
September, 1814, and was at the
battle, serving in Capt. Edmund B.
Hill's Company, Sumner's Regt. Ref:
R. & L. 1812, AGO Page 51; Book
51, AGO Page 13.

‡*HARRINGTON, ASA.
Served in Capt. Mason's Company,
Col. Fifield's Regt. Detached Militia
in U. S. service 6 months. 1812. Pen-
sion Certificate of widow, Lucretia,
No. 15888.

*HARRINGTON, DAVID.   Middlesex.
Served in Capt. Holden Putnam's
Company, 4 Regt. (Peck's) Vt. Mili-
tia.

*HARRINGTON, EDWARD F.
Served in 1 Regt. Vt. Militia commanded by Col. Judson.

HARRINGTON, IRA,   Cornwall.
Volunteered to go to Plattsburgh,
September, 1814, and was at the
battle, serving in Capt. Edmund B.
Hill's Company, Sumner's Regt. Ref:
Book 51, AGO Page 13.

*HARRINGTON, ISAAC R.
Served in 1 Regt. Vt. Militia commanded by Col. Judson.

*HARRINGTON, JAMES.
Served in 1 Regt. Vt. Militia commanded by Col. Martindale.

‡*HARRINGTON, JOB, Corporal.
Served in Capt. Strait's Company,
Col. Martindale's Regt. Detached
Militia in U. S. service 2 months
and 13 days, 1812. Pension Certifi-
cate of widow, Mary M., No. 7077.

*HARRINGTON, JOEL,   Cornwall.
Enlisted May 1, 1813 and served 1
month and 16 days in Capt. Simeon
Wright's Company, Col. Martindale's
Regt. Volunteered to go to Platts-
burgh, September, 1814, and was at
the battle, serving in Capt. Edmund
B. Hill's Company, Sumner's Regt.
Ref: Book 51, AGO Page 13.

*HARRINGTON, JOHN.
Served with Hospital Attendants, Vt.

*HARRINGTON, JONATHAN.
Served in Capt. Needham's Company,
Col. Martindale's Regt. Detached
Militia in U. S. service 2 months
and 14 days, 1812.

HARRINGTON, JOSHUA,   Clarendon.
Volunteered to go to Plattsburgh,
September, 1814, and served 4 days
in Capt. Durham Sprague's Company,
as a teamster. Ref: Book 52, AGO
Page 128.

*HARRINGTON, LEVI B.,   Corporal,
Shoreham. Served from April 12,
1814 to May 20, 1814 in Capt. George
Fisher's Company, Sumner's Regt.
Volunteered to go to Plattsburgh,
September, 1814, and served 6 days
in Capt. Samuel Hand's Company.
Ref: Rev. J. F. Goodhue's History
of Shoreham, Page 107.

HARRINGTON, NAHUM.
Served in Capt. Bingham's Company,
Col. Jonathan Williams' Regt. Detached Militia in U. S. service 2
months and 9 days, 1812. Ref: Book
53. AGO Page 19.

HARRINGTON, TIMOTHY. Ticonderoga.
Served from Oct. 31, 1814 to June
19, 1815 in Capt. Taylor's Company,
30th Inf. Ref: R. & L. 1812, AGO
Page 23.

‡HARRINGTON, WILLIAM.
Enlisted Sept. 20, 1813 in Capt. John
Wood's Company. Also served in
Capt. Thomas Hall's Company. Pen-
sion Certificate No. 28754.

*HARRINGTON, WINSLOW.
Served in Capt. O. Lowry's Company,
Col. Wm. Williams' Regt. Detached
Militia in U. S. service 4 months
and 26 days, 1812.

*HARRIS, ASA.
Served from April 12, 1814 to April
21, 1814 in Capt. Edmund B. Hill's
Company, Sumner's Regt.

HARRIS, DANIEL.   Barre.
Volunteered to go to Plattsburgh,
September, 1814, and served 10 days
in Capt. Warren Ellis' Company.
Ref: Book 52, AGO Page 242.

*HARRIS, DANIEL, Fifer,   Barre.
Volunteered to go to Plattsburgh
and was at the battle Sept. 11, 1814
serving in Capt. David Robinson's
Company 8 days. Also served in 2
Regt. (Fifield's) Vt. Militia. Ref:
Book 52, AGO Pages 2, 8, 10.

*HARRIS. DANIEL.
Served in Corning's Detachment, Vt.
Militia.

HARRIS. DARIUS.
Enlisted March 27, 1814 for duration
of the war in Capt. Gideon Spencer's
Company, 30th Regt.; on Muster Roll
from Dec. 30, 1813 to June 30, 1814;
joined June 30, 1814. Ref: R. & L.
1812, AGO Page 56.

HARRIS, DAVID.
Served in Capt. Wheeler's Company,
Col. Fifield's Regt. Detached Militia
in U. S. service 2 months and 26 days,
1812. Ref: Book 53, AGO Page 7.

‡*HARRIS, EBENEZER.
Served in Capt. Barns' Company. Col.
Wm. Williams' Regt. Detached Militia in U. S. service 4 months and
27 days. 1812. Also served in Capt.
Mansfield's Company. Pension Certificate of widow, Eunice, No. 29085.

HARRIS, ELISHA.
Enlisted June 5, 1813 for 1 year in
Capt. Simeon Wright's Company. Ref:
R. & L. 1812, AGO Page 51.

HARRIS, HENRY. Musician.
Served from May 1 to June 30, 1814
in Capt. Alexander Brooks' Corps of
Artillery. Ref: R. & L. 1812, AGO
Page 31.

*HARRIS. ISAAC.
Served from June 11. 1813 to June
14. 1813 in Lieut. Bates' Company,
1 Regt. (Judson's) Vt. Militia. Enlisted Sept. 23. 1813 in Capt. Amasa
Mansfield's Company, Dixon's Regt.

HARRIS. JACOB.
Volunteered to go to Plattsburgh,
September, 1814, and served 4 days
in Capt. Aaron Kidder's Company.
Ref: Book 52, AGO Page 65.

‡HARRIS. JAMES.
Served in Capt. Bethrong's Company.
Pension Certificate No. 25054.

HARRIS, JEDEDIAH H., Captain, Strafford. Volunteered to go to Plattsburgh, September, 1814, and served
6 days in command of company from
Strafford. Ref: Book 52, AGO Pages
43 and 99.

‡*HARRIS, JOHN.
Served from March 9, 1813 to June
8, 1813 in Capt. Charles Follett's Company, 11th Regt. Served with Hospital Attendants, Vt. Also served
in Capt. Morrill's Company (2 Regt.).

Pension Certificate of widow, Sarah,
No. 2724. Ref: R. & L. 1812, AGO
Page 13.

*HARRIS, JOHN B., Sergeant.   Stowe.
Volunteered to go to Plattsburgh,
September, 1814, and was at the
battle, serving in Capt. Nehemiah
Perkins' Company, 4 Regt. (Peck's).
Also served in Corning's Detachment,
Vt. Militia.

HARRIS, JOHN N.,   Lansingburg.
Served from Oct. 3, 1814 to June 19,
1815 in Capt. Taylor's Company, 30th
Inf. Ref: R. & L. 1812, AGO Page
23.

*HARRIS, JONATHAN.
Enlisted Sept. 23, 1813 in Capt.
Amasa Mansfield's Company, Dixon's
Regt.

HARRIS, LEONARD, Sergeant.
Served in company of Capt. Samuel
H. Holly, 11th Regt.; on Pay Roll
for January and February, 1813.
Ref: R. & L. 1812, AGO Page 25.

*HARRIS, LIBIUS (or Libins, Jr.?)
Served from April 12, 1814 to April
21, 1814 in Lieut. Justus Foote's Company, Sumner's Regt.

HARRIS, THOMAS.
Served in company of Capt. Charles
Follett, 11th Regt.; on Pay Roll for
January and February, 1812. Ref:
R. & L. 1812, AGO Page 12.

HARRIS, TRACY.
Served from Feb. 9, 1813 to May 8,
1813 in Capt. Edgerton's Company,
11th Regt. Ref: R. & L. 1812, AGO
Page 3.

*HARRIS. WILLIAM, Sergeant.
Served in 4 Regt. Vt. Militia commanded by Col. Peck.

HART, BENJAMIN,   Fairfax.
Served in 1813 and 1814 in Capt.
Joseph Beeman's Company. Ref: Hemenway's Vt. Gazetteer, Vol. 2, Page
402.

*HART, ERASTUS.
Served from April 12, 1814 to May
20, 1814, in Capt. George Fisher's
Company, Sumner's Regt.

*HART, JOHN.
Served from April 12, 1814 to April
21, 1814 in Capt. Eseck Sprague's
Company, Sumner's Regt.

*HART, JOHN.
Served in Lieut. Wm. S. Foster's
Company, 11th Regt.; on Pay Roll
for January and February, 1813.
Served from April 12, 1814 to April
21, 1814 in Capt. Eseck Sprague's
Company, Sumners' Regt. Also serv-
ed with Hospital Attendants, Vt.
Ref: R. & L. 1812, AGO Page 7;
Book 52, AGO Page 263.

*HART, ORANGE, Corporal.
Enlisted Sept. 25, 1813 in company
of Capt. Jonathan Prentiss, Jr. Dixon's Regt.

*HART, ROBERT.
Served in Capt. Morrill's Company,
Col. Fifield's Regt. Detached Militia
in U. S. service 5 months and 27
days, 1812.

*HART, WILLIAM.
Served in 4 Regt. (Peck's) Vt. Militia.

HARTFORD, HIRAM.
Served from May 1 to June 30, 1814
in Capt. Alexander Brooks' Corps of
Artillery. Ref: R. & L. 1812, AGO
Page 31.

HARTLEY, SAMUEL.
Enlisted Feb. 27, 1813 in Lieut. V.
R. Goodrich's Company, 11th Regt.;
on Pay Roll for January and Feb-
ruary, 1813. Ref: R. & L. 1812, AGO
Page 11.

*HARTSHORN, DARIUS.
Served in Capt. Wilson's Company,
Col. Wm. Williams' Regt. Detached
Militia in U. S. service 24 days,
1812.

HARTSHORN, DAVID, Corporal.
Served in Capt. Samul Gordon's Company, 11th Regt.; on Pay Roll for
January and February, 1813. Served
from May 1st to June 30, 1814 as a
carpenter in Alexander Parris' Company of Artificers. Ref: R. & L.
1812, AGO Page 9; and page 24.

*HARTSHORN, EPHRAIM.   Danville.
Served in Capt. Morrill's Company,
Col. Fifield's Regt. Detached Militia
in U. S. service 3 months and 2
days, 1812. Served from May 1st to
June 30, 1814 in Capt. Haig's Corps
of Light Dragoons.

HARTSHORN, LEONARD.
Enlisted May 10, 1813 for 1 year in
Capt. James Taylor's Company, 30th
Regt. Ref: R. & L. 1812, AGO Page 52.

‡*HARTSHORN, SILAS.
Served from June 11, 1813 to June
14, 1813 in Capt. Samuel Blinn's Company, 1st Regt. Also served in Capt.
Wilson's Company. Pension Certificate of widow, Dorcas, No. 30128.

HARTSHORN, WILLIAM.
Served in Capt. Dorrence's Company,
Col. Wm. Williams' Regt. Detached
Militia in U. S. service 4 months and
23 days, 1812. Served from April 12,
1814 to April 21, 1814 in Capt. Ed-
mund B. Hill's Company, Sumner's
Regt. Ref: Book 52. AGO Page 283;
Book 53, AGO Page 13.

*HARVEY, APOLUS.
Enlisted Sept. 20, 1813 in Capt. John
Weed's Company, Col. Clark's Rifle
Corps.

HARVEY, EZRA C., Franklin County.
Volunteered to go to Plattsburgh
Sept. 11, 1814 and served in 15th or
22nd Regt. Ref: Hemenway's Vt. Gazetteer, Vol. 2, Page 391.

HARVEY, JAMES.
Served from April 4, 1813 to July 3,
1813 in Lieut. Wm. S. Foster's Company, 11th Regt. Ref: R. & L. 1812,
AGO Page 6.

HARVEY, JAMES.
Served from Jan. 12, 1813 to June 8,
1813 in Capt. John W. Weeks' Company, 11th Regt. Ref: R. & L. 1812,
AGO Pages 4 and 5.

HARVEY, NATHAN B., Corporal.
Served from May 1, 1814 to June 30,
1814 in Corps of Light Dragoons. Ref:
R. & L. 1812, AGO Page 20.

HARVEY, NATHANIEL B.
Served from Nov. 1, 1812 to Feb. 28,
1813 in Capt. Samuel H. Holly's Company, 11th Regt. Ref: R. & L. 1812,
AGO Page 25.

HARVEY, THOMAS.
Served from May 1st to June 30, 1814
in Capt. Haig's Corps of Light Dragoons. Ref: R. & L. 1812, AGO Page
20.

*HARVEY, WILLIAM.
Served in Capt. Mason's Company,
Col. Fifield's Regt. Detached Militia
in U. S. service 5 months and 29
days, 1812. Served in Capt. Phineas
Williams' Company, 11th Regt.; on
Pay Roll for January and February,
1813.

HARWARD, JOHN,   Franklin County.
Volunteered to go to Plattsburgh
Sept. 11, 1814 and served in 15th or
22nd Regt. Ref: Hemenway's Vt. Gazetteer, Vol. 2, Page 391.

HARWOOD, AARON,   Braintree.
Marched to Plattsburgh Sept. 10, 1814,
serving in Capt. Lot Hudson's Company. Ref: Book 52, AGO Page 24.

HARWOOD, ABIJAH.
Born in Bennington and served in
War of 1812; captured by gunboats
May 28, 1813 at Henderson's Harbor;
escaped Sept. 3, 1813. Ref: Records
of Naval Records and Library, Navy
Dept.

‡HARWOOD, AHEL.
Served in Capt. Jordan's Company.
Pension Certificate No. 19211.

*HARWOOD, DOLPHE.
Served in 1 Regt. Vt. Militia commanded by Col. Martindale.

*HARWOOD, HIRAM, Sergeant.
Served in Capt. Cross' Company, Col.
Martindale's Regt. Detached Militia
in U. S. service 2 months and 14
days, 1812. Served in Capt. Charles
Follett's Company, 11th Regt.; on Pay
Roll for January and February, 1813
as a Sergeant.

HARWOOD, JAMES J.,   Wilmington.
Enlisted at New York Nov. 18, 1811
in U. S. Marine Corps. Ref: Book
52, AGO Page 294.

HARWOOD, JASON, Corporal, Pittsford.
Volunteered to go to Plattsburgh,
September, 1814, and served 8 days
in Capt. Caleb Hendee's Company.
Ref: Book 52, AGO Page 124.

*HARWOOD, NATHAN,   Braintree.
Enlisted Sept. 20, 1813 in Capt. John
Weed's Company, Col. Clark's Rifle

Corps. Marched to Plattsburgh Sept. 10, 1814 and served in Capt. Lot Hudson's Company.

HARWOOD, SAMUEL, Sergeant, Braintree. Marched to Plattsburgh Sept. 10, 1814 and served 9 days in Capt. Lot Hudson's Company. Ref: Book 51, AGO Page 295; Book 52, AGO Pages 24 and 33.

*HARWOOD, ZACK, Corporal. Served in Capt. Hopkins' Company, Col. Martindale's Regt. Detached Militia in U. S. service 2 months and 13 days, 1812.

HASCALL, PRINCE (or Prinn), Waitsfield. Volunteered to go to Plattsburgh, September, 1814, and served 4 days in Capt. Mathias S. Jones' Company. Ref: Book 52, AGO Page 170.

‡HASEL, GILES. Served in Capt. Wright's Company. Pension Certificate of widow, Julia A., No. 32207.

*HASELTINE, ABRAHAM. Served in Corning's Detachment, Vt. Militia.

‡*HASELTINE, URIAL (or Uriah) Lieutenant. Served in Capt. Sabin's Company, 3 Regt. (Williams') Vt. Militia. Pension Certificate of widow, Amy, No. 1844.

HASKELL, JOB, Tunbridge. Volunteered to go to Plattsburgh, September, 1814, and served 4 days in Capt. Ephraim Hackett's Company. Ref: Book 52, AGO Page 71.

*HASKELL, WILLIAM, Calais. Volunteered to go to Plattsburgh, September, 1814, and served 10 days in Capt. Gideon Wheelock's Company.

*HASKINS, ASAPH, Dover. Served in Capt. Preston's Company, Col. Jonathan Williams' Regt. Detached Militia in U. S. service 2 months and 6 days, 1812.

*HASKINS, CHESTER. Served in Sumner's Regt. Vt. Militia.

*HASKINS, ELI. Served in 1 Regt. Vt. Militia commanded by Col. Judson.

*HASKINS, JAMES. Served as Corporal in Capt. Willson's Company, Col. Wm. Williams' Regt. Detached Militia in U. S. service 3 months and 11 days, 1812. Also served in 3 Regt. (Tyler's) Vt. Militia.

‡HASKINS, JEDUTHAN, Middlesex. Volunteered to go to Plattsburgh, September, 1814, and served 10 days in Capt. Holden Putnam's Company, 4 Regt. (Peck's). Also served in Capt. O. Lowry's Company. Pension Certificate No. 28544.

*HASKINS, JOHN. Served in 1 Regt. Vt. Militia commanded by Col. Martindale.

*HASKINS, JONATHAN. Served in 4 Regt. Vt. Militia commanded by Col. Peck.

*HASKINS, LUTHER, Middlesex. Volunteered to go to Plattsburgh, September, 1814, and served 10 days in Capt. Holden Putnam's Company, 4 Regt. (Peck's).

*HASKINS, NATHAN JR. Served in 3 Regt. Vt. Militia commanded by Col. Tyler.

*HASKINS, SAMUEL. Served in 4 Regt. Vt. Militia commanded by Col. Peck.

*HASKINS, SELON. Served in 1 Regt. Vt. Militia commanded by Col. Martindale.

‡HASKINS, SOTON. Served in Capt. Richardson's Company. Pension Certificate of widow, Sophia, No. 2621.

HASKINS, THOMAS, Franklin County. Volunteered to go to Plattsburgh Sept. 11, 1814 and served in 15th or 22nd Regt. Ref: Hemenway's Vt. Gazetteer, Vol. 2, Page 391.

‡HASKINS, WILLIAM, Richmond. Volunteered to go to Plattsburgh, September, 1814, and served 9 days in Capt. Roswell's Hunt's Company, 3 Regt. (Tyler's). Pension Certificate of widow, Ruth, No. 27158.

HASTINGS, LEWIS. Served in company of Lieut. Wm. S. Foster, 11th Regt.; on Pay Roll for January and February, 1813. Ref: R. & L. 1812, AGO Page 7.

HASTINGS, SEYMOUR. Enlisted May 8, 1813 for 1 year in Capt. Simeon Wright's Company. Ref: R. & L. 1812, AGO Page 51.

HATCH, ARTEBAN. Enlisted March 1, 1813 in Lieut. V. R. Goodrich's Company, 11th Regt.; on Pay Roll to May 31, 1813. Ref: R. & L. 1812, AGO Page 10.

HATCH, ASA, Williamstown. Volunteered to go to Plattsburgh, September, 1814, and went as far as Burlington, serving in Capt. David Robinson's Company. Ref: Book 52, AGO Page 2.

HATCH, DANIEL. Volunteered to go to Plattsburgh, September, 1814, and served in company of Capt. Jonathan Jennings of Chelsea. Ref: Book 52, AGO Page 79.

*HATCH, DAVID. Served in 4 Regt. Vt. Militia commanded by Col. Peck.

*HATCH, DEXTER. Served in Capt. Persons' Company Col. Jonathan Williams' Regt. Detached Militia in U. S. service 2 months and 13 days, 1812.

‡*HATCH, EZEKIEL.
Enlisted Sept. 25, 1813 in Capt. Jesse Post's Company, Dixon's Regt. and served to Nov. 15, 1813. Also served in Capt. Elijah B. Wood's Company, Dixon's Regt. Pension Certificate of widow, Eliza A., No. 12879.

*HATCH, HARRY.
Served with Hospital Attendants, Vt.

HATCH, JOHN, Lieutenant.
Appointed 2 Lieutenant 31 Inf. April 30, 1813; 1 Lieutenant Feb. 2, 1814; honorably discharged June 15, 1815. Ref: Heitman's Historical Register & Dictionary USA.

*HATCH, JOSEPH.
Enlisted Sept. 25, 1813 and served 1 month and 23 days in Capt. Elijah Birge's Company, Col. Dixon's Regt.

HATCH, LUTHER, Ensign.
Volunteered to go to Plattsburgh, September, 1814, and served in company of Capt. David Robinson of Williamstown. Ref: Book 52, AGO Pages 7 and 10.

HATCH, MARTIN.
Served from March 11, 1813 to June 10, 1813 in Lieut. V. R. Goodrich's Company, 11th Regt. Ref: R. & L. 1812, AGO Page 10.

HATCH, MOSES.
Served from Feb. 12 to May 11, 1813 in Capt. Samul Gordon's Company, 11th Regt. Ref: R. & L. 1812, AGO Page 8.

HATCH, OBED S., Corporal.
Served in Capt. Weeks' Company, 11th Regt.; on Pay Roll for January and February, 1813. Ref: R. & L. 1812, AGO Page 5.

HATCH, OLIVER,   Williamstown.
Volunteered to go to Plattsburgh, September, 1814, and went as far as Burlington, serving in Capt. David Robinson's Company. Ref: Book 52, AGO Page 2.

HATCH, RUFUS, Lieutenant.
Appointed 1 Lieutenant 11 Inf. March 12, 1812; resigned Aug. 10, 1813. Served as Asst. Dep. Quartermaster in Capt. Samuel H. Holly's Company, 11th Regt.; on Pay Roll for January and February, 1814. Ref: Heitman's Historical Register & Dictionary USA; R. & L. 1812, AGO Page 25.

HATCH, TIMOTHY.
Served in Lieut. V. R. Goodrich's Company, 11th Regt. from Feb. 5, 1813 to date of death April 24, 1813. Ref. R. & L. 1812, AGO Pages 10 and 11.

HATCH, WARD.
Served from May 1 to June 30, 1814 as a laborer in company of Artificers commanded by Alexander Parris. Ref: R. & L. 1812, AGO Page 24.

HATCH, WILLIAM,   Williamstown.
Volunteered to go to Plattsburgh, September, 1814, and went as far as Burlington, serving 4 or 5 days in Capt. David Robinson's Company. Ref: Book 52, AGO Pages 2 and 4.

*HATHAWAY, ABRAHAM, Corporal.
Enlisted Sept. 25, 1813 and served 1 month and 23 days in Capt. Jesse Post's Company, Col. Dixon's Regt.

*HATHAWAY, AUSTIN.
Served in Capt. L. Robinson's Company, Col. Dixon's Regt. Detached Militia in U. S. service 2 months, 1813.

HATHAWAY, JOSIAH H.,   Swanton.
Enlisted April 24, 1813 for 1 year and served in Capt. James Taylor's Company and Capt. Gideon Spencer's Company, 30th Regt.; discharged April 27, 1814. Volunteered to go to Plattsburgh and was at the battle Sept. 11, 1814, serving 8 days in 30th Regt. Ref: R. & L. 1812, AGO Pages 52, 57, 59; Book 51, AGO Page 184; Book 52, AGO Page 119.

*HATHAWAY, LEVI JR., Ensign Lieutenant, Swanton. Appointed Ensign Sept. 27, 1813 in Capt. Asahel Langworthy's Company, Col. Clark's Volunteer Riflemen in U. S. service. Volunteered to go to Plattsburgh, September, 1814, and served 8 days as Lieutenant in Capt. S. W. Farnsworth's Company, Dixon's Regt. Ref: Book 51, AGO Pages 128, 184, 293.

HATHAWAY, PAUL,   Montpelier.
Volunteered to go to Plattsburgh, September, 1814, and served 8 days in Capt. Timothy Hubbard's Company. Ref: Book 52, AGO Pages 241, 246, 256.

*HATHAWAY, SALATHIEL.
Served from April 12, 1814 to April 15, 1814 in Lieut. Justus Foote's Company, Sumner's Regt.

*HATHAWAY, SHADRACK, Brig. Major.
Served from Sept. 25, 1813 to Oct. 9, 1813 on staff of Gen. Elias Fasset. Also served as Major in 4 Regt. (Williams') Vt. Militia.

*HATHAWAY, SHADRACH, JR.
Served as Major and Brigade Inspector in 1 Regt. 3 Brig 3 Div. Vt. Militia.

HATHAWAY, SILAS,   St. Albans.
Enlisted May 3, 1813 for 1 year in Capt. John Wires' Company, 30th Regt. Ref: R. & L. 1812, AGO Page 40.

‡HATHAWAY, SIMEON, Lieutenant, Swanton. Served in Capt. Dorrance's Company, Col. Wm. Williams' Regt. Detached Militia in U. S. service 4 months and 24 days, 1812. Appointed Ensign 30 Inf. April 30, 1813; 3 lieutenant Dec. 31, 1813; 2 Lieutenant Aug. 1, 1814; honorably discharged June 15, 1815. Served as Ensign in Capt. James Taylor's Company, 30th Regt. Volunteered to go to Plattsburgh, September, 1814, and served as Lieutenant in 10th Company, 30th Regt. American Army. Also served

in Capt. Brown's Company. Pension Certificate of widow, Eunice, No. 5859. Ref: Book 53, AGO Page 88; R. & L. 1812, AGO Pages 52 and 58; Heitman's Historical Register & Dictionary USA; Book 51, AGO Pages 140 and 184.

HATHAWAY, THOMAS, Calais.
Volunteered to go to Plattsburgh, September, 1814, and served 5 days in Capt. Gideon Wheelock's Company. Ref: Book 52, AGO Page 171.

HATLEY, SAMUEL.
Served from March 18, 1813 to June 17, 1813 in Lieut. V. R. Goodrich's Company, 11th Regt. Ref: R. & L. 1812, AGO Page 10.

*HAVEN, HEZEKIAH.
Served in Capt. Adams' Company, Col. Jonathan Williams' Regt. Detached Militia in U. S. service 2 months and 7 days, 1812.

*HAVEN, LUTHER.
Served from April 12, 1814 to April 21, 1814 in Capt. Shubael Wales' Company, Col. W. B. Sumner's Regt.

HAVERLAND, DENNIS.
Served from May 1 to June 30, 1814 in Capt. Alexander Brooks' Corps of Artillery. Ref: R. & L. 1812, AGO Page 31.

HAVILAND, JOSEPH.
Served from June 11, 1813 to June 14, 1813 in Capt. Moses Jewett's Company, 1st Regt. 2nd Brig. 3rd Div. Ref: R. & L. 1812, AGO Page 42.

HAVILAND, SAMUEL.
Served from Jan. 1 to June 30, 1814 in Capt. Haig's Corps of Light Dragoons. Ref: R. & L. 1812, AGO Pages 20 and 29.

HAWES, ELEAZER.
Served in Capt. Benjamin S. Edgerton's Company, 11th Regt.; on Pay Roll for September and October, 1812 and January and February, 1813. Ref: R. & L. 1812, AGO Pages 1 and 2.

*HAWES, JOSEPH, Sergeant Major.
Served in 2 Regt. Vt. Militia commanded by Col. Fifield.   •

*HAWKES, IRA.
Served in 4 Regt. (Peck's) Vt. Militia.

‡*HAWKINS, ABRAM.
Served in Capt. Durkee's Company, Col. Fifield's Regt. Detached Militia in U. S. service 2 months and 26 days, 1812. Pension Certificate No. 16915.

*HAWKINS, ADOLPHUS.
Served from April 12, 1814 to April 21, 1814 in Capt. Edmund B. Hill's Company, Sumner's Regt.

HAWKINS, DANIEL.
Enlisted Feb. 15, 1814 for duration of the war in Capt. Wm. Miller's Company, 30th Regt. Ref: R. & L. 1812, AGO Pages 1, 54, 57.

HAWKINS, GILBERT, Sergeant.
Served in Corps of Light Dragoons; on Pay Roll to June 30, 1814; prisoner of War. Ref: R. & L. 1812, AGO Page 20.

*HAWKINS, JOHN.
Served in Capt. Wheeler's Company, Col. Fifield's Regt. Detached Militia in U. S. service 6 months and 4 days, 1812.

*HAWKINS, ROSWELL.
Served in Sumner's Regt. Vt. Militia.

HAWKINS, SAMUEL.
Served from Feb. 23, 1813 to May 22, 1813 in Capt. Edgerton's Company, 11th Regt. Also served in 2 Regt. (Fifield's) Vt. Militia. Ref: R. & L. 1812, AGO Page 3.

*HAWKS, IRA JR.
Served in Corning's Detachment, Vt. Militia. Served in 4 Regt. (Peck's) Vt. Militia.

*HAWKS, ORRIN.
Served in Sumner's Regt. Vt. Militia.

*HAWKS, REUBEN JR.
Served in Capt. O. Lowry's Company, Col. Wm. Williams' Regt. Detached Militia in U. S. service 4 months and 26 days, 1812. Also served in Corning's Detachment, Vt. Militia.

*HAWLEY, ABIJAH.
Served in Capt. Needham's Company, Col. Martindale's Regt. Detached Militia in U. S. service 2 months and 14 days, 1812. Served from April 28, 1813 to April 28, 1814 in Capt. Simeon Wright's Company.

HAWLEY, DANIEL, Beon.
Served from May 1 to July 1, 1814 in Capt. Lynd's Company, 29th Inf. Ref: R. & L. 1812, AGO Page 30.

*HAWLEY, ELISHA JR. (or Elisha),
Sergeant. Served from Sept. 25 to Sept. 30, 1813 in Capt. Charles Bennett's Company, Dixon's Regt.

*HAWLEY, EMON (or Emor).
Served from June 11, 1813 to June 14, 1813 in Capt. Moses Jewett's Company, 1st Regt. 2nd Brig. 3rd Div.

HAWLEY, GIDEON, Lieutenant.
Appointed 2 Lieutenant 30 Inf. April 30, 1813; 1 Lieutenant March 5, 1814; honorably discharged June 15, 1815; died June 3, 1816. Ref: Heitman's Historical Register & Dictionary USA.

HAWLEY, IRA, Cambridge.
Enlisted April 28, 1813 for 1 year in Capt. John Wires' Company, 30th Regt. Ref: R. & L. 1812, AGO Page 40.

‡*HAWLEY, ISAAC, Lieutenant.
Served in Capt. O. Lowry's Company, Col. Wm. Williams' Regt. Detached Militia in U. S. service 4 months and 26 days, 1812. Served as Lieutenant in 4 Regt. (Williams'). Also served in Capt. Spencer's Company. Pension Certificate of widow, Nancy, No. 5242.

*HAWLEY, JABEZ JR., Ensign.
Served in 1st Regt. of Detached Militia of Vt. in U. S. service at Champlain Nov. 18 to Nov. 19, 1812.

*HAWLEY, JAMES, Corporal.
Served in Capt. Lowry's Company, Col. Wm. Williams' Regt. Detached Militia in U. S. service 4 months and 26 days, 1814. Also served as Sergeant in 1 Regt. (Judson's) Vt. Militia.

HAWLEY, JAMES C.
Served in Capt. Chadwick's Company. Ref: R. & L. 1812, AGO Page 32.

*HAWLEY, JOSIAH JR.
Served in Capt. Phelps' Company, Col. Jonathan Williams' Regt. Detached Militia in U. S. service 1 month and 16 days, 1812.

*HAWLEY, PAUL, Drummer.
Served in Capt. Phelps' Company, Col. Wm. Williams' Regt. Detached Militia in U. S. service 5 months, 1812.

*HAWLEY, PHINEHAS D.
Enlisted Sept. 25, 1813 and served 1 month and 23 days in Capt. N. B. Eldridge's Company, Col. Dixon's Regt.

*HAWLEY, PIERRE, Sergeant.
Served in Sumner's Regt. Vt. Militia.

‡*HAWLEY, RICHARD H.
Enlisted Sept. 25, 1813 and served 1 month and 23 days in Capt. Charles Bennett's Company, Col. Dixon's Regt. Pension Certificate of widow, Amelia, No. 15368.

*HAWLEY, TRUMAN, Lieutenant.
Served from June 11, 1813 to June 14, 1813 in Capt. Samuel Blinn's Company, 1 Regt. (Judson's).

‡HAWTHORNE, DAVID.
Served in Capt. Bartholomew's Company. Pension Certificate No. 9964.

‡*HAY, CLAUDIUS.
Enlisted Sept. 20, 1813 in Capt. John Weed's Company, Col. Clark's Rifle Corps. Also served in Capt. E. Hopkins' Company. Pension Certificate of widow, Fanny, No. 11778.

HAY, HENRY,   Vergennes.
Volunteered to go to Plattsburgh, September, 1814, and was at the battle, serving 10 days in Capt. Gideon Spencer's Company. Ref: Book 51, AGO Page 1.

HAY, WILLIAM,   Pittsford.
Volunteered to go to Plattsburgh, September, 1814, and discharged Sept. 11 by reason of old age; enlisted in Capt. Caleb Hendee's Company. Ref: Book 52, AGO Page 125.

*HAYDEN, SAMUEL.
Served in Corning's Detachment, Vt. Militia.

HAYDEN, WARREN,   Stockbridge.
Volunteered to go to Plattsburgh, September, 1814, and served 7 days in Capt. Elias Keyes' Company. Ref: Book 51, AGO Page 241.

HAYES, ADAM, Hospital Surgeon.
Served on General Staff of the Northern Army commanded by Major General George Izard; on Pay Roll to July 31, 1814. Ref: R. & L. 1812, AGO Page 28.

*HAYES, MICHAEL D.
Served from April 12, 1814 to April 21, 1814 in Capt. Eseck Sprague's Company, Sumner's Regt.

*HAYES, SEYMOUR.
Served from April 12, 1814 to April 21, 1814 in Capt. Eseck Sprague's Company, Sumner's Regt. Volunteered to go to Plattsburgh, September, 1814, and served 10 days in Capt. Gideon Spencer's Company. Ref: Book 51, AGO Page 1.

HAYFORD, SAMUEL.
Served from May 1 to June 30, 1814 as a carpenter in company of Artificers commanded by Alexander Parris. Ref: R. & L. 1812, AGO Page 24.

HAYNES, ABRAHAM J.,   Roxbury.
Volunteered to go to Plattsburgh, September, 1814, and served 7 days in Capt. Samuel M. Orcutt's Company. Ref: Book 52, AGO Pages 166 and 250.

‡HAYNES, VINE.
Served in Capt. Coleman's Company. Pension Certificate No. 24067.

HAYS, ELAM.
Born in Simsbury, Conn.; aged 35 years; 5 feet 11 inches high; dark complexion; dark hair; black eyes; by profession a cardwainer. Enlisted at Addison March 28, 1814 for the period of the war and served in Capt. Wm. Miller's Company and Capt. Gideon Spencer's Company, 30th Regt. Ref: R. & L. 1812, AGO Pages 54, 55, 57.

‡*HAYS, HARVEY (or Harry).
Served from Oct. 8 to Nov. 18, 1813 in Capt. Isaac Finch's Company, Col. Clark's Rifle Corps. Also served in Sumner's Regt. Vt. Militia and in Capt. Waddam's Company. Pension Certificate No. 19718.

HAYWAR, JOSEPH.
• Enlisted June 10, 1813 for 1 year in Capt. John Wires' Company, 30th Regt. Ref: R. & L. 1812, AGO Page 40.

*HAYWARD, ALLAN.
Served in Capt. Robbins' Company, Col. Wm. Williams' Regt. Detached Militia in U. S. service 4 months and 29 days, 1812.

*HAYWARD, EBENEZER.
Served in Capt. Robbins' Company, Col. Wm. Williams' Regt. Detached Militia in U. S. service 4 months and 29, days, 1812.

*HAYWARD, HARRY.
Served with Hospital Attendants, Vt.

*HAYWARD, JOSEPH,   St. Albans.
Served in Capt. John Wires' Company, 30th Regt., which was raised

in St. Albans and went into the
service Nov. 30, 1813. Also served
in Sumner's Regt. Vt. Militia. Ref:
Hemenway's Vt. Gazetteer, Vol. 2,
Page 433.

*HAYWARD, SAMUEL, Corporal.
Enlisted Sept. 25, 1813 and served
1 month and 23 days in Capt. Thomas
Waterman's Company, Col. Dixon's
Regt.

*HAYWOOD, JOHN, Corporal.
Served in Capt. Adams' Company,
Col. Jonathan Williams' Regt. Detached Militia in U. S. service 2
months and 7 days, 1812.

*HAYWOOD, PAUL.
Served in Capt. Persons' Company,
Col. Jonathan Williams' Regt. Detached Militia in U. S. service 2
months and 13 days, 1812.

*HAYWOOD, ZIBA.
Served in 3 Regt. (Williams') Vt.
Militia.

*HAZARD, DAVID.
Served in Sumner's Regt. Vt. Militia.

*HAZARD, JOHN.
Served with Hospital Attendants, Vt.

‡HAZELL, BENNETT.
Served in Capt. Allen's Company.
Pension Certificate of widow, Nancy
E., No. 32688.

*HAZELTINE, DANIEL,   Middletown.
Served in Capt. Scovell's Company,
Col. Martindale's Regt. Detached
Militia in U. S. service 1 month and
14 days, 1812.

*HAZELTON, JOSEPH, Sergeant, Bakers-
field. Served in Capt. Morrill's Company, Col. Fifield's Regt. Detached
Militia in U. S. service 6 months and
5 days, 1812. Served from June 11,
1813 to June 14, 1813 in Capt.
Moses Jewett's Company, 1st Regt.
2nd Brig. 3rd Div. Volunteered and
was at the battle of Plattsburgh
Sept. 11, 1814, serving in Capt. M.
Stearns' Company. Ref: Hemenway's
Vt. Gazetteer, Vol. 2, Page 394.

‡HAZEN, HENRY H.
Served in Capt. Pettis' Company.
Pension Certificate of widow, Abigail,
No. 24189.

‡HAZEN, JEDEDIAH.
Served in Capt. Pettis' Company.
Pension Certificate of widow, Sally,
No. 25111.

‡*HAZEN, JOHN.
Served with Hospital Attendants, Vt.
Also served in Capt. Joseph Hazen's
Company. Pension Certificate of
widow, Charlotty, No. 27402.

HAZEN, JOSEPH, Captain, North Hero.
Volunteered to go to Plattsburgh
Sept. 11, 1814 and commanded com-
pany raised at North Hero. Ref:
Hemenway's Vt. Gazetteer Vol. 2,
Page 565.

HAZLETON, DAVID,   Troy.
Served from July 4 to July 16, 1812
at Troy in company commanded by
Major A. Warner. Ref: Vol. 51, Vt.
State Papers, Page 107.

HAZLETON, MANSIL.
Enlisted March 29, 1813 in Capt. Ed-
gerton's Company, 11th Regt. Ref:
R .& L. 1812, AGO Page 3.

‡*HAZLETON, SILAS B., Ensign.
Served in 3 Regt. (Bowdish) Vt.
Militia. Also served in Capt. Dorm's
Company. Pension Certificate No.
33321.

HAZLETON, THOMAS,   Strafford.
Volunteered to go to Plattsburgh,
September, 1814, and served 5 days
in Capt. Joseph Barrett's Company.
Ref: Book 52, AGO Page 41.

HEAD, JAMES JR.
On Pay Roll of company of Capt.
John McNeil Jr., 11th Regt. for
January and February, 1813; never
mustered and never paid. Ref: R. &
L. 1812, AGO Page 17.

*HEADEN, SMITH.
Served with Hospital Attendants, Vt.

HEADER, SMITH.
Served from March 19, 1813 to June
8, 1813 in Capt. Charles Follett's
Company, 11th Regt. Ref: R. & L.
1812, AGO Page 13.

*HEADINGS, JAMES JR.
Served in Capt. Phelps' Company,
Col. Wm. Williams' Regt. Detached
Militia in U. S. service 5 months,
1812.

‡HEALD, IRA.
Served in Capt. Utley's Company.
Pension Certificate No. 13841.

*HEALD, JOHN, Sergeant.
Served in Capt. Parsons' Company,
Col. Jonathan Williams' Regt. Detached Militia in U. S. service 2
months and 13 days, 1812.

HEALEY, BENJAMIN JR.,   Shoreham.
Served from April 12, 1814 to May
20, 1814 in company of Capt. James
Gray Jr., Sumner's Regt. Volunteered to go to Plattsburgh September,
1814, and served 6 days in Capt.
Samuel Hand's Company. Ref: Book
52, AGO Page 279; Rev. J. F. Goodhue's History of Shoreham, Page 108.

HEALEY, JEREMIAH S.,   Shoreham.
Served from April 12, 1814 to May
20, 1814 in company of Capt. James
Gray Jr., Sumner's Regt. Volunteered to go to Plattsburgh, September,
1814, and served 6 days in Capt.
Samuel Hand's Company. Ref. Book
52, AGO Page 280; Rev. J. F. Goodhue's History of Shoreham, Page 108.

HEALEY, JOSHUA,   Shoreham.
Served with Vergennes Volunteers
under Capt. James Gray Jr. Ref:
Rev. J. F. Goodhue's History of
Shoreham, Page 107.

HEALEY, WILLIAM.
Enlisted Feb. 10, 1813 in Capt. Jonathan Starks' Company, 11th Regt.; on Pay Roll to May 31, 1813. Ref: R. & L. 1812, AGO Page 19.

*HEALY, SAMUEL, Sergeant.
Served in Capt. Burnap's Company, Col. Jonathan Williams' Regt. Detached Militia in U. S. service 2 months and 13 days, 1812.

HEARN, DANIEL.
Served from May 1 to June 30, 1814 as a laborer in Alexander Parris' Company of Artificers. Ref: R. & L. 1812, AGO Page 24.

*HEARSLEY, ELI.
Served in 3 Regt. Vt. Militia commanded by Col. Williams.

HEARTSHORN, LEONARD.
Served from May 10, 1813 to May 23, 1814 in Capt. Gideon Spencer's Company and Capt. James Taylor's Company, 30th Regt. Ref: R. & L. 1812, AGO Pages 57 and 58.

*HEATH, BRADBURY.
Served in Capt. Durkee's Company, Col. Fifield's Regt. Detached Militia in U. S. service 2 months and 21 days, 1812.

HEATH, CALEB,   Corinth.
Volunteered to go to Plattsburgh, September, 1814, and served in company of Capt. Ebenezer Spencer of Vershire. Ref: Book 52, AGO Page 48.

*HEATH, DANIEL, Fifer.
Enlisted Sept. 25, 1813 in Capt. Charles Bennett's Company, Dixon's Regt.

HEATH, DAVID,   Corinth.
Volunteered to go to Plattsburgh, September, 1814, and served in company of Capt. Ebenezer Spencer of Vershire. Ref: Book 52, AGO Page 48.

*HEATH, EPHRAIM.
Served in Col. Fifield's Regt. Detached Militia in U. S. service 2 months and 21 days, 1812.

*HEATH, ISAAC,   Corinth.
Served from April 12, 1814 to April 21, 1814 in Capt. Shubael Wales' Company, Col. W. B. Sumner's Regt. Volunteered to go to Plattsburgh, September, 1814, and served in company of Capt. Ebenezer Spencer, Vershire. Ref: Book 52, AGO Pages 48 and 49.

*HEATH, JACOB.
Served in Capt. Dodge's Company, Col. Fifield's Regt. Detached Militia in U. S. service 2 months and 21 days, 1812.

‡HEATH, JAMES,   Groton.
Served in Capt. Morrell's Company, Col. Fifield's Regt. Pension Certificate No. 19996.

*HEATH, JEREMIAH.
Served in Capt. Morrill's Company, Col. Fifield's Regt. Detached Militia

in U. S. service 26 days, 1812. Served from Feb. 11, 1813 to May 10, 1813 in Capt. Samul Gordon's Company, 11th Regt.

*HEATH, JOHN, Drummer,   Groton.
Served in Capt. Morrill's Company, Col. Fifield's Regt. Detached Militia in U. S. service 2 months and 18 days, 1812. Served in Corps of Light Dragoons commanded by Capt. Haig; on Pay Roll to June 30, 1814; prisoner of war. Ref: R. & L. 1812, AGO Page 20.

‡*HEATH, MOSES,   Groton.
Served in Capt. Morrill's Company, Col. Fifield's Regt. Detached Militia in U. S. service 5 months, 1812. Served in Capt. Samul Gordon's Company, 11th Regt.; on Pay Roll for January and February 1813; joined Feb. 14, 1813. Pension Certificate No. 14367.

‡*HEATH, MOULTON, Corporal, Groton.
Served in Capt. Morrill's Company, Col. Fifield's Regt. Detached Militia in U. S. service 6 months and 5 days, 1812. Pension Certificate of widow, Azubah, No. 7129.

*HEATH, PETER,   Danville.
Served in Capt. Morrill's Company, Col. Fifield's Regt. Detached Militia in U. S. service 4 months and 27 days, 1812. Served from Feb. 11 to May 10, 1813 in Capt. Samul Gordon's Company, 11th Regt. Ref: R. & L. 1812, AGO Page 8.

*HEATH, SAMUEL L., Corporal.
Served from April 12. 1814 to April 21, 1814 in Capt. Othniel Jewett's Company, Sumner's Regt.

‡HEATH, WELLS, Drummer, Johnson.
Served in Capt. Taylor's Company, Col. Williams' Regt. in U. S. service at Swanton in 1812. Served in Capt. Toby's Company. Pension Certificate No. 5275. Ref: Vol. 52, Vt. State Papers, Page 199.

*HEATH, WILLIAM L.,   Danville.
Served in Capt. Morrill's Company, Col. Fifield's Regt. Detached Militia in U. S. service 1 month and 10 days, 1812.

HEATH, WILLIAM, S.
Served from Feb. 11 to May 10, 1813 in Capt. Samul Gordon's Company, 11th Regt. Ref: R. & L. 1812, AGO Page 8.

‡HEATON, ALVA,   Thetford.
Volunteered to go to Plattsburgh, September, 1814, and served 12 days in Capt. Joseph Barrett's Company. Pension Certificate of widow, Laura, No. 29288.

HEATON, JAMES,   Thetford.
Volunteered to go to Plattsburgh, September, 1814, and served in Capt. Joseph Barrett's Company. Ref: Book 52, AGO Page 41.

*HEATON, JOHN.
Served in Capt. Robbins' Company, Col. Wm. Williams' Regt. Detached

Militia in U. S. service 4 months and 29 days, 1812. Served from April 12, 1814 to May 20, 1814 in Capt. George Fisher's Company, Sumner's Regt.

HEATON, JOSEPH.
Enlisted May 6, 1812 for 5 years in Capt. White Youngs' Company, 15th Regt.; on Muster Roll from Aug. 31, 1814 to Dec. 31, 1814; killed Sept. 11, 1814. Ref: R. & L. 1812, AGO Page 27.

*HEATON, NATHAN, Corporal.
Served in Capt. Wright's Company, Col. Martindale's Regt. Detached Militia in U. S. service 2 months and 14 days, 1812. Served in 1st Regt. of Detached Militia of Vt. in U. S. service Nov. 18 to Nov. 19, 1812.

HEATON, NATHANIEL,   Pittsford.
Volunteered to go to Plattsburgh, September, 1814, and served 8 days in Capt. Caleb Hendee's Company. Ref: Book 52, AGO Page 125.

*HEATON, SAMUEL.
Served in Corning's Detachment, Vt. Militia.

*HEATH, WILLIS (or Wells), Drummer.
Served in 4 Regt. Vt. Militia commanded by Col. Williams.

HEATON, WILLIAM S., Lieutenant.
Appointed 2 Lieutenant 11 Inf. March 12, 1812; 1 Lieutenant March 13, 1813; died Nov. 19, 1813 of wounds received Nov. 11, 1813 in battle of Chrystlers Fields, Upper Canada. On Pay Roll for Capt. Benjamin S. Edgerton's Company, 11th Regt. for September and October, 1812, and January and February, 1813. Ref: Heitman's Historical Register & Dictionary USA; R. & L. 1812, AGO Page 2.

*HEBARD, DIAH,   Randolph.
Volunteered to go to Plattsburgh, September, 1814, and served in Capt. Lebbeus Egerton's Company.

*HEBARD, ENOCH,   Randolph.
Volunteered to go to Plattsburgh, September, 1814, and served in Capt. Lebbeus Egerton's Company.

*HEBARD, SAMUEL,   Randolph.
Volunteered to go to Plattsburgh, September, 1814, and served in Capt. Lebbeus Egerton's Company.

*HEDGE, BARNABAS, Enosburgh or Richford. Enlisted Sept. 25, 1813 in Capt. Martin D. Folett's Company, Dixon's Regt.

‡*HEDGE, NATHAN, Enosburgh or Richford. Enlisted Sept. 25, 1813 in Capt. Martin D. Folett's Company, Dixon's Regt. Pension Certificate No. 25059; Pension Certificate of widow, Sally, No. 14785.

‡*HEDGE, SAMUEL, Enosburgh or Fairfield. Served in Capt. Kendall's Company, Col. Wm. Williams' Regt. Detached Militia in U. S. service 4 months and 23 days, 1812. Enlisted Sept. 25, 1813 in Capt. Martin D.

Folett's Company, Dixon's Regt. Pension Certificate No. 15322. Pension Certificate of widow, Rachel, No. 18000. Ref: Book 52, AGO Page 268.

HEERMAN, TIMOTHY,   Coventry.
Served in Capt. Masons' Company, Col. Fifield's Regt. stationed at Derby Line from Sept. 16, 1812 to March 16, 1813. Ref: Hemenway's Vt. Gazetteer, Vol. 3, Page 144.

*HEERS, SAMUEL.
Served in 1 Regt. Vt. Militia commanded by Col. Martindale.

HEFFERNAN, JAMES, Corporal .
Served from May 1 to June 30, 1814 in Capt. Alexander Brooks' Corps of Artillery. Ref: R. & L. 1812, AGO Page 31.

*HEIBLER, WEIGHT, Sergeant.
Served in Dixon's Regt. Vt. Militia.

HEIGHT, ALVIN.
Served from May 1 to June 30, 1814 in Capt. Haig's Corps of Light Dragoons. Ref: R. & L. 1812, AGO Page 20.

HEILEMAN, JULIUS FREDERICK.
Appointed Captain May 5, 1813; transferred to Artillery Corps May 12, 1814; died June 27, 1836. Ref: Heitman's Historical Register & Dictionary USA.

*HELEY, JEREMIAH S.
Served in Sumner's Regt. Vt. Militia.

‡*HELMS, NILES.
Served in 4 Regt. (Williams') Vt. Militia, Capt. Petty's Company. Pension Certificate of widow, Susan, No. 2727.

‡HELMS, SAMUEL.
Served in Capt. Pettis' Company. Pension Certificate No. 23689.

‡HELMS, SANDS.
Served in Capt. S. Pettis' Company. Pension Certificate of widow, Cynthia, No. 22985.

HELPWORTH, TRILLIS, Franklin County. Volunteered to go to Plattsburgh, Sept. 11, 1814 and served in 15th or 22nd Regt. Ref: Hemenway's Vt. Gazetteer, Vol. 2, Page 392.

*HEMENWAY, FRANCIS S., Sergeant.
Served from April 12, to May 20, 1814 in Capt. George Fisher's Company, Sumner's Regt.

HEMING, JOSEPH.
Served in Capt. Taylor's Company, Col. Wm. Williams' Regt. Detached Militia in U. S. service 4 months and 24 days, 1812. Ref: Book 53, AGO Page 14.

*HEMINGWAY, E. G.,   Fairfield.
Served in Capt. George W. Kindall's Company, Col. Wm. Williams' Regt. 4 months and 23 days, 1812.

*HEMINGWAY, SAMUEL.
Served in Capt. Wheeler's Company, Col. Fifield's Regt. Detached Militia in U. S. service 6 months and 4 days, 1812.

‡HEMINGWAY, STEPHEN F.
Served from May 1 to June 30, 1814 in Capt. Haig's Corps of Light Dragoons. Also served under Captains Butler and Hall. Pension Certificate of widow, Deborah, No. 15122. Ref: R. & L. 1812, AGO Page 20.

*HEMINGWAY, WILLIAM.
Served from April 12, 1814 to April 21, 1814 in Capt. Edmund B. Hill's Company, Sumner's Regt.

HEMINGWAY, ELBRIDGE G.
Served in Capt. George W. Kindall's Company, Col. Wm. Williams' Regt.; on Muster Roll from Aug. 31 to Oct. 31. 1812 and from Nov. 1 to Dec. 8, 1812; on Pay Roll to Sept. 10, 1812. Served in Capt. Haig's Corps of Light Dragoons; on Pay Roll to June 30. 1814. Ref: R. & L. 1812, AGO Pages 20, 37, 38, 39.

*HEMINGWAY, VASHNE.
Served from April 12, 1814 to May 20, 1814 in Capt. George Fisher's Company, Sumner's Regt.

HENDEE, ABNER, Waggoner, Pittsford.
Volunteered to go to Plattsburgh, September, 1814, and served 8 days in Capt. Caleb Hendee's Company. Ref: Book 52, AGO Page 125.

*HENDEE, ASEL (or Azel), Randolph.
Volunteered to go to Plattsburgh, September, 1814, and served in Capt. Lebbeus Egerton's Company.

HENDEE, CALEB JR., Captain, Pittsford. Volunteered to go to Plattsburgh, September, 1814, and served 8 days in command of company from Pittsford. Ref: Book 52, AGO Pages 124 and 126.

HENDEE, DANIEL, Pittsford.
Volunteered to go to Plattsburgh, September, 1814, and served 8 days in Capt. Caleb Hendee's Company. Ref: Book 52, AGO Page 125.

*HENDEE, JESSE.
Served from April 12, 1814 to April 21, 1814 in Capt. Othniel Jewett's Company, Sumner's Regt.

HENDEE, SAMUEL, Pittsford.
Volunteered to go to Plattsburgh, September, 1814, and served 4 days in Capt. Horton's Company. Ref: Book 52, AGO Page 162.

*HENDERSON, CHESTER.
Served in Tyler's Regt. Vt. Militia.

‡HENDERSON, HENRY.
Served in Capt. M. Cornas' Company. Pension Certificate No. 29232.

HENDERSON, JOHN, Franklin County.
Volunteered to go to Plattsburgh Sept. 11, 1814 and served in 15th or 22nd Regt. Ref: Hemenway's Vt. Gazetteer, Vol. 2, Page 391.

‡HENDERSON, JOSEPH.
Served from Jan. 30, 1813 to June 8, 1813 in Capt. Weeks' Company, 11th Regt. Pension Certificate No. 17617.

HENDERSON, TIMOTHY B.
Served from Feb. 5 to May 4, 1813 in Lieut. V. R. Goodrich's Company, 11th Regt. Ref: R. & L. 1812, AGO Pages 10 and 11.

HENDRICK, JABEZ, Ripton.
Volunteered to go to Plattsburgh, September, 1814, and served 10 days; no organization given. Ref: Book 51, AGO Page 36.

HENDRICK, TALMA, Enosburgh or Richford. Served in Capt. Follet's Company, Col. Dixon's Regt. Detached Militia in U. S. service 1 month and 23 days, 1813. Enlisted Sept. 25, 1813 in Capt. Martin D. Folett's Company, Dixon's Regt.

HENDRICKSON, CORNELIUS.
Enlisted Dec. 16, 1812 for 5 years in company of late Capt. J. Brooks commanded by Lieut. John I. Cromwell, Corps of U. S. Artillery; on Muster Roll from April 30, 1814 to June 30, 1814. Ref: R. & L. 1812, AGO Page 18.

HENDRIX, HENRY, Lieutenant.
Appointed Ensign 30th Inf. April 30, 1813; 3 Lieutenant Sept. 18, 1813; 2 Lieutenant Aug. 1, 1814; honorably discharged June 15, 1815. Served in Capt. James Taylor's Company, 30th Regt.; on Muster Roll to Feb. 28, 1814. Ref: Heitman's Historical Register & Dictionary USA; R. & L. 1812, AGO Page 53.

HENKSON, WILLIAM.
Served from Oct. 11, 1813 to Oct. 17, 1813 in Capt. John Munson's Company, 3 Regt. (Tyler's). Ref: R. & L. 1812, AGO Page 36.

*HENNESY, WILLIAM.
Enlisted Feb. 11, 1813 for 5 years in company of late Capt. J. Brooks, commanded by Lieut. John I. Cromwell, Corps of U. S. Artillery; on Muster Roll from April 30, 1814 to June 30, 1814. Served in 4 Regt. (Williams') and 2 Regt. (Fifield's) Vt. Militia. Ref: R. & L. 1812, AGO Page 18.

HENNING, PHILIP.
Served from May 1 to June 30, 1814 in Capt. Haig's Corps of Light Dragoons. Ref: R. & L. 1812, AGO Page 20.

HENRY, DAVID, Fifer, Jefferson, Mass.
Enlisted at Burlington Feb. 22, 1814 for duration of the war and served in Capt. Wm. Miller's Company, Capt. Gideon Spencer's Company and Capt. James Taylor's Company, 30th Regt. Ref: R. & L. 1812, AGO Pages 53, 54, 55, 56.

*HENRY, JOSEPH.
Served from June 11, 1813 to June 14, 1813 in Lieut. Bates' Company, 1st Regt.

HENRY, SAMUEL.
Served in Capt. Weeks' Company, 11th Regt.; on Pay Roll for January and February, 1813. Ref: R. & L. 1812, AGO Page 5.

HENRY, WILLIAM.
Served in Capt. Walker's Company,
Col. Fifield's Regt. Detached Militia
in U. S. service 3 months and 9 days,
1812. Ref: Book 53, AGO Page 70.

HENRY. ZIMRI O.
Served from Feb. 15, 1814 to June
30, 1814 in Regt. of Light Dragoons.
Ref: R. & L. 1812, AGO Page 21.

HENSEY, STEPHEN,   Sanborton.
Served in Capt. Poland's Company,
34th Inf.; discharged July 4, 1814.
Ref: R. & L. 1812, AGO Page 30.

HENTON, RICHARD,   Franklin County.
Volunteered to go to Plattsburgh
Sept. 11, 1814, and served in 15th or
22nd Regt. Ref: Hemenway's Vt. Gazetteer, Vol. 2, Page 391.

*HERICKSON, GEORGE W.
Served in Corning's Detachment, Vt.
Militia.

*HERRICK, ANDREW T.
Served from April 12, 1814 to April
21, 1814 in Capt. Othniel Jewett's
Company, Sumner's Regt.

HERRICK, DANIEL,   Highgate.
Volunteered to go to Plattsburgh,
September, 1814, and served 4 days
in Capt. Conrad Saxe's Company, 4
Regt. (Williams'). Ref: Book 51, AGO
Pages 100 and 101.

*HERRICK, DAVID,   Highgate.
Served in Capt. Saxe's Company,
Col. Wm. Williams' Regt. Detached
Militia in U. S. service 4 months
and 24 days, 1812.

‡*HERRICK, ELIJAH, Corporal.
Enlisted Sept. 25, 1813 in company
of Capt. Jonathan Prentiss Jr., Dixon's Regt. Pension Certificate of
widow, Harriet, No. 18701.

*HERRICK, EPHRAIM.
Enlisted Sept. 25, 1813 in company
of Capt. Jonathan Prentiss Jr., Dixon's Regt.

*HERRICK, ERASTUS.
Served from Sept. 23, 1813 to Sept.
29, 1813 in Capt. Amasa Mansfield's
Company, Dixon's Regt.

*HERRICK. ERVIN (or Erwin).
Served in Capt. Dorrance's Company,
Col. Wm. Williams' Regt. Detached
Militia in U. S. service 4 months
and 23 days, 1812.

HERRICK, JOHN.
Served from March 22 to June 21,
1813 in Capt. Samul Gordon's Company, 11th Regt. Ref: R. & L. 1812,
AGO Page 8.

‡HERRICK, MARTIN.
Served in Capt. Mendock's Company.
Pension Certificate No. 12893.

HERRICK, RUFUS,   Franklin County.
Volunteered to go to Plattsburgh
Sept. 11, 1814 and served in 15th or
22nd Regt. Ref: Hemenway's Vt. Gazetteer, Vol. 2, Page 392.

HERRICK. SIMEON. Corporal.
Served from March 15, 1813 to June
14, 1813 in Capt. Samul Gordon's
Company, 11th Regt. Ref: R. & L.
1812, AGO Page 8.

HERRIMAN, JOHN.
Enlisted Jan. 21, 1813 in Capt.
Samul Gordon's Company, 11th Regt.;
on Pay Roll to May 31, 1813. Ref:
R. & L. 1812, AGO Pages 8 and 9.

HERRIN, DAVID.
Appointed Ensign July 6, 1814; 3
Lieutenant Oct. 1, 1814, in 26th Regt.
of Riflemen. Ref: Governor and
Council Vt., Vol. 6, Page 477.

HERRIN, HENRY E.,   Franklin County.
Volunteered to go to Plattsburgh,
Sept. 11, 1814 and served in 15th or
22nd Regt. Ref: Hemenway's Vt.
Gazetteer, Vol. 2, Page 392.

*HERRIN, JOHN, Ensign.
Served in 1 Regt. Vt. Militia commanded by Col. Martindale.

HERRINGTON, ESAKEL.
Served in War of 1812 and was cap-
tured by troops June 26, 1813 at
Beaver Dams; discharged Aug. 10th.
Ref: Records of Naval Records and
Library, Navy Dept.

*HERWOOD. CYRUS.
Served in 4 Regt. (Williams') Vt.
Militia.

‡*HEWES. SAMUEL, Sergeant.
Served in Dixon's Regt. Vt. Militia.
Also served in Capt. Burnap's Com-
pany. Pension Certificate No. 18208.

‡HEWETT. ALVEN,   Pittsford.
Volunteered to go to Plattsburgh,
September, 1814, and served 8 days
in Capt. Caleb Hendee's Company.
Pension Certificate No. 28209.

*HEWETT, EZEKIEL.
Served in Capt. Barns' Company,
Col. Wm. Williams' Regt. Detached
Militia in U. S. service 5 months.
Served from Oct. 4, 1813 to Oct. 13,
1813 in Capt. John Palmer's Com-
pany, 1st Regt. 2nd Brig. 3rd Div.

‡*HEWETT, PITT E.
Served in Capt. Brown's Company,
Col. Martindale's Regt. Detached
Militia in U. S. service 2 months
and 14 days, 1812. Pension Certificate No. 13417. Pension Certificate
of widow, Lucy W., No. 18806.

*HEWEY. HENRY.
Served with Hospital Attendants, Vt.

*HEWEY, JOSEPH.
Served in 1 Regt. Vt. Militia commanded by Col. Judson.

*HEWITT. HANNANIAH, Corporal.
Served from April 12, 1814 to April
21, 1814 in Capt. Othniel Jewett's
Company, Sumner's Regt.

HEWITT, ISRAEL,   Chittenden.
Served from Oct. 31, 1812 to Feb. 28,
1813 in Capt. Samuel H. Holly's Company, 11th Regt. Ref: R. & L.
1812. AGO Page 25.

HEWITT, MARCUS D.,   Shoreham.
Served from Nov. 1, 1812 to Feb. 28,
1813 in Capt. Samuel H. Holly's Company, 11th Regt. Belonged to the 2nd
Regt. Light Artillery and died at
Sackett's Harbor the winter after his
enlistment. Ref: R. & L. 1812, AGO
Page 25; Rev. J. F. Goodhue's History of Shoreham, Page 102.

*HIBBARD, ABIAL, Fairfield or Swanton.
Served in Capt. George W. Kindall's
Company, 4 Regt. (Williams') Detached Militia in U. S. service 4 months
and 23 days, 1812.

*HIBBARD, ELIHUE.
Served in Corning's Detachment, Vt.
Militia.

*HIBBARD, ELIJAH.
Served in Corning's Detachment, Vt.
Militia.

*HIBBARD, ELISHA.
Served in 4 Regt. Vt. Militia commanded by Col. Peck.

*HIBBARD, ISAAC, Georgia or Highgate.
Served about 5½ months in Capt.
Conrade Saxe's Company, Col. Wm.
Williams' Regt. Detached Militia.

*HIBBARD, JOHN JR.
Served in Capt. Wheatly's Company,
Col. Fifield's Regt. Detached Militia
in U. S. service 2 months and 21
days, 1812.

HIBBARD, JOHN B.
Served from Jan. 18, 1813 to May 14,
1813 in Capt. Edgerton's Company,
11th Regt. Ref: R. & L. 1812, AGO
Pages 2 and 3.

‡HIBBARD, JONATHAN F.
Enlisted May 1, 1813 for 1 year in
Capt. Daniel Farrington's Company
(also commanded by Capt. Simeon
Wright), 30th Regt.; on Muster Roll
March 1, 1814 to April 30, 1814. Pension Certificate No. 10724.

HIBBARD, JOSEPH L.,   Charleston.
Served from Sept. 1, 1814 to June 16,
1815 in Capt. Sanford's Company,
30th Inf. Ref: R. & L. 1812, AGO
Page 23.

‡HIBBARD, ORLIN.
Served in Capt. S. Farnsworth's
Company. Pension Certificate of widow, Chloe, No. 26823.

HIBBARD, TIMOTHY,   Orwell.
Volunteered to go to Plattsburgh,
September, 1814, and served 11 days
in Capt. Wait Branch's Company.
Ref: Book 51, AGO Pages 16 and 17.

HICKS, COMFORT.
Enlisted Sept. 23, 1813 and served 1
month and 23 days in Capt. Amasa
Mansfield's Company, Col. Dixon's
Regt. Served in War of 1812 and was
captured by troops Sept. 17, 1814 at
Fort Erie; discharged Nov. 8, 1814.
Ref: Book 52, AGO Page 269; Book
53, AGO Page 112; Records of Naval
Records and Library, Navy Dept.

‡*HICKS, ISAAC.
Served in 1 Regt. (Judson's) and
4 Regt. (Williams') Vt. Militia. Also
served in Capt. Barnes' Company.
Pension Certificate No. 16911.

HICKS, JOHN.
Served from Jan. 19, 1813 to May 10,
1813 in Capt. John W. Weeks' Company, 11th Regt. Ref: R. & L. 1812,
AGO Page 4.

HICKS, LEVI.
Served in Capt. Benjamin S. Edgerton's Company, 11th Regt. from Nov.
1, 1812 to date of death Jan. 26,
1813. Ref: R. & L. 1812, AGO Pages
1 and 2.

‡*HICKS, LEVI JR.
Served from June 11, 1813 to June
14, 1813 in Capt. Moses Jewett's Company, 1st Regt. 2nd Brig. 3rd Div.
Also served in Capt. Barnes' Company, 4 Regt. (Williams') Vt. Militia. Pension Certificate No. 8299.

HICKS, SYLVANUS.
Enlisted June 12, 1813 for 5 years in
company of late Capt. J. Brooks
commanded by Lt. John I. Cromwell,
Corps of U. S. Artillery; on Muster
Roll from April 30, 1814 to June 30,
1814. Ref: R. & L. 1812, AGO Page
18.

HICOK, OLIVER C.
Served from Dec. 24, 1812 to Feb. 28,
1813. in Capt. Samuel H. Holly's
Company, 11th Regt. Ref: R. & L.
1812, AGO Page 25.

*HICOK, SELAH.
Served in Capt. Phelps' Company,
Col. Wm. Williams' Regt. Detached
Militia in U. S. service 5 months,
1812.

*HIDE, PAUL.
Served from April 12, 1814 to April
15, 1814 in Capt. Jonathan P. Stanley's Company, Col. W. B. Sumner's
Regt.

*HIGBEE, JOEL, Corporal.
Served from June 11, 1813 to June 14,
1813 in Capt. Samuel Blinn's Company, 1st Regt.

HIGBEE, LEVI.
Enlisted Nov. 11, 1813 for 1 year in
Capt. Wm. Miller's Company, 30th
Regt. Ref: R. & L. 1812, AGO
Page 54.

‡*HIGGINS, CORNELIUS,   Fairfax.
Enlisted Sept. 25, 1813 and served
1 month and 23 days in Capt. Asa
Wilkins' Company, Col. Dixon's Regt.
Also served in Capt. Scott's Company.
Pension Certificate No. 7542. Pension Certificate of widow, Almyra,
No. 29296.

*HIGGINS, JESSE, Corporal,   Fairfax.
Enlisted Sept. 25, 1813 in Capt. Asa
Wilkins' Company, Dixon's Regt.
Volunteered to go to Plattsburgh,
September, 1814, and served 8 days
as a Sergeant in Capt. Josiah Grout's
Company. Ref: Book 51, AGO Page
103; Hemenway's Vt. Gazetteer, Vol.
2, Page 408.

HIGGINS, SIMEON.
Served in Capt. Taylor's Company, Col. Wm. Williams' Regt. Detached Militia in U. S. service 4 months and 24 days, 1812. Enlisted May 17, 1813 for 1 year and served in Capt. James Taylor's Company and Capt. Gideon Spencer's Company, 30th Regt.; discharged May 17, 1814. Ref: Book 53, AGO Page 19; R. & L. 1812, AGO Pages 52, 57, 58.

HIGGINS, URIAH.
Served from March 24, 1813 to June 23, 1813 in Capt. Samul Gordon's Company, 11th Regt. Ref: R. & L. 1812, AGO Page 8.

HIGHT, GEORGE WASHINGTON, Lieutenant. Appointed Cadet Military Academy March 20, 1807; 2 Lieutenant Light Artillery Jan. 3, 1812; 1 Lieutenant Aug. 10, 1813; Major Asst. Inspector General July 17, 1814; honorably discharged June 15, 1815; died April 20, 1845. Ref: Heitman's Historical Register & Dictionary USA.

*HIGLEY, JESSE C.
Served from April 12, 1814 to April 21, 1814 in Capt. Eseck Sprague's Company, Sumner's Regt.

*HILBOURN, BENJAMIN.
Served in Sumner's Regt. Vt. Militia.

*HILDRETH, ALVIN.
Served from Sept. 25, 1813 to Oct. 1, 1813 in Capt. Elijah Birge's Company, Dixon's Regt.

*HILDRETH, ELDAD, Corporal.
Served in Capt. Wheatley's Company, Col. Fifield's Regt. Detached Militia in U. S. service 2 months and 21 days, 1812.

‡*HILDRETH, JARED.
Served in Capt. Wheatly's Company, Col. Fifield's Regt. Detached Militia in U. S. service 6 months, 1812. Pension Certificate of widow, Arathusa, No. 1112.

HILDRETH, JOEL,   Roxbury.
Volunteered to go to Plattsburgh, September, 1814, and served 8 days in Capt. Samuel M. Orcutt's Company. Ref: Book 52, AGO Page 250.

HILDRETH, PETER, Corporal.
Served in company of Capt. John McNeil Jr., 11th Regt.; on Pay Roll for January and Februray, 1813. Ref: R. & L. 1812, AGO Page 17.

‡*HILDRETH, SAMUEL.
Served in Corning's Detachment, Vt. Militia. Also served in Capt. Hunt's Company. Pension Certificate of widow, Polly, No. 9261.

*HIGGINS, SIMEON.
Served in 4 Regt. Vt. Militia commanded by Col. Williams.

HILL, AARON,   Waitsfield.
Volunteered to go to Plattsburgh, September, 1814, and served 4 days in Capt. Mathias S. Jones' Company. Ref: Book 52, AGO Page 170.

*HILL, ABNER.
Served from April 12, 1814 to April 21, 1814 in Capt. Edmund B. Hill's Company, Sumner's Regt.

*HILL, ALDEN.
Enlisted Sept. 25, 1813 in Capt. Elijah W. Wood's Company, Col. Dixon's Regt.; transferred to Capt. Asahel Langworthy's Company, Col. Isaac Clark's Regt. Oct. 28, 1813.

HILL, ASA.
Served from April 14, 1813 to July 13, 1813 in Capt. Samul Gordon's Company, 11th Regt. Ref: R. & L. 1812, AGO Page 8.

*HILL, BARNABAS.
Served in Capt. Phelps' Company, Col. Wm. Williams' Regt. Detached Militia in U. S. service 5 months, 1812.

*HILL, BENJAMIN, Musician.
Served from June 11, 1813 to June 14, 1813 in Capt. Moses Jewett's Company, 1st Regt. 2nd Brig. 3rd Div.

*HILL, CALEB,   Richford.
Enlisted Sept. 25, 1813 and served 1 month and 23 days in Capt. Martin D. Folett's Company, Col. Dixon's Regt.

*HILL, CHARLES.
Served from Oct. 4, 1813 to Oct. 13, 1813 in Capt. John Palmer's Company, 1st Regt. 2nd Brig. 3rd Div. Served from April 12, 1814 to May 20, 1814 in company of Capt. James Gray Jr., Sumner's Regt.

HILL, CHESTER C.
Enlisted May 15, 1813 for 1 year in Capt. Simeon Wright's Company; served as waiter for Lieutenant Johnson. Ref: R. & L. 1812, AGO Page 51.

*HILL, DAVID.
Enlisted May 3, 1813 for 1 year in Capt. Daniel Farrington's Company (also commanded by Capt. Simeon Wright) 30th Regt.; on Muster Roll March 1, 1814 to April 30, 1814. Also served in Sumner's Regt. Vt. Militia. Ref: R. & L. 1812, AGO Pages 50 and 51.

HILL, EBENEZER,   Highgate.
Volunteered to go to Plattsburgh, September, 1814, and served 6 days in Capt. Conrad Sax's Company, 4 Regt. (Williams'). Ref: Book 51, AGO Pages 100 and 101.

*HILL EDMUND B., Captain, Cornwall.
Served from April 12 to April 21, 1814 in command of a company in Sumner's Regt.. in service by order of Governor Chittenden. Volunteered to go to Plattsburgh, September, 1814, and was at the battle, serving as captain of his company.

HILL, FESTUS,   St. Albans.
Volunteered and was in the action at Plattsburgh Sept. 11, 1814 serving in Capt. Samuel H. Farnsworth's Company. Ref: Hemenway's Vt. Gazetteer, Vol. 2, Page 434.

HILL, GAIUS,   Georgia.
Volunteered to go to Plattsburgh,
September, 1814, and served 8 days
in Capt. Jesse Post's Company, Dixon's Regt. Ref: Book 51, AGO Pages
102 and 149.

‡*HILL, HARRY,   Cornwall.
Served from April 12, 1814 to April
21, 1814 in Capt. Edmund B. Hill's
Company, Sumner's Regt. Volunteered to go to Plattsburgh, September,
1814, and was at the battle, serving
in the same company. Pension Certificate of widow, Electa, No. 26280.

‡*HILL, HEMAN (or Herman).
Enlisted Sept. 25, 1813 and served
1 month and 23 days in Capt. Elijah
W. Wood's Company, Col. Dixon's
Regt. Also served in Capt. Saxe's
Company, 4 Regt. Pension Certificate
of widow, Charlotte, No. 11308.

*HILL, HIRA, Surgeon's Mate, Georgia.
Appointed Surgeon's Mate Sept. 25,
1813 in Consolidated Regt. of Vt.
Militia in U. S. service. Also served
as Corporal in Dixon's Regt. Vt.
Militia.

HILL, HUBBARD D.
Served in Capt. Samuel H. Holly's
Company, 11th Regt. from Jan. 1,
1813 to date of death Feb. 10, 1813.
Ref: R. & L. 1812, AGO Page 25.

‡*HILL, IRA, Lieutenant, Isle-La-Motte.
Served from July 22 to Dec. 9, 1812
in Capt. Pettes' Company, Col. Wm.
Williams' Regt. Detached Militia. Appointed 2nd Lieutenant Sept. 22, 1813
in Capt. Asahel Langworthy's Company, Col. Isaac Clark's Volunteer
Riflemen in U. S. service. Pension
Certificate No. 16143.

*HILL, ISAAC.
Served in 1 Regt. Vt. Militia commanded by Col. Martindale.

*HILL, ISRAEL.
Served in Capt. Hotchkiss' Company,
Col. Martindale's Regt. Detached
Militia in U. S. service 2 months
and 13 days, 1812.

*HILL, JAMES.
Served from Oct. 10 to Oct. 17, 1813
in Capt. Stephen Brown's Company,
3 Regt. (Tyler's).

*HILL, JOHN,   Wilmington.
Served in Tyler's Regt. Vt. Militia.

*HILL, JONATHAN.
Served in Capt. Start's Company, Col.
Martindale's Regt. Detached Militia
in U. S. service 2 months and 13
days, 1812.

HILL, JOSEPH, Corporal.
Served as Corporal in Capt. Noyce's
Company, Col. Jonathan Williams'
Regt. Detached Militia in U. S. serv-
ice 2 months and 6 days, 1812. Also
served as private in Sumner's Regt.
Vt. Militia.

*HILL, JOSHUA.
Served in 4 Regt. Vt. Militia commanded by Col. Peck.

HILL, LEVI.
Enlisted May 20, 1813 for 1 year in
Capt. Daniel Farrington's Company
(also commanded by Capt. Simeon
Wright) 30th Regt.; on Muster Roll
from March 1, 1814 to April 30, 1814.
Ref: R. & L. 1812, AGO Pages 50
and 51.

*HILL, LEWIS, Lieutenant.
Served in 4 Regt. Vt. Militia commanded by Col. Williams.

HILL, LOVEL.
Enlisted June 16, 1813 for 1 year in
Capt. Daniel Farrington's Company
(also commanded by Capt. Simeon
Wright) 30th Regt. Ref: R. & L.
1812, AGO Pages 50 and 51.

*HILL, LUCIUS (or Lumas).
Served in Capt. Preston's Company,
Col. Jonathan Williams' Regt. Detached Militia in U. S. service 2
months and 6 days, 1812.

*HILL, LYMAN.
Enlisted Sept. 25, 1813 and served
1 month and 23 days in Capt. Elijah
W. Wood's Company, Col. Dixon's
Regt.

HILL, NATHAN.
Served in Capt. Chadwick's Company.
Ref: R. & L. 1812, AGO Page 32.

*HILL, OLDEN.
Served in Capt. Langworthy's Com-
pany, Col. Dixon's Regt. Detached
Militia in U. S. service 21 days, 1813.

*HILL, RICHARD.
Served from April 12, 1814 to April
21, 1814 in Capt. Eseck Sprague's
Company, Sumner's Regt.

*HILL, RICHARD, Sergeant, Greensboro.
Served in Capt. Mason's Company,
Col. Fifield's Regt. Detached Militia
in U. S. service at Derby 6 months
in 1812.

‡HILL, RICHARD,   Starksboro.
Volunteered to go to Plattsburgh,
September, 1814, and served 4 days
in Capt. Moulton's Company. Pension Certificate No. 33092.

*HILL, RODRICK.
Enlisted Sept. 25, 1813 in company
of Capt. Jonathan Prentiss Jr., Dixon's Regt.

HILL, SAMUEL,   Danville.
Volunteered to go to Plattsburgh,
September, 1814, and served 3 days
in Capt. Solomon Langmaid's Company. Ref: Book 51, AGO Pages 75
and 76.

‡*HILL, SAMUEL JR., Musician, Starksboro. Served from June 11, 1813 to
June 14, 1813 in Capt. Moses Jewett's
Company, 1st Regt. 2nd Brig. 3rd
Div. Volunteered to go to Plattsburgh, September, 1814, and served
4 days in Capt. Moulton's Company.
Also served in Capt. Phelps' Company, 4 Regt. (Williams') Vt. Militia
and in Sumner's Regt. Vt. Militia.
Pension Certificate No. 7520. Pension Certificate of widow, Elizabeth,
No. 33026.

*HILL, SAMUEL H.
Served in Sumner's Regt. Vt. Militia.

*HILL, SAXTON.
Served in 1 Regt. (Judson's) Vt. Militia.

*HILL, THOMAS, Sergeant,   Richford.
Enlisted Sept. 25, 1813 and served 1 month and 23 days in Capt. Martin D. Folett's Company, Col. Dixon's Regt.

*HILL, THOMAS.
Served from April 12, 1814 to April 21, 1814 in Lieut. Justus Foote's Company, Sumner's Regt.

HILL, THOMAS.
Served from May 16, 1813 to May 15, 1814 in Capt. James Taylor's Company and Capt. Gideon Spencer's Company, 30th Regt. Ref: R. & L. 1812, AGO Pages 52, 57, 59.

*HILL, THOMAS C., Corporal.
Served from June 11, 1813 to June 14, 1813 in Capt. Hezekiah Barns' Company, 1st Regt. 2nd Brig. 3rd Div.

*HILL, TIMOTHY.
Served in Capt. O. Lowery's Company, Col. Wm. Williams' Regt. Detached Militia in U. S. service 4 months and 26 days, 1812. Also served with 4 Regt. (Peck's) Vt. Militia.

*HILL, TITUS JR., Sergeant.
Served from April 12, 1814 to April 21, 1814 in Capt. Edmund B. Hill's Company, Sumner's Regt.

*HILL, TRUMAN.
Enlisted Sept. 20, 1813 in Capt. John Weed's Company, Col. Clark's Rifle Corps; transferred to Capt. Jesse Post's Company, Dixon's Regt. Sept. 25, 1813.

‡*HILL, WILLIAM JR.
Served in Capt. Farr's Company, 3 Regt. (Tyler's) Vt. Militia. Pension Certificate No. 14454. Pension Certificate of widow, Anna, No. 30161.

*HILL, WYMAN, Sergeant.
Served from June 11, 1813 to June 14, 1813 in Lieut. Bates' Company, 1st Regt.

‡*HILLERY, JOHN (or John Jr.)
Served in Capt. E. Walker's Company, Col. Fifield's Regt. Detached Militia in U. S. service 6 months and 3 days, 1812. Pension Certificate No. 5205. Pension Certificate of widow, Hitty, No. 5913.

HILLERY, SAMUEL,   Berlin.
Volunteered to go to Plattsburgh, September, 1814, and served 8 days in Capt. Cyrus Johnson's Company. Ref: Book 52, AGO Page 202.

*HILLIARD, CLARKE, Sergeant, Richmond. Served from Oct. 5, 1813 to Oct. 16, 1813 in Capt. Hinman's Company, 3 Regt. (Tyler's); volunteered to go to Plattsburgh, Sep-

tember, 1814, and served 9 days in same company. Also served in Corning's Detachment, Vt. Militia.

*HILLIARD, MINOR,   Isle-La-Motte.
Served in Capt. Pettes' Company, Col. Wm. Williams' Regt. Detached Militia in U. S. service 4 months and 17 days, 1812.

HILLIARD, SAMUEL,   Shrewsbury.
Volunteered to go to Plattsburgh, September, 1814, and served 4 days in Capt. Robert Reed's Company. Ref: Book 52, AGO Page 138.

HILLS, SAMUEL.
Served in Capt. Start's Company, Col. Martindale's Regt. Detached Militia in U. S. service 2 months and 13 days, 1812. Ref: Book 53, AGO Page 24.

*HILLS, SIMEON.
Served in Corning's Detachment and 4 Regt. (Peck's) Vt. Militia.

HILLYARD, JACOB.
Enlisted June 16, 1812 for 5 years in Capt. White Youngs' Company, 15th Regt.; on Muster Roll from Aug. 31, 1814 to Dec. 31, 1814. Ref: R. & L. 1812, AGO Page 27.

HILLYARD, MINARD.
Served from Feb. 3, 1813 to May 22, 1813 in Capt. Charles Follett's Company, 11th Regt. Ref: R. & L. 1812, AGO Page 13.

‡HILMAN, FREDERICK.
Served in Capt. Sabin's Company. Pension Certificate No. 26621.

HILTON, DANIEL,   Frederick, N. Y.
Enlisted at Middletown Feb. 6, 1814 for period of the war and served in Capt. Wm. Miller's Company and Capt. Gideon Spencer's Company, 30th Regt.; on Muster Roll to Aug. 31, 1814. Ref: R. & L. 1812, AGO Pages 54, 55, 57.

‡*HILTON, JOSIAH, Corporal.
Enlisted Sept. 25, 1813 and served 1 month and 23 days in Capt. Elijah Birge's Company, Col. Dixon's Regt. Pension Certificate No. 9991.

HIMES, JAMES.
Served in Lt. Wm. S. Foster's Company, 11th Regt.; on Pay Roll for January and February, 1813. Ref: R. & L. 1812, AGO Page 7.

‡*HINDS, DAVID C.
Served from March 11, 1813 to June 10, 1813 in Capt. Charles Follett's Company, 11th Regt. Served from April 20, 1814 to April 21, 1814 in Capt. Eseck Sprague's Company, Sumner's Regt: Also served in Capt. Sexton's Company. Pension Certificate No. 28739. Ref: R. & L. 1812, AGO Page 13.

*HINDS, ELI,   Eden.
Served in 2 Regt. Vt. Militia commanded by Col. Fifield.

*HINDS, ISAAC.
Served from April 12, 1814 to May 20, 1814 in Capt. George Fisher's Company, Sumner's Regt.

*HINDS, MOSES.
Served from April 20. 1814 to April
21, 1814 in Capt. Eseck Sprague's
Company, Sumner's Regt.

*HINDS, NATHAN S.
Served from March 12, 1813 to June
11, 1813 in Capt. Edgerton's Company, 11th Regt.; was at the battle
of Chrystler's Farm Nov. 11, 1813
and was reported missing after the
battle. Also served in 2 Regt.
(Fifield's) Vt. Militia. Ref: R. & L.
1812, AGO Page 3; Governor and
Council Vt. Vol. 6, Page 490.

‡HINES, ABRAM WOOD.
Served in Capt. Farrington's Company (30th Regt.). Pension Certificate No. 6097.

HINES, COGSWELL H.
Served in Capt. Chadwick's Company.
Ref: R. & L. 1812, AGO Page 32.

*HINES, JOHN.
Served from Oct. 2 to Nov. 4, 1813
in Capt. Asahel Langworthy's Company, Col. Isaac Clark's Rifle Corps.

HINES, NATHANIEL S.
Served in Capt. Mason's Company,
Col. Fifield's Regt. Detached Militia
in U. S. service 3 months and 16
days, 1812. Ref: Book 53, AGO Page
68.

HINKLEY, IRA,   Georgia.
Volunteered to go to Plattsburgh,
September, 1814, and served 8 days
in Capt. Jesse Post's Company, Dixon's Regt. Ref: Book 51, AGO Page
102.

‡HINKLEY, STALHAN.
Pension Certificate No. 18388. Served
in Capt. Gorden's Company.

HINKSON, ABRAM,   Cabot.
Volunteered to go to Plattsburgh,
September, 1814, and served 3 days
in Capt. Anthony Perry's Company.
Ref: Book 52, AGO Pages 252, 253
and 254.

*HINKSON, ELIJAH.
Served from Oct. 5, 1813 to Oct. 16,
1813 in Capt. Roswell Hunt's Company, 3 Regt. (Tyler's).

*HINKSON, GEORGE W.
Served in Corning's Detachment, Vt.
Militia; also served in Tyler's Regt.
Vt. Militia.

‡*HINKSON, WILLIAM,   Richmond.
Volunteered to go to Plattsburgh,
September, 1814, and served 9 days
in Capt. Roswell Hunt's Company,
3 Regt. (Tyler's). Pension Certificate of widow, Sarah, No. 26809.

*HINMAN, BENJAMIN D.
Served from June 11, 1813 to June
14, 1813 in Lieut. Bates' Company,
1 Regt. (Judson's).

HINMAN, DAVID.
Enlisted May 1, 1813 for 1 year in
Capt. Simeon Wright's Company. Ref:
R. & L. 1812, AGO Page 51.

‡HINMAN. SETH.
Served from April 24, 1813 to April
26, 1814 in Capt. James Taylor's
Company and Capt. Gideon Spencer's
Company, 30th Regt. Ref: R. & L.
1812, AGO Pages 52, 57, 59. Also
served in Col. Clark's Company. Pension Certificate No. 2589.

‡HINMAN, SOLOMON.
Enlisted May 15, 1813 for 1 year
in Capt. Simeon Wright's Company.
Pension Certificate No. 5288.

‡HIPES, SAMUEL.
Served in Capt. Rowan's Company.
Pension Certificate of widow, Cath-
arine, No. 28584.

*HITCHCOCK, AMOS (or Hicock).
Served from June 11. 1813 to June
14, 1813 in Capt. Hezekiah Barns'
Company, 1st Regt. 2nd Brig. 3rd
Div. Served from April 12, 1814 to
April 21, 1814 in Capt. Othniel Jew-
ett's Company, Sumner's Regt.

*HITCHCOCK, ASA.
Served in Capt. Hiram Mason's Com-
pany, Col. Fifield's Regt. Detached
Militia in U .S. service 11 days, 1812.

‡HITCHCOCK, DAVID.
Served in Capt. Spencer's Company.
Pension Certificate No. 32580.

HITCHCOCK, ETHAN ALLEN.
Appointed Cadet Military Academy
Oct. 11, 1814. Ref: Heitman's His-
torical Register & Dictionary USA.

*HITCHCOCK, HENRY, 1st Corporal.
Served from June 11, 1813 to June
14, 1813 in Capt. Moses Jewett's Company, 1st Regt. 2nd Brig. 3rd Div.

HITCHCOCK, MANNA,   Kingsbury.
Served from May 1 to July 15, 1814
in Capt. Spencer's Company, 29th
Inf. Ref: R. & L. 1812, AGO Page
30.

*HITCHCOCK, STEBBINS,   Waitsfield.
Volunteered to go to Plattsburgh,
September, 1814, and served 4 days
in Capt. Mathias S. Jones Company.
Also served in Corning's Detachment
Vt. Militia. Ref: Book 52, AGO Page
170.

*HITCHCOCK, WELLS,   Waitsfield.
Served in 4 Regt. (Peck's) Vt. Militia.

*HITCHEL, JOSEPH.
Served in Sumner's Regt. Vt. Militia.

HIX, WILLIAM,   West Haven.
Volunteered to go to Plattsburgh,
September, 1814, and served 4 days
in Capt. David B. Phippeney's Company. Ref: Book 52, AGO Page 146.

*HIXON, JOSEPH,   Roxbury.
Served in Capt. Wheatly's Company,
Col. Fifield's Regt. Detached Militia
in U. S. service 6 months, 1812.
Volunteered to go to Plattsburgh,
September, 1814, and served 8 days
in Capt. Samuel M. Orcutt's Com-
pany. Ref: Book 52, AGO Page 250.

*HIXON, JOSEPH JR.
Served in 2 Regt. Vt. Militia commanded by Col. Fifield.

*HOAHAM, DANIEL.
Served in Tyler's Regt. Vt. Militia.

HOAR, DAVID,   Georgia.
Served from May 11, 1813 to May 21, 1814 in Capt. Taylor's Company and Capt. Gideon Spencer's Company, 30th Regt. Volunteered to go to Plattsburgh, September, 1814, and served 8 days in Capt. Jesse Post's Company, Dixon's Regt. Ref: R. & L. 1812, AGO Pages 52, 57, 59; Book 51, AGO Pages 102 and 163.

HOARD, SETH,   St. Albans.
Enlisted June 7, 1813 for 1 year in Capt. John Wires' Company, 30th Regt. Ref: R. & L. 1812, AGO Page 40.

HOBART, JOHN,   Middlesex.
Volunteered to go to Plattsburgh, September, 1814, and served 10 days in Capt. Holden Putnam's Company. Ref: Book 52, AGO Page 251.

‡*HOBART, JONAS, Captain.
Served in 2 Regt. 3 Brig. 3 Div. Vt. Militia. Pension Certificate No. 24870.

HOBART, JOSEPH,   Franklin County.
Enlisted Oct. 1, 1812 for 5 years in Capt. White Youngs' Company, 15th Regt.; on Muster Roll from Aug. 31, 1814 to Dec. 31, 1814. Ref: R. & L. 1812, AGO Page 27.

*HOBART, LUTHER.
Served in 3 Regt. (Tyler's) Vt. Militia.

HOBBES, ABRAM.
Served from March 16th to June 15, 1813 in Capt. Samul Gordon's Company, 11th Regt. Ref: R. & L. 1812, AGO Page 8.

*HOBBS, BENJAMIN.
Served with Hospital Attendants, Vt.

‡*HOBBS, JAMES.
Served in Capt. Lowry's Company, Col. Wm. Williams' Regt. Detached Militia in U. S. service 4 months and 26 days, 1812. Also served in Corning's Detachment, Vt. Militia. Pension Certificate No. 12725. Pension Certfiicate of widow, Charlotte, No. 32435.

*HOBERT, NOAH.
Served in 1 Regt. Vt. Militia commanded by Col. Judson.

*HOBSON, LEONARD KEEP.
Served in Capt. Howard's Company, Vt. Militia.

*HOCUM, CHARLES.
Served in 3 Regt. Vt. Militia commanded by Col. Williams.

‡*HODGDEN, SILAS W.
Served from April 12, 1814 to April 21, 1814 in Capt. Eseck Sprague's Company, Sumner's Regt. Also serv-

ed in Capt. Sexton's Company, Sumner's Regt. Pension Certificate of widow, Fanny, No. 29579.

HODGDON, NICHOLAS.
Served from Jan. 2, 1813 to March 5, 1813 in Capt. Jonathan Starks' Company, 11th Regt. Ref: R. & L. 1812, AGO Page 19.

HODGEKINS, JERRY, Sergeant, Belvidere. Volunteered to go to Plattsburgh, September, 1814, and served 7 days in Capt. Moody Shattuck's Company. Ref: Book 51, AGO Page 210.

HODGEKINS, JOHN,   Belvidere.
Volunteered to go to Plattsburgh, September, 1814, and served 7 days in Capt. Moody Shattuck's Company. Ref: Book 51, AGO Page 210.

*HODGES, JOHN, Sergeant.
Served in Sumner's Regt. Vt. Militia.

HODGING, REUBEN.
Served from May 1 to Aug. 21, 1814; no organization given. Ref: R. & L. 1812, AGO Page 29.

‡HODGKINS, HIRAM,   Rochester.
Volunteered to go to Plattsburgh, September, 1814, and served 7 days in Capt. Oliver Mason's Company. Pension Certificate No. 32807.

*HODGKINS, JERA (or Jena), Sergeant.
Enlisted Sept. 25, 1813 in Capt. Asa Wilkins' Company, Dixon's Regt.

HODGKINS, JOEL,   Fairfax.
Served from Sept. 12, 1813 in Capt. Asa Wilkins' Company, Dixon's Regt. Ref: Hemenway's Vt. Gazetteer, Vol. 2, Page 402.

‡*HODGKINS, STICKNEY,   Fairfax.
Served in Capt. Taylor's Company, Col. Wm. Williams' Regt. Detached Militia in U. S. service 4 months and 24 days, 1812. Enlisted Sept. 25, 1813 and served 1 month and 23 days in Capt. Asa Wilkins' Company, Col. Dixon's Regt. Served in Capt. M. Shattuck's Company. Pension Certificate of widow, Nancy, No. 28961.

HODGKINS, THOMAS, Adjutant, Rochester. Volunteered to go to Plattsburgh, September, 1814, and served 7 days in Capt. Oliver Mason's Company. Ref: Book 51, AGO Page 263.

HODGKINS, WILLIAM, St. Albans or Grand Isle. Enlisted May 3, 1813 for 1 year in Capt. John Wires' Company, 30th Regt. Ref: R. & L. 1812, AGO Page 40.

*HODGMAN, DAVID.
Served in Capt. Dodge's Company, Col. Fifield's Regt. Detached Militia in U. S. service 2 months and 21 days, 1812.

*HODGMAN, JONATHAN.
Served in Capt. Dodge's Company, Col. Fifield's Regt. Detached Militia in U. S. service 2 months and 21 days, 1812.

*HODGMAN, OLIVER, Musician.
Served in 2 Regt. Vt. Militia commanded by Col. Fifield.

*HOEUM, EZEKIEL JR.
Served in Regt. of Riflemen from September to November, 1813.

‡HOFF, JAMES.
Served in Capt. Thomas Hall's Company. Pension Certificate of widow, Philanda, No. 25127.

HOFFMAN, JOHN.
Served in Capt. Wheeler's Company, Col. Fifield's Regt. Detached Militia in U. S. service 2 months and 18 days, 1812. Ref: Book 53, AGO Page 81.

HOGABOOM, JAMES,   Manchester.
Enlisted May 1, 1813 for 1 year in Capt. Daniel Farrington's Company (also commanded by Capt. Simeon Wright), 30th Regt. Also served under Capt. Gideon Spencer, Capt. James Taylor and Capt. William Miller, 30th Regt. Ref: R. & L. 1812, AGO Pages 50 to 56.

‡HOGAN, JOHN.
Served in Capt. Reynolds' Company. Pension Certificate No. 22574.

HOGER, THOMAS.
Served in Capt. White Youngs' Company, 15th Regt.; on Muster Roll from Aug. 31, 1814 to Dec. 31, 1814. Ref: R. & L. 1812, AGO Page 27.

HOGERDOEN, PETER.
Served from May 1 to June 30, 1814 in Capt. Alexander Brooks' Corps of Artillery. Ref: R. & L. 1812, AGO Page 31.

HOGERMAN, JOHN, Musician.
Served from May 1 to June 30, 1814 in Capt. Alexander Brooks' Corps of Artillery. Ref: R. & L. 1812, AGO Page 31.

HOGG, ABRAHAM,   Franklin County.
Volunteered to go to Plattsburgh Sept. 11, 1814 and served in 15th or 22nd Regt. Ref: Hemenway's Vt. Gazetteer, Vol. 2, Pages 391 and 392.

‡HOHSTADT, JOHN, Sergeant.
Served from Sept. 25, 1813 to Nov. 15, 1813 in Capt. Elijah W. Wood's Company, Dixon's Regt. Also served in Captain Sawyer's Company. Pension Certificate No. 25504; pension certificate of widow, Mary Ann, No. 32358.

*HOISINGTON, GEORGE.
Served from April 12, 1814 to April 21, 1814 in Capt. Eseck Sprague's Company, Sumner's Regt.

‡HOIT, DAVID.
Served in Capt. Asahel Story's Company. Pension Certificate No. 29422.

HOIT, ELISHA, Corporal, Fairfax or Swanton. Served in Lieut. V. R. Goodrich's Company, 11th Regt.; on Pay Roll for January and February, 1813. Served from Aug. 8, 1812 in

company of Capt. Joseph Beeman, Jr., 11th Regt. U. S. Inf. under Col. Ira Clark. Ref: R. & L. 1812, AGO Page 11; Hemenway's Vt. Gazetteer, Vol. 2, Page 402.

*HOIT, GILBERT.
Served in 4 Regt. Vt. Militia commanded by Col. Williams.

*HOIT, HEMAN, Lieutenant,   Highgate.
Served from Sept. 1, 1812 in Capt. Conrade Saxe's Company, 4 Regt. (Williams'). Also served in Dixon's Regt. Vt. Militia.

HOIT, NATHANIEL,   Castleton, Vt.
Served in company of Capt. John McNeil Jr.. 11th Regt.; on Pay Roll for January and February, 1813. Ref: R. & L. 1812, AGO Page 17.

HOIT, THOMAS, Lieutenant.
Appointed Lieutenant Sept. 25, 1813 in Capt. Amos Robinson's Company. Dixon's Regt. Ref: Book 52, AGO Page 271.

HOLABIRD, HYMAN, Ensign, Shelburne.
Volunteered to go to Plattsburgh, September, 1814, and served in Major Judson's command (1 Regt.). Ref: Book 51, AGO Page 80.

HOLABIRD, TIMOTHY,   Shelburne.
Volunteered to go to Plattsburgh, September, 1814, and served in Major Luman Judson's command. Ref: Book 51, AGO Page 78.

*HOLBERT, LUTHER.
Served in 3 Regt. (Tyler's) Vt. Militia.

*HOLBROOK, ALANSON.
Served in Capt. Durkee's Company. Col. Fifield's Regt. Detached Militia in U. S. service 2 months and 16 days, 1812.

HOLBROOK, LUKE.
Served from May 1 to June 30, 1814 in Capt. Haig's Corps of Light Dragoons. Ref: R. & L. 1812, AGO Page 20.

*HOLBROOK, NATHANIEL.
Served in Capt. S. Pettes' Company, Col. Wm. Williams' Regt. Detached Militia in U. S. service from July 22 to Dec. 6, 1812.

HOLBROOK, ORIN,   Bakersfield.
Volunteered and was at the battle of Plattsburgh Sept. 11, 1814, serving in Capt. M. Stearns' Company. Ref: Hemenway's Vt. Gazetteer, Vol. 2, Page 394.

‡HOLBROOK, PELATIAH.
Served in Capt. Barns' Company, Col. Wm. Williams' Regt. Detached Militia in U. S. service 4 months and 27 days, 1812. Served from June 11, 1813 to June 14, 1813 in Capt. Moses Jewett's Company, 1st Regt. 2nd Brig. 3rd Div. Ref: Book 53, AGO Page 13.

HOLBROOK, SHELDON.
Served from Feb. 18, 1813 to July 16, 1813 in Capt. John W. Weeks' Company, 11th Regt. Ref: R. & L. 1812, AGO Page 4.

*HOLBROOK, WILLIAM.
Served in Capt. Walker's Company,
Col. Fifield's Regt. Detached Militia
in U. S. service 2 months and 21
days, 1812. Served from April 12,
1814 to April 15, 1814 in Capt. John
Hackett's Company, Sumner's Regt.

HOLCOMB, AMOS,   Isle-La-Motte.
Served in Capt. James Taylor's Com-
pany and Capt. Gideon Spencer's
Company, 30th Regt., from May 28,
1813 to date of death at Vergennes,
May, 1814. Ref: R. & L. 1812, AGO
Pages 52, 57, 58.

HOLCOMB, CHARLES C.
Enlisted Nov. 1, 1812 in Capt. Phineas
Williams' Company, 11th Regt.; died
Dec. 10, 1812. Ref: R. & L. 1812,
AGO Page 15.

*HOLCOMB, DAVID.
Served from April 12, 1814 to April
21, 1814 in Capt. Othniel Jewett's
Company, Sumner's Regt.

*HOLCOMB, ISAAC JR.
Served from April 19, 1814 to April
21, 1814 in Capt. Othniel Jewett's
Company, Sumner's Regt.

*HOLCOMB, MILO.
Served in Sumner's Regt. Vt. Militia.

*HOLCOMB, NOAH JR.
Served in Sumner's Regt. Vt. Militia.

*HOLCOMB, OBED.
Served from April 12, 1814 to April
21, 1814 in Capt. Othniel Jewett's
Company, Sumner's Regt.

*HOLCOMB, PHINEAS,   Panton.
Served in Capt. Robbins' Company,
Col. Wm. Williams' Regt. Detached
Militia in U. S. service 4 months
and 29 days, 1812. Volunteered to
go to Plattsburgh, September, 1814,
and was at the battle, serving 10
days in Capt. Gideon Spencer's Company. Ref: Book 51, AGO Pages 4
and 61.

‡HOLCOMB, SAMUEL, Drummer, Pittsford. Volunteered to go to Plattsburgh, September, 1814, and served
8 days in Capt. Caleb Hendee's Company. Pension Certificate of widow,
Verona, No. 42179.

*HOLCOMB, TITUS.
Served in Sumner's Regt. Vt. Militia.

HOLDEN, AARON.
Served from April 29, 1814 to June
16, 1814 in Capt. Gideon Spencer's
Company, 30th Regt. Ref: R. & L.
1812, AGO Page 57.

‡*HOLDEN, AMBROSE.
Enlisted Sept. 25, 1813 and served
1 month and 23 days in Capt. Amos
Robinson's Company, Col. Dixon's
Regt. Also served in Capt. Fifield's
Company. Pension Certificate of wid-
ow, Abigail, No. 19807.

*HOLDEN, EBENEZER A.
Served in Capt. S. Pettes' Company,
Col. Wm. Williams' Regt. Detached
Militia in U. S. service 4 months
and 17 days, 1812.

‡*HOLDEN, ELIJAH, Sergeant.
Served in Capt. Parsons' Company,
Col. Jonathan Williams' Regt. De-
tached Militia in U. S. service 2
months and 13 days, 1812. Pension
Certificate No. 3859.

HOLDEN, ELIJAH,   Shrewsbury.
Volunteered to go to Plattsburgh,
September, 1814, and served 4 days
in Capt. Robert Reed's Company. Ref:
Book 52, AGO Pages 138 and 140.

‡*HOLDEN, GILES H.,   Waterbury.
Volunteered to go to Plattsburgh,
September, 1814, and was at the
battle, serving in Capt. George Atkins' Company, 4 Regt. (Peck's).
Also served in Corning's Detachment,
Vt. Militia. Pension Certificate of
widow, Susan, No. 21077. (Was a
son of Richard Holden).

*HOLDEN, GUY I. A., Sergeant, Water-
bury. Volunteered to go to Plattsburgh, September, 1814, and was in
the battle, serving 11 days in Capt.
George Atkins' Company, 4 Regt.
(Peck's). Also served in Corning's
Detachment, Vt. Militia. (Was a son
of Richard Holden).

‡HOLDEN, HANNABAL,   Shrewsbury.
Volunteered to go to Plattsburgh,
September, 1814, and served 4 days
in Capt. Robert Reed's Company.
Pension Certificate of widow, Achsah,
No. 21542.

‡*HOLDEN, HORACE, Musician.
Volunteered to go to Plattsburgh,
September, 1814, and served 10 days
in Capt. Holden Putnam's Company,
4 Regt. (Peck's). Pension Certificate
of widow, Betsey, No. 29026.

HOLDEN, JOEL,   Barre.
Volunteered to go to Plattsburgh,
September, 1814, and served 9 days
in Capt. Warren Ellis' Company. Ref:
Book 52, AGO Pages 233 and 242.

*HOLDEN, JOHN (or John 2nd?) Brook-
line. Served in Capt. Noyes' Company, Col. Jonathan Williams' Regt.
Detached Militia in U. S. service 2
months and 6 days, 1812. Also served in Capt. Sabin's Company, Col.
Jonathan Williams' Regt. Detached
Militia in U. S. service 2 months
and 6 days, 1812.

*HOLDEN, JOSIAH.
Served in 4 Regt. Vt. Militia commanded by Col. Peck.

‡*HOLDEN, LYMAN.
Served in Capt. Parsons' Company,
Col. Jonathan Williams' Regt. De-
tached Militia in U. S. service 2
months and 13 days, 1812. Pension
Certificate No. 13760.

*HOLDEN, MOSES.
Served in Capt. Willson's Company,
Col. Wm. Williams' Regt. Detached
Militia in U. S. service 4 months
and 24 days, 1812.

‡*HOLDEN, RICHARD W.,   Waterbury.
Volunteered to go to Plattsburgh,
September, 1814, and was in the

battle, serving 11 days in Capt.
George Atkins' Company, 4 Regt.
(Peck's). Also served in Corning's
Detachment, Vt. Militia. Pension Cer-
tificate of widow, Mariah, No. 9858.
(Was a son of Richard Holden.)

*HOLDEN, STEPHEN, Fifer.
Served in Capt. Needham's Company,
Col. Martindale's Regt. Detached
Militia in U. S. service 2 months and
14 days, 1812.

*HOLDEN, SYLVESTER.
Served in Capt. Parsons' Company,
Col. Jonathan Williams' Regt. Detached Militia in U. S. service 2
months and 13 days, 1812.

*HOLDEN, TIMOTHY.
Served in Capt. Sabin's Company,
Col. Jonathan Williams' Regt. Detached Militia in U. S. service 2
months and 6 and days, 1812.

‡*HOLDEN, WILLARD.
Served in Capt. Briggs' Company,
Col. Jonathan Williams' Regt. De-
tached Militia in U. S. service 2
months and 13 days, 1812. Pension
Certificate No. 1308.

‡*HOLDEN, WILLIAM H., Musician, Middlesex. Volunteered to go to Plattsburgh, September, 1814, and served
10 days in Capt. Holden Putnam's
Company, 4 Regt. (Peck's). Pension
Certificate of widow, Eliza, No. 29443.

HOLDEN, XERXES,   Middlesex.
Volunteered to go to Plattsburgh,
September, 1814, and served in Capt.
Holden Putnam's Company, 4th Regt.
(Peck's). Ref: Hemenway's Vt. Ga-
zetter, Vol. 4, Page 250.

‡HOLDING, SAMUEL S.
Served in Capt. Hart's Company.
Pension Certificate No. 10294.

HOLDRIDGE, JEHIEL.
Served in Capt. Robinson's Company,
Col. Dixon's Regt. Detached Militia
in U. S. service 1 month and 23
days, 1813. Ref: Book 53, AGO Page
107.

‡*HOLDRIDGE, JOHN.
Enlisted Sept. 25, 1813 in Capt. Amos
Robinson's Company, Dixon's Regt.
Pension Certificate of widow, Content,
No. 34066.

HOLDRIDGE, SYLVESTER.
Served from March 17, 1813 to June
16, 1813 in Capt. Charles Follett's
Company, 11th Regt. Ref: R. & L.
1812, AGO Page 13.

*HOLGATE, SAMUEL JR. Ensign.
Served from Sept. 23, 1813 to Sept.
29, 1813 in Capt. Amasa Mansfield's
Company, Dixon's Regt.

HOLLADAY, NEHEMIAH.
Enlisted May 1, 1813 for 1 year in
Capt. Simeon Wright's Company.
Ref: R. & L. 1812, AGO Page 51.

‡HOLLAND, JONATHAN.
Served in Capt. E. Keyes' Company.
Pension Certificate of widow, Mary,
No. 17416.

*HOLLAND, REUBEN,   Pittsfield.
Served under Captains Durkee and
Wright, Col. Fifield's Regt. Detached
Militia in U. S. service 6 months,
1812. Volunteered to go to Platts-
burgh, September, 1814, and served
7 days in Capt. Calvin Fairbanks'
Company. Also served in 3 Regt.
(Williams') Vt. Militia.

*HOLLEMBECK, RAMINE F.
Served in Tyler's Regt. Vt. Militia.

‡*HOLLENBACK, BENJAMIN F.
Served in 4 Regt. (Williams') Vt.
Militia. Also served in Capt. Wil-
liams' Company. Pension Certificate
No. 11290.

*HOLLENBACK, LUCIUS.
Served in Corning's Detachment, Vt.
Militia.

HOLLENBECK, ABRAHAM, Sergeant,
Richmond. Volunteered to go to
Plattsburgh, September, 1814, and
served in Capt. Roswell Hunt's Com-
pany, Tyler's Regt. Ref: Book 51,
AGO Page 82.

‡*HOLLENBECK, JOHN B.
Served from June 11 to June 14, 1813
in Capt. Ithiel Stone's Company, 1st
Regt. 2nd Brig. 3rd Div. Also serv-
ed in Capt. Jehial Stone's Company.
Pension Certificate No. 25466.

‡HOLLEY, BENJAMIN JR.
Served in Capt. Samuel H. Holly's
Company, 11th Regt.; on Pay Roll
for January and February, 1813.
Pension Certificate of widow, Hezzi-
bah, No. 28512.

*HOLLEY, SAMUEL H., Captain, Shore-
ham. Appointed Captain 11 Inf.
March 12, 1812; Resigned March 15,
1813; died March 21, 1858. Also
served as 1st Lieutenant in Capt.
Edmund B. Hill's Company, Sumner's
Regt. Ref: Heitman's Historical Register & Dictionary USA.

HOLLEY, W. H.,   Bristol.
Volunteered to go to Plattsburgh,
September, 1814, and was at the
battle, serving 9 days in Capt. Jehiel
Saxton's Company, Sumner's Regt.
Ref: Book 51, AGO Page 18.

*HOLLIS, LYMAN.
Served in Capt. Barns' Company,
Col. Wm. Williams' Regt. Detached
Militia in U. S. service 5 months.
Served from June 11 to June 14,
1813 and from Oct. 4 to Oct. 13,
1813 in Capt. John Palmer's Com-
pany, 1st Regt. 2nd Brig. 3rd Div.
Ref: R. & L. 1812, AGO Pages 47
and 48.

*HOLLIS, PLAT.
Served from Oct. 4th to Oct. 13,
1813 in Capt. John Palmer's Company,
1st Regt. 2nd Brig. 3rd Div.

*HOLLIS, STODDARD.
Served in 1 Regt (Judson's) Vt. Militia.

HOLLISTER, JESSE W., Sergeant.
Served from May 1 to June 30, 1814
in Capt. Alexander Brooks' Corps
of Artillery. Ref: R. & L. 1812, AGO
Page 31.

HOLLY, JOHN V., Sergeant.
Served from April 25, 1813 to April
25, 1814 in Capt. Simeon Wright's Company. Ref: R. & L. 1812, AGO Page
51.

‡HOLLY, PAUL P.
Served in Capt. Spencer's Company.
Pension Certificate of widow, Elmina,
No. 31306.

*HOLMAN, ABEL.
Served from April 12, 1814 to April
21, 1814 in Lieut. James S. Morton's
Company, Sumner's Regt.

HOLMAN, IRA.
Enlisted May 1, 1813 for 1 year in
Capt. Simeon Wright's Company. Ref:
R. & L. 1812, AGO Page 51.

HOLMAN, SOLOMON,   Braintree.
Volunteered to go to Plattsburgh,
September, 1814, and served 7 days
in Capt. Frederick Griswold's Com-
pany, raised in Brookfield, Vt. Ref:
Book 52, AGO Pages 52 and 55.

HOLMES, ABNER, Ensign,   Fairfax.
Volunteered to go to Plattsburgh,
September, 1814, and served 8 days
in Capt. Josiah Grout's Company.
Ref: Book 51, AGO Pages 103 and 271.

‡HOLMES, BENJAMIN, Corporal, Fairfax.
Volunteered to go to Plattsburgh,
September, 1814, and served 8 days
in Capt. Josiah Grout's Company.
Pension Certificate of widow, Julia,
A., No. 28141.

HOLMES, CHANDLER,   Strafford.
Volunteered to go to Plattsburgh,
September, 1814, and served in Capt.
Cyril Chandler's Company. Ref: Book
52, AGO Page 42.

HOLMES, CHARLES.
Served in company of late Capt. J.
Brooks, commanded by Lt. John I.
Cromwell, Corps of U. S. Artillery;
on Muster Roll from April 30, 1814
to June 30, 1814; prisoner of war
on parole; transferred from Capt.
Leonard's Company. Ref: R. & L.
1812, AGO Page 18.

HOLMES, DANIEL.
Served in Capt. John W. Weeks' Company, 11th Regt. from Feb. 23, 1813
to date of death May 6, 1813. Ref:
R. & L. 1812, AGO Page 4.

*HOLMES, ISAAC.
Served from June 11 to June 14, 1813
in Capt. Moses Jewett's Company,
1st Regt. 2nd Brig. 3rd Div.

‡*HOLMES, JOHN B.
Enlisted Sept. 25, 1813 in Capt. Elijah
Birge's Company, Col. Dixon's Regt.;
transferred to Capt. Asahel Lang-
worthy's Company, Col. Isaac Clark's
Rifle Corps, Oct. 22, 1813. Pension
Certificate of widow, Mary Elizabeth,
No. 22551.

HOLMES, JOHN M.
Served from Feb. 6, 1813 to May 10,
1813 in Capt. John W. Weeks' Company, 11th Regt. Ref: R. & L.
1812, AGO Pages 4 and 5.

*HOLMES, LEVI,   Cambridge.
Enlisted Sept. 25, 1813 in Capt.
Charles Bennett's Company, Dixon's
Regt. Volunteered to go to Plattsburgh, September, 1814, serving 8
days in Capt. Salmon Green's Company.

‡*HOLMES, MANLY.
Served in Capt. Taylor's Company,
Col. Wm. Williams' Regt. Detached
Militia in U. S. service 4 months and
24 days, 1812. Pension Certificate of
widow, Sarah, No. 2675.

HOLMES, NATHAN,   Fairfax.
Served in 1813 and 1814 in Capt.
Joseph Beeman's Company. Ref: Hemenway's Vt. Gazetteer, Vol. 2, Page
402.

‡*HOLMES, NATHAN,   Stowe.
Volunteered to go to Plattsburgh,
September, 1814, and was at the
battle, serving in Capt. Nehemiah
Perkins' Company, 4 Regt. (Peck's).
Also served in Corning's Detachment,
Vt. Militia. Pension Certificate of
widow, Julia R., No. 30773.

*HOLMES, NATHAN L., Major
Served in 2 Regt. 3 Brig 3 Div. Vt.
Militia.

HOLMES, NILES.
Served in Capt. Pettes' Company, Col.
Wm. Williams' Regt. Detached Mili-
tia in U. S. service 4 months and
17 days, 1812. Ref: Book 53, AGO
Page 69.

HOLMES, SHIVRECK,   Georgia.
Volunteered to go to Plattsburgh,
September, 1814, and served 8 days
in Capt. Jesse Post's Company, Dixon's Regt. Ref: Book 51, AGO Page
102.

HOLMES, STEPHEN,   St. Albans.
Volunteered to go to Plattsburgh,
Sept. 11, 1814 and served in Capt.
Samuel H. Farnsworth's Company.
Ref: Military Records of Franklin
County, Vt.; Hemenway's Vt. Ga-
zetteer, Vol. 2, Page 434.

HOLMES, STEPHEN,   Georgia.
Volunteered to go to Plattsburgh,
September, 1814, and served 8 days
in Capt. Jesse Post's Company, Dixon's Regt. Ref: Book 51, AGO Page
102.

‡*HOLMES, THERON, Corporal.
Enlisted Sept. 25, 1813 and served
1 month and 23 days in Capt. Bennett's Company,, Col. Dixon's Regt.
Pension Certificate No. 22464; Pension Certificate of widow, Amanda,
No. 27648.

*HOLT, AMOS,   Barre.
Volunteered to go to Plattsburgh,
September, 1814, and served 10 days
in Capt. Warren Ellis' Company. Also
served in 4 Regt. (Peck's) Vt. Militia. Ref: Book 52, AGO Page 242.

HOLT, JEREMIAH.
Enlisted April 5, 1814 for duration
of the war; deserted from rendezvous

at Poultney April 14, 1814. Ref:
Recruiting Acct. of Capt. Wm. Miller,
30th Regt., R. & L. 1812, AGO
Page 1.

HOLT, NOAH,   Barre.
Volunteered to go to Plattsburgh,
September, 1814, serving 10 days
in Capt. Warren Ellis' Company. Ref:
Book 52, AGO Page 242.

*HOLT, SAMUEL.
Served from April 12, 1814 to April
21, 1814 in Lieut. James S. Morton's
Company, Col. W. B. Sumner's Regt.

HOLT, STEPHEN.
Volunteered to go to Plattsburgh,
September. 1814; no organization giv-
en. Ref: Book 52, AGO Page 155.

*HOLT, UZIEL (or Uriel).
Served in Col. Fifield's Regt. under
Captains Taylor and Walker, Detached Militia in U. S. service 6 months,
1812.

HOMES, WILLIAM.
Served in Capt. Chadwick's Company.
Ref. R . & L. 1812, AGO Page 32.

HONSINGER, BENJAMIN, Sergeant.
Served in Capt. Pettes' Company,
Col. Wm. Williams' Regt. stationed
at Swanton Falls in 1812. Ref: Vol.
49 Vt. State Papers, Page 119.

*HONTLY, ALLEN, Drummer.
Served in Corning's Detachment, Vt.
Militia.

HOOD, EZRA.
Volunteered to go to Plattsburgh,
September. 1814, and served in com-
pany of Capt. Jonathan Jennings,
Chelsea. Ref: Book 52, AGO Pages
79 and 80.

*HOOKER, JOHN,   Ferrisburg.
Served from Sept. 1, 1814 to June 16,
1815 in Capt. Sanford's Company, 30th
Inf. Also served in Sumner's Regt.
Vt. Militia. Ref: R. & L. 1812, AGO
Page 23.

HOOKER, NOAH.
Served from April 10th to June 30,
1814 in Regt. of Light Dragoons.
Ref: R. & L. 1812, AGO Page 21.

HOOKER, ORIS.
Was born at Poultney. Served in
the War of 1812 and was captured by
troops Feb. 22, 1813 at Stoney Point;
died Sept. 9, 1813. Ref: Records of Naval Records and Library, Navy Dept.

‡HOOKER, RALPH.
Served from Feb. 21, to June 30,
1814 in Regt. of Light Dragoons.
Also served in Capt. McFarland's
Company. Pension Certificate No.
7313. Ref: R. & L. 1812, AGO Page
21.

HOONIN, EZEKIEL JR.
Enlisted Sept. 20, 1813 in Capt. John
Weed's Company. Ref: Book 52, AGO
Page 292.

HOOPER, JOHN, Sergeant.
Served in Capt. Charles Follett's
Company, 11th Regt.; on Pay Roll
for January and February, 1813.
Ref: R. & L. 1812, AGO Page 12.

*HOOPER, THOMAS, Corporal.
Served in Capt. Taylor's Company,
Col. Wm. Williams' Regt. Detached
Militia in U. S. service 4 months
and 24 days, 1812.

*HOOPER, ZEBAH, Musician, Franklin
County. Enlisted May 20, 1812 for
5 years in Capt. White Youngs' Company, 15th Regt.; on Muster Roll
from Aug. 31, 1814 to Dec. 31, 1814.
Ref: R. & L. 1812, AGO Page 27.

‡HOOSE, ALBERN.
Served in Capt. Talcott's Company.
Pension Certificate No. 25402; Pension Certificate of widow, Gratia, No.
32767.

*HOOSE, ISAAC.
Served in 1 Regt. (Judson's) Vt.
Militia.

*HOPKINS, AMOS, Sergeant.
Served in Capt. Hopkins' Company,
Col. Martindale's Regt. Detached
Militia in U. S. service 2 months
and 13 days, 1812.

*HOPKINS, ASA.
Served from March 13 to June 12,
1813 in Capt. Phineas Williams' Com-
pany, 11th Regt. Also served in 2
Regt. (Fifield's) Vt. Militia. Ref: R.
& L. 1812, AGO Page 14.

*HOPKINS, BENJAMIN, Sergeant.
Served in Capt. Taylor's Company,
Col. Wm. Williams' Regt. Detached
Militia stationed at Swanton Falls,
in U. S. service 4 months and 24
days, 1812. Served in Capt. Benja-
min Bradford's Company; on Muster
Roll from May 31 to Aug. 31, 1813.
Ref: R. & L. 1812, AGO Page 26.

HOPKINS, DAVID, Sergeant.
Served in 1st Regt. of Detached Militia of Vt. in U. S. service at Champlain Nov. 18 to Nov. 19, 1812.

*HOPKINS, ELISHA, Lieutenant Captain.
Appointed Sept. 20, 1813 for 90 days
in Capt. John Weed's Company, Col.
Clark's Rifle Corps. Served as Captain of a company in 1st Regt. (Martindale's) Vt. Militia.

‡HOPKINS, FAY,   Enosburgh.
Volunteered to go to Plattsburgh,
September, 1814; no organization giv-
en. Served in Capt. M. D. Follett's
Company (Dixon's Regt.). Pension
Certificate No. 32582.

HOPKINS, HENRY,   Montgomery.
Volunteered to go to Plattsburgh,
September, 1814, and served 6 days
in Capt. Martin D. Follett's Com-
pany, Dixon's Regt. Ref: Book 51,
AGO Page 99.

HOPKINS, HENRY,   Enosburgh.
Volunteered to go to Plattsburgh,
September, 1814; no organization giv-
en. Ref: Book 51, AGO Page 188.

‡HOPKINS, HIRAM,   Cambridge.
Volunteered to go to Plattsburgh,
September, 1814, and served 8 days
in Capt. Salmon Green's Company.
Pension Certificate No. 25463.

*HOPKINS, JAMES,   Williamstown.
Enlisted Sept. 20, 1813 in Capt. John
Weed's Company, Col. Clark's Rifle
Regt. Volunteered to go to Platts-
burgh, September, 1814 and served
in Capt. David Robinson's Company.

HOPKINS, JOSEPH, Sergeant.
Served from Nov. 1, 1812 to Feb. 28,
1813 in Lieut. Wm. S. Foster's Company, 11th Regt. Ref: R. & L. 1812,
AGO Page 7.

*HOPKINS, JOSEPH W.
Enlisted Sept. 25, 1813 in Capt. Jesse
Post's Company, Dixon's Regt.; trans-
ferred to Rifle Corps Oct. 13, 1813.

‡HOPKINS, LUKE.
Served in Capt. Jesse Post's Company, Dixon's Regt. Pension Certificate of widow, Eunice, No. 34742.

HOPKINS, NATHANIEL,   Williamstown.
Volunteered to go to Plattsburgh,
September, 1814, and was at the
battle Sept. 11, 1814, serving 8 days
in Capt. David Robinson's Company.
Ref: Book 52, AGO Page 2.

‡HOPKINS, PERRY G., Ensign,   Cabot.
Volunteered to go to Plattsburgh,
September, 1814, and served 4 days
in Capt. Anthony Perry's Company.
Pension Certificate of widow, Alice,
No. 21549.

‡*HOPKINS, RUFUS, Corporal.
Enlisted Sept. 20, 1813 in Capt. John
Weed's Company, Col. Clark's Rifle
Corps. Pension Certificate No. 29669.

HOPKINS, SAFFORD.
Served in Capt. Chadwick's Company.
Ref: R. & L. 1812, AGO Page 32.

*HOPKINS, WAIT,   Fairfield.
Served in Capt. Kendall's Company,
Col. Wm. Williams' Regt. Detached
Militia in U. S. service 4 months
and 23 days, 1812.

*HORHAM, DANIEL,   Barton.
Served in Capt. Mason's Company,
Col. Fifield's Regt. Detached Militia
in U. S. service 5 months and 26
days, 1812.

HORLBOT, ELI.
Served from Jan. 1, to June 30, 1814
in Regt. of Light Dragoons. Ref:
R. & L. 1812, AGO Page 21.

HORLBOT, NEWMAN.
Served from Sept. 1, 1813 to June
30, 1814 in Regt. of Light Dragoons.
Ref: R. & L. 1812, AGO Page 21.

*HORNER, WILLIAM, Corporal.
Served from Sept. 25, 1813 to Oct. 10,
1813 in Capt. Charles Bennett's Company, Dixon's Regt.

*HORNSBY, ASA.
Served with Hospital Attendants, Vt.

*HORRINGTON, EDWARD F.
Served in 1 Regt. (Judson's) Vt. Militia.

*HORSFORD, JOSEPH.
Served in Capt. Howard's Company,
Vt. Militia.

*HORSFORD, WILLIAM.
Served in Capt. Howard's Company,
Vt. Militia.

HORTON, HENRY J., Captain, Hubbardton. Volunteered to go to Plattsburgh, September, 1814, and served
8 days in command of Hubbardton
company. Ref: Book 52, AGO Pages
142 and 161.

HORTON, LEVI, Sergeant.
Served from June 11, 1813 to June
14, 1813 in Capt. Hezekiah Barns'
Company, 1st Regt. 2nd Brig. 3rd
Div. Ref: R. & L. 1812, AGO Page
43.

‡*HORTON, LOVEL, Sergeant.
Served in Capt. Barnes' Company, 1
Regt. (Judson's) Vt. Militia. Pension Certificate of widow, Sylvia, No.
16639.

HOSFORD, ALFRED,   Poultney.
Volunteered to go to Plattsburgh,
September, 1814, and served 2 days
in Capt. Briant Ransom's Company.
Ref: Book 52, AGO Page 147.

HOSFORD, CALVIN,   Thetford.
Marched for Plattsburgh, September,
1814 and went as far as Bolton, Vt.,
serving 6 days in Capt. Salmon Howard's Company, 2nd Regt. Ref: Book
52, AGO Pages 15 and 16.

‡*HOSFORD, DANIEL D.
Served from Oct. 14 to Nov. 18, 1813
in Capt. Isaac Finch's Company, Col.
Clark's Rifle Corps. Pension Certificate of widow, Catharine, No. 25123.

HOSFORD, HARRIS,   Poultney.
Volunteered to go to Plattsburgh,
September, 1814, and served 2 days
in Capt. Briant Ransom's Company.
Ref: Book 52, AGO Page 147.

*HOSFORD, HERMAN, Drummer.
Served from June 11 to June 14,
1813 in Capt. Ithiel Stone's Company,
1st Regt. 2nd Brig. 3rd Div. Volunteered to go to Plattsburgh, September, 1814, and served in 2nd Regt.
2nd Brig. 4th Div. 6 days as Adjutant with rank of Captain. Ref:
Book 52, AGO Page 98.

*HOSFORD, JARED,   Thetford.
Marched for Plattsburgh, September,
1814, and went as far as Bolton,
Vt., serving 6 days in Capt. Salmon
Howard's Company, 2nd Regt.

*HOSFORD, JEDEDIAH.
Served from June 11, 1813 to June
14, 1813 in Capt. Ithiel Stone's Company, 1st Regt. 2nd Brig. 3rd Div.

‡*HOSFORD, JOHN,   Charlotte.
Served in Capt. Willson's Company,
Col. Wm. Williams' Regt. Detached

Militia in U. S. service 4 months and 23 days, 1812. Also served in Capt. Howard's Company, Vt. Militia. Volunteered to go to Plattsburgh, September, 1814, and served 8 days in Capt. Daniel Haugh's Company. Pension Certificate No. 17804. Ref: Book 51, AGO Pages 85 and 96.

HOSFORD, PHILO,   Poultney. Volunteered to go to Plattsburgh, September, 1814, and served 2 days in Capt. Briant Ransom's Company. Ref: Book 52, AGO Page 147.

HOSKINS, ELI. Served from June 11 to June 14, 1813 in Capt. John Palmer's Company, 1st Regt. 2nd Brig. 3rd Div. Ref: R. & L. 1812, AGO Page 48.

*HOSKINS, JAMES. Served in 3 Regt. Vt. Militia commanded by Col. Tyler.

*HOSKINS, SAMUEL. Served in 4 Regt. Vt. Militia commanded by Col. Peck.

‡HOSKINS, TIMOTHY. Served in Capt. Goodman's Company. Pension Certificate No. 4882.

‡HOSLEY, ELI. Served in Capt. Parsons' Company, Col. Jonathan Williams' Regt. Detached Militia in U. S. service 2 months and 13 days, 1812. Pension Certificate of widow, Angeline, No. 2992.

‡HOSMER, SYLVESTER. Served in Capt. Smith's Company. Pension Certificate of widow, Mabel, No. 10822.

HOSTARD, JOHN,   Highgate. Served in New York State from Sept. 25 to Nov. 18, 1813; no organization given. Ref: Vol. 50, Vt. State Papers, Page 94.

*HOSTAT, JOHN, Sergeant. Served in Dixon's Regt. Vt. Militia.

HOTCHKISS, ELISHA, Captain. Served in Artillery of Detached Militia of Vt. in U. S. service at Champlain from Nov. 18 to Nov. 19, 1812.

*HOTCHKISS, JEREMIAH. Served from April 12, 1814 to April 21, 1814 in Capt. Othniel Jewett's Company, Sumner's Regt.

*HOTCHKISS, MARCUS. Served in Capt. S. Pettes' Company, Col. Wm. Williams' Regt. Detached Militia in U. S. service 3 months and 15 days, 1812. Served from April 26, 1813 to April 30, 1814 in Capt. James Taylor's Company and Capt. Gideon Spencer's Company, 30th Regt. Ref: R. & L. 1812, AGO Pages 52, 57, 59.

*HOTCHKISS, RAYMOND, Captain. Served in 1st Regt. of Detached Militia of Vt. in U. S. service at Champlain from Nov. 18 to Nov. 19, 1812.

HOUGH, DANIEL (or Haugh), Sergeant. Served from Oct. 4, 1813 to Oct. 13, 1813 in Capt. John Palmer's Company, 1st Regt. 2nd Brig. 3rd Div. Ref: R. & L. 1812, AGO Page 47.

*HOUGH, JOHN, Corporal. Served in 3 Regt. (Williams') Vt. Militia.

HOUGHTAIL, JAMES, Franklin County. Volunteered to go to Plattsburgh Sept. 11, 1814 and served in 15th or 22nd Regt. Ref: Hemenway's Vt. Gazetteer, Vol. 2, Page 391.

HOUGHTON, CALVIN. Born in Lemington, Mass.; aged 44 years; 6 feet high; light complexion; sandy hair; grey eyes; by profession a farmer. Enlisted Oct. 6, 1813 at Plattsburgh and served in Capt. Wm. Miller's Company and Capt. Gideon Spencer's Company; on board the navy; probably discharged at Burlington, Vt., 1815. Ref: R. & L. 1812, AGO Pages 54, 55, 57.

HOUGHTON, IRA,   Woodstock. Served from July 1 to Sept. 5, 1812 and from Sept. 11, 1812 to Feb. 28, 1813 in Capt. Phineas Williams' Company, 11th Regt. Ref: R. & L. 1812, AGO Page 15.

*HOUGHTON, ISRAEL,   Woodstock. Served in Capt. Briggs' Company, Col. Jonathan Williams' Regt. Detached Militia in U. S. service 2 months and 13 days, 1812. Served from Feb. 12, 1813 to May 11, 1813 in Capt. Phineas Williams' Company, 11th Regt. Also served with Hospital Attendants, Vt. Ref: R. & L. 1812, AGO Page 14.

*HOUGHTON, JOSEPH. Served in Capt. Cross' Company, Col. Martindale's Regt. Detached Militia in U. S. service 2 months and 13 days, 1812.

HOUGHTON, NEHEMIAH. Enlisted May 17, 1812 in Capt. Weeks' Company, 11th Regt.; on Pay Roll for January and February, 1813. Ref: R. & L. 1812, AGO Page 5.

*HOUGHTON, PETER. Served in Capt. Robbins' Company, Col. Wm. Williams' Regt. Detached Militia in U. S. service 4 months and 29 days, 1812.

*HOUGHTON, RIPLEY. Served in Corning's Detachment, Vt. Militia.

*HOUGHTON, THOMAS. Served from Sept. 29, 1812 to Feb. 12, 1813 in Capt. Benjamin S. Edgerton's Company, 11th Regt. Also served in 2 Regt. (Fifield's) Vt. Militia. Ref: R. & L. 1812, AGO Pages 1 and 2.

*HOUGHTON, WALTER,   Pittsford. Served in Capt. Needham's Company, Col. Martindale's Regt. Detached Militia in U. S. service 2 months and 14 days, 1812. Served from June 20, 1814 to June 19, 1815 in Capt. Taylor's Company, 30th Inf.

HOUSE, BENJAMIN.
Volunteered to go to Plattsburgh,
September, 1814, and served 4 days
in Capt. Aaron Kidder's Company.
Ref: Book 52, AGO Page 65.

*HOUSE, ISRAEL.
Served in 2 Regt. (Fifield's) Vt.
Militia.

HOUSE, ISRAEL JR.,   Berlin.
Served from Sept. 1, 1812 to March
16, 1813 in Capt. Walker's Company,
Col. Fifield's Regt. Ref: Book 53,
AGO Page 71; Vol. 50 Vt. State
Papers, Page 224.

*HOUSE, ORSON.
Served from June 11, 1813 to June
14, 1813 in Capt. Ithiel Stone's Company, 1st Regt. 2nd Brig. 3rd Div.

HOUSE, SAMUEL.
Served in Capt. Hotchkiss' Company,
Col. Martindale's Regt. Detached
Militia in U. S. service 2 months
and 13 days, 1812. Ref: Book 53,
AGO Page 49.

HOUSE, WILLIAM.
Served from May 1 to July 18, 1813;
no organization given. Ref: R. & L.
1812, AGO Page 29.

HOUSTON, BENJAMIN G., Sergeant.
Enlisted Oct. 15, 1812 in Capt. Ben-
jamin S. Edgerton's Company, 11th
Regt.; on Pay Roll for September
and October, 1812, and January and
February, 1813. Ref: R. & L. 1812,
AGO Pages 1 and 2.

HOUTZELL, JACOB.
Served from May 1 to June 30, 1814
as an Armorer in Alexander Parris'
Company of Artificers. Ref: R. &
L. 1812, AGO Page 24.

*HOVEY, ALFRED,   Thetford.
Marched for Plattsburgh, September,
1814, and went as far as Bolton,
Vt., serving 6 days in Capt. Salmon
Howard's Company, 2nd Regt.

*HOVEY, JAMES.
Served in 2 Regt. (Fifield's) Vt. Militia.

HOVEY, JOHN,   Morristown.
Volunteered to go to Plattsburgh,
September, 1814, and served 8 days
in Capt. Denison Cook's Company.
Ref: Book 51, AGO Pages 202 and
206.

HOWARD, ABIJAH,   Montpelier.
Volunteered to go to Plattsburgh,
September, 1814, and served in Capt.
Timothy Hubbard's Company. Ref:
Book 52, AGO Pages 212 and 256.

*HOWARD, ALLEN.
Served in 4 Regt. (Williams'). Vt.
Militia.

HOWARD, ANTIPAS.
Enlisted May 27, 1813 for 1 year in
Capt. Daniel Farrington's Company,
30th Regt. (also comanded by Capt.
Simeon Wright). Ref: R. & L. 1812,
AGO Pages 50 and 51.

‡*HOWARD, AUGUSTUS C.,   Musician.
Served in Capt. Dodge's Company,
Col. Fifield's Regt. Detached Militia
in U. S. service 2 months and 21
days, 1812. Pension Certificate No.
11396. Pension Certificate of widow, Mary G., No. 18395.

HOWARD, BUEL,   Waltham.
Volunteered to go to Plattsburgh,
September, 1814, and was in the
battle, serving 10 days in Capt.
Gideon Spencer's Company. Ref: Book
51, AGO Page 3.

‡HOWARD, CHARLES.
Served in Capt. Danforth's Company.
Pension Certificate No. 12707.

*HOWARD, CHESTER.
Served from April 12, 1814 to April
15, 1814 in Lieut. Justus Foote's Company, Sumner's Regt.

HOWARD, DELPHA.
Served in Capt. Richardson's Company, Col. Martindale's Regt. Detached Militia in U. S. service 2 months
and 13 days, 1812. Ref: Book 53,
AGO Page 98.

*HOWARD, EBENEZER.
Served in 4 Regt. Vt. Militia commanded by Col. Williams.

HOWARD, EDWARD.
Served in Capt. Haig's Corps of Light
Dragoons; on Pay Roll to June 30,
1814. Ref: R. & L. 1812, AGO Page
20.

*HOWARD, ELIAS.
Served in company of Capt. Jonathan
Prentiss, Jr., Dixon's Regt., from
Sept. 30, 1813 as a substitute for
Archibald Cook. Ref: Book 52, AGO
Page 270.

HOWARD, EPHRAIM.
Served from May 1 to June 30, 1814
in Capt. Alexander Brooks' Corps of
Artillery. Ref: R. & L. 1812, AGO
Page 31.

*HOWARD, HARRY.
Served in 1 Regt. (Judson's) Vt.
Militia.

HOWARD, HENRY.
Served from June 11, 1813 to June
14, 1813 in Capt. Thomas Dorwin's
Company, 1st Regt. 2nd Brig. 3rd
Div. Ref: R. & L. 1812, AGO Pages
45 and 46.

HOWARD, ISAIAH.   West Fairlee.
Volunteered to go to Plattsburgh,
September, 1814, and served in Capt.
Aaron Kidder's Company. Ref: Book
52, AGO Pages 106 and 108.

HOWARD, JOEL.
Enlisted May 5, 1813 in Capt. Daniel
Farrington's Company, 30th Regt.; on
Muster Roll March 1, 1814 to April
30, 1814. Ref: R. & L. 1812, AGO
Pages 50 and 51.

*HOWARD, JONATHAN.
Served in Capt. Preston's Company,
Col. Jonathan Williams' Regt. Detached Militia in U. S. service 2
months and 6 days, 1812.

‡*HOWARD, JOSEPH.
Served from April 12, 1814 to April
21, 1814 in Capt. Shubael Wales'
Company, Col. W. B. Sumner's Regt.
Also served in 1 Regt. (Judson's) Vt.
Militia and in Capt. Utley's Com-
pany. Pension Certificate No. 2301.
Pension Certificate of widow, Lavina,
No. 33284.

*HOWARD, LYMAN.
Served in Capt. Howard's Company,
Vt. Militia.

HOWARD, MARSHALL, Fairfax.
Volunteered to go to Plattsburgh,
September, 1814, and served 8 days
in Capt. Josiah Grout's Company.
Also served in Capt. Joseph Beeman's
Company in 1813 and 1814. Ref:
Book 51, AGO Page 103; Hemenway's
Vt. Gazetteer, Vol. 2, Pages 402 and
403.

‡HOWARD, MORRIS.
Enlisted June 2, 1813 for 1 year in
Capt. Daniel Farrington's Company,
30th Regt.; on Muster Roll from
March 1, 1814 to April 30, 1814. Also
served in Capt. Willey's Company.
Pension Certificate of widow, Jane,
No. 15775. Ref: R. & L. 1812, AGO
Pages 50 and 51.

HOWARD, NATHANIEL, Waltham.
Volunteered to go to Plattsburgh,
September, 1814, and was in the
battle, serving 14 days in Capt.
Gideon Spencer's Company. Ref: Book
51, AGO Pages 2 and 3.

HOWARD, NATHANIEL, Franklin County. Volunteered to go to Plattsburgh Sept. 11, 1814 and served in
15th or 22nd Regt. Ref: Hemenway's
Vt. Gazetteer, Vol. 2, Page 391.

*HOWARD, SALMON, Captain. Thetford.
Volunteered to go to Plattsburgh,
September, 1814, and went as far as
Bolton, Vt., serving 6 days in com-
mand of company in 2nd Regt. 2nd
Brig. 4th Div. Vt. Militia. Also
served as Ensign in 2 Regt. (Fifield's)
Vt. Militia.

HOWARD, SAMUEL, Corporal.
Served in Capt. Chadwick's Company.
Ref: R. & L. 1812, AGO Page 32.

HOWARD, STEPHEN, Sergeant, Fairfax
or Swanton. Served in Lieut. V. R.
Goodrich's Company, 11th Regt.; on
Pay Roll for January and February,
1813. Served from Aug. 8, 1812 in
Company of Capt. Joseph Beeman Jr.,
11th Regt. U. S. Inf. under Col. Ira
Clark. Ref: R. & L. 1812, AGO
Page 11; Hemenway's Vt. Gazetteer,
Vol. 2, Page 402. Also served in
Capt. Joseph Beeman's Company in
1813 and 1814.

HOWARD, STEPHEN JR., Fairfax.
Served from Aug. 8, 1812 in company
of Capt. Joseph Beeman, Jr. 11th
Regt. U. S. Inf. under Col. Ira
Clark. Also served in Capt. Joseph
Beeman's Company in 1813 and 1814.
Ref: Hemenway's Vt. Gazetteer, Vol.
2, Page 402.

HOWARD, STEPHEN J., Fairfax or
Swanton. Served from Aug. 8, 1812 in
company of Capt. Joseph Beeman Jr.,
11th Regt. U. S. Inf. under Col.
Ira Clark. Also served in Lieut. V.
R. Goodrich's Company, 11th Regt.;
on Pay Roll for January and Febru-
ary, 1813. Ref: R. & L. 1812, AGO
Page 11; Hemenway's Vt. Gazetteer,
Vol. 2, Page 402.

HOWARD, WILLIAM, Barre.
Volunteered to go to Plattsburgh,
September, 1814, and served 10 days
in Capt. Warren Ellis' Company.
Ref: Book 52, AGO Page 242 .

HOWARD, ZETMAN C., Fairfax.
Served from Aug. 8, 1812 in company
of Capt. Joseph Beeman, Jr., 11th
Regt. U. S. Inf. under Col. Ira
Clark. Ref: Hemenway's Vt. Gazet-
teer, Vol. 2, Page 402.

‡*HOWDEN, HENRY C.
Served in Capt. Saxton's Company,
Sumner's Regt. Vt. Militia. Pen-
sion Certificate No. 28481.

‡HOWE, AMOS A.
Volunteered to go to Plattsburgh,
September, 1814, and served in Capt.
Jonathan Jennings' Company, Chel-
sea. Also served in Capt. Martin
Galusha's Company. Pension Certifi-
cate No. 30141. Pension Certificate
of widow, Melinda, No. 23550.

‡HOWE, BARSABEL, Sergeant.
Served from April 22, 1813 to April
28, 1814 in Capt. Simeon Wright's
Company. Pension Certificate No.
14910.

HOWE, BENJAMIN.
Served from Jan. 23, 1813 to April 6,
1813 in company of Capt. John Mc-
Neil Jr., 11th Regt. Ref: R. & L.
1812, AGO Page 16.

*HOWE, BRIGHAM, Jericho.
Served from Oct. 11, 1813 to Oct. 17,
1813 in Capt. John Munson's Company, 3 Regt. (Tyler's). Also took
part in the battle at Plattsburgh
Sept. 11, 1814. Ref: History of Jericho, Page 142.

*HOWE, CALVIN.
Served in 1st Regt. (Martindale's)
Vt. Militia.

*HOWE, CHARLES, 1st Lieutenant, Jeri-
cho. Served from Oct. 5, 1813 to
Oct. 17, 1813 in Capt. John Munson's Company, 3 Regt. (Tyler's).
Also took part in the battle at Plattsburgh Sept. 11, 1814. Ref: History
of Jericho, Page 142.

*HOWE, DANIEL, Sergeant.
Served in 1 Regt. (Judson's). Vt.
Militia .

HOWE, ERI.
Served from March 6 to June 5, 1813
in Capt. Samul Gordon's Company,
1th Regt. Ref: R. & L. 1812, AGO
Page 8.

*HOWE, FRANCIS.
Served from June 11, 1813 to June
14, 1813 in Capt. Moses Jewett's
Company, 1st Regt. 2nd Brig. 3rd
Div.

*HOWE, HENRY,   Jericho.
Served from Oct. 11, 1813 to Oct. 17,
1813 in Capt. John Munson's Company. 3 Regt. (Tyler's). Also took
part in the battle of Plattsburgh,
September 11, 1814. Ref: History of
Jericho, Page 142.

‡HOWE, HEZEKIAH,   Williamstown.
Volunteered to go to Plattsburgh,
September, 1814, and served 8 days
in Capt. David Robinson's Company.
Pension Certificate of widow, Nancy,
No. 34417.

*HOWE, JEREMIAH.
Served in Capt. Durkee's Company,
Col. Fifield's Regt. Detached Militia
in U. S. service 2 months and 21
days, 1812.

‡*HOWE, LUTHER, Corporal.
Served in Capt. Durkee's Company,
Col. Fifield's Regt. Detached Militia
in U. S. service 6 months, 1812. Pension Certificate of widow, Abigal, No.
2885.

‡HOWE, PORTER.
Served in Capt. Butler's Company.
Pension Certificate No. 13761. Pen-
sion Certificate of widow, Freelove J.,
No. 33995.

‡HOWE, READ P.,   Thetford.
Volunteered to go to Plattsburgh,
September, 1814, and served in Capt.
Orange Hubbard's Company. Pension
Certificate No. 32815.

*HOWE, RUFUS, Cornet.
Served in 3 Regt. (Williams') Vt.
Militia.

*HOWE, SAMUEL.
Served in Capt. Bingham's Company,
Col. Jonathan Williams' Regt. Detach-
ed Militia in U. S. service 2 months
and 9 days, 1812. Also served in 1
Regt. (Martindale's) Vt. Militia.

HOWE, WAIT.
Served from May 10, 1813 to May 10,
1814 in Capt. James Taylor's Company and Capt. Gideon Spencer's
Company, 30th Regt. Ref: R. & L.
1812, AGO Pages 52, 57, 59.

*HOWE, WILLIAM.
Served from April 12, 1814 to May
20, 1814 in company of Capt. James
Gray Jr., Sumner's Regt.

*HOWE, ZIMRI.
Served in Capt. Wright's Company,
Col. Martindale's Regt. Detached
Militia in U. S. service 2 months
and 14 days, 1812.

*HOWELL, EDWARD.
Enlisted Sept. 20, 1813 in Capt. John
Weed's Company, Col. Clark's Rifle
Corps.

HOWELL, EPHRAIM.
Served from Feb. 24 to June 4, 1814
in Capt. Alexander Brooks' Corps of
Artillery. Ref: R. & L. 1812, AGO
Page 31.

HOWELL, WILLIAM B., 2nd Lieutenant,
Franklin County. Enlisted Aug. 19,
1813 in Capt. White Youngs' Company, 15th Regt.; on Muster Roll
from Aug. 31, 1814 to Dec. 31, 1814.
Ref: R. & L. 1812, AGO Page 27.

*HOWER, JOSEPH, Drummer.
Enlisted Sept. 20, 1813 in Capt. John
Weed's Company, Col. Clark's Rifle
Corps.

‡*HOWES, CALEB H.
Served in Capt. Walker's Company,
2 Regt. (Fifield's) Vt. Militia in U.
S. service 2 months and 26 days, 1812.
Pension Certificate No. 9460.

HOWES, CALVIN,   Barre.
Volunteered to go to Plattsburgh,
September, 1814, and served in Capt.
Warren Ellis' Company. Ref: Hemen-
way's Vt. Gazetteer, Vol. 4, Page 42.

‡*HOWES, CHARLES.
Served in Capt. Wheatly's Company,
Col. Fifield's Regt. Detached Militia
in U. S. service 2 months and 21
days, 1812. Enlisted Jan. 27, 1813
in Lieut. V. R. Goodrich's Company,
11th Regt. Also served with Hospital
Attendants, Vt. Pension Certificate
No. 2743.

*HOWES, ISRAEL JR.
Served in 2 Regt. (Fifield's) Vt.
Militia.

HOWES, JOSEPH, Lieutenant, Montpelier.
Served in Capt. Walker's Company,
2 Regt. (Fifield's) Detached Militia,
in U. S. service 2 months and 26
days, 1812. Volunteered to go to
Plattsburgh, September, 1814, and
served as Lieutenant in Capt. Timothy Hubbard's Company. Ref: Book
53, AGO Page 2; Book 52, AGO Pages
197, 256, 212.

*HOWLAND, AMOS N.
Served in Capt. E. Walker's Company, Col. Fifield's Regt. Detached
Militia in U. S. service 2 months and
26 days, 1812.

*HOWLAND, CHARLES.
Served in Capt. Ormsbee's Company,
Col. Martindale's Regt. Detached
Militia in U. S. service 2 months and
14 days, 1812.

HOWLAND, ELISHA W.
Served from May 1 to June 30, 1814
as a carpenter in Alexander Parris'
Company of Artificers. Ref: R. & L.
1812, AGO Page 24.

HOWLAND, JOHN,   Barre.
Volunteered to go to Plattsburgh,
September, 1814, and served 10 days
in Capt. Warren Ellis' Company.
Ref: Book 52, AGO Pages 242 and 233.

HOYLE, JOHN,   Shoreham.
Volunteered to go to Plattsburgh,
September, 1814, and served 6 days
in Capt. Samuel Hand's Company.
Ref: Rev. J. F. Goodhue's History
of Shoreham. Page 108.

HOYT, ABNER.
Enlisted April 22, 1813 and served in Capt. James Taylor's Company and Capt. Gideon Spencer's Company, 30th Regt.; died at Westford, Vt., Jan. 13, 1814. Ref: R. & L. 1812, AGO Pages 52, 57, 58.

*HOYT, BENAH, Sergeant.
Served in 1 Regt. (Judson's) Vt. Militia.

HOYT, BENJAMIN,   Cabot.
Volunteered to go to Plattsburgh, September, 1814, and served 3 days in Capt. Anthony Perry's Company. Ref: Book 52, AGO Pages 252 and 254.

‡*HOYT, CLEMENT,   Richmond.
Served 3 months beginning, September, 1812, in 6th Company, 3rd Regt. 2nd Brig., commanded by Brig. Gen. Newell. Also served in Capt. Lowery's Company, 4 Regt. (Willimas') Vt. Militia. Pension Certificate of widow, Permelia, No. 30741.

HOYT, DANIEL .
Enlisted Aug. 22, 1813 for 1 year in Capt. Gideon Spencer's Company, 30th Regt.; on Muster Roll from Dec. 30, 1813 to June 30, 1814. Ref: R. & L. 1812, AGO Page 57.

‡HOYT, DAVID.
Served in Capt. Woster's Company. Pension Certificate No. 25520.

HOYT, EZRA.   Cabot.
Volunteered to go to Plattsburgh, September, 1814; no organization given. Ref: Book 51, AGO Page 72; Book 52, AGO Pages 188 and 206.

‡HOYT, JAMES,   Strafford.
Volunteered to go to Plattsburgh, September, 1814, and served 6 days in Capt. Jedediah H. Harris' Company. Pension Certificate No. 24108.

‡*HOYT, LUMAS T., (or Hoit).
Enlisted Sept. 25, 1813 in Capt. Amos Robinson's Company, Dixon's Regt.; transferred to Capt. N. B. Eldridge's Company, Col. Dixon's Regt. Sept. 28, 1813 and served 1 month and 23 days. Pension Certificate No. 11374.

HOYT, O.,   Swanton.
Served from July 15 to Dec. 8, 1813 in Capt. V. R. Goodrich's Company, 11th Regt.; was in action at the battle of Lundy's Lane. Ref: Hemenway's Vt. Gazetteer, Vol. 2, Page 444.

*HOYT, OREN.
Served from April 12, 1814 to April 21, 1814 in Capt. Eseck Sprague's Company, Sumner's Regt.

*HOYT, SETH JR.
Served from April 12, 1814 to April 21, 1814 in Capt. Eseck Sprague's Company, Sumner's Regt.

HOYT, TRISTAM C.,   Cabot.
Volunteered to go to Plattsburgh, September, 1814, and served 4 days in Capt. Anthony Perry's Company. Ref: Book 51, AGO Page 72; Book 52, AGO Pages 177, 252, 254.

HOYT, TRUMAN,   St. Albans.
Served from April 22, 1813 to April 25, 1814 in Capt. James Taylor's Company and Capt. Gideon Spencer's Company, 30th Regt. Volunteered to go to Plattsburgh and was at the battle Sept. 11, 1814, serving in Capt. Samuel H. Farnsworth's Company. Ref: R. & L. 1812, AGO Pages 52, 57, 58; Hemenway's Vt. Gazetteer, Vol. 2,, Page 434.

HOYT, TRUMAN,   Westford.
Volunteered to go to Plattsburgh, September, 1814, and served 8 days in company of Capt. Joseph Beeman of Fairfax. Ref: Book 51, AGO Page 119.

‡*HOYT, ZINA W.
Enlisted Sept. 25, 1813 in Capt. Amos Robinson's Company, Dixon's Regt.; transferred to Capt. N. B. Eldridge's Company, Dixon's Regt. Sept. 28, 1813 and served 1 month and 23 days. Pension Certificate No. 5279.

*HUBBARD, ADAM,   Randolph.
Volunteered to go to Plattsburgh, September, 1814, and served in Capt. Lebbeus Egerton's Company.

HUBBARD, ARNA,   Rochester.
Volunteered to go to Plattsburgh, September, 1814, and served 7 days in Capt. Oliver Mason's Company. Ref: Book 51, AGO Page 253.

*HUBBARD, CALVIN, Sergeant, Whiting.
Served from April 13, 1814 to April 16, 1814 in Capt. Salmon Foster's Company, Sumner's Regt.; volunteered to go to Plattsburgh, September, 1814, and served 9 days in same company.

HUBBARD, CROSS, Corporal.
Served from April 8, 1813 to July 1, 1813 in Lieut. Wm. S. Foster's Company, 11th Regt. Ref: R. & L. 1812, AGO Page 6.

HUBBARD, DAVID.
Enlisted May 10, 1813 for 1 year in Capt. Simeon Wright's Company. Ref: R. & L. 1812, AGO Page 51.

HUBBARD, EBEN (or Eben'zr).
Served from Dec. 23, 1812 to April 6, 1813 in company of Capt. John McNeil Jr., 11th Regt. Ref: R. & L. 1812, AGO Pages 16 and 17.

*HUBBARD, ELI (or Elihu).
Served in 1st Regt. of Detached Militia of Vt. in U. S. service at Champlain from Nov. 18 to Nov. 19, 1812.

*HUBBARD, JOSEPH.
Served in Corning's Detachment, Vt. Militia.

HUBBARD, PETER,   Rochester.
Volunteered to go to Plattsburgh, September, 1814, and served 7 days in Capt. Oliver Mason's Company. Ref: Book 51, AGO Page 257.

HUBBARD, R.,   Fairfax.
Served from Aug. 8, 1812 in company of Capt. Joseph Beeman, Jr., 11th

Regt. U. S. Inf. under Col. Ira Clark. Ref: Hemenway's Vt. Gazetteer, Vol. 2, Page 402.

HUBBARD, ROGER, Sergeant, Montpelier. Volunteered to go to Plattsburgh, September, 1814, and served 8 days in Capt. Timothy Hubbard's Company. Ref: Book 52, AGO Page 256.

HUBBARD, SAMUEL,   Berlin. Volunteered to go to Plattsburgh, September, 1814, and served 7 days in Capt. Cyrus Johnson's Company. Ref: Book 52, AGO Page 255.

HUBBARD, TIMOTHY, Captain, Montpelier. Volunteered to go to Plattsburgh, September, 1814, and served 8 days in command of company raised at Montpelier. Ref: Book 52, AGO Page 256.

HUBBARD, ZEBINA. Served in Lieut. V. R. Goodrich's Company, 11th Regt.; on Pay Roll for January and February, 1813. Ref: R. & L. 1812, AGO Page 11.

HUBBEL, ELIJAH D., Corporal. Served in Cavalry of Detached Militia of Vt. in U. S. service at Champlain from Nov. 18 to Nov. 19, 1812.

*HUBBELL, ABIJAH. Enlisted Sept. 23, 1813 and served 1 month and 25 days in Capt. Asahel Langworthy's Company, Col. Isaac Clark's Rifle Corps.

‡*HUBBELL, CHARLES, Sergeant. Served from June 11 to June 14, 1813 in Capt. John Palmer's Company, 1st Regt. 2nd Brig. 3rd Div. and from Oct. 4, 1813 to Oct. 13, 1813 in same company. Pension Certificate of widow, Rebecca S., No. 14735.

*HUBBELL, HIRAM. Served from Sept. 25, 1813 to Nov. 3, 1813 in Capt. Charles Bennett's Company, Col. Dixon's Regt.

*HUBBELL, SAMUEL,   Highgate. Served in Capt. Saxe's Company, Col. Wm. Williams' Regt. Detached Militia in U. S. service 4 months and 24 days, 1812.

*HUCKINS, WILLIAM.   Waterbury. Volunteered to go to Plattsburgh, September, 1814, and served 11 days in Capt. George Atkins' Company, 4 Regt. (Peck's).

HUDSON, AARON. Enlisted May 4, 1810 at New York in U. S. Marine Corps. Ref: Book 52, AGO Page 294.

*HUDSON, EBENEZER. Served in Capt. O. Lowry's Company, Col. Wm. Williams' Regt. Detached Militia in U. S. service 4 months and 26 days, 1812.

‡HUDSON, ELI,   Pittsford. Volunteered to go to Plattsburgh, September, 1814, and served 8 days in Capt. Caleb Hendee's Company. Pension Certificate of widow, Sarah, No. 40996.

HUDSON, JOSEPH. Served from Nov. 1, 1812 to Feb. 28, 1813 in Capt. Samuel H. Holly's Company, 11th Regt. Also served in Capt. McNeil's Company, 11th Inf. Ref. R. & L. 1812, AGO Pages 25 and 30.

HUDSON, LOT, Captain,   Braintree. Marched to Plattsburgh Sept. 10, 1814, serving in Capt. Lot Hudson's Company. Ref: Book 51, AGO Page 295; Book 52, AGO Page 24.

*HUDSON, SAMUEL. Served with Hospital Attendants, Vt.

HUDSON, WILLIAM,   Franklin County. Volunteered to go to Plattsburgh Sept. 11, 1814 and served in 15th or 22nd Regt. Ref: Hemenway's Vt. Gazetteer, Vol. 2, Page 392.

*HUFF, DAVID. Served in Sumner's Regt. Vt. Militia.

*HUFFMAN, JOHN, Corporal. Served in 2 Regt. (Fifield's) Vt. Militia.

*HUGGINS, DAVID. Served in Capt. Dodge's Company, Col. Fifield's Regt. Detached Militia in U. S. service 2 months and 21 days, 1812.

HUGHES, SAMUEL, Sergeant. Enlisted Sept. 23, 1813 in Capt. Amasa Mansfield's Company. Dixon's Regt. Ref: Book 52, AGO Page 269.

‡HULL, ANSON. Served in Capt. Follett's Company. Pension Certificate of widow, Mary H., No. 29442.

*HULL, CALEB 2nd, Corporal. Served in Capt. Barns' Company, Col. Wm. Williams' Regt. Detached Militia in U. S. service 5 months, 1812. Also served from June 11, 1813 to June 14, 1813 in Capt. Thomas Dorwin's Company, 1st Regt. 2nd Brig. 3rd Div.

*HULL, EDMON, Corporal. Served in Sumner's Regt. Vt. Militia.

‡*HULL, HIRAM. Served in 1 Regt. (Martindale's) Vt. Militia. Also served in Capt. A. Scovill's Company. Pension Certificate of widow, Nancy, No. 31307.

HULL, JOHN,   Montpelier. Volunteered to go to Plattsburgh, September, 1814, and served 8 days in Capt. Timothy Hubbard's Company. Ref: Book 52, AGO Page 256.

*HULL, JOSEPH. Served from Oct. 8, 1813 to Nov. 18, 1813 in Capt. Isaac Finch's Company, Col. Clark's Rifle Corps.

HULL, LYMAN, Fifer. Served from March 27, 1813 to June 26, 1813 in Capt. Charles Follett's Company, 11th Regt. Ref: R. & L. 1812, AGO Page 13.

*HULL, SAMUEL. Served in Dixon's Regt. Vt. Militia.

HUMPHREY, ARCHIBALD,   Orwell.
Volunteered to go to Plattsburgh,
September, 1814, and served 11 days
in Capt. Wait Branch's Company.
Ref: Book 51, AGO Page 16.

*HUMPHREY, EDD.
Served in 3 Regt. (Tyler's) Vt. Militia.

HUMPHREY, EDY,   Jericho.
Took part in Battle of Plattsburgh
and was granted pension. Ref: History of Jericho, Page 142.

*HUMPHREY, JAMES, Corporal.
Served in 3 Regt. (Tyler's) Vt. Militia.

*HUMPHREY, JONAS.
Served from June 11, 1813 to June
14, 1813 in Lieut. Bates' Company,
1st Regt. (Judson's).

HUMPHREY, WILLIAMS, Corporal .
Served in company of Capt. Phineas
Williams' 11th Regt.; on Pay Roll
for January and February, 1813.
Ref: R. & L. 1812, AGO Page 15.

*HUNKIN, ROBERT.
Served in 2 Regt. (Fifield's) Vt. Militia.

‡*HUNKINS, HASTINGS T.
Enlisted Sept. 25, 1813 and served 1
month and 23 days in Capt. Thomas
Waterman's Company, Col. Dixon's
Regt. Pension Certificate No. 23125.

HUNKINS, ROBERT.
Served in Capt. Rogers' Company,
Col. Fifield's' Regt. Detached Militia
in U. S. service 10 days, 1812. Enlisted Sept. 25, 1813 as a corporal in
Capt. N. B. Eldridge's Company, Dixon's Regt. Ref: Book 52, AGO Page
267; Book 53, AGO Page 97.

HUNSDEN, ALLEN JR., Corporal, Shoreham. Volunteered to go to Plattsburgh, September, 1814, and served
6 days in Capt. Samuel Hand's Company. Ref: Rev. J. F. Goodhue's
History of Shoreham, Page 107.

HUNT, ALANSON,   Shoreham.
Volunteered to go to Plattsburgh,
September, 1814, and served 6 days
in Capt. Samuel Hand's Company.
Ref: Rev. J. F. Goodhue's History
of Shoreham, Page 108.

‡*HUNT, BENJAMIN.
Served in 1 Regt. (Martindale's) Vt.
Militia. Pension Certificate of widow,
Thankful, No. 10141.

HUNT, BUSHNELL.
Served from Sept. 23 and Sept. 29,
1813 in Capt. Amasa Mansfield's
Company, Dixon's Regt. Ref: Book
52, AGO Page 269.

HUNT, CLARK.
Volunteered to go to Plattsburgh,
September, 1814, and served in company of Capt. Jonathan Jennings,
Chelsea. Ref: Book 52, AGO Pages
79 and 104.

HUNT, DANIEL,   St. Albans.
Enlisted June 1, 1813 in Capt. John
Wires' Company, 30th Regt. Ref: R.
& L. 1812, AGO Page 40.

‡HUNT, ELIJAH.
Served in Capt. Mead's Company.
Pension Certificate No. 5284.

HUNT, EPHRAIM.
Served from May 1 to June 30, 1814
in Capt. Alexander Brooks' Corps of
Artillery. Ref: R. & L. 1812, AGO
Page 31.

‡*HUNT, HARRY, Corporal.
Enlisted Oct. 2, 1813 in Capt. Asahel
Langworthy's Company, Col. Isaac
Clark's Rifle Corps; transferred to
Capt. Post's Company, Dixon's Regt.
Oct. 3, 1813. Volunteered to go to
Plattsburgh, September, 1814, and
served 1 week as a corporal in Capt.
Jesse Post's Company, Dixon's Regt.;
was at the battle. Pension Certificate
No. 18575.

*HUNT, HARVEY.
Served from April 12, 1814 to April
21, 1814 in Capt. Shubael Wales' Company, W. B. Sumner's Regt.

HUNT, HENRY,   Georgia.
Served in Capt. Langworthy's Company, Col. Dixon's Regt. Detached
Militia in U. S. service 1 month and
24 days, 1813. Volunteered to go to
Plattsburgh, September, 1814, and
served in Capt. Jesse Post's Company,
Dixon's Regt. Ref: Book 53, AGO
Page 111; Hemenway's Vt. Gazetteer,
Vol. 2, Page 417.

HUNT, ISAAC.
Served from May 1 to June 4, 1814
in Capt. Alexander Brooks' Corps of
Artillery. Died June 5, 1814. Ref:
R. & L. 1812, AGO Page 31.

*HUNT, JAMES.
Served in Dixon's Regt. Vt. Militia.

*HUNT, JASPER.
Served in Capt. Parsons' Company,
Col. Jonathan Williams' Regt. Detached Militia in U. S. service 2
months and 13 days, 1812.

HUNT, JOHN.
Enlisted March 20, 1813 in Capt. Jonathan Starks' Company, 11th Regt.;
on Pay Roll to May 31, 1813; captured June 3, 1813 on Lake Champlain. Ref: R. & L. 1812, AGO Page
19.

HUNT, JOHN.
Served from March 10 to June 9,
1813 in Capt. Samul Gordon's Company, 11th Regt. Ref: R. & L. 1812,
AGO Page 8.

‡*HUNT, JOHN.
Served in Capt. Cross' Company, Col.
Martindale's Regt. Detached Militia
in U. S. service 2 months and 13
days, 1812. Also served in Sumner's
Regt. Vt. Militia. Pension Certificate No. 3006.

‡*HUNT, JOSEPH, Corporal,   Fairfax.
Enlisted Sept. 25, 1813 and served 1 month and 23 days in Capt. Asa Wilkins' Company, Col. Dixon's Regt. Served from April 12, 1814 to May 20. 1814 in company of Capt. James Gray Jr., Sumner's Regt. Volunteered to go to Plattsburgh, September, 1814, and served 8 days in Capt. Josiah Grout's Company. Pension Certificate No. 23857. Pension Certificate of widow, Naomi, No. 27696.

‡HUNT, LEWIS,   Shoreham.
Volunteered to go to Plattsburgh, September, 1814, and served 6 days in Capt. Samuel Hand's Company. Pension Certificate of widow, Millitiah, No. 34418.

*HUNT, LUTHER,   Georgia.
Enlisted Sept. 25, 1813 in Capt. N. B. Eldridge's Company, Dixon's Regt.; transferred to Capt. Asahel Langworthy's Company, Col. Isaac Clark's Rifle Corps Sept. 27, 1813. Volunteered to go to Plattsburgh, September, 1814, and served in Capt. Jesse Post's Company. Dixon's Regt.

HUNT, LUTHER,   New Haven.
Volunteered to go to Plattsburgh, September, 1814, and served in Capt. Wheeler's Company. Ref: Book 51, AGO Page 26.

*HUNT, LYMAN.
Served from April 12. 1814 to May 20, 1814 in company of Capt. James Gray, Jr. Sumner's Regt.

HUNT, NATHANIEL.
Served from January 9. 1813 to Feb. 10, 1813 in Lieut. Wm. S. Foster's Company, 11th Regt. Ref: R. & L. 1812, AGO Page 6.

*HUNT, ROSWELL, Captain,   Richmond.
Served from Oct. 5, 1813 to Oct. 16, 1813 in command of company of 52 men raised in Richmond, Vt., assigned to 3rd U. S. Regt. commanded by Col. George Tyler, 2nd Brig. Volunteered to go to Plattsburgh. September, 1814, and commanded same company.

*HUNT, SILAS,   Richmond.
Served from Oct. 11, 1813 to Oct. 16, 1813 in Capt. Roswell Hunt's Company, 3 Regt. (Tyler's). Volunteered to go to Plattsburgh, September, 1814, and served 9 days in same company.

HUNT, SIMEON,   Tunbridge.
Volunteered to go to Plattsburgh, September, 1814, and served 4 days in Capt. Ephraim Hackett's Company. Ref: Book 52, AGO Pages 71 and 75.

HUNT, SIMON.
Volunteered to go to Plattsburgh, September, 1814, and served in company of Capt. Jonathan Jennings, Chelsea. Ref: Book 52, AGO Page 79.

HUNT, STODDARD.
Volunteered to go to Plattsburgh, September, 1814, and served in company of Capt. Jonathan Jennings, Chelsea. Ref: Book 52, AGO Page 104.

*HUNT, WARD.
Served from April 12. 1814 to May 20, 1814 in company of Capt. James Gray Jr., Sumner's Regt.

*HUNT, WILLIAM,   Stowe.
Volunteered to go to Plattsburgh, September, 1814, and was at the battle, serving in Capt. Nehemiah Perkins' Company, 4th Regt. (Peck's).

*HUNT, WILLIAM C.
Served in Sumner's Regt. Vt. Militia.

HUNT, ZACHEUS,   Vershire.
Volunteered to go to Plattsburgh, September, 1814, and served 3 days in Capt. Ira Corse's Company. Ref: Book 52, AGO Page 91.

*HUNTER, CHARLES,   Grand Isle.
Served under Captains Wheatly and Wright, Col. Fifield's Regt. Detached Militia in U. S. service 6 months, 1812.

HUNTER, JONATHAN.
Served from Feb. 13. 1813 to May 12, 1813 in Capt. Charles Follett's Company, 11th Regt. Ref: R. & L. 1812, AGO Page 13.

‡*HUNTER, JONATHAN D., (or W.)
Served from April 12. 1814 to May 20, 1814 in Capt. George Fisher's Company, Sumner's Regt. Volunteered to go to Plattsburgh, September, 1814, and served 6 days in Capt. Samuel Hand's Company. Pension Certificate No. 28278.

HUNTER, JOSEPH,   Shoreham.
Volunteered to go to Plattsburgh, September, 1814, and served 6 days in Capt. Samuel Hand's Company. Ref: Rev. J. F. Goodhue's History of Shoreham, Page 108.

*HUNTER, NOAH (or Manoah).
Served from April 12. 1814 to May 20, 1814 in Capt. George Fisher's Company, Sumner's Regt. Volunteered to go to Plattsburgh, September, 1814, and served 6 days in Capt. Samuel Hand's Company.

*HUNTER, TIMOTHY P.
Served in Capt. Wheelers' Company, Col. Fifield's Regt. Detached Militia in U. S. service 6 months and 4 days, 1812.

HUNTER, WILLIAM.
Served from March 1 to June 30. 1814 in Capt. Alexander Brooks' Corp of Artillery. Ref: R. & L. 1812, AGO Page 31.

*HUNTING, HARRY.
Served in 4 Regt. (Williams') Vt. Militia.

*HUNTINGTON, ABNER JR.
Served from April 12, 1814 to April 21, 1814 in Capt. Eseck Sprague's Company, Sumner's Regt.

HUNTINGTON, CHARLES M.. Montpelier.
Volunteered to go to Plattsburgh, September, 1814, and served 9 days in Capt. Timothy Hubbard's Company. Ref: Book 52, AGO Page 244.

*HUNTINGTON, FORDYCE, Ensign.
Served from April 12, 1814 to April
21, 1814 in Capt Eseck Sprague's
Company, Sumner's Regt.

*HUNTINGTON, HARRY.
Served in Capt. Phelps' Company,
Col. Wm. Williams' Regt. Detached
Militia in U. S. service 5 months,
1812.

*HUNTINGTON, JONATHAN.
Served from April 12, 1814 to April
15, 1814 in Lieut. Justus Foote's
Company, Sumner's Regt.

*HUNTINGTON, MILLER, Randolph.
Volunteered to go to Plattsburgh,
September, 1814, and served in Capt.
Lebbeus Egerton's Company.

*HUNTINGTON, ROSWELL, Fifer.
Served in Capt. Bingham's Company,
Col. Jonathan Williams' Regt. Detached Militia in U. S. service 2
months and 9 days, 1812.

*HUNTLEY, ALLEN, Drummer.
Served in Corning's Detachment, Vt.
Militia.

*HUNTLEY, EZEKIEL.
Served in Capt. Cross' Company,
Col. Martindale's Regt. Detached
Militia in U. S. service 2 months
and 14 days, 1812.

*HUNTLEY, IRA, Highgate.
Served in Capt. Saxe's Company, Col.
William Williams' Regt. Detached
Militia in U. S. service 2 months
and 26 days, 1812. Enlisted Sept.
25, 1813 in Company of Capt. Jonathan Prentiss Jr., Dixon's Regt.

*HUNTLEY, ISAIAH, Corporal.
Served in Capt. Lowry's Company,
Col. Wm. Williams' Regt. Detached
Militia in U. S. service 4 months
and 26 days, 1812. Also served in
4 Regt. (Peck's) Vt. Militia.

‡HUNTLEY, JACOB.
Served in Capt. Daniel M. Stearns'
Company. Pension Certificate No.
25479. Pension Certificate of widow,
Sarah, No. 35373.

*HUNTLEY, JOEL.
Served from April 12, 1814 to April
21, 1814 in Capt. Edmund B. Hill's
Company, Sumner's Regt.

HUNTLEY, NATHAN, Middlesex.
Volunteered to go to Plattsburgh,
September, 1814, and served in Capt.
Holden Putnam's Company, 4 Regt.
(Peck's). Ref: Hemenway's Vt. Ga-
zetteer, Vol. 4, Page 250.

‡HUNTLEY, SAMUEL H.
Served in Capt. Butler's Company.
Pension Certificate No. 28244.

‡*HUNTLEY, SMYTON.
Enlisted Sept. 25, 1813 in company
of Capt. Jonathan Prentiss Jr., Dixon's Regt. Pension Certificate of
widow, Lorena, No. 18646.

*HUNTOON, CHARLES.
Served in Capt. Rogers Company,
Fifield's Regt., Detached Militia in
U. S. service 5 months and 27 days,
1812.

HUNTOON, GEORGE.
Served from March 8, 1813 to June 7,
1813 in Capt. John W. Weeks' Company, 11th Regt. Ref: R. & L. 1812,
AGO Page 4.

HUNTOON, GREENLIEF.
Served from Feb. 21, 1813 to May
20, 1813 in Capt. John W. Weeks'
Company, 11th Regt. Ref: R. & L.
1812, AGO Page 4.

*HUNTOON, ISAAC F.
Served in Capt. Adams' Company,
Col. Jonathan Williams' Regt. Detached Militia in U. S. service 2
months and 7 days, 1812.

HUNTOON, WILLARD.
Served in Capt. Weeks' Company, 11th
Regt.; on Pay Roll for January and
February, 1813. Ref: R. & L. 1812,
AGO Page 5.

‡HUNTSLEY, LUTHER.
Served in Capt. Leonard's Company.
Pension Certificate No. 33337.

*HURD, GUILDERSLEVES.
Served in Capt. Strait's Company,
Col. Martindale's Regt. Detached
Militia in U. S. service 1 month and
16 days, 1812.

‡*HURD, ISAAC.
Served in Capt. Strait's Company,
Col. Martindale's Regt. Detached
Militia in U. S. service 2 months
and 13 days, 1812. Pension Certificate No. 1858. Pension Certificate
of daughter Amanda Hurd, No. 45447.

HURD, ISAAC.
Served in Capt. Cross' Company, Col.
Martindale's Regt. Detached Militia
in U. S. service 2 months and 14
days, 1812.

HURD, JOHN.
Enlisted Feb. 21, 1814 for period of
the war in Capt. Gideon Spencer's
Company, 30th Regt.; on Muster Roll
Dec. 30, 1813 to June 30, 1814; joined
June 1, 1814. Ref: R. & L. 1812,
AGO Page 57.

*HURD, JOHN C.
Served from April 12, 1814 to April
21, 1814 in Lieut. Justus Foote's Company, Sumner's Regt.

‡HURLBERT, CALVIN.
Served in Capt. Butler's Company.
Pension Certificate No. 24116.

‡HURLBURT, CHARLES.
Served in Capt. Scoville's Company.
Pension Certificate of widow, Eliza-
beth, No. 3005.

‡*HURLBURT, DAVID.
Served in Capt. Needham's Company,
Col. Martindale's Regt. Detached
Militia in U. S. service 2 months
and 14 days, 1812. Pension Certificate No. 16151. Pension Certificate
of widow, Clarissa, No. 31505.

*HURLBURT, ELIAS.
Served from April 12, 1814 to April 21, 1814 in Capt. Eseck Sprague's Company, Sumner's Regt.

HURLBURT, HARRY,   Huntington.
Volunteered to go to Plattsburgh, September, 1814, and was at the battle, serving in Capt. Josiah N. Barrows' Company. Ref: Book 51, AGO Page 77.

‡HURLBURT, JOHN.
Served in Capt. Ransom's Company. Pension Certificate of widow, Sarah F. W. No. 15538.

*HURLBURT, JOSEPH.
Enlisted Sept. 25, 1813 and served 1 month and 23 days in Capt. Elijah Birge's Company, Col. Dixon's Regt.

*HURLBURT, WILLIAM.
Enlisted Sept. 25, 1813 in company of Capt. Jonathan Prentiss Jr., Dixon's Regt. Served from April 12, 1814 to April 21, 1814 in Capt. Shubael Wales' Company, Col. W. B. Sumner's Regt. Volunteered to go to Plattsburgh, September, 1814, and was at the battle, serving in Capt. Edmund B. Hill's Company, Sumner's Regt. Ref: Book 51, AGO Page 13.

HURLBURT, WILLIAM (or Hurlbert), Cornwall. Volunteered to go to Plattsburgh, September, 1814, and served 6 days in Capt. Silas Wright's Company. Ref: Book 51, AGO Page 12.

*HURLBURT, WRIGHT, Sergeant.
Enlisted Sept. 25, 1813 and served 1 month and 23 days in Capt. Elijah Birge's Company, Col. Dixon's Regt.

*HURLBUSH, DANIEL.
Served in 1 Regt. (Martindale's) Vt. Militia.

*HURLBUT, ADAM JR.
Served in Capt. Taylor's Company, Col. Wm. Williams' Regt. Detached Militia in U. S. service 4 months and 24 days, 1812.

*HURLBUT, CHAUNCEY.
Served in Capt. Barns' Company, Col. Wm. Williams' Regt. Detached Militia in U. S. service 5 months, 1812. Served from June 11 to June 14, 1813 in Lieut. Bates' Company, 1 Regt. (Judson's).

*HURLBUT, DANIEL, Ensign.
Served in 1 Regt. (Judson's) Vt. Militia.

*HURLBUT, ELIJAH.
Served in 3 Regt. (Tyler's) Vt. Militia.

‡*HURLBUT, HERMAN,   Jericho.
Served from June 11 to June 14, 1813 in Capt. John Palmer's Company, 1st Regt. 2nd Brig. 3rd Div. Served from Oct. 5 to Oct. 17, 1813 in Capt. Stephen Brown's Company, 3 Regt. (Tyler's). Also served in Capt. Sinclair's Company. Pension Certificate No. 25274.

HURLBUT, ISAAC.
Served in Capt. Saxe's Company, Col. Wm. Williams' Regt. Detached Militia in U. S. service 4 months and 24 days, 1812. Ref: Book 53, AGO Page 70.

*HURLBUT, LEVI.
Enlisted Sept. 25, 1813 and served 1 month and 23 days in Capt. N. B. Eldridge's Company, Col. Dixon's Regt.

HUSE, MOSES M., Musician, West Fairlee. Volunteered to go to Plattsburgh, September, 1814, and served 4 days in Capt. Aaron Kidder's Company. Ref: Book 51, AGO Page 201; Book 52, AGO Pages 105 and 108.

*HUSKINS, ROBERT.
Served in 2 Regt. (Fifield's) Vt. Militia.

‡HUTCHINGS, JOSEPH.
Served in Capt. Joseph Hazen's Company. Pension Certificate No. 32825.

HUTCHINS, ALPHEUS.
Enlisted Nov. 1, 1812 in Capt. Weeks' Company, 11th Regt.; on Pay Roll for January and February, 1813. Ref: R. & L. 1812, AGO Page 5.

HUTCHINS, AMASA,   Vershire.
Volunteered to go to Plattsburgh, September, 1814, and served 3 days in Capt. Ira Corse's Company. Ref: Book 52, AGO Pages 91 and 102.

*HUTCHINS, BENJAMIN,   Pawlet.
Enlisted Oct. 2, 1813 and served 78 days in Capt. John Weed's Company, Col. Clark's Rifle Corps.

‡HUTCHINS, CALEB D.
Served in Capt. Warner's Company. Pension Certificate No. 19029. Pension Certificate of widow, Mindwell, No. 25922.

*HUTCHINS, DYER.
Served from April 12, 1814 to April 21, 1814 in Capt. Edmund B. Hill's Company, Sumner's Regt.

HUTCHINS, E. S., Assistant Surgeon, Jericho. Volunteered to go to Plattsburgh, September, 1814; no organization given. Ref: Book 51, AGO Page 278.

*HUTCHINS, EDWARD F.
Served in 3 Regt. (Tyler's) Vt. Militia.

HUTCHINS, ELEAZER, Surgeon, Jericho. Volunteered to go to Plattsburgh, September, 1814, and served in Col. Tyler's Regt. A pension was granted his widow, Betsy Hutchins. Ref: Book 51, AGO Page 278; History of Jericho, Page 142.

‡*HUTCHINS, ELISHA.
Served in Capt. Scovell's Company, Col. Martindale's Regt. Detached Militia in U. S. service 1 month and 14 days, 1812. Pension Certificate of widow, Lucinda, No. 9485.

*HUTCHINS, GEORGE.
Served with Hospital Attendants, Vt.

‡HUTCHINS, PARLEY.
Served in Capt. Johnson's Company.
Pension Certificate of widow, Polly,
No. 26193.

‡HUTCHINS, SAMUEL.
Served in Capt. Melvin's Company.
Pension Certificate No. 30059.

HUTCHINSON, AMBROSE,   Roxbury.
Volunteered to go to Plattsburgh,
September, 1814, and served 8 days
in Capt. Samuel M. Orcutt's Company. Ref: Book 52, AGO Page 250.

HUTCHINSON, ELISHA, Sergeant.
Enlisted Sept. 22, 1809 at New York
in U. S. Marine Corps. Ref: Book
52, AGO Page 294.

‡*HUTCHINSON, ELISHA.
Served in Capt. Burnap's Company,
Jonathan Williams' Regt. Detached
Militia in U. S. service 17 days.
Pension Certificate No. 20028. Pen-
sion Certificate of widow, Nancy S.,
No. 31161.

*HUTCHINSON, ISRAEL.
Served in Capt. Hiram Mason's Company, Col. Fifield's Regt. Detached
Militia in U. S. service 5 months
and 26 days, 1812.

HUTCHINSON, JOHN,   Thetford.
Volunteered to go to Plattsburgh,
September, 1814, and served in Capt.
Joseph Barrett's Company. Ref: Book
52, AGO Page 41.

‡*HUTCHINSON, LUTHER.
Served in Capt. Parsons' Company,
Col. Jonathan Williams' Regt. Detached Militia in U. S. service 2
months and 13 days, 1812. Pension
Certificate No. 9856. Pension Certificate of widow, Maria L., No. 8955.

HUTCHINSON, NATHANIEL, Braintree.
Marched to Plattsburgh Sept. 10, 1814
and served in Capt. Lot Hudson's
Company. Ref: Book 51, AGO Page
300; Book 52, AGO Pages 24 and 26.

‡*HUTCHINSON, RUFUS,   Braintree.
Served in Col. Fifield's Regt. De-
tached Militia in U. S. service 6
months, 1812. Marched to Plattsburgh
Sept. 10, 1814 and served 9 days in
Capt. Lot Hudson's Company. Ref:
Book 51, AGO Page 295; Book 52,
AGO Pages 24 and 33. Also served
in Capt. Wheatley's Company. Pen-
sion Certificate No. 1849.

HYDE, CYRIL.
Volunteered to go to Plattsburgh,
September, 1814, and served 7 days
in company of Capt. Frederick Gris-
wold, raised in Brookfield. Ref:
Book 52, AGO Page 52.

*HYDE, DAVID.
Served in 3 Regt. (Tyler's) Vt. Militia.

*HYDE, ELI, Corporal.
Served in Capt. Mansfield's Company,
Col. Dixon's Regt. Detached Militia

in U. S. service 1 month and 23
days; enlisted Sept. 23, 1813.

*HYDE, ENY (or Emy).
Served from Oct. 5 to Oct. 13, 1813
in Capt. Stephen Brown's Company,
3 Regt. (Tyler's).

*HYDE, GEORGE.
Served from Feb. 5, 1813 to May 4,
1813 in Lieut. V. R. Goodrich's Com-
pany, 11th Regt. Also served in 4
Regt. (Williams') Vt. Militia. Ref:
R. & L. 1812, AGO Page 10.

HYDE, ISAAC T.
Served in Capt. Barns' Company, Col.
Wm. Williams' Regt. Detached Mili-
tia in U. S. service 5 months, 1812.
Ref: Book 53, AGO Page 13.

HYDE, JOHN.
Served in Capt. Edgerton's Company,
11th Regt.; on Pay Roll for January
and February, 1813. Served from
Jan. 1st to June 30, 1814 in Capt.
Haig's Corps of Light Dragoons. Ref:
R. & L. 1812, AGO Pages 2, 3, 20.

HYDE, JOSHUA.
Served in Capt. Edgerton's Company,
11th Regt. from Jan. 18, 1813 to
date of death April 19, 1813. Ref:
R. & L. 1812, AGO Pages 2 and 3.

HYDE, LATHE,   Strafford.
Volunteered to go to Plattsburgh,
September, 1814, and served in com-
pany of Capt. Jedediah H. Harris.
Ref: Hemenway's Vt. Gazetteer, Vol.
2, Page 1083.

*HYDE, LEONARD.
Served in 1 Regt. (Judson's) Vt.
Militia.

*HYDE, LIGRAND.
Served from June 11-14, 1813 and
from Oct. 4-13, 1813 in Capt. John
Palmer's Company, 1st Regt. 2nd Brig.
3rd Div.

‡*HYDE, MARTIN.
Served in Tyler's Regt. Vt. Militia.
Pension Certificate of widow, Celin-
da, No. 20090.

HYDE, REUBEN. B., Lieutenant.
Appointed 3 Lieutenant April 30, 1813,
30th Inf. and 2nd Lieutenant Feb.
18, 1814. 30th Inf. Ref: Governor
and Council, vi., Vol. 6, Page 475.

HYDE, REUBEN C., Sergeant.
Served in Capt. Samul Gordon's Com-
pany, 11th Regt.; on Pay Roll for
January and February, 1813. Ref:
R. & L. 1812, AGO Page 9.

‡*HYDE, RUSSELL B., Lieutenant, Hyde
Park? Appointed 3 Lieutenant 30
Inf. April 30, 1813; 2 Lieutenant
Feb. 18, 1814; dismissed Oct. 25,
1814; reinstated Dec. 10, 1814; died
Aug. 22, 1851. Served as Ensign in
2 Regt. (Fifield's) Vt. Militia and
served in Capt. H. Mason's Company. Pension Certificate of widow,
Carolina N.. No. 9991. Ref: Heitman's Historical Register & Dictionary USA. (For biographical sketch
see Hemenway's Vt. Gazetteer, Vol.
2, Page 654.)

*HYDE, SEPTY.
Served in Capt. Wright's Company,
Col. Fifield's Regt. Detached Militia
in U. S. service 3 months and 9
days, 1812.

HYDE, THOMAS W.,   Sudbury.
Volunteered to go to Plattsburgh,
September, 1814, and served 6 days
in Capt. Thomas Hall's Company. Ref:
Book 52, AGO Page 122.

HYDE, WILLIAM.
Served from April 23, 1813 to April
26, 1814 in Capt. James Taylor's Company and Capt. Gideon Spencer's
Company, 30th Regt. Ref: R. & L.
1812, AGO Pages 52 and 57.

HYDE, WILLIAM.
Born in Norwich, Conn.; aged 47
years; 5 feet 7 inches high; light com-
plexion; grey hair; blue eyes; by
profession a farmer. Enlisted at
Plattsburgh, Feb. 10, 1814 for the
period of the war and served in Capt.
Wm. Miller's Company and Capt.
James Taylor's Company, 30th Regt.
Discharged at Burlington, Vt. in 1815.
Ref: R. & L. 1812, AGO Pages 54,
55, 59.

‡*HYDE, WILLIAM JR., Sergeant.
Served from June 11 to June 14, 1813
in Lieut. Bates Company, 1 Regt.
(Judson's). Pension Certificate of
widow, Hannah, No. 15637.

*HYER, FREDERICK.
Served from April 12, 1814 to May
20, 1814 in company of Capt. James
Gray Jr., Sumner's Regt.

HYMER, JACOB.
Served in Capt. Haig's Corps of Light
Dragoons; on Pay Roll to June 30,
1814; prisoner of war. Ref: R. &
L. 1812, AGO Page 20.

HYNDS, ELI.
Served in Capt. Mason's Company,
Col. Fifield's Regt. Detached Militia
in U. S. service 6 months, 1812. Served from March 12, 1813 to June 11,
1813 in Capt. Edgerton's Company,
11th Regt. Ref: Book 53, AGO Page
41; R. & L. 1812, AGO Page 3.

‡IDE, DANIEL.
Served in Capt. Howard's Company
(2 Regt.). Pension Certificate No.
33339.

ILHENNY, A. W., Captain and Brig. Major. Served from June 1 to July 31,
1814 on General Staff of the Northern Army commanded by Maj. Gen.
George Izard. Ref: R. & L. 1812,
AGO Page 28.

*INGALLS, HARVEY, Corporal.
Served in Capt. A. Robinson's Company, Col. Dixon's Regt. Detached
Militia in U. S. service 1 month and
23 days, 1813; enlisted Sept. 25, 1813.

INGALLS, PARKER,   Fairfax.
Volunteered to go to Plattsburgh,
September, 1814, and served 8 days
in Capt. Josiah Grout's Company.
Ref: Book 51, AGO Page 103.

INGERSOL, GEORGE.
Served in Capt. John W. Weeks' Company, 11th Regt. from Jan. 16, 1813
to date of death April 13, 1813. Ref:
R. & L. 1812, AGO Page 4.

INGERSOL, THOMAS.
Served from March 1 to June 30,
1814; no organization given. Ref:
R. & L. 1812, AGO Page 29.

INGERSON, JOHN.
On Pay Roll for Capt. John Weeks'
Company, 11th Regt.; never mustered
or paid. Ref: R. & L. 1812, AGO
Page 5.

‡INGRAHAM, CHESTER.
Served in Capt. J. Sinclair's Com-
pany. Pension Certificate of widow,
Esther, No. 33194.

*INGRAHAM, DANIEL.
Served in Capt. Wright's Company,
Col. Martindale's Regt. Detached
Militia in service 15 days, 1812. Also
served in Sumner's Regt. Vt. Militia.

INGRAHAM, ROSWELL,   Barre.
Volunteered to go to Plattsburgh,
September, 1814, and served 10 days
in Capt. Warren Ellis' Company.
Ref: Book 52, AGO Page 242.

INGRAHAM, SETH.
Served from Nov. 1, 1812 to Feb. 28,
1813 in Capt. Phineas Williams' Company, 11th Regt. Ref: R. & L. 1812,
AGO Page 15.

INGRAM, LUCIUS,   Washington.
Volunteered to go to Plattsburgh,
September, 1814, and was at the
battle Sept. 11th, serving in Capt.
David Robinson's Company. Ref:
Book 52, AGO Pages 2 and 8.

INGRAM, MARTIN,   Washington.
Volunteered to go to Plattsburgh,
September, 1814, and was at the
battle Sept. 11th, serving in Capt.
David Robinson's Company. Ref:
Book 52, AGO Page 2.

*IRELAND, JOHN.
Served from April 12, 1814 to April
21, 1814 in Lieut. Justus Foote's Company, Sumner's Regt.

‡*IRISH, ABEL,   Leicester.
Served in Capt. Simeon Wright's Com-
pany, Col. Stephen Martindale's Regt.
Detached Militia in U. S. service from
Sept. 17 to Dec. 1, 1812. Pension
Certificate No. 1785.

*IRISH, JEDEDIAH.
Enlisted Sept. 25, 1813 and served
1 month and 20 days in Capt. Amos
Robinson's Company, Dixon's Regt.

*IRISH, WILLIAM, Musician, Enosburgh.
Enlisted Sept. 25, 1813 in company
of Capt. Jonathan Prentiss Jr., Dixon's Regt.

IRVINE, JAMES.
Served in Capt. Alexander Brooks'
Corps of Artillery; on Pay Roll to
June 30, 1814. Ref: R. & L. 1812,
AGO Page 31.

*ISHAM, ANSEL, Corporal.
Enlisted Sept. 25, 1813 in Capt. N.
B. Eldridge's Company, Dixon's Regt.

‡*ISHAM, ASAHEL, Sergeant, St. Albans. Enlisted Sept. 25, 1813 and
served 1 month and 23 days in Capt.
N. B. Eldridge's Company, Dixon's
Regt. Volunteered to go to Plattsburgh, September, 1814, and served 8
days; no organization given. Pension
Certificate No. 21249. Ref: Book 51,
AGO Page 115.

ISHAM, DANIEL.
Served from Oct. 5 to Oct. 17, 1813
in Capt. Stephen Brown's Company,
3rd Regt. Ref: R. & L. 1812, AGO
Page 34.

*ISHAM, DAVID.
Served in 3 Regt. (Tyler's) Vt. Militia.

*ISHAM, ELISHA.
Served in 1 Regt. (Judson's) Vt. Militia.

*ISHAM, EPHORODITUS.
Enlisted Sept. 25, 1813 in Capt. Mar-
tin D. Follett's Company, Dixon's
Regt.

*ISHAM, JEREMIAH.
Served in Capt. Morrill's Company,
Col. Fifield's Regt. Detached Militia
in U. S. service 6 months and 5 days,
1812.

*ISHAM, JOHN, Musician.
Served in 1 Regt. (Judson's) Vt.
Militia.

‡*ISHAM, JOSHUA, Drummer.
Served from Oct. 5 to Oct. 17, 1813
in Capt. Stephen Brown's Company,
3 Regt. (Tyler's). Also served in
Capt. Eldridge's Company (Dixon's
Regt). Pension Certificate No. 1698.

*ISHAM, SAMUEL.
Served in 1 Regt. (Judson's) Vt. Militia.

‡*ISHAM, SELDEN (or Shelden)
Enlisted Sept. 25, 1813 in Capt. N.
B. Eldridge's Company, Dixon's Regt.
Pension Certificate No. 23672.

*IVES, AMOS.
Served in 1 Regt. (Martindale's) Vt.
Militia.

IVES, ANSON, Sergeant.
Served in 1 Regt. of Detached Militia of Vt. in U. S. service at Champlain from Nov. 18 to Nov. 19, 1812.

*IVES, JESSE.
Served from April 12, 1814 to April
21, 1814 in Capt. Shubael Wales' Company, Col. W. B. Sumner's Regt.

*IVES, JOHN.
Served from April 12, 1814 to April
21, 1814 in Lieut. Justus Foote's Company, Sumner's Regt.

JACKMAN, ABEL, Captain, Corinth. Volunteered to go to Plattsburgh, September, 1814, and commanded company
of volunteers from Corinth. Ref:
Book 52, AGO Page 44.

JACKMAN, WINTHROP T., Sergeant,
Corinth. Volunteered to go to Platts-
burgh, September, 1814, and served
7 days in company of Capt. Ebenezer
Spencer of Vershire. Ref: Book 52,
AGO Pages 48, 49, 120.

JACKSON, AARON,   Richford.
Served in Capt. Martin D. Follett's
Company, Dixon's Regt. on duty on
northern frontier in 1813. Ref: Hemenway's Vt. Gazetteer, Vol. 2, Page
428.

JACKSON ABRAHAM.   Richmond.
Enlisted Jan. 27, 1813 in Capt.
Phineas Williams' Company, 11th
Regt.; on Pay Roll to May 31, 1813.
Volunteered to go to Plattsburgh,
September, 1814, and served 9 days
in Capt. Roswell Hunt's Company,
3 Regt. Ref: R. & L. 1812, AGO
Pages 14 and 15; Book 51, AGO Page
82.

JACKSON, ASA,   Rutland.
Served from June 24, 1814 to June
19, 1815 in Capt. Taylor's Company,
30th Inf. Ref: R. & L. 1812, AGO
Page 23.

JACKSON, ASA, Corporal,   Richmond.
Volunteered to go to Plattsburgh,
September, 1814, and served 9 days
in Capt. Roswell Hunt's Company,
3rd Regt. Ref: Book 51, AGO Page
82.

*JACKSON, ASA JR.,   Richmond.
Served from Oct. 8, 1813 to Oct. 17,
1813 in Capt. Roswell Hunt's Company, 3rd Regt.; volunteered to go
to Plattsburgh, September, 1814, and
served 9 days in same company. Also
served in Corning's Detachment, Vt.
Militia.

JACKSON, BENJAMIN, Franklin County.
Enlisted June 1, 1812 for 5 years in
Capt. White Youngs' Company, 15th
Regt.; on Muster Roll from Aug. 31,
1814 to Dec. 31, 1814. Ref: R. & L.
1812, AGO Page 27.

JACKSON, DAVID,   Pittsford.
Volunteered to go to Plattsburgh,
September, 1814, and served 8 days
in Capt. Caleb Hendee's Company.
Ref: Book 52, AGO Page 125.

JACKSON, DAVID A.,   Pittsford.
Volunteered to go to Plattsburgh,
September, 1814, and served 8 days
in Capt. Caleb Hendee's Company.
Ref: Book 52, AGO Page 125.

‡*JACKSON, EPHRAM H., Corporal, Addison. Served in Capt. Robbins' Company, Col. Wm. Williams' Regt. Detached Militia in U. S. service 4
months and 29 days, 1812. Served
from April 12, 1814 to May 20, 1814
in Capt. George Fisher's Company,
Sumner's Regt.; volunteered to go
to Plattsburgh September, 1814, and
was at the battle Sept. 11th, serving
9 days in same company. Also served
in Capt. J. Robinson's Company.
Pension Certificate No. 1229. Pension Certificate of widow, Matilda,
No. 21204.

*JACKSON, FREDERICK (or Freedom?),
1st Sergeant. Served in Sumner's
Regt. Vt. Militia.

*JACKSON, FREEDOM, Sergeant, Ad-
dison. Volunteered to go to Plattsburgh Sept. 7, 1814 and was at the
battle, serving 9 days in Capt. George
Fisher's Company, Sumner's Regt.;
served from April 12, 1814 to May
20, 1814 in same company.

‡JACKSON, GRATAN, Rutland or Pittsford. Served from June 24, 1814 to
June 19, 1815 in Capt. Taylor's Company, 30th Inf. Pension Certificate
of widow, Melina H., No. 3601.

*JACKSON, HEZEKIAH.
Served from April 12, 1814 to May
20, 1814 in Capt. George Fisher's
Company, Sumner's Regt.

JACKSON, JAMES.
Served from April 29, 1813 to April
29, 1814 in Capt. Simeon Wright's
Company. Ref: R. & L. 1812, AGO
Page 51.

JACKSON, JOHN,   Sudbury.
Volunteered to go to Plattsburgh,
September, 1814, and served 6 days
in Capt. Thomas Hall's Company.
Ref: Book 52, AGO Page 122.

*JACKSON, JOHN JR.
Enlisted Sept. 23, 1813 and served
1 month and 23 days in Capt. Amasa
Mansfield's Company, Col. Dixon's
Regt.

*JACKSON, JUSTUS (or Justice).
Served from April 12, 1814 to May
20, 1814 in Capt. George Fisher's
Company, Sumner's Regt.

*JACKSON, MICHAEL,   Randolph.
Volunteered to go to Plattsburgh,
September, 1814, and served in Capt.
Lebbeus Egerton's Company.

‡*JACKSON, PETER.
Served in Capt. Robbins' Company,
Col. Wm. Williams' Regt. Detached
Militia in U. S. service 4 months
and 29 days, 1812. Pension Certifi-
cate No. 18175.

JACKSON, REUBEN, Corporal, Pittsford.
Volunteered to go to Plattsburgh,
September. 1814, and served 8 days
in Capt. Caleb Hendee's Company.
Ref: Book 52, AGO Page 124.

JACKSON, RIEL,   Richmond.
Volunteered to go to Plattsburgh,
September. 1814, and served 9 days
in Capt. Roswell Hunt's Company,
3 Regt. Ref: Book 51, AGO Page 82.

‡JACKSON. SAMUEL.
Enlisted May 7, 1813 for 1 year in
Capt. Simeon Wright's Company. Pen-
sion Certificate No. 10723.

*JACKSON, STEPHEN B.
Served from April 12, 1814 to May
20, 1814 in Capt. George Fisher's Company, Sumner's Regt.

JACKSON, WILLIAM.
Served from Sept. 1, 1814 to June 16,
1815 in Capt. Sanford's Company,
30th Inf. Ref: R. & L. 1812, AGO
Page 23.

*JACKSON, WILLIAM,   Addison.
Served from April 12, 1814 to May
20, 1814 in Capt. George Fisher's
Company, Sumner's Regt.; volunteered to go to Plattsburgh, September,
1814, and was at the battle, serving
9 days in same company.

JACKSON, WILLIAM.
Enlisted Feb. 24, 1814 for 5 years
in company of late Capt. J. Brooks,
commanded by Lieut. John I. Crom-
well, Corps of U. S. Artillery; on
Muster Roll from April 30, 1814 to
June 30, 1814. Ref: R. & L. 1812,
AGO Page 18.

JACKWOOD, LEVI.
Volunteered to go to Plattsburgh,
September, 1814, and served 8 days
in Capt. Josiah Grout's Company.
Ref: Book 51, AGO Page 103.

*JACOBS, DANIEL.
Served in Capt. Strait's Company,
Col. Martindale's Regt. Detached
Militia in U. S. service 2 months and
13 days, 1812.

JACOBS, JOHN.
Enlisted Aug. 27, 1813 for 1 year in
Capt. Simeon Wright's Company.
Ref: R. & L. 1812, AGO Page 51.

*JACOBS, JOSEPH,   Guilford.
Served in 4 Regt. (Peck's) Vt. Militia.

JACOBS, JOSEPH K., Lieutenant.
Private and Sergeant 9 Inf. Jan. 8,
1813 to July, 1814; appointed Ensign
9 Inf. July 12, 1814; 2 Lieutenant
Sept. 1, 1814; transferred to 5 Inf.
May 17, 1815; resigned Dec. 1, 1815.
Ref: Heitman's Historical Register &
Dictionary USA.

JACOBS, JOSEPHUS, Corporal.
Served from April 29, 1813 to April
29, 1814 in Capt. Daniel Farrington's
Company (also commanded by Capt.
Simeon Wright), 30th Regt. Ref: R.
& L. 1812, AGO Pages 50 and 51.

*JACOBS, JUSTIN.
Served in 4 Regt. (Peck's) Vt. Militia.

*JACOBS, LEWIS JR.
Served in Sumner's Regt. Vt. Militia.

‡JACOBS, NATHAN.
Served in Capt. Reed's Company. Pen-
sion Certificate of widow, Amelia A.,
No. 41418.

JACOBS, STEPHEN,   Montpelier.
Volunteered to go to Plattsburgh,
September, 1814, and served 8 days
in Capt. Timothy Hubbard's Company. Ref: Book 52, AGO Page 256.

JAGUAY, SYLVESTER,   Vergennes.
Volunteered to go to Plattsburgh,
September, 1814, and was at the
battle, serving 10 days in Capt.
Gideon Spencer's Company. Ref: Book
51, AGO Page 1.

JAME, JOSEPH.
Served from April 12, 1814 to May 20, 1814 in company of Capt. James Gray Jr., Sumner's Regt. Ref: Book 52, AGO Page 280.

JAMES, HENRY N.
Served in Capt. Eldridge's Company, Col. Dixon's Regt. Detached Militia in U. S. service 1 month and 23 days, 1813. Ref: Book 53, AGO Page 107.

*JAMES, ISAAC.
Served from April 12, 1814 to April 21, 1814 in Capt. Eseck Sprague's Company, Sumner's Regt.

‡*JAMES, JOHN.
Served from April 12, 1814 to May 20, 1814 in Capt. George Fisher's Company, Sumner's Regt. Also served in Capt. Pickett's Company. Pension Certificate No. 25328.

*JAMES, JULIUS, Corporal.
Served in Sumner's Regt. Vt. Militia.

‡*JAMES, MOSES.
Served in 4 Regt. ((Williams') Vt. Militia. Also served in Capt. Philip's Company. Pension Certificate of widow, Affar, No. 2177.

*JAMES, SAMUEL, Sergeant.
Served in Sumner's Regt. Vt. Militia.

*JANES, DANIEL.
Served from Sept. 25, 1813 to Nov. 12, 1813 in Capt. Amos Robinson's Company, Dixon's Regt.

*JANES, ELIJAH JR.
Served from Sept. 25, 1813 to Oct. 31, 1813 in Capt. Jesse Post's Company, Dixon's Regt.

*JANES, HENRY.
Enlisted Sept. 25, 1813 in Capt. N. B. Eldridge's Company, Dixon's Regt.

‡JANES, HENRY F., Montpelier.
Volunteered to go to Plattsburgh, September, 1814, and served 8 days in Capt. Timothy Hubbard's Company. Pension Certificate No. 32831.

JANES, HENRY FISKE, Ensign, Waterbury. Appointed Ensign in Capt. Gideon Wheelock's Company by Governor Galusha Feb. 6, 1813. (Was son-in-law of Ezra Butler and father of Dr. Henry Janes). Ref: Theo. G. Lewis' History of Waterbury, Pages 42 and 43.

*JANES, HORACE, Corporal.
Served in 1 Regt. (Martindale's) Vt. Militia.

JANES, JAMES.
Served from May 1 to Sept. 2, 1814; no organization given. Ref: R. & L. 1812, AGO Page 29.

*JANES, JONATHAN, Sergeant.
Served in Capt. Edgerton's Company, Vt. Volunteers.

JANES, JOSEPH H., Fairfax.
Served from Sept. 12, 1813 in Capt. Asa Wilkins' Company, Col. Dixon's Regt. Ref: Hemenway's Vt. Gazetteer, Vol. 2, Page 402.

*JANES, PARDON, Calais.
Volunteered to go to Plattsburgh, September, 1814, and served 10 days in Capt. Gideon Wheelock's Company.

*JANNE, LYMAN.
Served from April 12, 1814 to April 14, 1814 in Capt. Jonathan P. Stanley's Company, Col. W. B. Sumner's Regt.

‡*JAQUAYS, JOHN.
Served in Sumner's Regt. Vt. Militia. Also served in Capt. Hawley's Company. Pension Certificate No. 10031.

*JAQUAYS, SYLVESTER.
Served in Capt. Phelps' Company, Col. Wm. Williams' Regt. Detached Militia, in U. S. service 5 months, 1812. Also served as drummer in Sumner's Regt. Vt. Militia.

JAQUES, AMOS, Barnard.
Volunteered to go to Plattsburgh, September, 1814, and served 8 days in Capt. John S. Bicknell's Company. Ref: Book 51, AGO Page 250.

‡JAQUISH, HAZEN.
Served in Capt. Dickinson's Company. Pension Certificate No. 13826.

JAQUITH, JAMES, Vershire.
Volunteered to go to Plattsburgh, September, 1814, and served 3 days in Capt. Ira Corse's Company. Ref: Book 52, AGO Page 91.

JARVIS, WILLIAM.
Appointed Dep. Com. Aug. 18, 1812. Ref: Governor and Council Vt. Vol. 6, Page 478.

JASMYN, PETER.
Served in Lieut. V. R. Goodrich's Company, 11th Regt.; on Pay Roll for January and February, 1813. Ref: R. & L. 1812, AGO Page 11.

*JASPER, ASA JR.
Served in Corning's Detachment, Vt. Militia.

JAY, JOHN D., Franklin County.
Volunteered to go to Plattsburgh Sept. 11, 1814 and served in 15th or 22nd Regt. Ref: Hemenway's Vt. Gazetteer, Vol. 2, Page 392.

JAY, ZELAH.
Served in Capt. Mason's Company, Col. Fifield's Regt. Detached Militia in U. S. service 5 months and 26 days, 1812. Ref: Book 53, AGO Page 24.

JEFFORDS, COLONEL P.
Volunteered to go to Plattsburgh, September, 1814, and served 7 days in Capt. Frederick Griswold's Company, raised in Brookfield, Vt. Ref: Book 52, AGO Page 52.

*JEFFORDS, WILLIAM.
Served in 4 Regt. (Williams') Vt. Militia.

JEFTS, FRANCIS.
Served in Capt. Samul Gordon's Company, 11th Regt.; on Pay Roll for January and February, 1813. Ref: R. & L. 1812, AGO Page 9.

JENKINS, BENJAMIN, Artificer.
Enlisted Aug. 6, 1813 for 5 years in
company of late Capt. J. Brooks,
commanded by Lieut. John I. Crom-
well, Corps of U. S. Artillery; on
Muster Roll from April 30, 1814 to
June 30, 1814. Ref: R. & L. 1812,
AGO Page 18.

JENNE, GEORGE.
Served from Nov. 1, 1812 to Feb. 28,
1813 in Capt. Samul Gordon's Company, 11th Regt. Ref: R. & L. 1812,
AGO Page 9.

*JENNE, THOMAS.
Served from April 12, 1814 to April
21, 1814 in Lieut. James S. Morton's Company, Col. W. B. Sumner's
Regt.

*JENNER, SAMUEL.
Served in 1 Regt. (Martindale's) Vt.
Militia.

JENNESS, JONATHAN, Ensign.
Volunteered to go to Plattsburgh,
September, 1814, and served 4 days
in company of Capt. James George
of Topsham. Ref: Book 52, AGO
Page 70.

*JENNEY, EBENEZER, Captain, Leicester.
Served from April 12, 1814 to April
21, 1814 as 1st Lieutenant in Capt.
Jonathan P. Stanley's Company, Col.
W. B. Sumner's Regt. Volunteered
to go to Plattsburgh, September, 1814,
and served 8 days in command of
company raised at Leicester. Ref:
Book 51, AGO Pages 34 and 56; Book
52, AGO Page 160.

‡JENNINGS, ALEXANDER, Sergeant, St.
Albans. Enlisted May 5, 1813 for 1
year in Capt. John Wires' Company,
30th Regt. Also served under Captains Miller and Sanford. Pension
Certificate of widow, Catharine, No.
10746. Ref: R. & L. 1812, AGO Page
40.

*JENNINGS, GEORGE.
Served in Capt. Wheeler's Company,
Col. Fifield's Regt. Detached Militia
in U. S. service 6 months and 4
days, 1812.

*JENNINGS, ISRAEL.
Served in Sumner's Regt. Vt. Militia.

JENNINGS, JEBESH,   Hubbardton?
Served from April 27, 1813 to April
28, 1814 in Capt. Daniel Farrington's
Company (also commanded by Capt.
Simeon Wright) 30th Regt. Ref: R.
& L. 1812, AGO Pages 50 and 51.

‡JENNINGS, JONATHAN, Captain, Chelsea. Volunteered to go to Plattsburgh, September, 1814, and commanded company from Chelsea. Pension Certificate of widow, Sally, No.
1889.

*JENNINGS, PAUL.
Served from April 12, 1814 to April
21, 1814 in Capt. Eseck Sprague's
Company, Sumner's Regt.

‡*JENNINGS, WILLIAM.
Served in Capt. Burnap's Company,
Col. Jonathan Williams' Regt. De-

tached Militia in U. S. service 2
months and 13 days, 1812. Pension
Certificate of widow, Jane, No. 2343.

JENNISON, JOSIAH,   Shrewsbury.
Volunteered to go to Plattsburgh,
September, 1814, and served 4 days
in Capt. Robert Reed's Company.
Ref: Book 52, AGO Page 138.

*JEPHERSON, JEDEDIAH.
Served in Capt. Wright's Company,
Col. Fifield's Regt. Detached Militia
in U. S. service 6 months, 1812.

*JEPHERSON, ROSWELL.
Served in Capt. Durkee's Company,
Col. Fifield's Regt. Detached Militia
in U. S. service 2 months and 24
days, 1812.

*JEPHERSON, RUSSEL.
Served from April 20, 1813 to April
19, 1814 in Capt. Simeon Wright's
Company, Col. Fifield's Regt.

*JEPSON, HARVEY (or Henry).
Served in Capt. Cross' Company, Col.
Martindale's Regt. Detached Militia
in U. S. service 2 months and 14
days, 1812.

JERKINS, SAMUEL,   Franklin County.
Volunteered to go to Plattsburgh
Sept. 11, 1814 and served in 15th or
22nd Regt. Ref: Hemenway's Vt. Gazetteer, Vol. 2, Page 391.

JEROME, ELI,   Georgia.
Volunteered to go to Plattsburgh,
September, 1814, and served 8 days
in Capt. Jesse Post's Company, Dixon's Regt. Ref: Book 51, AGO Page
102.

JESMYER, PETER, Fairfax or Swanton.
Served from Aug. 8, 1812 in company
of Capt. Joseph Beeman, Jr. 11th
Regt. U. S. Inf. under Col. Ira
Clark. Ref: Hemenway's Vt. Gazet-
teer, Vol. 2, Page 402.

JEWELL, DAVID.
Served in Capt. Benjamin S. Edger-
ton's Company, 11th Regt.; on Pay
Roll for September and October, 1812.
Ref: R. & L. 1812, AGO Page 1.

JEWELL, DAVID.
Served in Capt. Samul Gordon's Com-
pany, 11th Regt.; on Pay Roll for
January and February, 1813; died
Feb. 17, 1813. Ref: R. & L. 1812,
AGO Page 9.

*JEWELL, JESSE, Ensign,   Bolton.
Served in 4 Regt. (Peck's) Vt. Militia. (For biographical sketch see Hemenway's Vt. Gazetteer, Vol. 1, Page
937.)

*JEWELL, JONATHAN,   Richmond.
Served in Capt. Dorrance's Company,
Col. Wm. Williams' Regt. Detached
Militia in U. S. service 4 months
and 7 days, 1812. Served from Oct.
11 to Oct. 17, 1813 in Capt. John
Munson's Company of Cavalry. Volunteered to go to Plattsburgh, September, 1814, and served in Capt. Roswell Hunt's Company, 3 Regt. Ref:
Book 51, AGO Page 82.

JEWELL, SAWYER,   Richmond.
Volunteered to go to Plattsburgh,
September, 1814, and served 9 days
in Capt. Roswell Hunt's Company,
3 Regt. Ref: Book 51, AGO Page 82.

*JEWETT, ALPHEUS, Ensign.
Served in 4 Regt. (Williams') Vt.
Militia.

*JEWETT, DAVID,   Fairfield.
Served in Capt. George W. Kindall's
Company, 4 Regt. (Williams') Vt.
Militia in U. S. service 4 months and
23 days, 1812.

JEWETT, DAVID.
Served in Capt. Benjamin S. Edger-
ton's Company, 11th Regt.; on Pay
Roll for January and February, 1813.
Ref: R. & L. 1812, AGO Page 2.

*JEWETT, DAVID.
Enlisted Oct. 29, 1813 in Capt. Asahel
Langworthy's Company, Col. Isaac
Clark's Regt. Also served in Dixon's
Regt. Vt. Militia.

JEWETT, ISAAC,   Strafford.
Volunteered to go to Plattsburgh,
September, 1814, and served in Capt.
Joseph Barrett's Company. Ref: Book
52, AGO Page 41.

*JEWETT, JARED, Captain.
Served in 3 Regt. (Bowdish) Vt.
Militia.

JEWETT, JONATHAN,   Rochester.
Volunteered to go to Plattsburgh,
September, 1814, and served 7 days
in Capt. Oliver Mason's Company.
Ref: Book 51, AGO Page 256.

*JEWETT. MOSES, Captain.
Served from June 11, 1813 to June
14, 1813 in command of company in
1st Regt. 2nd Brig. 3rd Div.

*JEWETT, OTHNIEL, Captain.
Served from April 12 to April 21,
1814 in command of company in Col.
W. B. Sumner's Regt.

JEWETT, PETER.
Served from Nov. 1, 1812 to Feb. 28,
1813 in Capt. Charles Follett's Company, 11th Regt. Ref: R. & L. 1812,
AGO Page 12.

‡*JEWETT, THOMAS, Sergeant.
Served from April 12, 1814 to April
21, 1814 in Capt. Shubael Wales' Company, Col. W. B. Sumner's Regt.
Also served in Capt. Wright's Company. Pension Certificate No. 16581.

JEWITT, EZEKEIL, Ensign.
Served in Lieut. Foster's Company,
11th Regt.; on Pay Roll for January and February, 1813. Ref: R. &
L. 1812, AGO Page 7.

*JILSON, CHARLES.
Served in Capt. Wright's Company,
Col. Martindale's Regt. Detached
Militia in U. S. service 19 days, 1812.

JOHN, CHRISTOPHER.
Served from April 7, 1813 to July 6,
1813 in Capt. Edgerton's Company,
11th Regt. Ref: R. & L. 1812, AGO
Page 3.

JOHN. JOHN F.
Served from April 7 to July 6, 1813
in Capt. Edgerton's Company, 11th
Regt. Ref: R. & L. 1812, AGO
Page 3.

*JOHNS, J. S., Sergeant.
Served in 2 Regt. (Fifield's) Vt. Militia.

*JOHN, JAMES.
Served in Dixon's Regt. Vt. Militia.

‡*JOHNS, JEHIEL JR.
Served in 3 Regt. (Tyler's) Vt. Mili-
tia. Also served in Capt. Artemus
Farr's Company. Pension Certificate
No. 32832.

*JOHNS, SILAS, Corporal.
Served in 3 Regt. (Tyler's) Vt. Militia.

*JOHNSON, AARON.
Served in Capt. Adams' Company,
Col. Jonathan Williams' Regt. Detached Militia in U. S. service 2
months and 7 days, 1812.

*JOHNSON, ABEL,   Fairfield.
Served in Capt. Kendall's Company,
Col. Wm. Williams' Regt. Detached
Militia in U. S. service 4 months and
23 days, 1812.

JOHNSON, ABEL JR.   Berkshire.
Served in Capt. Washington Kendal's
Company, Col. Wm. Williams' Regt.
5 months in 1812. Ref: Vol. 50 Vt.
State Papers, Page 102.

*JOHNSON, ABRAHAM.
Served in Capt. Brown's Company,
Col. Martindale's Regt. Detached
Militia in U. S. service 1 month,
1812.

JOHNSON, ADAM, Sergeant.
Enlisted Nov. 1, 1812 in Lieut. Fos-
ter's Company, 11th Regt.; on Pay
Roll for January and February, 1813.
Ref: R. & L. 1812, AGO Page 7.

‡JOHNSON, ANDREW.
Served in Capt. Young's Company.
Pension Certificate No. 34316.

JOHNSON, ASAHEL,   Ira.
Volunteered to go to Plattsburgh,
September, 1814, and served 4 days
in Capt. Matthew Anderson's Company. Ref: Book 52, AGO Page 144.

*JOHNSON, ALEXANDER.
Served in Sumner's Regt. Vt. Militia.

*JOHNSON, BEMAN.
Served from June 11 to June 14,
1813 in Lieut. Bates' Company, 1
Regt. (Judson's).

‡JOHNSON, BRAMIN.
Served in Capt. Kendall's Company
(4th Regt.). Pension Certificate No.
4940. Pension Certificate of widow,
Mary B., No. 24373.

JOHNSON, CHAUNCEY R., Sergeant,
Middlebury. Served from April 20,
1813 to April 19, 1814 in Capt. Simeon
Wright's Company. Served from Sept.
1, 1814 to June 16, 1815 in Capt.
Sanford's Company, 30th Inf. Ref:
R. & L. 1812, AGO Pages 23 and 51.

JOHNSON, CYRUS,   Berlin.
Appointed Captain 31 Inf. April 30,
1813; resigned Jan. 11, 1814. Volunteered to go to Plattsburgh, September, 1814, and served 9 days in command of company from Berlin. Ref:
Heitman's Historical Register & Dictionary USA; Book 52, AGO Pages
184 and 255.

JOHNSON, CYRUS,   Enosburgh.
Volunteered to go to Plattsburgh,
September, 1814; no organization giv-
en. Ref: Book 51, AGO Page 188.

JOHNSON, DANIEL.
Served from Feb. 18 to June 30, 1814
in Regt. of Light Dragoons. Ref:
R. & L. 1812, AGO Page 21.

‡*JOHNSON, DAVID, Enosburgh or Fairfax. Served from Oct. 15 to Nov. 17,
1813 in Capt. Asahel Scoville's Company, Col. Clark's Regt. of Riflemen.
Served from July 5, 1814 to June 19,
1815 in Capt. Taylor's Company, 30th
Inf. Pension Certificate of widow,
Elizabeth, No. 1384. Ref: R. & L.
1812, AGO Page 23.

*JOHNSON, DAVID.
Served in Capt. S. Pettes' Company,
Col. Wm. Williams' Regt. Detached
Militia in U. S. service 4 months
and 19 days, 1812. Also served in
Corning's Detachment, Vt. Militia.

*JOHNSON, DAVID JR.
Served in Capt. Walker's Company,
Col. Fifield's Regt. Detached Militia
in U. S. service 2 months and 26
days, 1812.

*JOHNSON, DAVID 2nd.
Served from April 12, 1814 to May 20,
1814 in Company of Capt. James
Gray Jr., Sumner's Regt.

*JOHNSON, EBENEZER.
Served from June 11 to June 14, 1813
in Lieut. Bates' Company, 1 Regt.
(Judson's). Also served in Corning's
Detachment, Vt. Militia.

*JOHNSON, EDWARD.
Served in Capt. Bingham's Company,
Col. Jonathan Williams' Regt. Detached Militia in U. S. service 2
months and 9 days, 1812.

‡*JOHNSON, ELISHA.
Served from April 12, 1814 to April
21, 1814 in Capt. Shubael Wales' Company, Col. W. B. Sumner's Regt.
Also served under Captains Wright
and Hill. Pension Certificate of widow, Philena, No. 1053.

JOHNSON, ENDURING,   Castleton.
Volunteered to go to Plattsburgh,
September, 1814, and served 9 days;
no organization given. Ref: Book
52, AGO Page 154.

‡JOHNSON, EZRA.
Served from March 19th to June 30,
1814 in Regt. of Light Dragoons.
Also served in Capt. Sweat's Com-
,pany. Pension Certificate No. 18064.

JOHNSON, FREEMAN,   Ira.
Volunteered to go to Plattsburgh,
September, 1814, and served 4 days
in Capt. Matthew Anderson's Company. Ref: Book 52, AGO Page 144.

JOHNSON, GEORGE,   Franklin County.
Volunteered to go to Plattsburgh
Sept. 11, 1814 and served in 15th or
22nd Regt. Ref: Hemenway's Vt. Gazetteer, Vol. 2, Page 391.

JOHNSON, HENRY,   St. Albans.
Enlisted April 30, 1813 for 1 year
in Capt. John Wires' Company, 30th
Regt. Ref: R. & L. 1812, AGO Page
40.

*JOHNSON, HENRY.
Served from June 11, 1813 to June 14,
1813 in Capt. Moses Jewett's Company, 1st Regt., 2nd Brig., 3rd Div.

JOHNSON, IRA.
Served in Capt. Benjamin S. Edgerton's Company, 11th Regt.; on Pay
Roll for September and October, 1812
and January and February, 1813.
Ref: R. & L. 1812, AGO Pages 1
and 2.

*JOHNSON, JAMES, Sergeant, Berkshire
or Fairfield. Served in Capt. Kendall's Company, Col. Wm. Williams'
Regt. Detached Militia in U. S. service 4 months and 23 days, 1812.

‡*JOHNSON, JAMES, Drummer, Highgate.
Served in Capt. Conrade Saxe's Company, 4 Regt. (Williams') from Sept.
1, 1812. Enlisted Sept. 25, 1813 and
served 1 month and 23 days in Capt.
Elijah W. Wood's Company, Col. Dixon's Regt. Detached Militia in U. S.
service. Pension Certificate No. 12423.

JOHNSON, JAMES, Lieutenant.
Appointed 2 Lieutenant 30 Inf. April
30, 1813; 1 Lieutenant July 10, 1814;
honorably discharged June 15, 1815.
Ref: Heitman's Historical Register &
Dictionary USA.

*JOHNSON, JAMES (or Johnston?)
Born in Hallowell, Mass.; aged 39
years; dark complexion; black hair;
black eyes; by profession a hatter;
5 feet 8 inches high. Enlisted March
19, 1814 for the period of the war
and served in Capt. Wm. Miller's
Company, and Capt. Gideon Spencer's
Company, 30th Regt.

JOHNSON, JESSE,   Middlesex?
Served from May 1 to June 30, 1814
in Capt. Haig's Corps of Light Dragoons. Ref: R. & L. 1812, AGO
Page 20.

JOHNSON, JOHN.
Served from March 29, 1813 to June
28, 1813 in Capt. Phineas Williams'
Company, 11th Regt. Ref: R. & L.
1812, AGO Page 14.

JOHNSON, JOHN.
Served from Feb. 10 to June 30, 1814
in Regt. of Light Dragoons. Ref:
R. & L. 1812, AGO Page 21.

‡JOHNSON, JOHN, Fairfield.
Served in Capt. Kendall's Company,
Col. Wm. Williams' Regt. Detached
Militia in U. S. service 4 months
and 23 days, 1812. Pension Certifi-
cate of widow, Hannah, No. 4242.

*JOHNSON, JOHN.
Served from June 11 to June 14, 1813
in Capt. Samuel Blinn's Company, 1st
Regt. (Judson's).

*JOHNSON, JOHN JR., Sergeant.
Served in Capt. Rogers' Company,
Col. Fifield's Regt. Detached Militia
in U. S. service 5 months and 27
days, 1812.

‡*JOHNSON, JOHN S., Sergeant.
Served in Capt. Wheeler's Company,
Col. Fifield's Regt. Detached Militia
in U. S. service 6 months and 4
days, 1812. Pension Certificate of
widow, Lydia, No. 1634.

*JOHNSON, JOSHUA, Musician.
Served from June 11 to June 14, 1813
in Capt. John M. Eldridge's Company, 1st Regt. 2nd Brig., 3rd Div.

JOHNSON, JOSIAH (or Johnston).
Served from April 12, 1814 to May
20, 1814 in Capt. George Fisher's Company, Sumner's Regt. Ref: Book 52,
AGO Page 278.

*JOHNSON, LEWIS, Lieutenant, Jericho.
Appointed 3 Lieutenant 26 Inf. June
25, 1814; honorably discharged June
15, 1815; died Aug. 7, 1847. Appointed Quartermaster Sept. 15, 1813 in
Col. Isaac Clark's Volunteer Rifle
Corps. Also took part in the Battle
of Plattsburgh. Ref: Heitman's Historical Register & Dictionary USA;
History of Jericho, Page 142.

*JOHNSON, MOSES.
Served from June 11 to June 14,
1813 in Lieut. Bates' Company, 1
Regt. (Judson's).

*JOHNSON, NATHANIEL (or Johnston),
Highgate. Served in Capt. Conrade
Saxe's Company, Col. Wm. Williams'
Regt. Detached Militia in U. S.
service 4 months and 24 days, 1812.
Served in New York State from Sept.
25 to Nov. 15, 1813 in Capt. Elijah
Wood's Company, Dixon's Regt. Also
served in Corning's Detachment.

*JOHNSON, NOAH, Huntington.
Volunteered to go to Plattsburgh,
September, 1814, and served 8 days
in Capt. Artemus Farr's Company, 3
Regt. (Tyler's).

‡JOHNSON, OBEDIAH.
Served as a teamster; no organization
given. Pension Certificate No. 10037.

JOHNSON, PETER.
Served in Capt. James Taylor's Com-
pany, 30th Regt. Ref: R. & L. 1812,
AGO Page 59.

JOHNSON, SALMON, Sergeant.
Served in Capt. Simeon Wright's Company; enlisted April 27, 1813 for 1
year. Ref: R. & L. 1812, AGO Page
51.

*JOHNSON, SAMUEL.
Served from April 12, 1814 to April
15, 1814 in Capt. John Hackett's Company, Sumner's Regt.

*JOHNSON, SAMUEL.
Served in 3 Regt. (Tyler's) Vt. Militia.

‡*JOHNSON, SAMUEL, Fairfield.
Served in Capt. Kendall's Company,
Col. Wm. Williams' Regt. Detached
Militia in U. S. service 4 months
and 14 days, 1812. Pension Certi-
ficate of widow, Polly, No. 6539.

JOHNSON, SAMUEL.
Served from June 11 to June 14, 1813
in Capt. John M. Eldridge's Company, 1st Regt. 2nd Brig., 3rd Div.
Ref: R. & L. 1812, AGO Page 35.

JOHNSON, SETH.
Served from Feb. 18th to June 30,
1814 in Regt. of Light Dragoons. Ref:
R. & L. 1812, AGO Page 21.

JOHNSON, SIMEON (or Simeon Jr.) Williamstown. Volunteered to go to
Plattsburgh, September, 1814, and
served 8 days in Capt. David Robinson's Company. Ref: Book 52, AGO
Pages 8 and 10.

JOHNSON, SMITH, Ira.
Volunteered to go to Plattsburgh,
September, 1814, and served 4 days
in Capt. Matthew Anderson's Company. Ref: Book 52, AGO Page 144.

JOHNSON, THOMAS, St. Albans.
Enlisted April 30, 1813 for 1 year in
Capt. John Wires' Company, 30th
Regt. Ref: R. & L. 1812, AGO Page
40.

JOHNSON, THOMAS.
Enlisted April 30, 1812 for 5 years
in Capt. White Youngs' Company,
15th Regt.; on Muster Roll from
Aug. 31, 1814 to Dec. 31, 1814. Ref:
R. & L. 1812, AGO Page 27.

*JOHNSON, ULYSSES.
Served in Capt. Burnap's Company,
Col. Jonathan Williams' Regt. Detached Militia in U. S. service 2
months and 13 days, 1812.

*JOHNSON, WAITSTILL A.
Served under Captains Taylor and
Walker, Col. Fifield's Regt. Detached
Militia in U. S. service 6 months,
1812.

‡JOHNSON, WILLIAM (or Johnston?),
Corporal. Served in Capt. Morrill's
Company, Col. Fifield's Regt. De-
tached Militia in U. S. service 2
months and 18 days, 1812. Pension
Certificate No. 17236.

‡*JOHNSON, WILLIAM C., (or Johnston). Served in Capt. S. Pettes' Company, Col. Wm. Williams' Regt. Detached Militia in U. S. service 4
months and 19 days, 1812. Pension
Certificate No. 722.

JOHNSON, ZENAS, Montpelier.
Volunteered to go to Plattsburgh,
September, 1814, and served 8 days
in Capt. Timothy Hubbard's Company. Ref: Book 52, AGO Page 256.

*JOHNSON, ZUR.
Served as a farrier in Capt. Dorrance's Company, Col. Wm. Williams'
Regt. Detached Militia in U. S.
service 4 months and 24 days, 1812.

JOHNSTON, ELISHA .
Enlisted in U. S. Marine Corps June
12, 1812 at Boston. Ref: Book 52,
AGO Page 294.

JOHNSTON, GIDEON.
Enlisted Nov. 6, 1812 for 5 years in
company of late Capt. J. Brooks, commanded by Lieut. John I. Cromwell,
Corps of U. S. Artillery; on Muster
Roll from April 30, 1814 to June 30,
1814. Ref: R. & L. 1812, AGO Page
18.

JOHNSTON, JAMES H.
Served in War of 1812 and was cap-
tured by troops July 17, 1814 at Fort
Erie; discharged March 16, 1815. Ref:
Records of Naval Records and Li-
brary, Navy Dept.

JOHONNETT, PETER.   Barre.
Volunteered to go to Plattsburgh,
September, 1814, serving 9 days in
Capt. Warren Ellis' Company. Ref:
Book 52, AGO Pages 225 and 242.

JOICE, AMBRA.   Hubbardton.
Volunteered to go to Plattsburgh,
September, 1814, serving 8 days in
Capt. Henry J. Horton's Company.
Ref: Book 52, AGO Page 142.

JONES, ABRAHAM.   Franklin County.
Volunteered to go to Plattsburgh
Sept. 11, 1814, serving in 15th or
22nd Regt. Ref: Hemenway's Vt. Gazetteer, Vol. 2, Page 392.

JONES, ALEXANDER.
Served in company of Capt. John
McNeil Jr., 11th Regt.; on Pay Roll
for January and February, 1813. Ref:
R. & L. 1812, AGO Page 17.

JONES, AMOS.   Barre.
Volunteered to go to Plattsburgh,
September, 1814, serving 10 days in
Capt. Warren Ellis' Company. Ref:
Book 52, AGO Page 242.

JONES, AMOS.
Enlisted March 30, 1814 during the
war in Capt. Gideon Spencer's Company, 30th Regt.; on Muster Roll
from Dec. 30, 1813 to June 30, 1814.
Ref: R. & L. 1812, AGO Page 57.

JONES, ANTHONY, Sergeant.
Enlisted June 24, 1813 for 1 year in
Capt. Daniel Farrington's Company,
30th Regt. (also commanded by Capt.
Simeon Wright); on Muster Roll from
March 1 to April 30, 1814. Ref: R.
& L. 1812, AGO Pages 50 and 51.

JONES, ASA.   Shoreham.
Volunteered to go to Plattsburgh,
September, 1814, and served in Capt.
Nathaniel North's Company of Caval-
ry. Ref: Rev. J. F. Goodhue's His-
tory of Shoreham, Page 107.

*JONES, BENJAMIN.   Randolph.
Volunteered to go to Plattsburgh,
September, 1814, and served in Capt.
Lebbeus Egerton's Company.

JONES, DANIEL,   Panton.
Age 19 years; 5 feet 6½ inches high;
light complexion; grey eyes; brown
hair; by profession a farmer; born
in Clarendon, Vt.; was enlisted by
Lieut. Spaulding in the town of Panton, Vt., on the 30th day of March,
1814; discharged at Burlington, 1815.
Served in Capt. Miller's Company
and Capt. Gideon Spencer's Company.
Ref: Paper in custody of Vt. Historical Society; R. & L. 1812, AGO
Pages 54, 55, 57.

*JONES, DAVID, Sergeant.
Served in Capt. Durkee's Company,
Col. Fifield's Regt. Detached Militia
in U. S. service 2 months and 21
days, 1812.

*JONES, EDWARD.
Served from April 12, 1814 to May
20, 1814 in Capt. George Fisher's
Company, Sumner's Regt.

*JONES, GEORGE.
Served in Capt. Walker's Company,
Col. Fifield's Regt. Detached Militia
in U. S. service 3 months and 26
days, 1812.

‡JONES, GILEAD.
Served in Capt. Taylor's Company.
Pension Certificate of widow, Anne,
No. 3258.

JONES, HANNANIAH, Franklin County.
Volunteered to go to Plattsburgh
Sept. 11, 1814 and served in 15th or
22nd Regt. Ref: Hemenway's Vt. Gazetteer, Vol. 2, Page 392.

*JONES, HENRY.
Served in Sumner's Regt. Vt. Militia.

JONES, HENRY,   St. Albans.
Volunteered and was in the action
at Plattsburgh Sept. 11, 1814, serving
in Capt. Samuel H. Farnsworth's
Company. Ref: Hemenway's Vt. Gazetteer, Vol. 2, Page 434.

JONES, HENRY, Sergeant,   Shoreham.
Enlisted under Captain Holley, March,
1813, with the rank of sergeant; was
in the skirmishes at Odeltown and
Chateaugay River under General
Hampton, in Scott's Brigade at Lundy's Lane, Chippewa and Fort Erie
in 1814; was wounded in the right
arm in the siege of the latter. Ref:
Rev. J. F. Goodhue's History of
Shoreham, Page 102.

JONES, HENRY.
Born at Middlebery; served in War
of 1812; captured by troops Feb. 22,
1813 at Stoney Point; discharged Oct.
31, 1814. Ref: Records of Naval Records and Library, Navy Dept.

JONES, HIRAM.
Enlisted March 25, 1813 during the
war and served in company of late
Capt. J. Brooks, commanded by
Lieut. John I. Cromwell, Corps of
U. S. Artillery; on Muster Roll from
April 30, 1814 to June 30, 1814. Ref:
R. & L. 1812, AGO Page 18.

JONES, HORACE.
Served in Capt. Wright's Company,
Col. Martindale's Regt. Detached

Militia in U. S. service 2 months and 14 days, 1812. Ref: Book 53, AGO Page 78.

JONES, HUMPHREY.
Enlisted May 11, 1812 for 5 years in Capt. White Youngs' Company, 15th Regt.; on Muster Roll from Aug. 31, 1814 to Dec. 31, 1814. Ref: R. & L. 1812, AGO Page 27.

‡JONES, IRA. ·
Served in Capt. Birge's Company (Dixon's Regt.). Pension Certificate No. 14493.

JONES, ISAAC, Stockbridge.
Volunteered to go to Plattsburgh, September, 1814, serving 7 days in Capt. Elias Keyes' Company. Ref: Book 51, AGO Pages 244 and 246.

*JONES, ISRAEL JR.
Served in 4 Regt. (Peck's) Vt. Militia.

‡*JONES, JACOB.
Served from April 12, 1814 to April 21, 1814 in Capt. Edmund B. Hill's Company, Sumner's Regt. Also served in Capt. James Gray's Company, Sumner's Regt. Pension Certificate of widow, Rizpah, No. 14995.

JONES, JAMES, Washington.
Volunteered to go to Plattsburgh, September, 1814, and was at the battle, serving 8 days in Capt. David Robinson's Company. Ref: Book 52, AGO Page 2.

*JONES, JAMES F.
Served in Capt. Rogers' Company, Col. Fifield's Regt. Detached Militia in U. S. service 5 months and 27 days, 1812.

‡*JONES, JOHN.
Served in Tyler's Regt. Vt. Militia and in Capt. Fillmore's Company. Pension Certificate No. 30509. Pension Certificate of widow, Lucinda, No. 32084.

*JONES, JONATHAN, Sergeant, Randolph. Volunteered to go to Plattsburgh, September, 1814, and served in Capt. Lebbeus Egerton's Company.

*JONES, JOSEPH.
Served from June 11 to June 14, 1813 in Capt. Samuel Blinn's Company, 1st Regt. (Judson's). Volunteered to go to Plattsburgh, September, 1814, and served 4 days in company of Capt. James George of Topsham.

*JONES, JOSIAH, Sergeant.
Enlisted Sept. 25, 1813 and served 1 month and 23 days in Capt. Thomas Waterman's Company, Col. Dixon's Regt.

JONES, JOSIAH, Franklin County.
Volunteered to go to Plattsburgh Sept. 11, 1814 and served in 15th or 22nd Regt. Ref: Hemenway's Vt. Gazetteer, Vol. 2, Page 392.

JONES, JOSIAH.
Born in Chapley, Mass.; aged 18 years; 5 feet 7 inches high; light complexion; brown hair; grey eyes; by profession a farmer. Enlisted and served in Capt. Wm. Miller's Company, Capt. James Taylor's Company and Capt. Gideon Spencer's Company, 30th Regt.; discharged at Burlington, Vt. in 1815. Ref: R. & L. 1812, AGO Pages 52, 54, 55, 57, 59.

JONES, MARVIN, Panton, Vt.
Born in Crown Point N. Y.; aged 18 years; 5 feet 5 inches high; light complexion; brown hair; blue eyes; by profession a farmer. Enlisted at Panton April 22, 1814 and served in Capt. Miller's Company and Capt. Gideon Spencer's Company, 30th Regt. Ref: R. & L. 1812, AGO Pages 54, 55, 57.

JONES, MATHIAS S., Captain, Waitsfield.
Volunteered to go to Plattsburgh, September, 1814, and commanded company raised at Waitsfield. Ref: Book 52, AGO Page 170.

*JONES, NATHAN, Orange.
Volunteered to go to Plattsburgh Sept. 11, 1814, and went part way, serving 5 days in Capt. David Rising's Company. Also served in 2 Regt. (Fifield's) Vt. Militia. Ref: Book 52, AGO Pages 19 and 23.

*JONES, NATHAN, Orange.
Served in Capt. Walker's Company, Col. Fifield's Regt. Detached Militia in U. S. service 6 months and 3 days, 1812. Volunteered to go to Plattsburgh, September, 1814, and served in Capt. David Rising's Company.

‡*JONES, NATHANIEL, Vershire.
Served in Capt. Ormsbee's Company, Col. Martindale's Regt. Detached Militia in U. S. service 2 months and 14 days, 1812. Volunteered to go to Plattsburgh, September, 1814, and served 3 days in Capt. Ira Corse's Company. Also served in 3 Regt. (Tyler's) Vt. Militia. Pension Certificate of widow, Diantha, No. 9720. Ref: Book 52, AGO Page 91.

JONES, NOAH, Shoreham.
Volunteered to go to Plattsburgh, September, 1814, and served 6 days in Capt. Nathaniel North's Company of Cavalry. Ref: Rev. J. F. Goodhue's History of Shoreham, Page 107.

‡JONES, OTIS G., Shrewsbury.
Volunteered to go to Plattsburgh, September, 1814, and served 4 days in Capt. Robert Reed's Company. Pension Certificate of widow, Fanny, No. 26661.

JONES, PILASTER.
Was born at Middleberry and served in the War of 1812; captured by troops Feb. 22, 1813 at Hogdensburgh; discharged Aug. 10, 1813. Ref: Records of Naval Records and Library, Navy Dept.

*JONES, REUBEN, Surgeon.
Appointed Sept. 15, 1813 for 60 days surgeon in Col. Isaac Clark's Rifle Corps.

‡*JONES, REUBEN.
Served from June 11 to June 14, 1813 in Lieut. Bates' Company, 1 Regt. (Judson's). Served from April 12, 1814 to April 21, 1814 in Capt. Edmund B. Hill's Company, Sumner's Regt. Pension Certificate No. 1344. Pension Certificate of widow, Lydia, No. 29530.

*JONES, RICHARD.
Served in Capt. Ormsbee's Company, Col. Martindale's Regt. Detached Militia in U. S. service 2 months and 14 days, 1812.

*JONES, SAMUEL.
Served in Capt. Rogers' Company, Col. Fifield's Regt. Detached Militia in U. S. service 6 months, 1812.

JONES, SIDNEY.
Volunteered to go to Plattsburgh, September, 1814, and went as far as Bolton, Vt., serving 4 days in Lieut. Phineus Kimball's Company, West Fairlee. Ref: Book 52, AGO Page 46.

‡JONES, SIMON.
Served in Capt. Sanford's Company. Pension Certificate No. 29638.

‡*JONES, SIMON.
Served in Capt. Stephen Jones' Company, 4 Regt. (Peck's). Also served in Corning's Detachment, Vt. Militia. Pension Certificate No. 24963.

JONES, SIMON.
Served in Capt. Benjamin S. Edgerton's Company, 11th Regt.; on Pay Roll for September and October, 1812 and January and February, 1813. Ref: R. & L. 1812, AGO Pages 1 and 2.

*JONES, STEPHEN, Captain.
Served as Lieutenant in Corning's Detachment, Vt. Militia and as Lieutenant in 4 Regt. (Williams') and Captain in 4 Regt. (Peck's) Vt. Militia.

*JONES, WATSON.
Served in Capt. Dodge's Company, Col. Fifield's Regt. Detached Militia in U. S. service 2 months and 21 days, 1812.

JONES, WILLIAM,   St. Albans.
Enlisted June 8, 1813 for 1 year in Capt. John Wires' Company, 30th Regt. Ref: R. & L. 1812, AGO Page 40.

*JONES, WILLIAM,   Randolph.
Volunteered to go to Plattsburgh, September, 1814, and served in Capt. Lebbeus Egerton's Company.

‡JONES, WILLIAM, Drummer.
Served in Capt. Phelps' Company, Col. Jonathan Williams' Regt. Detached Militia in U. S. service 2 months and 21 days, 1812. Pension Certificate No. 40. Pension Certificate of widow, Sarah, No. 22983.

*JONES, WILLIAM 3rd, Corporal .
Served from April 12, 1814 to May 20, 1814 in Capt. George Fisher's Company, Sumner's Regt.

JONES, ZENOS.
Served from March 4, 1813 to June 3, 1813 in Capt. Charles Follett's Company, 11th Regt. Ref: R. & L. 1812, AGO Page 13.

JONES, ZENOS JR.
Served from March 10, 1813 to June 9, 1813 in Capt. Charles Follett's Company, 11th Regt. Ref: R. & L. 1812, AGO Page 13.

JONSON, OBEDIAH,   Braintree.
Volunteered and went to Plattsburgh Sept. 10, 1814, serving in Capt. Lot Hudson's Company. Ref: Book 52, AGO Page 24.

JORDAN, ANDREW,   Franklin County.
Volunteered to go to Plattsburgh Sept. 11, 1814 and served in 15th or 22nd Regt. Ref: Hemenway's Vt. Gazetteer, Vol. 2, Page 391.

*JORDAN, ISAAC.
Served with Hospital Attendants, Vt.

‡*JORDAN, JEREMIAH.
Served in Capt. Wright's Company, Col. Fifield's Regt. Detached Militia in U. S. service 5 months and 25 days, 1812. Also served in Capt. Stewart's Company. Pension Certificate No. 13354.

*JORDAN, PETER.
Served in Capt. Phelps' Company, Col. Wm. Williams' Regt. Detached Militia in U. S. service 5 months, 1812.

*JORDAN, SAMUEL.
Served in Corning's Detachment, Vt. Militia.

JORDAN, WILLIAM,   Woodstock.
Served from May 22, 1814 to June 19, 1815 in Capt. Taylor's Company, 30th Inf. Ref: R. & L. 1812, AGO Page 23.

‡JOSLIN, HOOKER.
Served in Capt. M. S. Jones' Company. Pension Certificate of widow, Lucia, No. 33263.

*JOSLIN, ISRAEL.
Served in 3 Regt. (Tyler's) Vt. Militia.

JOSLIN, JAMES.   Waitsfield.
Volunteered to go to Plattsburgh, September, 1814, serving 4 days in Capt. Mathias S. Jones' Company. Ref: Book 52, AGO Page 170.

JOSLIN, SAMUEL,   Morristown.
Volunteered to go to Plattsburgh, September, 1814, and served 8 days in Capt. Denison Cook's Company. Ref: Book 51, AGO Pages 202 and 206.

*JOSLIN, SAMUEL,   Randolph.
Volunteered to go to Plattsburgh, September, 1814, and served in Capt. Lebbeus Egerton's Company.

*JOSLIN, WANTON.
Served from June 11 to June 14, 1813 in Capt. Thomas Dorwin's Company, 1st Regt. 2nd Brig. 3rd Div.

JOSLYN, ISAAC.
Served from May 1 to May 31, 1814 as laborer in Alexander Parris' Company of Artificers. Ref: R. & L. 1812, AGO, Page 24.

*JOURDAN, JOHN H.
Served in Capt. Wright's Company, Col. Martindale's Regt. Detached Militia in U. S. service 14 days, 1812.

JOURDIN, PETER,   Hubbardton.
Volunteered to go to Plattsburgh, September, 1814, and served 8 days in Capt. Henry J. Horton's Company. Ref: Book 52, AGO Page 142.

*JOY, COMFORT,   Putney.
Served in Capt. • Sabin's Company, Col. Jonathan Williams' Regt. Detached Militia in U. S. service 2 months and 6 days, 1812.

JOY, JOHN D.,   Plattsburgh.
Served from Dec. 23, 1813 to June 16, 1815 in Capt. Sanford's Company, 30th Inf. Ref: R. & L. 1812, AGO Page 23.

*JOY, OBEDIAH, Ensign.
Served in 3 Regt. (Williams') Vt. Militia.

*JOY, WATERMAN, Corporal,   Putney.
Served in Capt. Noyce's Company, Col. Jonathan Williams' Regt. Detached Militia in U. S. service 2 months' and 6 days, 1812.

*JOY, ZEBAH, Corporal.
Served in 2 Regt. (Fifield's) Vt. Militia.

JOYSLIN, CALVIN.
Volunteered to go to Plattsburgh, September, 1814; no organization given. Ref: Book 52, AGO Page 155.

JUDD, ANZY (or Ainza).
Served from Feb. 8, 1813 to May 7, 1813 in Lieut. V. R. Goodrich's Company, 11th Regt. Ref: R. & L. 1812, AGO Pages 10 and 11.

*JUDD, GILMAN.
Served in Capt. Taylor's Company, Col. Fifield's Regt. Detached Militia in U. S. service 2 months and 21 days, 1812.

*JUDD, JOHN.
Served from June 11, 1813 to June 14, 1813 in Capt. Ithiel Stone's Company, 1st Regt. 2nd Brig. 3rd Div.

*JUDD, WILLIAM H.
Served from Nov. 1, 1812 to Feb. 28, 1813 in Capt. Samuel H. Holly's Company, 11th Regt. Served from April 12, 1814 to April 21, 1814 in Capt. Edmund B. Hill's Company, Sumner's Regt. Was captured by troops July 17, 1814 at Fort Erie; died Nov. 7, 1814. Ref: R. & L. 1812, AGO Page 25; Records of Naval Records and Library, Navy Dept.

‡JUDKINS, JAMES,   Marshfield.
Volunteered to go to Plattsburgh, September, 1814, and served 8 days in Capt. James English's Company. Pension Certificate of widow, Betsey, No. 16332.

*JUDKINS, SAMUEL.
Served in Capt. Walker's Company, Col. Fifield's Regt. Detached Militia in U. S. service 6 months and 3 days, 1812.

*JUDSON, HENRY.
Served from June 11, 1813 to June 14, 1813 in Capt. Moses Jewett's Company, 1st Regt. 2nd Brig. 3rd Div.

*JUDSON, JAMES.
Served in 1 Regt. (Judson's) Vt. Militia.

*JUDSON, LEMON (or Luman), Major, Shelburne. Volunteered to go to Plattsburgh, September, 1814, and served in 1st Regt.

*JUDSON, ORLA, Sergeant.
Served in 3 Regt. (Tyler's) Vt. Militia.

JUNE, HEZEKIAH,   Pittsford.
Volunteered to go to Plattsburgh, September, 1814, and served 8 days in Capt. Caleb Hendee's Company. Ref: Book 52, AGO Pages 125 and 126.

JUSTISON, LAWRENCE, (or Juttson), Franklin County. Enlisted May 20, 1812 for 5 years in Capt. White Youngs' Company, 15th Regt.; on Muster Roll from Aug. 31, 1814 to Dec. 31, 1814. Ref: R. & L. 1812, AGO Page 27.

KASSON, WARREN.
Enlisted Nov. 1, 1812 in Capt. Weeks' Company, 11th Regt.; on Pay Roll for January and February, 1813. Ref: R. & L. 1812, AGO Page 5.

KEASER, LEONARD.
Served in Capt. Benjamin Bradford's Company; on Muster Roll from May 31 to Aug. 31, 1813. Ref: R. & L. 1812, AGO Page 26.

KEECH, JAMES (or Keach).
Served in Capt. Follett's Company, Col. Dixon's Regt. Detached Militia in U. S. service 1 month and 23 days, 1813; enlisted Sept. 25, 1813. Ref: Book 52, AGO Page 268; Book 53, AGO Page 106.

‡*KEECH, SALISBURY G., (or Keach), Highgate or St. Albans. Served in Capt. Saxe's Company, Col. Wm. Williams' Regt. Detached Militia in U. S. service 4 months and 24 days, 1812. Enlisted Sept. 27, 1813 and served 1 month and 21 days in Capt. Asahel Langworthy's Company in Col. Dixon's or Col. Isaac Clark's Regt. Volunteered to go to Plattsburgh, September, 1814, and served 8 days in Capt. David Dutcher's Company. Pension Certificate No. 9648. Ref: Book 52, AGO Page 261; Book 51, AGO Page 169.

KEELER, ABNER, Captain, South Hero. Volunteered to go to Plattsburgh, September, 1814, and commanded company raised at Grand Isle and South Hero. Ref: Hemenway's Vt. Gazetteer, Vol. 2, Page 534.

-*KEELER, ALLEN.
Served in Capt. Barns' Company, Col.
Wm. Williams' Regt. Detached Militia in U. S. service 5 months. Also
served in 1 Regt. (Judson's) Vt. Militia.

‡*KEELER, ANDREW S., Sergeant.
Served from June 11 to June 14, 1813
in Capt. Ithiel Stone's Company, 1st
Regt. 2nd Brig. 3rd Div. Pension
Certificate No. 23008.

*KEELER, BROWNSON.
Served in 1 Regt. (Judson's) Vt.
Militia.

*KEELER, ELISHA, Corporal.
Served from June 11 to June 14, 1813
in Capt. John Palmer's Company, 1st
Regt. 2nd Brig. 3rd Div.

*KEELER, JACOB.
Served in 1 Regt. (Judson's) Vt.
Militia.

‡KEELER, JESSE, Cornwall.
Volunteered to go to Plattsburgh,
September, 1814, and served in Capt.
Edmund B. Hill's Company, Sumner's
Regt. Pension Certificate of widow,
Sally, No. 26915.

*KEELER, JOHN.
Served in 1 Regt. (Judson's) Vt.
Militia.

KEELER, LOTT, Pittsford.
Volunteered to go to Plattsburgh,
September, 1814, and served 8 days
in Capt. Caleb Hendee's Company.
Ref: Book 52, AGO Page 125.

*KEELER, MARQUIS.
Enlisted Sept. 25, 1813 and served
1 month and 23 days in Capt. Elijah
W. Wood's Company, Col. Dixon's
Regt.

KEELER, SETH, Sergeant.
Served in 1st Regt. of Detached Militia of Vt. in the service of the U. S.
at Champlain for 2 days commencing
Nov. 18 and ending Nov. 19, 1812.

KEELER, SOLOMON, H., Charlotte.
Volunteered to go to Plattsburgh,
September, 1814, and served 8 days
in Capt. Daniel Hough's Company.
Ref: Book 51, AGO Page 94.

‡*KEELER, THOMAS A.
Served in Capt. Stone's Company,
1 Regt. (Judson's) Vt. Militia. Pension Certificate of widow, Sarah, No.
8374.

‡KEEN, ANDREW.
Served in Capt. Danforth's Company.
Pension Certificate of widow, Hannah, No. 1419.

KEEP, JABEZ, Fairfield.
Served in Capt. Geo. W. Kendall's
Company, Col. Wm. Williams' Regt.
Detached Militia in U. S. service 4
months and 23 days, 1812. Enlisted
Sept. 25, 1813 and served 1 month
and 23 days in Capt. Martin D.
Folett's Company, in Col. Dixon's
Regt. Volunteered to go to Platts-

burgh, September, 1814, and served 8
days in Capt. Samuel Farnsworth's
Company. Ref: R. & L. 1812, AGO
Pages 37, 38, 39; Book 51, AGO Pages
141, 192, 198; Book 52, AGO Page
268; Book 53, AGO Pages 20 and 106.

KEEP, JABEZ, Franklin or Swanton.
Volunteered to go to Plattsburgh,
September, 1814, and served in Capt.
Amasa I. Brown's Company. Ref:
Book 51, AGO Page 187.

*KEET, JABEZ.
Served in Dixon's Regt. Vt. Militia.

KEISER, CALVIN, Morristown.
Volunteered to go to Plattsburgh,
September, 1814, and served 8 days
in Capt. Denison Cook's Company.
Ref: Book 51, AGO Pages 202 and
206.

KEISER, JOHN, Morristown.
Volunteered to go to Plattsburgh,
September, 1814, and served 8 days
in Capt. Denison Cook's Company.
Ref: Book 51, AGO Pages 202, 203,
206.

‡*KEITH, BARNABAS, Woodstock.
Served in Capt. Phelps' Company,
Col. Jonathan Williams' Regt. Detached Militia in U. S. service 2
months and 21 days. 1812. Served
from Feb. 20 to May 19, 1813 in
Capt. Phineas Williams' Company,
11th Regt. Pension Certificate of widow, Seviah, No. 8448. Ref: R. & L.
1812, AGO Page 14.

*KEITH, GEORGE.
Served in Capt. Walker's Company,
Col. Fifield's Regt. Detached Militia
in U. S. service 23 days, 1812.

KEITH, ROSWELL R., Barre.
Volunteered to go to Plattsburgh,
September, 1814, serving 9 days in
Capt. Warren Ellis' Company. Ref:
Book 52, AGO Pages 223 and 242.

KEITH, WILLARD.
Volunteered to go to Plattsburgh,
September, 1814, and served in Capt.
Warren Ellis' Company. Ref: Hemenway's Vt. Gazetteer, Vol. 4, Page 41.

*KEIZER, PAUL (Keeser or Keezer).
Served from June 11 to June 14, 1813
in Lieut. Bates' Company, 1 Regt.
(Judson's). Served from Aug. 16,
1813 to Aug. 15, 1814 in Capt. James
Taylor's Company, 30th Regt.

*KELEY, CHARLES, Musician.
Served in Sumner's Regt. Vt. Militia.

*KELEY, JOHN.
Served from April 13 to April 16, 1814
in Capt. Salmon Foster's Company,
Sumner's Regt.

*KELLER, GEORGE.
Served with Hospital Attendants, Vt.

KELLEY, DANIEL.
Volunteered to go to Plattsburgh,
September, 1814, serving 4 days in
Capt. Aaron Kidder's Company. Ref:
Book 52, AGO Page 65.

KELLEY, DENNIS.
Served from May 1 to June 30, 1814
in Capt. Alexander Brooks' Corps of
Artillery. Ref: R. & L. 1812, AGO
Page 31.

‡*KELLEY, JAMES.
Served in Capt. Burnap's Company,
Col. Jonathan Williams' Regt. Detached Militia in U. S. service 2
months and 13 days, 1812. Also
served in Capt. Burnett's Company.
Pension Certificate No. 12024. Pension Certificate of widow, Maria, No.
33128.

KELLEY, WILLIAM, Sandy Hill, N. Y.
Served from Oct. 25, 1814 to June
19, 1815 in Capt. Taylor's Company,
30th Inf. Ref: R. & L. 1812, AGO
Page 23.

KELLOGG, AMOS, Waggoner, Pittsford.
Volunteered to go to Plattsburgh,
September, 1814, serving 8 days in
Capt. Caleb Hendee's Company. Ref:
Book 52, AGO Page 125.

KELLOGG, CHARLES,   St. Albans.
Enlisted April 27, 1813 for 1 year in
Capt. John Wires' Company, 30th
Regt. Ref: R. & L. 1812, AGO
Page 40.

*KELLOGG, DANIEL.
Served from April 12, 1814 to May
20, 1814 in Capt. George Fisher's
Company, Sumner's Regt.

KELLOGG, DAVID,   Starksboro.
Volunteered to go to Plattsburgh,
September, 1814, and served 4 days
in Capt. Moulton's Company. Ref:
Book 51, AGO Page 29.

*KELLOGG, ELIAS W.
Served in Corning's Detachment, Vt.
Militia.

*KELLOGG, ENOS JR.
Served in Corning's Detachment, Vt.
Militia.

KELLOGG, FRANCES,   Starksboro.
Volunteered to go to Plattsburgh,
September, 1814, and served 4 days
in Capt. Moulton's Company. Ref:
Book 51, AGO Page 29.

*KELLOGG, GEORGE.
Served in 1 Regt. (Judson's) Vt.
Militia.

KELLOGG, GIDEON,   Burlington.
Volunteered to go to Plattsburgh,
September, 1814, and served in Capt.
Henry Mayo's Company. Ref: Book
51, AGO Page 81.

KELLOGG, ISAAC,   St. Albans.
Enlisted May 3, 1813 for 1 year in
Capt. John Wires' Company, 30th
Regt. Ref: R. & L. 1812, AGO Page
40.

‡KELLOGG, MEDAD,   Cavendish.
Served from Feb. 27, 1814 to June
16, 1815 in Capt. Sanford's Company,
30th Inf. Also served in Capt.
Wright's Company. Pension Certificate of widow, Sophia, No. 3667.

*KELLOGG, OTIS, Sergeant.
Served in 3 Regt. (Tyler's) Vt. Militia.

*KELLOGG, PHILANDER,   Burlington.
Served from June 11 to June 14, 1813
in Capt. Moses Jewett's Company, 1st
Regt. 2nd Brig. 3rd Div. Volun-
teered to go to Plattsburgh, Septem-
ber, 1814, and served in Capt. Henry
Mayo's Company. Ref: Book 51, AGO
Page 81.

KELLOGG, PLINEY.
Volunteered to go to Plattsburgh,
September, 1814, and served 7 days
in company of Capt. Frederick Gris-
wold, raised in Brookfield, Vt. Ref:
Book 52, AGO Page 52.

KELLOGG, ROWLAND,   Middlebury.
Served from Sept. 1, 1813 to July 2,
1814 in Capt. Vanbunn's Company,
29th Inf. Ref: R. & L. 1812, AGO
Page 30.

KELLOGG, STEPHEN,   Stowe.
Volunteered to go to Plattsburgh,
September, 1814, and served in Capt.
Nehemiah Perkins' Company, 4th
Regt. (Peck's). Ref: Hemenway's
Vt. Gaz., Vol. 2, Page 742.

‡*KELLOGG, THOMAS.
Served in Capt. Bingham's Company,
Col. Jonathan Williams' Regt. De-
tached Militia in U. S. service 2
months and 9 days, 1812. Pension
Certificate No. 5627.

*KELLOGG, WAITSTILL.
Served from April 12 to April 15,
1814 in Capt. John Hackett's Company, Sumner's Regt.

*KELLOGG, WARNER.
Served in Corning's' Detachment, Vt.
Militia.

*KELLOGG, WILLIAM, 2nd Lieutenant,
Stowe. Served from Feb. 2 to Feb.
28, 1813 in Capt. Samuel H. Holly's
Company, 11th Regt. Served from
Sept. 18 to Nov. 18 as 2nd Lieuten-
ant in Capt. Isaac Finch's Company,
Col. Clark's Rifle Regt. Volunteered
to go to Plattsburgh, September, 1814,
and served in Capt. Nehemiah Per-
kins' Company, 4th Regt. (Peck's).
Also served in Corning's Detachment,
Vt. Militia.

*KELLY, GEORGE.
Served in 1 Regt. (Judson's). Vt.
Militia.

*KELLY, HENRY.
Served in Tyler's Regt. Vt. Militia.

KELSEY, CHARLES, Drummer.
Served from April 12 to April 21,
1814 in Capt. Shubael Wales' Company, Col. W. B. Sumner's Regt.
Ref: Book 52, AGO Page 288.

*KELSEY, CHARLES, Fifer,   Whiting.
Served from April 12 to April 21,
1814 in Capt. Salmon Foster's Company, Sumner's Regt.; volunteered
to go to Plattsburgh, September, 1814,
and served 9 days in same company.

*KELSEY. DANIEL, Corporal.
Served from April 13 to April 16,
1814 in Capt. Salmon's Foster's Company, Sumner's Regt.

KELSEY, ELIAS, Salisbury.
Volunteered to go to Plattsburgh,
September, 1814, and served 4 days
in Capt. John Morton's Company.
Ref: Book 52, AGO Page 141.

‡*KELSEY, HARVEY, Danville.
Served in Capt. Morrill's Company,
Col. Fifield's Regt. Detached Militia
in U. S. service 6 months and 5 days,
1812. Pension Certificate No. 4564.

KELSEY, JAMES JR., Danville.
Volunteered to go to Plattsburgh,
September, 1814, and served 3 days
in Capt. Solomon Langmaid's Company. Ref: Book 51, AGO Pages 75
and 76.

*KELSEY, JOSIAH, Corporal.
Served in 4 Regt. (Peck's) Vt. Militia.

*KELSEY, STEPHEN, Sergeant, Stowe.
Volunteered to go to Plattsburgh,
September, 1814, and was at the
battle, serving in Capt. Nehemiah Perkins' Company, 4 Regt. (Peck's) Vt.
Militia.

KELTER, JOSEPH, Franklin County.
Volunteered to go to Plattsburgh
Sept. 11, 1814 and served in 15th or
22nd Regt. Ref: Hemenway's Vt.
Gazetteer, Vol. 2, Page 392.

*KELTON, ENOCH, Calais or E. Montpelier. Volunteered to go to Plattsburgh, September, 1814, serving 10
days in Capt. Gideon Wheelock's
Company.

KELTON, JOHN B., E. Montpelier.
Served from May 1 to June 30, 1814
in Capt. Alexander Brooks' Corps
of Artillery. Ref: R. & L. 1812,
AGO Page 31.

*KELTON, NATHAN. Quartermaster,
E. Montpelier. Volunteered to go
to Plattsburgh, September, 1814, and
served 8 days in Capt. Timothy Hubbard's Company. Also served as
Quartermaster in 2 Regt. (Fifield's)
Vt. Militia. Ref: Book 52, AGO
Pages 198 and 256.

*KEMP, OLIVER P.
Served from Oct. 4, 1813 to Dec. 23,
1813 in Capt. Asahel Langworthy's
Company, Col. Isaac Clark's Rifle
Corps.

‡*KEMP, PARKER.
Served in 3 Regt. (Tyler's) Vt. Militia. Also served in Capt. Reed's Company. Pension Certificate, No. 25453.

KENADY, DAVID, Richmond.
Volunteered to go to Plattsburgh,
September, 1814, and served 9 days
in Capt. Roswell Hunt's Company.
Ref: Book 51, AGO Page 82.

KENCY, EBENEZER.
Served in Capt. Adams' Company,
Col. Jonathan Williams' Regt. De-

tached Militia in U. S. service 2
months and 6 days, 1812. Ref: Book
53, AGO Page 31.

‡KENDALL, CALEB.
Served in Capt. Picket's Company.
Pension Certificate of widow, Emily
A., No. 28453.

*KENDALL, GEORGE WASHINGTON (or
Kindall), Captain. Appointed 1 Lieutenant 30 Inf. April 30, 1813; Captain
Aug. 1, 1814; honorably discharged
June 15, 1815. Commanded company
in Col. Wm. Williams' Regt. about
6 months in 1812. Entered service
April 24, 1813 and served as 1st
Lieutenant in Capt. Wm. Miller's
Company and Capt. Gideon Spencer's
Company, 30th Regt.

*KENDALL, ISAAC, Calais.
Volunteered to go to Plattsburgh,
September, 1814, and served 10 days
in Capt. Gideon Wheelock's Company.

KENDALL, JONATHAN, Wagon-master,
Pittsford. Served from May 1, 1813
to May 1, 1814 in Capt. Daniel Farrington's Company (also commanded
by Capt. Simeon Wright) 30th Regt.
Volunteered to go to Plattsburgh,
September, 1814, and served 8 days
in Capt. Caleb Hendee's Company.
Ref: R. & L. 1812, AGO Pages 50
and 51; Book 52, AGO Page 124.

‡*KENDALL, SAMUEL, Enosburgh.
Enlisted Sept. 25, 1813 and served
1 month and 23 days in Capt. Martin
D. Folett's Company, Col. Dixon's
Regt. Also served in Capt. Robbins'
Company, 4 Regt. Pension Certificate No. 17255.

*KENDALL, TIMOTHY (or Kemball?).
Served from April 13 to April 21,
1814 in Capt. Salmon Foster's Company, Sumner's Regt.

*KENEDY, JOHN.
Served in Corning's Detachment, Vt.
Militia and in 4 Regt. (Peck's) Vt.
Militia.

KENFIELD, WILLIAM, Cambridge.
Enlisted Sept. 25, 1813 in Capt. Thomas Waterman's Company, Dixon's
Regt. Volunteered to go to Plattsburgh, September, 1814, and served
8 days in Capt. Salmon Green's Company. Ref: Book 51, AGO Page 207;
Book 52, AGO Page 291.

KENFORD, WHITING.
Served from June 11 to June 14, 1813
in Capt. Hezekiah Barns' Company,
1st Regt. 2nd Brig. 3rd Div. Ref: R.
& L. 1812, AGO Page 43.

‡*KENISON, BENJAMIN.
Served in Capt. Prentiss' Company,
Dixon's Regt. Pension Certificate No.
11421. Pension Certificate of widow,
Arminda, No. 39183.

KENISON. JOHN.
Served from March 1 to May 31, 1813
in Capt. Jonathan Starks' Company,
11th Regt. Ref: R. & L. 1812, AGO
Page 19.

KENISON, JONA.
Served from March 11 to June 10, 1813 in Capt. Jonathan Starks' Company, 11th Regt. Ref: R. & L. 1812, AGO Page 19.

‡*KENISON, SAMUEL, Corporal.
Served in Capt. John Prentiss' Company, Dixon's Regt. Pension Certificate No. 22008. Pension Certificate of widow, Nancy, No. 32189.

KENISTON, PHILIP (or Kineston?), Milton. Served from Sept. 1, 1814 to June 16, 1815 in Capt. Sanford's Company, 30th Inf. Ref: R. & L. 1812, AGO Page 23.

KENNAN, JUSTUS,   Waterbury.
Volunteered to go to Plattsburgh, September, 1814, serving 11 days in Capt. George Atkins' Company. Ref: Book 52, AGO Page 249.

*KENNEDY, DAVID, Corporal.
Served in Corning's Detachment, Vt. Militia and in 4 Regt. (Peck's) Vt. Militia.

KENNEDY, MOSES,   Franklin County.
Volunteered to go to Plattsburgh Sept. 11, 1814 and served in 15th or 22nd Regt. Ref: Hemenway's Vt. Gazetteer, Vol. 2, Page 392.

*KENNEDY, SAMUEL B., Sergeant, Bolton. Volunteered to go to Plattsburgh, September, 1814. Served as Sergeant in 4 Regt. (Peck's) Vt. Militia.

KENNEY, ASA.
Enlisted Feb. 15, 1813 in Capt. Phineas Williams' Company, 11th Regt.; on Pay Roll to May 31, 1813. Ref: R. & L. 1812, AGO Page 14.

*KENNISON, DAVID, Corporal.
Enlisted Sept. 18, 1813 in Capt. Isaac Finch's Company, Col. Clark's Rifle Corps.

*KENNON, JUSTUS.
Served in 4 Regt. (Peck's) Vt. Militia.

KENNY, BURNETT,   Franklin County.
Volunteered to go to Plattsburgh Sept. 11, 1814 and served in 15th or 22nd Regt. Ref: Hemenway's Vt. Gazetteer, Vol. 2, Page 391.

*KENNY, EBENEZER.
Served in 3 Regt. (Williams') Vt. Militia.

*KENT, AMASA.
Enlisted Sept. 20, 1813 in Capt. John Weed's Company, Col. Clark's Rifle Corps.

KENT, BENJAMIN,   Franklin County.
Volunteered to go to Plattsburgh Sept. 11, 1814 and served in 15th or 22nd Regt. Ref: Hemenway's Vt. Gazetteer, Vol. 2, Page 391.

*KENT, BUSHNEL.
Served in Dixon's Regt. Vt. Militia.

*KENT, ELIAS.
Served in Capt. Wheeler's Company, Col. Fifield's Regt. Detached Militia in U. S. service 3 months and 16 days, 1812.

*KENT, JACOB.
Served in Capt. Wheeler's Company, Col. Fifield's Regt. Detached Militia in U. S. service 3 months and 16 days, 1812.

*KENT, JOHN.
Served from June 11 to June 14, 1813 and from Oct. 4 to Oct. 13, 1813 in Capt. John Palmer's Company, 1st Regt. 2nd Brig. 3rd Div.

*KENT, ROBERT.
Served from April 12 to May 20, 1814 in company of Capt. James Gray Jr., Sumner's Regt.

‡*KENT, SAMUEL, Corporal.
Enlisted Sept. 20, 1813 in Capt. John Weed's Company, Col. Clark's Rifle Corps. Pension Certificate of widow, Mary, No. 41001.

KENTFICK, WILLIAM.
Served in Capt. Chadwick's Company. Ref: R. & L. 1812, AGO Page 32.

*KENYON, ARNOLD.
Served from June 11 to June 14, 1813 in Capt. John M. Eldridge's Company, 1st Regt. 2nd Brig. 3rd Div.

‡*KENYON, GILES 2nd.
Served in Capt. John M. Eldridge's Company, 1st Regt. (Judson's) Vt. Militia. Pension Certificate No. 24395.

*KENYON, JARED.
Served in 1 Regt. (Judson's) Vt. Militia.

*KENYON, SYLVESTER A.
Served in Capt. Barns' Company, Col. William Williams' Regt. Detached Militia in U. S. service 5 months, 1812. Served from June 11 to June 14, 1813 in Capt. Thomas Dorwin's Company, 1st Regt. 2nd Brig. 3rd Div.

*KERR, AARON T.
Served in 3 Regt. (Williams') Vt. Militia.

KERRIL, HARVEY.
Enlisted June 12, 1813 for 1 year in Capt. Daniel Farrington's Company (also commanded by Capt. Simeon Wright) 30th Regt.; on Muster Roll from March 1 to April 30, 1814. Ref: R. & L. 1812, AGO Pages 50 and 51.

*KETCHAM, BARNARD, 1st Lieutenant, Sudbury or Enosburgh. Appointed Oct. 14th and served to Nov. 17, 1813 as 1st Lieutenant in Capt. Scoville's Company; volunteered to go to Plattsburgh, September, 1814, and served 15 days in same company.

KETCHAM, BENJAMIN, Franklin County.
Enlisted April 21, 1812 for 5 years in Capt. White Youngs' Company, 15th Regt.; on Muster Roll from Aug. 31 to Dec. 31, 1814. Ref: R. & L. 1812, AGO Page 27.

KETCHAM, ELIAS,   Sudbury.
Volunteered to go to Plattsburgh,
September, 1814, and served 6 days
in Capt. Thomas Hall's Company.
Ref: Book 52, AGO Page 122.

‡KETCHAM, IRA,   Sudbury.
Volunteered to go to Plattsburgh,
September, 1814, and served 6 days
in Capt. Thomas Hall's Company.
Also served in Capt. Winslow's Com-
pany. Pension Certificate of widow,
Hannah, No. 32809.

*KETCHAM, ISAAC, Sudbury or Enos-
burgh. Served in Capt. Asahel Scoville's Company from Oct. 14 to Nov.
17, 1813; volunteered to go to Plattsburgh, September, 1814, and served
15 days in same company. Served
from April 12 to April 21, 1814 as
a fifer in Capt. Shubael Wales' Company, Col. W. B. Sumner's Regt.

KETCHAM, WILLIAM.
Served from April 13, 1814 to April
21, 1814 in Capt. Salmon Foster's
Company, Sumner's Regt. Ref: Book
52, AGO Page 284.

KETCHUM, R. W.,   .   Barre.
Volunteered to go to Plattsburgh,
September, 1814, and served 10 days
in Capt. Warren Ellis' Company. Ref:
Book 52, AGO Page 242.

KETLER, JOSEPH.
Enlisted April 25, 1812 for 5 years
in Capt. White Youngs' Company,
15th Regt. Ref: R. & L. 1812, AGO
Page 27.

*KETTY, HENRY.
Served in 3 Regt. (Tyler's) Vt. Militia.

KEYES, ELIAS, Captain,   Stockbridge.
Volunteered to go to Plattsburgh,
September, 1814, and served 8 days
in command of company of Militia.
Ref: Book 51, AGO Pages 237, 238 and
239.

KEYES, EPHRAIM,   Middlesex.
Volunteered to go to Plattsburgh,
September, 1814, and served in Capt.
Holden Putnam's Company, 4th Regt.
(Peck's). Ref: Hemenway's Vt. Ga-
zetteer, Vol. 4, Page 250.

*KEYES, JOSIAH.
Served in Capt. Walker's Company,
Col. Fifield's Regt. Detached Militia
in U. S. service 6 months and 3
days, 1812.

*KEYES, WILLARD.
Served in Capt. Noyes' Company,
Col. Jonathan Williams' Regt. Detached Militia in U. S. service 2
months and 6 days, 1812.

‡*KEYS, WILLIAM,   Strafford.
Enlisted March 29, 1813 in Capt.
Edgerton's Company, 11th Regt. Also
served in 3 Regt. (Williams') Vt.
Militia. Pension Certificate No. 16691.

KEZER, OREN.
Served in Capt. Mason's Company,
Col. Fifield's Regt. Detached Militia
in U. S. service 5 months and 28
days, 1812. Ref: Book 53, AGO Page
27.

‡*KEZER, PAUL.
Served in Capt. Barns' Company, Col.
Wm. Williams' Regt. Detached Mili-
tia in U. S. service 5 months, 1812.
Also served in Capt. Spencer's Com-
pany. Pension Certificate No. 8503.

*KIBBE, EDWARD.
Served in Capt. Burnap's Company,
Col. Jonathan Williams' Regt. Detached Militia in U. S. service 2
months and 13 days, 1812.

*‡KIBBEY, ISAAC.
Enlisted Oct. 14, 1813 in Capt. Asahel
Langworthy's Company, Col. Isaac
Clark's Rifle Corps. Also served in
Dixon's Regt. Pension Certificate No.
30511.

*KIBBY, IRA.
Served from June 11 to June 14, 1813
in Capt. Hezekiah Barns' Company,
1st Regt. 2nd Brig. 3rd Div.

KIBBY, NOADIAH (or Kibbey) Lieutenant. Appointed Ensign March 28,
1814, 31st Inf.; appointed 2nd Lieutenant Oct. 25, 1814. Ref: Governor
and Council Vt., Vol. 6, Page 478.

KIBLING, JACOB,   Strafford.
Volunteered to go to Plattsburgh,
September, 1814, and served 5 days
in Capt. Joseph Barrett's Company.
Ref: Book 52, AGO Page 41.

KIBLINGER, JOHN,   Strafford.
Volunteered to go to Plattsburgh,
September, 1814, and served in Capt.
Joseph Barrett's Company. Ref: Book
52, AGO Page 41.

KIDDER, AARON, Captain.
Volunteered to go to Plattsburgh,
September, 1814, and served 5 days
in command of company raised in
Fairlee and W. Fairlee. Ref: Book
52, AGO Page 65.

KIDDER, DAVID.
Volunteered to go to Plattsburgh,
September, 1814, and served 4 days
in Capt. Aaron Kidder's Company.
Ref: Book 52, AGO Page 65.

*KIDDER, JOHN.
Enlisted Oct. 4, 1813 in Capt. Asahel
Langworthy's Company, Col. Isaac
Clark's Rifle Corps.

‡KIDDER, LUTHER H.
Served in Capt. Labaree's Company.
Pension Certificate No. 27759.

KIDDER, LYMAN, 2nd Lieutenant, Braintree. Marched to Plattsburgh Sept.
10, 1814 and served in Capt. Lot
Hudsons' Company. Ref: Book 51,
AGO Page 295; Book 52, AGO Page
24.

KIDDER, LYMAN,   Braintree.
Marched to Plattsburgh Sept. 10, 1814
and served in Capt. Lot Hudson's
Company. Ref: Book 52, AGO Page
24.

KILBORN, ARTEMUS,   Whiting.
Volunteered to go to Plattsburgh,
September, 1814, and served 9 days
in Capt. Salmon Foster's Company,
Sumner's Regt. Ref: Book 51, AGO
Page 7.

*KILBOURN, BENJAMIN.
Served from April 12, 1814 to May
20, 1814 in Capt. George Fisher's
Company, Sumner's Regt.

*KILBURN, AUGUSTUS.
Served in Capt. Strait's Company,
Col. Martindale's Regt. Detached
Militia in U. S. service .2 months
and 13 days, 1812.

*KILBURN, CYRENIUS.
Served in Capt. Richardson's Company, Col. Martindale's Regt. Detached Militia in U. S. service 2
months and 13 days, 1812.

KILBURN, IRA.
Enlisted April 28, 1813 for 1 year in
Capt. Simeon Wright's Company. Ref:
R. & L. 1812, AGO Page 51.

‡*KILBURN, JOEL,   Waterbury.
Volunteered to go to Plattsburgh,
September, 1814, serving 11 days in
Capt. George Atkins' Company, 4
Regt. (Peck's). Pension Certificate
No. 23538.

KILLAM, CHARLES.
Served in Capt. Samuel H. Holly's
Company, 11th Regt.; on Pay Roll for
January and February, 1813. Ref:
R. & L. 1812, AGO Page 25.

*KILLIPS, JOHN.
Served in 1 Regt. (Judson's) Vt. Militia.

*KILLUM, JOSEPH,   Morgan.
Served in Capt. Hiram Mason's Company, Col. Fifield's Regt. Detached
Militia in U. S. service at Derby 5
months and 15 days, 1812.

*KIMBALL, ABEL.
Served in Capt. Robbins' Company,
Col. Wm. Williams' Regt. Detached
Militia in U. S. service 3 months and
21 days, 1812. Served in Capt. Haig's
Corps of Light Dragoons; on Pay Roll
to June 30, 1814. Ref: R. & L.
1812, AGO Page. 20.

*KIMBALL, AMOS, Lieutenant.
Served in Corning's Detachment, Vt.
Militia.

KIMBALL, ANDREW,   Stowe.
Volunteered to go to Plattsburgh,
September, 1814, and served in Capt.
Nehemiah Perkins' Company, 4th
Regt. (Peck's). Ref: Hemenway's Vt.
Gazetteer, Vol. 2, Page 742.

KIMBALL, BARTHOLOMEW, Montpelier.
Volunteered to go to Plattsburgh,
September, 1814, and served 8 days
in Capt. Timothy Hubbard's Company.
Ref: Book 52, AGO Page 256.

*KIMBALL, ELI, Sergeant, Burlington.
Served in Capt. Barns' Company, Col.
Wm. Williams' Regt. Detached Militia in U. S. service 5 months. Served
from June 11 to June 14, 1813 in
Capt. Moses Jewett's Company, 1st
Regt. 2nd Brig. 3rd Div. Volunteered to go to Plattsburgh, September,
1814, and served 10 days as Sergeant in Capt. Henry Mayo's Company. Ref: Book 51, AGO Page 81.

KIMBALL, GEORGE (or Kindall?) Fairfield. Commanded company from
Fairfield stationed at Swanton in
1813. Ref: Hemenway's Vt. Gazetteer, Vol. 2, Page 408.

‡*KIMBALL, GEORGE.
Served in Capt. Durkee's Company,
Col. Fifield's Regt. Detached Militia
in U. S. service 2 months and 21
days, 1812. Also served in Capt.
Wright's Company, Col. Fifield's Regt.
Detached Militia in U. S. service
3 months and 9 days, 1812. Pension
Certificate No. 10891. Ref: Book 53,
AGO Page 100.

*KIMBALL, HARRY.
Served in Capt. Dodge's Company,
Col. Fifield's Regt. Detached Militia
in U. S. service 2 months and 21
days, 1812.

KIMBALL, JEREMIAH, Sergeant.
Served in Lieut. Wm. S. Foster's
Company, 11th Regt.; on Pay Roll
for January and February, 1813. Ref:
R. & L. 1812, AGO Page 7.

*KIMBALL, JOHN H.,   Randolph.
Volunteered to go to Plattsburgh,
September, 1814, and served in Capt.
Lebbeus Egerton's Company.

KIMBALL, JOSEPH.
Volunteered to go to Plattsburgh,
September, 1814, and went as far as
Bolton, Vt., serving 4 days in Lieut.
Phineus Kimball's Company of West
Fairlee. Ref: Book 52, AGO Page
46.

‡*KIMBALL, LEVI.
Served in Capt. Lowry's Company,
Col. Wm. Williams' Regt. Detached
Militia in U. S. service 4 months
and 26 days, 1812. Pension Certifi-
cate No. 7100.

*KIMBALL, MOSES.
Served from June 11 to June 14, 1813
in Capt. Moses Jewett's Company,
1st Regt. 2nd Brig. 3rd Div.

KIMBALL, NATHAN, Sergeant, Royalton.
Volunteered to go to Plattsburgh,
September, 1814, and served 5 days
in Capt. Nehemiah Noble's Company.
Ref: Book 51, AGO Page 227.

KIMBALL, PHINEUS, Lieutenant, West
Fairlee. Volunteered to go to Plattsburgh, September, 1814, and went as
far as Bolton, Vt., serving 5 days
in command of company from West
Fairlee and vicinity. Ref: Book 52,
AGO Pages 46 and 47. (For biographical sketch see Hemenway's Vt. Gazetteer, Vol. 2, Page 913).

*KIMBALL, REUBEN.
Served in Corning's Detachment, Vt.
Militia.

KIMBALL, ROBERT,   Morristown.
Volunteered to go to Plattsburgh,
September, 1814, and served 8 days
in Capt. Denison Cook's Company.
Ref: Book 51, AGO Pages 202 and
206.

KIMBALL, ROSWELL.
Enlisted Dec. 19, 1813 for period of the war and served in Capt. Wm. Miller's Company and Capt. Gideon Spencer's Company. 30th Regt.; on board the Navy. Ref: R. & L. 1812, AGO Pages 54 and 57.

*KIMBALL, STEPHEN, Cornet.
Served in 4 Regt. (Williams') Vt. Militia.

*KIMBALL, THOMAS.
Served from Oct. 11 to Oct. 17, 1813 in Capt. John Munson's Company, 3 Regt. (Tyler's).

*KIMBALL, TIMOTHY.
Served from April 12 to April 21, 1814 in Capt. Shubael Wales' Company, Col. W. B. Sumner's Regt.

*KIMBALL, WILLIAM S.
Served in Capt. Richardson's Company, Col. Martindale's Regt. Detached Militia in U. S. service 2 months and 13 days, 1812.

*KIMPTON, JOHN, Sergeant.
Served from Oct. 5 to Oct. 16, 1813 in Capt. Roswell Hunt's Company, 3 Regt. (Tyler's).

*KINASTON, DAVID.
Served in 2 Regt. (Fifield's) Vt. Militia.

*KINDALL, ELISHA.
Served with Hospital Attendants, Vt.

KINDALL, NATHANIEL.
Served in Capt. George W. Kindall's Company, Col. Wm. Williams' Regiment; on Muster Roll from Nov. 1 to Dec. 8, 1812. Ref: R. & L. 1812, AGO Page 38.

‡*KING, CALEB H.
Enlisted Sept. 20, 1813 in Capt. John Weed's Company, Col. Clark's Rifle Corps. Pension Certificate No. 21936. Pension Certificate of widow, Roxy L., No. 10158.

‡KING, CHESTER C.
Served in Capt. Scofield's Company. Pension Certificate of widow, Eunice M., No. 23737.

*KING, DANIEL.
Served in Capt. Barns' Company, Col. Wm. Williams' Regt. Detached Militia in U. S. service 5 months, 1812. Served from June 11 to June 14, 1813 in Capt. Thomas Dorwin's Company, 1st Regt. 2nd Brig. 3rd Div.

KING, EBENEZER.
Served from May 1 to June 30, 1814 in Capt. Haig's Corps of Light Dragoons. Ref: R. & L. 1812, AGO Page 20.

*KING, ELEAZER.
Served in Capt. Strait's Company, Col. Martindale's Regt. Detached Militia in U. S. service 2 months and 13 days, 1812.

KING, GEORGE W.,   Fairfax.
Served in Capt. Charles Follett's Company, 11th Regt.; on Pay Roll

for January and February, 1812. Served in 1813 and 1814 in Capt. Joseph Beeman's Company. Ref: R. & L. 1812, AGO Page 12; Hemenway's Vt. Gazetteer, Vol. 2, Page 402.

KING, HORACE, Ensign.
Volunteered to go to Plattsburgh, September, 1814, and served in company of Capt. Joel Barnes of Chelsea. Ref: Book 52, AGO Pages 69 and 77.

‡*KING, JAMES.
Served in Capt. Strait's Company, Col. Martindale's Regt. Detached Militia in U. S. service 2 months and 13 days, 1812. Pension Certificate No. 9840. Pension Certificate of widow, Polly, No. 24163.

KING, JAMES.
Served in Capt. Weeks' Company, 11th Regt.; on Pay Roll for January and February, 1813; died at Amherst, N. H. Ref: R. & L. 1812, AGO Page 5.

KING, JESSE F.,   Tunbridge.
Volunteered to go to Plattsburgh, September, 1814, serving 4 days in Capt. Ephraim Hackett's Company. Ref: Book 52, AGO Pages 71 and 72.

*KING, JOHN,   Shoreham.
Served from April 12 to May 20, 1814 in company of Capt. James Gray Jr., Sumner's Regt. Volunteered to go to Plattsburgh, September, 1814, and served 6 days in Capt. Samuel Hand's Company. Ref: Rev. J. F. Goodhue's History of Shoreham, Page 107.

*KING, JOHN.
Served in Capt. Strait's Company, Col. Martindale's Regt. Detached Militia in U. S. service 2 months and 13 days, 1812. Served from March 4th to June 30, 1814 in Regt. of Light Dragoons. Volunteered to go to Plattsburgh, September, 1814, serving in company of Capt. Joel Barnes of Chelsea. Ref: R. & L. 1812, AGO Page 21; Book 52, AGO Pages 69 and 77.

‡KING, MARTIN.
Served in Capt. Thornton's Company. Pension Certificate No. 16692.

‡KING, NATHANIEL, C., Surgeon, E. Montpelier. Volunteered to go to Plattsburgh, September, 1814, and served 7 days in Col. Parley Davis' Regt. Pension Certificate No. 31039.

KING, NATHANIEL,   Tunbridge.
Born in Tunbridge; aged 19 years; 5 feet 3 inches high; light complexion; blue eyes; brown hair; by profession a farmer. Enlisted Aug. 10, 1813 for 1 year in the Army of the U. S. unless sooner discharged; enlistment approved by father, Joshua King. Ref: Enlistment contract in custody of Vt. Historical Society.

KING, NATHANIEL 2nd,   Tunbridge.
Volunteered to go to Plattsburgh, September, 1814, and served 4 days in Capt. Ephraim Hackett's Company. Ref: Book 52, AGO Pages 71 and 72.

KING, PARDON,   Shoreham.
Served from April 3, 1813 to July
2, 1813 in Capt. Jonathan Starks'
Company, 11th Regt.; was in the
Niagara campaign in the battles under Brown and Scott; at the sortie
of Fort Erie was wounded in the
ankle by the explosion of a shell,
from which he never fully recovered;
discharged at Greenbush at the close
of the war and returned to Shoreham. Ref: R. & L. 1812, AGO Page
19; Rev. J. F. Goodhue's History of
Shoreham, Page 102.

KING, SAMUEL,   Tunbridge, Vt.
Born in Tunbridge, Vt.; aged 18
years; 5 feet 9 inches high; light
complexion; blue eyes; light hair;
by profession a farmer. Enlisted
July 25, 1813 in U. S. Army for 1
year; enlistment approved by father,
Joshua King. Ref: Paper in custody
of Vt. Historical Society.

*KING, SILAS, 3rd Corporal.
Served from June 11 to June 14,
1813 in Capt. Moses Jewett's Company, 1st Regt. 2nd Brig. 3rd Div.

KING, SYREL.
Served in Capt. Phelps' Company,
Col. Jonathan Williams' Regt. Detached Militia in U. S. service 2
months and 21 days, 1812. Ref: Book
53, AGO Page 79.

‡KING, THEODORE JR.,   St. Albans.
Enlisted April 23, 1813 for 1 year in
Capt. John Wires' Company, 30th
Regt. Also served in Capt. William
Miller's Company (30th Regt). Pen-
sion Certificate of widow, Mary G.,
No. 8414.

KING, THOMAS, Lieutenant.
Volunteered to go to Plattsburgh,
September, 1814, and served 7 days
in Capt. Asaph Smith's Company.
Ref: Book 51, AGO Page 20.

KING, WILLIAM,   Fairfax.
Served from Aug. 8, 1812 in company of Capt. Joseph Beeman Jr.,
11th Regt. U. S. Inf. under Col. Ira
Clark. Ref: Hemenway's Vt. Gazetteer, Vol. 2, Page 402.

‡KINGON, ARNOLD.
Served in Capt. Eldridge's Company.
Pension Certificate No. 18125.

*KINGMAN, MITCHEL, Corporal.
Served from April 12 to May 20, 1814
in company of Capt. James Gray,
Jr., Sumner's Regt.

*KINGMAN, N. W., Lieutenant.
Served in 1 Regt. 3 Brig. 3 Div. Vt.
Militia.

KINGSBURY, JOSEPH,   Fairfax.
Volunteered to go to Plattsburgh,
September, 1814, serving 8 days in
Capt. Josiah Grout's Company. Ref:
Book 51, AGO Page 103.

*KINGSBURY, WILLIAM.
Served with Hospital Attendants, Vt.

*KINGSLAND, EDMUND,   Addison.
Volunteered to go to Plattsburgh,
September, 1814, and served 10 days

in Capt. William H. Pickett's Company, Col. Forsyth's Regt. Also served in Sumner's Regt. Vt. Militia.

KINGSLEY, ALPHA, Captain.
Appointed Captain 1st Inf. Jan. 20,
1813; honorably discharged June 15,
1815. Ref: Heitman's Historical Register & Dictionary USA.

KINGSLEY, BENJAMIN A.
Served in Capt. Chadwick's Company.
Ref: R. & L. 1812, AGO Page 32.

*KINGSLEY, EDMUND.
Served from April 12 to May 20, 1814
in Capt. George Fisher's Company,
Sumner's Regt.

‡*KINGSLEY, ENOS.
Served in Capt. Walker's Company,
Col. Fifield's Regt. Detached Militia
in U. S. service 3 months' and 14
days, 1812. Pension Certificate No.
632.

*KINGSLEY, JONATHAN JR., Lieuten-
ant, Woodstock. Served in 3 Regt.
(Williams') Vt. Militia.

*KINGSLEY, JOSEPH.
Served in Capt. Ormsbee's Company,
Col. Martindale's Regt. Detached
Militia in U. S. service 2 months
and 14 days, 1812.

KINGSLEY, SALMON,   St. Albans.
Enlisted April 23, 1813 for 1 year in
Capt. John Wires' Company, 30th
Regt. Ref: R. & L. 1812, AGO Page
40.

*KINNERSON, DAVID.
Served in 2 Regt. (Fifield's) Vt. Militia.

‡*KINNEY, ALVAN.
Served in Capt. Noyce's Company,
Col. Jonathan Williams' Regt. Detached Militia in U. S. service 2
months and 6 days, 1812. Pension
Certificate No. 15548. Pension Certificate of widow, Betsey, No. 5639.

KINNEY, DAVID,   Plainfield.
Volunteered to go to Plattsburgh,
September, 1814, and served 7 days
in Capt. James English's Company.
Ref: Book 52, AGO Pages 199 and
248.

‡KINNEY, EBENEZER.
Served in Capt. Adams' Company.
Pension Certificate No. 1413.

KINNEY, JAMES,   Barre.
Volunteered to go to Plattsburgh,
September, 1814, and served 9 days
in Capt. Warren Ellis' Company. Ref:
Book 52, AGO Pages 226 and 242.

‡*KINNEY, JOEL.
Served in Capt. Strait's Company,
Col. Martindale's Regt. Detached
Militia in U. S. service 2 months
and 13 days, 1812. Served in 1st
Regt. of Detached Militia in U. S.
service at Champlain from Nov. 18
to Nov. 19, 1812. Pension Certificate of widow, Clarissa, No. 3813.

*KINNEY, JOSEPH, Ensign,   Thetford.
Marched for Plattsburgh, September,
1814, and went as far as Bolton, Vt.,
serving 6 days in Capt. Salmon Howard's Company.

*KINNEY, NAHUM,   Braintree.
Served in Capt. Wright's Company,
Col. Fifield's Regt. Detached Militia
in U. S. service 6 months, 1812.
Marched to Plattsburgh September,
1814, serving 11 days in Capt. Lot
Hudson's Company. Ref: Book 52,
AGO Pages 24 and 26.

*KINNEY, NATHAN, Sergeant, Braintree.
Marched to Plattsburgh, September 10,
1814, serving 11 days in Capt. Lot
Hudson's Company. Also served in
2 Regt. (Fifield's) Vt. Militia. Ref:
Book 51, AGO Page 295; Book 52,
AGO Pages 24 and 33.

KINNEY, WILLIAM W. V.
Enlisted Sept. 23, 1813 in Capt.
Asahel Langworthy's Company, Col.
Isaac Clark's Volunteer Rifle Corps.
Ref: Book 52, AGO Page 260.

*KINNEY, ZACHEUS,   Fairfield.
Served in Capt. Taylor's Company,
Col. Wm. Williams' Regt. Detached
Militia in U. S. service 4 months and
24 days, 1812. Volunteered to go to
Plattsburgh, September, 1814, and
served 8 days in Capt. Josiah Grout's
Company. Ref: Book 51, AGO Pages
103 and 108.

*KINNY, JAMES, Sergeant.
Served in 1 Regt. (Judson's) Vt. Militia.

KINSLEY, BEN ALVAH,   Cambridge.
Enlisted April 27, 1813 for 1 year in
Capt. John Wires' Company, 30th
Regt.; was at the battle of Lacole
Mill, Odelltown, Canada, where he
was wounded. Ref: R. & L. 1812,
AGO Page 40; Hemenway's Vt. Ga-
zetteer, Vol. 2, Page 211.

KINSMAN, AARON,   Williamstown.
Volunteered to go to Plattsburgh,
September, 1814, and served in Capt.
David Robinson's Company. Ref: Book
52, AGO Page 114.

‡KINSMAN, ESBON,   Shrewsbury.
Volunteered to go to Plattsburgh,
September, 1814, and served 4 days
in Capt. Robert Reed's Company.
Pension Certificate No. 30945.

‡*KINSMAN, JAMES.
Served in Capt. Cross' Company, Col.
Martindale's Regt. Detached Militia
in U. S. service 2 months and 14
days, 1812. Pension Certificate No.
5578.

*KINSON, SYLVESTER A.
Served in 1 Regt. (Judson's) Vt.
Militia.

*KIRKUM, HENRY (or Harry) Cornwall.
Served from April 12 to April 21,
1814 in Capt. Shubael Wales' Com-
pany, Col. W. B. Sumner's Regt.
Volunteered to go to Plattsburgh,
September, 1814, and was at the
battle, serving in Capt. Edmund B.
Hill's Company, Sumner's Regt.

*KISER, ORIN.
Served in 2 Regt. (Fifield's Vt. Militia).

*KITCHELL, JOSEPH,   Bridport.
Served from April 12 to May 20, 1814
in company of Capt. James Gray Jr.,
Sumner's Regt.; volunteered to go
to Plattsburgh, September, 1814, and
served in same company.

*KITCHELL, MULFORD,   Bridport.
Volunteered to go to Plattsburgh,
September, 1814; no organization giv-
en. Ref: Book 51, AGO Page 39.

KITROUGH, JOHN, Corporal, Franklin
County. Enlisted June 13, 1812 for
5 years in Capt. White Youngs' Company, 15th Regt.; on Muster Roll
from Aug. 31 to Dec. 31, 1814. Ref:
R. & L. 1812, AGO Page 27.

KITTICUT, BEALS.
Enlisted Feb. 1, 1813 in Capt. Edgerton's Company, 11th Regt.; on
Pay Roll for January and February,
1813. Ref: R. & L. 1812, AGO Pages
2 and 3.

KIZER, PAUL.
Enlisted Aug. 16, 1813 for 1 year in
Capt. Gideon Spencer's Company, 30th
Regt.; on Muster Roll Dec. 30, 1813
to June 30, 1814. Ref: R. & L. 1812,
AGO Page 57.

KNAPP, CYRUS.
Served from Feb. 19, 1813 to May
18, 1813 in Lieut. V. R. Goodrich's
Company, 11th Regt. Ref: R. & L.
1812, AGO Pages 10 and 11.

*KNAPP, DANIEL.
Served from April 12 to April 21,
1814 in Capt. Eseck Sprague's Company, Sumner's Regt.

KNAPP, DAVID,   Barre.
Volunteered to go to Plattsburgh,
September, 1814, and served 7 days
in Capt. Frederick Griswold's Com-
pany, raised in Brookfield, Vt. Ref:
Book 52, AGO Pages 52 and 60.

*KNAPP, FRANCIS.
Served in Corning's Detachment, Vt.
Militia.

‡KNAPP, HENRY,   Waitsfield?
Volunteered to go to Plattsburgh
and served from Sept. 10 to Sept.
13, 1814 in Capt. Mathias Jones' Company. Pension Certificate of widow,
Lucy, No. 21162.

*KNAPP, JABEZ JR.,   Shoreham.
Volunteered to go to Plattsburgh,
September, 1814, and served 6 days
in Capt. Samuel Hand's Company.
Also served in Sumner's Regt. Vt.
Militia.

*KNAPP, JACOB JR.
Served from April 12 to May 20, 1814
in Capt. George Fisher's Company,
Sumner's Regt.

*KNAPP, JOHN.
Served in 1 Regt. (Martindale's) Vt.
Militia.

‡KNAPP, JOHN R.
Served in Capt. N. Parkins' Company, Pension Certificate No. 33518.

KNAPP, JOSHUA.
Enlisted March 19, 1813 in Capt.
John W. Weeks' Company, 11th Regt.
Ref: R. & L. 1812, AGO Page 4.

KNAPP, MASON,   Berlin.
Volunteered to go to Plattsburgh,
September, 1814, and served 7 days
in Capt. Frederick Griswold's Com-
pany, raised in Brookfield, Vt. Ref:
Book 52, AGO Pages 52 and 60.

*KNAPP, PETER.
Served from June 11 to June 14,
1813 in Capt. John M. Eldridge's
Company, 1st Regt. 2nd Brig. 3rd
Div.

*KNAPP, RANDALL, Drummer.
Served in Capt. Morrill's Company,
Col. Fifield's Regt. Detached Militia
in U. S. service 3 months and 17
days, 1812.

‡*KNAPP, WILLIAM, Sergeant.
Served in Capt. Prentiss' Company,
Col. Dixon's Regt. Detached Militia
in U. S. service 1 month and 23
days, 1813. Also served in Capt.
Bullard's Company. Pension Certificate No. 26429.

*KNEELAND, BARTHOLOMEW, Water-
bury. Volunteered to go to Plattsburgh, September. 1814, and served
11 days in Capt. George Atkins' Company, 4 Regt. (Peck's).

KNICKERBOCKER, HENRY.
Born in Canaan, Conn.; age 18 years;
5 feet 7 inches tall; light complexion;
brown hair; blue eyes; farmer. Enlisted at Addison March 24, 1814
for period of the war and served in
Capt. William Miller's Company and
Capt. Gideon Spencer's' Company,
30th Regt.; discharged at Burlington,
Vt. in 1815. Ref: R. & L. 1812, AGO
Pages 54, 55, 57.

KNIGHT, AMAZIAH (or Knights) Sergeant. Served in Capt. Weeks' Company, 11th Regt.; on Pay Roll for
January and February, 1813. Ref:
R. & L. 1812, AGO Page 5.

KNIGHT, ELIJAH (or Knights)
Served in Capt. Burnap's Company,
Col. Jonathan Williams' Regt. Detached Militia in U. S. service 2
months and 13 days, 1812. Ref: Book
53, AGO Page 14.

*KNIGHT, ELISHA.
Served in 3 Regt. (Williams') Vt.
Militia.

*KNIGHT, ISAAC.
Served in Capt. Walker's Company,
Col. Fifield's Regt. Detached Militia
in U. S. service 6 months and 3
days, 1812. Served from May 10,
1813 to May 9, 1814 in Capt. Simeon
Wright's Company. Ref: R. & L.
1812, AGO Page 51.

‡KNIGHT, JOHN.
Served in Capt. Pettis' Company.
Pension Certificate No. 14977.

‡KNIGHT, JOHN.
Served in Capt. Hoyt's Company. Pension Certificate No. 32849.

*KNIGHT, JOHN, Ensign.
Served in Corning's Detachment, Vt.
Militia.

*KNIGHT, JOHN.
Served in Capt. Adams' Company,
Col. Jonathan Williams' Regt. Detached Militia in U. S. service 2
months and 7 days, 1812.

*KNIGHT, JOHN (or Knights) Sergeant.
Served in Capt. O. Lowry's Company, Col. Wm. Williams' Regt. Detached Militia in U. S. service 4
months and 26 days, 1812; stationed
at Swanton Falls.

*KNIGHT, JOHN JR., Lieutenant.
Served in 4 Regt. (Williams') Vt.
Militia.

*KNIGHT, JOHN C. (or G?) Lieutenant,
Waterbury. Volunteered to go to
Plattsburgh, September, 1814, and was
at the battle, serving 11 days in
Capt. George Atkins' Company, 4
Regt. (Peck's).

KNIGHT, JOSIAH W., Musician.
Served from Feb. 6 to Feb. 28, 1813
in Capt. Samuel H. Holly's Company, 11th Regt. Ref: R. & L. 1812,
AGO Page 25.

KNIGHT, LUTHER,   Shrewsbury.
Volunteered to go to Plattsburgh,
September, 1814, and served 4 days
in Capt. Robert Reed's Company.
Ref: Book 52, AGO Pages 138 and
140.

‡KNIGHT, MILTON.
Served in Capt. Atkins' Company,
4 Regt. (Peck's) Vt. Militia. Pension Certificate of widow, Nancy, No.
10156.

KNIGHT, NATHANIEL.
Served in Capt. Samuel H. Holly's
Company, 11th Regt.; on Pay Roll
for January and February, 1813.
Ref: R. & L. 1812, AGO Page 25.

KNIGHT, SIMEON, Captain.
Appointed Captain 1 Inf. Jan. 20,
1813; Colonel Quartermaster General
Feb. 7, 1815; honorably discharged
June 15, 1815. Ref: Heitman's His-
torical Register & Dictionary USA.

‡*KNIGHT, WILLIAM.
Served from June 11 to June 14,
1813 in Lieut. Bates' Company, 1
Regt. (Judson's). Pension Certificate
of widow, Abigail, No. 29920.

*KNOTTON, BENJAMIN, Corporal.
Served from Oct. 14 to Nov. 17,
1813 in Capt. Asahel Scoville's Company, Col. Clark's Rifle Corps.

‡*KNOWLS, ADOLPHUS.
Served in Col. Wm. Williams' Regt.
Capt. Pettis' Company, Detached
Militia in U. S. service 4 months
and 17 days, 1812. Also served in
Tyler's Regt. Vt. Militia. Pension
Certificate of widow, Betsey, No.
22903.

KNOWLS, JOSEPH (or Knowles).
Served from Feb. 7, to Feb. 28, 1813
in Capt. Charles Follett's Company,
11th Regt. Ref: R. & L. 1812, AGO
Page 12.

‡*KNOWLTON, BENJAMIN, Enosburgh. Enlisted April 12, 1814 in Capt. Shubael Wales' Company, Col. W. B. Sumner's Regt.; transferred to Capt. Salmon Foster's Company, Col. Sumner's Regt. April 13, 1814 and served to April 21, 1814. Also served in Capt. A. Scoville's Company. Pension Certificate of widow, Polly, No. 22925.

‡KNOWLTON, SEWALL. Served in Captain Culver's Company. Pension Certificate of widow, Deborah, No. 35167.

*KNOWLTON, THOMAS, Corporal. Served in Capt. Needham's Company, Col. Martindale's Regt. Detached Militia in U. S. service 2 months and 14 days, 1812.

KNOWLTON, THOMAS,   Sudbury. Volunteered to go to Plattsburgh, September, 1814, and served 6 days in Capt. Thomas Hall's Company. Ref: Book 52, AGO Page 122.

‡*KNOWLTON, WILLIAM. Served in Capt. Morrill's Company, Col. Fifield's Regt. Detached Militia in U. S. service 6 months and 5 days, 1812. Pension Certificate No. 5878. Pension Certificate of widow, Abby S., No. 32149.

KNOX, DANIEL,   Franklin County. Volunteered to go to Plattsburgh Sept. 11, 1814 and served in 15th or 22nd Regt. Ref: Hemenway's Vt. Gazetteer, Vol. 2, Page 391.

KNOX, DAVID, Captain,   Tunbridge. Volunteered to go to Plattsburgh, September, 1814, and went as far as Bolton, Vt. serving 4 days. Ref: Book 52, AGO Pages 93 and 116.

*KNOX, JOHN, Lieutenant,   Shoreham. Served in Capt. Robbins' Company, Col. Wm. Williams' Regt. Detached Militia in U. S. service 4 months and 29 days, 1812. Served at Vergennes under Capt. James Gray Jr. from April 12 to May 20, 1814. Volunteered to go to Plattsburgh, September, 1814 and served 6 days in Capt. Samuel Hand's Company. Appointed Ensign in 26th Regt. June 25, 1814 and 3rd Lieutenant Oct. 1, 1814. Ref: Rev. J. F. Goodhue's History of Shoreham, Page 107; Governor and Council, Vt., Vol. 6, Page 477.

KORTY, HENRY,   Franklin County. Volunteered to go to Plattsburgh Sept. 11, 1814 and served in 15th or 22nd Regt. Ref: Hemenway's Vt. Gazetteer, Vol. 2, Page 391.

*KULER, LOT (or Culver?) Served in Sumner's Regt. Vt. Militia.

KULLER, ALLIN. Served from June 11 to June 14, 1813 in Capt. Ithiel Stone's Company, 1st Regt. 2nd Brig. 3rd Div. Ref: R. & L. 1812, AGO Page 44.

*KYES, JOSEPH. Served in 2 Regt. (Fifield's) Vt. Militia.

KYLE, AMOS. Served in Capt. Benjamin S. Edgerton's Company, 11th Regt.; on Pay Roll for September and October, 1812 and January and February, 1813. Ref: R. & L. 1812, AGO Pages 1 and 2.

*LABAIR, JOSEPH. Served in 4 Regt. (Williams') Vt. Militia.

LABARE, JOSEPH. Served in Capt. Weeks' Company, 11th Regt.; on Pay Roll for January and February, 1813. Ref: R. & L. 1812, AGO Page 5.

LABARE, PETER. Enlisted Jan. 18, 1813 in Capt. Weeks' Company, 11th Regt.; on Pay Roll for January and February, 1813. Ref: R. & L. 1812, AGO Page 5.

LACCOUR, VINCENT, Musician. Enlisted May 14, 1812 for 5 years in Capt. White Youngs' Company, 15th Regt.; on Muster Roll from Aug. 31, 1814 to Dec. 31, 1814. Ref: R. & L. 1812, AGO Page 27.

LACK, JACOB. Served in Capt. Charles Bennett's Company, Col. Dixon's Regt. Detached Militia in U. S. service 1 month and 23 days, 1813. Ref: Book 53, AGO Page 108.

LACKEY, ISHAM. Enlisted May 21, 1813 for 1 year in Capt. James Taylor's Company, 30th Regt.; on Muster Roll Nov. 30 to Dec. 31, 1813. Ref: R. & L. 1812, AGO Page 52.

LACKEY, ISOM. Served from May 21, 1813 to May 21, 1814 in Capt. Gideon Spencer's Company and Capt. James Taylor's Company, 30th Regt. Ref: R. & L. 1812, AGO Pages 57 and 59.

*LACKEY, LEVI. Enlisted Sept. 25, 1813 and served 1 month and 23 days in Capt. Amos Robinson's Company, Col. Dixon's Regt.

*LACKEY, SIMEON. Enlisted Sept. 25, 1813 and served 1 month and 23 days in Capt. Amos Robinson's Company, Col. Dixon's Regt.

LACKEY, THOMAS,   Swanton. Served from July 15 to Dec. 8, 1813 in Capt. V. R. Goodrich's Company, 11th Regt.; was in battle of Lundy's Lane. Ref: Hemenway's Vt. Gazetteer, Vol. 2, Page 444.

*LACLAIR, FRANCIS. Served in Capt. Needham's Company, Col. Martindale's Regt. Detached Militia in U. S. service 1 month and 19 days, 1812.

*LACLAIR, JOSHUA. Served in Capt. Needham's Company, Col. Martindale's Regt. Detached Militia in U. S. service 2 months and 14 days, 1812.

LACOUSE, WILLIAM.
Enlisted Aug. 14, 1812 in Capt.
Phineas Williams' Company, 11th
Regt.; on Pay Roll to May 31, 1813.
Ref: R. & L. 1812, AGO Page 14.

*LACY, SAMUEL, Lieutenant.
Served in 1 Regt. (Martindale's) Vt.
Militia.

LADD, ALPHEUS,   Thetford.
Volunteered to go to Plattsburgh,
September, 1814, serving in Capt.
Joseph Barrett's Company. Ref: Book
52, AGO Pages 41 and 100.

‡*LADD, ASA,   Enosburgh.
Served in Capt. Kendall's Company,
Col. Wm. Williams' Regt. Detached
Militia in U. S. service 4 months
and 23 days, 1812. Pension Certifi-
cate of widow, Lovisa, No. 3365.

LADD, ASA JR.,   Fairfield.
Served in Capt. George W. Kindall's
Company, 4 Regt. (Williams') 6
months in 1812. Ref: R. & L. 1812,
AGO Pages 37, 38, 39; Book 51, AGO
Page 199.

LADD, ELSWORTH.
Served in Capt. George W. Kindall's
Company, 4 Regt. (Williams'); on
Pay Roll to Sept. 10, 1812. Ref: R.
& L. 1812, AGO Page 37.

‡*LADD, FREDERIC.
Served in Capt. Bingham's Company,
Col. Jonathan Williams' Regt. De-
tached Militia in U. S. service 2
months and 9 days, 1812. Pension
Certificate No. 7705.

*LADD, JOHN, Corporal, Lansingburgh.
Served from Oct. 2, 1814 to June 19,
1815 in Capt. Taylor's Company, 30th
Inf. Also served with Hospital At-
tendants, Vt. Ref: R. & L. 1812,
AGO Page 23.

*LADD, JOSEPH,   Fairfield.
Served in Capt. Kendall's Company,
Col. Wm. Williams' Regt. Detached
Militia in U. S. service 4 months and
23 days, 1812. Also served in Lieut.
V. R. Goodrich's Company, 11th
Regt.; on Pay Roll for January and
February, 1813. Ref: R. & L. 1812,
AGO Page 11.

*LADD, MOSES.
Served in 2 Regt. (Fifield's) Vt. Militia.

LADD, OTIS.
Served from May 1 to June 30, 1814
in Capt. Haig's Corps of Light Dragoons. Ref: R. & L. 1812, AGO
Page 20.

LADD, ROGER,   Pittsford.
Volunteered to go to Plattsburgh,
September, 1814, serving 8 days in
Capt. Caleb Hendee's Company. Ref:
Book 52, AGO Page 125.

‡LADUE, ABRAM.
Served in Capt. Reynold's Company.
Pension Certificate No. 15939.

‡LADUE, SAMUEL.
Served in Capt. Reynold's Company.
Pension Certificate No. 19070.

*LAFFERTY, JAMES.
Served in Capt. Lowry's Company,
Col. Wm. Williams' Regt. Detached
Militia in U. S. service 4 months
and 26 days, 1812.

LAFLAME, JOHN,   Highgate.
Served from Sept. 1, 1812 in Capt.
Conrade Saxe's Company, Col. Wm.
Williams' Regt. Ref: Hemenway's
Vt. Gazetteer, Vol. 2, Page 420.

‡*LAFLIN, ABEL,   Georgia or Fairfax.
Enlisted Sept. 25, 1813 and served
1 month and 23 days as a fifer in
Capt. Jesse Post's Company, Col.
Dixon's Regt.; volunteered to go to
Plattsburgh, September, 1814, serving
8 days in same company. Served
in Capt. Joseph Beeman's Company
in 1813 and 1814. Ref: Hemenway's
Vt. Gazetteer, Vol. 2, Page 402. Pension Certificate of widow, Pattie, No.
4979.

LAFLIN, HENRY.
Served from May 1 to June 30, 1814
in Capt. Haig's Corps of Light Dragoons. Ref: R. & L. 1812, AGO
Page 20.

*LAFLIN, JOHN.
Enlisted Sept. 25, 1813 in Capt.
Jesse Post's Company, Dixon's Regt.

LAFURGY, WILLIAM.
Served from May 1 to June 30, 1814
in Capt. Alexander Brooks' Corps of
Artillery. Ref: R. & L. 1812, AGO
Page 31.

*LAGGAN, MATHEW.
Served in 1 Regt. (Martindale's) Vt.
Militia.

LAHAY, THOMAS,   Franklin County.
Volunteered to go to Plattsburgh
Sept. 11, 1814 and served in 15th or
22nd Regt. Ref: Hemenway's Vt. Gazetteer, Vol. 2, Page 392.

LAILIN, SILAS W.
Served from Oct. 11 to Oct. 17, 1813
in Capt. John Munson's Company,
3 Regt. Ref: R. & L. 1812, AGO
Page 36.

*LAISDEL, EZARIAH.
Served from Sept. 25 to Sept. 30,
1813 in Capt. Amos Robinson's Company, Dixon's Regt.

LAISDEL, SALAN.
Served from Sept. 25 to Sept. 28,
1813 in Capt. Amos Robinson's Company, Dixon's Regt. Ref: Book 52,
AGO Page 271.

LAISDELL, BENJAMIN.
Served from May 10, 1813 to May
16, 1814 in Capt. Gideon Spencer's
Company and Capt. James Taylor's
Company, 30th Regt. Ref: R. & L.
1812, AGO Pages 57 and 59.

LAITON, WILLIAM,   Schohani, N. Y.
Served from Sept. 10, 1814 to June
19, 1815 in Capt. Taylor's Company,
30th Inf. Ref: R. & L. 1812, AGO
Page 23.

*LAKE, HENRY.
Served in Capt. Hotchkiss' Company, Col. Martindale's Regt. Detached Militia in U. S. service 1 month and 20 days, 1812.

LAKE, JAMES.
Enlisted Aug. 6, 1813 for 5 years in company of late Capt. J. Brooks, commanded by Lieut. John I. Cromwell, Corps of U. S. Artillery; on Muster Roll from April 30, 1814 to June 30, 1814. Ref: R. & L. 1812, AGO Page 18.

*LAKE, JOHN.
Served in Capt. Hotchkiss' Company, Col. Martindale's Regt. Detached Militia in U. S. service 2 months and 13 days, 1812.

*LAKE, WILLARD.
Served in Capt. Brown's Company, Col. Martindale's Regt. Detached Militia in U. S. service 16 days, 1812.

LAKIN, SIMEON, Sergeant.
Served in Capt. Benjamin Bradford's Company; on Muster Roll from May 31 to Aug. 31, 1813. Ref: R. & L. 1812, AGO Page 26.

LAMB, ALPHEUS.
Volunteered to go to Plattsburgh, September, 1814, and served 7 days in Capt. Asaph Smith's Company. Ref: Book 51, AGO Page 20.

*LAMB, ASA.
Served in Capt. Rogers' Company, Col. Fifield's' Regt. Detached Militia in U. S. service 2 months and 21 days, 1812.

LAMB, CHARLES 2nd,   Granville.
Volunteered to go to Plattsburgh, September, 1814, and served 7 days in Capt. Asaph Smith's Company. Ref: Book 51, AGO Page 20.

*LAMB, ELIJAH.
Served in Capt. Walker's Company, Col. Fifield's Regt. Detached Militia in U. S. service 6 months.

*LAMB, HEMAN,   Georgia.
Served in Capt. Dorrance's Company, Col. Wm. Williams' Regt. Detached Militia in U. S. service 4 months and 24 days, 1812.

*LAMB, HERMAN.
Served in Dixon's Regt. Vt. Militia.

LAMB, JOHN.
Served from May 23, 1813 to May 23, 1814 in Capt. James Taylor's Company and Capt. Gideon Spencer's Company, 30th Regt. Ref: R. & L. 1812, AGO Pages 52, 57, 59.

LAMB, JONATHAN,   Granville.
Volunteered to go to Plattsburgh, September, 1814, and served 7 days in Capt. Asaph Smith's Company. Ref: Book 51, AGO Pages 20 and 21.

LAMB, ORMOND.
Served in Capt. L. Robinson's Company, Col. Dixon's Regt. Detached Militia in U. S. service 2 months, 1813. Ref: Book 53, AGO Page 110.

*LAMB, OSMUND,   Georgia.
Volunteered to go to Plattsburgh, September, 1814, and served 8 days in Capt. Jesse Post's Company, Dixon's Regt.

LAMB, REUBEN,   Barre?
Volunteered to go to Plattsburgh, September, 1814, and served 7 days in Capt. Asaph Smith's Company. Ref: Book 51, AGO Page 20.

‡LAMB, SAMUEL,   Braintree.
Marched to Plattsburgh, Sept. 10, 1814 and served in Capt. Lot Hudson's Company. Pension Certificate of widow, Polly, No. 18772.

LAMBERT, HEZEKIAH H.
Served from Feb. 20, 1813 to May 19, 1813 in Capt. Charles Follett's Company, 11th Regt. Ref: R. & L. 1812, AGO Page 13.

*LAMBERT, SOLOMON.
Served in 3 Regt. (Williams') Vt. Militia.

‡LAMKIN, ISAAC.
Served in Capt. Stewart's Company. Pension Certificate No. 13769.

*LAMPHEAR, DAVID.
Served in Capt. Strait's Company, Col. Martindale's Regt. Detached Militia in U. S. service 2 months and 13 days, 1812.

LAMPHEAR, JABEZ.
Volunteered to go to Plattsburgh, September, 1814, and served 4 days in Capt. Aaron Kidder's Company. Ref: Book 52, AGO Page 65.

LAMPHERE, JOHN,   Swanton.
Served in Lieut. V. R. Goodrich's Company, 11th Regt.; on Pay Roll for January and February, 1813. Ref: R. & L. 1812, AGO Page 11.

‡LAMPHERE, LYMAN.
Served in Capt. Waterman's Company. Pension Certificate of widow, Susan, No. 10737.

LAMPHIER, CHARLES.
Served in Capt. Phineas Williams' Company, 11th Regt.; on Pay Roll for January and February, 1813. Ref: R. & L. 1812, AGO Page 15.

LAMPHIER, JASON.
Served from April 21, 1813 to April 27, 1814 in Capt. Gideon Spencer's Company and Capt. James Taylor's Company, 30th Regt. Ref: R. & L. 1812, AGO Pages 52, 57, 59.

LAMPHIER, LUKE.
Served from Jan. 1, 1813 to Feb. 7, 1813 in Capt. Phineas Williams' Company, 11th Regt. Ref: R. & L. 1812, AGO Page 15.

LAMPHIER, ROSWELL.
Enlisted Dec. 22, 1812 in Capt. Phineas Williams' Company, 11th Regt.; on Pay Roll to May 31, 1813. Ref: R. & L. 1812, AGO Page 14.

LAMPHIER, SHUBAL,   Mendon.
Served from Feb. 2, 1813 to May 1, 1813 in Capt. Phineas Williams' Company, 11th Regt. Ref: R. & L. 1812, AGO Page 14.

‡LAMPHIRE, WILLIAM.
Served in Capt. Arnold's Company.
Pension Certificate No. 34381.

*LAMPKIN, NEWCOM, Captain.
Served in 1 Regt. 3 Brig. 3 Div. Vt.
Militia.

LAMPMAN, ABRAHAM.
Served from Feb. 2 to Feb. 28, 1813
in Capt. Samuel H. Holly's Company, 11th Regt. Ref: R. & L. 1812,
AGO Page 25.

‡*LAMPSON, HARVEY,   Randolph.
Volunteered to go to Plattsburgh,
September, 1814, and served in Capt.
Lebbeus Egerton's Company. Pension
Certificate No. 30610.

*LAMPSON, JOHN,   Pittsford.
Served in Capt. Scovell's Company,
Col. Martindale's Regt. Detached
Militia in U. S. service 2 months
and 21 days, 1812. Served from May
4, 1813 to May 3, 1814 in Capt.
Simeon Wright's Company.

LAMPSON, JOHN JR..
Volunteered to go to Plattsburgh,
September, 1814, and served 8 days
in Capt. Caleb Hendee's Company.
Ref: Book 52, AGO Page 125.

*LAMPSON, JOSEPH.
Served in Col. Wm. Williams' Regt.
Detached Militia in U. S. service 4
months and 26 days, 1812.

LAMPSON, SILAS,   Poultney.
Volunteered to go to Plattsburgh,
September, 1814 and served 2 days
in Capt. Briant Ransom's Company.
Ref: Book 52, AGO Page 147.

*LAMPSON, THOMAS,   Randolph.
Volunteered to go to Plattsburgh,
September, 1814, and served in Capt.
Lebbeus Egerton's Company.

*LAMPSON, WILLIAM JR., Corporal.
Served in Sumner's Regt. Vt. Militia.

*LAMSON, JOEL.
Served in Tyler's Regt. Vt. Militia.

LAMSON. JOSEPH,   Plainfield.
Volunteered to go to Plattsburgh
in September, 1814; no organization
given. Ref: Book 52, AGO Page 195.

LAMSON, SAMUEL,   Franklin County.
Volunteered to go to Plattsburgh
Sept. 11, 1814 and served in 15th or
22nd Regt. Ref: Hemenway's Vt.
Gazetteer, Vol. 2, Page 391.

LANDER, DAVID,   Randolph.
Volunteered to go to Plattsburgh,
September, 1814, and served in Capt.
Lebbeus Egerton's Company. Ref:
Book 52, AGO Page 82.

LANDERS, BENJAMIN.   Shoreham.
Volunteered to go to Plattsburgh,
September, 1814, and served 6 days
in Capt. Nathaniel North's Company
of Cavalry. Ref: Rev. J. F. Goodhue's History of Shoreham, Page 107.

LANDERS, LEVI,   Shoreham.
Volunteered to go to Plattsburgh,
September, 1814, and served 6 days

in Capt. Samuel Hand's Company.
Ref: Rev. J. F. Goodhue's History
of Shoreham, Page 108.

*LANDON, ALSON, Sergeant.
Served in Capt. Pettes' Company,
Col. Wm. Williams' Regt. Detached
Militia in U. S. service 4 months
and 17 days, 1812.

*LANDON. DAVID.
Served in Capt. Edgerton's Company,
Vt. Volunteers.

*LANDON, HORACE.
Served from April 12 to April 21,
1814 in Capt. Shubael Wales' Company, Col. W. B. Sumner's Regt.

LANDON, JAMES.
Served from May 1 to June 30, 1814
in Capt. Haig's Corps of Light Dragoons. Ref: R. & L. 1812, AGO
Page 20.

‡LANDON, JESSE.
Served in Capt. Keeler's Company.
Pension Certificate No. 34938.

‡LANDON, JULIUS C.
Served in Capt. Kinney's Company.
Pension Certificate No. 25327.

*LANDON. THOMAS.
Served from April 12 to April 21,
1814 in Capt. Shubael Wales' Company, Col. W. B. Sumner's Regt.

*LANDRUS. LEVI (or Landers?)
Served in Sumner's Regt. Vt. Militia.

*LANE, AMOS.
Served in Capt. Briggs' Company,
Col. Jonathan Williams' Regt. Detached Militia in U. S. service 2
months and 13 days, 1812.

LANE, CHARLES C.
Served in Capt. Charles Follett's Com-
pany, 11th Regt.; on Pay Roll for
January and February, 1812. Ref:
R. & L. 1812, AGO Page 12.

*LANE, DAVID.
Served in Capt. Taylor's Company,
Col. Fifield's Regt. Detached Militia
in U. S. service 2 months and 21
days, 1812.

LANE. GEORGE.
Served from May 1 to June 30, 1814
in Alexander Parris' Company of
Artificers. Ref: R. & L. 1812, AGO
Page 24.

*LANE, HARRY.
Served in 1 Regt. (Judson's) Vt.
Militia.

‡LANE. HENRY.
Served in Capt. H. Mayo's Company.
Pension Certificate of widow, Susan
E., No. 28232.

LANE, JEDEDIAH,   Jericho.
Enlisted May 1, 1813 for 1 year in
Capt. Simeon Wright's Company. Also
took part in the battle of Platts-
burgh, September, 1814. Ref: R. &
L. 1812, AGO Page 51; History of
Jericho, Page 142.

LANE, JOB, Teamster, Cornwall.
Volunteered to go to Plattsburgh,
September, 1814, and served in Capt.
Edmund B. Hill's Company, Sumner's
Regt. Ref: Rev. Lyman Mathews'
History of Cornwall, Page 345.

LANE, LEVI.
Served from Feb. 19 to Feb. 28, 1813
and from March 30 to June 29, 1813
in Lieut. V. R. Goodrich's Company,
11th Regt. Ref: R. & L. 1812, AGO
Pages 10 and 11.

LANE, STEPHEN, Jericho.
Took part in the Battle of Plattsburgh. Ref: History of Jericho, Page
142.

*LANE, STEPHEN B.
Served in 3 Regt. (Tyler's) Vt. Militia.

LANE, WILLIAM, Cornwall.
Volunteered to go to Plattsburgh,
September, 1814, and was at the
battle, serving in Capt. Edmund B.
Hill's Company, Sumner's Regt. Ref:
Book 51, AGO Page 13.

*LANGDON, HIRAM.
Served from April 12 to April 21,
1814 in Capt. Othniel Jewett's Company, Sumner's Regt.

‡*LANGMAID, SAMUEL, Danville.
Served in Capt. Morrill's Company,
Col. Fifield's Regt. Detached Militia
in U. S. service 2 months and 18
days, 1812. Pension Certificate No.
7050.

‡LANGMAID, SOLOMON , Danville.
Served from May 1 to June 30, 1814
in Capt. Haig's Corps of Light Dragoons. Also served in Capt. Hall's
Company. Pension Certificate No.
7285.

‡*LANGMAID, WLLIAM.
Served in Capt. Morrill's Company,
Col. Fifield's Regt. Detached Militia
in U. S. service 6 months and 5
days, 1812. Pension Certificate of
widow, Laura A., No. 17558.

*LANGWORTHY, ASAHEL, Captain, St.
Albans. Appointed Captain of company of Riflemen in U. S. service
under command of Col. Isaac Clark.
Volunteered to go to Plattsburgh
and was at the battle Sept. 11, 1814,
serving in Capt. Samuel H. Farnsworth's Company.

LAPELL, BRIGHAM.
Served in Capt. Langworthy's Com-
pany, Col. Dixon's Regt. Detached
Militia in U. S. service 1 month and
12 days, 1813. Ref: Book 53, AGO
Page 110.

*LAPHAM, HORACE.
Served from April 12 to May 20,
1814 in Capt. George Fisher's Company, Sumner's Regt.

LAQUE, JOSEPH.
Served from April 22, 1813 to April
25, 1814 in Capt. Simeon Wright's
Company. Ref: R. & L. 1812, AGO
Page 51.

*LARD, JOHN.
Served in Sumner's Regt. Vt. Militia.

LARD, JONAS.
Enlisted April 13, 1813 for duration
of the war and served in Capt. Wm.
Miller's Company and Capt. Gideon
Spencer's Company, 30th Regt. Ref:
R. & L. 1812, AGO Pages 54 and 57.

LARGLEY, STEPHEN.
Served in Capt. Benjamin Bradford's
Company; on Muster Roll from May
31 to Aug. 31, 1813; joined by trans-
fer July 22, 1813. Ref: R. & L. 1812,
AGO Page 26.

LARKINS, RUSSEL, Franklin County.
Volunteered to go to Plattsburgh
Sept. 11, 1814 and served in 15th or
22nd Regt. Ref: Hemenway's Vt.
Gazetteer, Vol. 2, Page 392.

LAROUSE, WILLIAMS.
Served from Nov. 1, 1812 to Feb. 28,
1813 in Capt. Phineas Williams' Company, 11th Regt. Ref: R. & L. 1812,
AGO Page 15.

LARRABEE, BENJAMIN, Shoreham.
Volunteered to go to Plattsburgh,
September, 1814, and served 6 days
in Capt. Samuel Hand's Company.
Ref: Rev. J. F. Goodhue's History
of Shoreham, Page 107.

*LARRABEE, CHARLES H.
Enlisted Sept. 25, 1813 and served
1 month and 23 days in Capt. Martin
D. Follett's Company, Col. Dixon's
Regt.

*LARRABEE, LYMAN, Sergeant.
Enlisted Sept. 25, 1813 and served
1 month and 23 days in Capt. Follett's Company, Col. Dixon's Regt.

‡*LARRABEE, WILLIAM.
Enlisted Sept. 25, 1813 and served
1 month and 23 days in Capt. Thomas Waterman's Company, Col. Dixon's
Regt. Pension Certificate No. 24609.

LARU, GEORGE.
Served as a carpenter in Alexander
Parris' Company of Artificers; on Pay
Roll for May and June, 1814. Ref:
R. & L. 1812, AGO Page 24.

LARY, SAMUEL, Lieutenant.
Served in 1st Regt. of Detached Militia of Vermont in U. S. service at
Champlain from Nov. 18 to Nov. 19,
1812.

*LASDEL, LABEN.
Served in Dixon's Regt. Vermont
Militia.

‡LASELL, AZARIAH.
Served in Capt. Phelps' Company.
Pension Certificate of widow, Joanna,
No. 24737.

*LASELL, BINGHAM.
Enlisted Sept. 25, 1813 in Capt.
Jesse Post's Company, Dixon's Regt.;
transferred to Capt. Asahel Lang-
worthy's Company, Col. Clark's Rifle
Corps Oct. 8, 1813.

‡LASELL, LABAN.
Served in Capt. Farnsworth' Company. Pension Certificate of widow,
Hepsebeth, No. 28102.

*LATHAM, BENJAMIN.
Enlisted Sept. 25, 1813 and served
1 month and 23 days in Capt. Amos
Robinson's Company, Col. Dixon's
Regt.

LATHAM, JAMES,   Waitsfield.
Volunteered to go to Plattsburgh,
September, 1814, and served 4 days
in Capt. Mathias S. Jones' Company. Ref: Book 52, AGO Pages
170 and 207.

*LATHAM, JOSEPH,   St. Johnsbury.
Served in Capt. Wheeler's Company,
Col. Fifield's Regt. Detached Militia
in U. S. service 3 months and 19
days, 1812 at Derby, Vt.

*LATHAM, SIMEON.
Served in Capt. Adams' Company,
Col. Jonathan Williams' Regt. Detached Militia in U. S. service 2
months and 7 days, 1812.

*LATHE, ASA,   Salem, Vt.
Served in Capt. Hiram Mason's Company, Col. Fifield's Regt. Detached
Militia in U. S. service 6 months
and 26 days, 1812; was at the battles
at Bridgewater and Fort Erie, in the
latter of which he received a wound;
was the father of Moses and David
Lathe, both of whom served in the
war. Ref: Book 52, AGO Page 2;
Hemenway's Vt. Gazetteer, Vol. 3,
Pages 307 and 308.

*LATHE, DAVID,   Salem. Vt.
Served in Capt. Wheeler's Company,
Col. Fifield's Regt. Detached Militia
in U. S. service 3 months and 16
days, 1812. Served from Feb. 11 to
May 10, 1813 in Capt. Edgerton's
Company, 11th Regt.; was in the
battles at Chippewa and Williamsburgh and was wounded at the latter; was a son of Asa Lathe. Ref:
R. & L. 1812, AGO Page 3; Hemenway's Vt. Gazetteer, Vol. 3, Pages
307 and 308.

LATHE, MOSES,   Salem, Vt.
Served at the Battle of Plattsburgh;
was a son of Asa Lathe. Ref: Hemenway's Vt. Gazetteer, Vol. 3, Pages
307 and 308.

LATHROP, ADGATE,   Pittsford.
Volunteered to go to Plattsburgh,
September, 1814, and served 8 days
as a waggoner in Capt. Caleb Hendee's Company. Ref: Book 52, AGO
Page 125.

*LATHROP, CHARLES.
Served in Col. Fifield's Regt. Detached Militia in U. S. service 6 months,
1812.

*LATHROP, ERASTUS (or Lothrop) Sergeant. Served from Sept. 25 to Nov.
6, 1813 in Capt. Amos Robinson's
Company, Dixon's Regt.

*LATHROP, GIDEON C., Corporal.
Served from June 11 to June 14,
1813 in Capt. Moses Jewett's Company, 1st Regt. 2nd Brig. 3rd Div.
Also served as a Corporal in 4 Regt.
(Williams') Vt. Militia.

‡LATHROP, HOWLAND.
Served in Capt. Kies' Company. Pension Certificate No. 31062.

*LATHROP, JOHN (or Lothrop) Burlington. Served from June 11 to
June 14, 1813 in Capt. Moses Jewett's
Company, 1st Regt. 2nd Brig. 3rd
Div. Volunteered to go to Plattsburgh,
September, 1814, and served in Capt.
Henry Mayo's Company.

LATHROP, NATHAN.
Served in Capt. Barns' Company,
Col. Wm. Williams' Regt. Detached
Militia in U. S. service 5 months,
1812. Ref: Book 53, AGO Page 67;
Vol. 51, Vt. State Papers, Page 115.

*LATHROP, NATHANIEL.
Served in 3 Regt. (Tyler's) Vt. Militia.

LATHROP, RUSSELL.
Enlisted Sept. 25, 1813 and served
1 month and 17 days in Capt. Amos
Robinson's Company, Col. Dixon's
Regt. Ref: Book 52, AGO Page 271;
Book 53, AGO Page 113.

LATHROP, URBANA.
Volunteered to go to Plattsburgh,
September, 1814, and served in company of Capt. Joel Barnes of Chelsea. Ref: Book 52, AGO Pages 77
and 78.

*LATHROP, URIEL or AZARIAH?
Served in Capt. Hotchkiss' Company, Col. Martindale's Regt. Detached Militia in U. S. service 2
months and 13 days, 1812.

LATHROP, WELLS.
Served from Jan. 6, 1813 to July 1,
1813 in Lieut. Wm. S. Foster's Company, 11th Regt.; served as a musician. Ref: R. & L. 1812, AGO
Page 6.

LATHROPE, MIJAH, Sergeant.
Enlisted April 26, 1813 for 1 year in
Capt. Daniel Farrington's Company,
30th Regt. (also commanded by
Capt. Simeon Wright); on Muster
Roll from March 1 to April 30, 1814.
Ref: R. & L. 1812, AGO Page 50.

*LAUGHLIN, FREDERICK (or Laflin)
Georgia or St. Albans. Served in
Capt. Willson's Company, Col. Wm.
Williams' Regt. Detached Militia in
U. S. service 4 months and 24 days,
1812. Served from April 23, 1813
to April, 1814, in Capt. John Wires'
Company, 30th Regt. Served from
Oct. 11, 1814 to June 19, 1815 in Capt.
Taylor's Company, 30th Inf. Ref:
R. & L. 1812, AGO Pages 23 and 40.

LAUGHLIN, HENRY.
Enlisted Sept. 25, 1813 in Capt. Elijah
W. Wood's Company, Dixon's Regt.
Ref: Book 52, AGO Page 273.

*LAUGHLIN, JOHN,   Georgia.
Served in Capt. Saxe's Company,
Col. Wm. Williams' Regt. Detached

Militia in U. S. service 2 months and 25 days, 1812. Also served in Corps of Artillery; on Pay Roll to June 30, 1814. Ref: R. & L. 1812, AGO Page 31.

LAUGHLIN, WILLIAM.
Served at Troy from July 15 to Aug. 13, 1812 in company of recruits commanded by Seth Warner, Lieutenant. Ref: Vol. 50, Vt. State Papers, Page 15.

*LAUGHTON, SOLOMON.
Served in Capt. Noyce's Company, Col. Jonathan Williams' Regt. Detached Militia in U. S. service 27 days.

*LAUKS, HENRY, Highgate.
Served from Sept. 1, 1812 in Capt. Conrade Saxe's Company, 4 Regt. (Williams').

LAUKS, JACOB, Highgate.
Volunteered to go to Plattsburgh, September, 1814, and served 5 days in Capt. Conrade Saxe's Company, 4 Regt. (Williams'). Ref: Book 51, AGO Page 100.

LAURENCE, THOMAS.
Volunteered to go to Plattsburgh, September, 1814, and went as far as Bolton, Vt., serving 4 days in Lieut. Phineus Kimball's Company, West Fairlee. Ref: Book 52, AGO Page 46.

LAURY, TILLEY, Franklin County.
Volunteered to go to Plattsburgh Sept. 11, 1814 and served in 15th or 22nd Regt. Ref: Hemenway's Vt. Gazetteer, Vol. 2, Page 391.

LAVENE, PAUL.
Served in Capt. Follet's Company, Col. Dixon's Regt. Detached Militia in U. S. service 1 month & 23 days, 1813. Ref: Book 53, AGO Page 105.

‡*LAW, JOSEPH H., Sergeant.
Enlisted Sept. 25, 1813 and served 1 month in Capt. Asa Wilkins' Company. Col. Dixon's Regt. Pension Certificate of widow, Lamoille, No. 9760.

*LAWRENCE, ANDREW.
Served from April 12 to April 15, 1814 in Capt. John Hackett's Company, Sumner's Regt.

*LAWRENCE, HARVEY H.
Enlisted April 12, 1814 in Capt. John Hackett's Company, Sumner's Regt.; transferred to Capt. Shubael Wales' Company, Sumner's Regt. April 15, 1814 and served to April 21, 1814.

*LAWRENCE, ISAAC, Corporal, Cornwall. Served in Capt. Robbins' Company, Col. Wm. Williams' Regt. Detached Militia in U. S. service 4 months and 29 days, 1812. Enlisted at Panton March 24, 1814 for the period of the war and served as a Corporal in Capt. Wm. Miller's Company, Capt. Gideon Spencer's Company and Capt. James Taylor's Company, 30th Regt. Ref: R. & L. 1812, AGO Pages 53, 54, 55, 56.

*LAWRENCE, JAMES.
Served in Capt. Willson's Company, Col. Wm. Williams' Regt. Detached Militia in U. S. service 4 months and 24 days, 1812.

*LAWRENCE, JOHN, Plainfield or Marshfield? Volunteered to go to Plattsburgh, September, 1814, and went as far as Burlington; no organization given. Served in 1 Regt. (Judson's) Vt. Militia.

LAWRENCE, JONATHAN.
Served in Capt. Samuel H. Holly's Company, 11th Regt.; on Pay Roll for January and February, 1813. Ref: R. & L. 1812, AGO Page 25.

LAWRENCE, LEVI.
Volunteered to go to Plattsburgh, September, 1814, and went as far as Bolton, Vt., serving 4 days in Lieut. Phineus Kimball's Company, West Fairlee. Ref: Book 52, AGO Page 46.

LAWRENCE, NATHANIEL, Carpenter.
Served from May 1 to June 30, 1814 in Alexander Parris' Company of Artificers. Ref: R. & L. 1812, AGO Page 24.

‡LAWRENCE, PETER.
Served in Capt. Richardson's Company, Col. Martindale's Regt. Detached Militia in U. S. service 2 months and 13 days, 1812. Pension Certificate No. 7954. Pension Certificate of widow, Phylynda, No. 24054.

‡*LAWRENCE, RUSSELL, St. Albans or Highgate. Served in Capt. Saxe's Company, Col. Wm. Williams' Regt. Detached Militia in U. S. service 4 months and 24 days, 1812. Served from Sept. 25, 1813 to Oct. 20, 1813 in Capt. Amos Robinson's Company, Dixon's Regt. Pension Certificate No. 945.

*LAWRENCE, STEPHEN, St. Albans.
Served from Sept. 25 to Oct. 11, 1813 in Capt. N. B. Eldredge's Company. Dixon's Regt. Volunteered to go to Plattsburgh, September, 1814, and served in Capt. Samuel H. Farnsworth's Company, Dixon's Regt.

LAWRENCE, THOMAS.
Served in Capt. Alexander Brooks' Corps of Artillery; on Pay Roll to June 30, 1814. Ref: R. & L. 1812, AGO Page 31.

*LAWRENCE, VILLE, 2nd Lieutenant.
Served from April 12 to April 21, 1814 in Capt. Eseck Sprague's Company, Sumner's Regt.

‡LAWSON, MARTIN, Cabot.
Volunteered to go to Plattsburgh, September, 1814, and served 4 days in Capt. Anthony Perry's Company. Pension Certificate of widow, Dorcas B., No. 27906.

LAWSON, SAMUEL, Barre.
Volunteered to go to Plattsburgh, September, 1814, and served 10 days in Capt. Warren Ellis' Company. Ref: Book 52, AGO Page 242.

LAYER, WILLIAM, Sergeant.
Served from May 1 to June 30, 1814
in Corps of Light Dragoons. Ref: R.
& L. 1812, AGO Page 20.

LAYMAN, GEORGE.
Served from May 9 to June 30, 1814
in Capt. Alexander Brooks' Corps
of Artillery. Ref: R. & L. 1812.
AGO Page 31.

LAYON, JONATHAN, Sergeant.
Served in Capt. Samuel Blinn's Com-
pany, from June 11 to June 14, 1813.
Ref: R. & L. 1812, AGO Page 49.

LAYTON, DAVID,   Sudbury.
Volunteered to go to Plattsburgh.
Sepember, 1814, serving 6 days in
Capt. Thomas Hall's Company. Ref:
Book 52, AGO Page 122.

LAYTON, JOHN,   Sudbury.
Volunteered to go to Plattsburgh.
September, 1814, and served 6 days
in Capt. Thomas Hall's Company.
Ref: Book 52, AGO Page 122.

*LAWSON, JAMES, Musician.
Served in Corning's Detachment, Vt.
Militia. Served as a musician in 4
Regt. (Peck's) Vt. Militia.

LEACH, ANDREW,   Pittsford.
Volunteered to go to Plattsburgh.
September, 1814, and served 8 days
as waggoner in Capt. Caleb Hendee's
Company. Ref: Book 52, AGO Page
125.

LEACH, BERIAH,   Middletown.
Volunteered to go to Plattsburgh.
September, 1814. and served 4 days
in Capt. Reuben Wood's Company.
Ref: Book 52, AGO Page 143.

*LEACH, GEORGE.
Served from Sept. 25 to Sept. 29,
1813 in Capt. N. B. Eldridge's Company, Dixon's Regt.

*LEACH, LEWIS, Corporal.
Served in Capt. Dorrance's Company.
Col. Wm. Williams' Regt. Detached
Militia in U. S. service 4 months
and 24 days, 1812. Served from
April 25, 1813 to April 29, 1814 in
Capt. James Taylor's Company, 30th
Regt. Ref: R. & L. 1812, AGO Pages
52, 57, 59.

*LEACH, LYMAN,   Fairfield.
Served in Capt. Kendall's Company.
Col. Wm. Williams' Regt. Detached
Militia in U. S. service 3 months and
28 days, 1812.

*LEACH, SHEREBIAH, Quartermaster
Sergeant. Served in 3 Regt. (Bowdish) Vt. Militia.

*LEACH, STEPHEN D., Drummer.
Served from Sept. 25 to Oct. 7, 1813
in Capt. Charles Bennett's Company,
Dixon's Regt.

LEACH, ZEBADIAH,   Swanton.
Served in Capt. George W. Kindall's
Company, 4 Regt. (Williams') 6
months in 1812. Ref: Book 51. AGO
Page 198.

*LEACH, ZEBULON,   Fairfield.
Served in Capt. Kendall's Company.
Col. Wm. Williams' Regt. Detached
Militia in U. S. service 4 months
and 23 days, 1812. Enlisted Oct.
15, 1813 and served 1 month and 3
days in Capt. Asahel Langworthy's
Company, Col. Dixon's Regt. or Col.
Isaac Clark's Rifle Corps. Ref: Book
52, AGO Page 261; Book 53, AGO
Page 108.

*LEALAND, JEREMIAH JR.
Served in 4 Regt (Peck's) Vt. Militia.

*LEAR, JACOB.
Served in Sumner's Regt. Vt. Militia.

*LEARNARD, MOSES.
Served in Capt. Richardson's Company, Col. Martnidale's Regt. Detached Militia in U. S. service 1
month and 9 days, 1812.

LEARNARD, NATHANIEL,   Fairfax.
Served in 1813 and 1814 in Capt.
Joseph Beeman's Company. Ref: Hemenway's Vt. Gazetteer, Vol. 2, Page
402.

LEARNED, DAVID.
Served from Jan. 4 to April 5, 1813
in company of Capt. John McNeil, Jr..
11th Regt. Ref: R. & L. 1812, AGO
Pages 16 and 17.

LEARNED, ISAAC,   Pawlet.
Served from Sept. 1, 1814 to June
16, 1815 in Capt. Sanford's Company,
30th Inf. Ref: R. & L. 1812, AGO
Page 23.

LEARNED. SYLVANUS.
Served in company of Capt. John Mc-
Neil Jr., 11th Regt.; on Pay Roll
for January and February, 1813.
Ref: R. & L. 1812, AGO Page 17.

LEASE, ERASTUS,   Williamstown.
Volunteered to go to Plattsburgh.
September, 1814, and was at the
battle, serving 8 days in Capt. David
Robinson's Company. Ref: Book 52,
AGO Page 2.

LEASE, JOHN,   Williamstown?
Served in Capt. Walker's Company,
Col. Fifield's Regt. Detached Militia
in U. S. service 6 months and 3
days, 1812. Ref: Book 53, AGO Page 5.

‡*LEASE, JOHN JR.,   Williamstown.
Served in Capt. Walker's Company,
2 Regt. (Fifield's). Also volunteered
to go to Plattsburgh, September, 1814,
and served 8 days in Capt. David
Robinson's Company. Pension Certificate No. 9706. Ref: Loose Rolls
Book 52, AGO.

LEASON, ARTIMAS.
Enlisted June 17, 1813 for 1 year in
Capt. Daniel Farrington's Company
(also commanded by Capt. Simeon
Wright) 30th Regt.; on Muster Roll
from March 1 to April 30, 1814. Ref:
R. & L. 1812, AGO Pages 50 and 51.

LEASON, BENJAMIN.
Enlisted June 15, 1813 for 1 year
in Capt. Daniel Farrington's Company (also commanded by Capt.

Simeon Wright) 30th Regt.; on Muster Roll from March 1 to April 30, 1814. Ref: R. & L. 1812, AGO Pages 50 and 51.

*LEASON, NATHAN.
Served in 3 Regt. (Williams') Vt. Militia.

‡LEATHEROW, JOHN.
Served in Capt. Fulks' Company. Pension Certificate No. 6193.

LEAVITT, MILES.
Served in Capt. Benjamin Bradford's Company; on Muster Roll from May 31 to Aug. 31, 1813; joined by transfer July 22, 1813. Ref: R. & L. 1812, AGO Page 26.

*LEAVY, JOHN (or Seavy?)
Served in 1 Regt. (Judson's) Vt. Militia.

LEBANON, ANSEL,   Fairfax.
Served from Aug. 8, 1812 in company of Capt. Joseph Beeman Jr., 11th Regt. U. S. Inf. under Col. Ira Clark. Ref: Hemenway's Vt. Gazetteer, Vol. 2, Page 402.

LEBARD, JOSEPH.
Served in Capt. Pettes' Company, Col. Wm. Williams' Regt. Detached Militia in U. S. service 4 months and 17 days, 1812. Ref: Book 53, AGO Page 30.

LEBARRON, ISAAC,   Montpelier.
Volunteered to go to Plattsburgh, September, 1814, and served 8 days in Capt. Timothy Hubbard's Company. Ref: Book 52, AGO Page 256.

‡*LEE, ALFRED, Ensign.
Served in 3 Regt. (Williams') Vt. Militia. Also served in Major Whitney's Company. Pension Certificate of widow, Asenath, No. 3955.

LEE, AMHERST,   Pittsford.
Volunteered to go to Plattsburgh, September, 1814, and served 8 days in Capt. Caleb Hendee's Company. Ref: Book 52, AGO Page 125.

LEE, ARSA (or Arza),   Pittsford.
Enlisted April 24, 1813 for 1 year in Capt. Simeon Wright's Company; lost a leg in the battle of Wililamsburgh. Was a son of Ashbel Lee. Ref: R. & L. 1812, AGO Page 51; A. M. Caverly's History of Pittsford, Page 366.

LEE, AZARIAH,   Colchester.
Volunteered to go to Plattsburgh, September, 1814, and served 8 days; no organization given. Ref: Book 51, AGO Pages 88 and 275.

LEE, AZRA,   Rutland.
Served from Jan. 1 to June 4, 1814 in Capt. Wright's Company, 30th Inf. Ref: R. & L. 1812, AGO Page 30.

*LEE, CHANCY G.
Served from June 11 to June 14, 1813 in Capt. Moses Jewett's Company, 1st Regt. 2nd Brig. 3rd Div.

LEE, DANIEL.
Served from May 14 to June 30, 1813 in Lieut. Wm. S. Foster's Company, 11th Regt. Ref: R. & L. 1812, AGO Page 6.

LEE, ELIJAH.
Enlisted Dec. 24, 1812 for 5 years in company of late Capt. J. Brooks commanded by Lieut. John I. Cromwell, Corps of U. S. Artillery; on Muster Roll from April 30, 1814 to June 30, 1814. Ref: R. & L. 1812, AGO Page 18.

*LEE, GEORGE.
Served from April 12 to May 20, 1814 in company of Capt. James Gray Jr., Sumner's Regt.

‡LEE, JACOB.
Served in Capt. Johnson's Company. Pension Certificate No. 10307.

*LEE, JOEL, Sergeant.
Served in Capt. Morrill's Company, Col. Fifield's Regt. Detached Militia in U. S. service 6 months and 5 days, 1812.

*LEE, JOHN.
Served in 3 Regt. (Tyler's) Vt. Militia.

LEE, JOSEPH,   Franklin County.
Volunteered to go to Plattsburgh Sept. 11, 1814 and served in 15th or 22nd Regt. Ref: Hemenway's Vt. Gazetteer, Vol. 2, Page 391.

*LEE, LINAS.
Served in 3 Regt. (Tyler's) Vt. Militia.

LEE, MARSHALL,   Whitehall, N. Y.
Served from Sept. 1, 1814 to June 16, 1815 in Capt. Sanford's Company, 30th Inf. Ref: R. & L. 1812, AGO Page 23.

LEE, MARSHALL.
Enlisted Feb. 7, 1814 for period of the war in Capt. Gideon Spencer's Company, 30th Regt.; on Muster Roll from Dec. 30, 1813 to June 30, 1814; joined June 1, 1814; on board the navy. Ref: R. & L. 1812, AGO Page 57.

LEE, MARTIAL.
Enlisted Feb. 25, 1814 for duration of the war in Capt. Daniel Farrington's Company, 30th Regt.; on Muster Roll from March 1 to April 30, 1814. Ref: R. & L. 1812, AGO Page 50.

LEE, SAMUEL, Artificer.
Enlisted March 24, 1813 for 5 years in company of late Capt. J. Brooks commanded by Lieut. John I. Cromwell, Corps of U. S. Artillery; on Muster Roll from April 30 to June 30, 1814. Ref: R. & L. 1812, AGO Page 18.

*LEE, STEPHEN.
Served in Capt. Phelps' Company, Col. Wm. Williams' Regt. Detached Militia in U. S. service 5 months, 1812. Served from April 12 to April 21, 1814 in Lieut. Justus Foote's Company, Sumner's Regt.

‡LEE, THEODORE S.
Served in Capt. Smith's Company.
Pension Certificate No. 28817.

*LEE, WILLIAM C.
Served in Capt. Noyce's Company,
Col. Jonathan Williams' Regt. Detached Militia in U. S. service 2
months and 6 days, 1812.

*LEEMAN, SAMUEL.
Served with Hospital Attendants, Vt.

LEFFINGWELL, DYER,   Middletown.
Volunteered to go to Plattsburgh,
September, 1814, and served 4 days
in Capt. Reuben Wood's Company.
Ref: Book 52, AGO Page 143.

*LEISTER, EDWARD,   Enosburgh.
Served from Oct. 15 to Nov. 17, 1813
in Capt. Asahel Scovell's Company,
Col. Clark's Rifle Corps.

*LELAND, JEREMIAH,   Middlesex.
Volunteered to go to Plattsburgh,
September, 1814, and served 10 days
in Capt. Holden Putnam's Company,
4 Regt. (Peck's).

*LELAND, RUFUS, Lieutenant, Middle-
sex. Volunteered to go to Plattsburgh, September, 1814, and served
10 days in Capt. Holden Puntam's
Company, 4 Regt. (Peck's).

LEMOND, BENJAMIN, Corporal.
Served from Oct. 4 to Oct. 13, 1813
in Capt. John Palmer's Company,
1st Regt. 2nd Brig. 3rd Div. Ref:
R. & L. 1812, AGO Page 47.

LENINGTON, HENRY.
Enlisted Sept. 26, 1812 for 5 years
in Capt. White Youngs' Company.
15th Regt.; on Muster Roll from
Aug. 31 to Dec. 31, 1814. Ref: R.
& L. 1812, AGO Page 27.

LENT, JOHN.
Enlisted Dec. 1, 1812 for 5 years
in company of late Capt. J. Brooks
commanded by Lieut. John I. Crom-
well, Corps of U. S. Artillery; on
Muster Roll from April 30, 1814 to
June 30, 1814. Ref: R. & L. 1812,
AGO Page 18.

*LEONARD, AARON.
Served in Sumner's Regt. Vt. Militia.

LEONARD, ALFRED.
Served in Capt. Samul Gordon's Com-
pany, 11th Regt.; on Pay Roll for
January and February, 1813. Ref:
R. & L. 1812, AGO Page 9.

LEONARD, ASHLEY,   Shoreham.
Volunteered to go to Plattsburgh,
September, 1814, and served 6 days
in Capt. Samuel Hand's Company.
Ref: Rev. J. F. Goodhue's History
of Shoreham, Page 108.

LEONARD, CROMWELL.
Served in Capt. Briggs' Company,
Col. Jonathan Williams' Regt. Detached Militia in U. S. service 2
months and 13 days, 1812. Ref: Book
53, AGO Page 27.

LEONARD, EPHRAIM,   Lansingburgh.
Served in Capt. Benjamin S. Edgerton's Company, 11th Regt.; on Pay
Roll for September and October, 1812
and January and February, 1813.
Served from Oct. 4, 1814 to June 19,
1815 in Capt. Taylor's Company, 30th
Inf. Ref: R. & L. 1812, AGO Pages
1 and 2 and 23.

LEONARD, EZEKIEL.
Served from March 19, 1813 to June
18, 1813 in Capt. Charles Follett's
Company, 11th Regt. Ref: R. & L.
1812, AGO Page 13.

*LEONARD, GIDEON M.,   Shoreham.
Served from April 12, 1814 to May 20,
1814 in Capt. George Fisher's Company, Sumner's Regt. Volunteered to
go to Plattsburgh, September, 1814,
and served 6 days in Capt. Samuel
Hand's Company.

LEONARD, JACOB.
Served from May 1 to June 30, 1814
in Capt. Alexander Brooks' Corps of
Artillery. Ref: R. & L. 1812, AGO
Page 31.

LEONARD, JOHN,   Orwell.
Volunteered to go to Plattsburgh,
September, 1814, and served 11 days
in Capt. Wait Branch's Company.
Ref: Book 51, AGO Page 16.

LEONARD, JOSIAH,   Barre.
Volunteered to go to Plattsburgh,
September, 1814, and served 10 days
in Capt. Warren Ellis' Company.
Ref: Book 52, AGO Page 242.

LEONARD, LUTHER, Captain.
Appointed Captain Light Artillery
July 6, 1812; honorably discharged
June 15, 1815. Ref: Heitman's His-
torical Register & Dictiony USA.

LEONARD, LYMAN.
Served in Capt. Samul Gordon's Com-
pany, 11th Regt.; on Pay Roll for
January and February, 1813; died
Jan. 5, 1813. Ref: R. & L. 1812, AGO
Page 9.

LEONARD, NATHANIEL, Captain.
Appointed Captain, 2 Artillerists and
Engineers Dec. 1, 1804; transferred
to 1 Artillery March 12, 1812; honorably discharged June 1, 1814. Ref:
Heitman's Historical Register & Dictionary USA.

‡LEONARD, WILLIAM.
Served in Capt. Hanborn's (probably
Sanborn's) Company. Pension Certi-
ficate of widow, Jane, No. 37514.

‡*LEROY, BENJAMIN.
Served in Capt. Parson's Company,
Col. Jonathan Williams' Regt. De-
tached Militia in U. S. service 2
months and 13 days, 1812. Pension
Certificate No. 269.

*LESHUR, JAN.
Served in 1 Regt. (Martindale's) Vt.
Militia.

LESLIE, DAVID.
Served in Capt. Benjamin Bradford's
Company; on Muster Roll from May
31 to Aug. 31, 1813. Ref: R. & L.
1812, AGO Page 26.

LESLIE, GEORGE.
Served in Capt. Benjamin Bradford's Company; on Muster Roll from May 31, 1813 to Aug. 31, 1813. Ref: R. & L. 1812, AGO Page 26.

LEVAKE, AUGUSTUS JR., Lieutenant.
Appointed 3rd Lieutenant 48 Inf. April 21, 1814; transferred to 26 Inf. May 12, 1814; appointed 2nd Lieutenant Aug. 1, 1814; honorably discharged June 15, 1815. Ref: Heitman's Historical Register & Dictionary USA; Governor and Council Vt. Vol. 6, Page 477.

*LEVAKE, HENRY.
Served in Corning's Detachment, Vt. Militia.

LEVAKE, JOHN, Captain.
Appointed Ensign 11 Inf. July 29, 1813; 1st Lieutenant Aug. 15, 1813; Captain 48 Inf. April 21, 1814; transferred to 26 Inf. May 12, 1814; honorably discharged June 15, 1815. Ref: Heitman's Historical Register & Dictionary USA.

LEVAKE, THOMAS, Lieutenant.
Appointed Ensign 11 Inf. March 12, 1812; 2nd Lieutenant March 13, 1813; 1st Lieutenant Aug. 15, 1813; honorably discharged June 15, 1815. Served as Ensign in Lieut. V. R. Goodrich's Company, 11th Regt.; on Pay Roll for January and February, 1813. Ref: Heitman's Historical Register & Dictionary USA; R. & L. 1812, AGO Page 11.

LEVINS, CALVIN.
Enlisted March 20, 1813 in Capt. Charles Follett's Company, 11th Regt.; on Pay Roll to May 31, 1813. Ref: R. & L. 1812, AGO Page 13.

*LEVINS, PANUEL.
Enlisted Sept. 25, 1813 in Capt. Martin D. Folett's Company, Dixon's Regt.

*LEVITT, JOSEPH JR.
Enlisted Sept. 20, 1813 in Capt. John Weed's Company, Col. Clark's Rifle Corps.

LEWELDER, JAMES, Franklin County.
Volunteered to go to Plattsburgh Sept. 11, 1814 and served in 15th or 22nd Regt. Ref: Hemenway's Vt. Gazetteer, Vol. 2, Page 391.

*LEWIS, ALANSON.
Served from April 12 to April 21, 1814 in Capt. Edmund B. Hill's Company, Sumner's Regt.

*LEWIS, ASA.
Served in Corning's Detachment, Vt. Militia. Served in 4 Regt. (Peck's) Vt. Militia.

*LEWIS, DAVID.
Served in Capt. Richardson's Company, Col. Martindale's Regt. Detached Militia in U. S. service 1 month and 3 days, 1812. Also served in Capt. Chadwick's Company. Ref: R. & L. 1812, AGO Page 32.

LEWIS, ELI JR.,   Hancock.
Volunteered to go to Plattsburgh, September, 1814, and served 7 days in Capt. Asaph Smith's Company. Ref: Book 51, AGO Pages 20 and 21.

LEWIS, ELISHA,   Shoreham.
Volunteered to go to Plattsburgh, September, 1814, and served 6 days as Aide to Timothy F. Chipman, Brig. Gen. of Vt. Militia. Ref: Rev. J. F. Goodhue's History of Shoreham, Page 105.

‡*LEWIS, EMERSON.
Served in Capt. Pettie's Company, Col. Wm. Williams' Regt. Detached Militia in U. S. service 4 months and 17 days, 1812. Also served in 3 Regt. (Tyler's) Vt. Militia. Pension Certificate No. 10072.

LEWIS, GEORGE, Sergeant, Burlington.
Served from June 11 to June 14, 1813 in Capt. Moses Jewett's Company, 1st Regt. 2nd Brig. 3rd Div. Volunteered to go to Plattsburgh, September, 1814, and served 10 days in Capt. Henry Mayo's Company, 1st Regt. (Martindale's).

LEWIS, HORACE H.
Enlisted May 20, 1813 for 1 year in Capt. Daniel Farrington's Company (also commanded by Capt. Simeon Wright) 30th Regt.; on Muster Roll from March 1 to April 30, 1814. Ref: R. & L. 1812, AGO Pages 50 and 51.

*LEWIS, ISAAC, Sergeant Major.
Served in Col. Wm. Williams' Regt. of Detached Militia stationed at Swanton Falls in 1812.

‡LEWIS, JACOB (colored).
Served in Capt. Wesley Beagle's Company. Pension Certificate No. 29670.

LEWIS, JOHN,   Poultney.
Volunteered to go to Plattsburgh, September, 1814, serving 2 days in Capt. Briant Ransom's Company. Ref: Book 52, AGO Page 147.

*LEWIS, JOHN.
Served in Capt. Ormsbee's Company, Col. Martindale's Regt. Detached Militia in U. S. service 19 days, 1812.

LEWIS, JOHN, Ensign,   Richford.
Enlisted Sept. 25, 1813 and served 1 month and 23 days in Capt. Martin D. Follett's Company, Col. Dixon's Regt.

*LEWIS, JOHN.
Served in Capt. Hopkins' Company, Col. Martindale's Regt. Detached Militia in U. S. service 2 months and 13 days, 1812.

LEWIS, JOHN,   Orwell.
Volunteered to go to Plattsburgh, September, 1814, and served 11 days in Capt. Wait Branch's Company. Ref: Book 51, AGO Page 16.

*LEWIS, JONATHAN.
Served in Corning's Detachment, Vt. Militia and 1 Regt. (Judson's) Vt. Militia.

LEWIS, JONATHAN,   Williamstown.
Volunteered to go to Plattsburgh,
September, 1814, and served 8 days
in Capt. David Robinson's Company.
Ref: Book 52, AGO Page 8.

LEWIS, JONATHAN, Sergeant.
Volunteered to go to Plattsburgh,
September, 1814, and served in Capt.
Ebenezer Spencer's Company, Ver-
shire. Ref: Book 52, AGO Page 48.

*LEWIS, JOSEPH.
Served with Hospital Attendants, Vt.
Also served with Corning's Detach-
ment, Vt. Militia and 4th Regt.
(Peck's) Vt. Militia.

‡*LEWIS, LABAN, Sergeant,   Georgia.
Volunteered to go to Plattsburgh,
September, 1814, and served 8 days
in Capt. Jesse Post's Company, Dixon's Regt. Pension Certificate of
widow, Abigail, No. 6246.

LEWIS, LYMAN, Fifer,   Weathersfield.
Served from Aug. 26, 1813 to March
8, 1814 in Capt. Daniel Farrington's
Company (also commanded by Capt.
Simeon Wright) 30th Regt. Served
from Sept. 25, 1814 to June 16, 1815
in Capt. Sanford's Company, 30th
Inf. Ref: R. & L. 1812, AGO Pages
23, 50, 51.

*LEWIS, MARTIN.
Served from April 12, 1814 to April
21, 1814 in Capt. Edmund B. Hill's
Company, Sumner's Regt.

LEWIS, NATHAN,   Burlington.
Served from March 1 to July 6, 1814
in Capt. Clark's Company, 30th Inf.
Ref: R. & L. 1812, AGO Page 30.

*LEWIS, NATHANIEL.
Served in Capt. Wheatley's Company,
Col. Fifield's Regt. Detached Militia
in U. S. service 6 months, 1812. Ap-
pointed Ensign 11th Inf. July 7, 1813
but probably did not accept. Ref:
Governor and Council, Vt., Vol. 6,
Page 478.

*LEWIS, ORANGE.
Served in Corning's Detachment, Vt.
Militia.

LEWIS, PETER.
Served in Capt. Benjamin S. Edgerton's Company, 11th Regt.; on Pay
Roll for September and October, 1812
and January and February, 1813.
Ref: R. & L. 1812, AGO Pages 1
and 2.

*LEWIS, REUBEN, Ensign.
Served in 1 Regt. (Martindale's) Vt.
Militia.

LEWIS, ROBERT.
Enlisted Sept. 16, 1812 in Capt. Ben-
jamin S. Edgerton's. Company, 11th
Regt.; on Pay Roll for September
and October 1812 and January and
February, 1813. Ref: R. & L. 1812,
AGO Pages 1 and 2.

LEWIS, SALAN, Sergeant.
Enlisted Sept. 25, 1813 in Capt. Jesse
Post's Company, Dixon's Regt. Ref:
Book 52, AGO Page 290.

LEWIS, SAMUEL.
Enlisted March 12, 1814 for 1 year
in Capt. Clark's Company, 30th Regt.
Ref: R. & L. 1812, AGO Page 1.

*LEWIS, SETH.
Served from April 12 to May 20, 1814
in company of Capt. James Gray Jr.,
Sumner's Regt.

LEWIS, SHUBAL,   Calais.
Volunteered to go to Plattsburgh,
September, 1814, and served 8 days
in Capt. Samuel M. Orcutt's Company. Ref: Book 52, AGO Pages
182 and 250.

‡*LEWIS, SIMON,   Enosburgh.
Served from Oct. 15 to Nov. 17, 1813
in Capt. Asahel Scoville's Company,
Col. Clark's Rifle Corps. Pension
Certificate No. 10110.

*LEWIS, WILLIAM.
Served in 4 Regt. (Peck's) Vt. Militia.

LEWIS, ZACARIAH, Sergeant.
Enlisted Nov. 18, 1812 for 5 years
in company of late Capt. J. Brooks
commanded by Lieut. John I. Crom-
well, Corps of U. S. Artillery; on
Muster Roll from April 30, 1814 to
June 30, 1814. Ref: R. & L. 1812,
AGO Page 18.

*LEWIS, ZEBION.
Served in Corning's Detachment, Vt.
Militia.

LIBBEY, JOSEPH, Sergeant.
Served in Capt. Benjamin Bradford's
Company; on Muster Roll from May
31 to Aug. 31, 1813; joined by transfer July 22, 1813. Ref: R. & L.
1812, AGO Page 26.

LIGHTHULL, WILLIAM, Franklin County. Volunteered to go to Plattsburgh Sept. 11, 1814, serving in 15th
or 22nd Regt. Ref: Hemenway's Vt.
Gazetteer, Vol. 2, Page 391.

LILLIE, DANIEL,   Bethel.
Volunteered to go to Plattsburgh,
September, 1814, and served 8 days
in Capt. Nehemiah Noble's Company.
Ref: Book 51, AGO Pages 223 and 224.

LILLIE, JOHN,   Tunbridge.
Volunteered to go to Plattsburgh,
September, 1814, and served in Capt.
David Knox's Company. Ref: Book
52, AGO Page 115.

*LILLIE, JOSEPH JR.
Served in Capt. Bingham's Company,
Col. Jonathan Williams' Regt. Detached Militia in U. S. service 2
months and 9 days, 1812.

LILLIE, RUFUS T., Sergeant.
Served in Capt. Phineas Williams'
Company, 11th Regt.; on Pay Roll
for January and February, 1813.
Ref: R. & L. 1812, AGO Page 15.

*LILLIE, SAMUEL,   Bethel.
Served in Capt. Bingham's Company,
Col. Jonathan Williams' Regt. Detached Militia in U. S. service 2
months and 9 days, 1812. Volunteer-

ed to go to Plattsburgh, September,
1814, and served 7 days in Capt.
Nehemiah Noble's Company.

*LINCOLN, ABIATHAN.
Served in 1 Regt. (Judson's) Vt.
Militia.

LINCOLN, BENJAMIN, Poultney.
Volunteered to go to Plattsburgh.
September, 1814, and served 2 days
in Capt. Briant Ransom's Company.
Ref: Book 52, AGO Page 147.

*LINCOLN, GOODWIN, Sergeant, Wil-
mington. Served in Capt. Preston's
Company, Col. Jonathan Williams'
Regt. Detached Militia in U. S.
service 2 months and 6 days, 1812.

*LINCOLN, GURDON (or Gordan).
Served in Capt. Wright's Company,
Col. Fifield's Regt. Detached Militia
in U. S. service 2 months and 21
days, 1812.

LINCOLN, JOHN H., Sergeant, Pittsford.
Enlisted Aug. 24, 1813 for 1 year
in Capt. Simeon Wright's Company.
Volunteered to go to Plattsburgh.
September, 1814, and served 8 days
in Capt. Caleb Hendee's Company.
Ref: R. & L. 1812, AGO Page 51;
Book 52, AGO Page 124.

*LINCOLN, JOSEPH.
Served in 1 Regt. (Martindale's) Vt.
Militia.

*LINCOLN, LINAS.
Served from Oct. 5 to Oct. 17, 1813
in Capt. Stephen Brown's Company,
3 Regt. (Tyler's).

*LINCOLN, LUTHER.
Served in Capt. Lowry's Company,
Col. Wm. Williams' Regt. Detached
Militia in U. S. service 4 months
and 26 days, 1812.

*LINCOLN, OBED.
Served in 1 Regt. (Martindale's) Vt.
Militia.

*LINCOLN, SAMUEL.
Served from June 11 to June 14, 1813
in Capt. Hezekiah Barns' Company,
1st Regt. 2nd Brig. 3rd Div.

LINCOLN, TISDALE, Pittsfield.
Volunteered to go to Plattsburgh,
September, 1814, and served 7 days
in Capt. Elias Keyes' Company. Ref:
Book 52, AGO Page 156.

*LINCOLN, WILLIAM, Shrewsbury.
Served from June 11 to June 14,
1813 in Capt. Hezekiah Barns' Com-
pany, 1st Regt. 2nd Brig. 3rd Div.
Volunteered to go to Plattsburgh.
September, 1814, and served 4 days
in Capt. Robert Reed's Company.
Ref: Book 52, AGO Pages 138 and 140.

‡LINDSAY, RUFUS H.
Served in Capt. S. Potter's Com-
pany. Pension Certificate of widow,
Julia, No. 21614.

*LINDSLEY, HORACE, 2nd Lieutenant.
Served from April 12 to April 21,
1814 in Capt. Shubael Wales' Company, Col. W. B. Sumner's Regt.

LINES, SAMUEL.
Served from March 1 to May 31, 1813
in Capt. Charles Follett's Company,
11th Regt. Ref: R. & L. 1812, AGO
Page 13.

LINES, WILLIAM, Williamstown, Mass.
Enlisted April 2, 1814 at Burlington
for 5 years and served in Capt. Wm.
Miller's Company and Capt. Gideon
Spencer's Company. Ref: R. & L.
1812, AGO Pages 54, 55, 57.

LINGHAM, THOMAS.
Served from Feb. 8 to June 30, 1814
in Regt. of Light Dragoons. Ref: R.
& L. 1812, AGO Page 21.

*LINGHAM, WILLIAM.
Served in Sumner's Regt. Vt. Militia.

LINKIN, OBADIAH.
Enlisted Sept. 27, 1812 for 5 years
in Capt. White Youngs' Company,
15th Regt.; on Muster Roll from Aug.
31, 1814 to Dec. 31, 1814. Ref: R.
& L. 1812, AGO Page 27.

LINNING, PATRICK (or Limry).
Served in Capt. Pettes' Company,
Col. Wm. Williams' Regt. Detached
Militia in U. S. service 4 months
and 17 days, 1812. Ref: Book 53,
AGO Page 69.

LINSEY, SAMUEL.
Served from Feb. 12, 1813 to May
10, 1813 in Capt. John W. Weeks'
Company, 11th Regt. Ref: R. & L.
1812, AGO Page 4.

LINSLEY, DAVID.
Served from Jan. 12 to Feb. 28,
1813 in Capt. Samuel H. Holly's
Company, 11th Regt. Ref: R. & L.
1812, AGO Page 25.

*LINSLEY, GILBERT, Cornwall.
Volunteered to go to Plattsburgh,
September, 1814, and served in Capt.
Edmund B. Hill's Company, Sumner's
Regt.

*LINSLEY, JOHN.
Served in 1 Regt. (Judson's) Vt. Militia.

LIONS, CHARLEY, Corporal.
Served in 1st Regt. of Detached Militia of Vt. in U. S. service at Champlain from Nov. 18 to Nov. 19, 1812.

*LISCOMB, FRANCIS.
Served in 4 Regt. (Peck's) Vt. Militia.

LISCUM, SOLOMON, Franklin County.
Volunteered to go to Plattsburgh
Sept. 11, 1814 and served in 15th or
22nd Regt. Ref: Hemenway's Vt.
Gazetteer, Vol. 2, Page 391.

LITTLE, ENOCH.
Served from April 7 to July 6, 1813
in Capt. Edgerton's Company, 11th
Regt. Ref: R. & L. 1812, AGO
Page 3.

*LITTLE, EPHRAIM, Surgeon.
Appointed Surgeon Sept. 25, 1813 in
Col. Dixon's consolidated Regt. of
Vt. Militia in U. S. service.

LITTLE, ERASTUS.
Enlisted April 22, 1814 for the dur-
ation of the war in Capt. Gideon
Spencer's Company, 30th Regt. On
Muster Roll from Dec. 30 to June 30,
1814. Ref: R. & L. 1812, AGO
Page 57.

LITTLE, ISAIAH,   Barre.
Volunteered to go to Plattsburgh,
September, 1814, and served 10 days
in Capt. Warren Ellis' Company. Ref:
Book 52, AGO Page 242.

LITTLE, JOHN.
Served from April 28, 1813 to April
27, 1814 in Capt. James Taylor's
Company and Capt. Gideon Spencer's
Company, 30th Regt. Ref: R. & L.
1812, AGO Pages 52, 57, 59.

*LITTLE, JOHN,   Irasburgh.
Served in Capt. Mason's Company,
Col. Fifield's Regt. Detached Militia
in U. S. service at Derby 5 months
and 21 days, 1812.

*LITTLE, JOSEPH (or Lillie?).
Served in 3 Regt. (Williams') Vt.
Militia.

*LITTLE, SAMUEL (or Lillie?).
Served in 3 Regt. (Williams') Vt.
Militia.

*LITTLEFIELD, DANIEL, Sergeant.
Served in Tyler's Regt. Vt. Militia.

LITTLEFIELD, ELIJAH, Surgeon's Mate.
Appointed Surgeon's Mate 31st Inf.
July 14, 1813; resigned Dec. 31, 1813.
Ref: Heitman's Historical Register &
Dictionary USA.

*LITTLEFIELD, TIMOTHY.
Served in Capt. Durkee's Company,
Col. Fifield's Regt. Detached Militia
in U. S. service 2 months and 16
days, 1812. Also served in Capt.
Wright's Company, Col. Fifield's Regt.
Detached Militia in U. S. service 3
months and 9 days, 1812.

LITTLEHALE, ISAAC.
Served in company of Capt. John
McNeil Jr., 11th Regt.; on Pay Roll
for January and February, 1813.
Ref: R. & L. 1812, AGO Page 17.

*LIVERMORE, CHARLES, Lieutenant.
Appointed 2nd Lieutenant 31 Inf.
April 30, 1813; resigned Nov. 23,
1813. Also served as Lieutenant and
Adjutant in 3 Regt. (Williams') Vt.
Militia. Ref: Heitman's Historical
Register & Dictionary USA.

LIVERMORE, WILLIAM, Corporal.
Served in Lieut. Wm. S. Foster's
Company, 11th Regt.; on Pay Roll
for January and February, 1813.
Ref: R. & L. 1812, AGO Page 7.

LIVINGSTON, BENJAMIN.
Enlisted Jan. 20, 1813 in Lieut. Wm.
S. Foster's Company, 11th Regt.;
on Pay Roll for January and Febru-
ary, 1813. Ref: R. & L. 1812, AGO
Pages 6 and 7.

‡*LIVINGSTON, JAMES, Ensign, Dorset.
Served in 1st Regt. of Detached Militia of Vt. in U. S. service at Cham-

plain from Nov. 18 to Nov. 19, 1812.
Also served as Captain of a com-
pany. Pension Certificate of widow,
Sabrina, No. 778.

*LLOYD, JAMES, Sergeant.
Served in 3 Regt. (Tyler's) Vt.
Militia.

LOCK, ISAAC.
Served from March 18 to June 17,
1813 in Lieut. Wm. S. Foster's Company, 11th Regt. Ref: R. & L. 1812,
AGO Page 6.

*LOCK, JACOB.
Enlisted Sept. 25, 1813 in Capt.
Charles Bennett's Company, Dixon's
Regt.

‡LOCK, JAMES.
Served in Capt. Stewart's Company.
Pension Certificate No. 291.

LOCK, JOHN.
Enlisted May 28, 1813 for 1 year
in Capt. Daniel Farrington's Company (also commanded by Capt.
Simeon Wright) 30th Regt.; on Muster Roll from March 1, 1814 to April
30, 1814. Ref: R. & L. 1812, AGO
Pages 50 and 51.

LOCK, JOHN.
Born in Stonington, Mass.; aged 39
years; 5 feet 6 inches high; dark complexion; black hair, black eyes; by
profession a farmer. Enlisted at
Plattsburgh Feb. 15, 1814 and served
in Capt. Wm. Miller's Company and
Capt. Gideon Spencer's Company,
30th Regt. Discharged at Burlington,
Vt., 1815. Ref: R. & L. 1812, AGO
Pages 54, 55, 57.

*LOCK, JOHN, Sergeant.
Served in Capt. Phelps' Company,
Col. Jonathan Williams' Regt. Detached Militia in U. S. service 1
month and 16 days, 1812.

*LOCK, JONATHAN.
Served in Corning's Detachment, Vt.
Militia.

‡*LOCK, JOSIAH,   Fairfax or Belvidere.
Served in Capt. Brush's Company,
Col. Dixon's Regt. Detached Militia
in U. S. service 1 month and 23
days, 1813. Served from Sept. 25 to
Nov. 13, 1813 in Capt. Asa Wilkins'
Company, Dixon's Regt. Volunteered
to go to Plattsburgh, September, 1814,
and served 7 days in Capt. Moody
Shattuck's Company. Pension Certificate of widow, Sally, No. 7203.

‡*LOCK, NATHANIEL R.
Served in Capt. Cross' Company, Col.
Martindale's Regt. Detached Militia
in U. S. service 2 months and 14
days, 1812. Pension Certificate of
widow, Almira D., No. 35359.

‡*LOCK, WILLIAM N., Musician.
Served in Capt. Dorrance's Company,
Col. Wm. Williams' Regt. Detached
Militia in U. S. service 4 months
and 14 days, 1812. Also served in
4 Regt. (Peck's) Vt. Militia. Pension Certificate No. 217.

LOCKEY, CHILLION W.
Served in Capt. Charles Follett's
Company, 11th Regt.; on Pay Roll
for January and February, 1812.
Ref: R. & L. 1812, AGO Page 12.

*LOCKHART, LEMUEL.
Served in 4 Regt. (Peck's) Vt. Militia.

LOCKLIN, JOSEPH.
Served from May 1 to June 30, 1814
in Capt. Haig's Corps of Light Dragoons. Ref: R. & L. 1812, AGO
Page 20.

*LOCKWOOD, BOSTWICK, Musician.
Served from June 11 to June 14, 1813
in Capt. Thomas Dorwin's Company,
1st Regt. 2nd Brig. 3rd Div.

‡*LOCKWOOD, EDMUND.
Served in Capt. Parsons' Company,
Col. Jonathan Williams' Regt. Detached Militia in U. S. service 2
months and 13 days, 1812. Pension
Certificate No. 7329.

‡*LOCKWOOD, JAMES.
Served in Capt. Adams' Company,
Col. Jonathan Williams' Regt. Detached Militia in U. S. service 2
months and 7 days, 1812. Pension
Certificate of widow, Eleanor, No.
9752.

LOCKWOOD, LEVI, Fairfax or St. Albans.
Volunteered to go to Plattsburgh,
September, 1814, and served 8 days
in Capt. Josiah Grout's Company.
Ref: Book 51, AGO Page 103.

LOCKWOOD, LEVI, St. Albans.
Volunteered to go to Plattsburgh
and was at the battle, serving in
Capt. Samuel H. Farnsworth's Company. Ref: Hemenway's Vt. Gazetteer, Vol. 2, Page 434.

*LOCKWOOD, LUMAN E.. Corporal.
Served in 3 Regt. (Tyler's) Vt. Militia.

‡*LOCKWOOD, LURAD (or Alured?),
Fairfield. Served in Capt. Kendall's
Company, Col. Wm. Williams' Regt.
Detached Militia in U. S. service 3
months and 28 days, 1812. Pension
Certificate No. 17866.

*LOCKWOOD, SAMUEL.
Served in 3 Regt. (Williams') Vt.
Militia.

LOCKWOOD, SHELDON.
Served in Capt. Samul Gordon's Company, 11th Regt.; on Pay Roll for
January and February, 1813. Ref: R.
& L. 1812, AGO Page 9.

*LOGAN, MATHEW.
Served in Capt. Richardson's Company, Col. Martindale's Regt. Detached Militia in U. S. service 2
months and 13 days, 1812.

LOGAN, ZEBINA.
Served from Feb. 12 to May 11,
1813 in Capt. Phineas Williams' Company, 11th Regt. Ref: R. & L. 1812,
AGO Page 14.

LOGGE, FRANCIS.
Served from May 1 to June 30, 1814
in Capt. Alexander Brooks' Corps of
Artillery. Ref: R. & L. 1812, AGO
Page 31.

LOID, JAMES, Franklin County.
Volunteered to go to Plattsburgh
Sept. 11, 1814 and served in 15th or
22nd Regt. Ref: Hemenway's Vt. Gazetteer, Vol. 2, Page 392.

*LOMBARD, ALVAN, Corporal.
Served in Capt. Hotchkiss' Company,
Col. Martindale's Regt. Detached
Militia in U. S. service 2 months
and 13 days, 1812.

‡LOMBARD, BENJAMIN.
Served in Capt. Hotchkiss' Company,
Col. Martindale's Regt. Detached
Militia in U. S. service 2 months
and 13 days, 1812. Pension Certificate No. 12709.

‡LOMBARD, SULLIVAN.
Served in Capt. Burnap's Company.
Pension Certificate of widow, Annie
R., No. 430.

LONG, ISAAC.
Enlisted June 9, 1813 for 5 years
in company of late Capt. J. Brooks,
commanded by Lieut. John I. Cromwell, Corps of U. S. Artillery; on
Muster Roll from April 30, 1814 to
June 30, 1814. Ref: R. & L. 1812,
AGO Page 18.

‡*LONG, RUFUS, Mendon.
Served in Capt. Scovell's Company,
Col. Martindale's Regt. Detached
Militia in U. S. service 2 months
and 21 days, 1812. Pension Certificate No. 5761. Pension Certificate
of widow, Susan, No. 7798.

*LONG, SAMUEL, Corporal, Danville.
Served in Capt. Morrill's Company,
Col. Fifield's Regt. Detached Militia
in U. S. service 4 months and 6
days, 1812.

*LONGLEY, JOHN.
Served in Sumner's Regt. Vt. Militia.

*LONGLEY. JOSEPH.
Served in Sumner's Regt. Vt. Militia.

LOOKADOE, WILLIAM, Sergeant.
Served from May 1 to June 30, 1814
in Corps of Light Dragoons. Ref: R.
& L. 1812, AGO Page 20.

LOOKER, JOHN, Cornwall.
Volunteered to go to Plattsburgh,
September, 1814, and served in Capt.
Wait Branch's Company. Ref: Book
51, AGO Page 16.

*LOOKER, JOHN. Addison.
Served from April 12 to May 20, 1814
in Capt. George Fisher's Company,
Sumner's Regt.; volunteered to go
to Plattsburgh, September, 1814, and
was in the battle, serving in the
same company.

LOOMIS, ALDEN, Roxbury.
Volunteered to go to Plattsburgh,
September, 1814, and served 8 days
in Capt. Samuel M. Orcutt's Company. Ref: Book 52, AGO Pages 183
and 250.

LOOMIS, AUGUSTINE, Franklin County.
Volunteered to go to Plattsburgh
Sept. 11, 1814 and served in 15th or
22nd Regt. Ref: Hemenway's Vt.
Gazetteer, Vol. 2, Page 392.

LOOMIS, AZRO, Quartermaster, E. Montpelier. Volunteered to go to Plattsburgh, September, 1814, and served
in Col. Parley Davis' Regt. Ref:
Book 52, AGO Page 178.

*LOOMIS, DANIEL.
Served from Sept. 25 to Oct. 30,
1813 in Capt. Jesse Post's Company,
Dixon's Regt.

LOOMIS, GUSTAVUS, Captain, Thetford
or Montpelier. Appointed 1st Lieutenant May 5, 1813; Captain assistant
deputy quartermaster general April
19 to September, 1813; transferred
to Artillery Corps May 12, 1814; died
March 5, 1872. Ref: Heitman's Historical Register & Dictionary USA.

*LOOMIS, JOHN, Lieutenant.
Served from Sept. 25 to Oct. 5, 1813
in Capt. Jesse Post's Company, Dixon's Regt.

*LOOMIS, JONAH,   Georgia.
Served from Sept. 25 to Oct. 30,
1813 in Capt. Jesse Post's Company,
Dixon's Regt.; volunteered to go to
Plattsburgh, September, 1814, and
served 8 days in same company.

*LOOMIS, JOSEPH JR.
Served from June 11 to June 14
and from Oct. 4 to Oct. 13, 1813,
in Capt. John Palmer's Company,
1st Regt. 2nd Brig. 3rd Div.

LOOMIS, NATHANIEL.
Enlisted Feb. 22, 1813 for duration
of the war in company of late Capt.
J. Brooks, commanded by Lieut.
John I. Cromwell, Corps of U. S.
Artillery; on Muster Roll from April
30, 1814 to June 30, 1814. Ref: R.
& L. 1812, AGO Page 18.

*LOOMIS, NOAH, Sergeant.
Enlisted Sept. 27, 1813 and served
1 month and 21 days in Capt. Jesse
Post's Company, Col. Dixon's Regt.

*LOOMIS, REUBEN.
Enlisted Sept. 23, 1813 and served
1 month and 23 days in Capt. Amasa
Mansfield's Company, Col. Dixon's
Regt.

*LOOMIS, ROGER.
Served from June 11 to June 14,
1813 in Lieut. Bates' Company, 1st
Regt. (Judson's).

*LOOMIS, ROSWELL, Lieutenant.
Served in Dixon's Regt. Vt. Militia.

*LOOMIS, SAMUEL.
Served in Capt. Walker's Company,
Col. Fifield's Regt. Detached Militia
in U. S. service 6 months.

LOOMIS, SILAS,   Waterbury.
Volunteered to go to Plattsburgh,
September, 1814, and served 8 days
in Capt. Timothy Hubbard's Company. Ref: Book 52, AGO Pages 198
and 256.

*LORD, BENJAMIN, Sergeant.
Served in Capt. Needham's Company,
Col. Martindale's Regt. Detached
Militia in U. S. service 2 months and
14 days, 1812.

LORD, DAN,   Roxbury.
Volunteered to go to Plattsburgh,
September, 1814, and served 8 days
in Capt. Samuel M. Orcutt's Company. Ref: Book 52, AGO Page 250.

LORD, HORATIO.
Served in Capt. Benjamin S. Edgerton's Company, 11th Regt.; on Pay
Roll for September and October, 1812,
and January and February, 1813; was
at the battle of Chrystler's Farm
Nov. 11, 1813 and was reported
missing after the battle; captured by
troops Dec. 19, 1813 at Fort Niagara
and discharged May 4, 1814. Ref: R.
& L. 1812, AGO Pages 1 and 2; Governor and Council Vt. Vol. 6, Page
490; Records of Naval Records and
Library, Navy Dept.

LORD, ICHOBOD.
Volunteered to go to Plattsburgh,
September, 1814, and served 7 days
in Capt. Frederick Griswold's Com-
pany, raised in Brookfield, Vt. Ref:
Book 52, AGO Page 52.

LORD, JAMES.
Served from Feb. 14 to June 30,
1814 in Regt. of Light Dragoons. Ref:
R. & L. 1812, AGO Page 21.

LORD, JOHN.
Served from April 12 to April 21,
1814 in Lieut. Justus Foote's Company, Sumner's Regt. Ref: Book 52,
AGO Page 285.

*LORD. PHILIP.
Served in Capt. Hopkins' Company,
Col. Martindale's Regt. Detached
Militia in U. S. service 2 months
and 13 days, 1812.

*LORD, RICHARD,   Thetford.
Marched for Plattsburgh, September,
1814, and went as far as Bolton,
Vt., serving 6 days in Capt. Salmon
Howard's Company, 2nd Regt.

LORD, RUBEN.
Served in Capt. Chadwick's Company.
Ref: R. & L. 1812, AGO Page 32.

*LORD, SAMUEL.
Served in 4 Regt. (Peck's) Vt. Militia.

LORING, IRA,   Franklin County.
Volunteered to go to Plattsburgh
Sept. 11, 1814 and served in 15th or
22nd Regt. Ref: Hemenway's Vt.
Gazetteer, Vol. 2, Page 391.

LOTHROP, GEORGE.
Served from May 1 to June 30, 1814
in Capt. Haig's Corps of Light Dragoons. Ref: R. & L. 1812, AGO
Page 20.

*LOTHROP, RUSSEL.
Served in Dixon's Regt. Vt. Militia.

‡LOUDON, JAMES W.
Served in Capt. Chandler's Company.
Pension Certificate No. 11463.

‡LOUGEE, JOHN,   Tunbridge.
Volunteered to go to Plattsburgh,
September, 1814, and served 4 days
in Capt. Ephraim Hackett's Company.
Pension Certificate of widow, Lydia,
No. 33215.

*LOUKS, HENRY.
Enlisted Oct. 11, 1813 in Capt. Asahel
Langworthy's Company, Col. Isaac
Clark's Rifle Corps.

*LOUKS, HENRY JR.
Served in Capt. Langworthy's Company, Col. Dixon's Regt. Detached
Militia in U. S. service 1 month and
7 days, 1813.

*LOUKS, WILLIAM.
Served from Sept. 25 to Oct. 7, 1813
in Capt. Elijah W. Wood's Company,
Dixon's Regt.

*LOVE, GEORGE W., Corporal.
Served from June 11 to June 14, 1813
in Capt. John M. Eldridge's Company,
1st Regt. 2nd Brig. 3rd Div.

*LOVE, HARRY .
Served in 1 Regt. (Judson's) Vt.
Militia.

LOVE, JAMES.
Enlisted May 20, 1812 for 5 years
in Capt. White Youngs' Company,
15th Regt.; on Muster Roll from Aug.
31 to Dec. 31, 1814. Ref: R. & L.
1812, AGO Page 27.

LOVEGROVE, EDGAR,   Fairfax.
Served in 1813 and 1814 in Capt.
Joseph Beeman's Company. Ref: Hemenway's Vt. Gazetteer, Vol. 2, Page
402.

‡LOVEGROVE, REUBEN,   Fairfax.
Served in 1813 and 1814 in Capt.
Joseph Beeman's Company. Also serv-
ed in Capt. Grout's Company. Pen-
sion Certfiicate of widow, Polly L.,
No. 28221.

‡*LOVEJOY, PETER C. (or E.), Stowe
or Montpelier. Volunteered to go to
Plattsburgh, September, 1814, and was
at the battle, serving in Capt. Nehemiah Perkins' Company; also served
in 1812. Pension Certificate of widow,
Jenny, No. 24376.

*LOVEJOY, RICHARD.
Served in Capt. O. Lowry's Company, Col. Wm. Williams' Regt. Detached Militia in U. S. service 4
months and 26 days, 1812.

‡LOVEJOY, WILLIAM.
Enlisted May 7, 1813 for 1 year in
Capt. Simeon Wright's Company. Pen-
sion Certificate No. 5629.

LOVELAND, ALLEN,   Fairfax.
Volunteered to go to Plattsburgh,
September, 1814, and served in Capt.
Josiah Grout's Company. Ref: Hem-
enway's Vt. Gazetteer Vol. 2, Page
403.

LOVELAND, CHESTER,   Salisbury.
Served in regular Army in 1812. Ref:
History of Salisbury.

LOVELAND, MEMBER.
Volunteered to go to Plattsburgh,
September, 1814, and served 8 days
in Capt. Josiah Grout's Company.
Ref: Book 51, AGO Page 103.

LOVELAND, REMEMBRANCE.
Served from April 22, 1813 to April
26, 1814 in Capt. James Taylor's
Company and Capt. Gideon Spencer's
Company, 30th Regt. Ref: R. & L.
1812, AGO Pages 52, 57, 58.

LOVELAND, ROBERT L.,   Pittsford.
Volunteered to go to Plattsburgh,
September, 1814, and served 8 days
in Capt. Caleb Hendee's Company.
Ref: Book 52, AGO Page 125.

*LOVELL, HORACE.
Served from April 12 to April 21,
1814 in Capt. Eseck Sprague's Company, Sumner's Regt.

LOVELL, JOHN.
Served from Feb. 13 to May 12, 1813
in Capt. Samul Gordon's Company,
11th Regt. Ref: R. & L. 1812, AGO
Pages 8 and 9.

*LOVELL, JOSEPH.
Served in Sumner's Regt. Vt. Militia.

*LOVELL, NEHEMIAH.
Served in Dixon's Regt. Vt. Militia.

LOVELL, ROBERT,   St. Albans.
Served at the battle of Plattsburgh
Sept. 11, 1814 in Capt. Samuel H.
Farnsworth's Company. Ref: Hemen-
way's Vt. Gazetteer, Vol. 2, Page 434.

LOVELL, SILAS.
Served in Capt. Samul Gordon's Company, 11th Regt.; on Pay Roll for
January and February, 1813. Also
served in 2 Regt. (Fifield's) Vt. Militia.

LOVELL, SILAVOUS.
Served in War of 1812 and was cap-
tured by troops July 25, 1814 at
Londer's Lane; discharged Oct. 8,
1814. Records of Naval Records and
Library, Navy Dept.

LOVERING, JEREMIAH, Franklin County. Volunteered to go to Plattsburgh Sept. 11, 1814 and served in
15th or 22nd Regt. Ref: Hemenway's Vt. Gazetteer, Vol. 2, Page
392.

LOVETT, SIMON.
Served in Capt. Benjamin Bradford's
Company; on Muster Roll from May
31 to Aug. 31, 1813; joined by transfer July 22, 1813. Ref: R. & L.
1812, AGO Page 26.

LOVEWELL, MOODY B.,   Orange.
Marched for Plattsburgh Sept. 11,
1814 and went part way, serving 5
days in Capt. David Rising's Company. Ref: Book 52, AGO Page 19.

‡LOVEWELL, ROBERT.
Served in Capt. Robinson's Company.
Pension Certificate No. 24193. Pen-
sion Certificate of widow, Hannah,
No. 29169.

LOW, JOHN.
Enlisted Feb. 15, 1813 in Capt.
Charles Follett's Company, 11th Regt.
and served until date of death March
20, 1813. Ref: R. & L. 1812, AGO
Page 13.

LOW, JOSEPH, 2nd Lieutenant.
Served in Capt. Benjamin Bradford's
Company; on Muster Roll from May
31 to Aug. 31, 1813. Ref: R. & L.
1812, AGO Page 26.

LOW, THOMAS, Townsend.
Served in Capt. Charles Follett's Com-
pany, 11th Regt.; on Pay Roll for
January and February, 1812. Ref:
R. & L. 1812, AGO Page 12.

LOWEL, EVANTINE, Lieutenant.
Served in Capt. Chadwick's Company.
Ref: R. & L. 1812, AGO Page 32.

*LOWELL, BRANT.
Served from April 12 to April 21,
1814 in Lieut. Justus Foote's Company, Sumner's Regt.

‡*LOWELL, MARTIN L., Corporal, Braintree. Served in Capt. Wheatley's
Company, Col. Fifield's Regt. Detached Militia in U. S. service 6
months, 1812. Pension Certificate No.
6125.

‡LOWELL, WILLARD.
Served in Capt. Maston's Company.
Pension Certificate No. 2798.

LOWHORN, CHARLES, Franklin County.
Volunteered to go to Plattsburgh
Sept. 11, 1814 and served in 15th or
22nd Regt. Ref: Hemenway's Vt.
Gazetteer, Vol. 2, Page 391.

LOWNSBURY, DANIEL, Franklin County.
Volunteered to go to Plattsburgh
Sept. 11, 1814 and served in 15th or
22nd Regt. Ref: Hemenway's Vt.
Gazetteer, Vol. 2, Page 392.

*LOWREY, OLIVER, Captain.
Served in 3 Regt. (Tyler's) Vt. Militia and 4 Regt. (Williams') Vt. Militia.

*LOWRY, JAMES.
Served in Capt. Lowry's Company,
Col. Wm. Williams' Regt. Detached
Militia in U. S. service 4 months
and 26 days, 1812.

LUCAS, GEORGE W.
Served from Feb. 16 to May 10, 1813
in Capt. John W. Weeks' Company,
11th Regt. Ref: R. & L. 1812, AGO
Page 4.

LUCAS, JAMES, Haverhill, N. H.
Served from May 1 to July 19, 1814
in Capt. Haig's Company of Light
Dragoons. Ref: R. & L. 1812, AGO
Pages 20 and 30.

LUCAS, JESSE.
Served in Capt. Strait's Company,
Col. Martindale's Regt. Detached
Militia in U. S. service 2 months
and 13 days, 1812. Ref: Book 53,
AGO Page 29.

*LUCAS, REUBEN.
Served in Capt. Burnap's Company,
Col. Jonathan Williams' Regt. Detached Militia in U. S. service 1
month and 26 days, 1812.

*LUCE, ANDREW 2nd, Stowe.
Volunteered to go to Plattsburgh,
September, 1814, and was at the
battle, serving in Capt. Nehemiah
Perkins' Company, 4th Regt.

*LUCE, CHESTER, Stowe or Montpelier.
Volunteered to go to Plattsburgh,
September, 1814, and was at the
battle, serving in Capt. Nehemiah
Perkins' Company, 4 Regt. (Peck's).

LUCE, EPHRAIM, Williamstown.
Volunteered to go to Plattsburgh,
September, 1814, and served 8 days
in Capt. David Robinson's Company.
Ref: Book 52, AGO Page 8.

*LUCE, IVORY, Stowe.
Volunteered to go to Plattsburgh,
September, 1814, and served in Capt.
Nehemiah Perkins' Company, 4 Regt.
(Peck's). Ref: Hemenway's Vt. Ga-
zetteer, Vol. 2, Page 742.

‡LUCE, JONAS.
Served in Capt. Arnold's Company.
Pension Certificate of widow, Betsey,
No. 5065.

*LUCE, JONATHAN, Stowe.
Volunteered to go to Plattsburgh,
September, 1814, and was at the
battle, serving in Capt. Nehemiah
Perkins' Company, 4 Regt. (Peck's).
Also served in Corning's Detachment,
Vt. Militia.

LUCE, JOSHUA, Waitsfield.
Volunteered to go to Plattsburgh,
September, 1814, and served 4 days
in Capt. Mathias S. Jones' Company.
Ref: Book 52, AGO Page 170.

‡*LUCE, ORANGE,   Stowe.
Volunteered to go to Plattsburgh,
September, 1814, and was at the
battle, serving in Capt. Nehemiah
Perkins' Company, 4 Regt. (Peck's).
Also served in Corning's Detachment,
Vt. Militia. Pension Certificate of
widow, Eunice, No. 7211.

*LUCE, ZEBINA (or Sebina?), Stowe.
Volunteered to go to Plattsburgh,
September, 1814, and was at the
battle, serving in Capt. Nehemiah
Perkins' Company, 4 Regt. (Peck's).
Also served in Corning's Detachment,
Vt. Militia.

*LUCUS, JESSEE.
Served in 1 Regt. (Martindale's) Vt.
Militia.

*LUIS, REUBIN.
Served in 3 Regt. (Williams') Vt.
Militia.

LULL, FRANCIS, Montpelier.
Volunteered to go to Plattsburgh,
September, 1814, and served 8 days
in Capt. Timothy Hubbard's Company. Ref: Book 52, AGO Page 256.

*LULL, ISAAC.
Served in Capt. Burnap's Company,
Col. Jonathan Williams' Regt. Detached Militia in U. S. service 2
months and 13 days, 1812.

*LULL, SALMON.
Served in Capt. Needham's Company,
Col. Martindale's Regt. Detached
Militia in U. S. service 2 months
and 14 days, 1812.

‡LUMBARD, BENJAMIN.
Served in Capt. Hodgkins' Company.
Pension Certificate of widow, Ellen,
No. 34745.

‡LUMBARD, CLARK,   Montpelier.
Volunteered to go to Plattsburgh,
September, 1814, and served 8 days
in Capt. Timothy Hubbard's Com-
pany. Pension Certificate of widow,
Lucinda, No. 29559.

‡*LUMBARD, JOSHUA.
Served in Capt. Phelps' Company,
Col. Jonathan Williams' Regt. Detached Militia in U. S. service 2
months and 21 days, 1812. Pension
Certificate No. 3139. Pension Certificate of widow, Persis, No. 18805.

LUMBARD, SOLOMON.
Served in Capt. Burnap's Company,
Col. Jonathan Williams' Regt. Detached Militia in U. S. service 2
months and 13 days, 1812. Ref: Book
53, AGO Page 61.

LUND, THOMAS,   Corinth.
Volunteered to go to Plattsburgh,
September, 1814, and served 3 days
in Capt. Abel Jackman's Company.
Ref: Book 52, AGO Pages 44 and 45.

LUND, WILLIAM JR.
Served in Capt. Richardson's Company. Col. Martindale's Regt. Detached Militia in U. S. service 2 months
and 13 days, 1812. Ref: Book 53,
AGO Page 58.

*LUNNEY, PATRICK.
Served in 4 Regt. (Williams') Vt.
Militia.

LUNTIN, JONATHAN.
Served in Capt. Chadwick's Company.
Ref: R. & L. 1812, AGO Page 32.

*LURD, WILLIAM JR.
Served in 1 Regt. (Martindale's) Vt.
Militia.

LUSH, STEPHEN JR., Judge Advocate.
Served on General Staff of the North-
ern Army commanded by Major Gen-
eral George Izard; on Pay Roll to
July 31, 1814. Ref: R. & L. 1812,
AGO Page 28.

LUSK, SAMUEL,   Montgomery.
Volunteered to go to Plattsburgh,
September, 1814, and served 6 days
in Capt. Martin D. Follett's Company,
Dixon's Regt. Ref: Book 51, AGO
Pages 99, 154, 188.

LUSK, SOLOMON, Lieutenant, Poultney.
Volunteered to go to Plattsburgh,
September, 1814, and served 2 days
in Capt. Briant Ransom's Company.
Ref: Book 52, AGO Page 147.

*LUTHER, JAMES JR.
Served under Captains Durkee and
Wright, Col. Fifield's Regt. Detached
Militia in U. S. service 5 months
and 25 days, 1812.

‡LUTHER, MARTIN,   Addison.
Volunteered to go to Plattsburgh,
September, 1814, and was in the
battle, serving 9 days in Capt. George
Fisher's Company, Sumner's Regt.
Pension Certificate of widow, L.
Louisa, No. 29769.

LUYON, JONATHAN, Sergeant.
Served from June 11 to June 14, 1813
in Capt. Samuel Blinn's Company.
Ref: R. & L. 1812, AGO Page 49.

LYFORD, FIFIELD, Lieutenant.
Appointed 2nd Lieutenant 31st Regt.
April 30, 1813; resigned Jan. 11,
1814. Ref: Governor and Council,
Vt., Vol. 6, Page 476; Heitman's
Historical Register & Dictionary USA.

‡LYFORD, PETER,   Cabot.
Served in Capt. Merrill's Company.
Pension Certificate of widow, Lois,
No. 2210.

LYMAN, ABEL JR.
Volunteered to go to Plattsburgh,
September, 1814, and served 7 days
in Capt. Frederick Griswold's Com-
pany, raised in Brookfield, Vt. Ref:
Book 52, AGO Page 52.

*LYMAN, CHESTER.
Served from April 12 to April 15, 1814
in Capt. John Hackett's Company,
Sumner's Regt.

*LYMAN, DANIEL, Ensign.
Served in 3 Regt. (Tyler's) Vt. Militia.

LYMAN, EBENEZER.
Enlisted May 17, 1813 for 1 year in
Capt. Daniel Farrington's Company
(also commanded by Capt. Simeon
Wright) 30th Regt.; on Muster Roll
from March 1 to April 30, 1814. Ref:
R. & L. 1812, AGO Pages 50 and 51.

*LYMAN, ELIHU, Corporal.
Served in Capt. Dodge's Company,
Col. Fifield's Regt. Detached Militia
in U. S. service 1 month and 8
days, 1812.

*LYMAN, HARVEY JR.
Served in 3 Regt. (Tyler's) Vt. Militia.

*LYMAN, JAMES .
Served in 4 Regt. (Williams') Vt.
Militia.

*LYMAN, JESSE, Colonel, Charlotte or
Vergennes. Volunteered to go to
Plattsburgh, September, 1814, with
company from Cornwall and vicinity.
Also served as Major in 4th Regt.
(Williams') Vt. Militia. Resided at
Monkton for several years and later
moved to Vergennes. Ref: Rev. Ly-
man Mathews' History of Cornwall,
Page 343; Hemenway's Vt. Gazet-
teer, Vol. 1, Page 66.

*LYMAN, JOHN, Surgeon.
Served in 4 Regt. (Williams') Vt.
Militia.

*LYMAN, JOSEPH.
Served from June 11 to June 14, 1813
in Capt. Moses Jewett's Company,
1st Regt. 2nd Brig. 3rd Div.

‡*LYMAN, NOAH JR.
Served in Col. Wm. Williams' Regt.,
Capt. Pettis' Company, Detached
Militia in U. S. service 4 months and
17 days, 1812. Also served in 3
Regt. (Tyler's) Vt. Militia. Pen-
sion Certificate No. 15404.

*LYMAN, PHINEHAS.
Served in 1 Regt. (Judson's) Vt.
Militia.

*LYMAN, SIMEON, Corporal.
Served in 3 Regt. (Tyler's) Vt. Militia.

*LYMAN, STEPHEN,   Jericho.
Served in 3 Regt. (Tyler's') Vt. Militia. Volunteered at Jericho Sept.
7, 1814 and took part in the battle
of Plattsburgh. Ref: History of
Jericho, Page 142.

*LYMAN, WARREN, Corporal.
Served in Sumner's Regt. Vt. Militia.

*LYMAN, WILLIAM.
Served from April 12 to April 21,
1814 in Capt. Shubael Wales' Company, Col. W. B. Sumner's Regt.

*LYNDE, AMASA.
Served in 3 Regt. (Williams') Vt.
Militia.

LYNDE, BENJAMIN.
Enlisted April 7, 1813 in Capt. Samul
Gordon's Company, 11th Regt.; on
Pay Roll to May 31, 1813. Ref: R.
& L. 1812, AGO Page 8.

*LYNDE, LEWIS.
Served in Capt. Parson's Company,
Col. Jonathan Williams' Regt. Detached Militia in U. S. service 2
months and 13 days, 1812.

*LYNN, JAMES.
Served in Capt. Dorrance's Company.
Col. Wm. Williams' Regt. Detached
Militia in U. S. service 4 months
and 6 days, 1812.

*LYON, ABEL.
Enlisted Sept. 25, 1813 and served
1 month and 23 days in Capt. Jesse
Post's Company, Col. Dixon's Regt.

*LYON, ARANNAH (or Aruna) Fife Ma-
jor. Served in 4 Regt. (Peck's) Vt.
Militia.

LYON, ASAHEL, Corporal, Fairfax or
Swanton. Served in Lieut. V. R.
Goodrich's Company, 11th Regt.; on
Pay Roll for January and February,
1813. Served from Aug. 8, 1812 in
company of Capt. Joseph Beeman
Jr., 11th Regt. U. S. Inf. under
Col. Ira Clark. Ref: R. & L. 1812,
AGO Page 11; Hemenway's Vt. Ga-
zetteer, Vol. 2, Page 402.

LYON, ASAHEL,   Montpelier.
Volunteered to go to Plattsburgh,
September, 1814, serving 8 days in
Capt. Timothy Hubbard's Company.
Ref: Book 52, AGO Page 256.

*LYON, JACOB.
Served in 2 Regt. (Fifield's) Vt.
Militia.

*LYON, JAMES.
Served in Capt. Taylor's Company,
Col. Fifield's Regt. Detached Militia
in U. S. service 2 months and 21
days, 1812.

LYON, JESSE.
Born in Lanesborough, Mass.; aged
20 years; 5 feet 6 inches high; dark
complexion; dark hair; dark eyes; by
profession a schoolmaster. Enlisted
at Bridport April 11, 1814 and served
in Capt. Wm. Miller's Company and
Capt. Gideon Spencer's Company,
30th Regt.; discharged at Burlington, Vt. in 1815. Ref: R. & L.
1812, AGO Pages 54, 55, 57.

*LYON, JOEL.
Served in Capt. Rogers' Company,
Col. Fifield's Regt. Detached Militia
in U. S. service 3 months and 9 days,
1812. Served in Capt. Taylor's Company, Col. Fifield's Regt. Detached
Militia in U. S. service 2 months and
21 days, 1812.

*LYON, JOHN, Fifer.
Served from June 11 to June 14,
1813 in Capt. Samuel Blinn's Company, 1st Regt. (Judson's).

‡*LYON, JONATHAN, Sergeant.
Served in Capt. Barns' Company, Col.
Wm. Williams' Regt. Detached Militia in U. S. service 5 months, 1812,
at Swanton Falls. Also served in
1 Regt. (Judson's). Pension Certificate No. 615.

‡LYON, MELZEAR A.
Served from April 24, 1813 to May 1,
1814 in Capt. Gideon Spencer's Company and Capt. James Taylor's Company, 30th Regt. Pension Certificate
No. 14919.

*LYON, SAMUEL.
Served in Corning's Detachment, Vt.
Militia.

*LYON, SIMON.
Served in Capt. Howard's Company,
Vt. Militia.

LYONS, WILLIAM.
Served from May 1 to June 30, 1814
in Capt. Haig's Corps of Light Dragoons. Ref: R. & L. 1812, AGO
Page 20.

MACGUIRE, HUGH,   Franklin County.
Volunteered to go to Plattsburgh
Sept. 11, 1814 and served in 15th or
22nd Regt. Ref: Hemenway's Vt.
Gazetteer, Vol. 2, Page 392.

*MACK, ABNER JR.
Served from June 11 to June 14, 1813
in Lieut. Bates' Company, 1 Regt.
(Judson's).

MACK, ELISHA, Ensign,   Marshfield.
Volunteered to go to Plattsburgh,
September, 1814, and served 9 days
in Capt. James English's Company.
Ref: Book 52, AGO Page 248.

MACK, JACOB,   Franklin County.
Enlisted May 16, 1812 for 5 years in
Capt. White Youngs' Company, 15th
Regt.; on Muster Roll from Aug. 31
to Dec. 31, 1814. Ref: R. & L. 1812,
AGO Page 27.

‡MACK, STEPHEN.
Served in Capt. Follett's Company.
Pension Certificate No. 24592.

MACKAY, SAMUEL MICHAEL, Lieutenant. Appointed 3 Lieutenant Light
Artillery April 4, 1813; 2 Lieutenant May 27, 1813; 1 Lieutenant Oct.
10, 1814; resigned Oct. 31, 1819. Ref:
Heitman's Historical Register & Dictionary USA.

*MACKINTIRE, BENJAMIN.
Served in 1 Regt. (Martindale's) Vt.
Militia.

*MACLALEM, WILLIAM.
Served in 4 Regt. (Williams') Vt.
Militia.

MACMONEY, THOMAS, Franklin County.
Volunteered to go to Plattsburgh
Sept. 11, 1814 and served in 15th or
22nd Regt. Ref: Hemenway's Vt.
Gazetteer, Vol. 2, Page 392.

MACOMB, ALEXANDER, Brig. General.
Served from May 1 to July 31, 1814
on General Staff of the Northern
Army commanded by Maj. Gen.
George Izard. Ref: R. & L. 1812,
AGO Page 28.

*MACUMBER, DAVID.
Served from Sept. 25 to Oct. 6, 1813
in Capt. Elijah Birge's Company,
Dixon's Regt.

‡*MACUMBER, JACOB.
Served in Capt. Taylor's Company,
Col. Wm. Williams' Regt. Detached
Militia in U. S. service 4 months
and 24 days, 1812. Pension Certi-
ficate of widow, Elmirah, No. 23299.

MADISON, JOHN,   Franklin County.
Volunteered to go to Plattsburgh
Sept. 11, 1814 and served in 15th or
22nd Regt. Ref: Hemenway's Vt.
Gazetteer, Vol. 2, Page 391.

MAGEE, FREEMAN.
Served from Feb. 12 to May 11, 1813
in Lieut. V. R. Goodrich's Company,
11th Regt. Ref: R. & L. 1812, AGO
Page 10.

*MAGIS, JULIUS.
Served in 1 Regt. (Judson's) Vt.
Militia.

*MAGOON, ELI B.
Served in Capt. Wheeler's Company,
Col. Fifield's Regt. Detached Militia
in U. S. service 6 months and 4
days, 1812.

MAGOON, JOHN,   Corinth.
Volunteered to go to Plattsburgh,
September, 1814, and served 3 days
in Capt. Abel Jackman's Company.
Ref: Book 52, AGO Pages 44 and 45.

MAGRAHAM, DANIEL.
Served from April 12 to April 21,
1814 in Capt. Shubael Wales' Company. Col. W. B. Sumner's Regt.
Ref: Book 52, AGO Page 288.

MAINAMARE, ASA.
Served from March 11 to June 10,
1813 in Lieut. V. R. Goodrich's
Company, 11th Regt. Ref: R. & L.
1812, AGO Page 10.

MAINWEARING, GEORGE, Musician,
Franklin County. Served from May
9 to June 30, 1814 in Capt. Alexander Brooks' Corps of Artillery.
Ref: R. & L. 1812, AGO Page 31.

*MAITLAND, WILLIAM, Corporal.
Served in Capt. Taylor's Company,
Col. Fifield's Regt. Detached Militia
in U. S. service 1 month and 14
days, 1812.

*MAJORS, GEORGE,   Fairfax.
Enlisted Oct. 26, 1813 in Capt. Asahel
Langworthy's Company, Col. Isaac
Clark's Rifle Corps; transferred to
Capt. Wilkins' Company, Col. Dixon's
Regt.; served 1 month and 23 days.

MAJORS, GEORGE JR.,   Fairfax.
Volunteered to go to Plattsburgh,
September, 1814, and served 8 days
in Capt. Josiah Grout's Company.
Ref: Book 51, AGO Page 103.

MAJORS, JOHN,   Fairfax.
Served from April 22, 1813 to April
25, 1814 in Capt. James Taylor's
Company and Capt. Gideon Spencer's
Company, 30th Regt. Volunteered to
go to Plattsburgh, September, 1814,
and served 8 days in Capt. Josiah
Grout's Company. Ref: R. & L.
1812, AGO Pages 52, 57, 58; Book 51,
AGO Page 103.

MAJORS, MOSES.
Enlisted April 24, 1813 for 1 year
in Capt. James Taylor's Company,
30th Regt. Ref: R. & L. 1812, AGO
Page 59.

MAJORS, PETER.
Served in Lieut. Wm. S. Foster's
Company, 11th Regt.; on Pay Roll
for January and February, 1813. Ref:
R. & L. 1812, AGO Page 7.

*MAKER, JUSTIN B.
Served from April 12 to April 21, 1814
in Capt. Shubael Wales' Company,
Col. W. B. Sumner's Regt.

MALLARY, CALVIN,   Poultney.
Volunteered to go to Plattsburgh.
September, 1814, and served 2 days
in Capt. Briant Ransom's Company.
Ref: Book 52, AGO Page 147.

MALLARY, DANIEL, Sergeant, Poultney.
Volunteered to go to Plattsburgh,
September, 1814, and served 2 days
in Capt. Briant Ransom's Company.
Ref: Book 52, AGO Page 147.

*MALLORY, JAMES B.
Served from Oct. 8 to Nov. 18, 1813
in Capt. Isaac Finch's Company,
Col. Clark's Regt. of Riflemen.

*MALLORY, LEVERET.
Served from Sept. 25 to Nov. 18,
1813 in Capt. Isaac Finch's Company,
Col. Clark's Rifle Corps.

*MALLORY, ROSWELL.
Served in Capt. Saxe's Company,
Col. Wm. Williams' Regt. Detached
Militia in U. S. service 4 months
and 24 days, 1812.

MALTBY, BENJAMIN.
Volunteered to go to Plattsburgh,
September, 1814, and served in company of Capt. Ebenezer Spencer, Vershire. Ref: Book 52, AGO Page 48.

MALTBY, GEORGE W., Sergeant.
Volunteered to go to Plattsburgh,
September, 1814, and served in company of Capt. Ebenezer Spencer, Vershire. Ref: Book 52 AGO Pages 48
and 120.

‡MANCHESTER, ABEL.
Served in Capt. Danforth's Company.
Pension Certificate No. 14834.

MANCHESTER, DAVID.
Served from March 17 to June 16,
1813 in Capt. Charles Follett's Company, 11th Regt. Ref: R. & L. 1812,
AGO Page 13.

‡MANCHESTER, MARCENA.
Served in Capt. Danforth's Company.
Pension Certificate No. 30794.

*MANCHESTER, NOAH.
Enlisted Sept. 18, 1813 in Capt. Isaac
Finch's Company, Col. Clark's Rifle
Corps. Also served in 4 Regt. (Williams') Vt. Militia. Was captured by
troops Dec. 19, 1813 at Fort Niagara;
discharged March 11, 1814.

*MANCHESTER, THOMAS.
Served in Capt. Cross' Company, Col.
Martindale's Regt. Detached Militia
in U. S. service 2 months and 13
days, 1812.

MANING, MARTIN,   Poultney.
Volunteered to go to Plattsburgh,
September, 1814, and served 2 days
in Capt. Briant Ransom's Company.
Ref: Book 52, AGO Page 147.

MANISTER, JOHN S.,   Strafford.
Volunteered to go to Plattsburgh,
September, 1814, and served in Capt.
Cyril Chandler's Company. Ref: Book
52, AGO Page 42.

MANLEY, ELI.
Enlisted May 13, 1813 in Capt. Daniel
Farrington's Company (also commanded by Capt. Simeon Wright) 30th
Regt.; on Muster Roll from March
1 to April 30, 1814. Ref: R. & L.
1812, AGO Pages 50 and 51.

‡MANLEY, ELI JR.,   Pittsford.
Volunteered to go to Plattsburgh,
September, 1814, and served 8 days
in Capt. Caleb Hendee's Company.
Pension Certificate of widow, Han-
nah, No. 26184.

*MANLEY, L. B.
Served with Hospital Attendants, Vt.

*MANLY, HARMON.
Enlisted Sept. 27, 1813 in Capt.
Asahel Langworthy's Company, Col.
Isaac Clark's Rifle Corps.

MANLY, HEMAN.
Served in Capt. Langworthy's Com-
pany, Col. Dixon's Regt. Detached
Militia in U. S. service 1 month and
21 days, 1813. Ref: Book 53, AGO
Page 112.

‡*MANN, BENJAMIN.
Served in Capt. Adams' Company,
Col. Jonathan Williams' Regt. De-
tached Militia in U. S. service 2
months and 7 days, 1812. Pension
Certificate No. 1253.

MANN, ISAAC,   Plainfield.
Volunteered to go to Plattsburgh,
September, 1814, and served 1 day;
no organization given. Ref: Book 52,
AGO Pages 193 and 200.

*MANN, LEONARD JR. (or Larned)
Served from April 12, 1814 to April
15, 1814 in Capt. John Hackett's Company, Sumner's Regt.

‡MANN, THOMAS J.
Served in Capt. Danforth's Company.
Pension Certificate No. 2598.

*MANNING, JOSEPH.
Served from July 22 to Dec. 9, 1812
in Capt. S. Pettes' Company, Col.
Wm. Williams' Regt. Detached Militia in U. S. service.

MANNIS, JAMES,   Randolph.
Volunteered to go to Plattsburgh,
September, 1814, and served in Capt.
Lebbeus Egerton's Company. Ref:
Book 52, AGO Page 82.

MANOR, JOSEPH.
Enlisted Oct. 11, 1812 in Capt. Ben-
jamin S. Edgerton's Company, 11th
Regt.; on Pay Roll for September
and October, 1812 and January and
February, 1813. Ref: R. & L. 1812,
AGO Pages 1 and 2.

*MANSFIELD, AMASA, Captain.
Commanded company in Col. Luther
Dixon's Regt.; appointed Sept. 23,
1813.

*MANSFIELD, AMBROSE.
Enlisted Sept. 23, 1813 and served 1
month and 23 days in Capt. Mansfield's Company, Col. Dixon's Regt.
Detached Militia in U. S. service.

MANSFIELD, AMOS.
Served from April 24, 1813 to April
11, 1814 in Capt. James Taylor's
Company and Capt. Gideon Spencer's
Company, 30th Regt. Ref: R. & L.
1812, AGO Pages 52, 57, 59.

‡MANSFIELD, AMOSA.
Served in Capt. Johnson's Company.
Pension Certificate No. 1777.

MANSFIELD, STEPHEN.
Served from April 24, 1813 to April
26, 1814 in Capt. James Taylor's
Company and Capt. Gideon Spencer's
Company, 30th Regt. Ref: R. & L.
1812, AGO Pages 52, 57, 59.

MANSFIELD, WILLIAM.
Served in Capt. Wilkins' Company,
Col. Dixon's Regt. Detached Militia
in U. S. service 1 month and 23
days, 1813. Ref: Book 53, AGO Page
112.

*MANWELL, PETER (or Manuel), Lieutenant, Richmond. Volunteered to go to Plattsburgh, September, 1814, and served in Capt. Roswell Hunt's Company, 3 Regt. (Tyler's).

‡*MANZER, ABRAM. Served in Capt. Prentiss' Company, Col. Dixon's Regt. Detached Militia in U. S. service 1 month and 23 days, 1813. Pension Certificate of widow, Ruth, No. 35550.

*MANZER, ISAAC, Corporal. Served in Capt. Prentiss' Company, Col. Dixon's Regt. Detached Militia in U. S. service 1 month and 23 days, 1813.

*MARBLE, JOSEPH, Waitsfield. Served in Capt. Durkee's Company, Col. Fifield's Regt. Detached Militia in U. S. service 2 months and 21 days, 1812. Volunteered to go to Plattsburgh, September, 1814, and served 4 days in Capt. Mathias S. Jones' Company.

MARBREDO, LEWIS, Fairfax. Served from Aug. 8, 1812 in company of Capt. Joseph Beeman Jr., 11th Regt. U. S. Inf. under Col. Ira Clark. Ref: Hemenway's Vt. Gazetteer, Vol. 2, Page 402.

MARCH, DAVID, Surgeon's Mate. Appointed Hospital Surgeon's Mate March 1, 1813; resigned Jan. 25, 1815. Ref: Heitman's Historical Register & Dictionary USA.

*MARCY, THOMAS, Corporal. Served in 3 Regt. (Williams') Vt. Militia.

‡*MARCY, WILLARD. Served in Capt. Dodge's Company, Col. Fifield's Regt. Detached Militia in U. S. service 2 months and 21 days, 1812. Pension Certificate No. 1850.

MARKELL, JOHN. Geneva. Served from May 1 to July 2, 1814 in Capt. Spencer's Company. 29th Inf. Ref: R. & L. 1812, AGO Page 30.

MARKER, BENJAMIN. Served in company of late Capt. J. Brooks, commanded by Lieut. John I. Cromwell, Corps of U. S. Artillery; on Muster Roll from April 30, 1814 to June 30, 1814. Ref: R. & L. 1812, AGO Page 18.

MARKER, CORNELIUS. Served from May 1 to June 30, 1814 in Capt. Alexander Brooks' Corps of Artillery. Ref: R. & L. 1812, AGO Page 31.

*MARKHAM, DAVID. Served from April 12 to April 21, 1814 in Capt. Edmund B. Hill's Company, Sumner's Regt.

*MARKHAM, ISAAC E. Served from April 12 to April 21, 1814 in Capt. Edmund B. Hill's Company, Sumner's Regt.

MARKHAM, JONATHAN, Barre. Volunteered to go to Plattsburgh. September, 1814, and served 9 days in Capt. Warren Ellis' Company. Ref: Book 52, AGO Pages 220 and 235.

*MARKS, ELUNA. Served from April 20 to April 21, 1814 in Capt. Eseck Sprague's Company, Sumner's Regt.

MARLO, AVERY, Sergeant. Served from June 11 to June 14, 1813 in Capt. Ithiel Stone's Company, 1st Regt. 2nd Brig. 3rd Div. Ref: R. & L. 1812, AGO Page 44.

*MARRINER, JAMES, Stowe. Volunteered to go to Plattsburgh, September, 1814, and was at the battle, serving in Capt. Nehemiah Perkins' Company, 4 Regt. (Peck's) Vt. Militia.

MARROW, WILLIAM. Served from March 3 to June 30, 1814 in Regt. of Light Dragoons. Ref: R. & L. 1812, AGO Page 21.

MARSEMAU, TIMOTHY (or Marsenow), Pittsford. Volunteered to go to Plattsburgh, September, 1814, and served in Capt. Henry Horton's Company, 1st Regt. 2nd Brig. 2nd Div. Ref: Book 52, AGO Page 161.

*MARSH, AVERY, Sergeant. Served in 1 Regt. (Judson's) Vt. Militia.

‡MARSH, DANIEL, Woodstock. Pension Certificate of widow, Nancy, No. 15371.

MARSH, DAVID, Surgeon's Mate. Appointed Surgeon's Mate, 13th Inf. April 1, 1813. Ref: Governor and Council, Vt., Vol. 6, Page 478.

MARSH, DWIGHT, Fifer, Calais or Swanton. Served from Feb. 12 to May 11, 1813 in Lieut. V. R. Goodrich's Company, 11th Regt. Ref: R. & L. 1812, AGO Pages 10 and 11.

*MARSH, FREDERICK. Served in Capt. Strait's Company, Col. Martindale's Regt. Detached Militia in U. S. service 2 months and 13 days, 1812.

‡*MARSH, HENRY, Sergeant. Served in Capt. Needham's Company, Col. Martindale's Regt. Detached Militia in U. S. service 2 months and 14 days, 1812. Also served as sergeant in 1st Regt. of Detached Militia of Vt. in U. S. service at Champlain from Nov. 18 to Nov. 19, 1812. Pension Certificate of widow, Sarah, No. 4804.

MARSH, JASON, Calais. Served from Feb. 12 to May 11, 1813 in Lieut. V. R. Goodrich's Company, 11th Regt. Ref: R. & L. 1812, AGO Pages 10 and 11.

MARSH, JOHN, Montpelier. Volunteered to go to Plattsburgh. September, 1814, and served 8 days in Capt. Timothy Hubbard's Company. Ref: Book 52, AGO Page 256.

*MARSH, JONAS,   Jericho.
Took part in the battle of Platts-
burgh and served in Capt. Myron
Reed's Company, 3 Regt. (Tyler's).

*MARSH, JOSEPH, Drummer.
Served from Nov. 1, 1812 to Feb. 28,
1813 in Capt. Charles Follett's Com-
pany, 11th Regt. Also served in 3
Regt. (Williams') Vt. Militia. Ref:
R. & L. 1812, AGO Page 12.

‡MARSH, MOSES M.
Served in Capt. Hall's Company. Pension Certificate of widow, Mary, No.
2260.

MARSH, PELEG S.,   Bethel.
Volunteered to go to Plattsburgh.
September, 1814, and served 6 days
in Capt. Nehemiah Noble's Company.
Ref: Book 51, AGO Page 227.

‡MARSH, PERRY,   Calais.
Served in Capt. Foster's Company.
Pension Certificate No. 866.

MARSH, ROBERT, Corporal.
Served in Capt. Benjamin Bradford's
Company; on Muster Roll from May
31 to Aug. 31, 1813. Ref: R. & L.
1812, AGO Page 26.

*MARSH, ROYAL, Corporal.
Served in Capt. Sabin's Company,
Col. Jonathan Williams' Regt. Detached Militia in U. S. service 2
months and 6 days, 1812.

‡*MARSH, SYLVANUS.
Served in Capt. Richardson's Company, Col. Martindale's' Regt. Detached Militia in U. S. service 2
months and 13 days, 1812. Also served in Capt. Mardson's Company. Pension Certificate No. 12835. Pension
Certificate of widow, Sarah D., No.
10578.

*MARSH, WALTER.
Enlisted Sept. 25, 1813 in Capt. Amos
Robinson's Company, Dixon's Regt.

*MARSHAL, JOHN.
Served from June 11 to June 14.
1813 in Capt. John M. Eldridge's
Company, 1st Regt. 2nd Brig. 3rd
Div. Vt. Militia.

MARSHALL, CHESTER,   Waitsfield.
Volunteered to go to Plattsburgh.
September, 1814, and served in Capt.
Mathias S. Jones' Company; also
commanded company formed at
Waitsfield, being a part of a com-
pany in the 4 Regt. 2 Brig., 3 Div.
Ref: Book 52, AGO Pages 169, 170,
187.

*MARSHALL, CLEMENT.
Served in Capt. Lowry's Company,
Col. Wm. Williams' Regt. Detached
Militia in U. S. service 4 months and
26 days, 1812.

*MARSHALL, DAVIS, Ensign, Waterbury.
Volunteered to go to Plattsburgh.
September, 1814, and was at the
battle, serving 11 days in Capt.
George Atkins' Company, 4 Regt.
(Peck's).

*MARSHALL, IRA.
Volunteered to go to Plattsburgh.
September, 1814, and was at the
battle, serving in Capt. Nehemiah
Perkins' Company, 4 Regt. (Peck's).

*MARSHALL, IRA.
Served in Capt. Taylor's Company,
Col. Fifield's Regt. Detached Militia
in U. S. service 6 months.

MARSHALL, IRA,   Vershire.
Volunteered to go to Plattsburgh.
September, 1814, and served 3 days
in Capt. Ira Corse's Company. Ref:
Book 52, AGO Page 91.

MARSHALL, JESSE, Corporal.
Served in company of Capt. John
McNeil Jr., 11th Regt.; on Pay Roll
for January and February, 1813. Ref:
R. & L. 1812, AGO Page 17.

MARSHALL, JOSEPH,   Morristown.
Volunteered to go to Plattsburgh.
September, 1814, and served 8 days
in Capt. Denison Cook's Company.
Ref: Book 51, AGO Page 202.

*MARSHALL, JOSEPH,   Stowe.
Volunteered to go to Plattsburgh.
September, 1814, and was at the
battle, serving in Capt. Nehemiah
Perkins' Company, 4 Regt. (Peck's).
Also served in Corning's Detachment,
Vt. Militia.

*MARSHALL, LUTHER.
Served in Capt. Ormsbee's Company,
Col. Martindale's Regt. Detached
Militia in U. S. service 10 days, 1812.
Served from June 12, 1813 to June,
1814, in Capt. John Wires' Company,
30th Regt. Also served with Hospital Attendants, Vt. Ref: R. & L.
1812, AGO Page 40.

MARSHALL, MOSES,   Corinth.
Volunteered to go to Plattsburgh.
September, 1814, and served in Capt.
Abel Jackman's Company. Ref: Book
52, AGO Page 44.

‡*MARSHALL, ORA,   Stowe.
Volunteered to go to Plattsburgh.
September, 1814, and was at the
battle, serving in Capt. Nehemiah
Perkins' Company, 4 Regt. (Peck's).
Also served in Capt. D. Moodys' Com-
pany. Pension Certificate of widow,
Polly, No. 31473.

MARSHALL, SAMUEL W., Carpenter.
Served from June 10 to June 30,
1814 in Alexander Parris' Company
of Artificers. Ref: R. & L. 1812,
AGO Page 24.

MARSHALL, SILAS.
Served from May 10, 1813 to date
of death Jan. 8, 1814, in Capt. James
Taylor's Company and Capt. Gideon
Spencer's Company, 30th Regt. Ref:
R. & L. 1812, AGO Pages 52, 57, 59.

MARSHALL, STEARNS,   Poultney.
Volunteered to go to Plattsburgh.
September, 1814, and served 2 days
in Capt. Briant Ransom's Company.
Ref: Book 52, AGO Page 147.

*MARSHALL, WILLIAM O.
Served with Hospital Attendants, Vt.

MARSTIN, CALEB.
Enlisted Feb. 25, 1813 in Capt. Jonathan Starks' Company, 11th Regt.; on Pay Roll to May 31, 1813. Ref: R. & L. 1812, AGO Page 19.

MARSTIN, WILLIAM,   Richford.
Served in Capt. Martin D. Follett's Company, Dixon's Regt. on duty on Canadian Frontier in 1813. Ref: Hemenway's Vt. Gazetteer, Vol. 2, Page 428.

‡MARSTON, ASA.
Volunteered to go to Plattsburgh, September, 1814, and served 4 days in Capt. Aaron Kidder's Company. Pension Certificate of widow, Matilda, No. 23005.

MARSTON, JOHN.
Volunteered to go to Plattsburgh, September, 1814, and served 4 days in Capt. Aaron Kidder's Company. Ref: Book 52, AGO Pages 65 and 66.

MARSTON, JOSEPH T. W.
Volunteered to go to Plattsburgh, September, 1814, and served 4 days in Capt. Aaron Kidder's Company. Ref: Book 52, AGO Page 65.

MARSTON, NATHANIEL.   Deerfield.
Served from May 1 to July 24, 1814 in Capt. Goodenoe's Company, 33rd Inf. Ref: R. & L. 1812, AGO Page 30.

MARSTON, RUSSELL,   Vershire.
Volunteered to go to Plattsburgh, September, 1814, and served 3 days in Capt. Ira Corse's Company. Ref: Book 52, AGO Page 91.

MARSTON, WILLIAM.
Served in Capt. Charles Follett's Company, 11th Regt.; on Pay Roll for January and February, 1812. Ref: R. & L. 1812, AGO Page 12.

*MARTHEN, ASHER (or Mathew).
Served from April 12 to April 21, 1814 in Capt. Shubael Wales' Company, Col. W. B. Sumner's Regt.

MARTIN, AARON,   Richford.
Served in Capt. Barns' Company, Col. Wm. Williams' Regt. Detached Militia in U. S. service 5 months, 1812. Served in Capt. Martin D. Follett's Company, Dixon's Regt. on duty on northern frontier in 1813. Ref: Book 53, AGO Page 73; Hemenway's Vt. Gazetteer, Vol. 2, Page 428.

‡MARTIN, ASA, Orderly Sergeant, Orwell. Volunteered to go to Plattsburgh, September, 1814, and served 15 days in Capt. Asahel Scovell's Company. Pension Certificate of widow, Sally, No. 33582.

*MARTIN, CALEB.
Served in Capt. Wright's Company, Col. Martindale's Regt. Detached Militia in U. S. service 2 months and 14 days, 1812. Served from April 12 to April 21, 1814 in Capt. Edmund B. Hill's Company, Sumner's Regt.

*MARTIN, CHESTER.
Served in Capt. Barns' Company, Col. Wm. Williams' Regt. Detached Militia in U. S. service 4 months and 25 days, 1812. Served from June 11 to June 14, 1813 in Capt. John Palmer's Company, 1st Regt. 2nd Brig. 3rd Div. Ref: Book 53, AGO Page 13.

MARTIN, CHRISTOPHER.
Served from March 1 to Aug. 22, 1814; no oraginzation given. Ref: R. & L. 1812, AGO Page 29.

MARTIN, CHRISTOPHER.
Enlsited Aug. 9, 1813 in Capt. Daniel Farrington's Company (also commanded by Capt. Simeon Wright) 30th Regt.; on Muster Roll from March 1 to April 30, 1814; wounded. Ref: R. & L. 1812, AGO Pages 50 and 51.

MARTIN, DANIEL O.
Served from April 12 to April 15, 1814 in Capt. John Hackett's Company, Sumner's Regt. Ref: Book 52, AGO Page 281.

*MARTIN, DAVID,   Highgate.
Served in Capt. Saxe's Company, Col. Wm. Williams' Regt. Detached Militia in U. S. service 4 months and 24 days, 1812. Served from March 1 to May 31, 1813 in Lieut. V. R. Goodrich's Company, 11th Regt.

‡MARTIN, EBENEZER,   Rochester.
Volunteered to go to Plattsburgh, September, 1814, and served 7 days in Capt. Elias Keyes' Company. Pension Certificate No. 33357.

*MARTIN, EDWARD,   Randolph.
Volunteered to go to Plattsburgh, September, 1814, and served in Capt. Lebbeus Egerton's Company.

‡*MARTIN, ELIAS.
Served in Capt. Morrill's Company, Col. Fifield's Regt. Detached Militia in U. S. service 6 months and 5 days, 1812. Pension Certificate No. 3022. Pension Certificate of widow, Elizabeth, No. 35221.

‡MARTIN, ENOCH,   Orwell.
Volunteered to go to Plattsburgh, September, 1814, and served 15 days in Capt. Asahel Scovell's Company. Pension Certificate of widow, Fanny No. 26648.

*MARTIN, GASHERN.
Served in 1 Regt. (Martindale's) Vt. Militia.

*MARTIN, GEORGE.
Served in 3 Regt. (Tyler's) Vt. Militia.

*MARTIN, GEORGE W.
Served in Capt. Durkee's Company, Col. Fifield's Regt. Detached Militia in U. S. service 2 months and 21 days, 1812.

‡MARTIN, GURDIN,   Williamstown.
Volunteered to go to Plattsburgh, September, 1814, and served 8 days in Capt. David Robinson's Company; was in the battle. Pension Certificate of widow, Sarah, No. 28819.

*MARTIN, ISAIAH, Sergeant.
Served in Capt. Mansfield's Company,
Col. Dixon's Regt. Detached Militia
in U. S. service 1 month and 23
days, 1813.

MARTIN, JENNIAH.
Served from March 20 to June 19,
1813 in Capt. Charles Follett's Company, 11th Regt. Ref: R. & L.
1812, AGO Page 13.

*MARTIN, JEREMIAH.
Served in 4 Regt. (Peck's) Vt. Militia.

‡*MARTIN, JESSE,   Randolph.
Volunteered to go to Plattsburgh,
September, 1814, and served in Capt.
Lebbeus Egerton's Company. Also
served in Capt. Wheatley's Company.
Pension Certificate of widow, Betsey,
No. 34476.

‡MARTIN, JOHN,   Fairfax or Swanton.
Served from Aug. 8, 1812 in com-
pany of Capt. Joseph Beeman, Jr.,
11th Regt. U. S. Inf. under Col. Ira
Clark. Served from Nov. 1, 1812 to
Feb. 28, 1813 in Lieut. V. R. Good-
rich's Company, 11th Regt. Pension
Certificate No. 1546.

MARTIN, JOHN,   Franklin County.
Volunteered to go to Plattsburgh
Sept. 11, 1814 and served in 15th or
22nd Regt. Ref: Hemenway's Vt.
Gazetteer, Vol. 2, Page 392.

MARTIN, JOHN.
Born in Mastins, Ireland; aged 41
years; 5 feet 9 inches high; dark
complexion; gray hair; blue eyes;
by profession a weaver. Served from
May 4 to May 13, 1813 in Capt. Simeon
Wright's Company. Enlisted June 3,
1814 and served in Capt. William
Miller's Company and Capt. Gideon
Spencer's Company, 30th Regt.; discharged at Burlington, Vt., in 1815.

MARTIN, JOHN.
Served from May 1 to June 30, 1814
as a carpenter in Alexander Parris'
Company of Artificers. Ref: R. & L.
1812, AGO Page 24.

MARTIN, JOHN.
Enlisted March 22, 1813 in Capt.
Samul Gordon's Company, 11th Regt.;
deserted before joined. Ref: R. &
L. 1812, AGO Page 8.

*MARTIN, JOHN G., Enosburgh or Rich-
ford. Enlisted Sept. 25, 1813 and
served in Capt. Follet's Company,
Col. Dixon's Regt. Detached Militia
in U. S. service.

*MARTIN, LEVI.
Served under Captains Wheatly and
Wright, Col. Fifield's Regt. Detached
Militia in U. S. service 6 months,
1812.

MARTIN, MENDON, Sergeant, Albany,
N. Y. Served from May 1 to July 6,
1814 in Lieut. Hanson's Company,
29th Inf. Ref: R. & L. 1812, AGO
Page 30.

*MARTIN, NATHAN.
Served in Capt. Rogers' Company,
Col. Fifield's Regt. Detached Militia
in U. S. service 5 months and 27
days, 1812.

‡*MARTIN, NATHANIEL,   Sheldon.
Served in Capt. Walker's Company,
Col. Fifield's Regt. Detached Militia
in U. S. service 6 months and 3
days, 1812. Served from June 11 to
June 14, 1813 as a corporal in Capt.
Ithiel Stone's Company, 1st Regt. 2nd
Brig. 3rd Div. Volunteered to go to
Plattsburgh, September, 1814, and
served in Capt. Samuel Weed's Com-
pany. Ref: Book 51, AGO Pages 125,
152, 172. Pension Certificate No. 16718.

‡*MARTIN, REUBEN.
Served from June 1, 1813 to May 31,
1814 in Capt. Simeon Wright's Company. Also served in 1 Regt. (Martindale's) Vt. Militia. Pension Certificate No. 1726.

*MARTIN, ROBERT,   Richmond.
Volunteered to go to Plattsburgh.
September, 1814, and served 9 days
in Capt. Roswell Hunt's Company,
3 Regt. Also served in 4 Regt. (Williams') Vt. Militia. Ref: Book 51,
AGO Page 82.

*MARTIN, RUFUS S.
Served from June 11 to June 14 and
from Oct. 4 to Oct. 13, 1813 in Capt.
John Palmer's Company, 1st Regt.
2nd Brig. 3rd Div.

MARTIN, SAMUEL,   Williamstown.
Volunteered to go to Plattsburgh,
September, 1814, and served in Capt.
David Robinson's Company; was at
the battle. Ref: Book 52, AGO
Page 2.

*MARTIN, STANLY F.
Served in 1 Regt. (Judson's) Vt.
Militia.

*MARTIN, STEDMAN,   Williamstown.
Served in Capt. Walker's Company,
Col. Fifield's Regt. Detached Militia
in U. S. service 6 months and 3
days, 1812. Volunteered to go to
Plattsburgh, September, 1814, and was
in the battle, serving 8 days in Capt.
David Robinson's Company. Ref: Book
52, AGO Page 2.

‡*MARTIN, STRATTON.
Served from June 11 to June 14, 1813
in Capt. Ithiel Stone's Company, 1st
Regt. 2nd Brig. 3rd Div. Pension
Certificate No. 16403.

*MARTIN, THOMAS,   Fairfield.
Served in Capt. Kendall's Company,
Col. Wm. Williams' Regt. Detached
Militia in U. S. service 4 months
and 23 days, 1812. Volunteered to
go to Plattsburgh, September, 1814,
and served 4 days in Capt. Aaron
Kidder's Company. Ref: Book 52,
AGO Pages 65 and 108.

*MARTIN, VINE,   Randolph.
Volunteered to go to Plattsburgh,
September, 1814, and served in Capt.
Lebbeus Egerton's Company.

*MARTIN, WAIT.
Served in 1 Regt. (Judson's) Vt.
Militia.

MARTIN, WILLIAM, Corporal.
Enlisted Oct. 22, 1812 for 5 years
in company of late Capt. J. Brooks,
commanded by Lieut. John I. Cromwell, Corps of U. S. Artillery; on
Muster Roll from April 30 to June
30, 1814. Ref: R. & L. 1812, AGO
Page 18.

*MARTIN, WILLIAM, Corporal.
Served from June 11 to June 14,
1813 in Capt. Ithiel Stone's Company,
1st Regt. 2nd Brig. 3rd Div.

*MARTIN, WILLIAM.
Served from June 11 to June 14, 1813
and from Oct. 4 to Oct. 13, 1813 in
Capt. John Palmer's Company, 1st
Regt. 2nd Brig. 3rd Div.

‡MARTIN.WILLIAM,   Plainfield.
Volunteered to go to Plattsburgh,
September, 1814, and served 7 days
in Capt. James English's Company.
Pension Certificate No. 32163.

*MARTIN, WILLIAM B.
Served in Sumner's Regt. Vt. Militia.

*MARTINDALE, ELISHA.
Served in Capt. Willson's Company,
Col. Wm. Williams' Regt. Detached
Militia in U. S. service 4 months
and 24 days, 1812. Enlisted Jan. 19,
1813 in Lieut. V. R. Goodrich's Company, 11th Regt.; on Pay Roll for
January and February, 1813. Also
served in 2 Regt. (Fifield's) Vt. Militia. Ref: R. & L. 1812, AGO Page 11.

*MARTINDALE, GERSHAM.
Served in Capt. Richardson's Company, Col. Martindale's Regt. Detached Militia in U. S. service 2
months and 13 days, 1812.

*MARTINDALE, MOSES,   Highgate.
Served in Capt. Saxe's Company, Col.
Wm. Williams' Regt. Detached Mili-
tia in U. S. service 4 months and
24 days, 1812. Also served in 2 Regt.
(Fifield's) Vt. Militia.

*MARTINDALE, STEPHEN, Colonel, Dor-
set. Served in 1st Regt. of Detached
Militia of Vt. in U. S. service at
Champlain from Nov. 18 to Nov. 19,
1812. Also served as Lieutenant-
Colonel in 1 Regt. (Martindale's) Vt.
Militia.

*MARTINDALE. STEPHEN JR., Sergeant
Major, Dorset. Served in Col. Martindale's Regt. Detached Militia in
U. S. service 2 months and 14 days,
1812.

MARVELADOO, LEWIS (or Marbredo?).
Served in Lieut. V. R. Goodrich's
Company, 11th Regt.; on Pay Roll
for January and February, 1813. Ref:
R. & L. 1812, AGO Page 11.

‡MARVIN, HENRY.
Served in Capt. Kinney's Company
(4 Regt.). Pension Certificate of
widow. Betsey, No. 30774.

*MARVIN, MATTHIAS.
Served in Tyler's Regt. Vt. Militia.

*MARVIN, MATTHIUS JR. (or Mathew).
Served from Oct. 5 to Oct. 17, 1813
in Capt. Stephen Brown's Company,
3 Regt. (Tyler's).

‡MARVIN, STEPHEN.
Born in Northfield, Conn.; aged 28
years; 5 feet 10 inches high; dark
complexion; dark hair; black eyes;
by profession a farmer. Enlisted June
7, 1813 and served in Capt. James
Taylor's Company, Capt. Wm. Miller's
Company and Capt. Gideon Spencer's
Company. Also served in Capt. Kindall's Company. Pension Certificate
of widow, Melissa, No. 7217. Ref: R.
& L. 1812, AGO Pages 52, 53, 54, 55,
57, 59.

*MARVIN, WYLLIS.
Enlisted Sept. 28, 1813 in Capt.
Asahel Langworthy's Company, Col.
Isaac Clark's Rifle Corps.

MASON, BHOMAN (or Beman).
Served in Capt. Phelps' Company,
Col. Wm. Williams' Regt. Detached
Militia in U. S. service 5 months,
1812. Ref: Book 53, AGO Page 15.

‡MASON, CHARLES A.
Served in Capt. Arnold's Company.
Pension Certificate of widow, Amanda
M., No. 26489.

*MASON, DAVID.
Served in Capt. Phelps' Company, Col.
Wm. Williams' Regt. Detached Militia in U. S. service 5 months, 1812.
Served from April 19 to April 21,
1814 in Capt. Othniel Jewett's Company, Sumner's Regt.

‡MASON, ELIJAH.
Pension Certificate of widow, Betsey,
No. 15643; no organization given.

MASON, HENRY,   Franklin County.
Enlisted May 12, 1812 for 5 years
in Capt. White Youngs' Company,
15th Regt.; on Muster Roll from
Aug. 31, 1814 to Dec. 31, 1814. Ref:
R. & L. 1812, AGO Page 27.

*MASON, HIRAM. Captain, Craftsbury.
Commanded company of Militia in 2
Regt. (Fifield's) in service at Derby,
Vt., 6 months in 1812.

MASON, ISAIAH,   Ira.
Volunteered to go to Plattsburgh,
September, 1814, and served 4 days
in Capt. Matthew Anderson's Company. Ref: Book 52, AGO Page 144.

MASON, JAMES,   Sheldon.
Volunteered to go to Plattsburgh,
September, 1814, and served in Capt.
Samuel Weed's Company. Ref: Book
51, AGO Pages 152, 155, 172.

MASON, JOHN,   Ira.
Volunteered to go to Plattsburgh,
September, 1814, and served 4 days
in Capt. Matthew Anderson's Company. Ref: Book 52, AGO Page 144.

MASON, JOHN L.,   Fairfax.
Volunteered to go to Plattsburgh,
September, 1814, and served in com-
pany of Capt. Josiah Grout. Ref:
Book 51, AGO Page 271.

*MASON, JOSEPH,   Enosburgh.
Served from Oct. 15 to Nov. 17, 1813
in Capt. Asahel Scovell's Company,
Col. Clark's Regt. of Riflemen.

MASON, JOSHUA.
Served from April 12 to April 21,
1814 in Lieut. James S. Morton's
Company, Col. W. B. Sumner's Regt.
Ref: Book 52, AGO Page 286.

MASON, LEONARD,   Ira.
Volunteered to go to Plattsburgh,
September, 1814, and served 4 days
in Capt. Matthew Anderson's Company. Ref: Book 52, AGO Page 144.

MASON, LOT,   Fairfax.
Volunteered to go to Plattsburgh,
September, 1814, and served in Capt.
Josiah Grout's Company. Ref: Book
51, AGO Page 271.

MASON, MILO, Lieutenant.
Appointed 1st Lieutenant Artillerists
Feb. 29, 1812; transferred to Artillery Corps May 12, 1814; died Feb. 4,
1837. Ref: Heitman's Historical Register & Dictionary USA.

*MASON, MOSES,   St. Albans.
Served in Capt. Mason's Company,
Col. Fifield's Regt. Detached Militia
in U. S. service 3 months and 16
days, 1812. Served from April 24,
1813 to April, 1814 in Capt. John
Wires' Company, 30th Regt. Also
served in Capt. Amasa Brown's Company. Pension Certificate No. 21110.

MASON, OLIVER, Major,   Rochester.
Volunteered to go to Plattsburgh,
September, 1814, and commanded company raised in Rochester. Ref: Book
51, AGO Page 249.

*MASON, PAUL, Sergeant.
Served in 4 Regt. (Peck's) Vt. Militia.

MASON, PELEG S. (or Peter S.) Sur-
geon. Appointed Surgeon 30 Inf.
June 29, 1813; transferred to 31 Inf.
Dec. 30, 1813; honorably discharged
June 15, 1815. Ref: Heitman's His-
torical Register & Dictionary USA;
Governor and Council, Vt., Vol. 6,
Page 475.

*MASON, ROMAN.
Served in 4 Regt. (Williams') Vt.
Militia.

*MASON, SOLOMON.
Served from April 12 to April 21,
1814 in Capt. Edmund B. Hill's Company, Sumner's Regt.

*MASON, WILLIAM, Corporal.
Served in 2 Regt. (Fifield's) Vt.
Militia.

*MASSEY, WOODBURY.
Served in Capt. Phelps' Company, Col.
Jonathan Williams' Regt. Detached
Militia in U. S. service 2 months
and 21 days, 1812.

MASTENS, JAMES.
Served in company of Capt. John Mc-
Neil Jr., 11th Regt.; on Pay Roll
for January and February, 1813. Ref:
R. & L. 1812, AGO Page 17.

*MASTER, JOSIAH.
Served in Capt. Howard's Company,
Vt. Militia.

MASTERS, BENJAMIN, Franklin County.
Volunteered to go to Plattsburgh
Sept. 11, 1814 and served in 15th or
2nd Regt. Ref: Hemenway's Vt. Gazetteer, Vol. 2, Page 391.

‡MASTERS, WILLIAM.
Served in Capt. Melvin's Company.
Pension Certificate No. 4884.

*MASTICK, WILLIAM.
Served in Capt. Sabin's Company,
Col. Jonathan Williams' Regt. Detached Militia in U. S. service 2
months and 6 days, 1812.

MASTIN, THOMAS.
Enlisted Jan. 11, 1813 in company of
Capt. John McNeil Jr., 11th Regt.;
on Pay Roll to May 31, 1813. Ref:
R. & L. 1812, AGO Pages 16 and 17.

‡MATCHETT, WILLIAM.
Served in Capt. B. Church's Company. Pension Certificate No. 23873.

*MATHER, ENOS.
Served in Capt. Preston's Company,
Col. Jonathan Williams' Regt. Detached Militia in U. S. service 2
months and 6 days, 1812.

‡*MATHER, LUTHER.
Served in Capt. Preston's Company,
Col. Jonathan Williams' Regt. Detached Militia in U. S. service 2
months and 6 days, 1812. Pension
Certificate of widow, Clarissa, No.
22745.

*MATHER, WILLIAM.
Served in Capt. Preston's Company,
Col. Jonathan Williams' Regt. Detached Militia in U. S. service 2
months 6 days, 1812.

MATHEWSON, MARK, Franklin County.
Volunteered to go to Plattsburgh
Sept. 11, 1814 and served in 15th or
22nd Regt. Ref: Hemenway's Vt.
Gazetteer, Vol. 2, Page 392.

MATHEWSON, THOMAS, Captain.
Commanded Detachment of Militia
sent to Derby from Caledonia County
in July 1812 to protect the town. Ref:
Vol. 49 Vt. State Papers, Page 223.

MATSIGAR, GEORGE.
Enlisted June 7, 1813 for duration
of the war in Capt. White Youngs'
Company; on Muster Roll from Aug.
31 to Dec. 31, 1814. Ref: R. & L.
1812, AGO Page 27.

MATSON, AARON, Lieutenant.
Appointed Ensign 31 Inf. April 30,
1813; 3 Lieutenant Jan. 11, 1814; 2
Lieutenant May 2, 1814; honorably
discharged June 15, 1815. Ref: Heitman's Historical Register & Dictionary USA.

MATSON, AMOS,   Vershire.
Volunteered to go to Plattsburgh,
September, 1814, and served 3 days
in Capt. Ira Corse's Company. Ref:
Book 52, AGO Page 91.

*MATTHEWS, AMOS.
Served from April 12 to April 21,
1814 in Capt. Othniel Jewett's Company, Sumner's Regt.

MATTHEWS, DAVID.
Served from Sept. 1, 1813 to June 30,
1814 in Regt. of Light Dragoons.
Ref: R. & L. 1812, AGO Page 21.

‡MATTHEWS, DAVID.
Enlisted May 6, 1813 for 1 year in
Capt. Simeon Wright's Company. Pen-
sion Certificate No. 6164.

*MATTHEWS, DAVID.
Served in 1 Regt. (Martindale's) Vt.
Militia.

*MATTHEWS, ELEAZUR.
Served in 4 Regt. (Peck's) Vt. Militia.

*MATTHEWS, ELI,   Middlebury.
Served from April 12 to April 15,
1814 in Capt. John Hackett's Company, Sumner's Regt. Volunteered to
go to Plattsburgh, September, 1814,
and served 7 days in same company.

*MATTHEWS, HARMON.
Served from April 12 to April 21,
1814 in Capt. Shubael Wales' Company, Col. W. B. Sumner's Regt.

‡MATTHEWS, JABEZ.
Served in Capt. Parker's Company.
Pension Certificate No. 13906.

*MATTHEWS, JAMES.
Served from April 12 to April 21,
1814 in Capt. Othniel Jewett's Company, Sumner's Regt.

*MATTHEWS, JAMES R., Sergeant.
Served in Capt. Phelps' Company, Col.
Wm. Williams' Regt. Detached Militia in U. S. service at Swanton Falls
5 months in 1812.

*MATTHEWS, JEREMIAH.
Served in 3 Regt. (Tyler's) Vt. Miliita.

*MATTHEWS, JONAS, Corporal.
Served from April 12 to April 21,
1814 in Capt. Edmund B. Hill's Company, Sumner's Regt.

*MATTHEWS, JOSEPH.
Served from April 12 to April 21,
1814 in Capt. Othniel Jewett's Company, Sumner's Regt.

MATTHEWS, ROBERT.
Served in Capt. Benjamin Bradford's
Company; on Muster Roll from May
31 to Aug. 31, 1813. Ref: R. & L.
1812, AGO Page 26.

MATTHEWS, TIMOTHY, Ensign.
Appointed Ensign 30 Inf. April 30,
1813; dismissed Oct. 9, 1813. Ref:
Heitman's Historical Register & Dictionary USA.

*MATTHEWS, WATROUS.
Served in 4 Regt. (Peck's) Vt. Militia.

*MATTHEWS, WILLIAM.
Served from May 1 to June 30, 1814
in Capt. Haig's Corps of Light Dra-

goons. Also served in 4 Regt.
(Peck's) Vt. Militia. Ref: R. & L.
1812, AGO Page 20.

*MATTISON, HEZEKIAH.
Served in Capt. Cross' Company, Col.
Martindale's Regt. Detached Militia
in U. S. service 2 months and 14
days, 1812.

*MATTISON, REUBEN.
Served in Capt. Strait's Company,
Col. Martindale's Regt. Detached
Militia in U. S. service 2 months
and 13 days, 1812.

*MATTISON, SAMUEL.
Served in Capt. Cross' Company, Col.
Martindale's Regt. Detached Militia
in U. S. service 2 months and 9
days, 1812.

*MATTOKS, JOHN.
Served from April 12 to April 15,
1814 in Lieut. Justus Foote's Company, Sumner's Regt.

MATTOON, PHILIP.
Volunteered to go to Plattsburgh,
September, 1814, and went as far as
Bolton, Vt., serving 4 days in Lieut.
Phineus Kimball's Company of West
Fairlee. Ref: Book 52, AGO Pages
46 and 47.

MAXELL, STEPHEN.
Served from Feb. 16 to May 15, 1813
in Capt. Jonathan Starks' Company,
11th Regt. Ref: R. & L. 1812, AGO
Page 19.

*MAXFIELD, ELIPHALET.
Served in Capt. Phineas Williams'
Company, 11th Regt.; on Pay Roll
for January and February, 1813. Also
served with Hospital Attendants. Ref:
R. & L. 1812, AGO Page 15.

‡MAXFIELD, HARVEY.
Served in Capt. I. Grout's Company.
Pension Certificate of widow, Sophia,
No. 28292.

*MAXFIELD, ISAAC.
Enlisted Sept. 25, 1813 in Capt. Jesse
Post's Company, Dixon's Regt.

*MAXFIELD, JOHN.
Served in Capt. Phelps' Company, Col.
Wm. Williams' Regt. Detached Mili-
tia in U. S. service 5 months, 1812.

‡*MAXFIELD, JOHN.
Served in Capt. Willson's Company,
Col. Wm. Williams' Regt. Detached
Militia in U. S. service 4 months
and 24 days, 1812. Pension Certificate No. 2403. Pension Certificate
of widow, Joanna P., No. 26002.

*MAXFIELD, LEVI.
Served from March 26 to June 25,
1813 in Capt. Phineas Williams' Company, 11th Regt. Ref: R. & L. 1812,
AGO Page 14.

*MAXFIELD, MOSES.
Enlisted Feb. 10, 1813 in Capt. Jonathan Starks' Company, 11th Regt.;
on Pay Roll to May 31, 1813. Enlisted Sept. 25, 1813 and served 1
month and 23 days in Capt. Elijah

W. Wood's Company, Col. Dixon's
Regt. Also served with Hospital Attendants, Vt.

*MAXFIELD, WILLIAM.
Enlisted Sept. 25, 1813 in Capt. Asa
Wilkins' Company, Dixon's Regt.

MAXHAM, ELLIS.
Served in Capt. Samuel H. Holly's
Company, 11th Regt.; on Pay Roll
for January and February, 1813. Ref:
R. & L. 1812, AGO Page 25.

MAXNALLY, JNO.
Served in War of 1812 and was cap-
tured by troops Dec. 19, 1813 at Fort
Niagara; discharged Feb. 24, 1814.
Ref: Records of Naval Records and
Library, Navy Dept.

‡*MAY, ANDREW,   Berlin.
Served in Capt. E. Walker's Company, Col. Fifield's Regt. Detached
Militia in U. S. service 6 months
and 3 days, 1812. Volunteered to
go to Plattsburgh, September, 1814,
and served 6 days in Capt. Timothy
Hubbard's Company. Pension Certificate No. 1052.

MAY, ELISHA.
Volunteered to go to Plattsburgh,
September, 1814, and served 4 days
in Capt. Aaron Kidder's Company.
Ref: Book 52, AGO Page 65.

MAY, IRA.
Volunteered to go to Plattsburgh,
September, 1814, and served 8 days
in Capt. Timothy Hubbard's Company.
Ref: Book 52, AGO Page 256.

*MAY, SAMUEL G.,   Richmond.
Volunteered to go to Plattsburgh,
September, 1814, and served 9 days
in Capt Roswell Hunt's Company, 3
Regt. Also served in 1 Regt. (Jud-
son's) Vt. Militia.

‡*MAY, STEPHEN.
Served in Capt. Rogers' Company,
Col. Fifield's Regt. Detached Militia
in U. S. service 6 months. Also
served in Capt. Oliver Taylor's Company, 2 Regt. (Fifield's). Pension
Certificate No. 20600. Pension Certificate of widow, Rhoda, No. 6085.

MAYAGEN, MARKLE.
Served from April 10 to June 30,
1814 in Regt. of Light Dragoons.
Ref: R. & L. 1812, AGO Page 21.

MAYERS, GEORGE,   Fairfax.
Served from Aug. 8, 1812 in company
of Capt. Joseph Beeman, Jr., 11th
Regt. U. S. Inf. commanded by Col.
Ira Clark. Served in Capt. Taylor's
Company, Col. Wm. Williams' Regt.
Detached Militia in U. S. service 4
months and 24 days, 1812. Ref: Hem-
enway's Vt. Gazetteer, Vol. 2, Page
402.

‡*MAYNARD, ABNER.
Served in Capt. Ormsbee's Company.
Col. Martindale's Regt. Detached
Militia in U. S. service 2 months
and 14 days, 1812. Also served in
Capt. Cook's Company. Pension Cer-
tificate of widow, Margurett, No.
21093.

*MAYNARD, SILAS.
Served in Capt. Ormsbee's Company,
Col. Martindale's Regt. Detached
Militia in U. S. service 2 months
and 14 days, 1812.

‡MAYNARD, STEPHEN.
Served in Capt. Samul Gordon's Company, 11th Regt.; on Pay Roll for
January and February, 1813. Pension Certificate No. 15221.

MAYNARD, WINSLOW.
Enlisted May 31, 1813 for 1 year in
Capt. Benjamin Bradford's Company;
on Muster Roll from May 31 to Aug.
31, 1813. Ref: R. & L. 1812, AGO
Page 26.

‡*MAYO, DAVID,   Burlington.
Served from April 12 to April 21,
1814 in Lieut. Justus Foote's Company, Sumner's Regt. Volunteered to
go to Plattsburgh, September, 1814,
and served 10 days in Capt. Henry
Mayo's Company. Pension Certificate
of widow, Maria Julia, No. 26176.

*MAYO, HENRY, Captain, Burlington.
Volunteered to go to Plattsburgh,
September, 1814, and served 10 days
in command of company raised in
Burlington and vicinity. Also served
as Lieutenant in 1 Regt. (Judson's)
Vt. Militia.

MAZIER, MILLER.
Served in Capt. Pettes' Company.
Col. Wm. Williams' Regt. Detached
Militia in U. S. service 4 months and
17 days, 1812. Ref: Book 53, AGO
Page 8.

MAZOOZEN, MARK W.,   Fairfax.
Served from April 28, 1814 to June 16,
1815 in Capt. Sanford's Company,
30th Inf. Ref: R. & L. 1812, AGO
Page 23.

‡MAZOUSON, ERASTUS,   Shoreham.
Volunteered to go to Plattsburgh,
September, 1814, and served 6 days
in Capt. Samuel Hand's Company.
Pension Certificate of widow, Betsey,
No. 26490.

MC ALISTER, DAVID.
Volunteered to go to Plattsburgh,
September, 1814, and served 7 days
in Frederick Griswold's Company
raised in Brookfield, Vt. Ref: Book
52, AGO Page 52.

MC ALLISTER, JAMES.
Served from May 1 to June 30, 1814
in Capt. Haig's Corps of Light Dragoons. Ref: R. & L. 1812, AGO
Page 20.

*MC ALLISTER, JOHN,   Stowe.
Volunteered to go to Plattsburgh,
September, 1814, and was at the
battle, serving in Capt. Nehemiah
Perkins' Company, 4 Regt. (Peck's).

MC ANDREWS, JOHN, Franklin County.
Volunteered to go to Plattsburgh
Sept. 11, 1814, and served in 15th or
22nd Regt. Ref: Hemenway's Vt.
Gazetteer, Vol. 2, Page 391.

*MC ARTHU, CHARLES, Sergeant.
Served in 4 Regt. (Williams') Vt.
Militia.

*MC ARTHUR, ALEXANDER.
Served in Capt. Strait's Company, Col.
Martindale's Regt. Detached Militia
in U. S. service 2 months and 13
days, 1812. Enlisted Sept. 20, 1813
in Capt. John Weed's Company, Col.
Clark's Regt. of Riflemen.

*MC ARTHUR, CHARLES.
Served in Tyler's Regt. Vt. Militia.

MC ARTHUR, JOHN B.
Served in Capt. Dorrance's Company,
Col. Wm. Williams' Regt. Detached
Militia in U. S. service 4 months and
24 days, 1812. Ref: Book 53, AGO
Page 13.

MCBLUNK, JOHN.
Enlisted April 21, 1814 for duration
of the war in Capt. Gideon Spencer's
Company; on Muster Roll Dec. 30,
1813 to June 30, 1814. Ref: R. & L.
1812, AGO Page 57.

MCBRIDE, DENNIS.
Served from March 22 to June 21,
1813 in Capt. Charles Follett's Company, 11th Regt. Ref: R. & L. 1812,
AGO Page 13.

MC CALL, JOHN.
Served from March 9 to June 30, 1814
in Capt. Alexander Brooks' Corps of
Artillery. Ref: R. & L. 1812, AGO
Page 31.

MC CAMMON, THOMAS W., Corporal.
Served from May 1 to June 30, 1814
in Capt. Alexander Brooks' Corps of
Artillery. Ref: R. & L. 1812, AGO
Page 31.

MC CANN, THOMAS.
Enlisted May 5, 1812 for 5 years in
Capt. White Youngs' Company, 15th
Regt.; on Muster Roll from Aug. 31
to Dec. 31, 1814. Ref: R. & L. 1812,
AGO Page 27.

MC CARTY, DANIEL.
Born in Londonderry, Ireland. Enlisted at Middletown March 26, 1814
for duration of the war and served
in Capt. Wm. Miller's Company and
Capt. Gideon Spencer's Company, 30th
Regt. Ref: R. & L. 1812, AGO Pages
54, 55, 57.

*MC CARTY, JOHN B.
Served as a saddler in 4 Regt. (Williams') Vt. Militia.

MC-CASSELL, WILLIAM.
Born at Philadelphia, Pa. Enlisted
at Burlington March 29, 1814 for
duration of the war and served in
Capt. Wm. Miller's Company and
Capt. Gideon Spencer's Company, 30th
Regt. Ref: R. & L. 1812, AGO Pages
54, 55, 57.

*MC CAY, DAVID.
Served in Capt. Needham's Company,
Col. Martindale's Regt. Detached
Militia in U. S. service 2 months and
14 days, 1812.

*MC CLARY, ANDREW, Groton.
Served in Capt. Rogers' Company,
Col. Fifield's Regt. Detached Militia
in U. S. service 5 months and 27
days, 1812.

MC CLARY, SILAS C., Corporal.
Served in Capt. Benjamin S. Edgerton's Company, 11th Regt.; on Pay
Roll for September and October, 1812
and January and February, 1813.
Ref: R. & L. 1812, AGO Pages 1
and 2.

*MC CLENTHEN, ORIN.
Served in Capt. Strait's Company, Col.
Martindale's Regt. Detached Militia
in U. S. service 2 months and 13
days, 1812.

*MC CLOUD, DAVID,   Middlesex.
Served in Capt. Walker's Company,
Col. Fifield's Regt. Detached Militia
in U. S. service 6 months and 5
days, 1812. Volunteered to go to
Plattsburgh, September, 1814, and
served 10 days in Capt. Holden Putnam's Company. Ref: Book 52, AGO
Page 251.

*MC CLOUD, JOHN.   Middlesex.
Served in Capt. Phineas Williams'
Company, 11th Regt.; on Pay Roll
for January and February, 1813.
Volunteered to go to Plattsburgh,
September, 1814, and served 10 days
in Capt. Holden Putnam's Company,
4 Regt. (Peck's). Also served in 2
Regt. (Fifield's) Vt. Militia. Ref:
Book 52, AGO Page 251.

MC CLARY, JESSE,   Thetford.
Volunteered to go to Plattsburgh
September, 1814, and went as far as
Bolton, Vt., serving 6 days in Capt.
Salmon Howard's Company, 2nd Regt.
Ref: Book 52, AGO Pages 15 and 16.

*MC CLARY, JOHN,   Thetford.
Volunteered to go to Plattsburgh,
September, 1814, and went as far as
Bolton, Vt., serving 6 days in Capt.
Salmon Howard's Company, 2nd Regt.

MC COLLAND, DANIEL.
Served from March 16 to June 15,
1813 in Capt. Charles Follett's Company, 11th Regt. Ref: R. & L. 1812,
AGO Page 13.

MC COLLOM, HENRY.
Served from May 1, 1813 to May 1,
1814 in Capt. Daniel Farrington's
Company (also commanded by Capt.
Simeon Wright) 30th Regt. Ref: R.
& L. 1812, AGO Pages 50 and 51.

MC COLLOM, ROBERT, Corporal.
Served from May 12, 1813 to May 12,
1814 in Capt. James Taylor's Company and Capt. Gideon Spencer's
Company, 30th Regt. Ref: R. & L.
1812, AGO Pages 52, 57, 58.

*MC COLLUM, JOHN.
Served in Capt. Parsons' Company,
Col. Jonathan Williams' Regt. Detached Militia in U. S. service 2
months and 13 days, 1812.

*MC COMBER, JONATHAN.
Served in 1 Regt. (Judson's) Vt. Militia.

MC CORMAR, ARCHIBALD.
Enlisted July 20, 1813 for 1 year in
Capt. Daniel Farrington's Company
(also commanded by Capt. Simeon

Wright) 30th Regt.; on Muster Roll from March 1 to April 30, 1814. Ref: R. & L. 1812, AGO Pages 50 and 51.

*MC CORMICK, PETER.
Served with Hospital Attendants, Vt.

MC COTTER, ALEXANDER,   Benson.
Enlisted June 4, 1813 ·for 1 year in Capt. John Wires' Company, 30th Regt. Served from April 23, 1814 to June 19, 1815 in Capt. Taylor's Company, 30th Inf. Ref: R. & L. 1812, AGO Pages 23 and 40.

MC COY, AMASA.
Served in Capt. Charles Follett's Company, 11th Regt.; on Pay Roll for January and February, 1812. Ref: R. & L. 1812, AGO Page 12.

‡*MC COY, DANIEL,   St. Albans.
Served in Capt. Taylor's Company, Col. Wm. Williams' Regt. Detached Militia in U. S. service 4 months and 24 days, 1812. Served from April 30, 1813 to May, 1814. in Capt. John Wires' Company, 30th Regt.

‡MC COY, DANIEL (alias Over or Ober. Peter S). Served in Capt. Taylor's Company. Pension Certificate No. 12313.

MC COY, DAVID,   Dorset.
Served from April 13 to July 12, 1813 in Capt. Samul Gordon's Company, 11th Regt. Served from July 14, 1814 to June 19, 1815 in Capt. Taylor's Company, 30th Inf. Ref: R. & L. 1812, AGO Pages 8 and 23.

MC COY, JAMES.
Enlisted Feb. 16, 1814 for duration of the war in company of late Capt. J. Brooks, commanded by Lieut. John I. Cromwell's Corps of U. S. Artillery; on Muster Roll from April 30 to June 30, 1814. Ref: R. & L. 1812, AGO Page 18.

*MC COY. JOHN.
Served in Capt. Strait's Company, Col. Martindale's Regt. Detached Militia in U. S. service 2 months and 13 days. 1812. Enlisted Oct. 18, 1813 and served 62 days in Capt. John Weed's Company, Regt. of Riflemen.

*MC CRAW. JOSEPH.
Served in Sumner's Regt. Vt. Militia.

*MC CULLEN, DAVID.
Served in Dixon's Regt. Vt. Militia.

MC CULLOUGH, BENJAMIN, Annapolis.
Served from May 1 to July 4, 1814 in Capt. McIlvains' Company. 14th Inf. Ref: R. & L. 1812, AGO Page 30.

*MC CULLOUGH, JOHN (or McCollough), Ensign, Highgate. Appointed Ensign in Capt. Elijah W. Wood's Company Oct. 13, 1813 and served to Nov. 18, 1813.

*MC CUTCHIN, HUGH,   Stowe.
Volunteered to go to Plattsburgh. September, 1814, and was at the battle, serving in Capt. Nehemiah Perkins' Company, 4 Regt. (Peck's).

*MC DANIELS, ROBERT.
Enlisted Sept. 25, 1813 and served 1 month and 23 days in Capt. Waterman's Company, Col. Dixon's Regt.

*MC DOLE, DAVID.
Served in Capt. Lowry's Company. Col. Wm. Williams' Regt. Detached Militia in U. S. service 4 months and 26 days, 1814.

*MC DOLE, THOMAS, Corporal.
Served in Capt. Rogers' Company, Col. Fifield's Regt. Detached Militia in U. S. service 5 months and 27 days, 1812.

*MC DOLE, WILLIAM.
Served in Capt. Lowry's Company, Col. Wm. Williams' Regt. Detached Militia in U. S. service 4 months and 26 days, 1812.

MC DONALD, CHRISTOPHER.
Enlisted May 12, 1813 for 1 year in Capt. Daniel Farrington's Company, 30th Regt. (also commanded by Capt. Simeon Wright); on Muster Roll from March 1 to April 30, 1814. Ref: R. & L. 1812, AGO Pages 50 and 51.

*MC DONALD, GEORGE (or McDaniel?), Standish. Served from May 1 to Aug. 11, 1814 in Capt. Goodenou's Company, 33d Inf. Also served with Hospital Attendants, Vt.

MC DONALD, ICHABOD, Corporal.
Enlisted May 12, 1813 for 1 year in Capt. Daniel Farrington's Company (also commanded by Capt. Simeon Wright) 30th Regt.; on Muster Roll March 1 to April 30, 1814. Ref: R. & L. 1812, AGO Pages 50 and 51.

MC DONALD, JOHN,   Brandon.
Volunteered to go to Plattsburgh. September, 1814, and served 8 days in Capt. Micah Brown's Company. Ref: Book 52, AGO Page 136.

MC DONALD, WILLIAM C.
Served from May 1 to June 30, 1814 in Capt. Haig's Corps of Light Dragoons. Ref: R. & L. 1812, AGO Page 20.

MC ELVIN, WILLIAM,   Philadelphia.
Served from May 1 to July 29, 1814 in Capt. Vandalion's Company, 15th Inf. Ref: R. & L. 1812, AGO Page 30.

*MC ERVIN, CARLETON (or McEwen?). Ensign. Served from June 11 to June 14, 1813 in Capt. Thomas Dorwin's Company, 1st Regt. 2nd Brig. 3rd Div.

MC EVER, JOHN,   Franklin County.
Volunteered to go to Plattsburgh Sept. 11, 1814 and served in 15th or 22nd Regt. Ref: Hemenway's Vt. Gazetteer, Vol. 2, Page 392.

‡*MC EWEN, AUGUSTUS, Sergeant.
Served in Capt. Dorwin's Company, 1 Regt. (Judson's) Vt. Militia. Pension Certificate of widow, Balina, No. 21262.

*MC EWEN. GEORGE.
Served in 1 Regt. (Judson's) Vt. Militia.

*MC FALL, ROBERT.
Served with Hospital Attendants, Vt.

MC FARLAND, ANDREW, Lieutenant.
Appointed Cornet 2 Light Dragoons March 12, 1812; 3rd Lieutenant April 29, 1813; honorably discharged June 1, 1814. Ref: Heitman's Historical Register & Dictionary USA.

*MC FARLAND, JAMES, Sergeant, Danville. Served in Capt. Morrill's Company, Col. Fifield's Regt. Detached Militia in U. S. service from Sept. 16, 1812 to March 17, 1813.

MC FARSON, MOSES.
Enlisted Jan. 27, 1813 in Capt. Phineas Williams' Company, 11th Regt.; on Pay Roll to May 31, 1813. Ref: R. & L. 1812, AGO Page 14.

MC GEE, ALEXANDER.
Served from May 1 to June 30, 1814 in Capt. Haig's Corps of Light Dragoons. Ref: R. & L. 1812, AGO Page 20.

MC GEE, TRUMAN.
Was born at Gerrica and served in War of 1812; captured by boats and troops June 13, 1813 on Lake Champlain and exchanged May 4, 1815. Ref: Records of Naval Records and Library, Navy Dept.

*MC GOLPHLIN, HENRY (or McGlofflin).
Served in Capt. Wood's Company, Col. Dixon's Regt. Detached Militia in U. S. service 1 month and 23 days, 1813.

MC GONIGAL, JOHN (or McGouigal).
Born in Ireland; aged 36 years; 5 feet 5½ inches high; light complexion; sandy hair; grey eyes; by profession a paper maker. Enlisted at Burlington March 17, 1814 for the period of the war in Capt. Wm. Miller's Company; discharged at Burlington in 1815. Ref: R. & L. 1812, AGO Pages 54 and 55.

MC GOOCH, ROBERT, Franklin County.
Volunteered to go to Plattsburgh Sept. 11, 1814 and served in 15th or 22nd Regt. Ref: Hemenway's Vt. Gazetteer, Vol. 2, Page 392.

MC GOWAN, JOHN.
Enlisted June 7, 1812 for 5 years in Capt. White Youngs' Company, 15th Regt.; on Muster Roll from Aug. 31 to Dec. 31, 1814. Ref: R. & L. 1812, AGO Page 27.

MC GREGER, CAMERON, Pittsford.
Volunteered to go to Plattsburgh, September, 1814, and served 8 days in Capt. Caleb Hendee's Company. Ref: Book 52, AGO Page 125.

*MC GREGER, HUGH C.
Served in 1 Regt. (Martindale's) Vt. Militia.

MC GREGOR, DUNCAN.
Served from May 1 to June 30, 1814 in Capt. Alexander Brooks' Corps of Artillery. Ref: R. & L. 1812, AGO Page 31.

MC GREGORE, CAMRON.
Served from April 24, 1813 to April 24, 1814 in Capt. Simeon Wright's Company. Ref: R. & L. 1812, AGO Page 51.

MC GUIRE, HUGH, Franklin County.
Enlisted April 26, 1812 for 5 years in Capt. White Youngs' Company, 15th Regt.; on Muster Roll from Aug. 31 to Dec. 31, 1814. Ref: R. & L. 1812, AGO Page 27.

MC HURIN, SETH.
Served in Capt. Scovell's Company, Col. Martindale's Regt. Detached Militia in U. S. service 2 months and 21 days, 1812. Ref: Book 53, AGO Page 42.

MC INTIRE, JACOB.
Served in Capt. Weeks' Company, 11th Regt.; on Pay Roll for January and February, 1813. Ref: R. & L. 1812, AGO Page 5.

*MC INTIRE, JOHN.
Served in Col. Fifield's Regt. Detached Militia in U. S. service 6 months, 1812.

‡MC INTOSH, DONALD, Surgeon.
Served as Surgeon in U. S. Navy. Pension Certificate of widow, Susan, No. 25204.

MC INTOSH, MILO.
Served from May 1 to June 30, 1814 in Capt. Haig's Corps of Light Dragoons. Ref: R. & L. 1812, AGO Page 20.

MC INTOSH, MILO, Corporal.
Served in 1st Regt. of Detached Militia of Vt. in U. S. service at Champlain from Nov. 18 to Nov. 19, 1812.

MC INTYRE, ROBERT, Franklin County.
Volunteered to go to Plattsburgh Sept. 11, 1814 and served in 15th or 22nd Regt. Ref: Hemenway's Vt. Gazetteer, Vol. 2, Page 392.

MC KEE, EPHRAIM.
Served in Capt. Strait's Company, Col. Martindale's Regt. Detached Militia in U. S. service 2 months and 13 days, 1812. Ref: Book 53, AGO Page 86.

MC KEE, MICHAEL.
Served from May 1 to June 30, 1814 in Capt. Alexander Brooks' Corps of Artillery. Ref: R. & L. 1812, AGO Page 31.

MC KEE, WILLIAM.
Served from Jan. 26, 1813 to date of death, March 20, 1813, in company of Capt. John McNeil Jr., 11th Regt. Ref: R. & L. 1812, AGO Page 16.

*MC KELLEPS, MOSES.
Served in Sumner's Regt. Vt. Militia.

MC KENNEY, SCOTT (or McKinney), Sheldon or Berkshire. Volunteered to go to Plattsburgh, September, 1814, and served in Capt. Samuel Weed's Company. Ref: Book 51, AGO Page 109.

‡MC KENNEY, WILLIAM (or McKinney), Sheldon. Served in Capt. Langworthy's Company, Col. Dixon's Regt. Detached Militia in U. S. service 1 month and 25 days, 1813. Volunteered to go to Plattsburgh, September, 1814, and served in Capt. Samuel Weed's Company. Pension Certificate No. 13189. Ref: Book 51, AGO Pages 172 and 180.

MC KENZIE, WILLIAM, Waltham. Volunteered to go to Plattsburgh, September, 1814, and was in the battle, serving 14 days in Capt. Gideon Spencer's Company. Ref: Book 51, AGO Page 2.

MC KEVER, JOHN. Enlisted March 3, 1812 for 5 years in Capt. White Youngs' Company, 15th Regt.; on Muster Roll from Aug. 31 to Dec. 31, 1814. Ref: R. & L. 1812, AGO Page 27.

MC KINLEY, JOHN. Served from Feb. 26 to June 30, 1814 in Regt. of Light Dragoons. Ref: R. & L. 1812, AGO Page 21.

‡MC KINNEY, AARON. Served in Capt. Hall's Company. Pension Certificate No. 13754.

MC KINNEY, JOHN, Franklin County. Enlisted June 12, 1812 for 5 years in Capt. White Youngs' Company, 15th Regt.; on Muster Roll from Aug. 31 to Dec. 31, 1814. Ref: R. & L. 1812, AGO Page 27.

*MC KINZEY, ISAAC. Served in Sumner's Regt. Vt. Militia.

MC KNIGHT, DAVID. Served from Feb. 27 to 28, 1813 and from April 1 to June 30, 1813, in Lieut. V. R. Goodrich's Company, 11th Regt. Ref: R. & L. 1812, AGO Pages 10 and 11.

MC KNIGHT, JAMES. Enlisted Feb. 27, 1813 in Lieut. V. R. Goodrich's Company, 11th Regt.; on Pay Roll for advance pay and retained bounty to May 31, 1813. Ref: R. & L. 1812, AGO Pages 10 and 11.

MC KNIGHT, JAMES JR. Enlisted Feb. 27, 1813 in Lieut. V. R. Goodrich's Company, 11th Regt.; on Pay Roll to May 31, 1813. Ref: R. & L. 1812, AGO Pages 10 and 11.

MC KNIGHT, LEMUEL, Montpelier. Volunteered to go to Plattsburgh, September, 1814, and served 8 days in Capt. Timothy Hubbard's Company. Ref: Book 52, AGO Page 256.

MC KNIGHT, THOMAS, Montpelier. Volunteered to go to Plattsburgh, September, 1814, and served 8 days in Capt. Timothy Hubbard's Company. Ref: Book 52, AGO Page 256.

MC LANE, JAMES. Served in Lieut. Wm. S. Foster's Company, 11th Regt.; on Pay Roll for January and February, 1813. Ref: R. & L. 1812, AGO Page 7.

MC LANE, WILLIAM. Served from Nov. 1, 1812 to Dec. 13, 1812 in Lieut. V. R. Goodrich's Company, 11th Regt. Ref: R. & L. 1812, AGO Page 11.

‡*MC LAUGHLIN, CYRUS. Served in 1 Regt. (Judson's) Vt. Militia. Also served in Capt. Kinney's Company. Pension Certificate No. 11164.

*MC LAUGHLIN, HENRY, Georgia. Volunteered to go to Plattsburgh, September, 1814, and served 8 days in Capt. Jesse Post's Company, Dixon's Regt.

MC LAUGHLIN, HEZK. Enlisted Nov. 21, 1812 in Lieut. Wm. S. Foster's Company, 11th Regt.; on Pay Roll for January and February, 1813. Ref: R. & L. 1812, AGO Page 7.

MC LAUGHLIN, HIRAM. Served from May 31 to June 30, 1814 in Regt. of Light Dragoons. Ref: R. & L. 1812, AGO Page 21.

*MC LAUGHLIN, SILAS. Served in 3 Regt. (Tyler's) Vt. Militia.

MC LEAN, HUGH, Franklin County. Volunteered to go to Plattsburgh Sept. 11, 1814 and served in 15th or 22nd Regt. Ref: Hemenway's Vt. Gazetteer, Vol. 2, Page 391.

*MC LEAN, JOHN. Served in Capt. S. Pettes' Company, Col. Wm. Williams' Regt. Detached Militia in U. S. service 4 months and 17 days, 1812.

‡*MC LELLAN, SILAS, Huntington. Served in Capt. Dorrance's Company, Col. Wm. Williams' Regt. Detached Militia in U. S. service 4 months and 23 days, 1812. Volunteered to go to Plattsburgh, September, 1814, and was at the battle, serving in Capt. Josiah N. Barrows' Company.

MC MANNING, THOMAS. Enlisted May 27, 1812 for 5 years in Capt. White Youngs' Company, 15th Regt.; on Muster Roll from Aug. 31 to Dec. 31, 1814. Ref: R. & L. 1812, AGO Page 27.

MC MANNAS, JOHN, Corporal. Served in company of late Capt. J. Brooks, commanded by Lieut. John I. Cromwell, Corps of U. S. Artillery; on Muster Roll from April 30, 1814 to June 30, 1814. Ref: R. & L. 1812, AGO Page 18.

MC MASTER, SAMUEL, Strafford. Served in Capt. Benjamin S. Edgerton's Company, 11th Regt.; on Pay Roll for September and October, 1812 and January and February, 1813; enlisted Nov. 1, 1812. Ref: R. & L. 1812, AGO Pages 1 and 2.

MC MELLY, JOHN JR. Served with Capt. Benjamin Edgerton's Company, 11th Regt., at Battle of Chrystler's Field Nov. 11, 1813 and was reported missing after the battle. Ref: Governor and Council Vt., Vol. 6, Page 490.

*MC MENAS, PATRICK.
Served in Capt. Wheeler's Company,
Col. Fifield's Regt. Detached Militia
in U. S. service 6 months and 4
days, 1812.

‡MC NAMARA, ASA.
Served in Capt. Beeman's Company.
Pension Certificate No. 2756.

*MC NAUGHTON, DANIEL, Corporal.
Served in 1 Regt. (Martindale's) Vt.
Militia.

*MC NEAL, JOHN, Corporal.
Served from June 11 to June 14,
1813 in Capt. Ithiel Stone's Company,
1st Regt. 2nd Brig. 3rd Div.

*MC NEAL, ISRAEL,   Cornwall.
Volunteered to go to Plattsburgh,
September, 1814, and was at the
battle, serving in Capt. Edmund B.
Hill's Company, Sumner's Regt.

MC NEAL, JOHN,   Cornwall.
Volunteered to go to Plattsburgh,
September, 1814, and was at the
battle, serving in Capt. Edmund B.
Hill's Company, Sumner's Regt.
Ref: Book 51, AGO Page 13.

MC NEIL. JOHN JR., Captain.
Served in company of Capt. John
McNeil Jr., 11th Regt.; on Pay Roll
for January and February, 1813. Ref:
R. & L. 1812, AGO Page 17.

MC NELLY, JOHN,   Strafford.
Served from March 10 to June 9,
1813 in Capt. Edgerton's Company,
11th Regt. Ref: R. & L. 1812, AGO
Page 3.

MC NELLY, JOHN J.
Served from March 23 to June 22,
1813 in Capt. Edgerton's Company,
11th Regt. Ref: R. & L. 1812, AGO
Page 3.

*MC NIEL. THOMAS P.,   Whiting.
Served from July 9 to Dec. 8, 1812
in Col. Wm. Williams' Regt. of Detached Militia in U. S. service.

MC NORTON, DANIEL.
Served in Capt. Hopkins' Company,
Col. Martindale's Regt. Detached
Militia in U. S. service 2 months and
13 days, 1812. Ref: Book 53, AGO
Page 29.

MC PHERSON, JOSIAH,   Shoreham.
Volunteered to go to Plattsburgh,
September, 1814, and served 3 days
in company of Militia Cavalry. Ref:
Book 51, AGO Page 33.

MC PHERSON, JOSIAH JR.,   Shoreham.
Volunteered to go to Plattsburgh,
September. 1814, and served 3 days
in Company of Militia Cavalry. Ref:
Book 51, AGO Page 33.

‡MC PHERSON, MOSES.
Served in Capt. Jones' Company. Pension Certificate of widow, Sarah, No.
5566.

*MC RAY, RICHARD.
Served in 4 Regt. (Peck's) Vt. Militia.

*MC REA, EPHRAIM.
Served in 1 Regt. (Martindale's) Vt.
Militia.

*MC READY, WILLIAM.
Served in Sumner's Regt. Vt. Militia.

MC TRIMMER, DONALD, Sergeant, Franklin County. Volunteered to go to
Plattsburgh Sept. 11, 1814 and served in 15th or 22nd Regt. Ref: Hemenway's Vt. Gazetteer, Vol. 2, Page
391.

*MC WADE, WILLIAM.
Served in Capt. Phelps' Company,
Col. Wm. Williams' Regt. Detached
Militia in U. S. service 5 months,
1812.

MC WAID, EDWARD.
Served from March 1 to June 30, 1814
in Capt. Alexander Brooks' Corps of
Artillery. Ref: R. & L. 1812, AGO
Page 31.

MC WILLIAMS, WILLIAM.
Served in Capt. Alexander Brooks'
Corps of Artillery; on Pay Roll to
June 30, 1814. Ref: R. & L. 1812,
AGO Page 31.

‡*MEACHAM, ELIJAH.
Served in Capt. Phelps' Company,
Col. Jonathan Williams' Regt. De-
tached Militia in U. S. service 2
months and 21 days, 1812. Pension
Certificate of widow, Lydia, No. 693.

*MEACHAM, JEREMIAH, Corporal, Rich-
ford or Fairfield. Served in Capt.
Kendall's Company, Col. Wm. Williams' Regt. Detached Militia in U.
S. service 4 months and 23 days, 1812.

*MEAD, ABEL.
Served in Sumner's Regt. Vt. Militia.

‡*MAD, EZRA, Ensign,   Cornwall.
Served from April 12 to April 21,
1814 in Capt. Edmund B. Hill's Company. Sumner's Regt. Volunteered to
go to Plattsburgh, September. 1814,
and was in the battle, serving in
the same company. Pension Certificate of widow, Anna, No. 32407.

*MEAD, HELON,   Cornwall.
Served from April 12 to April 21,
1814 in Capt. Edmund B. Hill's Company, Sumner's Regt.; volunteered to
go to Plattsburgh, September. 1814,
and was at the battle, serving in
same company.

‡*MEAD. HENRY.
Served in Capt. Hopkins' Company,
Col. Martindale's Regt. Detached
Militia in U. S. service 1 month and
3 days, 1812. Also served in Sumner's Regt. Vt. Militia. Pension Certificate No. 23843. Pension Certificate of widow, Malinda Hopkins,
No. 31185.

MEAD, IRA, Sergeant.
Served in 1st Regt. of Detached Militia of Vt. in U. S. service at Champlain from Nov. 18 to Nov. 19, 1812.

‡MEAD, JOEL,   Montpelier.
Volunteered to go to Plattsburgh,
September, 1814, and served 8 days

in Capt. Timothy Hubbard's Company. Pension Certificate of widow, Lucy, No. 22395.

*MEAD, JOSIAH, Sergeant.
Enlisted Sept. 25, 1813 and served 1 month and 23 days in Capt. Elijah Birge's Company, Col. Dixon's Regt. Detached Militia in U. S. service.

‡*MEAD, MARTIN.
Served from June 11 to June 14, 1813 in Capt. Thomas Dorwin's Company, 1st Regt. 2nd Brig. 3rd Div. Pension Certificate No. 24857.

MEAD, RUFUS, Sergeant,   Cornwall.
Volunteered to go to Plattsburgh, September, 1814, and was at the battle, serving in Capt. Edmund B. Hill's Company, Sumner's Regt. Ref: Book 51, AGO Page 13.

*MEAD, RUFUS JR.
Served in Capt. Wright's Company, Col. Martindale's Regt. Detached Militia in U. S. service 2 months and 14 days, 1812. Served from April 12 to April 21, 1814 as a corporal in Capt. Edmund B. Hill's Company, Sumner's Regt.

MEAD, SAMUEL, Montpelier or Middlesex. Volunteered to go to Plattsburgh, September, 1814, and served 8 days in Capt. Timothy Hubbard's Company. Ref: Book 52, AGO Page 256.

‡*MEAD, SILAS, Drummer.
Served in Capt. Wright's Company, 1 Regt. (Martindale's) Vt. Militia. Pension Certificate No. 4771. Pension Certificate of widow, Betsey, No. 14701.

MEAD, THOMAS JR.,   Montpelier.
Volunteered to go to Plattsburgh, September, 1814, and served 8 days in Capt. Timothy Hubbard's Company. Ref: Book 52, AGO Page 256.

*MEAD, WILLIAM.
Served in 1 Regt. (Judson's) Vt. Militia.

MEAD, WILLIAM.
Enlisted May 9, 1812 for 5 years in Capt. White Youngs' Company, 15th Regt.; on Muster Roll from Aug. 31 to Dec. 31, 1814. Ref: R. & L. 1812, AGO Page 27.

‡MEAD, ZEBULON.
Served in Capt. Burbank's Company. Pension Certificate of widow, Delia, No. 18031.

‡MEADER, STEPHEN.
Served in Capt. Stewart's Company. Pension Certificate of widow, Mary, No. 1843.

MEADS, ELISHA.
Served from March 29 to June 30, 1813 in Lieut. Wm. S. Foster's Company, 11th Regt. Ref: R. & L. 1812, AGO Page 6.

*MEAKER, JOHN.
Served from June 11 to June 14, 1813 in Capt. Samuel Blinn's Company, 1 Regt. (Judson's).

MEARS, JOSEPH D.,   Danville.
Volunteered to go to Plattsburgh, September, 1814, and served 2 days in company commanded by Capt. James Kelsey Jr., and Capt. Solomon Langmaid. Ref: Book 51, AGO Pages 71, 75, 76.

*MEARS, ROSWELL.
Enlisted Oct. 26, 1813 and served 23 days in Capt. Asahel Langworthy's Company, Col. Isaac Clark's Regt. Detached Militia in U. S. service.

‡MEARS, ROSWELL JR.
Served in Capt. Post's Company, Col. Dixon's Regt. Detached Militia in U. S. service 1 month, 1813. Pension Certificate No. 20643. Pension Certificate of widow, Lucy House, No. 42589.

*MEDCALF, LACY.
Served in Sumner's Regt. Vt. Militia.

MEDCALF, LYMAN.
Served from April 12 to April 15, 1814 in Capt. Jonathan P. Stanley's Company, Col. W. B. Sumner's Regt. Ref: Book 52, AGO Page 287.

‡*MEECH, AVERY, Sergeant.
Served in 1 Regt. (Judson's) Vt. Militia. Also served as captain of a company. Pension Certificate of widow, Sarah Mariah, No. 17721.

‡MEECH, ERASTUS.
Served in Capt. Barns' Company, Col. Wm. Williams' Regt. Detached Militia in U. S. service 5 months, 1812. Also served in Capt. Newell's Company. Pension Certificate of widow, Annis, No. 2567. Ref: Book 53, AGO Page 21.

MEEKER, DANIEL,   Hubbardton.
Volunteered to go to Plattsburgh, September, 1814, and served 8 days in Capt. Henry J. Horton's Company. Ref: Book 52, AGO Page 142.

MEEKER, WILLIAM, Corporal. Weybridge, Vt. Enlisted at Plattsburgh and served in Capt. James Taylor's Company, Capt. Gideon Spencer's Company and Capt. Wm. Miller's Company. 30th Regt. Ref: R. & L. 1812, AGO Pages 53, 54, 55, 56.

*MEEKUM, JUSTIN B.
Served in Sumner's Regt. Vt. Militia.

MEGANAGAL, JOHN.
Enlisted March 17, 1814 during the war in Capt. Gideon Spencer's Company, 30th Regt.; on Muster Roll from Dec. 30, 1813 to June 30, 1814. Ref: R. & L. 1812, AGO Page 57.

*MEHURIN, SETH.
Served in 1 Regt. (Martindale's) Vt. Militia.

*MEIGS, GUY, Sergeant.
Served from Sept. 25 to Oct. 29, 1813 as Quartermaster Sergeant in Dixon's Regt. of Vt. Militia in U. S. service. Served in Lieut. V. R. Goodrich's Company, 11th Regt.; on Pay Roll for January and February, 1813. Ref: R. & L. 1812, AGO Page 11.

*MEIGS, JULIUS.
Served in Capt. Barns' Company,
Col. Wm. Williams' Regt. Detached
Militia in U. S. service 4 months
and 21 days, 1812.

‡*MEIGS, LUMAS.
Enlisted Sept. 25, 1813 in Capt.
Elijah W. Wood's Company, Dixon's
Regt.; re-enlisted Oct. 11 for 1 year.
Pension Certificate No. 23268.

*MEIGS, LUTHER.
Enlisted Sept. 25, 1813 and served 1
month and 23 days in Capt. Elijah
W. Wood's Company, Col. Dixon's
Regt. Detached Militia in U. S. serv-
ice.

‡*MELCHER, SAMUEL.
Served in Capt. Merrill's Company,
2 Regt. (Fifield's) Vt. Militia. Pension Certificate of widow, Zeruah, No.
22602.

MELLALLEN, DAVID.
Enlisted Sept. 25, 1813 in Capt. N.
B. Eldridge's Company, Dixon's Regt.
Ref: Book 52, AGO Page 267.

*MELLEN, EBENEZER,   Waterbury.
Volunteered to go to Plattsburgh,
September, 1814, and was in the
battle, serving 11 days in Capt.
George Atkins' Company, 4 Regt.
(Peck's).

*MELLEN, JAMES.
Served in 2 Regt. (Fifield's) Vt. Militia.

MELONER, CORNELIUS.
Served from May 1 to June 30, 1814
as a carpenter in company of Artificers commanded by Alexander Parris. Ref: R. & L. 1812, AGO Page
24.

*MELTIMORE, JAMES (or Miltimore).
Served in Capt. Richardson's Company, Col: Martindale's Regt. Detached Militia in U. S. service 2
months and 13 days, 1812.

MENOW, DAVID,   Franklin County.
Volunteered to go to Plattsburgh
Sept. 11, 1814 and served in 15th or
22nd Regt. Ref: Hemenway's Vt. Gazetteer, Vol. 2, Page 392.

‡*MERIAM, GUSTAVUS.
Served in Capt. Dodge's Company,
Col. Fifield's Regt. Detached Militia
in U. S. service 1 month and 25
days, 1812.

*MERILS, TOMAS.
Served in Capt. Howard's Company,
Vt. Militia.

*MERRIAM, JAMES.
Served in 4 Regt. (Peck's) Vt. Militia.

MERRIAM, WILLIAM.
Served from Feb. 15 to July 16, 1813
in Capt. John W. Weeks' Company,
11th Regt. Ref: R. & L. 1812, AGO
Page 4.

*MERRICK, JOHN.
Served in 1 Regt. (Martindale's) Vt.
Militia.

*MERRICK, ROSWELL, Drum Major.
Served in 4 Regt. (Williams') Vt.
Militia.

*MERRIFIELD, CHAUNCY.
Served from June 11 to June 14, 1813
in Capt. Hezekiah Barns' Company,
1st Regt. 2nd Brig. 3rd Div.

‡*MERRIFIELD, HIRAM.
Served in Capt. Mason's Company,
Col. Fifield's Regt. Detached Militia
in U. S. service 1 month and 17
days, 1812. Pension Certificate of
widow, James, No. 6988.

*MERRILL, ABEL.
Served in Corning's Detachment, Vt.
Militia.

MERRILL, ASA, Lieutenant,   Corinth.
Volunteered to go to Plattsburgh,
September, 1814, and served in Capt.
Abel Jackman's Company. Ref: Book
52, AGO Page 44.

*MERRILL, BENJAMIN,   Richmond.
Enlisted Sept. 25, 1813 in Capt.
Thomas Waterman's Company, Dix-
on's Regt. Volunteered to go to
Plattsburgh, September, 1814, served
9 days in Capt. Roswell Hunt's Com-
pany, Tyler's Regt. Ref: Book 51,
AGO Page 82.

MERRILL, DAVID,   Franklin County.
Volunteered to go to Plattsburgh,
Sept. 11, 1814 and served in 15th or
22nd Regt. Ref: Hemenway's Vt.
Gazetteer, Vol. 2, Page 392.

*MERRILL, DAVID,   Washington.
Served in Capt. Walker's Company,
Col. Fifield's Regt. Detached Militia
in U. S. service 6 months and 3
days, 1812. Volunteered to go to
Plattsburgh, September, 1814, and
served in Capt. Amos Stiles' Company.

MERRILL, ELIPHALET,   Corinth.
Volunteered to go to Plattsburgh,
September, 1814, and served 3 days
in Capt. Abel Jackman's Company.
Ref: Book 52, AGO Pages 44, 45, 113.

‡*MERRILL, HENRY L..   Irasburgh.
Served in Capt. Mason's Company,
Col. Fifield's Regt. Detached Militia
in U. S. service 5 months and 26
days, 1812, at Derby. Pension Certificate No. 9511.

‡MERRILL, JAMES.
Volunteered to go to Plattsburgh,
September, 1814, and served in Capt.
Jonathan Jennings' Company, of Chel-
sea. Pension Certificate No. 33128.

‡*MERRILL, JOHN, Lieutenant.
Appointed 1st Lieutenant 31 Inf.
April 30, 1813; resigned Feb. 21, 1814.
Served as Ensign in Capt. Bingham's
Company, 3 Regt. (Williams') Vt.
Militia. Pension Certificate No. 13929.
Ref: Heitman's Historical Register &
Dictionary USA.

MERRILL, ORSAMUS C., Lt. Colonel,
Bennington. Appointed Major 11th
Inf. March 3, 1813; transferred to
26th Inf. June 7, 1814; Lieutenant

Colonel Sept. 4, 1814; honorably discharged June 15, 1815; died April 11, 1865. Ref: Heitman's Historical Register & Dictionary USA.

MERRILL, REUBEN,   St. Albans.
Enlisted May 19, 1813 for 1 year in Capt. John Wires' Company. 30th Regt. Ref: R. & L. 1812, AGO Page 40.

*MERRITT, GILES,   Calais.
Volunteered to go to Plattsburgh, September, 1814, and served 10 days in Capt. Gideon Wheelock's Company.

MERRITT, JONA P.
Served from April 2 to July 1, 1813 in Capt. Samul Gordon's Company, 11th Regt. Ref: R. & L. 1812, AGO Page 8.

MERRITT, JOSEPH E., Sergeant.
Enlisted Jan. 1, 1813 and appointed Paymaster Jan. 25, 1813 in company of Capt. John McNeil Jr., 11th Regt.; on Pay Roll for January and February, 1813. Served on General Staff of the Northern Army commanded by Major Gen. George Izard; on Pay Roll to July 31, 1814. Ref: R. & L. 1812, AGO Pages 17 and 28.

*MERRITT, SEWALL.
Served from April 12, 1814 to April 21, 1814 in Capt. Othniel Jewett's Company, Sumner's Regt.

*MERRITT, THOMAS,   Cornwall.
Served from April 12 to April 21, 1814 in Capt. Shubael Wales' Company, Col. W. B. Sumner's Regt. Served from Sept. 1, 1814 to June 16, 1815 in Capt. Sanford's Company, 30th Inf.

*MESERVY, JOSEPH.
Served in Capt. Wheeler's Company, Col. Fifield's Regt. Detached Militia in U. S. service 3 months and 16 days, 1812.

MESSENGER, WILLIAM S.
Served in Capt. Phineas Williams' Company, 11th Regt.; on Pay Roll for January and February, 1813. Ref: R. & L. 1812, AGO Page 15.

MESSEREAU, JOHN.
Served from May 1 to June 30, 1814 in Capt. Alexander Brooks' Corps of Artillery. Ref: R. & L. 1812, AGO Page 31.

METCALF, ELIAS,   Montpelier.
Volunteered to go to Plattsburgh, September, 1814, and served 8 days in Capt. Timothy Hubbard's Company. Ref: Book 52, AGO Page 256.

METCALF, JASON.
Served from May 1 to June 30, 1814 in Capt. Haig's Corps of Light Dragoons. Ref: R. & L. 1812, AGO Page 20.

METSINGUIRE, GEORGE, Franklin County. Volunteered to go to Plattsburgh Sept. 11, 1814 and served in 15th or 22nd Regt. Ref: Hemenway's Vt. Gazetteer, Vol. 2, Page 392.

MICKELON, WILLIAM,   Fairfax.
Served from Aug. 8, 1812 in company of Capt. Joseph Beeman Jr., 11th Regt. U. S. Inf. under Col. Ira Clark. Ref: Hemenway's Vt. Gazetteer, Vol. 2, Page 402.

MIDDLETON, MASON W.
Served in Capt. Alexander Brook's Corps of Artillery; on Pay Roll to June 30, 1814. Ref: R. & L. 1812, AGO Page 31.

MIGHILL, J. W.
Served from March 18 to June 19, 1813 in Capt. Samul Gordon's Company, 11th Regt. Ref: R. & L. 1812, AGO Page 8.

MILCHER, SAMUEL.
Served in Capt. Hiram Mason's Company, Col. Fifield's Regt. Detached Militia in U. S. service 6 months, 1812. Ref: Book 53, AGO Page 8.

*MILES, DANIEL S., Corporal.
Served in Capt. Rogers' Company, Col. Fifield's Regt. Detached Militia in U. S. service 5 months and 29 days, 1812.

*MILES, JONAS.
Served from Sept. 25 to Sept. 29, 1813 in Capt. N. B. Eldridge's Company, Dixon's Regt.

‡*MILES, SAMUEL, Drummer.
Served in Capt. Wheeler's Company, Col. Fifield's Regt. Detached Militia in U. S. service 2 months and 18 days, 1812. Also served in Capt. Arnold's Company. Pension Certificate No. 2248.

*MILES, THEODUS (or Thaddeus or Theodore), Middlesex. Volunteered to go to Plattsburgh, September, 1814, and served 10 days in Capt. Holden Putnam's Company, 4 Regt. (Peck's).

MILES, THOMAS JR.
Served from Nov. 1, 1812 to Feb. 28, 1813 in Capt. Samuel H. Holly's Company, 11th Regt. Ref: R. & L. 1812, AGO Page 25.

*MILES, WILLIAM JR.
Served in 1 Regt. (Judson's) Vt. Militia.

MILLARD, ASHLEY.
Served from May 1 to June 30, 1814 in Capt. Haig's Corps of Light Dragoons. Ref: R. & L. 1812, AGO Page 20.

‡*MILLARD, SOL. E. D. Y., Corporal.
Served in Capt. Strait's Company, Col. Martindale's Regt. Detached Militia in U. S. service 2 months 13 days, 1812. Served as Corporal in 1st Regt. of Detached Militia of Vt. in U. S. service at Champlain from Nov. 18 to Nov. 19, 1812. Pension Certificate of widow, Anna A., No. 4245.

*MILLER, ADAM K., Sergeant.
Served in Sumner's Regt. Vt. Militia.

MILLER, BERNARD, Corporal.
Served in Corps of Light Dragoons; on Pay Roll to June 30, 1814. Ref: R. & L. 1812, AGO Page 20.

MILLER, CALVIN S.
Served in Capt. Samul Gordon's Company, 11th Regt.; on Pay Roll for January and February, 1813. Ref: R. & L. 1812, AGO Page 9.

‡*MILLER, CHESTER, Sergeant, Highgate. Served in Capt. Saxe's Company, Col. Wm. Williams' Regt. in U. S. service at Swanton Falls 4 months and 24 days, 1812. Enlisted Oct. 11, 1813 and served in Capt. Elijah W. Wood's Company, Col. Dixon's Regt. and in Capt. Asahel Langworthy's Company, Col. Isaac Clark's Rifle Corps. Pension Certificate of widow, Sarah, No. 18991.

*MILLER, CONSIDER, Corporal.
Served in Capt. Adams' Company, Col. Jonathan Williams' Regt. Detached Militia in U. S. service 2 months and 7 days, 1812.

MILLER, DANA, Sergeant, Williamstown.
Volunteered to go to Plattsburgh, September, 1814, and served in Capt. David Robinson's Company 8 days. Ref: Loose Rolls, Book 52, AGO.

MILLER, ELIHU,   Wallingford?
Enlisted Feb. 11, 1814 during the war in Capt. Clark's Company, 30th Regt. Ref: R. & L. 1812, AGO Page 1.

MILLER, ELIHU,   Cornwall.
Enlisted May 27, 1813 for 1 year in Capt. Sanford's Company, 30th Regt. Ref: R. & L. 1812, AGO Page 1.

‡*MILLER, ELISHA, Sergeant, Highgate.
Enlisted Sept. 25, 1813 in Capt. Jesse Post's Company, Dixon's Regt. Also served in Capt. Lampkin's Company. Pension Certificate of widow, Amy, No. 2770.

‡*MILLER, ELISHA JR., Sergeant.
Served in Capt. Lowry's Company, Col. Wm. Williams' Regt. Detached Militia in U. S. service 4 months and 25 days, 1812, at Swanton Falls. Pension Certificate No. 600.

*MILLER, ETHENY.
Served in Capt. Bingham's Company, Col. Jonathan Williams' Regt. Detached Militia in U. S. service 2 months and 9 days, 1812. Also served in Capt. Phineas Williams' Company, 11th Regt., from March 5, 1813 to June 4, 1813. Ref: R. & L. 1812, AGO Page 14.

MILLER, GEORGE,   Franklin County.
Volunteered to go to Plattsburgh Sept. 11, 1814 and served in 15th or 22nd Regt. Ref: Hemenway's Vt. Gazetteer, Vol. 2, Page 392.

*MILLER, GILBERT.
Served in Capt. Robbins' Company, Col. Wm. Williams' Regt. Detached Militia in U. S. service 4 months and 29 days, 1812.

MILLER, HAWLEY.
Served in Capt. Wood's Company, Col. Dixon's Regt. Detached Militia in U. S. service 1 month and 23 days, 1813. Ref: Book 53, AGO Page 113.

MILLER, ISAAC,   Enosburgh.
Served from Oct. 15 to Nov. 17, 1813 in Capt. Asahel Scovell's Company. Ref: R. & L. 1812, AGO Page 22; Book 52, AGO Page 274.

MILLER, J. BROOK.
Served from Feb. 14 to May 25, 1813 in Capt. Charles Follett's Company, 11th Regt. Ref: R. & L. 1812, AGO Page 13.

‡*MILLER, JACOB.
Served in Capt. Sinclair's Company, Tyler's Regt. Vt. Militia. Pension Certificate of widow, Susey Barnett, No. 29992.

‡*MILLER, JAMES, Enosburg or Richford. Served in Capt. Rogers' Company, Col. Fifield's Regt. Detached Militia in U. S. service 10 days, 1812. Enlisted Nov. 1, 1812 in Capt. Weeks' Company, 11th Regt.; on Pay Roll for January and February, 1813. Enlisted Sept. 25, 1813 and served 1 month and 23 days in Capt. Martin D. Folett's Company, Col. Dixon's Regt. Pension Certificate No. 13206. Pension Certificate of widow, Polly Ann, No. 11844.

*MILLER, JOHN, Enosburgh or Richford. Enlisted Sept. 25, 1813 and served 1 month and 23 days in Capt. Martin D. Folett's Company, Col. Dixon's Regt. Detached Militia in U. S. service.

MILLER, JOHN,   Pittsford.
Volunteered to go to Plattsburgh, September, 1814, and served 3 days in Capt. Caleb Hendee's Company. Ref: Book 52, AGO Page 125.

*MILLER, JONATHAN P.,   Randolph.
Volunteered to go to Plattsburgh, September, 1814, and served in Capt. Lebbeus Egerton's Company.

MILLER, LEVI.
Served in company of Capt. John McNeil Jr., 11th Regt.; on Pay Roll for January and February, 1813. Ref: R. & L. 1812, AGO Page 17.

MILLER, ROBERT, Fairfax or Swanton. Served from Aug. 8, 1812 in company of Capt. Joseph Beeman Jr., 11th Regt. U. S. Inf. under Col. Ira Clark. Served in Lieut. V. R. Goodrich's Company, 11th Regt.; on Pay Roll for January and February, 1813. Ref: R. & L. 1812, AGO Page 11; Hemenway's Vt. Gazetteer, Vol. 2, Page 402.

MILLER, SAMUEL A.
Served in Capt. Phineas Williams' Company, 11th Regt.; on Pay Roll for January and February, 1813. Served from May 1 to June 30, 1814 in Capt. Haig's Corps of Light Dragoons. Ref: R. & L. 1812, AGO Pages 15 and 20.

MILLER, SETH.
Served from May 1 to June 30, 1814 in Capt. Haig's Corps of Light Dragoons. Ref: R. & L. 1812, AGO Page 20.

*MILLER, STEPHEN, Sergeant.
Served in 4 Regt. (Peck's) Vt. Militia.

MILLER, TOLMAN,   Richford.
Served in Capt. Martin D. Follett's
Company, Dixon's Regt. on duty on
Canadian Frontier in 1813. Ref:
Hemenway's Vt. Gazetteer, Vol. 2,
Page 428.

*MILLER, WILLIAM,   Enosburgh.
Enlisted Sept. 25, 1813 and served
1 month and 23 days in Capt. Martin D. Folett's Company, Col. Dixon's
Regt. Detached Militia in U. S. service.

MILLER, WILLIAM, Captain. Poultney.
Appointed 1st Lieutenant 30th Inf.
April 30, 1813; Captain Jan. 31, 1814;
honorably discharged June 15, 1815.
Ref: Heitman's Historical Register &
Dictionary USA.

MILLER, WILLIAM.
Enlisted Dec. 9, 1812 for 5 years in
company of late Capt. J. Brooks,
commanded by Lieut. John I. Cromwell. Corps of U. S. Artillery; on
Muster Roll from April 30, 1814 to
June 30, 1814. Ref: R. & L. 1812,
AGO Page 18.

*MILLER, WILLIAM, Corporal.
Served in Capt. S. Pettes' Company.
Col. Wm. Williams' Regt. Detached
Militia in U. S. service 4 months and
17 days, 1812.

*MILLER, SILAS.
Served in Capt. Bingham's Company,
Col. Jonathan Williams' Regt. Detached Militia in U. S. service 1
month and 7 days, 1812.

MILLET, WILLIAM A.,   Stockbridge.
Volunteered to go to Plattsburgh,
September, 1814, and served 8 days
in Capt. Elias Keyes' Company. Ref:
Book 51, AGO Page 239.

*MILLIKEN, ALEXANDER.
Served in Capt. Briggs' Company, Col.
Jonathan Williams' Regt. Detached
Militia in U. S. service 2 months and
13 days, 1812.

MILLIKIN, JAMES.
Served as a carpenter in Alexander
Parris' Company of Artificers; on Pay
Roll for May and June, 1814. Ref:
R. & L. 1812, AGO Page 24.

MILLIKIN, STERLING F.
Served from June 10 to June 30, 1814
in Alexander Parris' Company of Artificers. Ref: R. & L. 1812, AGO
Page 24.

MILLINGTON, HIRAM,   Pittsford.
Volunteered to go to Plattsburgh,
September, 1814, and served 8 days
in Capt. Caleb Hendee's Company.
Ref: Book 52, AGO Page 125.

MILLS, AMOS S.
Served in Capt. Samuel H. Holly's
Company, 11th Regt.; on Pay Roll
for January and February, 1813. Ref:
R. & L. 1812, AGO Page 25.

MILLS, CLARK M.,   Johnson.
Volunteered to go to Plattsburgh,
September, 1814, and served in Capt.
Thomas Waterman's Company, Dixon's Regt. Ref: Book 51, AGO Page
208.

*MILLS, COLLINS.
Served in Capt. Ormsbee's Company,
Col. Martindale's Regt. Detached
Militia in U. S. service 2 months
and 14 days, 1812.

*MILLS, DANIEL.
Served in 1 Regt. (Judson's) Vt.
Militia.

*MILLS, DAVID.
Served from June 11 to June 14,
1813 in Capt. Hezekiah Barns' Company, 1st Regt. 2nd Brig. 3rd Div.

MILLS, ELIAS.
Served in Capt. Alexander Brooks'
Corps of Artillery; on Pay Roll to
June 30, 1814. Ref: R. & L. 1812,
AGO Page 31.

*MILLS, EPHRAIM.
Served in Capt. Barns' Company, Col.
Wm. Williams' Regt. Detached Militia in U. S. service 4 months and
26 days, 1812 Served from June 11
to June 14, 1813 in Capt. Moses
Jewett's Company, 1st Regt. 2nd Brig.
3rd Div. Ref: Book 53, AGO Page
13.

‡MILLS, EZEKIEL.
Served in Capt. Utley's Company.
Pension Certificate No. 22474.

MILLS, JOSEPH,   Waitsfield.
Volunteered to go to Plattsburgh,
September, 1814, and served 4 days
in Capt. Mathias S. Jones' Company.
Ref: Book 52, AGO Page 170.

‡MILLS, REUBEN.
Served in Capt. D. Hough's Company. Pension Certificate of widow,
Louisa, No. 31877.

‡*MILLS, SAMUEL, Ensign.
Served from June 11 to June 14,
1813 in Capt. Moses Jewett's Company, 1st Regt. 2nd Brig. 3rd Div.
Pension Certificate of widow, Rebecca, No. 8171.

*MINARD, DANIEL.
Served in Capt. Morrill's Company,
Col. Fifield's Regt. Detached Militia
in U. S. service 2 months and 18
days, 1812.

*MINER, ALEXANDER.
Served in Sumner's Regt. Vt. Militia.

*MINER, ANDREW B., Lieutenant.
Served in 4 Regt. (Peck's) Vt. Militia.

‡*MINER, CLEMENT S.
Served from Feb. 8 to May 7, 1813
in Capt. Benjamin S. Edgerton's Company, 11th Regt. Served from April
12 to May 20, 1814 in company of
Capt. James Gray Jr., Sumner's Regt.
Pension Certificate No. 3721.

MINER, HENRY, Sergeant.
Served in Capt. Phineas Williams'
Company, 11th Regt.; on Pay Roll for
January and February, 1813. Ref: R.
& L. 1812, AGO Page 15.

MINER, JOSEPH JR.
Born at Plattsburgh, N. Y. Enlisted
at Burlington April 13, 1814 and serv-
ed in Capt. James Taylor's Company,
Capt. Gideon Spencer's Company and
Capt. Wm. Miller's Company, 30th
Regt. Ref: R. & L. 1812, AGO Pages
53, 54, 55, 57.

*MINOR, FREDERICK T.
Served in Corning's Detachment, Vt.
Militia and in 4 Regt. (Peck's) Vt.
Militia.

*MINOR, ISAAC.
Served from April 12, 1814 to April
21, 1814 in Capt. Edmund B. Hill's
Company, Sumner's Regt.

*MINOR, JOSEPH, Sergeant.
Served from April 12 to May 20,
1814 in company of Capt. James
Gray Jr., Sumner's Regt.

‡*MINOR, SAMUEL.
Served from June 11 to June 14,
1813 in Capt. Samuel Blinn's Company, 1st Regt. (Judson's). Pension
Certificate of widow, Patience, No.
11560.

MINOR, WILLIAM,   Middletown.
Volunteered to go to Plattsburgh,
September, 1814, and served 4 days
in Capt. Reuben Wood's Company.
Ref: Book 52, AGO Page 143.

*MINOTT, BENJAMIN.
Served in Capt. Wheeler's Company,
Col. Fifield's Regt. Detached Militia
in U. S. service 3 months and 7
days, 1812.

*MINOTT, ROSWELL (or Minot).
Served in 1 Regt. (Judson's) Vt.
Militia.

*MIRES, JOHN.
Served in Sumner's Regt. Vt. Militia.

MITCHELL, ABIAL.
Enlisted May 10, 1813 for 1 year in
Capt. Daniel Farrington's Company,
30th Regt.; on Muster Roll from
March 1 to April 30, 1814. Ref: R.
& L. 1812, AGO Pages 50 and 51.

‡MITCHELL, DAVID,   Fairfield.
Served in Capt. Kendall's Company,
Col. Wm. Williams' Regt. Detached
Militia in U. S. service 4 months
and 23 days, 1812. Pension Certifi-
cate of widow, Polly, No. 5671. Ref:
Book 53, AGO Page 67.

MITCHELL, EBENEZER,   Pittsford.
Volunteered to go to Plattsburgh,
September, 1814, and served 8 days
in Capt. Caleb Hendee's Company.
Ref: Book 52, AGO Page 125.

*MITCHELL, ELIPHALET.
Served from April 12 to April 21,
1814 in Lieut. Justus Foote's Company, Sumner's Regt.

*MITCHELL, HENRY.
Served from Sept. 25 to Sept. 29,
1813 in Capt. Amos Robinson's Company, Dixon's Regt.

*MITCHELL, HUBBEL.   Fairfield.
Served in Capt. Kendall's Company,
Col. Wm. Williams' Regt. Detached
Militia in U. S. service 16 days.

*MITCHELL, JOHN B.,   Fairfield.
Served in Capt. Kendall's Company,
Col. Wm. Williams' Regt. Detached
Militia in U. S. service 4 months
and 23 days, 1812.

*MITCHELL, PHILANDER, Sergeant,
Highgate. Served in Capt. Saxe's
Company, Col. Wm. Williams' Regt.
Detached Militia in U. S. service 4
months and 24 days, 1812; held rank
of Corporal. Enlisted Sept. 23, 1813
as a Sergeant in Capt. Asahel Langworthy's Company, Col. Isaac Clark's
Volunteer Riflemen.

*MITCHELL, SAMUEL,   Barre.
Served from June 11 to June 14, 1813
in Capt. Moses Jewett's Company,
1st Regt. 2nd Brig. 3rd Div. Volunteered to go to Plattsburgh, September, 1814, and served in Capt. Warren Ellis' Company.

‡MITCHELL, SILAS.
Served in Capt. Kendall's Company,
4 Regt. Pension Certificate No. 2143.

MITCHELL, THOMAS.
Enlisted May 1, 1813 for 1 year in
Capt. Simeon Wright's Company. Ref:
R. & L. 1812, AGO Page 51.

*MITCHELL, WELLS.
Enlisted Sept. 25, 1813 and served
1 month and 23 days in Capt. A. Robinson's Company, Col. Dixon's Regt.

MITRENBEECHER, JACOB, Franklin
County. Volunteered to go to Plattsburgh Sept. 11, 1814 and served in
15th or 22nd Regt. Ref: Hemenway's
Vt. Gazetteer, Vol. 2, Page 391.

MIX, IRA, Sergeant,   St. Albans.
Enlisted Nov. 30, 1813 in Capt. John
Wires' Company, 30th Regt. Ref:
Hemenway's Vt. Gazetteer, Vol. 2,
Page 433.

MIXTER, DANIEL.
Served in Lieut. Wm. S. Foster's
Company, 11th Regt.; on Pay Roll
for January and February, 1813. Ref:
R. & L. 1812, AGO Page 7.

MOFFITT, ENOCH,   Hadley, N. Y.
Served from May 1 to July 24, 1814
in Capt. Lynd's Company, 29th Inf.
Ref: R. & L. 1812, AGO Page 30.

MOLTON, SAMUEL, Ensign.
Served in 1st Regt. of Detached Militia of Vt. in U. S. service at Champlain from Nov. 18 to Nov. 19, 1812.

*MONGER, AUGUSTUS.
Served from April 13 to April 21,
1814 in Capt. Salmon Foster's Company, Sumner's Regt.

*MONSON, BENJAMIN.
Enlisted Sept. 20, 1813 in Capt. John
Weed's Company, Regt. of Riflemen.

MONTAGUE, JOSEPH,   Cambridge.
Volunteered to go to Plattsburgh,
September, 1814, and served 8 days
in Capt. Salmon Green's Company.
Ref: Book 51, AGO Page 207.

MONTAGUE, JOSEPH A.,   Pittsford.
Volunteered to go to Plattsburgh,
September, 1814, and served 8 days
in Capt. Caleb Hendee's' Company.
Ref: Book 52, AGO Page 125.

*MONTAGUE, SAMUEL,   Fairfax.
Enlisted Sept. 25, 1813 and served
1 month and 23 days in Capt. Asa
Wilkins' Company, Col. Dixon's Regt.

‡*MONTAGUE, SOLOMON, Sergeant, Cambridge. Enlisted Sept. 25, 1813 and
served 1 month and 23 days in Capt.
Charles Bennett's Company, Col. Dixon's Regt. Detached Militia in U. S.
service. Volunteered to go to Plattsburgh, September, 1814, and served
9 days in Capt. Salmon Green's Company. Pension Certificate No. 20305.
Ref: Book 51, AGO Page 207.

MONTAGUE, THOMAS,   Cambridge.
Volunteered to go to Plattsburgh,
September, 1814, and served 8 days
in Capt. Salmon Green's Company.
Ref: Book 51, AGO Page 207.

MONTEY, ABRAHAM.
Enlisted Feb. 14, 1814 for 5 years in
company of late Capt. J. Brooks,
commanded by Lieut.. John I. Cromwell, Corps of U. S. Artillery; on
Muster Roll from April 30 to June 30,
1814. Ref: R. & L. 1812, AGO
Page 18.

*MONTGOMERY, HUGH,   Pawlet.
Served in Capt. Hotchkiss' Company.
Col. Martindale's Regt. Detached
Militia in U. S. service 2 months
and 13 days, 1812.

*MONTY, JOSEPH (or Montey).
Enlisted Oct. 4, 1813 in Capt. Asahel
Langworthy's Company, Col. Clark's
Rifle Corps. Enlisted Feb. 12, 1814
for 5 years in company of late Capt.
J. Brooks, commanded by Lieut. John
I. Cromwell, Corps of U. S. Artillery;
on Muster Roll from April 30, 1814
to June 30. 1814. Ref: R. & L.
1812, AGO Page 18.

*MOODY, ABEL, Fifer.
Served from April 12 to April 21,
1814 in Lieut. Justus Foote's Company, Sumner's Regt.

‡*MOODY, DAVID.
Served in Capt. Bingham's Company,
Col. Jonathan Williams' Regt. De-
tached Militia in U. S. service 2
months and 9 days, 1812. Pension
Certificate No. 7780.

‡MOODY, DAVID.
Pension Certificate of widow, Priscilla,
No. 3170; no organization given.

*MOODY, DAVID. Corporal,   Swanton.
Served from Feb. 11 to May 10, 1813
in Lieut. V. R. Goodrich's Company,

11th Regt. Also served with Hospital Attendants, Vt. Ref: R. & L.
1812, AGO Pages 10 and 11.

MOODY, DAVID, Sergeant,   Tunbridge.
Volunteered to go to Plattsburgh,
September, 1814, and served 4 days
in Capt. Ephraim Hackett's Company.
Ref: Book 52, AGO Pages 71 and 72.

MOODY, DUDLEY,   Tunbridge.
Volunteered to go to Plattsburgh,
September, 1814, and served 4 days
in Capt. Ephraim Hackett's Company.
Ref: Book 52, AGO Pages 71 and 72.

MOODY, JOHN,   Tunbridge.
Enlisted Feb. 12, 1813 in Capt. Ben-
jamin Edgerton's Company, 11th
Regt. Volunteered to go to Platts-
burgh, September, 1814, and served
4 days in Capt. Ephraim Hackett's
Company. Ref: R. & L. 1812, AGO
Pages 2 and 3; Book 52, AGO Page 71.

*MOODY, ROBERT.
Served from April 12 to April 21,
1814 in Lieut Justus Foote's Company, Sumner's Regt.

*MOODY. ROSWELL.
Served in Capt. Lowry's Company,
Col. Wm. Williams' Regt. Detached
Militia in U. S. service 4 months
and 26 days, 1812.

*MOODY, WILLIAM,   Stowe.
Served in company of Capt. John
McNeil Jr., 11th Regt.; on Pay Roll
for January and February, 1813.
Volunteered to go to Plattsburgh, Sep-
tember, 1814, and was at the battle,
serving as a corporal in Capt. Nehe-
miah Perkins' Company, 4 Regt.
(Peck's). Also served in Corning's
Detachment, Vt. Militia. Ref: R. &
L. 1812, AGO Page 17.

*MOON. DAVID.
Served in Dixon's Regt. Vt. Militia.

‡MOON, HAZARD A.
Served in Capt. Foster's Company.
Pension Certificate No. 1375.

MOON, JESSE.   Pittsford.
Volunteered to go to Plattsburgh.
September, 1814, and served 8 days
in Capt. Caleb Hendee's Company.
Ref: Book 52, AGO Page 125.

‡*MOON, RANSOM,   Wallingford?
Served in 1 Regt. (Martindale's) Vt.
Militia, Capt. Hotchkiss' Company.
Pension Certificate of widow, Lydia
G., No. 15228.

*MOON, SILAS.
Served in Dixon's Regt. Vt. Militia.

MOONEY, CHARLES.
Enlisted June 15, 1813 for 5 years in
company of late Capt. J. Brooks,
commanded by Lieut. John I. Cromwell, Corps of U. S. Artillery; on
Muster Roll from April 30 to June 30,
1814. Ref: R. & L. 1812, AGO
Page 18.

*MOONEY, HUGH.   .
Enlisted Sept. 25, 1813 and served 1
month and 23 days in Capt. N. B.

Eldridge's Company, Col. Dixon's Regt. Detached Militia in U. S. service.

MOONTS, JOHN.
Enlisted Sept. 27, 1813 in Capt. Asahel Langworthy's Company, Col. Isaac Clark's Rifle Corps. Ref: Book 52, AGO Page 260.

*MOORE, ASHEL.
Served from June 11 to June 14, 1813 in Capt. Moses Jewett's Company, 1st Regt. 2nd Brig. 3rd Div.

*MOORE, DANIEL.
Served in Capt. Adams' Company, Col. Jonathan Williams' Regt. Detached Militia in U. S. service 2 months and 7 days, 1812.

MOORE, DARIUS,   Thetford.
Volunteered to go to Plattsburgh, September, 1814, and served 6 days in Capt. Orange Hubbard's Company. Ref: Book 52, AGO Page 51.

‡*MOORE, DAVID C.,   Highgate.
Served in Capt. Conrade Saxe's Company, Col. Wm. Williams' Regt. Detached Militia in U. S. service 4 months and 1 day, 1812. Also served with Hospital Attendants, Vt. Pension Certificate No. 3143.

‡*MOORE, ELAM.
Served in Capt. Hopkins' Company. Col. Martindale's Regt. Detached Militia in U. S. service 2 months and 13 days, 1812. Pension Certificate No. 3090.

*MOORE, FRED A.
Served in Capt. Phelps' Company, Col. Wm. Williams' Regt. Detached Militia in U. S. service 5 months, 1812.

MOORE, HARVEY.
Enlisted Sept. 1, 1812 in Capt. Weeks' Company, 11th Regt.; on Pay Roll for January and February, 1813. Ref: R. & L. 1812, AGO Page 5.

*MOORE, HEZEKIAH.
Served in Capt. Briggs' Company, Col. Jonathan Williams' Regt. Detached Militia in U. S. service 2 months and 13 days, 1812.

*MOORE, JABEZ.
Served in Capt. Walker's Company, Col. Fifield's Regt. Detached Militia in U. S. service 20 days, 1812.

*MOORE, JAMES 3rd.
Served in Capt. Howard's Company, Vt. Militia.

MOORE, JEREMIAH,   Edgecombe.
Served from May 1 to July 5, 1814 in Capt. Poland's Company, 34th Inf. Ref: R. & L. 1812, AGO Page 30.

‡MOORE, JOHN.
Served in Capt. John Morton's Company. Pension Certificate No. 32873.

*MOORE, JOHN (or More).
Served with Hospital Attendants, Vt.

MOORE. JOHN,   Plainfield.
Volunteered to go to Plattsburgh, September, 1814, and served 9 days in Capt. James English's Company. Ref: Book 52, AGO Pages 199 and 248.

MOORE, JOHN JR.
Served in Capt. Phelps' Company, Col. Jonathan Williams' Regt. Detached Militia in U. S. service 2 months and 21 days, 1812. Ref: Book 53, AGO Page 79.

MOORE, JOHN W.
Served from Feb. 3, 1813 to date of death, May 2, 1813, in Capt. John W. Weeks' Company, 11th Regt. Ref: R. & L. 1812, AGO Page 4.

MOORE, N.
Served from May 1 to July 31, 1814 as barrack master on General Staff of the Northern Army commanded by Maj. Gen. George Izard. Ref: R. & L. 1812, AGO Page 28.

*MOORE, NATHAN.
Served in Capt. Rogers' Company, Col. Fifield's Regt. Detached Militia in U. S. service 4 months and 20 days, 1812.

‡*MOORE, PAUL,   Cornwall.
Served from April 12 to May 20, 1814 in company of Capt. James Gray Jr., Sumner's Regt. Volunteered to go to Plattsburgh, September, 1814, and was at the battle, serving in Capt. Edmund B. Hill's Company, Sumner's Regt. Pension Certificate of widow, Eunice, No. 28243.

*MOORE, RANSOM.
Served in Capt. Hotchkiss' Company, Col. Martindale's Regt. Detached Militia in U. S. service 2 months and 13 days, 1812.

‡*MOORE, SAMUEL,   Shoreham.
Volunteered to go to Plattsburgh, September, 1814, and served in Capt. Nathaniel North's Company of Cavalry. Also served in Capt. Howard's Company. Pension Certificate of widow, Maria, No. 32696.

MOORE. STEWART (or More).
Served from May 1 to June 30, 1814 in Capt. Alexander Brooks' Corps of Artillery. Ref: R. & L. 1812, AGO Page 31.

MOORE. ZEBULON.
Volunteered to go to Plattsburgh, September. 1814, and served in company of Capt. Joel Barnes of Chelsea. Ref: Book 52, AGO Page 69.

MOORES, JACOB P.
Served from Feb. 3 to May 10, 1813 in Capt. John W. Weeks' Company, 11th Regt. Ref: R. & L. 1812, AGO Page 4.

MOORITS, JOHN.
Served in Capt. Langworthy's Company. Col. Dixon's Regt. Detached Militia in U. S. service 1 month and 21 days, 1813. Ref: Book 53, AGO Page 110.

‡MOORS, WILLIAM.
Served in Capt. Johnson's Company.
Pension Certificate No. 19338.

MOREN, JOHN.
Served in War of 1812 and was cap-
tured by troops Sept. 6, 1814 at
Plattsburgh; discharged Oct. 8, 1814.
Ref: Records of Naval Records and
Library Navy Dept.

*MORES, JONATHAN.
Served in 3 Regt. (Tyler's) Vt. Militia.

MORES, NATHAN.
Served from Feb. 11 to May 10, 1813
in Capt. John W. Weeks' Company,
11th Regt. Ref: R. & L. 1812, AGO
Page 4.

*MORETON, DANIEL O.
Served in Sumner's Regt. Vt. Militia.

MOREY, EPHRAIM,   Vershire.
Volunteered to go to Plattsburgh,
September, 1814, and served 3 days
as a drummer in Capt. Ira Corse's
Company. Ref: Book 52, AGO Page
91.

MOREY, KINGSLEY.
Enlisted May 22, 1813 for 1 year and
served in Capt. Sanford's Company
and Capt. John Wires' Company, 30th
Regt. Ref: R. & L. 1812, AGO Pages
1 and 40.

‡MOREY, MOSES D.
Served in Capt. Jewett's Company.
Pension Certificate No. 24649.

MOREY, REUBEN,   Strafford.
Volunteered to go to Plattsburgh,
September, 1814, and served 5 days
in Capt. Cyril Chandler's Company.
Ref: Book 52, AGO Page 42.

MOREY, THOMAS.
Served in Capt. Preston's Company,
Col. Jonathan Williams' Regt. Detached Militia in U. S. service 2
months and 6 days, 1812. Ref: Book
53, AGO Page 64.

MOREY, STEPHEN.
Enlisted April 26, 1813 for 1 year
in Capt. John Wires' Company, 30th
Regt. Ref: R. & L. 1812, AGO Page
40.

‡MOREY, THOMAS.
Pension Certificate of widow, Laura,
No. 6226; no organization given.

MOREY, WILLIAM P.
Served from Feb. 8 to May 7, 1813
in Capt. Samul Gordon's Company,
11th Regt. Ref: R. & L. 1812, AGO
Pages 8 and 9.

*MORGAN, CALEB.
Enlisted Sept. 25, 1813 and served
1 month and 23 days in Capt. Thomas
Waterman's Company, Col. Dixon's
Regt. Detached Militia in U. S. serv-
ice.

MORGAN, DAVID.
Enlisted April 7, 1813 for period of
the war in company of late Capt.
J. Brooks, commanded by Lieut. John

I. Cromwell, Corps of U. S. Artillery; on Muster Roll from April 30
to June 30, 1814. Ref: R. & L. 1812,
AGO Page 18.

*MORGAN, GEORGE,   Fairfax.
Enlisted Sept. 25, 1813 in Capt. Asa
Wilkins' Company, Dixon's Regt.;
transferred to Rifle Company Oct. 20,
1813.

MORGAN, GUY.
Served in Capt. Samul Gordon's Com-
pany, 11th Regt.; on Pay Roll for
January and February, 1813. Ref:
R. & L. 1812, AGO Page 9.

*MORGAN, HARVEY.
Served in Capt. Wilson's Company.
Col. Wm. Williams' Regt. Detached
Militia in U. S. service 4 months
and 24 days, 1812.

*MORGAN, JOSIAH.
Served in Capt. Waterman's Company, Col. Dixon's Regt. Detached
Militia in U. S. service 1 month and
23 days, 1813.

MORGAN, JOSIAH JR.
Served in Capt. Thomas Waterman's
Company, Dixon's Regt.; enlisted
Sept. 25, 1813. Ref: Book 25, AGO
Page 291.

MORGAN, JUSTIN, Sergeant, Stockbridge.
Volunteered to go to Plattsburgh,
September, 1814, and served 8 days
in Capt. Elias Keyes' Company.
Ref: Book 51, AGO Page 237; Book
52, AGO Page 155.

*MORGAN, PARKER.
Served with Hospital Attendants, Vt.

*MORGAN, REUBEN, D.
Enlisted Sept. 25, 1813 and served
in Capt. Thomas Waterman's Company, Col. Dixon's Regt. Detached
Militia in U. S. service 1 month and
23 days.

*MORGAN, RUSSELL.
Served in 1 Regt. (Judson's) Vt.
Militia.

MORGAN, SKIFF.
Served from May 23, 1813 to March
15, 1814 in Capt. James Taylor's Company and Capt. Gideon Spencer's
Company, 30th Regt. Ref: R. & L.
1812, AGO Pages 52, 57, 59.

MORGAN, SOLOMON,   New Haven.
Volunteered to go to Plattsburgh,
September, 1814, and served 8 days;
no organization given. Ref: Book 51,
AGO Page 30.

*MORGAN, THOMAS.
Served from April 18 to April 21,
1814 in Capt. Eseck Sprague's Company, Sumner's Regt.

MORGAN, TIMOTHY,   Rochester.
Volunteered to go to Plattsburgh,
September, 1814, and served 7 days
in Capt. Oliver Mason's Company.
Ref: Book 51, AGO Page 255.

MORGAN, WILLIAM,   Pittsford.
Volunteered to go to Plattsburgh,
September, 1814, and served 8 days
in Capt. Caleb Hendee's Company.
Ref: Book 52, AGO Page 125.

*MORGAN, WILLIAMS.
Served in 1 Regt. (Judson's) Vt.
Militia.

MORGIN, CALEB.
Served in Capt. Chadwick's Company.
Ref: R. & L. 1812, AGO Page 32.

*MORRELL, ABEL.
Served in Corning's Detachment, Vt.
Militia.

MORRILL, DAVID,   Strafford.
Volunteered to go to Plattsburgh,
September, 1814, and served 6 days
in Capt. Jedediah H. Harris' Company. Was a son of Smith Morrill.
Ref: Book 52, AGO Page 43; Hemenway's Vt. Gazetteer, Vol. 2, Page
1070.

MORRILL, JAMES,   Danville.
Volunteered to go to Plattsburgh,
September, 1814, and served 3 days
in Capt. Solomon Langmaid's Company. Ref: Book 51, AGO Pages 75
and 76.

*MORRILL, JESSE.
Served in Capt. Morrill's Company,
Col. Fifield's Regt. Detached Militia
in U. S. service 6 months and 5
days, 1812.

MORRILL, JOHN,   Danville.
Volunteered to go to Plattsburgh,
September, 1814, and served 3 days
in Capt. Solomon Langmaid's Company. Ref: Book 51, AGO Pages 75
and 76.

MORRILL, JOSEPH,   Strafford.
Volunteered to go to Plattsburgh,
September, 1814, and served 6 days
in Capt. Jedediah H. Harris' Company. Was a son of Smith Morrill.
Ref: Book 52, AGO Page 43; Hemenway's Vt. Gazetteer, Vol. 2, Page
1070.

*MORRILL, JOSEPH 2nd, Captain, Dan-
ville. Appointed Captain 31 Inf.
April 30, 1813; resigned Dec. 1, 1814.
Also served as Captain in 2nd Regt.
(Fifield's) Vt. Militia. Ref: Heitman's Historical Register & Dictionary USA. (For biographical sketch
see Hemenway's Vt. Gazetteer, Vol.
1, Page 318).

*MORRILL, JOSHUA.
Served in Capt. Morrill's Company,
Col. Fifield's Regt. Detached Militia
in U. S. service 3 months and 17
days, 1812. Served in Capt. Wheeler's Company. Col. Fifield's Regt.
Detached Militia in U. S. service 2
months and 18 days, 1812.

MORRILL, NATHANIEL,   Strafford.
Volunteered to go to Plattsburgh,
September, 1814, and served 6 days
in Capt. Jedediah H. Harris' Com-
pany. Was a son of Smith Morrill.
Ref: Book 52, AGO Pages 43 and 99;
Hemenway's Vt. Gazetteer, Vol. 2,
Page 1070.

MORRILL, PAUL, Sergeant.
Served in Capt. Benjamin Bradford's
Company; on Muster Roll from May
31 to Aug. 31, 1813. Ref: R. & L.
1812, AGO Page 26.

MORRILL, SAMUEL,   Danville.
Volunteered to go to Plattsburgh,
September, 1814, and served 3 days
in Capt. Solomon Langmaid's Company. Ref: Book 51, AGO Pages 75
and 76.

MORRILL, SIMON S., Blacksmith.
Served from May 1 to June 30, 1814
in Capt. Haig's Corps of Light Dragoons. Ref: R. & L. 1812, AGO
Page 20.

MORRILL, SMITH,   Strafford.
Volunteered to go to Plattsburgh,
September, 1814, and went as far as
Burlington, serving as a teamster in
Capt. Jedediah H. Harris' Company.
Was the father of Joseph, Nathaniel,
Stephen and David who were also
volunteers. Ref: Hemenway's Vt.
Gazetteer, Vol. 2, Pages 1070 and
1083.

MORRILL, STEPHEN,   Strafford.
Volunteered to go to Plattsburgh,
September, 1814, and served in Capt.
Jedediah H. Harris' Company. Was
a son of Smith Morrill. Ref: Hemenway's Vt. Gazetteer, Vol. 2, Pages
1070 and 1083.

*MORRILL, TIMOTHY.
Served in Capt. Phelps' Company,
Col. Wm. Williams' Regt. Detached
Militia in U. S. service 5 months,
1812.

*MORRILL, WILLIAM. Cornet.
Served in Dixon's Regt. Vt. Militia.

‡*MORRIS, AUGUSTUS.
Served in Capt. Walker's Company,
Col. Fifield's Regt. Detached Militia
in U. S. service 2 months and 21
days, 1812. Also served in Capt.
Taylor's Company. Pension Certificate of widow, Susan, No. 17447.

MORRIS, GODFREY.
Volunteered to go to Plattsburgh,
September, 1814, and served 4 days
in Capt. Aaron Kidder's Company.
Ref: Book 52, AGO Page 65.

*MORRIS, HORACE, 1st Lieutenant and
Adjutant. Served from Sept. 15 to
Nov. 11. 1813 as Adjutant in Col.
Isaac Clark's Volunteer Rifle Corps.

*MORRIS, JAMES JR.,   Randolph.
Volunteered to go to Plattsburgh,
September, 1814, and served in Capt.
Lebbeus Egerton's Company.

MORRIS, JESSE,   Barre.
Volunteered to go to Plattsburgh,
September, 1814, and served in Capt.
Warren Ellis' Company. Ref: Hemen-
way's Vt. Gazetteer, Vol. 4, Page 41.

MORRIS, OLIVER.
Served from May 1 to June 30, 1814
in Capt. Haig's Corps of Light Dragoons. Ref: R. & L. 1812, AGO
Page 20.

MORRIS, PARK.
Volunteered to go to Plattsburgh,
September, 1814, and went as far as
Bolton, Vt., serving 4 days in Lieut.
Phineus Kimball's Company, West
Fairlee. Ref: Book 52, AGO Page 46.

*MORRIS, RUSSEL,   Randolph.
Volunteered to go to Plattsburgh,
September, 1814, and served in Capt.
Lebbeus Egerton's Company.

*MORRIS, SAMUEL W., Corporal, Fair-
field. Served in Capt. Kimball's (or
Kindall's) Company, Col. Wm. Williams' Regt. Detached Militia in U.
S. service 4 months and 23 days.
1812.

MORRIS, WILLIAM M.
Volunteered to go to Plattsburgh,
September, 1814, and went as far as
Bolton, Vt., serving 4 days in Lieut.
P. Kimball's Company, West Fairlee.
Ref: Book 52, AGO Pages 46 and 47.

*MORRISON, JAMES,   Philadelphia.
Served from April 12 to April 21,
1814 in Capt. Edmund B. Hill's Company, Sumner's Regt. Served from
May 1 to July 29, 1814 in Capt.
Youngs' Company. 15th Inf. Volunteered to go to Plattsburgh, September, 1814, and served 4 days in Capt.
Aaron Kidder's Company. Ref: Book
52, AGO Page 65.

MORRISON, JONATHAN.
Served from May 1 to June 30, 1814
in Capt. Alexander Brooks' Corps of
Artillery. Ref: R. & L. 1812, AGO
Page 31.

MORRISON, JOSEPH, Lieutenant, Franklin County. Volunteered to go to
Plattsburgh, Sept. 11, 1814 and served in 15th or 22nd Regt. Ref: Hemenway's Vt. Gazetteer, Vol. 2, Page
391.

MORRISON, MOSES B.
Served in company of Capt. John
McNeil Jr., 11th Regt.; on Pay Roll
for January and Februray, 1813.
Ref: R. & L. 1812, AGO Page 17.

‡*MORRISON, WILLIAM, Sergeant.
Served in Capt. Dodge's Company,
Col. Fifield's Regt. Detached Militia
in U. S. service 2 months and 21
days, 1812. Served in company of
late Capt. J. Brooks, commanded by
Lieut. John I. Cromwell, Corps of U.
S. Artillery; on Muster Roll from
April 30 to June 30, 1814. Pension
Certificate No. 8563. Ref: R. & L.
1812, AGO Page 18.

*MORRITS, JOHN.
Served from September to November,
1813 in Regiment of Riflemen.

MORROW, JAMES,   Franklin County.
Volunteered to go to Plattsburgh,
Sept. 11, 1814, and served in 15th
or 22nd Regt. Ref: Hemenway's Vt.
Gazetteer, Vol. 2, Page 392.

MORROW, JOSEPH.
Enlisted March 2, 1814 for period of
the war in Capt. Gideon Spencer's
Company, 30th Regt.; on Muster Roll
from Dec. 30, 1813 to June 30, 1814.
Ref: R. & L. 1812, AGO Page 57.

MORSE, AARON,   Shoreham.
Entered the army for 5 years; was
stationed at Burlington; died in St.
Lawrence County, N. Y. Ref: Rev.
J. F. Goodhue's History of Shore-
ham, Page 102.

*MORSE, AMASA.
Served with Hospital Attendants, Vt.

MORSE, BENJAMIN.
Served from April 20 to June 30,
1813 in Lieut. Wm. S. Foster's Company, 11th Regt. Ref: R. & L.
1812, AGO Page 6.

MORSE, CALEB,   Montpelier.
Volunteered to go to Plattsburgh,
September, 1814, and served 8 days
in Capt. Timothy Hubbard's Company. Ref: Book 52, AGO Page 256.

MORSE, CALVIN.
Served from March 5 to June 4, 1813
in Capt. Edgerton's Company, 11th
Regt. Ref: R. & L. 1812, AGO
Page 3.

‡*MORSE, CHARLES.
Served in Capt. Aikin's Company.
Also served with Hospital Attendants,
Vt. Pension Certificate No. 14979.

*MORSE, DANIEL,   Fairfield.
Served in Capt. Kendall's Company,
Col. Wm. Williams' Regt. Detached
Militia in U. S. service 4 months
and 23 days, 1812. Served from
April 25, 1813 to April 24, 1814 in
Capt. Simeon Wright's Company.
Ref: R. & L. 1812, AGO Page 51.

‡MORSE, EBENEZER W.
Served in Capt. Stewart's Company.
Pension Certificate No. 10373.

MORSE, JAMES,   Burlington.
Volunteered to go to Plattsburgh,
September, 1814, and served 10 days
in Capt. Henry Mayo's Company.
Ref: Book 51, AGO Page 81.

‡*MORSE, JOHN.
Served in Capt. Pineo's Company, 4
Regt. (Peck's) Vt. Militia. Pension
Certificate of widow, Hannah, No.
7757.

*MORSE, JOHN JR.
Served in Corning's Detachment, Vt.
Militia.

*MORSE, JOHN M.
Served in 1 Regt. (Judson's) Vt.
Militia.

*MORSE, JONA.
Served in 1 Regt. (Martindale's) Vt.
Militia.

MORSE, JONATHAN.
Served in Capt. Wright's Company,
Col. Martindale's Regt. Detached
Militia in U. S. service 2 months
and 14 days, 1812. Ref: Book 53,
AGO Page 56.

*MORSE, JOSEPH.
Served in Corning's Detachment, Vt.
Militia. Also served in 4 Regt.
(Peck's) Vt. Militia.

*MORSE, JOSIAH.
Served in 3 Regt. (Williams') Vt.
Militia.

MORSE, LEONARD,   Williamstown.
Volunteered to go to Plattsburgh,
September, 1814, and was at the
battle, serving 8 days in Capt. David
Robinson's Company. Ref: Book 52,
AGO Page 2.

*MORSE, LEVI.
Served from April 22, 1813 to April
25, 1814 in Capt. Simeon Wright's
Company. Also served in 4 Regt.
(Peck's) Vt. Militia. Ref: R. & L.
1812, AGO Page 51.

*MORSE, MATHEW.
Served in 4 Regt. (Peck's) Vt. Militia.

MORSE, MOSES,   Williamstown.
Volunteered to go to Plattsburgh,
September, 1814, and was at the
battle, serving 8 days in Capt. David
Robinson's Company. Ref: Book 52,
AGO Page 2.

MORSE, PETER,   Fairfax.
Served from Aug. 8, 1812 in com-
pany of Capt. Joseph Beeman Jr.,
11th Regt. U. S. Inf. under Col.
Ira Clark. Ref: Hemenway's Vt.
Gazetteer, Vol. 2, Page 402.

*MORSE, ROBERT,   Barre.
Served in Capt. Walker's Company,
Col. Fifield's Regt. Detached Militia
in U. S. service 2 months and 24
days, 1812.

MORSE, SHEPPARD.
Served in Capt. Weeks' Company,
11th Regt.; on Pay Roll for January
and February, 1813. Ref: R. & L.
1812, AGO Page 5.

‡*MORSE, WALTER.
Served in Capt. Briggs' Company,
Col. Jonathan Williams' Regt. Detached Militia in U. S. service 2
months and 13 days, 1812. Also served in 4 Regt. (Peck's) Vt. Militia.
Pension Certificate No. 14884.

MORSE, WILLIAM.
Volunteered to go to Plattsburgh,
September, 1814, and served 4 days
in Capt. Aaron Kidder"s Company.
Ref: Book 52, AGO Page 65.

MORTON, DANIEL O.,   Middlebury.
Served from April 12 to April 15,
1814 in Capt. John Hackett's Company, Sumner's Regt. Volunteered to
go to Plattsburgh, September, 1814,
and served 6 days in Capt. Elias
Keyes' Company. Ref: Vol. 50 Vt.
State Papers, Page 219; Book 51, AGO
Pages 35, 52, 53.

MORTON, ISAIAH, Sergeant.
Enlisted Sept. 23, 1813 in Capt.
Amasa Mansfield's Company, Dixon's
Regt. Ref: Book 52, AGO Page 269.

‡MORTON, JAMES,   Sudbury.
Served in Capt. Hale's Company.
Volunteered to go to Plattsburgh,
September, 1814, and served 42 days;
no organization given. Pension Cer-
tificate of widow, Zeruah, No. 27608.

*MORTON, JAMES L. 3d Lieutenant.
Served from April 12 to April 21,
1814, part of the time in Capt. Eseck
Sprague's Company, Sumner's Regt.
and part of the time in command of
a company in the same regiment.

MORTON, JOHN, Captain,   Georgia.
Volunteered to go to Plattsburgh,
September, 1814, and served 10 days

in command of company raised at
Georgia. Ref: Book 52, AGO Pages
111 and 186.

MORTON, JOHN JR.   Salisbury.
Served in Regular Army in 1812.
Ref: History of Salisbury.

MORTON, JOHN JR.,   Georgia.
Volunteered to go to Plattsburgh,
September, 1814, and served 10 days
in company of Capt. John Morton Sr.
Ref: Book 51, AGO Page 111.

*MORTON, JOSEPH,   Randolph.
Volunteered to go to Plattsburgh,
September, 1814, and served in Capt.
Lebbeus Egerton's Company.

*MORTON, MARTIN, Corporal.
Served in 3 Regt. (Tyler's) Vt. Militia.

*MORTON, OWEN.
Served from Oct. 16 to Oct. 17, 1813
in Capt. Stephen Brown's Company,
3 Regt. (Tyler's).

*MORTON, ROSWELL, Captain.
Served in 3 Regt. (Tyler's) Vt. Militia.

MORTON, SETH.
Served in War of 1812 and was cap-
tured by troops Sept. 17, 1814 at
Fort Erie; discharged Nov. 8, 1814.
Ref: Records of Naval Records and
Library, Navy Dept.

*MORTON, WILLIAM.
Served from April 12 to April 15, 1814
in Capt. John Hackett's Company,
Sumner's Regt.

*MOSES, AMASA,   Shoreham.
Served from April 12 to May 20, 1814
in company of Capt. James Gray
Jr., Sumner's Regt. Volunteered to
go to Plattsburgh, September, 1814,
and served 6 days in Capt. Samuel
Hand's Company.

MOSES, CHARLES.
Served as drummer in the War of
1812; was captured by troops June
26, 1813 at Beaver Dams; discharged
Aug. 10th. Ref: Records of Naval
Records and Library, Navy Dept.

*MOSES, EMERSON (or Morse?).
Served in Capt. Durkee's Company,
Col. Fifield's Regt. Detached Militia
in U. S. service 2 months and 21
days, 1812.

MOSES, JAMES.
Served in Capt. Phelps' Company,
Col. Wm. Williams' Regt. Detached
Militia in U. S. service 5 months,
1812. Ref: Book 53, AGO Page 73.

MOSES, JOHN.
Served from Feb. 26 to May 25, 1813
in Capt. Charles Follett's Company,
11th Regt. Served in the war and
was captured by troops July 25, 1814
at Londers Lane; discharged Oct. 8,
1814. Ref: R. & L. 1812, AGO Page
13; Records of Naval Records and
Library, Navy Dept.

‡*MOSES, JONATHAN.
Served in Capt. Pettis' Company, Col.
Wm. Williams' Regt. Detached Militia in U. S. service 4 months and
17 days, 1812. Pension Certificate
of widow, Mercy, No. 3907.

*MOSES, ORRIN.
Served from April 12 to April 21,
1814 in Capt. Edmund B. Hill's Company, Sumner's Regt.

*MOSES, SILAS.
Served in Capt. Barns' Company, Col.
Wm. Williams' Regt. Detached Militia in U. S. service 5 months, 1812.
Served from Feb. 26 to May 25,
1813 in Capt. Charles Follett's Company, 11th Regt. Ref: R. & L. 1812,
AGO Page 13.

MOSHER, ISAAC,　　　Lansingburgh.
Served from Oct. 10, 1814 to June
19, 1815 in Capt. Taylor's Company,
30th Inf. Ref: R. & L. 1812, AGO
Page 23.

MOSHER, JOHN.
Served from March 22 to June 21,
1813 in Capt. Samul Gordon's Company, 11th Regt. Ref: R. & L. 1812,
AGO Page 8.

*MOSIER, CALVIN.
Served from Sept. 25 to Sept. 28,
1813 in Capt. Amos Robinson's Company, Dixon's Regt.

MOSIER, JONATHAN.
Served in Capt. Samuel H. Holly's
Company, 11th Regt.; on Pay Roll
for January and February, 1813.
Ref: R. & L. 1812, AGO Page 25.

*MOSIER, MILLER.
Served in 4 Regt. (Williams') Vt.
Militia.

MOSLEY, KINGSLEY,　　　St. Albans.
Entered service Nov. 30, 1813 in
Capt. John Wires' Company, 30th
Regt. Ref: Hemenway's Vt. Gazetteer, Vol. 2, Page 433.

MOSLEY, STEPHEN,　　　St. Albans.
Entered service Nov. 30, 1813 in
Capt. John Wires' Company, 30th
Regt. Ref: Hemenway's Vt. Gazetteer, Vol. 2, Page 433.

*MOSLEY, THOMAS. Sergeant.
Enlisted Sept. 25, 1813 in company
of Capt. Jonathan Prentiss Jr., Dixon's Regt.

MOSS, SILAS W.
Served from May 1 to June 30, 1814
in Capt. Haig's Corps of Light Dragoons. Ref: R. & L. 1812, AGO
Page 20.

MOSSI, PETER.
Served in Lieut. V. R. Goodrich's
Company. 11th Regt.; on Pay Roll
for January and February, 1813.
Ref: R. & L. 1812, AGO Page 11.

MOSSO, FRANCIS.
Enlisted March 23, 1814 for 5 years
in company of late Capt. J. Brooks,
commanded by Lieut. John I. Cromwell, Corps of U. S. Artillery; on

Muster Roll from April 30 to June 30,
1814. Ref: R. & L. 1812, AGO Page
18.

MOTT, ELIHU.
Served in company of Capt. John
McNeil Jr., 11th Regt.; on Pay Roll
for January and February, 1813. Ref:
R. & L. 1812, AGO Page 17.

MOTT, JESSE, Corporal, Franklin County.
Enlisted Jan. 1, 1813 for period of
the war in Capt. White Youngs' Company, 15th Regt.; on Muster Roll
from Aug. 31 to Dec. 31, 1814. Ref:
R. & L. 1812, AGO Page 27.

*MOULD. ASA.
Served in Capt. Scovell's Company,
Col. Martindale's Regt. Detached
Militia in U. S. service 1 month and
14 days, 1812.

‡MOULTON, AMASA,　　　Corinth.
Volunteered to go to Plattsburgh,
September, 1814, and served in Capt.
Abel Jackman's Company. Pension
Certificate No. 34267.

*MOULTON, BENJAMIN.
Served in Capt. Phelps' Company, Col.
Jonathan Williams' Regt. Detached
Militia in U. S. service 2 months and
21 days, 1812.

MOULTON, FREEMAN,　　　Randolph.
Volunteered to go to Plattsburgh,
September, 1814, and served in Capt.
Lebbeus Egerton's Company. Ref:
Book 52, AGO Page 82.

*MOULTON, HOWARD.
Served in Capt. Wright's Company,
Col. Fifield's Regt. Detached Militia
in U. S. service 6 months, 1812.

*MOULTON, JOHN.
Served in Capt. Willson's Company,
Col. Wm. Williams' Regt. Detached
Militia in U. S. service 4 months
and 24 days, 1812.

MOULTON, JOHN .
Enlisted May 11, 1812 for 5 years in
company of late Capt. J. Brooks, commanded by Lieut. John I. Cromwell,
Corps of U. S. Artillery; on Muster
Roll from April 30 to June 30, 1814;
transferred from Capt. Watson's
Company. Ref: R. & L. 1812, AGO
Page 18.

MOULTON, JOSIAH.
Served in Capt. Benjamin Bradford's
Company; on Muster Roll from May
31 to Aug. 31, 1813; joined by transfer July 22, 1813. Ref: R. & L. 1812,
AGO Page 26.

MOULTON, PATRICK, Franklin County.
Volunteered to go to Plattsburgh
Sept. 11, 1814 and served in 15th or
22nd Regt. Ref: Hemenway's Vt.
Gazetteer, Vol. 2, Page 392.

*MOULTON, PHINEAS JR.,　　　Randolph.
Volunteered to go to Plattsburgh,
September, 1814, and served in Capt.
Lebbeus Egerton's Company.

MOULTON, RICHARD.
Served in Capt. Benjamin Bradford's
Company; on Muster Roll from May
31 to Aug. 31, 1813; joined by transfer July 22, 1813. Ref: R. & L.
1812, AGO Page 26.

‡*MOULTON, STILLMAN,   Randolph.
Volunteered to go to Plattsburgh,
September, 1814, and served in Capt.
Lebbeus Egerton's Company. Also
served in Capt. Nathaniel Wheaton's
Company. Pension Certificate No.
29611.

*MOULTON, TRUMAN.
Served in Capt. Edgerton's Company,
Vt. Volunteers.

‡MOULTON, ZEBINA,   Montpelier.
Volunteered to go to Plattsburgh,
September, 1814, and served 8 days
in Capt. Timothy Hubbard's Company.
Pension Certificate of widow, Hannah,
No. 30426.

MOUNTFORD, JOHN, 1st Lieutenant.
Served in company of Capt. J.
Brooks commanded by Lieut. John
I. Cromwell, Corps of U. S. Artil-
lery; on Muster Roll from April 30
to June 30, 1814; joined June 6, 1814.
Ref: R. & L. 1812, AGO Page 18.

*MOULTHROP, TIMOTHY.
Served in 1 Regt. (Judson's) Vt. Militia.

*MOWER, JABEZ, Orderly Sergeant,
Calais. Volunteered to go to Plattsburgh, September, 1814, and served
8 days in Capt. Gideon Wheelock's
Company.

*MOWER, JOHN.
Served in 3 Regt. (Williams') Vt.
Militia.

MOWER, THOMAS.   Barre.
Volunteered to go to Plattsburgh,
September, 1814, and served 9 days
in Capt. Warren Ellis' Company. Ref:
Book 52, AGO Pages 227 and 242.

MUDGE, EBENEZER.
Served in Capt. Weeks' Company,
11th Regt.; on Pay Roll for January and February, 1813. Ref: R.
& L. 1812, AGO Page 5.

MUDGET, JESSE.
Served in Capt. Chadwick's Company.
Ref: R. & L. 1812, AGO Page 32.

MUDGETT, JOHN.
Served in Capt. Haig's Corps of Light
Dragoons; on Pay Roll to June 30,
1814. Ref: R. & L. 1812, AGO Page
20.

*MUDGETT, JONATHAN, Corporal.
Served from Sept. 25 to Oct. 4, 1813
in Capt. Charles Bennett's Company,
Dixon's Regt.

‡MUDGETT, THOMAS,   Cambridge.
Volunteered to go to Plattsburgh,
September, 1814, and served 8 days
in Capt. Salmon Green's Company.
Pension Certificate of widow, Saman-
tha, No. 28219.

MUGGETT, SAMUEL.
Served in Capt. Benjamin Bradford's
Company; on Muster Roll from May
31 to Aug. 31, 1813; discharged by
reason of disability Aug. 18, 1813.
Ref: R. & L. 1812, AGO Page 26.

MULLIKIN, JOSEPH.
Served in Capt. Weeks' Company,
11th Regt.; on Pay Roll for Janu-
ary and February, 1813; deserted
Jan. 1, 1813. Ref: R. & L. 1812,
AGO Page 5.

*MUMFORD, JERAH.
Served from April 12 to April 21,
1814 in Capt. Eseck Sprague's Company, Sumner's Regt.

*MUNGER, AUGUSTUS.
Served from April 12 to April 21,
1814 in Capt. Shubael Wales' Company, Col. W. B. Sumner's Regt.

MUNGER, IRA,   Orwell.
Volunteered to go to Plattsburgh,
September, 1814, and served 11 days
in Capt. Wait Branch's Company.
Ref: Book 51, AGO Page 16.

MUNN, REUBEN, Fifer,   Vershire.
Volunteered to go to Plattsburgh,
September, 1814, and served 3 days
in Capt. Ira Corse's Company. Ref:
Book 52, AGO Page 91.

MUNRO, BOHON S.
Served in Capt. Samuel H. Holly's
Company, 11 Regt. On Pay Roll for
January and February, 1813. Ref:
R. & L. 1812, AGO Page 25.

MUNRO, JESSE.
Served in 3 Regt. (Tyler's) Vt. Militia.

MUNROE, DAVID.
Served in Capt. Benjamin Bradford's
Company; on Muster Roll from May
31 to Aug. 31, 1813. Ref: R. & L.
1812, AGO Page 26.

*MUNROE, ROYAL.
Enlisted Oct. 4, 1813 in Capt. Asahel
Langworthy's Company, Col. Isaac
Clark's Rifle Corps.

‡*MUNSEL, THOMAS JR.
Served in Capt. Robbins' Company,
Col. Wm. Williams' Regt. Detached
Militia in U. S. service 4 months and
29 days, 1812. Pension Certificate No.
5109.

*MUNSELL, GURDON, Sergeant.
Served from April 12 to April 21,
1814 in Capt. Othniel Jewett's Company, Sumner's Regt.

*MUNSELL, HARRY.
Served from April 12 to April 21,
1814 in Capt. Edmund B. Hill's Company, Sumner's Regt.

*MUNSON, AMNA.
Served in 4 Regt. (Peck's) Vt. Militia.

‡MUNSON, BENJAMIN.
Served in Capt. Weed's Company.
Pension Certificate No. 22743. Pen-
sion Certificate of widow, Maritta,
No. 7205.

*MUNSON, CALEB, Captain.
Served as Lieutenant in Corning's
Detachment, Vt. Militia and Captain
in 4 Regt. (Peck's) Vt. Militia.

*MUNSON, EPHRAIM, 1st Lieutenant.
Served from April 12 to April 21,
1814 in Capt. Othniel Jewett's Company, Sumner's Regt.

*MUNSON, JOHN, Captain.
Served from Oct. 5 to Oct. 17, 1813
in Capt. John Munson's Company, 3
Regt. (Tyler's).

MUNSON, NOBLE,   Bristol.
Volunteered to go to Plattsburgh,
September, 1814, and was at the
battle, serving 9 days in Capt. Jehiel
Saxton's Company, Sumner's Regt.
Ref: Book 51, AGO Page 18.

*MUNSON, REUBEN.
Served in Corning's Detachment, Vt.
Militia. Also served in 4 Regt.
(Peck's) Vt. Militia.

*MUNSON, WILLIAM C., Captain.
Served in Sumner's Regt. Vt. Militia.

*MURCH, ADEN.
Served in Capt. Brown's Company,
Col. Martindale's Regt. Detached
Militia in U. S. service 2 months
and 14 days, 1812.

*MURPHY, CHESTER.
Served in Capt. Phelps' Company,
Col. Wm. Williams' Regt. Detached
Militia in U. S. service 5 months,
1812.

MURPHY, PAUL.
Enlisted May 8, 1812 for 5 years in
Capt. White Youngs' Company 15th
Regt.; on Muster Roll from Aug. 31
to Dec. 31, 1814. Ref: R. & L.
1812, AGO Page 27.

‡*MURRAY, AMASA.
Served in Capt. Brown's Company,
Col. Martindale's Regt. Detached
Militia in U. S. service 2 months
and 14 days, 1812. Also served in
Capt. Hall's Company. Pension Cer-
tificate of widow, Adosha, No. 6611.

‡*MURRAY, EBER R.,   Sudbury.
Served from Oct. 14 to Nov. 17, 1813
in Capt. Asahel Scoville's Company,
Col. Clark's Rifle Corps. Volunteered
to go to Plattsburgh, September, 1814,
and served 6 days in Capt. Thomas
Hall's Company. Pension Certificate
of widow, Deidamia, No. 25163.

*MURRAY, MANUS, Sudbury or Enos-
burgh. Served from Oct. 14 to Nov.
17, 1813 in Capt. Asahel Scoville's
Company. Volunteered to go to
Plattsburgh, September. 1814, and
served 6 days in Capt. Thomas Hall's
Company.

MURRAY, ROBERT.
Served in Capt. Barns' Company,
Col. Wm. Williams' Regt. Detached
Militia in U. S. service 4 months and
23 days, 1812. Ref: Book 53, AGO
Page 13.

MURRY, IRAM,   Moreau.
Served from May 1 to June 28, 1814
in Capt. Spencer's Company, 29th
Inf. Ref: R. & L. 1812, AGO Page 30.

MURRY, MONUS.
Enlisted Oct. 15, 1813 in Capt. Asahel
Scovell's Company. Ref: Book 52,
AGO Page 274.

*MURRY, TRUMAN,   Waterbury.
Volunteered to go to Plattsburgh,
September, 1814, and was in the
battle, serving 11 days in Capt.
George Atkins' Company, 4 Regt.
(Peck's). Also served in Corning's
Detachment, Vt. Militia.

MYERS, JAMES.
Served from March 9 to June 7, 1813
in Capt. Edgerton's Company, 11th
Regt. Ref: R. & L. 1812, AGO
Page 3.

*MYERS, JOHN.
Enlisted Dec. 23, 1813 for period of
the war in Capt. Simeon Wright's
Company. Also served in Sumner's
Regt. Vt. Militia. Ref: R. & L.
1812, AGO Page 51.

MYERS, PETER.
Served from Jan. 30 to Feb. 28,
1813 in Capt. Samuel H. Holly's Company, 11th Regt. Ref: R. & L. 1812,
AGO Page 25.

*MYRICK, BARNABAS, Cornet, Enos-
burgh. Served from Oct. 14 to Nov.
17, 1813 in Capt. Asahel Scoville's
Company, Col. Clark's Rifle Corps.

*MYRICK, BARNABAS, Lieutenant. Brid-
port. Served from April 12 to May
20, 1814 in company of Capt. James
Gray Jr., Sumner's Regt.

MYRICK, JOHN.
Served in Capt. Start's Company,
Col. Martindale's Regt. Detached
Militia in U. S. service 2 months
and 13 days, 1812. Served in Lieut.
V. R. Goodrich's Company, 11th
Regt.; on Pay Roll for January and
February, 1813. Ref: Book 53, AGO
Page 24; R. & L. 1812, AGO Page 11.

‡*MYRICK, NATHAN,   Enosburgh.
Served in Capt. Robbins' Company,
Col. Wm. Williams' Regt. Detached
Militia in U. S. service 4 months
and 29 days, 1812. Served from Oct.
14 to Nov. 17, 1813 in Capt. Asahel
Scovell's Company, Col. Clark's Rifle
Corps. Pension Certificate of widow,
Harriet R., No. 23292.

*MYRICK, RUSSELL, Drum Major.
Served in Col. Wm. Williams' Regt.
Detached Militia in U. S. service 5
months, 1812. Served from Feb. 18
to May 17, 1813 in Lieut. V. R.
Goodrich's Company, 11th Regt.

MYRICK, WILLIAM, Captain.
Appointed 1st Lieutenant 30th Inf.
April 30, 1813; Captain June 23,
1814; honorably discharged June 15,
1815. Served in Capt. James Taylor's Company, 30th Regt. Ref: Heitman's Historical Register & Dictionary USA; R. & L. 1812, AGO Page 53.

*NAMES, WILLIAM.
Served in Capt. Robbins' Company,
Col. Wm. Williams' Regt. Detached
Militia in U. S. service 3 months and
21 days, 1812.

NARSE, JOHN.
Served from March 27 to June 26, 1813 in Capt. Charles Follett's Company, 11th Regt. Ref: R. & L. 1812, AGO Page 13.

‡NASH, ABRAHAM.
Served in Capt. Allen's Company. Pension Certificate of widow, Elizabeth, No. 21208.

NASH, BARTLETT, Corporal.
Served in Capt. Haig's Corps of Light Dragoons; on Pay Roll to June 30, 1814. Ref: R. & L. 1812, AGO Page 20.

*NASH, CALEB JR.
Served in 3 Regt. (Tyler's) Vt. Militia.

*NASH, DAVID P., Lt. Colonel.
Served in Sumner's Regt. Vt. Militia.

*NASH, ELIAS.
Served from Sept. 25 to Sept. 30, 1813 in Capt. Elijah Birge's Company, Dixon's Regt.

‡NASH, JOHN.
Served in Capt. Kinney's Company. Pension Certificate No. 25625.

NASH, THOMAS.
Served in Capt. Benjamin S. Edgerton's Company, 11th Regt.; on Pay Roll for September and October, 1812 and January and February, 1813. Ref: R. & L. 1812, AGO Pages 1 and 2.

*NASH, VINSON.
Served in 3 Regt. (Tyler's) Vt. Militia.

*NASH, WILLIAM, Quartermaster.
Served in Sumner's Regt. Vt. Militia.

NASMITH, JAMES.
Enlisted January, 1813, in company of Capt. John McNeil Jr., 11th Regt.; on Pay Roll to May 31, 1813. Ref: R. & L. 1812, AGO Page 16.

‡NASMITH, ROBERT.
Served in Capt. Walker's Company. Pension Certificate of widow, Sally, No. 11122.

NASMITH, STEPHEN.
Served from Feb. 15 to May 14, 1813 in company of Capt. John McNeil Jr., 11th Regt. Ref: R. & L. 1812, AGO Page 16.

‡NASON, HORACE.
Pension Certificate of widow, Mary, No. 37711; no organization given.

NASON, WILLIAM.
Served in Capt. Durkee's Company, Col. Fifield's Regt. Detached Militia in U. S. service 2 months and 21 days, 1812. Ref: Book 53, AGO Pages 66 and 67.

*NAY, AARON.
Served from Sept. 25, to Oct. 1, 1813 in Capt. Jesse Post's Company, Dixon's Regt.

*NAY, JAMES JR.
Served from Sept. 25 to Sept. 28, 1813 in company of Capt. Jonathan Prentiss Jr., Dixon's Regt.

*NAY, JOHN.
Served from Sept. 25 to Oct. 3, 1813 in Capt. Jesse Post's Company, Dixon's Regt.

NAY, NATHAN.
Served from March 22 to June 21, 1813 in Lieut. V. R. Goodrich's Company, 11th Regt. Ref: R. & L. 1812, AGO Page 10.

NAY, ROBERT.
Served from May 5, 1813 to May 5, 1814 in Capt. Gideon Spencer's Company and Capt. James Taylor's Company, 30th Regt. Ref: R. & L. 1812, AGO Pages 52, 57, 59.

*NAY, WILLIAM A., Fife Major.
Appointed Fife Major in company of Capt. Jonathan Prentiss, Jr. Dixon's Regt. Sept. 25, 1813; joined Oct. 5, 1813; transferred to Capt. Amasa Mansfield's Company, Dixon's Regt. Nov. 17, 1813.

*NAYSMITH, ROBERT.
Served in Capt. E. Walker's Company, Col. Fifield's Regt. Detached Militia in U. S. service 6 months and 5 days, 1812.

*NEAL, ISRAEL M.
Served from April 12 to April 21, 1814 in Capt. Edmund B. Hill's Company, Sumner's Regt.

NEAL, JOSEPH B.
Served in Capt. Samuel H. Holly's Company, 11th Regt.; on Pay Roll for January and February, 1813. Ref: R. & L. 1812, AGO Page 25.

*NEAL, THOMAS.
Served from April 12 to April 21, 1814 in Capt. Edmund B. Hill's Company, Sumner's Regt.

NEALEY, BENJAMIN.   Montpelier.
Volunteered to go to Plattsburgh, September, 1814, and served 8 days in Capt. Timothy Hubbard's Company. Ref: Book 52, AGO Page 256.

NEALEY, SAMUEL B.
Served from May 1 to June 30, 1814 in Capt. Haig's Corps of Light Dragoons. Ref: R. & L. 1812, AGO Page 20.

*NEALY, ANDREW,   Calais.
Volunteered to go to Plattsburgh, September, 1814, and served 10 days in Capt. Gideon Wheelock's Company.

NEEDHAM, ABNER.
Served from April 19, 1813 to April 25. 1814 in Capt. Daniel Farrington's Company, 30th Regt. Ref: R. & L. 1812, AGO Page 50.

*NEEDHAM, BENJAMIN, Captain.
Served in 1st Regt. of Detached Militia of Vt. in U. S. service at Champlain from Nov. 18 to Nov. 19, 1812.

NEEDHAM, BENJAMIN, Sergeant.
Enlisted May 1, 1813 for 1 year in Capt. Simeon Wright's Company. Ref: R. & L. 1812, AGO Page 51.

*NEEDHAM, DANFORD, Musician.
Served from April 13 to April 16,
1814 in Capt. Salmon Foster's Company, Sumner's Regt.

*NEEDHAM, ELIAS, Corporal.
Served from April 12 to April 21,
1814 in Capt. Shubael Wales' Company, Col. W. B. Sumner's Regt.

‡NEEDHAM, HORATIO,   Whiting.
Volunteered to go to Plattsburgh,
September, 1814, and served 21 days
in Capt. Salmon Foster's Company,
Sumner's Regt. Pension Certificate of
widow, Betsey, No. 29719.

*NEEDHAM, L., Corporal.
Served from April 13 to April 21,
1814 in Capt. Salmon Foster's Company, Sumner's Regt.

NEEDHAM, LIBER.
Served from April 12 to April 21,
1814 in Capt. Shubael Wales' Company, Col. W. B. Sumner's Regt.
Ref: Book 52, AGO Page 289.

NEEDHAM, LINUS, Sergeant,   Whiting.
Volunteered to go to Plattsburgh,
September, 1814, and served 21 days
in Capt. Salmon Foster's Company,
Sumner's Regt. Ref: Book 51, AGO
Pages 7, 8, 9.

*NEEDHAM, NEHEMIAH.
Served in Capt. Parsons' Company,
Col. Jonathan Williams' Regt. Detached Militia in U. S. service 2
months and 13 days, 1812.

NEEDHAM, WILLIAM A., Surgeon's
Mate. Appointed Surgeon's Mate
30th Inf. July 19, 1813; out July,
1814. Ref: Heitman's Historical Register & Dictionary USA.

*NEEDHAM, ZIBA,   Whiting.
Served from April 13, 1814 to April
21, 1814 in Capt. Salmon Foster's
Company, Sumner's Regt.; volunteered to go to Plattsburgh, September,
1814, and served 9 days in same company.

*NEELS, JOHN.
Served in Lieut. V. R. Goodrich's
Company, 11th Regt.; on Pay Roll
for January and February, 1813.
Also served in 4 Regt. (Williams')
Vt. Militia.

‡*NEFF, JAMES,   Braintree.
Served in Col. Fifield's Regt. Detached Militia in U. S. service 6
months, 1812. Pension Certificate No.
15279.

*NELSON, CHARLES.
Served in Capt. Mason's Company,
Col. Fifield's Regt. Detached Militia
in U. S. service 2 months and 14
days, 1812.

*NELSON, DANIEL.
Served in 4 Regt. (Peck's) Vt. Militia.

NELSON, DAVID,   Orange.
Marched for Plattsburgh Sept. 11,
1814 and went part way, serving 5
days in Capt. David Rising's Company. Ref: Book 52, AGO Page 19.

‡NELSON, JAMES.
Served in Capt. S. C. Cotton's Company. Pension Certificate of widow,
Lucy, No. 29937.

‡*NELSON, JAMES Y.
Served in Capt. Hopkins' Company,
Col. Martindale's Regt. Detached
Militia in U. S. service 2 months
and 13 days, 1812. Pension Certificate No. 5547.

*NELSON, JAMES Y. JR.
Enlisted Oct. 2, 1813 and served 78
days in Capt. John Weed's Company,
Rifle Regt.

*NELSON, JOHN,   Strafford.
Volunteered to go to Plattsburgh,
September, 1814, and served 6 days
in Capt. Jedediah H. Harris' Company. Also served in 1 Regt. (Judson's) Vt. Militia. Ref: Book 52,
AGO Page 43.

‡*NELSON, MOSES,   Waterbury.
Volunteered to go to Plattsburgh,
September, 1814, and was in the
battle, serving 11 days in Capt.
George Atkins' Company, 4 Regt.
(Peck's). Pension Certificate No.
24196.

*NELSON, PETER,   Montpelier.
Served in Capt. Walker's Company,
Col. Fifield's Regt. Detached Militia
in U. S. service 6 months and 5
days, 1812. Volunteered to go to
Plattsburgh, Sept. 1814, and served 8
days in Capt. Timothy Hubbard's Company. Also served in Capt. Johnson's
Company. Pension Certificate of widow, Polly, No. 1981.

NELSON, THOMAS.
Served in Capt. Alexander Brooks'
Corps of Artillery; on Pay Roll to
June 30, 1814. Ref: R. & L. 1812,
AGO Page 31.

NELSON, WASHINGTON.
Enlisted March 11, 1814 for the period
of the war and served in Capt.
James Taylor's Company, Capt. Wm.
Miller's Company and Capt. Gideon
Sepncer's Company, 30th Regt. Ref:
R. & L. 1812, AGO Pages 53, 54, 57.

NESMITH, JAMES.
Served in Capt. Weeks' Company,
11th Regt.; on Pay Roll for January and February, 1813. Ref: R. &
L. 1812, AGO Page 5.

*NEW, JOHN.
Served from April 12 to April 21,
1814 in Capt. Edmund B. Hill's Company, Sumner's Regt.

*NEWCOMB, JACOB.
Served in Capt. Howard's Company,
Vt. Militia.

NEWCOMB, SMITH, Sergeant,
Served in Capt. Charles Follett's Company, 11th Regt.; on Pay Roll for
January and February, 1813. Ref:
R. & L. 1812, AGO Page 12.

*NEWCOMB, WILLIAM.
Served with Hospital Attendants, Vt.

‡NEWELL, DANIEL.
Served in Capt. Brownell's Company.
Pension Certificate of widow, Patience,
No. 7930.

*NEWELL, JASON, Lieutenant.
Served in 1 Regt. 3rd Brig. 3rd Div.
Vt. Militia.

*NEWELL, ORRIN.
Served from June 11 to June 14,
1813 in Capt. Ithiel Stone's Company,
1st Regt. 2nd Brig. 3rd Div.

NEWELL, SULLIVAN, Franklin County.
Volunteered to go to Plattsburgh
Sept. 11, 1814 and served in 15th or
22nd Regt. Ref: Hemenway's Vt. Gazetteer, Vol. 2, Page 392.

*NEWELL, TRUMAN.
Enlisted Sept. 25, 1813 in company
of Capt. Jonathan Prentiss Jr., Dixon's Regt.

*NEWLAND, JAMES.
Served in Capt. Mason's Company,
Col. Fifield's Regt. Detached Militia
in U. S. service 6 months, 1812.

*NEWMAN, ABEL,   Williamstown.
Served in Capt. Walker's Company,
Col. Fifield's Regt. Detached Militia
in U. S. service 6 months and 3
days, 1812.

*NEWMAN, BENJAMIN, Sergeant.
Enlisted Sept. 23, 1813 and served
1 month and 23 days in Capt. Amasa
Mansfield's Company, Col. Dixon's
Regt. Detached Militia in U. S. serv-
ice.

*NEWMAN, CHRISTOPHER.
Served from April 12 to May 20,
1814 in Capt. George Fisher's Company, Sumner's Regt.

NEWMAN, JOHN.
Served in Capt. Taylor's Company,
Col. Fifield's Regt. Detached Militia
in U. S. service 6 months, 1812.

NEWMAN, JOSEPH.
Served in Capt. Samul Gordon's Com-
pany, 11th Regt.; on Pay Roll for
January and February, 1813. Ref:
R. & L. 1812, AGO Page 9.

‡NEWMAN, THOMAS,   Strafford.
Served in Capt. Clark's Company.
Pension Certificate of widow, Fannie,
No. 35413.

*NEWMAN, WILLIAM,   Williamstown.
Served in Capt. Samul Gordon's Company, 11th Regt.; on Pay Roll for
January and February, 1813. Also
served in 2 Regt. (Fifield's) Vt. Militia. Ref: R. & L. 1812, AGO Page 9.

*NEWTON, ALVIN.
Enlisted Sept. 25, 1813 and served
1 month and 23 days in Capt. Amos
Robinson's Company, Col. Dixon's
Regt. Detached Militia in U. S. serv-
ice.

*NEWTON, ANSON,   Barnard.
Served in Capt. Bingham's Company,
Col. Jonathan Williams' Regt. Detached Militia in U. S. service 2
months and 9 days, 1812.

*NEWTON, ASAHEL.
Served from April 12 to April 21,
1814 in Lieut. James S. Morton's
Company, Col. W. B. Sumner's Regt.

*NEWTON, EARL, Corporal,   Barnard.
Served in Capt. Phelps' Company,
Col. Jonathan Williams' Regt. Detached Militia in U. S. service 2
months and 21 days, 1812. Volunteered to go to Plattsburgh, September, 1814, and served 8 days in Capt.
John S. Bicknell's Company.

NEWTON, EBEN,   Thetford.
Volunteered to go to Plattsburgh,
September, 1814, and served in Capt.
Joseph Barrett's Company. Ref:
Book 52, AGO Page 41.

NEWTON, EDMUND,   Shoreham.
Volunteered to go to Plattsburgh,
September, 1814, and served 6 days
in Capt. Samuel Hand's Company.
Ref: Rev. J. F. Goodhue's History
of Shoreham, Page 108.

NEWTON, EZEKIEL.
Served from May 18 to June 8, 1813
in Capt. Simeon Wright's Company.
Ref: R. & L. 1812, AGO Page 51.

NEWTON, GEORGE.
Served in Capt. Alexander Brooks'
Corps of Artillery; on Pay Roll to
June 30, 1814. Ref: R. & L. 1812,
AGO Page 31.

*NEWTON, ISAAC, Sergeant.
Served in Capt. Brown's Company,
Col. Martindale's Regt. Detached
Militia in U. S. service 2 months and
14 days, 1812.

NEWTON, JASON,   Ira.
Volunteered to go to Plattsburgh,
September, 1814, and served 4 days
in Capt. Matthew Anderson's Company. Also served in Sumner's Regt.
Vt. Militia. Ref: Book 52, AGO Page
144.

‡NEWTON, JASON JR., Sergeant, Ira.
Served in 1st Regt. of Detached Militia of Vt. in U. S. service at Champlain from Nov. 18 to Nov. 19, 1812.
Also served in Capt. Brown's Company. Pension Certificate No. 19622.

NEWTON, JOHN.
Served in Capt. Benjamin S. Edgerton's Company, 11th Regt.; on Pay
Roll for September and October, 1812
and January and February, 1813.
Ref: R. & L. 1812, AGO Pages 1
and 2.

*NEWTON, JOSEPH, Corporal.
Served in Sumner's Regt. Vt. Militia.

NEWTON, JOSIAH,   St. Albans.
Volunteered and was in the action
at Plattsburgh Sept. 11, 1814, serving in Capt. Samuel H. Farnsworth's
Company. Ref: Hemenway's Vt. Gazetteer, Vol. 2, Page 434.

*NEWTON, LUTHER.
Enlisted Sept. 25, 1813 in Capt.
Thomas Waterman's Company, Dix-
on's Regt.

‡NEWTON, LYMAN H.
Served in Capt. J. Merrill's Company. Pension Certificate of widow, Sophia, No. 26544.

NEWTON, MARSHALL, Corporal, Shoreham. Volunteered to go to Plattsburgh, September, 1814, and served 6 days in Capt. Samuel Hand's Company. Ref: Rev. J. F. Goodhue's History of Shoreham, Page 107.

NEWTON, RUFUS,   Salisbury. Volunteered to go to Plattsburgh, September, 1814, and served 10 days in Capt. John Morton's Company. Ref: Book 51, AGO Page 55.

NEWTON, SAMUEL.
Served from June 11 to June 14, 1813 in Capt. Moses Jewett's Company, 1st Regt. 2nd Brig. 3rd Div. Ref: R. & L. 1812, AGO Page 42.

*NEWTON, SEWELL.
Enlisted Sept. 25, 1813 and served 1 month and 23 days in Capt. Thomas Waterman's Company, Col. Dixon's Regt. Detached Militia in U. S. service.

NEWTON, THOMAS C.,   Ira.
Volunteered to go to Plattsburgh September, 1814, and served in Capt. Matthew Anderson's Company. Ref: Hemenway's Vt. Gazetteer, Vol. 3, Page 783.

*NEWTON, WINSOR.
Served in Capt. Rogers' Company, Col. Fifield's Regt. Detached Militia in U. S. service 2 months and 18 days, 1812.

NICHOLAS, TRUMAN,   Fairfax.
Served from Aug. 8, 1812 in company of Capt. Joseph Beeman, Jr. 11th Regt. U. S. Inf. under Col. Ira Clark. Ref: Hemenway's Vt. Gazetteer, Vol. 2, Page 402.

NICHOLAS, WARREN.
Enlisted May 28, 1813 and served 5 years in company of late Capt. J. Brooks commanded by Lieut. John I. Cromwell, Corps of U. S. Artillery; on Muster Roll from April 30 to June 30, 1814. Ref: R. & L. 1812, AGO Page 18.

‡*NICHOLS, AARON.
Served in Capt. Hiram Mason's Company, Col. Fifield's Regt. Detached Militia in U. S. service 3 months and 17 days, 1812. Also served in Capt. Morrill's Company. Pension Certificate No. 9305. Pension Certificate of widow, Ruth, No. 26973.

‡*NICHOLS, ALFRED E., (or Nicholls).
Served from April 12 to May 20, 1814 in company of Capt. James Gray Jr., Sumner's Regt. Pension Certificate of widow, Mary Ann, No. 15792.

*NICHOLS, ALLEN.
Served in Capt. Brown's Company, Col. Martindale's Regt. Detached Militia in U. S. service 2 months, 1812.

*NICHOLS, CHARLES H.
Served from Oct. 5 to Oct. 16, 1813 in Capt. Roswell Hunt's Company, 3 Regt. (Tyler's). Also served in Corning's Detachment, Vt. Militia.

NICHOLS, DAVID, Corporal, Braintree. Marched to Plattsburgh Sept. 10, 1814 and served in Capt. Lot Hudson's Company. Ref: Book 52, AGO Pages 24 and 26.

*NICHOLS, DEWEY, Fletcher or Fairfax.
Enlisted Sept. 25, 1813 and served 1 month and 23 days in Capt. Asa Wilkins' Company, Col. Dixon's Regt. Detached Militia in U. S. service. Volunteered to go to Plattsburgh, September, 1814, and served 6 days in Capt. Amasa J. Brown's Company. Ref: Book 51, AGO Page 144.

‡NICHOLS, GEORGE WASHINGTON, Braintree. Volunteered to go to Plattsburgh, September, 1814, and served 8 days in Capt. Lot Hudson's Company. Pension Certificate No. 31620.

NICHOLS, GUY C.,   Barre.
Served from April 24, 1813 to April 28, 1814 in Capt. Simeon Wright's Company. Volunteered to go to Plattsburgh, September, 1814, and served 10 days in Capt. Warren Ellis' Company. Ref: R. & L. 1812, AGO Page 51; Book 52, AGO Page 242.

*NICHOLS, JAMES.
Served from June 11 to June 14, 1813 in Lieut. Bates' Company, 1st Regt.

NICHOLS, JAMES.
Enlisted April 18, 1814 for 5 years and served in Capt. James Taylor's Company, Capt. Wm. Miller's Company and Capt. Gideon Spencer's Company, 30th Regt. Ref: R. & L. 1812, AGO Pages 53, 54, 57.

*NICHOLS, JAMES H.
Served from Oct. 5 to Oct. 16, 1813 in Capt. Roswell Hunt's Company, 3 Regt. Also served in Corning's Detachment. Ref: R. & L. 1812, AGO Page 41.

*NICHOLS, JAMES N.
Served in Capt. Ormsbee's Company, Col. Martindale's Regt. Detached Militia in U. S. service 2 months and 14 days, 1812.

NICHOLS, JESSE,   Barre.
Volunteered to go to Plattsburgh, September, 1814, and served 10 days in Capt. Warren Ellis' Company. Ref: Book 52, AGO Page 242.

NICHOLS, JOHN.
Served from March 22 to June 21, 1813 in Capt. Edgerton's Company, 11th Regt. Ref: R. & L. 1812, AGO Page 3.

*NICHOLS, JOHN (or Nicholls).
Served from April 12 to May 20, 1814 in company of Capt. James Gray Jr., Sumner's Regt.

NICHOLS, JOHN,   St. Albans.
Enlisted May 3 1813 for 1 year in
Capt. John Wires' Company, 30th
Regt. Ref: R. & L. 1812, AGO
Page 40.

NICHOLS, JOHN.
Enlisted June 23, 1813 for 1 year
in Capt. Daniel Farrington's Company (also commanded by Capt.
Simeon Wright) 30th Regt.; on Muster Roll from March 1 to April 30,
1814. Ref: R. & L. 1812, AGO Pages
50 and 51.

NICHOLS, JOHN L.
Served from March 5 to June 30,
1814 in Regt. of Light Dragoons.
Ref: R. & L. 1812, AGO Page 21.

NICHOLS, JONATHAN.
Served in company of Capt. John
McNeil Jr., 11th Regt.; on Pay Roll
for January and February, 1813. Ref:
R. & L. 1812, AGO Page 17.

*NICHOLS, JOSEPH.
Served in Capt. Walker's Company,
Col. Fifield's Regt. Detached Militia
in U. S. service 14 days, 1812.

*NICHOLS, JOSIAH,   Middlebury.
Served from June 10 to June 30,
1814 as an armorer in Alexander
Parris' Company. Also served in
Capt. Taylor's Company, 30th Inf.;
on Pay Roll of discharged men to
Dec. 30, 1815. Ref: R. & L. 1812,
AGO Pages 23 and 24. Also served
in 1 Regt. (Judson's) Vt. Militia.

*NICHOLS, LEVI.
Served in Capt. Taylor's Company,
Col. Wm. Williams' Regt. Detached
Militia in U. S. service 4 months
and 24 days, 1812. Enlisted Sept.
25, 1813 in Capt. Thomas Waterman's
Company, Dixon's Regt.

NICHOLS, LEVI JR.,   Johnson.
Volunteered to go to Plattsburgh,
September, 1814, and served in Capt.
Thomas Waterman's Company, Dix-
on's Regt. Ref: Book 51, AGO Page
208.

NICHOLS, MOSES.
Served from April 2 to July 1, 1813
in Capt. Samul Gordon's Company,
11th Regt. Ref: R. & L. 1812, AGO
Page 8.

‡NICHOLS, OTIS W.
Served in Capt. Smith's Company.
Pension Certificate of widow, Asenath,
No. 42476.

NICHOLS, PETER, Ensign,   Barre.
Volunteered to go to Plattsburgh,
September, 1814, and served 8 days
in Capt. Warren Ellis' Company. Ref:
Book 52, AGO Pages 168, 215, 242.

*NICHOLS, REUBEN.
Served in 2 Regt. (Fifield's') Vt.
Militia.

NICHOLS, SAMUEL, Sergeant,   Barre.
Volunteered to go to Plattsburgh,
September, 1814, and served 10 days
in Capt. Warren Ellis' Company.
Ref: Book 52, AGO Page 242.

*NICHOLS, TIMOTHY.
Served in Capt. Adams' Company,
Col. Jonathan Williams' Regt. Detached Militia in U. S. service 2
months and 7 days, 1812. Also served
in Corning's Detachment, Vt. Militia.

NICHOLS, WASHINGTON,   Braintree.
Marched to Plattsburgh Sept. 10, 1814,
serving in Capt. Lot Hudson's Company. Ref: Book 52, AGO Page 24.

NICHOLSON, GEORGE, Corporal.
Served in 1st Regt. of Detached Militia of Vt. in U. S. service at Champlain from Nov. 18 to Nov. 19, 1812.

NICKINSON, FREEMAN, Lieutenant.
Appointed 3rd Lieutenant 31st Inf.
April 30, 1813; dismissed Nov. 1,
1813; appointed 2nd Lieutenant Jan.
11, 1814. Ref: Heitman's Historical
Register & Dictionary USA; Governor and Council Vt., Vol. 6, Page
476.

*NIEMAN, BENJAMIN. Sergeant.
Served in Dixon's Regt. Vt. Militia.

*NILES, ABIEL.
Served in Capt. Rogers' Company,
Col. Fifield's Regt. Detached Militia
in U. S. service 1 month and 23
days, 1812.

‡*NILES, DAVID.
Served in Capt. Preston's Company,
Col. Jonathan Williams' Regt. De-
tached Militia in U. S. service 2
months and 6 days, 1812. Pension
Certificate of widow, Anna, No. 14435.

*NILES, EPHRAIM.
Served in 2 Regt. (Fifield's) Vt. Militia.

*NILES, NATHANIEL.
Served in Capt. O. Taylor's Company, Col. Fifield's Regt. Detached
Militia in U. S. service 2 months and
3 days, 1812.

NILES. SAMUEL.
Volunteered to go to Plattsburgh,
September, 1814, and served 4 days
in Capt. Aaron Kidder's Company.
Ref: Book 52, AGO Page 65.

NILES, WILLIAM.
Volunteered to go to Plattsburgh,
September, 1814, and served 4 days
in Capt. Aaron Kidder's Company.
Ref: Book 52, AGO Page 65.

NILES, WILLIAM JR.
Served from June 11 to June 14, 1813
in Capt. Ithiel Stone's Company, 1st
Regt. 2nd Brig. 3rd Div. Ref: R.
& L. 1812, AGO Page 44.

*NIMBLET, DANIEL.
Served with Hospital Attendants, Vt.

*NIMBLET, JOSEPH.
Served with Hospital Attendants, Vt.

NITE. WILLIAM.
Served in Capt. Barns' Company, Col.
Wm. Williams' Regt. Detached Mili-
tia in U. S. service 5 months, 1812.
Ref: Book 53, AGO Page 13.

NOBLE, ENOCH,   Richmond.
Served from Oct. 5 to Oct. 16, 1813
in Capt. Roswell Hunt's Company,
3 Regt. (Tyler's); volunteered to go
to Plattsburgh, September, 1814, and
served 9 days in same company. Ref:
R. & L. 1812, AGO Page 41; Book 51,
AGO Pages 82 and 277.

*NOBLE, ENOS.
Served in 3 Regt. (Tyler's) Vt. Militia.

‡NOBLE, JOHN,   Bethel.
Volunteered to go to Plattsburgh,
September, 1814, and served 9 days
in Capt. Nehemiah Noble's Company. Also served in Capt. Cross'
Company. Pension Certificate No.
31621. Pension Certificate of widow,
Sarah, No. 2887.

NOBLE, JONATHAN.
Volunteered to go to Plattsburgh,
September, 1814, and served 7 days
in Capt. Asaph Smith's Company.
Ref: Book 51, AGO Page 20.

NOBLE, NEHEMIAH, Captain,   Bethel.
Appointed Captain 31st Inf. April
30, 1813; resigned Jan. 11, 1814.
Volunteered to go to Plattsburgh,
September, 1814, and served 10 days
in command of company raised at
Bethel, Vt. Ref: Heitman's Historical
Register & Dictionary USA; Book 51,
AGO Page 219.

‡*NOBLE, PERCY B.
Served in Capt. Bingham's Company,
Col. Jonathan Williams' Regt. Detached Militia in U. S. service 2
months and 9 days, 1812. Pension
Certificate No. 6307. Pension Certificate of widow, Abigail, No. 35225.

*NOBLE, ROGER, Sergeant.
Served from April 12 to April 21,
1814 in Capt. Othniel Jewett's Company, Sumner's Regt.

*NOBLES, HARVEY, Sergeant.
Served from Oct. 5 to Oct. 17, 1813
in Capt. Stephen Brown's Company,
3 Regt. (Tyler's).

*NOBLES, JOHN,   Enosburgh.
Served from Oct. 14 to Nov. 17, 1813
in Capt. Asahel Scoville's Company.

*NOBLES, JOHN 2nd, Ensign.
Served in 1st Regt. of Detached Militia of Vt. in U. S. service at Champlain from Nov. 18 to Nov. 19, 1812.

NOLES, JOHN,   Fairfax.
Served from Aug. 8, 1812 in company of Capt. Joseph Beeman Jr.,
11th Regt. U. S. Inf. under Col. Ira
Clark. Ref: Hemenway's Vt. Gazetteer, Vol. 2, Page 402.

*NOLTON, BENJAMIN, Corporal.
Appointed Corporal Oct. 14, 1813 in
Capt. Asahel Scovell's Company, Col.
Clark's Rifle Corps.

*NOLTON, JOSEPH.
Served from April 12 to April 15,
1814 in Capt. Jonathan P. Stanley's
Company, Col. W. B. Sumner's Regt.

*NORRIS, CLARK D.,   Danville.
Served in Capt. Mason's Company,
Col. Fifield's Regt. Detached Militia
in U. S. service 3 months and 16
days, 1812. Volunteered to go to
Plattsburgh, September, 1814, and
served 3 days in Capt. Solomon Langmaid's Company.

*NORRIS, DANIEL,   Corinth.
Served in Capt. Rogers' Company,
Col. Fifield's Regt. Detached Militia
in U. S. service 2 months and 18
days, 1812. Volunteered to go to
Plattsburgh, September, 1814, and
served in Capt. Abel Jackman's Company.

NORRIS, DAVID.
Served in Capt. Benjamin S. Edgerton's Company, 11th Regt.; on Pay
Roll for September and October, 1812
and January and February, 1813.
Ref: R. & L. 1812, AGO Pages 1
and 2.

‡NORRIS, EZEKIEL.
Served in Capt. F. Eaton's Company.
Pension Certificate No. 33938.

NORRIS, JAMES,   Corinth.
Volunteered to go to Plattsburgh,
September, 1814, and served in Capt.
Abel Jackman's Company. Ref: Book
52, AGO Page 44.

NORRIS, JOHN,   Corinth.
Volunteered to go to Plattsburgh,
September, 1814, and served in Capt.
Abel Jackman's Company. Ref: Book
52, AGO Page 44.

*NORRIS, JONATHAN,   Stockbridge.
Served in Capt. Durkee's Company,
Col. Fifield's Regt. Detached Militia
in U. S. service 2 months and 21
days, 1812. Volunteered to go to
Plattsburgh, September, 1814, and
served 7 days in Capt. Elias Keyes'
Company.

‡*NORRIS, MOSES,   Vershire.
Volunteered to go to Plattsburgh,
September, 1814, and served 3 days
in Capt. Ira Corse's Company. Also
served in 2 Regt. (Fifield's) Vt.
Militia and in Capt. Taylor's Company. Pension Certificate of widow,
Sally, No. 1244.

‡*NORRIS, SAMUEL,   Corinth?
Served in Capt. Mason's Company,
Col. Fifield's Regt. Detached Militia
in U. S. service 3 months and 20
days, 1812. Pension Certificate No.
116.

‡NORMANDIN, M. LEE.
Served in Capt. Towle's Company.
Pension Certificate No. 202.

‡*NORRIS, NATHANIEL JR.
Served in Capt. Hiram Mason's Company, Col. Fifield's Regt. Detached
Militia in U. S. service 5 months and
14 days, 1812. Pension Certificate
No. 12552.

NORTHAWAY, DANIEL O.
Served in Capt. Taylor's Company.
Pension Certificate No. 7068.

NORTH, GAD,   Shoreham.
Volunteered to go to Plattsburgh,
September, 1814, and served about 6
days in Capt. Samuel Hand's Com-
pany. Ref: Rev. J. F. Goodhue's
History of Shoreham, Page 108.

NORTH, NATHANIEL,   Shoreham.
Volunteered to go to Plattsburgh,
September, 1814, marched to Burlington and crossed the lake but did not
take part in the battle; commanded
company of cavalry from Shoreham.
Ref: Rev. J. F. Goodhue's History
of Shoreham, Page 104.

‡NORTHROP, STEPHEN.
Served from March 31 to June 30,
1813 in Capt. Samul Gordon's Company, 11th Regt. Pension Certificate
No. 15342.

‡NORTHROP, WILLIS, Fairfield, Sheldon
or Fairfax. Volunteered to go to
Plattsburgh, September, 1814, and
served 7 days in Capt. Joseph Beeman's Company. Also served in Capt.
Asahel Story's Company. Pension Certificate No. 29645. Pension Certificate of widow, Caroline, No. 27914.
Ref: Book 51, AGO Page 127.

NORTHRUP, SAMUEL,   Shoreham.
Volunteered to go to Plattsburgh,
September, 1814, and served 6 days
in Capt. Nathaniel North's Company
of Cavalry. Ref: Rev. J. F. Goodhue's History of Shoreham, Page 107.

*NORTHWAY, ASAHEL.
Enlisted Sept. 25, 1813 and served
1 month and 23 days in Capt. Elijah
Birge's Company, Col. Dixon's Regt.
Detached Militia in U. S. service.

*NORTHWAY, FRANCIS JR., Lieutenant.
Appointed Lieutenant Sept. 25, 1813
in Capt. Elijah Birge's Company, Dixon's Regt.; joined from 4th Company
of Militia.

‡NORTHWAY, GEORGE.
Served in Capt. Beeman's Company.
Pension Certificate of widow, Amy,
No. 28285.

NORTHWAY, OWEN.
Served from April 22, 1813 to April 25,
1814 in Capt. James Taylor's Company and Capt. Gideon Spencer's
Company, 30th Regt. Ref: R. & L.
1812, AGO Pages 52, 57, 58.

*NORTON, CHARLES.
Served in 3 Regt. (Tyler's) Vt. Militia.

NORTON, ELISHA.   Strafford.
Served from March 23 to June 21,
1813 in Capt. Edgerton's Company,
11th Regt. Ref: R. & L. 1812, AGO
Page 3.

NORTON, ERASTUS.
Served in Capt. Samul Gordon's Com-
pany, 11th Regt.; on Pay Roll for
January and February, 1813. Ref:
R. & L. 1812, AGO Page 9.

*NORTON, HENRY A.
Served in Capt. Willson's Company,
Col. Wm. Williams' Regt. Detached
Militia in U. S. service 4 months
and 24 days, 1812.

NORTON, JACOB,   Hadley, N. Y.
Served from March 1, 1814 to July
7, 1814 in Capt. Spencer's Company,
29th Inf. Ref: R. & L. 1812, AGO
Page 30.

NORTON, JAMES R.,   Poultney.
Volunteered to go to Plattsburgh,
September. 1814, and served 2 days
in Capt. Briant Ransom's Company.
Ref: Book 52, AGO Page 147.

*NORTON, JOHN.
Served in 3 Regt. (Williams') Vt.
Militia.

NORTON, MARTIN, Lt. Colonel.
Appointed Lt. Colonel 30th Inf. Feb.
23, 1813; resigned July 24, 1814.
Ref: Heitman's Historical Register &
Dictionary USA.

*NORTON, NATHANIEL.
Served in 3 Regt. (Tyler's) Vt. Militia.

*NORTON, PORTER.
Served from April 12 to April 21,
1814 in Capt. Eseck Sprague's Company, Sumner's Regt.

*NORTON, SOLOMON (or Salmon), Ad-
jutant, Fair Haven. Served in 1st
Regt. of Detached Militia of Vt. in
U. S. service at Champlain from Nov.
18 to Nov. 19, 1812.

‡NOURSE, TIMOTHY,   Shrewsbury.
Volunteered to go to Plattsburgh,
September, 1814, and served 4 days
in Capt. Robert Reed's Company.
Also served in Capt. N. Crary's
Company. Pension Certificate of wid-
ow, Lucretia M., No. 22432.

NOYES, DANIEL.
Enlisted March 19, 1813 in Capt.
Samul Gordon's Company, 11th Regt.;
deserted before joined. Ref: R. & L.
1812, AGO Page 8.

*NOYES, ELIJAH.
Served in Capt. Walker's Company,
Col. Fifield's Regt. Detached Militia
in U. S. service 6 months and 3 days,
1812.

*NOYES, GILBERT.
Served from April 12 to April 21,
1814 in Capt. Edmund B. Hill's Company, Sumner's Regt.

NOYES, ISAAC.   Salisbury.
Volunteered to go to Plattsburgh,
September, 1814, and served 4 days
in Capt. John Morton's Company.
Ref: Book 52, AGO Page 141.

*NOYES, ISAAC, Sergeant.
Served from April 12 to April 21,
1814 in Lieut. James S. Morton's
Company, Sumner's Regt. Also served as a Captain in 3 Regt. (Williams') Vt. Militia.

NOYES, JACOB.
Served from May 1 to June 30, 1814
as a carpenter in Alexander Parris'
Company of Artificers. Ref: R. & L.
1812, AGO Page 24.

NOYES, JACOB,　　　　Poultney.
Served from April 14, 1814 to June
19, 1815 in Capt. Taylor's Company,
30th Inf. Ref: R. & L. 1812, AGO
Pages 1 and 23.

NOYES JOHN,　　　　Tunbridge.
Volunteered to go to Plattsburgh,
September, 1814, and served in Capt.
David Knox's Company. Ref: Book
52, AGO Page 116.

‡NOYES, JOSEPH.
Served in Capt. Denison Noyes' Com-
pany. Pension Certificate of widow,
Grace B., No. 9273.

*NOYES, OLIVER.
Served in Capt. Barns' Company,
Col. Wm. Williams' Regt. Detached
Militia in U. S. service 5 months.
Served from June 11, 1813 to June
14, 1813 in Capt. Hezekiah Barns'
Company, 1st Regt. 2nd Brig. 3rd
Div.

NOYES, RICHARD,　　　Tunbridge.
Volunteered to go to Plattsburgh,
September, 1814, and served 4 days
in Capt. Ephraim Hackett's Company. Ref: Book 52, AGO Page 71.

NOYES, SAMUEL,　　　Tunbridge.
Volunteered to go to Plattsburgh,
September, 1814, and served 4 days
in Capt. Ephraim Hackett's Company. Ref: Book 52, AGO Pages
71 and 74.

*NOYES, WILLIAM, Fife Major.
Served in Dixon's Regt. Vt. Militia.

NUNN, JONATHAN.
Served in company of late Capt. J.
Brooks, commanded by Lt. John I.
Cromwell, Corps of U. S. Artillery;
on Muster Roll from April 30 to June
30, 1814; prisoner of war on parole;
transferred from Capt. Leonard's
Company. Ref: R. & L. 1812, AGO
Page 18.

NUTT, JOHN.
Volunteered to go to Plattsburgh,
September, 1814, and served 4 days
in company of Capt. James George
of Topsham. Ref: Book 52, AGO
Pages 67 and 70.

*NUTT, JOHN JR.
Served in Capt. Rogers' Company,
Col. Fifield's Regt. Detached Militia
in U. S. service 1 month and 16
days, 1812.

NUTT, WILLIAM, Lieutenant.
Volunteered to go to Plattsburgh,
September, 1814, and served 4 days
in company of Capt. James George
of Topsham. Ref: Book 52, AGO
Page 70.

*NUTTER, SAMUEL.
Served with Hospital Attendants, Vt.

NUTTING, JONATHAN,　　Roxbury.
Volunteered to go to Plattsburgh,
September, 1814, and served in Capt.
Samuel Orcutt's Company. Ref: Hem-
enway's Vt. Gazetteer, Vol. 4, Page
753.

NUTTING, JOSEPH, Drummer, Roxbury.
Volunteered to go to Plattsburgh,
September, 1814, and served 9 days
in Capt. Samuel M. Orcutt's Company. Ref: Book 52, AGO Pages
182 and 250.

*NUTTING, NATHANIEL.
Served in Capt. Noyce's Company,
Col. Jonathan Williams' Regt. Detached Militia in U. S. service 2
months and 6 days, 1812.

*NUTTING, TALCOT G., Corporal.
Served from Sept. 25 to Sept. 27,
1813 in Capt. N. B. Eldredge's Company, Dixon's Regt.

NYE, EPHRAIM,　　　Montpelier.
Volunteered to go to Plattsburgh,
September, 1814, and served 8 days
in Capt. Timothy Hubbard's Company.
Ref: Book 52, AGO Page 256.

NYE, IRAM,　　　Montpelier.
Volunteered to go to Plattsburgh,
September, 1814, and served 8 days
in Capt. Timothy Hubbard's Company. Ref: Book 52, AGO Page 256.
*NYE, ZENUS.
Served from Sept. 25 to Oct. 6, 1813
in Capt. Elijah Birge's Company, Dixon's Regt.

‡NYES, FLAVEL J.
Served in Capt. Partridge's Com-
pany. Pension Certificate of widow,
Aurellia, No. 28464.

‡*OAK, EBENEZER.
Served in Capt. Noyce's Company,
Col. Jonathan Williams' Regt. Detached Militia in U. S. service 2
months and 6 days, 1812. Pension
Certificate of widow, Betsey, No.
12007.

OATMAN, JOHN.
Served from Nov. 1, 1812 to Feb. 28,
1813 in Capt. Charles Follett's Company, 11th Regt. Ref: R. & L. 1812,
AGO Page 12.

*OBER, BENJAMIN.
Enlisted Sept. 25, 1813 and served
1 month and 23 days in Capt. Thomas
Waterman's Company, Col. Dixon's
Regt. Detached Militia in U. S. serv-
ice.

*OBER, DAVID.
Served in Capt. Sabins' Company,
Col. Jonathan Williams' Regt. Detached Militia in U. S. service 2
months and 6 days, 1812.

‡*OBER, ISRAEL.
Enlisted Sept. 25, 1813 in Capt.
Thomas Waterman's Company, Dixon's Regt. Pension Certificate No.
25312.

‡*OBER, PETER S. (alias Daniel Mc-
Coy?), Johnson. Served in Capt.
Taylor's Company, Col. Wm. Williams' Regt. Detached Militia in U.
S. service 4 months and 24 days,
1812. Volunteered to go to Plattsburgh, September, 1814, and served
10 days in Capt. Thomas Waterman's Company, Dixon's Regt. Pension Certificate No. 12313. Pension
Certificate of widow, Sally Toothaker,
No. 19214.

*O'BRIEN, DANIEL, Sergeant.
Served in 1 Regt. (Judson's) Vt.
Militia.

*O'BRIEN, JOHN.
Served in 4 Regt. (Williams') Vt.
Militia.

O'CONNER, JOHN M., Asst. Adjutant
General. Served in General Staff
of the Northern Army commanded
by Maj. Gen. George Izard; on Pay
Roll to July 31, 1814. Ref: R. & L.
1812, AGO Page 28.

*ODELL, ABRAHAM.
Served from April 12 to April 21,
1814 in Capt. Eseck Sprague's Company, Sumner's Regt.

*ODELL, ELI.
Served from Sept. 25 to Oct. 30,
1813 in Capt. Jesse Post's Company,
Dixon's Regt.

*ODELL, ISAAC.
Served from April 20, 1814 to April
21, 1814 in Capt. Eseck Sprague's
Company, Sumner's Regt.

‡ODELL, WILLIAM.
Served under Captains Utley and
Wright. Pension Certificate No.
14354.

ODIT, JOSEPH.
Enlisted Oct. 22, 1813 for 1 year in
Capt. Wires' Company, 30th Regt.
Ref: R. & L. 1812, AGO Page 1.

ODLE, EZEKIAL.
Served from April 24, 1813 to April
25, 1814 in Capt. Daniel Farrington's
Company (also commanded by Capt.
Simeon Wright) 30th Regt. Ref: R.
& L. 1812, AGO Pages 50 and 51.

ODLE, JEREMIAH.
Enlisted May 28, 1813 for 1 year in
Capt. Daniel Farrington's Company
(also commanded by Capt. Simeon
Wright) 30th Regt.; on Muster Roll
from March 1 to April 30, 1814. Ref:
R. & L. 1812, AGO Pages 50 and 51.

OGDEN, SAMUEL.
Enlisted Nov. 11, 1812 for 5 years in
company of late Capt. J. Brooks
commanded by Lt. John I. Cromwell, Corps of U. S. Artillery; on
Muster Roll from April 30 to June 30,
1814. Ref: R. & L. 1812, AGO
Page 18.

OLCOTT, HENRY, Lieutenant.
Appointed 2nd Lieutenant Marines in
1813 and 1st Lieutenant June 18,
1814. Ref: Governor and Council,
Vt., Vol. 6, Page 478.

OLDER, DAVID, W., Shoreham.
Served in Lt. V. R. Goodrich's Com-
pany, 11th Regt.; on Pay Roll for
January and February, 1813. Ref:
R. & L. 1812, AGO Page 11.

*OLDFIELD, ABRAHAM.
Served with Hospital Attendants, Vt.

‡OLDHAM, THADDEUS.
Served in Capt. Danforth's Company.
Pension Certificate of widow, Celia,
No. 952.

OLDS, ELIAS.
Enlisted Sept. 25, 1813 in Capt. Amos
Robinson's Company, Dixon's Regt.
Ref: Book 52, AGO Page 271.

*OLDS, HARVEY, Morristown.
Served in Capt. Mason's Company,
Col. Fifield's Regt. Detached Militia
in U. S. service 2 months and 20
days, 1812.

*OLDS, JAMES.
Served 10 days in Capt. Birge's Com-
pany, Col. Dixon's Regt. Detached
Militia in U. S. service. Oct. 2, 1813 in Capt. Asahel Lang-
worthy's Company, Col. Isaac Clark's
Rifle Corps.

*OLDS, WILLIAM.
Served in Dixon's Regt. Vt. Militia.

*OLEDS, ELIAS.
Served in Dixon's Regt. Vt. Militia.

‡*OLIN, ARCHIBALD.
Served in Capt. Cross' Company, Col.
Martindale's Regt. Detached Militia
in U. S. service 2 months and 14
days, 1812. Pension Certificate No.
11059.

*OLIN, JUSTIN.
Served from April 12 to May 20, 1814
in Capt. George Fisher's Company,
Sumner's Regt.

‡OLIN, PELEG G.
Served in Capt. M. Galusha's Com-
pany. Pension Certificate of widow,
Samanda, No. 35266.

*OLIVER, CHARLES, Shoreham.
Served from April 12 to May 20, 1814
in company of Capt. James Gray Jr.,
Sumner's Regt. Volunteered to go
to Plattsburgh, September, 1814, and
served 6 days in Capt. Samuel Hand's
Company.

OLIVER, NATHANIEL.
Enlisted March 4, 1813 in Capt.
Charles Follett's Company, 11th
Regt.; on Pay Roll to May 31, 1813.
Ref: R. & L. 1812, AGO Page 13.

OLMSTEAD, DAVID.
Enlisted April 24, 1813 for 1 year
in Capt. Daniel Farrington's Com-
pany (also commanded by Capt.
Simeon Wright) 30th Regt.; on Muster
Roll March 1 to April 30, 1814;
wounded. Ref: R. & L. 1812, AGO
Pages 50 and 51.

OLMSTEAD, JEREMIAH. St. Albans.
Enlisted in August, 1813, for 1 year
in Capt. John Wires' Company, 30th
Regt. Ref: R. & L. 1812, AGO Page
40.

*OLMSTEAD, JOHN, (or Omsted), Fair-
fax. Enlisted Sept. 25, 1813 in Capt.
Asa Wilkins' Company, Dixon's Regt.

‡*OLMSTEAD, STEPHEN JR.
Served in Capt. Ormsby's Company,
1st Regt. (Martindale's) Vt. Militia.
Pension Certificate No. 22087.

OLMSTEAD, WILLIAM.
Served from Feb. 13 to May 12, 1813
in Capt. Phineas Williams' Company,
11th Regt. Ref: R. & L. 1812, AGO
Page 14.

OLMSTED, IRA.
Served in Capt. Chadwick's Company.
Ref: R. & L. 1812, AGO Page 32.

O'NEIL, JOHN, Sandy Hill, N. Y.
Served from Dec. 13, 1814 to June
19, 1815 in Capt. Taylor's Company,
30th Inf. Ref: R. & L. 1812, AGO
Page 23.

‡O'NEIL, PATRICK.
Served in Capt. Boardman's Company. Pension Certificate No. 22081.

*ORCUTT, FRANKLIN.
Served in Capt. Wright's Company,
Col. Fifield's Regt. Detached Militia
in U. S. service 6 months, 1812.

‡ORCUTT, SAMUEL M., Captain, Roxbury. Volunteered to go to Plattsburgh, September, 1814, and served
7 days in command of company raised in Roxbury. Pension Certificate
of widow, Mary, No. 23836.

ORCUTT, ZEBINA.
Enlisted April 25, 1813 for 1 year in
Capt. Simeon Wright's Company. Ref:
R. & L. 1812, AGO Page 51.

ORDWAY, BENJAMIN H.
Enlisted Jan. 14, 1813 in Capt.
Phineas Williams' Company, 11th
Regt.; on Pay Roll to May 31, 1813.
Ref: R. & L. 1812, AGO Page 14.

ORDWAY, JAMES, Strafford.
Volunteered to go to Plattsburgh,
September, 1814, and served 4 days
in Capt. Joseph Barrett's Company.
Ref: Book 52, AGO Page 100.

‡ORDWAY, NEHEMIAH.
Served in Capt. Robertson's Company. Pension Certificate No. 20212.

*ORDWAY, PETER.
Served in Capt. Brigham's Company,
Col. Jonathan Williams' Regt. Detached Militia in U. S. service 2
months and 9 days, 1812.

*ORLIN, JAMES.
Served in Capt. Taylor's Company,
Col. Wm. Williams' Regt. Detached
Militia in U. S. service 3 months
and 15 days, 1812.

ORMES, ALLEN, West Haven.
Volunteered to go to Plattsburgh,
September, 1814, and served 4 days
in Capt. David B. Phippeney's Company. Ref: Book 52, AGO Page 146.

*ORMS, JONATHAN, Brig. General.
Served on Staff of Vt. Militia.

*ORMSBEE, MASON, Major.
Appointed Major 31st Inf. Feb. 23,
1813; resigned Feb. 21, 1814. Served
as Captain in 1st Regt. (Martindale's)
Detached Militia of Vt. in U. S.
service at Champlain from Nov. 18
to Nov. 19, 1812. Ref: Heitman's
Historical Register & Dictionary USA.

ORMSBEE, THOMAS.
Volunteered to go to Plattsburgh,
September, 1814, and served 4 days
in Capt. Aaron Kidder's Company.
Ref: Book 52, AGO Page 65.

*ORMSBY, GIDEON.
Served in 1 Regt (Judson's) Vt.
Militia.

ORMSTEAD, HENRY, Goshen.
Volunteered to go to Plattsburgh,
September, 1814, and served 5 days
in Capt. Durham Sprague's Company.
Ref: Book 52, AGO Page 129.

ORMSTEAD, MOSES, Goshen.
Volunteered to go to Plattsburgh,
September, 1814, and served 5 days
in Capt. Durham Sprague's Company.
Ref: Book 52, AGO Page 129.

ORNE, EBENEZER.
Enlisted Oct. 10, 1812 in Capt. Benjamin S. Edgerton's Company, 11th
Regt.; served at the battle of
Chrystler's Farm Nov. 11, 1813 and
was reported missing after the battle;
was captured by troops Dec. 19, 1813
at Fort Niagara; discharged May 4,
1814. Ref: R. & L. 1812, AGO
Pages 1 and 2; Governor and Council
Vt. Vol. 6, Page 490; Records of
Naval Records and Library, Navy
Dept.

ORNE, JOSEPH.
Served in Capt. Benjamin S. Edgerton's Company, 11th Regt.; on Pay
Roll for September and October, 1812,
and January and February, 1813; was
at the battle of Chrystler's Farm
Nov. 11, 1813 and reported missing
after the battle. Ref: R. & L. 1812,
AGO Pages 1 and 2; Governor and
Council Vt., Vol. 6, Page 490.

*ORR, ALEXANDER, Highgate.
Served in Capt. Saxe's Company, Col.
Wm. Williams' Regt. Detached Militia in U. S. service 4 months and
24 days, 1812. Served from May
17, 1813 to May 16, 1814 in Capt.
John Wires' Company, 30th Regt.
Ref: R. & L. 1812, AGO Page 40.

*ORR, JAMES.
Served in 3 Regt. (Tyler's) Vt. Militia.

*ORR, STEPHEN.
Served in Capt. Pettes' Company, Col.
Wm. Williams' Regt. Detached Militia in U. S. service 4 months and
17 days, 1812. Enlisted Jan. 13,
1813 in Capt. John W. Weeks' Company, 11th Regt.; on Pay Roll to
July 16, 1813. Ref: R. & L. 1812,
AGO Pages 4 and 5.

ORTON, DAVID.
Served from April 27, 1813 to April
28, 1814 in Capt. Gideon Spencer's
Company and Regt. James Taylor's
Company, 30th Regt. Ref: R. & L.
1812, AGO Pages 52, 57, 59.

‡*ORVIS, JOHN M., Sergeant.
Served in Capt. Noyes' Company,
Col. Jonathan Williams' Regt. Detached Militia in U. S. service 2
months and 6 days, 1812. Pension
Certificate of widow, Anna, No. 5058.

‡OSBORN, ERASMUS.
Served in Capt. Benjamin S. Edgerton's Company, 11th Regt.; on Pay
Roll for September and October, 1812

and January and February 1813. Also served in Capt. Copp's Company. Pension Certificate No. 15241. Ref: R. & L. 1812, AGO Pages 1 and 2.

OSBORNE, JOHN,   Enosburgh.
Served in Capt. Martin D. Folett's Company. Ref: Hemenway's Vt. Gazetteer, Vol. 2, Page 155.

OSBORNE, OZIAS,   Franklin County.
Volunteered to go to Plattsburgh Sept. 11, 1814 and served in 15th or 22nd Regt. Ref: Hemenway's Vt. Gazetteer, Vol. 2, Page 392.

‡*OSBURN, WILLIAM T.,   Richford.
Enlisted Sept. 25, 1813 and served 1 month and 23 days in Capt. Martin D. Folett's Company, Col. Dixon's Regt. Detached Militia in U. S. service. Pension Certificate No. 22904.

‡*OSGOOD, JESSE.
Served in Capt. Morrill's Company, Col. Fifield's Regt. Detached Militia in U. S. service 6 months and 5 days. 1812. Pension Certificate No. 12682.

OSGOOD, SAMUEL,   Boston, Mass.
Served from Sept. 1, 1814 to June 16, 1815 in Capt. Sanford's Company, 30th Inf. Ref: R. & L. 1812, AGO Page 23.

O'STUND, JOHN.
Served from April 12 to May 20, 1814 in Capt. George Fisher's Company, Sumner's Regt. Ref: Book 52, AGO Page 278.

*OSYER, JAMES.
Served from April 12 to April 15, 1814 in Capt. Jonathan P. Stanley's Company. Col. W. B. Sumner's Regt. Ref: Book 52, AGO Page 287.

*OTHELTHORP, JOHN T. (or Y).
Served from April 12 to May 20, 1814 in company of Capt. James Gray Jr., Sumner's Regt.

OTIS, DANIEL.
Served from May 1 to June 30, 1814 in Capt. Haig's Corps of Light Dragoons. Ref: R. & L. 1812, AGO Page 20.

‡OTIS, HEZEKIAH.
Served in Capt. Morrill's Company. Pension Certificate No. 11871.

*OTIS, JOHN.
Enlisted Sept. 18, 1813 for 2 months in Capt. Isaac Finch's Company, Col. Clark's Rifle Corps.

*OTIS, JOSEPH, Ensign.
Served from April 12 to April 21, 1814 in Lieut. Justus Foote's Company, Sumner's Regt.

OTIS, JOSH,   Danville.
Served in Capt. Morrill's Company, Col. Fifield's Regt. Detached Militia in U. S. service 6 months. Ref: Hemenway's Vt. Gazetteer, Vol. 1, Page 314.

*OTIS, SAMUEL, Sergeant.
Served in Capt. Wheeler's Company, Col. Fifield's Regt. Detached Militia in U. S. service 6 months and 4 days, 1812.

OTIS, SOLOMON.
Served from March 5 to June 4, 1813 in Lieut. Wm. S. Foster's Company, 11th Regt. Ref: R. & L. 1812, AGO Page 6.

OUDERCARRICK, JOHN.
Enlisted July 5, 1813 for 5 years in company of late Capt. J. Brooks, commanded by Lt. John I. Cromwell, Corps of U. S. Artillery; on Muster Roll from April 30 to June 30, 1814. Ref: R. & L. 1812, AGO Page 18.

*OVIT, WILLIAM, Sergeant.
Served in Capt. Kendall's Company, Col. Wm. Williams' Regt. Detached Militia in U. S. service 4 months and 23 days, 1812.

*OWEN, ABEL.
Served from June 11 to June 14, 1813 in Capt. Moses Jewett's Company, 1st Regt. 2nd Brig. 3rd Div.

OWEN, ABRAHAM,   Pittsford.
Volunteered to go to Plattsburgh, September, 1814, and served 8 days in Capt. Caleb Hendee's Company. Ref: Book 52, AGO Page 125.

OWEN, AMASA,   Pittsford.
Enlisted July, 1812, for 5 years in Capt. Hawley's Company, Col. Clark's (11th) Regt.; was at Sackett's Harbor at the time of the British attack May 29, 1813; was also in the battle of Williamsburgh Nov. 11th, was wounded in the thigh by a musket ball and captured by the enemy. Was captured by troops Dec. 19, 1813 at Fort Niagara and discharged March 12, 1814. Ref: R. & L. 1812, AGO Page 25; A. M. Caverly's History of Pittsford, Page 366; Records of Naval Records and Library, Navy Dept.

‡OWEN, IRA, Corporal,   Montpelier.
Volunteered to go to Plattsburgh, September, 1814, and served 8 days in Capt. Timothy Hubbard's Company. Pension Certificate of widow, Harriet M., No. 30213.

*OWEN, JESSE, Drummer.
Served in Capt. Hotchkiss' Company. Col. Martindale's Regt. Detached Militia in U. S. service 2 months and 13 days, 1812.

*OWEN, LEONARD.
Served with Hospital Attendants, Vt.

*OWEN, WILLIAM, Corporal.
Served from April 13 to April 16, 1814 in Capt. Salmon Foster's Company, Sumner's Regt.

OWENS, EPHRAIM,   Pittsford.
Served from June 29, 1814 to June 19, 1815 in Capt. Taylor's Company, 30th Inf. Ref: R. & L. 1812, AGO Page 23.

OWENS. MICHAEL, Sandy Hill, N. Y.
Served from Oct. 14, 1814 to June
19, 1815 in Capt. Taylor's Company,
30th Inf. Ref: R. & L. 1812, AGO
Page 23.

*PACKARD, ANDREW.
Served from June 11 to June 14,
1813 in Lieut. Bates' Company, 1st
Regt. (Judson's).

PACKARD, ELIJAH, Woodstock.
Served from March 26, 1813 to June
1, 1813 in Capt. Phineas Williams'
Company, 11th Regt. Ref: R. & L.
1812, AGO Page 14.

*PACKARD. JUDSON.
Enlisted Sept. 25, 1813 in company
of Capt. Jonathan Prentiss, Jr., Dixon's Regt.

*PACKARD, MELZER.
Served in 1 Regt. (Judson's) Vt.
Militia.

*PACKARD, ZEBEDEE, Jericho.
Served in 3 Regt. (Tyler's) Vt. Mili-
tia. Took part in the battle of
Plattsburgh. Ref: History of Jericho,
Page 142.

‡PACKER, JOSHUA.
Served in Capt. Noyes' Company.
Pension Certificate No. 32185.

PADDOCK, ROBERT, Barre.
Volunteered to go to Plattsburgh,
September, 1814, and served 10 days
in Capt. Warren Ellis' Company.
Ref: Book 52, AGO Page 242.

‡PADDOCK. WILLIAM.
Appointed Surgeon's Mate 30th Inf.
June 29, 1813; transferred to 31st
Inf. Dec. 30, 1813; resigned Sept.
29, 1814. Served in Capt. Ways'
Company. Pension Certificate No.
23853. Ref: Heitman's Historical
Register & Dictionary USA.

*PAGE, BENJAMIN, Calais.
Volunteered to go to Plattsburgh,
September, 1814, and served 10 days
in Capt. Gideon Wheelock's Company.

‡*PAGE, BENJAMIN, Groton.
Served in Capt. Morrill's Company,
Col. Fifield's Regt. Detached Militia in U. S. service 6 months and
5 days, 1812. Pension Certificate No.
7317.

*PAGE. CALVIN.
Served in Capt. Howard's Company,
Vt. Militia.

PAGE. CHARLES.
Served from May 1 to May 31, 1814
as a laborer in Alexander Parris'
Company of Artificers. Ref: R. &
L. 1812, AGO Page 24.

*PAGE, HENRY (or Harry).
Served in Capt. Parsons' Company,
Col. Jonathan Williams' Regt. Detached Militia in U. S. service 2
months and 13 days, 1812.

*PAGE. HARVEY, Shoreham.
Served from April 12 to May 20, 1814
in Capt. George Fisher's Company,

Sumner's Regt. Volunteered to go
to Plattsburgh, September, 1814, and
served 6 days in Capt. Samuel Hand's
Company.

*PAGE, JOHN, Groton?
Served in Capt. Wheeler's Company,
Col. Fifield's Regt. Detached Militia
in U. S. service 6 months and 4
days, 1812.

*PAGE. JOSEPH.
Served in Capt. Wheeler's Company,
Col. Fifield's Regt. Detached Militia
in U. S. service 6 months and 4
days, 1812. Volunteered to go to
Plattsburgh, September, 1814, and
served 7 days in Capt. Asaph Smith's
Company.

‡*PAGE, JOSIAH.
Served in Capt. Morrill's Company,
Col. Fifield's Regt. Detached Militia
in U. S. service 4 months and 2
days, 1812. Pension Certificate No.
21781.

*PAGE, LEMUEL. Lieutenant.
Served in 1 Regt. (Judson's) Vt.
Militia.

*PAGE, LEVERETT, Groton.
Served in Capt. Morrill's Company,
Col. Fifield's Regt. Detached Militia
in U. S. service 6 months and 5
days, 1812.

PAGE, ORSMUS.
Enlisted Feb. 19, 1813 in Capt. John
W. Weeks' Company, 11th Regt. and
served to date of death, April 8, 1813.
Ref: R. & L. 1812, AGO Page 4.

PAGE, PARKER.
Served in Capt. Chadwick's Company.
Ref: R. & L. 1812, AGO Page 32.

PAGE, RICHARD.
Served in Capt. Chadwick's Company.
Ref: R. & L. 1812, AGO Page 32.

‡*PAGE, SAMUEL, Lieutenant. Essex.
Served as Ensign in Capt. Pettis'
Company, 4 Regt. (Williams') Vt.
Militia and in 3 Regt. (Tyler's) Vt.
Militia. Served as 3rd Lieutenant in
Tyler's Regt. Vt. Militia. Pension
Certificate of widow, Hannah, No.
1196.

PAGE, STEPHEN, Hancock.
Volunteered to go to Plattsburgh,
September, 1814, and served 7 days
in Capt. Asaph Smith's Company.
Ref: Book 51, AGO Page 20.

*PAGE, WILLIAM.
Served from Sept. 25 to Nov. 9, 1813
in Capt. Thomas Waterman's Company, Dixon's Regt.

‡PAIGE. JOHN .
Served in Capt. Morrill's Company.
Pension Certificate of widow, Sally,
No. 6120.

*PAIN, AMOS, Stowe.
Volunteered to go to Plattsburgh,
September, 1814, and served in Capt.
Nehemiah Perkins' Company, 4th
Regt. (Peck's).

*PAINE, AHIRA.
Served in Capt. S. Pettes' Company,
Col. Wm. Williams' Regt. Detached
Militia in U. S. service 4 months
and 17 days, 1812.

PAINE, AMOS, Morristown.
Volunteered to go to Plattsburgh,
September, 1814, and served in Capt.
Denison Cook's Company. Ref: Book
51, AGO Page 202.

PAINE, DAVID.
Volunteered to go to Plattsburgh,
September, 1814, and went as far as
Bolton, Vt., serving 4 days in Lieut.
Phineus Kimball's Company of West
Fairlee. Also appears on roll of
Capt. Ebenezer Spencer's Company.
Ref: Book 52, AGO Pages 46, 48, 49.

PAINE, EARL J., Fifer, Vershire.
Volunteered to go to Plattsburgh,
September, 1814, and served 3 days
in Capt. Ira Corse's Company. Ref:
Book 52, AGO Page 91.

PAINE, EARL P.
Volunteered to go to Plattsburgh,
September, 1814, and went as far as
Bolton, Vt., serving 4 days in Lieut.
Phineus Kimball's Company, West
Fairlee. Ref: Book 52, AGO Page 46.

PAINE, JOHN, Roxbury.
Volunteered to go to Plattsburgh,
September, 1814, and served 8 days
in Capt. Samuel M. Orcutt's Company. Ref: Book 52, AGO Page 250.

PAINE, JOSEPH, Vershire.
Volunteered to go to Plattsburgh,
September, 1814, and went as far as
Bolton, Vt., serving 4 days in Lieut.
Phineus Kimball's Company of West
Fairlee. Also appears on roll of
Capt. Ebenezer Spencer's Company.
Ref: Book 52, AGO Pages 46, 48,
49, 50.

*PAINTER, LYMAN, 1st Sergeant.
Served in Sumner's Regt. Vt. Militia.

PALADAY, MICHAEL.
Enlisted Dec. 22, 1812 in Capt.
Phineas Williams' Company, 11th
Regt.; discharged Feb. 15, 1813. Ref:
R. & L. 1812, AGO Page 15.

PALMER, AHBEL, St. Albans.
Enlisted May 11, 1813 for 1 year in
Capt. John Wires' Company, 30th
Regt. Ref: R. & L. 1812, AGO
Page 40.

*PALMER, ALLEN, Musician.
Served in Capt. Brown's Company,
Col. Martindale's Regt. Detached
Militia in U. S. service 2 months and
14 days, 1812.

*PALMER, ALVA (or Parmer?)
Served from June 11 to June 14,
1813 in Capt. Samuel Blinn's Company, 1st Regt.

‡*PALMER, AMOS.
Served in Capt. Wright's Company,
Col. Martindale's Regt. Detached
Militia in U. S. service 2 months
and 14 days, 1812. Served from April
12 to April 21, 1814 in Capt. Shubael

Wales' Company, Col. W. B. Sumner's Regt. Pension Certificate of
widow, Adelia M., No. 22304.

*PALMER, ASA P.
Served in Capt. Phelps' Company,
Col. Wm. Williams' Regt. Detached
Militia in U. S. service 5 months,
1812.

*PALMER, CLEMONS C.
Served from April 12, to April 21,
1814 in Capt. Eseck Sprague's Company, Sumner's Regt.

*PALMER, CORNELIUS.
Enlisted Sept. 25, 1813 and served
1 month and 23 days in Capt. Elijah
Birge's Companyy, Col. Dixon's Regt.
Detached Militia in U. S. service.

*PALMER, DANIEL.
Served from April 12 to April 21,
1814 in Capt. Shubael Wales Company, Col. W. B. Sumner's Regt.

PALMER, DAVID, Fairfax.
Volunteered to go to Plattsburgh,
September, 1814, and served 8 days
in Capt. Josiah Grout's Company.
Ref: Book 51, AGO Page 103.

*PALMER, EBENEZER.
Served from April 12 to April 21,
1814 in Capt. Othniel Jewett's Company, Sumner's Regt.

*PALMER, ELIAS.
Served in Capt. Wright's Company,
Col. Martindale's Regt. Detached
Militia in U. S. service 2 months and
14 days, 1812. Served from April
12 to April 21, 1814 in Capt. Shubael
Wales' Company, Col. W. B. Sum-
ner's Regt.

PALMER, GEORGE.
Served from July 14, 1813 to May
10, 1814 in Capt. James Taylor's
Company, 30th Regt. Ref: R. & L.
1812, AGO Pages 52, 53, 57, 59.

*PALMER, HARVEY, Richford.
Enlisted Sept. 25, 1813 and served
1 month and 23 days in Capt. Martin D. Folett's Company, Col. Dixon's
Regt. Detached Militia in U. S. service.

*PALMER, HEMAN.
Served from April 12 to May 20, 1814
in Capt. George Fisher's Company,
Sumner's Regt.

*PALMER, JOHN, Captain.
Served from June 11 to June 14,
1813 and from Oct. 4 to Oct. 13, 1813
in command of company in 1st Regt.
2nd Brig. 3rd Div.

PALMER, JOHN.
Served from Feb. 19 to May 18, 1813
in Capt. Edgerton's Company, 11th
Regt. Ref: R. & L. 1812, AGO Page 3.

PALMER, JOSEPH.
Enlisted June 12, 1813 for 1 year
in Capt. Daniel Farrington's Company (also commanded by Capt.
Simeon Wright) 30th Regt.; on Muster Roll from March 1 to April 30,
1814. Also served in Capt. Howard's

Company and in Corning's Detachment and with Hospital Attendants, Vt. Ref: R. & L. 1812, AGO Pages 50 and 51.

*PALMER, JOSHUA,   Randolph.
Volunteered to go to Plattsburgh, September, 1814, and served in Capt. Lebbeus Egerton's Company.

PALMER, L. G.,   Swanton.
Served in Capt. V. R. Goodrich's Company, 11th Regt.; on Pay Roll from July 15 to Dec. 8, 1813; was in action at the battle of Lundy's Lane. Ref: Hemenway's Vt. Gazetteer, Vol. 2, Page 444.

PALMER, NATHANIEL.
Enlisted Jan. 9, 1813 in Capt. Jonathan Starks' Company, 11th Regt., on Pay Roll to May 31, 1813. Ref: R. & L. 1812, AGO Page 19.

‡*PALMER, RICHARD S., Corporal.
Served in Capt. Phelps' Company, Col. Wm. Williams' Regt. Detached Militia in U. S. service 5 months, 1812. Pension Certificate of widow, Sarah, No. 2810.

*PALMER, ROBERT.
Served in Capt. Barns' Company, Col. Wm. Williams' Regt. Detached Militia in U. S. service 5 months, 1812. Also served in 1 Regt. (Judson's) Vt. Militia.

PALMER, SAMUEL,   St. Albans.
Enlisted May 8, 1813 for 1 year in Capt. John Wires' Company, 30th Regt. Ref: R. & L. 1812, AGO Page 40.

PALMER, SAMUEL.
Served in Capt. Wm. Miller's Company and Capt. James Taylor's Company, 30th Regt. from March 30, 1814 to date of death, Aug. 28, 1814. Ref: R. & L. 1812, AGO Pages 53, 54, 57.

*PALMER, STEPHEN.
Served in Capt. Saxe's Company, Col. Wm. Williams' Regt. Detached Militia in U. S. service 4 months and 24 days, 1812.

‡*PALMER, THOMAS.
Served in Capt. Bingham's Company, Col. Jonathan Williams' Regt. Detached Militia in U. S. service 2 months and 9 days, 1812. Also served in Capt. Stewart's Company. Pension Certificate of widow, Elsie, No. 6530.

*PALMER, WILLIAM, Fifer.
Served in 1 Regt. (Judson's) Vt. Militia.

PALMER, ZALMON C.,Sergeant.
Served in Lt. V. R. Goodrich's Company, 11th Regt.; on Pay Roll for January and February, 1813. Ref: R. & L. 1812, AGO Page 11.

PANE, REUBEN.
Served in Lt. Wm. S. Foster's Company, 11th Regt.; on Pay Roll for January and February, 1813. Ref: R. & L. 1812, AGO Page 7.

*PANERS, ELAM (or Powers?)
Served in 4 Regt. (Williams') Vt. Militia.

‡PANGBORN, HOSEAH.
Enlisted March 30, 1814 during the war in Capt. James Taylor's Company, 30th Regt. Also served in Capt. Sanford's Company. Pension Certificate of widow, Christina, No. 35431. Ref: R. & L. 1812, AGO Page 53.

*PANGBORN, NATHANIEL, Ensign.
Served from April 12 to April 21, 1814 in Col. W. B. Sumner's Regt.

*PANGBOURN, NOAH.
Served from April 12 to May 20, 1814 in Capt. George Fisher's Company, Sumner's Regt.

*PANGBOURN, TRUMAN.
Served from April 12 to May 20, 1814 in Capt. George Fisher's Company, Sumner's Regt.

PANGBOURN, ZEBA.
Served from April 12 to April 21, 1814 in Capt. Edmund B. Hill's Company, Sumner's Regt. Ref: Book 52, AGO Page 283.

PANGBURN, HOSEA,   Elizabeth, N. Y.
Enlisted March 29, 1814 during the war and served in Capt. Wm. Miller's Company and Capt. Gideon Spencer's Company, 30th Regt. Ref: R. & L. 1812, AGO Pages 54, 55, 57.

*PANGMAN, LUTHER.
Served from June 11 to June 14, 1813 in Capt. Moses Jewett's Company, 1st Regt. 2nd Brig. 3rd Div.

PANO, LAWRENCE.
Served from March 4 to June 3, 1813 in Lieut. V. R. Goodrich's Company, 11th Regt. Ref: R. & L. 1812, AGO Page 10.

PARCELS, ISAAC.
Enlisted Dec. 4, 1812 for 5 years in company of late Capt. J. Brooks, commanded by Lieut. John I. Cromwell, Corps of U. S. Artillery; on Muster Roll from April 30 to June 30, 1814. Ref: R. & L. 1812, AGO Page 18.

*PARCHER, TIMOTHY.
Served in 4 Regt. (Williams') Vt. Militia.

PARDIT, EPHRAIM.
Was one of the Vermont men on board the British prison ship "San Antonio" at Chatam, England. Ref: Records of Naval Records and Library, Navy Dept.

*PARDO, JAMES.
Served in 1 Regt. (Judson's) Vt. Militia.

PARIS, CALEB.
Served in Capt. Brown's Company, Col. Martindale's Regt. Detached Militia in U. S. service 2 months and 14 days, 1812. Ref: Book 53, AGO Page 98.

*PARISH, DANIEL,   Randolph.
Volunteered to go to Plattsburgh,
September, 1814, and served in Capt.
Lebbeus Egerton's Company.

PARISH, ELISHA,   Randolph.
Volunteered to transport men and
supplies at time of battle at Platts-
burgh and served about 4 days in
Capt. Lebbeus Egerton's Company.
Ref: Book 52, AGO Page 87.

*PARISH, GUY.
Served in Dixon's Regt. Vt. Militia.

‡*PARISH, JACOB K.,   Randolph.
Served in Capt. Wright's Company,
Col. Fifield's Regt. Detached Militia
in U. S. service 6 months, 1812.
Volunteered to go to Plattsburgh, September, 1814, and served as 1st Sergeant in Capt. Lebbeus Egerton's
Company. Also served in Capt.
Wheatley's Company. Pension Certificate No. 2119. Pension Certificate
of widow, Mary A., No. 32535.

PARISH, JOHN,   Morristown.
Volunteered to go to Plattsburgh,
September, 1814, and served 8 days
in Capt. Denison Cook's Company.
Ref: Book 51, AGO Pages 202 and 206.

PARISH, LEVI, Corporal.
Served in 1st Regt. of Detached Militia of Vt. in U. S. service at Champlain from Nov. 18 to Nov. 19, 1812.

‡*PARISH, LUTHER, Sergeant, Highgate.
Served in Capt. Saxe's Company, Col.
Wm. Williams' Regt. stationed at
Swanton Falls in 1812. Enlisted Sept.
25, 1813 in company of Capt. Jon-
athan Prentiss, Jr., Dixon's Regt.
Pension Certificate No. 15123.

*PARISH. RODNEY.
Served in 1 Regt. (Judson's) Vt.
Militia.

*PARK, STEPHEN.
Served in Sumner's Regt. Vt. Militia.

*PARKEL, JESSE, Lieutenant.
Served in 1 Regt. (Martindale's) Vt.
Militia.

*PARKER, AARON.
Enlisted Sept. 25, 1813 and served
1 month and 23 days in Capt. Elijah
Birge's Company, Col. Dixon's Regt.
Detached Militia in U. S. service.

PARKER, ABRAHAM,   Hancock.
Volunteered to go to Plattsburgh.
September, 1814, and served 7 days
as teamster in Capt. Asaph Smith's
Company. Ref: Book 51, AGO Page
20.

PARKER, AMOS.
Enlisted Sept. 19, 1812 for 5 years
in company of late Capt. J. Brooks,
commanded by Lt. John I. Cromwell,
Corps of U. S. Artillery; on Muster
Roll from April 30 to June 30, 1814.
Ref: R. & L. 1812, AGO Page 18.

PARKER, DANIEL,   St. Albans.
Enlisted May 29, 1813 for 1 year in
Capt. John Wires' Company, 30th
Regt. Ref: R. & L. 1812, AGO Page
40.

‡*PARKER, DAVID, Corporal.
Served in Capt. Hopkins' Company,
Col. Martindale's Regt. Detached
Militia in U. S. service 2 months and
13 days, 1812. Also served in Capt.
Harper's Company. Pension Certifi-
cate No. 3083. Pension Certificate of
widow, Olive, No. 24539.

*PARKER, DENNIS,   Highgate.
Served from Sept. 1, 1812 in Capt.
Conrade Saxe's Company, 4 Regt.
(Williams') Vt. Militia.

*PARKER, DEXTER,   Stowe.
Volunteered to go to Plattsburgh,
September, 1814, and was at the
battle, serving in Capt. Nehemiah
Perkins' Company, 4 Regt. (Peck's).

‡PARKER, EBENEZER P.,   Vershire.
Volunteered to go to Plattsburgh,
September, 1814, and served 3 days
in Capt. Ira Corse's Company. Pension Certificate of widow, Laura, No.
21670.

PARKER, FRANCIS B.,   Bakersfield.
Volunteered and was at the battle
of Plattsburgh Sept. 11, 1814, serving in Capt. M. Stearns' Company.
Ref: Hemenway's Vt. Gazetteer, Vol.
2, Page 393.

PARKER, GEORGE..
Volunteered to go to Plattsburgh,
September, 1814, and served 7 days
in Capt. Frederick Griswold's Com-
pany, raised in Brookfield, Vt. Ref:
Book 52, AGO Page 52.

*PARKER, HARVY.
Served from April 12 to April 15,
1814 in Lieut. Justus Foote's Company, Sumner's Regt.

*PARKER, HENRY (or Harry).
Served in Capt. Wright's Company,
Col. Martindale's Regt. Detached
Militia in U. S. service 2 months
and 14 days, 1812.

PARKER, JAMES..
Served from May 1st to June 30,
1814 in Alexander Parris' company
of Artificers.

PARKER, JAMES W.
Volunteered to go to Plattsburgh,
September, 1814, and served 7 days
in Capt. Asaph Smith's Company.
Ref: Book 51, AGO Page 20.

*PARKER, JOHN.
Served in 3 Regt. (Williams') Vt.
Militia.

PARKER, JOHN,   South Richford.
Served from March 29 to June 28,
1813 in Capt. Samul Gordon's Detachment of Recruits, 11th Regt. Ref:
R. & L. 1812, AGO Page 8.

PARKER, JOHN.
Served from May 1 to June 30, 1814
in Capt. Alexander Brooks' Corps of
Artillery. Ref: R. & L. 1812, AGO
Page 31.

‡PARKER, JOHN B.
Served in Capt. Silas Dickinson's
Company. Pension Certificate of wid-
ow, Fanny, No. 5964.

PARKER, JONAS,   Williamstown.
Volunteered and was at the battle
of Plattsburgh Sept. 11, 1814 serving 8 days in Capt. David Robinson's
Company. Ref: Book 52, AGO Pages
2 and 10.

PARKER, JONATHAN,   Clarendon.
Enlisted Aug. 20, 1813 for 1 year
and served in Capt. Daniel Farrington's Company (also commanded by
Capt. Simeon Wright) 30th Regt.;
on Muster Roll from March 1 to
April 30, 1814. Served from Sept. 1,
1814 to June 16. 1815 in Capt. Sanford's Company, 30th Inf. Ref: R.
& L. 1812, AGO Pages 23, 50, 51.

PARKER, JONATHAN C.
Served from March 3 to June 2, 1813
in Capt. Phineas Williams' Company,
11th Regt. Ref: R. & L. 1812, AGO
Page 14.

PARKER, JOSEPH.
Served to Feb. 4, 1813 in Capt.
Weeks' Company, 11th Regt.; on
Pay Roll for January and February.
Ref: R. & L. 1812, AGO Page 5.

PARKER, JOSIAH.   Weybridge.
Volunteered to go to Plattsburgh.
September, 1814, and served 8 days
in Capt. Silas Wright's Company. Ref:
Book 51, AGO Page 11.

*PARKER, LEWIS.
Served from Sept. 25 to Nov. 2, 1813
in Capt. N. B. Eldridge's Company,
Col. Dixon's Regt. Detached Militia in
U. S. service.

*PARKER, MORRILL, Sergeant, Whiting.
Served from April 13 to April 16,
1814 in Capt. Salmon Foster's Company. Sumner's Regt.; volunteered
to go to Plattsburgh, September. 1814,
and served 9 days in same company.

*PARKER, NAHAM, Sergeant.
Served from April 12 to April 21,
1814 in Lieut. Justus Foote's Company, Sumner's Regt.

PARKER, NATHAN. Londonderry, N. H.
Enlisted at Burlington Feb. 7, 1814
for 5 years in Capt. Wm. Miller's
Company. 30th Regt; on Muster Roll
to Aug. 31, 1814. Ref: R. & L. 1812,
AGO Pages 54 and 55.

PARKER, NATHANIEL, Musician. Fair-
fax? Served from Aug. 8, 1812 in
company of Capt. Joseph Beeman
Jr., 11th Regt. U. S. Inf. under
Col. Ira Clark. Served in Capt.
Samuel H. Holly's Company, 11th
Regt.; on Pay Roll for January and
February, 1813. Ref: R. & L. 1812,
AGO Page 25; Hemenway's Vt. Ga-
zetteer, Vol. 2. Page 402.

*PARKER, ORIN.
Served from Sept. 25 to Sept. 30,
1813 in Capt. Elijah Birge's Company, Dixon's Regt.

*PARKER, RUFUS.   Clarendon.
Served in Capt. Needham's Company,
Col. Martindale's Regt. Detached
Militia in U. S. service 2 months
and 14 days. 1812. Enlisted May 1,

1813 for 1 year in Capt. Daniel Farrington's Company, 30th Regt. (also
commanded by Capt. Simeon Wright);
on Muster Roll March 1 to April 30,
1814.

‡PARKER, SIMON.
Served in Capt. Wright's Company.
Pension Certificate No. 5731.

*PARKER, STERLING. Captain.
Served in 3 Regt. (Bowdish) Vt.
Militia.

*PARKER, SYLVANUS,   Waterbury.
Served in Capt. O. Lowry's Company, Col. Wm. Williams' Regt. Detached Militia in U. S. service 4
months and 26 days, 1812. Volunteered to go to Plattsburgh, September,
1814, and served 11 days in Capt.
George Atkins' Company, 4th Regt.
(Peck's).

PARKER, THOMAS, Sergeant.
Served from May 12, 1813 to May 23,
1814 in Capt. Gideon Spencer's Company, 30th Regt. Ref: R. & L. 1812,
AGO Page 56.

PARKER, THOMAS, Corporal.
Enlisted April 26, 1813 for 1 year in
Capt. James Taylor's Company, 30th
Regt.; on Muster Roll Nov. 30 to
Dec. 31, 1813. Ref: R. & L. 1812,
AGO Pages 52 and 58.

PARKER, THOMAS,   Montpelier.
Volunteered to go to Plattsburgh,
September, 1814, and served 8 days
in Capt. Timothy Hubbard's Company. Ref: Book 52, AGO Page 256.

*PARKER, THOMAS.
Served in Capt. Mason's Company,
Col. Fifield's Regt. Detached Militia
in U. S. service 5 months and 8 days,
1812.

PARKER, THOMAS G.,   Barre.
Volunteered to go to Plattsburgh,
September, 1814, and served 8 days
in Capt. Warren Ellis' Company. Ref:
Book 52, AGO Pages 230, 233, 242.

PARKER, TIMOTHY.
Served in Capt. Lowry's Company,
Col. Wm. Williams' Regt. Detached
Militia in U. S. service 4 months and
26 days, 1812. Ref: Book 53, AGO
Page 12.

*PARKER, WILLIAM.
Served in Tyler's Regt. Vt. Militia.

PARKHURST, JABEZ, Lieutenant.
Appointed Cadet Military Academy
July 21, 1813; 3rd Lieutenant Light
Artillery July 21, 1814; transferred
to Artillery Corps May 17, 1815. Ref:
Heitman's Historical Register & Dic-
tionary USA.

*PARKHURST, LEMUEL, Corporal.
Served as corporal in Corning's Detachment, Vt. Militia and as a private in 4 Regt. (Peck's) Vt. Militia.

*PARKILL, DAVID.
Served from April 12 to April 21,
1814 in Capt. Edmund B. Hill's Company, Sumner's Regt.

*PARKS, ABIJAH.
Served in Capt. Sabin's Company,
Col. Jonathan Williams' Regt. Detached Militia in U. S. service 2
months and 6 days, 1812.

PARKS, BENJAMIN M.
Served from April 8 to July 7, 1813
in Capt. Samul Gordon's Company,
11th Regt. Ref: R. & L. 1812, AGO
Page 8.

*PARKS, HORATIO,   Enosburgh.
Served from Oct. 15 to Nov. 17, 1813
in Capt. Asahel Scovell's Company,
Col. Clark's Rifle Corps.

*PARKS, JACOB P.
Served with Hospital Attendants, Vt.

‡*PARKS, JOHN B., Fifer.
Served in Capt. Ormsbie's Company,
1st Regt. (Martindale's) Vt. Militia. Pension Certificate of widow, Rebecca, No. 14056.

*PARKS, SILAS LEONARD.
Served in Capt. Utley's Company.
Pension Certificate No. 14715.

PARLIMENT, JAMES.
Served from July 1 to Dec. 2, 1813;
no organization given. Ref: R. & L.
1812, AGO Page 29.

*PARLIN, ELISHA,   Barton.
Served in Capt. Mason's Company,
Col. Fifield's Regt. Detached Militia
in U. S. service 5 months and 26
days, 1812.

*PARLING, ABEL.
Served in 2 Regt. (Fifield's) Vt.
Militia.

*PARMELEE, MILTON.
Served from April 19 to April 21,
1814 in Capt. Othniel Jewett's Company, Sumner's Regt.

PARMENTER, VALENTINE, Drummer.
Served from April 2 to July 1, 1813
in Capt. Charles Follett's Company,
11th Regt. Ref: R. & L. 1812, AGO
Page 13.

‡PARMENTERE, ABEL.
Served in Capt. Carpenter's Company. Pension Certificate No. 23333.

PARMERTON, ICHABOD.
Enlisted Jan. 1, 1813 in company
of late Capt. J. Brooks commanded
by Lt. John I. Cromwell, Corps of
U. S. Artillery; re-enlisted June 3,
1814; on Muster Roll from April 30
to June 30, 1814. Ref: R. & L. 1812,
AGO Page 18.

*PARMETER, MARTIN.
Served in Capt. Durkee's Company,
Col. Fifield's Regt. Detached Militia
in U. S. service 6 months.

*PARMETER, WALTER.
Served in Capt. Durkee's Company,
Col. Fifield's Regt. Detached Militia
in U. S. service 6 months.

*PARQUET, LEMUEL. Corporal.
Served in Corning's Detachment, Vt.
Militia.

*PARR, STEPHEN.
Served from Sept. 23 to Nov. 3, 1813
in Capt. Amasa Mansfield's Company,
Dixon's Regt.

PARRETT, JOHN.
Enlisted March 18, 1813 in Capt.
Charles Follett's Company, 11th Regt.;
on Pay Roll to May 31, 1813. Ref:
R. & L. 1812, AGO Page 13.

PARRINGTON, STEPHEN.
Served from Feb. 20 to May 9, 1813
in Capt. Charles Follett's Company,
11th Regt. Ref: R. & L. 1812, AGO
Page 13.

*PARRIS, CALEB.
Served in 1 Regt. (Martindale's) Vt.
Militia.

*PARSONS, ABIAL, Drum Major.
Served in 3 Regt. (Williams') Vt.
Militia.

PARSONS, DANIEL, Lieutenant.
Appointed Ensign March 28, 1814 and
3rd Lieutenant May 1, 1814 31st
Inf. Ref: Governor and Council Vt.,
Vol. 6, Page 478.

PARSONS, DAVID,   Montpelier.
Volunteered to go to Plattsburgh,
September, 1814, and served 8 days
in Capt. Timothy Hubbard's Company.
Ref: Book 52, AGO Page 256.

PARSONS, EBEN.
Enlisted Sept. 30, 1813 for 1 year
in Capt. James Taylor's Company,
30th Regt. Ref: R. & L. 1812, AGO
Page 53.

‡PARSONS, ELDAD.
Served in Capt. B. Holmes' Company.
Pension Certificate of widow, Abigail,
No. 30708.

‡*PARSONS, ELIAS S.,   Randolph.
Volunteered to go to Plattsburgh,
September, 1814, and served in Capt.
Lebbeus Egerton's Company. Pension
Certificate of widow, Laurenia, No.
3469.

*PARSONS, JOSHUA, Corporal.
Served in Capt. Burnap's Company,
Col. Jonathan Williams' Regt. Detached Militia in U. S. service 2
months and 13 days, 1812.

*PARSONS, LUKE, Captain.
Served in 3 Regt. (Williams') Vt.
Militia.

PARSONS, PHINEHAS,   Montpelier.
Volunteered to go to Plattsburgh,
September, 1814, and served 8 days
in Capt. Timothy Hubbard's Company. Ref: Book 52, AGO Pages 246
and 256.

‡*PARSONS, SAMUEL.
Served in Capt. Amos Robinson's
Company, Dixon's Regt. Vt. Militia.
Also served in Capt. Hoyle's Com-
pany. Pension Certificate No. 13260.
Pension Certificate of widow, Sarah,
No. 24047.

PARSONS, SYLVANUS,   Jericho.
Volunteered Sept. 7, 1814 and served
in Peter L. Allen's Company, Col.
George Tyler's Regt. Ref: History
of Jericho, Page 143.

*PARTCH. DOCTOR.
Served from June 11 to June 14.
1813 in Capt. Thomas Dorwin's Company, 1st Regt. 2nd Brig. 3rd Div.

*PARTCH, JAMES.
Served from June 11 to June 14,
1813 in Capt. John M. Eldridge's
Company, 1st Regt. 2nd Brig. 3rd
Div.

*PARTCH. JOHN, Musician.
Served from June 11 to June 14,
1813 in Capt. Thomas Dorwin's Company, 1st Regt. 2nd Brig. 3rd Div.

PARTRIDGE, AMOS,   Braintree.
Volunteered and went to Plattsburgh
Sept. 10, 1814, serving in Capt. Lot
Hudson's Company. Ref: Book 52,
AGO Page 24.

PARTRIDGE. ALDEN, Captain.
Appointed Captain Engineers July 23,
1810; resigned April 15, 1818; died
Jan. 17, 1854. Ref: Heitman's Historical Register & Dictionary USA.

*PARTRIDGE, APPOLLOS, Sergeant.
Enlisted Sept. 25, 1813 in Capt. Elijah
Birge's Company, Dixon's Regt.

PARTRIDGE. ASA.   Barre.
Volunteered to go to Plattsburgh.
September. 1814, and served 10 days
in Capt. Warren Ellis' Company. Ref:
Book 52, AGO Pages 228, 236, 242.

PARTRIDGE. ASA. Lieutenant.
Appointed Sergeant and Quartermaster Sergeant 14th Inf. May 3 to
September, 1813; Ensign 14th Inf.
Sept. 24, 1813; 3 Lieutenant Nov.
14, 1813; resigned May 30, 1814. Ref:
Heitman's Historical Register & Dictionary USA.

‡*PARTRIDGE, ISAAC N.
Served in Capt. Burnap's Company.
Col. Jonathan Williams' Regt. Detached Militia in U. S. service 5
days, 1812. Pension Certificate of
widow, Mary E., No. 32423.

‡PARTRIDGE. SAMUEL.
Served in Capt. Alden Partridge's
Company. Pension Certificate No.
2376. Pension Certificate of widow.
Emma G., No. 33438.

PARTRIDGE. STEPHEN.
Volunteered to go to Plattsburgh.
September. 1814, and served 7 days
in Capt. Frederick Griswold's Company, raised in Brookfield, Vt. Ref:
Book 52, AGO Page 52.

PARTRIDGE. WILLIAM. Captain.
Appointed Captain Engineers July 1,
1812; died Sept. 20, 1812. Ref: Heitman's Historical Register & Dictionary USA.

PASSWATERS, JENMIAH.   Delaware.
Served from Feb. 1 to Aug. 11, 1814
in Capt. Gilders' Company. 14th Inf.
Ref: R. & L. 1812. AGO Page 30.

PATCH. DAVID.
Served from March 16 to June 15.
1813 in Capt. Jonathan Starks' Company. 11th Regt. Ref: R. & L. 1812,
AGO Page 19.

PATCH. REUBEN.
Served from May 31 to Aug. 31, 1813
in Capt. Benjamin Bradford's Company. Ref: R. & L. 1812, AGO
Page 26.

*PATCH. SAMUEL.
Enlisted Sept. 25. 1813 in Capt.
Thomas Waterman's Company, Dixon's Regt.

PATNOE, LEWIS.
Served from April 23 to June 30,
1814 in Regt. of Light Dragoons. Ref:
R. & L. 1812, AGO Page 21.

PATRICK. JOSEPH JR.
Volunteered to go to Plattsburgh,
September, 1814, and served 7 days
in Capt. Asaph Smith's Company.
Ref: Book 51, AGO Page 20.

PATRICK, MATHEW JR., Lieutenant.
Appointed 3rd Lieutenant 40th Inf.
Feb. 10, 1814; honorably discharged
June 15. 1815. Ref: Heitman's Historical Register & Dictionary USA.

*PATT, OLNEY.
Served in 1 Regt. (Martindale's) Vt.
Militia.

*PATTEN. MARK T.
Served with Hospital Attendants, Vt.

PATTERSON, ANSEL.   Barre.
Volunteered to go to Plattsburgh,
September. 1814, and served 10 days
in Capt. Warren Ellis' Company. Ref:
Book 52, AGO Page 242.

*PATTERSON. ISAAC.   Stowe.
Volunteered to go to Plattsburgh,
September, 1814, and served in Capt.
Nehemiah Perkins' Company, 4th
Regt. (Peck's). Also served in Sumner's Regt. Vt. Militia. Ref: Hemenway's Vt. Gazetteer, Vol. 2, Page
742.

PATTERSON, JAMES.   Addison.
Volunteered to go to Plattsburgh,
September. 1814, and was in the
battle. serving 9 days in Capt. George
Fisher's Company. Sumner's Regt.
Ref: Book 51. AGO Page 5.

PATTERSON, JAMES.   Strafford.
Volunteered to go to Plattsburgh,
September. 1814, and served in Capt.
Joseph Barrett's Company. Ref: Book
52, AGO Pages 111 and 112.

PATTERSON. JEREMIAH.
Enlisted Oct. 28. 1812 for 5 years in
company of late Capt. J. Brooks, commanded by Lt. John I. Cromwell,
Corps of U. S. Artillery; on Muster
Roll from April 30 to June 30, 1814.
Ref: R. & L. 1812. AGO Page 18.

PATTERSON, JOSEPH.
Served in Capt. Phineas Williams'
Company. 11th Regt.; on Pay Roll
for January and February, 1813. Ref:
R. & L. 1812, AGO Page 15.

*PATTERSON. LEWIS. Lieutenant. Stowe.
Volunteered to go to Plattsburgh.
September, 1814, and was at the
battle. serving in Capt. Nehemiah
Perkins' Company. 4 Regt. (Peck's).
Also served as Sergeant in Corning's
Detachment, Vt. Militia.

PATTERSON, NELSON.
Served in Capt. Benjamin Bradford's
Company; on Muster Roll from May
31 to Aug. 31, 1813. Ref: R. & L.
1812, AGO Page 26.

*PATTERSON, WILLIAM.
Served in Capt. Sanford's Company.
Pension Certificate No. 2642.

PATTISON, WILLIAM,   St. Albans.
Enlisted May 1, 1813 for 1 year in
Capt. John Wires' Company, 30th
Regt. Ref: R. & L. 1812, AGO
Page 40.

*PATTISON, WILLIAM, Brigade Chap-
lain. Served with General and Staff
(Orms') Vt. Militia.

PAUL, ALPHIUS.
Served from Feb. 8 to May 7, 1813
in Lieut. V. R. Goodrich's Company,
11th Regt. Ref: R. & L. 1812, AGO
Page 10.

PAUL, BENONI O.
Enlisted May 7, 1813 in Capt. Simeon
Wright's Company and served to date
of death, March 7, 1814. Ref: R. &
L. 1812, AGO Page 51.

*PAYN, ROSWELL.
Served from April 12 to April 21,
1814 in Capt. Shubael Wales' Company, Col. W. B. Sumner's Regt.

*PAYN, SAMUEL.
Served from June 11 to June 14,
1813 in Capt. Samuel Blinn's Company, 1st Regt.

*PAYNE, ASEL.
Served in Capt. Wheeler's Company,
Col. Fifield's Regt. Detached Militia
in U. S. service 3 months and 16
days, 1812.

*PAYNE, JAMES H.
Served from April 12 to April 21,
1814 in Capt. Othniel Jewett's Company, Sumner's Regt.

PAYNE, SAMUEL,   Fairfield.
Volunteered to go to Plattsburgh,
September, 1814, and served 3 days
in Capt. Benjamin Wooster's Com-
pany. Ref: Book 51, AGO Page 188;
Hemenway's Vt. Gazetteer, Vol. 2,
Page 408.

*PAYNE, STEPHEN.
Served in Capt. Pettis' Company.
Pension Certificate No. 24690.

*PAYSON, ALONSON.
Served in 3 Regt. (Tyler's) Vt. Militia.

PAYSON, EDWARD.
Served from May 1 to May 31, 1814
in Alexander Parris' Company of Artificers. Ref: R. & L. 1812, AGO
Page 24.

*PAYSON, SAMUEL.
Served in 1 Regt. (Martindale's) Vt.
Militia.

PEABODY, ASA. Ensign.
Appointed Ensign 31st Inf. April 30,
1813; resigned April 27, 1814. Also

served in Capt. Stuart's Company.
Pension Certificate No. 19869. Ref:
Heitman's Historical Register & Dic-
tionary USA.

PEABODY, LOUIS F.
Served in Capt. Benjamin Bradford's
Company; on Muster Roll from May
31 to Aug. 31, 1813. Ref: R. & L.
1812, AGO Page 26.

‡*PEACH, THOMAS, Surgeon.
Served in 2 Regt. (Fifield's) Vt. Militia. Pension Certificate No. 16195.

*PEACOCK, GEORGE W., Corporal.
Served from Sept. 23 to Nov. 8, 1813
in Capt. Amasa Mansfield's Company,
Dixon's Regt.

*PEAKE, MARCUS.
Served in Capt. Briggs' Company,
Col. Jonathan Williams' Regt. Detached Militia in U. S. service 2
months and 13 days, 1812.

PEAKE, THOMAS.   Sheldon.
Volunteered to go to Plattsburgh,
September, 1814, and served in Capt.
Samuel Weed's Company. Ref: Book
51, AGO Pages 152, 155, 176.

*PEARCE, PHINEAS.
Served in 1 Regt. (Martindale's) Vt.
Militia.

*PEARCE, SOLOMON.
Served in Capt. Morrill's Company,
Col. Fifield's Regt. Detached Militia
in U. S. service 6 months and 5
days, 1812.

*PEARCH, WARREN.
Served in Sumner's Regt. Vt. Militia.

PEARL, SIMON.
Enlisted Dec. 29, 1812 in Capt. Jonathan Starks' Company, 11th Regt.;
on Pay Roll to May 31, 1813. Ref:
R. & L. 1812, AGO Page 19.

‡PEARSON, ABIAL.
Served in Capt. Phelps' Company.
Pension Certificate No. 20543.

‡*PEARSON, CHESTER (or Chesterfield),
Fifer. Served in Capt. Phelps' Company, Col. Jonathan Williams' Regt.
Detached Militia in U. S. service 2
months and 21 days, 1812. Pension
Certificate of widow, Mary Ann, No.
8956.

‡*PEARSON, JAMES G.
Served in Capt. Mason's Company,
Col. Fifield's Regt. Detached Militia
in U. S. service 3 months and 16
days, 1812. Pension Certificate of
widow, Polly, No. 7259.

‡PEARSON, LEONARD.
Served in Capt. Akin's Company. Pension Certificate No. 6064.

PEARSONS, SAMUEL.
Served in Capt. Robinson's Company,
Col. Dixon's Regt. Detached Militia
in U. S. service 1 month and 23 days,
1813. Ref: Book 53, AGO Page 107.

*PEAS, GOYAS.
Served in 3 Regt. (Tyler's) Vt. Militia.

*PEASE, EBENEZER.
Served in 1 Regt. (Judson's) Vt. Militia.

PEASE, EDWARD.
Volunteered to go to Plattsburgh, September, 1814, and served 7 days in company of Capt. Frederick Griswold of Brookfield. Ref: Book 52, AGO Page 52.

*PEASE, ELIJAH.
Served from June 11 to June 14, 1813 in Capt. John Palmer's Company, 1st Regt. 2nd Brig. 3rd Div.

*PEASE, ENOCH,   Enosburgh.
Enlisted Sept. 25, 1813 and served 1 month and 23 days in Capt. Martin D. Folett's Company, Col. Dixon's Regt. Detached Militia in U. S. service.

*PEASE, ENOS.
Enlisted Sept. 25, 1813 in Capt. Jesse Post's Company, Dixon's Regt.

*PEASE, LEICESTER.
Served from June 11 to June 14, 1813 in Capt. Hezekiah Barns' Company, 1st Regt. 2nd Brig. 3rd Div.

‡*PEASE, LYMAN.
Served from June 11 to June 14, 1813 in Capt. Ithiel Stone's Company, 1st Regt. 2nd Brig. 3rd Div. Pension Certificate No. 34624.

*PEASELEE, SAMUEL.
Served in 1 Regt. (Judson's) Vt. Militia.

PEAVY, JACOB,   Pessenfield.
Served from May 1 to Aug. 12, 1814 in 11th Inf. Ref: R. & L. 1812, AGO Page 30.

*PECK, ALANSON, Sergeant.
Enlisted April 12, 1814 in Capt. Shubael Wales' Company, Col. W. B. Sumner's Regt.; transferred to Capt. Salmon Foster's Company, Sumner's Regt. April 13, 1814 and served to April 21, 1814.

‡*PECK, ARAD.
Served in Capt. Phelps' Company, Col. Wm. Williams' Regt. Detached Militia in U. S. service 5 months, 1812. Also served in Sumner's Regt. Vt. Militia. Pension Certificate No. 2783. Pension Certificate of widow, Nancy, No. 29836.

‡*PECK, BENJAMIN.
Served in Capt. Barns' Company, Col. Wm. Williams' Regt. Detached Militia in U. S. service 5 months, 1812. Also served in 1 Regt. (Judson's) Vt. Militia. Pension Certificate of widow, Anna, No. 672.

PECK, CHARLES. Sergeant.
Served from May 7, 1813 to May 15, 1814 in Capt. Gideon Spencer's Company and Capt. James Taylor's Company, 30th Regt. Ref: R. & L. 1812. AGO Pages 56 and 58.

*PECK, EP.
Served in 1 Regt. (Martindale's) Vt. Militia.

PECK, HENRY.   St. Albans.
Enlisted May 5, 1813 for 1 year in Capt. John Wires' Company, 30th Regt. Ref: R. & L. 1812, AGO Page 40.

*PECK, HIRAM, 1st Major.
Served in 4 Regt. (Peck's) Vt. Militia.

PECK, HIRAM,   Clarendon.
Volunteered to go to Plattsburgh, September, 1814, and served 7 days in Capt. Durham Sprague's Company. Ref: Book 52, AGO Page 128.

*PECK, JEDEDIAH.
Served from April 12 to April 21, 1814 in Capt. Eseck Sprague's Company, Sumner's Regt.

*PECK, JOEL.
Served from June 11 to June 14, 1813 in Capt. John M. Eldridge's Company, 1st Regt. 2nd Brig. 3rd Div.

PECK, JOHN, Colonel and Brig. General, Waterbury. Served as Lt. Colonel in 4 Regt. (Peck's) Vt. Militia. Also served as Brig. General of Vt. Militia at the Battle of Plattsburgh. (For biographical sketch see Theo. G. Lewis' History of Waterbury, Pages 44 and 47.)

‡*PECK, JOHN.
Served from Oct. 5 to Oct. 16, 1813 in Capt. Roswell Hunt's Company, 3 Regt. (Tyler's). Also served in Capt. Spencer's Company. Pension Certificate of widow, Amy, No. 29444.

PECK, LEWIS,   Barre.
Volunteered to go to Plattsburgh, September, 1814, and served 10 days in Capt. Warren Ellis' Company. Ref: Book 52, AGO Page 242.

*PECK, NATHAN (or Pike?), Drummer.
Served in Sumner's Regt. Vt. Militia.

*PECK, NIRAM.
Served from April 12 to April 21, 1814 in Capt. Eseck Sprague's Company, Sumner's Regt.

PECK, NOAH,   Clarendon.
Volunteered to go to Plattsburgh, September, 1814, and served 7 days in Capt. Durham Sprague's Company. Ref: Book 52, AGO Page 128.

PECK, NOAH,   Ira.
Volunteered to go to Plattsburgh, September, 1814, and served 4 days in Capt. Matthew Anderson's Company. Ref: Book 52, AGO Page 144.

*PECK, PETHRO.
Served in 1 Regt. (Martindale's) Vt. Militia.

*PECK, RULUF.
Served in 1 Regt. (Judson's) Vt. Militia.

*PECK, SOLOMON.
Served in Capt. Rogers' Company, Col. Fifield's Regt. Detached Militia in U. S. service 2 months and 18 days, 1812.

*PECK, WILLIAM.
Served from April 12 to April 21,
1814 in Capt. Edmund B. Hill's Company, Sumner's Regt.

*PECK, ZERA.
Served from June 11 to June 14,
1813 in Capt. John M. Eldridge's Company, 1st Regt. 2nd Brig. 3rd Div.
Ref: R. & L. 1812, AGO Page 35.

*PECKHAM, GEORGE,   Fairfield.
Served in Capt. Kendall's Company,
Col. Wm. Williams' Regt. Detached
Militia in U. S. service 4 months and
8 days, 1812. Ref: Book 53, AGO
Page 20.

PECORE, FRANCIS.
Served from Feb. 5, 1813 to June 30,
1814 in Regt. of Light Dragoons.
Ref: R. & L. 1812, AGO Page 21.

*PEESHO, PETER.
Served with Hospital Attendants, Vt.

*PEET, FREDERICK.
Served in Sumner's Regt. Vt. Militia.

*PEET, WALKER.
Served in Sumner's Regt. Vt. Militia.

PELKEY, FRANCIS.
Served in Capt. Benjamin S. Edgerton's Company, 11th Regt.; on Pay
Roll for September, and October, 1812,
and January and February, 1813.
Ref: R. & L. 1812, AGO Pages 1
and 2.

PELLET, CALEB.
Served in Capt. Langworthy's Company. Col. Dixon's Regt. Detached
Militia in U. S. service 1 month and
1 day, 1813. Ref: Book 53, AGO Page
110.

PELSUE, GEORGE.
Served in Capt. Samuel Gordon's Com-
pany, 11th Regt.; on Pay Roll for
January and February, 1813. Ref:
R. & L. 1812, AGO Page 9.

PELTON, CHARLES,   Pawlet.
Served in Capt. Hotchkiss' Company,
Col. Martindale's Regt. Detached
Militia in U. S. service 2 months
and 13 days, 1812. Ref: Book 53,
AGO Page 25.

*PELTON, MOSES.   Richmond.
Volunteered to go to Plattsburgh,
September, 1814, and served in Capt.
Roswell Hunt's Company, 3 Regt.
(Tyler's), 9 days. Also served in 1
Regt. (Judson's) Vt. Militia. Ref:
Book 51, AGO Page 82.

*PELTON, SAMUEL.
Served in Tyler's Regt. Vt. Militia.

PELTON, STEPHEN.
Enlisted at Erie April 29, 1813 in
U. S. Marine Corps. Ref: Book 52,
AGO Page 294.

PELVES, LYMAN.
Enlisted May 11, 1813 for 1 year in
Capt. James Taylor's Company, 30th
Regt. Ref: R. & L. 1812, AGO Page
58.

*PEMBERTON, WILLIAM.
Served in Sumner's Regt. Vt. Militia.

*PENGREE, WILLIAM, Corporal.
Served in Capt. Cross' Company,
Col. Martindale's Regt. Detached
Militia in U. S. service 2 months and
14 days, 1812.

PENN, THOMAS, Musician.
Served from July 1 to Aug. 15, 1814;
no organization given. Ref: R. & L.
1812, AGO Page 29.

*PENNIMAN, UDNEY H.
Served from April 12 to April 15,
1814 in Lieut. Justus Foote's Company, Sumner's Regt.

PENNOCK, ISAAC,   Strafford.
Volunteered to go to Plattsburgh,
September, 1814, and served in Capt.
Cyril Chandler's Company. Ref: Book
52, AGO Page 42.

PENNOCK, LEWIS, 1st Sergeant, Strafford. Volunteered to go to Plattsburgh, September, 1814, and served 5
days in Capt. Cyril Chandler's Company. Ref: Book 52, AGO Page 42.

PENNOCK, PETER.   Strafford.
Volunteered to go to Plattsburgh,
September, 1814, and served in Capt.
Joseph Barrett's Company. Ref: Book
52, AGO Page 41.

PENNY, RICHARD.
Served in Capt. Chadwick's Company.
Ref: R. & L. 1812, AGO Page 32.

PENOYER, AMOS,   Cornwall.
Volunteered to go to Plattsburgh,
September, 1814, and was at the
battle, serving in Capt. Edmund B.
Hill's Company, Sumner's Regt. Ref:
Book 51, AGO Page 13.

PERCH, WARREN.
Served from April 17 to April 21,
1814 in Capt. Othniel Jewett's Company, Sumner's Regt. Ref: Book 52,
AGO Page 265.

PERCIVAL, PAUL,   Franklin County.
Volunteered to go to Plattsburgh
Sept. 11, 1814 and served in 15th or
22nd Regt. Ref: Hemenway's Vt.
Gazetteer, Vol. 2, Page 392.

PERG, JOHN B.
Enlisted Jan. 8, 1814 for 5 years in
company of late Capt. J. Brooks,
commanded by Lt. John I. Cromwell,
Corps of U. S. Artillery; on Muster
Roll from April 30 to June 30, 1814.
Ref: R. & L. 1812, AGO Page 18.

*PERHAM, JESSEY, Ensign, Belvidere.
Appointed Ensign Sept. 25, 1813 in
Capt. Asa Wilkins' Company, Dixon's
Regt. Volunteered to go to Platts-
burgh, September, 1814, and served
7 days in Capt. Moody Shattuck's
Company. Ref: Book 51, AGO Page
210.

PERHAM, JOEL W., Sergeant, Belvidere.
Volunteered to go to Plattsburgh,
September, 1814, and served 7 days
in Capt. Moody Shattuck's Company.
Ref: Book 51, AGO Page 210.

PERIGO, ELIAS.
Volunteered to go to Plattsburgh,
September, 1814, and served in company of Capt. Jonathan Jennings
of Chelsea. Ref: Book 52, AGO Page
79.

*PERIGO, JOHN.
Served in 1 Regt. (Martindale's) Vt.
Militia.

PERIGO, ORRIN.
Volunteered to go to Plattsburgh,
September, 1814, and served in company of Capt. Jonathan Jennings
of Chelsea. Ref: Book 52, AGO Page
79.

PERKINS, ABIZER.
Served from March 20 to June 9,
1813 in Capt. Phineas Williams' Company, 11th Regt. Ref: R. & L. 1812,
AGO Page 14.

*PERKINS, AUGUSTUS.
Served from April 12 to April 21,
1814 in Lieut. James S. Morton's
Company, W. B. Sumner's Regt.
Also served in 1 Regt. (Martindale's)
Vt. Militia.

*PERKINS, BENJAMIN.
Served with Hospital Attendants, Vt.

PERKINS, DANIEL,   St. Albans.
Enlisted May 8, 1813 for 1 year in
Capt. John Wires' Company. 30th
Regt. Ref: R. & L. 1812, AGO Page
40.

PERKINS, DANIEL.
Enlisted Nov. 1, 1812 in Capt. Weeks'
Company. 11th Regt.; on Pay Roll
for January and February, 1813. Ref:
R. & L. 1812, AGO Page 5.

*PERKINS, EBENEZER.
Served in Capt. Burnap's Company,
Col. Jonathan Williams' Regt. Detached Militia in U. S. service 2
months and 13 days, 1812.

‡*PERKINS, EDMUND, Drummer.
Served in Capt. N. Perkins' Company, 4th Regt. Also served in Corning's Detachment, Vt. Militia. Pension Certificate of widow, Jerusha L.,
No. 36393.

PERKINS, EZRA,   Tunbridge.
Volunteered to go to Plattsburgh,
September. 1814, and served 4 days
in Capt. Ephraim Hackett's Company.
Ref: Book 52, AGO Pages 71 and 76.

PERKINS, GEORGE,   Strafford.
Volunteered to go to Plattsburgh,
September, 1814, and served 6 days
in Capt. Jedediah H. Harris' Company. Ref: Book 52, AGO Page 43.

PERKINS, GEORGE.
Volunteered to go to Plattsburgh,
September, 1814, and served 7 days
in Capt. Frederick Griswold's Company of Brookfield, Vt. Ref: Book
52, AGO Page 52.

*PERKINS, JACOB, Sergeant.
Served in Capt. Ormsbee's Company.
Col. Martindale's Regt. Detached
Militia in U. S. service 2 months

and 14 days, 1812. Served as Sergeant in 1st Regt. of Detached Militia in U. S. service at Champlain
from Nov. 18 to Nov. 19, 1812.

‡PERKINS, JAMES.
Served in Capt. Weeks' Company,
11th Regt.; on Pay Roll for January and February, 1813. Also served
in Capt. Hendee's Company. Pension
Certificate of widow, Sarah, No. 32781.

*PERKINS, JOHN.
Enlisted Sept. 25, 1813 and served
1 month and 23 days in Capt. Jesse
Post's Company, Col. Dixon's Regt.
Detached Militia in U. S. service.

*PERKINS, JOHN, Corporal.
Served in Capt. Adams' Company,
Col. Jonathan Williams' Regt. Detached Militia in U. S. srevice 2
months and 7 days, 1812.

PERKINS, JOHN.
Served from March 6 to June 5, 1813
in Capt. Jonathan Starks' Company,
11th Regt. Ref: R. & L. 1812, AGO
Page 19.

PERKINS, JOHN JR.
Enlisted March 5, 1813 in Capt.
Phineas Williams' Company, 11th
Regt. and served until date of death
April 24, 1813. Ref: R. & L. 1812,
AGO Page 14.

PERKINS, JOHN S.
Served in Capt. Phineas Williams'
Company, 11th Regt.; on Pay Roll
for January and February, 1813.
Ref: R. & L. 1812, AGO Page 15.

PERKINS, LUTHER, Corporal.
Served in 1st Regt. of Detached Militia of Vt. in U. S. service at Champlain from Nov. 18 to Nov. 19, 1812.

PERKINS, MOSES,   Shrewsbury.
Volunteered to go to Plattsburgh,
September, 1814, and served 4 days
in Capt. Robert Reed's Company.
Ref: Book 52, AGO Pages 138 and
140.

*PERKINS, NATHANIEL, Corporal,
Waterbury. Served in Capt. Lowry's
Company, Col. Wm. Williams' Regt.
Detached Militia in U. S. service 4
months and 26 days. Volunteered to
go to Plattsburgh, September. 1814,
and served 11 days in Capt. George
Atkins' Company, 4th Regt. (Peck's).

PERKINS, NEHEMIAH, Captain, Stowe.
Volunteered to go to Plattsburgh,
September, 1814, and was at the
battle, serving in command of com-
pany raised at Stowe. Served as
Captain in Corning's Detachment and
4 Regt. (Peck's) Vt. Militia. Ref.
Book 51, AGO Page 214.

*PERKINS, ORAN.
Served in Corning's Detachment, Vt.
Militia.

‡PERKINS, RALPH.
Served in Captain Colton's Company.
Pension Certificate of widow, Polly,
No. 23849.

*PERKINS, REUBEN, Corporal.
Served in Capt. O. Lowry's Company, Col. Wm. Williams' Regt. Detached Militia in U. S. service 4 months and 26 days, 1812.

PERKINS, ROBERT, Strafford.
Volunteered to go to Plattsburgh, September, 1814, and served in Capt. Cyril Chandler's Company. Ref: Book 52, AGO Page 42.

*PERKINS, RUFUS.
Served from April 12 to April 15, 1814 in Capt. John Hackett's Company, Sumner's Regt.

PERKINS, SAMUEL, Lieutenant.
Appointed Ensign 31st Inf. April 30, 1813, 2nd Lieutenant Feb. 21, 1814; resigned June 14. 1814. Ref: Heitman's Register & Dictionary USA.

*PERKINS, THOMAS.
Served in Capt. Phineas Williams' Company, 11th Regt.; on Pay Roll for January and February, 1813. Served from April 17 to April 21, 1814 in Capt. Othniel Jewett's Company, Sumner's Regt. Ref: R. & L. 1812, AGO Page 15.

PERLEY, JAMES. Berlin.
Volunteered to go to Plattsburgh, September, 1814, and served 7 days in Capt. Cyrus Johnson's Company. Ref: Book 52, AGO Page 255.

PERLEY, SAMUEL. Berlin.
Volunteered to go to Plattsburgh, September, 1814, and served 7 days in Capt. Cyrus Johnson's Company. Ref: Book 52, AGO Page 255.

PERMOND, MATTHEW, Franklin County.
Volunteered to go to Plattsburgh, Sept. 11, 1814, and served in 15th or 22nd Regt. Ref: Hemenway's Vt. Gazetteer, Vol. 2, Page 392.

‡PERO, JOHN.
Served in Capt. Boardman's Company. Pension Certificate of widow. Mary, No. 26726.

*PERRIGO, DAVID, Corporal.
Appointed Corporal Sept. 25. 1813 and served 1 month and 23 days in Capt. Elijah W. Wood's Company, Col. Dixon's Regt.

*PERRIGO, LYMAN.
Served in 3 Regt. (Tyler's) Vt. Militia.

*PERRY, AARON, Ensign.
Served from April 12 to April 15, 1814 in Capt. Jonathan P. Stanley's Company, Col. W. B. Sumner's Regt.

*PERRY, EBIJAH.
Served from April 12 to April 15. 1814 in Capt. Jonathan P. Stanley's Company, Col. W. B. Sumner's Regt.

*PERRY, ALFRED.
Served in Sumner's Regt. Vt. M'litia.

PERRY, ANTHONY, Captain. Cabot.
Volunteered to go to Plattsburgh, September, 1814, and served 4 days

in command of company raised at Cabot. Ref: Book 52, AGO Pages 188 and 205.

‡PERRY, BEERS.
Served in Capt. Colton's Company. Pension Certificate of widow, Eleanor, No. 12765.

*PERRY, BENJAMIN, Waterbury.
Volunteered to go to Plattsburgh, September, 1814, and was in the battle, serving 11 days in Capt. George Atkins' Company, 4 Regt. (Peck's).

*PERRY, BENJAMIN JR.
Served in Corning's Detachment, Vt. Militia.

*PERRY, BOOTH.
Served in Sumner's Regt. Vt. Militia.

PERRY, CHARLES, Highgate.
Served from Sept. 1, 1812 in Capt. Conrade Saxe's Company, Col. Wm. Williams' Regt. Ref: Hemenway's Vt. Gazetteer, Vol. 2, Page 420.

PERRY, DANIEL, Montpelier.
Volunteered to go to Plattsburgh, September, 1814, and served 8 days in Capt. Timothy Hubbard's Company. Ref: Book 52, AGO Page 256.

PERRY, ELIJAH, Musician, Montpelier.
Volunteered to go to Plattsburgh, September, 1814, and served 8 days in Capt. Timothy Hubbard's Company. Ref: Book 52, AGO Page 256.

PERRY, ELIJAH 2nd, Fifer, Marshfield.
Volunteered to go to Plattsburgh, September, 1814, and served 9 days in Capt. James English's Company. Ref: Book 52, AGO Page 248.

‡*PERRY, FULLAM.
Served in Capt. Phelps' Company, Col. Jonathan Williams' Regt. Detached Militia in U. S. service 2 months and 21 days, 1812. Pension Certificate No. 15380.

PERRY, GUY, Swanton.
Served in Capt. V. R. Goodrich's Company, 11th Regt.; on Pay Roll from July 15 to Dec. 8, 1813; in action at the battle of Lundy's Lane. Ref: Hemenway's Vt. Gazetteer, Vol. 2, Page 444.

PERRY, HENRY.
Served from Feb. 10 to Feb. 28, 1813 and from March 17 to June 16, 1813 in Lieut. V. R. Goodrich's Company, 11th Regt. Ref: R. & L. 1812, AGO Pages 10 and 11.

‡PERRY, ISRAEL B., Charlotte.
Served in Capt. Stone's Company, Pension Certificate of widow, Elizabeth, No. 30309.

PERRY, JAMES JR., Marshfield.
Volunteered to go to Plattsburgh, September, 1814, and served 9 days in Capt. James English's Company. Ref: Book 52, AGO Page 248.

*PERRY, JOHN C., Montpelier.
Volunteered to go to Plattsburgh, September, 1814, and served 8 days

in Capt. Timothy Hubbard's Company. Also served in Corning's Detachment and 4 Regt. (Peck's) Vt. Militia. Ref: Book 52, AGO Page 256.

*PERRY, LEMUEL, Lieutenant, Calais. Volunteered to go to Plattsburgh, September, 1814, and served 8 days in Capt. Gideon Wheelock's Company.

‡PERRY, NATHAN. Served in Capt. Hiram Mason's Company, 2 Regt. Pension Certificate No. 25527.

PERRY, NATHANIEL, 1st Sergeant. Volunteered to go to Plattsburgh, September, 1814, and served in company of Capt. Joel Barnes of Chelsea. Ref: Book 52, AGO Pages 69 and 77.

*PERRY, NATHANIEL A. Served in Capt. Phelps' Company, Col. Wm. Williams' Regt. Detached Militia in U. S. service 5 months, 1812.

‡PERRY, NATHANIEL G. Served in Capt. Buck's Company. Pension Certificate No. 2247.

‡PERRY, OLIVER H. Served in Capt. Robinson's Company. Pension Certificate of widow, Lucretia, No. 8322..

PERRY, PHILO, Sergeant. Served from Nov. 1, 1812 to Feb. 28, 1813 in Capt. Samuel H. Holly's Company, 11th Regt. Ref: R. & L. 1812, AGO Page 25.

*PERRY, RICHARD. Enlisted Sept. 25, 1813 and served 1 month and 14 days in Capt. Thomas Waterman's Company, Col. Dixon's Regt. Detached Militia in U. S. service.

*PERRY, SAMUEL. Served in Corning's Detachment, Vt. Militia. Also served in 4 Regt. (Peck's) Vt. Militia.

*PERRY, SHUBEL. Served in Capt. Richardson's Company, Col. Martindale's Regt. Detached Militia in U. S. service 2 months and 13 days, 1812.

‡*PERSONS, AMASA (or Pearsons). Randolph. Volunteered to go to Plattsburgh. September, 1814, and served in Capt. Lebbeus Egerton's Company, Pension Certificate No. 32623.

PERSONS, EBEN. Enlisted Sept. 30, 1813 for 1 year in Capt. Daniel Farrington's Company (commanded by Capt. Simeon Wright) 30th Regt.; on Muster Roll from March 1 to April 30, 1814. Ref: R. & L. 1812, AGO Pages 50 and 51.

PERSONS, IRA, Pittsford. Volunteered to go to Plattsburgh, September, 1814, and served 8 days in Capt. Caleb Hendee's Company. Ref: Book 52, AGO Page 125.

PERSONS JAMES, Pittsford. Volunteered to go to Plattsburgh, September, 1814, and served 8 days

in Capt. Caleb Hendee's Company. Ref: Book 52, AGO Page 125.

*PERSONS, JOHN (or Pearson). Served in Capt. Rogers' Company, Col. Fifield's Regt. Detached Militia in U. S. service 5 months and 27 days, 1812.

*PERSONS, JOSHUA, Corporal. Served in 3 Regt. (Williams') Vt. Militia.

PERSONS, JOSIAH, Pittsford. Volunteered to go to Plattsburgh, September, 1814, and served 8 days as waggoner in Capt. Caleb Hendee's Company. Ref: Book 52, AGO Page 125.

PERSONS, SAMUEL. Enlisted Sept. 25, 1813 in Capt. Amos Robinson's Company, Dixon's Regt. Ref: Book 52, AGO Page 271.

‡*PERSONS, WILLIAM JR. Served in 1 Regt. (Judson's) Vt. Militia, Lieutenant Bates' Company. Pension Certificate No. 24584.

*PETERS, COMFORT. Enlisted April 12, 1814 in Capt. Shubael Wales' Company, Col. W. B. Sumner's Regt.; transferred to Capt. Salmon Foster's Company, Sumner's Regt. April 13 and served to April 21, 1814.

‡PETERS, JOSEPH. Served in Capt. Keeler's Company. Pension Certificate No. 6732.

PETERS, LEVI. Enlisted June 4, 1812 for 5 years and served in Capt. White Young's Company, 15th Regt.; on Muster Roll from Aug. 31 to Dec. 31, 1814. Ref: R. & L. 1812, AGO Page 27.

PETERS, LEWIS, Franklin County. Volunteered to go to Plattsburgh Sept. 11, 1814 and served in 15th or 22nd Regt. Ref: Hemenway's Vt. Gazetteer, Vol. 2, Page 392.

*PETERS, LYMAN. Served in Capt. S. Pettes' Company, Col. Wm. Williams' Regt. Detached Militia in U. S. service 4 months and 17 days, 1812.

PETERS, REUBEN, St. Albans. Enlisted July 24, 1813 for 1 year in Capt. John Wires' Company, 30th Regt. Ref: R. & L. 1812, AGO Page 40.

PETERS, SAMUEL, Hinesburgh. Volunteered to go to Plattsburgh, September, 1814, and served in Capt. Stone's Company. Ref: Book 51, AGO Page 95.

‡PETERSON, TURNER, Roxbury. Volunteered to go to Plattsburgh, September, 1814, and served 8 days in Capt. Samuel M. Orcutt's Company. Pension Certificate of widow, Mary, No. 36934.

‡PETTENGILL, JAMES. Served in Capt. Bradley's Company. Pension Certificate No. 20591. Pension Certificate of widow, Lois, No. 25282.

*PETTES. JOHN.
Served in Capt. S. Pettes' Company,
Col. Wm. Williams' Regt. Detached
Militia in U. S. service from July
22 to Dec. 9, 1812.

*PETTIBONE, AZEL.
Served in Capt. Hopkins' Company,
Col. Martindale's Regt. Detached
Militia in U. S. service 13 days, 1812.

PETTIBONE, JOHN R., Lieutenant.
Appointed Ensign 30 Inf. April 30,
1813; 3 Lieutenant Feb. 18, 1814;
resigned Oct. 8, 1814. Ref: Heitman's
Historical Register & Dictionary USA.

*PETTIBONE, JOHN S., 2nd Lieutenant,
Manchester. Appointed 2nd Lieuten-
ant Sept. 20, 1813 in Capt. John
Weed's Company, Col. Clark's Rifle
Corps.

‡PETTIBONE. ROSWELL. Corporal.
Served from April 29, 1813 to April
24, 1814 in Capt. Daniel Farrington's
Company (also commanded by Capt.
Simeon Wright) 30th Regt. Also serv-
ed in Capt. Utley's Company. Pen-
sion Certificate No. 10370. Ref: R.
& L. 1812, AGO Pages 50 and 51.

*PETTIFACE, SILAS.
Served from June 11 to June 14,
1813 in Capt. Moses Jewett's Company, 1st Regt. 2nd Brig. 3rd Div.

PETTINGELL, SAMUEL. Corporal.
Enlisted May 23, 1813. for 1 year in
Capt. Daniel Farrington's Company
(also commanded by Capt. Simeon
Wr ght) 30th Regt.; on Muster Roll
from March 1 to April 30, 1814. Ref:
R. & L. 1812, AGO Pages 50 and 51.

*PETTIS. STEPHEN, Captain.
Served in 4 Regt. (Williams') Vt.
Militia.

PETTIT, STEPHEN,   Fishkills, N. Y.
Enlisted at Burlington March 22, 1814
for the period of the war and served
in Capt. Wm. Miller's Company, Capt.
G deon Spencer's Company and Capt.
James Taylor's Company. 30th Regt.
Ref: R. & L. 1812, AGO Pages 53,
54, 55, 57.

*PETTON, CHARLES.
Served in 1 Regt. (Martindale's) Vt.
Militia.

PETTON. MOSES,   Richmond.
Volunteered to go to Plattsburgh,
September, 1814, and served 9 days
in Capt. Roswell Hunt's Company,
3 Regt. (Tyler's). Ref: Book 51, AGO
Page 82.

*PETTON, SAMUEL.
Served in 3 Regt. (Tyler's) Vt. Militia.

*PETTYBONE. LORIN.
Served from April 12 to April 15,
1814 in Lieut. Justus Foote's Company, Sumner's Regt.

‡PHELPS, ABEL A. (or M).
Served in Capt. A. Keeler's Company.
Pension Certificate No. 25528. Pen-
sion Certificate of widow, Theodotia,
No. 33262.

*PHELPS, BURNHAM.
Served from April 12 to April 21,
1814 in Lieut. Justus Foote's Company, Sumner's Regt.

*PHELPS, DANIEL L., Captain.
Served in 3 Regt. (Williams') Vt.
Militia.

*PHELPS. DAVID JR.
Served in 4 Regt. (Peck's) Vt. Militia.

PHELPS, ELNATHAN.
Enlisted April 24, 1813 for 1 year in
Capt. Daniel Farrington's Company
(also commanded by Capt. Simeon
Wright) 30th Regt.; on Muster Roll
from March 1 to April 30, 1814 .Ref:
R. & L. 1812, AGO Pages 50 and 51.

PHELPS, HORACE JAMES, Sergeant.
Served in 1st Regt. of Detached Militia of Vt. in U. S. service at Champlain from Nov. 18 to Nov. 19, 1812.

*PHELPS, JOSEPH.
Enlisted Oct. 15, 1813 in Capt. Asahel
Scovell's Company, Col. Clark's Rifle
Corps.

PHELPS. JOSEPH JR.
Served from Oct. 14 to Nov. 17, 1813
in Capt. Asahel Scoville's Company.
Ref: R. & L. 1812, AGO Page 22.

*PHELPS, MATTHEW JR., Major, New
Haven. Appointed Major 31st Inf.
Feb. 23, 1813; died Sept. 5, 1813.
Served as Captain in 4 Regt. (Wil-
liams') Vt. Militia. Ref: Heitman's
Historical Register & Dictionary USA.

‡*PHELPS, ORANGE.
Enlisted Sept. 3, 1813 and served 1
month and 23 days in Capt. Amasa
Mansfield's Company, Col. Dixon's
Regt. Pension Certificate No. 20312.

*PHELPS, PAUL, Corporal.
Served from Sept. 25 to Oct. 28,
1813 in Capt. Jesse Post's Company,
Dixon's Regt.

*PHELPS, SAMUEL SHETHAR. Sergeant
Major, Middlebury. Appointed Dis-
trict Paymaster Aug. 21, 1812; honor-
ably discharged June 15, 1815; died
March 25, 1855. Served as Sergeant
Major in Sumner's Regt. Vt. M litia.
Ref: Heitman's Historical Register &
Dictionary USA.

PHELPS, THEODORE.
Served in Capt. Weeks' Company,
11th Regt.; on Pay Roll for January and February, 1813. Ref: R. &
L. 1812, AGO Page 5.

‡PHELPS. WALTER.
Pension Certificate of widow, Celinda,
No. 32578; no organization given.

PHIFER, FREDERICK, Franklin County.
Volunteered to go to Plattsburgh
Sept. 11, 1814 and served in 15th or
22nd Regt. Ref: Hemenway's Vt.
Gazetteer, Vol. 2, Page 392.

PHILBRICK, EPHRAIM.
Served in Capt. Benjamin Bradford's
Company; on Muster Roll from May
31 to Aug. 31, 1813. Ref: R. & L.
1812, AGO Page 26.

*PHILBROOK, DAVID.
Served in Capt. Mason's Company,
Col. Fifield's Regt. Detached Militia
in U. S. service 12 days, 1812.

*PHILBROOK, JOSEPH.
Served in 1 Regt. (Judson's) Vt.
Militia.

*PHILIMORE, ADAM.
Enlisted Sept. 25, 1813 in Capt. Amos
Robinson's Company, Dixon's Regt.

PHILLIPS, AMOS.
Enlisted Feb. 2, 1813 in Capt. Ed-
gerton's Company, 11th Regt. Ref:
R. & L. 1812, AGO Pages 2 and 3.

PHILLIPS, ANTHONY,   St. Albans.
Enlisted May 13, 1813 for 1 year in
Capt. John Wires' Company, 30th
Regt. Ref: R. & L. 1812, AGO Page
40.

‡PHILLIPS, ANTHONY,   Ira.
Served from January 1, 1814 to June
16, 1815 in Capt. Ira Sanford's Company, 30th Inf. Pension Certificate
No. 3180.

*PHILLIPS, ANTHONY.
Served in 1 Regt. (Martindale's) Vt.
Militia.

*PHILLIPS, CALEB.
Enlisted Sept. 25, 1813 in company
of Capt. Jonathan Prentiss, Jr., Dixon's Regt.

PHILLIPS, CHRISTOPHER.
Served from May 1 to June 30, 1814
as ship carpenter in Alexander Parris' Company of Artificers. Ref: R.
& L. 1812, AGO Page 24.

‡PHILLIPS, DAVID.
Served in Capt. Hall's Company. Pension Certificate of widow, Gratis, No.
33097.

‡PHILLIPS, ELAM.
Served in Capt. Straight's Company.
Pension Certificate No. 25937.

‡PHILLIPS, ELEZER.
Served from April 21, 1813 to April
25, 1814 in Capt. Daniel Farrington's
Company (also commanded by Capt.
Simeon Wright) 30th Regt. Pension
Certificate No. 7052.

PHILLIPS, ELI.
Served from Aug. 10, 1813 to Jan.
18, 1814 in Capt. Daniel Farrington's
Company (also commanded by Capt.
Simeon Wright) 30th Regt. Ref: R.
& L. 1812, AGO Pages 50 and 51.

*PHILLIPS, EZRA.
Served in Capt. Scovell's Company,
Col. Martindale's Regt. Detached
Militia in U. S. service 2 months
and 21 days, 1812.

PHILLIPS, JOSEPH, Fifer,   Vershire.
Volunteered to go to Plattsburgh,
September, 1814, and served 3 days
in Capt. Ira Corse's Company. Ref:
Book 52, AGO Page 91.

PHILLIPS, JOSEPH.
Volunteered to go to Plattsburgh,
September, 1814, and went as far as

Bolton, Vt., serving 4 days in Lt.
Phineus Kimball's Company, West
Fairlee. Ref: Book 52, AGO Page 46.

*PHILLIPS, JOSEPH.
Served in Corning's Detachment, Vt.
Militia.

‡*PHILLIPS, JOSEPH G.
Served in 3 Regt. (Tyler's) Vt. Militia. Also served in Capt. Thompson's
Company. Pension Certificate of widow, Lois, No. 8537.

PHILLIPS, JOSEPH M.
Volunteered to go to Plattsburgh,
September, 1814, and served in com-
pany of Capt. Ebenezer Spencer of
Vershire. Ref: Book 52, AGO Page
48.

PHILLIPS, JOSHUA,   Marlboro.
Killed Sept. 17, 1814 at Sackett's Harbor. Ref: History of Marlboro.

*PHILLIPS, MICHAEL (or Philip), Cor-
poral. Served in Capt. Waterman's
Company, Col. Dixon's Regt. Detached Militia in U. S. service 1 month
and 23 days, 1813. Enlisted Sept. 25,
1813 for 3 months in said company.
Also served in Capt. Chadwick's Company. Volunteered to go to Plattsburgh, September, 1814, and went as
far as Bolton, Vt., serving 4 days in
Lt. Phineas Kimball's Company, West
Fairlee. Ref: R. & L. 1812, AGO
Page 32; Book 52, AGO Pages 46 and
47.

*PHILLIPS, MOSES.
Served in 4 Regt. (Peck's) Vt. Militia.

*PHILLIPS, NEHEMIAH,   Fairfield.
Served in Capt. Kendall's Company,
Col. Wm. Williams' Regt. Detached
Militia in U. S. service 4 months and
23 days, 1812.

*PHILLIPS, REUBEN.
Served in Capt. Morrill's Company,
Col. Fifield's Regt. Detached Militia
in U. S. service 5 months, 1812. En-
listed Sept. 25, 1813 in Capt. Thomas
Waterman's Company, Dixon's Regt.
Also served in Capt. Chadwick's Com-
pany. Served from Feb. 12, 1813 to
May 11, 1813 in Lieut. V. R. Good-
rich's Company, 11th Regt. Ref: R.
& L. 1812, AGO Page 32; and page 10.

PHILLIPS, SEBA.
Volunteered to go to Plattsburgh,
September, 1814, and went as far as
Bolton, Vt., serving 4 days in Lt.
Phineus Kimball's Company, West
Fairlee. Ref: Book 52, AGO Pages
46 and 47.

*PHILLIPS, STEPHEN.
Served from Sept. 25 to Oct. 25,
1813 in Capt. N. B. Eldridge's Company, Dixon's Regt.

*PHILLIPS, WILLIAM.
Served in Capt. Walker's Company,
Col. Fifield's Regt. Detached Militia
in U. S. service 18 days, 1812. Enlisted Sept. 29, 1812 in Capt. Benjamin S. Edgerton's Company, 11th
Regt.; on Pay Roll for September
and October, 1812, and January and
February, 1813.

PHINNEY, BENJAMIN, Sergeant, Montpelier. Volunteered to go to Plattsburgh, September, 1814, and served 8 days in Capt. Timothy Hubbard's Company. Ref: Book 52, AGO Page 256.

PICKETT, LEICESTER.
Enlisted April 7, 1814 for period of the war and served in Capt. Wm. Miller's Company and Capt. James Taylor's Company, 30th Regt. Was captured by troops Sept. 6, 1814 at Plattsburgh; discharged Oct. 8, 1814. Ref: R. & L. 1812, AGO Pages 53 and 54; Records of Naval Records and Library, Navy Dept.

*PICKETT, WILLIAM, Captain.
Served from April 12 to April 21, 1814 in Col. W. B. Sumner's Regt.

*PIER, MANFORD, Musician.
Served from April 19 to April 21, 1814 in Capt. Othniel Jewett's Company, Sumner's Regt.

PIERCE, ABEL,   St. Albans.
Enlisted April 16, 1813 for 1 year in Capt. John Wires' Company, 30th Regt. Ref: R. & L. 1812, AGO Page 40.

‡*PIERCE, ABEL.
Served in Capt. Charles Bennett's Company, Col. Dixon's Regt. Detached Militia in U. S. service 1 month and 23 days, 1813; enlisted Sept. 25, 1813. Also served in Capt. Saxe's Company. Pension Certificate No. 19413.

*PIERCE, AMOS.
Served in Corning's Detachment and 4 Regt. (Peck) Vt. Militia.

‡PIERCE, CHAUNCY.
Served in Capt. James Kinney's Company. Pension Certificate of widow, Mahala, No. 29022.

*PIERCE, CYRUS,   Fairfax.
Served from Aug. 8, 1812 in company of Capt. Joseph Beeman Jr., 11th Regt. U. S. Inf. under Col. Ira Clark. Served in Lt. V. R. Goodrich's Company, 11th Regt.; on Pay Roll for January and February, 1813. Also served in 3 Regt. (Williams') Vt. Militia. Ref: R. & L. 1812, AGO Page 11; Hemenway's Vt. Gazetteer, Vol. 2, Page 402.

‡*PIERCE, DANIEL H.
Served in Capt. Cross' Company, Col. Martindale's Regt. Detached Militia in U. S. service 2 months and 16 days, 1812. Pension Certificate of widow, Levina, No. 8470.

PIERCE, EBENEZER.
Served from Feb. 20 to May 9, 1813 in Capt. Charles Follett's Company, 11th Regt. Ref: R. & L. 1812, AGO Page 13.

*PIERCE, JASON C.
Served in Dixon's Regt. Vt. Militia.

PIERCE, JOHN.
Served from May 1 to July 11, 1814 as a carpenter in Alexander Parr's Company of Artificers. Ref: R. & L. 1812, AGO Page 24.

PIERCE, JOHN.
Served in company of Capt. John McNeil Jr., 11th Regt.; on Pay Roll for January and February, 1813. Ref: R. & L. 1812, AGO Page 17.

PIERCE, JOHN H.,   Sudbury.
Volunteered to go to Plattsburgh, September, 1814, and served 6 days in Capt. Thomas Hall's Company. Ref: Book 52, AGO Page 122.

PIERCE, NICHOLAS.
Served from Feb. 3, 1813 to March, 1813 in Capt. Edgerton's Company, 11th Regt. Ref: R. & L. 1812, AGO Page 3.

*PIERCE, LEONARD (or Peirce).
Served in Capt. Walker's Company, Col. Fifield's Regt. Detached Militia in U. S. service 19 days, 1812.

‡PIERCE, PHILEMON.
Served in Capt. Richardson's Company, Col. Martindale's Regt. Detached Militia in U. S. service 1 month and 3 days, 1812. Pension Certificate of widow, Laura Ann, No. 31358.

*PIERCE, RICHARD.
Served from Sept. 25 to Oct. 28, 1813 in Capt. Jesse Post's Company, Dixon's Regt.

PIERCE, ROBERT,   Sudbury.
Volunteered to go to Plattsburgh, September, 1814, and served 6 days in Capt. Thomas Hall's Company. Ref: Book 52, AGO Page 122.

*PIERCE, RODNEY.
Served from April 12 to April 21, 1814 in Lieut. James S. Morton's Company, Col. W. B. Sumner's Regt.

PIERCE, RUFUS,   Sudbury.
Volunteered to go to Plattsburgh, September, 1814, and served 6 days in Capt. Thomas Hall's Company. Ref: Book 52, AGO Page 122.

*PIERCE, SHERMAN, Quartermaster Sergeant. Served in Col. Martindale's Regt. Detached Militia in U. S. service 2 months and 14 days, 1812.

‡*PIERCE, SIMON.
Served in 2 Regt. (Fifield's) Vt. Militia. Also served in Capt. Stewart's Company. Pension Certificate of widow, Lydia, No. 4431.

PIERCE, STEPHEN, Surgeon.
Marched to Burlington and served 8 days in April, 1814, in Col. John Peck's Regt. Ref: Vol. 50 Vt. State Papers, Page 220.

‡*PIERCE, THOMAS,   Georgia.
Enlisted Sept. 25, 1813 and served 1 month and 23 days in Capt. Jesse Post's Company, Col. Dixon's Regt. Volunteered to go to Plattsburgh, September, 1814, and served 8 days in same company. Pension Certificate No. 17256.

PIERCE, THOMAS,   St. Albans.
Volunteered and was in the battle at Plattsburgh Sept. 11, 1814, serving in Capt. Samuel H. Farnsworth's Company. Ref: Hemenway's Vt. Gazetteer, Vol. 2, Page 434.

*PIERCE, WILLIAM.
Served in Capt. Noyce's Company,
Col. Jonathan Williams' Regt. Detached Militia in U. S. service 2
months and 6 days, 1812.

*PIERPOINT, SAMUEL, Corporal.
Served from June 11 to June 14,
1813 in Capt. Samuel Blinn's Company, 1st Regt. (Judson's).

*PIERPONT, DAVID, 3rd Lieutenant.
Served from April 12 to April 21,
1814 in Capt. Edmund B. Hill's Company, Sumner's Regt.

PIERSON, SAMUEL.
Enlisted May 6, 1812 for 5 years in
Capt. White Youngs' Company, 15th
Regt.; on Muster Roll from Aug.
31 to Dec. 31, 1814. Ref: R. & L.
1812, AGO Page 27.

*PIKE, AMBROSE.
Served in Capt. Preston's Company,
Col. Jonathan Williams' Regt. Detached Militia in U. S. service 2
months and 6 days, 1812.

*PIKE, CHESTER,   Corinth.
Served in Capt. Rogers' Company,
Col. Fifield's Regt. Detached Militia
in U. S. service 2 months and 18
days, 1812.

*PIKE, JAMES,   Randolph.
Volunteered to go to Plattsburgh,
September, 1814, and served in Capt.
Lebbeus Egerton's Company. Ref:
Book 52, AGO Page 82.

PIKE, JOHN,   Marshfield.
Volunteered to go to Plattsburgh,
September, 1814, and served 4 days;
no organization given. Ref: Book
52, AGO Page 195.

*PIKE, NATHAN, Drummer.
Served from April 12 to April 21,
1814 in Capt. Edmund B. Hill's Company, Sumner's Regt.

*PILLSBURY, NATHAN.
Served in Capt. Morrill's Company,
Col. Fifield's Regt. Detached Militia
in U. S. service 6 months and 3
days, 1812.

PILOT, SIMON.
Served from Feb. 9 to May 8, 1813
in Capt. Charles Follett's Company,
11th Regt. Ref: R. & L. 1812, AGO
Pages 12 and 13.

*PINCHER, CLIFFORD.
Served from April 12 to May 20,
1814 in company of Capt. James
Gray Jr., Sumner's Regt.

*PINE, DANIEL, Corporal.
Served from Oct. 5 to Oct. 17, 1813
in Capt. Stephen Brown's Company,
3 Regt. (Tyler's).

‡*PINE, JAMES.   Montpelier.
Served in Capt. Walker's Company,
Col. Fifield's Regt. Detached Militia
in U. S. service 3 months and 9
days, 1812. Pension Certificate No.
12990. Pension Certificate of widow,
Lydia, No. 6835. Volunteered to go
to Plattsburgh, September, 1814, and

served 8 days in Capt. Timothy Hubbard's Company. Ref: Book 52, AGO
Page 256.

‡*PINE, SAMUEL.
Served in Capt. Wilson's Company,
4 Regt. (Williams') Vt. Militia.

‡*PINEO, ANDREW.
Served in 4 Regt. (Peck's) Vt. Mili-
tia, Capt. John Pinneo's Company.
Pension Certificate of widow, Sarah
A., No. 30415.

*PINEO, DANIEL, Sergeant.
Served in 4 Regt. (Peck's) Vt. Militia.

*PINEO, GILES.
Served in 4 Regt. (Peck's) Vt. Mili-
tia and Corning's Detachment, Vt.
Militia.

PINGREE, JAMES.
Served from Feb. 16 to May 15, 1813
in Capt. Edgerton's Company, 11th
Regt. Ref: R. & L. 1812, AGO
Page 3.

PINGRY, JOHN,   Strafford.
Volunteered to go to Plattsburgh,
September, 1814, and served 6 days
in Capt. Jedediah H. Harris' Company. Ref: Book 52, AGO Page 43.

PINGRY, WILLIAM, Corporal.
Served in 1st Regt. of Detached Militia of Vt. in U. S. service at Champlain from Nov. 18 to Nov. 19, 1812.

PINKHAM, CHARLES.
Served from May 1 to June 1, 1814
as a carpenter in Alexander Parris'
Company of Artificers. Ref: R. & L.
1812, AGO Page 24.

PINKHAM, DANIEL.
Served from Feb. 25 to May 24, 1813
in Capt. John W. Weeks' Company,
11th Regt. Ref: R. & L. 1812, AGO
Page 4.

PINKNEY, NINIAN, Inspector General.
Served on General Staff of the North-
ern Army commanded by Maj. Gen.
George Izard. Ref: R. & L. 1812,
AGO Page 28.

*PINNEY, ALMON.
Served in Sumner's Regt. Vt. Militia.

‡*PINNEY, AMIEL.
Served in Capt. Briggs' Company,
Col. Jonathan Williams' Regt. De-
tached Militia in U. S. service 2
months and 13 days, 1812. Pension
Certificate No. 664.

‡PINNEY, BENJAMIN.
Served in Capt. A. Smith's Company.
Pension Certificate of widow, Mary
W., No. 24727.

*PINNEY, JOSEPH.
Served in Capt. Dodge's Company,
Col. Fifield's Regt. Detached Militia
in U. S. service 2 months and 21
days, 1812.

‡*PINNEY, SOLOMON.
Served in Capt. Briggs' Company,
Col. Jonathan Williams' Regt. De-

tached Militia in U. S. service 2 months and 13 days, 1812. Pension Certificate of widow, Anna, No. 12202.

*PINNO, JOHN, Captain,   Bolton.
Served in 4 Regt. (Peck's) Vt. Militia as a Captain. Volunteered to go to Plattsburgh, September, 1814.

PINNY, JOB,   Franklin County.
Volunteered to go to Plattsburgh Sept. 11, 1814 and served in 15th or 22nd Regt. Ref: Hemenway's Vt. Gazetteer, Vol. 2, Page 392.

‡PIPER. AARON.
Served in Capt. A. Smith's Company. Pension Certificate No. 33155.

‡PIPER, AMASA.
Volunteered to go to Plattsburgh, September, 1814, and served 7 days in Capt. Asaph Smith's Company as a teamster. Also served in Capt. Durkee's Company. Pension Certificate No. 6161. Ref: Book 51, AGO Page 20.

‡*PIPER, AMASA JR.
Served in Capt. Wright's Company, Col. Fifield's Regt. Detached Militia in U. S. service 6 months, 1812. Also served in Capt. Durkee's Company. Pension Certificate No. 12360.

*PIPER, REUBEN.
Served in Capt. Wright's Company, Col. Fifield's Regt. Detached Militia in U. S. service 6 months, 1812.

‡PITCHER, ALEXANDER M.
Pension Certificate of widow, Clarinda, No. 31090; no organization given.

*PITCHER, DANIEL.
Served in Corning's Detachment, Vt. Militia.

*PITCHER, WILLIAM.
Served from June 11 to June 14, 1813 in Capt. Samuel Blinn's Company, 1st Regt. (Judson's).

PITKIN, HANEY,   Marshfield.
Volunteered to go to Plattsburgh, September, 1814, and served 9 days in Capt. James English's Company. Ref: Book 52, AGO Page 248.

‡PITKIN, JOHN,   St. Albans.
Enlisted June 7, 1813 for 1 year in Capt. John Wires' Company and Capt. Sanford's Company, 30th Regt. Also served in Capt. Spencer's Company. Pension Certificate No. 17285. Ref: R. & L. 1812, AGO Pages 1 and 40.

PITKIN, JOSEPH,   Poultney.
Volunteered to go to Plattsburgh, September, 1814, and served 2 days in Capt. Briant Ransom's Company. Ref: Book 52, AGO Page 147.

*PITKIN, RUSSELL,   Poultney.
Served in Capt. Brown's Company, Col. Martindale's Regt. Detached Militia in U. S. service 2 months and 14 days, 1812.

PITTKIN, RUSSEL,   St. Albans.
Enlisted April 27, 1813 for 1 year in Capt. John Wires' Company, 30th Regt. Ref: R. & L. 1812, AGO Page 40.

*PITTON, MOSES.
Served from June 11 to June 14, 1813 in Capt. Thomas Dorwin's Company, 1st Regt. 2nd Brig. 3rd Div.

PITTSLEY, JAMES,   Montpelier.
Volunteered to go to Plattsburgh, September, 1814, and served 8 days in Capt. Timothy Hubbard's Company. Ref: Book 52, AGO Page 256.

‡*PIXLEY, JOHN.
Served in Capt. S. Pettes' Company, Col. Wm. Williams' Regt. Detached Militia in U. S. service 4 months and 11 days, 1812. Pension Certificate of widow, Sally, No. 12752.

PIXLEY, ORANGE.
Served in Capt. Weeks' Company, 11th Regt.; on Pay Roll for January and February, 1813. Ref: R. & L. 1812, AGO Page 5.

*PLACE, ARCHIBALD.
Served in Sumner's Regt. Vt. Militia.

*PLACE. ARNOLD.
Served from April 19 to April 21, 1814 in Capt. Othniel Jewett's Company, Sumner's Regt.

PLACE, AUGUSTUS.
Served from March 26 to June 25, 1813 in Capt. Edgerton's Company, 11th Regt. Ref: R. & L. 1812, AGO Page 3.

PLACE, EBENEZER.
Served from March 9 to June 8, 1813 in Lieut. Wm. S. Foster's Company, 11th Regt. Ref: R. & L. 1812, AGO Page 6.

*PLACE, JOSEPH.
Served in Capt. Barns' Company, Col. Wm. Williams' Regt. Detached Militia in U. S. service 5 months, 1812.

*PLACE. KINYON.
Served from June 11 to June 14, 1813 in Capt. John M. Eldridge's Company, 1st Regt. 2nd Brig. 3rd Div.

PLACE, SANFORD.
Served in Capt. Edgerton's Company, 11th Regt.; on Pay Roll to June 25, 1813. Ref: R. & L. 1812, AGO Page 3.

PLACE, SHADRACK.
Served from March 3 to June 2, 1813 in Capt. Edgerton's Company, 11th Regt. Ref: R. & L. 1812, AGO Page 3.

*PLAICE, JOHN JR.
Served from June 11 to June 14, 1813 in Lt. Bates' Company, 1 Regt. (Judson's).

PLAISTED, OLIVER.
Served in Capt. Phineas Williams' Company, 11th Regt. from Feb. 20, 1813 to date of death April 4, 1813. Ref: R. & L. 1812, AGO Page 14.

PLANT, SAMUEL,   Sandy Hill, N. Y.
Served from Oct. 28, 1814 to June 19, 1815 in Capt. Taylor's Company, 30th Inf. Ref: R. & L. 1812, AGO Page 23.

PLASS, ANTWINE.
Enlisted March 12, 1814 for period of the war and served in Capt. James Taylor's Company, 30th Regt.; died June 6, 1814 at Burlington. Ref: R. & L. 1812, AGO Pages 53 and 57.

‡PLATT, ANTOINE.
Served in Capt. Pollard's Company. Pension Certificate No. 29413.

*PLATT, BARZILLA (or Plate).
Served from April 20 to April 21, 1814 in Capt. Eseck Sprague's Company, Sumner's Regt.

‡PLATT, DAVID,   Vershire.
Volunteered to go to Plattsburgh, September, 1814, and served 3 days in Capt. Ira Corse's Company. Pension Certificate of widow, Eleanor, No. 23858.

PLATT, FRANCIS.
Enlisted July 11, 1812 for 5 years in company of late Capt. J. Brooks, commanded by Lt. John I. Cromwell, Corps of U. S. Artillery; on Muster Roll from April 30, 1814 to June 30, 1814. Ref: R. & L. 1812, AGO Page 18.

*PLATT, HARRY.
Served in 1 Regt. (Judson's) Vt. Militia.

PLATT, HEWE (or Hue).
Enlisted Jan. 1, 1813 in Capt. Edgerton's Company, 11th Regt.; on Pay Roll for January and February, 1813. Ref: R. & L. 1812, AGO Pages 2 and 3.

*PLATT, PARMERSON T.
Served in Capt. Sabin's Company, Col. Jonathan Williams' Regt. Detached Militia in U. S. service 2 months and 6 days, 1812.

*PLEER, PETER.
Served from June 11 to June 14, 1813 in Capt. Hezekiah Barns' Company, 1st Regt. 2nd Brig. 3rd Div.

*PLOOF, ALEXANDER.
Enlisted Sept. 23, 1813 in Capt. Asahel Langworthy's Company Col. Isaac Clark's Regt. of Riflemen in U. S. service.

PLUMB, ELISHA.
Served in Capt. Samul Gordon's Company, 11th Regt.; on Pay Roll for January and February, 1813. Ref: R. & L. 1812, AGO Page 9.

*PLUMB, GEORGE.
Served in Capt. Dodge's Company, Col. Fifield's Regt. Detached Militia in U. S. service 2 months and 21 days, 1812.

*PLUMB, GREEN.
Served in Capt. Pettes' Company, Col. Wm. Williams' Regt. Detached Militia in U. S. service 4 months and 17 days, 1812.

‡*PLUMB, WILLIAM, Sergeant.
Served in Capt. Preston's Company, Col. Jonathan Williams' Regt. Detached Militia in U. S. service 2 months and 6 days, 1812. Pension Certificate No. 15231.

*PLUMBLY, SILAS.
Served in Capt. Phelps' Company, Col. Wm. Williams' Regt. Detached Militia in U. S. service 5 months, 1812.

*PLUMLEY, ERASTUS.
Served from April 12 to April 21, 1814 in Capt. Othniel Jewett's Company, Sumner's Regt.

PLUMLEY, JOHN,   Franklin County.
Enlisted Aug. 26, 1812 for 5 years in Capt. White Youngs' Company, 15th Regt.; on Muster Roll from Aug. 31 to Dec. 31, 1814. Ref: R. & L. 1812, AGO Page 27.

*PLUMLEY, LEVI.
Served in Capt. Hopkins' Company, Col. Martindale's Regt. Detached Militia in U. S. service 2 months and 13 days, 1812.

*PLUMLEY, RICHARD C., Sergeant.
Served in Capt. Strait's Company, Col. Martindale's Regt. Detached Militia in U. S. service 2 months and 13 days, 1812. Served in 1st Regt. of Detached Militia of Vt. in U. S. service at Champlain from Nov. 18 to Nov. 19, 1812.

PLUMMER, JOSEPH .
Served from Feb. 6 to May 5, 1813 in Lieut. Wm. S. Foster's Company, 11th Regt. Ref: R. & L. 1812, AGO Page 6.

*PLUMMER, SAMUEL.
Served from April 12, 1814 to April 21, 1814 in Capt. Eseck Sprague's Company, Sumner's Regt.

*PODGE, BENJAMIN.
Served from Oct. 5 to Oct. 17, 1813 in Capt. Stephen Brown's Company, 3 Regt. (Tyler's).

*POLLARD, JAMES, Sergeant.
Served in Capt. Briggs' Company, Col. Jonathan Williams' Regt. Detached Militia in U. S. service 2 months and 13 days, 1812.

‡*POLLARD, JOSEPH,   Enosburgh.
Enlisted Sept. 25, 1813 and served 1 month and 23 days in Capt. Martin D. Folett's Company, Col. Dixon's Regt. Pension Certificate of widow, Anna, No. 14248.

*POLLY, JOSEPH.
Served in 1 Regt. (Martindale's) Vt. Militia.

POMARAY, HARTWELL,   Vergennes.
Volunteered to go to Plattsburgh, September, 1814, and served 8 days in Capt. Gideon Spencer's Company as a waggoner. Ref: Book 51, AGO Page 1.

‡POMEROY, JACOB.
Pension Certificate of widow, Sophia W., No. 8207; no organization given.

POMEROY, RICHARD C., Lieutenant.
Appointed 2nd Lieutenant Ordnance Dec. 26, 1814; 1st Lieutenant Sept. 1, 1818. Ref: Heitman's Historical Register & Dictionary USA.

POMEROY, THADDEUS, Schenectady.
Served from May 1 to May 27, 1814
in Capt. Leonard's Company Light
Artillery. Ref: R. & L. 1812, AGO
Page 30.

POMEROY, THOMAS.
Served to June 28, 1814 in Capt.
Alexander Brooks' Corps of Artillery.
Ref: R. & L. 1812, AGO Page 31.

*POMROY, JOHN, Surgeon.
Served in 1 Regt. (Judson's) Vt.
Militia.

POMROY, OLIVER, Corporal.
Served from Feb. 18 to May 17,
1813 in Capt. Charles Follett's Company, 11th Regt. Ref: R. & L. 1812,
AGO Page 13.

POND, DAN, Poultney.
Volunteered to go to Plattsburgh,
September, 1814, and served 2 days
in Capt. Briant Ransom's Company.
Ref: Book 52, AGO Page 147.

POND, HARVEY C., Poultney.
Volunteered to go to Plattsburgh,
September, 1814 ,and served 4 days
in Capt. Briant Ransom's Company.
Ref: Book 52, AGO Page 148.

*POND, JARED, Corporal.
Enlisted Sept. 18, 1813 in Capt. Isaac
Finch's Company, Col. Clark's Rifle
Corps.

POND, JOHN, Shoreham.
Volunteered to go to Plattsburgh,
September, 1814, and served 6 days
in Capt. Samuel Hand's Company.
Ref: Rev. J. F. Goodhue's History
of Shoreham, Page 108.

POND, JOSIAH, Sergeant, Cornwall.
Volunteered to go to Plattsburgh,
September, 1814, and was at the
battle, serving in Capt. Edmund B.
Hill's Company. Sumner's Regt. Ref:
Book 51, AGO Page 13.

‡*POND, NATHANIEL JR.
Served from April 12 to May 20,
1814 in company of Capt. James
Gray Jr., Sumner's Regt. Also served in Capt. Sheldon's Company. Pension Certificate No. 25684.

POND, PHILIP, Poultney.
Volunteered to go to Plattsburgh,
September, 1814, and served 2 days
in Capt. Briant Ransom's Company.
Ref: Book 52, AGO Page 147.

*POND, SAMUEL, Addison.
Served from April 12 to May 20,
1814 in Capt. George Fisher's Company, Sumner's Regt. Volunteered
to go to Plattsburgh, September, 1814,
and was in the battle, serving 9
days in same company.

*POND, SAMUEL L. (or S).
Served from April 17 to April 21,
1814 in Capt. Othniel Jewett's Company, Sumner's Regt.

POND, SYLVESTER, Addison.
Served from Nov. 1, 1812 to Feb.
28, 1813 in Capt. Samul Gordon's
Company, 11th Regt. Volunteered to

go to Plattsburgh, September, 1814,
and was in the battle, serving 9
days in Capt. George Fisher's Company, Sumner's Regt. Ref: R. & L.
1812, AGO Page 9; Book 51, AGO
Page 5.

*POND, WILLIAM, Sergeant.
Enlisted Sept. 18, 1813 in Capt. Isaac
Finch's Company, Col. Clark's Rifle
Corps.

*POND, WILLIAM JR.
Served in Capt. Ormsbee's Company,
Col. Martindale's Regt. Detached
Militia in U. S. service 2 months
and 14 days, 1812.

POND, ZEBULON, Pittsford.
Enlisted May 29, 1813 for 1 year in
Capt. Daniel Farrington's Company,
30th Regt. (also commanded by Capt.
Simeon Wr:ght); on Muster Roll from
March 1 to April 30, 1814. Volun-
teered to go to Plattsburgh, Septem-
ber, 1814, and served 8 days in Capt.
Caleb Hendee's Company. Ref: R.
& L. 1812, AGO Pages 50 and 51;
Book 52, AGO Page 125.

POOL, GALEN.
Served as a carpenter in Alexander
Parris' Corps of Artificers; on Pay
Roll for May and June, 1814. Ref:
R. & L. 1812, AGO Page 24.

‡POOR, BENJAMIN.
Served in Capt. Stewart's Company.
Pension Certificate No. 14523.

POOR, JOHN, Berlin.
Volunteered to go to Plattsburgh,
September, 1814, and served 7 days
in Capt. Frederick Griswold's Com-
pany, raised in Brookfield, Vt. Ref:
Book 52, AGO Pages 52 and 53.

POPE, SAMUEL.
Served from April 30, 1813 to April
30, 1814 in Capt. Daniel Farrington's
Company, 30th Regt. (also command-
ed by Capt. Simeon Wright). Ref:
R. & L. 1812, AGO Pages 50 and 51.

POPE, SIMEON.
Served from April 20 to July 19,
1813 in Capt. Charles Follett's Company, 11th Regt. Ref: R. & L. 1812,
AGO Page 13.

*PORTER, ARUNAH.
Served from April 12 to April 21,
1814 in Capt. Othniel Jewett's Company, Sumner's Regt.

‡PORTER, BENONI.
Served in Capt. Spencer's Company.
Pension Certificate No. 1186.

PORTER, EBENEZER.
Enlisted May 17, 1813 for 1 year in
Capt. Daniel Farrington's Company,
30th Regt. (also commanded by Capt.
Simeon Wright); on Muster Roll from
March 1 to April 30, 1814 as waiter
for paymaster. Ref: R. & L. 1812,
AGO Pages 50 and 51.

‡PORTER, EZRA.
Served from Nov. 1, 1812 to Feb.
28, 1813 in Capt. Gordon's Company,
11th Regt. Also served under Major
Oliver Mason. Pension Certificate of
widow, Adah, No. 15963.

*PORTER, HEZECIAH.
Served in Capt. Howard's Company,
Vt. Militia.

‡PORTER, JOHN,   Jericho.
Served in Capt. P. A. Allen's Company. Took part in the battle of
Plattsburgh. Pension Certificate of
widow, Lemira, No. 28415. Ref: History of Jericho, Page 142.

PORTER JOHN JR.,   Jericho.
Took part in the Battle of Plattsburgh. Ref: History of Jericho, Page
142.

*PORTER, JOSEPH.
Served in Capt. Noyce's Company,
Col. Jonathan Williams' Regt. Detached Militia in U. S. service 2
months and 6 days, 1812.

*PORTER, NOAH W.
Served in Sumner's Regt. Vt. Militia.

*PORTER, SIMEON J.
Served from April 12 to April 21,
1814 in Capt. Othniel Jewett's Company, Sumner's Regt.

*PORTER, SMITH.   Randolph.
Volunteered to go to Plattsburgh,
September, 1814, and served in Capt.
Lebbeus Egerton's Company.

*PORTER, TIMOTHY.
Served in Col. Wm. Williams' Regt.
Detached Militia in U. S. Service
4 months and 26 days, 1812. Served
from May 1, 1813 to April 30, 1814
in Capt. Simeon Wright's Company.
Ref: R. & L. 1812, AGO Page 51.

*PORTER, WILLIAM,   Randolph.
Volunteered to go to Plattsburgh,
September, 1814, and served in Capt.
Lebbeus Egerton's Company.

‡PORTER, ZERAH.
Served in Capt. A. Jewett's Company.
Pension Certificate of widow, Sophro-
nia, No. 22470.

*PORTERFIELD, JAMES.
Served from June 11 to June 14, 1813
in Capt. Moses Jewett's Company,
1st Regt. 2nd Brig. 3rd Div.

*POST, ABEL,   Highgate.
Served in Capt. Saxe's Company, Col.
Williams' Regt. Detached Militia in
U. S. service 4 months and 24 days,
1812.

‡POST, DAVID H.,   Addison.
Volunteered to go to Plattsburgh,
September, 1814, and served 9 days
in Capt. George Fisher's Company,
Sumner's Regt.; was in the battle.
Pension Certificate of widow, Hannah,
No. 31933.

‡POST, HARLOW.
Served in Capt. Jesse Post's Company. Pension Certificate No. 34791.

POST, HARRY.
Volunteered to go to Plattsburgh,
September, 1814, and served in Capt.
Jesse Post's Company. Dixon's Regt.
Ref: Book 51, AGO Page 25.

*POST, HARVEY.
Served from April 12 to May 20, 1814
in Capt. George Fisher's Company,
Sumner's Regt.

*POST, HENRY.
Served in 3 Regt. (Tyler's) Vt. Militia.

POST, JACOB,   Addison.
Volunteered to go to Plattsburgh,
September, 1814, and served 9 days
in Capt. George Fisher's Company,
Sumner's Regt.; was in the battle.
Ref: Book 51, AGO Page 5.

*POST, JESSE, Captain,   Georgia.
Entered service Sept. 25, 1813 as
Captain of a company in Col. Luther
Dixon's Regt. Volunteered to go to
Plattsburgh, September 1814 and serv-
ed 8 days in same regiment.

‡*POST, JOHN C.
Enlisted Sept. 25, 1813 and served 1
month and 23 days in Capt. Jesse
Post's Company, Col. Dixon's Regt.
Pension Certificate No. 17762.

*POST, JOHN S.
Served from March 27 to June 26,
1813 in Capt. Charles Follett's Com-
pany, 11th Regt. Also served with
Hospital Attendants, Vt. Ref: R. &
L. 1812, AGO Page 13.

POST, JUSTUS, Colonel Quartermaster
General. Appointed 1st Lieutenant
Artillerists July 1, 1811; transferred
to 1st Artillery March 12, 1812; trans-
ferred to Artillery Corps May 12,
1814; Colonel Quartermaster General
Nov. 22, 1814; honorably discharged
June 15, 1815; died March 14, 1846.
Ref: Heitman's Historical Register &
Dictionary USA.

‡POST, MAJOR, Corporal, Georgia.
Enlisted Sept. 25, 1813 in Capt. Jesse
Post's Company, Dixon's Regt. Volunteered to go to Plattsburgh, September, 1814, and served 8 days in same
company. Pension Certificate No.
17761.

*POST, STEPHEN.
Served from April 12 to April 21,
1814 in Capt. Eseck Sprague's Company, Sumner's Regt.

POST, WICKLIFFE G., Corporal, Addison.
Served in Capt. Robbins' Company,
Col. Wm. Williams' Regt. Detached
Militia in U. S. service 4 months
and 29 days, 1812. Served from
April 12 to May 20, 1814 in Capt.
George Fisher's Company, Sumner's
Regt.; volunteered to go to Platts-
burgh, September, 1814, and served
in same company. Ref: Book 51, AGO
Page 5; Book 52, AGO Page 277;
Book 53, AGO Page 54.

POTTER, BENONI.
Served in Capt. Weeks' Company,
11th Regt.; on Pay Roll for January and February, 1813. Ref: R. &
L. 1812, AGO Page 5.

POTTER, BYRON,   Barre.
Volunteered to go to Plattsburgh,
September, 1814, and served in Capt.
Warren Ellis' Company. Ref: Hemen-
way's Vt. Gazetteer, Vol. 4, Page 41.

POTTER, CALEB M.
Served in Capt. Barns' Company, Col.
Wm. Williams' Regt. Detached Militia in U. S. service 4 months and
26 days, 1812. Ref: Book 53, AGO
Page 76.

POTTER, DAVID,   Clarendon.
Volunteered to go to Plattsburgh,
September, 1814, and served 7 days
in Capt. Durham Sprague's Company.
Also served in 4 Regt. (Williams')
Vt. Militia. Ref: Book 52, AGO
Page 128.

POTTER, FREEBORN,   St. Albans.
Volunteered and was in the action
at Plattsburgh Sept. 11, 1814, serving in Capt. Samuel H. Farnsworth's
Company. Ref: Hemenway's Vt. Gazetteer, Vol. 2, Page 434.

POTTER, JEREMIAH,   Swanton.
Volunteered and was at the Battle
of Plattsburgh Sept. 11, 1814, and
served in Capt. Amasa J. Brown's
Company. Ref: Hemenway's Vt. Gazetteer, Vol. 2, Page 445.

POTTER, JNO.
Was captured by troops July 17,
1814 at Fort Erie; died Dec. 7, 1814.
Ref: Records of Naval Records and
Library, Navy Dept.

*POTTER. JOSEPH M.,   Fairfield.
Served in Capt. Robbins' Company,
Col. Wm. Williams' Regt. Detached
Militia in U. S. service 4 months
and 29 days, 1812. Served in Capt.
George Kimball's Company. 4 Regt.
(Williams') stationed at Swanton in
1813.

*POTTER. JOSIAH W.,   Richford.
Served in Capt. Kendall's Company,
Col. Wm. Williams' Regt. Detached
Militia in U. S. service 4 months
and 23 days at Swanton Falls in
1812. Enlisted Sept. 25, 1813 and
served 1 month and 23 days in Capt.
Follett's Company, Col. Dixon's Regt.
Detached Militia in U. S. service.

POTTER. MILTON,   Pittsford.
Volunteered to go to Plattsburgh.
September. 1814, and served 8 days
in Capt. Caleb Hendee's Company as
a waggoner. Ref: Book 52, AGO Page
125.

‡*POTTER. MOSELY,   St. Albans.
Enlisted Sept. 25, 1813 and served
1 month and 23 days in Capt. Eldridge's Company, Col. Dixon's Regt.
Detached Militia in U. S. service.
Volunteered to go to Plattsburgh,
September, 1814, and served 8 days
in Capt. Samuel H. Farnsworth's
Company. Pension Certificate of widow, Polly H., No. 23627. Ref: Book
51. AGO Page 121; Hemenway's Vt.
Gazetteer, Vol. 2, Page 434.

*POTTER. MOSES.
Enlisted Sept. 23, 1813 and served
1 month and 23 days in Capt. Amasa
Mansfield's Company, Dixon's Regt.
Detached Militia in U. S. service.

POTTER, NAEB.
Enlisted Feb. 10, 1813 in Lieut. V.
R. Goodrich's Company, 11th Regt.;
on Pay Roll to May 31, 1813. Ref:
R. & L. 1812, AGO Page 10.

POTTER, NOEL,   Clarendon.
Volunteered to go to Plattsburgh,
September, 1814, and served 7 days
in Capt. Durham Sprague's Company.
Ref: Book 52, AGO Page 128.

POTTER, OLIVER,   Swanton.
Volunteered to go to Plattsburgh,
September, 1814, and served 7 days
in Capt. Amasa I. Brown's Company.
Ref: Book 51, AGO Pages 139 and
148.

*POTTER, ORRIN.
Enlisted Sept. 25, 1813 in company
of Capt. Jonathan Prentiss Jr., Dixon's Regt.

‡*POTTER, THEOPHILUS,   Bakersfield.
Served in Capt. Kendall's Company,
Col. Wm. Williams' Regt. Detached
Militia in U. S. service 4 months
and 23 days, 1812. Volunteered and
was at the Battle of Plattsburgh Sept.
11, 1814, serving in Capt. M. Stearns'
Company. Pension Certificate No.
4951. Ref: Hemenway's Vt. Gazetteer, Vol. 2, Page 394.

POTTER, THOMAS.   Franklin County.
Enlisted Feb. 25, 1812 for 5 years in
Capt. White Youngs' Company, 15th
Regt.; on Muster Roll from Aug. 31
to Dec. 31, 1814. Ref: R. & L. 1812,
AGO Page 27.

POTTER, THOMAS,   Fairfield.
Served in Capt. George W. Kindal's
Company, 4 Regt. (Williams') 6
months in 1812. Ref: Book 51, AGO
Page 198.

*POTTER, THOMAS.
Served in Capt. Hotchkiss' Company,
Col. Martindale's Regt. Detached
Militia in U. S. service 2 months
and 13 days, 1812.

POTTER, THOMAS,   Plainfield.
Volunteered to go to Plattsburgh,
September, 1814, and served 10 days;
not assigned to any company. Ref:
Book 52, AGO Pages 193 and 200.

‡POTTER, THOMPSON.
Pension Certificate of widow, Sarah,
No. 15063; no organization given.

‡POWELL, ALANSON.
Served in Capt. Newell's Company.
Pension Certificate of widow, Huldah,
No. 43093.

*POWELL. CALVIN.
Served from June 11 to June 14,
1813 in Capt. Hezekiah Barns' Company, 1st Regt. 2nd Brig. 3rd Div.

POWELL. EBENEZER.
Volunteered to go to Plattsburgh,
September, 1814, and went as far as
Bolton, Vt.. serving 4 days in Lieut.
Phineus Kimball's Company, West
Fairlee. Ref: Book 52, AGO Pages
46 and 47.

*POWELL, EGBERT, Lieutenant, Cambridge. Volunteered to go to Plattsburgh, September, 1814, and served
8 days in Capt. Salmon Green's Company. Also served as Lieutenant in
2 Regt. 3 Brig. 3 Div. Vt. Militia.
Ref: Book 51, AGO Page 207.

*POWELL, ELIJAH (or Powel), Sergeant. Served from June 11 to June 14, 1813 in Capt. Ithiel Stone's Company, 1st Regt. 2nd Brig. 3rd Div.

‡*POWELL, ERASTUS, Lieutenant. Served in Capt. Chadwick's Company, 2 Regt. 3 Brig. 3 Div. Pension Certificate of widow, Sally, No. 1609.

POWELL, HORACE. Served from Aug. 28, 1813 to Aug. 27, 1814 in Capt. James Taylor's Company and Capt. Wm. Miller's Company, 30th Regt. Ref: R. & L. 1812, AGO Pages 52, 53, 54, 57.

POWELL, JOHN JR.,   Strafford. Volunteered to go to Plattsburgh, September, 1814, and served 6 days in Capt. Jedediah H. Harris' Company. Ref: Book 52, AGO Page 43.

‡*POWELL, MILES. Served in Capt. Dorrance's Company, Col. Wm. Williams' Regt. Detached Militia in U. S. service 4 months and 23 days. 1812. Pension Certificate of widow, Polly, No. 6440.

*POWELL, MYRON, Corporal. Served in Capt. Willson's Company, Col. Wm. Williams' Regt. Detached Militia in U. S. service 4 months and 7 days, 1812.

POWELL, PERLEY,   Strafford. Served in War of 1812 and was captured by troops July 25, 1814 at Londers Lane; discharged Nov. 8, 1814. Ref: Records of Naval Records and Library, Navy Dept.

‡POWELL, PROSPER. Served in Capt. Parker's Company. Pension Certificate No. 33996.

*POWELL, SEYMOUR, Sergeant. Served from April 22, 1813 to April 25, 1814 in Capt. Gideon Spencer's Company and Capt. James Taylor's Company, 30th Regt. Also served as lieutenant in 4 Regt. (Williams') Vt. Militia. Ref: R. & L. 1812, AGO Pages 56 and 58.

POWELL, TRUEMAN, Surgeon. Appointed Surgeon 31st Inf. July 19. 1813; transferred to 30th Inf. Dec. 30, 1813; resigned Jan. 11, 1814. Ref: Heitman's Historical Register & Dictionary USA.

*POWELL, WILLIAM JR. Enlisted Sept. 25, 1813 in company of Capt. Jonathan Prentiss, 'Jr., Dixon's Regt.

‡*POWERS, ASAHEL . Served in Capt. Adams' Company, Col. Jonathan Williams' Regt. Detached Militia in U. S. service 2 months and 7 days, 1812. Pension Certificate of widow, Sophia, No. 1307.

POWERS, AUGUSTUS, Sergeant. Served from Sept. 1, 1812 to Feb. 28, 1813 in Capt. Samul Gordon's Company, 11th Regt. Ref: R. & L. 1812. AGO Page 9.

*POWERS, ELAM. Served in Capt. Phelps' Company, Col. Wm. Williams' Regt. Detached Militia in U. S. service 5 months, 1812.

*POWERS, GEORGE W., Corporal. Appointed Corporal Sept. 29, 1813 in Capt. Asahel Langworthy's Company, Col. Isaac Clark's Volunteer Riflemen in U. S. service.

‡*POWERS, HARTWELL. Served in Capt. Phelps' Company, Col. Wm. Williams' Regt. Detached Militia in U. S. service 5 months, 1812. Also served in Sumner's Regt. Vt. Militia. Pension Certificate of widow, Philura, No. 11029.

*POWERS, JAMES,   Randolph. Volunteered to go to Plattsburgh, September, 1814, serving in Capt. Lebbeus Egerton's Company.

POWERS, JOAB,   Pittsford. Volunteered to go to Plattsburgh, September, 1814, and served 8 days in Capt. Caleb Hendee's Company. Ref: Book 52, AGO Page 125.

POWERS, JOHN. Served from May 1 to June 30, 1814 in Capt. Samuel H. Holly's Company, 11th Regt. Ref: R. & L. 1812, AGO Page 25.

POWERS, JOHN. Served as blacksmith in Capt. Haig's Corps of Light Dragoons. Ref: R. & L. 1812, AGO Page 20.

POWERS, JUSTUS,   Pittsford. Volunteered to go to Plattsburgh, September, 1814, and served 8 days in Capt. Caleb Hendee's Company. Ref: Book 52, AGO Page 125.

POWERS, LEVI, Captain. Appointed 1st Lieutenant 31st Inf. April 30. 1813; Captain Jan. 11, 1814; honorably discharged June 15, 1815. Ref: Heitman's Historical Register & Dictionary USA.

‡*POWERS, LEVI. Served in Capt. Wheeler's Company, Col. Fifield's Regt. Detached Militia in U. S. service 6 months and 4 days, 1812. Pension Certificate No. 1326.

*POWERS, LEVI H. Served from Sept. 25 to Oct. 11, 1813 in Capt. N. B. Eldridge's Company, Dixon's Regt.

*POWERS, NAHAM. Served in Capt. Taylor's Company, Col. Fifield's Regt. Detached Militia in U. S. service 6 months, 1812.

*POWERS, OLIVER,   Woodstock. Served in Capt. Phelps' Company, Col. Jonathan Williams' Regt. Detached Militia in U. S. service 2 months and 21 days, 1812.

*POWERS, PETER,   Pittsford. Served in Capt. Wheeler's Company, Col. Fifield's Regt. Detached Militia in U. S. service 3 months and 19 days, 1812. Volunteered to go to Plattsburgh, September, 1814, and served 8 days in Capt. Caleb Hendee's Company.

POWERS, RICHARD M.,   Pittsford.
Volunteered to go to Plattsburgh, September, 1814, and served 8 days in Capt. Caleb Hendee's Company. Ref: Book 52, AGO Page 125.

POWRS, RICHARD M.,   Pittsford.
Served from April 24, 1813 to April 25, 1814 in Capt. Simeon Wright's Company. Ref: R. & L. 1812, AGO Page 51.

POWERS, WILLIAM, Lieutenant, Rochester. Volunteered to go to Plattsburgh, September, 1814; no organization given. Was captured by troops Sept. 17, 1814 at Fort Erie; discharged Nov. 8, 1814. Ref: Book 51, AGO Page 249; Records of Naval Records and Library, Navy Dept.

PRAGER, WILLIAM C., Sergeant.
Enlisted July 6, 1812 for 5 years in Capt. White Youngs' Company, 15th Regt.; on Muster Roll from Aug. 31 to Dec. 31, 1814. Ref: R. & L. 1812, AGO Page 27.

PRAGERS, JOEL, Sergeant.
Served in Capt. Barnes' Company, Col. Wm. Williams' Regt. stationed at Swanton Falls in 1812. Ref: Vol. 49, Vt. State Papers, Page 119.

*PRATT, ALLEN,   Fairfield.
Served in Capt. George W. Kindall's Company, 4 Regt. (Williams') Detached Militia in U. S. service 4 months and 23 days, 1812.

PRATT, BENJAMIN, Lieutenant.
Appointed 1st Lieutenant 2nd Light Dragoons March 12, 1812; resigned May 16, 1813. Ref: Heitman's Historical Register & Dictionary USA.

PRATT, DAVID, Sergeant.
Served in company of Capt. John McNeil Jr., 11th Regt.; on Pay Roll for January and February, 1813. Ref: R. & L. 1812, AGO Page 17.

‡PRATT, DAVID.
Served in Capt. Burnap's Company. Pension Certificate No. 8767.

PRATT, DAVID I.
Enlisted Nov. 1, 1812 in company of Capt. John McNeil Jr., 11th Regt.; on Pay Roll for January and February, 1813. Ref: R. & L. 1812, AGO Page 17.

‡*PRATT, EBENEZER.
Served in Capt. Brown's Company, Col. Martindale's Regt. Detached Militia in U. S. service 2 months and 14 days, 1812. Pension Certificate No. 14915.

‡*PRATT, EPHRAIM,   Cornwall.
Served from April 12 to April 21, 1814 in Capt. Edmund B. Hill's Company, Sumner's Regt.; volunteered to go to Plattsburgh, September, 1814, and was at the battle, serving in same company. Pension Certificate of widow, Loraine, No. 27261.

*PRATT, EZEKIEL, Sergeant.
Enlisted Sept. 25, 1813 in company of Capt. Jonathan Prentiss Jr., Dixon's Regt.

PRATT, HEMAN, Fifer Corporal.
Enlisted April 22, 1813 for 1 year and served in Capt. Gideon Spencer's Company and Capt. James Taylor's Company, 30th Regt. Ref: R. & L. 1812, AGO Pages 52, 56, 58.

‡PRATT, IRA ALLEN.
Served in Capt. G. W. Kendall's Company. Pension Certificate of widow, Asenath Hyde, No. 31354.

*PRATT, ISAAC.
Served in Capt. Lowry's Company, Col. Wm. Williams' Regt. Detached Militia, in U. S. service 4 months and 26 days, 1812.

*PRATT, JEREMIAH.
Served in Capt. Phelps' Company, Col. Jonathan Williams' Regt. Detached Militia in U. S. service 2 months and 21 days, 1813.

PRATT, JOHN.
Served in Capt. L. Robinson's Company, Col. Dixon's Regt. Detached Militia in U. S. service 2 months, 1813. Ref: Book 53, AGO Page 108.

PRATT, JOHN,   Shrewsbury.
Volunteered to go to Plattsburgh, September, 1814, and served 4 days in Capt. Robert Reed's Company. Ref: Book 52, AGO Page 138.

*PRATT, JOHN A., Corporal, Woodstock.
Served in Capt. Briggs' Company, Col. Jonathan Williams' Regt. Detached Militia in U. S. service 2 months and 12 days, 1812. Also served in 4 Regt. (Williams') Vt. Militia.

*PRATT, JOHN JR., Lieutenant.
Appointed 3rd Lieutenant 31st Inf. April 30, 1813; 2nd Lieutenant Jan. 11, 1814; 1st Lieutenant May 2, 1814; Regimental Quartermaster Aug. 1814; to Jan. 1, 1815; honorably discharged June 15. 1815. Served as Sergeant in Dixon's Regt. Vt. Militia. Ref: Heitman's Historical Register & Dictionary USA.

*PRATT, JONATHAN,   Addison.
Served from April 12 to May 20, 1814 in Capt. George Fisher's Company, Sumner's Regt.; volunteered to go to Plattsburgh, September, 1814, and was in the battle, serving 9 days in same company.

*PRATT, JOSHUA,   Braintree.
Served under Captains Wheatly and Wright, Col. Fifield's Regt. Detached Militia in U. S. service 6 months, 1812. Volunteered to go to Plattsburgh Sept. 10, 1814 and served as Sergeant in Capt. Lot Hudson's Company. Also served with Hospital Attendants. Vt. Ref: Book 51, AGO Page 295; Book 52, AGO Page 24.

*PRATT, LEVI.
Served in Capt. Needham's Company, Col. Martindale's Regt. Detached

Militia in U. S. service 2 months and 14 days, 1812. Served from Feb. 28, 1813 to May 27, 1813 in Capt. John W. Weeks' Company, 11th Regt. Ref: R. & L. 1812, AGO Page 4.

‡*PRATT, LYMAN S.
Served from April 12 to May 20, 1814 in company of Capt. James Gray Jr., Sumner's Regt. Pension Certificate of widow, Sally E., No. 13388.

PRATT, OLNEY.
Served in Capt. Cross' Company, Col. Martindale's Regt. Detached Militia in U. S. service 2 months and 14 days, 1812. Ref: Book 53, AGO Page 38.

*PRATT, SAMUEL.
Enlisted Oct. 23, 1813 and served 26 days. in Capt. Asahel. Langworthy's Company, Dixon's Regt. and Col. Isaac Clark's Rifle Corps; transferred to Capt. Jesse Post's Company, Dixon's Regt. and served 28 days.

PRATT, SANFORD.
Served from April 22, 1813 to April 25, 1814 in Capt. James Taylor's Company and Capt. Gideon Spencer's Company. 30th Regt. Ref: R. & L. 1812, AGO Pages 52, 57, 59.

*PRATT, SIMEON.
Served in 4 Regt. (Peck's) Vt. Militia and in Corning's Detachment, Vt. Militia.

‡*PRATT, SOL. C., Sergeant.
Served in Capt. Noyes' Company, Col. Jonathan Williams' Regt. Detached Militia in U. S. service 2 months and 6 days, 1812. Pension Certificate No. 1542.

PRAY, EPHRAIM.   Calais.
Served from May 1 to June 30, 1814 in Capt. Alexander Brooks' Corps of Artillery. Ref: R. & L. 1812, AGO Page 31.

*PRAY, JONATHAN.   Calais.
Volunteered to go to Plattsburgh, September, 1814, and served 10 days in Capt. Gideon Wheelock's Company.

*PRAY. MOSES.
Served with Hospital Attendants, Vt.

*PREBLE, ABRAHAM.
Served from April 12 to May 20, 1814 in Capt. George Fisher's Company, Sumner's Regt.

PRELMES, CHARLES, Franklin County.
Volunteered to go to Plattsburgh Sept. 11, 1814 and served in 15th or 22nd Regt. Ref: Hemenway's Vt. Gazetteer, Vol. 2, Page 391.

*PRENTICE. ELI.
Served in 1 Regt. (Martindale's) Vt. Militia.

PRENTISS, ANSON D.,   St. Albans.
Volunteered and was in the action at Plattsburgh Sept. 11, 1814; serving in Capt. Samuel H. Farnsworth's Company. Ref: Hemenway's Vt. Gazetteer, Vol. 2, Page 434.

PRENTISS, JOHN,   Bakersfield.
Volunteered and was at the battle of Plattsburgh Sept. 11, 1814, serving in Capt. M. Stearns' Company. Ref: Hemenway's Vt. Gazetteer, Vol. 2, Page 394.

*PRENTISS. JONATHAN JR., Captain.
Enlisted Sept. 25, 1813 in Col. Luther Dixon's Regt.

PRESBURY, WILLIAM.
Served in Capt. Benjamin Bradford's Company; on Muster Roll from May 31 to Aug. 31, 1813. Ref: R. & L. 1812, AGO Page 26.

PRESCOTT, ELISHA,   Strafford.
Volunteered to go to Plattsburgh, September, 1814, and served in Capt. Joseph Barrett's Company. Ref: Book 52, AGO Page 41.

PRESCOTT, JOSEPH,   Montpelier.
Served from March 1, 1814 to June 19, 1815 in Capt. Taylor's Company, 30th Inf. Ref: R. & L. 1812, AGO Page 23.

PRESCOTT, SHERBURN,   Strafford.
Volunteered to go to Plattsburgh, September, 1814, and served in Capt. Joseph Barrett's Company. Ref: Book 52, AGO Page 41.

*PRESCOTT, WILLIAM, Sergeant, Vershire. Served in Capt. Taylor's Company, Col. Fifield's Regt. Detached Militia in U. S. service 2 months and 21 days, 1812. Served in Capt. Walker's Company, Col. Fifield's Regt. Detached Militia in U. S. service 3 months and 9 days, 1812. Volunteered to go to Plattsburgh, September, 1814, and served 3 days in Capt. Ira Corse's Company. Ref: Book 52, AGO Page 91.

PRESTON, AMBROSE,   Strafford.
Volunteered to go to Plattsburgh, September, 1814, and served in Capt. Cyril Chandler's Company.   Ref: Book 52, AGO Page 42.

PRESTON, AMOS.
Enlisted April 21, 1813 for 1 year in Capt. Simeon Wright's Company. Ref: R. & L. 1812, AGO Page 51.

*PRESTON, ASAHEL.
Served in Capt. Morrill's Company, Col. Fifield's Regt. Detached Militia, in U. S. service 3 months and 10 days, 1812.

*PRESTON, HERNAN.
Served in 4 Regt. (Peck's) Vt. Militia.

*PRESTON, ISAIAH.
Served in Corning's Detachment, Vt. Militia and in 4 Regt. (Peck's) Vt. Militia.

*PRESTON, JOHN.
Served in Capt. Rogers' Company, Col. Fifield's Regt. Detached Militia in U. S. service 3 days, 1812. Served in Capt. Taylor's Company, Col. Fifield's Regt. Detached Militia in U. S. service 2 months and 21 days, 1812.

PRESTON, MOSES N.
Served in Capt. Barns' Company.
Col. Wm. Williams' Regt. Detached
Militia in U. S. service 4 months
and 22 days, 1812. Ref: Book 53,
AGO Page 13.

*PRESTON. NOAH, Corporal.
Served in 4 Regt. (Peck's) Vt. Militia.

PRESTON. ORMOND.
Served in War of 1812 and was captured by troops June 26, 1813 at
Beaver Dams; discharged Aug. 10th.
Ref: Records of Naval Records and
Library, Navy Dept.

*PRESTON, REUBEN, Lieutenant.
Served in 3 Regt. (Bowdish) Vt.
Militia.

*PRESTON, SAMUEL, Captain.
Served in 3 Regt. (Williams') Vt.
Militia.

PRICE, DAVID. Corporal.
Served in Capt. Samuel H. Holly's
Company, 11th Regt.; on Pay Roll
for January and February, 1813. Ref:
R. & L. 1812, AGO Page 25.

*PRICE, WILLIAM JR.
Served in Dixon's Regt. Vt. Militia.

*PRIER. DANIEL.
Served in Dixon's Regt. Vt. Militia.

*PRIER, LEVI.
Enlisted Sept. 25, 1813 and served
1 month and 23 days in Capt. Elijah
Birge's Company, Col. Dixon's Regt.

*PRIEST. JOSEPH,   Coventry.
Served in Capt. Hiram Mason's Company, Col. Fifield's Regt. Detached
Militia in U. S. service from Sept.
19, 1812 to March 16, 1813.

PRILL, JOHN.
Served in Capt. Samuel H. Holly's
Company, 11th Regt.; on Pay Roll
for January and February, 1813. Ref:
R. & L. 1812, AGO Page 25.

*PRIM. NATHANIEL.
Served from April 12 to April 21,
1814 in Capt. Othniel Jewett's Company, Sumner's Regt.

PRIME. GRANT,   Bristol.
Volunteered to go to Plattsburgh,
September, 1814, and was at the
battle, serving 8 days in Capt. Jehiel
Saxton's Company, Sumner's Regt.
Ref: Book 51, AGO Page 19.

PRIME, JOHN.
Served from Feb. 13 to May 12, 1813
in company of Capt. John McNeil
Jr., 11th Regt. Ref: R. & L. 1812,
AGO Pages 16 and 17.

PRIME. JONATHAN.
Served from March 3 to June 2,
1813 in Capt. Jonathan Starks' Company, 11th Regt. Ref: R. & L. 1812,
AGO Page 19.

PRINDLE. MARTIN, Fairfield or Fairfax.
Served in 1813 and 1814 in Capt. Joseph Beeman's Company. Volunteer-

ed to go to Plattsburgh, September,
1814, and served 8 days in Capt.
Josiah Grout's Company. Ref: Book
51, AGO Page 159; Hemenway's Vt.
Gazetteer, Vol. 2, Page 402.

‡PRIOR, ALVA.   Cambridge.
Volunteered to go to Plattsburgh,
September, 1814, and served 8 days
in Capt. Salmon Green's Company.
Pension Certificate of widow, Experience, No. 26972.

PRIOR. DANIEL,   Cambridge.
Volunteered to go to Plattsburgh,
September, 1814, and served 8 days
in Capt. Salmon Green's Company.
Ref: Book 51, AGO Pages 207 and 277.

‡*PRIOR. WILLIAM.
Served in Capt. Willson's Company,
Col. Wm. Williams' Regt. Detached
Militia in U. S. service 4 months and
24 days, 1812. Pension Certificate No.
11405.

*PRIOR, WILLIAM JR.
Enlisted Oct. 2, 1813 in Capt. Asahel
Langworthy's Company, Col. Isaac
Clark's Rifle Corps. Served in Capt.
Eldridge's Company, Col. Dixon's
Regt. Detached Militia in U. S. service 1 month and 24 days, 1813.

PRITCHARD, HARVEY,   Middlebury.
Volunteered to go to Plattsburgh,
September, 1814, and served 7 days;
no organization given. Ref: Book 51,
AGO Pages 49 and 51.

PRITCHARD, JOHN,   Franklin County.
Volunteered to go to Plattsburgh
Sept. 11, 1814, and served in 15th or
22nd Regt. Ref: Hemenway's Vt. Gazetteer, Vol. 2, Page 392.

‡*PRITCHARD, JOSEPH.
Served in Capt. Phelps' Company,
4 Regt. (Williams') Vt. Militia. Pension Certificate No. 11076.

*PROCTOR, ASA.
Served from Sept. 25 to Nov. 13,
1813 in Capt. Thomas Waterman's
Company, Dixon's Regt.

*PROCTOR, ASA.
Served in Capt. Wilkins' Company,
Col. Dixon's Regt. Detached Militia
in U. S. service 1 month and 18 days,
1813.

PROCTOR. ASA.
Served in Capt. Chadwick's Company.
Ref: R. & L. 1812, AGO Page 32.

*PROCTOR. HANIBAL.
Enlisted May 11, 1813 for 1 year in
Capt. James Taylor's Company, 30th
Regt.; on Muster Roll from Nov. 30
to Dec. 31, 1813. Also served as
drummer in 4 Regt. (Williams') Vt.
Militia. Ref: R. & L. 1812, AGO
Pages 52 and 57.

PROCTOR, JOHN.
Served from April 23 to July 22, 1813
in Capt. Phineas Williams' Company,
11th Regt. Also served in Capt.
James Taylor's Company, 30th Regt.;
on Muster Roll from Nov. 30 to Dec.
31, 1813. Ref: R. & L. 1812, AGO
Pages 14 and 52.

PROCTOR, JOHN, Drummer, Littletown, Mass. Enlisted at Burlington Jan. 28, 1814 in Capt. Wm. Miller's Company, 30th Regt.; transferred to Capt. James Taylor's Company, 30th Regt. March 8, 1814. Joined Capt. Gideon Spencer's Company, 30th Regt. June 1, 1814; on Muster Roll Dec. 30, 1813 to June 30, 1814. Ref: R. & L. 1812, AGO Pages 53, 54, 55, 56.

PROCTOR, NATHANIEL, Montpelier. Volunteered to go to Plattsburgh, September, 1814, and served 8 days in Capt. Timothy Hubbard's Company. Ref: Book 52, AGO Pages 246 and 256.

*PROCTOR, OLIVER. Served from April 12 to May 20, 1814 in Capt. George Fisher's Company, Sumner's Regt.

*PROCTOR, SAMUEL. Served in 1 Regt. (Judson's) Vt. Militia.

‡*PROCTOR, WILLIAM. Served in 3 Regt. (Tyler's) Vt. Militia. Also served in Capt. Howe's Company. Pension Certificate of widow, Polly, No. 39843.

PROPER, JOHN. Served from May 1 to May 31, 1814; no organization given. Ref: R. & L. 1812, AGO Page 29.

‡PROUBY, NATHANIEL. Served in Capt. Johnson's Company. Pension Certificate No. 11172.

PROUT, JAMES. Served from March 12 to June 30, 1814 in Regt. of Light Dragoons. Ref: R. & L. 1812, AGO Page 21.

*PROUTY, CALEB. Served in Capt. Weeks' Company, 11th Regt.; on Pay Roll for January and February, 1813. Also served in 4 Regt. (Williams') Vt. Militia. Ref: R. & L. 1812, AGO Page 5.

*PROUTY, JAMES, Sergeant. Served in Capt. Preston's Company, Col. Jonathan Williams' Regt. Detached Militia in U. S. service 2 months and 6 days, 1812.

*PROUTY, LUTHER. Sergeant, Jericho. Served as a Sergeant in Capt. Myron Reed's Company, 3 Regt. (Tyler's) Vt. Militia and took part in the battle of Plattsburgh. Died in 1856 or 1857 leaving widow Hepzebah. Ref: History of Jericho, Page 142.

*PROUTY, NATHANIEL. Served from April 12 to April 15, 1814 in Lieut. Justus Foote's Company, Sumner's Regt.

PROWTER, CALEB, Highgate. Served from Sept. 1, 1812 in Capt. Conrade Saxe's' Company, 4 Regt. (Williams'). Ref: Hemenway's Vt. Gazetteer, Vol. 2, Page 420.

PROWTY, NATHANIEL, Middlebury. Served from Sept. 1, 1814 to June 16, 1815 in Capt. Sanford's Company, 30th Inf. Ref: B. & L. 1812, AGO Page 28.

PRUN, DANIEL. Served from Sept. 25 to Sept. 30, 1813 in Capt. N. B. Eldridge's Company, Dixon's Regt. Ref: Book 52, AGO Page 267.

PRUN, WILLIAM JR. Enlisted Sept. 25, 1813 in Capt. N. B. Eldridge's Company, Dixon's Regt. Ref: Book 52, AGO Page 267.

PUAN, FRANCIS, Shoreham. Enlisted in Capt. Samuel H. Holly's Company. Ref: Rev. J. F. Goodhue's History of Shoreham, Page 102.

*PUBLEE, LUMAN (or Rublee?) Served in 1 Regt. (Judson's) Vt. Militia.

PUDNEY, JUSTIS. Served from May 1 to June 1, 1814 as blacksmith in Alexander Parris' Company of Artificers. Ref: R. & L. 1812, AGO Page 24.

‡PUFFER, ERASMUS. Served in Capt. Parker's Company. Pension Certificate No. 31999.

*PUFFER, PETER. Served from April 12 to April 21, 1814 in Capt. Eseck Sprague's Company, Sumner's Regt.

PULSIFER, GANISH. Served from May 1 to June 30, 1814 in Capt. Haig's Corps of Light Dragoons. Ref: R. & L. 1812, AGO Page 20.

*PULSIFER, SALMON. Served in Capt. Durkee's Company, Col. Fifield's Regt. Detached Militia in U. S. service 2 months and 14 days, 1812.

PUNER, JASON C. Served from Sept. 25 to Oct. 13, 1813 in Capt. N. B. Eldridge's Company, Dixon's Regt. Ref: Book 52, AGO Page 267.

PURINGTON, JOHN, Gosstown. Served from May 1 to July 3, 1814 in Capt. Goodenor's Company, 33rd Inf. Ref: R. & L. 1812, AGO Page 30.

*PURMONT, JOSHUA. Enlisted Sept. 18, 1813 in Capt. Isaac Finch's Company, Col. Clark's Rifle Regt.

PURPLE, ROBERT. Served in company of Capt. John McNeil Jr., 11th Regt.; on Pay Roll for January and February, 1813. Ref: R. & L. 1812, AGO Page 17.

PURSE, WILLIAM. Served in War of 1812 and was captured by troops June 26, 1813 at Beaver Dams; discharged Aug. 10th. Ref: Records of Naval Records and Library, Navy Dept.

PUTNAM, ABEL. Served in Capt. Richardson's Company, Col. Martindale's Regt. Detached Militia in U. S. service 2 months and 13 days, 1812. Pension Certificate No. 3860. Pension Certificate of widow, Laura A., No. 18615.

‡*PUTNAM, ARCHELAUS, Woodstock.
Served in Capt. Phelps' Company,
Col. Jonathan Williams' Regt. De-
tached Militia in U. S. service 2
months and 21 days, 1812. Pension
Certificate No. 1137.

‡PUTNAM, ASA, Cambridge.
Volunteered to go to Plattsburgh,
September, 1814, and served 8 days
in Capt. Salmon Green's Company.
Also served in Capt. Chadwick's Com-
pany. Pension Certificate of widow,
Elizabeth, No. 27315. Ref: R. & L.
1812, AGO Page 32.

PUTNAM, BENJAMIN, Sergeant.
Served in Capt. Phineas Williams'
Company, 11th Regt.; on Pay Roll for
January and February, 1813. Ref:
R. & L. 1812, AGO Page 15.

*PUTNAM, CALVIN.
Served in Capt. Walker's Company,
Col. Fifield's Regt. Detached Militia
in U. S. service 6 months and 5 days,
1812.

PUTNAM, DAVID, Vergennes.
Served from Dec. 20, 1814 to June
19, 1815 in Capt. Taylor's Company,
30th Inf. Also served in Capt. Chadwick's Company. Ref: R. & L. 1812,
AGO Pages 23 and 32.

*PUTNAM, HOLDEN, Captain, Middlesex.
Marched to Burlington and served 8
days in April, 1814, in Col. John
Peck's Regt. of Militia.

PUTNAM, HORACE, Middlesex.
Volunteered to go to Plattsburgh,
September, 1814, and served 10 days
in Capt. Holden Putnam's Company,
4 Regt. (Peck's). Ref: Book 52, AGO
Page 251.

PUTNAM, ISAAC, 1st Lieutenant, Montpelier. Volunteered to go to Plattsburgh, September, 1814, and served 8
days in Capt. Timothy Hubbard's Company. Ref: Book 52, AGO Page 256.

PUTNAM, JOHN, Lieutenant, Montpelier.
Appointed 2nd Lieutenant 31st Inf.
April 30, 1813; resigned Feb. 17,
1814. Ref: Heitman's Historical Register & Dictionary USA.

‡*PUTNAM, JOHN.
Served in Capt. Adams' Company,
Col. Jonathan Williams' Regt. De-
tached Militia in U. S. service 2
months and 7 days, 1812. Pension
Certificate No. 3793.

*PUTNAM, JOHN JR.
Served in Capt. Rogers' Company,
Col. Fifield's Regt. Detached Militia
in U. S. service 2 months and 18
days, 1812.

*PUTNAM, JOHN.
Served in Capt. Rogers' Company,
Col. Fifield's Regt. Detached Militia
in U. S. service 5 months and 6
days, 1812.

*PUTNAM, JOSEPH, Thetford.
Served in Capt. Taylor's Company,
Col. Fifield's Regt. Detached Militia
in U. S. service 2 months and 21

days, 1812. Volunteered to go to
Plattsburgh, September, 1814, and
served 5 days in Capt. Orange Hubbard's Company.

*PUTNAM, LEWIS, Middlesex.
Served in Capt. Holden Putnam's
Company, 4 Regt. (Peck's) Vt. Mili-
tia.

‡*PUTNAM, THOMAS.
Served in Capt. Wheeler's Company,
Col. Fifield's Regt. Detached Militia
in U. S. service 2 months and 10
days, 1812. Pension Certificate No.
8856.

*PUTNEY, BAILEY, Tunbridge.
Born in Tunbridge, Vt.; aged 19
years; 5 feet 7 inches high; light complexion; blue eyes; light hair; by
profession a farmer. Served in Capt.
Bingham's Company, Col. Jonathan
Williams' Regt. Detached Militia in
U. S. service 2 months and 9 days,
1812. Enlisted at Tunbridge May 17,
1813 in U. S. Army for 1 year. Name
of father James Putney. Ref: Paper
in custody of Vt. Historical Society.

*PUTNEY, EZRA.
Served in Capt. Sabin's Company,
Col. Jonathan Williams' Regt. Detached Militia in U. S. service 2
months and 6 days, 1812.

PUTNEY, JOSEPH.
Served from April 1 to June 30, 1813
in Lieut. Wm. S. Foster's Company,
11th Regt. Ref: R. & L. 1812, AGO
Page 6.

*QUIMBY, JOHN.
Served with Hospital Attendants, Vt.

QUIMBY, JONATHAN.
Served in Capt. Benjamin Bradford's
Company; joined by transfer July
22, 1813; on Muster Roll from May
31 to Aug. 31, 1813. Volunteered
to go to Plattsburgh, September, 1814,
and served 7 days in company of
Capt. Frederick Griswold of Brookfield. Ref: R. & L. 1812, AGO Page
26; Book 52, AGO Pages 52 and 62.

QUIMBY, JOSEPH.
Served in Capt. Benjamin Bradford's
Company; joined by transfer July 22,
1813; on Muster Roll from May 31
to Aug. 31, 1813. Ref: R. & L.
1812, AGO Page 26.

QUIMBY, STEPHEN.
Enlisted Feb. 8, 1813 in Capt. Jonathan Starks' Company, 11th Regt.;
on Pay Roll to May 31, 1813. Ref:
R. & L. 1812, AGO Page 19.

QUIMBY, THOMAS.
Volunteered to go to Plattsburgh,
September, 1814, and served in Capt.
Ebenezer Spencer's Company of Ver-
shire. Ref: Book 52, AGO Pages 48
and 49.

QUIN, MICHAEL, Franklin County.
Enlisted Dec. 18, 1812 for 5 years in
Capt. White Youngs' Company, 15th
Regt.; on Muster Roll from Aug. 31
to Dec. 31, 1814. Ref: R. & L. 1812,
AGO Page 27.

*QUINCEY, SAMUEL, Corporal.
Served in 3 Regt. (Tyler's) Vt. Militia.

QUIRE, RAYMOND.
Served in Capt. Haig's Corps of Light Dragoons; on Pay Roll to June 30, 1814. Ref: R. & L. 1812, AGO Page 20.

*RACE, LUTHER.
Served from April 12 to April 21, 1814 in Lieut. James S. Morton's Company, Col. W. B. Sumner's Regt.

RACE, MILTON, Trumpeter, Salisbury.
Served from May 1 to June 30, 1814 in Capt. Haig's Corps of Light Dragoons. Ref: R. & L. 1812, AGO Page 20.

*RALPH, DAVID, Randolph.
Volunteered to go to Plattsburgh, September, 1814, and served in Capt. Lebbeus Egerton's Company.

*RALPH, JACOB, Chelsea?
Served from June 11 to June 14, 1813 in Lieut. Bates' Company, 1 Regt. (Judson's). Volunteered to go to Plattsburgh, September, 1814 and served 4 days in Capt. Jonathan Jennings' Company.

*RAMOND, PAUL JR. (or Raymond, Ruel Jr.?) Served in Sumner's Regt. Vt. Militia.

‡*RAMSDELL, DAVID, Shoreham.
Served from April 12 to May 20, 1814 in company of Capt. James Gray, Jr., Sumner's Regt. Volunteered to go to Plattsburgh, September, 1814, and served 6 days in Capt. Samuel Hand's Company. Pension Certificate of widow, Deborah, No. 32130.

RAMSDELL, FARRINGTON, Shoreham.
Volunteered to go to Plattsburgh, September, 1814, and served 6 days in Capt. Samuel Hand's Company. Ref: Rev. J. F. Goodhue's History of Shoreham, Page 107.

*RAND, JOHN.
Served in Capt. Rogers' Company, Col. Fifield's Regt. Detached Militia in U. S. service 5 months and 27 days, 1812.

*RAND, NATHANIEL, Sergeant, Pittsford. Served as Sergeant and Cornet in 1 Regt. (Martindale's) Vt. Militia.

*RAND, ROBERT.
Served in Capt. Rogers' Company, Col. Fifield's' Regt. Detached Militia in U. S. service 2 months and 20 days, 1812.

RAND, S., Stowe.
Volunteered to go to Plattsburgh, September, 1814, and served in Capt. Nehemiah Perkins' Company. 4th Regt. (Peck's). Ref: Hemenway's Vt. Gazetteer, Vol. 2, Page 742.

*RANDALL, ELIAS, Woodstock.
Served in Capt. Phelps' Company, Col. Jonathan Williams' Regt. Detached Militia in U. S. service 2 months and 21 days, 1812.

RANDALL, ELIJAH, Franklin County.
Volunteered to go to Plattsburgh, Sept. 11, 1814, and served in 15th or 22nd Regt. Ref: Hemenway's Vt. Gazetteer, Vol. 2, Page 392.

‡*RANDALL, GORDON, Braintree.
Served in Capt. Wheatley's Company, Col. Fifield's Regt. Detached Militia in U. S. service 6 months. Pension Certificate of widow, Laura S., No. 12094.

RANDALL, JARVIS.
Served in Capt. Benjamin S. Edgerton's Company, 11th Regt.; on Pay Roll for September and October, 1812. Ref: R. & L. 1812, AGO Page 1.

*RANDALL, JESSE.
Served from Sept. 25 to Oct. 3, 1813 in Capt. Jesse Post's Company, Dixon's Regt.

RANDALL, JOHN, Fairfax.
Volunteered to go to Plattsburgh, September, 1814, and served 8 days in Capt. Josiah Grout's Company.

*RANDALL, JONAS.
Served from April 12 to April 21, 1814 in Capt. Edmund B. Hill's Company, Sumner's Regt.

RANDALL, JOSIAH, Fifer, Richford.
Enlisted Sept. 25, 1813 and served 1 month and 23 days in Capt. Martin D. Follett's Company, Col. Dixon's Regt. Detached Militia in U. S. service. Ref: Book 52, AGO Page 268; Book 53, AGO Page 106.

RANDALL, THOMAS, Danville.
Volunteered to go to Plattsburgh, September, 1814, and served 3 days in Capt. Solomon Langmaid's Company. Ref: Book 51, AGO Pages 75 and 76.

*RANDALL, WILLIAM, Musician.
Served in Capt. Mason's Company, Col. Fifield's Regt. Detached Militia in U. S. service 6 months, 1812.

RANDELP, AMOS.
Served from Feb. 17 to May 6, 1813 in Capt. Charles Follett's Company, 11th Regt. Ref: R. & L. 1812, AGO Page 13.

RANDOLPH, ELIJAH, Franklin County.
Volunteered to go to Plattsburgh Sept. 11, 1814 and served in 15th or 22nd Regt. Ref: Hemenway's Vt. Gazetteer, Vol. 2, Page 391.

RANDOLPH, FRANCIS.
Served from March 1, 1813 to Feb. 18, 1814 in Lt. Chatterfield's Company, 4th Inf. Ref: R. & L. 1812, AGO Page 30.

RANGER, JOEL, Sudbury.
Volunteered to go to Plattsburgh, September, 1814, and served 6 days in Capt. Thomas Hall's Company. Ref: Book 52, AGO Page 122.

RANSALEAR, JOHN.
Served from March 8 to June 7, 1813 in Capt. Charles Follett's Company, 11th Regt. Ref: R. & L. 1812, AGO Page 13.

*RANSLARE, KELLEY.
Served from June 11 to June 14, 1813 in Capt. Hezekiah Barns' Company, 1st Regt. 2nd Brig. 3rd Div.

*RANSLOW, CALEY.
Served in Capt. Willson's Company, Col. Wm. Williams' Regt. Detached Militia in U. S. service 4 months and 24 days, 1812.

‡RANSLOW, KELLEY.
Served in Capt. Willson's Company. Pension Certificate No. 2129. Pension Certificate of widow, Jerusha, No. 16530.

RANSOM, AMI R. C.
Served in Capt. Benjamin S. Edgerton's Company, 11th Regt.; on Pay Roll for September and October, 1812 and January and February, 1813. Ref: R. & L. 1812, AGO Pages 1 and 2.

RANSOM, BRIANT, Captain, Poultney.
Volunteered to go to Plattsburgh, September, 1814, and served 2 days in command of company raised in Poultney. Ref: Book 52, AGO, Page 147.

RANSOM, MOSES.
Enlisted Feb. 17, 1813 in Capt. Charles Follett's Company, 11th Regt. and served to date of death, April 10, 1813. Ref: R. & L. 1812, AGO Page 13.

RANSOM, SAMUEL.
Served in Capt. Benjamin S. Edgerton's Company, 11th Regt.; on Pay Roll for September and October, 1812 and January and February, 1813. Ref: R. & L. 1812, AGO Page 2.

RANSOM, WARREN.
Served from March 3 to June 2, 1813 in Capt. Phineas Williams' Company, 11th Regt. Served from May 1 to June 30, 1814 in Capt. Alexander Brooks' Corps of Artillery. Ref: R. & L. 1812, AGO Pages 14 and 31.

RASSOM, BENJAMIN.
Served from May 1 to June 30, 1814 in Capt. Haig's Corps of Light Dragoons. Ref: R. & L. 1812, AGO Page 20.

RATHBONE, ALBERT, Ensign.
Served as private, corporal and sergeant 11th Inf. May 18, 1812 to April, 1815; appointed Ensign 11th Inf. April 7, 1815; honorably discharged June 15, 1815. Also served in Capt. Weeks' Company, 11th Regt.; on Pay Roll for January and February, 1813. Ref: Heitman's Historical Register & Dictionary USA; R. & L. 1812, AGO Page 5.

RATHBORN, JAMES.
Served from April 27, 1813 to April 27, 1814 in Capt. James Taylor's Company and Capt. Gideon Spencer's Company, 30th Regt. Ref: R. & L. 1812, AGO Pages 52, 57, 59.

RAULINGS, JOHN.
Served from May 1 to June 30, 1814 in Capt. Haig's Corps of Light Dragoons. Ref: R. & L. 1812, AGO Page 20.

RAWLING, DAVID, Corinth.
Volunteered to go to Plattsburgh, September, 1814, and served 3 days in Capt. Abel Jackman's Company. Ref: Book 52, AGO Pages 44 and 45.

RAWLINGS, JONATHAN, Corinth.
Volunteered to go to Plattsburgh, September, 1814, and served in Capt. Abel Jackman's Company. Ref: Book 52, AGO Page 44.

‡RAWSON, LOWELL.
Served in Capt. Hammond's Company. Pension Certificate of widow, Sally, No. 27664.

*RAY, CALVIN.
Served in 1 Regt. (Judson's) Vt. Militia.

*RAY, ELEZER.
Served from April 12 to April 21, 1814 in Lieut. Justus Foote's Company, Sumner's' Regt.

*RAYMOND, ASAHEL, Captain, Stowe.
Served as Ensign in Corning's Detachment, Vt. Militia and Captain in 4 Regt. (Peck's) Vt. Militia.

*RAYMOND, ELEAZER T., Randolph.
Volunteered to go to Plattsburgh, September, 1814, and served in Capt. Lebbeus Egerton's Company. Also served in 1 Regt. (Judson's) Vt. Militia.

*RAYMOND, JONATHAN.
Served from April 12 to April 21, 1814 in Capt. Eseck Sprague's Company, Sumner's Regt.

*RAYMOND, LYSANDER, Sergeant, Woodstock. Served in Capt. Phelps' Company, Col. Jonathan Williams' Regt. Detached Militia in U. S. service 2 months and 21 days, 1812.

*RAYMOND, PERIS.
Served in Sumner's Regt. Vt. Militia.

*RAYMOND, RUEL JR.
Served in Sumner's Regt. Vt. Militia.

RAYMOND, SILAS.
Enlisted June 22, 1812 for 5 years in company of late Capt. J. Brooks, commanded by Lt. John I. Cromwell. Corps of U. S. Artillery; on Muster Roll from April 30 to June 30, 1814. Ref R. & L. 1812, AGO Page 18.

*RAYMOND, SMITH.
Served in Corning's Detachment, Vt. Militia.

READ, DANIEL, Fairfield.
Volunteered to go to Plattsburgh, Sept. 11, 1814, and served in Capt. Benjamin Wooster's Company. Ref: Hemenway's' Vt. Gazetteer, Vol. 2, Page 408.

*READ, DANIEL, Lieutenant, Wardsboro.
Volunteered to go to Plattsburgh, September, 1814, and served 7 days in Capt. L. Scott's Company. Also served in 2 Regt. 3 Brig. 3 Div. Vt. Militia. Ref: Book 51, AGO Page 153.

*READ, DAVID.
Served in Capt. Rogers' Company, Col. Fifield's Regt. Detached Militia in U. S. service 2 months and 18 days, 1812.

*READ, ELIJAH (or Reed), Corporal.
Served in Capt. Parsons' Company, Col. Jonathan Williams' Regt. Detached Militia in U. S. service 2 months and 13 days, 1812.

‡*READ, HORACE (or Reed).
Enlisted Sept. 25, 1813 in Capt. N. B. Eldridge's Company, Dixon's Regt. Pension Certificate of widow, Almira P., No. 34980.

*READ, LOWELL.
Served in Capt. Sabins' Company, Col. Jonathan Williams' Regt. Detached Militia in U. S. service 2 months and 6 days, 1812.

*READ, LUTHER, Corporal.
Served in 4 Regt. (Williams') Vt. Militia.

READ, RUFUS, Thetford.
Volunteered to go to Plattsburgh, September, 1814, and served 6 days in Capt. Orange Hubbard's Company. Ref: Book 52, AGO Page 51.

*READ, SIMEON.
Served in 1 Regt. (Judson's) Vt. Militia.

‡*READER, WILLIAM.
Served from April 12 to April 21, 1814 in Capt. Eseck Sprague's Company, Sumner's Regt. Also served in Capt. Manson's Company. Pension Certificate No. 22207.

READING, THOMAS.
Served in company of late Capt. J. Brooks commanded by Lt. John I. Cromwell, Corps of U. S. Artillery; on Muster Roll from April 30, 1814 to June 30, 1814; prisoner of war on parole; transferred from Capt. Leonard's Company. Ref: R. & L. 1812, AGO Page 18.

REDFIELD, ANTHONY C.
Served from Jan. 25 to June 8, 1813 in Capt. John W. Weeks' Company, 11th Regt. Ref: R. & L. 1812, AGO Pages 4 and 5.

REDMAN, JAMES. Thetford.
Marched for Plattsburgh, September, 1814, and went as far as Bolton. serving 6 days in Capt. Salmon Howard's Company, 2nd Regt. Ref: Book 52, AGO Page 15.

*REDWAY, TIMOTHY, Calais.
Volunteered to go to Plattsburgh, September, 1814, and served 10 days in Capt. Gideon Wheelock's Company.

REE, ROBERT W., Herpesfield.
Served from May 1 to July 9, 1814 in Capt. Spencer's Company, 29th Inf. Ref: R. & L. 1812, AGO Page 30.

REECE, WILLIAM.
Enlisted May 4, 1813 for 1 year in Capt. John Wires' Company, 30th Regt. Ref: R. & L. 1812, AGO Page 40.

‡*REED, ABIHU.
Served in Capt. Dorrance's Company, 4 Regt. (Williams') Vt. Militia. Pension Certificate of widow, Phebe, No. 8879.

REED, ANDRUS.
Volunteered to go to Plattsburgh, September, 1814, and served 7 days in Capt. Frederick Griswold's Company raised in Brookfield, Vt. Ref: Book 52, AGO Pages 52 and 58.

‡REED, AUGUSTUS.
Served in Capt. Gordon's Company. Pension Certificate No. 25609.

*REED, CALVIN.
Served in Capt. Preston's Company, Col. Jonathan Williams' Regt. Detached Militia in U. S. service 2 months and 6 days, 1812.

REED, DANFORTH, Barre.
Volunteered to go to Plattsburgh, September, 1814, and served in Capt. Warren Ellis' Company. Ref: Hemenway's Vt. Gazetteer, Vol. 4, Page 41.

*REED, DAVID, Plainfield.
Served from June 11 to June 14, 1813 in Capt. Moses Jewett's Company, 1st Regt. 2nd Brig. 3rd Div. Volunteered to go to Plattsburgh, September, 1814, and served 9 days in Capt. James English's Company.

‡REED, BAYLEY (Frye B.)
Volunteered to go to Plattsburgh, September, 1814, and served 7 days in Capt. Frederick Griswold's Company raised in Brookfield, Vt. Also served in Capt. Collamer's Company. Pension Certificate of widow, Asenath S., No. 42391.

*REED, ISAAC, Randolph.
Volunteered to go to Plattsburgh, September, 1814, and served in Capt. Lebbeus Egerton's Company.

REED, JACOB.
Served in Lt. Wm. S. Foster's Company, 11th Regt.; on Pay Roll for January and February, 1813. Ref: R. & L. 1812, AGO Page 7.

REED, JOHN B., Corporal, Shoreham.
Served in Capt. Samuel H. Holly's Company, 11th Regt.; on Pay Roll for January and February, 1813; lost his left hand at the siege of Fort Erie. Ref: R. & L. 1812, AGO Page 25; Rev. J. F. Goodhue's History of Shoreham, Page 102.

*REED, JOSEPH F., Sergeant.
Served in Capt. Willson's Company, Col. Wm. Williams' Regt. Detached Militia in U. S. service 4 months and 24 days, 1812. Pension Certificate of widow, Harriet, No. 1815.

*REED, JOSHUA JR., Sergeant.
Served from June 11 to June 14, 1813 in Capt. Samuel Blinn's Company, 1st Regt. (Judson's).

REED, JOSIAH.
Served from April 27, 1813 to April 27, 1814 in Capt. James Taylor's Company and Capt. Gideon Spencer's Company, 30th Regt. Ref: R. & L. 1812, AGO Pages 52, 57, 59.

REED, JOSIAH, Corporal.
Served in Capt. Weeks' Company,
11th Regt.; on Pay Roll for January and February, 1813. Ref: R. &
L. 1812, AGO Page 5.

*REED, MATTHIAS.
Served in Capt. Strait's Company, Col.
Martindale's Regt. Detached Militia
in U. S. service 2 months and 13
days, 1812.

*REED, MOSES,   Plainfield.
Served in Capt. Rogers' Company,
Col. Fifield's Regt. .Detached Militia in U. S. service from Dec. 8,
1812 to March 17, 1813.

‡*REED, MYRON, Captain.
Served in 3 Regt. (Tyler's) Vt. Mili-
tia. Pension Certificate of widow,
Ann, No. 34105.

‡*REED, NATHANIEL JR. (or Read),
Quartermaster Sergeant. Cambridge.
Appointed Quartermaster Sergeant
Sept. 25, 1813 in Col. Dixon's Consolidated Regt. of Vt. Militia. Also
served in Capt. Chadwick's Company.
Born at Warren, Worcester County,
Mass., the son of Nathaniel Read
and Anna Keyes Read. Volunteered
to go to Plattsburgh, September, 1814,
and was in the battle. Pension Certificate No. 2110. Ref: Hemenway's'
Vt. Gazetteer, Vol. 2, Page 616.

REED, PETER,   Tunbridge.
Volunteered to go to Plattsburgh,
September, 1814, and served 4 days
in Capt. Ephraim Hackett's Company. Ref: Book 52, AGO Page 71.

*REED, RENSELLIER, Lieutenant.
Served in 3 Regt. (Bowdish) Vt.
Militia.

REED, SAMUEL.
Served in company of Capt. John
McNeil Jr., 11th Regt.; on Pay Roll
for January and February, 1813. Ref:
R. & L. 1812, AGO Page 17.

*REED, SAMUEL A. (or H.). Lieutenant.
Served in 3 Regt. (Williams') Vt.
Militia.

REED, THOMAS,   Jericho.
Served in Capt. Myron Reed's Company, 3 Regt. (Tyler's); took part in
the Battle of Plattsburgh.

‡REED. THOMAS JR.,   Montpelier.
Volunteered to go to Plattsburgh,
September, 1814, and served 8 days
in Capt. Timothy Hubbard's Com-
pany. Pension Certificate of widow,
Mary L. W., No. 30927.

REED, THOMAS B., Fairfax or Swanton.
Served from Aug. 8, 1812 in com-
pany of Capt. Joseph Beeman Jr.,
11th Regt. U. S. Inf. under Col. Ira
Clark. Served in Lt. V. R. Good-
rich's Company, 11th Regt.; on Pay
Roll for January and February, 1813.
Ref: R. & L. 1812, AGO Page 11;
Hemenway's Vt. Gazetteer, Vol. 2,
Page 402.

REED, WILLIAM,   Plainfield.
Served from Feb. 8 to May 7, 1813
in Lieut. V. R. Goodrich's Com-

pany, 11th Regt. Volunteered to go
to Plattsburgh, September, 1814, and
served 7 days in Capt. James English's Company. Ref: R. & L. 1812,
AGO Page 10; Book 52, AGO Pages
194 and 248.

REES, JAMES, Deputy Quartermaster
General. Served on General Staff
of the Northern Army commanded
by Major General George Izard; on
Pay Roll to July 31, 1814. Ref: R.
& L. 1812, AGO Page 28.

REEVE, ERASTUS, 2nd Lieutenant, Cornwall.. Volunteered to go to Plattsburgh, September, 1814, and was at
the Battle, serving in Capt. Edmund
B. Hill's Company, Sumner's Regt.
Ref: Book 51, AGO Page 13.

‡REITH, BARNABAS (or Keith?)
Served in Capt. Phelps' Company.
Pension Certificate of widow, Leviah,
No. 17655.

*REMELEE, SAMUEL H.
Enlisted April 12, 1814 in Capt.
Shubael Wales' Company, Col. W. B.
Sumner's Regt.; transferred to Capt.
Salmon Foster's Company, Sumner's
Regt.; April 13, 1814 and served to
April 21, 1814.

REMINGTON, HOSEA.
Served in Capt. Phineas Williams'
Company, 11th Regt.; on Pay Roll for
January and February, 1813. Ref:
R. & L. 1812, AGO Page 15.

REMINGTON, IRA.
Served in Capt. Samul Gordon's Company, 11th Regt.; on Pay Roll for
January and February, 1813. Was
captured by troops July 25, 1814 at
Londers Lane; discharged Oct. 8,
1814. Ref: R. & L. 1812. AGO Page
9; Records of Naval Records and
Records and Library, Navy Dept.

‡REMINGTON, JOHN.
Served in Capt. O. Stafford's Company. Pension Certificate No. 34371.

‡REMINGTON, JONATHAN.
Served in Capt. Phineas Williams'
Company, 11th Regt.; on Pay Roll
for January and February, 1813. Pension Certificate of widow, Rachel, No.
22734.

‡REMINGTON, RUFUS.
Enlisted Sept. 8, 1813 for 1 year in
Capt. Simeon Wright's Company. Pen-
sion Certificate of widow, Rebecca,
No. 6521.

‡*REMINGTON, SILAS, Surgeon's Mate,
Rupert. Served in Capt. Hopkins'
Company, Col. Martindale's Regt. Detached Militia in U. S. service 2
months and 13 days, 1812. Served
from June 15, 1814 to June 19, 1815
in Capt. Taylor's Company, 30th Inf.
Pension Certificate of widow, Margaret, No. 39717.

*REMINGTON, WILLIAM.
Served in Capt. Strait's Company,
Col. Martindale's Regt. Detached
Militia in U. S. service 2 months
and 13 days, 1812.

RENELL, AMBROSE.
Served from Feb. 4 to May 3, 1813
in Lt. Wm. S. Foster's Company,
11th Regt. Ref: R. & L. 1812, AGO
Page 6.

REVAUGH, DANIEL.
Enlisted June 3, 1812 for 5 years in
Capt. White Youngs' Company, 15th
Regt.; on Muster Roll from Aug.
31 to Dec. 31, 1814. Ref: R. & L.
1812, AGO Page 27.

*REXFORD, WHITING.
Served in 1 Regt. (Judson's) Vt.
Militia.

REYNOLDS, AARON, St. Albans.
Enlisted May 30, 1813 for 1 year in
Capt. John Wires' Company, 30th
Regt. Ref: R. & L. 1812, AGO Page
40.

‡*REYNOLDS, ALEXANDER, Shoreham.
Served from April 12 to May 20, 1814
in Capt. George Fisher's Company,
Sumner's Regt. Also served in Capt.
Hawley's Company. Pension Certifi-
cate No. 15531.

‡*REYNOLDS, DAVID, Shoreham.
Served in Capt. Richardson's Company, Col. Martindale's Regt. Detached Militia in U. S. service 2
months and 13 days, 1812. Served
from April 12 to May 20, 1814 in
Capt. George Fisher's Company, Sumner's Regt. Volunteered to go to
Plattsburgh, September, 1814, and
served in Capt. Samuel Hand's Company, 6 days. Pension Certificate No.
5532. Pension Certificate of widow,
Sarah, No. 10497.

REYNOLDS, EBENZO.
Served from Feb. 9 to Feb. 28, 1813
in Capt. Samuel H. Holly's Company, 11th Regt. Ref: R. & L. 1812,
AGO Page 25.

*REYNOLDS, ENON.
Served in 4 Regt. (Williams') Vt.
Militia.

‡*REYNOLDS, FOLLETT, Cambridge.
Enlisted Sept. 25, 1813 and served
1 month and 23 days in Capt. Ben-
nett's Company, Col. Dixon's Regt.
Detached Militia in U. S. service.
Volunteered to go to Plattsburgh,
September, 1814, and served 8 days
in Capt. Salmon Green's Company.
Pension Certificate of widow, Hannah,
No. 26247.

*REYNOLDS, HARRY.
Enlisted Sept. 25, 1813 and served
1 month and 23 days in Capt. Charles
Bennett's Company, Col. Dixon's Regt.
Detached Militia in U. S. service.

REYNOLDS, HARVEY.
Served from March 15 to June 30,
1814 in Regt. of Light Dragoons.
Ref: R. & L. 1812, AGO Page 21.

*REYNOLDS, HENRY W.
Served from April 12 to April 21,
1814 in Capt. Eseck Sprague's Company, Sumner's Regt.

‡*REYONLDS, JAMES B.
Served from April 12 to April 21,
1814 in Capt. Shubael Wales' Company, Col. W. B. Sumner's Regt.
Served from May 1 to June 18, 1814;
no organization given. Also served
in Capt. Silas Wright's Company.
Pension Certificate of widow, Mary,
No. 10384.

*REYNOLDS, JOHN.
Served in 3 Regt. (Tyler's) Vt. Militia.

REYNOLDS, JOHN.
Enlisted April 2, 1814 for period of
the war in Capt. Gideon Spencer's
Company, 30th Regt.; on Muster Roll
from Dec. 30, 1813 to June 30, 1814;
transferred to Capt. Clark's Company, 30th Regt. Ref: R. & L. 1812,
AGO Page 57.

*REYNOLDS, JOHN.
Enlisted Sept. 25, 1813 and served 1
month and 23 days in Capt. Amos
Robinson's Company, Col. Dixon's
Regt.

‡REYNOLDS, JOHN D.
Served in Capt. Reynolds' Company.
Pension Certificate No. 15838.

REYNOLDS, JOSEPH.
Enlisted April 2, 1814 during the
war in Capt. James Taylor's Company, 30th Regt. Ref: R. & L. 1812,
AGO Page 53.

REYNOLDS, JOSEPH JR.
Enlisted June 10, 1813 for 1 year in
Capt. Daniel Farrington's Company
(also commanded by Capt. Simeon
Wright) 30th Regt. Ref: R. & L.
1812, AGO Pages 50 and 51.

REYNOLDS, LYMAN.
Enlisted Aug. 16, 1813 for 1 year and
served in Capt. James Taylor's Company and Capt. Gideon Spencer's
Company, 30th Regt. Re-enlisted Feb.
24, 1814 in Light Dragoons; served
in Capt. Haig's Corps of Light Dragoons from May 1 to June 30, 1814.
Ref: R. & L. 1812, AGO Pages 20,
52, 57, 59.

*REYNOLDS, PHILIP, Shoreham.
Served in Capt. Robbins' Company,
Col. Wm. Williams' Regt. Detached
Militia in U. S. service 4 months
and 29 days, 1812. Volunteered to
go to Plattsburgh, September, 1814,
and served 6 days in Capt. Samuel
Hand's Company.

‡REYNOLDS, RAYMOND.
Served from Feb. 18th to June 30,
1814 in Regt. of Light Dragoons,
Capt. A. McFarland's Company. Pen-
sion Certificate of widow, Hannah,
No. 5384. Ref: R. & L. 1812, AGO
Page 21.

‡REYNOLDS, ROBERT.
Served in Capt. J. D. Reynolds'
Company. Pension Certificate of wid-
ow, Mary, No. 37088.

‡*REYNOLDS, ROSWELL.
Served from April 17 to April 21,
1814 in Capt. Othniel Jewett's Com-

pany, Sumner's Regt. Also served
under Captains Munson, Stevens, and
Spencer. Pension Certificate No.
30062.

REYNOLDS, SILAS,   Whiting.
Enlisted July 5, 1813 for 1 year in
Capt. Simeon Wright's Company.
Served from September, 1813, to July
6, 1814 in Capt. Taylor's Company,
30th Inf. Ref: R. & L. 1812, AGO
Pages 23 and 51.

‡*REYNOLDS, SYLVANUS.
Served in Capt. Strait's Company,
Col. Martindale's Regt. Detached
Militia in U. S. service 1 month
and 5 days, 1812. Pension Certifi-
cate of widow, Margaret, No. 33864.

‡*REYNOLDS, THOMAS P., Corporal.
Served in Capt. Pettis' Company, 4
Regt. (Williams') Vt. Militia. Pension Certificate of widow, Elsie, No.
28249.

*REYNOLDS, TYLER.
Served in Capt. Phelps' Company,
Col. Wm. Williams' Regt. Detached
Militia in U. S. service 5 months,
1812.

*REYNOLDS, WILLIAM,   Shoreham.
Served from Oct. 5 to Oct. 16, 1813
in Capt. Roswell's Hunt's Company,
3 Regt. (Tyler's). Also served in
Capt. John Robbins' Company, Col.
Wm. Williams' Regt.

*REYNOLDS, WILLIAM JR.
Served from April 12 to May 20, 1814
in Capt. George Fisher's Company,
Sumner's Regt.

‡*RHOADS, DANIEL.
Served in Capt. Parsons' Company,
Col. Jonathan Williams' Regt. De-
tached Militia in U. S. service 2
months and 13 days, 1812. Pension
Certificate of widow, Mary, No. 2352.

RHODES, JAMES.   Franklin County.
Volunteered to go to Plattsburgh
Sept. 11, 1814 and served in 15th or
22nd Regt. Ref: Hemenway's Vt.
Gazetteer, Vol. 2, Page 391.

RHODES, WILLIAM,   Richmond.
Volunteered to go to Plattsburgh,
September, 1814, and served 9 days
in Capt. Roswell Hunt's Company, 3
Regt. (Tyler's). Ref: Book 51, AGO
Pages 82 and 84.

*RIBBY, IRA.
Served in 1 Regt. (Judson's) Vt.
Militia.

*RICE, ABIJAH,   Enosburgh.
Enlisted Sept. 25, 1813 and served
1 month and 23 days in Capt. Martin
D. Folett's Company, Col. Dixon's
Regt. Detached Militia in U. S. serv-
ice.

RICE, ALPHEUS, Ensign,   Orwell.
Volunteered to go to Plattsburgh,
September, 1814, and served 11 days
in Capt. Wait Branch's Company.
Ref: Book 51, AGO Page 16.

RICE, ANTHONY C., Sergeant, Pittsford.
Volunteered to go to Plattsburgh,
September, 1814, and served 8 days
in Capt. Caleb Hendee's Company.
Ref: Book 52, AGO Page 124.

*RICE, ARA B.,   Woodstock.
Served in Capt. Phelps' Company,
Col. Jonathan Williams' Regt. Detached Militia in U. S. service 2
months and 2 days, 1812.

*RICE, ARTEMUS, Fairfax or Belvidere.
Enlisted Sept. 25, 1813 in Capt. Asa
Wilkins' Company, Dixon's Regt. Vol-
unteered to go to Plattsburgh, Sep-
tember, 1814, and served 7 days in
Capt. Moody Shattuck's Company.

RICE, BENJAMIN,   Enosburgh.
Volunteered to go to Plattsburgh,
September, 1814, and served 6 days;
no organization given. Ref: Book
51, AGO Page 156.

*RICE, CALEB.
Served in Capt. Needham's Company,
Col. Martindale's Regt. Detached
Militia in U. S. service 2 months and
14 days, 1812.

*RICE, CALEB.
Served in Capt. Durkee's Company,
Col. Fifield's Regt. Detached Militia
in U. S. service 2 months and 16
days, 1812.

*RICE, CHARLES.
Served in Capt. Phelps' Company,
Col. Jonathan Williams' Regt. Detached Militia in U. S. service 2
months and 21 days, 1812.

*RICE, EDMUND.
Served in 4 Regt. (Peck's) Vt. Militia.

RICE, ELI,   Sudbury.
Volunteered to go to Plattsburgh,
September, 1814, and served 6 days
in Capt. Thomas Hall's Company.
Ref: Book 52, AGO Page 122.

RICE, EWEL,   Bakersfield.
Volunteered and was at the battle
of Plattsburgh Sept. 11, 1814, serving
in Capt. M. Stearns' Company. Ref:
Hemenway's Vt. Gazetteer, Vol. 2,
Page 394.

*RICE, ISAAC.
Served in Capt. Noyce's Company,
Col. Jonathan Williams' Regt. Detached Militia in U. S. service 2
months and 6 days, 1812.

RICE, JACOB.
Enlisted Jan. 23, 1813 for 5 years
in Capt. White Youngs' Company,
15th Regt.; on Muster Roll from
Aug. 31 to Dec. 31, 1814. Ref: R.
& L. 1812, AGO Page 27.

RICE, JAMES.
Served from April 12 to May 20, 1814
in company of Capt. James Gray Jr.,
Sumner's Regt. Ref: Book 52, AGO
Page 280.

*RICE, JOEL,   Granville.
Served in Capt. O. Lowry's Company, Col. Wm. Williams' Regt. De-

tached Militia in U. S. service 4
months and 26 days, 1812. Volunteered to go to Plattsburgh, September,
1814, and served 7 days in Capt.
Asaph Smith's Company.

*RICE, JOHN,   Highgate.
Served in Capt. Saxe's Company, Col.
Wm. Williams' Regt. Detached Militia in U. S. service 4 months and
24 days, 1812. Served from April 12
to May 20, 1814 in Capt. George
Fisher's Company, Dixon's Regt.

*RICE, JONAS.
Served in Sumner's Regt. Vt. Militia.

RICE, JOSEPH,   Franklin County.
Volunteered to go to Plattsburgh
Sept. 11, 1814 and served in 15th or
22nd Regt. Ref: Hemenway's Vt.
Gazetteer, Vol. 2, Page 391.

*RICE, NATHAN, Corporal.
Enlisted Sept. 29, 1813 in Capt.
Charles Bennett's Company, Dixon's
Regt.

RICE, NATHANIEL.
Served in Lt. Wm. S. Foster's Com-
pany, 11th Regt.; on Pay Roll for
January and February, 1813.   Ref:
R. & L. 1812, AGO Page 7.

‡RICE, OLIVER,   Pittsford.
Volunteered to go to Plattsburgh,
September, 1814, and served 8 days
in Capt. Caleb Hendee's Company.
Pension Certificate of widow, Emillie,
No. 37231.

RICE, S. JR.,   Barre.
Volunteered to go to Plattsburgh,
September, 1814, and served in Capt.
Warren Ellis' Company. Ref: Hemen-
way's Vt. Gazetteer, Vol. 4, Page 42.

*RICE, SAMUEL, Fairfax or Belvidere.
Served in Capt. Taylor's Company,
Col. Wm. Williams' Regt. Detached
Militia in U. S. service 4 months and
24 days, 1812.
Served in Lt. Wm. S. Foster's Com-
pany, 11th Regt.; on Pay Roll for
January and February, 1813. Served
from Sept. 25 to Oct. 5, 1813 in Capt.
Asa Wilkins' Company, Dixon's Regt.
Volunteered to go to Plattsburgh,
September, 1814, and served 7 days
in Capt. Moody Shattuck's Company.
Served in 1 Regt. (Judson's) Vt.
Militia.

‡*RICE, SAMUEL B.
Served in Capt. Parsons' Company,
Col. Jonathan Williams' Regt. De-
tached Militia in U. S. service 2
months and 13 days, 1812. Pension
Certificate No. 9969.

RICE, SILAS,   Barre.
Volunteered to go to Plattsburgh,
September, 1814, and served 10 days
in Capt. Warren Ellis' Company.
Ref: Book 52, AGO Page 242.

‡RICE, STEPHEN.
Served in Capt. S. Danforth's Company. Pension Certificate No. 7007.

RICE, STEPHEN,   Barre.
Volunteered to go to Plattsburgh,

September, 1814, and served 10 days
in Capt. Warren Ellis' Company.
Ref: Book 52, AGO Page 242.

RICE, STEPHEN 2nd.
Served in Capt. Cross' Company, Col.
Martindale's Regt. Detached Militia
in U. S. service 2 months and 14
days, 1812. Ref: Book 53, AGO Page
38.

*RICE, WILLIAM.   St. Albans.
Served from Oct. 4 to Oct. 13, 1813
in Capt. John Palmer's Company, 1st
Regt. 2nd Brig. 3rd Div. (Judson's).
Served as sergeant in 1st Regt. Detached Militia of Vt. in U. S. service
at Champlain from Nov. 18 to Nov.
19, 1812. Served in Capt. John Wires'
Company, 30th Regt., raised in St.
Albans, which went into service Nov.
30, 1813. Ref: Hemenway's Vt. Gazetteer, Vol. 2, Page 434.

‡RICH, DAVID.
Served in Capt. Chandler's Company.
Pension Certificate No. 32316.

RICH, DAVID,   Shoreham.
Volunteered to go to Vergennes in
1814 and served in company of Capt.
James Gray Jr., Sumner's Regt. Vol-
unteered to go to Plattsburgh, Sep-
tember, 1814, and served 6 days in
Capt. Samuel Hand's Company. Ref:
Rev. J. F. Goodhue's History of
Shoreham, Page 107.

‡*RICH, EZRA,   Shoreham.
Served in Capt. Robbins' Company,
Col. Wm. Williams' Regt. Detached
Militia in U. S. service 4 months and
29 days, 1812. Volunteered to go to
Plattsburgh, September, 1814, and
served 6 days in Capt. Samuel Hand's
Company. Pension Certificate of wid-
dow, Esther, No. 7216.

RICH. GEORGE, Sergeant,   Montpelier.
Volunteered to go to Plattsburgh,
September, 1814, and served 8 days
in Capt. Timothy Hubbard's Company. Ref: Book 52, AGO Page 256.

*RICH, HYSON.
Served from June 11 to June 14, 1813
and from Oct. 4 to Oct. 13, 1813
in Capt. John Palmer's Company, 1st
Regt. 2nd Brig. 3rd Div.

RICH, JAMES.
Served from April 13 to July 12, 1813
in Capt. Phineas Williams' Company,
11th Regt. Ref: R. & L. 1812, AGO
Page 14.

RICH, JOHN,   Shoreham.
Entered service for 5 years and died
in Greenbush, N. Y. Ref: Rev. J. F.
Goodhue's History of Shoreham, Page
102.

RICH. JONATHAN.
Served from May 1 to June 26, 1814;
no organization given. Ref: R. & L.
1812, AGO Page 29.

RICH, SAMUEL, Lieutenant, Shoreham.
Appointed 3rd Lieutenant 26th Regt.
April 21, 1814; 2nd Lieutenant May
20, 1814. Served as Lieutenant under
Capt. Holley; was stationed at Bur-

lington under command of General
Hampton; died in St. Lawrence County, N. Y . Ref: Governor and Council, Vt. Vol. 6, Page 477; Rev. J. F.
Goodhue's History of Shoreham, Page
102.

RICH. SAMUEL,   Montpelier.
Volunteered to go to Plattsburgh,
September, 1814, and served 8 days
in Capt. Timothy Hubbard's Company. Ref: Book 52, AGO Page 256.

RICHARD, A.,   St. Albans.
Entered service Nov. 30, 1813 in
Capt. John Wires' Company, 30th
Regt. Ref: Hemenway's Vt. Gazetteer Vol. 2, Page 433.

*RICHARD, BOSWELL.
Served with Hospital Attendants, Vt.

RICHARDS, ABRAHAM.
Served from March 11 to June 16, 1813
in Lt. Wm. S. Foster's Company,
11th Regt. Ref: R. & L. 1812, AGO
Page 6.

*RICHARDS, BENJAMIN,   Barre?
Served from April 12 to April 21,
1814 in Capt. Shubael Wales' Company, Col. W. B. Sumner's Regt.

*RICHARDS, CALVIN.
Served from April 12 to April 21,
1814 in Capt. Shubael Wales' Company, Col. W. B. Sumner's Regt.

RICHARDS, JAMES.
Served from Feb. 5 to May 4, 1813
in Lt. Wm. S. Foster's Company,
11th Regt. Ref: R. & L. 1812, AGO
Page 6.

RICHARDS, JASON.
Served from Jan. 5 to June 30, 1814
in Capt. Alexander Brooks' Corps of
Artillery. Ref: R. & L. 1812, AGO
Page 31.

RICHARDS, JE'K (or Jack?),   Barre.
Volunteered to go to Plattsburgh,
September, 1814, and served in Capt.
Warren Ellis' Company. Ref: Hemenway's Vt. Gazetteer, Vol. 4, Page
41.

RICHARDS, JOHN,   Barre.
Volunteered to go to Plattsburgh,
September, 1814, and served 10 days
in Capt. Warren Ellis' Company. Ref:
Book 52, AGO Page 242.

RICHARDS, JONA.
Served from Feb. 9 to May 8, 1813
in Lt. Wm. S. Foster's Company,
11th Regt. Ref: R. & L. 1812, AGO
Page 6.

*RICHARDS, NICHOLAS.
Served in 1 Regt. (Judson's) Vt.
Militia.

‡RICHARDS, PAUL S.
Served in Capt. J. Post's Company,
Dixon's Regt. Pension Certificate of
widow, Hester Ann, No. 26865.

‡*RICHARDS, RUSSELL,   Cornwall.
Served from April 12 to April 21,
1814 in Capt. Edmund B. Hill's Company, Sumner's Regt. Volunteered to

go to Plattsburgh, September, 1814,
and was at the battle, serving in
same company. Pension Certificate
No. 14018.

RICHARDS, SAMUEL,   Cornwall.
Volunteered to go to Plattsburgh,
September, 1814, and was at the
battle, serving in Capt. Edmund B.
Hill's Company, Sumner's Regt. Ref:
Book 51, AGO Page 13.

*RICHARDS, SAMUEL JR .
Served from April 12 to April 21,
1814 in Capt. Edmund B. Hill's Company, Sumner's Regt.

‡*RICHARDS, SAMUEL 1st.
Served in Capt. Wheeler's Company,
Col. Fifield's Regt. Detached Militia
in U. S. service 6 months and 4
days, 1812. Pension Certificate No.
3472. Pension Certificate of widow,
Rachel, No. 30981.

*RICHARDS, SAMUEL 2nd.
Served in 2nd Regt. (Fifield's) Vt.
Militia.

RICHARDS, STEPHEN.
Served from Jan. 20 to May 8, 1813
in Lt. Wm. S. Foster's Company,
11th Regt. Ref: R. & L. 1812, AGO
Page 6.

RICHARDS, WILLIAM.
Enlisted May 6, 1813 for 1 year in
Capt. Simeon Wright's Company. Ref:
R. & L. 1812, AGO Page 51.

*RICHARDSON, ABIAL, Captain.
Served in 1st Regt. of Detached Militia of Vt. in U. S. service at Champlain from Nov. 18 to Nov. 19, 1812
under Col. Martindale.

*RICHARDSON, ABIEL.
Served from Oct. 15 to Nov. 17, 1813
in Capt. Asahel Scoville's Company,
Col. Clark's Rifle Corps.

*RICHARDSON, AMOS.
Served in Capt. Burnap's Company,
Col. Jonathan Williams' Regt. Detached Militia in U. S. service 2
months and 13 days, 1812.

‡*RICHARDSON, ASA.
Enlisted Sept. 25, 1813 and served
1 month and 23 days in Capt. Elijah
Birge's Company, Col. Dixon's Regt.
Also served in Capt. J. A. Prentis'
Company, Dixon's Regt. Pension Certificate of widow, Betsey, No. 24622.

RICHARDSON, BENJAMIN,   Barre.
Volunteered to go to Plattsburgh,
September, 1814, and served 10 days
in Capt. Warren Ellis' Company. Ref:
Book 52, AGO Page 242.

‡RICHARDSON, BENJAMIN A.
Served in Capt. Levake's Company.
Pension Certificate No. 21313.

‡*RICHARDSON, DANIEL.
Served in company of Capt. John
McNeil Jr., 11th Regt.; on Pay Roll
for January and February, 1813. Served from March 11, 1813 to June 10,
1813 in Lt. R. V. R. Goodrich's Company, 11th Regt. Enlisted Sept. 25,
1813, and served 1 month and 23 days

in Capt. Elijah Birge's Company, Col. Dixon's Regt. Pension Certificate No. 4199. Pension Certificate of widow, Julia, No. 10408.

RICHARDSON, DAVID,   Barre. Served from July 1 to Aug. 31, 1813 and from May 1 to July 4, 1814 in Capt. Chadwick's Company, 34th Inf. Volunteered to go to Plattsburgh, September, 1814, and served 9 days in Capt. Warren Ellis' Company. Ref: R. & L. 1812, AGO Page 30; Book 52, AGO Pages 231 and 242.

‡RICHARDSON, DIAH,   Montpelier. Volunteered to go to Plattsburgh, September, 1814, and served 8 days in Capt. Timothy Hubbard's Company. Pension Certificate of widow, Louisa H., No. 12416.

RICHARDSON, EBENEZER. Served from May 1 to June 30, 1814 in Capt. Haig's Corps of Light Dragoons. Ref: R. & L. 1812, AGO Page 20.

RICHARDSON, EDWARD, Carpenter. Served from May 1 to June 30, 1814 in Alexander Parris' Company of Artificers. Ref: R. & L. 1812, AGO Page 24.

*RICHARDSON, ELIJAH, Sergeant, Pittsford. Served in Capt. Taylor's Company, Col. Wm. Williams' Regt. Detached Militia in U. S. service 4 months and 24 days, 1812, at Swanton Falls. Volunteered to go to Plattsburgh, September, 1814, and served 8 days in Capt. Caleb Hendee's Company. Ref: Book 52, AGO Page 125.

RICHARDSON, EZEKIEL,   Fairfax. Volunteered to go to Plattsburgh, September, 1814, and served 8 days in Capt. Josiah Grout's Company. Ref: Book 51, AGO Page 103.

*RICHARDSON, EZRA T., Corporal. Served in Capt. Walker's Company, Col. Fifield's Regt. Detached Militia in U. S. service 6 months and 3 days, 1812.

‡*RICHARDSON, GEORGE, Corporal, Waitsfield. Volunteered to go to Plattsburgh, September, 1814, and served 4 days in Capt. Mathias S. Jones' Company. Served as corporal in Corning's Detachment and private in 4 Regt. (Peck's) Vt. Militia. Pension Certificate of widow, Betsey, No. 8752.

*RICHARDSON, GODFREY. Served from June 11 to June 14, 1813 in Capt. Moses Jewett's Company, 1st Regt. 2nd Brig. 3rd Div. (Judson's Regt.)

RICHARDSON, HARRY,   Montpelier. Volunteered to go to Plattsburgh, September, 1814, and served 8 days in Capt. Timothy Hubbard's Company. Ref: Book 52, AGO Pages 246 and 256.

‡*RICHARDSON, IRA, Sergeant. Served in Corning's Detachment and 4 Regt. (Peck's) Vt. Militia. Also

served in Capt. Campbell's Company. Pension Certificate of widow, Rachel, No. 9164.

RICHARDSON, JAMES,   Irasburgh. Captain Richardson served in the army during the War of 1812 and died in the service. Ref: Heemnway's Vt. Gazetteer, Vol. 3, Page 247.

RICHARDSON, JOEL. Served from Feb. 11 to May 10, 1813 in Capt. Edgerton's Company, 11th Regt. Ref: R. & L. 1812, AGO Page 3.

RICHARDSON, JOHN,   Waitsfield. Volunteered to go to Plattsburgh, September, 1814, and served 4 days in Capt. Mathias S. Jones' Company. Ref: Book 52, AGO Page 170.

RICHARDSON, JOHN,   Barre. Volunteered to go to Plattsburgh, September, 1814, and served 10 days in Capt. Warren Ellis' Company. Ref: Book 52, AGO Page 242.

RICHARDSON, JONAS. Served in company of Capt. John McNeil Jr., 11th Regt.; on Pay Roll for January and February, 1813. Ref: R. & L. 1812, AGO Page 17.

‡*RICHARDSON, JOSEPH W. Served in Capt. Pettes' Company, Col. Wm. Williams' Regt. Detached Militia in U. S. service 4 months and 18 days, 1812. Pension Certificate of widow, Lucy B., No. 24135.

RICHARDSON, JOSIAH. Served from Feb. 17 to May 16, 1813 in Capt. Samul Gordon's Company, 11th Regt. Ref: R. & L. 1812, AGO Page 8.

RICHARDSON, KIMBALL. Volunteered to go to Plattsburgh, September, 1814, and went as far as Bolton, Vt., serving 4 days in Lt. Phineus Kimball's Company, West Fairlee. Ref: Book 52, AGO Page 46.

*RICHARDSON, MOSES. Served in Capt. Burnap's Company, Col. Jonathan Williams' Regt. Detached Militia in U. S. service 2 months and 13 days, 1812.

RICHARDSON, NATHAN. Served in Capt. Benjamin S. Edgerton's Company, 11th Regt.; on Pay Roll for September and October, 1812. Ref: R. & L. 1812, AGO Page 1.

‡RICHARDSON, NATHANIEL. Pension Certificate of widow, Florella, No. 43371; no organization given.

*RICHARDSON, NATHANIEL, Corporal. Served in Capt. Walker's Company, Col. Fifield's Regt. Detached Militia in U. S. service 2 months and 24 days, 1812.

RICHARDSON, NATHANIEL, Lieutenant, Waitsfield. Volunteered to go to Plattsburgh, September, 1814, and served 4 days in Capt. Mathias S. Jones' Company. Ref: Book 52, AGO Pages 170 and 207.

RICHARDSON, NATHANIEL, Orange.
Marched for Plattsburgh Sept. 11,
1814 and marched part way, serving
5 days in Capt. David Rising's Company. Ref: Book 52, AGO Page 19.

*RICHARDSON, NOAH F., Fairfax.
Served from Sept. 25 to Nov. 10,
1813 in Capt. Asa Wilkins' Company,
Dixon's Regt. Volunteered to go to
Plattsburgh, September, 1814, and
served 8 days in Capt. Josiah Grout's
Company.

RICHARDSON, OBED, Enosburgh.
Served from Oct. 14 to Nov. 17,
1813 in Capt. Asahel Scovel's Com-
pany, Col. Clark's Rifle Corps. Ref:
Hemenway's Vt. Gazetteer, Vol. 2,
Page 398.

RICHARDSON, ROBERT, Orange.
Marched for Plattsburgh Sept. 11,
1814 and went part way, serving 5
days as a wagoner in Capt. David
Rising's Company. Ref: Book 52,
AGO Pages 19 and 22.

RICHARDSON, ROBERT, Strafford.
Volunteered to go to Plattsburgh,
September, 1814, and served in Capt.
Cyril Chandler's Company. Ref: Book
52, AGO Page 42.

*RICHARDSON, ROBERT.
Served in Capt. Taylor's Company,
Col. Fifield's Regt. Detached Militia
in U. S. service 6 months, 1812.

RICHARDSON, SAMUEL, Roxbury.
Volunteered to go to Plattsburgh,
September, 1814, and went as far as
Montpelier, serving 2 days in Capt.
Samuel M. Orcutt's Company. Ref:
Book 52, AGO Page 167.

RICHARDSON, SAMUEL, Corinth.
Volunteered to go to Plattsburgh,
September, 1814, and served in Capt.
Abel Jackman's Company. Ref: Book
52, AGO Page 44.

RICHARDSON, SETH.
Enlisted April 6, 1813 for 5 years in
company of late Capt. J. Brooks
commanded by Lt. John I. Cromwell, Corps of U. S. Artillery; on
Muster Roll from April 30 to June 30,
1814; served to June 13, 1814. Ref:
R. & L. 1812, AGO Page 18.

*RICHARDSON, STEPHEN.
Served with Hospital Attendants. Vt.

*RICHARDSON, THOMAS.
Served from Sept. 25 to Oct. 23, 1813
in Capt. Elijah Birge's Company, Col.
Dixon's Regt.

‡*RICHARDSON, WILLIAM.
Served in Capt. Mason's Company,
Col. Fifield's Regt. Detached Militia
in U. S. service 3 months and 17
days, 1812. Served from Feb. 11 to
May 10, 1813 in Capt. Edgerton's
Company, 11th Regt. Enlisted Sept.
25, 1813 and served 1 month and 23
days in Capt. Asa Wilkins' Company,
Col. Dixon's Regt. Pension Certificate
of widow, Hannah, No. 26240. Ref:
R. & L. 1812, AGO Page 3.

RICHARDSON, WILLIAM, Jericho.
Took part in the battle of Plattsburgh. Ref: History of Jericho, Page
142.

RICHARDSON, WILLIAM P., Sergeant.
Age 28; height 6 feet; eyes blue; hair
brown; complexion dark; occupation
farmer. Served from April 22, 1813
to April 25, 1814 in Capt. Gideon
Spencer's Company and Capt. James
Taylor's Company, 30th Regt. Ref:
R. & L. 1812, AGO Pages 52, 56, 58.

RICHARDSON, ZEBEDIAH, Bethel.
Volunteered to go to Plattsburgh,
September, 1814, and served 7 days
in Capt. Nehemiah Noble's Company.
Ref: Book 51, AGO Pages 248, 276,
282.

*RICHMOND, ALLEN, Barnard.
Served in Capt. Brigg's Company,
Col. Jonathan Williams' Regt. Detached Militia in U. S. service 2
months and 13 days, 1812.

‡*RICHMOND, ANSON.
Served in Capt. Briggs' Company,
Col. Jonathan Williams' Regt. Detached Militia in U. S. service 2
months and 13 days, 1812. Pension
Certificate of widow, Betsey, No.
30022.

‡*RICHMOND, JOHN, Barnard.
Served in Capt. Phelps' Company,
Col. Jonathan Williams' Regt. De-
tached Militia in U. S. service 2
months and 21 days, 1812. Pension
Certificate No. 11628.

RICHMOND, LEMUEL, Barnard.
Volunteered to go to Plattsburgh,
September, 1814, and served 8 days
in Capt. John S. Bicknell's Company.
Ref: Book 51, AGO Page 250.

*RICHMOND, NATHANIEL.
Served in Capt. Phelps' Company,
Col. Jonathan Williams' Regt. Detached Militia in U. S. service 1
month and 15 days, 1812.

RICHMOND, THOMAS, Barnard.
Enlisted May 10, 1813 in Capt. Nehemiah Noble's Company, 31st U. S.
Inf. Ref: Wm. M. Newton's History
of Barnard, Vol. 1, Page 95.

RICKARD, AMBROS.
Enlisted May 6, 1813 for 1 year in
Capt. John Wires' Company, 30th
Regt. Ref: R. & L. 1812, AGO Page
40.

*RICKARD, IRA.
Served in 4 Regt. (Peck's) Vt. Militia.

*RICKARD, JARED, Woodstock.
Served in Capt. Phelps' Company,
Col. Jonathan Williams' Regt. Detached Militia in U. S. service 2
months and 21 days, 1812.

RICKETS, FRANCIS.
Served from March 19 to June 30,
1814 in Regt. of Light Dragoons. Ref:
R. & L. 1812, AGO Page 21.

RIDDALL, JOHN, Lieutenant, Tunbridge.
Volunteered to go to Plattsburgh,
September, 1814, and served 4 days
in Capt. Ephraim Hackett's Company.
Ref: Book 52, AGO Page 71.

RIDDIN, WILLIAM.
Enlisted Sept. 19, 1813 during the
war in Capt. White Youngs' Company, 15th Regt. Served to Oct. 1,
1814. Ref: R. & L. 1812, AGO Page
27.

RIDDLE, SAMUEL, 3rd Lieutenant.
Enlisted Oct. 19, 1813 in Capt. White
Youngs' Company, 15th Regt.; on
Muster Roll from Aug. 31 to Dec. 31,
1814. Ref: R. & L. 1812, AGO Page
27.

*RIDER, ASAHEL.
Served in Corning's Detachment, Vt.
Militia.

*RIDER, HORATIO, Corporal, Waitsfield.
Volunteered to go to Plattsburgh,
September, 1814, and served 4 days
in Capt. Mathias S. Jones' Company. Also served in Corning's Detachment, Vt. Militia. Ref: Book 52,
AGO Page 170.

‡*RIDER, JOHN G.
Served in Capt. Phelps' Company,
Col. Wm. Williams' Regt. Detached
Militia in U. S. service 5 months.
Pension Certificate No. 11731. Pen-
sion Certificate of widow, Betsey, No.
6517.

RIDER, PHINEAS,   Waitsfield.
Volunteered to go to Plattsburgh,
September, 1814, and served 4 days
in Capt. Mathias S. Jones' Company.
Ref: Book 52, AGO Page 170.

RIDER, SAMUEL B.,   Braintree.
Volunteered to go to Plattsburgh,
September, 1814, and served 8 days
in Capt. Lot Hudson's Company.
Ref: Book 52, AGO Page 31.

RIDETTE, ELIHU.
Served in Capt. Follett's Company,
11th Regt.; on Pay Roll for January and February, 1812. Ref: R. &
L. 1812, AGO Page 12.

RIDGWAY, SAMUEL.
Served from May 1 to June 30, 1814
as a carpenter in Alexander Parris'
Company of Artificers. Ref: R. & L.
1812, AGO Page 24.

*RIDLEY, MATHIAS.
Served in 2 Regt. (Fifield's) Vt.
Militia.

RIDLON, MATTHIAS.
Served in Capt. Walker's Company,
Col. Fifield's Regt. Detached Militia
in U. S. service 3 months and 9
days, 1812. Ref: Book 53, AGO Page
21.

RIFORD, LAZARUS.   Braintree.
Marched to Plattsburgh Sept. 10,
1814, serving in Capt. Lot Hudson's
Company. Ref: Book 52, AGO Pages
24 and 26.

RIFORD, SETH,   Braintree.
Marched to Plattsburgh Sept. 10, 1814,
serving in Capt. Lot Hudson's Company. Ref: Book 52, AGO Page 24.

RIGGS, JAMES,   Falmoth, Mass.
Enlisted at Burlington Feb. 11, 1814
during the war and served in Capt.
Wm. Miller's Company, Capt. Gideon
Spencer's Company, and Capt. James
Taylor's Company, 30th Regt. Ref:
R. & L. 1812, AGO Pages 53, 54,
55, 57.

RIGHTER, JACOB.
Enlisted April 1, 1809 for 5 years in
Capt. White Youngs' Company, 15th
Regt.; on Muster Roll from Aug. 31
to Dec. 31, 1814. Ref: R. & L. 1812,
AGO Page 27.

RILEY, BARTHOLOMEW, Franklin County. Enlisted April 9, 1813 during the
war in Capt. White Youngs' Company, 15th Regt.; on Muster Roll
from Aug. 31 to Dec. 31, 1814. Ref:
R. & L. 1812, AGO Page 27.

RILEY, EPHRAIM,   Franklin County.
Volunteered to go to Plattsburgh
Sept. 11, 1814 and served in 15th or
22nd Regt. Ref: Hemenway's Vt. Gazetteer, Vol. 2, Page 391.

*RILLS, SAMUEL.
Served in 1 Regt. (Martindale's) Vt.
Militia.

RING, DANIEL.
Served from May 1 to June 30, 1814
in Capt. Haig's Corps of Light Dragoons. Ref: R. & L. 1812, AGO
Page 20.

RING, JOHN.
Enlisted May 1, 1813 for 5 years in
company of late Capt. J. Brooks com-
manded by Lt. John I. Cromwell,
Corps of U. S. Artillery; on Muster
Roll from April 30 to June 30, 1814.
Ref: R. & L. 1812, AGO Page 18.

*RINGE, NATHAN,   Randolph.
Volunteered to go to Plattsburgh,
September, 1814, and served in Capt.
Lebbeus Egerton's Company.

*RIPLEY, ELIAS.
Served as Waiter in Corning's Detachment, Vt. Militia.

*RIPLEY, SAMUEL P., Corporal.
Served from April 12 to April 21,
1814 in Lt. Justus Foote's Company,
Sumner's Regt.

*RIPLEY, SHUBAL.
Served from April 12 to April 15,
1814 in Lt. Justus Foote's Company,
Sumner's Regt.

RIPLEY, WILLIAM, Corporal,   Barre.
Volunteered to go to Plattsburgh,
September, 1814, and served 8 days
in Capt. Warren Ellis' Company. Ref:
Book 52, AGO Pages 229 and 242.

*RISING, AMOS.
Served in 4 Regt. (Peck's) Vt. Militia.

RISING, DAVID. Captain,   Orange.
Marched for Plattsburgh, September,
1814, and went part way, serving
about a week in command of company from Orange. Ref: Book 52,
AGO Page 19.

*RISING, SIMEON, Ensign.
Appointed Ensign Sept. 20, 1813 in
Capt. John Weed's Company, Col.
Clark's Rifle Corps.

RISLEY, WILLIAM, Lieutenant.
Appointed Ensign 11th Inf. March
13, 1813; 3 Lieutenant May 20, 1813;
2 Lieutenant Aug. 15, 1813; 1 Lieutenant Sept. 17, 1814; honorably discharged June 15, 1815. Ref: Heitman's Historical Register & Dictionary USA.

RITTERBUSH, WILLIAM,   Fairfax.
Enlisted Sept. 25, 1813 and served 1
month and 23 days in Capt. Asa
Wilkins' Company, Col. Dixon's Regt.
Ref: Book 52, AGO Page 272; Book
53, AGO Page 112.

RIX, JAMES.
Enlisted Jan. 18, 1813 in Capt. Jonathan Starks' Company, 11th Regt.
and served to date of death May 8,
1813. Ref: R. & L. 1812, AGO Page
19.

ROACH. PATRICK.
Enlisted Feb. 13, 1813 in Capt.
Charles Follett's Company, 11th Regt.;
on Pay Roll to May 31, 1813. Ref:
R. & L. 1812, AGO Page 13.

*ROADES, ELIZER.
Served from April 12 to April 21,
1814 in Capt. Eseck Sprague's Company, Sumner's Regt.

ROADES, SILAS.
Served in Capt. Benjamin Bradford's
Company; on Muster Roll from May
31 to Aug. 31, 1813. Ref: R. & L.
1812, AGO Page 26.

ROBBINS, JOHN.   Wallingford?
Served in Capt. Benjamin Bradford's
Company; on Muster Roll from May
31 to Aug. 31, 1813. Ref: R. & L.
1812, AGO Page 26.

*ROBBINS, JOHN.   Shoreham.
Commanded company in Col. Wm.
Williams' Regt. about 4 months in
1812. Volunteered to go to Platts-
burgh, September, 1814, and served
6 days as 3rd Lieutenant in Capt.
Samuel Hand's Company. Ref: Rev.
J. F. Goodhue's History of Shoreham,
Page 107.

*ROBBINS, JONATHAN.
Served in Capt. Noyce's Company,
Col. Jonathan Williams' Regt. Detached Militia in U. S. service 2
months and 6 days, 1812.

*ROBBINS, JOTHAM,   Waterbury.
Volunteered to go to Plattsburgh,
September, 1814, and served 11 days
in Capt. George Atkins' Company, 4
Regt. (Peck's).

ROBBINS, LYMAN.
Served in Capt. Benjamin Bradford's
Company; on Muster Roll from May
31 to Aug. 31, 1813. Ref: R. & L.
1812, AGO Page 26.

‡*ROBBINS, ZADOC B.,   Cornwall.
Served from April 12 to April 21,
1814 in Capt. Shubael Wales' Company, Col. W. B. Sumner's Regt.
Volunteered to go to Plattsburgh,
September, 1814, and was at the
battle, serving in Capt. Edmund B.
Hill's Company, Sumner's Regt. Pension Certificate No. 23551. Pension
Certificate of widow, Sarah A., No.
29392.

*ROBERSON, LEONARD, Lieutenant.
Served in 4 Regt. (Williams') Vt.
Militia.

*ROBERTS, ELISHA,   Bristol.
Served from April 19 to April 21,
1814 in Capt. Othniel Jewett's Company, Sumner's Regt. Volunteered
to go to Plattsburgh, September, 1814,
and served in Capt. Jehiel Saxton's
Company, Sumner's Regt.

ROBERTS, GEORGE.
Served in Capt. Samul Gordon's Com-
pany, 11th Regt.; on Pay Roll for
January and February, 1813. Ref:
R. & L. 1812, AGO Page 9.

‡*ROBERTS, HORACE R.,   Swanton.
Served in Capt. L. Robinson's Company, Col. Dixon's Regt. Detached
Militia in U. S. service 1 month,
1813. Volunteered to go to Plattsburgh, September, 1814, and served
7 days; no organization given. Pension Certificate No. 23813. Ref: Book
51, AGO Page 145.

*ROBERTS, HOSEA.
Served in 4 Regt. (Peck's) Vt. Militia.

‡*ROBERTS, JAMES.
Served in Capt. Persons' Company,
Col. Jonathan Williams' Regt. De-
tached Militia in U. S. service 2
months and 13 days, 1812. Pension
Certificate No. 18438.

*ROBERTS, JEDUTHAN.
Served in 3 Regt. (Williams') Vt.
Militia.

ROBERTS, JESSE,   Franklin County.
Volunteered to go to Plattsburgh
Sept. 11, 1814 and served in 15th or
22nd Regt. Ref: Hemenway's Vt. Gazetteer, Vol. 2, Page 392.

ROBERTS, JONATHAN.
Served in Capt. Preston's Company,
Col. Jonathan Williams' Regt. Detached Militia in U. S. service 2
months and 6 days, 1812. Ref: Book
53, AGO Page 55.

*ROBERTS, JONATHAN, Sergeant. Straf-
ford. Served in Capt. Wheeler's Company, Col. Fifield's Regt. Detached
Militia in U. S. service 2 months and
18 days, 1812. Served in Capt. Morrill's Company, Col. Fifield's Regt.
Detached Militia in U. S. service 3
months and 17 days, 1812. Volunteered to go to Plattsburgh, September,
1814, and served 6 days in Capt.
Jedediah H. Harris' Company. Ref:
Book 52, AGO Page 43.

‡ROBERTS, JOSEPH,   Strafford.
Served in Capt. Patridge's Company.
Pension Certificate No. 10766.

*ROBERTS, ORIN.
Served in Capt. Adams' Company,
Col. Jonathan Williams' Regt. Detached Militia in U. S. service 1
month and 16 days, 1812.

*ROBERTS, ROSWELL.
Served in Corning's Detachment, Vt.
Militia.

*ROBERTS, SAMUEL.
Served in Capt. Preston's Company,
Col. Jonathan Williams' Regt. Detached Militia in U. S. service 2
months and 6 days, 1812.

*ROBERTS, SAMUEL R.
Served in 4th Regt. (Williams') Vt.
Militia.

*ROBERTS, TRUMAN.
Served in 3 Regt. (Tyler's) Vt. Militia.

ROBERTSON, ISAAC.
Served in Capt. Benjamin S. Edgerton's Company, 11th Regt.; on Pay
Roll for September and October, 1812
and January and February 1813; enlisted Sept. 30, 1812. Ref: R. & L.
1812, AGO Pages 1 and 2.

ROBERTSON, JEDEDIAH H.
Enlisted Nov. 1, 1812 in Capt. Benjamin S. Edgerton's Company; on
Pay Roll for January and February,
1813. Ref: R. & L. 1812, AGO Pages
1 and 2.

ROBERTSON, ROBERT H.
Served in Capt. Weeks' Company,
11th Regt.; on Pay Roll for January and February, 1813. Ref: R. &
L. 1812, AGO Page 5.

*ROBERTSON, SAMUEL.
Served in 4th Regt. (Williams') Vt.
Militia.

ROBERTSON, SAMUEL,   Roxbury.
Volunteered to go to Plattsburgh,
September, 1814, and served 7 days
in Capt. Samuel M. Orcutt's Company. Ref: Book 52, AGO Pages 166
and 250.

*ROBERTSON, SAMUEL R.
Served in 4 Regt. (Williams') Vt.
Militia.

*ROBINS, AARON.
Served from April 12 to April 14, 1814
in Capt. Jonathan P. Stanley's Company, Col. W. B. Sumner's Regt.

*ROBINS, DANIEL JR.
Served from Oct. 5 to Oct. 16, 1813
in Capt. Roswell Hunt's Company, 3
Regt. (Tyler's). Also served in Corning's Detachment, Vt. Militia.

*ROBINS, ELIAS.
Served in Corning's Detachment, Vt.
Militia.

*ROBINS, GEORGE.
Served from April 12 to April 21,
1814 in Capt. Shubael Wales' Company, Col. W. B. Sumner's Regt.

ROBINS, SETH L.
Served in Capt. Samuel H. Holly's
Company, 11th Regt.; on Pay Roll
for January and February, 1813. Ref:
R. & L. 1812, AGO Page 25.

‡*ROBINSON, ALMON.
Served in Capt. Walker's Company,
Col. Fifield's Regt. Detached Militia
in U. S. service 2 months and 24
days, 1812. Pension Certificate of
widow, Mercy, No. 10558.

*ROBINSON, AMOS, Captain.
Appointed Captain Sept. 25, 1813 in
Lt. Col. Luther Dixon's Regt.

*ROBINSON, ANDREW,   Barre.
Enlisted Sept. 25, 1813 as drummer
in Capt. Jesse Post's Company, Dixon's Regt. Volunteered to go to
Plattsburgh, September, 1814, and served 10 days in Capt. Warren Ellis'
Company. Ref: Book 52, AGO Page
242.

ROBINSON, AUGUSTUS.
Volunteered to go to Plattsburgh,
September, 1814, and served 7 days
in Capt. Frederick Griswold's Com-
pany from Brookfield. Ref: Book 52,
AGO Page 52.

*ROBINSON, BENJAMIN, Adjutant.
Served in 3 Regt. (Williams') Vt.
Militia.

ROBINSON, CHARLES,   Barre.
Volunteered to go to Plattsburgh,
September, 1814, and served 10 days
in Capt. Warren Ellis' Company. Ref:
Book 52, AGO Page 242.

ROBINSON, CHASE.
Served from May 1 to June 30, 1814
in Capt. Haig's Corps of Light Dragoons. Ref: R. & L. 1812, AGO
Page 20.

*ROBINSON, DANIEL,   Stowe.
Volunteered to go to Plattsburgh,
September, 1814, and was at the
battle, serving in Capt. Nehemiah Perkins' Company, 4 Regt. (Peck's). Also
served in Corning's Detachment, Vt.
Militia.

‡ROBINSON, DANIEL D., Musician.
Volunteered to go to Plattsburgh,
September, 1814, and served 7 days
in Capt. Frederick Griswold's Company from Brookfield. Pension Certificate of widow, Electa, No. 30908.
Ref: Book 52, AGO Pages 52 and 59.

‡ROBINSON, DAVID, Captain, Williamstown. Volunteered to go to Plattsburgh, September, 1814, and was in
the battle, serving 8 days in command
of company from Williamstown. Also
served in Capt. R. B. Brown's Company. Pension Certificate of widow,
Lenda, No. 29066. Ref: Book 52,
AGO Pages 3 and 10.

ROBINSON, ELIJAH,   Barre.
Volunteered to go to Plattsburgh,
September, 1814, and served in Capt.
Warren Ellis' Company. Ref: Hem-
enway's Vt. Gazetteer, Vol. 4, Page
41.

*ROBINSON, ELIJAH, Captain.
Served as Ensign in 4 Regt. (Wil-
liams') Vt. Militia; Lieutenant in
Corning's Detachment, Vt. Militia;
Captain in 4 Regt. (Peck's) Vt.
Militia.

ROBINSON, ELISHA, Shoreham.
Volunteered to go to Plattsburgh.
September, 1814, and served 6 days
in Capt. Samuel Hand's Company.
Ref: Rev. J. F. Goodhue's History
of Shoreham, Page 108.

*ROBINSON, FRANKLIN, Corporal.
Served in 1 Regt. (Judson's) Vt. Militia.

*ROBINSON, GEORGE.
Served in Capt. Mason's Company,
Col. Jonathan Williams' Regt. Detached Militia in U. S. service 3
months and 15 days, 1812. Also
served in 2 Regt. (Fifield's) Vt. Militia. Ref: Book 53, AGO Page 37.

‡ROBINSON, HARRY.
Served in Capt. Wood's Company.
Pension Certificate No. 22930.

*ROBINSON, HARTWELL.
Served as a waiter in Corning's Detachment, Vt. Militia.

‡*ROBINSON, HENRY.
Enlisted Sept. 25, 1813 and served
1 month and 23 days in Capt. Elijah
W. Wood's Company, Col. Dixon's
Regt. Also served in Capt. Elihu Emmens' Company. Pension Certificate
No. 18549.

ROBINSON, HENRY.
Appointed Assistant District Paymaster Oct. 15, 1814; honorably discharged June 15, 1815. Ref: Heitman's Historical Register & Dictionary USA.

*ROBINSON, ISAAC, Ensign.
Served as Ensign in 2 Regt. (Fifield's)
Vt. Militia. Also served in 1 Regt.
(Judson's) Vt. Militia.

*ROBINSON, ISAIAH, Fifer.
Enlisted Sept. 25, 1813 in Capt. Amos
Robinson's Company, Dixon's Regt.;
transferred to Capt. Asahel Langworthy's Company, Col. Clark's Rifle
Corps Sept. 28, 1813; discharged Oct.
20, 1813.

ROBINSON, JAMES, Fairfax.
Volunteered to go to Plattsburgh,
September, 1814, and served 8 days
in Capt. Josiah Grout's Company.
Ref: Book 51, AGO Pages 103 and
175.

*ROBINSON, JOEL, Calais.
Volunteered to go to Plattsburgh.
September. 1814, and served 10 days
in Capt. Gideon Wheelock's Company.

‡*ROBINSON, JOHN W., Corporal Sergeant, Manchester. Served in Capt.
Strait's Company, Col. Martindale's
Regt. Detached Militia in U. S. service 2 months and 13 days, 1812. Enlisted May 1, 1813 for 1 year in Capt.
Daniel Farrington's Company (also
commanded by Capt. Simeon Wright)
30th Regt. Enlisted Feb. 24, 1814 and
served in Capt. Gideon Spencer's Company and Capt. James Taylor's Company, 30th Regt. Served from Sept.
1, 1814 to June 16, 1815 in Capt.
Sanford's Company, 30th Inf. Pension
Certificate No. 21544. Ref: R. & L.
1812, AGO Pages 23, 50, 51, 53, 56.

‡ROBINSON, JOSEPH, Fairfax.
Volunteered to go to Plattsburgh,
September, 1814, and served 8 days
in Capt. Josiah Grout's Company.
Pension Certificate of widow, Junia,
No. 27192.

*ROBINSON, JOSEPH JR.
Served in Capt. L. Robinson's Company, Col. Dixon's Regt. Detached
Militia in U. S. service 1 month, 1813.

*ROBINSON, JOSIAH, Fifer.
Served in Dixon's Regt. Vt. Militia.

‡ROBINSON, JUDGE, Northfield.
Volunteered to go to Plattsburgh,
September. 1814, and served 8 days
in Capt. David Robinson's Company;
took part in the battle. Pension Certificate No. 29813. Pension Certificate
of widow, Marcia B., No. 34303.

ROBINSON, JUSTIN L., Barre.
Volunteered to go to Plattsburgh,
September, 1814, and served 9 days
in Capt. Warren Ellis' Company.
Ref: Book 52, AGO Pages 232 and 242.

*ROBINSON, LEONARD, Captain.
Served in Dixon's Regt. Vt. Militia.

*ROBINSON, LEONARD JR., Lieutenant.
Served in 4 Regt. (Williams') Vt.
Militia.

ROBINSON, LEVI.
Served from Jan. 13 to Feb. 17,
1813 in Lt. V. R. Goodrich's Company, 11th Regt. Died March 12,
1813. Ref: R. & L. 1812, AGO
Pages 10 and 11.

ROBINSON, MAJOR, Captain, Walden.
Volunteered to go to Plattsburgh,
September, 1814, and served 5 days
in command of company. Ref: Book
51, AGO Page 74.

ROBINSON, NATHAN.
Born at Wales; served in War of
1812 and was captured by troops June
6, 1813 at Stoney Point; discharged
Oct. 10, 1814. Ref: Records of Naval
Records and Library, Navy Dept.

*ROBINSON, NATHAN.
Enlisted Sept. 25, 1813 in Capt.
Thomas Waterman's Company, Dixon's Regt.

‡*ROBINSON, NATHAN JR., Sergeant
Major, Stowe. Volunteered to go to
Plattsburgh. September, 1814, and was
at the battle, serving in Capt. Nehemiah Perkins' Company, 4 Regt.
(Peck's). Also served in Corning's
Detachment, Vt. Militia. Pension Certificate No. 23437. Pension Certificate
of widow, Emily, No. 30116.

*ROBINSON, NATHANIEL.
Served in Capt. Burnap's Company,
Col. Jonathan Williams' Regt. Detached Militia in U. S. service 2
months and 13 days, 1812.

‡*ROBINSON, PAUL JR.
Enlisted Sept. 25, 1813 in Capt. Amos
Robinson's Company, Dixon's Regt.;
served as waiter for Major Hathaway. Pension Certificate of widow,
Betsey, No. 3787.

ROBINSON, PHILETAS, Waitsfield.
Volunteered to go to Plattsburgh,
September, 1814, and served 4 days
in Capt. Mathias S. Jones' Company.
Ref: Book 52, AGO Page 170.

ROBINSON, R. S.
Served from March 27 to June 26,
1813 in Capt. Samul Gordon's Company, 11th Regt. Ref: R. & L. 1812,
AGO Page 8.

*ROBINSON, RANSOM, Cornwall.
Served from April 12 to April 21,
1814 in Capt. Edmund B. Hill's
Company, Sumner's Regt.; volunteered to go to Plattsburgh, September,
1814, and was at the battle, serving
in same company.

*ROBINSON, ROYAL.
Served in Corning's Detachment, Vt.
Militia.

‡ROBINSON, RUSSELL.
Served in Capt. Partridge's Company.
Pension Certificate No. 5116.

*ROBINSON, SAFFORD. Sergeant.
Served in Capt. Hopkins' Company,
Col. Martindale's Regt. Detached
Militia in U. S. service 2 months
and 13 days, 1812. Served as sergeant in Artillery of Detached Militia
of Vt. in U. S. service at Champlain
from Nov. 18 to Nov. 19, 1812.

‡*ROBINSON, SAMUEL B, Shoreham.
Served in Capt. Taylor's Company,
Col. Wm. Williams' Regt. Detached
Militia in U. S. service 4 months
and 24 days, 1812. Served from
April 12 to May 20, 1814 in company
of Capt. James Gray Jr., Sumner's
Regt. Pension Certificate No. 18616.

‡ROBINSON. SILAS A.
Served in Capt. Partridge's Company.
Pension Certificate of widow, Eunice,
No. 25461.

ROBINSON, SIMEON, Captain.
Appointed 1st Lieutenant 30th Inf.
April 30, 1813; Captain March 5,
1814; resigned June 23, 1814. Served
as 1st Lieutenant in Capt. James
Taylor's Company, 30th Regt. Ref:
Heitman's Historical Register & Dic-
tionary USA; Governor and Council
Vt. Vol. 6, Page 475; R. & L. 1812,
AGO Page 58.

*ROBINSON, STEPHEN, Sergeant.
Enlisted Sept. 25, 1813 in Capt. Amos
Robinson's Company, Dixon's Regt.

ROBINSON, STEPHEN JR.
Served in Capt. Robinson's Company,
Col. Dixon's Regt. Detached Militia
in U. S. service 1 month and 23
days, 1813. Ref: Book 53, AGO Page
107.

ROBINSON, THOMAS.
Born in Ireland. Served from March
18 to June 17, 1813 in Capt. Charles
Follett's Company, 11th Regt. En-
listed at Burlington Dec. 17, 1813 for
period of the war in Capt. Wm.
Miller's Company, 30th Regt. Ref:
R. & L. 1812, AGO Pages 13, 54, 55.

‡*ROBINSON, TIMOTHY.
Served in Capt. Noble's Company, 3
Regt. (Williams') Vt. Militia. Pension Certificate of widow, Olive, No.
35778.

*ROBY, JONATHAN (or Robee).
Served in Capt. Rogers' Company,
Col. Fifield's Regt. Detached Militia
in U. S. service 2 months and 18
days, 1812.

‡ROBY, MOODY.
Served in Capt. Utley's Company.
Pension Certificate No. 25842.

ROCHE, PETER.
Served from Feb. 17 to June 30, 1814
in Regt. of Light Dragoons. Ref:
R. & L. 1812, AGO Page 21.

ROCK, FRANCIS.
Enlisted Feb. 17, 1813 in Lieut. V.
R. Goodrich's Company, 11th Regt.;
on Pay Roll to May 31, 1813. Ref:
R. & L. 1812, AGO Pages 10 and 11.

*ROCKWELL, HARVEY.
Served from April 12 to April 21,
1814 in Capt. Shubael Wales' Company, Col. W. B. Sumner's Regt.

*ROCKWELL, HENRY.
Served in Sumner's Regt. Vt. Militia.

*ROCKWELL, JOSEPH.
Served from April 12 to April 21,
1814 in Capt. Shubael Wales' Company, Col. W. B. Sumner's Regt.

*ROCKWELL, MOSES.
Served from April 12 to April 21,
1814 in Capt. Edmund B. Hill's Company, Sumner's Regt.

ROCKWELL. NIRAM W., Cornwall.
Served from Sept. 1, 1814 to June 16,
1815 in Capt. Sanford's Company,
30th Inf. Ref: R. & L. 1812, AGO
Page 23.

*ROCKWELL, NOAR.
Served from April 12 to April 15,
1814 in Capt. Jonathan P. Stanley's
Company, Col. W. B. Sumner's Regt.

*ROCKWELL, WILLARD, Sergeant.
Served in 1 Regt. (Judson's) Vt. Militia.

ROCKWELL. AMIEL 2nd Lieutenant,
Barre. Volunteered to go to Plattsburgh. September, 1814, and served
10 days in Capt. Warren Ellis' Company. Ref: Book 52, AGO Page 242.

ROCKWOOD, CEPHAS L., Captain.
Appointed 1st Lieutenant 31st Inf.
April 30, 1813; Captain January 11,
1814; honorably discharged June 15,
1815. Ref: Heitman's Historical Register & Dictionary USA.

*ROCKWOOD. JOHN.
Served in Corning's Detachment, Vt.
Militia.

ROE, BENJAMIN.
Served in company of Capt. John
McNeil Jr., 11th Regt.; on Pay Roll
for January and February, 1813. Ref:
R. & L. 1812, AGO Page 17.

ROGERS, ABRAHAM.
Served from March 1 to May 31,
1813 in Capt. John W. Weeks' Company, 11th Regt. Ref: R. & L. 1812,
AGO Page 4.

‡ROGERS, ALANSON.
Enlisted at Poultney April 9, 1814
during the war and served in Capt.
Wm. Miller's Company, Capt. Gideon
Spencer's Company and Capt. James
Taylor's Company, 30th Regt. Pen-
sion Certificate No. 3128. Ref: R. &
L. 1812, AGO Pages 1, 53, 54, 55, 57.

ROGERS, BENJAMIN, Corporal.
Served from Nov. 1 to Feb. 28, 1813
in Capt. Samul Gordon's Company,
11th Regt. Ref: R. & L. 1812, AGO
Page 9.

*ROGERS, EBENEZER.
Served in Capt. Phineas Williams'
Company, 11th Regt.; on Pay Roll
for January and February, 1813.
Also served in 2 Regt. (Fifield's) Vt.
Militia. Ref: R. & L. 1812, AGO
Page 15.

*ROGERS, ERASTUS.
Served in 1 Regt. (Judson's) Vt.
Militia.

ROGERS, EZEKIEL.
Served from Nov. 1, 1812 to Feb.
28, 1813 in Capt. Samuel H.. Holly's
Company, 11th Regt. Ref: R. & L.
1812, AGO Page 25.

*ROGERS, HARRY.
Served in 4 Regt. (Williams') Vt.
Militia.

*ROGERS, HENRY, Corporal.
Served in Capt. Phelps' Company,
Col. Wm. Williams' Regt. Detached
Militia in U. S. service 5 months,
1812.

‡*ROGERS, JASON.
Served in Capt. Dorrance's Company,
Col. Wm. Williams' Regt. Detached
Militia in U. S. service 4 months and
23 days, 1812. Pension Certificate
of widow, Nancy, No. 1616.

*ROGERS, JOEL, Sergeant.
Served in Capt. Barns' Company, Col.
Wm. Williams' Regt. Detached Mili-
tia in U. S. service 5 months, 1812.
Also served in 1 Regt. (Judson's) Vt.
Militia.

*ROGERS, JOSEPH.
Served from April 12 to May 20, 1814
in Capt. George Fisher's Company,
Sumner's Regt. Volunteered to go
to Plattsburgh, September, 1814, and
served 4 days in company of Capt.
James George of Topsham. Ref: Book
52, AGO Page 68.

‡ROGERS, JOSEPH G.
Enlisted April 23, 1813 for 1 year in
Capt. Simeon Wright's Company. Pen-
sion Certificate No. 18511. Pension
Certificate of widow, Minerva, No.
18049.

*ROGERS, LEVI. Captain.
Served in 2 Regt. (Fifield's) Vt.
Militia.

ROGERS, M. DELA, Sergeant.
Served in Capt. Samuel H. Holly's
Company, 11th Regt.; on Pay Roll
for January and February, 1813. Ref:
R. & L. 1812, AGO Page 25.

ROGERS, MARTIN.
Served from March 19 to June 18,.
1813 in Capt. Phineas Williams' Company, 11th Regt. Ref: R. & L. 1812,
AGO Page 14.

ROGERS, MICAJAH.
Volunteered to go to Plattsburgh,
September, 1814, and went as far as
Bolton, Vt., serving 4 days in Lt.
Phineus Kimball's Company of West
Fairlee. Ref: Book 52, AGO Page 46..

*ROGERS, NATHANIEL.
Served in Capt. Bingham's Company,
Col. Jonathan Williams' Regt. Detached Militia in U. S. service 2
months and 9 days, 1812.

ROGERS, ROBERT.
Served from March 1 to June 30,
1814 in Capt. Alexander Brooks' Corps
of Artillery. Ref: R. & L. 1812,
AGO Page 31.

ROGERS, RUSSELL P.
Served from Nov. 1, 1812 to Feb. 28,
1813 in Capt. Samuel H. Holly's Company, 11th Regt. Ref: R. & L. 1812,
AGO Page 25.

*ROGERS, SAMUEL.
Served in Corning's Detachment. Vt.
Militia. May have lived in Holland
at one time.

ROGERS, THOMAS P., Corporal.
Served from Jan. 1 to June 30, 1814
in Regt. of Light Dragoons. Ref:
R. & L. 1812, AGO Page 21.

ROGERS, URIAH, Sergeant, St. Albans.
Enlisted April 29, 1813 for 1 year in
Capt. John Wires' Company, 30th
Regt. Ref: R. & L. 1812, AGO Page
40.

ROGERS, WILLIAM C., Franklin County.
Volunteered to go to Plattsburgh
Sept. 11, 1814 and served in 15th or
22nd Regt. Ref: Hemenway's Vt.
Gazetter. Vol. 2, Page 391.

ROLDINS, JOHN,   Franklin County.
Volunteered to go to Plattsburgh
Sept. 11, 1814 and served in 15th or
22nd Regt. Ref: Hemenway's Vt.
Gazetteer, Vol. 2, Page 392.

*ROLF, BENJAMIN,   Thetford.
Marched for Plattsburgh, September,
1814, and went as far as Bolton, Vt.,.
serving 6 days in Capt. Salmon Howard's Company, 2nd Regt.

*ROLF, CHARLES,   Thetford.
Marched for Plattsburgh, September,
1814, and went as far as Bolton, Vt.,
serving 6 days in Capt. Salmon Howard's Company.

ROLF, WILLIAM,   Thetford.
Marched for Plattsburgh, September,
1814, and went as far as Bolton, Vt.,.
serving 6 days in Capt. Salmon Howard's Company, 2nd Regt. Ref: Book
52, AGO Page 15.

‡ROLFE, JACOB.
Volunteered to go to Plattsburgh,
September, 1814, and served in Capt.
Jonathan Jennings' company of Chel-
sea. Also served under Captains
Massey and White. Pension Certi-
ficate of widow, Betsey, No. 16872.
Ref: Book 52, AGO Pages 79 and 104.

ROLL, WILLIAM.
Enlisted Jan. 6, 1813 for 5 years in
company of late Capt. J. Brooks
commanded by Lt. John I. Cromwell, Corps of U. S. Artillery; on
Muster Roll from April 30 to June
30, 1814; died June 13, 1814 at Plattsburgh. Ref: R. & L. 1812, AGO Page
18.

*ROLLINS, JAMES.
Served in Capt. Rogers' Company,
Col. Fifield's Regt. Detached Militia
in U. S. service 10 days, 1812.

*ROLLINS, JOHN.
Served in Capt. Needham's Company,
Col. Martindale's Regt. Detached
Militia in U. S. service 2 months
and 14 days, 1812. Served from May
1 to May 15, 1813 in Capt. Simeon
Wright's Company. Served as musi-
cian in 2 Regt. (Fifield's) Vt. Militia.

ROLLINS, JOSIAH.   Corinth.
Volunteered to go to Plattsburgh,
September, 1814, and served in Capt.
Ebenezer Spencer's Company. Ref:
Book 52, AGO Page 48.

‡ROLLINS, MYHEW.
Served in Capt. Brown's Company.
Pension Certificate of widow, Lydia,
No. 28557.

ROLLINS, NATHAN, Corporal.
Served in 1st Regt. of Detached Militia of Vt. in U. S. service at Champlain from Nov. 18 to Nov. 19, 1812.

ROLLINS, WILLIAM.
Served in Capt. Mason's Company,
Col. Fifield's Regt. Detached Militia
in U. S. service 6 months, 1812. Ref:
Book 53, AGO Page 21.

*ROLPH, NATHAN.
Served in Capt. Howard's Company,
Vt. Militia.

ROOD, AARON,   Barre.
Volunteered to go to Plattsburgh,
September, 1814, and served in Capt.
Warren Ellis' Company. Ref: Hemen-
way's Vt. Gazetteer, Vol. 4, Page 41.

‡ROOD, GILES.
Volunteered to go to Plattsburgh,
September, 1814, and served 7 days
in Capt. Frederick Griswold's Company raised in Brookfield, Vt. Pension Certificate of widow, Catharine,
No. 30070.

ROOD, JAMES,   Jericho.
Took part in the battle of Plattsburgh. Ref: History of Jerchio, Page
142.

ROOD, MOSES JR., Sergeant,   Barre.
Volunteered to go to Plattsburgh,
September, 1814, and served 10 days
in Capt. Warren Ellis' Company. Ref:
Book 52, AGO Page 242.

*ROOD, OLIVER C.,   Waterbury.
Volunteered to go to Plattsburgh,
September, 1814, and was in the
battle, serving 11 days in Capt.
George Atkins' Company, 4 Regt.
(Peck's).

‡*ROOD, SILAS S.,   Jericho.
Served from Sept. 23 to Sept. 29,
1813 in Capt. Amasa Mansfield's Company, Dixon's Regt. Also served under Capt. Beeman. Took part in the
battle of Plattsburgh. Pension Certificate of widow, Sally P., No. 29088.

ROOD, WILLIAM,   Jericho.
Took part in the battle of Plattsburgh.
Ref: History of Jericho, Page 142.

*ROOLIN, MANLY.
Served in 3 Regt. (Tyler's) Vt. Militia.

ROOT, A. L.
Served in War of 1812 and was cap-
tured by troops Sept. 17, 1814 at Fort
Erie; discharged Nov. 8, 1814. Ref:
Records of Naval Records and Li-
brary, Navy Dept.

ROOT, AUSTIN, Sergeant, Fairfax or
Swanton. Served from Aug. 8, 1812
in company of Capt. Joseph Beeman
Jr., 11th Regt. U. S. Inf. under
Col. Ira Clark. Enlisted Nov. 1,
1812 in Lt. V. R. Goodrich's Com-
pany, 11th Regt.; died Jan. 10, 1813.
Ref: R. & L. 1812, AGO Page 11;
Hemenway's Vt. Gazetteer, Vol. 2,
Page 402.

ROOT, CHESTER, 1st Lieutenant and Aid.
Served on General Staff of the North-
ern Army commanded by Major Gen-
eral George Izard; on Pay Roll to
July 31, 1814. Ref: R. & L. 1812,
AGO Page 28.

ROOT, FRANKLIN, Corporal.
Enlisted May 7, 1813 during the war
in company of late Capt. J. Brooks,
commanded by Lt. John I. Cromwell, Corps of U. S. Artillery; on
Muster Roll from April 30 to June 30,
1814; promoted from private May 1,
1814. Ref: R. & L. 1812, AGO Page
18.

*ROOT, HORACE.
Enlisted Sept. 20, 1813 in Capt. John
Weed's Company, Col. Clark's Rifle
Corps.

‡ROOT, OLIVER.
Served in Capt. McKensie's Company.
Pension Certificate No. 20840.

*ROOT, SETH, Corporal.
Served in 4 Regt. (Williams') Vt.
Militia.

ROSCO, JOSEPH.
Enlisted Dec. 1, 1812 for 5 years in
company of late Capt. J. Brooks com-
manded by Lt. John I. Cromwell,
Corps of U. S. Artillery; on Muster
Roll from April 30 to June 30, 1814.
Ref: R. & L. 1812, AGO Page 18.

ROSE, AMOS.
Enlisted June 12, 1813 for 1 year
in Capt. James Taylor's Company,

30th Regt. ; also served in Capt. Spencer's Company, 30th Regt. to July 12, 1814. Ref: R. & L. 1812, AGO Pages 52 and 57.

*ROSE, CHANDLER, Weybridge. Served from April 12 to April 21, 1814 in Capt. Edmund B. Hill's Company, Sumner's Regt. Volunteered to go to Plattsburgh, September, 1814 and served in Capt. Silas Wright's Company. Ref: Book 51, AGO Page 70.

ROSE, DENISON R. Served from Jan. 1 to June 30, 1814 in Capt. Haig's Corps of Light Dragoons. Ref: R. & L. 1812, AGO Page 20.

ROSE, JONATHAN, W. Chester. Served from May 1 to July 4, 1814 in Capt. McIlvains' Company, 14th Inf. Ref: R. & L. 1812, AGO Page 30.

ROSE, NATHANIEL, Lancaster. Served from May 1 to Aug. 5, 1814 in Capt. McIlwain's Company, 14th Inf. Ref: R. & L. 1812, AGO Page 30.

*ROSE, NEWTON, Weybridge. Served from April 12 to April 21, 1814 in Capt. Shubael Wales' Company, Col. W. B. Sumner's Regt. Volunteered to go to Plattsburgh, September, 1814, and served 15 days in Capt. Silas Wright's Company.

‡*ROSS, HIRAM. Served in Capt. Wheeler's Company, Col. Fifield's Regt. Detached Militia in U. S. service 6 months and 4 days, 1812. Pension Certificate No. 6657.

ROSS, JOHN. Served from Feb. 5 to May 4, 1813 in Capt. Charles Follett's Company, 11th Regt. Ref: R. & L. 1812, Page 13.

*ROSS, JOSEPH. Served in Capt. Hopkins' Company. Col. Martindale's Regt. Detached Militia in U. S. service 2 months and 13 days, 1812.

*ROSWALT, JACOB, Drummer. Served in Capt. Pettes' Company. Col. Wm. Williams' Regt. Detached Militia in U. S. service 4 months and 17 days, 1812.

ROUND, LINSAY, Clarendon. Volunteered to go to Plattsburgh, September, 1814, and served 7 days in Capt. Durham Sprague's Company. Ref: Book 52, AGO Page 128.

ROUND, OZIAL H., Orderly Sergeant, Clarendon. Volunteered to go to Plattsburgh, September, 1814, and served 7 days in Capt. Durham Sprague's Company. Ref: Book 52, AGO Page 128.

ROUND, ROBERT I., Clarendon. Volunteered to go to Plattsburgh, September, 1814, and served 7 days in Capt. Durham Sprague's Company. Ref: Book 52, AGO Page 128.

ROUNDS, DANIEL. Enlisted Oct.. 15, 1813 in Capt. Asahel Langworthy's Company, Col. Isaac Clark's Rifle Corps. Ref: Book 52, AGO Page 261.

‡*ROUNDS, JOSEPH. Served from April 12 to April 21, 1814 in Capt. Othniel Jewett's Company, Sumner's Regt. Also served in Capt. Sterling Parker's Company. Pension Certificate No. 33173.

‡*ROUNDS, STEPHEN, Drummer. Served from June 11 to June 14, 1813. in Capt. John Palmer's Company, 1st Regt. 2nd Brig. 3rd Div. Also served in Capt. Daniel Hough's Company. Pension Certificate No. 33174.

‡*ROUNDY, DANIEL. Served from September to November, 1813 in Regt. of Riflemen. Also served in Capt. Gates' Company. Pension Certificate No. 44875.

ROUSE, ALVIN, Sandy Hill, N. Y. Served from Dec. 1, 1814 to June 19, 1815 in Capt. Taylor's Company, 30th Inf. Ref: R. & L. 1812, AGO Page 23.

ROUSE, AZARIAH. Jericho. Took part in the battle of Plattsburgh. Ref: History of Jericho, Page 142.

‡ROUSE, OLIVER, Jericho. Took part in the Battle of Plattsburgh. Served in Capt. Peter Allen's Company. Pension Certificate No. 25239.

*ROUSE, WILLIAM, Jericho. Served in 3 Regt. (Tyler's) Vt. Militia. Took part in the battle of Plattsburgh.

‡*ROW, MARTIN. Served in Capt. Phelps' Company, Col. Jonathan Williams' Regt. Detached Militia in U. S. service 2 months and 21 days, 1812. Pension Certificate of widow, Anna, No. 25626.

*ROWBOTTOM, PEACE, Corporal. Served in Capt. Saxe's Company, Col. Wm. Williams' Regt. Detached Militia in U. S. service 4 months and 24 days, 1812.

*ROWE, ELIJAH, Lieutenant. Served in 2 Regt. (Fifield's) Vt. Militia.

ROWE, HORACE. Served in Capt. Eldridge's Company, Col. Dixon's Regt. Detached Militia in U. S. service 1 month and 23 days, 1813. Ref: Book 53, AGO Page 111.

*ROWE, LEBEUS. Served from April 12 to April 21, 1814 in Capt. Shubael Wales' Company, Col. W. B. Sumner's Regt.

‡ROWELL, DAVID, Tunbridge. Volunteered to go to Plattsburgh, September, 1814, and served 3 days in Capt. David Knox's Company. Pension Certificate of widow, Annis, No. 31367.

ROWELL, JOHN,   Strafford.
Volunteered to go to Plattsburgh,
September, 1814, and served in Capt.
Cyril Chandler's Company. Ref: Book
52, AGO Page 42.

ROWELL, ROBERT,   Vershire.
Volunteered to go to Plattsburgh,
September, 1814, and served 3 days
in Capt. Ira Corse's Company. Ref:
Book 52, AGO Page 91.

ROWELL, STEPHEN.
Volunteered to go to Plattsburgh,
September, 1814, and went as far as
Bolton, Vt., serving 4 days in Lt.
Phineus Kimball's Company of West
Fairlee. Ref: Book 52, AGO Page 46.

‡*ROWLEY, AARON, Corporal, Shelburne.
Appointed corporal Sept. 27, 1813 in
Capt. Asahel Langworthy's Company,
Col. Isaac Clark's Volunteer Riflemen
in U. S. service. Volunteered to go
to Plattsburgh, September, 1814, and
served in Major Luman Judson's command. Also served in Capt. Kinney's
Company. Pension Certificate of widow, Betsey T., No. 29701.

*ROWLEY, ERASTUS, Musician.
Served in 1 Regt. (Judson's) Vt.
Militia.

ROWLEY, HEMAN, Musician.
Served from June 11 to June 14, 1813
in Lt. Bates' Company, 1st Regt.
Ref: R. & L. 1812, AGO Page 33.

ROWLEY, HIRAM,   Shoreham.
Volunteered to go to Plattsburgh,
September, 1814, and served 6 days
in Capt. Samuel Hand's Company.
Ref: Rev. J. F. Goodhue's History of
Shoreham, Page 108.

ROWLEY, JOHN.
Served from Nov. 1, 1812 to Feb. 28,
1813 in Capt. Samuel H. Holly's
Company, 11th Regt. Ref: R. & L.
1812, AGO Page 25.

ROWLEY, REUBEN.
Served from March 15 to June 30,
1814 in Regt. of Light Dragoons.
Ref: R. & L. 1812, AGO Page 21.

ROWLEY, SILAS, Corporal,   Shoreham.
Enlisted May 1, 1813 for 1 year in
Capt. Simeon Wright's Company.
Fought at LaCole and on Chateaugay
River. Volunteered to go to Platts-
burgh, September, 1814, and served 6
days in Capt. Samuel Hand's Com-
pany. Ref: R. & L. 1812, AGO Page
51; Rev. J. F. Goodhue's History of
Shoreham, Pages 102 and 108.

ROWLEY, SYLVESTER.
Enlisted May 10, 1813 during the war
in company of late Capt. J. Brooks,
commanded by Lt. John I. Cromwell,
Corps of U. S. Artillery; on Muster
Roll from April 30 to June 30, 1814.
Ref: R. & L. 1812, AGO Page 18.

*ROXFORD, BOYCE, (or Royce).
Served in 1 Regt. (Judson's) Vt.
Militia.

*ROYCE, ABIJAH.
Served in Dixon's Regt. Vt. Militia.

*ROYCE, CALEB, Major.
Served in 1 Regt. (Martindale's) Vt.
Militia. Served as a Major in 3
Regt. (Bowdish) Vt. Militia.

ROYCE, CHARLES,   Berlin.
Volunteered to go to Plattsburgh,
September, 1814, and served 8 days
in Capt. Cyrus Johnson's Company.
Ref: Book 52, AGO Page 202.

ROYCE, JOHN,   Shoreham.
Volunteered to go to Plattsburgh,
September, 1814, and served 6 days
in Capt. Samuel Hand's Company.
Ref: Rev. J. F. Goodhue's History
of Shoreham, Page 108.

*ROYCE, STEPHEN 2nd.
Served in 1 Regt. (Martindale's) Vt.
Militia.

RUBLEE, ANDREW, Lieutenant.
Appointed 2nd Lieutenant 30th Inf.
April 30, 1813; discharged Sept. 18,
1813. Served as 2nd Lieutenant in
Capt. James Taylor's Company, 30th
Regt. Ref: Heitman's Historical Reg-
ister & Dictionary USA; R. & L. 1812,
AGO Page 58.

‡RUBLEE, DAN.
Served in Capt. Brown's Company.
Pension Certificate No. 14418.

*RUBLEE, JOHN B., Lieutenant.
Served in 3 Regt. (Bowdish) Vt.
Militia.

‡*RUBLEE, LUMAN.
Served in 1 Regt. (Judson's) Vt.
Militia. Also served in Capt. Mayo's
Company. Pension Certificate No.
32206.

‡RUDD, LEVI.
Enlisted May 6, 1814 during the war
and served in Capt. James Taylor's
Company, Capt. Wm. Miller's Company and Capt. Gideon Spencer's Company, 30th Regt. Was captured by
troops Sept. 6, 1814 at Plattsburgh;
discharged Nov. 8, 1814. Pension
Certificate No. 6664. Ref: Records
of Naval Records and Library, Navy
Dept.

RUDE, THOMAS B.,   Fairfax.
Served from Aug. 8, 1812 in company
of Capt. Joseph Beeman Jr., 11th
Regt. U. S. Inf. under Col. Ira
Clark. Ref: Hemenway's Vt. Gazet-
teer, Vol. 2, Page 402.

RUE, STEPHEN.
Enlisted Jan. 4, 1813 in Capt. Charles
Follett's Company, 11th Regt. and
served to date of death April 22,
1813. Ref: R. & L. 1812, AGO Page
13.

RUGG, E.,   Fairfax.
Served in 1813 and 1814 in Capt.
Joseph Beeman's Company. Ref: Hemenway's Vt. Gazetteer, Vol. 2, Page
402.

RUGG, JONAS,   Coventry.
Served from Sept. 16, 1812 to March
16, 1813 in Capt. Mason's Company,
Col. Fifield's Regt. stationed at Derby Line. Ref: Hemenway's Vt. Gazetteer, Vol. 3, Page 144.

*RUGGLES, BARNABAS, Musician.
Served in 2 Regt. (Fifield's) Vt. Militia.

‡RUGGLES, BARNEY .
Served in Capt. Mason's Company.
Pension Certificate No. 11368. Pension Certificate of widow, Charlotte, No. 33249.

*RUGGLES, JONATHAN F., Randolph.
Volunteered to go to Plattsburgh, September, 1814, and served in Capt. Lebbeus Egerton's Company.

‡*RULE, JOHN H. (or R.)
Served in Capt. Richardson's Company, Col. Martindale's Regt. Detached Militia in U. S. service 2 months and 13 days, 1812. Pension Certificate of widow, Deborah, No. 14728.

*RULEY, BROWNSON or Keeler?)
Served from June 11 to June 14, 1813 in Capt. Hezekiah Barns' Company, 1st Regt. 2nd Brig. 3rd Div.

RUMERY, DAVID.
Enlisted Jan. 4, 1813 in Capt. Jonathan Stark's Company, 11th Regt.; on Pay Roll to May 31, 1813. Ref: R. & L. 1812, AGO Page 19.

RUMRILL, WILLIAM, Sergeant.
Served in Capt. Benjamin Bradford's Company; on Muster Roll from May 31 to Aug. 31, 1813; on command on board Montgomery Sloop. Ref: R. & L. 1812, AGO Page 26.

*RUMSAY, AARON.
Served in Capt. Samuel H. Holly's Company, 11th Regt.; on Pay Roll for January and February, 1813. Also served with Hospital Attendants, Vt. Ref: R. & L. 1812, AGO Page 25.

RUMSEY, DAVID.   Hubardton.
Volunteered to go to Plattsburgh, September, 1814, and served 6 days in Capt. Henry J. Horton's Company as a teamster. Ref: Book 52, AGO Page 142.

*RUMSEY, JOHN,   St. Albans.
Served in Capt. Ormsbee's Company, Col. Martindale's Regt. Detached Militia in U. S. service 1 month and 21 days, 1812. Served from May 6, 1813 to May 5, 1814 in Capt. John Wires' Company, 30th Regt.

*RUMSEY, NATHAN,   Hubbardton.
Served in 1 Regt. (Martindale's) Vt. Militia. Was taken a prisoner in September, 1814, and died a prisoner at Halifax in March, 1815. Ref: Hemenway's Vt. Gazetteer, Vol. 3, Pages 757 and 772.

*RUMSEY, STEPHEN, Lieutenant, Hubbardton. Appointed 2nd Lieutentnt 30th Inf. April 30, 1813; 1st Lieutenant Jan. 31, 1814; honorably discharged June 15, 1815. Served as 2nd Lieutenant in Capt. Daniel Farrington's Company, 30th Regt. (also commanded by Capt. Simeon Wright). Served as Ensign in 1st Regt. of Detached Militia of Vt. in U. S. service at Champlain from Nov. 18 to 19, 1812. Served as Lieutenant in 1 Regt. (Martindale's) Vt. Militia. Ref: Heitman's Historical Register & Dictionary USA; R. & L. 1812, AGO Page 50.

RUMSEY, TIMOTHY, Corporal, Hubbardton. Enlisted April 23, 1813 for 1 year in Capt. Daniel Farrington's Company, 30th Regt. (also commanded by Capt. Simeon Wright); killed in action March 30, 1814. Ref: R. & L. 1812, AGO Pages 50 and 51.

*RUNDALL, JOSIAH, Fifer.
Served in Dixon's Regt. Vt. Militia.

RUNLET, JONATHAN.
Served in Capt. Benjamin Bradford's Company; on Muster Roll from May 31 to Aug. 31, 1813. Ref: R. & L. 1812, AGO Page 26.

RUNOLDS, BENJAMIN.
Served in Capt. Phineas Williams' Company, 11th Regt.; on Pay Roll for January and February, 1813. Ref: R. & L. 1812, AGO Page 15.

*RUSCO, NATHANIEL.
Served in Capt. Phelps' Company, Col. Wm. Williams' Regt. Detached Militia in U. S. service 5 months, 1812.

*RUSH, HYSON.
Served in 1 Regt. (Judson's) Vt. Militia.

‡*RUSS, AMASA,   Waitsfield.
Volunteered to go to Plattsburgh, September, 1814, and served 4 days in Capt. Mathias S. Jones' Company. Also served in Corning's Detachment, Vt. Militia. Pension Certificate of widow, Harriet F., No. 25190.

RUSS, JAMES.
Volunteered to go to Plattsburgh, September, 1814, and went as far as Bolton, Vt., serving 4 days in Lt. Phineus Kimball's Company, West Fairlee. Ref: Book 52, AGO Page 46.

RUSS, JOHN, Ensign.
Volunteered to go to Plattsburgh, September, 1814, and went as far as Bolton, Vt., serving 4 days in company of Lt. Phineus Kimball of W. Fairlee. Ref: Book 52, AGO Pages 46 and 47.

‡RUSS, JOSEPH.
Served in Capt. Jones' Company. Pension Certificate of widow, Aurelia, No. 26120.

*RUSSELL, ASA.
Served in Capt. Morrill's Company, Col. Fifield's Regt. Detached Militia in U. S. service 4 months and 28 days, 1812. Served from Feb. 10 to May 9, 1813 in Capt. Samul Gordon's Company, 11th Regt. Ref: R. & L. 1812, AGO Pages 8 and 9.

RUSSELL, BENJAMIN, Franklin County.
Volunteered to go to Plattsburgh Sept. 11, 1814, and served in 15th or 22nd Regt. Ref: Hemenway's Vt. Gazetteer, Vol. 2, Page 391.

*RUSSELL, ELEAZER.
Served from April 12 to April 21, 1814 in Capt. Othniel Jewett's Company, Sumner's Regt.

RUSSELL, EBENEZER, Solmontown.
Served from July 11 to Aug. 31, 1813 and from May 1 to July 10, 1814 in Capt. Poland's Company, 34th Inf. Ref: R. & L. 1812, AGO Page 30.

RUSSELL, ELIJAH.
Served in Capt. James Taylor's Company, 30th Regt. Ref: R. & L. 1812, AGO Page 59.

*RUSSELL, GIDEON R. (or G.)
Served in Capt. Burnap's Company, Col. Jonathan Williams' Regt. Detached Militia in U. S. service 1 month and 26 days, 1812.

*RUSSELL, HARTWELL.
Served in Corning's Detachment, Vt. Militia.

RUSSELL, JAMES.
Enlisted Oct. 4, 1813 for 1 year in Capt. Daniel Farrington's Company, 30th Regt. (also commanded by Capt. Simeon Wright); on Muster Roll from March 1 to April 30, 1814. Ref: R. & L. 1812, AGO Pages 50 and 51.

*RUSSELL, JOEL.
Served in Capt. Taylor's Company, Col. Fifield's Regt. Detached Militia in U. S. service 2 months and 21 days, 1812.

*RUSSELL, JOHN, Swanton.
Served from June 11 to June 14, 1813 in Capt. Hezekiah Barns' Company, 1st Regt. 2nd Brig. 3rd Div. Served from July 15 to Dec. 8, 1813 in Capt. V. R. Goodrich's Company, 11th Regt. Ref: Hemenway's Vt. Gazetteer, Vol. 2, Page 444.

*RUSSELL, JOHN JR.
Served in Capt. Morrill's Company, Col. Fifield's Regt. Detached Militia in U. S. service 6 months and 3 days, 1812.

RUSSELL, JONAH.
Enlisted Oct. 28, 1813 for 1 year in Capt. Simeon Wright's Company. Ref: R. & L. 1812, AGO Page 51.

‡RUSSELL, JONATHAN.
Served in Capt. Longmaid's Company. Pension Certificate No. 26378.

RUSSELL, JOSEPH PYNCHON, Surgeon.
Appointed Surgeon's Mate 4th Inf. May 25, 1814; transferred to 5th Inf. May 17, 1815; Post Surgeon Aug. 10, 1818; died Sept. 19, 1849. Ref: Heitman's Historical Register & Dictionary USA.

*RUSSELL, JOSIAH, Stowe.
Volunteered to go to Plattsburgh, September, 1814, and was at the battle, serving in Capt. Nehemiah Perkins' Company, 4 Regt. (Peck's). Also served in Corning's Detachment, Vt. Militia.

RUSSELL, METZER, Barre.
Volunteered to go to Plattsburgh, September, 1814, and served 10 days in Capt. Warren Ellis' Company. Ref: Book 52, AGO Page 242.

*RUSSELL, NATHANIEL, Stowe.
Volunteered to go to Plattsburgh, September, 1814, and was at the battle, serving in Capt. Nehemiah Perkin's Company, 4 Regt. (Peck's).

*RUSSELL, PERRY, Corporal.
Served from June 11 to June 14, 1813 in Capt. John M. Eldridge's Company, 1st Regt. 2nd Brig. 3rd Div.

‡*RUSSELL, ROBERT.
Served in 3 Regt. (Tyler's) Vt. Militia. Also served in Capt. T. Leslie's Company. Pension Certificate of widow, Mary, No. 27200.

‡*RUSSELL, SETH, Ira.
Served in Capt. Brown's Company, Col. Martindale's Regt. Detached Militia in U. S. service 2 months and 14 days, 1812. Pension Certificate No. 6661.

*RUSSELL, STEPHEN F., Corporal, Stowe. Volunteered to go to Plattsburgh, September, 1814, and was at the battle, serving in Capt. Nehemiah Perkins' Company, 4 Regt. (Peck's).

*RUSSELL, THOMAS P., Randolph.
Volunteered to go to Plattsburgh, September, 1814, and served in Capt. Lebbeus Egerton's Company.

‡*RUSSELL, WILLIAM JR.
Served in Capt. Robbins' Company, Col. Wm. Williams' Regt. Detached Militia in U. S. service 4 months and 29 days, 1812. Pension Certificate of widow, Cynthia, No. 7444.

*RUST. JOHN F.
Served in Capt. Burnap's Company, Col. Jonathan Williams' Regt. Detached Militia in U. S. service 2 months and 13 days, 1812.

*RUTHERFORD, JOHN.
Served in 1 Regt. (Judson's) Vt. Militia.

‡*RUTHERFORD, OLIVER.
Served from June 11 to June 14, 1813 in Capt. Hezekiah Barns' Company, 1st Regt. 2nd Brig. 3rd Div. Pension Certificate of widow, Polly, No. 35745.

*RUTTER, JOHN.
Served in 3 Regt. (Tyler's) Vt. Militia.

*RUTTER, WILLIAM.
Served in 3 Regt. (Tyler's) Vt. Militia.

RYDER, SAMUEL B., Braintree.
Marched to Plattsburgh Sept. 10, 1814 and served in Capt. Lot Hudson's Company. Ref: Book 52, AGO Page 24.

RYNO, WILLIAM.
Enlisted Nov. 25, 1812 for 5 years in company of late Capt. J. Brooks, commanded by Lt. John I. Cromwell, Corps of U. S. Artillery; on Muster Roll from April 30 to June 30, 1814. Ref: R. & L. 1812, AGO Page 18.

‡*SABIN, ALVAH, Lieutenant, Georgia. Enlisted in Capt. Jesse Post's Company, Dixon's Regt.; transferred to Capt. Asahel Langworthy's Company, Col. Isaac Clark's Rifle Corps Oct. 23, 1813. Volunteered to go to Plattsburgh, September, 1814, and served 8 days as a corporal in Capt. Post's Company. Pension Certificate No. 20612.

‡SABIN, DANIEL,   Georgia. Volunteered to go to Plattsburgh, September, 1814, and served 8 days in Capt. Jesse Post's Company, Dixon's Regt. Pension Certificate No. 25292.

SABIN, JAMES,   Wallingford? Served in Capt. Hotchkiss' Company, Col. Martindale's Regt. Detached Militia in U. S. service 2 months and 13 days, 1812. Ref: Book 53, AGO Page 64.

*SABIN, LEMUEL D., Captain. Served in 3 Regt. (Williams') Vt. Militia.

SABREY, STEPHEN. Served in War of 1812 and was captured by troops Sept. 17, 1814 at Fort Erie; discharged Nov. 8, 1814. Ref: Records of Naval Records and Library, Navy Dept.

*SACKET, RICHARD.   St. Albans. Served from Sept. 25 to Oct. 9, 1813 in Capt. N. B. Eldridge's Company, Dixon's Regt. Volunteered and was at the battle of Plattsburgh Sept. 11, 1814, serving in Capt. Samuel H. Farnsworth's Company.

*SACKETT, ISAAC. Served in 1 Regt. (Judson's) Vt. Militia.

SAFFORD, JOHN, Sergeant, Cambridge. Volunteered to go to Plattsburgh. September, 1814, and served 8 days in Capt. Salmon Green's Company. Ref: Book 51, AGO Page 207.

SAFFORD, JONAS. Enlisted May 13, 1813 for 1 year in Capt. Daniel Farrington's Company, 30th Regt. (also commanded by Capt. Simeon Wright); on Muster Roll from March 1 to April 30, 1814. Ref: R. & L. 1812, AGO Pages 50 and 51.

*SAFFORD, OEL. Served in Capt. Charles Bennett's Company, Col. Dixon's Regt. Detached Militia in U. S. service 28 days, 1813.

*SAFFORD, ORSON, Ensign. Served from Sept. 25 to Nov. 6, 1813 in Capt. Charles Bennett's Company, Dixon's Regt.

SAFFORD, SAMUEL G., Fifer, St. Albans. Enlisted May 5, 1813 for 1 year in Capt. John Wires' Company, 30th Regt. Ref: R. & L. 1812, AGO Page 40.

SAGE, DAVID,   Worthington, Conn. Enlisted at Burlington March 15, 1814 during the war and served in Capt.

Wm. Miller's Company, Capt. Gideon Spencer's Company and Capt. James Taylor's Company, 30th Regt. Ref: R. & L. 1812, AGO Pages 53, 54, 55, 57.

*SAGER, DAVID,   Highgate. Served in Capt. Conrade Saxe's Company, 4 Regt. (Williams') Detached Militia in U. S. service at Swanton Falls 6 or 9 months in 1812.

*ST. CLAIR, MICHAEL. Served in Capt. Pettes' Company, Col. Wm. Williams' Regt. Detached Militia in U. S. service 4 months and 17 days, 1812.

‡ST. JOHN, THOMAS P.,   St. Albans. Volunteered to go to Plattsburgh, September, 1814, and served 8 days in Capt. Samuel H. Farnsworth's Company. Pension Certificate No. 32943.

SALISBURY, ANDREW. Served from May 1 to May 14, 1814; no organization given. Ref: R. & L. 1812, AGO Page 29.

*SALISBURY, BELCHER,   Randolph. Volunteered to go to Plattsburgh, September, 1814, and served in Capt. Lebbeus Egerton's Company.

*SALISBURY, JOHN. Served from April 12 to April 21, 1814 in Capt. Othniel Jewett's Company, Sumner's Regt.

*SALISBURY, JOSEPH.   Randolph. Volunteered to go to Plattsburgh, September, 1814, and served in Capt. Lebbeus Egerton's Company.

SALISBURY, REUBEN, Lieutenant, St. Albans. Appointed 1st Lieutenant 30th Inf. April 30, 1813; resigned Feb. 18, 1814. Enlisted April 13, 1813 in Capt. John Wires' Company, 30th Regt. Ref: Heitman's Historical Register & Dictionary USA; R. & L. 1812, AGO Page 40.

SALTER, ISAAC,   Barre. Volunteered to go to Plattsburgh, September, 1814, and served in Capt. Warren Ellis' Company. Ref: Hemenway's Vt. Gazetteer, Vol. 4, Page 42.

*SALVIN, JAMES. Served in 1 Regt. (Martindale's) Vt. Militia.

SAMPCIE, JOHN,   Fairfax. Served from Aug. 8, 1812 in company of Capt. Joseph Beeman Jr., 11th Regt. U. S. Inf. under Col. Ira Clark. Ref: Hemenway's Vt. Gazetteer, Vol. 2, Page 402.

*SAMPLIN, ELISHA. Served in 1 Regt. (Martindale's) Vt. Militia.

*SAMPSON, JOEL. Served in 3 Regt. (Tyler's) Vt. Militia.

‡*SAMPSON, JONATHAN JR. Served under Captains Wheatly and Wright, Col. Fifield's Regt. Detached

Militia in U. S. service 6 months, 1812. Pension Certificate of widow, Lois, No. 30358.

SAMPSON, WILLIAM JR., Corporal. Served from April 12 to April 21, 1814 in Capt. Othniel Jewett's Company, Sumner's Regt. Ref: Book 52, AGO Page 264.

SAMSON, BENJAMIN,   Roxbury. Volunteered to go to Plattsburgh, September, 1814, and served 8 days in Capt. Samuel M. Orcutt's Company. Ref: Book 52, AGO Page 250.

SAMSON, CHARLES, Sergeant, Roxbury. Volunteered to go to Plattsburgh, September, 1814, and served 7 days in Capt. Samuel M. Orcutt's Company. Ref: Book 52, AGO Pages 167 and 250.

*SAMSON, EMERY. Served in Capt. Durkee's Company, Col. Fifield's Regt. Detached Militia in U. S. service 1 month and 12 days, 1812..

SANBORN, ABRAM. Served from March 24 to June 23, 1813 in Capt. John W. Weeks' Company, 11th Regt. Ref: R. & L. 1812, AGO Page 4.

SANBORN, BENJAMIN, Franklin County. Volunteered to go to Plattsburgh Sept. 11, 1814. and served in 15th or 22nd Regt. Ref: Hemenway's Vt. Gazetteer, Vol. 2, Page 391.

*SANBORN, DANIEL,   Danville. Served in Capt. Morrill's Company, Col. Fifield's Regt. Detached Militia in U. S. service 6 months and 5 days, 1812.

SANBORN, EDMOND. Served in Capt. Weeks' Company, 11th Regt.; on Pay Roll for January and February, 1813. Ref: R. & L. 1812, AGO Page 5.

SANBORN, JESSE,   Franklin County. Volunteered to go to Plattsburgh Sept. 11, 1814 and served in 15th or 22nd Regt. Ref: Hemenway's Vt. Gazetteer, Vol. 2, Page 391.

SANBORN, JOSEPH,   Corinth. Volunteered to go to Plattsburgh, September, 1814, and served 3 days in Capt. Abel Jackman's Company. Ref: Book 52, AGO Pages 44 and 45.

‡SANBORN, JOSEPH,   Strafford. Volunteered to go to Plattsburgh, September, 1814, and served 6 days in Capt. Jedediah H. Harris' Company. Pension Certificate of widow, Polly, No. 28529.

SANBORN, JOSEPH N., Musician. Served from Nov. 1, 1812 to Dec. 31, 1812 in Capt. Benjamin S. Edgerton's Company, 11th Regt.; on Pay Roll for September and October, 1812, and January and February, 1813. Ref: R. & L. 1812, AGO Pages 1 and 2.

SANBORN, PAUL,   Stowe. Volunteered to go to Plattsburgh, September, 1814, and served in Capt. Nehemiah Perkins' Company, 4th Regt. (Peck's). Ref: Hemenway's Vt. Gazetteer, Vol. 2, Page 742.

SANBORN, SIMEON. Enlisted March 12, 1813 in Capt. Charles Follett's Company, 11th Regt. and served to date of death, April 30, 1813. Ref: R. & L. 1812, AGO Page 13.

SANBORN, WILLARD,   Sanburton. Served from July 11 to Aug. 31, 1813 and from May 1 to July 10, 1814 in Capt. Chadwick's Company, 34th Inf. Ref: R. & L. 1812, AGO Page 30.

‡SANDERS, GEORGE. Served in Capt. Coser's Company. Pension Certificate No. 7475.

SANDERS, JABEZ. Served in Capt. Wheeler's Company, Col. Fifield's Regt. Detached Militia in U. S. service 2 months and 12 days, 1812. Ref: Book 53, AGO Page 71.

*SANDERS. LEVI. Served from April 12 to May 20, 1814 in company of Capt. James Gray Jr., Sumner's Regt.

*SANDERS, WILLIAM,   Fairfield. Served in Capt. George W. Kindal's Company, 4 Regt. (Williams') Detached Militia in U. S. service 4 months and 23 days, 1812.

SANDERSON, ABEL,   Woodstock. Served in Capt. Phineas Williams' Company, 11th Regt.; on Pay Roll for January and February, 1813. Ref: R. & L. 1812, AGO Page 15.

‡SANDERSON, ABRAHAM, Shrewsbury. Volunteered to go to Plattsburgh, September, 1814. and served 4 days in Capt. Robert Reed's Company. Pension Certificate of widow, Arathusa, No. 28376.

SANDERSON, EBENEZER,   St. Albans. Volunteered and was in the action at Plattsburgh Sept. 11, 1814, serving in Capt. Samuel H. Farnsworth's Company. Ref: Hemenway's Vt. Gazetteer, Vol. 2, Page 434.

SANDERSON, EBENEZER,   Highgate. Served in Capt. Saxe's Company, Col. Wm. Williams' Regt. Detached Militia in U. S. service 4 months and 24 days. 1812. Enlisted Sept. 25, 1813 in Capt. N. B. Eldridge's Company, Dixon's Regt.; furloughed Sept. 28th, sick; died Oct. 10, 1813. Ref: Book 52, AGO Page 267; Book 53, AGO Page 73.

*SANDERSON, HIRAM. Enlisted Sept. 25, 1813 in company of Capt. Jonathan Prentiss, Jr., Dixon's Regt.

SANDERSON, ISRAEL. Served from March 27 to June 26, 1813 in Capt. John W. Weeks' Company, 11th Regt. Ref: R. & L. 1812, AGO Page 4.

*SANDERSON, JABEZ.
Served in 2 Regt. (Fifield's) Vt. Militia.

SANDERSON, JAMES,   Morristown.
Served from May 6, 1813 to May 10,
1814 in Capt. Gideon Spencer's Company and Capt. James Taylor's Company, 30th Regt. Volunteered to go
to Plattsburgh, September, 1814, and
served 8 days in Capt. Denison Cook's
Company. Ref: R. & L. 1812, AGO
Pages 52, 57, 59; Book 51, AGO Pages
202 and 206.

*SANDERSON, JESSE.
Served in 1 Regt. (Judson's) Vt.
Militia.

*SANDERSON, JOEL,   Woodstock.
Served in Capt. Wheatley's Company, Col. Fifield's Regt. Detached
Militia in U. S. service 1 month and
27 days, 1812. Also served in 3
Regt. (Williams') Vt. Militia.

SANDERSON, JOHN.
Was born in Woodstock; served in
War of 1812; captured by troops June
6, 1813 at Stoney Point; discharged
Oct. 10, 1814. Ref: Records of Naval
Records and Library, Navy Dept.

*SANDERSON, LEVI, Musician.
Served from Sept. 23 to Sept. 29,
1813 in Capt. Amasa Mansfield's Company, Dixon's Regt.

SANDERSON, THOMAS.
Served from May 1 to June 30, 1814
in Capt. Haig's Corps of Light Dragoons. Ref: R. & L. 1812, AGO
Page 20.

*SANDERSON, WILLIAM.
Served in 2 Regt. (Fifield's) Vt. Militia.

*SANDFORD, CARR N.
Served from April 12 to April 21,
1814 in Capt. Eseck Sprague's Company, Sumner's Regt.

*SANDFORD, ELIAS, Corporal.
Served from Oct. 8 to Nov. 18, 1813
in Capt. Isaac Finch's Company, Col.
Clark's Rifle Corps.

SANFORD, AARON,   Woodbury, Conn.
Enlisted at Pawlet Feb. 26, 1814 during the war and served in Capt.
Wm. Miller's Company, Capt. Gideon
Spencer's Company and Capt. James
Taylor's Company, 30th Regt. Ref:
R. & L. 1812, AGO Pages 53, 54,
55, 56.

*SANFORD, DANIEL,   Cornwall.
Served in Capt. Bingham's Company,
Col. Jonathan Williams' Regt. Detached Militia in U. S. service 2
months and 9 days, 1812. Served from
April 12 to April 21, 1814 in Capt.
Edmund B. Hill's Company, Sumner's
Regt.; volunteered to go to Plattsburgh, September, 1814, and was at
the battle, serving as orderly sergeant
in same company.

SANFORD, DAVID, Captain.
Appointed Captain 30th Inf. April
30, 1813; honorably discharged June

15, 1815. Ref: Heitman's Historical
Register & Dictionary USA.

SANFORD, IRA H.
Enlisted March 31, 1814 for 5 years
and served in Capt. Gideon Spencer's
Company, Capt. Clark's Company and
Capt. James Taylor's Company, 30th
Regt. Ref: R. & L. 1812, AGO Pages
53 and 56.

*SANFORD, ISRAEL.
Served from June 11 to June 14, 1813
in Capt. John M. Eldridge's Company,
1st Regt. 2nd Brig. 3rd Div.

*SANFORD, JOHN,   Cornwall.
Served in Capt. Weeks' Company,
11th Regt.; on Pay Roll for January and February, 1813. Served from
April 12 to April 21, 1814 in Capt.
Edmund B. Hill's Company, Sumner's
Regt.; volunteered to go to Plattsburgh, September, 1814, and was at
the battle, serving in same company.
Ref: R. & L. 1812, AGO Page 5.

‡*SANFORD, JONAH,   Cornwall.
Served from April 12 to April 21,
1814 in Capt. Edmund B. Hill's Company, Sumner's Regt.; volunteered
to go to Plattsburgh, September, 1814,
and was at the battle, serving in
same company. Also served in Capt.
Scoville's Company. Pension Certificate of widow, Harriet E., No. 28036.

*SANFORD, NATHANIEL,   Sergeant,
Sandgate. Served in Capt. Strait's
Company, Col. Martindale's Regt. Detached Militia in U. S. service 2
months and 13 days, 1812. Enlisted
June 5, 1813 for 1 year in Capt.
Daniel Farrington's Company, 30th
Regt.; on Muster Roll from March
1 to April 30, 1814. Served from
Sept. 1, 1814 to June 16, 1815 in
Capt. Sanford's Company, 30th Inf.
Ref: R. & L. 1812, AGO Pages 50
and 51.

*SANFORD, OZIAS,   Cornwall.
Served in Capt. Wright's Company,
Col. Martindale's Regt. Detached
Militia in U. S. service 2 months
and 14 days, 1812. Volunteered to
go to Plattsburgh, September, 1814,
and served as a Corporal in Capt.
Edmund B. Hill's Company, Sumner's
Regt.

SANFORD, PEREZ S., Lieutenant.
Appointed Sergeant 11th Inf. May
18, 1812; Ensign Aug. 23, 1813; 3rd
Lieutenant Dec. 12, 1813; 2nd Lieutenant May 2, 1814; honorably discharged June 15, 1815. Served in
Capt. Samul Gordon's Company, 11th
Regt. as a sergeant; on Pay Roll for
January and February, 1813. Ref:
Heitman's Historical Register & Dictionary USA; R. & L. 1812, AGO
Page 9.

SANTER, LOYD,   Panton.
Served from Sept. 1, 1814 to June
16, 1815 in Capt. Sanford's Company,
30th Inf. Ref: R. & L. 1812, AGO
Page 23.

*SARGEANT, JACOB.
Served in Capt. Parsons' Company,
Col. Jonathan Williams' Regt. De-

tached Militia in U. S. service 2 months and 13 days, 1812.

SARGEANT, JOHN P., Plainfield. Volunteered to go to Plattsburgh, September, 1814, and served 8 days in Capt. James English's Company. Ref: Book 52, AGO Pages 199 and 248.

‡*SARGENT, LEONARD, Manchester. Served in Capt. Richardson's Company, Col. Martindale's Regt. Detached Militia in U. S. service 21 days, 1812. Pension Certificate No. 9717.

‡SARGENT, ROBERT, Tunbridge or Strafford. Volunteered to go to Plattsburgh, September, 1814, and served 4 days in Capt. Ephraim Hackett's Company. Also served in Capt. Buck's Company. Pension Certificate No. 10203. Ref: Book 52, AGO Page 71.

SARGENT, ISAAC. Served in Capt. Benjamin Bradford's Company; on Muster Roll from May 31 to Aug. 31, 1813. Ref: R. & L. 1812, AGO Page 26.

*SARGENT, LEVI, Orange. Served in Capt. Walker's Company, Col. Fifield's Regt. Detached Militia in U. S. service 2 months and 24 days, 1812.

*SARGENT, MOSES, Randolph. Volunteered to go to Plattsburgh, September, 1814, and served in Capt. Lebbeus Egerton's Company.

SARGENT, NOAH, Strafford. Volunteered to go to Plattsburgh, September, 1814, and served 2 days in Capt. Cyril Chandler's Company. Ref: Book 52, AGO Page 42.

SARGENT, SAMUEL, Franklin County. Volunteered to go to Plattsburgh Sept. 11, 1814 and served in 15th or 22nd Regt. Ref: Hemenway's Vt. Gazetteer, Vol. 2, Page 391.

‡SARGENT, STEPHEN L. Served in Capt. John Campbell's Company. Pension Certificate of widow, Bridget, No. 11293.

*SARTWELL, AARON. Served in Capt. Walker's Company, Col. Fifield's Regt. Detached Militia in U. S. service 6 months and 3 days, 1812.

SARTWELL, WARREN, Sergeant. Served from Nov. 1, 1812 to Feb. 28, 1813 in Lt. Wm. S. Foster's Company, 11th Regt. Ref: R. & L. 1812, AGO Page 7.

SATTER, ISAAC, Barre. Volunteered to go to Plattsburgh, September, 1814, and served 10 days in Capt. Warren Ellis' Company. Ref: Book 52, AGO Page 242.

SATTERFIELD, JOHN, Corporal, Franklin County. Enlisted April 23, 1812 for 5 years in Capt. White Youngs' Company, 15th Regt.; on Muster Roll from Aug. 31 to Dec. 31, 1814. Ref: R. & L. 1812, AGO Page 27.

SAVAGE, GIBSON, Sergenat, St. Albans. Enlisted May 3, 1813 for 1 year in Capt. John Wires' Company, 30th Regt. Ref: R. & L. 1812, AGO Page 40.

SAVAGE, MARTIN. Enlisted Feb. 28, 1812 for 5 years in Capt. White Youngs' Company, 15th Regt.; on Muster Roll from Aug. 31 to Dec. 31, 1814. Ref: R. & L. 1812, AGO Page 27.

*SAVERY, HARVEY. Served from April 12, 1814 to April 21, 1814 in Lieut. James S. Morton's Company, Col. W. B. Sumner's Regt.

‡SAWTELL, ABEL. Served under Captains Martin and Robinson. Pension Certificate No. 23170. Pension Certificate of widow, Drusilla, No. 36452.

SAWYER, BENJAMIN. Volunteered to go to Plattsburgh, September, 1814, and served 4 days in Capt. Aaron Kidder's Company. Ref: Book 52, AGO Page 65.

*SAWYER, EBENEZER, Thetford. Served in Capt. Morrill's Company, Col. Fifield's Regt. Detached Militia in U. S. service 6 months and 5 days, 1812. Served from April 12 to April 14, 1814 in Capt. Jonathan P. Stanley's Company, Col. W. B. Sumner's Regt. Volunteered to go to Plattsburgh, September, 1814, and went as far as Bolton, serving 6 days in Capt. Salmon Howard's Company, 2nd Regt. Ref: Book 52, AGO Page 287.

‡SAWYER, ELIJAH W., Montpelier. Served from June 17, 1814 to June 19, 1815 in Capt. Taylor's Company, 30th Inf. Also served in Capt. Aken's Company. Pension Certificate of widow, Sally, No. 5425. Ref: R. & L. 1812, AGO Page 23.

SAWYER, ELISHA. Enlisted Oct. 18, 1812 in Capt. Benjamin S. Edgerton's Company, 11th Regt.; on Pay Roll for January and February, 1813. Ref: R. & L. 1812, AGO Pages 1 and 2.

‡SAWYER, ENOS. Volunteered to go to Plattsburgh, September, 1814, and served 4 days in Capt. Aaron Kidder's Company. Pension Certificate No. 31101.

*SAWYER, EZRA. Served from April 12 to April 15, 1814 in Capt. Jonathan P. Stanley's Company, Col. W. B. Sumner's Regt.

SAWYER, FREDERICK AUGUSTUS, Lieutenant. Appointed Ensign 11th Inf. March 12, 1812; 2nd Lieutenant June 26, 1813; 1st Lieutenant Dec. 12, 1813; died April 28, 1831. Served as Ensign in Capt. Benjamin S. Edgerton's Company, 11th Regt.; on Pay Roll for September and October, 1812 and January and February, 1813. Ref: Heitman's Historical Register & Dictionary USA; R. & L. 1812, AGO Pages 1 and 2.

SAWYER, HORACE B., Midshipman, Burlington. Appointed a Midshipman June 4, 1812; served on Lake Champlain during the early part of the war; wounded, taken prisoner and sent to Canada; served from Dec. 14, 1814 to July 3, 1815 on U. S. Frigate CONSTITUTION and participated in the capture of the CYANE and LEVANT Feb. 20, 1815; remained in Navy until Sept. 13, 1855 when he was placed on reserve list with rank of Captain; died Feb. 14, 1860. Ref: Records of Naval Records and Library, Navy Dept.

SAWYER, JOHN, Highgate. Volunteered to go to Plattsburgh, September, 1814, and served 5 days in Capt. Conrade Saxe's Company, 4th Regt. (Williams'). Ref: Book 51, AGO Page 100.

SAWYER, JOHN Y., Lieutenant. Appointed Ensign 31st Inf. April 30, 1813; 2nd Lieutenant April 18, 1814; 1st Lieutenant Dec. 1, 1814; honorably discharged June 15, 1815. Ref: Heitman's Historical Register & Dictionary USA.

‡*SAWYER, JOSEPH, Drummer. Served in Capt. Willson's Company, Col. Wm. Williams' Regt. Detached Militia in U. S. service 4 months and 24 days, 1812. Served from Sept. 25 to Nov. 8, 1813 in Capt. N. B. Eldridge's Company, Dixon's Regt. Pension Certificate No. 13451.

*SAWYER, JOSHUA. Served in Capt. Briggs' Company, Col. Jonathan Williams' Regt. Detached Militia in U. S. service 2 months and 13 days, 1812.

*SAWYER, MOSES H., Berlin. Served in Capt. Walker's Company, Col. Fifield's Regt. Detached Militia in U. S. service 6 months and 3 days, 1812. Volunteered to go to Plattsburgh, September, 1814, and served 7 days in Capt. Cyrus Johnson's Company.

SAWYER, NATHANIEL, Carpenter. Served from May 1 to June 30, 1814 in Alexander Parris' Company of Artificers. Ref: R. & L. 1812, AGO Page 24.

*SAWYER, NOAHDIAH. Served from Sept. 25 to Sept. 28, 1813 in Capt. Amos Robinson's Company, Dixon's Regt.

SAWYER, PLUMMER, Danville. Served in Capt. Morrill's Company, Col. Fifield's Regt. Detached Militia in U. S. service 6 months. Ref: Hemenway's Vt. Gazetteer, Vol. 1, Page 314.

‡*SAXE, CONRADE, Captain, Highgate. Served from Sept. 1, 1812 as Captain of a company in 4 Regt. (Williams'). Volunteered to go to Plattsburgh, September, 1814, and served 5 days in command of company from Highgate. Pension Certificate No. 4816.

*SAXTON, HARRY. Served from April 12 to April 21, 1814 in Capt. Edmund B. Hill's Company, Sumner's Regt.

*SAXTON, HORACE, Captain. Served in 1 Regt. (Judson's) Vt. Militia.

*SAXTON, JAMES, 2nd Lieutenant, Bristol. Served from April 12 to April 21, 1814 in Capt. Othniel Jewett's Company, Sumner's Regt. Volunteered to go to Plattsburgh, September, 1814, and was at the battle, serving 9 days in Capt. Jehiel Saxton's Company, Sumner's Regt.

‡SAXTON, JOSIAH, Captain. Pension Certificate of widow, Polly, No. 221; no organization given.

*SAYER, ABIJAH B. Served from June 11 to June 14, 1813 in Capt. Moses Jewett's Company, 1st Regt. 2nd Brig. 3rd Div.

*SCHANK, HARMONIUS. Served in Capt. Brown's Company, Col. Martindale's Regt. Detached Militia in U. S. service 2 months and 14 days, 1812.

SCHMICK, PETER. Served from May 1 to June 30, 1814 in Capt. Alexander Brooks' Corps of Artillery. Ref: R. & L. 1812, AGO Page 31.

SCHOFF, HENRY D., Brunswick. Served from May 1 to June 30, 1814 in Capt. Haig's Corps Corps of Light Dragoons. Ref: R. & L. 1812, AGO Page 20.

SCHOMP, PETER. Served from May 1 to June 30, 1814 in Capt. Alexander Brooks' Corps of Artillery. Ref: R. & L. 1812, AGO Page 31.

SCHOOLCRAFT, JAMES, Georgia. Volunteered to go to Plattsburgh, September, 1814, and served 7 days in Capt. Elijah Dee's Company. Ref: Book 51, AGO Page 217.

*SCOFIELD, DANIEL. Served in 1 Regt. (Judson's) Vt. Militia.

*SCOFIELD, DAVID. Served in 1 Regt. (Judson's) Vt. Militia.

*SCOFIELD, HORACE. Served from April 12 to May 20, 1814 in Capt. George Fisher's Company, Sumner's Regt.

SCOFIELD, JOSEPH, 1st Lieutenant. Appointed 1st Lieutenant in Capt. White Youngs' Company, 15th Regt. March 14, 1812; on Muster Roll from Aug. 31 to Dec. 31, 1814. Ref: R. & L. 1812, AGO Page 27.

SCOFIELD, PELEG, 1st Sergeant, Morristown. Volunteered to go to Plattsburgh, September, 1814, and served 8 days in Capt. Danison Cook's Company. Ref: Book 51, AGO Pages 202, 203, 205.

*SCOFIELD, SAMUEL.
Served from Sept. 25 to Nov. 15,
1813 in Capt. Elijah W. Woods' Company, Dixon's Regt.
*SCOTT, AARON.

Served in Capt. Mason's Company,
Col. Fifield's Regt. Detached Militia
in U. S. service 6 months, 1812. Serv-
ed from Feb. 11 to May 10, 1813 in
Capt. Edgerton's Company, 11th Regt.
Ref: R. & L. 1812, AGO Page 3.

*SCOTT. AMOS.   Georgia.
Enlisted Sept. 25, 1813 and served 1
month and 6 days in Capt. Jesse
Post's Company, Col. Dixon's Regt.

*SCOTT. AMOS JR.
Served in Sumner's Regt. Vt. Militia.

SCOTT, BANFIELD.
Served in company of Capt. John
McNeil Jr., 11th Regt.; on Pay Roll
of company for January and Febru-
ary, 1813. Ref: R. & L. 1812, AGO
Page 17.

‡SCOTT, CHARLES.
Served in Capt. Aiken's Company.
Pension Certificate No. 12165.

SCOTT, EBENEZER B..   Bakersfield.
Volunteered and was at the battle of
Plattsburgh Sept. 11, 1814, serving in
Capt. M. Stearns' Company. Ref:
Hemenway's Vt. Gazetteer, Vol. 2,
Page 394.

SCOTT, ELIJAH.
Enlisted Jan. 1, 1814 for 1 year and
served in Capt. Gideon Spencer's Company and Capt. James Taylor's Company, 30th Regt.; mustered for discharge at Burlington June 3, 1814.
Ref: R. & L. 1812, AGO Pages 53
and 56.

‡SCOTT, ISAAC.
Served in Capt. McKeon's Company.
Pension Certificate of widow, Sophia,
No. 31870.

SCOTT. JACOB.   Barre.
Volunteered to go to Plattsburgh,
September, 1814, and served 10 days
in Capt. Warren Ellis' Company.
Ref: Book 52, AGO Page 242.

SCOTT. JOHN.
Enlisted May 13, 1812 for 5 years
in Capt. White Youngs' Company,
15th Regt.; on Muster Roll from Aug.
31 to Dec. 31, 1814. Ref: R. & L.
1812, AGO Page 27.

*SCOTT, JONATHAN.
Enlisted Oct. 31, 1813 in Capt. Asa
Wilkins' Company, Dixon's Regt. Vol-
unteered to go to Plattsburgh, Sep-
tember, 1814, and served 8 days in
Capt. Josiah Grout's Company.

SCOTT, JOSEPH.
Served 15 days at Troy in 1812; no
organization given. Ref: Vol. 51, Vt.
State Papers, Page 107.

*SCOTT. JOSHUA, Fifer.
Served from April 12 to April 21,
1814 in Capt. Edmund B. Hill's Company, Sumner's Regt.

SCOTT, JOTHAM,   Fairfax.
Served from Sept. 12, 1813 in Capt.
Asa Wilkins' Company, Dixon's Regt.
in U. S. service. Ref: Hemenway's
Vt. Gazetteer, Vol. 2, Page 402.

*SCOTT, LEMUEL, Captain.
Served in 2 Regt. 3 Brig. 3 Div. Vt.
Militia.

SCOTT, LEMUEL JR., Sergeant, Fairfax.
Volunteered to go to Plattsburgh,
September, 1814, and served 8 days
in Capt. Josiah Grout's Company.
Ref: Book 51, AGO Page 103.

SCOTT, LINES.
Enlisted Jan. 15, 1814 for 1 year and
served in Capt. Gideon Spencer's Company, Capt. Wm. Miller's Company
and Capt. James Taylor's Company,
30th Regt. Ref: R. & L. 1812, AGO
Pages 53, 54, 56.

SCOTT, MARTIN, Lieutenant, Bennington.
Appointed 2nd Lieutenant 26th Inf.
April 21, 1814; 1st Lieutenant Aug.
1, 1814; honorably discharged June
15, 1815. Ref: Heitman's Historical
Register & Dictionary USA; Governor
and Council Vt. Vol. 6, Page 477.

*SCOTT, RICHARD, Sergeant.
Served in Capt. Strait's Company. Col.
Martindale's Regt. Detached Militia
in U. S. service 1 month and 5 days,
1812. Served from May 1 to June 30,
1814 in Corps of Light Dragoons.
Ref: R. & L. 1812, AGO Page 20.

*SCOTT, SAMUEL.   Montpelier.
Served from April 17, 1814 to April
21, 1814 in Capt. Othniel Jewett's
Company, Sumner's Regt. Volunteered to go to Plattsburgh, September,
1814, and served 8 days in Capt.
Timothy Hubbard's Company.

*SCOTT, SETH,   Fairfax.
Served in Capt. Taylor's Company,
Col. Wm. Williams' Regt. Detached
Militia in U. S. service 4 months and
24 days, 1812. Enlisted Sept. 25,
1813 and served 1 month and 23 days
in Capt. Asa Wilkins' Company, Dixon's Regt.

SCOTT. ZELOTES.   Berlin.
Volunteered to go to Plattsburgh,
September, 1814, and served 8 days
in Capt. Cyrus Johnson's Company.
Ref: Book 52, AGO Pages 202 and 255.

SCOVALL. SAMUEL.   Highgate.
Served in New York State from Sept.
25 to Nov. 18, 1813. Ref: Vol. 50
Vt. State Papers, Page 94.

*SCOVELL. ASAHEL, Captain. Orwell or
Enosburgh. Served in Cavalry of 1st
Regt. of Detached Militia of Vt. in
U. S. service at Champlain from Nov.
18 to Nov. 19, 1812. Served from
Oct. 14 to Nov. 17, 1813 in Col. Isaac
Clark's Regt. Volunteered to go to
Plattsburgh, September, 1814, and
served 15 days in company raised at
Orwell.

*SCOVELL, DANIEL.
Served from April 12 to April 21,
1814 in Capt. Edmund B. Hill's Company, Sumner's Regt.

‡*SCOVELL, DANIEL JR.
Served in Capt. Wright's Company,
Col. Martindale's Regt. Detached
Militia in U. S. service 2 months
and 14 days, 1812. Pension Certificate No. 2140.

*SCOVELL, EZEKIEL, Cornwall.
Served from April 12 to April 21,
1814 in Capt. Edmund B. Hill's Company, Sumner's Regt.; volunteered
to go to Plattsburgh, September, 1814,
and was at the battle, serving in
same company.

SCOVELL, EZRA, Cornwall.
Volunteered to go to Plattsburgh,
September, 1814, and served as a
teamster in Capt. Edmund B. Hill's
Company, Sumner's Regt. Ref: Lyman
Mathews' History of Cornwall, Page
345.

‡*SCOVELL, HOLSEY B., Enosburgh.
Served from Oct. 15 to Nov. 17, 1813
in Capt. Asahel Scovell's Company.
Pension Certificate No. 24534.

*SCOVILL, HOMER.
Served in Sumner's Regt. Vt. Militia.

*SCRANTON, NATHAN, Sergeant, Jericho. Served in Capt. Pettes' Company, Col. Wm. William's Regt. Detached Militia in U. S. service at
Swanton Falls 4 months and 17 days.
1812. Took part in the battle of
Plattsburgh. Ref: History of Jericho,
Page 142.

SCRIBNER, JOSIAH, Washington.
Volunteered to go to Plattsburgh,
September, 1814, and served in Capt.
Amos Stiles' Company. Ref: Book
52, AGO Page 113.

*SCRIBNER, NOAH.
Served in Corning's Detachment, Vt.
Militia.

SCRIME, MATTHEW.
Enlisted March 22, 1813 for 5 years
in Capt. White Youngs' Company,
15th Regt.; on Muster Roll from Aug.
31 to Dec. 31, 1814. Ref: R. & L.
1812, AGO Page 27.

SCRIPTURE, ELIJAH.
Enlisted Sept. 2, 1813 for 1 year and
served in Capt. James Taylor's Company and Capt. Gideon Spencer's
Company, 30th Regt. Ref: R. & L.
1812, AGO Pages 52, 53, 57.

SCRIVER, MATT, Franklin County.
Volunteered to go to Plattsburgh
Sept. 11, 1814 and served in 15th or
22nd Regt. Ref: Hemenway's Vt.
Gazetteer, Vol. 2, Page 392.

*SCUTT, ABRAM.
Served in Capt. Pettes' Company,
Col. Wm. Williams' Regt. Detached
Militia in U. S. service 4 months
and 17 days, 1812.

*SCUTT, ABRAM 3rd.
Served in 4 Regt. (Williams') Vt.
Militia.

*SEABURY, CALEB.
Served in Corning's Detachment, Vt.
Militia.

‡*SEABURY, JOHN JR.
Served in Corning's Detachment, Vt.
Militia. Served in Capt. N. Perkins'
Company, 4 Regt. Pension Certificate No. 32917.

SEALEY, BENJAMIN.
Enlisted May 8, 1813 for 1 year in
Capt. Daniel Farrington's Company,
30th Regt. (also commanded by Capt.
Simeon Wright); on Muster Roll from
March 1 to April 30, 1814. Ref: R.
& L. 1812, AGO Pages 50 and 51.

*SEALEY, JONATHAN JR.
Enlisted April 12, 1814 in Capt.
Shubael Wales' Company, Col. W. B.
Sumner's Regt.; transferred to Capt.
Salmon Foster's Company, Sumner's
Regt. April 13, 1814 and served to
April 21, 1814.

‡SEAMANS, WILLIAM.
Pension Certificate of widow, Berthena, No. 31447; no organization
given.

SEAMONS, CHARLES, Clarendon.
Volunteered to go to Plattsburgh,
September, 1814, and served 7 days
in Capt. Durham Sprague's Company.
Ref: Book 52, AGO Page 128.

SEAMONS DANIEL, Sergeant, Clarendon.
Volunteered to go to Plattsburgh,
September, 1814, and served 7 days
in Capt. Durham Sprague's Company.
Ref: Book 52, AGO Page 128.

*SEARL, PHILIP, 1st Major.
Served in Sumner's Regt. Vt. Militia.

‡SEARLES, JOHN L.
Served in Capt. Brown's Company.
Pension Certificate No. 14253.

*SEARLES, SHELDON, Drum Major.
Enlisted Sept. 25, 1813 in Capt. Martin D. Folett's Company, Dixon's
Regt.

SEARLS, JOHN.
Enlisted April 30, 1813 for 1 year
and served in Capt. Gideon Spencer's
Company and Capt. James Taylor's
Company, 30th Regt. Ref: R. & L.
1812, AGO Pages 52, 57, 59.

SEARS, DAVID, Sergeant.
Served from Feb. 22 to May 21, 1813
in Capt. Charles Follett's Company,
11th Regt. Ref: R. & L. 1812, AGO
Page 13.

‡*SEARS, JAMES C.
Served in Capt. Willson's Company,
Col. Wm. Williams' Regt. Detached
Militia in U. S. service 4 months
and 24 days, 1812. Pension Certificate No. 10468.

SEARS, JOSEPH, Sergeant, Morristown.
Volunteered to go to Plattsburgh,
September, 1814, and served 8 days
in Capt. Denison Cook's Company.
Ref: Book 51, AGO Pages 202, 203,
205, 206.

*SEARS, NATHAN.
Served from Feb. 19 to May 18,
1813 in Lieut. V. R. Goodrich's Com-

pany, 11th Regt. Also served in 4 Regt. (Williams') Vt. Militia. Ref: R. & L. 1812, AGO Page 10.

‡*SEARS, OTIS, Corporal,   ˙Dover.
Served in Capt. Parsons' Company, Col. Jonathan Williams' Regt. Detached Militia in U. S. service 2 months and 13 days, 1812. Pension Certificate of widow, Lazelle, No. 4787.

SEARS, PHILIP, Major,   Bridport.
Volunteered to go to Plattsburgh, September, 1814; no organization given. Ref: Book 51, AGO Page 40.

‡*SEARS, SILAS, Ensign.
Served as Ensign in 2 Regt. 3 Brig. 3 Div. Vt. Militia. Also served as Captain; no organization given. Pension Certificate No. 14048.

SEARS, WILLIAM.
Served from Feb. 19 to May 18, 1813 in Lt. V. R. Goodrich's Company, 11th Regt. Ref: R. & L. 1812, AGO Pages 10 and 11.

SEARS, ZEBULON.
Served in Capt. George W. Kindall's Company, Col. Wm. Williams' Regt.; on Pay Roll to Sept. 10, 1812. Ref: R. & L. 1812, AGO Page 37.

SEATON, JAMES P.
Served in Capt. Charles Follett's Company, 11th Regt.; on Pay Roll for January and February, 1812; died Feb. 26, 1813. Ref: R. & L. 1812, AGO Page 12.

*SEAVER, AARON.
Served in Capt. Burnap's Company, Col. Jonathan Williams' Regt. Detached Militia in U. S. service 2 months and 13 days, 1812.

*SEAVER, CALVIN.
Served in Capt. Howard's Company, Vt. Militia.

‡SEAVER, THOMAS.
Served in Capt. Russell's Company. Pension Certificate of widow, Deborah, No. 1479.

SEAVEY, BENJAMIN.
Enlisted Feb. 9, 1813 in Capt. Jonathan Starks' Company, 11th Regt.; on Pay Roll to May 31, 1813. Ref: R. & L. 1812, AGO Page 19.

*SEAVY, JOHN.
Served from June 11 to June 14, 1813 in Capt. John M. Eldridge's Company, 1st Regt. 2nd Brig. 3rd Div.

SEEGAR, DAVID.
Served in Capt. Saxe's Company, Col. Wm. Williams' Regt. Detached Militia in U. S. service 4 months and 24 days, 1812. Ref: Book 53, AGO Page 20.

SEEGAR, ELIJAH.
Served from April 20, 1813 to April 24, 1814 in Capt. Daniel Farringtno's Company, 30th Regt. (also commanded by Capt. Simeon Wright). Ref: R. & L. 1812, AGO Pages 50 and 51.

*SEEGER, RODERIC.
Served from Sept. 25 to Oct. 20, 1813 in Capt. Jesse Post's Company, Dixon's Regt.

‡SEELEY, BENJAMIN.
Served in Capt. Harkness' Company. Pension Certificate No. 22254.

SEELEY, GILMORE,   Jericho.
Enlisted at Middlebury in Capt. Danforth's Company in the spring of 1813. Ref: History of Jericho, Page 143.

SEELEY, JONATHAN,   Middlebury.
Volunteered to go to Plattsburgh, September, 1814, and served 6 days; no organization given. Ref: Book 51, AGO Page 58.

*SEEMAN, SAMUEL.
Served with Hospital Attendants, Vt.

SEERS, JESSE.
Served in Capt. Chadwick's Company. Ref: R. & L. 1812, AGO Page 32.

SEGAR, ISAAC,   Pittsford.
Volunteered to go to Plattsburgh, September, 1814, and served 8 days in Capt. Caleb Hendee's Company as a waggoner. Ref: Book 52, AGO Page 125.

SELDEN, MARTIUS L., Lieutenant.
Appointed 3rd Lieutenant 30th Inf. April 30, 1813; 2nd Lieutenant Aug. 15, 1813; 1st Lieutenant Aug. 1, 1814; honorably discharged June 15, 1815. Ref: Heitman's Historical Register & Dictionary USA.

‡*SELLECK, HENRY, Musician, Enosburgh. Served in Capt. Scovell's Company, Col. Martindale's Regt. Detached Militia in U. S. service 2 months and 21 days, 1812. Served from Oct. 14 to Nov. 17, 1813 in Capt. Asahel Scovell's Company, Col. Isaac Clark's Rifle Corps. Pension Certificate of widow, Polly, No. 1408.

SELLECK, MOSES,   Hubbardton.
Volunteered to go to Plattsburgh, September, 1814, and served 8 days in Capt. Henry J. Horton's Company. Ref: Book 52, AGO Page 142.

SENTER, ISAAC,   Vershire.
Volunteered to go to Plattsburgh. September, 1814, and went as far as Bolton, serving 6 days; did not belong to any organized company. Ref: Book 52, AGO Page 96.

SERGEANTS, STERLIN.
Served in company of Capt. John McNeil Jr., 11th Regt.; on Pay Roll for January and February, 1813. Ref: R. & L. 1812, AGO Page 17.

SESSIONS, THOMAS.
Enlisted July 27, 1813 for 1 year in Capt. Gideon Spencer's Company, 30th Regt.; discharged July 26, 1814. Ref: R. & L. 1812, AGO Pages 29 and 56.

*SEVER, JOSHUA.
Served from April 12 to April 21, 1814 in Lieut. James S. Morton's Company, Col. W. B. Sumner's Regt.

*SEVERANCE, ASAPH, Corporal, Bristol.
Volunteered to go to Plattsburgh,
Sept. 11, 1814 no organization given.
Served as corporal in Sumner's Regt.
Vt. Militia. Ref: Vol. 54 Vt. State
Papers, Page 183.

SEVERY, IRA.   Merideth.
Served from July 10 to Aug. 31, 1813
and from May 1 to July 9, 1814 in
Capt. Poland's Company, 34th Inf.
Ref: R. & L. 1812, AGO Page 30.

*SEWARD, ANSON.
Served in Capt. Phelps' Company.
Col. Wm. Williams' Regt. Detached
Militia in U. S. service 5 months,
1812. Also served in Sumner's Regt.
Vt. Militia.

‡*SEWARD, WILLIAM.
Served in Capt. Phelps' Company,
Col. Wm. Williams' Ret. Detached
Militia in U. S. service 5 months,
1812. Also served in Sumner's Regt.
Pension Certificate of widow, Lois,
No. 4904.

*SEXTON, HENRY.
Served in Sumner's Regt. Vt. Militia.

SEXTON, HIRAM, Sergeant.
Volunteered to go to Plattsburgh,
September, 1814, and served 7 days
in Capt. Frederick Griswold's Company from Brookfield, Vt. Ref: Book
52, AGO Page 52.

SEYMOUR, HAYES,   Vergennes.
Volunteered to go to Plattsburgh,
September, 1814, and was in the
battle, serving 10 days in Capt.
Gideon Spencer's Company. Ref: Book
51, AGO Page 1.

*SEYMOUR, WARREN, Corporal.
Served from April 12 to April 21,
1814 in Capt. Eseck Sprague's Company, Sumner's Regt.

*SEYMOUR, WILLIAM I.
Served in 1 Regt. (Judson's) Vt.
Militia.

SHALLARD, GEORGE.
Served from Dec. 26, 1812 to June
8, 1813 in Capt. John W. Weeks'
Company, 11th Regt. Ref: R. & L.
1812, AGO Page 4.

*SHALLOCK, SYLVANUS.
Served in 2 Regt. (Fifield's) Vt. Militia.

SHAMPAR, WILLIAM.   Fairfax.
Served from Aug. 8, 1812 in company
of Capt. Joseph Beeman Jr., 11th
Regt. U. S. Inf. under Col. Ira
Clark. Ref: Hemenway's Vt. Gazet-
teer, Vol. 2, Page 402.

SHANKS, THOMAS, Ensign.
Appointed Ensign 26th Inf. Aug. 7,
1813; died in 1814. Ref: Heitman's
Historical Register & Dictionary USA.

SHARLAND, GEORGE.
Enlisted Dec. 26, 1812 in Capt. Weeks'
Company, 11th Regt.; on Pay Roll
for January and February, 1813. Ref:
R. & L. 1812, AGO Page 5.

‡SHARPE, ABRAHAM.
Served in Capt. Gordon's Company.
Pension Certificate No. 17377.

SHARP, DANIEL,   Barnard.
Volunteered to go to Plattsburgh,
September, 1814, and served 8 days
in Capt. John S. Bicknell's Company.
Ref: Book 51, AGO Page 250.

SHARP, ROBERT,   Franklin County.
Enlisted May 8, 1812 for 5 years in
Capt. White Youngs' Company, 15th
Regt.; on Muster Roll from Aug. 31
to Dec. 31, 1814. Ref: R. & L. 1812,
AGO Page 27.

SHARP, SOLOMON.
Served from Feb. 2 to May 1, 1813
in Capt. Charles Follett's Company,
11th Regt. Ref: R. & L. 1812, AGO
Page 13.

‡*SHARP, STEPHEN, Sergeant.
Served in Capt. Dorrance's Company,
Col. Wm. Williams' Regt. Detached
Militia in U. S. service 4 months
and 7 days, 1812. Enlisted June 13,
1813 for 1 year in Capt. Simeon
Wright's Company. Also served in
Capt. Pratt's Company. Pension Cer-
tificate No. 18683.

SHARP, WILLIAM, Sergeant.
Served from May 1 to June 30, 1814
in Capt. Alexander Brooks' Corps of
Artillery. Ref: R. & L. 1812, AGO
Page 31.

*SHATTOCK, PETER (or Shattuck?)
Served in 3 Regt. (Tyler's) Vt. Militia.

SHATTUCK, BENJAMIN, Corporal, Townshend. Served from April 30, 1813
to May 1, 1814 in Capt. James Taylor's Company and Capt. Gideon Spencer's Company, 30th Regt. Ref: R. &
L. 1812, AGO Pages 52, 56, 58.

*SHATTUCK, BENJAMIN,   Highgate.
Served in Capt. Saxe's Company, Col.
Wm. Williams' Regt. Detached Militia in U. S. service 4 months and 1
day, 1812.

*SHATTUCK, JEREMIAH, Belvidere or
Fairfax. Served in Capt. Taylor's
Company, Col. Wm. Williams' Regt.
Detached Militia in U. S. service 4
months and 24 days, 1812. Served
in Capt. Wilkins' Company, Col. Dix-
on's Regt. Detached Militia in U.
S. service 28 days, 1813. Enlisted
Oct. 23, 1813 in Capt. Asahel Lang-
worthy's Company, Col. Isaac Clark's
Rifle Corps. Volunteered to go to
Plattsburgh, September, 1814, and
served 7 days in Capt. Moody Shat-
tuck's Company. Ref: Book 51, AGO
Page 210.

*SHATTUCK, JOHN,   Townshend.
Served in 1 Regt. (Martindale's) Vt.
Militia.

‡*SHATTUCK, LEVI.
Served in Capt. Lowry's Company,
Col. Wm. Williams' Regt. Detached
Militia in U. S. service 4 months and
26 days, 1812. Also served in 3 Regt.
(Tyler's) Vt. Militia. Pension Cer-
tificate of widow, Mary, No. 1775.

*SHATTUCK, MOODY, Captain, Belvidere.
Volunteered to go to Plattsburgh,
September, 1814, and served 7 days
in command of company from Belvidere. Served as Captain in 2 Regt.
3 Brig. 3 Div. Vt. Militia. Ref: Book
51, AGO Pages 210 and 212.

SHATTUCK, ZEBEDIAH. Corporal.
Served in Capt. Benjamin Bradford's
Company; on Muster Roll from May
31 to Aug. 31, 1813. Ref: R. & L.
1812, AGO Page 26.

SHAW, AARON.
Served from April 12 to April 21,
1814 in Lieut. Justus Foote's Company, Sumner's Regt. Ref: Book 52,
AGO Page 285.

‡*SHAW, BARTON, Fife Major, Richford.
Served in Capt. Follet's Company,
Col. Dixon's Regt. Detached Militia
in U. S. service 1 month and 23
days, 1813. Also served in Capt.
Rublee's Company. Pension Certificate No. 17713.

SHAW, BENNONI,   Morristown.
Volunteered to go to Plattsburgh,
September, 1814, and served 3 days
in Capt. Dennison Cook's Company.
Ref: Book 51, AGO Page 205.

*SHAW, CHARLES.
Served in Capt. Dorrance's Company,
Col. Wm. Williams' Regt. Detached
Militia in U. S. service 4 months and
24 days, 1812. Served from May 1
to June 30, 1814 in Capt. Haig's Corps
of Light Dragoons.

SHAW, CRISPUS, Corporal, Morristown.
Volunteered to go to Plattsburgh,
September, 1814, and served 8 days
in Capt. Denison Cook's Company.
Ref: Book 51, AGO Page 202.

SHAW, EARL.
Enlisted Feb. 11, 1814 for duration
of the war; deserted June 12, 1814
from rendezvous, Poultney. Ref: R.
& L. 1812, AGO Page 1.

SHAW, ELIJAH, Lieutenant.
Volunteered to go to Plattsburgh,
September, 1814, and served in company of Capt. Joel Barnes of Chelsea. Ref: Book 52, AGO Pages 69
and 77.

SHAW, HAZARD.
Served from Nov. 1, 1812 to Feb. 28,
1813 in Capt. Samuel H. Holly's Company, 11th Regt. Ref: R. & L. 1812,
AGO Page 25.

‡SHAW, JOHN.
Served in Capt. E. Wood's Company.
Pension Certificate No. 28525.

SHAW, JONATHAN W., Surgeon.
Appointed Surgeon 11th Inf. Sept.
29, 1812; resigned Aug. 25, 1813. Ref:
Heitman's Historical Register & Dictionary USA.

*SHAW, NAPTHALI.
Served in 2 Regt. (Fifield's) Vt.
Militia.

*SHAW, ORRIN.
Served in Sumner's Regt. Vt. Militia.

SHAW, SAMUEL, Hospital Surgeon.
Appointed Hospital Surgeon, 9 Mil.
Div. Right Wing, April 6, 1813; hon-
orably discharged June 15, 1815. Ref:
Heitman's Historical Register & Dic-
tionary USA.

SHAW, STEPHEN H.
Served in Capt. Phineas Williams'
Company, 11th Regt.; on Pay Roll
for January and February, 1813. Ref:
R. & L. 1812, AGO Page 15.

*SHAYS, JOHN.
Served with Hospital Attendants, Vt.

SHEA, WILLIAM.
Enlisted April 12, 1814 during the
war in Capt. Wm. Miller's Company,
30th Regt. Ref: R. & L. 1812, AGO
Page 1.

*SHED, JEPTHA.
Served from April 12 to April 21,
1814 in Capt. Eseck Sprague's Company, Sumner's Regt.

*SHED, NATHANIEL.
Served with Hospital Attendants, Vt.

SHED, WILLIAM,   Lebanon, N. H.
Enlisted at Plainfield April 12, 1814
during the war and served in Capt.
Wm. Miller's Company, Capt. Gideon
Spencer's Company and Capt. James
Taylors' Company, 30th Regt. Ref:
R. & L. 1812, AGO Pages 53, 54,
55, 56.

*SHEFFIELD, GEORGE.
Served in 1 Regt. (Judson's) Vt. Mili-
tia and in 4 Regt. (Williams') Vt.
Militia.

*SHELDON, AMBROSE.
Served in Capt. Dorrance's Company,
Col. Wm. Williams' Regt. Detached
Militia in U. S. service 4 months and
23 days, 1812.

‡*SHELDON, CALEB.
Served in 4 Regt. (Peck's) Vt. Militia, Capt. A. Atkins' Company. Pension Certificate of widow, Mary S.,
No. 23010.

*SHELDON, CHANCY, Sergeant.
Served from June 11 to June 14, 1813
in Capt. Hezekiah Barns' Company,
1st Regt. 2nd Brig. 3rd Div.

‡*SHELDON, DAVID.
Served in Corning's Detachment, Vt.
Militia. Served in Capt. Dorrance's
Company, 4th Regt. Pension Certifi-
cate of widow, Eliza P., No. 32940.

*SHELDON, ELIAKIM.
Served in Capt. Preston's Company,
Col. Jonathan Williams' Regt. Detached Militia in U. S. service 2
months and 6 days, 1812.

*SHELDON, ERASTUS.
Served from Sept. 25 to Oct. 4, 1813
in Capt. Elijah Birge's Company, Dixon's Regt.

SHELDON, GEORGE B., 2nd Lieutenant.
Served in Capt. Alexander Brooks'
Corps of Artillery; on Pay Roll to
June 30, 1814; transferred to 4th
Rifle Regt. Ref: R. & L. 1812, AGO
Page 31.

SHELDON, GIDEON. Pittsford.
Served from April 25, 1813 to April
26, 1814 in Capt. Simeon Wright's
Company. Ref: R. & L. 1812, AGO
Page 51.

SHELDON, HEZE F., Danville.
Volunteered to go to Plattsburgh,
September, 1814, and served 3 days
in Capt. Solomon Langmaid's Company. Ref: Book 51, AGO Pages 75
and 76.

*SHELDON, ISRAEL.
Served in 1 Regt. (Martindale's) Vt.
Militia.

*SHELDON, JAMES.
Enlisted Sept. 20, 1813 in Capt. John
Weed's Company, Rifle Corps. Pen-
sion Certificate No. 24261.

SHELDON, JOSIAH, Fairfield.
Served in Capt. George W. Kindall's
Company, Col. Wm. Williams' Regt.
Detached Militia in U. S. service 4
months and 23 days, 1812.

*SHELDON, MICAH, Sergeant.
Served in Capt. Phelps' Company.
Col. Wm. Williams' Regt. Detached
Militia in U. S. service 5 months.

*SHELDON, NATHANIEL.
Served in Capt. Barns' Company, Col.
Wm. Williams' Regt. Detached Militia
in U. S. service 5 months. Served
from June 11 to June 14, 1813 in
Capt. Hezekiah Barns' Company, 1st
Regt. 2nd Brig. 3rd Div.

SHELDON, OBED, St. Albans.
Served from Sept. 1, 1814 to June
16, 1815 in Capt. Sanford's Company,
30th Inf. Ref: R. & L. 1812, AGO
Page 23.

*SHELDON, RODNEY.
Served with Hospital Attendants, Vt.

SHELDON, SAMUEL, Salisbury.
Volunteered to go to Plattsburgh,
September, 1814, and served 4 days
in Capt. John Morton's Company.
Ref: Book 52, AGO Page 139.

*SHELDON, SAMUEL R.
Served in 1 Regt. (Martindale's) Vt.
Militia.

‡SHELDON, STEPHEN.
Served in Capt. Masters' Company.
Pension Certificate No. 23187.

‡*SHELDON, TRUMAN.
Served in 3 Regt. (Tyler's) Vt. Militia. Served in Capt. Bliss' Company.
Pension Certificate No. 8082. Pension Certificate of widow, Polly, No.
31908.

SHELDON, WALTER, Captain, Salisbury.
Appointed 2nd Lieutenant 11th Inf.
March 12, 1812; 1st Lieutenant March
13, 1813; Regimental Paymaster Sept.
18, 1812 to Aug. 4, 1813; District
Paymaster Aug. 4, 1813; Captain Dec.
12, 1813 to June 30, 1814; died June
16, 1816. Ref: Heitman's Historical
Register & Dictionary USA; R. & L.
1812, AGO Pages 25 and 28.

SHELLER, GAMEL.
Served from March 1 to June 30, 1814
in Capt. Alexander Brooks' Corps of
Artillery. Ref: R. & L. 1812, AGO
Page 31.

‡SHELLER, SAMUEL.
Pension Certificate of widow, Jane.
No. 39939; no organization given.

SHELLY, JOHN.
Served from May 1 to June 30, 1814
in Capt. Alexander Brooks' Corps of
Artillery. Ref: R. & L. 1812, AGO
Page 31.

*SHEPARD, AARON.
Served in 1 Regt. (Judson's) Vt.
Militia.

SHEPARD, ASEL , Georgia.
Volunteered to go to Plattsburgh,
September, 1814, and served 15 days;
no organization given. Ref: Book 51,
AGO Page 151.

‡*SHEPARD, DANIEL.
Served in Capt. Taylor's Company,
Col. Fifield's Regt. Detached Militia
in U. S. service 2 months and 21
days, 1812. Pension Certificate No.
12686.

SHEPARD, DAVID, St. Albans.
Enlisted April 19, 1813 for 1 year in
Capt. John Wires' Company, 30th
Regt. Ref: R. & L. 1812, AGO
Page 40.

SHEPARD, JONATHAN, Montpelier.
Volunteered to go to Plattsburgh,
September, 1814, and served 8 days
in Capt. Timothy Hubbard's Company.
Ref: Book 52, AGO Pages 246 and
256.

SHEPARD, LEVI, Georgia.
Volunteered to go to Plattsburgh,
September, 1814, and served 15 days
in Capt. Jesse Post's Company, Dixon's Regt. Ref: Book 51, AGO Pages
102 and 151.

SHEPARD, LEVI B., Georgia.
Volunteered to go to Plattsburgh,
September, 1814, and served 8 days
in Capt. Jesse Post's Company, Dixon's Regt. Ref: Book 51, AGO Pages
102 and 150.

*SHEPARD, LYMAN, Salisbury or Pan-
ton. Served from April 19 to April
21, 1814 in Capt. Othniel Jewett's
Company, Sumner's Regt. Volunteered to go to Plattsburgh, September,
1814 and served in Capt. John Morton's Company 4 days. Ref: Book
51, AGO Page 61; Book 52, AGO
Page 141.

‡SHEPARD, MASON.
Served in Capt. Hubbard's Company.
Pension Certificate of widow, Jane,
No. 40916.

SHEPARD, RUSSELL, Georgia.
Volunteered to go to Plattsburgh,
September, 1814, and served 15 days;
no organization given. Ref: Book
51, AGO Page 151.

*SHEPARD. SAMUEL, Enosburgh.
Served from Oct. 15 to Nov. 17, 1813
in Capt. Asahel Scovell's Company,
Col. Clark's Rifle Corps.

SHEPARD. SAMUEL, Salisbury or Panton. Volunteered to go to Plattsburgh, September, 1814, and served 4
days in Capt. John Morton's Company. Ref: Book 51, AGO Page 66;
Book 52, AGO Page 141.

‡SHEPARD, THOMAS, Poultney or St.
Albans. Enlisted May 3, 1813 for 1
year in Capt. John Wires' Company,
30th Regt. Served in Capt. Miller's
Company. Pension Certificate of widow, Mary, No. 6909. Ref: R. & L.
1812, AGO Page 40.

SHEPARDSON, ANSEL. Fairfax.
Served in 1813 and 1814 in Capt.
Joseph Beeman's Company. Ref: Hemenway's Vt. Gazetteer, Vol. 2, Page
402.

‡*SHEPARDSON, REUBEN.
Served in Capt. Noyes' Company,
3 Regt. (Williams') Vt. Militia. Pension Certificate No. 4790.

SHEPHARD, IRA, Franklin County.
Volunteered to go to Plattsburgh
Sept. 11, 1814 and served in 15th or
22nd Regt. Ref: Hemenway's Vt.
Gazetteer, Vol. 2, Page 391.

SHEPHEARD, SAMUEL.
Served in War of 1812 and was captured by troops May 5, 1814 at Rappids; exchanged May 4, 1815. Ref:
Records of Naval Records and Library, Navy Dept.

SHEPHERD, ELIAS, Musician.
Served in company of late Capt. J.
Brooks, commanded by Lt. John I.
Cromwell, Corps of U. S. Artillery;
on Muster Roll from April 30 to June
30, 1814; paroled prisoner; trans-
ferred from Capt. Lind's Company.
Ref: R. & L. 1812, AGO Page 18.

‡*SHEPHERD. HENRY.
Served in Capt. Ormsbee's Company,
Col. Martindale's Regt. Detached
Militia in U. S. service 14 days,
1812. Also served in Capt. Young's
Company. Pension Certificate No.
20087.

*SHEPHERD, JONATHAN.
Served in Capt. Brown's Company,
Col. Martindale's Regt. Detached
Militia in U. S. service 2 months
and 14 days, 1812.

*SHEPHERD. PHILIP.
Served under Captains Taylor and
Rogers, Col. Fifield's Regt. Detached
Militia in U. S. service 2 months
and 21 days, 1812.

‡*SHEPHERD, SAMUEL, Enosburgh?
Served in Capt. Scovell's Company,
Col. Martindale's Regt. Detached
Militia in U. S. service 2 months and
21 days, 1812. Pension Certificate No.
5262. Pension Certificate of widow,
Sarah, No. 21615.

SHERBURN, DAVID, Orange.
Volunteered to go to Plattsburgh.
September, 1814, and served 9 days
in Capt. Warren Ellis' Company. Ref:
Book 52, AGO Pages 236, 239, 242.

SHERMAN, ASAPH, Adjutant. Barre.
Volunteered to go to Plattsburgh.
September, 1814, and served 10 days
in Capt. Warren Ellis' Company. Ref:
Book 52, AGO Page 242.

*SHERMAN, CALEB.
Served in Sumner's Regt. Vt. Militia.

SHERMAN, EBENEZER, Sergeant.
Served in Artillery of Detached Militia of Vt. in U. S. service at Champlain from Nov. 18 to Nov. 19, 1812.

*SHERMAN, EDMUND. Lieutenant.
Served from June 11 to June 14 and
from Oct. 4 to Oct. 13, 1813 in Capt.
John Palmer's Company, 1st Regt.
2nd Brig. 3rd Div.

*SHERMAN, ELEZER, Corporal.
Served in Capt. Hopkins' Company,
Col. Martindale's Regt. Detached
Militia in U. S. service 2 months
and 13 days, 1812.

*SHERMAN, ELI, Sergeant, Fairfield.
Enlisted Sept. 25, 1813 and served 1
month and 23 days in Capt. Martin
D. Folett's Company, Col. Dixon's
Regt. Detached Militia in U. S. serv-
ice. Volunteered to go to Plattsburgh,
September, 1814 and served 8 days in
Capt. Benjamin Wooster's Company.

*SHERMAN, GEORGE.
Served from Oct. 5 to Oct. 8, 1813
in Capt. Roswell Hunt's Company, 3
Regt. (Tyler's).

SHERMAN, IRA.
Served in Capt. Walker's Company,
Col. Fifield's Regt. Detached Militia
in U. S. service 2 months and 26
days, 1812. Ref: Book 53, AGO Page
74.

*SHERMAN, JACOB.
Enlisted May 4, 1813 for 1 year in
Capt. Simeon Wright's Company. Also
served in 1 Regt. (Martindale's) Vt.
Militia. Ref: R. & L. 1812, AGO
Page 51.

*SHERMAN, JONATHAN JR., Corporal,
Barre. Served in Capt. Walker's
Company, Col. Fifield's Regt. Detached Militia in U. S. service 6 months
and 3 days, 1812. Volunteered to go
to Plattsburgh. September, 1814, and
served 9 days in Capt. Warren Ellis'
Company.

*SHERMAN, NATHAN, Sergeant.
Served in 3 Regt. (Tyler's) Vt. Militia.

SHERMAN, NATHANIEL, Sergeant,
Barre. Volunteered to go to Plattsburgh. September, 1814, and served
9 days in Capt. Warren Ellis' Company. Ref: Book 52, AGO Pages 234
and 242.

SHERMAN, REUBEN JR.
Enlisted Jan. 19, 1813 and served in
company of Capt. John McNeil Jr.,
11th Regt. Ref: R. & L. 1812, AGO
Page 16.

*SHERMAN, RODNEY.
Served from June 11 to June 14, 1813
in Capt. John M. Eldridge's Company, 1st Regt. 2nd Brig. 3rd Div.

*SHERMAN, SMITH.
Served in Capt. Walker's Company,
Col. Fifield's Regt. Detached Militia
in U. S. service 2 months and 24
days, 1812.

SHERMAN, STEPHEN.
Served from Jan. 11 to May 2, 1813
in company of Capt. John McNeil
Jr., 11th Regt. Ref: R. & L. 1812,
AGO Page 16.

‡SHERMAN, WHEELER.
Pension Certificate of widow, Jane,
No. 28148; no organization given.

*SHERRELL, ELLIOTT.
Served from April 12 to April 21,
1814 in Capt. Eseck Sprague's Company, Sumner's Regt.

*SHERWIN, BILDAD.
Enlisted Sept. 20, 1813 in Capt. John
Weed's Company, Col. Clark's Rifle
Corps.

‡*SHERWOOD, AARON,   Fairfield.
Served in Capt. Follett's Company,
Col. Dixon's Regt. Detached Militia
in U. S. service 1 month and 3 days,
1813. Enlisted Oct. 23, 1813 and served 26 days in Capt. Asahel Langworthy's Company, Col. Dixon's Regt.
or Col. Isaac Clark's Rifle Corps.
Volunteered to go to Plattsburgh,
September, 1814, and served 8 days
in Capt. Benjamin Wooster's Company. Also served in Capt. Foster's
Company. Pension Certificate of widow, Calista, No. 32084.

SHERWOOD, ANSON,   Richford.
Served in Capt. Martin D. Follett's
Company, Col. Dixon's Regt. on duty
on Canadian Frontier in 1813. Ref:
Hemenway's Vt. Gazetteer, Vol. 2,
Page 426.

SHERWOOD, DYER.   Fairfield.
Volunteered to go to Plattsburgh,
September, 1814, and served 8 days
in Capt. Benjamin Wooster's Company. Ref: Book 51, AGO Page 182.

SHERWOOD, ELI,   Fairfield.
Volunteered to go to Plattsburgh,
Sept. 11, 1814 and served in Capt.
Benjamin Wooster's Company. Ref:
Hemenway's Vt. Gazetteer, Vol. 2,
Page 408.

SHERWOOD, ELIAS,   Fairfield.
Volunteered to go to Plattsburgh
Sept. 11, 1814 and served in Capt.
Benjamin Wooster's Company. Ref:
Hemenway's Vt. Gazetteer, Vol. 2,
Page 408.

*SHERWOOD, JOSIAH.
Served from April 12 to April 21,
1814 in Capt. Edmund B. Hill's Company, Sumner's Regt.

*SHERWOOD, MARSTON (or Maston),
Cornwall. Served in Capt. Wright's
Company, Col. Martindale's Regt. De-

tached Militia in U. S. service 2
months and 14 days, 1812. Served
from April 12 to April 21, 1814 in
Capt. Edmund B. Hill's Company.
Sumner's Regt.; volunteered to go
to Plattsburgh, September, 1814, and
was at the battle, serving in the same
company.

*SHERWOOD, NATHAN, Sergeant.
Served as private in 4 Regt. (Williams') Vt. Militia and as sergeant
in Dixon's Regt. Vt. Militia.

*SHERWOOD, NATHANIEL,   Cornwall.
Served from April 12 to April 21,
1814 in Capt. Edmund B. Hill's Company, Sumner's Regt.; volunteered to
go to Plattsburgh, September, 1814,
and was at the battle, serving in
same company.

*SHERWOOD, OBEDIAH, Fairfield or
Richford. Served in Capt. Follet's
Company, Col. Dixon's Regt. Detach
ed Militia in U. S. service 1 month
and 23 days, 1813. Served 26 days
in Capt. Langworthy's Company, Col.
Dixon's Regt. Enlisted Oct. 23, 1813
in Capt. Asahel Langworthy's Company, Col. Isaac Clark's Rifle Corps.
Volunteered to go to Plattsburgh,
September, 1814, and served 8 days
in Capt. Benjamin Wooster's Company. Ref: Book 51, Pages 120 and
182.

*SHERWOOD, WYMAN.
Served in Capt. Taylor's Company,
Col. Wm. Williams' Regt. Detached
Militia in U. S. service 4 months and
24 days, 1812. Enlisted Sept. 25,
1813 and served 1 month and 23
days in Capt. Elijah Birge's Company, Col. Dixon's Regt.

‡SHERWOOD, ZALMON,   Fairfield.
Volunteered to go to Plattsburgh,
September, 1814, and served 7 days
in Capt. Benjamin Wooster's Com-
pany. Pension Certificate of widow,
Emily, No. 29803.

SHIELD, JOSIAH, Lieutenant.
Appointed Ensign 11th Inf. April 15,
1814; 3rd Lieutenant May 1, 1814;
2nd Lieutenant Sept. 1, 1814. Ref:
Heitman's Historical Register & Dictionary USA.

*SHIPMAN, ADRIEL.
Served in Tyler's Regt. Vt. Militia.

‡SHIPMAN, ALVIN.
Served in Capt. Fuller's Company.
Pension Certificate of widow, Sophia,
No. 8365.

SHIPMAN, LEVI,   Waitsfield.
Volunteered to go to Plattsburgh,
September, 1814, and served 4 days
in Capt. Mathias S. Jones' Company. Ref: Book 52, AGO Page 170.

SHIPP, E., Captain and Brigade Major.
Served from May 1 to July 31, 1814
on General Staff of the Northern
Army commanded by Major General
Geroge Izard. Ref: R. & L. 1812,
AGO Page 28.

SHIPPA, CALVIN.   Shrewsbury.
Volunteered to go to Plattsburgh,
September, 1814, and served 4 days
in Capt. Robert Reed's Company. Ref:
Book 52, AGO Page 140.

*SHIPPEE, NATHAN.
Served in Capt. Richardson's Company, Col. Martindale's Regt. Detached Militia in U. S. service 1
month and 5 days, 1812.

‡*SHIPPEY, MOREY.
Served in Capt. Needham's Company,
Col. Martindale's Regt. Detached
Militia in U. S. service 2 months
and 13 days, 1812. Pension Certifi-
cate No. 13766.

SHIRLEY, DANIEL.
Served in Capt. Weeks' Company,
11th Regt.: on Pay Roll for Janu-
ary and February, 1813; deserted
Jan. 1, 1813. Ref: R. & L. 1812,
AGO Page 5.

SHIRLEY, JOHN.
Served in Capt. Weeks' Company,
11th Regt.; on Pay Roll for January and February, 1813. Ref: R. &
L. 1812, AGO Page 5.

SHIRTLIFF, JOHN, Corporal.
Served from April 30, 1813 to April
30, 1814 in Capt. James Taylor's Company and Capt. Gideon Spencer's
Company, 30th Regt. Ref: R. & L.
1812, AGO Pages 52, 56, 58.

*SHIRTLIFF, JOHN JR.
Served in Capt. Scovell's Company.
Col. Martindale's Regt. Detached
Militia in U. S. service 1 month and
6 days, 1812.

SHIRTLIFF, OTIS, Sergeant.
Served in Artillery of Detached Militia of Vt. in U. S. service from Nov.
18 to Nov. 19, 1812.

*SHIRTLIFF, WILLIAM.
Served in Dixon's Regt. and 4 Regt.
(Williams') Vt. Militia.

*SHOALS, PERLEY.
Served in Capt. Wheeler's Company,
Col. Fifield's Regt. Detached Militia
in U. S. service 4 months and 8 days,
1812.

SHOOT, JOHN.
Served in Capt. Haig's Corps of Light
Dragoons; on Pay Roll to June 30,
1814. Ref: R. & L. 1812, AGO Page
20.

SHOOTS, THOMAS,   Franklin County.
Volunteered to go to Plattsburgh
Sept. 11, 1814 and served in 15th or
22nd Regt. Ref: Hemenway's Vt. Gazetteer, Vol. 2, Page 392.

*SHORT, CYRENUS,   Calais.
Served in Capt. Walker's Company,
Col. Fifield's Regt. Detached Militia
in U. S. service 5 months and 17
days, 1812.

SHORT, JAMES,   Montpelier.
Volunteered to go to Plattsburgh,
September, 1814, and served 8 days
in Capt. Timothy Hubbard's Company. Ref: Book 52, AGO Page 256.

SHORT, SHUBAL.
Served in Capt. Alexander Brooks'
Corps of Artillery; on Pay Roll to
June 30, 1814. Ref: R. & L. 1812,
AGO Page 31.

*SHORT, WILLIAM.
Served in Capt. Morrill's Company,
Col. Fifield's Regt. Detached Militia
in U. S. service 6 months and 5 days,
1812.

‡SHORY, SAMUEL.
Served in Capt. Winslow's Company.
Pension Certificate of widow, Sylvina,
No. 12578.

*SHROND, BILLINGS.
Served in 3 Regt. (Tyler's) Vt. Militia.

‡SHULTIS, PHILIP.
Served in Capt. C. Saxe's Company.
Pension Certificate No. 29000.

SHUMWAY, DRUSES.
Enlisted Jan. 1, 1813 in Capt. Samuel
H. Holly's Company, 11th Regt.; died
Feb. 22, 1813. Ref: R. & L. 1812,
AGO Page 25.

SHUMWAY, JOHN, Ensign,   Poultney.
Volunteered to go to Plattsburgh,
September, 1814, and served 2 days
in Capt. Briant Ransom's Company.
Ref: Book 52, AGO Page 147.

*SHUMWAY, SALUM.
Served in Capt. Parsons' Company,
Col. Jonathan Williams' Regt. Detached Militia in U. S. service 2
months and 13 days, 1812.

*SHUMWAY, THOMAS.
Served in Capt. Preston's Company,
Col. Jonathan Williams' Regt. Detached Militia in U. S. service 2
months and 6 days, 1812.

SHUTLACK, JOHN, Corporal.
Served from Feb. 15 to April 28,
1813 in Lt. V. R. Goodrich's Company, 11th Regt. Ref: R. & L. 1812,
AGO Page 10.

*SIAS, JAMES,   Derby.
Served in Capt. Mason's Company,
Col. Fifield's Regt. Detached Militia
in U. S. service 5 months and 27
days, 1812.

‡*SIAS, JOHN,   Derby.
Served in Capt. Mason's Company,
Col. Fifield's Regt. Detached Militia
in U. S. service 5 months and 27
days, 1812. Served in Capt. Morrill's
Company, Col. Fifield's Regt. Detached Militia in U. S. service 3 months
and 17 days, 1812. Pension Certificate No. 13289. Pension Certificate
of widow, Lucretia, No. 13862.

SIAS, NATHANIEL.
Served from March 4 to June 3, 1813
in Capt. Edgerton's Company, 11th
Regt.; was at battle of Chrystler's
Farm Nov. 11, 1813 and reported
missing after the battle. Ref: R. &
L. 1812, AGO Page 3; Governor and
Council Vt., Vol. 6, Page 490.

*SIBLEY, ASA.
Served in Capt. Robbins' Company,
Col. .Wm. Williams' Regt. Detached
Militia in U. S. service 4 months and
29 days, 1812.

SIBLEY, CALEB,   Enosburgh.
Volunteered to go to Plattsburgh,
September, 1814, and served 6 days;
no organization given. Ref: Book
51, AGO Page 107.

*SIBLEY, EDWIN.
Enlisted Sept. 25, 1813 and served
1 month and 23 days in Capt. Elijah
Birge's Company, Col. Dixon's Regt.
Detached Militia in U. S. service.

‡SIBLEY, JOHN.
Served in Capt. Wright's Company.
Pension Certificate of widow, Lucy,
No. 8275.

SIBLEY, WILLIAM.
Enlisted Sept. 25, 1813 in Capt. Elijah
Birge's Company, Dixon's Regt. Ref:
Book 52, AGO Page 275.

SIDDON, THOMAS.
Served from May 1 to June 30, 1814
in Capt. Alexander Brooks' Corps of
Artillery. Ref: R. & L. 1812, AGO
Page 31.

SIEVER, JONATHAN,   Waitsfield.
Volunteered to go to Plattsburgh,
September, 1814, and served 4 days
in Capt. Mathias S. Jones' Company.
Ref: Book 52, AGO Page 170.

*SIKES, HARRY.
Served in Capt. Start's Company,
Col. Martindale's Regt. Detached
Militia in U. S. service 2 months
and 13 days, 1812.

*SILLOWAY, JOSEPH.
Served in 4 Regt. (Peck's) Vt. Militia.

*SILSBEE, LAZEL.
Served in Corning's Detachment, Vt.
Militia.

SILVER, BENJAMIN.
Served in Capt. Phineas Williams'
Company, 11th Regt.; on Pay Roll
for January and February, 1813. Ref:
R. & L. 1812, AGO Page 15.

SILVER, CHRISTOPHER.
Served from March 27 to June 26,
1813 in Capt. Edgerton's Company,
11th Regt. Ref: R. & L. 1812, AGO
Page 3.

SILVER, PUTNAM.
Served from Feb. 27 to May 27,
1813 in Capt. Edgerton's Company,
11th Regt. Ref: R. & L. 1812, AGO
Page 3.

SILVER, ZEBEDIAH.
Served from March 29 to June 28,
1813 in Capt. Edgerton's Company,
11th Regt. Ref: R. & L. 1812, AGO
Page 3.

SIMLIN, JOHN C.
Served from May 1 to June 30, 1814
in Alexander Parris' Company of Artificers. Ref: R. & L. 1812, AGO
Page 24.

‡*SIMMONS, AARON.
Served in Capt. Phelps' Company,
Col. Jonathan Williams' Regt. Detached Militia in U. S. service 2
months and 21 days, 1812. Pension
Certificate No. 11798. Pension Certificate of widow, Sibyl, No. 33206.

*SIMMONS, DANIEL.
Served in Capt. Needham's Company,
Col. Martindale's Regt. Detached
Militia in U. S. service 2 months and
14 days, 1812.

SIMMONS, JACOB,   Pittsford.
Volunteered to go to Plattsburgh,
September, 1814, and served 8 days
in Capt. Caleb Hendee's Company.
Ref: Book 52, AGO Page 125.

SIMMONS, JOHN,   Pittsford.
Volunteered to go to Plattsburgh,
September, 1814, and served 8 days
in Capt. Caleb Hendee's Company.
Ref: Book 52, AGO Page 125.

SIMMONS, LEVI,   St. Albans.
Enlisted April 30, 1813 for 1 year
in Capt. John Wires' Company, 30th
Regt. Ref: R. & L. 1812, AGO
Page 40.

SIMMONS, THOMAS,   Cheshire, Mass.
Served from Sept. 1, 1814 to June 16,
1815 in Capt. Sanford's Company,
30th Inf. Ref: R. & L. 1812, AGO
Page 23.

*SIMONDS, ASA M., Ensign.
Enlisted as private 29th Inf. June 5,
1813; appointed Ensign 11th Inf.
April 18, 1814; struck off July 28,
1814. Served as Ensign in 1st Regt.
of Detached Miliita of Vt. in U. S.
service at Champlain from Nov. 18
to Nov. 19, 1812. Served as Ensign
in 2 Regt. (Fifield's) Vt. Militia.
Ref: Heitman's Historical Register &
Dictionary USA.

‡*SIMONDS, BENJAMIN, Corporal.
Served in Capt. Barns' Company, Col.
Wm. Williams' Regt. Detached Militia
in U. S. service 5 months. Served
from June 11 to June 14, 1813 in
Capt. John Palmer's Company, 1st
Regt. 2nd Brig. 3rd Div. Pension
Certificate No. 3004. Pension Certi-
ficate of widow, Abigail M., No. 33095.

*SIMONDS, EZEKIAL.
Served in 1 Regt. (Judson's) Vt.
Militia.

*SIMONDS, LUMAN.
Served in Capt. John Palmer's Company, 1st Regt. 2nd Brig. 3rd Div.
from June 11 to June 14, 1813 and
from Oct. 4 to Oct. 13, 1813.

*SIMONS, ASA (or Simonds),   Randolph.
Volunteered to go to Plattsburgh,
September, 1814, and served in Capt.
Lebbeus Egerton's Company.

SIMONS, ELEM.
Served in Capt. Samul Gordon's Com-
pany, 11th Regt.; on Pay Roll for
January and February, 1813. Ref:
R. & L. 1812, AGO Page 9.

*SIMONS, RUFUS, Lieutenant, Williamstown. Volunteered to go to Plattsburgh, September, 1814, and served in Capt. David Robinson's Company. Also served in 2 Regt. (Fifield's) Vt. Militia.

SIMONS, THOMAS.
Enlisted June 17, 1813 for 1 year in Capt. Daniel Farrington's Company 30th Regt. (also commanded by Capt. Simeon Wright) on Muster Roll from March 1 to April 30, 1814. Ref: R. & L. 1812, AGO Pages 50 and 51.

*SIMPSON, ALEXANDER.
Served in Capt. Rogers' Company, Col. Fifield's Regt. Detached Militia in U. S. service 2 months and 18 days, 1812.

*SIMPSON, CAMPBELL.
Served in Capt. Phelps' Company, Col. Wm. Williams' Regt. Detached Militia in U. S. service 2 months and 21 days, 1812.

*SIMPSON, JOSEPH,   Sheffield.
Served in Capt. Wheeler's Company, Col. Fifield's Regt. Detached Militia in U. S. service 6 months and 4 days, 1812, stationed at Derby.

SIMPSON, LEWIS.   Franklin County.
Volunteered to go to Plattsburgh Sept. 11, 1814 and served in 15th or 22nd Regt. Ref: Hemenway's Vt. Gazetteer, Vol. 2, Page 392.

SIMPSON, ROBERT,   St. Albans.
Enlisted Aug. 12, 1813 for 1 year in Capt. John Wires' Company, 30th Regt. Ref: R. & L. 1812, AGO Page 40.

*SIMPSON, THOMAS.
Served in Capt. Lowry's Company, Col. Wm. Williams' Regt. Detached Militia in U. S. service 17 days, 1812.

*SIMPSON, WILLIAM.
Served in 1 Regt. (Judson's) Vt. Militia.

‡SIMS, JOSIAH.
Served in Capt. Crary's Company. Pension Certificate No. 24278.

*SINCLAIR, CONNER, Corporal.
Served in Tyler's Regt. Vt. Militia.

*SINCLAIR, EBENEZER.
Served from June 11 to June 14, 1813 in Capt. Moses Jewett's Company, 1st Regt. 2nd Brig. 3rd Div.

*SINCLAIR, JOSEPH, Corporal.
Served in Capt. Hiram Mason's Company, Col. Fifield's Regt. Detached Militia in U. S. service 4 months and 19 days, 1812. Also served in 3 Regt. (Tyler's) Vt. Militia.

SINCLAIR, JOSEPH, Sergeant, Morristown. Volunteered to go to Plattsburgh. September, 1814, and served 8 days in Capt. Denison Cook's Company. Ref: Book 51, AGO Pages 202 and 206.

*SINCLAIR, MASON.
Served in 3 Regt. (Tyler's) Vt. Militia.

‡SINCLAIR, MICHAEL.
Served in Capt. Pettie's Company. Pension Certificate No. 15171.

*SINCLAIR, NOAH, Corporal.
Served from May 1 to July 29, 1814; no organization given. Served in 1 Regt. (Judson's) Vt. Militia. Ref: R. & L. 1812, AGO Page 29.

*SINCLEAR, DAVID.
Served in Tyler's Regt. Vt. Militia.

*SINCLEAR, HAZEN.
Served in Tyler's Regt. Vt. Militia.

*SINCLEAR, JOSEPH, Captain.
Served as Lieutenant and Captain in Tyler's Regt. Vt. Militia.

*SINCLEAR, JOSEPH 2nd.
Served in Tyler's Regt. Vt. Militia.

*SINCLEAR, SIMON.
Served in 1 Regt. (Judson's) Vt. Militia.

SINDER, JACOB.
Served from June 11 to June 14, 1813 in Capt. John M. Eldridge's Company, 1st Regt. 2nd Brig. 3rd Div. Ref: R. & L. 1812, AGO Page 35.

SIRVER, JONATHAN,   Waitsfield.
Volunteered to go to Plattsburgh, September, 1814, and served 4 days in Capt. Mathias S. Jones' Company. Ref: Book 52, AGO Page 170.

SISCO, MICHAEL F.,   West Haven.
Volunteered to go to Plattsburgh, September, 1814, and served 4 days in Capt. David B. Phippeney's Company. Ref: Book 52, AGO Page 146.

*SISCO, URIAH.
Enlisted Oct. 3, 1813 and served 1 month and 23 days in Capt. Langworthy's Company, Col. Dixon's Regt. and Col. Clark's Rifle Corps.

SISSON, DANIEL, Corporal. Berne, N. Y.
Served from Aug. 5, 1814 to June 19, 1815 in Capt. Taylor's Company, 30th Inf. Ref: R. & L. 1812, AGO Page 23.

SKATES, JACOB,   Franklin County.
Enlisted May 7, 1812 for 5 years in Capt. White Youngs' Company, 15th Regt.; on Muster Roll from Aug. 31 to Dec. 31, 1814. Ref: R. & L. 1812, AGO Page 27.

*SKINNER, AMASA.
Served in Corning's Detachment, Vt. Militia.

*SKINNER, CALVIN.
Served from April 12 to May 20, 1814 in Capt. George Fisher's Company, Sumner's Regt.

*SKINNER, DAVID B.
Served in 3 Regt. (Tyler's) Vt. Militia.

*SKINNER, ELIPHALET.
Served in Capt. Noyce's Company, Col. Jonathan Williams' Regt. Detached Militia in U. S. service 2 months and 6 days, 1812.

SKINNER, HENRY.
Served from March 11 to June 10,
1813 in Capt. Edgerton's Company,
11th Regt. Ref: R. & L. 1812, AGO
Page 3.

*SKINNER, JOEL.
Served in 4 Regt. (Peck's) Vt. Militia.

SKINNER, JONATHAN,   Strafford.
Volunteered to go to Plattsburgh,
September, 1814, and served in Capt.
Cyril Chandler's Company. Ref: Book
52, AGO Page 42.

*SKINNER, LUTHER.
Served from April 12 to May 20, 1814
in company of Capt. James Gray Jr.,
Sumner's Regt.

SKINNER, NATHAN,   Marshfield.
Volunteered to go to Plattsburgh,
September, 1814, and served 9 days
in Capt. James English's Company.
Ref: Book 52, AGO Page 248.

SKINNER, ORSON,   Waterbury.
Volunteered to go to Plattsburgh,
September, 1814, and served 7 days
in Capt. Chester Marshall's Company
of Cavalry. Ref: Book 52, AGO Page
169.

‡SKINNER, SILAS,   Plainfield.
Volunteered to go to Plattsburgh,
September, 1814, and served 8 days
in Capt. James English's Company.
Pension Certificate of widow, Sarah
E., No. 26322.

‡SKINNER, THOMAS.
Served in Capt. Follett's Company.
Pension Certificate No. 2339.

‡SKINNER, TIMOTHY,   Montpelier.
Served from Sept. 17, 1814 to June
19, 1815 in Capt. Taylor's Company,
30th Inf. Pension Certificate of widow, Hannah, No. 7872. Ref: R. &
L. 1812, AGO Page 23.

SKINNER, ZUINLIUS.
Served in company of Capt. John
McNeil Jr., 11th Regt.; on Pay Roll
for January and February, 1813. Ref:
R. & L. 1812, AGO Page 17.

*SLADE, BENJAMIN.
Served in 2 Regt. (Fifield's) Vt.
Militia.

‡*SLADE, ENOCH, Corporal.
Served in Capt. Wheatly's Company,
Col. Fifield's Regt. Detached Militia
in U. S. service 2 months and 21
days, 1812. Pension Certificate of
widow, Mary T., No. 22009 .

*SLADE, JOHN.
Served in 2 Regt. (Fifield's) Vt.
Militia.

*SLADE, STEPHEN.
Served in 2 Regt. (Fifield's) Vt.
Militia.

SLADE, WILLIAM, Baggage Master,
Cornwall. Volunteered to go to
Plattsburgh, September, 1814, and was
at the battle, serving in Capt. Edmund B. Hill's Company, Sumner's
Regt. Ref: Book 51, AGO Page 13.

SLAPOR, JONATHAN,   Sudbury.
Volunteered to go to Plattsburgh,
September, 1814, and served 6 days
in Capt. Thomas Hall's Company.
Ref: Book 52, AGO Page 122.

*SLATER, CHAUNCEY.
Served in Capt. Barns' Company,
Col. Wm. Williams' Regt. Detached
Militia in U. S. service 5 months,
1812. Also served in 3 Regt. (Tyler's) Vt. Militia.

*SLATER, SAMUEL.
Served in 3 Regt. (Tyler's) Vt.
Militia.

SLAUGHTER, JONATHAN.
Served from March 1 to June 30,
1814 in Capt. Alexander Brook's
Corps of Artillery. Ref: R. & L.
1812, AGO Page 31.

*SLAYTON, BUCKLIN,   Calais.
Volunteered to go to Plattsburgh,
September, 1814, and served 10 days
in Capt. Gideon Wheelock's Company.

‡*SLAYTON, DARIUS,   Calais.
Volunteered to go to Plattsburgh,
September, 1814, and served 10 days
in Capt. Gideon Wheelock's Company.
Pension Certificate No. 29709.

*SLAYTON, HARVEY.   Calais.
Volunteered to go to Plattsburgh,
September, 1814, and served 10 days
in Capt. Gideon Wheelock's Company.

*SLAYTON, JESSE JR.,   Calais.
Volunteered to go to Plattsburgh,
September, 1814, and served 10 days
in Capt. Gideon Wheelock's Company.

*SLAYTON, PHINEAS,   Calais.
Volunteered to go to Plattsburgh,
September, 1814, and served 10 days
in Capt. Gideon Wheelock's Company.

SLAYTON, ROBERT,   Franklin County.
Volunteered to go to Plattsburgh
Sept. 11, 1814 and served in 15th or
22nd Regt. Ref: Hemenway's Vt.
Gazetteer, Vol. 2, Page 391.

SLEEPER, BENJAMIN, Sergeant, Corinth.
Volunteered to go to Plattsburgh,
September, 1814, and served 3 days
in Capt. Abel Jackman's Company.
Ref: Book 52, AGO Pages 44 and 45.

SLEEPER, DAVID,   Corinth.
Volunteered to go to Plattsburgh,
September, 1814, and served in Capt.
Abel Jackman's Company. Ref: Book
52, AGO Page 44.

SLEEPER, DAVID,   Vershire.
Volunteered to go to Plattsburgh,
September, 1814, and served 3 days
in Capt. Ira Corse's Company. Ref:
Book 52, Page 91.

SLEEPER, DAVID.
Volunteered to go to Plattsburgh,
September, 1814, and served in company of Capt. Ebenezer Spencer, Vershire. Ref: Book 52, AGO Page 48.

SLEEPER, EZEKIEL,   Corinth.
Volunteered to go to Plattsburgh,
September, 1814, and served in Capt.
Abel Jackman's Company. Ref: Book
52, AGO Page 44.

SLEEPER, EZRA,   Corinth.
Volunteered to go to Plattsburgh,
September, 1814, and served in Capt.
Abel Jackman's Company. Ref: Book
52, AGO Page 44.

SLEEPER, GEORGE,   Corinth.
Volunteered to go to Plattsburgh,
September, 1814, and served 3 days
in Capt. Abel Jackman's Company.
Ref: Book 52, AGO Pages 44 and 45.

SLEEPER, JETHRO,   Corinth.
Volunteered to go to Plattsburgh,
September, 1814, and served in Capt.
Abel Jackman's Company. Ref: Book
52, AGO Page 44.

‡*SLEEPER, JOHN, Sergeant, Corinth.
Served in Capt. Rogers' Company,
Col. Fifield's Regt. Detached Militia
in U. S. service 5 months and 27
days, 1812. Volunteered to go to
Plattsburgh, September, 1814, and
served as sergeant in Capt. Abel
Jackman's Company. Pension Certificate of widow, Julia G., No. 16636.

*SLEEPER, JOSEPH.
Served in Capt. Rogers' Company,
Col. Fifield's Regt. Detached Militia
in U. S. service 5 months and 2 days,
1812.

SLEEPER, ROBERT JR.,   Corinth.
Volunteered to go to Plattsburgh,
September, 1814, and served 3 days
in Capt. Abel Jackman's Company.
Ref: Book 52, AGO Pages 44 and 45.

‡SLOAN, ALFRED,   Strafford.
Served in Capt. Benjamin S. Edger-
ton's Company, 11th Regt.; on Pay
Roll for September and October, 1812
and January and February, 1813.
Pension Certificate of widow, Lima
H.. No. 4919. Ref: R. & L. 1812,
AGO Pages 1 and 2.

SLOAN, DAVID.
Enlisted June 3, 1813 for 1 year and
served in Capt. Gideon Spencer's
Company and Capt. James Taylor's
Company, 30th Regt.; re-enlisted Feb.
21, 1814 into Capt. Burnap's Com-
pany, 36th Inf. Ref: R. & L. 1812,
AGO Pages 52, 57, 59.

*SLOAT, PLATT.
Served in Capt. Phelps' Company,
Col. Wm. Williams' Regt. Detached
Militia in U. S. service 5 months,
1812.

*SLOCUM, SAMUEL.
Served from April 12 to April 21,
1814 in Capt. Edmund B. Hill's Company, Sumner's Regt.

SLOCUM, SAMUEL, Schoghticoke, N. Y.
Enlisted May 20, 1813 for 1 year in
Capt. Daniel Farrington's Company
(also commanded by Capt. Simeon
Wright) 30th Regt. Served from Sept.
1, 1814 to June 16, 1815 as corporal
in Capt. Sanford's Company, 30th
Inf. Ref: R. & L. 1812, AGO Pages
23, 50, 51.

‡*SLOPER, DANIEL.
Enlisted Sept. 25, 1813 and served
1 month and 23 days in Capt. Thomas

Waterman's Company, Col. Dixon's
Regt. Pension Certificate No. 22239.
Pension Certificate of widow, Rhoda,
No. 34453.

‡*SLOPER, JOHN.
Served in Capt. Taylor's Company,
Col. Wm. Williams' Regt. Detached
Militia in U. S. service 4 months and
24 days, 1812. Pension Certificate of
widow, Lucy, No. 8164.

*SLOPER, SAMUEL.
Served in 4 Regt. (Williams') Vt.
Militia.

*SLY, JOHN, JR.
Served in Capt. Morrill's Company,
Col. Fifield's Regt. Detached Militia
in U. S. service 1 month and 7 days,
1812.

*SMALL, AARON.
Served in Capt. Burnap's Company,
Col. Jonathan Williams' Regt. Detached Militia in U. S. service 2
months and 13 days, 1812.

*SMALL, DANIEL.
Served in Corning's Detachment, Vt.
Militia.

SMALL, DAVID, Musician.
Served in company of Capt. John
McNeil Jr., 11th Regt.; on Pay Roll
for January and February, 1813. Ref:
R. & L. 1812, AGO Page 17.

SMALL, EDWARD.
Served in company of Capt. John
McNeil Jr., 11th Regt.; on Pay Roll
for January and February, 1813. Ref:
R. & L. 1812, AGO Page 17.

SMALL, JOHN D.
Served in company of Capt. John
McNeil Jr., 11th Regt.; on Pay Roll
for January and February, 1813. Ref:
R. & L. 1812, AGO Page 17.

SMALL, LUTHER,   Morristown.
Volunteered to go to Plattsburgh,
September, 1814, and served 8 days
in Capt. Denison Cook's Company.
Ref: Book 51, AGO Pages 202 and
203.

SMALL, MOSES S.
Served from May 1 to July 18, 1814;
no organization given. Ref: R. &
L. 1812, AGO Page 29.

SMALL, SAMUEL.
Served in company of Capt. John
McNeil Jr., 11th Regt.; on Pay Roll
for January and February, 1813. Ref:
R. & L. 1812, AGO Page 17.

*SMALLEY, BENJAMIN.
Served in Capt. Wheatly's Company,
Col. Fifield's Regt. Detached Militia
in U. S. service 2 months and 21
days, 1812.

SMALLEY, DAVID.
Enlisted April 28, 1813 for 1 year in
Capt. Sanford's Company, 30th Regt.
Served from June 1 to Aug. 20, 1814
in Capt. Wm. Miller's Company, 30th
Regt., as servant to Capt. Miller.
Ref: R. & L. 1812, AGO Pages 1
and 54.

*SMALLEY, FRANCIS JR.
Served in Capt. Burnap's Company,
Col. Jonathan Williams' Regt. Detached Militia in U. S. service 2
months and 13 days, 1812.

*SMALLEY, ISAAC, Lieutenant, Waits-
field. Served 8 days in April, 1814,
as Ensign in Col. John Peck's Regt.
Also served as Lieutenant in 4 Regt.
(Peck's). Volunteered to go to Plattsburgh, September, 1814, and served
4 days in Capt. Mathias S. Jones'
Company. Ref: Book 52, AGO Page
170; Vol. 50 Vt. State Papers, Page
220.

*SMALLEY, JAMES. 2nd Major.
Served in 4 Regt. (Peck's) Vt. Militia.

‡SMART, JEREMIAH.
Served in Capt. Morrison's Company.
Pension Certificate No. 9096.

SMART, JOHN.
Served from April 1 to June 30, 1813
in Lieutenant Wm. S. Foster's Company, 11th Regt. Ref: R. & L. 1812,
AGO Page 6.

*SMALLEY, ZACHEUS.
Served from June 11 to June 14,
1813 in Lt. Bates' Company, 1 Regt.
(Judson's).

SMEAD, BENJAMIN, Captain.
Appointed 1st Lieutenant 11th Inf.
March 12, 1812; Captain Aug. 15,
1813; honorably discharged June 15,
1815. Served as 1st Lieutenant in
Capt. Charles Follett's Company, 11th
Regt.; on Pay Roll for January and
February, 1813. Ref: Heitman's His-
torical Register & Dictionary USA;
R. & L. 1812, AGO Page 12.

*SMEAD, CHESTER, Corporal.
Served from April 12 to April 21,
1814 in Capt. Shubael Wales' Company, Col. W. B. Sumner's Regt.

*SMEAD, ELISHA.
Served from April 12 to April 21,
1814 in Capt. Shubael Wales' Company, Col. W. B. Sumner's Regt.

SMEAD, REUBEN, Captain.
Appointed Captain 11th Inf. Aug.
15, 1813. Ref: Governor and Council,
Vt., Vol. 6, Page 474.

*SMEAD, RUFUS, Drummer.
Served from April 12 to April 21,
1814 in Capt. Shubael Wales' Company, Col. W. B. Sumner's Regt.

SMEADLEY, LEMUEL, Williamstown,
Mass. Served from June 24, 1814 to
June 19, 1815 in Capt. Taylor's Com-
pany, 30th Inf. Ref: R. & L. 1812,
AGO Page 23.

SMEDES, BENJAMIN, Sergeant.
Enlisted Feb. 1, 1813 for 5 years in
company of late Capt. J. Brooks, com-
manded by Lt. John I. Cromwell,
Corps of U. S. Artillery; on Muster
Roll from April 30 to June 30, 1814;
promoted from Corporal June 1, 1814.
Ref: R. & L. 1812, AGO Page 18.

*SMEDLEY, JOSHUA K.
Enlisted Sept. 25, 1813 and served 1
month and 23 days in Capt. Amos
Robinson's Company, Col. Dixon's
Regt.

*SMEDLY, WILLAM, Sergeant, St. Al-
bans. Served in Capt. Taylor's Company, Col. Wm. Williams' Regt. Detached Militia in U. S. service 4
months and 24 days, 1812. Enlisted
April 27, 1813 for 1 year as a corporal in Capt. John Wires' Company,
30th Regt. Served as Sergeant in
Capt. Chadwick's Company. Ref: R.
& L. 1812, AGO Page 32.

SMIDLEY, MOSES.
Served in Capt. Samul Gordon's Com-
pany, 11th Regt.; on Pay Roll for
January and February, 1813. Ref:
R. & L. 1812, AGO Page 9.

SMILEY, JAMES.
Served in Capt. Chadwick's Company.
Ref: R. & L. 1812, AGO Page 32.

SMILIE, NATHAN,   Cambridge.
Volunteered to go to Plattsburgh,
September, 1814, and served 8 days
in Capt. Salmon Green's Company.
Also served in Capt. Chadwick's
Company. Ref: Book 51, AGO Page
207; R. & L. 1812, AGO Page 32.

*SMITH, AARON.
Served from Oct. 8 to Nov. 18, 1813
in Capt. Isaac Finch's Company, Col.
Clark's Regt. of Riflemen.

*SMITH, ABIAL, Sergeant.
Served in Sumner's Regt. Vt. Militia.

‡*SMITH, ABIJAH.
Enlisted Sept. 25, 1813 and served
1 month and 23 days in Capt. Thomas
Watermans' Company, Col. Dixon's
Regt. Detached Militia in U. S. serv-
ice. Pension Certificate of widow,
Thankful, No. 4922.

‡*SMITH, ABIJAH JR.
Served in Capt. Wheatly's Company,
Col. Fifield's Regt. Detached Militia
in U. S. service 2 months and 21
days, 1812. Pension Certificate No.
2120.

‡*SMITH, ADIN.
Served in Capt. Wheatly's Company,
Col. Fifield's Regt. Detached Militia
in U. S. service 2 months and 21
days, 1812. Pension Certificate No.
9046.

SMITH, ALBA,   Williamstown.
Volunteered to go to Plattsburgh,
September, 1814, and was at the
battle, serving 8 days in Capt. David
Robinson's Company. Ref: Book 52,
AGO Page 2.

‡SMITH, ALLEN.
Served in Capt. Pickett's Company.
Pension Certificate of widow, Paulina
D., No. 28421.

*SMITH, ALLEN, Quartermaster Ser-
geant. Served in Sumner's Regt. Vt.
Militia.

SMITH, ALLEN, Musician.
Served in Capt. Week's Company.
11th Regt.; on Pay Roll for January and February, 1813. Ref: R. &
L. 1812, AGO Page 5.

SMITH, ALMERIN, Lieutenant.
Appointed 3rd Lieutenant 30 Inf.
April 30, 1813; 2nd Lieutenant March
5, 1814; honorably discharged June
15, 1815. Ref: Heitman's Historical
Register & Dictionary USA.

SMITH, ALPHEUS.
Served from March 12 to June 11,
1813 in Capt. Charles Follett's Company, 11th Regt. Ref: R. & L. 1812,
AGO Page 13.

*SMITH, AMOS,   Addison.
Volunteered to go to Plattsburgh,
September, 1814, and was in the
battle, serving 9 days in Capt. George
Fisher's Company, Sumner's Regt.
Served from April 12 to May 20,
1814 in same company.

*SMITH, ANDREW.
Served in Capt. Rogers' Company,
Col. Fifield's Regt. Detached Militia
in U. S. service 5 months and 27
days, 1812.

*SMITH, ARAD.
Served in Capt. Walker's Company,
Col. Fifield's Regt. Detached Militia
in U. S. service 5 months and 17
days, 1812.

*SMITH, ARCHIBALD.
Served from April 12 to April 21,
1814 in Capt. Othniel Jewett's Company, Sumner's Regt.

*SMITH, ARNOLD.
Served in Capt. Wright's Company,
Col. Fifield's Regt. Detached Militia
in U. S. service 3 months and 9 days,
1812.

*SMITH, ARTEMAS.
Served in Sumner's Regt. Vt. Militia.

SMITH, ASA,   Sudbury.
Volunteered to go to Plattsburgh,
September, 1814, and served 6 days
in Capt. Thomas Hall's Company.
Ref: Book 52, AGO Page 122.

‡SMITH, ASA SAMUEL STILLWELL.
Served in Capt. Oliver Lowry's Company (4 Regt.). Pension Certificate
No. 21377.

‡*SMITH, ASAHEL,   Poultney.
Served in Capt. Scovell's Company,
Col. Martindale's Regt. Detached
Militia in U. S. service 2 months and
21 days, 1812. Volunteered to go to
Plattsburgh, September, 1814, and
served 2 days in Capt. Briant Ransom's Company. Pension Certificate
No. 30734. Pension Certificate of
widow, Abigail, No. 44619.

SMITH, ASAPH, Captain,   Hancock.
Volunteered to go to Plattsburgh,
September, 1814, and served 7 days
in command of company raised in
Hancock and Granville. Ref: Book
51, AGO Page 20.

‡*SMITH, BARTHOLOMEW C.,   Barre.
Served in Capt. Walker's Company,
Col. Fifield's Regt. Detached Militia
in U. S. service 2 months and 24
days, 1812. Pension Certificate of
widow, Emma, No. 3421.

SMITH, BENJAMIN.
Served from April 2 to July 1, 1813
in Lieut. Wm. S. Foster's Company,
11th Reg. Ref: R. & L. 1812, AGO
Page 6.

SMITH, BENJAMIN.
Served from May 1 to June 30, 1814
in Capt. Haig's Corps of Light Dragoons. Ref: R. & L. 1812, AGO Page
20.

SMITH, BENJAMIN.
Enlisted March 2, 1813 during the
war and served in company of late
Capt. J. Brooks, commanded by Lt.
John I. Cromwell, Corps of U. S.
Artillery; on Muster Roll from April
30 to June 30, 1814. Ref: R. & L.
1812, AGO Page 18.

SMITH, BENJAMIN,   Cabot.
Volunteered to go to Plattsburgh,
September, 1814, and served 3 days
in Capt. Anthony Perry's Company.
Ref: Book 52, AGO Pages 252 and
254.

SMITH, CALVIN,   Barre.
Volunteered to go to Plattsburgh,
September, 1814, and served 10 days
in Capt. Warren Ellis' Company. Ref:
Book 52, AGO Page 242.

*SMITH, CHAUNCEY,   Georgia.
Enlisted Sept. 25, 1813 and served
1 month and 23 days in Capt. Post's
Company, Col. Dixon's Regt. Detached Militia in U. S. service.

SMITH, CHESTER.
Volunteered to go to Plattsburgh,
September, 1814, and served 7 days
in Capt. Frederick Griswold's Company, raised in Brookfield, Vt. Ref:
Book 52, AGO Page 52.

SMITH, CLARK. Lieutenant.
Served as private, Sergeant and Sergeant Major, 31st Inf. June 15, 1813
to March, 1814; appointed Ensign
31st Inf. March 30, 1814; 2nd Lieutenant May 1, 1814; 3rd Lieutenant
June 23, 1814; honorably discharged
June 15, 1815. Ref: Heitman's Historical Register & Dictionary USA.

SMITH, COMFORT.   Barre.
Volunteered to go to Plattsburgh,
September, 1814, and served 10 days
in Capt. Warren Ellis' Company. Ref:
Book 52, AGO Page 242.

*SMITH, CURTIS.
Served in Sumner's Regt. Vt. Militia.

‡SMITH, CYRUS,   Washington.
Volunteered to go to Plattsburgh,
September, 1814, and was in the
battle, serving 8 days in Capt. David
Robinson's Company. Pension Certificate No. 27928. Also served in
Capt. Carter's Company. Pension Certificate of widow, Fanny A., No.
39510.

*SMITH, DANIEL.
Served from April 12 to April 15,
1814 in Capt. Jonathan P. Stanley's
Company, Col. W. B. Sumner's Regt.

SMITH, DANIEL,   Cabot.
Volunteered to go to Plattsburgh,
September, 1814, and served 4 days
in Capt. Anthony Perry's Company.
Ref: Book 52, AGO Page 179.

SMITH, DANIEL,   Addison.
Volunteered to go to Plattsburgh,
September, 1814, and was in the
battle, serving 9 days in Capt. George
Fisher's Company, Sumner's Regt.;
served from April 12 to May 20, 1814
in same company. Ref: Book 51,
AGO Page 5; Book 52, AGO Page 277.

*SMITH, DAVID.
Served from June 11 to June 14,
1813 in Capt. John Palmer's Company, 1st Regt. 2nd Brig. 3rd Div.

SMITH, DAVID,   Leicester.
Volunteered to go to Plattsburgh,
September, 1814, and served 8 days
in Capt. Ebenezer Jenney's Company.
Ref: Book 52, AGO Page 160.

*SMITH, DAVID.
Served in Capt. Barns' Company,
Col. Wm. Williams' Regt. Detached
Militia in U. S. service 5 months,
1812.

SMITH, DAVID.
Served in Capt. Benjamin Bradford's
Company; on Muster Roll from May
31 to Aug. 31, 1813. Ref: R. & L.
1812, AGO Page 26.

SMITH, EBENEZER,   Fairfax.
Served from April 24, 1813 to April
24, 1814 in Capt. Daniel Farrington's
Company, 30th Regt. (also commanded by Capt. Simeon Wright). Volunteered to go to Plattsburgh, September, 1814, and served 8 days in Capt.
Josiah Grout's Company. Ref: R. &
L. 1812, AGO Pages 50 and 51; Book
51, AGO Page 103.

‡SMITH, ELEAZER.
Served in Capt. Partridge's Company. Pension Certificate No. 7670.

*SMITH, ELI. ENSIGN.
Served in 3 Regt. (Tyler's) Vt. Militia.

‡*SMITH, ELI JR.,   Lyndon.
Served in Capt. Wheeler's Company,
Col. Fifield's Regt. Detached Militia
in U. S. service 6 months and 4 days,
1812. Pension Certificate No. 9705.
Pension Certificate of widow, Clarissa, No. 29877.

*SMITH, ELIJAH.
Served in Capt. Robbins' Company,
Col. Wm. Williams' Regt. Detached
Militia in U. S. service 3 months
and 21 days, 1812. Enlisted Oct. 8,
1813 in Capt. Isaac Finch's Company,
Col. Clark's Rifle Regt.

SMITH, ELIJAH,   Waitsfield.
Volunteered to go to Plattsburgh,
September, 1814, and served 4 days
in Capt. Mathias S. Jones' Company.
Ref: Book 52, AGO Pages 170 and
207.

*SMITH, ELISHA, Sergeant,   Pawlet.
Served in Capt. Hotchkiss' Company,
Col. Martindale's Regt. Detached
Militia in U. S. service 2 months
and 13 days, 1812. Served in 1st
Regt. of Detached Militia of Vt. in
U. S. service at Champlain from
Nov. 18 to Nov. 19, 1812.

SMITH, ELISHA, Lieutenant, St. Albans.
Appointed 2nd Lieutenant 30th Inf.
April 30, 1813; 1st Lieutenant June
23, 1814; honorably discharged June
15, 1815. Served as 2nd Lieutenant
in Capt. James Taylor's Company,
30th Regt. and Capt. John Wires'
Company, 30th Regt. Ref: Heitman's
Historical Register & Dictionary USA;
R. & L. 1812, AGO Pages 40 and 53.

SMITH, ENOCH.
Enlisted March 8, 1813 in Capt.
Charles Follett's Company, 11th Regt.;
on Pay Roll to May 31, 1813. Ref:
R. & L. 1812, AGO Page 13.

SMITH, ENOCH JR., Sergeant, Sudbury.
Volunteered to go to Plattsburgh,
September, 1814, and served 6 days
in Capt. Thomas Hall's Company.
Ref: Book 52, AGO Page 122.

‡SMITH, ENOCH P.
Served in Capt. Reed's Company.
Pension Certificate of widow, Lydia
L., No. 26331.

SMITH, EPHRAIM.
Served in Capt. Benjamin Bradford's
Company; on Muster Roll from May
31 to Aug. 31, 1813. Ref: R. & L.
1812, AGO Page 26.

*SMITH, EPHRAIM.
Enlisted Sept. 25, 1813 in Capt. Amos
Robinson's Company, Dixon's Regt.;
transferred to Rifle Corps Oct. 3,
1813.

SMITH, EZRA, Lieutenant.
Appointed 2nd Lieutenant 1st Artil-
lery March 12, 1813; 1st Lieutenant
May 11, 1813; transferred to Artil-
lery Corps May 12, 1814; Captain
Asst. Deputy Quartermaster General
April 19, 1813 to June 15, 1815; honor-
ably discharged June 15, 1815; died
Dec. 17, 1867. Ref: Heitman's His-
torical Register & Dictionary USA;
R. & L. 1812, AGO Page 28.

SMITH, EZRA.
Served from Nov. 1, 1812 to Feb. 28,
1813 in Capt. Phineas Williams' Company, 11th Regt. Ref: R. & L. 1812,
AGO Page 15.

SMITH, FREDERICK,   Strafford.
Volunteered to go to Plattsburgh,
September, 1814, and served 6 days
in Capt. Jedediah H. Harris' Company. Ref: Book 52, AGO Pages 43
and 99.

*SMITH, FREDERICK.
Served from April 12 to May 20, 1814
in Capt. George Fisher's Company,
Sumner's Regt.

*SMITH, GEORGE.
Served from April 12 to April 21,
1814 in Capt. Othniel Jewett's Company, Sumner's Regt.

*SMITH, GEORGE 2nd, Corporal.
Served in Capt. Phelps' Company,
Col. Wm. Williams' Regt. Detached
Militia in U. S. service 1 month and
22 days, 1812.

SMITH, GRANT, Sergeant.
Volunteered to go to Plattsburgh,
September, 1814, and served 4 days
in Capt. Aaron Kidder's Company.
Ref :Book 52, AGO Page 65.

SMITH, HARRY.
Enlisted Jan. 24, 1813 in Capt.
Charles Follett's Company, 11th Regt.;
died April 22, 1813. Ref: R. & L.
1812, AGO Page 13.

SMITH, HENRY,   Washington.
Volunteered to go to Plattsburgh,
September, 1814, and served 9 days
in Capt. Warren Ellis' Company.
Ref: Book 52, AGO Page 220.

SMITH, HENRY.
Served from Nov. 1, 1812 to Jan. 22,
1813 in Capt.. Weeks' Company, 11th
Regt. Ref: R. & L. 1812, AGO
Page 5.

SMITH, HENRY,   Addison.
Volunteered to go to Plattsburgh,
September, 1814, and was in the
battle, serving 9 days in Capt. George
Fisher's Company. Sumner's Regt.
Ref: Book 51, AGO Page 5.

‡*SMITH, HIRAM.
Served from April 12 to May 20, 1814
in company of Capt. James Gray Jr.,
Sumner's Regt. Also served in Capt.
Ormsbury's Company, 1st Regt. (Martindale's). Pension Certificate No.
21584.

‡*SMITH, ISAAC.
Served from April 5 to July 1, 1813
in Lieut. Wm. S. Foster's Company,
11th Regt. Enlisted Sept. 25, 1813
as a corporal in Capt. Elijah Birge's
Company, Dixon's Regt. Also served
in Lieut. Dunham's Company. Pension Certificate No. 28478.

SMITH, ISAIAH,   St. Albans.
Enlisted May 6, 1813 for 1 year in
Capt. John Wires' Company, 30th
Regt. Ref: R. & L. 1812, AGO Page
40.

*SMITH, ISRAEL, Captain.
Appointed 1st Lieutenant 30th Inf.
April 30, 1813; Regimental Paymaster
May 15, 1813 to July 10, 1814; re-
signed July 10, 1814. Served as 1st
Lieutenant in Capt. James Taylor's
Company, 30th Regt. Served as Cap-
tain and Aide de Camp with General
and Staff (Orms') Vt. Militia. Ref:
Heitman's Historical Register & Dic-
tionary USA; R. & L. 1812, AGO
Page 58.

SMITH, ISRAEL,   Orwell.
Volunteered to go to Plattsburgh,
September, 1814, and served 11 days
in Capt. Wait Branch's Company.
Also served in 1 Regt. (Martindale's)
Vt. Militia. Ref: Book 51, AGO
Page 16.

SMITH, J. C., Lieutenant,   Tunbridge.
Volunteered to go to Plattsburgh,
September, 1814, and went as far as
Bolton, serving 4 days. Went with
Capt. David Knox but did not join
any organization. Ref: Book 52, AGO
Pages 93 and 116.

*SMITH, JAMES,   Wilmington.
Served in Capt. Preston's Company,
Col. Jonathan Williams' Regt. Detached Militia in U. S. service 2
months and 6 days, 1812.

SMITH, JAMES,   Franklin County.
Volunteered to go to Plattsburgh
Sept. 11, 1814, and served in 15th
or 22nd Regt. Ref: Hemenway's Vt.
Gazetteer, Vol. 2, Page 391.

*SMITH, JAMES.
Served in 4 Regt. (Williams') Vt.
Militia.

‡*SMITH, JAMES.
Served in Capt. E. Walker's Company. Col. Fifield's Regt. Detached
Militia in U. S. service 6 months and
3 days, 1812. Pension Certificate No.
21762.

SMITH, JAMES.
Served from Feb. 22 to May 21,
1813 in Capt. Charles Follett's Company, 11th Regt. Ref: R. & L. 1812,
AGO Page 13.

SMITH, JAMES,   Berlin.
Volunteered to go to Plattsburgh,
September, 1814, and served 7 days
in Capt. Cyrus Johnson's Company.
Ref: Book 52, AGO Page 255.

SMITH, JAMES, Lieutenant.
Appointed 3rd Lieutenant 30th Inf.
April 30, 1813; 2nd Lieutenant June
23, 1814; honorably discharged June
15, 1815. Ref: Heitman's Historical
Register & Dictionary USA.

SMITH, JAMES.
Served in Capt. Benjamin Bradford's
Company; on Muster Roll from May
31 to Aug. 31, 1813. Ref: R. & L.
1812, AGO Page 26.

SMITH, JAMES.
Served from April 19, 1813 to April 6,
1814 in Capt. Daniel Farrington's
Company, 30th Regt. (also command-
ed by Capt. Simeon Wright). Ref:
R. & L. 1812, AGO Pages 50 and 51.

SMITH, JAMES N.
Served in Capt. Haig's Corps of
Light Dragoons; on Pay Roll to June
30, 1814. Ref: R. & L. 1812, AGO
Page 20.

*SMITH, JARAD, Sergeant.
Served in Capt. Barns' Company, Col.
Wm. Williams' Regt. Detached Militia in U. S. service 5 months, 1812,
at Swanton Falls. Served from June
11 to June 14, 1813 in Capt. Hezekiah
Barns' Company, 1st Regt. 2nd Brig.
3rd Div.

*SMITH, JARED C.
Served from Oct. 5 to Oct. 16, 1813
in Capt. Roswell Hunt's Company,
3 Regt. (Tyler's).

*SMITH, JESSE, Acting Orderly Sergeant, Addison. Volunteered to go to Plattsburgh, September, 1814, and was in the battle, serving 9 days in Capt. George Fisher's Company, Sumner's Regt. Also served with Hospital Attendants, Vt. Ref: Book 51, AGO Page 5.

SMITH, JETHRO, Corporal.
Served in Capt. Charles Follett's Company, 11th Regt.; on Pay Roll for January and February, 1813. Ref: R. & L. 1812, AGO Page 12.

SMITH, JOB.
Served in Capt. Weeks' Company, 11th Regt.; on Pay Roll for January and February, 1813. Ref: R. & L. 1812, AGO Page 5.

SMITH, JOHN.
Served from April 1 to June 30, 1813 in Lieut. Wm. S. Foster's Company, 11th Regt. Ref: R. & L. 1812, AGO Page 6.

*SMITH, JOHN.
Served in 1 Regt. (Judson's) Vt. Militia.

*SMITH, JOHN, Major.
Served in 2 Regt. (Fifield's) Vt. Militia.

SMITH, JOHN G., Shoreham.
Volunteered to go to Plattsburgh, September, 1814, serving 6 days in Capt. Samuel Hand's Company. Ref: Rev. J. F. Goodhue's History of Shoreham, Page 107.

SMITH, JOHN.
Served from March 1 to June 30, 1814 in Capt. Alexander Brooks' Corps of Artillery. Ref: R. & L. 1812, AGO Page 31.

*SMITH, JOHN.
Served from April 12 to April 21, 1814 in Capt. Othniel Jewett's Company, Sumner's Regt.

‡*SMITH, JOHN.
Served in Capt. Durkee's Company, Col. Fifield's Regt. Detached Militia in U. S. service 2 months and 16 days, 1812. Pension Certificate of widow, Sarah T., No. 23691.

*SMITH, JOHN.
Served in Capt. Parsons' Company, Col. Jonathan Williams' Regt. Detached Militia in U. S. service 2 months and 13 days, 1812.

*SMITH, JOHN JR.
Served in Capt. Wheeler's Company, Col. Fifield's Regt. Detached Militia in U. S. service at Derby 6 months and 4 days, 1812.

‡SMITH, JOHN C.
Served in Capt. Perry's Company. Pension Certificate No. 1725.

SMITH, JONATHAN JR., Barre.
Volunteered to go to Plattsburgh, September, 1814, and served 10 days in Capt. Warren Ellis' Company. Ref: Book 52, AGO Page 242.

*SMITH, JOSEPH.
Served in Capt. Preston's Company, Col. Jonathan Williams' Regt. Detached Militia in U. S. service 2 months and 6 days, 1812.

SMITH, JOSEPH.
Served from Feb. 18 to May 17, 1813 in Capt. Edgerton's Company, 11th Regt. Ref: R. & L. 1812, AGO Page 3.

*SMITH, JOSEPH.
Served from April 12 to April 21, 1814 in Lieut. James S. Morton's Company, Col. W. B. Sumner's Regt.

SMITH, JOSEPH 1st, Shoreham.
Volunteered to go to Plattsburgh, September, 1814, and served 6 days in Capt. Samuel Hand's Company. Ref: Rev. J. F. Goodhue's History of Shoreham, Page 108.

SMITH, JOSEPH 2nd, Shoreham.
Volunteered to go to Plattsburgh, September, 1814, and served 6 days in Capt. Samuel Hand's Company. Ref: Rev. J. F. Goodhue's History of Shoreham, Page 108.

*SMITH, JOSIAH.
Served from April 12 to April 21, 1814 in Capt. Edmund B. Hill's Company, Sumner's Regt.

‡*SMITH, JOSIAH, Georgia.
Enlisted Sept. 25, 1813 and served in Capt. N. B. Eldridge's Company, Col. Dixon's Regt. Detached Militia in U. S. service. Volunteered to go to Plattsburgh, September, 1814, and served 7 days in Capt. S. Farnsworth's Company. Pension Certificate of widow, Deborah, No. 28226.

SMITH, JOSIAH 2nd, Tunbridge.
Volunteered to go to Plattsburgh, September, 1814, and served 4 days in Capt. Ephraim Hackett's Company. Ref: Book 52, AGO Page 71.

SMITH, LEMUEL, Bethel.
Volunteered to go to Plattsburgh, September, 1814, and served 8 days in Capt. Nehemiah Noble's Company. Ref: Book 51, AGO Pages 226 and 234.

SMITH, LEVI, Strafford.
Served from March 8 to June 7, 1813 in Capt. Edgerton's Company, 11th Regt. Ref: R. & L. 1812, AGO Page 3.

‡SMITH, LEVI.
Served in Capt. Round's Company. Pension Certificate of widow, Prudence, No. 22062.

SMITH, LEVI, Clarendon.
Volunteered to go to Plattsburgh, September, 1814, and served in Capt. Durham Sprague's Company. Ref: Book 52, AGO Page 128.

*SMITH, LEVI.
Enlisted Sept. 25, 1813 in company of Capt. Jonathan Prentiss, Jr., Dixon's Regt.

*SMITH, LEVI JR.
Served from April 19 to April 21, 1814 in Capt. Othniel Jewett's Company, Sumner's Regt.

‡SMITH, LEWIS,   Shoreham.
Served in Capt. Holley's Company
and in Capt. Burnap's Company. Pension Certificate No. 16965.

SMITH, LUCIUS.
Served in Capt. Samuel H. Holly's
Company, 11th Regt.; on Pay Roll
for January and February, 1813. Ref:
R. & L. 1812, AGO Page 25.

‡SMITH, LYMAN.
Served in Capt. Partridge's Company.
Pension Certificate No. 15529.

‡SMITH, LYMAN.
Served in Capt. Morrill's Company.
Pension Certificate No. 17007.

‡*SMITH, LYSAMORE.
Served in Capt. Hotchkiss' Company,
Col. Martindale's Regt.   Detached
Militia in U. S. service 2 months
and 13 days, 1812. Pension Certificate
of widow, Almy, No. 20796.

SMITH, MARTIN,   Arlington.
Served from Sept. 1, 1814 to June 16,
1815 in Capt. Sanford's Company,
30th Inf. Ref: R. & L. 1812, AGO
Page 23.

*SMITH, MARTIN.
Served in 4 Regt. (Williams') Vt.
Militia.

SMITH, MARTIN.
Enlisted Jan. 12, 1814 for 1 year in
Capt. Daniel Farrington's Company,
30th Regt.; on Muster Roll from
March 1 to April 30, 1814. Ref: R.
& L. 1812, AGO Page 50.

*SMITH, MORRIS.
Served from April 12 to April 21,
1814 in Capt. Othniel Jewett's Company, Sumner's Regt.

SMITH, NATHAN, Sergeant, Shrewsbury.
Served from May 16, 1814 to June
19, 1815 in Capt. Taylor's Company,
30th Inf. Ref: R. & L. 1812, AGO
Page 23.

‡SMITH, NATHAN.
Served in Capt. Cummings' Company.
Pension Certificate No. 21274.

*SMITH, NATHAN.
Enlisted Sept. 25, 1813 in Capt.
Charles Bennett's Company, Dixon's
Regt.

SMITH, NATHAN.
Enlisted May 9, 1813 for 1 year in
Capt. Daniel Farrington's Company,
30th Regt. (also commanded by Capt.
Simeon Wright). Ref: R. & L. 1812,
AGO Pages 50 and 51.

SMITH, NATHAN,   Jericho.
Took part in the Battle of Plattsburgh. Ref: History of Jericho, Page
142.

*SMITH, NEWELL B.
Served from April 19 to April 21,
1814 in Capt. Othniel Jewett's Company, Sumner's Regt.

SMITH, OBED C.,   Pittsford.
Volunteered to go to Plattsburgh,
September, 1814, and served 8 days
in Capt. Caleb Hendee's Company.
Ref: Book 52, AGO Page 125.

*SMITH, OLIVER.
Served from April 12 to April 15,
1814 in Capt. John Hackett's Company, Sumner's Regt.

*SMITH, ORIMEL L.
Served in Capt. Howard's Company,
Vt. Militia.

*SMITH, ORRIN (or Orange).
Served in Capt. Durkee's Company,
Col. Fifield's Regt. Detached Militia
in U. S. service 2 months and 16
days, 1812.

SMITH, ORSON,   Barre.
Volunteered to go to Plattsburgh,
September, 1814, and served in Capt.
Warren Ellis' Company. Ref: Hemenway's Vt. Gazetteer, Vol. 4, Page
41.

SMITH, PETER,   Fairfax.
Volunteered to go to Plattsburgh,
September, 1814, and served 8 days
in Capt. Josiah Grout's Company.
Ref: Book 51, AGO Pages 103 and 134.

SMITH, PETER JR.
Served from May 1 to June 30, 1814
in Capt. Alexander Brooks' Corps of
Artillery. Ref: R. & L. 1812, AGO
Page 31.

‡SMITH, PHELPS, Lieutenant.
Appointed 3rd Lieutenant 30th Inf.
April 30, 1813; 2nd Lieutenant March
5, 1814; honorably discharged June
15, 1815. Served under Captains
James Taylor, Gideon Spencer, William Miller, 30th Regt. and under
Captains Wood and Scoville. Pension
Certificate of widow, Marilla, No.
28982. Ref: Heitman's Historical
Register & Dictionary USA; R. & L.
1812, AGO Pages 52, 54, 56, 58.

‡SMITH, PHILANDER.
Served in Capt. Shell's Company.
Pension Certificate of widow, Mary,
No. 43163.

SMITH, PHILIP, Lieutenant, Shoreham
or Enosburgh. Appointed 1st Lieutenant 48th Inf. April 21, 1814; 26th
Inf. May 12, 1814; honorably discharged June 15, 1815. Served from
Oct. 14 to Nov. 17, 1813 in Capt.
Asahel Scovell's Company. Col. Clark's
Rifle Corps. Ref: Heitman's Historical Register & Dictionary USA;
R. & L. 1812, AGO Page 22.

‡*SMITH, PHILIP, Sergeant,   Stowe.
Volunteered to go to Plattsburgh,
September, 1814, and was at the
battle, serving as Sergeant in Capt.
Nehemiah Perkins' Company, 4 Regt.
(Peck's). Also served in Corning's
Detachment, Vt. Militia. Pension Certificate of widow, Mary J., No. 26874.

SMITH, PHINEAS,   Randolph?
Enlisted Feb. 18, 1813 in Capt.
Charles Follett's Company, 11th Regt.;
died April 24, 1813. Ref: R. & L.
1812, AGO Page 13.

*SMITH, PHINEAS.
Volunteered to go to Plattsburgh,
September, 1814, and served in Capt.
Lebbeus Egerton's Company.

*SMITH, PROPERTY.
Served in Sumner's Regt. Vt. Militia.

SMITH, REUBEN, Teamster, Clarendon.
Volunteered to go to Plattsburgh,
September, 1814, and served 4 days
in Capt. Durham Sprague's Company.
Ref: Book 52, AGO Page 128.

SMITH, RICHARD,   Montgomery.
Served in Capt. Follet's Company,
Col. Dixon's Regt. Detached Militia
in U. S. service 1 month and 23
days, 1813. Volunteered to go to
Plattbsurgh, September, 1814, and
served 6 days in same company. Ref:
Book 53, AGO Page 106; Book 51,
AGO Pages 99, 106, 154, 188.

SMITH, RICHARD,   Barre.
Volunteered to go to Plattsburgh,
September, 1814, and served 9 days
in Capt. Warren Ellis' Company. Ref:
Book 52, AGO Pages 172, 236, 242.

SMITH, RICHARD,   Berlin.
Volunteered to go to Plattsburgh,
September, 1814, and served 7 days
in Capt. Cyrus Johnson's Company.
Ref: Book 52, AGO Page 255.

*SMITH, RICHARD JR.
Enlisted Sept. 25, 1813 in Capt. Mar-
tin D. Folett's Company, Dixon's
Regt.

‡*SMITH, RODNEY, Corporal, Waitsfield.
Volunteered to go to Plattsburgh,
September ,1814, and served 4 days
in Capt. Mathias S. Jones' Company.
Served as a corporal in Corning's De-
tachment, Vt. Militia. Served in
Capt. Campbell's Company. Pension
Certificate of widow, Betsey R., No.
22067.

*SMITH, RUFUS, Sergeant,   Addison.
Served from April 12 to May 20, 1814
in Capt. George Fisher's Company,
Sumner's Regt.; volunteered to go
to Plattsburgh, September, 1814, and
was in the battle, serving 9 days in
same company.

*SMITH, RUSSELL,   Addison.
Enlisted Oct. 18, 1813 and served 62
days in Capt. John Weed's Company,
Col. Clark's Rifle Corps. Served from
April 12 to May 20, 1814 in Capt.
George Fisher's Company, Sumner's
Regt.; volunteered to go to Platts-
burgh, September, 1814, and was in
the battle, serving 9 days in same
company.

*SMITH, SAMUEL R.,   Stowe.
Volunteered to go to Plattsburgh,
September, 1814, and was at the
battle, serving in Capt. Nehemiah
Perkins' Company, 4 Regt. (Peck's).
Also served in Corning's Detachment,
Vt. Militia.

‡*SMITH, SAMUEL.
Enlisted June 11, 1813 for 1 year
in Capt. Daniel Farrington's Company; on Muster Roll from March 1,
1814 to April 30, 1814; (company
was also commanded by Capt. Simeon
Wright.) Also served with Hospital
Attendants, Vt. Pension Certificate
No. 9922 and No. 24000.

*SMITH, SAMUEL,   Shoreham.
Served in 3 Regt. (Tyler's) Vt. Militia. Enlisted for eighteen months and
was killed in the battle of Bridgewater. Ref: Rev. J. F. Goodhue's
History of Shoreham, Page 102.

‡*SMITH, SANFORD.
Served in Capt. Wright's Company,
Col. Fifield's' Regt. Detached Militia
in U. S. service 6 months, 1812. Pension Certificate No. 3152.

SMITH, SELAH,   Waitsfield.
Volunteered to go to Plattsburgh,
September, 1814, and served 4 days
in Capt. Mathias S. Jones' Company.
Ref: Book 52, AGO Page 170.

SMITH, SHUBAL JR.,   Brookfield.
Volunteered to go to Plattsburgh,
September, 1814, and served 8 days
in Capt. Frederick Griswold's Com-
pany, raised in Brookfield, Vt. Ref:
Book 52, AGO Pages 52 and 57.

*SMITH, SILAS.
Enlisted Sept. 20, 1813 in Capt. John
Weed's Company, Col. Clark's Rifle
Corps.

SMITH, SHUBAEL,   Washington.
Volunteered to go to Plattsburgh,
September, 1814, and served 9 days
in Capt. Warren Ellis' Company. Ref:
Book 52, AGO Pages 220 and 235.

*SMITH, SIMEON,   Braintree.
Served in Capt. Wheatley's Company,
Col. Fifield's Regt. Detached Militia
in U. S. service 2 months and 21
days, 1812.

SMITH, SOLOMON,   Brookfield.
Volunteered to go to Plattsburgh,
September, 1814, and served 7 days
in Capt. Frederick Griswold's Company. Ref: Book 52, AGO Pages 52,
61, 121.

SMITH, STAFFORD,   Royalton.
Volunteered to go to Plattsburgh,
September, 1814, and served 9 days
in Capt. Warren Ellis' Company of
Barre. Ref: Book 51, Page 293; Book
52, Page 172.

*SMITH, STEPHEN.
Served from April 12 to April 15,
1814 in Capt. John Hackett's Company, Sumner's Regt. Volunteered to
go to Plattsburgh, September, 1814,
and served 6 days in Capt. Samuel
Hand's Company.

SMITH, STEPHEN,   Starksboro.
Volunteered to go to Plattsburgh,
September, 1814, and served 4 days
in Capt. Moulton's Company. Ref:
Book 51, AGO Page 29.

*SMITH, STILLMAN.
Served in Capt. Lowry's Company,
Col. Wm. Williams' Regt. Detached
Militia in U. S. service 4 months and
26 days, 1812.

‡SMITH, SYCAMORE.
Served in Capt. Hotchkiss' Company.
Pension Certificate No. 17336.

*SMITH, SYLVANUS,   Stowe.
Volunteered to go to Plattsburgh,
September, 1814, and was at the
battle, serving in Capt. Nehemiah
Perkins' Company, 4 Regt. (Peck's).

SMITH, TH. A., Brig. General.
Served on General Staff of the Northern Army commanded by Maj. Gen.
George Izard; on Pay Roll to July 31,
1814. Ref: R. & L. 1812, AGO Page
28.

SMITH, THOMAS.
Served from May 1 to June 30, 1814
in Capt. Alexander Brooks' Corps
of Artillery. Ref: R. & L. 1812, AGO
Page 31.

SMITH, THOMAS. Musician.
Served from Nov. 1, 1812 to Feb.
28, 1813 in company of Capt. John
McNeil Jr., 11th Regt. Ref: R. & L.
1812, AGO Page 17.

SMITH, TRUMAN, Corporal.
Enlisted May 15, 1813 for 1 year
in Capt. Daniel Farrington's Com-
pany, 30th Regt. (also commanded by
Capt. Simeon Wright). Ref: R. &
L. 1812, AGO Page 50.

SMITH, WAITSTILL.   Strafford.
Volunteered to go to Plattsburgh,
September, 1814, and served 4 days
in Capt. Cyril Chandler's Company.
Ref: Book 52, AGO Page 42.

*SMITH, WALTER, Ensign.
Served in 3 Regt. (Williams') Vt.
Militia.

*SMITH, WILLIAM.
Served with Hospital Attendants, Vt.

SMITH, WILLIAM,   Franklin County.
Volunteered to go to Plattsburgh
Sept. 11, 1814. and served in 15th or
22nd Regt. Ref: Hemenway's Vt.
Gazetteer, Vol. 2, Page 391.

SMITH, WILLIAM,   St. Albans.
Enlisted June 24, 1813 for 1 year in
Capt. John Wires' Company, 30th
Regt. Ref: R. & L. 1812, AGO Page
40.

*SMITH, WILLIAM, Corporal.
Served in Capt. Bingham's Company.
Col. Jonathan Williams' Regt. Detached Militia in U. S. service 2
month and 9 days, 1812.

SMITH, WILLIAM.
Served in War of 1812 and was cap-
tured by troops Sept. 10, 1814 at
Plattsburgh; discharged Oct. 8, 1814.
Ref: Records of Naval Records and
Library, Navy Dept.

*SMITH, WILLIAM, Ensign and Sergeant,
Stowe. Volunteered to go to Plattsburgh, September, 1814, and was at
battle, serving in Capt. Nehemiah
Perkins' Company, 4 Regt. (Peck's).
Served as Sergeant in Corning's Detachment, Vt. Militia.

*SMITH, WILLIAM, Drummer.
Served from Sept. 25 to Sept. 30,
1813 in Capt. Amos Robinson's Company, Dixon's Regt.

SMITH, WILLIAM, Sergeant.
Served in Capt. Weeks. Company,
11th Regt.; on Pay Roll for January
and February, 1813. Ref: R. & L.
1812, AGO Page 5.

SMITH, WILLIAM.
Served in Lt. Wm. S. Foster's Com-
pany, 11th Regt.; on Pay Roll for
January and February, 1813. Ref:
R. & L. 1812, AGO Page 7.

SMITH, WILLIAM, Sergeant, Tunbridge
or Strafford. Volunteered to go to
Plattsburgh, September, 1814, and
served 4 days in Capt. Ephraim
Hackett's Company. Ref: Book 52,
AGO Pages 71 and 73.

SMITH, WILLIAM.
Served from April 4 to July 3, 1813
in Capt. Charles Follett's Company,
11th Regt. Ref: R. & L. 1812, AGO
Page 13.

SMITH, WILLIAM.
Served in Capt. Alexander Brooks'
Corps of Artillery; on Pay Roll to
June 30, 1814. Ref: R. & L. 1812,
AGO Page 31.

SMITH, WILLIAM.
Served in War of 1812 and was cap-
tured by troops Sept. 17, 1814 at
Fort Erie; discharged Nov. 8, 1814.
Ref: Records of Naval Records and
Library, Navy Dept.

SMITH, WILLIAM.
Served from April 28, 1813 to April
28, 1814 in Capt. Simeon Wright's
Company. Ref: R. & L. 1812, AGO
Page 51.

SMITH, WILLIAM.   Jericho.
Took part in the battle of Plattsburgh. Ref: History of Jericho, Page
142.

SMITH, WILLIAM N., Carpenter.
Served from June 10 to 30, 1814 in
Alexander Parris' Company of Arti-
ficers. Ref: R. & L. 1812, AGO
Page 24.

*SMITH, WINDSOR.
Served in Capt. Adams' Company.
Col. Jonathan Williams' Regt. Detached Militia in U. S. service 1
month and 16 days, 1812.

*SMITH, ZENAS.
Served from April 12 to May 20,
1814 in Capt. George Fisher's Company, Sumner's' Regt.

SMYTH, HAROLD, 1st Lieutenant.
Served in Capt. Alexander Brooks'
Corps of Artillery; on Pay Roll to
June 30, 1814. Ref: R. & L. 1812,
AGO Page 31.

SNEFFIELD, JOSEPH.
Served in company of late Capt. J.
Brooks, commanded by Lt. John I.
Cromwell, Corps of U. S. Artillery;
on Muster Roll from April 30 to June
30, 1814; prisoner of War on parole;
transferred from Capt. Leonard's
Company. Ref: R. & L. 1812, AGO
Page 18.

‡*SNELL, JOHN.
Served from April 12 to May 20,
1814 in Capt. George Fisher's Company, Sumner's Regt. Pension Certificate of widow, Susan, No. 29025.

*SNELL, WINSLOW.
Served from April 12 to April 15,
1814 in Capt. John Hackett's Company, Sumner's Regt.

SNIDER, JOHN,   Huntington.
Volunteered to go to Plattsburgh,
September, 1814. Ref: Book 51, AGO
Page 277.

SNOW, ADAM.
Served in Capt. Adams' Company.
Col. Jonathan Williams' Regt. Detached Militia in U. S. service 2
months and 6 days, 1812. Ref: Book
53, AGO Page 31.

*SNOW, ADEN.
Served in Capt. Durkee's Company,
Col. Fifield's Regt. Detached Militia
in U. S. service 5 months and 25
days, 1812.

‡*SNOW, ALDEN.
Served in Capt. Adams' Company, 3
Regt. (Williams') Vt. Militia. Also
served in Capt. White's Company.
Pension Certificate No. 1194. Pension
Certificate of widow, Matilda, No.
30678.

SNOW, AMASA, Sergeant,   Shoreham.
Enlisted as a sergeant and served
under Wilkinson on the St. Lawrence
and in the battles of the Niagara
frontier. (Was a brother of Eli
Snow.) Ref: Rev. J. F. Goodhue's
History of Shoreham, Page 102.

SNOW, BERNICE.
Served from March 17 to June 16,
1813 in Capt. Edgerton's Company,
11th Regt. Ref: R. & L. 1812, AGO
Page 3.

*SNOW, CYRUS.
Served in Capt. Burnap's Company,
Col. Jonathan Williams' Regt. Detached Militia in U. S. service 2
months and 13 days, 1812.

SNOW, DANIEL, Dover or Wilmington.
Served in Capt. Hopkins' Company,
Col. Martindale's Regt. Detached Mili-
tia in U. S. service 2 months and
13 days, 1812. Ref: Book 53, AGO
Page 25.

*SNOW, EBEN, Quartermaster Sergeant.
Served in 3 Regt. (Williams') Vt.
Militia.

‡*SNOW, EBENEZER.
Served in Capt. Burnap's Company,
Col. Jonathan Williams' Regt. De-
tached Militia in ·U. S. service 2
months and 12 days, 1812. Pension
Certificate of widow, Polly, No. 4728.

SNOW, ELI,   Shoreham.
Served from Feb. 2 to Feb. 28, 1813
in Capt. Samuel H. Holly's Company,
11th Regt.; acted as recruiting sergeant and saw no active service. Died
in Shoreham. (Was a brother of
Amasa Snow.) Ref: R. & L. 1812,
AGO Page 25; Rev. J. F. Goodhue's
History of Shoreham, Page 102.

*SNOW, ELI A.
Served in Capt. Wheeler's Company,
Col. Fifield's Regt. Detached Militia
in U. S. service 2 months and 1 day,.
1812.

SNOW, ELIJAH.
Enlisted May 29, 1813 for 1 year in·
Capt. Daniel Farrington's Company,
30th Regt. (also commanded by Capt.
Simeon Wright); on Muster Roll from
March 1 to April 30, 1814. Ref: R.
& L. 1812, Pages 50 and 51.

*SNOW, EZRA JR.
Served from April 12 to May 20,
1814 in Capt. George Fisher's Company, Sumner's Regt. Volunteered to·
go to Plattsburgh, September, 1814,
and served 6 days in Capt. Samuel
Hand's Company.

SNOW, JOSEPH,   Wilmington.
Served from Feb. 12 to May 11, 1813
in Capt. Samul Gordon's Company,
11th Regt. Ref: R. & L. 1812, AGO·
Page 8.

SNOW, PLINY H.,   St. Albans.
Enlisted May 6, 1813 for 1 year in
Capt. John Wires, Company, 30th
Regt. Ref: R. & L. 1812, AGO Page
40.

*SNOW, SAMUEL, Corporal.
Served in Capt. Phelps' Company,
Col. Jonathan Williams' Regt. Detached Militia in U. S. service 2·
months and 21 days, 1812.

SNYDER, GEORGE R.
Served in Capt. Haig's Corps of Light
Dragoons; on Pay Roll to June 30,
1814. Ref: R. & L. 1812, AGO Page·
20.

*SNYDER, JACOB.
Served in 1 Regt. (Judson's) Vt.
Militia.

*SNYDER, JOHN.
Served in 3 Regt. (Tyler's) Vt. Mili--
tia

*SNYDER, JONATHAN.
Served in 3 Regt. (Tyler's) Vt. Mili--
tia

*SNYDER, JOSEPH.
Served in 1 Regt. (Judson's) Vt.
Militia.

*SOPER, BENJAMIN.
Served from April 12 to April 21,.
1814 in Capt. Eseck Sprague's Company and Lieut. James S. Morton's
Company, Col. W. B. Sumner's Regt.

*SOPER, ENOS, Sergeant.
Served in Capt. Robbins' Company,
Col. Wm. Williams' Regt. Detached
Militia in U. S. service 3 months and
25 days, 1812, at Swanton Falls.

*SOPER, ERASTUS.
Served from Sept. 23 to Oct. 1, 1813
in Capt. Amasa Mansfield's Company,
Dixon's Regt.

SOPER, JESSE,   Brandon.
Volunteered to go to Plattsburgh,
September. 1814, and served 8 days·
in Capt. Micah Brown's Company.
Ref: Book 52, AGO Page 132.

*SOPER, JOSEPH.
Enlisted Sept. 20, 1813 in Capt. John
Weed's Company, Col. Clark's Rifle
Corps; transferred to Capt. Mans-
field's Company, Col. Dixon's Regt.
Detached Militia in U. S. service 1
month and 23 days.

*SOPER, JOSIAH.
Served in Col. Clark's Rifle Corps
from September to November, 1813.

SOPER, MOSES.
Served from April 19, 1813 to April
19, 1814 in Capt. Daniel Farrington's
Company, 30th Regt. (also command-
ed by Capt. Simeon Wright). Ref:
R. & L. 1812, AGO Pages 50 and 51.

‡*SOPER, REMEMBER E.
Enlisted Sept. 23, 1813 and served 1
month and 23 days in Capt. Amasa
Mansfield's Company, Col. Dixon's
Regt. Detached Militia in U. S. serv-
ice. Pension Certificate No. 28344.

*SOULE, CHARLES W.
Served in Capt. Adams' Company,
Col. Jonathan Williams' Regt. Detached Militia in U. S. service 2
months and 7 days, 1812.

SOULE, HENRY,   Fairfax.
Served in 1813 and 1814 in Capt.
Joseph Beeman's Company. Ref: Hemenway's Vt. Gazetteer, Vol. 2, Page
402.

SOULE, JOSEPH,   Fairfield.
Volunteered to go to Plattsburgh,
September, 1814, and served 8 days
in Capt. Benjamin Wooster's Company. Ref: Book 51, AGO Pages 120,
170, 171, 182.

*SOULE, SALMON.
Enlisted Oct. 30, 1813 in Capt. Asahel
Langworthy's Company, Col. Isaac
Clark's Regt. or Col. Dixon's Regt.
Detached Militia in U. S. service and
served 18 days.

‡*SOULE, SALMON 2nd.   Fairfield.
Served 1 month and 23 days, 1813,
in Capt. Follet's Company, Col. Dixon's Regt. Detached Militia in U. S.
service. Volunteered to go to Plattsburgh, September, 1814, and served 8
days in Capt. Benjamin Wooster's
Company. Pension Certificate No.
19721. Pension Certificate of widow,
Salina B., No. 34344.

SOULE, TIMOTHY,   Fairfield.
Volunteered to go to Plattsburgh,
September, 1814, and served 5 days
in Capt. Benjamin Wooster's Company. Ref: Book 51, AGO Page 179.

‡*SOUTHARD, MOSES.
Served in Capt. Robbins' Company,
Col. Wm. Williams' Regt. Detached
Militia in U. S. service 4 months
and 29 days, 1812. Also served in
Capt. Howard's Company. Pension
Certificate No. 20667. Pension Certi-
ficate of widow, Phebe, No. 28325.

SOUTHARD, PRESSON,   Ira.
Volunteered to go to Plattsburgh,
September, 1814, and served 4 days
in Capt. Matthew Anderson's Company. Ref: Book 52, AGO Page 144.

*SOUTHERLAND, PETER.
Served in Capt. Scovell's Company,
Col. Martindale's Regt. Detached
Militia in U. S. service 1 month and
27 days, 1812.

*SOUTHWARD, ELIJAH.
Served from April 12 to May 20, 1814
in company of Capt. James Gray
Jr., Sumner's Regt.

*SOUTHWARD, JOSIAH.
Served in 2 Regt. (Fifield's) Vt. Militia.

SOUTHWARD, WILLIAM.
Served in company of late Capt. J.
Brooks, commanded by Lt. John I.
Cromwell, Corps of U. S. Artillery;
on Muster Roll from April 30 to June
30, 1814; prisoner of war on parole;
transferred from Capt. Leonard's
Company. Ref: R. & L. 1812, AGO
Page 18.

SOUTHWICK, CALEB.
Served from April 25, 1813 to April
26, 1814 in Capt. Gideon Spencer's
Company and Capt. James Taylor's
Company, 30th Regt. Ref: R. & L.
1812, AGO Pages 52, 57, 59.

SOUTHWICK, JAMES, East Montpelier.
Volunteered to go to Plattsburgh,
September, 1814, and served 5 days;
no organization given. Ref: Book
52, AGO Page 174.

*SOUTHWORTH, ALBA, Corporal.
Served in 4 Regt. (Williams') Vt.
Militia.

SOUTHWORTH, ASA, Corporal.
Volunteered to go to Plattsburgh,
September, 1814, and served 4 days
in Capt. Aaron Kidder's Company.
Ref: Book 52, AGO Page 65.

‡SOUTHWORTH, ELEAZAR.
Served in Capt. Kidder's Company.
Pension Certificate of widow, Ame,
No. 26343.

SOUTHWORTH, ELIOM.
Volunteered to go to Plattsburgh,
September, 1814, and served 4 days
in Capt. Aaron Kidder's Company.
Ref: Book 52, AGO Page 65.

SOUTHWORTH, IRA.
Volunteered to go to Plattsburgh,
September, 1814, and served 4 days
in Capt. Aaron Kidder's Company.
Ref: Book 52, AGO Page 65.

SOUTHWORTH, JOSIAH.
Volunteered to go to Plattsburgh,
September, 1814, and went as far as
Bolton, Vt., serving 4 days in Lt.
Phineus Kimball's Company, West
Fairlee. Ref: Book 52, AGO Pages
46 and 47.

*SOUTHWORTH, JOSIAH.
Served under Captains Walker and
Taylor, Col. Fifield's Regt. Detached
Militia in U. S. service 6 months.

SOUTHWORTH, JOSIAH.
Volunteered to go to Plattsburgh,
September, 1814, and served 4 days
in Capt. Aaron Kidder's Company.
Ref: Book 52, AGO Page 65.

*SOUTHWORTH. LUTHER.
Served in Capt. Walker's Company, Col. Fifield's Regt. Detached Militia in U. S. service 1 month and 20 days, 1812. Served in Capt. Weeks' Company, 11th Regt.; on Pay Roll for January and February, 1813; discharged Jan. 22, 1813. Ref: R. & L. 1812, AGO Page 5.

SOUTHWORTH, SETH A.
Volunteered to go to Plattsburgh, September, 1814, and served 4 days in Capt. Aaron Kidder's Company. Ref: Book 51, AGO Page 201; Book 52, AGO Page 65.

*SPAFFORD, OMRI.
Enlisted Sept. 25, 1813 in Capt. Charles Bennett's Company, Dixon's Regt.

SPAFFORD, SAMUEL, Lieutenant.
Appointed Sergeant 23rd Inf. March 26, 1813; Ensign Dec. 2, 1813; 2nd Lieutenant Sept. 1, 1814; honorably discharged June 15, 1815. Ref: Heitman's Historical Register & Dictionary USA.

*SPALDIN, CALVIN.
Served in 1 Regt. (Judson's) Vt. Militia.

SPALDING, ALVA, Musician, Morristown.
Volunteered to go to Plattsburgh, September, 1814, and served 8 days in Capt. Denison Cook's Company. Ref: Book 51, AGO Page 202.

*SPALDING, ANDREW.
Served from Oct. 11 to Oct. 17, 1813 in Capt. John Munson's Company, 3 Regt. (Tyler's).

SPALDING, EQUILLA,   Morristown.
Volunteered to go to Plattsburgh, September, 1814, and served 8 days in Capt. Denison Cook's Company. Ref: Book 51, AGO Pages 202 and 206.

SPALDING, BARSILLA, Corporal, Morristown. Volunteered to go to Plattsburgh, September, 1814, and served 8 days in Capt. Denison Cook's Company. Ref: Book 51, AGO Pages 202 and 206.

SPALDING, BEZABELL, Fifer, Roxbury.
Volunteered to go to Plattsburgh, September, 1814, and served 8 days in Capt. Samuel M. Orcutt's Company. Ref: Book 52, AGO Page 250.

SPALDING, DARIUS,   Roxbury.
Volunteered to go to Plattsburgh, September, 1814, and served 7 days in Capt. Samuel M. Orcutt's Company. Ref: Book 52, AGO Page 250.

SPALDING, DARIUS JR.,   Roxbury.
Volunteered to go to Plattsburgh, September, 1814, and served 7 days in Capt. Samuel M. Orcutt's Company. Ref: Book 52, AGO Pages 166 and 250.

SPALDING, GILBERT R., Lieutenant, Roxbury. Volunteered to go to Plattsburgh, September, 1814, and served in Capt. Samuel M. Orcutt's Company. Ref: Hemenway's Vt. Gazetteer, Vol. 4, Page 753.

SPALDING, JARED,   Swanton.
Volunteered to go to Plattsburgh, September, 1814; no organization given. Ref: Book 51, AGO Page 146.

*SPALDING, JEREMIAH.
Served from April 12 to April 21, 1814 in Capt. Othniel Jewett's Company, Sumner's Regt.

SPALDING, JOHN,   Panton.
Volunteered to go to Plattsburgh, September, 1814, and served 3 days; no organization given. Ref: Book 51, AGO Page 31.

‡SPALDING, JOHN M.,   Roxbury.
Volunteered to go to Plattsburgh, September, 1814, and served 7 days in Capt. Samuel M. Orcutt's Company. Pension Certificate of widow, Betsey, No. 37245.

*SPALDING, LEVI, Sergeant, Morristown.
Volunteered to go to Plattsburgh, September, 1814, and served 8 days in Capt. Denison Cook's Company. Served 8 days in April, 1814, as Ensign in Col. John Peck's Regt.; marched to Burlington.

*SPALDING, MARK.
Served in 4 Regt. (Peck's) Vt. Militia.

‡*SPALDING, MICAH.
Served in 4 Regt. (Peck's) Vt. Militia. Also served in Capt. Campbell's Company. Pension Certificate No. 18725.

*SPALDING, NATHAN, Lieutenant.
Served in 4 Regt. (Williams') Vt. Militia.

SPALDING, NATHAN, Lieutenant, Vergennes. Appointed 3rd Lieutenant 30th Inf. April 30, 1813; 2nd Lieutenant Jan. 31, 1814; dismissed Jan. 13, 1815. Volunteered to go to Plattsburgh, September, 1814, and was in the battle, serving 10 days in Capt. Gideon Spencer's Company. Ref: Heitman's Historical Register & Dictionary USA; Book 51, AGO Page 1.

‡SPALDING, NOAH.
Served in Capt. Stewart's Company. Pension Certificate No. 13296.

SPARHAWK, JUSTIN,   Richmond.
Volunteered to go to Plattsburgh, September, 1814, and served 9 days in Capt. Roswell Hunt's Company, 3 Regt. (Tyler's). Ref: Book 51, AGO Page 82.

*SPARKS, HARVEY.
Served from April 12 to April 15, 1814 in Capt. Jonathan P. Stanley's Company, Col. W. B. Sumner's Regt.

*SPARKS. JOHN,   Dover.
Served in Capt. Preston's Company, Col. Jonathan Williams' Regt. Detached Militia in U. S. service 2 months and 6 days, 1812.

‡SPAULDING, DANIEL.
Served in Capt. A. Scovill's Company. Pension Certificate No. 25117. Pension Certificate of widow, Isabel, No. 28631.

.SPAULDING, GILBERT R., Lieutenant, Roxbury. Volunteered to go to Plattsburgh, September, 1814, and served 7 days in Capt. Samuel M. Orcutt's Company. Ref: Book 52, AGO Pages 181 and 250.

*SPAULDING, IRA.
Served from April 12 to April 21, 1814 in Capt. Shubael Wales' Company, Col. W. B. Sumner's Regt. Also served in Capt. Salmon Foster's Company.

‡SPAULDING, ISAAC.
Served in Capt. G. Spencer's Company. Pension Certificate of widow, Phebe, No. 28601.

‡SPAULDING, JAMES.
Served in Capt. Spencer's Company. Pension Certificate of widow, Mandana, No. 22488.

*SPAULDING, JARED.
Served in Capt. L. Robinson's Company, Col. Dixon's Regt. Detached Militia in U. S. service 27 days, 1813.

*SPAULDING, JEDEDIAH.
Served in Capt. Rogers' Company, Col. Fifield's Regt. Detached Militia in U. S. service 5 months and 27 days, 1812.

‡*SPAULDING, JEREMIAH.
Served in Capt. Robbins' Company, Col. Wm. Williams' Regt. Detached Militia in U. S. service 4 months and 29 days, 1812. Pension Certificate of widow, Catharine, No. 5972.

*SPAULDING, JOSIAH, Drummer.
Served in Sumner's Regt. Vt. Militia.

‡SPAULDING, OZIAS, Morristown.
Volunteered to go to Plattsburgh, September, 1814, and served 3 days in Capt. Denison Cook's Company. Pension Certificate of widow, Caroline, No. 11843.

*SPAULDING, THOMAS, Fifer, Georgia.
Served in Capt. Saxe's Company, Col. Wm. Williams' Regt. Detached Militia in U. S. service 3 months and 20 days, 1812. Enlisted Oct. 1, 1813 in Capt. Elijah W. Wood's Company, Dixon's Regt.

.SPAULDING, THOMAS.
Served in Lt. Wm. S. Foster's Company, 11th Regt.; on Pay Roll for January and February, 1813. Ref: R. & L. 1812, AGO Page 7.

*SPEAR, ASAHEL, ENSIGN.
Served from June 11 to June 14, 1813 in Capt. Samuel Blinn's Company, 1 Regt. (Judson's).

*SPEAR, ARAM (Auron).
Served from June 11 to June 14, 1813 in Capt. Moses Jewett's Company, 1st Regt. 2nd Brig. 3rd Div.

:SPEAR, BENJAMIN, Corporal, Braintree.
Marched to Plattsburgh Sept. 10, 1814 and served 10 days in Capt. Lot Hudson's Company. Ref: Book 51, AGO Page 295; Book 52, AGO Pages .24 and 33.

*SPEAR, BARNABAS JR.
Served from June 11 to June 14, 1813 in Capt. Moses Jewett's Company, 1st Regt. 2nd Brig. 3rd Div.

‡SPEAR, CHARLES, Charlotte.
Volunteered to go to Plattsburgh, September, 1814, and served 10 days in Major Luman Judson's command. Also served in Capt. Kinney's Company. Pension Certificate of widow, Anna L., No. 28370. Ref: Book 51, AGO Page 80.

‡SPEAR, EBENEZER.
Served in Capt. Partridge's Company. Pension Certificate No. 12982.

*SPEAR, ELIAS, Musician.
Served in 1 Regt. (Judson's) Vt. Militia.

‡*SPEAR, FRANCIS.
Served from June 11 to June 14, 1813 in Capt. Thomas Dorwin's Company. 1st Regt. 2nd Brig. 3rd Div. Also served in Capt. Kinney's Company. Pension Certificate No. 21380.

*SPEAR, IRA.
Served in Capt. Morrill's Company, Col. Fifield's Regt. Detached Militia in U. S. service 3 months and 17 days, 1812.

*SPEAR, JACOB (John Edson, Substitute), Sergeant, Braintree. Served in Capt. Wright's Company, Col. Fifield's Regt. Detached Militia in U. S. service 6 months, 1812.

SPEAR, JACOB.
Volunteered to go to Plattsburgh, September, 1814, and served in Capt. Ebenezer Spencer's Company, Vershire. Ref: Book 52, AGO Page 48.

*SPEAR, MOSES.
Served from June 11 to June 14, 1813 in Capt. Moses Jewett's Company, 1st Regt. 2nd Brgi. 3rd Div.

SPEAR, SEVA.
Volunteered to go to Plattsburgh, September, 1814, and served in Capt. Ebenezer Spencer's Company, Vershire. Ref: Book 52, AGO Page 48.

SPEAR, SILAS, Barre.
Volunteered to go to Plattsburgh, September, 1814, and served in Capt. Warren Ellis' Company. Ref: Hemenway's Vt. Gazetteer, Vol. 4, Page 41.

‡*SPEAR, STEPHEN, Braintree.
Served in Capt. Wheatly's Company, Col. Fifield's Regt. Detached Militia in U. S. service 2 months and 21 days, 1812. Volunteered to go to Plattsburgh, September, 1814, and served in Capt. Lot Hudson's Company. Pension Certificate No. 1930. Pension Certificate of widow, Delia M., No. 11119.

*SPEAR, WILLIAM.
Served in Capt. Rogers' Company, Col. Fifield's Regt. Detached Militia in U. S. service 5 months and 27 days, 1812.

SPENCER, ABEL,   Ira.
Volunteered to go to Plattsburgh, September, 1814, and served 4 days in Capt. Matthew Anderson's Company. Ref: Book 52, AGO Page 144.

*SPENCER, CALVIN.
Served from April 12 to April 21, 1814 in Capt. Othniel Jewett's Company, Col. W. B. Sumner's Regt. Detached Militia in U. S. service.

*SPENCER, CHARLES.
Served from April 12 to May 20, 1814 in Capt. George Fisher's Company, Sumner's Regt.

SPENCER, EBEZENER, Captain.
Volunteered to go to Plattsburgh, September, 1814, and served 8 days in command of company raised in Vershire and Corinth. Ref: Book 52. AGO Pages 48, 49, 120.

SPENCER, ELIHU.
Served in Capt. Weeks' Company, 11th Regt.; on Pay Roll for January and February, 1813. Ref: R. & L. 1812, AGO Page 5.

SPENCER, ETHAN,   Williston.
Served from Sept. 1, 1814 to June 16, 1815 in Capt. Sanford's Company, 30th Inf. Ref: R. & L. 1812, AGO Page 23.

‡SPENCER, EZRA.   Pittsford.
Volunteered to go to Plattsburgh, September, 1814, and served 8 days in Capt. Caleb Hendee's Company. Pension Certificate No. 32939.

SPENCER, FRANKLIN.
Served from March 18 to June 17, 1813 in Capt. Samul Gordon's Company, 11th Regt. Ref: R. & L. 1812, AGO Page 8.

SPENCER, GIDEON JR., Captain.
Appointed Captain 30th Inf. April 30, 1813; resigned June 23, 1814. Ref: Heitman's Historical Register & Dictionary USA; R. & L. 1812, AGO Page 56.

*SPENCER, GOSHUM S. (or Gersham).
1st Sergeant. Enlisted Sept. 20, 1813 in Capt. John Weed's Company, Col. Clark's Rifle Corps.

SPENCER, GUSTAVUS, Franklin County.
Volunteered to go to Plattsburgh Sept. 11, 1814 and served in 15th or 22nd Regt. Ref: Hemenway's Vt. Gazetteer, Vol. 2, Page 391.

SPENCER, HENRY, Sergeant.
Enlisted June 22, 1814 during the war in Capt. Miller's Company, 30th Regt. Ref: R. & L. 1812, AGO Pages 1 and 54.

SPENCER, JOHN JR.,   Marshfield.
Volunteered to go to Plattsburgh, September, 1814, and served 9 days in Capt. James English's Company. Ref: Book 52, AGO Pages 248 and 195.

‡*SPENCER, JONATHAN B.
Served from April 12 to April 21, 1814 in Capt. Othniel Jewett's Company, Sumner's' Regt. Pension Certificate No. 11280. Pension Certificate of widow, Mary, No. 26724, shows service in Capt. Robbins' Company.

‡SPENCER, JOSEPH G.
Served in Capt. Bingham's Company. Pension Certificate of widow, Persis, No. 7173.

*SPENCER, LEWIS,   Randolph.
Volunteered to go to Plattsburgh, September, 1814, and served in Capt. Lebbeus Egerton's Company.

SPENCER, OBEDIAH.
Enlisted June 14, 1813 for 5 years in company of late Capt. J. Brooks, commanded by Lt. John I. Cromwell, Corps of U. S. Artillery; served to May 18, 1814. Ref: R. & L. 1812, AGO Page 18.

*SPENCER, PHINEAS.
Enlisted Sept. 20, 1813 in Capt. John Weed's Company, Col. Clark's Rifle Corps.

SPENCER, ROBERT,   Marshfield.
Volunteered to go to Plattsburgh, September, 1814, and served 9 days in Capt. James English's Company. Ref: Book 52, AGO Page 248.

*SPENCER, STEPHEN.
Served from April 12 to May 20, 1814 in Capt. George Fisher's Company, Sumner's Regt.

*SPENCER, STEPHEN W., Sergeant.
Served in Capt. Phelps' Company, Col. Wm. Williams' Regt. Detached Militia in U. S. service at Swanton Falls 5 months, 1812.

SPENCER, WILLIAM, Waggoner, Pittsford. Volunteered to go to Plattsburgh, September, 1814, and served 8 days in Capt. Caleb Hendee's Company. Ref: Book 52, AGO Page 125.

SPERRY, JACOB.
Served in Capt. Weeks' Company, 11th Regt.; on Pay Roll for January and February, 1813. Ref: R. & L. 1812, AGO Page 5.

*SPINK; WHITMAN.
Served in Capt. Cross' Company, Col. Martindale's' Regt. Detached Militia in U. S. service 2 months and 14 days, 1812.

*SPOONER, BARNEY,   Richmond.
Served from Oct. 5, to Oct. 16, 1813 in Capt. Roswell Hunt's Company, 3 Regt. (Tyler's); volunteered to go to Plattsburgh, September, 1814, and served 9 days in same company.

*SPOONER, BARNIA.
Served in Corning's Detachment, Vt. Militia.

SPOONER, BENJAMIN.
Enlisted Aug. 1, 1813 for 1 year in Capt. James Taylor's Company, 30th Regt.; died at Richmond, November, 1813. Ref: R. & L. 1812, AGO Pages 52 and 59.

*SPOONER, GARDNER.
Served in Capt. Phelps' Company,
Col. Jonathan Williams' Regt. Detached Militia in U. S. service 2
months and 21 days, 1812.

SPOONER, ISAAC,   Woodstock.
Enlisted Feb. 12, 1813 in Capt. Phineas
Williams' Company, 11th Regt.; on
Pay Roll to May 31, 1813. Ref: R.
& L. 1812, AGO Page 14.

SPOONER, JOSHUA,   Poultney.
Volunteered to go to Plattsburgh,
September, 1814, and served 2 days
in Capt. Briant Ransom's Company.
Ref: Book 52, AGO Page 147.

SPOONER, LEMUEL,   Woodstock.
Served in Capt. Phineas Williams'
Company, 11th Regt.; on Pay Roll
for January and February, 1813. Ref:
R. & L. 1812, AGO Page 15.

*SPOONER, REMEY.
Served in 3 Regt. (Tyler's) Vt. Militia.

‡SPOOR, ALMOND.
Served in Capt. Levenworth's Company. Pension Certificate No. 21381.

*SPOOR, ISAAC.
Enlisted Sept. 25, 1813 in Capt. Amos
Robinson's Company, Dixon's Regt.

SPRAGUE, BELA, Corporal.
Served from Nov. 1, 1812 to Feb. 28,
1813 in Capt. Phineas Williams' Company, 11th Regt. Ref: R. & L. 1812,
AGO Page 15.

SPRAGUE, DURHAM, Captain, Clarendon.
Volunteered to go to Plattsburgh,
September, 1814, and served 7 days
in command of company from Clarendon. Ref: Book 52, AGO Page 128.

‡SPRAGUE, ELI A.
Served in Capt. Pittbone's Company.
Pension Certificate No. 25187.

SPRAGUE, ELIAKIM,   Salisbury.
Served in Capt. Samuel H. Holly's
Company, 11th Regt.; on Pay Roll
for January and Februray, 1813. Ref:
R. & L. 1812, AGO Page 25.

*SPRAGUE, ESECK JR.,Captain.
Served from April 12 to April 27,
1814 in Sumner's Regt.

SPRAGUE, FRED A.
Served from May 1 to June 30, 1814
as a carpenter in Alexander Parris'
Company of Artificers. Ref: R. & L.
1812, AGO Page 24.

*SPRAGUE, HEMAN.
Served in 2 Regt. (Fifield's) Vt. Militia.

‡*SPRAGUE, HORACE.
Served from April 12 to April 21,
1814 in Capt. Eseck Sprague's Company, Sumner's Regt. Pension Certificate of widow, Zurviah, No. 29208.

‡SPRAGUE, HORATIO.
Served in Capt. Samuel H. Holly's
Company, 11th Regt.; on Pay Roll
for January and February, 1813. Also

served in Capt. Hanley's Company.
Pension Certificate No. 16309. Ref:
R. & L. 1812, AGO Page 25.

*SPRAGUE, ISIAH.
Served in Capt. Phelps' Company,
Col. Wm. Williams' Regt. Detached
Militia in U. S. service 5 months,
1812.

SPRAGUE, JEREMIAH.
Served in Capt. Samuel H. Holly's
Company, 11th Regt.; on Pay Roll
for January and February, 1813. Ref:
R. & L. 1812, AGO Page 25.

*SPRAGUE, MENASSAH (or Manossett).
Served from June 11 to June 14, 1813
in Capt. John M. Eldridge's Company,
1st Regt. 2nd Brig. 3rd Div.

*SPRAGUE, PARDON, Corporal.
Served in Capt. Dorrance's Company,
Col. Wm. Williams' Regt. Detached
Militia in U. S. service 4 months
and 29 days, 1812.

‡*SPRAGUE, RODOLPHUS, Corporal.
Served in Capt. Briggs' Company,
Col. Jonathan Williams' Regt. Detached Militia in U. S. service 2
months and 13 days, 1812. Pension
Certificate No. 531.

SPRAGUE, WILLIAM.
Served in Capt. Dodge's Company,
Col. Fifield's Regt. Detached Militia
in U. S. service 2 months and 21
days, 1812. Ref: Book 53, AGO Page
37.

SPRATT, JAMES.
Served in Capt. Haig's Corps of
Light Dragoons; on Pay Roll to June
30, 1814. Ref: R. & L. 1812, AGO
Page 20.

SPRAY, FRANCIS.
Served from June 11 to June 14, 1813
in Capt. Thomas Dorwin's Company,
1st Regt. 2nd Brig. 3rd Div. Ref:
R. & L. 1812, AGO Page 46.

SPRIGGS, LEVEN, Sergeant.
Served in company of late Capt. J.
Brooks, commanded by Lt. John I.
Cromwell, Corps of U. S. Artillery;
on Muster Roll from April 30 to June
30, 1814; prisoner of war; transferred from Capt. Leonard's Company.
Ref: R. & L. 1812, AGO Page 18.

SPRIGS, GEORGE, Seaman.
Captured by Earl Moira Aug. 10, 1813
on Lake Ontario; discharged Sept.
21st. Ref: Records of Naval Records
and Library, Navy Dept.

‡SPRING, SAMUEL H.
Served in Capt. F. Kebbens' Company. Pension Certificate No. 28943.

*SPROUT, ELI W., Corporal.
Served in Capt. Durkee's Company,
Col. Fifield's Regt. Detached Militia
in U. S. service 2 months and 24
days, 1812.

*SPURS, CHARLES.
Served in 1 Regt. (Judson's) Vt.
Militia.

*SPURS, ELIAS, Musician.
Served in 1 Regt. (Judson's) Vt.
Militia.

‡SQUIRE, HOSEA.
Served in Capt. Wright's Company.
Pension Certificate No. 20498.

*SQUIRE, RUBEN.
Served from Oct. 5 to Oct. 16, 1813
in Capt. Roswell Hunt's Company, 3
Regt. (Tyler's).

SQUIRES, DANIEL.
Served from April 12 to May 20, 1814
in Capt. George Fisher's Company,
Sumner's Regt. Ref: Book 52, AGO
Page 277.

‡*SQUIRES, EZEKIEL.
Served from Oct. 5 to Oct. 8, 1813
in Capt. Roswell Hunt's Company, 3
Regt. (Tyler's). Also served in Capt.
Talcott's Company. Pension Certifi-
cate of widow, Percy, No. 27384.
Ref: R. & L. 1812, AGO Page 41.

*STACKHOUSE, BENJAMIN.
Served in 1 Regt. (Judson's) Vt.
Militia.

STACKPOLE, SAMUEL.
Enlisted Jan. 1, 1813 in Capt. Edger-
ton's Company, 11th Regt. Ref: R.
& L. 1812, AGO Page 3.

STACKWELL, LUTHER L.
Served in War of 1812 and was captured by troops July 25, 1814 at
Londers Lane; discharged Oct. 8,
1814. Ref: Records of Naval Records
and Library, Navy Dept.

STACY, ASAHEL,   Huntington.
Volunteered to go to Plattsburgh,
September, 1814, and was at the
battle, serving in Capt. Josiah N.
Barrows' Company. Ref: Book 51,
AGO Page 77.

STACY, CHARLES H.,   Orange.
Served from Feb. 1 to May 31, 1813
in Capt. Benjamin S. Edgerton's Company, 11th Regt. Ref: R. & L. 1812,
AGO Pages 2 and 3.

*STACY, JOHN JR.,   Orange.
Served in Capt. Walker's Company,
Col. Fifield's Regt. Detached Militia
in U. S. service 2 months and 24
days, 1812.

STACY, MAHLON,   Barre.
Volunteered to go to Plattsburgh,
September, 1814, and served 10 days
in Capt. Warren Ellis' Company.
Ref: Book 52, AGO Page 242.

‡STACY, WILLIAM.
Served in Capt. Culver's Company.
Pension Certificate No. 32642.

*STAFFORD, ABEL.
Served in 2 Regt. (Fifield's) Vt.
Militia.

*STAGG, JOSIAH.
Served from April 12 to April 21,
1814 in Capt. Othniel Jewett's Company, Sumner's Regt.

STALTER, JOSEPH.
Enlisted Nov. 2, 1812 for 5 years in
company of late Capt. J. Brooks, com-

manded by Lt. John I. Cromwell,
Corps of U, S. Artillery; on Muster
Roll from April 30 to June 30, 1814.
Ref: R. & L. 1812, AGO Page 18.

STAMFORD, ABEL.
Served in Capt. Mason's Company,
Col. Fifield's Regt. Detached Militia
in U. S. service 1 month and 22
days, 1812. Ref: Book 53, AGO Page
46.

STANARD, ZINA.
Served from Sept. 25 to Sept. 30,
1813 in Capt. Jesse Post's Company,
Dixon's Regt. Ref: Book 52, AGO
Page 290.

STANBURY, JNO.
Served in War of 1812 and was cap-
tured by gun boats Aug. 15, 1814 at
Fort Erie; discharged Nov. 8, 1814.
Ref: Records of Naval Records and
Library, Navy Dept.

*STANFORD, JOHN.
Served in Sumner's Regt. Vt. Militia.

STANIFORD, THOMAS, Lieutenant.
Appointed Ensign 11th Inf. Oct. 12,
1812; 2nd Lieutenant June 26, 1813;
Regimental Paymaster Dec. 20, 1813
to August, 1814; 1st Lieutenant Sept.
1, 1814; Asst. Deputy Paymaster General Aug. 26, 1814 to June 15, 1815;
died Feb. 3, 1855. Served as Ensign
in Capt. Samul Gordon's Company,
11th Regt.; on Pay Roll for January and February, 1813. Ref: Heitman's Historical Register & Dictionary USA; R. & L. 1812, AGO Page 9.

*STANLEY, ABIJAH.
Served in 3 Regt. (Williams') Vt.
Militia.

STANLEY, AQUILLA,   Tunbridge.
Volunteered to go to Plattsburgh,
September, 1814, and served 4 days
in Capt. Ephraim Hackett's Company.
Ref: Book 52, AGO Page 71.

*STANLEY, BENJAMIN, Sergeant.
Served in Capt. Bingham's Company,
Col. Jonathan Williams' Regt. Detached Militia in U. S. service 2
months and 9 days, 1812.

STANLEY, JAMES P.
Enlisted Jan. 30, 1813 in Capt. John
W. Weeks' Company, 11th Regt.;
died May 16, 1813. Ref: R. & L.
1812, AGO Page 4.

‡STANLEY, JOHN.
Served in Capt. Dickinson's Company.
Pension Certificate No. 32643.

*STANLEY, JONATHAN P., Captain.
Served from April 12 to April 15,
1814 in Col. W. B. Sumner's Regt.

‡*STANLEY, LUTHER, Drummer.
Served in Capt. Bingham's Company,
Col. Jonathan Williams' Regt. De-
tached Militia in U. S. service 2
months and 9 days, 1812. Pension
Certificate No. 14718.

STANLEY, MOSES I.
Served from March 30 to June 30,
1814 in Regt. of Light Dragoons.
Ref: R. & L. 1812, AGO Page 21.

STANLEY, NATHAN.
Served from March 30 to June 30,
1814 in Regt. of Light Dragoons.
Ref: R. & L. 1812, AGO Page 21.

*STANLEY, PHINEAS.
Served with Hospital Attendants, Vt.
Served in 3 Regt. (Williams') Vt.
Militia.

*STANLEY, ROBERT.
Served in Capt. Sabin's Company, Col.
Jonathan Williams' Regt. Detached
Militia in U. S. service 2 months
and 6 days, 1812.

*STANLEY, ROSWELL B.
Served in Capt. Wheatly's Company,
Col. Fifield's Regt. Detached Militia
in U. S. service 6 months, 1812.
Served in Regt. of Light Dragoons
from March 15 to June 30, 1814. Ref:
R. & L. 1812, AGO Page 21.

STANLEY, SAMUEL.
Enlisted Feb. 6, 1813 in Capt. Jonathan Starks' Company, 11th Regt.;
on Pay Roll to May 31, 1813. Ref:
R. & L. 1812, AGO Page 19.

STANLY, JOHN.
Served in company of Capt. John
McNeil Jr., 11th Regt.; on Pay Roll
for January and February, 1813. Ref:
R. & L. 1812, AGO Page 17.

*STANNARD, ZINA (or Fina).
Served in Dixon's Regt. Vt. Militia.

‡*STANTON, ALEXANDER.
Enlisted Sept. 25, 1813 in Capt. Jesse
Post's Company, Dixon's Regt. Pen-
sion Certificate No. 4057. Pension
Certificate of widow, Polly, No. 11379.

*STANTON, ELIJAH, Quartermaster.
Served in 4 Regt. (Williams') Vt.
Militia.

STANTON, ERASTUS,   Danville.
Volunteered to go to Plattsburgh,
September, 1814, and served 3 days
in company commanded by Capt.
James Kelsey Jr. and Capt. Solomon
Langmaid. Ref: Book 51, AGO Pages
73, 75, 76.

STANTON, HENRY, Captain.
Appointed 3rd Lieutenant Light Artil-
lery June 29, 1813; 2nd Lieutenant
March 7, 1814; Captain Asst. Deputy
Quartermaster General July 12, 1813
to May 26, 1814; died Aug. 1, 1856.
Served as 2nd Lieutenant on Gen-
eral Staff of the Northern Army com-
manded by Major General George
Izard on Pay Roll to July 31, 1814.
Ref: Heitman's Historical Register &
Dictionary USA; R. & L. 1812, AGO
Page 28.

STANTON, ISAAC W.,   Danville.
Volunteered to go to Plattsburgh,
September, 1814, and served in Capt.
Solomon Langmaid's Company. Ref:
Book 51, AGO Pages 71, 75, 76.

*STANTON, JOHN A., Lieutenant, Dan-
ville. Served in Capt. Joseph Morrill's Company, 2 Regt. (Fifield's) Vt.
Militia.

*STANTON, STEPHEN.
Served in 1 Regt. (Judson's) Vt.
Militia.

STANTON, WILLIAM,   Williamstown.
Volunteered to go to Plattsburgh,
September, 1814, and was at the
battle September 11th, serving 8 days
in Capt. David Robinson's Company.
Ref: Book 52, AGO Page 2.

STAPLES, BASTIAN J.,   Berne.
Served from May 1 to June 30, 1814
in Capt. Lynd's Company, 29th Inf.
Ref: R. & L. 1812, AGO Page 30.

STAPLES, DAVID.
Served from May 1 to June 30, 1814
in Capt. Haig's Corps of Light Dragoons. Ref: R. & L. 1812, AGO
Page 20.

*STAPLES, FOXEL.
Served in 4 Regt. (Peck's) Vt. Militia.

STAPLES, JAMES.
Served in company of Capt. John Mc-
Neil Jr., 11th Regt.; on Pay Roll
for January and February, 1813. Ref:
R. & L. 1812, AGO Page 17.

STAPLES, PETER S. P.,   Roxbury.
Volunteered to go to Plattsburgh,
September, 1814, and served 7 days
in Capt| Samuel M. Orcutt's Com-
pany. Ref: Book 52, AGO Pages 166
and 250.

*STARKE, JONATHAN.
Enlisted Sept. 14, 1813 in Capt. Isaac
Finch's Company, Col. Clark's Regt.
of Riflemen.

STARKEY, NATHAN.
Served from Dec. 1, 1813 to Aug. 11,
1814; no organization given. Ref: R.
& L. 1812, AGO Page 29.

STARKS, WILLIAM T., Sergeant, Pownal.
Served from Sept. 1, 1814 to June
16, 1815 in Capt. Sanford's Company,
30th Inf. Ref: R. & L. 1812, AGO
Page 23.

STARKWEATHER, JOHN,   Waitsfield.
Volunteered to go to Plattsburgh,
September, 1814, and served 4 days
in Capt. Mathias S. Jones' Company.
Ref: Book 52, AGO Page 170.

‡STARLING, ELISHA.
Served in Capt. Lowry's Company.
Pension Certificate No. 12375.

*STARLING, JOHN.
Served with Hospital Attendants, Vt.

‡STARLING, SIMON.
Served in Capt. Campbell's Company.
Pension Certificate No. 28384.

‡STARNS, JAMES.
Served in Capt. Saxe's Company, 4
Regt. (Williams'). Pension Certifi-
cate of widow, Mariah, No. 23204.

*STARNS, JOHN.
Served from June 11 to June 14, 1813
in Capt. John M. Eldridge's Company, 1st Regt. 2nd Brig. 3rd Div.

*STARNS, JONATHAN.
Served from June 11 to June 14, 1813
in Capt. John M. Eldridge's Company, 1st Regt. 2nd Brig. 3rd Div.

*STATED, CHAUNCEY (or Slater?)
Served in 3 Regt. (Tyler's) Vt. Militia.

STAVENS, AMMA,   West Haven.
Volunteered to go to Plattsburgh,
September, 1814, and served 4 days
in Capt. David B. Phippeney's Company. Ref: Book 52, AGO Page 146.

STEADMAN, PORTER.
Served from May 1 to June 30, 1814
in Capt. Alexander Brooks' Corps of
Artillery. Ref: R. & L. 1812, AGO
Page 31.

‡STEARNS, ABEL.
Served from March 3 to June 2, 1813
in Lieut. V. R. Goodrich's Company,
11th Regt. Pension Certificate No.
2766.

*STEARNS, AMOS.
Served in Sumner's Regt. Vt. Militia.

*STEARNS, ASA,   Waterbury.
Volunteered to go to Plattsburgh,
September, 1814, and was in the
battle, serving 11 days in Capt. George
Atkins' Company, 4 Regt. (Peck's).

*STEARNS, BATEMAN, Corporal.
Served from June 11 to June 14, 1813
in Capt. Thomas Dorwin's Company,
1st Regt. 2nd Brig. 3rd Div.

*STEARNS, BENJAMIN.
Enlisted Sept. 25, 1813 in Capt. Amos
Robinson's Company, Dixon's Regt.;
transferred to Capt. Asahel Lang-
worthy's Company, Col. Clark's Rifle
Corps Oct. 3, 1813.

STEARNS, BILLEY.
Served from Feb. 3 to May 2. 1813
in company of Capt. John McNeil
Jr., 11th Regt. Ref: R. & L. 1812,
AGO Page 16.

‡STEARNS, CALVIN.
Served in Capt. Wright's Company.
Pension Certificate of widow, Mar-
garet K., No. 41541.

‡STEARNS, CHARLES.
Served in Capt. Churchill's Company.
Pension Certificate No. 16913.

*STEARNS, DANIEL M., 1st Lieutenant.
Served in 3 Regt. (Bowdish) Vt. Militia.

*STEARNS, EBENEZER JR.
Served from April 12 to April 21,
1814 in Capt. Eseck Sprague's Company, Sumner's Regt.

STEARNS, ERASTUS, Northampton. Mass.
Enlisted at Benson, Feb. 16, 1814 dur-
ing the war and served in Capt.
William Miller's Company, and Capt.
Gideon Spencer's Company, 30th Regt.
Ref: R. & L. 1812, AGO Pages 54,
55, 56.

*STEARNS, GEORGE.
Served in 3 Regt. (Williams') Vt.
Militia.

*STEARNS, ISAAC.
Served from April 12 to April 21,
1814 in Capt. Othniel Jewett's Company, Sumner's Regt.

*STEARNS, ISRAEL.
Served in 4 Regt. (Peck's) Vt. Militia.

‡STEARNS, JAMES.
Served in Capt. Wooster's Company.
Pension Certificate No. 20682.

*STEARNS, JOHN.
Served in 1 Regt. (Judson's) Vt.
Militia.

*STEARNS, JOHN E.
Served in Capt. Sabins' Company,
Col. Jonathan Williams' Regt. Detached Militia in U. S. service 2
months and 6 days, 1812.

*STEARNS, JONATHAN.
Served in 1 Regt. (Judson's) Vt. Militia.

‡*STEARNS, JONATHAN A.
Enlisted May 10, 1814 during the war
in Capt. Gideon Spencer's Company,
30th Regt.; joined June 30, 1814.
Also served in 1 Regt. (Martindale's)
Vt. Militia and in Capt. Miller's
Company. Pension Certificate No.
6854. Ref: R. & L. 1812, AGO Page
56.

STEARNS, M., Captain,   Bakersfield.
Commanded company of volunteers at
the battle of Plattsburgh Sept. 11,
1814. Ref: Hemenway's Vt. Gazetteer, Vol. 2, Page 393.

‡*STEARNS, NATHAN, Drummer.
Served in Capt. Lowry's Company,
Col. Wm. Williams' Regt. Detached
Militia in U. S. service 4 months and
26 days, 1812. Served from Feb. 12
to May 11, 1813 in Capt. Edgerton's
Company, 11th Regt. Also served in
3 Regt. (Tyler's) Vt. Militia. Pen-
sion Certificate No. 1335. Pension
Certificate of widow, Emily, No. 28224.
Ref: R. & L. 1812, AGO Page 3.

*STEARNS, NOAH.
Served in Capt. Adams' Company,
Col. Jonathan Williams' Regt. Detached Militia in U. S. service 2
months and 6 days, 1812.

*STEARNS, PHINEAS.
Enlisted Sept. 25, 1813 and served 1
month and 23 days in Capt. Charles
Bennett's Company, Col. Dixon's Regt.
Detached Militia in U..S. service.

STEARNS, SAMUEL.
Enlisted May 31, 1813 for 1 year in
Capt. Benjamin Bradford's Company;
on Muster Roll from May 31 to Aug.
31, 1813. Ref: R. & L. 1812, AGO
Page 26.

*STEARNS, SIDNEY O.
Served in Capt. Lowry's Company,
Col. Wm. Williams' Regt. Detached
Militia in U. S. service 4 months
and 26 days, 1813.

*STEARNS, SOLOMON.
Enlisted Oct. 11, 1813 in Capt. Asahel
Langworthy's Company, Col. Isaac

Clark's Rifle Corps. Also served in Dixon's Regt.

*STEARNS, STEPHEN, Drummer.
Served in 4 Regt. (Williams') Vt. Militia.

*STEARNS, WILLIAM.
Enlisted Sept. 27, 1813 and served 1 month and 21 days in Capt. Asahel Langworthy's Company, Col. Isaac Clark's Rifle Corps or Col. Dixon's Regt. Ref: Book 53, AGO Page 110.

STEBBINS, JOHN,   Franklin County.
Volunteered to go to Plattsburgh Sept. 11, 1814 and served in 15th or 22nd Regt. Ref: Hemenway's Vt. Gazetteer, Vol. 2, Page 391.

*STEBBENS, WALBRIDGE, 2nd Lieutenant. Served in 1 Regt. (Martindale's) Vt. Militia.

*STEBBINS, ALPHEUS.
Served in Capt. Rogers' Company, Col. Fifield's Regt. Detached Militia in U. S. service 10 days, 1812.

STEBBINS, BENJAMIN, 1st Lieutenant.
Served from July 4 to July 16, 1812 in Major A. Warner's Company at Troy. Ref: Vol. 51, Vt. State Papers, Page 107.

STEBBINS, BLISS,   Williamstown.
Volunteered to go to Plattsburgh, September, 1814, and went as far as Burlington, serving in Capt. David Robinson's Company. Ref: Book 52, AGO Pages 2 and 12.

STEBBINS, JOTHAN.
Served from Feb. 25 to May 24, 1813 in Lieut. V. R. Goodrich's Company, 11th Regt. Ref: R. & L. 1812, AGO Page 10.

‡*STEBBINS, LEVI, Drummer.
Served as drummer in Dixon's Regt. Vt. Militia. Served as private in 1 Regt. (Judson's) Vt. Militia. Pension Certificate of widow, Sarah, No. 14547.

STEBBINS, MILO,   Williamstown.
Volunteered to go to Plattsburgh, September, 1814, and was at the battle Sept. 11th, serving 8 days in Capt. David Robinson's Company. Ref: Book 52, AGO Page 2.

*STEBBINS, SAMUEL.
Served in Col. Clark's Regt. of Riflemen from September to November, 1813.

*STEBINS, ISRAEL J.
Served from Sept. 25 to Oct. 27, 1813 in Capt. Jesse Post's Company, Dixon's Regt.

STEBINS, SAMUEL.
Served from April 30, 1813 to Feb. 27, 1814 in Capt. Daniel Farrington's Company, 30th Regt. (also commanded by Capt. Simeon Wright). Ref: R. & L. 1812, AGO Pages 50 and 51.

*STEDMAN, EDMOND P.
Served in 1 Regt. (Judson's) Vt. Militia.

‡*STEDMAN, EMANUEL P.
Served from June 11 to June 14, 1813 and from Oct. 4 to Oct. 13, 1813 in Capt. John Palmer's Company, 1st Regt. 2nd Brig. 3rd Div. Also served in Capt. Hollenbeck's Company. Pension Certificate No. 2352. Pension Certificate of widow, Phebe J., No. 21286.

*STEEL, JOSIAH, Corporal.
Served from June 11 to June 14, 1813 in Capt. John M. Eldridge's Company, 1st Regt. 2nd Brig. 3rd Div. Ref: R. & L. 1812, AGO Page 35.

STEELE, ABEL,   Putney.
Served from Feb. 19 to May 18, 1813 in Lieut. V. R. Goodrich's Company, 11th Regt. Ref: R. & L. 1812, AGO Page 10.

*STEELE, JAMES,   Randolph.
Volunteered to go to Plattsburgh, September, 1814, and served in Capt. Lebbeus Egerton's Company.

‡STEELE, SAMUEL.
Served in Capt. Jones' Company. Pension Certificate No. 8485.

STEERE, SAMUEL.
Served from May 3, 1813 to April 26, 1814 in Capt. Simeon Wright's Company. Ref: R. & L. 1812, AGO Page 51.

*STEPHENS, ALONZO, Corporal.
Served in 3 Regt. (Tyler's) Vt. Militia.

*STEPHENS, BATEMAN, Corporal.
Served from June 11 to June 14, 1813 in Capt. Thomas Dorwin's Company, 1st Regt. 2nd Brig. 3rd Div.

STEPHENS, BENJAMIN,   Fairfax.
Served in Capt. Joseph Beeman's Company in 1813 and 1814. Ref: Hemenway's Vt. Gazetteer, Vol. 2, Page 402.

STEPHENS, BENJAMIN,   Fairfax.
Served from Aug. 8, 1812 in company of Capt. Joseph Beeman Jr., 11th Regt. U. S. Inf. under Col. Ira Clark. Served from Nov. 1, 1812 to Feb. 28, 1813 in Lt. V. R. Goodrich's Company, 11th Regt. Ref: R. & L. 1812, AGO Page 11; Hemenway's Vt. Gazetteer, Vol. 2, Page 402.

*STEPHENS, ROYAL.
Enlisted Sept. 25, 1813 and served 1 month and 23 days in Capt. Birge's Company, Col. Dixon's Regt. Detached Militia in U. S. service.

*STEPHENS, THOMAS.
Served in Capt. Robbins' Company, Col. Wm. Williams' Regt. Detached Militia in U. S. service 4 months and 29 days, 1812.

STEPHENS, THOMAS, Lieutenant.
Appointed 2nd Lieutenant 30th Inf. April 30, 1813; 1st Lieutenant June 23, 1814; honorably discharged June 15, 1815. Ref: Heitman's Historical Register & Dictionary USA.

‡STEPHENS, WILLARD.
Served in Capt. Morrill's Company.
Pension Certificate No. 10375.

STEPHENSON, BENJAMIN, Sergeant.
Served from Nov. 1, 1812 to February, 1813 in Capt. Weeks' Company, 11th Regt. Ref: R. & L. 1812, AGO Page 5.

STEPHENSON, ELI.
Served from May 1 to June 3, 1814 in Capt. Alexander Brooks Corps of Artillery. Ref: R. & L. 1812, AGO Page 31.

*STEPHENSON, JOHN.
Served from June 11 to June 14, 1813 in Capt. Moses Jewett's Company, 1st Regt. 2nd Brig. 3rd Div.

*STERLING, ELIJAH.
Served in 4 Regt. (Peck's) Vt. Militia.

*STERLING, ELISHA.
Served in Capt. O. Lowry's Company, Col. Wm. Williams' Regt. Detached Militia in U. S. service 4 months and 26 days, 1812.

‡*STERLING, JACOB.
Served in Corning's Detachment, Vt. Militia. Also served in Capt. J. Campbell's Company. Pension Certificate No. 34300.

*STERLING, JOSEPH (or Sterlin), Barre.
Served in Capt. E. Walker's Company, Col. Fifield's Regt. Detached Militia in U. S. service 4 months and 1 day, 1812. Volunteered to go to Plattsburgh, September, 1814, and served 9 days in Capt. Warren Ellis' Company.

STERLING, SAMUEL,   Woodstock.
Served in Capt. Phineas Williams' Company, 11th Regt.; on Pay Roll for January and February, 1813. Ref: R. & L. 1812, AGO Page 15.

*STERLING, SIMON.
Served in Corning's Detachment, Vt. Militia.

*STERNS, SAMUEL.
Served from April 12 to April 21, 1814 in Lieut. Justus Foote's Company, Sumner's Regt.

*STEVANS, JOHN E.
Served in 3 Regt. (Williams') Vt. Militia.

STEVENS, ABIAL,   Strafford.
Volunteered to go to Plattsburgh, September, 1814, and served 6 days in Capt. Jedediah H. Harris' Company. Ref: Book 52, AGO Page 43.

‡*STEVENS, ALBERT.
Served from Oct. 11 to Oct. 17, 1813 in Capt. John Munson's Company, 3 Regt. (Tyler's). Also served in Capt. Sinclair's Company. Pension Certificate of widow, Eunice, No. 28916.

*STEVENS, ANDREW.
Served in 3 Regt. (Tyler's) Vt. Militia.

*STEVENS, ASA, Sergeant,   Pawlet.
Served in Capt. Hopkins' Company, Col. Martindale's Regt. Detached Militia in U. S. service 2 months and 13 days, 1812. Served in Artillery of Detached Militia of Vt. in U. S. service at Champlain from Nov. 18 to Nov. 19, 1812.

*STEVENS, AUGUSTUS.
Served from April 12 to April 21, 1814 in Capt. Eseck Sprague's Company, Sumner's Regt.

‡*STEVENS, BENJAMIN, 3rd Lieutenant.
Served from April 12 to April 21, 1814 in Capt. Othniel Jewett's Company, Sumner's Regt. Pension Certificate No. 14647.

‡STEVENS, BENJAMIN. W., Surgeon.
Served in Col. Williams' Regt. Pension Certificate of widow, Lydia M., No. 19725.

*STEVENS, CARLOS, Corporal.
Served from Oct. 11 to Oct. 17, 1813 in Capt. John Munson's Company, 3 Regt. (Tyler's).

*STEVENS, CHARLES, Corporal.
Served from April 12 to April 21, 1814 in Capt. Othniel Jewett's Company, Sumner's Regt.

STEVENS, DANIEL,   Hartland.
Enlisted at Poultney Jan. 22, 1814 and served in Capt. William Miller's Company, Capt. James Taylor's Company and Capt. Gideon Spencer's Company, 30th Regt. Ref: R. & L. 1812, AGO Pages 1, 53, 54, 55, 57.

STEVENS, HENRY.
Volunteered to go to Plattsburgh, September, 1814, and served in Capt. Ebenezer Spencer's Company, Vershire. Ref: Book 52, AGO Page 48.

STEVENS, HIGHMAN.   Pittsford.
Volunteered to go to Plattsburgh, September, 1814, and served 8 days in Capt. Caleb Hendee's Company. Ref: Book 52, AGO Page 125.

STEVENS, HIRAM.
Served from March 9 to July 8, 1813 in Capt. Jonathan Starks' Company, 11th Regt. Ref: R. & L. 1812, AGO Page 19.

‡*STEVENS, HORACE.
Served from April 12 to April 21, 1814 in Capt. Eseck Sprague's Company, Sumner's Regt. Also served in Capt. Spencer's Company. Pension Certificate of widow, Susan R., No. 34442.

*STEVENS, HYMEN.
Served in 1 Regt. (Judson's) Vt. Militia.

*STEVENS, JAMES.
Served in Corning's Detachment, Vt. Militia.

‡STEVENS, JAMES.
Served in Capt. Lowery's Company. Pension Certificate of widow, Patty, No. 24858.

STEVENS, JAMES.
Served from Nov. 1, 1812 to Feb.
28, 1813 in Capt. Phineas Williams'
Company, 11th Regt. Ref: R. & L.
1812, AGO Page 15.

STEVENS, JAMES,   Danville.
Volunteered to go to Plattsburgh,
September, 1814, and served 2 days
in Capt. James Kelsey's Company.
Ref: Book 51, AGO Page 71.

STEVENS, JOHN.   Montpelier.
Volunteered to go to Plattsburgh,
September. 1814; no organization giv-
en. Ref: Book 52, AGO Pages 173 and
211.

*STEVENS, JOHN, Sergeant.
Served in Capt. Adams' Company,
Col. Jonathan Williams' Regt. Detached Militia in U. S. service 2
months and 7 days, 1812.

STEVENS, JOHN JR.,   Montpelier.
Volunteered to go to Plattsburgh,
September, 1814; no organization giv-
en. Ref: Book 52, AGO Page 211.

STEVENS, JOHN J.
Served from March 16, 1813 to June
15, 1813 in company of Capt. John
McNeil Jr., 11th Regt. Ref: R. & L.
1812, AGO Page 16.

STEVENS, JONATHAN,   Montpelier.
Volunteered to go to Plattsburgh,
September, 1814, and served in Capt.
Timothy Hubbard's Company. Ref:
Book 52, AGO Page 256.

STEVENS, JOSHUA.
Served from March 26 to June 23,
1813 in Capt. John W. Weeks' Company, 11th Regt. Ref: R. & L. 1812,
AGO Page 4.

STEVENS, JOTHAM.
Served from April 5 to July 4, 1813
in Capt. Edgerton's Company, 11th
Regt. Ref: R. & L. 1812, AGO
Page 3.

STEVENS, LEVI.
Served from March 29 to June 28,
1813 in Capt. Samul Gordon's Company, 11th Regt. Ref: R. & L. 1812,
AGO Page 8.

*STEVENS, MARTIN.
Enlisted Sept. 27, 1813 in Capt. Asahel
Langworthy's Company, Col. Isaac
Clark's Rifle Corps.

STEVENS, MATTHEW B.
Served from March 1 to April 16,
1814; no organization given. Ref:
R. & L. 1812, AGO Page 29.

*STEVENS, MICHAEL, Corporal, Corinth.
Served in Capt. Rogers' Company,
Col. Fifield's Regt. Detached Militia
in U. S. service 5 months and 27
days, 1812.

STEVENS, NATHAN,   Washington.
Volunteered to go to Plattsburgh,
September, 1814, and served 9 days
in Capt. Warren Ellis' Company. Ref:
Book 52, AGO Page 220.

*STEVENS, PETER.
Served in Capt. Hotchkiss' Company,
Col. Martindale's Regt. Detached
Militia in U. S. service 2 months
and 13 days, 1812.

STEVENS, REUBEN.
Served from March 18 to June 8, 1813
in Capt. John W. Weeks' Company,
11th Regt. Ref: R. & L. 1812, AGO
Page 4.

STEVENS, REUBEN.
Served from April 23, 1813 to April
25, 1814 in Capt. Simeon Wright's
Company. Ref: R. & L. 1812, AGO
Page 51.

*STEVENS, SAFFORD.
Served in 3 Regt. (Tyler's) Vt. Militia.

STEVENS, SAMUEL.
Served from March 26 to June 25,
1813 in Capt. Samul Gordon's Company, 11th Regt. Ref: R. & L. 1812,
AGO Page 8.

*STEVENS, SAMUEL.
Enlisted Oct. 18, 1813 in Capt. John
Weeds' Company, Col. Clark's Rifle
Corps.

*STEVENS, SAMUEL.
Served in Capt. Wheeler's Company,
Col. Fifield's Regt. Detached Militia
in U. S. service 6 months and 4
days, 1812.

*STEVENS, SAMUEL G.
Served in Capt. Briggs' Company,
Col. Jonathan Williams' Regt. Detached Militia in U. S. service 2
months and 13 days, 1812.

STEVENS, SAMUEL L.,   Effing, N. H.
Served from Sept. 1, 1814 to June 16,
1815 in Capt. Sanford's Company,
30th Inf. Ref: R. & L. 1812, AGO
Page 23.

STEVENS, SIMEON, Lieutenant.
Appointed Ensign 31st Inf. April 30,
1813; Regimental Paymaster April,
1813, to June, 1815; 2nd Lieutenant
May 1, 1814; honorably discharged
June 15, 1815. Ref: Heitman's Historical Register & Dictionary USA.

STEVENS, URIAH H.,   Strafford.
Volunteered to go to Plattsburgh,
September, 1814, and served 6 days
in Capt. Jedediah H. Harris' Company. Ref: Book 52, AGO Page 43.

*STEVENS, W., Surgeon.
Served in 3 Regt. (Williams') Vt.
Militia.

STEVENS, WAIT, Lieutenant, Washington. Volunteered to go to Plattsburgh, September, 1814, and served
in Capt. Amos Stiles' Company. Ref:
Book 52, AGO Page 36.

‡STEVENS, WILLIAM.
Served in Capt. G. Spencer's Company. Pension Certificate No. 25486.

STEVENS, WILLIAM,   Pittsford.
Volunteered to go to Plattsburgh,
September, 1814, and served 8 days
in Capt. Caleb Hendee's Company.
Ref: Book 52, AGO Page 125.

STEVENS, WILLIAM.
Served in Capt. Walker's Company, Col. Fifield's Regt. Detached Militia in U. S. service 13 days, 1812. Ref: Book 53, AGO Page 35.

*STEVENS, WILLIAM.
Served from April 17 to April 21, 1814 in Capt. Othniel Jewett's Company, Sumner's Regt.

*STEVENS, WYMAN, Stowe.
Volunteered to go to Plattsburgh, September, 1814, and was at the battle, serving in Capt. Nehemiah Perkins' Company, 4 Regt. (Peck's) Vt. Militia.

STEVENSON, BENJAMIN, Lieutenant.
Appointed Ensign 11th Inf. Sept. 21, 1813; 2nd Lieutenant June 30, 1814. Ref: Governor and Council Vt., Vol. 6, Page 474.

*STEWARD, JAMES P.
Served in 2 Regt. (Fifield's) Vt. Militia.

STEWARD, RUSSELL, Montpelier.
Volunteered to go to Plattsburgh, September, 1814, and served in Capt. Timothy Hubbard's Company 8 days. Ref: Book 52, AGO Page 256.

STEWARD, THOMAS W.
Served from March 22 to March 25, 1813 in Capt. Edgerton's Company, 11th Regt. Ref: R. & L. 1812, AGO Page 3.

‡STEWART, AUGUSTUS.
Served from May 9 to May 13, 1813 in Capt. Simeon Wright's Company. Also served in Capt. Taylor's Company. Pension Certificate No. 13157.

STEWART, CALVIN, Corporal.
Served from Nov. 1, 1812 to Feb. 28, 1813 in Capt. Samuel H. Holly's Company, 11th Regt. Was a sergeant in light troops; in the Indian slaughter on the Chateaugay was wounded in the neck. Ref: R. & L. 1812, AGO Page 25; Rev. J. F. Goodhue's History of Shoreham, Page 102.

*STEWART, CHAUNCY A.
Served from April 12 to April 21, 1814 in Capt. Edmund B. Hill's Company, Sumner's Regt.

STEWART, DANIEL, Corporal, Bristol, Mass. Served from Sept. 1, 1814 to June 16, 1815 in Capt. Sanford's Company, 30th Inf. Ref: R. & L. 1812, AGO Page 23.

*STEWART, DAVID.
Served in 4 Regt. (Peck's) Vt. Militia, Corning's Detachment, Vt. Militia, and 4 Regt. (Williams') Vt. Militia.

STEWART, ISAAC, Bridport, Vt.
Served from March 1 to July 10, 1814 in Capt. Spencer's Company, 30th Inf. Ref: R. & L. 1812, AGO Page 30.

STEWART, ISAAC.
Enlisted July 11, 1813 for 1 year in Capt. James Taylor's Company, 30th

Regt.; on Muster Roll to Feb. 28, 1814. Ref: R. & L. 1812, AGO Page 53.

STEWART, JOHN, Franklin County.
Volunteered to go to Plattsburgh Sept. 11, 1814 and served in 15th or 22nd Regt. Ref: Hemenway's Vt. Gazetteer, Vol. 2, Page 392.

*STEWART, JOHN.
Served in 4 Regt. (Williams') Vt. Militia. Also served with Hospital Attendants, Vt.

STEWART, JOHN.
Served in Capt. Benjamin Bradford's Company; on Muster Roll from May 31 to Aug. 31, 1813; on command on board the scows. Ref: R. & L. 1812, AGO Page 26.

STEWART, JOHN P.
Served in Capt. O. Durkee's Company, Col. Fifield's Regt. Detached Militia in U. S. service 2 months and 26 days, 1812. Ref: Book 53, AGO Page 3.

STEWART, JOHN, Lieutenant, Berlin.
Volunteered to go to Plattsburgh, September, 1814, and served 7 days in Capt. Cyrus Johnson's Company. Ref: Book 52, AGO Page 255.

‡*STEWART, LEMUEL.
Served in 1 Regt. (Martindale's) Vt. Militia. Also served in Capt. Schofield's Company. Pension Certificate of widow, Sally, No. 25262.

STEWART, LEVI.
Served from May 1 to July 18, 1814; no organization given. Ref: R. & L. 1812, AGO Page 29.

STEWART, LEWIS.
Served from April 23, 1813 to April 27, 1814 in Capt. James Taylor's Company and Capt. Gideon Spencer's Company, 30th Regt. Ref: R. & L. 1812, AGO Pages 52, 57, 58.

*STEWART, LUKE.
Served from Sept. 25 to Oct. 24, 1813 in Capt. N. B. Eldridge's Company, Col. Dixon's Regt. Detached Militia in U. S. service.

STEWART, RUFUS, Captain.
Appointed Captain 31st Inf. April 30, 1813; honorably discharged June 15, 1815. Ref: Heitman's Historical Register & Dictionary USA.

‡*STEWART, SAMUEL, Corporal.
Served from April 12 to April 21, 1814 in Capt. Eseck Sprague's Company, Sumner's' Regt. Also served in 1 Regt. (Martindale's) Vt. Militia. Pension Certificate of widow, Anice, No. 28336.

STEWART, WILLIAM, Corporal.
Served from April 23, 1813 to April 27, 1814 in Capt. James Taylor's Company and Capt. Gideon Spencer's Company, 30th Regt. Ref: R. & L. 1812, AGO Pages 52, 56, 58.

*STICKNEY, ALVIN.
Served from April 12 to April 21, 1814 in Capt. Shubael Wales' Company, Col. Sumner's Regt.

*STICKNEY, ASA.
Served from April 12 to April 21,
1814 in Capt. Shubael Wales' Company, Col. W. B. Sumner's Regt.

STICKNEY, DANIEL,   Shoreham.
Volunteered to go to Plattsburgh,
September, 1814, and served 6 days
in Capt. Samuel Hand's Company.
Ref: Rev. J. F. Goodhue's History
of Shoreham, Page 107.

‡*STICKNEY, DAVID, Corporal, Highgate.
Served in Col. Wm. Williams' Regt.
Capt. Saxe's Company, Detached Militia in U. S. service 4 months and
24 days, 1812. Enlisted Sept. 18,
1813 in Capt. Isaac Finch's Company,
Col. Clark's Rifle Corps. Pension Certificate No. 695. Pension Certificate
of widow, Clarissa, No. 20089.

*STICKNEY, JOHN.
Enlisted Oct. 11, 1813 in Capt. Asahel
Langworthy's Company, Col. Isaac
Clark's Rifle Corps.

*STICKNEY, JOSIAH.
Served in Sumner's Regt. Vt. Militia.

‡STILES, ALBERT,   South Hero.
Volunteered to go to Plattsburgh,
September, 1814, and was at the
battle, serving in Capt. Abner Keeler's
Company. Pension Certificate No.
25523. Pension Certificate of widow,
Sophia, No. 34387.

STILES, AMOS, Captain,   Washington.
Volunteered to go to Plattsburgh,
September, 1814, and served in Capt.
Amos Stiles' Company. Ref: Book 52,
AGO Page 36.

STILES, ASA.
Served from Feb. 16 to May 15, 1813
in Capt. Charles Follett's Company,
11th Regt. Ref: R. & L. 1812, AGO
Page 13.

‡*STILES, DANFORTH W.
Served in Capt. E. Robinson's Company. Also served in 4 Regt. (Peck's)
Vt. Militia. Pension Certificate of
widow, Emily, No. 19537.

STILES, EBEN.
Enlisted June 25, 1813 for 1 year in
Capt. Daniel Farrington's Company,
30th Regt. (also commanded by Capt.
Simeon Wright). Ref: R. & L. 1812,
AGO Pages 50 and 51.

*STILES, EPHRAIM.
Served in Capt. Mason's Company,
Col. Fifield's' Regt. Detached Militia
in U. S. service 5 months and 5
days, 1812.

STILES, EZRA.
Served from Feb. 17 to May 16, 1813
in Capt. Charles Follett's Company,
11th Regt. Ref: R. & L. 1812, AGO
Page 13.

STILES, HORACE.
Served from Sept. 25 to Sept. 29,
1813 in Capt. Elijah W. Wood's Company, Dixon's Regt. Ref: Book 52,
AGO Page 273.

STILES, HOSEA,   Rutland County.
Volunteered to go to Plattsburgh,
September, 1814, and served 18 days;
no organization given. Ref: Book 52,
AGO Page 151.

‡*STILES, JAMES, Corporal.
Served in Capt. Morrill's Company,
Col. Fifield's Regt. Detached Militia
in U. S. service 3 months and 17
days, 1812. Also served as corporal
in 3 Regt. (Williams') Vt. Militia.
Pension Certificate No. 12326.

‡STILES, JOSEPH.
Served in Capt. Burnap's Company,
Col. Jonathan Williams' Regt. Detached Militia in U. S. service 2
months and 13 days, 1812. Pension
Certificate of widow, Jemimah, No.
701.

‡STILES, JOSIAH,   Hubbardton.
Volunteered to go to Plattsburgh,
September, 1814, and served 8 days
in Capt. Henry J. Horton's Company.
Pension Certificate of widow, Char-
lotte, No. 30488.

‡*STILES, LEVI.
Served in 4 Regt. (Peck's) Vt. Militia. Also served in Capt. Robinson's
Company. Pension Certificate No.
2724.

STILES, LUTHER,   Bridgtown.
Served from May 1 to June 29,
1814 in Capt. Branch's Company of
Light Artillery. Ref: R. & L. 1812,
AGO Page 30.

STILES, NATHAN,   Bridgtown.
Served from May 1 to June 30, 1814
in Capt. Branch's Company of Light
Artillery. Ref: R. & L. 1812, AGO
Page 30.

STILES, REUBEN.
Served from Feb. 18 to May 17,
1813 in Capt. Charles Follett's Company, 11th Regt. Ref: R. & L. 1812,
AGO Page 13.

*STILES, WILLIAM, Corporal.
Served in Capt. Parsons' Company,
Col. Jonathan Williams' Regt. Detached Militia in U. S. service 2
months and 13 days, 1812.

STILKEY, HENRY,   Franklin County.
Volunteered to go to Plattsburgh
Sept. 11, 1814, and served in 15th or
22nd Regt. Ref: Hemenway's Vt.
Gazetteer, Vol. 2, Page 391.

STILL, PEMBER W.
Enlisted Dec. 11, 1813 for 5 years in
company of late Capt. J. Brooks com-
manded by Lt. John I. Cromwell,
Corps of U. S. Artillery; on Muster
Roll from April 30 to June 30, 1814.
Ref: R. & L. 1812, AGO Page 18.

*STILLWELL, SAMUEL.
Served in Capt. Ormsbee's Company,
Col. Martindale's Regt. Detached
Militia in U. S. service 2 months
and 14 days, 1812.

‡STILPHIN, CHARLES.
Served in Capt. A. J. Brown's Company. Volunteered to go to Platts-

burgh, September, 1814. Pension Certificate No. 31377. Pension Certificate of widow, Laura, No. 38259. Ref: Book 51, AGO Page 123.

*STIMPSON, I., Ensign.
Served in 4 Regt. (Peck's) Vt. Militia.

‡*STIMPSON, THOMAS.
Served in Capt. Rogers' Company, Col. Fifield's Regt. Detached Militia in U. S. service 5 months and 27 days, 1812. Pension Certificate No. 13438.

*STIMSON, EDWARD.
Served in Capt. Sabin's Company, Col. Jonathan Williams' Regt. Detached Militia in U. S. service 2 months and 6 days, 1812.

*STIMSON, ELIAS JR.
Served in 3 Regt. (Tyler's) Vt. Militia.

*STIMSON, JEPHTHAN, Ensign.
Served in 4 Regt. (Peck's') Vt. Militia.

‡STINEHOUR, LUTHER.
Served in Capt. Conrad Saxe's Company, 4 Regt. (Wm. Williams'). Pension Certificate No. 28615.

*STITES, HARRIS, Sergeant.
Served in Dixon's Regt. Vt. Militia.

*STOCKER, THADEUS.
Served with Hospital Attendants, Vt.

*STOCKHOUSE, BENJAMIN.
Served in 1 Regt. (Judson's) Vt. Militia.

*STOCKWELL, ASA.
Served in 4 Regt. (Peck's) Vt. Militia.

*STOCKWELL, DAVID, Corporal, Middlesex. Volunteered to go to Plattsburgh, September, 1814, and served 10 days in Capt. Holden Putnam's Company, 4 Regt. (Peck's).

*STOCKWELL, EBENEZER.
Enlisted Sept. 25, 1813 and served 1 month and 23 days in Capt. Elijah W. Wood's Company, Col. Dixon's Regt. Detached Militia in U. S. service.

STOCKWELL, EBENEZER,   Highgate.
Volunteered to go to Plattsburgh, September, 1814, and served in Capt. Conrade Saxe's Company, Col. Wm. Williams' Regt. Ref: Book 51, AGO Page 100.

*STOCKWELL, ELI.
Served in Capt. Dorrance's Company, Col. Wm. Williams' Regt. Detached Militia in U. S. service 4 months and 24 days, 1812. Ref: Book 53, AGO Page 75.

*STOCKWELL, EPHRAIM, Ensign.
Served in 2 Regt. (3rd Brig. 3rd Div.) Vt. Militia.

*STOCKWELL, JOHN.
Served from Oct. 5 to Oct. 15, 1813 in Capt. Roswell Hunt's Company, 3 Regt. (Tyler's). Also served in Corning's Detachment, Vt. Militia.

STOCKWELL, LUTHER, Shaftsbury or Williamstown. Served from March 27 to June 26, 1813 in Capt. Edgerton's Company, 11th Regt. Served in Capt. Gideon Spencer's Company; on Muster Roll from Dec. 30, 1813 to June 30, 1814. Served from Sept. 1, 1814 to June 16, 1815 in Capt. Sanford's Company, 30th Inf. Ref: R. & L. 1812, AGO Pages 3, 23 and 56.

‡*STOCKWELL, NATHANIEL, Corporal.
Served in Corning's Detachment, Vt. Militia. Served in 4 Regt. (Peck's) Vt. Militia. Also served in Capt. Pinneo's Company. Pension Certificate of widow, Malvina M., No. 23378.

STOCKWELL, WILLIAM, Williamstown. Served from Dec. 5, 1814 to June 19, 1815 in Capt. Taylor's Company, 30th Inf. Ref: R. & L. 1812, AGO Page 23.

STODARD, DAVID.
Served from March 9 to June 8, 1813 in Capt. John W. Weeks' Company, 11th Regt. Ref: R. & L. 1812, AGO Page 4.

STODDARD, EDWIN F.
Enlisted Aug. 2, 1813 for 1 year in Capt. Daniel Farrington's Company, 30th Regt. (also commanded by Capt. Simeon Wright); on Muster Roll from March 1 to April 30, 1814. Received pay from March 1 to Sept. 14, 1814; no organization given. Ref: R. & L. 1812, AGO Pages 29, 50, 51.

STODDARD, ISAAC, Lieutenant.
Appointed 2nd Lieutenant Inf. March, 1812. Ref: Governor and Council Vt., Vol. 6, Page 473.

*STODDARD, LATHROP T.
Served in Corning's Detachment, Vt. Militia.

STODDARD, NATHAN.
Served in Capt. Samuel H. Holly's Company, 11th Regt.; on Pay Roll for January and February, 1813. Ref: R. & L. 1812, AGO Page 25.

‡*STODDARD, ROBERT O. (or C.), Corporal. Served in Corning's Detachment, Vt. Militia. Served in 4 Regt. (Peck's) Vt. Militia. Also served in Capt. J. Campbell's Company. Pension Certificate of widow, Betsey, No. 28069.

*STODDARD, SAMUEL.
Served in Sumner's Regt. Vt. Militia.

*STODDARD, STEPHEN.
Served from June 11 to June 14, 1813 in Capt. Thomas Dorwin's Company, 1st Regt. 2nd Brig. 3rd Div.

STODDER, EDWIN,   Franklin County.
Volunteered to go to Plattsburgh Sept. 11, 1814 and served in 15th or 22nd Regt. Ref: Hemenway's Vt. Gazetteer, Vol. 2, Page 392.

*STOEL, CONSTANT,   Thetford.
Marched for Plattsburgh, September,
1814, and went as far as Bolton, Vt.,
serving 6 days in Capt. Salmon Howard's Company, 2nd Regt.

*STOEL, JOHN.
Served in 4 Regt. (Williams') Vt.
Militia.

*STOEL, NATHAN. Lieutenant.
Served from April 13 to April 21,
1814 in Capt. Salmon Foster's Company, Sumner's Regt.

*STOKES, JETHRO.
Served from April 12 to April 21,
1814 in Capt. Eseck Sprague's Company, Sumner's Regt.

STONE, A. F.,   Richford.
Served in Capt. Martin D. Follett's
Company, Dixon's Regt. on duty on
Canadian Frontier in 1813. Ref: Hem-
enway's Vt. Gazetteer, Vol. 2, Page
427.

STONE, ABEL,   Whiting.
Volunteered to go to Plattsburgh,
September, 1814, and served 9 days
in Capt. Salmon Foster's Company,
Sumner's Regt. Ref: Book 51, AGO
Page 8.

*STONE, DANIEL.
Enlisted April 12, 1814 in Capt.
Shubael Wales' Company, Col. W.
B. Sumner's Regt.; transferred to
Capt. Salmon Foster's Company, Sum-
ner's Regt. April 13, 1814 and served
to April 21, 1814.

‡STONE, HENRY.
Served in Capt. J. Gray's Company,
Sumner's Regt. Pension Certificate of
widow, Betsey, No. 28390.

*STONE, ISAAC.
Served from April 12 to April 21,
1814 in Capt. Shubael Wales' Company, Col. W. B. Sumner's Regt.

‡*STONE, ITHIEL, Captain,   Charlotte.
Served from June 11 to June 14, 1813
in command of company in 1st Regt.
2nd Brig. 3rd Div. Pension Certificate of widow, Electa, No. 28561.

STONE, JAMES.
Served from April 30, 1813 to April
29, 1814 in Capt. James Taylor's Company and Capt. Gideon Spencer's
Company, 30th Regt. Ref: R. & L.
1812, AGO Pages 52, 57, 59.

*STONE, JAMES.
Served from Aug. 31 to Dec. 8, 1812
in Capt. George W. Kindall's Company, 4 Regt. (Williams').

STONE, JAMES JR.   Fairfield.
Served in Capt. Kendall's Company.
Col. Wm. Williams' Regt. Detached
Militia in U. S. service 4 months
and 10 days, 1812. Ref: Book 51,
AGO Page 199; Book 53, AGO Page 55.

‡STONE, JAMES 2nd.
Served in Capt. Kendall's Company.
Pension Certificate of widow, Lucinda,
No. 21290.

‡STONE, JAMES C.
Served in Capt. Jewell's Company.
Pension Certificate No. 31259.

STONE, JOHN,   Richford.
Served in Capt. Follet's Company,
Col. Dixon's Regt. Detached Militia
in U. S. service 1 month and 23
days, 1813. Ref: Book 53, AGO Page
105.

STONE, JOHN.
Served from April 30, 1813 to April
30, 1814 in Capt. James Taylor's Company and Capt. Gideon Spencer's
Company, 30th Regt. Ref: R. & L.
1812, AGO Pages 52, 57, 59.

*STONE, JOHN JR., Corporal.
Enlisted Sept. 25, 1813 in Capt. Mar-
tin D. Folett's Company, Dixon's
Regt.

STONE, JOHN F. W.
Served in company of late Capt. J.
Brooks, commanded by Lt. John I.
Cromwell, Corps of U. S. Artillery;
on Muster Roll from April 30 to
June 30, 1814; prisoner of war on
parole; transferred from Capt. Leon-
ard's Company. Ref: R. & L. 1812,
AGO Page 18.

‡STONE, JOHN H.
Served in Capt. Bradford's Company.
Pension Certificate of widow, Hannah,
No. 6135.

STONE, NATHAN. Lieutenant,   Barre.
Volunteered to go to Plattsburgh,
September, 1814, and served 10 days
in Capt. Warren Ellis' Company. Ref:
Book 52, AGO Page 242.

STONE, NATHAN. Artificer.
Enlisted June 10, 1812 for 5 years in
company of late Capt. J. Brooks,
commanded by Lt. John I. Cromwell,
Corps of U. S. Artillery; on Muster
Roll from April 30 to June 30, 1814.
Ref: R. & L. 1812, AGO Page 18.

*STONE, REUBEN.
Served in 2 Regt. (Fifield's) Vt. Militia.

*STONE, RICHARD.
Served in 1 Regt. (Judson's) Vt.
Militia.

STONE, SOLOMON,   Montpelier.
Volunteered to go to Plattsburgh,
September, 1814, and served 8 days
in Capt. Timothy Hubbard's Company. Ref: Book 52, AGO Page 256.

STORES, ALMON.
Served from Feb. 18 to June 30, 1814
in Capt. Alexander Brooks' Corps of
Artillery. Ref: R. & L. 1812, AGO
Page 31.

STORES, CHIPMAN.
Served from Feb. 18 to June 30, 1814
in Capt. Alexander Brooks' Corps of
Artillery. Ref: R. & L. 1812, AGO
Page 31.

*STORES, ALVIN L., Corporal.
Served in Dixon's Regt. Vt. Militia.

STORES, DAVID.
Served from Feb. 18 to June 30, 1814
in Capt. Alexander Brooks' Corps of
Artillery. Ref: R. & L. 1812, AGO
Page 31.

*STORES, EDWIN.
Served from April 12 to April 21,
1814 in Lieut. Justus Foote's Company, Sumner's Regt.

STORES, WILLIAM.
Served from Feb. 18 to June 30, 1814
in Capt. Alexander Brooks' Corps of
Artillery. Ref: R. & L. 1812, AGO
Page 31.

*STOREY, ASAHEL, Captain.
Served in 3 Regt. (Bowdish) Vt.
Militia.

STORM, HENRY.
Served in Capt. James Taylor's Company and Capt. Gideon Spencer's
Company, 30th Regt. Ref: R. & L.
1812, AGO Pages 53 and 57.

STORM, SAMUEL.
Served in Capt. James Taylor's Com-
pany, 30th Regt. Ref: R. & L. 1812,
AGO Page 53.

‡STORRS, DAVID.
Served in Capt. Allen's Company. Pension Certificate of widow, Mary, No.
33872.

*STORRS, HIRAM,   Randolph.
Volunteered to go to Plattsburgh,
September. 1814, and served in Capt.
Lebbeus Egerton's Company.

*STORRS, HUCKENS, Colonel.
Appointed Lt. Colonel 31st Inf. Feb.
23, 1813; Colonel 34th Inf. Oct. 31,
1814; honorably discharged June 15,
1815. Served as Major in 2 Regt.
(Fifield's) Vt. Militia.

STORRS, STEPHEN.
Served from June 1 to June 30, 1814
as laborer in company of Artificers
commanded by Alexander Parris.
Ref: R. & L. 1812, AGO Page 24.

*STOREY, ALVIN L., Corporal.
Enlisted Sept. 23, 1813 in Capt.
Amasa Mansfield's Company, Dixon's
Regt.; transferred to Capt. Asahel
Langworthy's Company, Col. Isaac
Clark's Rifle Corps Oct. 30, 1813.

*STORY, ALVIN TICHENOR, Corporal.
Enlisted Sept. 25, 1813 and served
1 month and 23 days in Capt. Follet's
Company. Col. Dixon's Regt. Detached Militia in U. S. service.

STORY, ANDREW,   Fairfax.
Volunteered to go to Plattsburgh,
September, 1814, and served 8 days
in Capt. Josiah Grout's Company.
Ref: Book 51, AGO Page 103.

STORY, ELIJAH,   Fairfax.
Volunteered to go to Plattsburgh,
September, 1814, and served 8 days
in Capt. Josiah Grout's Company.
Ref: Book 51, AGO Page 103.

STORY, HIRAM, Sergeant,   Fairfax.
Volunteered to go to Plattsburgh,
September, 1814, and served 8 days
in Capt. Josiah Grout's Company.
Ref: Book 51, AGO Page 103.

STORY, ISAAC T., Corporal,   Fairfax.
Volunteered to go to Plattsburgh,
September, 1814, and served 8 days
in Capt. Josiah Grout's Company.
Ref: Book 51, AGO Page 103.

‡STORY, JOHN R.
Served under Captains Grout and
Beeman. Pension Certificate of wid-
ow, Mary, No. 34674.

‡*STORY, JOSEPH,   Fairfax.
Enlisted Sept. 25, 1813 and served 1
month and 23 days in Capt. Asa
Wilkins' Company, Col. Dixon's Regt.
Volunteered to go to Plattsburgh,
September, 1814, and served 8 days
in Capt. Josiah Grout's Company.
Ref: Book 51, AGO Page 103. Pension
Certificate No. 20909.

‡STORY, SAMUEL M., Corporal, Fairfax
or Swanton. Served from Aug. 8,
1812 in company of Capt. Joseph Beeman Jr., 11th Regt. U. S. Inf. under
Col. Ira Clark. Served in Lt. V. R.
Goodrich's Company, 11th Regt. Pension Certificate of widow, Elmira L.,
No. 27690. Ref: Hemenway's Vt. Gazetteer, Vol. 2, Page 402.

*STOUGHTON, JOSEPH.
Served in 4 Regt. (Peck's) Vt. Militia.

*STOW, BENJAMIN.
Served from April 12 to April 21,
1814 in Lieut. Justus Foote's Company, Sumner's Regt.

*STOW, DANIEL, Fifer.
Served in 1 Regt. (Martindale's) Vt.
Militia.

*STOW, DAVID.
Served from April 12 to April 21,
1814 in Capt. Othniel Jewett's Company, Sumner's Regt.

*STOW, JAMES.
Served in Capt. Phineas Williams'
Company, 11th Regt.; on Pay Roll
for January and February, 1813. Also
served in 1 Regt. (Martindale's) Vt.
Militia. Ref: R. & L. 1812, AGO
Page 15.

‡*STOW, JOSEPH.
Served in Capt. Richardson's Company, Col. Martindale's Regt. Detached Militia in U. S. service 2
months and 13 days, 1812. Pension
Certificate of widow, Mary E., No.
28266.

*STOW, MILO.
Served from April 12 to April 21,
1814 in Capt. Shubael Wales' Company, Col. W. B. Sumner's Regt.

*STOW, WARD.
Served from April 12 to April 21,
1814 in Capt. Eseck Sprague's Company, Sumner's Regt.

STOWE, REUBEN.
Served in Capt. Morrill's Company,
Col. Fifield's Regt. Detached Militia
in U. S. service 6 months and 5
days, 1812. Ref: Book 53, AGO
Page 7.

‡STOWELL, DANIEL.
Served in Capt. Perkins' Company.
Pension Certificate No. 33426.

STOWELL, ISAAC,   Whiting.
Volunteered to go to Plattsburgh,
September, 1814, and served 9 days
in Capt. Salmon Foster's Company,
Sumner's Regt. Ref: Book 51, AGO
Page 8.

‡*STOWELL, JOHN.
Served in Capt. Lowry's Company,
Col. Wm. Williams' Regt. Detached
Militia in U. S. service 4 months
and 26 days, 1812. Also served in
Corning's Detachment, Vt. Militia.
Also served as sergeant in 4 Regt.
(Peck's) Vt. Militia. Pension Certi-
ficate of widow, Alice, No. 32447.

*STOWELL, NATHAN, 3rd Lieutenant,
Whiting. Served from April 12 to
April 21, 1814 in Capt. Shubael Wales'
Company, Col. W. B. Sumner's Regt.
Volunteered to go to Plattsburgh,
September, 1814, and served 9 days
in Capt. Salmon Foster's Company,
Sumner's Regt.

‡*STOWELL, RATIO L.
Served in Sumner's' Regt. Vt. Militia. Also served in Capt. Munson's
Company. Pension Certificate No.
25373.

*STOWELL, THOMAS.
Served in 4 Regt. (Peck's) Vt. Militia.

*STOWELL, WILLIAM.
Served in 4 Regt. (Peck's) Vt. Militia.

*STRAIGHT, BURTON, Captain.
Served in 1st Regt. of Detached Mili-
tia of Vt. in U. S. service at Cham-
plain from Nov. 18 to Nov. 19, 1812.
Also served in 1 Regt. (Martindale's)
Vt. Militia.

STRAIGHT, HENRY.
Served from April 27, 1813 to April
27, 1814 in Capt. James Taylor's Company and Capt. Gideon Spencer's Company, 30th Regt. Ref: R. & L. 1812,
AGO Pages 52, 57, 59.

STRAND, BILLINGS,   Richmond.
Volunteered to go to Plattsburgh,
September, 1814, and served 9 days
in Capt. Roswell Hunt's Company, 3
Regt. (Tyler's). Ref: Book 51, AGO
Pages 82 and 84.

STRATON, THOMAS.
Volunteered to go to Plattsburgh,
September, 1814, and served 4 days
in Capt. Aaron Kidder's Company.
Ref: Book 52, AGO Page 65.

STRATTON, DANIEL.
Served from March 29 to June 28,
1813 in Capt. John W. Weeks' Company, 11th Regt. Ref: R. & L. 1812,
AGO Page 4.

*STRATTON, DAVID.
Served in 4 Regt. (Williams') Vt.
Militia.

*STRATTON, JOHN.
Served in Capt. Needham's Company,
Col. Martindale's Regt. Detached
Militia in U. S. service 2 months
and 14 days, 1812.

*STRATTON, MOSES.
Enlisted Sept. 25, 1813 in Capt. Amos
Robinson's Company, Dixon's Regt.

‡STRATTON, RICHARD.
Served in Capt. Wilson's Company.
Pension Certificate No. 26292.

‡STRATTON, THOMAS.
Served in Capt. Alexander Brooks'
Corps of Artillery; on Pay Roll to
June 30, 1814. Pension Certificate of
widow. Elizabeth, No. 27973. Ref:
R. & L. 1812, AGO Page 31.

*STRATTON, WILLIAM.
Served with Hospital Attendants, Vt.

*STRAW, DAVID.
Served from June 11 to June 14,
1813 in Capt. Samuel Blinn's Company, 1st Regt. (Judson's). Also
served in 4 Regt. (Williams') Vt.
Militia.

‡*STRAW, ISRAEL,   Waterbury.
Volunteered to go to Plattsburgh,
September, 1814, and was in the
battle, serving 11 days in Capt. George
Atkins' Company, 4 Regt. (Peck's).
Pension Certificate No. 23143.

STRAW, JOHN M.
Enlisted Feb. 27, 1813 in Capt. John
W. Weeks' Company, 11th Regt.; died
March 26, 1813. Ref: R. & L. 1812,
AGO Page 4.

*STRAW, JONATHAN, Ensign. Stowe.
Volunteered to go to Plattsburgh,
September, 1814, and was at the
battle, serving in Capt. Nehemiah
Perkins' Company, 4 Regt. (Peck's).
Also served as sergeant in Corning's
Detachment.

STRAY, JOHN,   Adams, Conn.
Enlisted at Plattsburgh May 1, 1813
and served in Capt. Gideon Spencer's Company, Capt. James Taylor's
Company and Capt. Wm. Miller's
Company, 30th Regt. Ref: R. & L.
1812, AGO Pages 52, 53, 54, 55, 57, 59.

*STREETER, DAVID.
Served in Capt. Wheeler's Company,
Col. Fifield's Regt. Detached Militia
in U. S. service 3 months and 23
days, 1812.

*STREETER, GROVE.
Served in Capt. Parsons' Company,
Col. Jonathan Williams' Regt. Detached Militia in U. S. service 2
months and 13 days, 1812.

*STREETER, HARRIS,   Richford.
Served in Capt. Wheeler's Company,
Col. Fifield's Regt. Detached Militia
in U. S. service 6 months and 4
days, 1812. Also served in Capt.
Martin D. Follett's Company, Dixon's
Regt. on duty on Northern Frontier
in 1813.

*STREETER, JOSEPH.
Served in 1 Regt. (Judson's) Vt.
Militia.

*STRICKLAND, JOSEPH.
Served in Capt. O. Lowry's Company,
Col. Wm. Williams' Regt. Detached
Militia in U. S. service 4 months
and 26 days, 1812.

STRICKLAND, RICHARD.
Served in War of 1812 and was cap-
tured by troops July 5, 1813 at Fort
Sclusher; discharged Oct. 31, 1814.
Ref: Records of Navy Records and
Library, Navy Dept.

STRONG, ABSALOM, ,   Orange.
Volunteered to go to Plattsburgh
Sept. 11, 1814 and went part way,
serving 5 days in Capt. David Ris-
ing's Company. Ref: Book 52, AGO
Page 19.

*STRONG, AMBROSE,   Thetford.
Served under Captains Taylor and
Walker, Col. Fifield's Regt. Detached
Militia in U. S. service 4 months
and 27 days, 1812. Marched for
Plattsburgh, September, 1814, and
went as far as Bolton, Vt., serving
6 days in Capt. Salmon Howard's
Company, 2nd Regt.

STRONG, AMOS,   Berlin.
Volunteered to go to Plattsburgh,
September, 1814, and served 9 days
in Capt. Cyrus Johnson's Company.
Ref: Book 52, AGO Page 202.

STRONG, HARMON,   Salisbury.
Volunteered to go to Plattsburgh,
September, 1814, and served 4 days
in Capt. John Morton's Company.
Ref: Book 52, AGO Page 141.

*STRONG, IRA, Corporal.
Served from April 12 to May 20,
1814 in Capt. George Fisher's Company, Sumner's Regt.

*STRONG, JACOB.
Served from June 11 to June 14,
1813 in Capt. Hezekiah Barns' Company, 1st Regt. 2nd Brig. 3rd Div.

STRONG, JASPER.
Appointed Cadet Military Academy
Aug. 11, 1814; died Nov. 6, 1865.
Ref: Heitman's Historical Register
and Dictionary USA.

*STRONG, JOEL JR.,   Thetford.
Marched for Plattsburgh, September,
1814, and went as far as Bolton, Vt.,
serving 6 days in Capt. Salmon Howard's Company, 2nd Regt.

‡*STRONG, JOHN M.
Served in Sumner's Regt. Vt. Mili-
tia. Pension Certificate of widow,
Olive Hanna, No. 24512.

*STRONG, RETURN, Lieutenant, Pawlet.
Served in Capt. Scovell's Company,
Col. Martindale's Regt. Detached
Militia in U. S. service 2 months
and 21 days, 1812. Appointed 3rd
Lieutenant, 30th Inf. April 30, 1813;
served in Capt. James Taylor's Company, 30th Regt.; resigned June 29,
1814. Ref: Heitman's Historical Register & Dictionary USA; R. & L.
1812, AGO Page 33.

*STRONG, REUBEN,   Thetford.
Served in Capt. Benjamin Edgerton's
Company, 11th Regt.; on Pay Roll
for September and October, 1812 and
January and February, 1813. Marched
for Plattsburgh, September, 1814, and
went as far as Bolton, Vt., serving
6 days in Capt. Salmon Howard's
Company, 2nd Regt. Ref: R. & L.
1812, AGO Pages 1 and 2.

STRONG, SAMUEL, General, Vergennes.
Volunteered to go to Plattsburgh,
September, 1814, in command of vol-
unteers from Cornwall. Ref: Rev.
Lyman Mathews' History of Corn-
wall, Page 343.

*STRONG, SAMUEL P., 2nd Lieutenant.
Served in Sumner's Regt. Vt. Militia.

*STRONG, SIDNEY.
Served from April 12 to May 20,
1814 in Capt. George Fisher's Company, Sumner's Regt.

*STRONG, TIMOTHY C., Sergeant.
Served from April 12 to April 15,
1814 in Capt. John Hackett's Company, Sumner's Regt.

*STRONG, WILLIAM H.,   Randolph.
Volunteered to go to Plattsburgh,
September, 1814, and served in Capt.
Lebbeus Egerton's Company.

*STROUD, BILLINGS,   Richmond.
Served from Oct. 11 to Oct. 16, 1813
in Capt. Roswell Hunt's Company,
3 Regt. (Tyler's); volunteered to go
to Plattsburgh, September, 1814, and
served 9 days in same company.

STROUD, JAMES,   Franklin County.
Enlisted June 3, 1812 for 5 years in
Capt. White Youngs' Company, 15th
Regt.; on Muster Roll from Aug.
31 to Dec. 31, 1814. Ref: R. & L.
1812, AGO Page 27.

*STUART, DAVID.
Served in Capt. Lowry's Company,
Col. Wm. Williams' Regt. Detached
Militia in U. S. service 4 months and
26 days, 1812.

*STUART, JOHN.
Served in Capt. S. Pettes' Company,
Col. Wm. Williams' Regt. Detached
Militia in U. S. service 3 months
and 13 days, 1812.

STUDSON, ROBERT.
Served from Feb. 26 to May 25, 1813
in Capt. Charles Follett's Company,
11th Regt. Ref: R. & L. 1812, AGO
Page 13.

STUERT, LUTHER.
Volunteered to go to Plattsburgh,
September, 1814, and served 7 days
in Capt. Frederick Griswold's Com-
pany, raised in Brookfield, Vt. Ref:
Book 52, AGO Page 52.

STUFF, JOHN,   Watervillet, N. Y.
Enlisted at Burlington Dec. 17, 1813
during the war in Capt. Wm. Miller's
Company, 30th Regt.; on Muster Roll
to Aug. 31, 1814. Ref: R. & L. 1812,
AGO Pages 54 and 55.

*STURD, JOHN O. (or Hurd).
Served in Sumner's Regt. Vt. Militia.

STURDEVANT, SILAS, Franklin County.
Volunteered to go to Plattsburgh
Sept. 11, 1814, and served in 15th or
22nd Regt. Ref: Hemenway's Vt.
Gazetteer, Vol. 2, Page 391.

*STURGES, SAMUEL.
Served from April 17 to April 21,
1814 in Capt. Othniel Jewett's Company, Sumner's Regt.

*STURLING. ELISHA.
Served in 4 Regt. (Peck's) Vt. Militia.

*STURTEVANT, ABNER.
Served from April 12 to April 21,
1814 in Capt. Shubael Wales' Company, Col. W. B. Sumner's Regt.

*STURTEVANT, AUGUSTUS.
Served from April 12 to April 21,
1814 in Capt. Shubael Wales' Company, Col. W. B. Sumner's Regt.

*STURTEVANT, JOHN.
Served from April 12 to April 21,
1814 in Capt. Shubael Wales' Company, Col. W. B. Sumner's Regt.

STURTEVANT, MARTIN.
Served from May 1 to June 1, 1814
as armorer in Alexander Parris' Company of Artificers. Ref: R. & L.
1812, AGO Page 24.

‡*STURTEVANT, NOAH.
Served from April 12 to April 21,
1814 in Capt. Shubael Wales' Company, Col. W. B. Sumner's Regt.
Also served in Capt. Britain's Company. Pension Certificate No. 33985.

STURTEVANT, ZOPHAR,   Marshfield.
Volunteered to go to Plattsburgh,
September, 1814, and served 8 days
in Capt. James English's Company.
Ref: Book 52, AGO Pages 199 and 248.

SULEY, ELEAZER.
Enlisted May 10, 1813 for 5 years in
company of late Capt. J. Brooks,
commanded by Lt. John I. Cromwell, Corps of U. S. Artillery; on
Muster Roll from April 30 to June
30, 1814. Ref: R. & L. 1812, AGO
Page 18.

SULLIVAN, JEREMIAH, Corporal.
Enlisted June 6, 1812 for 5 years
in Capt. White Young's Company,
15th Regt.; on Muster Roll from
Aug. 31 to Dec. 31, 1814. Ref: R.
& L. 1812, AGO Page 27.

SULLIVAN, TIMOTHY.
Served from March 1 to March 31,
1814; no organization given. Served
from May 1 to June 12, 1814 in Alexander Parris' Company of Artificers
as a carpenter. Ref: R. & L. 1812,
AGO Pages 24 and 29.

SUMMIX, JOSEPH.
Served from Feb. 24 to May 23, 1813
in Capt. Charles Follett's Company,
11th Regt. Ref: R. & L. 1812, AGO
Page 13.

*SUMNER, ADAM,   Morristown.
Served in Capt. Mason's Company,
Col. Fifield's Regt. Detached Militia
in U. S. service 4 months and 19
days, 1812. Served from May 6, 1813
to May 10, 1814 in Capt. James Taylor's Company and Capt. Gideon Spencer's Company. 30th Regt. Ref: R. &
L. 1812, AGO Pages 52, 57, 59.

*SUMNER, ASA.
Served from April 12 to April 15,
1814 in Lieut. Justus Foote's Company, Sumner's Regt.

‡SUMNER, CYRUS.
Served in Capt. Jewett's Company.
Pension Certificate No. 29858.

*SUMNER, GEORGE H.
Served from April 12 to April 21,
1814 in Capt. Edmund B. Hill's Company, Sumner's Regt.

*SUMNER, JOHN A., Ensign.
Served in Sumner's Regt. Vt. Militia.

SUMNER, SAMUEL   Bakersfield.
Volunteered to go to Plattsburgh
and was at the battle Sept. 11, 1814,
serving in Capt. M. Stearns' Company. Ref: Hemenway's Vt. Gazetteer, Vol. 2, Page 394.

SUMNER, SAMUEL G.
Served in Capt. Samuel H. Holly's
Company, 11th Regt.; on Pay Roll
for January and February, 1813. Ref:
R. & L. 1812, AGO Page 25.

*SUMNER, WILLIAM B., Colonel.
Served as Colonel of Sumner's Regt.
Vt. Militia.

*SUMRICKS, JOSEPH.
Served with Hospital Attendants, Vt.

SUMRISE, HENRY.
Served in Capt. Charles Follett's
Company, 11th Regt.; on Pay Roll
for January and February, 1812.
Ref: R. & L. 1812, AGO Page 12.

*SUNDERLAND, ASA (or Sunderlin),
Shoreham. Served from April 12 to
May 20, 1814 in Capt. George Fisher's
Company, Sumner's Regt.

*SUNDERLAND, NOAH.
Served from April 12 to May 20,
1814 in company of Capt. James Gray
Jr., Sumner's Regt.

SUNDERLIN. WATERMAN,   Shoreham.
Volunteered to go to Plattsburgh,
September, 1814, and served 6 days
in Capt. Nathaniel North's Company
of Cavalry. Ref: Rev. J. F. Goodhue's History of Shoreham, Page 107.

*SUNDERLINE, DANIEL.
Served in Capt. Scovell's Company.
Col. Martindale's Regt. Detached
Militia in U. S. service 2 months
and 21 days, 1812.

SUPP, BENJAMIN,   Franklin County.
Volunteered to go to Plattsburgh
Sept. 11, 1814, and served in 15th or
22nd Regt. Ref: Hemenway's Vt. Gazetteer, Vol. 2, Page 392.

SURRETT, AMBROSE.
Enlisted Jan. 19, 1813 in Lt. V. R.
Goodrich's Company, 11th Regt.; on
Pay Roll for January and February,
1813. Ref: R. & L. 1812, AGO Page
.11.

SUTHERLAND, DANIEL.
Enlisted June 9, 1813 for 1 year in
Capt. Daniel Farrington's Company,
30th Regt. (also commanded by Capt.
Simeon Wright); on Muster Roll from
March 1 to April 30, 1814. Ref: R.
& L. 1812, AGO Pages 50 and 51.

*SUTHERLAND, JAMES.
Served from April 12 to April 21,
1814 in Capt. Shubael Wales' Company, Col. W. B. Sumner's Regt.

*SUTTON, SAMUEL.
Served with Hospital Attendants, Vt.

‡*SUTTON, WILLIAM.
Served from June 11 to June 14,
1813 in Lt. Bates' Company, 1 Regt.
(Judson's). Pension Certificate No.
34742.

*SWAIN, JOHN C.
Served from March 18 to June 17,
1813 in Capt. John W. Weeks' Com-
pany, 11th Regt. Also served with
Hospital Attendants, Vt. Ref: R. &
L. 1812, AGO Page 4.

SWAN, HAZEAL,   Granville.
Volunteered to go to Plattsburgh,
September, 1814, and served 7 days
in Capt. Asaph Smith's' Company.
Ref: Book 51, AGO Page 20.

‡*SWAN, JOHN.
Enlisted Sept. 25, 1813 in company
of Capt. Jonathan Prentiss Jr., Dixon's Regt.; transferred Sept. 29, 1813
to Capt. Asahel Langworthy's Company, Col. Isaac Clark's Rifle Corps
of Col. Dixon's Regt. and served 1
month and 22 days in U. S. service.
Pension Certificate of widow, Philena,
No. 21404.

*SWARD, ANSON.
Served in Sumner's Regt. Vt. Militia.

SWASEY, JAROCK,   Franklin County.
Volunteered to go to Plattsburgh
Sept. 11, 1814 and served in 15th or
22nd Regt. Ref: Hemenway's Vt. Gazetteer, Vol. 2, Page 391.

SWEAT, JOHN, Corporal.
Served in Capt. Benjamin Bradford's
Company; joined by transfer July 22,
1813; on Muster Roll from May 31
to Aug. 31, 1813. Ref: R. & L.
1812, AGO Page 26.

SWEET, ABRAHAM.
Served in War of 1812 and was cap-
tured by troops Sept. 17, 1814 at
Fort Erie; discharged March 13, 1815.

*SWEET, EDWARD.
Served from April 12 to April 21,
1814 in Capt. Othniel Jewett's Company, Sumner's Regt.

‡*SWEET, EZEKIEL.
Served from June 11 to June 14, 1813
in Capt. Thomas Dorwin's Company,

1st Regt. 2nd Brig. 3rd Div. Pension Certificate of widow Cleora, No.
9039.

‡SWEET, THOMAS E.
Served in Capt. Pettis' Company (4th
Regt.). Pension Certificate of widow,
Anna, No. 4770.

*SWEETLAND, ELEAZER,   Thetford.
Marched for Plattsburgh September,
1814, and went as far as Bolton, Vt.,
serving 6 days in Capt. Salmon Howard's Company, 2nd Regt.

*SWEETLAND, NOAH S.,   Thetford.
Marched for Plattsburgh, September,
1814, and went as far as Bolton, Vt.,
serving 6 days in Capt. Salmon Howard's Company, 2nd Regt.

*SWEETLAND, PHILETUS.   Fairfield.
Served in Capt. Kendall's Company,
Col. Wm. Williams' Regt. Detached
Militia in U. S. service 4 months
and 23 days, 1812. Served from July
25, 1813 to July 24, 1814 in Capt.
Gideon Spencer's Company and Capt.
James Taylor's Company, 30th Regt.
Ref: R. & L. 1812, AGO Pages 52
and 57.

*SWEETZER, WILLIAM, Teamster. Serv-
ed in Capt. Dodge's Company, Col.
Fifield's Regt. Detached Militia in U.
S. service 2 months and 21 days, 1812.

*SWETT, LEVI.
Served from June 11 to June 14,
1813 in Capt. Thomas Dorwin's Company, 1st Regt. 2nd Brig. 3rd Div.

‡*SWETT, LUKE 2nd.,   Danville.
Served in Capt. Morrill's Company,
Col. Fifield's Regt. Detached Militia
in U. S. service 6 months and 5
days, 1812. Pension Certificate No.
2738. Pension Certificate of widow,
Hannah, No. 15753.

‡SWETT, WILLIAM.
Served in Capt. Sanborn's Company.
Pension Certificate of widow, Judith,
No. 32037.

*SWIFT, ERASTUS. Sergeant.
Served from April 12 to May 20,
1814 in Capt. George Fisher's Company, Sumner's Regt.

*SWINNERTON. BENJAMIN.
Served in Capt. Phelps' Company,
Col. Jonathan Williams' Regt. Detached Militia in U. S. service 2
months and 21 days, 1812.

SWISS, IRA T.
Enlisted Sept. 25, 1813 in Capt.
Charles Bennett's Company, Dixon's
Regt. Ref: Book 52, AGO Page 266.

SWITZER, STEPHEN.
Enlisted June 14, 1814 and served
in Capt. Gideon Spencer's Company
and Capt. Wm. Miller's Company,
30th Regt. Ref: R. & L. 1812, AGO
Pages 54 and 56.

‡*SYKES, HARRY.
Served in 1 Regt. (Martindale's) Vt.
Militia. Pension Certificate of wid-
ow, Orphe, No. 19397.

*SYLLICK. SEYMOUR.
Served from April 12 to April 21,
1814 in Lieut. Justus Foote's Company, Sumner's Regt.

SYLVESTER,   BARZILLA,   Corporal,
Stockbridge.   Volunteered to go to
Plattsburgh,   September,   1814,   and
served 8 days in Capt. Elias Keyes'
Company. Ref: Book 51, AGO Pages
239 and 243.

SYLVESTER, JOHN.
Served from April 22, 1813 to April 27,
1814 in Capt. Simeon Wright's Company. Ref: R. & L. 1812, AGO
Page 51.

*SYMONDS, BENJAMIN, Corporal.
Served in 1 Regt. (Judson's) Vt.
Militia.

*SYMONS, RUFUS (or Simons) Lieuten-
ant. Served in 2 Regt. (Fifield's) Vt.
Militia.

TABOR, ARDEN,   Mt. Tabor.
Served in Capt. Hotchkiss' Company,
Col.   Martindale's   Regt.   Detached
Militia in U. S. service 1 month and
1 day, 1812. Ref: Book 53, AGO
Page 60.

‡*TABOR, EDWARD C., Sergeant, Danby
or Mount Tabor. Served in Capt.
Hotchkiss' Company, Col. Martindale's
Regt.   Detached   Militia   in   U.   S.
service 2 months and 13 days, 1812.
Served in 1 Regt. of Detached Militia in U. S. service at Champlain
from Nov. 18 to Nov. 19, 1812. Pension Certificate of widow, Nancy A.,
No. 34122.

*TABOR, GIDEON, Musician.
Served in 1 Regt. (Judson's) Vt.
Militia.

TABOR, ISAAC.
Volunteered to go to Plattsburgh,
September, 1814, and served 4 days
in company of Capt. James George
of Topsham. Ref: Book 52, AGO
Page 68.

*TABOR, JOHN, Corporal and 2nd Major.
Served as corporal and 2nd Major
in 1 Regt. (Judson's) Vt. Militia.

TABOR, LEVI,   Topsham.
Volunteered to go to Plattsburgh,
September, 1814, and served 4 days
in Capt. James George's Company.
Ref: Book 52, AGO Page 68.

*TABOR, STEPHEN, Fifer.
Served in Capt. Rogers' Company,
Col. Fifield's Regt. Detached Militia
in U. S. service 5 months and 27
days, 1812.

‡TADDER, JAMES,   Pittsford.
Served from April 30, 1813 to May 1,
1814 in Capt. Daniel Farrington's
Company, 30th Regt. (also commanded by Capt. Simeon Wright). Volunteered to go to Plattsburgh, September, 1814, and served 8 days in Capt.
Caleb Hendee's Company. Pension
Certificate of widow, Margaret, No.
30023. Ref: Book 52, AGO Page 125.

*TAFT, BENJAMINE.
Served in 1 Regt. (Judson's) Vt. Militia.

*TAFT, GIDEON.
Served in 3 Regt. (Tyler's) Vt. Militia.

*TAFT, OTIS.
Served in 3 Regt. (Tyler's) Vt. Militia.

*TAGART, JONAS.
Served in 1 Regt. (Judson's) Vt. Militia.

TAGGART, JAMES.
Served from May 1 to June 30, 1814
in Alexander Parris' Company of Artificers. Ref: R. & L. 1812, AGO
Page 24.

*TAISEY, JAMES,   Groton.
Served in 2 Regt. (Fifield's) Vt. Militia.

‡*TAISEY, JOHN,   Groton.
Served in Capt. Morrill's Company,
Col. Fifield's Regt. Detached Militia
in U. S. service 6 months and 5
days, 1812. Pension Certificate No.
18725. Pension Certificate of widow,
Phebe, No. 14942.

TAITON, JOSEPH JR.
Served in Capt. Chadwicks' Company.
Ref: R. & L. 1812, AGO Page 32.

TALBOTT, JOHN H.,   Annapolis.
Served from May 1 to Aug. 15, 1814
in Capt. McIlwain's Company, 14th
Inf. Ref: R. & L. 1812, AGO Page
30.

*TALCOTT, JAMES, Ensign.
Served from Oct. 5 to Oct. 17, 1813
in Capt. Stephen Brown's Company,
3 Regt. (Tyler's).

*TALER, JOBE,   Calais.
Volunteered to go to Plattsburgh,
September, 1814, and served 10 days
in Capt. Gideon Wheelock's Company.

‡TALMADGE, JOHN.
Served in Capt. Seymour's Company.
Pension Certificate of widow, Fanny
L., No. 30696.

‡TAMBLIN, TIMOTHY.
Served in Capt. Hubberd's Company.
Pension Certificate No. 6508.

TAMBLING, ELISHA.
Served in Capt. Hopkins' Company,
Col.   Martindale's   Regt.   Detached
Militia in U. S. service 2 months and
13 days, 1812. Ref: Book 53, AGO
Page 72.

*TAME, JOSEPH.   Shoreham.
Volunteered to go to Vergennes and
served in company of Capt. James
Gray Jr.. Sumner's Regt. Volunteered
to go to Plattsburgh, September, 1814,
and served 6 days in Capt. Samuel
Hand's Company.

TAPLIN, WILLIAM,   Montpelier.
Volunteered to go to Plattsburgh,
September, 1814, and served 8 days
in Capt. Timothy Hubbard's Company.
Ref: Book 52, AGO Page 256.

*TAPPAN, SILAS.
Served from April 17 to April 21,
1814 in Capt. Othniel Jewett's Company, Sumner's Regt.

‡TARBELL, JAMES.
Served in Capt. Emmon's Company.
Pension Certificate No. 7336.

‡TARBELL, ZACHARIAH (or Tarbel).
Served in Capt. Wheeler's Company.
Pension Certificate of widow, Anna
M., No. 28613.

TARBLE, JAMES.
Enlisted Feb. 13, 1813 in Capt.
Phineas Williams' Company, 11th
Regt.; on Pay Roll to May 31, 1813.
Ref: R. & L. 1812, AGO Page 14.

*TARBLE, SAMUEL.
Served in 3 Regt. (Williams') Vt.
Militia.

*TARBOX, ISAAC, Ensign,   Randolph.
Volunteered to go to Plattsburgh,
September, 1814, and served in Capt.
Lebbeus Egerton's Company.

TARBOX, WILLIAM,   Richmond.
Volunteered to go to Plattsburgh,
September, 1814, and served 9 days
in Capt. Roswell Hunt's Company, 3
Regt. (Tyler's). Ref: Book 51, AGO
Pages 82 and 84.

*TARRANCE, ORRAN.
Enlisted Sept. 18, 1813 in Capt. Isaac
Finch's Company, Col. Clark's Rifle
Corps.

*TASKER, JOHN,   Cabot.
Enlisted Sept. 25, 1813 in Capt.
Thomas Waterman's Company, Dixon's
Regt. Volunteered to go to Plattsburgh, September, 1814, and served
3 days in Capt. Anthony Perry's Company. Ref: Book 52, AGO Pages 252
and 253.

*TASKER, SILAS.
Served from Sept. 25 to Oct. 28,
1813 in Capt. Thomas Waterman's
Company, Dixon's Regt.

‡TASKETT, JAMES.
Served in Capt. R. B. Brown's Company. Pension Certificate No. 7888.

*TAYLOR, ALPHEUS, Corporal, Vernon.
Served in Capt. Noyce's Company,
Col. Jonathan Williams' Regt. Detached Militia in U. S. service 2
months and 6 days, 1812.

*TAYLOR, AMOS.
Enlisted Oct. 24, 1813 in Capt. Asahel
Langworthy's Company, Col. Isaac
Clark's Rifle Corps; transferred to
Capt. Elijah Birge's Company, Col.
Dixon's Regt. Detached Militia in
U. S. service 30 days.

TAYLOR, ANTHONY, Corporal.
Enlisted May 31, 1813 for 1 year in
Capt. Simeon Wright's Company. Ref:
R. & L. 1812, AGO Page 51.

TAYLOR, B. T.
Enlisted April 22. 1813 for 1 year in
Capt. James Taylor's Company, 30th
Regt. Ref: R. & L. 1812, AGO Page
58.

*TAYLOR, CHARLES B., Sergeant.
Enlisted Sept. 25, 1813 and served
1 month and 23 days in Capt. Thomas
Waterman's Company, Col. Dixon's
Regt. Detached Militia in U. S. serv-
ice.

*TAYLOR, DANIEL.
Served in 4 Regt. (Peck's' Vt. Militia).

*TAYLOR, DAVID.
Served in Capt. Morrill's Company,
Col. Fifield's Regt. Detached Militia
in U. S. service 2 months and 18
days, 1812. Served from June 11 to
June 14, 1813 in Capt. Moses Jewett's
Company, 1st Regt. 2nd Brig. 3rd
Div. Served from April 12 to April
21, 1814 in Lieut. James S. Morton's
Company, Col. W. B. Sumner's Regt.

TAYLOR, EDWARD.
Served from March 10 to June 9, 1813
in Lieut. V. R. Goodrich's Company,
11th Regt. Ref: R. & L. 1812, AGO
Page 10.

*TAYLOR, ELIAS, Sergeant.
Served in Capt. O. Lowry's Company,
Col. Wm. Williams' Regt. Detached
Militia in U. S. service at Swanton
Falls 4 months and 26 days, 1812.
Also served in 4 Regt. (Peck's) Vt.
Militia.

*TAYLOR, ELIAS JR., Ensign.
Served in 4 Regt. (Peck's) Vt. Militia.

TAYLOR, ELIPHALET.
Served from March 1 to May 26, 1813
in Capt. John W. Weeks' Company,
11th Regt. Ref: R. & L. 1812, AGO
Page 4.

TAYLOR, ELISHA, Corporal.
Served from March 20 to June 9,
1813 in Capt. Charles Follett's Company, 11th Regt. Ref: R. & L. 1812,
AGO Page 13.

TAYLOR, FOSTER.
Enlisted April 22, 1813 and served
in Capt. James Taylor's Company and
Capt. Gideon Spencer's Company, 30th
Regt. Ref: R. & L. 1812, AGO Pages
52 and 56.

*TAYLOR, GILES,   Fairfax.
Served in Capt. Taylor's Company,
Col. Wm. Williams' Regt. Detached
Militia in U. S. service 4 months and
24 days, 1812. Also served in Capt.
Wilkins' Company, Col. Dixon's Regt.
Detached Militia in U. S. service 1
month and 23 days, 1813.

*TAYLOR, HORATIO.
Served from Sept. 25 to Oct. 3, 1813
in Capt. Jesse Post's Company, Dixon's Regt.

TAYLOR, J.,   Richford.
Served in Capt. Martin D. Follett's
Company, Dixon's Regt. on duty on
Canadian Frontier in 1813. Ref: Hem-
enway's Vt. Gazetteer, Vol. 2, Page
428.

‡*TAYLOR, JAMES, Corporal.
Served in Capt. Willson's Company,
Col. Wm. Williams' Regt. Detached

Militia in U. S. service 4 months and 24 days, 1812. Also served in 4 Regt. (Peck's) Vt. Militia. Pension Certificate No. 4322.

*TAYLOR, JAMES, Captain,   Berlin. Served as Captain in 4 Regt. (Williams') Vt. Militia. Volunteered to go to Plattsburgh, September, 1814, and served 7 days in Capt. Cyrus Johnson's Company. Ref: Book 52, AGO Page 255.

TAYLOR, JAMES, Captain. Appointed Captain 30th Inf. April 30, 1813; honorably discharged June 15, 1815. Ref: Heitman's Historical Register & Dictionary USA; R. & L. 1812, AGO Pages 52, 53, 58.

TAYLOR, JOB JR.,   Marshfield. Volunteered to go to Plattsburgh, September, 1814, and served 9 days in Capt. James English's Company. Ref: Book 52, AGO Page 248.

‡TAYLOR, JOHN. Served in Capt. Bradley's Company. Pension Certificate No. 3763.

TAYLOR, JOHN,   Franklin County. Enlisted Dec. 28, 1812 for 5 years in Capt. White Youngs' Company, 15th Regt.; on Muster Roll from Aug. 31 to Dec. 31, 1814. Ref: R. & L. 1812, AGO Page 27.

TAYLOR, JOHN. Served in Capt. Phineas Williams' Company, 11th Regt.; on Pay Roll of company for January and February, 1813. Ref: R. & L. 1812, AGO Page 15.

TAYLOR, JOHN B., Corporal, Shoreham. Enlisted as corporal, saw much severe service, returned sick to Greenbush at the end of the war and was honorably discharged. Ref: Rev. J. F. Goodhue's History of Shoreham, Page 103.

*TAYLOR, JOSIAH P. Served in Capt. Morrill's Company, Col. Fifield's Regt. Detached Militia in U. S. service 3 months and 17 days, 1812. Also served in Capt. Howard's Company, 2 Regt. Vt. Militia.

*TAYLOR, LUTHER,   Richford. Served in Capt. Briggs' Company, Col. Jonathan Williams' Regt. Detached Militia in U. S. service 2 months and 13 days, 1812. Enlisted Sept. 25, 1813 in Capt. Martin D. Folett's Company, Dixon's Regt.

‡TAYLOR, NILES. Pension Certificate of widow, Martha, No. 44245; no organization given.

*TAYLOR, NOAH. Served in 4 Regt. (Williams') Vt. Militia.

TAYLOR, OBEDIAH. Served from May 1 to June 30, 1814 in Capt. Haig's Corps of Light Dragoons. Ref: R. & L. 1812, AGO Page 20.

*TAYLOR, OLIVER, Captain,   Thetford. Served in 2 Regt. (Fifield's) Vt. Militia.

TAYLOR, RODERICK. Enlisted Jan. 31, 1813 in Capt. Benjamin S. Edgerton's Company, 11th Regt.; on Pay Roll for January and February, 1813. Ref: R. & L. 1812, AGO Pages 2 and 3.

TAYLOR, SEBRIAN C., Sergeant. Served from May 12, 1813 to May 11, 1814 in Capt. Daniel Farrington's Company, 30th Regt. (also commanded by Capt. Simeon Wright). Ref: R. & L. 1812, AGO Pages 50 and 51.

*TAYLOR, STEPHEN. Served from April 12 to April 21, 1814 in Lieut. James S. Morton's Company, Col. W. B. Sumner's Regt.

TAYLOR, THOMAS,   Fairfield. Volunteered to go to Plattsburgh, September, 1814, and served 6 days in Capt. Benjamin Wooster's Company. Ref: Book 51, AGO Pages 112 and 158.

TAYLOR, TYLER. Enlisted Sept. 25, 1813 in Capt. Asa Wilkins' Company, Dixon's Regt. Ref: Book 52, AGO Page 272.

TAYLOR, WALTER. Enlisted June 10, 1813 for 1 year in Capt. Daniel Farrington's Company, 30th Regt. (also commanded by Capt. Simeon Wright); on Muster Roll from March 1 to April 30, 1814. Ref: R. & L. 1812, AGO Pages 50 and 51.

TAYLOR, WILLIAM,   Franklin County. Enlisted June 27, 1812 for 5 years in Capt. White Youngs' Company, 15th Regt.; on Muster Roll from Aug. 31 to Dec. 31, 1814. Ref: R. & L. 1812, AGO Page 27; Hemenway's Vt. Gazetteer, Vol. 2, Page 392.

*TAYLOR, WILLIAM. Served in Capt. Briggs' Company, Col. Jonathan Williams' Regt. Detached Militia in U. S. service 2 months and 13 days, 1812.

TEDDER, JAMES,   Franklin County. Volunteered to go to Plattsburgh Sept. 11, 1814 and served in 15th or 22nd Regt. Ref: Hemenway's Vt. Gazetteer, Vol. 2, Page 391.

TEMPLE, LOREN. Served in company of Capt. John McNeil Jr., 11th Regt.; on Pay Roll for January and February, 1813. Ref: R. & L. 1812, AGO Page 17.

‡TEMPLETON, JOEL H.,   Montpelier. Volunteered to go to Plattsburgh, September, 1814, and served 8 days in Capt. Timothy Hubbard's Company. Pension Certificate of widow, Abigail, No. 13621.

*TENANT, ARTHUR. Served in 2 Regt. (Fifield's) Vt. Militia.

*TENANT, RUFUS. Served in Capt. Wright's Company, Col. Fifield's Regt. Detached Militia

*TERRILL, IRA.
Served in 1 Regt. (Martindale's) Vt. Militia.

*TERRY, HENRY.
Served in 4 Regt. (Williams') Vt. Militia.

*TERRY, JEREMIAH.
Served from Oct. 5 to Oct. 17, 1813 in Capt. Roswell Hunt's Company, 3 Regt. (Tyler's). Also served in 4 Regt. (Williams') Vt. Militia.

TEWKSBURY, JACOB.
Served from April 12 to April 15, 1814 in Capt. John Hackett's Company, Sumner's Regt.

THAIR, JASON.
Served in Capt. Samuel H. Holly's Company, 11th Regt.; on Pay Roll for January and February, 1813. Ref: R. & L. 1812, AGO Page 25.

*THATCHER, ALVAN.
Served in 3 Regt. (Tyler's) Vt. Militia.

THATCHER, AMASA (or Ammissa), Poultney or St. Albans. Enlisted April 23, 1813 for 1 year in Capt. John Wires' Company, 30th Regt. Ref: R. & L. 1812, AGO Page 40.

THATCHER, COMFORT. Fifer, Granville. Enlisted May 4, 1813 for 1 year in Capt. Simeon Wright's Company. Volunteered to go to Plattsburgh, September, 1814, and served 7 days in Capt. Asaph Smith's Company. Ref: R. & L. 1812, AGO Page 51; Book 51, AGO Page 20.

*THATCHER, EPHRAIM.
Served from Oct. 5 to Oct. 17, 1813 in Capt. Stephen Brown's Company, 3 Regt. (Tyler's).

*THATCHER, PETER, Sergeant Major.
Served in 3 Regt. (Williams') Vt. Militia.

THATCHER, SAMUEL, Granville.
Volunteered to go to Plattsburgh, September, 1814, and served 7 days in Capt. Asaph Smith's Company. Ref: Book 51, AGO Page 20.

THAYER, ABEL, Braintree.
Marched to Plattsburgh, Sept. 10, 1814, serving in Capt. Lot Hudson's Company. Ref: Book 52, AGO Pages 24 and 26.

THAYER, ABRAM.
Served from March 15 to June 14, 1813 in Capt. Edgerton's Company, 11th Regt. Ref: R. & L. 1812, AGO Page 3.

*THAYER, ALBERT, Corporal.
Served in Capt. Sabin's Company, Col. Jonathan Williams' Regt. Detached Militia in U. S. service 2 months and 6 days, 1812.

*THAYER, ALVIN.
Served in Capt. Sabin's Company, Col. Jonathan Williams' Regt. Detached Militia in U. S. service 2 months and 6 days, 1812.

*THAYER, AMHERST, Lieutenant.
Served from Sept. 27 to Oct. 26, 1813 in Capt. Jesse Post's Company, Dixon's Regt.

THAYER, DAVID, Montpelier.
Volunteered to go to Plattsburgh, September, 1814, and served 8 days in Capt. Samuel M. Orcutt's Company. Ref: Book 52, AGO Pages 182, 196, 250.

THAYER, LEVI.
Enlisted Aug. 21, 1813 for 1 year and served in Capt. James Taylor's Company and Capt. Gideon Spencer's Company, 30th Regt. Ref: R. & L. 1812, AGO Pages 52, 53, 56, 59.

*THAYER, NATHAN.
Served in 4 Regt. (Peck's) Vt. Militia.

THAYER, SAMUEL.
Served in Capt. Cross' Company, Col. Martindale's Regt. Detached Militia in U. S. service 2 months and 14 days, 1812. Ref: Book 53, AGO Page 38.

*THAYER, WILLIAM.
Served from April 12 to April 15, 1814 in Capt. John Hackett's Company, Sumner's Regt. Also served in Capt. Howard's Company, 2 Regt.

THAYER, ZENAS, Musician, Braintree.
Marched to Plattsburgh Sept. 10, 1814, serving in Capt. Lot Hudson's Company. Ref: Book 52, AGO Pages 24 and 29.

*THEYER, NATHAN JR.
Served in 4 Regt. (Peck's) Vt. Militia.

THINK, DODRICH, Franklin County.
Volunteered to go to Plattsburgh Sept. 11, 1814 and served in 15th or 22nd Regt. Ref: Hemenway's Vt. Gazetteer, Vol. 2, Page 392.

THOMAS, ALLEN.
Served in company of late Capt. J. Brooks, commanded by Lt. John I. Cromwell, Corps of U. S. Artillery; on Muster Roll from April 30 to June 30, 1814; prisoner of war; transferred from Capt. Collins' Company. Ref: R. & L. 1812, AGO Page 18.

‡THOMAS, ASA, Salisbury.
Volunteered to go to Plattsburgh, September, 1814, and served 4 days in Capt. John Morton's Company. Also served in Capt. Moses Powers' Company. Pension Certificate No. 15889. Ref: Book 52, AGO Pages 139 and 141.

THOMAS, AUGUSTUS, Belvidere.
Volunteered to go to Plattsburgh, September, 1814, and served 7 days in Capt. Moody Shattuck's Company. Ref: Book 51, AGO Page 211.

THOMAS, BENJAMIN.
Served in Capt. White Youngs' Company, 15th Regt.; on Muster Roll from Aug. 31 to Dec. 31, 1814. Ref: R. & L. 1812, AGO Page 27.

THOMAS, CHAUNCY.
Served from May 1 to June 30, 1814 in Capt. Alexander Brooks' Corps of Artillery. Ref: R. & L. 1812, AGO Page 31.

THOMAS, DANIEL,   Franklin County.
Volunteered to go to Plattsburgh Sept. 11, 1814 and served in 15th or 22nd Regt. Ref: Hemenway's Vt. Gazetteer, Vol. 2, Page 391.

THOMAS, DAVID, Drummer, Middletown.
Volunteered to go to Plattsburgh, September, 1814, and served 4 days in Capt. Reuben Wood's Company. Ref: Book 52, AGO Page 143.

*THOMAS, DUDLEY.
Served in Capt. Parsons' Company, Col. Jonathan Williams' Regt. Detached Militia in U. S. service 2 months and 13 days, 1812.

THOMAS, EDWARD.
Served from May 1 to June 30, 1814 in Alexander Parris' Company of Artificers as a carpenter. Ref: R. & L. 1812, AGO Page 24.

*THOMAS, ELIJAH JR.
Served in Sumner's Regt. Vt. Militia.

THOMAS, GIDEON.
Served from Nov. 1, 1812 to Feb. 28, 1813 in company of Capt. John McNeil Jr., 11th Regt. Ref: R. & L. 1812, AGO Page 17.

THOMAS, HENRY,   Franklin County.
Volunteered to go to Plattsburgh Sept. 11, 1814, and served in 15th or 22nd Regt. Ref: Hemenway's Vt. Gazetteer, Vol. 2, Page 391.

*THOMAS, IRA.
Served in 3 Regt. (Tyler's) Vt. Militia.

‡THOMAS, ISAAC.
Pension Certificate of widow, Lydia, No. 39519; no organization given.

THOMAS, JAMES,   Boston, Mass.
Served from Sept. 1, 1814 to June 16, 1815 in Capt. Sanford's Company, 30th Inf. Ref: R. & L. 1812, AGO Page 23.

THOMAS, JEREMIAH, Ensign and Lieutenant. Appointed Sergeant 21st Inf. April 30, 1812; Ensign 21st Inf. June 24, 1814; 2nd Lieutenant Oct. 1, 1814; honorably discharged June 15, 1815. Ref: Heitman's Historical Register & Dictionary USA.

THOMAS, JOHN,   St. Albans.
Enlisted June 1, 1813 for 1 year in Capt. John Wires' Company, 30th Regt. Ref: R. & L. 1812, AGO Page 40.

‡*THOMAS, JOHN.
Served in Capt. Parsons' Company, Col. Jonathan Williams' Regt. De-

tached Militia in U. S. service 2 months and 13 days, 1812. Pension Certificate No. 12592.

THOMAS, JOHN,   Woodbury.
Volunteered to go to Plattsburgh, September, 1814, and served 7 days; no organization given. Ref: Book 52, AGO Page 210.

THOMAS, JOSEPH.
Enlisted April 25, 1813 for 1 year in Capt. Daniel Farrington's Company, 30th Regt. (also commanded by Capt. Simeon Wright); on Muster Roll from March 1 to April 30, 1814. Ref: R. & L. 1812, AGO Pages 50 and 51.

‡THOMAS, KEMP.
Served in Capt. Brown's Company. Pension Certificate of widow, Nancy, No. 31805.

THOMAS, LEMUEL.
Enlisted July 4, 1812 for 5 years in company of late Capt. J. Brooks, commanded by Lt. John I. Cromwell, Corps of U. S. Artillery; on Muster Roll from April 30 to June 30, 1814. Ref: R. & L. 1812, AGO Page 18.

*THOMAS, LINZA.
Served with Hospital Attendants, Vt.

‡*THOMAS, LUCAS, Corporal, Pittsford.
Served in Capt. Scovell's Company, Col. Martindale's Regt. Detached Militia in U. S. service 2 months and 21 days, 1812. Pension Certificate of widow, Susan, No. 2627.

THOMAS, MOSES.
Served from May 1 to May 31, 1814 as a carpenter in Alexander Parris' Company of Artificers. Ref: R. & L. 1812, AGO Page 24.

THOMAS, ROBERT.
Served from May 1 to June 30. 1814 as a carpenter in Alexander Parris' Company of Artificers. Ref: R. & L. 1812, AGO Page 24.

‡*THOMAS, SILAS.
Served in Capt. Phelps' Company, 3 Regt. (Williams') Vt. Militia. Pension Certificate of widow, Berthia, No. 1285.

THOMAS, THOMAS W.
Served in Capt. Benjamin Bradford's Company; on Muster Roll from May 31 to Aug. 31, 1813. Ref: R. & L. 1812, AGO Page 26.

THOMAS, VILAS.
Served in Capt. Mason's Company, Col. Fifield's Regt. Detached Militia in U. S. service 2 months and 21 days, 1812. Ref: Book 53, AGO Page 37.

THOMAS, WILLIAM,   Philadelphia.
Served from May 1 to July 28, 1814 in Capt. Young's Company, 15th Inf. Ref: R. & L. 1812, AGO Page 30.

*THOMPSON, BENJAMIN, Corporal, Barre? Served as musician and corporal in 3 Regt. (Tyler's) Vt. Militia.

THOMPSON, BENONIE, Ensign, Richmond. Volunteered to go to Plattsburgh, September, 1814, and served in Capt. Roswell Hunt's Company, 3 Regt. (Tyler's). Ref: Book 51, AGO Page 82.

THOMPSON, CHARLES.
Served from March 12 to June 30, 1814 in Regt. of Light Dragoons. Ref: R. & L. 1812, AGO Page 21.

‡*THOMPSON, DANIEL.
Served in Capt. Preston's Company, Col. Jonathan Williams' Regt. Detached Militia in U. S. service 2 months and 5 days, 1813. Also served in Capt. Samuel Pearson's Company. Pension Certificate No. 10492. Pension Certificate of widow, Sarah, No. 25114.

*THOMPSON, EBENEZER, Corporal.
Served in 1 Regt. (Judson's) Vt. Militia, 4 Regt. (Williams') Vt. Militia and 3 Regt. (Tyler's) Vt. Militia.

THOMPSON, FESTUS L., Lieutenant, Pawlet. Appointed Sergeant 11th Inf. Feb. 12, 1814; Ensign 26 Inf. June 25, 1814; 3 Lieutenant Oct. 1, 1814; 2 Lieutenant Dec. 10, 1814; honorably discharged June 15, 1815. Ref: Heitman's Historical Register & Dictionary USA.

*THOMPSON, FRANCIS.
Served from March 29 to June 28, 1813 in Capt. Charles Follett's Company, 11th Regt. Also served with Hospital Attendants, Vt. Ref: R. & L. 1812, AGO Page 13.

THOMPSON, HARRIS.
Enlisted May 20, 1813 for 1 year in Capt. Sanford's Company, 30th Regt. Ref: R. & L. 1812, AGO Page 1.

*THOMPSON, HENRY.
Enlisted Sept. 20, 1813 in Capt. John Weed's Company, Col. Clark's Rifle Corps.

THOMPSON, HORACE B., Poultney or St. Albans. Enlisted May 20, 1813 for 1 year in Capt. John Wires' Company, 30th Regt. Ref: R. & L. 1812, AGO Page 40.

THOMPSON, ISAAC S.,   Barre.
Volunteered to go to Plattsburgh, September, 1814, and served 10 days in Capt. Warren Ellis' Company. Ref: Book 52, AGO Page 242.

THOMPSON, JAMES,   Jericho.
Took part in the Battle of Plattsburgh. Ref: History of Jericho, Page 142.

*THOMPSON, JAMES.
Served from March 23 to June 22, 1813 in Capt. Samul Gordon's Company, 11th Regt. Enlisted Sept. 25, 1813 and served 1 month and 23 days in Capt. Elijah Birge's Company, Dixon's Regt. Detached Militia in U. S. service. Ref: R. & L. 1812, AGO Page 8.

*THOMPSON, JEDEDIAH, Corporal.
Served in 2 Regt. (Fifield's) Vt. Militia.

.*THOMPSON, JESSEE, Lieutenant.
Served in 3 Regt. (Tyler's) Vt. Militia.

THOMPSON, JOB,   Richford.
Served in Capt. Martin D. Follett's Company, Dixon's Regt. on duty on Canadian Frontier in 1813. Ref: Hemenway's Vt. Gazetteer, Vol. 2, Page 428.

*THOMPSON, JOEL.
Enlisted Sept. 25, 1813 and served 1 month and 23 days in Capt. Follet's Company, Col. Dixon's Regt. Detached Militia in U. S. Service.

THOMPSON, JOHN,   Richford.
Served in Capt. Martin D. Follett's Company, Dixon's Regt. on duty on Canadian Frontier in 1813. Ref: Hemenway's Vt. Gazetteer, Vol. 2, Page 428.

‡THOMPSON, JOHN.
Served in Capt. Joseph Sinchar's Company. Pension Certificate No. 25400.

THOMPSON, JOHN,   Jericho.
Took part in the battle of Plattsburgh. Ref: History of Jericho, Page 142.

*THOMPSON, JOHN.
Served from Oct. 11 to Oct. 17, 1813 in Capt. John Munson's Company of Cavalry, 3 Regt. (Tyler's).

‡THOMPSON, JOHN,   Barre.
Volunteered to go to Plattsburgh, September, 1814, and served 10 days in Capt. Warren Ellis' Company. Pension Certificate of widow, Sally, No. 14355.

THOMPSON, JOHN.
Served from Jan. 12 to Feb. 28, 1813 in Capt. Samuel H. Holly's Company, 11th Regt. Ref: R. & L. 1812, AGO Page 25.

THOMPSON, JOHN.
Served from April 7 to July 6, 1813 in Capt. Samul Gordon's Company, 11th Regt. Ref: R. & L. 1812, AGO Page 8.

THOMPSON, JOHN.
Enlisted Sept. 28, 1813 during the war in company of late Capt. J. Brooks, commanded by Lt. John I. Cromwell, Corps of U. S. Artillery; on Muster Roll from April 30 to June 30, 1814. Ref: R. & L. 1812, AGO Page 18.

*THOMPSON, JOHN JR.
Served in 3 Regt. (Tyler's) Vt. Militia.

‡THOMPSON, JONATHAN,   Richmond.
Volunteered to go to Plattsburgh, September, 1814, and served 9 days in Capt. Roswell Hunt's Company, 3 Regt. (Tyler's). Pension Certificate No. 12754.

*THOMPSON, JOSEPH.   Barre.
Served in Capt. Wright's Company,
Col. Fifield's Regt. Detached Militia
in U. S. service 2 months and 21
days, 1812.

THOMPSON, JOSEPH, Captain.
Appointed Captain 48 Inf. April 21,
1814; 26 Inf. May 12, 1814; honorably
discharged June 15, 1815. Ref: Heitman's Historical Register & Dictionary USA.

THOMPSON, JOSIAH,   Richmond.
Served from Oct. 5 to Oct. 16, 1813
in Capt. Roswell Hunt's Company,
3 Regt. (Tyler's). Volunteered to
go to Plattsburgh, September, 1814,
and served 9 days in same company.
Ref: R. & L. 1812, AGO Page 41;
Book 51, AGO Pages 82 and 277.

THOMPSON, MICHAEL.
Volunteered to go to Plattsburgh,
September, 1814, and served 4 days
in company of Capt. James George
of Topsham. Ref: Book 52, AGO
Pages 67, 68, 70.

THOMPSON, NATHAN, Lieutenant.
Appointed Sergeant 11 Inf. Feb.
20, 1813; Ensign 26 Inf. June 25,
1814; 3rd Lieutenant Oct. 1, 1814;
2nd Lieutenant Nov. 15, 1814; honorably discharged June 15, 1815. Served
from Feb. 20, 1813 to May 31, 1813
as Sergeant in Capt. Charles Follett's
Company, 11th Regt. Ref: Heitman's
Historical Register & Dictionary USA;
R. & L. 1812, AGO Page 13.

THOMPSON, ORPHEUS.
Enlisted May 3, 1813 for 1 year in
Capt. Simeon Wright's Company. Ref:
R. & L. 1812, AGO Page 51.

THOMPSON, OTIS.   Tunbridge, Vt.
Born in Norwich; aged 18 years; 5
feet 5 inches high; light complexion;
blue eyes; light sandy hair; by profession a farmer. Enlisted at Tunbridge May 6, 1813 for 1 year in
U. S. Army. Ref: Paper in custody
of Vt. Historical Society.

THOMPSON, PHINEAS, Corporal, Barre.
Volunteered to go to Plattsburgh,
September, 1814, and served 10 days
in Capt. Warren Ellis' Company.
Ref: Book 52, AGO Page 242.

*THOMPSON, ROGER.
Served in Capt. Richardson's Company, Col. Martindale's Regt. Detached Militia in U. S. service 2
months and 13 days, 1812. Also served in 3 Regt. (Tyler's) Vt. Militia.

THOMPSON, SAMUEL, Sergeant.
Served from Feb. 20 to May 19, 1813
in Capt. Charles Follett's Company,
11th Regt. Ref: R. & L. 1812, AGO
Page 13.

*THOMPSON, THOMAS.
Served with Hospital Attendants, Vt.

THOMPSON, THOMAS.   Marshfield.
Volunteered to go to Plattsburgh,
September, 1814, and served 9 days
in Capt. James English's Company.
Ref: Book 52, AGO Page 248.

THOMPSON, THOMAS.
Enlisted April 30, 1812 for 5 years in
Capt. White Youngs' Company, 15th
Regt.; on Muster Roll from Aug. 31
to Dec. 31, 1814. Ref: R. & L. 1812,
AGO Page 27.

*THOMPSON, TIMOTHY.
Enlisted Sept. 25, 1813 and served
1 month and 23 days in Capt. Bennett's Company, Col. Dixon's Regt.

*THOMPSON, TIMOTHY, Sergeant, Rich-
mond. Served from Oct. 5 to Oct.
16, 1813 in Capt. Roswell Hunt's Company, 3 Regt. (Tyler's); volunteered
to go to Plattsburgh, September, 1814,
and served in same company.

THOMPSON, WILLIAM.
Served in Lt. V. R. Goodrich's Com-
pany, 11th Regt.; on Pay Roll for
January and February, 1813; dis-
charged March 1, 1813. Ref: R. &
L. 1812, AGO Page 11.

*THOMPSON, ZEBADIAH, Corporal.
Served in Capt. Taylor's Company,
Col. Fifield's Regt. Detached Militia
in U. S. service 4 months and 17
days, 1812.

THOMPSON, ZEBULON.
Volunteered to go to Plattsburgh,
September, 1814, and served in company of Capt. Ebenezer Spencer, Vershire. Ref: Book 52, AGO Page 48.

*THOMSON, ARIEL.
Served from April 12 to April 21,
1814 in Capt. Othniel Jewett's Company, Sumner's Regt.

*THOMSON, ELI.
Served in Capt. E. Walker's Company, Col. Fifield's Regt. Detached
Militia in U. S. service 2 months and
24 days, 1812.

‡*THOMSON, JAMES.
Served in Capt. Walker's Company,
Col. Fifield's Regt. Detached Militia
in U. S. service 6 months and 3 days,
1812. Pension Certificate No. 11367.

*THOMSON, SAMUEL, Corporal.
Served in Capt. Richardson's Company, Col. Martindale's Regt. Detached Militia in U. S. service 2
months and 13 days, 1812.

*THORN, ISRAEL (or Thom?)
Served in Capt. Walker's Company,
Col. Fifield's Regt. Detached Militia
in U. S. service 6 months and 3 days,
1812.

*THORN, SAMUEL, Sergeant.
Served in Capt. Walker's Company,
Col. Fifield's Regt. Detached Militia
in U. S. service 2 months and 24
days, 1812.

‡THORTON, ASA.
Enlisted July 15, 1813 for 1 year and
served in Capt. James Taylor's Com-
pany and Capt. Gideon Spencer's
Company, 30th Regt. Also served in
Capt. Clark's Company. Pension Cer-
tificate No. 1848. Ref: R. & L. 1812,
AGO Pages 29, 52, 56, 59.

*THORNTON, JOHN, Richmond.
Served from Oct. 9 to Oct. 16, 1813
in Capt. Roswell Hunt's Company, 3
Regt. (Tyler's); volunteered to go
to Plattsburgh, September, 1814, and
served 9 days in same company. Also
served in Corning's Detachment, Vt.
Militia.

THORP, JOHN, Franklin County.
Volunteered to go to Plattsburgh
Sept. 11, 1814 and served in 15th or
22nd Regt. Ref: Hemenway's Vt.
Gazetteer, Vol. 2, Page 391.

THORP, NATHAN.
Served from May 1 to June 30, 1814
in Capt. Haig's Corps of Light Dragoons. Ref: R. & L. 1812, AGO
Page 20.

‡THORRINGTON, PHINEAS.
Served in Capt. Johnson's Company.
Pension Certificate No. 9587.

*THOYR, SAMUEL.
Served in 1 Regt. (Martindale's) Vt.
Militia.

‡THRALL, LEWIS G.
Served in Capt. H. Wade's Company.
Pension Certificate No. 34432.

‡THRALL, LUTHER.
Served in Capt. H. Mead's Company.
Pension Certificate of widow, Laura,
No. 26398.

*THRALL, REUBEN R.
Served in Capt. Brown's Company,
Col. Martindale's Regt. Detached
Militia in U. S. service 2 months
and 14 days, 1812.

‡*THRALL, WALTER, Corporal.
Served in Capt. Brown's Company,
Col. Martindale's Regt. Detached
Militia in U. S. service 2 months
and 14 days, 1812. Enlisted April 26,
1813 for 1 year in Capt. Simeon
Wright's Company, 30th Regt. Pension
Certificate No. 1348.

‡*THRASHER, COMFORT.
Served in Capt. Noyce's Company,
Col. Jonathan Williams' Regt. Detached Militia in U. S. service 2
months and 6 days, 1812. Pension
Certificate No. 12885. Pension Certificate of widow, Anna, No. 13234.

*THRASHER, SIMON, Sergeant.
Served in Capt. Sabin's Company,
Col. Jonathan Williams' Regt. Detached Militia in U. S. service 2
months and 6 days, 1812. Served
from March 8 to June 7, 1813 in
Lieut. V. R. Goodrich's Company,
11th Regt. Ref: R. & L. 1812, AGO
Page 10.

*THURBER, AMOS.
Served in Capt. Wheeler's Company,
Col. Fifield's Regt. Detached Militia
in U. S. service 6 months and 4
days, 1812.

THURBER, DOW.
Served in Capt. Haig's Corps of
Light Dragoons; on Pay Roll to June
30, 1814. Ref: R. & L. 1812, AGO
Page 20.

*THURSTIN, JESSE.
Served in Capt. Strait's Company,
Col. Martindale's Regt. Detached
Militia in U. S. service 2 months
and 13 days, 1812.

*THURSTIN, JOHN.
Served with Hospital Attendants, Vt.

THURSTON, JOHN, Corinth.
Volunteered to go to Plattsburgh,
September, 1814, and served in Capt.
Abel Jackman's Company. Ref: Book
52, AGO Page 44.

THURSTON, JOHN H., Orange.
Marched for Plattsburgh Sept. 11,
1814 and went part way, serving 5
days in Capt. David Rising's Company. Ref: Book 52, AGO Page 19.

‡*THURSTON, WILLIAM, Fife Major,
Orange? Served in Capt. Walker's
Company, Col. Fifield's Regt. Detach-
ed Militia in U. S. service 6 months
and 3 days, 1812. Also served under
Captains Dyer and Wait. Pension
Certificate No. 34773.

THWING, JOHN, Barre.
Volunteered to go to Plattsburgh,
September, 1814, and served 9 days
in Capt. Warren Ellis' Company. Ref:
Book 52, AGO Pages 233 and 242.

*TIBBETS, JOHN.
Served in Capt. Lowry's Company,
Col. Wm. Williams' Regt. Detached
Militia in U. S. service 4 months
and 26 days, 1812.

*TIBBITS, HENRY (or Tibbitts),
Served in Sumner's Regt. Vt. Militia.

‡TIBBITS, JOHN.
Served from Feb. 20 to May 19, 1813
in Capt. Charles Follett's Company,
11th Regt. Pension Certificate No.
4692.

‡TICHENOR, JOHN.
Pension Certificate of widow, Betsey,
No. 27502; no organization given.

TICHENOR, JOHN (or Tichoner).
Enlisted May 20, 1812 for 5 years in
Capt. White Youngs' Company, 15th
Regt.; on Muster Roll from Aug.
31 to Dec. 31, 1814. Ref: R. & L.
1812, AGO Page 27.

*TICHENOR, JOHN W.
Served in Capt. Willson's Company,
Col. Wm. Williams' Regt. Detached
Militia in U. S. service 3 months and
23 days, 1812.

*TIER, MOSES, Fifer.
Served in Capt. Dodge's Company,
Col. Fifield's Regt. Detached Militia
in U. S. service 2 months and 21
days, 1812.

TIFFANY, FREDERICK, Sergeant.
Served in Capt. Charles Follett's
Company, 11th Regt.; on Pay Roll
for January and February, 1813. Ref:
R. & L. 1812, AGO Page 12.

*TIFFANY, JOHN, Randolph.
Volunteered to go to Plattsburgh,
September, 1814, and served in Capt.
Lebbeus Egerton's Company. Ref:
Book 52, AGO Pages 82 and 85.

*TIFFANY, SAMUEL.
Enlisted Sept. 25, 1813 in Capt.
Thomas Waterman's Company, Dix-
on's Regt.

TILDEN, DIAH,   Williamstown.
Volunteered to go to Plattsburgh,
September, 1814, and went as far as
Burlington, serving 3 days in Capt.
David Robinson's Company. Ref:
Book 52, AGO Pages 2, 6 and 12.

‡*TILDEN, ELISHA.
Served in Capt. Burnap's Company,
Col. Jonathan Williams' Regt. Detached Militia in U. S. service 2
months and 13 days, 1812. Pension
Certificate of widow, Lucretia, No.
26152.

*TILDEN, JOHN.
Served in Capt. Howard's' Company,
Vt. Militia.

*TILDEN, LEVI F.,   Cornwall.
Served from April 12 to April 21,
1814 in Capt. Shubael Wales' Company, Col. W. B. Sumner's Regt.
Volunteered and was at the battle
of Plattsburgh. September, 1814, serving in Capt. Edmund B. Hill's Company, Sumner's Regt.

‡TILLETSON, ABNER.
Served in Capt. Hackett's Company.
Pension Certificate No. 23829.

*TILLOTSON, JONATHAN.
Served in Capt. Rogers' Company,
Col. Fifield's Regt. Detached Militia
in U. S. service 2 months and 18
days, 1812.

*TILLOTSON, SIMEON.
Served in Capt. Dorrance's Company,
Col. Wm. Williams' Regt. Detached
Militia in U. S. service 3 months
and 29 days, 1812. Served from April
12 to April 15, 1814 in Capt. John
Hackett's Company, Sumner's Regt.

TILSON, JOHN,   Franklin County.
Volunteered to go to Plattsburgh
Sept. 11, 1814 and served in 15th or
22nd Regt. Ref: Hemenway's Vt.
Gazetteer, Vol. 2, Page 391.

TILTON, DAVID.
Served from May 1 to June 30, 1814
in Capt. Haig's Corps of Light Dragoons. Ref: R. & L. 1812, AGO
Page 20.

TINGLEY, DANIEL, Corporal.
Enlisted Oct. 28, 1812 for 5 years in
company of late Capt. J. Brooks,
commanded by Lt. John I. Cromwell,
Corps of U. S. Artillery; on Muster
Roll from April 30 to June 30, 1814.
Ref: R. & L. 1812, AGO Page 18.

TINKER, JOEL.
Volunteered to go to Plattsburgh,
September, 1814, and served in company of Capt. Joel Barnes of Chelsea. Ref: Book 52, AGO Pages 69
and 77.

*TINKER, STEPHEN, Corporal.
Served in Capt. Edgerton's Company,
Vt. Volunteers.

*TINKHAM, ALMOND,   Randolph.
Volunteered to go to Plattsburgh,
September, 1814, and served in Capt.
Lebbeus Egerton's Company.

*TINKHAM, ANDREW.
Served in Corning's Detachment, Vt.
Militia.

*TINKHAM, LUTHER.
Served in Capt. Ormsbee's Company,
Col. Martindale's Regt. Detached
Militia in U. S. service 2 months and
14 days, 1812.

‡*TINKHAM, NOAH.
Served in Capt. E. Walker's Company, Col. Fifield's' Regt. Detached
Militia in U. S. service 6 months and
3 days, 1812. Pension Certificate of
widow, Sophia, No. 22103.

*TINKHAM, SETH, Corporal.
Served as private in Corning's Detachment, Vt. Militia and corporal
in 4 Regt. (Peck's) Vt. Militia.

TINNEY, JOHN.
Served from March 1 to May 31, 1813
in Capt. Charles Follett's Company,
11th Regt. Ref: R. & L. 1812, AGO
Page 13.

TINSLER, SOLOMON.
Enlisted March 2, 1814 for 5 years
in company of late Capt. J. Brooks,
commanded by Lt. John I. Cromwell,
Corps of U. S. Artillery; on Muster
Roll from April 30 to June 30, 1814;
transferred from Capt. Collins' Company. Ref: R. & L. 1812, AGO Page
18.

TIPHINY, SAMUEL.
Served in Capt. Chadwick's Company.
Ref: R. & L. 1812, AGO Page 32.

TIRRELL, JOHN.
Served in Capt. Richardson's Company, Col. Martindale's Regt. Detached Militia in U. S. service 2
months and 13 days, 1812. Ref: Book
53, AGO Page 58.

TITAS, ROBERT, Corporal.
Served from May 1 to June 30, 1814
in Corps of Light Dragoons. Ref: R.
& L. 1812, AGO Page 20.

TITUS, BEVERLY,   Thetford.
Volunteered to go to Plattsburgh,
September, 1814, and served in Capt.
Joseph Barrett's Company. Ref: Book
52, AGO Page 41.

TITUS, DANIEL, Fifer,   Vershire.
Volunteered to go to Plattsburgh,
September, 1814, and served 3 days
in Capt. Ira Corse's Company. Ref:
Book 52, AGO Page 91.

TITUS, JOHN JR.
Served from April 25 to July 24, 1813
in Capt. Charles Follett's Company,
11th Regt. Ref: R. & L. 1812, AGO
Page 13.

TITUS, MICHAEL.
Volunteered to go to Plattsburgh,
September, 1814, and went as far as
Bolton, Vt., serving 4 days in Lt.
Phineus Kimball's Company. West
Fairlee. Ref: Book 52, AGO Page 46.

TITUS, NATHAN, Corinth.
Volunteered to go to Plattsburgh,
September, 1814, and served 3 days
in Capt. Abel Jackman's Company.
Ref: Book 52, AGO Pages 44 and 45.

TITUS, NOAH.
Volunteered to go to Plattsburgh,
September, 1814, and went as far as
Bolton, Vt., serving 4 days in Lt.
Phineus Kimball's Company or Capt.
Ebenezer Spencer's Company, West
Fairlee. Ref: Book 52, AGO Pages
46 and 49.

TOBES, LUTHER, Sergeant.
Served from April 12 to April 21,
1814 in Capt. Edmund B. Hill's Company, Sumner's Regt. Ref: Book 52,
AGO Page 282.

*TOBEY, SYLVANUS.
Served in Capt. Parsons' Company,
Col. Jonathan Williams' Regt. Detached Militia in U. S. service 2
months and 13 days, 1812.

*TOBY, ALDEN.
Served in Capt. Parsons' Company,
Col. Jonathan Williams' Regt. Detached Militia in U. S. service 2
months and 13 days, 1812.

*TOBY, LEMUEL.
Served in Capt. Preston's Company,
Col. Jonathan Williams' Regt. Detached Militia in U. S. service 2
months and 6 days, 1812.

TOHN, CHRISTOPHER.
Served with Capt. Benjamin Edgerton's Company, 11th Regt. at the
Battle of Chrystler's Farm Nov. 11,
1813 and was reported missing after
the battle. Ref: Governor and Council Vt., Vol. 6, Page 490.

TOLE, CHARLES.
Served from May 1 to June 30, 1814
in Capt. Haig's Corps of Light Dragoons. Ref: R. & L. 1812, AGO
Page 20.

TOLLAND, ROBERT.
Served from May 1 to June 30, 1814
in Capt. Alexander Brooks' Corps of
Artillery. Ref: R. & L. 1812, AGO
Page 31.

TOMLIN, RICHARD.
Served from May 1 to June 30, 1814
in Capt. Alexander Brooks' Corps of
Artillery. Ref: R. & L. 1812, AGO
Page 31.

TOMPKINS, WILLIAM S., Corporal.
Enlisted March 9, 1814 during the
war in Capt. James Taylor's Company, 30th Regt. Ref: R. & L. 1812,
AGO Page 53.

*TOMLINSON, AMOS, Musician.
Served from June 11 to June 14, 1813
as Fifer in Capt. Hezekiah Barns'
Company, 1st Regt. 2nd Brig. 3rd
Div.

TOMLINSON, CYRUS.
Enlisted Dec. 21, 1813 for 1 year in
Capt. Wm. Miller's Company, 30th
Regt.; on Muster Roll to Aug. 31,
1814. Ref: R. & L. 1812, AGO Page
54.

TOMPKINS, WILLIAM S., Sergeant.
Enlisted March 9, 1814 and served
in Capt. Gideon Spencer's Company
and Capt. Wm. Miller's Company,
30th Regt.; on Muster Roll to Aug.
31, 1814. Ref: R. & L. 1812, AGO
Pages 54, 55, 56.

TOMPSON, HIRAM, Lansingburgh.
Served from Oct. 30, 1814 to June
19, 1815 in Capt. Taylor's Company,
30th Inf. Ref: R. & L. 1812, AGO
Page 23.

*TOMPSON, JAMES.
Served in 1 Regt. (Judson's) Vt.
Militia.

*TOOT, JOHN.
Served in Sumner's Regt. Vt. Militia.

‡TOOTHAKER, ALLEN.
Served in Capt. Taylor's Company.
Pension Certificate of widow, Sally,
No. 19214.

TORREY, HENRY AUGUSTUS, Lieutenant. Appointed 2nd Lieutenant 3
Artillery March 12, 1812; struck off
Sept. 1, 1812. Ref: Heitman's Historical Register & Dictionary USA.

TORREY, JOHN, Bethel.
Volunteered to go to Plattsburgh,
September, 1814, and served 8 days
in Capt. Nehemiah Noble's Company.
Ref: Book 51, AGO Page 228.

TORRY, DAVID S., Orwell or Sudbury.
Volunteered to go to Plattsburgh,
September, 1814, and served 8 days
in Capt. Henry Culver's Company.
Ref: Book 51, AGO Page 47; Book 52,
AGO Page 153.

*TORRY, NATHANIEL M., Sergeant.
Served in Capt. L. Robinson's Com-
pany, Col. Dixon's Regt. Detached
Militia in U. S. service 1 month, 1813.

TOTTEN, JOSEPH G., Major Engineers.
Served on General Staff of the North-
ern Army commanded by Major Gen-
eral George Izard; on Pay Roll to
July 31, 1814. Ref: R. & L. 1812,
AGO Page 28.

TOTTINGHAM, JOSEPH, Pittsford.
Volunteered to go to Plattsburgh,
September, 1814, and served 8 days
as a waggoner in Capt. Caleb Hendee's
Company. Ref: Book 52, AGO Page
125.

‡*TOUSLEY, BOSTWICK, 2nd Corporal.
Served from June 11 to June 14, 1813
in Capt. Moses Jewett's Company of
Militia, 1st Regt. 2nd Brig. 3rd Div.
Also served in Capt. Kinney's Com-
pany. Pension Certificate No. 24838.
Pension Certificate of widow, Clarissa,
No. 31753.

TOUSLEY, REUBEN (or Towsley), Corporal, Dorset. Enlisted May 27, 1813
in Capt. Daniel Farrington's Company, 30th Regt. (also commanded
by Capt. Simeon Wright); on Muster
Roll from March 1 to April 30, 1814.
Served from Sept. 1, 1814 to June
16, 1815 in Capt. Sanford's Company,
30th Inf. Ref: R. & L. 1812, AGO
Pages 23, 50, 51.

‡TOUSLEY, ZARDENS.
Served in Capt. Jewett's Company.
Pension Certificate of widow, Mary,
No. 26090.

TOWER, BENJAMIN,   Shoreham.
Volunteered to go to Plattsburgh,
September, 1814, and served 6 days
in Capt. Samuel Hand's Company.
Ref: Rev. J. F. Goodhue's History
of Shoreham, Page 108.

TOWER, HORACE B.
Served in Capt. Samuel H. Holly's
Company, 11th Regt.; on Pay Roll
for January and February, 1813. Was
killed in the sanguinary battle of
Bridgwater and was buried in "the
corn field" as the soldiers were ac-
customed to denominate the grounds
where the slain were interred. Ref:
R. & L. 1812, AGO Page 25; Rev.
J. F. Goodhue's History of Shoreham, Page 103.

TOWER, THOMAS,   Ira.
Volunteered to go to Plattsburgh,
September, 1814, and served 4 days
in Capt. Matthew Anderson's Company. Ref: Book 52, AGO Page 144.

TOWER, THOMAS, Lieutenant. Clarendon.
Volunteered to go to Plattsburgh,
September, 1814, and served 7 days
in Capt. Durham Sprague's Company.
Ref: Book 52, AGO Page 128.

TOWL, PARLEY, Corporal.
Enlisted May 14, 1813 for 1 year in
Capt. Daniel Farrington's Company,
30th Regt. (also commanded by Capt.
Simeon Wright); on Muster Roll from
March 1 to April 30, 1814. Ref: R.
& L. 1812, AGO Pages 50 and 51.

*TOWN, ABIJAH, Corporal, Waterbury.
Volunteered to go to Plattsburgh,
September, 1814, and was in the
battle. serving 11 days in Capt. George
Atkins' Company, 4 Regt. (Peck's).

TOWN, ALLEN,   Barre.
Volunteered to go to Plattsburgh,
September, 1814, and served 10 days
as a teamster in Capt. Warren Ellis'
Company. Ref: Book 52, AGO Page
242.

*TOWN, ASA, Sergeant.
Served in Capt. Lowry's Company.
Col. Wm. Williams' Regt. Detached
Militia in U. S. service 4 months and
26 days, 1812. Served in 3 Regt.
(Williams') Vt. Militia. Served as
Sergeant in 4 Regt. (Peck's) Vt. Mili-
tia.

*TOWN, DANIEL.
Served in Capt. Lowry's Company.
Col. Wm. Williams' Regt. Detached
Militia in U. S. service 4 months and
26 days, 1812.

*TOWN. DAVID A., Sergeant, Waterbury.
Volunteered to go to Plattsburgh,
September, 1814, and was in the
battle, serving 11 days in Capt. George
Atkins' Company, 4 Regt. (Peck's).

*TOWN, EDMUND,   Waterbury.
Volunteered to go to Plattsburgh,
September, 1814, and was in the

battle, serving 11 days in Capt.
George Atkins' Company, 4 Regt.
(Peck's). Also served with Hospital
Attendants, Vt.

*TOWN, ELITHU.
Served in Corning's Detachment, Vt.
Militia.

TOWN, ENOS,   Barre.
Volunteered to go to Plattsburgh,
September, 1814, and served 10 days
in Capt. Warren Ellis' Company. Ref:
Book 52, AGO Page 242.

*TOWN, EPHRAIM.
Served in Corning's Detachment, Vt.
Militia.

TOWN, GEORGE,   Richmond.
Volunteered to go to Plattsburgh,
September, 1814, and served 9 days
in Capt. Roswell Hunt's Company. 3
Regt. (Tyler's). Ref: Book 51, AGO
Page 82.

*TOWN, HOSEA,   Waterbury.
Volunteered to go to Plattsburgh,
September. 1814, and was in the
battle, serving 11 days in Capt. George
Atkins' Company, 4 Regt. (Peck's).

*TOWN, IRA.
Served with Hospital Attendants, Vt.
Served in 4 Regt. (Peck's) Vt. Mili-
tia.

*TOWN, JABEZ.
Served in Capt. Stephen Pette's Company, Col. Wm. Williams' Regt. Detached Militia in service during summer of 1812.

*TOWN, JOHN.   Fairfax.
Volunteered to go to Plattsburgh,
September, 1814, and served 8 days
in Capt. Josiah Grout's Company.
Ref: Book 51, AGO Page 103.

*TOWN, MOSES.
Served in Corning's Detachment, Vt.
Militia.

*TOWN. SALEM,   Waterbury.
Volunteered to go to Plattsburgh,
September, 1814, and was in the
battle, serving 11 days in Capt.
George Atkins' Company, 4 Regt.
(Peck's).

‡TOWN, SAMUEL,   Morristown.
Volunteered to go to Plattsburgh,
September, 1814, and served 8 days
in Capt. Denison Cook's Company.
Pension Certificate of widow, Lucre-
tia, No. 11901.

*TOWN, SETH.
Served in Capt. Walker's Company,
Col. Fifield's Regt. Detached Militia
in U. S. service 6 months and 3
days, 1812.

*TOWN. STEPHEN.
Served with Hospital Attendants, Vt.

‡TOWN, THOMAS.   Barre.
Volunteered to go to Plattsburgh,
September. 1814, and served 9 days
in Capt. Warren Ellis' Company. Pension Certificate No. 31674.

*TOWN, WELCOME (or Tower?)
Served in Capt. Needham's Company,
Col. Martindale's Regt. Detached
Militia in U. S. service 2 months and
7 days, 1812.

‡TOWNE, WILLIAM.
Served from March 15 to June 14,
1813 in Lieut. V. R. Goodrich's Company, 11th Regt. Also served in Capt.
Crawford's Company. Pension Certificate No. 14967. Ref: R. & L. 1812,
AGO Page 10.

TOWNER, DYER, Sergeant.
Served in 1st Regt. of Detached Militia of Vt. in U. S. service at Champlain from Nov. 18 to Nov. 19, 1812.

‡TOWNER, JAMES S.
Served in Capt. Stone's Company.
Pension Certificate of widow, Harriet
C., No. 29916.

TOWNER, JOSIAH,   Sudbury, Vt.
Enlisted at Shoreham March 18, 1814
during the war and served in Capt.
Wm. Miller's Company, Capt. James
Taylor's Company, and Capt. Gideon
Spencer's Company, 30th Regt. Ref:
R. & L. 1812, AGO Pages 53, 54,
55, 56.

TOWNER, NORMAN, Ensign.
Served in 1st Regt. of Detached Militia of Vt. in U. S. service at Champlain from Nov. 18 to Nov. 19, 1812.

*TOWNER, RICHARD Z.
Served from June 11 to June 14, 1813
in Capt. John Palmer's Company, 1st
Regt. 2nd Brig. 3rd Div.; served
from Oct. 4 to Oct. 13, 1813 in same
company.

‡TOWNSEND, MARSHALL,   Barnard.
Volunteered to go to Plattsburgh,
September, 1814, and served 8 days
in Capt. John S. Bicknell's Company.
Pension Certificate of widow, Han-
nah, No. 45108.

TOWNSHEND, ABRAHAM,   Berlin.
Volunteered to go to Plattsburgh,
September, 1814, and served 9 days
in Capt. Cyrus Johnson's Company.
Ref: Book 52, AGO Pages 202 and 255.

TOWNSHEND, JONATHAN.
Served from May 1 to June 30, 1814
as a carpenter in Alexander Parris'
Company of Artificers. Ref: R. & L.
1812, AGO Page 24.

*TOWSLEY, ABIJAH, Corporal.
Served in Capt. Strait's Company,
Col. Martindale's Regt. Detached
Militia in U. S. service 18 days, 1812.

*TOWSLEY, MATHEW.
Served in Capt. Strait's Company,
Col. Martindale's' Regt. Detached
Militia in U. S. service 2 months and
13 days, 1812.

TOZER, BENJAMIN H., Sergeant.
Served in Capt. Samul Gordon's Com-
pany, 11th Regt.; on Pay Roll for
January and February, 1813. Ref:
R. & L. 1812, AGO Page 9.

*TRACEY, ERASTUS, Sergeant.
Served in 1 Regt. (Judson's) Vt.
Militia.

TRACEY, JAMES CARLETON, Ensign.
Appointed Ensign 11th Inf. March 12,
1812; struck off Sept. 2, 1812. Ref:
Heitman's Historical Register & Dictionary USA.

*TRACY, DIMIC,   Randolph.
Volunteered to go to Plattsburgh,
September, 1814, and served in Capt.
Lebbeus Egerton's Company.

‡TRACY, GARDNER.
Served in Capt. Joseph Hazen's Com-
pany. Pension Certificate of widow,
Phebe, No. 26933.

*TRACY, LUCIUS.
Served in Capt. Scovell's Company,
Col. Martindale's Regt. Detached
Militia in U. S. service 2 months and
7 days, 1812.

*TRACY, PEREZ,   Randolph.
Volunteered to go to Plattsburgh,
September, 1814, and served in Capt.
Lebbeus Egerton's Company.

TRASK, DART,   Rochester.
Volunteered to go to Plattsburgh,
September,.1814; no organization giv-
en. Ref: Book 51, AGO Page 249.

TRASK, JOHN, Fifer,   Rochester.
Volunteered to go to Plattsburgh,
September, 1814, and served 7 days
in Oliver Mason's Company. Ref:
Book 51, AGO Pages 249 and 265.

TREMBLE, JAMES.
Enlisted May 13, 1812 and served 5
years in Capt. White Youngs' Company, 15th Regt.; on Muster Roll
from Aug. 31 to Dec. 31, 1814. Ref:
R. & L. 1812, AGO Page 27.

TRESCOTT, GEORGE, 2nd Lieutenant Engineers. Served on General Army of
the Northern Army commanded by
Major General George Izard; on Pay
Roll to July 31, 1814. Ref: R. & L.
1812, AGO Page 28.

*TRESCOTT, SAMUEL.
Served in Capt. Howard's Company,
Vt. Militia.

TRIMBLER, JAMES,   Franklin County.
Volunteered to go to Plattsburgh
Sept. 11, 1814 and served in 15th or
22nd Regt. Ref: Hemenway's Vt. Gazetteer, Vol. 2, Page 392.

TRIMMER, NICHOLS.
Served in Capt. Phelps' Company,
Col. Wm. Williams' Regt. Detached
Militia in U. S. service 1 month and
22 days, 1812. Ref: Book 53, AGO
Page 50.

TRIPP, JACOB,   Franklin County.
Volunteered to go to Plattsburgh
Sept. 11, 1814 and served in 15th or
22nd Regt. Ref: Hemenway's Vt. Gazetteer, Vol. 2, Page 392.

*TRIPP, JESSE.
Served from Sept. 23 to Oct. 1, 1813
in Capt. Amasa Mansfield's Company,
Dixon's Regt.

TRIPP, THOMAS, Franklin County.
Volunteered to go to Plattsburgh
Sept. 11, 1814 and served in 15th or
22nd Regt. Ref: Hemenway's Vt. Gazetteer, Vol. 2, Page 392.

*TROBRIDGE, CHAUNCEY.
Served in Capt. Ormsbee's Company,
Col. Martindale's Regt. Detached
Militia in U. S. service 2 months and
14 days, 1812.

TROINER, ISAAC.
Served to June 29, 1814 in Capt. Alex-
ander Brooks' Corps of Artillery. Ref:
R. & L. 1812, AGO Page 31.

TROW, JOHN, Teamster, Barre.
Volunteered to go to Plattsburgh,
September, 1814, and served 10 days
in Capt. Warren Ellis' Company. Ref:
Book 52, AGO Page 242.

*TROWBRIDGE, DANIEL, Musician.
Served in 1 Regt. (Judson's) Vt.
Militia.

*TROWBRIDGE, JAMES.
Served in Capt. Burnap's Company,
Col. Jonathan Williams' Regt. Detached Militia in U. S. service 2
months and 13 days, 1812. Also served with Hospital Attendants, Vt.

*TROWBRIDGE, RICHARD.
Served in 4 Regt. (Peck's) Vt. Militia.

TRUE, EZEKIEL, Sergeant, Corinth.
Volunteered to go to Plattsburgh,
September, 1814, and served in Capt.
Abel Jackman's Company. Ref: Book
52, AGO Page 44.

‡*TRUE, HENRY C.
Served in Capt. Wheeler's Company,
Col. Fifield's Regt. Detached Militia
in U. S. service 2 months and 18
days, 1812. Pension Certificate No.
4085.

TRUE, JOSEPH, Rochester.
Volunteered to go to Plattsburgh,
September, 1814, and served 7 days
in Capt. Oliver Mason's Company.
Ref: Book 51, AGO Page 258.

TRUMBELL, EBENEZER.
Served from Feb. 3 to June 30, 1814
in Regt. of Light Dragoons. Ref:
R. & L. 1812, AGO Page 21.

TRUMBELL, ORIN.
Served from Feb. 15 to June 30, 1814
in Regt. of Light Dragoons. Ref:
R. & L. 1812, Page 21.

TRUMBELL, RUFUS.
Served in Capt. Strait's Company, Col.
Martindale's' Regt. Detached Militia
in U. S. service 2 months and 13
days, 1812. Ref: Book 53, AGO Page
25.

*TRUMBELL, SIMEON.
Served in Capt. Strait's Company, Col.
Martindale's Regt. Detached Militia
in U. S. service 2 months and 13
days, 1812.

*TRUMBLE, RUFUS.
Enlisted Sept. 20, 1813 in Capt. John
Weed's Company, Col. Clark's Rifle
Corps. Also served in 1 Regt. (Mar-
tindale's) Vt. Militia.

TRUSSELL, JACOB J.
Served in Capt. Weeks' Company,
11th Regt.; on Pay Roll for January
and February, 1813. Ref: R. & L.
1812, AGO Page 5.

*TRUSSELL, RHEUBEN.
Served from June 11 to June 14, 1813
in Capt. Moses Jewett's Company, 1st
Regt. 2nd Brig. 3rd Div.

TRYON, ELIJAH, Sergeant, West Haven.
Volunteered to go to Plattsburgh,
September, 1814, and served 4 days
in Capt. David B. Phippeney's Company. Ref: Book 52, AGO Page 146.

TRYON, ELIJAH JR., St. Albans.
Enlisted April 24, 1813 for 1 year in
Capt. John Wires' Company, 30th
Regt. Ref: R. & L. 1812, AGO Page
40.

*TRYON, JESSE St. Albans.
Enlisted Sept. 25, 1813 in Capt. Amos
Robinson's Company, Dixon's Regt.
Volunteered and was at the battle
of Plattsburgh, Sept. 11, 1814, serv-
ing in Capt. Samuel H. Farnsworth's
Company.

*TUBBS, BENJAMIN.
Served in 3 Regt. (Tyler's) Vt. Militia.

*TUBBS, FREDERICK.
Served in Tyler's Regt. Vt. Militia.

*TUBBS, IRA, Fifer.
Served in Capt. Lowry's Company,
Col. Wm. Williams' Regt. Detached
Militia in U. S. service 4 months
and 25 days, 1812.

*TUBS, RAMINE.
Served in Tyler's Regt. Vt. Militia.

TUCKER, DAVID.
Enlisted April 22, 1813 in Capt.
James Taylor's Company, 30th Regt.
Ref: R. & L. 1812, AGO Page 58.

*TUCKER, EDWARD, Calais.
Volunteered to go to Plattsburgh,
September, 1814, and served 10 days
in Capt. Gideon Wheelock's Company.

TUCKER, ENOS, St. Albans.
Enlisted May 3, 1813 for 1 year in
Capt. John Wires' Company, 30th
Regt. Ref: R. & L. 1812, AGO Page
40.

‡*TUCKER, IRA.
Served in Capt. Saxton's Company,
Sumner's Regt. Pension Certificate of
widow, Eliza, No. 27770.

TUCKER, ISAAC.
Served from May 1 to May 24, 1814;
no organization given. Ref: R. & L.
1812, AGO Page 29.

TUCKER, JOEL, Fairfax.
Served from Aug. 8, 1812 in company
of Capt. Joseph Beeman Jr., 11th
Regt. U. S. Inf. under Col. Ira Clark.
Ref: Hemenway's Vt. Gazetteer, Vol.
2, Page 402.

*TUCKER, JOHN.
Served from June 11 to June 14 and
from Oct. 4 to Oct. 13, 1813 in Capt.
John Palmer's Company, 1st Regt.
2nd Brig. 3rd Div.

TUCKER, JOSEPH.
Served from May 1 to June 20, 1814;
no organization given. Ref: R. & L.
1812, AGO Page 29.

*TUCKER, JOSEPH.
Served from June 11 to June 14, 1813
in Capt. Samuel Blinn's Company, 1st
Regt. (Judson's).

*TUCKER, NOYES.
Served in Capt. Robbins' Company,
Col. Wm. Williams' Regt. Detached
Militia in U. S. service 4 months and
29 days, 1812.

*TUCKER, OLIVER.
Served in Capt. Bingham's Company,
Col. Jonathan Williams' Regt. Detached Militia in U. S. service 2
months and 9 days, 1812.

TUCKER, RALPH.
Served from May 1 to June 30, 1814
in Capt. Haig's Corps of Light Dragoons. Ref: R. & L. 1812, AGO
Page 20.

‡*TUCKER, STEPHEN.
Served in Capt. Preston's Company,
Col. Jonathan Williams' Regt. De-
tached Militia in U. S. service 2
months and 6 days, 1812. Volunteer-
ed to go to Plattsburgh, September,
1814, and served as corporal in Capt.
Lebbeus Egerton's Company. Pension
Certificate No. 6692. Ref: Book 52,
AGO Pages 82 and 88.

*TUCKER, WALDO, Sergeant.
Served in Capt. Dodge's Company,
Col. Fifield's Regt. Detached Militia
in U. S. service 2 months and 21
days, 1812.

‡TULLAR, ALMON.
Served in Capt. Robinson's Company.
Pension Certificate of widow, Martha,
No. 22962.

TUPPER, CHARLES,   Barnard.
Enlisted May 17, 1813 in Capt. Nehemiah Noble's Company, 31st U. S.
Inf. Ref: Wm. M. Newton's History
of Barnard, Vol. 1, Page 95.

‡*TUPPER, ELAM.
Served from April 12 to April 21,
1814 in Capt. Edmund B. Hill's Company, Sumner's Regt. Pension Certificate No. 31425.

*TUPPER, GIDEON.
Served in Sumner's Regt. Vt. Militia.

*TUPPER, JOSEPH, Sergeant.
Served in 1 Regt. (Judson's) Vt.
Militia.

‡*TUPPER, NORMAN,   Middlebury.
Served from April 12 to April 21,
1814 in Lieut. Justus Foote's Company, Sumner's Regt. Volunteered to
go to Plattsburgh, September, 1814;
no organization given. Pension Certificate No. 31424. Pension Certificate
of widow, Adaline W., No. 40025.

*TUPPER, THOMAS, Captain.
Served from April 15 to July 14, 1813
in Capt. Charles Follett's Company,
11th Regt. as a Sergeant. Appointed

Ensign 11th Inf. Aug. 23, 1813; 2nd
Lieutenant May 2, 1814. Also served
as Captain in 3 Regt. (Bowdish) Vt.
Militia. Ref: R. & L. 1812, AGO
Page 13; Governor and Council Vt.,
Vol. 6, Page 474.

‡TURNER, EDMUND.
Served from April 29, 1813 to April
29, 1814 in Capt. Gideon Spencer's
Company, 30th Regt. Also served in
Capt. James Taylor's Company, 30th
Regt. and in Capt. Amasa J. Brown's
Company. Ref: R. & L. 1812, AGO
Pages 52, 56, 58. Pension Certificate
of widow, Betsey, No. 27556.

TURNER, HENRY.
Served from May 1 to June 30, 1814
in Capt. Alexander Brooks' Corps of
Artillery. Ref: R. & L. 1812, AGO
Page 31.

TURNER, MOSES, Sergeant, St. Albans.
Served in Capt. John Wires' Com-
pany, 30th Regt. which was raised
in St. Albans and went into service
Nov. 30, 1813. Ref: Hemenway's Vt.
Gazetteer, Vol. 2, Page 433.

*TURNER, STEPHEN, Drummer.
Served from April 21, 1813 to April
25, 1814 in Capt. Simeon Wright's
Company. Also served in Corning's
Detachment and 4 Regt. (Peck's) Vt.
Militia. Ref: R. & L. 1812, AGO
Page 51.

*TURNER, THOMAS,   Shoreham.
Served in Capt. Dodge's Company,
Col. Fifield's Regt. Detached Militia
in U. S. service 2 months and 21
days, 1812. Volunteered to go to
Plattsburgh, September, 1814, and
served 6 days in Capt. Samuel Hand's
Company.

TURNEY, MOSES, Sergeant.
Enlisted May 14, 1813 for 1 year in
Capt. John Wires' Company, 30th
Regt. Ref: R. & L. 1812, AGO
Page 40.

*TURRILL, JOHN.
Served in 1 Regt. (Martindale's) Vt.
Militia.

TUTTLE, CHAUNCY D.,   Clarendon.
Volunteered to go to Plattsburgh,
September, 1814, and served 7 days
as a teamster in Capt. Durham
Sprague's Company. Ref: Book 52,
AGO Page 128.

TUTTLE, EBENEZER,   Clarendon.
Volunteered to go to Plattsburgh,
September, 1814, and served 7 days
in Capt. Durham Sprague's Company,
as a teamster. Ref: Book 52, AGO
Page 128.

TUTTLE, HARVEY.   St. Albans.
Enlisted May 12, 1813 for 1 year in
Capt. John Wires' Company, 30th
Regt. Ref: R. & L. 1812, AGO Page
40.

*TUTTLE, ICHABOD, Adjutant.
Served as Adjutant and Sergeant Major in 1 Regt. (Judson's) Vt. Militia.

TUTTLE, NATHAN.
Served in Capt. Samuel H. Holly's
Company, 11th Regt.; on Pay Roll
for January and February, 1813. En-
listed May 5, 1813 for 1 year in Capt.
Simeon Wright's Company, 30th Regt.
Ref: R. & L. 1812, AGO Pages 25
and 51.

*TWISS, IRA.
Served in Capt. Charles Bennett's
Company, Col. Dixon's Regt. Detached Militia in U. S. service 1 month
and 23 days, 1813.

*TWITCHELL, DANIEL, Sergeant.
Served from April 12 to April 21,
1814 in Capt. Othniel Jewett's Company, Sumner's Regt.

TWITCHELL, EPHRAIM,   Stockbridge.
Volunteered to go to Plattsburgh,
September, 1814, and served 7 days
in Capt. Elias Keyes' Company. Ref:
Book 51, AGO Page 237.

*TWITCHELL, TIMOTHY.
Served from April 17 to April 21,
1814 in Capt. Othniel Jewett's Company, Sumner's Regt.

*TYLER, AARON.
Served from April 12 to April 21,
1814 in Lieut. Justus Foote's Company, Sumner's Regt.

*TYLER, AARON B., Sergeant.
Served in Capt. Scovell's Company,
Col. Martindale's Regt. Detached
Militia in U. S. service 2 months
and 21 days, 1812.

TYLER, ALVAH,   Shelburne.
Volunteered to go to Plattsburgh,
September, 1814, and served in Major
Luman Judson's command. Ref: Book
51, AGO Pages 78 and 79.

TYLER, AMASA B., Sergeant.
Served in Cavalry of Detached Militia
of Vt. in U. S. service at Champlain from Nov. 18 to Nov. 19, 1812.

TYLER, ARTEMUS.
Served in Capt. Samuel H. Holly's
Company, 11th Regt.; on Pay Roll
for January and February, 1813.
Ref: R. & L. 1812, AGO Page 25.

‡*TYLER, DANIEL.
Served in Tyler's Regt. Vt. Militia.
Also served in Capt. Sinclair's Com-
pany. Pension Certificate of widow,
Permelia, No. 28469.

TYLER, GEORGE, Colonel,   Essex.
Commanded a portion of the Vt.
Militia under General Strong at the
battle of Plattsburgh. Ref: Hemenway's Vt. Gazetteer, Vol. 1, Page
790.

*TYLER, JERIMAH.
Served in Capt. Howard's Company,
Vt. Militia.

TYLER, JOHN,   Thetford.
Marched for Plattsburgh, September,
1814, and went as far as Bolton,
Vt., serving 6 days in Capt. Salmon
Howard's Company, 2nd Regt. Ref:
Book 52, AGO Page 18.

TYLER, JOHN B.
Served in Capt. Samuel H. Holly's
Company, 11th Regt.; on Pay Roll
for January and February, 1813. Ref:
R. & L. 1812, AGO Page 25.

*TYLER, JOSEPH.
Served in Capt. Willson's Company.
Col. Wm. Williams' Regt. Detached
Militia in U. S. service 4 months and
24 days, 1812.

TYLER, PERLY,   Northfield.
Volunteered and was at the battle
of Plattsburgh, Sept. 11, 1814, serving
8 days in Capt. David Robinson's
Company. Ref: Book 52, AGO Pages
2 and 8.

TYLER, SAMUEL.
Served from Feb. 23 to June 16, 1814
in Capt. Sanford's Company, 30th Inf.
Ref: R. & L. 1812, AGO Page 23.

TYRREL, IRA.
Served in Capt. Ormsbee's Company,
Col. Martindale's Regt. Detached
Militia in U. S. service 2 months
and 14 days, 1812. Ref: Book 53,
AGO Page 53.

*TYRREL, JOSEPH.
Enlisted Oct. 11, 1813 in Capt. Asahel
Langworthy's Company, Col. Isaac
Clark's Rifle Corps.

‡*TYRREL, THOMAS M., Sergeant.
Served in Capt. Walker's Company,
Col. Fifield's Regt. Detached Militia
in U. S. service 6 months and 3
days, 1812. Pension Certificate of
widow, Susanna, No. 2178.

‡TYRREL, WILLIAM.
Served in Capt. Hotchkiss' Company,
1 Regt. Pension Certificate of widow,
Love, No. 10962.

*UNDERHILL, JACOB,   Burlington.
Served in Capt. Barns' Company,
Col. Wm. Williams' Regt. Detached
Militia in U. S. service 4 months
and 22 days, 1812. Volunteered to
go to Plattsburgh, September, 1814,
and served in Capt. Henry Mayo's
Company.

*UNDERWOOD, LITTLETON.
Served with Hospital Attendants, Vt.

UNDERWOOD, REUBEN,   Sudbury.
Volunteered to go to Plattsburgh,
September, 1814, and served 6 days
in Capt. Thomas Hall's Company.
Ref: Book 52, AGO Page 122.

*UNDERWOOD, SAMUEL.
Served in Capt. Wheeler's Company,
Col. Fifield's Regt. Detached Militia
in U. S. service 6 months and 4 days,
1812.

*UNDERWOOD, THAD.
Served in Capt. Parsons' Company,
Col. Jonathan Williams' Regt. Detached Militia in U. S. service 2
months and 13 days, 1812.

UPHAM, BENJAMIN,   Franklin County.
Volunteered to go to Plattsburgh
Sept. 11, 1814 and served in 15th or
22nd Regt. Ref: Hemenway's Vt. Gazetteer, Vol. 2, Page 392.

UPHAM, SAMUEL JR., Montpelier. Volunteered to go to Plattsburgh, September, 1814, and served in Capt. Timothy Hubbard's Company. Ref: Book 52, AGO Pages 208 and 256.

UTLEY, DANIEL. Served from March 21 to June 20, 1813 in Capt. John W. Weeks' Company, 11th Regt. Ref: R. & L. 1812, AGO Page 4.

‡UTLEY, HIRAM, Drummer. Served from April 21, 1813 to April 24, 1814 in Capt. Daniel Farrington's Company, 30th Regt. (also commanded by Capt. Simeon Wright). Pension Certificate of widow, Frances M., No. 12417. Ref: R. & L. 1812, AGO Pages 50 and 51.

UTLEY, PEABODY, Captain, Landgrove. Appointed Captain 30th Inf. April 30, 1813; resigned March 5, 1814. Ref: Heitman's Historical Register & Dictionary USA.

*VADICAN, PHILIP. Served in Sumner's Regt. Vt. Militia.

*VAIL, N. W. HULL, Jamaica. Served in Capt. Phelps' Company, Col. Jonathan Williams' Regt. Detached Militia in U. S. service 1 month and 15 days, 1812.

*VALLETT, RUSSELL. Served from April 12 to April 21, 1814 in Capt. Edmund B. Hill's Company, Sumner's Regt.

VANAUKIN, PHILIP S., Corporal. Enlisted Oct. 24, 1812 for 5 years in company of late Capt. J. Brooks, commanded by Lt. John I. Cromwell, Corps of U. S. Artillery; on Muster Roll from April 30 to June 30, 1814. Ref: R. & L. 1812, AGO Page 18.

‡VANCE, WILLIAM. Served in Capt. Green's Company. Pension Certificate No. 11994.

VANDEBOGERT, JAMES. Enlisted Dec. 19, 1812 for 5 years in company of late Capt. J. Brooks, commanded by Lt. John I. Cromwell, Corps of U. S. Artillery; on Muster Roll from April 30 to June 30, 1814. Ref: R. & L. 1812, AGO Page 18.

VANDERGRIPT, JONATHAN, Sergeant. Enlisted Nov. 16, 1812 for 5 years in company of late Capt. J. Brooks, commanded by Lt. John I. Cromwell, Corps of U. S. Artillery; on Muster Roll from April 30 to June 30, 1814. Ref: R. & L. 1812, AGO Page 18.

*VANDERLIP, WILLIAM. Served in 1 Regt. (Martindale's) Vt. Militia.

VANDEVENTER, JAMES, Franklin County. Enlisted May 20, 1812 for 5 years in Capt. White Youngs' Company, 15th Regt.; on Muster Roll from Aug. 31 to Dec. 31, 1814. Ref: R. & L. 1812, AGO Page 27.

VAN DOZEN, HARRY, 1st Lieutenant, Middlebury. Volunteered to go to Plattsburgh, September, 1814, and served 7 days in Capt. Silas Wright's Company. Ref: Book 51, AGO Page 10.

‡*VAN DUZEN, ABRAHAM. Served from April 12 to April 15, 1814 in Capt. John Hackett's Company, Sumner's Regt. Pension Certificate of widow, Louis, No. 22525.

VANHOSEN, JESSE. Enlisted May 30, 1812 for 5 years in Capt. White Youngs' Company, 15th Regt.; died Oct. 10, 1814 at Burlington. Ref: R. & L. 1812, AGO Page 27.

*VANORNAM, ETHAN. Served from June 11 to June 14, 1813 in Capt. Samuel Blinn's Company, 1 Regt. (Judson's).

*VANORNAM. HEMAN. Served from June 11 to June 14, 1813 in Capt. Samuel Blinn's Company, 1 Regt. (Judson's).

*VANORNEM, MILES. Served in 1 Regt. (Judson's) Vt. Militia.

VANPELT, TUNIS. Served from May 1 to June 30, 1814 in Capt. Alexander Brooks' Corps of Artillery. Ref: R. & L. 1812, AGO Page 31.

*VAN RANSELEAR, JOHN. Served in Capt. Strait's Company, Col. Martindale's Regt. Detached Militia in U. S. service 11 days.

VANSCHAICK, SAMUEL. Served in Capt. Weeks' Company, 11th Regt.; on Pay Roll for January and February, 1813. Ref: R. & L. 1812, AGO Page 5.

VAN VLIEK, PETER. Served from May 1 to June 30, 1814 in Capt. Alexander Brooks' Corps of Artillery. Ref: R. & L. 1812, AGO Page 31.

*VAN VLIET, CHRISTIAN. Served in Sumner's Regt. Vt. Militia.

*VAN WORET, WILLIAM. Served from April 12 to May 20, 1814 in Capt. George Fisher's Company, Sumner's Regt.

‡VARNEY, ALVIN. Served in Capt. Wooster's Company. Pension Certificate No. 32341.

*VARNEY, MOSES C., Fifer, Danville. Served in Capt. Morrill's Company, Col. Fifield's Regt. Detached Militia in U. S. service 6 months and 5 days, 1812. Moved to Barton some time after the war and died there. Ref: Hemenway's Vt. Gazetteer, Vol. 3, Page 76.

VARNEY. PAUL. Served from March 29 to June 28, 1813 in Capt. Edgerton's Company, 11th Regt. Ref: R. & L. 1812, AGO Page 3.

‡VAUGHAN, JIRAH.
Served in Capt. Penfield's Company.
Pension Certificate of widow, Ruth
W., No. 43356.

*VAUGHN, HARRY, Corporal.
Served in Sumner's Regt. Vt. Militia.

*VAUGHN, NEHEMIAH (or Nemiah)
Served from June 11 to June 14, 1813
in Capt. Moses Jewett's Company.
1st Regt. 2nd Brig. 3rd Div.

*VAUGHN, WASHINGTON.
Served in 1 Regt. (Judson's) Vt.
Militia.

*VAUGHN, WILLIAM.
Served in Capt. Hotchkiss' Company.
Col. Martindale's Regt. Detached
Militia in U. S. service 2 months
and 13 days, 1812. Served from Feb.
20 to May 19, 1813 in Capt. Phineas
Williams' Company, 11th Regt. Ref:
R. & L. 1812, AGO Page 14.

*VAUGHN, WILLIAM H., Corporal.
Served from April 12 to May 20, 1814
in company of Capt. James Gray Jr.,
Sumner's Regt.

*VENER, L., ARNOLD (or Venor)
Served in Capt. Phelps' Company,
Col. Wm. Williams' Regt. Detached
Militia in U. S. service 5 months,
1812.

*VENT, JOHN F. JR.
Served in Capt. Sabin's Company,
Col. Jonathan Williams' Regt. Detached Militia in U. S. service 2
months and 6 days, 1812.

VESEY, BENJAMIN,   Braintree.
Volunteered to go to Plattsburgh,
September, 1814, and served in Capt.
Lot Hudson's Company. Ref: Book
52, AGO Page 24.

VIRGINIA, JEREMIAH,   Fairfax.
Served at Plattsburgh and was wounded there Sept. 11, 1814. Was later
granted remuneration by Vt. Legislature for loss of services on account
of wound. (This man was a negro.)
Ref: Hemenway's Vt. Gazetteer, Vol.
2, Page 403.

‡VIRGINIA, WILLIAM C.
Served in Capt. Amasa Brown's Company. Pension Certificate No. 31429.

VIRTUE, GEORGE.
Served from May 1 to June 30, 1814
in Capt. Alexander Brooks' Corps
of Artillery. Ref: R. & L. 1812,
AGO Page 31.

*VITTUM, WILLIAM.
Served with Hospital Attendants, Vt.

VON, SAML.
Born at Waterberry; served in War
of 1812; captured June 6, 1813 at
Stoney Point; discharged Oct. 31,
1814. Ref: Records of Naval Records
and Library, Navy Dept.

‡VOSE, JOHN B.
Served in Capt. Walker's Company.
Pension Certificate of widow, Betsey,
No. 3529.

VOTER, JOHN, Sergeant, Lanesboro,.
Mass. Served from July 26, 1814 to
June 19, 1815 in Capt. Taylor's Com-
pany, 30th Inf. Ref: R. & L. 1812,
AGO Page 23.

VRANDENBURG, ABRAM.
Served from March 9 to June 8, 1813
in Lieut. V. R. Goodrich's Company,
11th Regt. Ref: R. & L. 1812, AGO
Page 10.

*VRANDENBURGH, HENRY,   Bristol.
Volunteered to go to Plattsburgh,
September, 1814, and was at the
battle, serving 9 days in Capt. Jehiel
Saxton's Company, Sumner's Regt.

‡*WADE, BENJAMIN.
Served in Capt. Wright's Company,
Col. Fifield's Regt. Detached Militia
in U. S. service 6 months, 1812.
Also served in Capt. Durkee's Com-
pany. Pension Certificate No. 1082.

WADE, JOSHUA.
Enlisted July 25, 1813 for 1 year in
Capt. Daniel Farrington's Company,
30th Regt. (also commanded by Capt.
Simeon Wright); on Muster Roll from
March 1 to April 30, 1814; wounded.
Ref: R. & L. 1812, AGO Pages 50
and 51.

WADE, SOLOMON.
Enlisted Oct. 23, 1813 for 1 year in
Capt. Simeon Wright's Company; new
recruit not accepted. Ref: R. & L.
1812, AGO Page 51.

‡*WADE STEPHEN.
Served in Capt. Wright's Company,
Col. Fifield's Regt. Detached Militia
in U. S. service 6 months, 1812. Also
served in Capt. Durkee's Company.
Pension Certificate No. 25303.

WADE, WILLIAM.
Enlisted July 25, 1813 for 1 year in
Capt. Daniel Farrington's Company,
30th Regt. (also commanded by Capt.
Simeon Wright); discharged July 24,
1814. Ref: R. & L. 1812, AGO Pages
29, 50, 51.

‡WADHAMS, HEMAN, Lieutenant.
Appointed 3rd Lieutenant 30th Inf.
April 30, 1813; 2nd Lieutenant June
23, 1814; resigned Sept. 15, 1814.
Served in Capt. Gideon Spencer's Company and Capt. William Miller's Company, 30th Regt. Pension Certificate
of widow, Lavina, No. 13115. Ref:
R. & L. 1812, AGO Pages 54 and
56; Heitman's Historical Register &
Dictionary USA.

*WADSON, JEFFREY.
Served in 4 Regt. (Williams') Vt.
Militia.

WADSWORTH, JAMES O.,   Pittsford.
Volunteered to go to Plattsburgh,
September, 1814, and served 8 days
in Capt. Caleb Hendee's Company.
Ref: Book 52, AGO Page 125.

WAGER, GEORGE T.
Served from May 1 to Aug. 11, 1814;
no organization given. Ref: R. & L.
1812, AGO Page 29.

*WAGGONER, CHRISTIAN A., (or I.)
Fifer. Served in Capt. Pettes' Company, Col. Wm. Williams' Regt. Detached Militia in U. S. service 4 months and 17 days, 1812.

‡WAGGONER, FRANCIS.
Served in Capt. John D. Reynolds' Company. Pension Certificate No. 20366. Pension Certificate of widow, Cyrene, No. 23349.

‡WAGGONER, STEPHEN.
Served in Capt. Reynolds' Company. Pension Certificate of widow, Polly, No. 6102.

WAIDE, THOMAS, Lieutenant.
Appointed Ensign 48th Inf. April 21, 1814; 26th Inf. May 12, 1814; 2nd Lieutenant Oct. 1, 1814; honorably discharged June 15, 1815. Ref: Heitman's Historical Register & Dictionary USA.

WAIDRIGHT, EZRA,   Burlington.
Volunteered to go to Plattsburgh, September, 1814, and served in Capt. Henry Mayo's Company. Ref: Book 51, AGO Page 81.

*WAINWRIGHT, JONATHAN JR.
Served from April 12 to April 15, 1814 in Capt. John Hackett's Company, Sumner's Regt.

*WAINWRIGHT, RUFUS.
Served from April 12 to April 21, 1814 in Lieut. Justus Foote's Company, Sumner's Regt.

*WAINWRIGHT, SAMUEL.
Served in 1 Regt. (Judson's) Vt. Militia.

*WAIT, BENJAMIN, Ensign.
Served in 1st Regt. 3rd Brig. 3rd Div. Vt. Militia.

‡WAIT, BOWEN.
Served in Capt. Lacey's Company. Pension Certificate of widow, Polly M., No. 28180.

‡*WAIT, DANIEL, Ensign.
Served in 3 Regt. (Williams') Vt. Militia, Capt. Adams' Company. Pension Certificate of widow, Cynthia, No. 13757.

*WAIT, DAVID,   Pawlet.
Served in Capt. Hotchkiss' Company, Col. Martindale's Regt. Detached Militia in U. S. service 2 months and 13 days, 1812.

‡*WAIT, ELI.
Served in Corning's Detachment, Vt. Militia and 4 Regt. (Peck's) Vt. Militia. Also served in Capt. Campbell's Company. Pension Certificate No. 24128.

*WAIT, HARRY,   Isle-La-Motte?
Served in 4 Regt. (Williams') Vt. Militia.

‡WAIT, HENRY S.,Corporal.
Served in Capt. Stephen Pette's Company, Col. Wm. Williams' Regt. Detached Militia in service during summer of 1812. Served in Capt. Phineas

Williams' Company, 11th Regt.; on Pay Roll for January and February, 1813. Pension Certificate No. 6817. Pension Certificate of widow, Sophia, No. 32919.

*WAIT, JOHN.
Served in Capt. Mansfield's Company, Col. Dixon's Regt. Detached Militia in U. S. service 1 month and 23 days; enlisted Sept. 23, 1813.

WAIT, JOHN JR.
Served from Feb. 8 to May 7, 1813 in Capt. Charles Follett's Company, 11th Regt. Ref: R. & L. 1812, AGO Page 13.

*WAIT, THOMAS (or Waite)
Served in Capt. Richardson's Company, Col. Martindale's Regt. Detached Militia in U. S. service 2 months and 13 days, 1812.

WAIT, WILLIAM,   Shoreham.
Resided on Five Mile Point; entered the army and was at the battles of Chippewa and Lundy's Lane. During the fifty days' siege of Fort Erie by the British and Canadian forces, his head was taken off by an eighteen pound shot. Ref: Rev. J. F. Goodhue's History of Shoreham, Page 103.

*WAKEFIELD, ELIAS.
Served in Capt. E. Wheeler's Company, Col. Fifield's Regt. Detached Militia in U. S. service 2 months and 26 days, 1812.

*WALBRIDGE, CHARLES.
Served in Capt. Scovell's Company, Col. Martindale's Regt. Detached Militia in U. S. service 2 months and 21 days, 1812.

*WALBRIDGE, HENRY, Sergeant Major.
Served from Sept. 25 to Nov. 4, 1813 in Dixon's Consolidated Regt. of Vt. Militia in U. S. service.

*WALBRIDGE, JOHN.
Enlisted Sept. 25 and served 1 month and 23 days in Capt. Charles Bennett's Company, Col. Dixon's Regt. Detached Militia in U. S. service.

WALBRIDGE, JOSEPH JR.
Served in Capt. Samuel H. Holly's Company, 11th Regt.; on Pay Roll for January and February, 1813. Ref: R. & L. 1812, AGO Page 25.

*WALBRIDGE, MARTIN, Adjutant.
Served from Sept. 25 to Nov. 4, 1813 in Dixon's Consolidated Regt. of Vt. Militia in U. S. service.

*WALBRIDGE, ROGER.
Served in Capt. Bingham's Company, Col. Jonathan Williams' Regt. Detached Militia in U. S. service 1 month and 18 days, 1812.

WALBRIDGE, SOLOMON,   St. Albans.
Volunteered to go to Plattsburgh, September, 1814, and served 8 days; no organization given. Ref: Book 51, AGO Page 118.

*WALBRIDGE, STEBBINS, Lieutenant.
Served as 1st Lieutenant in Cavalry of Detached Militia of Vt. in U. S.

service at Champlain from Nov. 18 to Nov. 19, 1812. Served as 2nd Lieutenant in 1 Regt. (Martindale's) Vt. Militia.

WALDRAM, JOHN.
Enlisted April 21, 1814 during the war in Capt. Gideon Spencer's Company, 30th Regt.; on Muster Roll from Dec. 30, 1813 to June 30, 1814. Ref: R. & L. 1812, AGO Page 56.

WALDRON, JABEZ L.
Served from May 1 to June 30, 1814 in Capt. Haig's Corps of Light Dragoons. Ref: R. & L. 1812, AGO Page 20.

WALDRON, PETER.
Enlisted Oct. 22, 1812 for 5 years in company of late Capt. J. Brooks, commanded by Lt. John I. Cromwell, Corps of U. S. Artillery; on Muster Roll from April 30 to June 30, 1814. Ref: R. & L. 1812, AGO Page 18.

WALDRON, RICHARD, Carpenter.
Served from June 10 to June 30, 1814 in Alexander Parris' Company of Artificers. Ref: R. & L. 1812, AGO Page 24.

*WALES, BENJAMIN, Lieutenant.
Served in 1 Regt. (Martindale's) Vt. Militia.

WALES, EDWARD, Ensign.
Appointed Ensign April 6, 1812. Ref: Governor and Council, Vt., Vol. 6, Page 478.

*WALES, SHUBAEL, Captain.
Served from April 12 to April 21, 1814 in Col. Wm. B. Sumner's Regt.

*WALES, SHUBAL,   Randolph.
Volunteered to go to Plattsburgh, September, 1814, and served in Capt. Lebbeus Egerton's Company.

*WALKER, ALDEN.
Served in Capt. Sabin's Company, Col. Jonathan Williams' Regt. Detached Militia in U. S. service 2 months and 6 days, 1812.

*WALKER, AMOS E.
Served from April 12 to April 21, 1814 in Capt. Shubael Wales' Company, Col. W. B. Sumner's Regt. Also served in Capt. Salmon Foster's Company.

*WALKER, DAVID.
Served in Capt. Morrill's Company, Col. Fifield's Regt. Detached Militia in U. S. service 2 months and 16 days, 1812.

*WALKER, EBENEZER, Lieutenant.
Served as 3rd Lieutenant in Sumner's Regt. Vt. Militia.

WALKER, ELISHA, Sergeant, Hubbardton. Served from April 26, 1813 to April 26, 1814 in Capt. Daniel Farrington's Company, 30th Regt. (also commanded by Capt. Simeon Wright). Ref: R. & L. 1812, AGO Pages 50, 51.

‡*WALKER, ENOS, Captain.
Appointed 1st Lieutenant 31st Inf. April 30, 1813; resigned April 18,

1814. Also served as Captain in 2 Regt. (Fifield's) Vt. Militia. Pension Certificate of widow, Hannah, No. 1678. Ref: Heitman's Historical Register & Dictionary USA.

WALKER, EPHRAIM.
Served in Capt. Charles Follett's Company, 11th Regt.; on Pay Roll for January and February, 1812. Ref: R. & L. 1812, AGO Page 12.

WALKER, FREEMAN,   Strafford.
Volunteered to go to Plattsburgh, September, 1814, and served in Capt. Cyril Chandler's Company. Ref: Book 52, AGO Page 42.

WALKER, HORATIO,   Pittsford.
Volunteered to go to Plattsburgh, September, 1814, and served 8 days in Capt. Caleb Hendee's Company. Ref: Book 52, AGO Page 125.

WALKER, JAMES O.,   Whiting.
Volunteered to go to Plattsburgh, September, 1814, and served 9 days in Capt. Salmon Foster's Company. Sumner's Regt. Ref: Book 51, AGO Page 7.

‡*WALKER, JEREMIAH,   Danville.
Served in Capt. Morrill's Company, Col. Fifield's Regt. Detached Militia in U. S. service 4 months and 24 days, 1812. Served from May 1 to June 30, 1814 in Capt. Haig's Corps of Light Dragoons. Pension Certificate No. 6334. Pension Certificate of widow, Hannah, No. 16483.

‡*WALKER, JESSE JR.
Served in Capt. Noyce's Company, Col. Jonathan Williams' Regt. Detached Militia in U. S. service 2 months and 6 days, 1812. Pension Certificate No. 13894.

‡WALKER, JOHN.
Served in Capt. Johnson's Company. Pension Certificate of widow, Mary, No. 3005.

WALKER, JOHN C., Lieutenant, Manchester. Appointed Ensign 11th Inf. July 19, 1813; 2nd Lieutenant Nov. 19, 1813; 1st Lieutenant 48th Inf. April 21, 1814; 26th Inf. May 12, 1814; honorably discharged June 15, 1815. Ref: Heitman's Historical Register & Dictionary USA.

WALKER, LUTHER.
Served from Sept. 25 to Oct. 8, 1813 in Capt. Jesse Post's Company, Dixon's Regt. Ref: Book 52, AGO Page 290.

WALKER, LYMAN.
Volunteered to go to Plattsburgh, September, 1814, and went as far as Bolton, Vt., serving 4 days in Lt. Phineus Kimball's Company of West Fairlee. Ref: Book 52, AGO Page 46.

WALKER, NATHANIEL.
Served from Feb. 25 to May 24, 1813 in Capt. Edgerton's Company, 11th Regt. Ref: R. & L. 1812, AGO Page 3.

*WALKER, SAMUEL.
Served in Capt. Sabin's Company, Col. Jonathan Williams' Regt. Detached Militia in U. S. service 2 months and 7 days, 1812.

WALKER. SIMEON, Cabot?
Served in War of 1812 and was captured by troops June 26, 1813 at Beaver Dams; discharged Aug. 10th. Ref: Records of Naval Records and Library, Navy Dept.

WALKER, TILLY, Pittsford.
Volunteered to go to Plattsburgh, September, 1814, and served 8 days in Capt. Caleb Hendee's Company. Ref: Book 52, AGO Page 125.

*WALKER, WHITEFIELD, Sergeant, Whiting. Served from April 13 to April 21, 1814 in Capt. Salmon Foster's Company, Sumner's Regt.; volunteered to go to Plattsburgh, September, 1814, and served 15 days in same company.

WALKER, WHITFORD, Sergeant.
Served from April 12 to April 21, 1814 in Capt. Shubel Wales' Company, Col. W. B. Sumner's Regt. Ref: Book 52, AGO Page 288.

WALKER, WILLIAM, Highgate.
Served from Sept. 1, 1812 in Capt. Conrade Saxe's Company, Col. Wm. Williams' Regt. Ref: Hemenway's Vt. Gazetteer, Vol. 2, Page 420.

‡WALKER, WILLIAM.
Served in Capt. Concord's Company. Pension Certificate No. 13846.

*WALKER, WILLIAM.
Served in Capt. Willson's Company, Col. Wm. Williams' Regt. Detached Militia in U. S. service 4 months and 24 days, 1812.

*WALKER, WILLIAM.
Enlisted Sept. 25, 1813 in Capt. N. B. Eldridge's Company, Dixon's Regt.

WALL, ASA, Sergeant.
Enlisted April 25, 1813 for 1 year in Capt. Simeon Wright's Company. Ref: R. & L. 1812, AGO Page 51.

WALLACE, ADOLPHUS, Sudbury.
Volunteered to go to Plattsburgh, September, 1814, and served 6 days in Capt. Thomas Hall's Company. Ref: Book 52, AGO Page 122.

WALLACE, GROSVENER, Sudbury.
Volunteered to go to Plattsburgh, September, 1814, and served 6 days in Capt. Thomas Hall's Company. Ref: Book 51, AGO Page 47; Book 52, AGO Page 122.

*WALLACE, GROVENOR, Corporal.
Served in Capt. Brown's Company, Col. Martindale's Regt. Detached Militia in U. S. service 2 months and 14 days, 1812.

*WALLACE, IRA.
Served in Capt. Robbins' Company, Col. Wm. Williams' Regt. Detached Militia in U. S. service 4 months and 29 days, 1812.

WALLACE, JAMES, Franklin County.
Volunteered .to go to Plattsburgh Sept. 11, 1814 and served in 15th or 22nd Regt. Ref: Hemenway's Vt. Gazetteer, Vol. 2, Page 392.

WALLACE, JOHN, Franklin County.
Enlisted Dec. 14, 1812 for 5 years in Capt. White Youngs' Company, 15th Regt.; on Muster Roll from Aug. 31 to Dec. 31, 1814. Ref: R. & L. 1812, AGO Page 27.

WALLACE, JOSEPH, Hospital Surgeon's Mate. Served from May 1 to July 31, 1814 on General Staff of the Northern Army commanded by Major General George Izard. Ref: R. & L. 1812, AGO Page 28.

WALLACE, JOSEPH.
Served in Capt. Samuel H. Holly's Company, 11th Regt.; on Pay Roll for January and February, 1813. Ref: R. & L. 1812, AGO Page 25.

*WALLACE, MAJOR D., Sergeant.
Served in Capt. Taylor's Company, Col. Fifield's Regt. Detached Militia in U. S. service 2 months and 21 days, 1812.

*WALLACE, MOSES, Richford.
Enlisted Sept. 25, 1813 in Capt. Martin D. Folett's Company, Dixon's Regt.

WALLACE, MOSES, 1st Sergeant.
Volunteered to go to Plattsburgh, September, 1814, and served 3 days in company of Capt. James George of Topsham. Ref: Book 52, AGO Pages 67, 68, 70.

*WALLACE, ROBERT.
Enlisted Sept. 28, 1813 and served 1 month and 21 days in Capt. Charles Bennett's Company, Col. Dixon's Regt.

‡WALLACE, SAMUEL, Vershire.
Volunteered to go to Plattsburgh, September, 1814, and served in Capt. Ira Corse's Company. Pension Certificate of widow, Maria F., No. 27765.

WALLACE, TIMOTHY.
Enlisted June 7, 1813 for 1 year and served in Capt. Gideon Spencer's Company and Capt. James Taylor's Company, 30th Regt. Ref: R. & L. 1812, AGO Pages 56 and 59.

*WALLACE, WILLIAM.
Served in Capt. Willson's Company, Col. Wm. Williams' Regt. Detached Militia in U. S. service 4 months and 24 days, 1812.

WALLBRIDGE WILLIAM, St. Albans.
Enlisted April 29, 1813 for 1 year in Capt. John Wires' Company, 30th Regt. Ref: R. & L. 1812, AGO Page 40.

*WALLER, WALTER.
Served from May 1 to June 30, 1814 in Capt. Haig's Corps of Light Dragoons. Also served in 2 Regt. (Fifield's) Vt. Militia. Ref: R. & L. 1812, AGO Page 20.

WALLIS, ELIPHA, Sergeant.
Served in Capt. Chadwick's Company. Ref: R. & L. 1812, AGO Page 32.

*WALLIS, FREDERICK, Corporal.
Served in Corning's Detachment, Vt. Militia.

‡*WALLIS, LUKE, Sergeant.
Served in Capt. O. Lowry's Company,
Col. Wm. Williams' Regt. Detached
Militia in U. S. service 4 months
and 26 days, 1812. Stationed at Swanton Falls. Pension Certificate of widow, Elizabeth, No. 31615.

WALLIS, TIMOTHY.
Enlisted June 7, 1813 for 1 year in
Capt. James Taylor's Company, 30th
Regt.; on Muster Roll from Nov. 30
to Dec. 31, 1813. Ref: R. & L. 1812,
AGO Page 52.

WALSH, BARTHOLOMEW.
Served from May 1 to June 30, 1814
in Capt. Alexander Brooks' Corps of
Artillery. Ref: R. & L. 1812, AGO
Page 31.

WALSTON, WILLIAM.
Served from Oct. 5 to Oct. 17, 1813 in
Capt. Stephen Brown's Company, 3
Regt. Ref: R. & L. 1812, AGO
Page 34.

*WALTER, ENOS.
Served in Capt. Wheeler's Company,
Col. Fifield's Regt. Detached Militia in U. S. service 2 months and
18 days, 1812.

WALTON, CALEB A.
Served in Capt. Samuel H. Holly's
Company, 11th Regt.; on Pay Roll
for January and February, 1813. Ref:
R. & L. 1812, AGO Page 25.

‡WANDALL, ROBERT L.
Served in Capt. Sylvanus Danforth's
Company. Pension Certificate of wid-
ow, Mary, No. 6520.

‡*WANDALL, ROBERT R.
Served in Capt. Cross' Company,
Col. Martindale's Regt. Detached
Militia in U. S. service 18 days, 1812.

‡WANYER, JOHN.
Served in Capt. Daine's Company.
Pension Certificate No. 10161.

*WANZER, JOHN, Fairfax.
Served in 1813 and 1814 in Capt.
Joseph Beeman's Company. Also serv-
ed in 4 Regt. (Williams') Vt. Mili-
tia. Ref: Hemenway's Vt. Gazetteer,
Vol. 2, Page 402.

*WARD, CHANDLER.
Served in Capt. Taylor's Company,
Col. Wm. Williams' Regt. Detached
Militia in U. S. service 4 months
and 24 days, 1812.

*WARD, CHARLES, Sergeant.
Served in Capt. Ormsbee's Company,
Col. Martindale's Regt. Detached
Militia in U. S. service 2 months and
14 days, 1812. Served as Sergeant
in 1st Regt. of Detached Militia of
Vt. in U. S. service at Champlain
from Nov. 18 to Nov. 19, 1812.

*WARD, CHAUNCY, Fifer.
Enlisted Sept. 20, 1813 in Capt. John
Weed's Company, Col. Clark's Rifle
Corps.

WARD, DAN.
Served from March 22 to June 21,
1813 in Capt. Samul Gordon's Company, 11th Regt. Ref: R. & L. 1812,
AGO Page 8.

WARD, DAVID, Shoreham.
Volunteered to go to Plattsburgh,
September, 1814, and served 6 days
in Capt. Samuel Hand's Company.
Ref: Rev. J. F. Goodhue's History
of Shoreham, Page 108.

WARD, GILES, Corporal.
Enlisted May 10, 1813 for 1 year in
Capt. Simeon Wright's Company. Ref:
R. & L. 1812, AGO Page 51.

‡*WARD, IRA.
Served in Sumner's Regt. Vt. Militia.
Also served in Capt. N. Munson's
Company. Pension Certificate No.
34015.

*WARD, ISAAC.
Served in 1 Regt. (Martindale's) Vt.
Militia.

WARD, JONATHAN.
Served from March 22 to June 21,
1813 in Capt. Samul Gordon's Company, 11th Regt. Ref: R. & L. 1812,
AGO Page 8.

*WARD, JOSIAH.
Served in 2 Regt. (Fifield's) Vt.
Militia.

WARD, LEWIS.
Served from Feb. 26 to May 25, 1813
in Lieut. V. R. Goodrich's Company,
11th Regt. Was captured by troops
July 25, 1814 at Londers Lane; discharged Oct. 8, 1814. Ref: R. & L.
1812, AGO Pages 10 and 11; Records
of Naval Records and Library, Navy
Dept.

WARD, LUTHER, Vershire.
Volunteered to go to Plattsburgh,
September, 1814, and served 3 days
in Capt. Ira Corse's Company. Ref:
Book 52, AGO Page 91.

*WARD, MATTES A., Corporal.
Served from April 12 to April 21,
1814 in Lieut. Justus Foote's Company, Sumner's Regt.

‡*WARD, PHINEAS.
Served in Capt. Strait's Company, Col.
Martindale's Regt. Detached Militia
in U. S. service 2 months and 13
days, 1812. Pension Certificate of
widow, Diana, No. 13330.

*WARD, SALMON.
Enlisted Sept. 25, 1813 and served 1
month and 23 days in Capt. Elijah
Birge's Company, Col. Dixon's Regt.
Detached Militia in U. S. service.

WARD, SOLOMON, Corinth.
Volunteered to go to Plattsburgh,
September, 1814, and served 3 days
in Capt. Abel Jackman's Company.
Ref: Book 52, AGO Pages 44 and 45.

*WARD, THOMAS, Hardwick.
Served 6 months in fall and winter
of 1812 at Derby in Capt. Hiram
Mason's Company, 2 Regt. (Fifield's)
Vt. Militia.

*WARD, TIMOTHY.
Served in 1 Regt. (Judson's) Vt.
Militia.

WARD, URIAH, Captain.
Appointed Captain 31st Inf. April
30, 1813; resigned Aug. 28, 1813.
Ref: Heitman's Historical Register &
Dictionary USA.

WARDSWELL, ALPHEUS, Franklin
County. Volunteered to go to Plattsburgh Sept. 11, 1814 and served in
15th or 22nd Regt. Ref: Hemenway's
Vt. Gazetteer, Vol. 2, Page 391.

WARE, CYRUS,   Montpelier.
Volunteered to go to Plattsburgh,
September, 1814, and served 8 days
in Capt. Timothy Hubbard's Company. Ref: Book 52, AGO Page 256.

*WARE, DANIEL H.
Served in 3 Regt. (Williams') Vt.
Militia.

WARE, GEORGE.
Served from May 1, 1813 to May 1,
1814 in Capt. Gideon Spencer's Company and Capt. James Taylor's Company, 30th Regt. Ref: R. & L. 1812,
AGO Pages 52 and 56.

*WARE, JOHN.   Calais.
Volunteered to go to Plattsburgh,
September, 1814, and served 10 days
in Capt. Gideon Wheelock's Company.

*WARE, JONATHAN, Quartermaster.
Served in Capt. Briggs' Company, Col.
Jonathan Williams' Regt. Detached
Militia in U. S. service 2 months and
13 days, 1812.

WARE, JOSEPH,   Thetford.
Marched for Plattsburgh, September,
1814, and went as far as Bolton, Vt.,
serving 6 days in Capt. Salmon Howard's Company, 2nd Regt. Ref: Book
52, AGO Page 15.

*WARE, THOMAS D.,   Thetford.
Marched for Plattsburgh, September,
1814, and went as far as Bolton,
Vt., serving 6 days in Capt. Salmon
Howard's Company, 2nd Regt.

*WARKER, LUTHER.
Served in Dixon's Regt. Vt. Militia.

WARNER, APPOLLUS,   Barnard.
Volunteered to go to Plattsburgh.
September, 1814, and served 8 days
in Capt. John S. Bicknell's Company.
Ref: Book 51, AGO Page 270.

*WARNER, CLARK.
Served from April 12 to May 20,
1814 in Capt. George Fisher's Company, Sumner's Regt.

‡*WARNER, DAN.
Served from April 12 to April 21,
1814 in Capt. Edmund B. Hill's Company, Sumner's Regt. Also served in
Capt. Hall's Company. Pension Certificate No. 32026.

*WARNER, GEORGE, Ensign.
Served from Sept. 25 to Nov. 4, 1813
in Capt. N. B. Eldridge's Company,
Dixon's Regt.

*WARNER, JABEZ.
Served in 3 Regt. (Tyler's) Vt. Militia.

‡WARNER, JAPHETH L.,   Corporal,
Pittsford. Volunteered to go to
Plattsburgh, September, 1814, and
served 8 days in Capt. Caleb Hendee's
Company. Pension Certificate of wid-
ow, Fila, No. 30496.

WARNER, JOHN.
Enlisted March 24, 1814 during the
war in company of late Capt. J.
Brooks, commanded by Lt. John I.
Cromwell, Corps of U. S. Artillery;
on Muster Roll from April 30 to June
30, 1814; transferred from Capt. Collins' Company. Ref: R. & L. 1812,
AGO Page 18.

WARNER, JOHN, Sergeant, Cambridge.
Volunteered to go to Plattsburgh,
September, 1814, and served 8 days
in Capt. Salmon Green's Company.
Ref: Book 51, AGO Page 207; Hemen-
way's Vt. Gazetteer, Vol. 2, Page 617.

WARNER, JOSEPH.
Enlisted in U. S. Marine Corps at
Boston Oct. 14, 1812. Ref: Book 52,
AGO Page 294.

WARNER, JOSEPH L.,   Shrewsbury.
Volunteered to go to Plattsburgh,
September, 1814, and served 4 days
in Capt. Robert Reed's Company.
Ref: Book 52, AGO Pages 138 and 140.

WARNER, JUSTIN, Fifer,   Vershire.
Volunteered to go to Plattsburgh,
September, 1814, and served 3 days
in Capt. Ira Corse's Company. Ref:
Book 52, AGO Page 91.

*WARNER, LEMUEL.
Served in 4 Regt. (Peck's) Vt. Militia.

*WARNER, LEVI, Surgeon.
Served in Sumner's Regt. Vt. Militia.

*WARNER, LEVI.
Served from Sept. 25 to Sept. 29,
1813 in Capt. Amos Robinson's Company, Dixon's Regt.

WARNER, MOSES.
Served from Feb. 12 to Feb. 22, 1813
in Lieut. Wm. S. Foster's Company,
11th Regt. Ref: R. & L. 1812, AGO
Page 6.

WARNER, OMRI,   Ira.
Volunteered to go to Plattsburgh,
September, 1814, and served in Capt.
Matthew Anderson's Company as a
teamster. Ref: Hemenway's Vt. Ga-
zetteer, Vol. 2, Page 783.

WARNER, PETER,   Pittsford.
Volunteered to go to Plattsburgh,
September, 1814, and served 8 days
in Capt. Caleb Hendee's Company.
Ref: Book 52, AGO Page 125.

‡WARNER, PHILO SAXTON,   Bristol.
Volunteered to go to Plattsburgh,
September, 1814, and was at the
battle, serving 9 days in Capt. Jehiel
Saxton's Company, Sumner's Regt.
Pension Certificate of widow, Melis-
sa, No. 29164.

WARNER, REVENES.
Enlisted Feb. 26, 1814 during the war in company of late Capt. J. Brooks, commanded by Lt. John I. Cromwell, Corps of U. S. Artillery; on Muster Roll from April 30 to June 30, 1814; transferred from Capt. Collins' Company. Ref: R. & L. 1812, AGO Page 18.

*WARNER, SEXTON.
Served from April 12 to April 21, 1814 in Capt. Edmund B. Hill's Company, Sumner's Regt.

WARNER, SIMEON.
Served from April 7 to July 6, 1813 in Capt. Samul Gordon's Company, 11th Regt. Ref: R. & L. 1812, AGO Page 8.

WARNER, SIMEON.
Served from Feb. 21 to May 20, 1813 in Capt. John W. Weeks' Company, 11th Regt. Ref: R. & L. 1812, AGO Page 4.

‡*WARNER, STEPHEN.
Served in Capt. Barns' Company, 4 Regt. (Williams') Vt. Militia. Pension Certificate of widow, Polly, No. 35197.

WARNER, WARREN, Sergeant, Sudbury.
Volunteered to go to Plattsburgh, September, 1814, and served 6 days in Capt. Thomas Hall's Company. Ref: Book 52, AGO Page 122.

WARNER, WILLIAM.
Served from March 31 to June 30, 1813 in Capt. Samul Gordon's Company, 11th Regt. Ref: R. & L. 1812, AGO Page 8.

WARNER, WILLIAM.
Enlisted May 12, 1813 in Capt. Daniel Farrington's Company, 30th Regt. (also commanded by Capt. Simeon Wright); died in service Dec. 6, 1813. Ref: R. & L. 1812, AGO Pages 50 and 51.

*WARR, JONATHAN.
Served in 3 Regt. (Williams') Vt. Militia.

‡WARREN, CALVIN,   Berlin.
Volunteered to go to Plattsburgh, September, 1814, and served 7 days in Capt. Cyrus Johnson's Company. Pension Certificate of widow, Lydia M., No. 33478.

*WARREN, CLARK.
Served in Sumner's Regt. Vt. Militia.

WARREN, DAVID, 1st Sergeant, Rochester. Volunteered to go to Plattsburgh, September, 1814, and served 7 days in Capt. N. Brown's Company. Ref: Book 51, AGO Page 249.

WARREN, EBENEZER.
Served from April 24, 1813 to April 26, 1814 in Capt. Daniel Farrington's Company, 30th Regt. (also commanded by Capt. Simeon Wright). Ref: R. & L. 1812, AGO Pages 50 and 51.

‡WARREN, EZRA.
Volunteered to go to Plattsburgh, September, 1814; no organization given. Also served in Capt. Keyes' Company. Pension Certificate of widow, Jemima, No. 27168. Ref: Book 52, AGO Page 155.

WARREN, GEORGE.
Served from April 2 to July 1, 1813 in Capt. John W. Weeks' Company, 11th Regt. Ref: R. & L. 1812, AGO Page 4.

WARREN, HARMON B.
Served from Jan. 10 to Feb. 28, 1813 in Capt. Samuel H. Holly's Company. 11th Regt. Ref: R. & L. 1812, AGO Page 25.

WARREN, HASTINGS, Colonel, Middlebury. Volunteered to go to Plattsburgh, September, 1814, with company of volunteers from Cornwall and vicinity. Ref: Rev. Lyman Mathews' History of Cornwall, Page 344.

*WARREN, JACOB.
Served in Corning's Detachment, Vt. Militia.

‡WARREN, JOHN,   Rochester.
Volunteered to go to Plattsburgh, September, 1814, and served 7 days in Capt. Oliver Mason's Company. Also served in Capt. Wade Hampton's Company. Pension Certificate No. 4837. Ref: Book 51, AGO Pages 249 and 252.

*WARREN, LEMUEL.
Served in 4 Regt. (Peck's) Vt. Militia.

*WARREN, OTIS.
Served in Capt. Wheeler's Company, Col. Fifield's Regt. Detached Militia in U. S. service 3 months and 24 days, 1812.

WARREN, PHILIP, Captain,   Orwell.
Volunteered to go to Plattsburgh, September, 1814, and served 11 days in command of company of Militia Artillery. Ref: Book 51, AGO Page 31.

WARREN, SAMUEL,   Morristown.
Volunteered to go to Plattsburgh, September, 1814, and served 8 days in Capt. Denison Cook's Company. Ref: Book 51, AGO Pages 202 and 206.

WARREN, WILLIAM.
Served in Capt. Alexander Brooks' Corps of Artillery; on Pay Roll to June 30, 1814. Ref: R. & L. 1812, AGO Page 31.

WARREN, ZEBINA,   Middlesex.
Volunteered to go to Plattsburgh, September, 1814, and served in Capt. Holden Putnam's Company, 4th Regt. (Peck's). Ref: Hemenway's Vt. Gazetteer, Vol. 4, Page 250.

*WARRINER, CONVERSE.
Served in Capt. Brown's Company, Col. Martindale's Regt. Detached Militia in U. S. service 1 month and 22 days, 1812.

WASBURN, SAMUEL, Lieutenant.
Corporal and Sergeant Light Artillery October, 1809 to May, 1813; appointed

3rd Lieutenant May 20, 1813; 2nd Lieutenant Dec. 13, 1813; died Aug. 23, 1821. Ref: Heitman's Historical Register & Dictionary USA.

*WASHBORN, SALMON 2nd.
Served in Dixon's Regt. Vt. Militia.

WASHBUN, ARTIMAS.
Served in Capt. Chadwick's Company. Ref: R. & L. 1812, AGO Page 32.

WASHBURN, ABIEZAR, Sergeant.
Born at Bridgewater, Mass. Enlisted at Burlington March 21, 1814 and served in Capt. Gideon Spencer's Company, Capt. James Taylor's Company and Capt. Wm. Miller's Company. 30th Regt. Ref: R. & L. 1812, AGO Pages 53, 54, 55, 56.

‡*WASHBURN, ASA, Corporal, Putney?
Served in Capt. Parsons' Company, Col. Jonathan Williams' Regt. Detached Militia in U. S. service 2 months and 13 days, 1812. Pension Certificate No. 9922. Pension Certificate of widow, Ruth, No. 16989.

*WASHBURN, EDWARD, Sergeant.
Served in Capt. Dorrance's Company, Col. Wm. Williams' Regt. Detached Militia in U. S. service 4 months and 19 days, 1812.

*WASHBURN, ELISHA.
Served in 1 Regt. (Judson's) Vt. Militia.

*WASHBURN, HEMAN.
Served from June 11 to June 14, 1813 in Lt. Bates' Company, 1 Regt. (Judson's).

*WASHBURN, JAMES.
Served in Capt. Rogers' Company, Col. Fifield's Regt. Detached Militia in U. S. service 5 months and 27 days, 1812.

*WASHBURN, JAMES.
Served under Captains Wheatly and Wright, Col. Fifield's Regt. Detached Militia in U. S. service 6 months, 1812.

WASHBURN, JOSIAH.
Served from April 5 to July 4, 1813 in Capt. John W. Weeks' Company, 11th Regt. Ref: R. & L. 1812, AGO Page 4.

*WASHBURN, JOSIAH JR., Randolph.
Served under Captains Wheatly and Wright, Col. Fifield's Regt. Detached Militia in U. S. service 6 months, 1812. Volunteered to go to Plattsburgh, September, 1814, and served in Capt. Lebbeus Edgerton's Company.

WASHBURN, LEVI.
Served from April 28, 1813 to April 28, 1814 in Capt. James Taylor's Company and Capt. Gideon Spencer's Company, 30th Regt. Ref: R. & L. 1812, AGO Pages 52, 56, 59.

WASHBURN, OMER.
Served from March 29 to June 28, 1813 in Capt. Samul Gordon's Company, 11th Regt. Ref: R. & L. 1812, AGO Page 8.

*WASHBURN, PETER, Sergeant.
Served in Capt. Durkee's Company, Col. Fifield's Regt. Detached Militia in U. S. service 2 months and 21 days, 1812.

‡*WASHBURN, PHINEAS,   Georgia.
Served in Capt. Saxe's Company, Col. Wm. Williams' Regt. Detached Militia in U. S. service 4 months and 24 days, 1812. Enlisted Oct. 1, 1813 and served 1 month and 23 days in Capt. Elijah W. Wood's Company, Col. Dixon's Regt. Pension Certificate of widow, Lucinda, No. 14315.

‡*WASHBURN, REUBEN,   Highgate.
Served in Capt. Saxe's Company, Col. Wm. Williams' Regt. Detached Militia in U. S. service 2 months and 1 day, 1812. Pension Certificate No. 14027.

*WASHBURN, REUBEN.
Enlisted Sept. 23, 1813 and served 1 month and 23 days in Capt. Amasa Mansfield's Company, Col. Dixon's Regt.

‡*WASHBURN, RUEBEN.
Served in Capt. Mason's Company, Col. Fifield's Regt. Detached Militia in U. S. service 5 months and 29 days, 1812; stationed at Derby . Pension Certificate of widow, Olive, No. 6108.

WASHBURN, RICHARD.
Served in Capt. Charles Follett's Company, 11th Regt.; on Pay Roll for January and February, 1813. Ref: R. & L. 1812, AGO Page 12.

*WASHBURN, SALATHIEL.
Enlisted Sept. 29, 1813 in Capt. Charles Bennett's Company, Dixon's Regt.

*WASHBURN. SALMON.
Served from Sept. 23 to Nov. 4, 1813 in Capt. Amasa Mansfield's Company, Dixon's Regt.

‡WASHBURN, SETH.
Served in Capt. Abel Farwell's Company. Pension Certificate of widow, Hannah, No. 40854.

*WASHBURN, SYLVANUS.
Enlisted Sept. 23, 1813 in Capt. Amasa Mansfield's Company, Dixon's Regt.

*WASHBURN, SYLVESTER.
Served in Capt. Mansfield's Company, Col. Dixon's Regt. Detached Militia in U. S. service 1 month and 10 days, 1813. Served from April 2 to July 1, 1813 in Capt. Edgerton's Company, 11th Regt.

‡*WASHBURN, THOMAS,   Troy.
Served in Capt. Morrill's Company, 2 Regt. (Fifield's) Detached Militia stationed at Derby in year 1812-1813. Pension Certificate No. 13849.

WASON, MOSES,   Corinth.
Volunteered to go to Plattsburgh, September, 1814, and served in Capt. Abel Jackman's Company. Ref: Book 52, AGO Page 44.

*WASSON, ROBERT, Corinth.
Served in Capt. Rogers' Company,
Col. Fifield's Regt. Detached Militia
in U. S. service 5 months and 27
days, 1812. Volunteered to go to
Plattsburgh, September, 1814, and
served in Capt. Abel Jackman's Company.

*WATERHOUSE, EDSON R.
Served in 1 Regt. (Judson's) Vt.
Militia.

*WATERHOUSE, ELEAZER.
Served in 1 Regt. (Judson's) Vt.
Militia.

*WATERHOUSE, HARRY, Sergeant.
Served from April 12 to April 15,
1814 in Capt. John Hackett's Company, Sumner's Regt.

*WATERHOUSE, IRA.
Served in Capt. Ormsbee's Company,
Col. Martindale's Regt. Detached
Militia in U. S. service 2 months and
14 days, 1812.

WATERHOUSE, JACOB.
Served from May 1 to June 30, 1814
in Alexander Parris' Company of Artificers. Ref: R. & L. 1812, AGO
Page 24.

WATERHOUSE, JOHN, Sergeant Major.
Served from May 1 to Aug. 18, 1814;
no organization given. Ref: R. & L.
1812, AGO Page 29.

WATERMAN, ARAUNAH, Montpelier.
Volunteered to go to Plattsburgh,
September, 1814, and served 5 days
in Capt. Timothy Hubbard's Company. Ref: Book 52, AGO Page 240.

*WATERMAN, ASA, Corporal, Johnson.
Enlisted Sept. 25, 1813 and served
1 month and 23 days in Capt. Thomas
Waterman's Company, Col. Dixon's
Regt.; volunteered to go to Plattsburgh, September, 1814, and served
4 days in same company.

*WATERMAN, AZARIAH, Johnson.
Enlisted Sept. 25, 1813 in Capt.
Thomas Waterman's Company, Dixon's
Regt.; volunteered to go to Plattsburgh, September, 1814, and served
4 days in same company.

WATERMAN, BENJAMIN, Orange.
Marched for Plattsburgh Sept. 11,
1814 and went part way, serving 5
days in Capt. David Rising's Company, as a wagoner. Ref: Book 52,
AGO Pages 19 and 22.

*WATERMAN, ELIAS.
Served in Capt. Dorrance's Company,
Col. Wm. Williams' Regt. Detached
Militia in U. S. service 3 months
and 23 days, 1812.

‡*WATERMAN, ELIJAH.
Served in Capt. Burnap's Company,
Col. Jonathan Williams' Regt. Detached Militia in U. S. service 2
months and 13 days, 1812. Pension
Certificate of widow, Polly, No. 26041.

WATERMAN, ELISHA.
Served in company of late Capt. J.
Brooks, commanded by Lt. John I.

Cromweil, Corps of U. S. Artillery;
on Muster Roll from April 30 to June
30, 1814; prisoner of war on parole;
transferred from Capt. Collins' Company. Ref: R. & L. 1812, AGO Page
18.

*WATERMAN, JOHN, Corporal.
Served in Capt. Needham's Company,
Col. Martindale's Regt. Detached
Militia in U. S. service 2 months
and 14 days, 1812.

WATERMAN, JOHN B., Shrewsbury.
Volunteered to go to Plattsburgh,
September, 1814, and served 4 days
in Capt. Robert Reed's Company. Ref:
Book 52, AGO Pages 138 and 140.

*WATERMAN, JOSEPH.
Enlisted Sept. 25, 1813 and served
1 month and 23 days in Capt. Thomas
Waterman's Company, Col. Dixon's
Regt.

WATERMAN, SILAS, St. Albans.
Enlisted May 6, 1813 for 1 year in
Capt. John Wires' Company, 30th
Regt. Ref: R. & L. 1812, AGO Page
40.

WATERMAN, SILAS, St. Albans.
Served from March 1 to May 30, 1814
in Capt. Sanford's Company, 30th Inf.
Ref: R. & L. 1812, AGO Page 30.

*WATERMAN, STEPHEN.
Served in Capt. Dodge's Company,
Col. Fifield's Regt. Detached Militia
in U. S. servcie 2 months and 21
days, 1812.

*WATERMAN, THOMAS, Captain, Johnson. Appointed Sept. 25, 1813, captain in Col. Luther Dixon's Regt.
Volunteered to go to Plattsburgh,
September, 1814, and served 8 days
in command of company in same
Regt.

WATEROUS, ELEAZER.
Served from June 11 to June 14, 1813
in Capt. Moses Jewett's Company,
1st Regt. 2nd Brig. 3rd Div. Ref:
R. & L. 1812, AGO Page 42.

WATERS, GARDNER.
Enlisted Feb. 17, 1813 in Lt. V. R.
Goodrich's Company, 11th Regt. on
Pay Roll for January and February,
1813. Ref: R. & L. 1812, AGO Page
11.

*WATERS, REUBEN D., Ass't Commissary, Calais. Volunteered to go to
Plattsburgh, September, 1814, and
served 8 days in Capt. Gideon
Wheelock's Company.

*WATKINS, ALVIN.
Served from April 12 to April 21,
1814 in Capt. Othniel Jewett's Company, Sumner's Regt.

*WATKINS, LYMAN, Sergeant.
Served in Capt. Adams' Company,
Col. Jonathan Williams' Regt. Detached Militia in U. S. service 2
months and 7 days, 1812.

WATSON, B., Fairfax.
Served from Aug. 8, 1812 in company
of Capt. Joseph Beeman Jr., 11th

Regt. U. S. Inf. under Col. Ira Clark. Ref: Hemenway's Vt. Gazetteer, Vol. 2, Page 402.

*WATSON, CLARK, Corporal.
Served in Capt. Brown's Company, Col. Martindale's Regt. Detached Militia in U. S. service 2 months and 14 days, 1812. Served as corporal in 1st Regt. Detached Militia in U. S. service at Champlain from Nov. 18 to Nov. 19, 1812.

WATSON, CLINTON,   Barre.
Volunteered to go to Plattsburgh, September, 1814, and served 10 days in Capt. Warren Ellis' Company. Ref: Book 52, AGO Page 242.

WATSON, DAVID,   Williamstown.
Volunteered to go to Plattsburgh, September, 1814, and served 8 days in Capt. David Robinson's Company. Ref: Book 52, AGO Pages 8 and 10.

WATSON, EBENEZER, Fifer.
Served in Lt. Wm. S. Foster's Company, 11th Regt.: on Pay Roll for January and February, 1813. Ref: R. & L. 1812, AGO Page 7.

WATSON, JAMES.   Fairfax.
Served in 1813 and 1814 in Capt. Joseph Beeman's Company. Ref: Hemenway's Vt. Gazetteer, Vol. 2, Page 402.

*WATSON, JAMES (or James Jr.), Danville. Served in Capt. Morrill's Company. Col. Fifield's Regt. Detached Militia in U. S. service 3 months and 22 days, 1812. Also served in Capt. Haig's Corps of Light Dragoons; on Pay Roll to June 30, 1813.

WATSON, JEFFREY.
Served in Capt. Taylor's Company, Col. Wm. Williams' Regt. Detached Militia in U. S. service 4 months and 24 days, 1812. Ref: Book 53, AGO Page 67.

WATSON, ROBERT,   Richford.
Served in Capt. Martin D. Follett's Company, Dixon's Regt. on duty on Canadian frontier in 1813. Ref: Hemenway's Vt. Gazetteer, Vol. 2, Page 428.

WATSON, SHERMAN.   Barre.
Volunteered to go to Plattsburgh, September, 1814, and served 10 days in Capt. Warren Ellis' Company. Ref: Book 52, AGO Page 242.

‡*WATSON, SIMEON, Corporal.
Served in Capt. Cross' Company, Col. Martindale's Regt. Detached Militia in U. S. service 2 months and 14 days, 1812. Pension Certificate of widow, Olive, No. 5606.

*WATSON, WILLIAM.
Served in 3 Regt. (Tyler's) Vt. Militia.

*WATTS, DANIEL.
Served in Corning's Detachment, Vt. Militia.

*WAUGH, JOHN,   Marshfield.
Served in Capt. Rogers' Company, Col. Fifield's Regt. Detached Militia in U. S. service 5 months and 27 days, 1812.

*WAUGH, JOHN D., Corporal.
Served in Capt. Bingham's Company, Col. Jonathan Williams' Regt. Detached Militia in U. S. service 2 months and 9 days, 1812.

*WAUGH, NATHANIEL.
Served in 4 Regt. (Peck's) Vt. Militia.

*WAVERY, GEORGE W.
Served in 2 Regt. (Fifield's) Vt. Militia.

*WAY, RUFUS M.
Served from Oct. 24 to Nov. 18, 1813 in Capt. Isaac Finch's Company, Col. Clark's Rifle Corps.

WEAD, SAMUEL, Captain.   Sheldon.
Volunteered to go to Plattsburgh, September, 1814, and commanded company raised in Sheldon. Ref: Book 51, AGO Pages 109, 125, 152; Hemenway's Vt. Gazetteer, Vol. 2, Page 373.

WEADON, WILLIAM.
Served from March 24 to June 23, 1813 in Capt. Samul Gordon's Company. 11th Regt. Ref: R. & L. 1812, AGO Page 8.

WEAL, BENJAMIN JR.
Served from Feb. 18 to May 17, 1813 in Lieut. V. R. Goodrich's Company. 11th Regt. Ref: R. & L. 1812, AGO Page 10.

*WEAST, REAN.
Served with Hospital Attendants, Vt.

*WEATHERBY, JOSHUA.
Served in Sumner's Regt. Vt. Militia.

*WEAVER, JAMES.
Enlisted Sept. 26, 1812 in Capt. Benjamin S. Edgerton's Company, 11th Regt.; on Pay Roll for September and October, 1812, and January and February, 1813. Also served in 3 Regt. (Williams') Vt. Militia. Ref: R. & L. 1812, AGO Pages 1 and 2.

WEAVER, JOHN,   Franklin County.
Volunteered to go to Plattsburgh Sept. 11, 1814 and served in 15th or 22nd Regt. Ref: Hemenway's Vt. Gazetteer, Vol. 2, Page 391.

WEAZLE, CONRAD,   Highgate.
Served in Capt. Langworthy's Company, Col. Dixon's Regt. Detached Militia in U. S. service 1 month and 21 days, 1813; enlisted Sept. 27, 1813. Volunteered to go to Plattsburgh, September, 1814, and served 5 days in Capt. Conrade Saxe's Company, 4 Regt. (Williams'). Ref: Book 51, AGO Page 100; Book 52, AGO Page 260; Book 53, AGO Page 110.

‡*WEBB, AARON B.
Served from June 11 to June 14, 1813 in Capt. Hezekiah Barns' Company, 1st Regt. 2nd Brig. 3rd Div. Pension Certificate No. 25529.

WEBB, JOHN.
Enlisted April 18, 1812 for 5 years in Capt. White Youngs' Company, 15th Regt.; on Muster Roll from Aug. 31 to Dec. 31, 1814. Ref: R. & L. 1812, AGO Page 27.

*WEBB, MELANTON B.
Served from Oct. 4 to Oct. 13, 1813
in Capt. John Palmer's Company, 1st
Regt. 2nd Brig. 3rd Div.

WEBB, REUBEN, Lieutenant, Hubbardton. Volunteered to go to Plattsburgh, September, 1814, and served
2 days in Capt. Henry J. Horton's
Company. Ref: Book 52, AGO Pages
142 and 158.

WEBB, STEPHEN HINSDALE, Lieutenant, St. Albans. Appointed Ensign,
30th Inf. April 30, 1813; 3rd Lieutenant June 23, 1814; honorably discharged June 15. 1815; died February, 1873. Served as Ensign in Capt.
John Wires' Company, 30th Regt. Ref:
Heitman's Historical Register & Dictionary USA; R. & L. 1812, AGO
Page 40.

*WEBB, THOMAS.
Served from Oct. 11 to Oct. 17, 1813
in Capt. Stephen Brown's Company, 3
Regt. (Tyler's).

*WEBBER, JAMES.
Served in Capt. Morrill's Company,
Col. Fifield's Regt. Detached Militia
in U. S. service 3 months and 18
days, 1812. Served from May 1 to
June 30, 1814 as corporal in Corps
of Light Dragoons. Ref: R. & L.
1812, AGO Page 20.

‡WEBBER, JOHN F.
Served in Capt. Morrill's Company.
Pension Certificate No. 20941.

‡WEBBER, JUSTICE.
Served in Capt. Keyes' Company.
Pension Certificate of widow, Julia,
No. 40628.

WEBSTER, AMOS.
Served in Capt. Weeks' Company, 11th
Regt.; on Pay Roll for January and
February, 1813; deserted Jan. 1, 1813.
Ref: R. & L. 1812, AGO Page 5.

*WEBSTER, EPHRAIM, Corporal, Bol-
ton. Volunteered to go to Plattsburgh, September, 1814, and served in
Capt. John Pinno's Company. Also
served in 4 Regt. (Peck's) Vt. Militia. Ref: Book 51, AGO Page 90.

WEBSTER, HARRY B., Corporal.
Served in Capt. Benjamin S. Edger-
ton's Company, 11th Regt.; on Pay
Roll for September and October, 1812
and January and February, 1813.
Ref: R. & L. 1812, Pages 1 and 2.

*WEBSTER, HIRAM.
Served in Capt. Taylor's Company.
Col. Wm. Williams' Regt. Detached
Militia in U. S. service 4 months and
24 days, 1812.

WEBSTER, HOPKINS, Fairfax.
Volunteered to go to Plattsburgh.
September, 1814, and served 8 days
in Capt. Josiah Grout's Company.
Ref: Book 51, AGO Page 103.

WEBSTER, HORACE.
Appointed Cadet Military Academy
Oct. 24. 1814. Ref: Heitman's His-
torical Register & Dictionary USA.

WEBSTER, HUMPHREY, Lieutenant.
Appointed Ensign 11th Inf. Sept. 22,
1813; 2nd Lieutenant July 25, 1814.
Ref: Governor and Council Vt.,
Vol. 6, Page 474.

WEBSTER, HYDE.
Enlisted Oct. 15, 1813 in Capt. Asahel
Scovell's Company. Ref: Book 52,
AGO Page 274.

WEBSTER, ISAAC, Fairfax.
Served in 1813 and 1814 in Capt.
Joseph Beemans' Company. Volunteer-
ed to go to Plattsburgh, September,
1814, and served in Capt. Josiah
Grout's Company. Ref: Hemenway's
Vt. Gazetteer, Vol. 2, Pages 402 and
403.

*WEBSTER, JAMES.
Served from June 11 to June 14, 1813
in Lt. Bates' Company, 1 Regt. (Judson's).

‡WEBSTER, JESSE, Cabot.
Volunteered to go to Plattsburgh,
September, 1814, and served 3 days
in Capt. Anthony Perry's Company.
Pension Certificate No. 32656. Pension Certificate of widow, Susan, No.
40098.

*WEBSTER, JOHN.
Served from June 11 to June 14, 1813
in Lt. Bates' Company, 1 Regt (Judson's).

*WEBSTER, JOSEPH, Fairfax.
Served in Capt. Taylor's Company,
Col. Wm. Williams' Regt. Detached
Militia in U. S. service 4 months
and 24 days, 1812. Volunteered to
go to Plattsburgh, September, 1814,
and served 8 days as a corporal in
Capt. Josiah Grout's Company.

*WEBSTER, SAMUEL.
Served in 4 Regt. (Peck's) Vt. Militia.

‡WEBSTER, SAMUEL, Fairfax.
Served in 1813 and 1814 in Capt.
Joseph Beeman's Company. Volunteered to go to Plattsburgh, September, 1814, and served 8 days in Capt.
Josiah Grout's Company. Pension Certificate of widow, Electa, No. 26192.
Ref: Hemenway's Vt. Gazetteer, Vol.
2, Pages 402 and 403.

*WEBSTER, SAMUEL JR.
Served in Corning's Detachment, Vt.
Militia.

*WEBSTER, SIMEON.
Served from Sept. 25 to Sept. 28,
1813 in Capt. Elijah W. Wood's Company, Dixon's Regt.

‡*WEBSTER, ZENAS.
Served in Capt. Burnap's Company,
Col. Jonathan Williams' Regt. De-
tached Militia in U. S. service 2
months and 21 days, 1812. Pension
Certificate of widow, Parnell, No. 1709.

WEDGWOOD, THOMAS.
Served from Feb. 20 to May 19, 1813
in Capt. Jonathan Starks' Company,
11th Regt. Ref: R. & L. 1812, AGO
Page 19.

WEED, BENJAMIN JR.
Enlsited Feb. 18, 1813 in Lt. V. R.
Goodrich's Company, 11th Regt.; on
Pay Roll for January and February,
1813. Ref: R. & L. 1812, AGO Page
11.

WEED, DANIEL.
Served in Capt. Benjamin S. Edgerton's Company, 11th Regt.; on Pay
Roll for September and October, 1812,
and January and February, 1813;
died Feb. 21, 1813. Ref: R. & L.
1812, AGO Pages 1 and 2.

*WEED, IRA. Sergeant.
Served in Capt. Strait's Company,
Col. Martindale's Regt. Detached
Militia in U. S. service 2 months and
13 days, 1812.

*WEED, JAMES.
Served from Feb. 6 to May 5, 1813
in Lieut. V. R. Goodrich's Company,
11th Regt. Enlisted Sept. 20, 1813
in Capt. John Weed's Company. Col.
Clark's Rifle Corps. Ref: R. & L.
1812, AGO Pages 10 and 11.

*WEED, JOHN, Captain.
Enlisted Sept. 20, 1813 in Col. Isaac
Clark's Rifle Corps.

WEED, JOSEPH.
Served from January 6 to June 8,
1813 in Capt. John W. Weeks' Company, 11th Regt. Ref: R. & L. 1812,
AGO Pages 4 and 5.

*WEED, LYMAN R.
Enlisted Sept. 25, 1813 and served
1 month and 23 days in Capt. Amos
Robinson's Company, Col. Dixon's
Regt. Detached Militia in U. S. serv-
ice.

*WEED, ORRIN. Sergeant,   Highgate.
Served in Capt. Saxe's Company, Col.
Wm. Williams' Regt. Detached Militia in U. S. service 3 months and
29 days, 1812. Also served as sergeant in Dixon's' Regt. Vt. Militia.

*WEEDING, SAMUEL.
Served in Capt. Dodge's Company,
Col. Fifield's Regt. Detached Militia
in U. S. service 2 months and 21
days, 1812.

WEEKS, EZRA.
Served from January 1 to January
26, 1813 in Capt. Phineas Williams'
Company, 11th Regt. Ref: R. & L.
1812, AGO Page 15.

*WEEKS, FREDERICK.
Enlisted Sept. 25, 1813 and served
1 month and 23 days in Capt. Post's
Company. Col. Dixon's Regt. Detached Militia in U. S. service.

*WEEKS, JOHN JR.
Served in 1 Regt. (Martindale's) Vt.
Militia.

WEEKS, JOHN.
Served from Sept. 1, 1812 to Jan.
22, 1813 in Capt. Weeks' Company.
11th Regt. Ref: R. & L. 1812, AGO
Page 5.

WEEKS, JOHN W., Captain.
Served in command of company in
11th Regt.; on Pay Roll for January and February, 1813. Ref: R. &
L. 1812, AGO Page 5.

*WEEKS, JOSEPH,   Georgia.
Enlisted Sept. 25, 1813 and served
1 month and 23 days in Capt. Jesse
Post's Company, Col. Dixon's Regt.;
volunteered to go to Plattsburgh, September, 1814, and served in same company.

‡*WEEKS, LYMAN.
Enlisted Sept. 25, 1813 and served 1
month and 23 days in Capt. Amos
Robinson's Company, Col. Dixon's
Regt. Detached Militia in U. S. serv-
ice. Pension Certificate No. 22416.

‡WEEKS, RICHARD,   Richmond.
Volunteered to go to Plattsburgh,
September, 1814, and served 9 days
in Capt. Roswell Hunt's Company,
3 Regt. (Tyler's). Pension Certificate No. 25230. Pension Certificate
of widow, Sophia, No. 27773.

WEEKS, SHEVERICK, Lieutenant.
Appointed 1st Lieutenant 30th Inf.
April 30, 1813; resigned Dec. 31, 1813.
Ref: Heitman's Historical Register &
Dictionary, USA.

‡WEEKS, WILLIAM.
Served in Lieut. Warner's Company.
Pension Certificate of widow, Sarah
E., No. 17784.

*WELCH, AARON JR.
Served in Capt. Morrill's Company,
Col. Fifield's Regt. Detached Militia
in U. S. service 6 months and 5 days,
1812.

*WELCH, DANIEL, Sergeant.
Served in Capt. Cross' Company, Col.
Martindale's Regt. Detached Militia
in U. S. service 2 months and 14
days, 1812. Served as Sergeant in
1st Regt. of Detached Militia of Vt.
in U. S. service at Champlain from
Nov. 18 to Nov. 19, 1812.

*WELCH, REUBEN.
Served in Capt. Walker's Company,
Col. Fifield's Regt. Detached Militia
in U. S. service 2 months and 24
days, 1812.

*WELCH, WALTER,   Pawlet.
Served in Capt. Scovell's Company,
Col. Martindale's Regt. Detached
Militia in U. S. service 2 months and
21 days, 1812.

WELLER, ARDIN, Fifer,   Pittsford.
Volunteered to go to Plattsburgh,
September, 1814, and served 8 days
in Capt. Caleb Hendee's Company.
Ref: Book 52, AGO Page 124.

*WELLER, TIMOTHY.
Served in 1 Regt. (Judson's) Vt.
Militia.

WELLINGTON, ASHLEY,   Braintree.
Marched for Plattsburgh, September,
1814, and served 9 days in Capt.
Lot Hudson's Company. Ref: Book
52, AGO Page 32.

‡*WELLMAN, LEMUEL. Sergeant.
Served in Capt. Noyce's Company,
Col. Jonathan Williams' Regt. De-
tached Militia in U. S. service 2
months and 6 days, 1812. Pension
Certificate No. 1925.

*WELLMAN, REUBEN, Drum Major, St.
Albans. Appointed Drum Major in
Capt. John Wires' Company, 30th
Regt. April 26, 1813; transferred to
Dixon's Consolidated Regt. of Vt.
Militia in U. S. service Sept. 25,
1813. Ref: R. & L. 1812, AGO Page
40.

*WELLS, AMBROSE.
Served in 4 Regt. (Peck's) Vt. Militia.

‡*WELLS, ASA.
Served from June 11 to June 14, 1813
in Capt. Thomas Dorwin's Company,
1st Regt. 2nd Brig. 3rd Div. Volunteered to go to Plattsburgh, September, 1814, and served 7 days in Capt.
Frederick Griswold's Company, raised in Brookfield. Also served in Capt.
Hezekiah Barnes' Company. Pension
Certificate No. 19006.

*WELLS, DANIEL.
Served in Col. Wm. Williams' Regt.
Detached Militia in U. S. service 4
months and 26 days, 1812. Enlisted
April 28, 1813 for 1 year in Capt.
Simeon Wright's Company.

*WELLS, EDWARD.
Served in Capt. Robbins' Company,
Col. Wm. Williams' Regt. Detached
Militia in U. S. service 4 months and
29 days, 1812.

WELLS, ELIPHALET, Lieutenant.
Appointed 1st Lieutenant 30th Inf.
April 30, 1813; resigned Aug. 15,
1813. Ref: Heitman's Historical Register & Dictionary USA.

*WELLS, HIRAM.   Calais.
Volunteered to go to Plattsburgh,
September, 1814, and served 10 days
in Capt. Gideon Wheelock's Company.

WELLS, ISAAC,   Salisbury.
Served in Regular Army in 1812. Ref:
History of Salisbury.

*WELLS, ISAAC,   Calais.
Volunteered to go to Plattsburgh,
September, 1814, and served 10 days
in Capt. Gideon Wheelock's Company.

*WELLS, ISRAEL.
Served in Sumner's Regt. Vt. Militia.

WELLS, JACOB (or Wills?)
Served from May 1 to Aug. 4, 1814;
no organization given. Ref: R. & L.
1812, AGO Page 29.

WELLS, JAMES, 2nd Lieutenant.
Served in Lt. Foster's Company, 11th
Regt.; on Pay Roll for January and
February, 1813. Ref: R. & L. 1812,
AGO Page 7.

*WELLS, JOHN.
Served from Oct. 5 to Oct. 17, 1813
in Capt. Stephen Brown's Company,
3 Regt. (Tyler's).

‡*WELLS, JOSEPH, Sergeant.
Served in Capt. Reed's Company, 3
Regt. (Tyler's) Vt. Militia. Pension
Certificate No. 20398.

WELLS, JOSEPH,   Marshfield.
Volunteered to go to Plattsburgh,
September, 1814, and served 9 days
in Capt. James English's Company.
Ref: Book 52, AGO Page 248.

WELLS, LEVI,   St. Albans.
Enlisted May 4, 1813 for 1 year in
Capt. John Wires' Company, 30th
Regt. Ref: R. & L. 1812, AGO Page
40.

WELLS, MICHAEL.
Served from May 1 to June 30, 1814
in Capt. Alexander Brooks' Corps of
Artillery. Ref: R. & L. 1812, AGO
Page 31.

*WELLS, NATHANIEL.
Served in Capt. Robbins' Company,
Col. Wm. Williams' Regt. Detached
Militia in U. S. service 4 months and
29 days, 1812.

WELLS, NICHOLAS C.,   Strafford.
Served from Feb. 12 to May 11, 1813
in Capt. Edgerton's Company, 11th
Regt. Ref: R. & L. 1812, AGO Page 3.

*WELLS, NOAH B.
Enlisted Sept. 25, 1813 in Capt. N.
B. Eldridge's Company, Dixon's Regt.

*WELLS, PELEG.
Served in 3 Regt. (Tyler's) Vt. Militia.

WELLS, RANSOM.
Volunteered to go to Plattsburgh,
September, 1814, and served in company of Capt. Joel Barnes of Chelsea. Ref: Book 52, AGO Page 77.

*WELLS, REUBEN,   Stowe.
Volunteered to go to Plattsburgh,
September, 1814, and was at the
battle, serving in Capt. Nehemiah
Perkins' Company, 4 Regt. (Peck's).

WELLS, RICHARD.
Volunteered to go to Plattsburgh,
September, 1814, and served in com-
pany of Capt. Jonathan Jennings,
Chelsea. Ref: Book 52, AGO Pages
79 and 104.

*WELLS, ROBERT.
Served in 4 Regt. (Peck's) Vt. Militia. Served as Sergeant in Corning's Detachment, Vt. Militia.

WELLS, REUBEN, Sergeant.
Enlisted Feb. 25, 1814 for 5 years in
company of late Capt. J. Brooks,
commanded by Lt. John I. Cromwell,
Corps of U. S. Artillery; on Muster
Roll from April 30 to June 30, 1814;
transferred from Capt. Collins' Company. Ref: R. & L. 1812, AGO
Page 18.

‡WELLS, RUSSEL.
Served from April 24, 1813 to May
23, 1814 in Capt. James Taylor's Company and Capt. Gideon Spencer's
Company, 30th Regt. Pension Certificate No. 15936. Ref: R. & L. 1812,
AGO Pages 52, 56, 59.

*WELLS, SYLVESTER,　　　Stowe.
Volunteered to go to Plattsburgh,
September, 1814, and was at the
battle, serving in Capt. Nehemiah Perkins' Company, 4 Regt. (Peck's).

*WELLS, THOMAS.
Served in 3 Regt. (Tyler's) Vt. Militia.

*WELLS, WANTON,　　　Richmond.
Served in Capt. Barns' Company, Col.
Wm. Williams' Regt. Detached Mili-
tia in U. S. service 5 months, 1812.
Volunteered to go to Plattsburgh,
September, 1814, and served 9 days
in Capt. Roswell Hunt's Company,
3 Regt. (Tyler's). Also served in 1
Regt. (Judson's) Vt. Militia. Ref:
Book 51, AGO Page 82; Book 53, AGO
Page 9.

*WELLS, WATERMAN.
Served in Capt. Morrill's Company,
Col. Fifield's Regt. Detached Militia
in U. S. service 6 months and 5
days, 1812.

*WELLS, WILLIAM.
Served in Lt. Wm. S. Foster's Company, 11th Regt.; on Pay Roll January and February, 1813. Also served
in Corning's Detachment, Vt. Militia.
Ref: R. & L. 1812, AGO Page 7.

*WELLS, WILLIAM JR.,　　Richmond.
Served from June 11 to June 14,
1813 in Capt. Thomas Dorwin's Com-
pany, 1st Regt. 2nd Brig. 3rd Div.
Volunteered to go to Plattsburgh,
September, 1814, serving 9 days in
Capt. Roswell Hunt's Company, 3
Regt. (Tyler's). Also served in 4
Regt. (Williams') Vt. Militia. Ref:
Book 51, AGO Page 82.

WELMAN, BENJAMIN.
Enlisted May 3, 1813 for 1 year in
Capt. Daniel Farrington's Company,
30th Regt. (also commanded by Capt.
Simeon Wright); on Muster Roll from
March 1 to April 30, 1814. Ref: R.
& L. 1812, AGO Pages 50 and 51.

WEMAN, EBENEZER.
Served from May 1 to June 30, 1814
as a carpenter in Alexander Parris'
Company of Artificers. Ref: R. & L.
1812, AGO Page 24.

*WENTWORTH, DANIEL.
Served in Capt. Bingham's Company,
Col. Jonathan Williams' Regt. Detached Militia in U. S. service 2
months and 9 days, 1812.

‡WENTWORTH, IRA,　　Cornwall.
Volunteered to go to Plattsburgh,
September, 1814, and was at the
battle, serving in Capt. Edmund B.
Hill's Company, Sumner's Regt. Pension Certificate of widow, Sabina, No.
27625.

WENTWORTH, JOHN.
Served from May 1 to June 30, 1814
in Capt. Haig's Corps of Light Dragoons. Ref: R. & L. 1812, AGO
Page 20.

WENTWORTH, JOHN,　　Sudbury.
Volunteered to go to Plattsburgh,

Septembebr, 1814, and served 6 days.
in Capt. Thomas Hall's Company.
Ref: Book 52, AGO Page 122.

WESCOTT, AMOS, Sergeant.
Re-enlisted Feb. 22, 1814 during the
war in Capt. Gideon Spencer's Company, 30th Regt.; on Muster Roll
from Dec. 30, 1813 to June 30, 1814;
joined June 1, 1814. Ref: R. & L.
1812, AGO Page 56.

WESCOTT, NATHANIEL H.,　　Pittsford.
Volunteered to go to Plattsburgh,
September, 1814, and served 8 days.
in Capt. Caleb Hendee's Company.
Ref: Book 52, AGO Page 125.

WESCOTT, THOMAS (or Wescot), St. Albans. Enlisted May 4, 1813 for 1
year in Capt. John Wires' Company,
30th Regt. Ref: R. & L. 1812, AGO.
Page 40.

‡*WESSON, AARON,　　　Barnet.
Served in Capt. Morril's Company,
Col. Fifield's Regt. in 1812. Pension.
Certificate No. 4563.

WESSON, CHARLES B.,　　Lieutenant,.
Sheldon. Volunteered to go to Plattsburgh, September, 1814, and served
5 days in Capt. Samuel Weed's Company. Ref: Book 51, AGO Pages.
109, 125 and 175; Hemenway's Vt.
Gazetteer, Vol. 2, Page 373.

*WEST, ABNER,　　Barre or Montpelier.
Served in Capt. E. Walker's Company,
Col. Fifield's Regt. Detached Militia
in U. S. service 6 months and 3 days,.
1812. Volunteered to go to Plattsburgh, September, 1814, and served 8
days in Capt. Timothy Hubbard's.
Company.

WEST, EBENEZER,　　　Strafford.
Volunteered to go to Plattsburgh,
September, 1814, and served in Capt.
Joseph Barrett's Company. Ref: Book
52, AGO Page 41.

*WEST, ELI.
Served in Capt. Ormsbee's Company,
Col. Martindale's Regt. Detached
Militia in U. S. service 2 months and
14 days, 1812.

*WEST, HEEN.
Served with Hospital Attendants, Vt.

WEST, HENRY L.,　　　Thetford.
Volunteered to go to Plattsburgh,.
September, 1814, and served in Capt.
Orange Hubbard's Company. Ref:
Book 52, AGO Page 51.

WEST, ISRAEL,　　　New Haven.
Volunteered to go to Plattsburgh,
September, 1814, and served in Capt.
Othaniel Jewett's Company, Sumner's
Regt. Ref: Book 51, AGO Pages 23
and 24.

*WEST, ISRAEL JR.
Served from April 12 to April 21,
1814 in Capt. Eseck Sprague's Company, Sumner's Regt.

‡*WEST, JEREMIAH.
Served in Capt. Taylor's Company,
2 Regt. (Fifield's) Vt. Militia. Pension Certificate No. 22427. Pension.
Certificate of widow, Nancy, No. 33521.

*WEST, JOHN, Sergeant Surgeon.
Enlisted Sept. 25, 1813 in Capt. Amos
Robinson's Company, Dixon's Regt.

*WEST, JONATHAN S.
Enlisted Sept. 25, 1813 in Capt. Amos
Robinson's Company, Dixon's Regt.

*WEST, LEWIS, Sergeant.
Served in Capt. Wheeler's Company,
Col. Fifield's Regt. Detached Militia
in U. S. service 6 months and 4
days, 1812.

*WEST, LYMAN.
Enlisted Oct. 23, 1813 in Capt. Asahel
Langworthy's Company, Col. Isaac
Clark's Rifle Corps; transferred to
Capt. Folett's Company, Col. Dixon's
Regt.

WEST, NATHAN.
Enlisted Feb. 20, 1813 in Capt.
Phineas Williams' Company, 11th
Regt.; on Pay Roll to May 31, 1813.
Ref: R. & L. 1812, AGO Page 14.

‡WEST, NATHANIEL.
Served in Capt. Taylor's Company.
Pension Certificate of widow, Sally,
No. 5318.

WEST, NEHIMIAH.
Enlisted Nov. 1, 1812 in Capt. Weeks'
Company, 11th Regt.; on Pay Roll
for January and February, 1813. Ref:
R. & L. 1812, AGO Page 5.

WEST, PRESBURY, Lieutenant, Montpelier. Appointed 1st Lieutenant 31st
Inf. April 30, 1813; dismissed Jan.
31, 1814. Ref: Heitman's Historical
Register & Dictionary USA.

*WEST, RUFUS.
Enlisted Sept. 25, 1813 in Capt. Amos
Robinson's Company, Col. Dixon's
Regt. Detached Militia in U. S. serv-
ice 1 month and 23 days, 1813.

WEST, STUTSON,   Danville.
Served in Capt. Morrill's Company,
Col. Fifield's Regt. Detached Militia
in U. S. service 6 months. Ref: Hemenway's Vt. Gazetteer, Vol. 1, Page
314.

‡WEST, THOMAS.
Served in Capt. Pettis' Company.
Pension Certificate No. 20404.

*WEST, WILLIAM.
Served in Capt. Ormsbee's Company,
Col. Martindale's Regt. Detached
Militia in U. S. service 2 months and
14 days, 1812.

*WEST, WILLIAM.
Served in Capt. Burnap's Company,
Col. Jonathan Williams' Regt. Detached Militia in U. S. service 2
months and 13 days, 1812.

WEST, WILLIAM.
Enlisted Feb. 10, 1813 in Capt.
Phineas Williams' Company, 11th
Regt.; on Pay Roll to May 31, 1813.
Ref: R. & L. 1812, AGO Page 14.

*WEST, WILLIAM C., Corporal.
Served in 4 Regt. (Williams') Vt.
Militia.

WESTBROOK, T. W.,   Sherburne.
Volunteered to go to Plattsburgh,
September, 1814, and served 10 days;
no organization given. Ref: Book 52,
AGO Pages 164 and 165.

WESTCOAT, BENJAMIN.
Served in Capt. Barns' Company, Col.
Wm. Williams' Regt. Detached Mili-
tia in U. S. service 5 months. Ref:
Book 53, AGO Page 65.

*WESTCOAT, JOHNSON.
Served in Capt. Needham's Company,
Col. Martindale's Regt. Detached
Militia in U. S. service 2 months and
14 days, 1812.

*WESTCOAT, NICHOLAS.
Served in Capt. Needham's Company,
Col. Martindale's Regt. Detached
Militia in U. S. service 2 months and
14 days, 1812. Enlisted April 21, 1813
in Capt. Simeon Wright's Company,
30th Regt.; died Dec. 27, 1813.

*WESTCOTT, BENJAMIN.
Served from June 11 to June 14, 1813
in Capt. John Palmer's Company,
1st Regt. 2nd Brig. 3rd Div.

‡*WESTCOTT, DYER, Sergeant.
Served in Capt. Barns' Company, Col.
Wm. Williams' Regt. Detached Mili-
tia in U. S. service 5 months at
Swanton Falls in 1812. Served from
June 11 to June 14, 1813 and from
Oct. 4 to Oct. 14, 1813 in Capt. John
Palmer's Company, 1st Regt. 2nd
Brig. 3rd Div. Pension Certificate of
widow, Harty, No. 5070.

*WESTCOTT, JOHN.
Served from June 11 to June 14, 1813
and from Oct. 4 to Oct. 13, 1813 in
Capt. John Palmer's Company, 1st
Regt. 2nd Brig. 3rd Div.

*WESTON, AARON.
Served in Capt. Morrill's Company,
Col. Fifield's Regt. Detached Militia
in U. S. service 6 months and 5 days,
1812.

*WESTON, SAMUEL H.
Served in Capt. Ormsbee's Company,
Col. Martindale's Regt. Detached
Militia in U. S. service 2 months and
14 days, 1812.

‡WESTOVER, DIODORUS S.
Served in Capt. Hale's Company. Pension Certificate of widow, Betsey, No.
16142.

‡*WESTOVER, HYDE,   Enosburgh.
Served from Oct. 14 to Nov. 17, 1813
in Capt. Asahel Scoville's Company,
Col. Clark's Rifle Corps. Pension Certificate No. 22123.

*WETHERBEE, ELIAS (or Witherbee).
Served from March 2 to June 1, 1813
in Lieut. V. R. Goodrich's Company,
11th Regt. Served as Corporal in 2
Regt. (Fifield's) Vt. Militia. Ref:
R. & L. 1812, AGO Page 10.

*WETHERBEE, JOHN.
Served in Capt. Wheeler's Company,
Col. Fifield's Regt. Detached Militia
in U. S. service 6 months and 4 days,
1812.

‡*WETHERBEE, JOSIAH.
Served in Capt. Briggs' Company,
Col. Jonathan Williams' Regt. De-
tached Militia in U. S. service 2
months and 13 days, 1812. Pension
Certificate No. 9978.

WETHERBEE, SAMUEL JR., Lieutenant.
Appointed 3rd Lieutenant 31st Inf.
April 30, 1813; 2nd Lieutenant Jan.
11, 1814; 1st Lieutenant Sept. 30,
1814; honorably discharged June 15,
1815. Ref: Heitman's Historical Register & Dictionary USA.

*WETHERBY, DANIEL.
Served in Capt. Phelps' Company,
Col. Jonathan Williams' Regt. Detached Militia in U. S. service 2
months and 21 days, 1812.

*WETHERBY, LUTHER.
Enlisted Sept. 25, 1813 in Capt. N.
B. Eldridge's Company, Dixon's Regt.

*WETTAIN, REXFORD (or Wettam).
Served in Capt. Cross' Company. Col.
Martindale's Regt. Detached Militia
in U. S. service 2 months and 13
days, 1812.

*WEYMOUTH, SHADRACK, Vershire.
Served in Capt. Taylor's Company,
Col. Fifield's Regt. Detached Militia
in U. S. service 6 months, 1812. Volunteered to go to Plattsburgh, September, 1814, and served 3 days in
Capt. Ira Corse's Company.

WHALEY, ELIAS.
Served in Capt. Samuel H. Holly's
Company, 11th Regt.; on Pay Roll
for January and February, 1813. Ref:
R. & L. 1812, AGO Page 25.

*WHEATLEY, JOHN, Captain, Randolph.
Served in 2 Regt. (Fifield's) Vt. Militia.

*WHEATON, HOSEA.
Served from April 12 to April 21,
1814 in Capt. Shubael Wales' Company, Col. W. B. Sumner's Regt.

WHEATON, ISAAC, 1st Lieutenant, Pittsford. Volunteered to go to Plattsburgh, September, 1814, and served 8
days in Capt. Caleb Hendee's Company. Ref: Book 52, AGO Pages 124
and 126.

*WHEATON, JOHN.
Served in Sumner's Regt. Vt. Militia.

WHEATON, PLINNY, Barre.
Volunteered to go to Plattsburgh,
September, 1814, and served 8 days
in Capt. Warren Ellis' Company.
Ref: Book 52, AGO Pages 233 and 242.

WHEELER, AARON, Shoreham.
Volunteered to go to Plattsburgh,
September, 1814, and served 6 days
in Capt. Samuel Hand's Company.
Ref: Rev. J. F. Goodhue's History
of Shoreham, Page 108.

WHEELER, ABEL, Pittsford.
Enlisted May 15, 1813 in Capt. Daniel
Farrington's Company (30th Regt.
(also commanded by Capt. Simeon
Wright); this boy, the son of Jesse

Wheeler, served as a waiter to Col.
Rumsey of Hubbardton and died of
wounds April 18, 1814. Ref: R. & L.
1812, AGO Pages 50 and 51; A. M.
Caverly's History of Pittsford, Page
366.

WHEELER, ABIATHER.
Served from Nov. 1, 1812 to Feb. 28,
1813 in Capt. Samuel H. Holly's Company, 11th Regt. Ref: R. & L. 1812,
AGO Page 25.

*WHEELER, ALFRED, Fairfax.
Enlisted Sept. 25, 1813 and served 1
month and 23 days in Capt. Asa
Wilkins' Company, Col. Dixon's Regt.
Served in 1813 and 1814 in Capt.
Joseph Beeman's Company. Ref:
Hemenway's Vt. Gazetteer, Vol. 2,
Page 402.

WHEELER, ALVIN, West Haven.
Volunteered to go to Plattsburgh,
September, 1814, and served 4 days
in Capt. David B. Phippeney's Company. Ref: Book 52, AGO Page 46.

*WHEELER, AMOS, Shoreham.
Served from April 12 to May 20, 1814
in Capt. George Fisher's Company,
Sumner's Regt. Volunteered to go to
Plattsburgh, September, 1814, and
served 6 days in Capt. Samuel Hand's
Company.

‡WHEELER, APPOLLUS, Cabot.
Volunteered to go to Plattsburgh,
September, 1814, and served 3 days
in Capt. Anthony Perry's Company.
Pension Certificate No. 28509.

WHEELER, AUGUSTUS, Ensign, Sudbury.
Volunteered to go to Plattsburgh,
September, 1814, and served 6 days
in Capt. Thomas Hall's Company.
Ref: Book 52, AGO Pages 122, 131
and 152.

*WHEELER, CHARLES H.
Served from June 11 to June 14, 1813
in Capt. Ithiel Stone's Company, 1st
Regt. 2nd Brig. 3rd Div.

‡*WHEELER, CHAUNCEY.
Enlisted Sept. 25, 1813 in company
of Capt. Jonathan Prentiss Jr., Dixon's Regt. Pension Certificate No.
32976.

*WHEELER, CHESTER.
Served in Capt. Barns' Company, Col.
Wm. Williams' Regt. Detached Mili-
tia in U. S. service 5 months, 1812.
Also served in 1 Regt. (Judson's)
Vt. Militia.

*WHEELER, DANIEL, Corporal.
Served from April 12 to May 20, 1814
in company of Capt. James Gray Jr.,
Sumner's Regt.

‡WHEELER, EDWARD, Pittsford.
Enlisted April 24, 1813 for 1 year
in Capt. Simeon Wright's Company,
30th Regt. Pension Certificate No.
1146.

WHEELER, ELISHA, Corporal.
Served from Oct. 4 to Oct. 14, 1813
in Capt. John Palmer's Company,
1st Regt. 2nd Brig. 3rd Div. Ref:
R. & L. 1812, AGO Page 47.

WHEELER, HARRY T., Lieutenant, Sudbury. Volunteered to go to Plattsburgh, September, 1814, and served 6 days in Capt. Thomas Hall's Company. Ref: Book 52, AGO Page 122.

WHEELER, HARVEY T., Highgate. Volunteered to go to Plattsburgh, September, 1814; no organization given. Ref: Book 51, AGO Page 131.

WHEELER, HENRY T. Served in Capt. Phineas Williams' Company, 11th Regt.; on Pay Roll for January and February, 1813. Ref: R. & L. 1812, AGO Page 15.

WHEELER, HEZEKIAH. Volunteered to go to Plattsburgh, September, 1814, and served 4 days in Capt. Aaron Kidder's Company. Ref: Book 52, AGO Page 65.

*WHEELER, HORACE, Randolph. Volunteered to go to Plattsburgh, September, 1814, and served in Capt. Lebbeus Egerton's Company.

WHEELER, JACOB. Served from March 3 to June 2, 1813 in Capt. Charles Follett's Company, 11th Regt. Ref: R. & L. 1812, AGO Page 13.

WHEELER, JACOB. Served from Feb. 28 to May 27, 1813 in Capt. Samul Gordon's Company, 11th Regt. Ref: R. & L. 1812, AGO Page 8.

‡*WHEELER, JAMES, Sergeant. Served in Capt. Pettes' Company, Col. Wm. Williams' Regt. Detached Militia in U. S. service 3 months and 22 days, 1812; stationed at Swanton Falls. Also served in 3 Regt. (Tyler's) Vt. Militia. Pension Certificate of widow, Betsey, No. 9576.

WHEELER, JAMES, Cabot. Volunteered to go to Plattsburgh, September, 1814, and served 3 days in Capt. Anthony Perry's Company. Ref: Book 52, AGO Page 253.

*WHEELER, JEDEDIAH. Enlisted Sept. 25, 1813 in company of Capt. Jonathan Prentiss Jr., Dixon's Regt.

*WHEELER, JEREMIAH. Served in Capt. Weeks' Company, 11th Regt.; on Pay Roll for January and February, 1813. Also served in 4 Regt. (Williams') Vt. Militia. Ref: R. & L. 1812, AGO Page 5.

‡WHEELER, JOHN R. Served in Capt. Tarr's Company. Pension Certificate No. 18601.

WHEELER, JOSEPH, Sergeant. Served from May 1 to June 30, 1814 in Corps of Light Dragoons. Ref: R. & L. 1812, AGO Page 20.

WHEELER, LEONARD, Thetford. Marched for Plattsburgh, September, 1814, and went as far as Bolton, Vt., serving 6 days in Capt. Salmon Howard's Company, 2nd Regt. Ref: Book 52, AGO Page 15.

WHEELER, LYMAN. Served from May 1 to June 30, 1814 in Capt. Haig's Corps of Light Dragoons. Ref: R. & L. 1812, AGO Page 20.

*WHEELER, MOSES F., Corporal. Served from April 12 to April 15, 1814 in Capt. John Hackett's Company, Sumner's Regt.

*WHEELER, NAHUM. Served in Capt. Robbins' Company, Col. Wm. Williams' Regt. Detached Militia in U. S. service 4 months and 29 days, 1812.

WHEELER, NATHAN. Served from May 31 to Aug. 11, 1813 in Capt. Benjamin Bradford's Company. Ref: R. & L. 1812, AGO Page 26.

*WHEELER, NICHOLAS. Served in 1 Regt. (Judson's) Vt. Militia.

*WHEELER, ORRIN. Enlisted Sept. 25, 1813 in company of Capt. Jonathan Prentiss, Jr., Dixon's Regt.

*WHEELER, PETER, Lieutenant, Charlotte. Served from April 12 to April 21, 1814 in Capt. Eseck Sprague's Company, Sumner's Regt.

‡*WHEELER, ROBERT. Served in Capt. Sabin's Company, Col. Jonathan Williams' Regt. Detached Militia in U. S. service 2 months and 6 days, 1812. Pension Certificate of widow, Jane, No. 32750.

*WHEELER, SAMUEL, North Hero. Served in Capt. Pettes' Company, Col. Wm. Williams' Regt. Detached Militia in U. S. service 4 months and 17 days, 1812.

WHEELER, SAMUEL, Pittsford. Volunteered to go to Plattsburgh, September, 1814, and served 8 days in Capt. Caleb Hendee's Company as a waggoner. Ref: Book 52, AGO Page 125.

*WHEELER, SAMUEL A., Captain. Served in 2 Regt. (Fifield's) Vt. Militia.

*WHEELER, SILAS, Glover. Served in Capt. Mason's Company, Col. Fifield's Regt. Detached Militia in U. S. service 6 months, 1812.

‡WHEELER, SILAS, Waitsfield or Faystony. Volunteered to go to Plattsburgh, September, 1814, and served 4 days in Capt. Mathias S. Jones' Company. Pension Certificate No. 33532.

‡WHEELER, WARREN, Cornwall. Volunteered to go to Plattsburgh, September, 1814, and was at the battle, serving in Capt. Edmund B. Hill's Company, Sumner's Regt. Pension Certificate No. 25326.

*WHEELER, WILLARD, Highgate. Served in Capt. Saxe's Company, Col. Wm. Williams' Regt. Detached Militia in U. S. service 4 months and 24 days, 1812.

‡WHEELER, WILLIAM, Waitsfield.
Volunteered to go to Plattsburgh,
September, 1814, and served 4 days
in Capt. Mathias S. Jones' Company.
Pension Certificate of widow, Sophia,
No. 28558.

WHEELER, WILLIAM, Poultney.
Volunteered to go to Plattsburgh,
September, 1814, serving 2 days in
Capt. Briant Ransom's Company. Ref:
Book 52, AGO Page 147.

WHEELOCK, DANIEL.
Served in Capt. Chadwick's Company.
Ref: R. & L. 1812, AGO Page 32.

WHEELOCK, EZRA.
Served from June 10 to June 30, 1814
in Alexander Parris' Company of Artificers as a carpenter. Ref: R. & L.
1812, AGO Page 24.

*WHEELOCK, GIDEON, Calais.
Volunteered to go to Plattsburgh,
September, 1814, in command of com-
pany of volunteers from Calais. Ref:
Hemenway's Vt. Gazetteer, Vol. 4,
Page 147.

WHEELOCK, HENRY, Johnson.
Volunteered to go to Plattsburgh,
September, 1814, and served 10 days
in Capt. Thomas Waterman's Com-
pany, Dixon's Regt. Ref: Book 51,
AGO Page 208.

‡*WHEELOCK, JONATHAN.
Served under Captains Durkee and
Walker, Col. Fifield's Regt. Detached
Militia in U. S. service 6 months
and 5 days, 1812. Also served in
Capt. Wright's Company. Pension
Certificate No. 1743.

*WHEELOCK, JONATHAN, Calais.
Volunteered to go to Plattsburgh,
September, 1814, and served 10 days
in Capt. Gideon Wheelock's Company.

*WHEELOCK, JOSEPH.
Served in Capt. Cross' Company, Col.
Martindale's Regt. Detached Militia
in U. S. service 2 months and 14
days, 1812.

‡WHEELOCK, JOSEPHUS.
Served under Captains Wright and
Warren. Pension Certificate No.
25915.

‡WHEELOCK, JOSEPHUS.
Served under Captains Warren and
Wright. Pension Certificate of widow,
Mehitable, No. 30643.

‡WHEELOCK, LUCIUS T., Lieutenant,
Townshend. Appointed Ensign 31st
Inf. March 28, 1814; 2nd Lieutenant
Sept. 30, 1814. Took part in battles
of Chateaugay, Stone Mill, and Platts-
burgh. Served in Capt. Dickinson's
Company. Pension Certificate No.
6062. Ref: Governor and Council Vt.,
Vol. 6, Page 478; James H. Phelps'
History of Townshend, Page 92.

*WHEELOCK, MARK.
Served in Capt. Sabins' Company,
Col. Jonathan Williams' Regt. Detached Militia in U. S. service 2
months and 6 days, 1812.

‡*WHEELOCK, NAHAR, Bridport.
Served in Capt. James Gray's Company, Sumner's Regt. Volunteered to
go to Plattsburgh, September, 1814;
no organization given. Pension Certificate of widow, Candace A., No.
22537.

*WHEELOCK, NATHAN.
Served from April 12 to May 20, 1814
in company of Capt. James Gray Jr.,
Sumner's Regt.

WHEELOCK, SALEM.
Served from Feb. 21 to May 25, 1813
in Lieut. V. R. Goodrich's Company,
11th Regt. Ref: R. & L. 1812, AGO
Pages 10 and 11.

*WHEELON, SAMUEL R.
Served in 1 Regt. (Martindale's) Vt.
Militia.

*WHEETEN, LEONARD.
Served in Capt. Howard's Company,
Vt. Militia.

*WHELEN, JOHN.
Served in Capt. Howard's Company,
Vt. Militia.

WHELPLY, JAMES, Lieutenant, Manchester. Appointed 1st Lieutenant
48th Inf. April 21, 1814; transferred
to 26th Inf. May 12, 1814; honorably
discharged June 15, 1815. Ref: Heitman's Historical Register & Dictionary USA.

*WHELPLEY, JAMES, Sergeant.
Served in Capt. Richardson's Company, Col. Martindale's Regt. Detached Militia in U. S. service 2
months and 13 days, 1812. Served
in 1st Regt. of Detached Militia of
Vt. in U. S. service at Champlain
from Nov. 18 to Nov. 19, 1812. Enlisted Sept. 20, 1813 in Capt. John
Weed's Company, Col. Clark's Rifle
Corps.

*WHERRY, XERXES.
Served in Capt. Dorrance's Company,
Col. Wm. Williams' Regt. Detached
Militia in U. S. service 3 months
and 23 days, 1812.

WHIPPLE, BARNEY P.
Enlisted Nov. 1, 1812 in Capt. Weeks'
Company, 11th Regt.; on Pay Roll
for January and February, 1813. Ref:
R. & L. 1812, AGO Page 5.

WHIPPLE, CALEB, Sergeant.
Enlisted April 25, 1813 for 1 year
in Capt. Simeon Wright's Company.
Ref: R. & L. 1812, AGO Page 51.

*WHIPPLE, JOHN, Sergeant.
Served in Capt. Noyce's Company,
Col. Jonathan Williams' Regt. Detached Militia in U. S. service 2
months and 6 days, 1812.

‡WHIPPLE, MOSES JR.
Enlisted May 10, 1813 for 1 year in
Capt. Simeon Wright's Company. Pen-
sion Certificate No. 5972.

*WHIPPLE, STEPHEN.
Enlisted March 4, 1813 and served to
June 3, 1813 in Capt. Jonathan Starks'

Company, 11th Regt. Also served with Hospital Attendants, Vt. Ref: R. & L. 1812, AGO Page 19.

*WHIPPLE, STEPHEN 2nd.
Served in Capt. Cross' Company, Col. Martindale's Regt. Detached Militia in U. S. service 2 months and 14 days, 1812.

WHIPPLE, THOMAS.
Enlisted Oct. 15, 1813 for 5 years in company of late Capt. J. Brooks, commanded by Lt. John I. Cromwell, Corps of U. S. Artillery; on Muster Roll from April 30 to June 30, 1814; transferred from Capt. Collins' Company. Ref: R. & L. 1812, AGO Page 18.

*WHIPPLE, WESTLEY (or Whiple).
Served from Oct. 13 to Oct. 17, 1813 in Capt. Stephen Brown's Company, 3 Regt. (Tyler's).

WHITAKER, JONATHAN.
Served in Capt. Phelps' Company, Col. Jonathan Williams' Regt. Detached Militia in U. S. service 2 months and 21 days, 1812. Ref: Book 53, AGO Page 41.

WHITAKER, PETER.
Served from May 31, 1813 to Aug. 31, 1813 in Capt. Benjamin Bradford's Company. Ref: R. & L. 1812, AGO Page 26.

*WHITCHER, JOHN.   Groton.
Served in Capt. Morrill's Company, Col. Fifield's Regt. Detached Militia in U. S. service 6 months and 5 days, 1812.

‡*WHITCHER, JOSEPH,   Groton.
Served in Capt. Morrill's Company, Col. Fifield's Regt. Detached Militia in U. S. service 6 months and 5 days, 1812. Pension Certificate No. 4132.

WHITCOMB, ISAAC.
Served in company of Capt. John McNeil Jr., 11th Regt.; on Pay Roll for January and February, 1813. Ref: R. & L. 1812, AGO Page 17.

‡WHITCOMB, JOHN.
Served in Capt. Elias Keys' Company. Pension Certificate No. 33217.

*WHITCOMB, JOSHUA, Ensign .
Served from Oct. 5 to Oct. 16, 1813 in Capt. Roswell Hunt's Company, 3 Regt. (Tyler's).

WHITCOMB, LOT,   Stockbridge.
Volunteered to go to Plattsburgh, September, 1814, and served 8 days in Capt. Elias Keyes' Company. Ref: Book 51, AGO Page 239.

WHITCOMB, PAUL.
Served from May 31 to Aug. 31, 1813 in Capt. Benjamin Bradford's Company. Ref: R. & L. 1812, AGO Page 26.

WHITCOMB, RUFUS.
Served from Feb. 22 to May 21, 1813 in Capt. Edgerton's Company, 11th Regt. Ref: R. & L. 1812, AGO Page 3.

WHITE, ABNER.
Born at Union, Conn. Enlisted at Middletown Jan. 25, 1814 during the war and served in Capt. Wm. Miller's Company and Capt. Gideon Spencer's Company. 30th Regt. Ref: R. & L. 1812, AGO Pages 54, 55, 56.

‡*WHITE, ALANSON,   Enosburgh.
Served from Oct. 14 to Nov. 17, 1813 in Capt. Asahel Scoville's Company, Col. Clark's Rifle Corps. Pension Certificate No. 18874. Pension Certificate of widow, Sarah, No. 33680.

‡*WHITE, ALEXANDER,   Clarendon.
Served in Capt. Needham's Company, Col. Martindale's Regt. Detached Militia in U. S. service 2 months and 14 days, 1812. Pension Certificate No. 6061. Pension Certificate of widow, Fanny, No. 8094.

WHITE, ALLEN.
Served from Dec. 26, 1812 to June 8, 1813 in Capt. John W. Weeks' Company, 11th Regt. Was at the battle of Plattsburgh, Sept. 11, 1814, serving 8 days in Capt. David Robinson's Company. Ref: R. & L. 1812, AGO Pages 4 and 5; Book 52, AGO Page 2.

*WHITE, AMASA.
Served in Capt. Strait's Company, Col. Martindale's Regt. Detached Militia in U. S. service 2 months and 13 days, 1812.

*WHITE, ASAHEL.
Served in Capt. Bingham's Company, Col. Jonathan Williams' Regt. Detached Militia in U. S. service 2 months and 9 days, 1812.

*WHITE, AUGUSTUS, Corporal.
Served from April 12 to April 21, 1814 in Capt. Othniel Jewett's Company, Sumner's Regt.

WHITE, BENJAMIN.
Served from Feb. 28 to May 27, 1813 in Capt. Phineas Williams' Company, 11th Regt. Ref: R. & L. 1812, AGO Page 14.

*WHITE, CALVIN, Lieutenant.
Served in Tyler's Regt. Vt. Militia.

WHITE, CEPHAS.
Served from April 5 to July 4, 1813 in Capt. Samul Gordon's Company, 11th Regt. Ref: R. & L. 1812, AGO Page 8.

WHITE, CHARLES,   Thetford.
Marched for Plattsburgh, September, 1814, and went as far as Bolton, serving 6 days in Capt. Salmon Howard's Company. Ref: Book 52, AGO Page 15.

‡WHITE, CHESTER.
Served in Capt. Butler's Company. Pension Certificate No. 8568.

WHITE, CORNELIUS.
Served in Capt. Phineas Williams' Company, 11th Regt.; on Pay Roll for January and February, 1813. Was captured by troops July 25, 1814 at Londer's Lane; discharged Oct. 8, 1814. Ref: R. & L. 1812, AGO Page 15; Records of Naval Records and Library, Navy Dept.

*WHITE, DAVID.
Served in Capt. Briggs' Company,
Col. Jonathan Williams' Regt. De-
tached Militia in U. S. service 2
months and 13 days, 1812. Served
from Nov. 1, 1812 to Feb. 28, 1813 in
Capt. Samul Gordon's Company, 11th
Regt. Served from Feb. 28, 1813 to
May 27, 1813 in Capt. Phineas Wil-
liams' Company, 11th Regt. Served
from April 12 to April 21, 1814 in
Capt. Edmund B. Hill's Company,
Sumner's Regt. Ref: R. & L. 1812,
AGO Pages 9 and 14.

WHITE, EBENEZER,   Strafford.
Enlisted Nov. 1, 1812 in Capt. Ben-
jamin S. Edgerton's Company, 11th
Regt.; on Pay Roll for January and
February, 1813. Ref: R. & L. 1812,
AGO Pages 1 and 2.

*WHITE, ELI, Corporal.
Served in Capt. Mason's Company,
Col. Fifield's Regt. Detached Militia
in U. S. service 2 months and 9
days, 1812.

‡*WHITE,ENOCH.
Served from Sept. 14 to Nov. 4, 1813
in Capt. Asahel Langworthy's Company, Col. Isaac Clark's Rifle Corps.
Also served in Capt. Wood's Company. Pension Certificate No. 17993.

*WHITE, HORACE.
Served in 3 Regt. (Tyler's) Vt. Militia.

WHITE, HUGH,   Franklin County.
Volunteered to go to Plattsburgh
Sept. 11, 1814 and served in 15th or
22nd Regt. Ref: Hemenway's Vt.
Gazetteer, Vol. 2, Page 392.

‡WHITE, IRA.
Served in Capt. Chandler's Company.
Pension Certificate No. 20415.

‡*WHITE, IRA.
Served in Capt. Briggs' Company,
Col. Jonathan Williams' Regt. De-
tached Militia in U. S. service 2
months and 13 days, 1812. Pension
Certificate No. 5760.

*WHITE, ISAAC.
Served in Capt. Phelps' Company,
Col. Jonathan Williams' Regt. Detached Militia in U. S. service 2
months and 21 days, 1812.

WHITE, JEREMIAH.
Served in Capt. Weeks' Company,
11th Regt.; on Pay Roll for January and February, 1813. Ref: R. &
L. 1812, AGO Page 5.

WHITE, JESSE,   Pownal.
Served from Sept. 1, 1814 to June
16, 1815 in Capt. Sanford's Company,
30th Inf. Ref: R. & L. 1812, AGO
Page 23.

WHITE, JESSE.
Served in Capt. Phineas Williams'
Company, 11th Regt.; on Pay Roll
for January and February, 1813. Ref:
R. & L. 1812, AGO Page 15.

*WHITE, JOEL.
Served in 3 Regt. (Williams') Vt.
Militia.

*WHITE, JOHN,   Thetford.
Marched for Plattsburgh, September,
1814, and went as far as Bolton, Vt.,
serving 6 days in Capt. Salmon Howard's Company.

‡*WHITE, JOHN JR.
Served from April 12 to April 21,
1814 in Capt. Othniel Jewett's Company, Sumner's Regt. Also served
under Captains Spencer and Howard.
Pension Certificate No. 25305. Pension Certificate of widow, Mary F.,
No. 27461.

*WHITE, JOSEPH.
Served in Capt. Scovell's Company,
Col. Martindale's Regt. Detached
Militia in U. S. service 2 months
and 21 days, 1812. Served from May
31 to Aug. 31, 1813 in Capt. Ben-
jamin Bradford's Company. Ref: R.
& L. 1812, AGO Page 26.

WHITE, JOSIAH,   Montpelier or Calais.
Volunteered to go to Plattsburgh,
September, 1814, and served 8 days
in Capt. Timothy Hubbard's Company. Ref: Book 52, AGO Page 256.

*WHITE, JOSIAH, Corporal,   Calais?
Served under Captains Durkee and
Wright, Col. Fifield's Regt. Detached
Militia in U. S. service 6 months
and 5 days, 1812.

WHITE, LYMAN.
Served from April 29, 1813 to April
29, 1814 in Capt. James Taylor's Company and Capt. Gideon Spencer's Company, 30th Regt. Ref: R. & L. 1812,
AGO Pages 52, 56, 59.

*WHITE, MARK.
Served from April 12 to April 14,
1814 in Capt. Jonathan P. Stanley's
Company, Col. W. B. Sumner's Regt.

WHITE, MAURICE,   Williamstown.
Volunteered to go to Plattsburgh,
September, 1814, and served 8 days
in Capt. David Robinson's Company.
Ref: Book 52, AGO Page 8.

WHITE, MOSES.
Enlisted May 3, 1813 for 1 year in
Capt. John Wires' Company, 30th
Regt. Ref: R. & L. 1812, AGO Page
40.

*WHITE, NOAH, Corporal,   Walden.
Served in Capt. Morrill's Company,
Col. Fifield's Regt. Detached Militia
in U. S. service 6 months and 3 days,
1812. Volunteered to go to Plattsburgh, September, 1814, and served 4
days in Capt. Major Robinson's Company. Ref: Book 51, AGO Page 74.

*WHITE, OLCUTT.
Served from April 12 to April 21,
1814 in Capt. Edmund B. Hill's Company, Sumner's Regt.

WHITE, PAUL,   St. Albans.
Enlisted May 4, 1813 for 1 year in
Capt. John Wires' Company, 30th
Regt. Ref: R. & L. 1812, AGO Page
40..

*WHITE, PLINY. Surgeon's Mate.
Served in 3 Regt. ((Williams') Vt.
Militia.

‡*WHITE, ROBERT. Lieutenant, Ryegate.
Served from Dec. 1, 1812 to Feb. 12,
1813 in Capt. Morrill's Company, Col.
Fifield's Regt. Served as Lieutenant
in 1 Regt. (Judson's) Vt. Militia
and 4 Regt. (Williams') Vt. Militia. Also served in Capt. Barnes'
Company. Pension Certificate No.
7330. Pension Certificate of widow,
Parthena, No. 5234.

*WHITE, RUFUS.
Served in Capt. Robinson's Company,
Col. Dixon's Regt. Detached Militia
in U. S. service 1 month and 23
days; enlisted Sept. 25, 1813.

WHITE, RULEFF,   Orwell.
Volunteered to go to Plattsburgh,
September, 1814, and served 11 days
in Capt. Wait Branch's Company.
Ref: Book 51, AGO Page 16.

WHITE, SAMUEL, Sheldon or Berkshire.
Volunteered to go to Plattsburgh,
September, 1814, and served 4 days
in Capt. Samuel Weed's Company.
Ref: Book 51, AGO Pages 125, 143,
155, 172.

WHITE, SAMUEL, Sergeant,   Goshen.
Volunteered to go to Plattsburgh,
September, 1814, and served 5 days
in Capt. Durham Sprague's Company.
Ref: Book 52, AGO Page 129.

*WHITE, SYLVESTER.
Enlisted Sept. 25, 1813 and served 1
month and 23 days in Capt. Elijah
W. Wood's Company, Col. Dixon's
Regt.

WHITE, THADDEUS,   Washington.
Volunteered to go to Plattsburgh,
September, 1814, and served in Capt.
Amos Stiles' Company. Ref: Book
52, AGO Pages 36, 37, 38.

WHITE, WILLIAM,   Huntington.
Volunteered to go to Plattsburgh,
September, 1814, and was at the
battle, serving in Capt. Josiah N.
Barrows' Company. Ref: Book 51,
AGO Page 77.

WHITE, WILLIAM,   Strafford.
Volunteered to go to Plattsburgh,
September, 1814, and served in Capt.
Cyril Chandler's Company. Ref: Book
52, AGO Page 42.

‡*WHITE, WILLIAM.
Served in Capt. Rogers' Company,
Col. Fifield's Regt. Detached Militia
in U. S. service 2 months and 18
days, 1812. Pension Certificate No.
5643.

*WHITE, WILLIAM.
Served from Oct. 11 to Oct. 17, 1813
in Capt. John Munson's Company, 3
Regt. (Tyler's).

‡*WHITE, WILLIAM G.
Enlisted Sept. 25, 1813 in Capt. Amos
Robinson's Company, Col. Dixon's
Regt.; transferred to Capt. Langworthy's Company, Col. Clark's Rifle
Corps Sept. 27, 1813. Pension Certificate No. 21999.

WHITE, ZIBA.
Served in Capt. Weeks' Company,
11th Regt.; on Pay Roll for January and February, 1813; deserted Jan.
1, 1813. Ref: R. & L. 1812, AGO
Page 5.

*WHITECAR, LEVI.
Served in 2 Regt. (Fifield's) Vt.
Militia.

WHITEHEAD, DAVID L.,   St. Albans.
Enlisted May 1, 1813 for 1 year in
Capt. John Wires' Company, 30th
Regt. Ref: R. & L. 1812, AGO Page
40.

WHITEHOUSE, JOHN B.
Served from April 14 to July 13, 1813
in Lieut. Wm. S. Foster's Company,
11th Regt. Ref: R. & L. 1812, AGO
Page 6.

*WHITFORD, DEAN.
Served in Capt. Willson's Company,
Col. Wm. Williams' Regt. Detached
Militia in U. S. service 5 months,
1812.

*WHITFORD, HIRAM.
Served from April 12 to April 21,
1814 in Capt. Othniel Jewett's Company, Sumner's Regt.

*WHITFORD, WILLIAM, Ensign, Addison. Served from April 12 to May
20, 1814 in Capt. George Fisher's
Company, Sumner's Regt.; volunteered to go to Plattsburgh, September,
1814, and was in the battle, serving
9 days in same company.

*WHITING, HOMER.
Served in 2 Regt. (Fifield's) Vt. Militia.

*WHITING, JOHN.
Served in Capt. Adams' Company, Col.
Jonathan Williams' Regt. Detached
Militia in U. S. service 2 months
and 7 days, 1812.

WHITING, SANDERS.
Served from June 11 to June 14, 1813
in Capt. Moses Jewett's Company,
1st Regt. 2nd Brig. 3rd Div. Ref:
R. & L. 1812, AGO Page 42.

WHITING, WINSLOW.
Served from April 3 to July 13, 1813
in Lieut. Wm. S. Foster's Company,
11th Regt. Ref: R. & L. 1812, AGO
Page 6.

*WHITING, ZACHARIAH,   Johnson.
Enlisted Sept. 25, 1813 and served
1 month and 23 days in Capt. Waterman's Company, Col. Dixon's Regt.
Detached Militia in U. S. service 1
month and 23 days; volunteered to
go to Plattsburgh, September, 1814,
and served 4 days in same company.

*WHITLOCK, JOSEPH.
Served in 1 Regt. (Judson's) Vt. Militia.

WHITLOCK, SALMON.
Served from Feb. 18 to May 17, 1813
in Lieut. V. R. Goodrich's Company,
11th Regt. Ref: R. & L. 1812, AGO
Pages 10 and 11.

WHITMAN, BENJAMIN,   Middletown.
Served from May 17, 1814 to June
19, 1815 in Capt. Taylor's Company,
30th Inf. Ref: R. & L. 1812, AGO
Page 23.

‡*WHITMAN, CHRISTOPHER.
Served in Capt. Briggs' Company, Col.
Jonathan Williams' Regt. Detached
Militia in U. S. service 2 months and
13 days, 1812. Pension Certificate of
widow, Eunice, No. 5766.

*WHITMAN, JAMES.
Served from April 12 to April 15,
1814 in Capt. Jonathan P. Stanley's
Company, Col. W. B. Sumner's Regt.

*WHITMAN. JOSEPH.
Served from April 12 to April 15,
1814 in Capt. Jonathan P. Stanley's
Company, Col. W. B. Sumner's Regt.

WHITMAN, LEVI.
Served from March 5 to June 4, 1813
in company of Capt. John McNeil Jr.,
11th Regt. Ref: R. & L. 1812, AGO
Page 16.

*WHITMAN, NATHAN, Sergeant, Lin-
coln. Served from April 12 to April
15, 1814 in Capt. Jonathan P. Stanley's Company, Col. W. B. Sumner's
Regt. Volunteered to go to Plattsburgh, September, 1814, and served
in Capt. Ebenezer Jenney's Company.
Pension Certificate of widow, Stella
W., No. 30386.

‡*WHITMAN, SAMUEL.
Served in Capt. Hotchkiss' Company,
Col. Martindale's Regt. Detached
Militia in U. S. service 2 months and
13 days, 1812. Pension Certificate
No. 2859. Pension Certificate of wid-
ow, Elizabeth, No. 6676.

WHITMORE, EDMUND,   Ira.
Volunteered to go to Plattsburgh,
September, 1814, and served 4 days
in Capt. Matthew Anderson's Company. Ref: Book 52, AGO Page 144.

WHITMORE, LEMUEL.   Pittsford.
Volunteered to go to Plattsburgh,
September, 1814, in Capt. Caleb Hen-
dee's Company. Ref: Book 52, AGO
Page 125.

‡*WHITMORE, RUFUS (or Whitman).
Served in Capt. Phelps' Company,
Col. Wm. Williams' Regt. Detached
Militia in U. S. service 5 months,
1812. Pension Certificate No. 3343.

WHITNEY, ABEL,   Tunbridge.
Volunteered to go to Plattsburgh,
September, 1814, and served 4 days
in Capt. Ephraim Hackett's Company.
Ref: Book 52, AGO Page 71.

*WHITNEY, BENJAMIN.
Served from April 12 to April 21,
1814 in Capt. Eseck Sprague's Company, Sumner's Regt.

*WHITNEY, CALEB.   Westminster, Vt.
Enlisted at Burlington April 11, 1814
during the war and served in Capt.
Wm. Miller's Company and Capt.
Gideon Spencer's Company, 30th Regt.
Also served in 1 Regt. (Judson's)
Vt. Militia. Ref: R. & L. 1812,
AGO Pages 54, 55, 56.

‡*WHITNEY, CALVIN, Corporal.
Served in Capt. Burnap's Company,
Col. Jonathan Williams' Regt. Detached Militia in U. S. service 2
months and 13 days, 1812. Also served in Capt. Dodge's Company. Pension Certificate of widow, Polly, No.
5294.

‡WHITNEY, DAVID JR.,   Tunbridge.
Volunteered to go to Plattsburgh,
September, 1814, and served 4 days
in Capt. Ephraim Hackett's Company.
Pension Certificate No. 32978.

WHITNEY, EPHRAIM.
Served in Capt. Alexander Brooks'
Corps of Artillery; on Pay Roll to
June 30, 1814. Ref: R. & L. 1812,
AGO Page 31.

WHITNEY, FREDERIC.
Enlisted July 28, 1813 in Capt. James
Taylor's Company, 30th Regt.; died
Nov. 27, 1813. Ref: R. & L. 1812,
AGO Page 52.

WHITNEY, HEZEKIAH.
Volunteered to go to Plattsburgh,
September, 1814, and served 7 days
in Capt. Frederick Griswold's Com-
pany of Brookfield. Ref: Book 52,
AGO Page 52.

*WHITNEY, HOLLIS.
Served in Capt. Preston's Company,
Col. Jonathan Williams' Regt. Detached Militia in U. S. service 2
months and 6 days, 1812.

WHITNEY, HOMER.
Served in Capt. Dodge's Company,
Col. Fifield's Regt. Detached Militia
in U. S. service 2 months and 21
days, 1812. Ref: Book 53, AGO Page
15.

*WHITNEY, IRA.
Served in Tyler's Regt. Vt. Militia.

WHITNEY, ISRAEL.
Served in Capt. Wright's Company,
Col. Fifield's Regt. Detached Militia
in U. S. service 3 months and 9 days,
1812. Ref: Book 53, AGO Page 75.

*WHITNEY, JAMES.
Served in Capt. Weeks' Company,
11th Regt.; on Pay Roll for January
and February, 1813. Served from Oct.
8 to Nov. 18, 1813 in Capt. Isaac
Finch's Company, Col. Clark's Rifle
Corps. Ref: R. & L. 1812, AGO
Page 5.

*WHITNEY, JERED, Drummer.
Served in 2 Regt. (Fifield's) Vt. Militia.

*WHITNEY, JOHN.
Served in Capt. Briggs' Company, Col.
Jonathan Williams' Regt. Detached
Militia in U. S. service 2 months and
13 days, 1812. Served from March 2
to June 1, 1813 in Capt. Edgerton's
Company, 11th Regt. Ref: R. & L.
1812, AGO Page 3.

WHITNEY, JOHN,   Tunbridge.
Volunteered to go to Plattsburgh,
September, 1814, and served 4 days
in Capt. Ephraim Hackett's Company.
Ref: Book 52, AGO Page 71.

WHITNEY, JOSIAH.
Served from May 1 to June 1, 1814
in Alexander Parris' Company of Artificers. Ref: R. & L. 1812, AGO
Page 24.

*WHITNEY, LUTHER.
Served in 1 Regt. (Judson's) Vt.
Militia.

*WHITNEY, NATHAN.
Served in Capt. Needham's Company.
Col. Martindale's Regt. Detached
Militia in U. S. service 1 month and
11 days, 1812. Served from May 23
to June 30, 1814 in Regt. of Light
Dragoons. Ref: R. & L. 1812, AGO
Page 21.

WHITNEY, OLIVER.
Volunteered to go to Plattsburgh,
September, 1814, and served 7 days
in Capt. Asaph Smith's Company.
Ref: Book 51, AGO Pages 20 and 27.

‡*WHITNEY, PETER.
Served in Capt. Sabins' Company, Col.
Jonathan Williams' Regt. Detached
Militia in U. S. service 2 months and
6 days, 1812. Also served in Capt.
J. Hazen's Company. Pension Cer-
tificate of widow, Laury, No. 26919.

WHITNEY, PHINEAS.
Served from Jan. 8 to Feb. 28, 1813
in Capt. Samuel H. Holly's Company,
11th Regt. Ref: R. & L. 1812, AGO
Page 25.

*WHITNEY, SANDERS.
Served in 1 Regt. (Judson's) Vt.
Militia.

WHITNEY, SILAS, Musician.
Served in Capt. Weeks' Company,
11th Regt.; on Pay Roll for January and February, 1813. Ref: R. &
L. 1812, AGO Page 5.

WHITNEY, SOLOMON,   Hubbardton.
Volunteered to go to Plattsburgh,
September, 1814, and served 8 days
in Capt. Henry J. Horton's Company.
Ref: Book 52, AGO Page 142.

‡WHITNEY, THOMAS,   Tunbridge.
Volunteered to go to Plattsburgh,
September, 1814, and served 4 days
in Capt. Ephraim Hackett's Company.
Pension Certificate of widow, Anna,
No. 22538.

*WHITNEY, TIMOTHY H., Major, Brook-
line. Served in 3 Regt. (Williams')
Vt. Militia.

‡WHITNEY, WILLIAM.
Served in Capt. William Prichett's
Company. Pension Certificate No.
12783.

*WHITNEY, WILLIAM.
Served in Capt. Briggs' Company, Col.
Jonathan Williams' Regt. Detached
Militia in U. S. service 2 months
and 13 days, 1812.

*WHITNEY, WILLIAM.
Served from April 12 to May 20, 1814
in Capt. George Fisher's Company,
Sumner's Regt.

‡WHITNEY, WILLIAM M.
Served in Capt. Pickett's Company.
Pension Certificate No. 25365.

WHITTAKER, JESSE W.
Served from May 1 to June 30, 1814
in Corps of Light Dragoons. Ref: R.
& L. 1812, AGO Page 20.

WHITTAKER, JOHN.
Served from Jan. 1 to March 10,
1814; no organization given. Ref:
R. & L. 1812, AGO Page 29.

‡WHITTEMORE, ALBERT G.
Served in Capt. Farnworth's Com-
pany. Pension Certificate of widow,
Abbey, No. 34112.

WHITTEMORE, BETA, Franklin County.
Volunteered to go to Plattsburgh
Sept. 11, 1814 and served in 15th or
22nd Regt. Ref: Hemenway's Vt.
Gazetteer, Vol. 2, Page 392.

WHITTEMORE, GEORGE.
Enlisted March 8, 1813 in Capt.
Charles Follett's Company, 11th Regt.;
on Pay Roll to May 31, 1813. Ref:
R. & L. 1812, AGO Page 13.

WHITTEMORE, PETER.
Born in Pembroke, N. H. Enlisted
at Plattsburgh Feb. 20, 1814 during
the war in Capt. Wm. Miller's Company, 30th Regt.; on Muster Roll to
Aug. 31, 1814; on board Navy. Ref:
R. & L. 1812, AGO Pages 54 and 55.

WHITTEMORE, PETER.
Enlisted Sept. 2, 1813 for 1 year; re-
enlisted Feb. 20, 1814 for duration
of the war; served in Capt. Gideon
Spencer's Company and Capt. James
Taylor's Company, 30th Regt. Ref:
R. & L. 1812, AGO Pages 52 and 56.

*WHITTEN, HAWLEY.
Served in Dixon's Regt. Vt. Militia.

WHITTIER, JOHN,   Cabot.
Volunteered to go to Plattsburgh,
September, 1814, and served 4 days
in Capt. Anthony Perry's Company.
Ref: Book 52, AGO Pages 177, 205,
252, 254.

*WHITTING, ABIJAH.
Served in Tyler's Regt. Vt. Militia.

*WHITTING, ELI.
Served in Tyler's Regt. Vt. Militia.

WHITTON, ABIJAH.   Jericho.
Took part in the battle of Plattsburgh. Ref: History of Jericho, Page
142.

WHITTON, THOMAS.
Served from Jan. 19 to May 10, 1813
in Capt. John W. Weeks' Company,
11th Regt. Ref: R. & L. 1812, AGO
Page 4.

WHITTREDGE, PELEG,   Montpelier.
Volunteered to go to Plattsburgh,
September, 1814, and served 8 days
in Capt. Timothy Hubbard's Company.
Ref: Book 52, AGO Page 256.

‡WICKER, BENAJAH P.,   Orwell.
Volunteered to go to Plattsburgh,
September, 1814, and served 11 days

in Capt. Wait Branch's Company. Also served in Capt. Culver's Company. Pension Certificate of widow, Angeline E., No. 23406. Ref: Book 51, AGO Page 16.

‡*WICKER, IRA.
Served from April 12 to May 20, 1814 in company of Capt. James Gray Jr., Sumner's Regt. Pension Certificate of widow, Louisa, No. 22214.

*WICKER, PLINY.
Served from April 12 to May 20. 1814 in company of Capt. James Gray Jr., Sumner's Regt.

*WICKWIRE, GILES.
Served from April 12 to May 20, 1814 in Capt. George Fisher's Company, Sumner's Regt.

WICKWIRE, OLIVER W.
Served from May 12, 1813 to May 12, 1814 in Capt. James Taylor's Company and Capt. Gideon Spencer's Company, 30th Regt. Ref: R. & L. 1812, AGO Pages 52, 56, 59.

WIER, GEORGE (or Ware).
Enlisted May 1, 1813 for 1 year in Capt. James Taylor's Company, 30th Regt. Ref: R. & L. 1812, AGO Page 59.

*WIGGIN, MESHACK.
Served in Capt. Wright's Company, Col. Fifield's Regt. Detached Militia in U. S. service 6 months, 1812.

*WIGHT, THRODUS.
Served in 1 Regt. (Martindale's) Vt. Militia.

‡WIGHTMAN, ABEL P.
Served in Capt. O. Jewett's Company. Pension Certificate of widow, Delia E., No. 24593.

*WIGHTON, DAVID (or Wrighton).
Served in 1 Regt. (Martindale's) Vt. Militia.

*WILBER, ITHEMOR.
Served in 1 Regt. (Judson's) Vt. Militia.

WILBUR, ISAAC. Corporal.
Served in 1 Regt. of Detached Militia of Vt. in U. S. service at Champlain from Nov. 18 to Nov. 19, 1812.

WILBUR, SAMUEL.
Served in Capt. Samuel H. Holly's Company, 11th Regt.; on Pay Roll for January and February, 1813. Ref: R. & L. 1812, AGO Page 25.

‡*WILCOX, AARON,   Thetford.
Served in Capt. Taylor's Company, Col. Fifield's Regt. Detached Militia in U. S. service 2 months and 21 days, 1812. Marched for Plattsburgh, September, 1814, and went as far as Bolton, serving 6 days in Capt. Salmon Howard's Company, 2nd Regt. Pension Certificate No. 11622.

WILCOX, ALANSEN.
Served from April 12 to May 20, 1814 in company of Capt. James Gray Jr., Sumner's Regt. Ref: Book 52, AGO Page 279.

‡*WILCOX, AMON, Fifer.
Served from April 12 to April 21, 1814 in Capt. Eseck Sprague's Company, Sumner's Regt. Pension Certificate No. 32987.

*WILCOX. ANSON.
Served in Sumner's Regt. Vt. Militia.

WILCOX, EDWARD.
Served from May 1 to June 30, 1814 as a farrier in Capt. Haig's Corps of Light Dragoons. Ref: R. & L. 1812, AGO Page 20.

WILCOX, ELISHA,   Roxbury.
Volunteered to go to Plattsburgh, September, 1814, and served 8 days in Capt. Samuel M. Orcutt's Company. Ref: Book 52, AGO Page 250.

‡*WILCOX, ERASTUS.
Served in Capt. Preston's Company, Col. Jonathan Williams' Regt. Detached Militia in U. S. service 2 months and 6 days, 1812. Pension Certificate of widow, Patty, No. 4183.

*WILCOX, IRAM.
Served in 3 Regt. (Williams') Vt. Militia.

WILCOX, JOHN,   Roxbury.
Volunteered to go to Plattsburgh, September, 1814, and served 8 days in Capt. Samuel M. Orcutt's Company. Ref: Book 52, AGO Page 250.

*WILCOX, JOSEPH,   Fairfax.
Enlisted Sept. 25, 1813 in company of Capt. Jonathan Prentiss, Jr., Dixon's Regt. Served from Aug. 8, 1812 in company of Capt. Joseph Beeman Jr., 11th Regt. U. S. Inf. under Col. Ira Clark. Ref: Hemenway's Vt. Gazetteer, Vol. 2, Page 402.

WILCOX, NOAH,   Colchester.
Volunteered to go to Plattsburgh, September, 1814, and served 4 days in Capt. Arad Merrill's Company. Ref: Book 51, AGO Page 164.

‡*WILCOX, STEPHEN.
Served in Capt. Preston's Company, 3 Regt. (Williams') Vt. Militia. Pension Certificate No. 18013.

WILCOX, THOMAS.
Served from April 19 to May 31, 1813 in Capt. Samul Gordon's Company, 11th Regt. Ref: R. & L. 1812, AGO Page 8.

*WILCOX, WILLIAM JR.
Enlisted Sept. 25, 1813 in company of Capt. Jonathan Prentiss, Jr., Dixon's Regt.

*WILD, ASA (or Wiles).
Served in Capt. Walker's Company, Col. Fifield's Regt. Detached Militia in U. S. service 6 months.

WILD, ELISHA.
Volunteered to go to Plattsburgh, September, 1814, and served 4 days in Capt. Aaron Kidder's Company. Ref: Book 52, AGO Page 65.

‡WILD, RANDALL H.
Volunteered to go to Plattsburgh, September, 1814, and served 4 days in Capt. Aaron Kidder's Company. Pension Certificate No. 32985.

*WILDER, ABEL.
Served in Sumner's Regt. Vt. Militia.

‡WILDER, BENJAMIN.
Served in Capt. Butler's Company.
Pension Certificate No. 19424.

‡*WILDER, FRANCIS,   Waitsfield.
Volunteered to go to Plattsburgh,
September, 1814, and served 5 or
6 days in company of Cavalry commanded by Chester Marshall, 4 Regt.
(Peck's) Vt. Militia. Pension Certificate of widow, Betsey, No. 30323.

WILDER, HARRY M.,   Jericho.
Took part in the battle of Plattsburgh. Ref: History of Jericho, Page
142.

*WILDER, JOHN.
Served in Capt. Preston's Company,
Col. Jonathan Williams' Regt. Detached Militia in U. S. service 2
months and 6 days, 1812.

*WILDER, OLIVER JR., Jericho or Wil-
mington? Served in 3 Regt. (Tyler's)
Vt. Militia. Took part in the battle
of Plattsburgh. Ref: History of Jericho, Page 142.

*WILDER, WILLIAM, Sergeant, Wilming-
ton. Served in Capt. Parson's Company, Col. Jonathan Williams' Regt.
Detached Militia in U. S. service 2
months and 13 days, 1812.

WILDS, BENJAMIN.
Served from September, 1812, to June
30, 1814 in Regt. of Light Dragoons.
Ref: R. & L. 1812, AGO Page 21.

‡*WILDS, MOSES.
Served in Capt., Rogers' Company,
Col. Fifield's Regt. Detached Militia
in U. S. service 2 months and 18
days, 1812. Pension Certificate No.
5125. Pension Certificate of widow,
Abigail, No. 29163.

WILEY, DAVID.
Enlisted May 2, 1813 for 1 year in
Capt. Simeon Wright's Company. Ref:
R. & L. 1812, AGO Page 51.

WILEY, EPHRAIM,   Alexandria.
Served from May 1 to June 23, 1813
in Capt. Montgomery's Company, 14th
Inf. Ref: R. & L. 1812, AGO Page 30.

WILEY, JAMES,   Weybridge.
Volunteered to go to Plattsburgh,
September, 1814, and was fatally
wounded; no organization given.
Ref: Rev. Lyman Mathews' History
of Cornwall, Page 345.

WILEY, JOHN.
Enlisted May 1, 1813 in Capt. Simeon
Wright's Company; re-enlisted and
transferred April 20, 1814. Ref: R.
& L. 1812, AGO Page 51.

*WILKINS, AARON, Musician,   Stowe.
Volunteered to go to Plattsburgh,
September, 1814, and was at the
battle, serving as musician in Capt.
Nehemiah Perkins' Company, 4 Regt.
(Peck's). Served as fifer in Corn-
ing's Detachment Vt. Militia. Also
served in 3 Regt. (Williams') Vt.
Militia.

*WILKINS, ASA, Captain.   Fairfax.
Appointed Captain in Lt. Col. Luther
Dixon's Regt. Sept. 25, 1813.

WILKINS, ASA JR., Lieutenant, Fairfax.
Volunteered to go to Plattsburgh,
September, 1814, and served 8 days
in Capt. Josiah Grout's Company.
Book 51, AGO Page 103; Hemenway's
Vt. Gazetteer, Vol. 2, Page 402.

WILKINS, DANIEL, Sergeant.
Volunteered to go to Plattsburgh,
September, 1814, and served 8 days
in Capt. Josiah Grout's Company.
Ref: Book 51, AGO Page 103.

WILKINS, DANIEL G.,   Addison.
Volunteered to go to Plattsburgh,
September, 1814, and was in the
battle, serving 9 days in Capt. George
Fisher's Company, Sumner's Regt.
Ref: Book 51, AGO Page 5.

WILKINS, DAVID,   Fairfax.
Volunteered to go to Plattsburgh,
September, 1814, and served in Capt.
Josiah Grout's Company. Ref: Hem-
enway's Vt. Gazetteer, Vol 2, Page
402.

WILKINS, FRANCIS C.
Served from April 26, 1813 to May 2,
1814 in Capt. James Taylor's Company and Capt. Gideon Spencer's Company, 30th Regt. Ref: R. & L. 1812,
AGO Pages 52, 56, 59.

WILKINS, GEORGE,   Orid, N. Y.
Served from May 1 to July 7, 1814
in Lt. Hanson's Company, 29th Inf.
Ref: R. & L. 1812, AGO Page 30.

*WILKINS, IRA.
Served in Capt. Hiram Mason's Com-
pany, Col. Fifield's Regt. Detached
Militia in U. S. service 5 months
and 8 days, 1812. Served from April
26, 1813 to April 27, 1814 in Capt.
James Taylor's Company and Capt.
Gideon Spencer's Company, 30th Regt.
Ref: R. & L. 1812, AGO Pages 52,
56, 59.

*WILKINS, JAMES,   Fairfax.
Served in Capt. Taylor's Company,
Col. Wm. Williams' Regt. Detached
Militia in U. S. service 4 months and
24 days, 1812. Enlisted Sept. 25, 1813
in Capt. Asa Wilkins' Company, Dix-
on's Regt. Volunteered to go to
Plattsburgh, September, 1814, and
served 8 days in Capt. Josiah Grout's
Company.

*WILKINS, JASON, Fifer,   Danville.
Served in Capt. Morrill's Company,
Col. Fifield's Regt. Detached Militia
in U. S. service 6 months and 5 days,
1812.

*WILKINS, JOHN,   Fairfax.
Served in Capt. Taylor's Company,
Col. Wm. Williams' Regt. Detached
Militia in U. S. service 4 months and
24 days, 1812. Enlisted Sept. 25, 1813
in Capt. Asa Wilkins' Company, Dixon's Regt.

*WILKINS, JONATHAN.
Served in Corning's Detachment, Vt.
Militia.

WILKINS, JOTHAM.
Served in Capt Weeks' Company, 11th
Regt.; on Pay Roll for January and
February, 1813. Ref: R. & L. 1812,
AGO Page 5.

WILKINS, PETER.
Served from May 1 to June 30, 1814
in Capt. Alexander Brooks' Corps of
Artillery. Ref: R. & L. 1812, AGO
Page 31.

WILKINS, RICHARD,   Northfield.
Volunteered to go to Plattsburgh
and was at the battle Sept. 11, 1814,
serving 8 days in Capt. David Robinson's Company. Ref: Book 52, AGO
Page 2.

*WILKINS, ROBERT B.,   Fairfax.
Served in Capt. Taylor's Company.
Col. Wm. Williams' Regt. Detached
Militia in U. S. service 2 months,
1812. Volunteered to go to Plattsburgh, September, 1814, and served 8
days in Capt. Josiah Grout's Company.

*WILKINS, URIAH,   Stowe.
Volunteered to go to Plattsburgh,
September, 1814, and was at the
battle, serving in Capt. Nehemiah
Perkins' Company, 4 Regt. (Peck's).
Also served in Corning's Detachment,
Vt. Militia. Ref: Book 51, AGO Page
215.

*WILKINS, URIAH JR.
Served in Corning's Detachment and
in 4 Regt. (Peck's) Vt. Militia.

WILKINSON, BENNING.
Served in Capt. Benjamin Bradford's
Company; on Muster Roll from May
31 to Aug. 31, 1813; joined by trans-
fer July 22, 1813. Ref: R. & L. 1812,
AGO Page 26.

WILKINSON, BRADBURY.
Served in Capt. Benjamin Bradford's
Company; on Muster Roll from May
31 to Aug. 31, 1813; joined by trans-
fer July 22, 1813. Ref: R. & L. 1812,
AGO Page 26.

WILKINSON, ICHABOD,   Bakersfield.
Volunteered and was at the battle
of Plattsburgh Sept. 11, 1814, serving in Capt. M. Stearns Company.
Ref: Hemenway's Vt. Gazetteer, Vol.
2, Page 393.

WILKINSON, JOHN.
Served from May 1 to July 5, 1814
in Capt. Smythe's Company, Rifle
Regt. Ref: R. & L. 1812, AGO Page
30.

WILKINSON, JOHN.
Served from May 1 to June 30, 1814
as a carpenter in Alexander Parris'
Company of Artificers. Ref: R. & L.
1812, AGO Page 24.

WILKINSON, JOHN.
Served in Capt. Weeks' Company, 11th
Regt.; on Pay Roll for January and
February, 1813. Ref: R. & L. 1812,
AGO Page 5.

‡*WILKINSON, MOSES S.
Served in 4 Regt. (Peck's) Vt. Mili-
tia. Pension Certificate of widow,
Sophia W., No. 18960.

WILLARD, AARON,   Pawlet, Vt.
Enlisted at Pawlet March 1, 1814 dur-
ing the war and served in Capt. Wm.
Miller's Company and Capt. Gideon
Spencer's Company, 30th Regt. Ref:
R. & L. 1812, AGO Pages 54, 55, 56.

‡WILLARD, CALEB,   Randolph.
Served from Feb. 2 to May 1, 1813
in Capt. Phineas Williams' Company,
11th Regt. Volunteered to go to
Plattsburgh, September, 1814, and
served in Capt. Lebbeus Egerton's
Company. Pension Certificate No.
20356. Ref: R. & L 1812, AGO Page
14; Book 52, AGO Page 82.

*WILLARD, CLARK, Sergeant.
Served in Corning's Detachment, Vt.
Militia.

*WILLARD, DANIEL.
Served in Capt. Stephen Pette's Company, Col. Wm. Williams' Regt. Detached Militia in service during summer of 1812.

*WILLARD, DENBARTUS JR.
Served from June 11 to June 14, 1813
in Capt. Moses Jewett's Company,
1st Regt. 2nd Brig. 3rd Div.

WILLARD, DUNBARTON, Ensign, Burlington. Volunteered to go to Plattsburgh. September, 1814, and served
10 days in Capt. Henry Mayo's Company. Ref: Book 51, AGO Page 81.

WILLARD, EBENEZER F.,   Barre.
Volunteered to go to Plattsburgh,
September, 1814, serving 10 days in
Capt. Warren Ellis' Company. Ref:
Book 52, AGO Page 242.

*WILLARD, GUSTAVUS V.
Served from June 11 to June 14, 1813
in Capt. Moses Jewett's Company, 1st
Regt. 2nd Brig. 3rd Div.

*WILLARD, HENRY.
Served in 3 Regt. (Williams') Vt.
Militia.

WILLARD, JACOB,   Franklin County.
Volunteered to go to Plattsburgh
Sept. 11, 1814, and served in 15th or
22nd Regt. Ref: Hemenway's Vt. Gazetteer, Vol. 2, Page 392.

WILLARD, JOHN M.,   Barre.
Volunteered to go to Plattsburgh,
September, 1814, serving 10 days in
Capt. Warren Ellis' Company. Ref:
Book 52, AGO Page 242.

WILLARD, JOHN S., Lieutenant, Hartland. Appointed 2nd Lieutenant 31st
Inf. April 30, 1813; resigned July,
1813. Served as 2nd Sergeant in Capt.
Dodge's Company. Col. Fifield's Regt.
Detached Militia in U. S. service 2
months and 21 days, 1812. Ref: Heitman's Historical Register & Dictionary USA; Book 53, AGO Page 19;
Vol. 50, Vt. State Papers, Page 136.

*WILLARD, LEMUEL,   Pawlet.
Served in 1 Regt. (Martindale's) Vt.
Militia.

‡*WILLARD, LEVI,   Burlington.
Served from June 11 to June 14, 1813
in Capt. Moses Jewett's Company, 1st

Regt. 2nd Brig. 3rd Div. Volunteered to go to Plattsburgh, September, 1814, and served 10 days in Capt. Henry Mayo's Company. Pension Certificate of widow, Samantha, No. 24927.

*WILLARD, LEWIS.
Served from June 11 to June 14, 1813 in Capt. Moses Jewett's Company, 1st Regt. 2nd Brig. 3rd Div.

WILLARD, MOSES T.
Served in company of Capt. John McNeil Jr., 11th Regt.; on Pay Roll for January and February, 1813. Ref: R. & L. 1812, AGO Page 17.

WILLARD, PRENTISS, Captain.
Appointed Captain, Engineers, July 6, 1812; died Oct. 12, 1813. Ref: Heitman's Historical Register & Dictionary USA.

WILLARD. REUBEN,   Highgate.
Volunteered to go to Plattsburgh, September. 1814, and served 5 days in Capt. Conrade Saxe's Company, 4 Regt. (Williams'). Ref: Book 51, AGO Page 100.

*WILLARD, SAMUEL.
Served in Capt. Bingham's Company, Col. Jonathan Williams' Regt. Detached Militia in U. S. service 2 months and 9 days, 1812.

WILLARD, SAMUEL.
Served in Capt. Hotchkiss' Company, Col. Martindale's Regt. Detached Militia in U. S. service 2 months and 13 days, 1812. Ref: Book 53, AGO Page 25.

*WILLARD. SAMUEL .
Enlisted Sept. 27, 1813 in Capt. Aashel Langworthy's Company, Col. Isaac Clark's Rifle Corps.

*WILLARD, SILAS, Corporal,   Pawlet.
Served in Capt. Hotchkiss' Company, Col. Martindale's Regt. Detached Militia, in U. S. service 2 months and 13 days, 1812.

WILLARD, SILAS,   Barre.
Volunteered to go to Plattsburgh, September, 1814, and served 10 days in Capt. Warren Ellis' Company. Ref: Book 52, AGO Page 242.

WILLARD, SIMON,   Burlington.
Volunteered to go to Plattsburgh, September. 1814, and served 10 days in Capt. Henry Mayo's Company. Ref: Book 51, AGO Page 81.

*WILLARD, WILLIAM.
Served from Oct. 11 to Nov. 18, 1813 in Capt. Isaac Finch's Company, Col. Clark's Rifle Corps.

*WILLARD, WILLIAM TELL, Lieutenant. Appointed 3rd Lieutenant 26th Inf. April 21, 1814; 2nd Lieutenant Oct. 1, 1814; honorably discharged June 15, 1815. Served from April 12 to April 21, 1814 in Capt. Edmund B. Hill's Company, Sumner's Regt. Ref: Heitman's Historical Register & Dictionary USA.

WILLCOX, DAVID, Lieutenant, Thetford. Marched for Plattsburgh, September, 1814, and went as far as Bolton, Vt., serving 6 days in Capt. Salmon Howard's Company. Ref: Book 52, AGO Pages 15 and 16.

‡*WILLCOX, JOHN.
Served from June 11 to June 14, 1813 in Capt. John M. Eldridge's Company, 1st Regt. 2nd Brig. 3rd Div. Pension Certificate of widow, Altha, No. 16987.

*WILLCOX, JOHN C.
Served from Sept. 23 to Sept. 29, 1813 in Capt. Amasa Mansfield's Company, Dixon's Regt.

*WILLCOX, MOSES.
Served in Sumner's Regt. Vt. Militia.

*WILLCOX, NATHANIEL.
Served in Sumner's Regt. Vt. Militia.

WILLER, TIMOTHY.
Served from June 11 to June 14, 1813 in Capt. John M. Eldridge's Company, 1st Regt. 2nd Brig. 3rd Div. Ref: R. & L. 1812, AGO Page 35.

*WILLET, ROBERT.
Served with Hospital Attendants, Vt.

WILLEY, AUSTIN.
Served in Capt. Phineas Williams' Company, 11th Regt.; on Pay Roll for January and February, 1813. Ref: R. & L. 1812, AGO Page 15.

*WILLEY, HUBBARD, Sergeant. Middlesex. Served as Sergeant in Capt. Holden Putnam's Company, 4 Regt. (Peck's) Vt. Militia.

WILLEY, JAMES,   Cornwall.
Volunteered to go to Plattsburgh. September, 1814, and was at the battle, serving in Capt. Edmund B. Hill's Company, Sumner's Regt. Ref: Book 51, AGO Page 13.

*WILLEY, JOHN JR..   Sheffield
Served in Capt. Wheeler's Company, Col. Fifield's Regt. Detached Militia in U. S. service 6 months and 4 days, 1812; stationed at Derby.

WILLEY, NOAH,   Danville.
Served in Capt. Morrill's Company Col. Fifield's Regt. Detached Militia in U. S. service 6 months. Ref: Hemenway's Vt. Gazetteer, Vol. 1, Page 314.

WILLEY, PAUL,   Georgia.
Volunteered to go to Plattsburgh, September, 1814, and served 8 days; no organization given. Ref: Book 51, AGO Pages 105 and 183.

WILLEY, PETER.
Served in Lt. Wm. S. Foster's Company, 11th Regt.; on Pay Roll for January and February, 1813. Ref: R. & L. 1812, AGO Page 7.

*WILLEY, ROBERT, Sergeant.
Served from Feb .19 to March 3, 1813 in Capt. Jonathan Starks' Company, 11th Regt. Served as Sergeant in Corning's Detachment. Vt. Militia. Ref: R. & L. 1812, AGO Page 19.

WILLEY, SAMUEL.
Served from Feb. 13 to May 12, 1813
in Capt. Edgerton's Company, 11th
Regt. Ref: R. & L. 1812, AGO
Page 3.

*WILLEY, SETH, Corporal Sergeant.
Served in Capt. Willson's Company,
Col. Wm. Williams' Regt. Detached
Militia in U. S. service 4 months
and 24 days, 1812; stationed at Swan-
ton Falls. Served from Sept. 25 to
Nov. 12, 1813 in Capt. N. B. El-
dridge's Company, Dixon's Regt.

‡*WILLEY, THEODORE,   Georgia.
Served from Sept. 25 to Oct. 8, 1813
in Capt. Jesse Post's Company, Dixon's Regt.; volunteered to go to
Plattsburgh, September, 1814 and served 8 days in same company. Pension
Certificate of widow, Hannah, No.
16678.

*WILLIAMS, ANTIPAS.
Served in Capt. Wheeler's Company,
Col. Fifield's Regt. Detached Militia
in U. S. service 6 months and 4
days, 1812.

*WILLIAMS, ASHER.
Served in Capt. Walker's Company,
Col. Fifield's Regt. Detached Militia
in U. S. service 3 months and 8 days,
1812.

‡*WILLIAMS, ASHER JR. (or Asher
2nd). Served in Capt. Walker's Company, Col. Fifield's Regt. Detached
Militia in U. S. service 6 months and
2 days, 1812. Pension Certificate No.
12097. Pension Certificate of widow,
Esther, No. 21934.

*WILLIAMS, BARZILLAI.
Served in Capt. Mason's Company,
Col. Fifield's Regt. Detached Militia
in U. S. service 6 months, 1812.

*WILLIAMS, BENJAMIN.
Served in Sumner's Regt. Vt. Militia.

WILLIAMS, CATO.
Served in Capt. Samuel H. Holly's
Company, 11th Regt.; on Pay Roll
for January and February, 1813.
Ref: R. & L. 1812, AGO Page 25.

*WILLIAMS, CHARLES K., Major.
Served in 1st Regt. of Detached Militia of Vt. in U. S. service at Champlain from Nov. 18 to Nov. 19, 1812.

‡WILLIAMS, CHESTER.
Served in Capt. Danforth's Company.
Pension Certificate of widow, Saman-
tha, No. 22959.

WILLIAMS, DANIEL, Sergeant.
Volunteered to go to Plattsburgh,
September, 1814, and served 7 days
in Capt. Frederick Griswold's Company raised in Brookfield. Ref: Book
52, AGO Page 52.

*WILLIAMS, DARIUS.
Served in Capt. Wheeler's Company,
Col. Fifield's Regt. Detached Militia
in U. S. service 6 months and 4 days,
1812.

*WILLIAMS, DAT,   Shoreham.
Served from April 12 to May 20, 1814
in company of Capt. James Gray
Jr., Sumner's Regt.

*WILLIAMS, DAVID or (William).
Served in Capt. Howard's Company,
Vt. Militia.

*WILLIAMS, EBENEZER.
Served in 1 Regt. (Judson's) Vt.
Militia.

WILLIAMS, EBENEZER.
Served from May 1 to June 4, 1814
as a carpenter in Alexander Parris'
Company of Artificers. Ref: R. &
L. 1812, AGO Page 24.

*WILLIAMS, EBENEZER L., Musician.
Served in Capt. Parsons' Company,
Col. Jonathan Williams' Regt. Detached Militia in U. S. service 2
months and 13 days, 1812.

‡WILLIAMS, ELEAZER,   Bakersfield.
Served in Capt. Stearns' Company.
Volunteered and was at the battle
of Plattsburgh Sept. 11, 1814. Pension Certificate No. 30391.

*WILLIAMS, ELISHA.
Served in 3 Regt. (Tyler's) Vt. Militia.

WILLIAMS, HAMILTON.
Enlisted March 30, 1813 in Capt.
Charles Follett's Company, 11th Regt.;
deserted same day. Ref: R. & L.
1812, AGO Page 13.

*WILLIAMS, HARRIS.
Served in Sumner's Regt. Vt. Militia.

*WILLIAMS, HORACE.
Served from April 12 to May 20, 1814
in company of Capt. James Gray Jr.,
Sumner's Regt.

WILLIAMS, HOSEA, Lieutenant.
Served in 1st Regt. of Detached Militia of Vt. in U. S. service at Champlain from Nov. 18 to Nov. 19, 1812.

WILLIAMS, IRA, Captain.
Appointed 2nd Lieutenant 2nd Light
Dragoons March 12, 1812; resigned
Jan. 31, 1814; Captain 48th Inf.
April 21, 1814; transferred to 26th
Inf. May 12, 1814; honorably dis-
charged June 15, 1815. Ref: Heit-
man's Historical Register & Dictionary
USA.

‡*WILLIAMS, ISAAC.
Served in Capt. Adams' Company,
Col. Jonathan Williams' Regt. Detached Militia in U. S. service 2
months and 7 days, 1812. Pension Certificate No. 2931.

WILLIAMS, JEREMIAH,   Providence,
R. I. Served from Sept. 1, 1814 to
June 16, 1815 in Capt. Sanford's
Company, 30th Inf. Ref: R. & L.
1812, AGO Page 23.

*WILLIAMS, JESSE.
Served in Capt. Wheeler's Company,
Col. Fifield's Regt. Detached Militia
in U. S. service 6 months and 4 days,
1812.

*WILLIAMS, JOHN.
Served in Capt. Wheeler's Company,
Col. Fifield's Regt. Detached Militia
in U. S. service 2 months and 18
days, 1812.

WILLIAMS, JOHN.
Enlisted April 21, 1813 for 1 year in
Capt. Simeon Wright's Company. Ref:
R. & L. 1812, AGO Page 51.

WILLIAMS, JOHN,   Springtown.
Served from Nov. 16, 1814 to June
19, 1815 in Capt. Taylor's Company,
30th Inf. Ref: R. & L. 1812, AGO
Page 23.

WILLIAMS, JOHN.
Enlisted Sept. 6, 1812 for 5 years in
Capt. White Youngs' Company, 15th
Regt.; on Muster Roll from Aug. 31
to Dec. 31, 1814. Ref: R. & L. 1812,
AGO Page 27.

WILLIAMS, JOHN.
Served from May 1 to June 30, 1814
in company of late Capt. J. Brooks,
commanded by Lt. John I. Cromwell,
Corps of U. S. Artillery; transferred
from Capt. Collins' Company. Ref: R.
& L. 1812, AGO Pages 18 and 31.

WILLIAMS, JOHN M.
Served from Dec. 21, 1812 to May 8,
1813 in Capt. John W. Weeks' Company, 11th Regt. Ref: R. & L. 1812,
AGO Pages 4 and 5.

*WILLIAMS, JONATHAN,   Lieutenant
Colonel. Served in command of 3
Regt. (Williams') Vt. Militia.

WILLIAMS, JOSEPH,   Waitsfield.
Volunteered to go to Plattsburgh,
September, 1814, and served 4 days
in Capt. Mathias S. Jones' Company.
Was one of the Vt. men on board
the British prison ship "San Antonio"
at Chatam, England. Ref: Book 52,
AGO Page 170; Records of Naval Records and Library, Navy Dept.

WILLIAMS, LEMUEL,   Chelsea, Vt.
Born at Plainfield, N. H.; aged 41
years; 5 feet 11 inches high; light
complexion; blue eyes; dark hair; by
profession a farmer; enlisted April 28,
1813 in U. S. Army for 1 year unless sooner discharged. Ref: Paper
in custody of Vt. Historical Society.

*WILLIAMS, LYMAN.
Served from June 11 to June 14, 1813
in Capt. John M. Eldridge's Company, 1st Regt. 2nd Brig. 3rd Div.

*WILLIAMS, PAUL.
Served in Capt. Wheeler's Company,
Col. Fifield's Regt. Detached Militia
in U. S. service 1 month and 2 days,
1812.

WILLIAMS, PHINEHAS JR., Captain,
Woodstock. Appointed Captain 11th
Inf. March 12, 1812; on Pay Roll of
company for January and February,
1813; dismissed, 1813. Ref: Heitman's
Historical Register & Dictionary USA;
R. & L. 1812, AGO Page 15.

WILLIAMS, ROBERT.
Served from May 1 to June 30, 1814

in Capt. Alexander Brooks' Corps of
Artillery. Ref: R. & L. 1812, AGO
Page 31.

*WILLIAMS, SAMUEL.
Served in 1 Regt. (Judson's) Vt.
Militia.

*WILLIAMS, SANDFORD.
Served in 3 Regt. (Tyler's) Vt. Militia.

‡WILLIAMS, SILAS JR.,   Marshfield.
Volunteered to go to Plattsburgh,
September, 1814, and served 9 days
in Capt. James English's Company.
Pension Certificate of widow, Mary
H., No. 40028.

*WILLIAMS, TIMOTHY, Musician.
Served in Capt. Adams' Company,
Col. Jonathan Williams' Regt. Detached Militia in U. S. service 2
months and 7 days, 1812.

*WILLIAMS, WILLIAM,   Lieutenant
Colonel. Commanded 4 Regt. (Williams') Vt. Militia.

*WILLIAMSON, CLARK.
Served from April 12 to April 21,
1814 in Capt. Shubael Wales' Company, Col. W. B. Sumner's Regt.

WILLIAMSON, REUBEN, Franklin County. Volunteered to go to Plattsburgh
Sept. 11, 1814 and served in 15th or
22nd Regt. Ref: Hemenway's Vt. Gazetteer, Vol. 2, Page 391.

WILLINGTON, ASHLEY,   Braintree.
Marched for Plattsburgh Sept. 10,
1814 and served in Capt. Lot Hudson's Company. Ref: Book 52, AGO
Page 24.

*WILLINGTON, HIRAM.
Served in Capt. Needham's Company,
Col. Martindale's Regt. Detached
Militia in U. S. service 17 days, 1812.

*WILLINGTON, IRA,   Williamstown.
Was an indentured apprentice of Cornelius Lynde.   Served in Capt.
Walker's Company, Col. Fifield's Regt.
Detached Militia in U. S. service,
from Sept. 12, 1812 to date of his
death at Swanton, Dec. 22, 1812.

WILLINGTON, JOSIAH,   Braintree.
Marched to Plattsburgh Sept. 10, 1814,
serving in Capt. Lot Hudson's Company. Ref: Book 52, AGO Page 24.

*WILLIS, DANIEL.
Served in 4 Regt. (Williams') Vt.
Militia.

*WILLIS, EZRA.
Served in Capt. Wheeler's Company,
Col. Fifield's Regt. Detached Militia
in U. S. service 5 months and 26
days, 1812.

*WILLIS, JACOB.
Served in Capt. Rogers' Company,
Col. Fifield's Regt. Detached Militia
in U. S. service 10 days, 1812. Serv-
ed in Capt. Phineas Williams' Com-
pany, 11th Regt.; on Pay Roll for
January and February, 1813. Ref:
R. & L. 1812, AGO Page 15.

*WILLIS, JAMES.
Served in 2 Regt. (Fifield's) Vt. Militia.

WILLIS, JOHN,　　　Plymouth, Vt.
Enlisted at Vergennes March 21, 1814 during the war and served in Capt. Wm. Miller's Company and Capt. Gideon Spencer's Company, 30th Regt. Ref: R. & L. 1812, AGO Pages 54, 55, 56.

‡WILLIS, NATHAN.
Served in Capt. Johnson's Company. Pension Certificate No. 24503.

*WILLIS, PETER.
Served in 2 Regt. (Fifield's) Vt. Militia.

*WILLIS, SECEL.
Served in 4 Regt. (Peck's) Vt. Militia.

*WILLIS, SILAS D., Musician.
Served in Capt. Scovell's Company, Col. Martindale's Regt. Detached Militia in U. S. service 1 month and 23 days, 1812.

*WILLMAN, GIDEON.
Served in 1 Regt. (Martindale's) Vt. Militia.

WILLMARTH, ABEL,　　　Addison.
Volunteered to go to Plattsburgh, September, 1814, and was in the battle, serving 9 days in Capt. George Fisher's Company, Sumner's Regt. Ref: Book 51, AGO Pages 5 and 6.

‡WILLMARTH, AMOS, Sergeant, Addison.
Volunteered to go to Plattsburgh, September, 1814 and was in the battle, serving 9 days in Capt. George Fisher's Company, Sumner's Regt. Pension Certificate No. 21217.

*WILLMOTT, DAVID,　　　Thetford.
Marched for Plattsburgh, September, 1814, and went as far as Bolton, Vt., serving 6 days in Capt. Salmon Howard's Company, 2nd Regt.

*WILLMOTT, JOSEPH,　　　Thetford.
Marched for Plattsburgh, September, 1814, and went as far as Bolton, Vt., serving 6 days in Capt. Salmon Howard's Company, 2nd Regt.

‡*WILLOBY, ABEL.
Served in Capt. Needham's Company, Col. Martindale's Regt. Detached Militia in U. S. service 2 months and 14 days, 1812. Pension Certificate No. 7179.

WILLS, EBENEZER,　　　Tunbridge.
Volunteered to go to Plattsburgh, September, 1814, and served in Capt. David Knox's Company. Ref: Book 52, AGO Page 117.

WILLS, ISAAC,　　　Calais.
Volunteered to go to Plattsburgh, September, 1814, and served 10 days in Capt. Gideon Wheelock's Company. Ref: Book 52, AGO Page 247.

WILLS, MERRILL,　　　Strafford.
Volunteered to go to Plattsburgh, September, 1814, and served in Capt. Cyril Chandler's Company. Ref: Book 52, AGO Page 42.

WILLS, WANTON.
Served from June 11 to June 14, 1813 in Capt. John M. Eldridge's Company, 1st Regt. 2nd Brig. 3rd Div. Ref: R. & L. 1812, AGO Page 35.

*WILLSON, BOSWELL, Captain.
Served in 4 Regt. (Williams') Vt. Militia.

*WILLSON, DAVID.
Served in 3 Regt. (Williams') Vt. Militia.

*WILLSON, EBENEZER,　　　Shoreham.
Served in Capt. Robbins' Company, Col. Wm. Williams' Regt. Detached Militia in U. S. service 4 months and 29 days, 1812.

WILLSON, EDWARD L.
Served from Sept. 26, 1812 to Feb. 27, 1813 in Capt. Benjamin S. Edgerton's Company, 11th Regt. Ref: R. & L. 1812, AGO Page 2.

*WILLSON, FESTUS.
Served in Capt. Wright's Company, Col. Martindale's Regt. Detached Militia in U. S. service 2 months and 14 days, 1812. Served from April 12 to April 21, 1814 in Capt. Shubael Wales' Company, Col. W. B. Sumner's Regt.

WILLSON, GIDEON.
Served in Capt. Start's Company, Col. Martindale's Regt. Detached Militia in U. S. service 2 months and 13 days, 1812. Ref: Book 53, AGO Page 21.

*WILLSON, HARVY.
Served from April 12 to April 21, 1814 in Lieut. Justus Foote's Company, Sumner's Regt.

WILLSON, JOHN,　　　Barre?
Enlisted April 14, 1814 during the war in Capt. Gideon Spencer's Company, 30th Regt.; on Muster Roll from Dec. 30, 1813 to June 30, 1814. Ref: R. & L. 1812, AGO Page 56.

*WILLSON, JOSIAH.
Enlisted Sept. 20, 1813 in Capt. John Weed's Company, Col. Clark's Rifle Corps.

‡WILLSON, LOTAN,　　　Fairfax.
Served in 1813 and 1814 in Capt. Joseph Beeman's Company. Pension Certificate of widow, Loedis, No. 30608. Ref: Hemenway's Vt. Gazetteer, Vol. 2,, Page 402.

*WILLSON, PETER.
Served in Capt. Sabins' Company, Col. Jonathan Williams' Regt. Detached Militia in U. S. service 2 months and 6 days, 1812.

*WILLSON, ROBERT.
Served from Feb. 15 to March 2, 1813 in Capt. Edgerton's Company, 11th Regt. Also served in 1 Regt. (Martindale's) Vt. Militia. Ref: R. & L. 1812, AGO Page 3.

*WILLSON, THOMAS.
Enlisted Sept. 25, 1813 and served 1 month and 23 days in Capt. Waterman's Company, Col. Dixon's Regt.

*WILLY, ROBERT, Sergeant.
Served in Corning's Detachment, Vt.
Militia.

*WILLYS, ELIJAH.
Served from Oct. 8 to Nov. 18, 1813
in Capt. Isaac Finch's Company, Col.
Clark's Rifle Corps.

*WILMARTH, ASA JR.,   Addison.
Volunteered to go to Plattsburgh,
September, 1814, and was in the
battle, serving 9 days in Capt. George
Fisher's Company, Sumner's Regt.

WILMARTH, DAVID,   Eaton, N. Y.
Served from March 1 to July 7, 1814
in Capt. Lynd's Company, 29th Inf.
Ref: R. & L. 1812, AGO Page 30.

‡*WILMARTH, GEORGE, Corporal, Addison. Served from April 12 to May
20, 1814 in Capt. George Fisher's Company, Sumner's Regt. Volunteered to
go to Plattsburgh, September, 1814,
and was in the battle, serving 9 days
in same company. Pension Certificate
No. 25225. Pension Certificate of
widow, Susan, No. 26205.

WILMARTH, HARTFORD.
Served from May 1 to June 30, 1814
in Capt. Alexander Brooks' Corps of
Artillery. Ref: R. & L. 1812, AGO
Page 31.

*WILMARTH, IRA, 1st Lieutenant, Ad-
dison. Served from April 12 to May
20, 1814 in Capt. George Fisher's
Company, Sumner's Regt.; volunteered to go to Plattsburgh, September,
1814, and was at the battle, serving
9 days in same company.

WILMARTH, NATHANIEL,   Ira.
Volunteered to go to Plattsburgh.
September, 1814, and served 4 days
in Capt. Matthew Anderson's Company. Ref: Book 52, AGO Page 144.

‡WILMOT, ELI T.
Served in Capt. J. Bishop's Company.
Pension Certificate of widow, Harriet
E., No. 32644.

*WILMOT, ORA, Corporal.
Served in 1 Regt. (Judson's) Vt.
Militia.

*WILMOTT, DAVID.
Served with Hospital Attendants, Vt.

*WILMOUTH, ASAHEL.
Served from April 12 to May 20, 1814
in Capt. George Fisher's Company,
Sumner's Regt.

WILSON, ABSOLEM.
Served in Capt. Weeks' Company, 11th
Regt.; on Pay Roll for January and
February, 1813. Ref: R. & L. 1812,
AGO Page 5.

*WILSON, ANTHONY.
Served from April 20 to April 21,
1814 in Capt. Eseck Sprague's Company, Sumner's Regt.

*WILSON, ASA.
Enlisted Sept. 25, 1813 in Capt. Amos
Robinson's Company, Dixon's Regt.

WILSON, BENJAMIN, Corporal.
Served in Capt. Weeks' Company, 11th
Regt.; on Pay Roll for January and
February, 1813. Ref: R. & L. 1812,
AGO Page 5.

WILSON, CALEB.
Volunteered to go to Plattsburgh,
September, 1814, and served 4 days
in company of Capt. James George
of Topsham. Ref: Book 52, AGO
Pages 67 and 70.

WILSON, DANIEL.
Served from May 1st to June 30,
1814 in Capt. Haig's Corps of Light
Dragoons. Ref: R. & L. 1812, AGO
Page 20.

‡WILSON, DANIEL HARVEY.
Served in Capt. Thompson's Company.
Pension Certificate No. 8254.

WILSON, DAVID.
Served from April 17, 1813 to April
13, 1814 in Capt. Simeon Wright's
Company. Ref: R. & L. 1812, AGO
Page 51.

*WILSON, DURFEE, Sergeant.
Enlisted Sept. 25, 1813 in Capt.
Charles Bennett's Company, Dixon's
Regt.

*WILSON, ELAM.
Served from Sept. 25 to Nov. 11,
1813 in Capt. Amos Robinson's Company, Dixon's Regt.

WILSON, GEORGE.
Served in Capt. Alexander Brooks'
Corps of Artillery; on Pay Roll to
June 30, 1814. Ref: R. & L. 1812,
AGO Page 31.

WILSON, HAMILTON.
Served in Capt. Alexander Brooks'
Corps of Artillery to June 29, 1814.
Ref: R. & L. 1812, AGO Page 31.

WILSON, IRAM.
Served in Capt. Preston's Company,
Col. Jonathan Williams' Regt. Detached Militia in U. S. service 2
months and 6 days, 1812. Ref: Book
53, AGO Page 84.

*WILSON, JAMES JR.,   Shoreham.
Served from April 12 to May 20, 1814
in company of Capt. James Gray Jr.,
Sumner's Regt. Volunteered to go to
Plattsburgh, September, 1814, and
served 6 days in Capt. Samuel Hand's
Company.

WILSON, JOHN.
Served from May 1 to June 30, 1814
in Capt. Haig's Corps of Light Dragoons. Ref: R. & L. 1812, AGO
Page 20.

*WILSON, JOHN.
Served from April 12 to April 21,
1814 in Capt. Othniel Jewett's Company, Sumner's Regt.

WILSON, JOHN.
Served in Capt. Weeks' Company, 11th
Regt.; on Pay Roll for January and
February, 1813. Ref: R. & L. 1812,
AGO Page 5.

‡WILSON, JONATHAN.
Served in Capt. Robbins' Company.
Pension Certificate of widow, Clarissa,
No. 926.

‡WILSON, JONATHAN.
Served in Capt. Robbins' Company.
Pension Certificate of widow, Betsey,
No. 16379.

*WILSON, JONATHAN.
Served in Capt. Robbins' Company,
Col. Wm. Williams' Regt. Detached
Militia in U. S. service 3 months and
21 days, 1812.

*WILSON, JONATHAN JR.,   Shoreham.
Served from April 12 to May 20, 1814
in company of Capt. James Gray Jr.,
Sumner's Regt.

‡*WILSON, NATHAN (or Nathaniel),
Shoreham. Served from April 12 to
May 20, 1814 in company of Capt.
James Gray Jr., Sumner's Regt. Pen-
sion Certificate of widow, Susan, No.
24931.

*WILSON, ROSWELL, Captain.
Served in 2nd Regt. 3rd Brig. 3rd
Div. Vt. Militia and in 4 Regt. (Wil-
liams') Vt. Militia.

WILSON, SAMUEL,   Franklin County.
Volunteered to go to Plattsburgh.
Sept. 11, 1814 and served in 15th
or 22nd Regt. Ref: Hemenway's Vt.
Gazetteer, Vol. 2, Page 392.

*WILSON, SIMEON.
Served in 4 Regt. (Peck's) Vt. Militia.

WILSON, THOMAS.
Served in Capt. Alexander Brooks'
Corps of Artillery to May 22, 1814.
Ref: R. & L. 1812, AGO Page 31.

WILSON, WILLIAM H., Surgeon.
Appointed Surgeon 45th Inf. April
12, 1814; promoted from Assistant
Surgeon. Was captured by troops
Sept. 6, 1814 at Plattsburgh; discharg-
ed Oct. 8, 1814. Ref: Governor and
Council, Vt., Vol. 6, Page 478; Rec-
ords of Naval Records and Library,
Navy Dept.

*WINANTS, JOSIAH.
Served from April 12 to April 21, 1814
in Capt. Edmund B. Hill's Company,
Sumner's Regt.

*WINCH, ABIJAH, Fifer.
Served in Capt. Wright's Company.
Col. Martindale's Regt. Detached
Militia in U. S. service 2 months and
8 days, 1812.

WINCH, ABIJAH JR.
Served in Capt. Willson's Company,
Col. Wm. Williams' Regt. Detached
Militia in U. S. service 5 months,
1812. Ref: Book 53, AGO Page 90.

*WINCHESTER, DAVID.
Served in Capt. Scovell's Company,
Col. Martindale's Regt. Detached
Militia in U. S. service 2 months and
22 days, 1812.

WINCHESTER, WALTER,   Marlboro.
Killed in battle of Black Rock aged
23. Ref: History of Marlboro.

*WINES, JOHN W.
Served from April 12 to May 20, 1814
in company of Capt. James Gray Jr.,
Sumner's Regt.

*WINES, WILLIAM.
Served from April 12 to May 20, 1814
in Capt. George Fisher's Company,
Sumner's Regt.

WING, JAMES,   Rochester.
Volunteered to go to Plattsburgh,
September, 1814, and served 7 days
in Capt. Oliver Mason's Company.
Ref: Book 51, AGO Page 259.

WING, JOSIAH,   Montpelier.
Volunteered to go to Plattsburgh,
September, 1814, and served 8 days
in Capt. Timothy Hubbard's Company. Ref: Book 52, AGO Page 256.

*WING, MATHEW.
Served from Sept. 23 to Sept. 29,
1813 in Capt. Amasa Mansfield's Company, Dixon's Regt.

WING, NATHANIEL,   Rochester.
Volunteered to go to Plattsburgh,
September, 1814; no organization giv-
en. Ref: Book 51, AGO Page 249.

*WINGATE, ELIJAH C., Sergeant, Bos-
ton, Mass. Served from Oct. 6, 1814
to June 19, 1815 in Capt. Taylor's
Company, 30th Inf. Served with Hospital Attendants, Vt. Ref: R. & L.
1812, AGO Page 23.

*WINGATE, JOHN.
Served in 3 Regt. (Tyler's) Vt. Militia.

WINN, DANIEL,   Mindon, N. Y.
Enlisted at Burlington March 20,
1814 during the war, serving in Capt.
Wm. Miller's Company and Capt.
Gideon Spencer's Company, 30th Regt.
Ref: R. & L. 1812, AGO Pages 54,
55, 56.

WINNE, PETER.
Enlisted in company of late Capt.
J. Brooks, commanded by Lt. John
I. Cromwell, Corps of U. S. Artil-
lery; period of enlistment; Nov. 2,
1812 to May 21, 1814; on Muster Roll
from April 30 to June 30, 1814. Ref:
R. & L. 1812, AGO Page 18.

WINNEY, PETER, Northumberland, N. Y.
Served from Dec. 7, 1814 to June 19,
1815 in Capt. Taylor's Company, 30th
Inf. Ref: R. & L. 1812, AGO Page
23.

*WINSHIP, ELIJAH.
Served from June 11 to June 14,, 1813
in Capt. Moses Jewett's Company,
1st Regt. 2nd Brig. 3rd Div.

WINSLOW, GEORGE A., Sergeant.
Served from Jan. 1 to June 30, 1814
in Regt. of Light Dragoons. Ref:
R. & L. 1812, AGO Page 21.

WINSLOW, JACOB, Corporal.
Served in Capt. Alexander Brooks'
Corps of Artillery; reduced to private

June 28, 1814. Ref: R. & L. 1812, AGO Page 31.

WINSLOW, JARAD.
Served in Capt. James Taylor's Company, 30th Regt. Ref: R. & L. 1812, AGO Page 59.

WINSLOW, JUSTIN, Brandon.
Volunteered to go to Plattsburgh. September, 1814, and served 8 days in Capt. Micah Brown's Company. Ref: Book 52, AGO Pages 130 and 132.

WINSLOW, K., Surgeon, Pittsford.
Volunteered to go to Plattsburgh, September, 1814, and served 8 days in Capt. Caleb Hendee's Company. Ref: Book 52, AGO Page 124.

‡WINSLOW, SAMUEL JR.
Served in Capt. Wheeler's Company. Pension Certificate No. 21709.

*WINSLOW, THERON, Drummer.
Served in 3 Regt. (Tyler's) Vt. Militia.

‡WINTERS, JOHN, Sergeant, Highgate.
Enlisted Sept. 25, 1813 in Capt. Elijah W. Wood's Company, Dixon's Regt. Volunteered to go to Plattsburgh, September, 1814, and served 6 days in Capt. Conrad Sax's Company, 4 Regt. (Williams'). Pension Certificate of widow, Hannah, No. 7162.

*WINTERS, NOAH.
Served in Dixon's Regt. Vt. Militia.

WINTERS, WILLIAM.
Enlisted April 11, 1814 for 5 years and served in Capt. Gideon Spencer's Company and Capt. Wm. Miller's Company, 30th Regt.; on Muster Roll to Aug. 31, 1814. Ref: R. & L. 1812, AGO Pages 54 and 56.

*WINTWORTH, WILLIAM.
Served in Capt. Needham's Company, Col. Martindale's Regt. Detached Militia in U. S. service 9 days, 1812.

WIRES, JOHN, St. Albans.
Appointed Captain 30th Inf. April 30, 1813; resigned Aug. 1, 1814. Ref: Governor and Council Vt., Vol. 6, Page 475; Heitman's Historical Register & Dictionary USA.

WISE, EBENEZER H.
Served from March 31 to June 30, 1813 in Lieut. V. R. Goodrich's Company, 11th Regt. Ref: R. & L. 1812, AGO Page 10.

WISE, JOHN, Franklin County.
Enlisted April 6, 1812 for 5 years in Capt. White Youngs' Company, 15th Regt.; on Muster Roll from Aug. 31 to Dec. 31, 1814. Ref: R. & L. 1812, AGO Page 27.

*WISE, JOHN.
Served from April 12 to April 15, 1814 in Capt. John Hackett's Company, Sumner's Regt.

WISE, JOHN H., Providence, R. I.
Served from Sept. 1, 1814 to June 16, 1815 in Capt. Sanford's Company, 30th Inf. Ref: R. & L. 1812, AGO Page 23.

‡WISEWELL, MOSES C.
Served in Capt. Burnes' Company. Pension Certificate No. 6401.

WISGARVER, JACOB, Berne, N. Y.
Served from Aug. 4, 1814 to June 19, 1815 in Capt. Taylor's Company, 30th Inf. Ref: R. & L. 1812, AGO Page 23.

WISGARVER, WILLIAM, Berne, N. Y.
Served from July 30, 1814 to June 19, 1815 in Capt. Taylor's Company, 30th Inf. Ref: R. & L. 1812, AGO Page 23.

WISHER, SAMUEL E.
Served from May 1 to June 30, 1814 as a laborer in Alexander Parris' Company of Artificers. Ref: R. & L. 1812, AGO Page 24.

WISHER, WILLIAM.
Served from June 1 to June 30, 1814 in Alexander Parris' Company of Artificers as a laborer. Ref: R. & L. 1812, AGO Page 24.

WITHERELL, HORACE, Shoreham.
Was with General Wilkinson on the St. Lawrence and in most of the battles under Brown and Scott on the Niagara frontier; returned and resided in Shoreham until his death in 1858. Ref: Rev. J. F. Goodhue's History of Shoreham, Page 103.

*WITHERELL, JAMES.
Served in Capt. Pettes' Company, Col. Wm. Williams' Regt. Detached Militia in U. S. service 4 months 17 days, 1812. Served from Oct. 29, 1812 to Feb. 28, 1813 in Capt. Weeks' Company, 11th Regt.

*WITHERELL, JOHN.
Served in Capt. Durkee's Company, Col. Fifield's Regt. Detached Militia in U. S. service 2 months and 21 days, 1812.

WITHERELL, JOSEPH.
Served from April 14 to June 30, 1814 in Regt. of Light Dragoons. Ref: R. & L. 1812, AGO Page 21.

‡WITHERELL, LEVI.
Served in Capt. J. Hazen's Company. Pension Certificate of widow, Nancy, No. 28669.

WITHERELL, MATHER.
Served from March 17 to June 16, 1813 in Lieut. V. R. Goodrich's Company, 11th Regt. Ref: R. & L. 1812, AGO Page 10.

‡*WITHERELL, NOAH (or Wetherell)
Served from Sept. 25 to Oct. 30, 1813 in Capt. Charles Bennett's Company, Col. Dixon's Regt. Also served in Capt. Winchester's Company. Pension Certificate No. 23054.

*WITHERELL, WARREN.
Served in Capt. Charles Bennett's Company, Dixon's Regt. from Sept. 25 to Oct. 27, 1813.

WITHERS, THOMAS, Franklin County.
Volunteered to go to Plattsburgh Sept. 11, 1814 and served in 15th or 22nd Regt. Ref: Hemenway's Vt. Gazetteer, Vol. 2, Page 391.

WITHEY, JOHN.
Served from March 27 to June 26, 1813 in Capt. Charles Follett's Company, 11th Regt. Ref: R. & L. 1812, AGO Page 13.

*WITHINGTON, JOHN.
Served in Capt. Sabin's Company, Col. Jonathan Williams' Regt. Detached Militia in U. S. service 2 months and 6 days, 1812.

WITHINGTON, JOSIAH,   Braintree.
Volunteered to go to Plattsburgh, September, 1814, and served in Capt. Lot Hudson's Company. Ref: Book 52, AGO Page 24.

*WITTER, HAWLEY,   Georgia.
Enlisted Sept. 25, 1813 in Capt. Elijah W. Wood's Company, Dixon's Regt. Volunteered to go to Plattsburgh, September, 1814, and served 8 days in Capt. Jesse Post's Company, Dixon's Regt.

WITTROUS, JASON,   Franklin County.
Volunteered to go to Plattsburgh Sept. 11, 1814 and served in 15th or 22nd Regt. Ref: Hemenway's Vt. Gazetteer, Vol. 2, Page 391.

WITTUM, RIXFORD (or Wettain, Rexford?)
Served from Feb. 4 to May 3, 1813 in Capt. Charles Follett's Company, 11th Regt. Was captured by troops July 25, 1814 at Londers Lane; discharged March 13, 1814. Ref: R. & L. 1812, AGO Page 13; Records of Naval Records and Library, Navy Dept.

WOLCOTT, ARIEL,   Shoreham.
Volunteered to go to Plattsburgh, Septmeber, 1814, and served 6 days in Capt. Samuel Hand's Company. Ref: Rev. J. F. Goodhue's History of Shoreham, Page 107; Book 51, AGO Page 44.

‡*WOLCOTT, GEORGE.
Served in Lieut. Bates' Company, 1 Regt. (Judson's) Vt. Militia. Pension Certificate of widow, Nancy, No. 20378.

*WOLCOTT, JOSEPH.
Served in 4 Regt. (Peck's) Vt. Militia.

‡*WOLCOTT, MOSES.
Served from April 12 to May 20, 1814 in Capt. George Fisher's Company, Sumner's Regt. Also served in Capt. Hand's Company. Pension Certificate of widow, Polly Ann, No. 34448.

‡WOLCOTT, NOAH.
Served in Capt. M. Bates' Company. Pension Certificate of widow, Harriet, No. 32597.

WOLCOTT, SEYMOUR,   Shoreham.
Was connected with the 2nd Regt. Light Artillery; acted as gunner at the repulse of Otter Creek, May 14, 1814, in the repulse of the British flotilla at that point. In March of the same year, he had directed one of the two field pieces in the affair

of the Stone Mill, and remained alone to give the enemy the last gun. He served also at the Beaver Dams, Little York and the capture of Fort George. He died at Little Falls. Ref: Rev. J. F. Goodhue's History of Shoreham, Page 103.

WONNEL, JAMES.
Served to June 26, 1814 in Capt. Alexander Brooks' Corps of Artillery. Ref: R. & L. 1812, AGO Page 31.

WOOD, ABEL,   Sudbury.
Volunteered to go to Plattsburgh, September, 1814, and served 6 days in Capt. Thomas Hall's Company. Ref: Book 52, AGO Page 122.

WOOD, ANSEL,   Georgia.
Volunteered to go to Plattsburgh, September, 1814, and served 8 days in Capt. Jesse Post's Company, Dixon's Regt. Ref: Book 51, AGO Page 102.

‡*WOOD, ARNA.
Served in Capt. Adams' Company, Col. Jonathan Williams' Regt. Detached Militia in U. S. service 2 months and 7 days, 1812. Pension Certificate No. 21674.

*WOOD, ASAPH,   Georgia.
Served in Capt. Saxe's Company, Col. Wm. Williams' Regt. Detached Militia in U. S. service 4 months and 24 days, 1812. Enlisted Sept. 25, 1813 and served 1 month and 23 days in Capt. Wood's Company, Col. Dixon's Regt. Detached Militia in U. S. service. Volunteered to go to Plattsburgh, September, 1814, and served 8 days in Capt. Jesse Post's Company, Dixon's Regt.

*WOOD, BENJAMIN.
Served in Corning's Detachment, Vt. Militia.

*WOOD, CHANDLER (or Ward?)
Served in 4 Regt. (Williams') Vt. Militia.

WOOD, CHARLES.
Enlisted May 10, 1813 for 1 year in Capt. Simeon Wright's Company. Ref: R. & L. 1812, AGO Page 51.

‡*WOOD, DANIEL.
Enlisted Sept. 25, 1813 in Capt. Jesse Post's Company, Dixon's Regt. Also served in Capt. E. W. Wood's Company, Dixon's Regt. Pension Certificate of widow, Sybil L., No. 28121.

WOOD, DANIEL,   Montpelier.
Volunteered to go to Plattsburgh, September, 1814, and served 8 days in Capt. Timothy Hubbard's Company. Ref: Book 52, AGO Page 256.

WOOD, DANIEL JR.
Served in Capt. Jesse Post's Company, Col. Dixon's Regt. Detached Militia in U. S. service 1 month and 23 days, 1813. Ref: Book 53, AGO Page 108.

*WOOD, DAVID.
Enlisted May 10, 1813 for 1 year in Capt. Simeon Wright's Company. Also served in Corning's Detachment, Vt. Militia. Ref: R. & L. 1812, AGO Page 51.

*WOOD, EBENEZER 3d.
Served in Capt. Wheeler's Company,
Col. Fifield's Regt. Detached Militia
in U. S. service 6 months and 4 days,
1812.

WOOD, ELIJAH W.,   Georgia.
Volunteered to go to Plattsburgh,
September, 1814, and served 8 days
in Capt. Jesse Post's Company, Dixon's Regt. Ref: Book 51, AGO Page
102.

*WOOD, ELIJAH W., Captain.
Appointed Captain in Lt. Col. Luther
Dixon's Regt. Sept. 25, 1813.

*WOOD, EPHRAIM,   Fairfax.
Served from Aug. 8, 1812 in com-
pany of Capt. Joseph Beeman Jr.,
11th Regt. U. S. Inf. under Col. Ira
Clark. Served in Lt. V. R. Good-
rich's Company, 11th Regt. Also serv-
ed with Hospital Attendants, Vt.
Ref: R. & L. 1812, AGO Page 11;
Hemenway's Vt. Gazetteer, Vol. 2,
Page 402.

WOOD, FREDERICK, Sergeant, Sullivan.
Served from Sept. 1, 1813 to July
27, 1814 in Lt. Hanson's Company,
29th Inf. Ref: R. & L. 1812, AGO
Page 30.

*WOOD, GIDEON H.
Served in Capt. Phelps' Company,
Col. Wm. Williams' Regt. Detached
Militia in U. S. service 5 months,
1812.

*WOOD. JACOB.
Served in Capt. Taylor's Company,
Col. Fifield's Regt. Detached Militia
in U. S. service 2 months and 21
days, 1812.

WOOD, JESSE, Lieutenant, Strafford.
Volunteered to go to Plattsburgh,
September, 1814, and served 7 days
in Capt. Joseph Barrett's Company.
Ref: Book 52, AGO Page 41.

‡WOOD, JOHN.
Served in Capt. Glass' Company. Also
in Quartermaster Dept. Pension Certificate No. 26100. Pension Certificate
of widow, Lucy, No. 35353.

*WOOD, JOHN JR.,   Barre?
Served from March 12 to June 11,
1813 in Lieut. V. R. Goodrich's Com-
pany, 11th Regt. Served from June
11 to June 14, 1813 in Capt. John M.
Eldridge's Company, 1st Regt. 2nd
Brig. 3rd Div. Ref: R. & L. 1812,
AGO Page 10.

*WOOD, JOSEPH.
Served from April 12 to April 21,
1814 in Lieut. Justus Foote's Company, Sumner's Regt.

‡*WOOD, JOSEPH JR., Sergeant, Woodstock. Served in Capt. Phelps' Company, Col. Jonathan Williams' Regt.
Detached Militia in U. S. service 2
months and 21 days, 1812. Pension
Certificate No. 1746. Pension Certificate of widow, Lucy B., No. 12636.

WOOD, JOSIAH JR.,   Sherburne.
Volunteered to go to Plattsburgh,
September, 1814, and served 10 days;
no organization given. Ref: Book
52, AGO Page 164.

WOOD, LISCOM.
Enlisted June 18, 1813 for 1 year in
Capt. Daniel Farrington's Company,
30th Regt. (also commanded by Capt.
Simeon Wright). Ref: R. & L. 1812,
AGO Pages 50 and 51.

*WOOD, LUTHER B.,   Pawlet.
Served in Capt. Hotchkiss' Company,
Col. Martindale's Regt. Detached
Militia in U. S. service 2 months and
13 days, 1812.

*WOOD, MARTIN,   Middlebury.
Served in Capt. Dorrance's Company,
Col. Wm. Williams' Regt. Detached
Militia in U. S. service 3 months and
29 days, 1812. Served from April 12
to April 15, 1814 in Capt. John
Hackett's Company, Sumner's Regt.

*WOOD, MORGAN.
Served in Capt. Ormsbee's Company,
Col. Martindale's Regt. Detached
Militia in U. S. service 1 month and
17 days, 1812.

WOOD, NATHANIEL, Corporal, Whitehall, N. Y. Served from Sept. 1,
1814 to June 16, 1815 in Capt. Sanford's Company, 30th Inf. Ref: R.
& L. 1812, AGO Page 23.

WOOD, NATHANIEL JR.
Enlisted March 2, 1814 during the
war in Capt. Clark's Company, 30th
Regt. Ref: R. & L. 1812, AGO
Page 1.

‡WOOD, ORRIN.
Served in Capt. Prentiss' Company,
Col. Dixon's Regt. Detached Militia
in U. S. service 1 month and 23 days,
1813. Pension Certificate of widow,
Minerva S., No. 44184.

WOOD, OTIS,   Thetford.
Marched for Plattsburgh, September,
1814, and went as far as Bolton, Vt.,
serving 6 days in Capt. Salmon Howard's Company, 2nd Regt. Ref: Book
52, AGO Pages 15 and 16.

‡WOOD, OTIS,   Poultney.
Volunteered to go to Plattsburgh,
September, 1814, and served 4 days
in Capt. Briant Ransom's Company.
Pension Certificate of widow, Esther,
No. 22558.

WOOD, PHILANDER.
Served in Capt. Samul Gordon's Com-
pany, 11th Regt.; on Pay Roll for
January and February, 1813. Ref:
R. & L. 1812, AGO Page 9.

WOOD, PRATT.
Served in War of 1812 and was cap-
tured by troops June 26, 1813 at
Beaver Dams; discharged Aug. 10th.
Ref: Records of Naval Records and
Library, Navy Dept.

*WOOD, REUBEN.
Served from June 11 to June 14,
1813 in Capt. Hezekiah Barns' Company, 1st Regt. 2nd Brig. 3rd Div.

WOOD, REUBEN, Captain, Middletown.
Volunteered to go to Plattsburgh,
September, 1814, and served 4 days
in command of company from Middletown. Ref: Book 52, AGO Page 143.

*WOOD, SAMUEL.
Served in 2 Regt. (Fifield's) Vt. Militia.

WOOD, SEWALL,   Shoreham.
Volunteered to go to Plattsburgh,
September, 1814, and served 6 days
in Capt. Nathaniel North's Company
of Cavalry. Ref: Rev. J. F. Goodhue's History of Shoreham, Page 107.

‡*WOOD, SILAS.
Served in Capt. Morrill's Company,
Col. Fifield's Regt. Detached Militia
in U. S. service 3 months and 17
days, 1812. Pension Certificate No.
2664. Pension Certificate of widow,
Cornelia H., No. 27793.

WOOD, SIMEON.
Served from April 15 to July 14, 1813
in Capt. Samul Gordon's Company,
11th Regt. Ref: R. & L. 1812, AGO
Page 8.

WOOD, SQUIRE,   Danby.
Served from April 12, 1814 to June
19, 1815 in Capt. Taylor's Company,
30th Inf. Ref: R. & L. 1812, AGO
Page 23.

WOOD, SQUIRE,   St. Albans.
Enlisted April 29, 1813 for 1 year in
Capt. John Wires' Company, 30th
Regt. Ref: R. & L. 1812, AGO Page
40.

WOOD, THOMAS.
Served in Capt. Mason's Company,
Col. Fifield's Regt. Detached Militia
in U. S. service 6 months, 1812.
Ref: Book 53, AGO Page 71.

*WOOD, THOMAS,   Randolph.
Volunteered to go to Plattsburgh,
September, 1814, in Capt. Lebbeus
Egerton's Company; did not appear
and probably deserted.

*WOOD, TIMOTHY,   Pawlet.
Served in Capt. Hotchkiss' Company,
Col. Martindale's Regt. Detached
Militia in U. S. service 2 months
and 13 days, 1812.

‡WOOD, URIAH.
Pension Certificate of widow, Sally,
No. 7001; no organization given.

WOOD, WILLIAM,   Pittsford.
Volunteered to go to Plattsburgh,
September, 1814, and served 8 days
in Capt. Caleb Hendee's Company.
Ref: Book 52, AGO Page 125.

‡*WOOD, WILLIAM JR.
Served in Capt. Mason's Company,
Col. Fifield's Regt. Detached Militia
n U. S. service 6 months, 1812. Pension Certificate of widow, Jane, No.
24951.

*WOODARD, AYERS.
Served in 3 Regt. (Williams') Vt.
Militia.

*WOODARD, DANIEL (or Woodward?)
Served from June 11 to June 14, 1813
in Lt. Bates' Company, 1 Regt. (Judson's).

*WOODARD, DAVID.
Served in Capt. Brown's Company,
Col. Martindale's Regt. Detached
Militia in U. S. service 2 months
and 14 days, 1812.

WOODARD, GEORGE S.,   Barre.
Volunteered to go to Plattsburgh,
September, 1814, and served 8 days
in Capt. Warren Ellis' Company. Ref:
Book 52, AGO Pages 221 and 242.

WOODARD, JOHN G.
Enlisted April 23, 1813 for 1 year in
Capt. John Wires' Company, 30th
Regt. Ref: R. & L. 1812, AGO Page
40.

*WOODARD, LEONARD,   Randolph.
Volunteered to go to Plattsburgh,
September, 1814, and served in Capt.
Lebbeus Egerton's Company.

*WOODARD, WILLIAM.
Served in Capt. Strait's Company,
Col. Martindale's Regt. Detached
Militia in U. S. service 2 months and
13 days, 1812.

*WOODBRIDGE, TIMOTHY.
Served from Sept. 25 to Sept. 29,
1813 in Capt. Amos Robinson's Company, Dixon's Regt.

WOODBURY, BENJAMIN.
Served from March 3 to June 2, 1813
in company of Capt. John McNeil
Jr., 11th Regt. Ref: R. & L. 1812,
AGO Page 16.

*WOODBURY, DANIEL.
Served in 1 Regt. (Martindale's) Vt.
Militia.

WOODBURY, DANIEL.
Enlisted Nov. 1, 1812 in Capt. Benjamin S. Edgerton's Company, 11th
Regt.; on Pay Roll for September
and October, 1812 and January and
February, 1813; was at the battle
of Chrystler's Farm Nov. 11, 1813
and was reported missing after the
battle. Ref: R. & L. 1812, AGO
Pages 1 and 2; Governor and Council Vt., Vol. 6, Page 490.

WOODBURY, DAVID,   Bethel.
Volunteered to go to Plattsburgh,
September, 1814, and served 9 days
in Capt. Nehemiah Noble's Company.
Ref: Book 51, AGO Page 220.

WOODBURY, JOHN,   Bethel.
Volunteered to go to Plattsburgh,
September, 1814, and served 8 days
in Capt. Nehemiah Noble's Company.
Ref: Book 51, AGO Page 232.

*WOODBURY, NATHAN.
Served in Capt. Phineas Williams'
Company, 11th Regt.; on Pay Roll
for January and February, 1813.
Served with Hospital Attendants, Vt.
Ref: R. & L. 1812, AGO Page 15.

WOODBURY, PHINEAS, Surgeon.
Appointed Surgeon's Mate 25th Inf.
July 6, 1812; Surgeon March 30, 1814;
transferred to 8th Inf. May 17, 1815;
died February, 1818. Ref: Heitman's
Historical Register & Dictionary USA.

WOODBURY, SAMUEL,   Bethel.
Volunteered to go to Plattsburgh,
September, 1814, and served 8 days
in Capt. Nehemiah Noble's Company.
Ref: Book 51, AGO Page 221.

*WOODFORD, AUSTIN,   Shoreham.
Served from April 12 to May 20,
1814 in company of Capt. James
Gray Jr., Sumner's Regt.

*WOODHOUSE, HENRY, Corporal.
Served in Capt. Brown's Company,
Col. Martindale's Regt. Detached
Militia in U. S. service 2 months and
14 days, 1812.

‡WOODMAN, BENJAMIN.
Served in Capt. Morrell's Company.
Pension Certificate of widow, Calenda,
No. 6038.

*WOODMAN, DANIEL.
Served in 1 Regt. (Judson's) Vt.
Militia.

WOODMAN, JEREMAH.
Served from May 1 to June 30, 1814
in Capt. Alexander Brooks' Corps
of Artillery. Ref: R. & L. 1812, AGO
Page 31.

*WOODRUFF, ELI, Sergeant.
Enlisted Sept. 25, 1813 in Capt. Elijah
Birge's Company, Col. Dixon's Regt.;
transferred to Capt. Asahel Langworthy's Company, Col. Isaac Clark's
Rifle Corps Oct. 22, 1813; served 1
month and 23 days.

‡*WOODRUFF, HENRY.
Enlisted Sept. 25, 1813 and served
1 month and 23 days in Capt. Elijah
Birge's Company, Col. Dixon's Regt.
Also served in 4 Regt. (Williams')
Vt. Militia. Pension Certificate No.
11060.

*WOODRUFF, HERVEY.
Served in Dixon's Regt. of Militia.

*WOODRUFF, JOEL.
Served in Dixon's Regt. of Militia.

*WOODRUFF, JOSIAH.
Served in 1 Regt. (Judson's) Vt.
Militia.

*WOODRUFF, NATHAN.
Served in Tyler's Regt. Vt. Militia.

‡*WOODRUFF, ROMANTA.
Served in Capt. Taylor's Company,
Col. Wm. Williams' Regt. Detached
Militia in U. S. service 4 months and
24 days, 1812. Pension Certificate No.
20890. Pension Certificate of widow,
Betsey, No. 31822.

WOODRUFF, RUSSEL, Musician.
Served from April 22, 1813 to April
25, 1814 in Capt. James Taylor's
Company and Capt. Gideon Spencer's
Company, 30th Regt. Ref: R. & L.
1812, AGO Pages 52, 56, 58.

WOODS, ANDREW.
Served from Feb. 9 to May 10, 1813
in Capt. John W. Weeks' Company,
11th Regt. Ref: R. & L. 1812, AGO
Pages 4 and 5.

‡*WOODS, ZEBA, Sergeant.
Served in Capt. Taylor's Company,
Col. Wm. Williams' Regt. Detached
Militia in U. S. service 4 months and
24 days, 1812. Also served in 1 Regt.
(Judson's) Vt. Militia. Pension Cer-
tificate of widow, Harriot, No. 3135.

*WOODWARD, AMIRIAH.
Served in Capt. Morrill's Company,
Col. Fifield's Regt. Detached Militia
in U. S. service 6 months and 5 days,
1812.

*WOODWARD, APPOLLOS.
Served in Capt. Morrill's Company,
Col. Fifield's Regt. Detached Militia
in U. S. service 3 months and 21 days,
1812.

*WOODWARD, ASAHEL.
Served in Capt. Wright's Company,
Col. Martindale's Regt. Detached
Militia in U. S. service 2 months and
14 days, 1812.

WOODWARD, AYERS.
Served in Capt. Briggs' Company, Col.
Jonathan Williams' Regt. Detached
Militia in U. S. service 2 months and
13 days, 1812. Ref: Book 53, AGO
Page 96.

WOODWARD, BILLEY, Ensign. Roxbury.
Volunteered to go to Plattsburgh,
September, 1814, and served 7 days
in Capt. Samuel M. Orcutt's Company. Ref: Book 52, AGO Pages 167
and 250.

WOODWARD, CLARK.
Volunteered to go to Plattsburgh,
September, 1814, and served 4 days
in Capt. Aaron Kidder's Company.
Ref: Book 52, AGO Page 65.

WOODWARD, LEONARD.
Volunteered to go to Plattsburgh,
September, 1814, and served 4 days
in Capt. Aaron Kidder's Company.
Ref: Book 52, AGO Page 65.

WOODWARD, NATHAN.
Enlisted May 28, 1813 for 1 year in
Capt. Daniel Farrington's Company,
30th Regt. (also commanded by Capt.
Simeon Wright); on Muster Roll from
March 1 to April 30, 1814. Ref: R.
& L. 1812, AGO Pages 50 and 51.

‡WOODWARD, NATHANIEL.
Served in Capt. Morrill's Company.
Pension Certificate of widow, Anna,
No. 5359.

*WOODWARD, NATHANIEL.   Danville.
Served in Capt. Morrill's Company,
Col. Fifield's Regt. Detached Militia
in U. S. service 4 months and 24
days, 1812.

*WOODWARD, NATHANIEL JR., Dan-
ville. Served in Capt. Morrill's Company, Col. Fifield's Regt. Detached
Militia in U. S. service 4 months and
15 days, 1812.

*WOODWARD, SAMUEL.
Served in Capt. Briggs' Company,
Col. Jonathan Williams' Regt. Detached Militia in U. S. service 2
months and 13 days, 1812.

WOODWARD, THEODORE, Surgeon's Mate. Appointed Surgeon's Mate 11th Inf. Aug. 9, 1813; honorably discharged June 15, 1815. Ref: Heitman's Historical Register & Dictionary USA.

*WOODWORTH, ASAPH.
Served in 3 Regt. (Tyler's) Vt. Militia.

WOODWORTH, BENJAMIN, St. Albans. Enlisted May 7, 1813 for 1 year in Capt. John Wires' Company, 30th Regt. Ref: R. & L. 1812, AGO Page 40.

*WOODWORTH, JABEZ JR.
Served in 3 Regt. (Tyler's) Vt. Militia.

WOODWORTH, JAMIN, Randolph. Volunteered to go to Plattsburgh, September, 1814, in Capt. Lebbeus Egerton's Company. Ref: Hemenway's Vt. Gazetteer, Vol. 2, Page 999; Book 52, AGO Pages 82 and 85.

*WOODWORTH, JOHN.
Served in Capt. Robinson's Company, Col. Dixon's Regt. Detached Militia in U. S. service 1 month and 20 days, 1813.

*WOODWORTH, JOHN.
Served in Capt. Taylor's Company. Col. Wm. Williams' Regt. Detached Militia in U. S. service 4 months and 24 days, 1812.

WOODWORTH, JOHN, St. Albans. Enlisted April 24, 1813 for 1 year in Capt. John Wires' Company, 30th Regt. Ref: R. & L. 1812, AGO Page 40.

*WOODWORTH, JONATHAN.
Served from Sept. 25 to Nov. 13, 1813 in Capt. Amos Robinson's Company, Dixon's Regt. Also served as fifer in 3 Regt. (Tyler's) Vt. Militia. Ref: Book 52, AGO Page 271.

WOODWORTH, JOSEPH, Montpelier. Volunteered to go to Plattsburgh, September, 1814, and served 8 days in Capt. Timothy Hubbard's Company. Ref: Book 52, AGO Page 256.

*WOODWORTH, LEMUEL.
Served in Capt. Bingham's Company, Col. Jonathan Williams' Regt. Detached Militia in U. S. service 2 months and 9 days, 1812.

WOODWORTH, LEONARD, Randolph. Volunteered to go to Plattsburgh. September, 1814, in Capt. Lebbeus Egerton's Company. Ref: Hemenway's Vt. Gazetteer, Vol. 2, Page 999.

‡*WOODWORTH, LYMAN.
Served in Capt. Bingham's Company, Col. Jonathan Williams' Regt. Detached Militia in U. S. service 2 months and 9 days, 1812. Pension Certificate No. 10078. Pension Certificate of widow, Elizabeth B., No. 20372.

*WOODWORTH, LYMAN.
Served in Capt. Walker's Company, Col. Fifield's Regt. Detached Militia in U. S. service 2 months and 26 days, 1812.

‡WOODWORTH, RAPHA, Adjutant. Served as Adjutant to Col. Tyler. Pension Certificate of widow, Abigail G., No. 27114.

WOOLCOT, OLIVER JR., Pittsford. Volunteered to go to Plattsburgh, September, 1814, and served 8 days in Capt. Caleb Hendee's Company. Ref: Book 52, AGO Page 125.

*WOOLCUT, ELIJAH JR.
Served from June 11 to June 14, 1813 in Lt. Bates' Company, 1 Regt. (Judson's).

*WOOLDRIDGE, AARON.
Served with Hospital Attendants, Vt.

*WOOLEY, ELEPHEUS (or Elaphus).
Served in Capt. Sabin's Company, Col. Jonathan Williams' Regt. Detached Militia in U. S. service 2 months and 6 days, 1812.

WOOLFE, JAMES Y., Roxbury. Volunteered to go to Plattsburgh, September, 1814, and served 8 days in Capt. Samuel M. Orcutt's Company. Ref: Book 52, AGO Page 250.

WOOLMAN, DAVID.
Enlisted May 10, 1813 for 1 year in Capt. Daniel Farrington's Company, 30th Regt. (also commanded by Capt. Simeon Wright); on Muster Roll from March 1 to April 30, 1814. Ref: R. & L. 1812, AGO Pages 50 and 51.

WOOLMAN, STEPHEN.
Enlisted Jan. 23, 1813 during the war in company of late Capt. J. Brooks, commanded by Lt. John I. Cromwell, Corps of U. S. Artillery; on Muster Roll from April 30 to June 30, 1814. Ref: R. & L. 1812, AGO Page 18.

WOOLSEY, FRANCIS P., 2nd Lieutenant. Appointed May 2, 1813, 2nd Lieutenant in company of late Capt. J. Brooks, commanded by Lt. John I. Cromwell. Corps of U. S. Artillery; on Muster Roll from April 30 to June 30, 1814; transferred to Capt. A. S. Brooks' Company. Ref: R. & L. 1812, AGO Pages 18 and 31.

*WOOLSON, SIMEON.
Served in 4 Regt. (Peck's) Vt. Militia.

WOOSTER, REV. BENJAMIN, Fairfield. Volunteered to go to Plattsburgh, September, 1814, and was at the battle. Recruited and commanded company from Sheldon. Ref: Vol. 3, History of Vt. Page 97; Book 51, AGO Pages 112 and 132; Hemenway's Vt. Gazetteer, Vol. 2, Pages 193-6.

*WOOSTER, GEORGE W.
Served from April 12 to April 21, 1814 in Capt. Edmund B. Hill's Company, Sumner's Regt.

*WOOSTER, JEREMY.
Served from Oct. 11 to Oct. 17, 1813 in Capt. John Munson's Company, 3 Regt. (Tyler's).

WOOSTER, MOSES,   Cornwall.
Volunteered to go to Plattsburgh,
September, 1814, and was at the
battle, serving in Capt. Edmund B.
Hill's Company. Sumner's Regt. Ref:
Book 51, AGO Page 13.

‡WOOSTER, RODERIC (or Broderick?),
Cornwall. Volunteered to go to Platts-
burgh, September, 1814, and was at
the battle, serving in Capt. Edmund
B. Hill's Company, Sumner's Regt.
Pension Certificate of widow, Olive
R., No. 29969.

*WORCESTER, PARKER.
Served in Corning's Detachment, Vt.
Militia and 4 Regt. (Peck's) Vt. Mili-
tia.

WORDEN, SAMUEL JR.
Served in Regt. of Light Dragoons;
on Pay Roll to June 30, 1814. Ref:
R. & L. 1812, AGO Page 21.

*WORKMAN, JOHN S.
Served from Sept. 1, 1813 to June
7, 1814 in Capt. Vanbunn's Company,
29th Inf. Also served with Hospital
Attendants, Vt. Ref: R. & L. 1812,
AGO Page 30.

WORKS, ALEXANDER,   Williamstown.
Volunteered to go to Plattsburgh
and was at the battle Sept. 11, 1814,
serving 8 days in Capt. David Robinson's Company. Ref: Book 52, AGO
Page 2.

*WORLY, ELDRIDGE.
Served in Capt. Dorrance's Company,
Col. Wm. Williams' Regt. Detached
Militia in U. S. service 3 months and
23 days, 1812.

*WORSTER, LYMAN, Lieutenant.
Served in 1 Regt. (Judson's) Vt.
Militia.

*WORTHEN, DAVID.
Enlisted Sept. 25, 1813 and served
1 month and 23 days in Capt. Elijah
Birge's Company, Col. Dixon's Regt.
Also served in Capt. Chadwick's Company. Ref: R. & L. 1812, AGO Page
32.

WORTHEN, JACOB,   Barre.
Volunteered to go to Plattsburgh,
September, 1814, and served 5 days
in Capt. Warren Ellis' Company. Ref:
Book 52, AGO Page 239.

WORTHEN, LYMAN, Lieutenant.
Served from June 11 to June 14, 1813
in Capt. Ithiel Stone's Company, 1st
Regt. 2nd Brig. 3rd Div. Ref: R. &
L. 1812, AGO Page 44.

WORTHINGTON, DANFORD.
Served in Lt. Wm. S. Foster's Com-
pany, 11th Regt.; on Pay Roll for
January and February, 1813. Ref:
R. & L. 1812, AGO Page 7.

*WRAY, CALVIN.
Served from June 11 to June 14, 1813
in Capt. Thomas Dorwin's Company,
1st Regt. 2nd Brig. 3rd Div.

*WRAY, OLIVER.
Served from June 11 to June 14, 1813
in Capt. Thomas Dorwin's Company,
1st Regt. 2nd Brig. 3rd Div.

*WRAY, PHILO, Corporal.
Served from June 11 to June 14, 1813
in Capt. Thomas Dorwin's Company,
1st Regt. 2nd Brig. 3rd Div.

WRIGHT, ALANSON,   Berlin.
Volunteered to go to Plattsburgh,
September, 1814, and served 7 days
in Capt. Cyrus Johnson's Company.
Ref: Book 52, AGO Page 255.

*WRIGHT, ALPHEUS, Corporal.
Served in Capt. Sabin's Company, Col.
Jonathan Williams' Regt. Detached
Militia in U. S. service 2 months and
6 days, 1812.

WRIGHT, ALVIN,   Pittsford.
Volunteered to go to Plattsburgh,
September, 1814, and served 8 days
in Capt. Caleb Hendee's Company.
Ref: Book 52, AGO Page 125.

*WRIGHT, ANDREW JR., Ensign.
Served from April 12 to May 20, 1814
in company of Capt. James Gray Jr.,
Sumner's Regt. Volunteered to go
to Plattsburgh, September, 1814, and
served 6 days in Capt. Samuel Hand's
Company as a 2nd Lieutenant.

‡*WRIGHT, BENJAMIN, Musician.
Served in 3 Regt. (Tyler's) Vt. Militia. Also served in Capt. Joseph
Sinclair's Company. Pension Certificate of widow, Margaret, No. 39227.

*WRIGHT, BENONI.
Served from Sept. 25 to Oct. 1, 1813
in Capt. Elijah W. Wood's Company,
Dixon's Regt.

*WRIGHT, BERIAH,   Thetford.
Marched for Plattsburgh, September,
1814, and went as far as Bolton, Vt.,
serving 6 days in Capt. Salmon Howard's Company, 2nd Regt.

‡WRIGHT, BINGHAM C.
Served in Capt. Talcott's Company.
Pension Certificate of widow, Urania,
No. 26931.

*WRIGHT, BRADLEY.
Served from April 12 to April 15, 1814
in Capt. John Hackett's Company,
Sumner's Regt.

‡WRIGHT, DANIEL, Lieutenant.
Pension Certificate of widow, Rachel,
No. 37937.

*WRIGHT, DANIEL,   Cornwall.
Served from April 12 to April 21,
1814 in Capt. Edmund B. Hill's Company, Sumner's Regt.

*WRIGHT, DANIEL, Sergeant.
Served from April 12 to April 21,
1814 in Capt. Shubael Wales' Company, Col. W. B. Sumner's Regt.

*WRIGHT, DANIEL M.
Served in Capt. Ormsbee's Company,
Col. Martindale's Regt. Detached
Militia in U. S. service 2 months and
14 days, 1812.

WRIGHT, DAVID.
Enlisted May 21, 1812 for 5 years in
Capt. White Youngs' Company, 15th
Regt.; on Muster Roll from Aug. 31
to Dec. 31, 1814. Ref: R. & L. 1812,
AGO Page 27.

*WRIGHT, EBENEZER JR.
Served in Capt. O. Durkee's Company,
Col. Fifield's Regt. Detached Militia
in U. S. service 2 months and 16
days, 1812.

*WRIGHT, ELIHU,   Glover.
Served in Capt. Mason's Company,
Col. Fifield's Regt. Detached Militia
in U. S. service 6 months, 1812.

WRIGHT, ELIJAH,   Shoreham.
Volunteered to go to Plattsburgh,
September, 1814, and served 6 days
in Capt. Samuel Hand's Company.
Ref: Rev. J. F. Goodhue's History
of Shoreham, Page 108.

‡WRIGHT, ELISHA.
Served in Capt. J. Talcott's Company.
Pension Certificate of widow, Semele,
No. 29227.

*WRIGHT, GARDNER,   Fairfax.
Served from Aug. 8, 1812 in company
of Capt. Joseph Beeman Jr., 11th
Regt. U. S. Inf. under Col. Ira
Clark. Served in Lt. V. R. Good-
rich's Company, 11th Regt.; on Pay
Roll for January and February, 1813.
Also served in 4 Regt. (Williams')
Vt. Militia. Ref: R. & L. 1812, AGO
Page 11; Vol. 50, Vt. State Papers.
Page 242; Hemenway's Vt. Gazetteer,
Vol. 2, Page 402.

‡WRIGHT, GEORGE.
Served in Capt. Reed's Company.
Pension Certificate of widow, Theresa
A., No. 32389.

WRIGHT, GIDEON,   Richmond.
Volunteered to go to Plattsburgh,
September, 1814, and served 9 days
in Capt. Roswell Hunt's Company, 3
Regt. (Tyler's). Ref: Book 51, AGO
Page 82.

*WRIGHT, GORDAN.
Served in Capt. Phelps' Company,
Col. Wm. Williams' Regt. Detached
Militia in U. S. service 5 months,
1812.

*WRIGHT, HENRY.
Served in 1 Regt. (Martindale's) Vt.
Militia.

WRIGHT, ISAAC, Musician.
Served in Capt. Samul Gordon's Com-
pany, 11th Regt.; on Pay Roll for
January and February, 1813. Ref:
R. & L. 1812, AGO Page 9.

WRIGHT, JEHIAL W.
Served from Sept. 28 to Nov. 15,
1813 in Capt. Elijah W. Wood's Company, Dixon's Regt. Ref: Book 52,
AGO Page 273.

WRIGHT, JN'O.
Served in Capt. Cross' Company,
Col. Martindale's Regt. Detached
Militia in U. S. service 2 months and
13 days, 1812. Ref: Book 53, AGO
Page 7.

WRIGHT, JOHN,   Richford.
Served in Capt. Martin D. Follett's
Company, Dixon's Regt. on duty on
northern frontier in 1813. Ref: Hemenway's Vt. Gazetteer, Vol. 2, Page
428.

WRIGHT, JOHN, Sergeant,   Pownal.
Served from March 24, 1814 to June
19, 1815 in Capt. Taylor's Company,
30th Inf. Ref: R. & L. 1812, AGO
Page 23.

‡*WRIGHT, JOHN.
Served in Capt. Cross' Company, 1
Regt. (Martindale's) Vt. Militia. Pension Certificate of widow, Nancy, No.
22852.

WRIGHT, JOHN, Lieutenant.
Appointed Cadet Military Academy
May 22, 1812; 2nd Lieutenant Engineers March 30, 1814; resigned July
23, 1818; died Sept. 10, 1860. Ref:
Heitman's Historical Register & Dictionary USA.

‡*WRIGHT, JOHN P., Sheldon or Fairfield. Enlisted Sept. 25, 1813 in Capt.
Martin D. Folett's Company, Dixon's
Regt. Volunteered to go to Plattsburgh. September. 1814, and served 9
days in Capt. Benjamin Wooster's
Company. Also served in Capt. Dorrance's Company, 4 Regt. (Williams').
Pension Certificate No. 6889.

*WRIGHT, JONATHAN,   Shoreham.
Volunteered to go to Plattsburgh,
September. 1814, and served 6 days
in Capt. Samuel Hand's Company.

*WRIGHT, JONATHAN.
Served from April 12 to May 20, 1814
in company of Capt. James Gray Jr.,
Sumner's Regt.

*WRIGHT, JONATHAN.
Served from April 12 to April 21,
1814 in Capt. Shubael Wales' Company, Sumner's Regt.

WRIGHT, JOSEPH,   Fairfield.
Served in Capt. George Kimball's
Company, stationed at Swanton in
1813. Ref: Hemenway's Vt. Gazetteer, Vol. 2, Page 408.

*WRIGHT, JOSEPH.
Served in Capt. Howard's Company,
Vt. Militia.

*WRIGHT, JOSHUA.
Enlisted Sept. 25, 1813 in Capt. Elijah
Birge's Company, Dixon's Regt.

*WRIGHT, JOSIAH.   Swanton.
Served in Capt. George W. Kindall's
Company, 4 Regt. (Williams') Detached Militia in U. S. service 4
months and 23 days, 1812.

*WRIGHT, JOTHAM.
Enlisted Oct. 3, 1813 in Capt. Asahel
Langworthy's Company, Col. Isaac
Clark's Rifle Corps. Also served in
Capt. Jesse Post's Company, Col. Dix-
on's Regt.

*WRIGHT, JUSTUS, Corporal Enosburgh.
Served from Oct. 14 to Nov. 17, 1813
in Capt. Asahel Scovell's Company,
Col. Clark's Rifle Corps.

*WRIGHT, KENT. Corporal,   Shoreham.
Served from April 12 to May 20, 1814
in company of Capt. James Gray
Jr., Sumner's Regt.

WRIGHT, LEWIS.
Served from April 4 to July 3, 1813
in Capt. Charles Follett's Company,
11th Regt. Ref: R. & L. 1812, AGO
Page 13.

WRIGHT, LUTHER,   Fairfield.
Volunteered to go to Plattsburgh,
September, 1814, and served 8 days
in Capt. Benjamin Wooster's Company. Ref: Book 51, AGO Pages 120,
178, 182.

*WRIGHT, MEDAD,   Calais.
Volunteered to go to Plattsburgh,
September, 1814, and served 10 days
in Capt. Gideon Wheelock's Company.

*WRIGHT, MOSES.
Served from April 12 to April 15,
1814 in Capt. Jonathan P. Stanley's
Company, Col. W. B. Sumner's Regt.

WRIGHT, OBED.
Served in Alexander Parris' Company
of Artificers; on Pay Roll for May
and June, 1814. Ref: R. & L. 1812,
AGO Page 24.

‡*WRIGHT, OLIVER.
Served in Capt. Brown's Company,
Col. Martindale's Regt. Detached
Militia in U. S. service 2 months and
14 days, 1812. Served from April 1
to June 30, 1813 in Capt. Samul Gordon's Company, 11th Regt. Also served in Capt. Wright's Company. Pension Certificate of widow, Laura P.,
No. 5228. Ref: R. & L. 1812, AGO
Page 8.

*WRIGHT, PRESERVED, 2nd Lieutenant.
Served in Artillery of Detached Militia of Vt. in U. S. service at Champlain from Nov. 18 to Nov. 19, 1812.

*WRIGHT, PETER.
Served in Capt. Adams Company, Col.
Jonathan Williams' Regt. Detached
Militia in U. S. service 2 months and
7 days, 1812.

WRIGHT, POTTER J.
Served from Nov. 1, 1812 to Feb. 28,
1813 in Capt. Samul Gordon's Company, 11th Regt. Ref: R. & L. 1812,
AGO Page 9.

*WRIGHT, RAWLIN (or Rolen).
Served with Hospital Attendants, Vt.

‡*WRIGHT, REUBEN, Corporal.
Served in Capt. Ormsbee's Company,
Col. Martindale's Regt. Detached
Militia in U. S. service 2 months and
14 days, 1812. Served as Corporal in
1st Regt. of Detached Militia of Vt.
in U. S. service at Champlain from
Nov. 18 to Nov. 19, 1812. Pension
Certificate of widow. Laura, No. 20480.

WRIGHT, ROBERT,   Pittsford.
Enlisted in U. S. Marine Corps Jan.
26, 1811 at New Orleans. Ref: Book
52, AGO Page 294.

WRIGHT, ROBERT,   Pittsford?
Served in Capt. Phineas Williams'
Company, 11th Regt; on Pay Roll for
January and February, 1813. Ref:
R. & L. 1812, AGO Page 15.

WRIGHT, ROGER.
Enlisted July 27, 1813 for 1 year in
Capt. James Taylor's Company, 30th
Regt.; on Muster Roll from Nov. 30
to Dec. 31, 1813. Ref: R. & L. 1812,
AGO Page 52.

WRIGHT, ROGER.
Enlisted June 27, 1813 for 1 year in
Capt. Gideon Spencer's Company,
30th Regt.; on Muster Roll from Dec.
30, 1813 to June 30, 1814; transferred
to Capt. Clark's Company, 30th Inf.
Ref: R. & L. 1812, AGO Page 56.

WRIGHT, SAMUEL,   Fairfax.
Volunteered to go to Plattsburgh,
September, 1814, and served 8 days
in Capt. Josiah Grout's Company.
Ref: Book 51, AGO Page 103.

WRIGHT, SAMUEL.
Enlisted May 29, 1813 for 1 year in
Capt. Daniel Farrington's Company,
30th Regt. (also commanded by Capt.
Simeon Wright); on Muster Roll from
March 1 to April 30, 1814. Ref: R.
& L. 1812, AGO Pages 50 and 51.

*WRIGHT, SAMUEL.
Served from April 12 to April 14,
1814 in Capt. Jonathan P. Stanley's
Company, Col. W. B. Sumner's Regt.

‡*WRIGHT, SAMUEL.
Served in Capt. Taylor's Company,
Col. Wm. Williams' Regt. Detached
Militia in U. S. service 4 months
and 24 days, 1812. Pension Certifi-
cate of widow, Leafy, No. 33866.

*WRIGHT, SAMUEL, 1st Lieutenant.
Served from April 12 to April 21,
1814 in Capt. Shubael Wales' Company, Col. W. B. Sumner's Regt.

‡WRIGHT, SAMUEL B.
Served in John Levake's Company.
Pension Certificate No. 6489.

WRIGHT, SAMUL C., Clerk.
Enlisted Nov. 2, 1812 for 5 years in
company of late Capt. J. Brooks,
commanded by Lt. John I. Cromwell,
Corps of U. S. Artillery; on Muster
Roll from April 30 to June 30, 1814;
appointed Clerk May 1, 1814. Ref:
R. & L. 1812, AGO Page 18.

‡WRIGHT SETH S.
Served in Capt. Danford's Company.
Pension Certificate No. 20728.

*WRIGHT, SIMEON, Captain.
Served in 1st Regt. of Detached Mili-
tia of Vt. in U. S. service at Cham-
plain from Nov. 18 to Nov. 19, 1812.
Served in 2 Regt. (Fifield's) Vt.
Militia. Appointed Captain 30th Inf.
April 30, 1813; honorably discharged
June 15, 1813. Ref: Heitman's His-
torical Register & Dictionary USA.

WRIGHT, SIMEON,   Pittsford.
Volunteered to go to Plattsburgh,
September, 1814, and served 8 days
in Capt. Caleb Hendee's Company.
Ref: Book 52, AGO Page 125.

WRIGHT, STEPHEN, Corporal, Berlin.
Volunteered to go to Plattsburgh,
September, 1814, and served 9 days
in Capt. Cyrus Johnson's Company.
Ref: Book 52, AGO Pages 202 and 255.

*WRIGHT, STIDMAN H., Sergeant.
Served from June 11 to June 14, 1813
in Capt. Thomas Dorwin's Company,
1st Regt. 2nd Brig. 3rd Div.

WRIGHT, THADDEUS.
Served in Capt. Richardson's Company, Col. Martindale's Regt. Detached Militia in U. S. service 2 months
and 13 days, 1812. Ref: Book 53, AGO
Page 14.

WRIGHT, THOMAS,   Franklin County.
Enlisted May 30, 1812 for 5 years in
Capt. White Youngs' Company, 15th
Regt.; on Muster Roll from Aug. 31
to Dec. 31, 1814. Ref: R. & L. 1812,
AGO Page 27.

WRIGHT, URIAH.
Served in Capt. Samul Gordon's Com-
pany, 11th Regt.; on Pay Roll for
January and February, 1813. Ref: R.
& L. 1812, AGO, Page 9.

‡*WRIGHT, URIAL, Drummer.
Served in Capt. Hopkins' Company,
Col. Martindale's Regt. Detached
Militia in U. S. service 2 months
and 13 days, 1812. Pension Certificate
of widow, Ann Gray, No. 16172.

*WRIGHT, WAIT, Lieutenant.
Served in 1st Regt. of Detached Militia of Vt. in U. S. service at Champlain from Nov. 18 to Nov. 19, 1812.

WRIGHT, WHITTLESEY,   Bristol.
Served from Sept. 1, 1814 to June 16,
1815 in Capt. Sanford's Company,
30th Inf. Ref: R. & L. 1812, AGO
Page 23.

*WRIGHT, WILLIAM,   Highgate.
Served in Capt. Dorrance's Company,
Col. Wm. Williams' Regt. Detached
Militia in U. S. service 4 months and
24 days, 1812. Served in New York
State from Sept. 25 to Nov. 18, 1813;
no organization given. Ref: Vol. 50,
Vt. State Papers, Page 94.

WRIGHT, WILLIAM,   Hubbardton.
Volunteered to go to Plattsburgh,
September, 1814, and served 8 days
in Capt. Henry J. Horton's Company.
Ref: Book 52, AGO Page 142.

*WRITE, JEHIAL W.
Served in Dixon's Regt. Vt. Militia.

*WROATH, ELISHA.
Served with Hospital Attendants, Vt.

*WROTHBONE, JAMES.
Served in 1 Regt. (Martindale's) Vt.
Militia.

WYAT, JOHN R.
Served in Capt. Weeks' Company,
11th Regt.; on Pay Roll for January and February, 1813. Ref: R. &
L. 1812, AGO Page 5.

WYERS, BENJAMIN,   Swanton.
Served in Capt. George W. Kindal's
Company, 4 Regt. (Williams') Vt.
Militia in U. S. service 6 months in
1812. Ref: Book 51, AGO Page 198.

*WYGHT, POTTER.
Served in Capt. Ormsbee's Company,
Col. Martindale's Regt. Detached
Militia in U. S. service 14 days, 1812.

*WYLIE, PETER JR.
Served in Capt. Mason's Company,
Col. Fifield's Regt. Detached Militia
in U. S. service 4 months and 21
days, 1812.

*WYLIE, SAMUEL.
Served in Capt. Mason's Company,
Col. Fifield's Regt. Detached Militia
in U. S. service 3 months and 16
days, 1812. Also served in 1 Regt.
(Judson's) Vt. Militia.

*WYMAN, ABIEL.
Served in 1 Regt. (Judson's) Vt.
Militia.

WYMAN, ARTEMUS,   West Haven.
Volunteered to go to Plattsburgh,
September, 1814, and served 4 days
in Capt. David B. Phippeney's Company. Ref: Book 52, AGO Page 146.

WYMAN, PARKER, Corporal.
Served in 1st Regt. of Detached Militia of Vt. in U. S. service at Champlain from Nov. 18 to Nov. 19, 1812.

*WYMAN, STEPHEN.
Served in Capt. Sabin's Company,
Col. Jonathan Williams' Regt. Detached Militia in U. S. service 2
months and 6 days, 1812.

YANCOOL, PETER W.
Enlisted March 21, 1814 during the
war in Capt. Gideon Spencer's Company, 30th Regt.; on Muster Roll
from Dec. 30, 1813 to June 30, 1814;
joined June 1, 1814. Ref: R. & L.
1812, AGO Pages 1 and 56.

*YATES, AXDILL.
Served in Sumner's Regt. Vt. Militia.

YATES, FRAS.
Served as private in War of 1812 and
was captured by troops Dec. 19, 1813
at Fort Niagara and exchanged May
4, 1814; captured by troops Sept. 6,
1814 at Plattsburgh; discharged Oct.
8, 1814. Ref: Records of Naval Records and Library, Navy Dept.

YAW, OLIVER,   Pittsford.
Volunteered to go to Plattsburgh,
September, 1814, and served 8 days
in Capt. Caleb Hendee's Company.
Ref: Book 52, AGO Page 125.

YORK, JEREMIAH, Lieutenant.
Appointed Ensign 31st Inf. April 30,
1813; 2nd Lieutenant Feb. 17, 1814;
1st Lieutenant Oct. 25, 1814; honorably discharged June 15, 1815. Ref:
Heitman's Historical Register & Dictionary USA.

YORKE, JOSEPH.
Enlisted May 31, 1813 for 1 year in
Capt. Benjamin Bradford's Company;
joined by transfer July 22, 1813. Ref:
R. & L. 1812, AGO Page 26.

‡*YOUNG, AGIL (or Agib?)
Served in Capt. Wheeler's Company,
Col. Fifield's Regt. Detached Militia
in U. S. service 6 months and 4 days,
1812. Pension Certificate of widow,
Etherlinda, No. 1579.

YOUNG, ASA,   Orwell.
Volunteered to go to Plattsburgh, September, 1814, serving 11 days in Capt. Wait Branch's Company. Ref: Book 51, AGO Page 16.

YOUNG, CALEB.
Served from April 14 to July 13, 1813 in Lieut. Wm. S. Foster's Company, 11th Regt. Ref: R. & L. 1812, AGO Page 6.

‡YOUNG, CHAUNCEY L.
Served in Lt. Young's Company. Pension Certificate No. 34869.

‡YOUNG, DANIEL.
Pension Certificate No. 24394; no organization given.

‡YOUNG, DANIEL.
Served in Capt. Phinney's Company. Pension Certificate No. 8845.

*YOUNG, DANIEL,   Calais.
Served in Capt. Walker's Company, Col. Fifield's Regt. Detached Militia in U. S. service 2 months and 24 days, 1812. Volunteered to go to Plattsburgh, September, 1814, and served 8 days in Capt. Samuel M. Orcutt's Company.

‡YOUNG, ENOS, Sergeant,   Roxbury.
Volunteered to go to Plattsburgh, September, 1814, and served 9 days in Capt. Samuel M. Orcutt's Company. Pension Certificate of widow, Laura, No. 31488.

YOUNG, JAMES, Lieutenant, Franklin County. Volunteered to go to Plattsburgh Sept. 11, 1814 and served in 15th or 22nd Regt. Ref: Hemenway's Vt. Gazetteer, Vol. 2, Page 391.

‡YOUNG, JESSE.
Served in Capt. Aikin's Company. Pension Certificate No. 17105. Pension Certificate of widow, Polly, No. 19286.

‡YOUNG, JOAB,   Strafford.
Served in Capt. A. Partridge's Company. Pension Certificate No. 848.

*YOUNG, JOB.
Served with Hospital Attendants, Vt.

YOUNG, JOHN.   Montpelier.
Volunteered to go to Plattsburgh, September, 1814, and served 8 days in Capt. Samuel M. Orcutt's Company. Ref: Book 52, AGO Pages 182 and 250.

YOUNG, JOHN,   Montpelier.
Volunteered to go to Plattsburgh, September, 1814, and served 8 days in Capt. Timothy Hubbard's Company. Ref: Book 52, AGO Page 256.

YOUNG, JONATHAN M., Captain.
Appointed 1st Lieutenant 30th Inf. April 30, 1813; Captain Aug. 1, 1814; honorably discharged June 15, 1815. Ref: Heitman's Historical Register & Dictionary USA.

YOUNG, JOSEPH E.
Served in Capt. Phineas Williams' Company, 11th Regt.; on Pay Roll for January and February, 1813. Ref: R. & L. 1812, AGO Page 15.

*YOUNG, LYMAN.
Served with Hospital Attendants, Vt.

YOUNG, MASON, Corporal.
Served in Capt. Samul Gordon's Company, 11th Regt.; on Pay Roll for January and February, 1813. Ref: R. & L. 1812, AGO Page 9.

YOUNG, NATHAN, Sergeant,   Strafford.
Served in Capt. Benjamin S. Edgerton's Company, 11th Regt.; on Pay Roll for September and October, 1812 and January and February, 1813. Ref: R. & L. 1812, AGO Pages 1 and 2.

*YOUNG, NATHAN.
Served in Capt. Dodge's Company, Col. Fifield's Regt. Detached Militia in U. S. service 2 months and 21 days, 1812.

YOUNG, NESTOR.
Served in Capt. Benjamin Bradford's Company; on Muster Roll from May 31 to Aug. 31, 1813. Ref: R. & L. 1812, AGO Page 26.

‡YOUNG, NOAH.
Served in Capt. Adams' Company. Pension Certificate No. 13834.

*YOUNG, RERRIUS.
Served in Sumner's Regt. Vt. Militia.

*YOUNG, SIMON.
Served with Hospital Attendants, Vt.

‡YOUNG, WILLIAM.
Served in Capt. Lowry's Company. Pension Certificate No. 18850.

YOUNG, WILLIAM.
Served from April 23, 1813 to April 26, 1814 in Capt. James Taylor's Company and Capt. Gideon Spencer's Company, 30th Regt. Ref: R. & L. 1812, AGO Pages 52, 56, 58.

YOUNG, WILLIAM,   Leicester.
Volunteered to go to Plattsburgh, September, 1814, and served 8 days in Capt. Ebenezer Jenney's Company. Ref: Book 52, AGO Page 160.

YOUNG, WINTHROP.
Served in Capt. Wheeler's Company, Col. Fifield's Regt. Detached Militia in U. S. service 6 months and 4 days, 1812. Ref: Book 53, AGO Page 55.

YOUNGS, GEORGE, Corporal.
Enlisted June 12, 1812 for 5 years in Capt. White Youngs' Company, 15th Regt.; on Muster Roll from Aug. 31 to Dec. 31, 1814. Ref: R. & L. 1812, AGO Page 27.

YOUNGS, WHITE, Captain, Franklin County. Appointed Captain March 12, 1812 in Col. David Bundy's 15th Regt.; on Muster Roll from Aug. 31 to Dec. 31, 1814. Ref: R. & L. 1812, AGO Page 27.

YOVELL, DANIEL THOMAS.
Enlisted March 21, 1814 during the war and served in Capt. Gideon Spencer's Company and Capt. Wm. Miller's Company, 30th Regt. Ref: R. & L. 1812, AGO Pages 54 and 56.